Dictionary of Literary Biography

1 *The American Renaissance in New England*, edited by Joel Myerson (1978)

2 *American Novelists Since World War II*, edited by Jeffrey Helterman and Richard Layman (1978)

3 *Antebellum Writers in New York and the South*, edited by Joel Myerson (1979)

4 *American Writers in Paris, 1920-1939*, edited by Karen Lane Rood (1980)

5 *American Poets Since World War II*, 2 parts, edited by Donald J. Greiner (1980)

6 *American Novelists Since World War II, Second Series*, edited by James E. Kibler Jr. (1980)

7 *Twentieth-Century American Dramatists*, 2 parts, edited by John MacNicholas (1981)

8 *Twentieth-Century American Science-Fiction Writers*, 2 parts, edited by David Cowart and Thomas L. Wymer (1981)

9 *American Novelists, 1910-1945*, 3 parts, edited by James J. Martine (1981)

10 *Modern British Dramatists, 1900-1945*, 2 parts, edited by Stanley Weintraub (1982)

11 *American Humorists, 1800-1950*, 2 parts, edited by Stanley Trachtenberg (1982)

12 *American Realists and Naturalists*, edited by Donald Pizer and Earl N. Harbert (1982)

13 *British Dramatists Since World War II*, 2 parts, edited by Stanley Weintraub (1982)

14 *British Novelists Since 1960*, 2 parts, edited by Jay L. Halio (1983)

15 *British Novelists, 1930-1959*, 2 parts, edited by Bernard Oldsey (1983)

16 *The Beats: Literary Bohemians in Postwar America*, 2 parts, edited by Ann Charters (1983)

17 *Twentieth-Century American Historians*, edited by Clyde N. Wilson (1983)

18 *Victorian Novelists After 1885*, edited by Ira B. Nadel and William E. Fredeman (1983)

19 *British Poets, 1880-1914*, edited by Donald E. Stanford (1983)

20 *British Poets, 1914-1945*, edited by Donald E. Stanford (1983)

21 *Victorian Novelists Before 1885*, edited by Ira B. Nadel and William E. Fredeman (1983)

22 *American Writers for Children, 1900-1960*, edited by John Cech (1983)

23 *American Newspaper Journalists, 1873-1900*, edited by Perry J. Ashley (1983)

24 *American Colonial Writers, 1606-1734*, edited by Emory Elliott (1984)

25 *American Newspaper Journalists, 1901-1925*, edited by Perry J. Ashley (1984)

26 *American Screenwriters*, edited by Robert E. Morsberger, Stephen O. Lesser, and Randall Clark (1984)

27 *Poets of Great Britain and Ireland, 1945-1960*, edited by Vincent B. Sherry Jr. (1984)

28 *Twentieth-Century American-Jewish Fiction Writers*, edited by Daniel Walden (1984)

29 *American Newspaper Journalists, 1926-1950*, edited by Perry J. Ashley (1984)

30 *American Historians, 1607-1865*, edited by Clyde N. Wilson (1984)

31 *American Colonial Writers, 1735-1781*, edited by Emory Elliott (1984)

32 *Victorian Poets Before 1850*, edited by William E. Fredeman and Ira B. Nadel (1984)

33 *Afro-American Fiction Writers After 1955*, edited by Thadious M. Davis and Trudier Harris (1984)

34 *British Novelists, 1890-1929: Traditionalists*, edited by Thomas F. Staley (1985)

35 *Victorian Poets After 1850*, edited by William E. Fredeman and Ira B. Nadel (1985)

36 *British Novelists, 1890-1929: Modernists*, edited by Thomas F. Staley (1985)

37 *American Writers of the Early Republic*, edited by Emory Elliott (1985)

38 *Afro-American Writers After 1955: Dramatists and Prose Writers*, edited by Thadious M. Davis and Trudier Harris (1985)

39 *British Novelists, 1660-1800*, 2 parts, edited by Martin C. Battestin (1985)

40 *Poets of Great Britain and Ireland Since 1960*, 2 parts, edited by Vincent B. Sherry Jr. (1985)

41 *Afro-American Poets Since 1955*, edited by Trudier Harris and Thadious M. Davis (1985)

42 *American Writers for Children Before 1900*, edited by Glenn E. Estes (1985)

43 *American Newspaper Journalists, 1690-1872*, edited by Perry J. Ashley (1986)

44 *American Screenwriters, Second Series*, edited by Randall Clark, Robert E. Morsberger, and Stephen O. Lesser (1986)

45 *American Poets, 1880-1945, First Series*, edited by Peter Quartermain (1986)

46 *American Literary Publishing Houses, 1900-1980: Trade and Paperback*, edited by Peter Dzwonkoski (1986)

47 *American Historians, 1866-1912*, edited by Clyde N. Wilson (1986)

48 *American Poets, 1880-1945, Second Series*, edited by Peter Quartermain (1986)

49 *American Literary Publishing Houses, 1638-1899*, 2 parts, edited by Peter Dzwonkoski (1986)

50 *Afro-American Writers Before the Harlem Renaissance*, edited by Trudier Harris (1986)

51 *Afro-American Writers from the Harlem Renaissance to 1940*, edited by Trudier Harris (1987)

52 *American Writers for Children Since 1960: Fiction*, edited by Glenn E. Estes (1986)

53 *Canadian Writers Since 1960, First Series*, edited by W. H. New (1986)

54 *American Poets, 1880-1945, Third Series*, 2 parts, edited by Peter Quartermain (1987)

55 *Victorian Prose Writers Before 1867*, edited by William B. Thesing (1987)

56 *German Fiction Writers, 1914-1945*, edited by James Hardin (1987)

57 *Victorian Prose Writers After 1867*, edited by William B. Thesing (1987)

58 *Jacobean and Caroline Dramatists*, edited by Fredson Bowers (1987)

59 *American Literary Critics and Scholars, 1800-1850*, edited by John W. Rathbun and Monica M. Grecu (1987)

60 *Canadian Writers Since 1960, Second Series*, edited by W. H. New (1987)

61 *American Writers for Children Since 1960: Poets, Illustrators, and Nonfiction Authors*, edited by Glenn E. Estes (1987)

62 *Elizabethan Dramatists*, edited by Fredson Bowers (1987)

63 *Modern American Critics, 1920-1955*, edited by Gregory S. Jay (1988)

64 *American Literary Critics and Scholars, 1850-1880*, edited by John W. Rathbun and Monica M. Grecu (1988)

65 *French Novelists, 1900-1930*, edited by Catharine Savage Brosman (1988)

66 *German Fiction Writers, 1885-1913*, 2 parts, edited by James Hardin (1988)

67 *Modern American Critics Since 1955*, edited by Gregory S. Jay (1988)

68 *Canadian Writers, 1920-1959, First Series*, edited by W. H. New (1988)

69 *Contemporary German Fiction Writers, First Series*, edited by Wolfgang D. Elfe and James Hardin (1988)

70 *British Mystery Writers, 1860-1919*, edited by Bernard Benstock and Thomas F. Staley (1988)

71 *American Literary Critics and Scholars, 1880-1900*, edited by John W. Rathbun and Monica M. Grecu (1988)

72 *French Novelists, 1930-1960,* edited by Catharine Savage Brosman (1988)

73 *American Magazine Journalists, 1741-1850,* edited by Sam G. Riley (1988)

74 *American Short-Story Writers Before 1880,* edited by Bobby Ellen Kimbel, with the assistance of William E. Grant (1988)

75 *Contemporary German Fiction Writers, Second Series,* edited by Wolfgang D. Elfe and James Hardin (1988)

76 *Afro-American Writers, 1940-1955,* edited by Trudier Harris (1988)

77 *British Mystery Writers, 1920-1939,* edited by Bernard Benstock and Thomas F. Staley (1988)

78 *American Short-Story Writers, 1880-1910,* edited by Bobby Ellen Kimbel, with the assistance of William E. Grant (1988)

79 *American Magazine Journalists, 1850-1900,* edited by Sam G. Riley (1988)

80 *Restoration and Eighteenth-Century Dramatists, First Series,* edited by Paula R. Backscheider (1989)

81 *Austrian Fiction Writers, 1875-1913,* edited by James Hardin and Donald G. Daviau (1989)

82 *Chicano Writers, First Series,* edited by Francisco A. Lomelí and Carl R. Shirley (1989)

83 *French Novelists Since 1960,* edited by Catharine Savage Brosman (1989)

84 *Restoration and Eighteenth-Century Dramatists, Second Series,* edited by Paula R. Backscheider (1989)

85 *Austrian Fiction Writers After 1914,* edited by James Hardin and Donald G. Daviau (1989)

86 *American Short-Story Writers, 1910-1945, First Series,* edited by Bobby Ellen Kimbel (1989)

87 *British Mystery and Thriller Writers Since 1940, First Series,* edited by Bernard Benstock and Thomas F. Staley (1989)

88 *Canadian Writers, 1920-1959, Second Series,* edited by W. H. New (1989)

89 *Restoration and Eighteenth-Century Dramatists, Third Series,* edited by Paula R. Backscheider (1989)

90 *German Writers in the Age of Goethe, 1789-1832,* edited by James Hardin and Christoph E. Schweitzer (1989)

91 *American Magazine Journalists, 1900-1960, First Series,* edited by Sam G. Riley (1990)

92 *Canadian Writers, 1890-1920,* edited by W. H. New (1990)

93 *British Romantic Poets, 1789-1832, First Series,* edited by John R. Greenfield (1990)

94 *German Writers in the Age of Goethe: Sturm und Drang to Classicism,* edited by James Hardin and Christoph E. Schweitzer (1990)

95 *Eighteenth-Century British Poets, First Series,* edited by John Sitter (1990)

96 *British Romantic Poets, 1789-1832, Second Series,* edited by John R. Greenfield (1990)

97 *German Writers from the Enlightenment to Sturm und Drang, 1720-1764,* edited by James Hardin and Christoph E. Schweitzer (1990)

98 *Modern British Essayists, First Series,* edited by Robert Beum (1990)

99 *Canadian Writers Before 1890,* edited by W. H. New (1990)

100 *Modern British Essayists, Second Series,* edited by Robert Beum (1990)

101 *British Prose Writers, 1660-1800, First Series,* edited by Donald T. Siebert (1991)

102 *American Short-Story Writers, 1910-1945, Second Series,* edited by Bobby Ellen Kimbel (1991)

103 *American Literary Biographers, First Series,* edited by Steven Serafin (1991)

104 *British Prose Writers, 1660-1800, Second Series,* edited by Donald T. Siebert (1991)

105 *American Poets Since World War II, Second Series,* edited by R. S. Gwynn (1991)

106 *British Literary Publishing Houses, 1820-1880,* edited by Patricia J. Anderson and Jonathan Rose (1991)

107 *British Romantic Prose Writers, 1789-1832, First Series,* edited by John R. Greenfield (1991)

108 *Twentieth-Century Spanish Poets, First Series,* edited by Michael L. Perna (1991)

109 *Eighteenth-Century British Poets, Second Series,* edited by John Sitter (1991)

110 *British Romantic Prose Writers, 1789-1832, Second Series,* edited by John R. Greenfield (1991)

111 *American Literary Biographers, Second Series,* edited by Steven Serafin (1991)

112 *British Literary Publishing Houses, 1881-1965,* edited by Jonathan Rose and Patricia J. Anderson (1991)

113 *Modern Latin-American Fiction Writers, First Series,* edited by William Luis (1992)

114 *Twentieth-Century Italian Poets, First Series,* edited by Giovanna Wedel De Stasio, Glauco Cambon, and Antonio Illiano (1992)

115 *Medieval Philosophers,* edited by Jeremiah Hackett (1992)

116 *British Romantic Novelists, 1789-1832,* edited by Bradford K. Mudge (1992)

117 *Twentieth-Century Caribbean and Black African Writers, First Series,* edited by Bernth Lindfors and Reinhard Sander (1992)

118 *Twentieth-Century German Dramatists, 1889-1918,* edited by Wolfgang D. Elfe and James Hardin (1992)

119 *Nineteenth-Century French Fiction Writers: Romanticism and Realism, 1800-1860,* edited by Catharine Savage Brosman (1992)

120 *American Poets Since World War II, Third Series,* edited by R. S. Gwynn (1992)

121 *Seventeenth-Century British Nondramatic Poets, First Series,* edited by M. Thomas Hester (1992)

122 *Chicano Writers, Second Series,* edited by Francisco A. Lomelí and Carl R. Shirley (1992)

123 *Nineteenth-Century French Fiction Writers: Naturalism and Beyond, 1860-1900,* edited by Catharine Savage Brosman (1992)

124 *Twentieth-Century German Dramatists, 1919-1992,* edited by Wolfgang D. Elfe and James Hardin (1992)

125 *Twentieth-Century Caribbean and Black African Writers, Second Series,* edited by Bernth Lindfors and Reinhard Sander (1993)

126 *Seventeenth-Century British Nondramatic Poets, Second Series,* edited by M. Thomas Hester (1993)

127 *American Newspaper Publishers, 1950-1990,* edited by Perry J. Ashley (1993)

128 *Twentieth-Century Italian Poets, Second Series,* edited by Giovanna Wedel De Stasio, Glauco Cambon, and Antonio Illiano (1993)

129 *Nineteenth-Century German Writers, 1841-1900,* edited by James Hardin and Siegfried Mews (1993)

130 *American Short-Story Writers Since World War II,* edited by Patrick Meanor (1993)

131 *Seventeenth-Century British Nondramatic Poets, Third Series,* edited by M. Thomas Hester (1993)

132 *Sixteenth-Century British Nondramatic Writers, First Series,* edited by David A. Richardson (1993)

133 *Nineteenth-Century German Writers to 1840,* edited by James Hardin and Siegfried Mews (1993)

134 *Twentieth-Century Spanish Poets, Second Series,* edited by Jerry Phillips Winfield (1994)

135 *British Short-Fiction Writers, 1880-1914: The Realist Tradition,* edited by William B. Thesing (1994)

136 *Sixteenth-Century British Nondramatic Writers, Second Series,* edited by David A. Richardson (1994)

137 *American Magazine Journalists, 1900-1960, Second Series,* edited by Sam G. Riley (1994)

138 *German Writers and Works of the High Middle Ages: 1170-1280,* edited by James Hardin and Will Hasty (1994)

139 *British Short-Fiction Writers, 1945-1980,* edited by Dean Baldwin (1994)

140 *American Book-Collectors and Bibliographers, First Series,* edited by Joseph Rosenblum (1994)

141 *British Children's Writers, 1880-1914,* edited by Laura M. Zaidman (1994)

142 *Eighteenth-Century British Literary Biographers,* edited by Steven Serafin (1994)

143 *American Novelists Since World War II, Third Series,* edited by James R. Giles and Wanda H. Giles (1994)

144 *Nineteenth-Century British Literary Biographers,* edited by Steven Serafin (1994)

145 *Modern Latin-American Fiction Writers, Second Series,* edited by William Luis and Ann González (1994)

146 *Old and Middle English Literature,* edited by Jeffrey Helterman and Jerome Mitchell (1994)

147 *South Slavic Writers Before World War II,* edited by Vasa D. Mihailovich (1994)

148 *German Writers and Works of the Early Middle Ages: 800-1170,* edited by Will Hasty and James Hardin (1994)

149 *Late Nineteenth- and Early Twentieth-Century British Literary Biographers,* edited by Steven Serafin (1995)

150 *Early Modern Russian Writers, Late Seventeenth and Eighteenth Centuries,* edited by Marcus C. Levitt (1995)

151 *British Prose Writers of the Early Seventeenth Century,* edited by Clayton D. Lein (1995)

152 *American Novelists Since World War II, Fourth Series,* edited by James R. Giles and Wanda H. Giles (1995)

153 *Late-Victorian and Edwardian British Novelists, First Series,* edited by George M. Johnson (1995)

154 *The British Literary Book Trade, 1700-1820,* edited by James K. Bracken and Joel Silver (1995)

155 *Twentieth-Century British Literary Biographers,* edited by Steven Serafin (1995)

156 *British Short-Fiction Writers, 1880-1914: The Romantic Tradition,* edited by William F. Naufftus (1995)

157 *Twentieth-Century Caribbean and Black African Writers, Third Series,* edited by Bernth Lindfors and Reinhard Sander (1995)

158 *British Reform Writers, 1789-1832,* edited by Gary Kelly and Edd Applegate (1995)

159 *British Short-Fiction Writers, 1800-1880,* edited by John R. Greenfield (1996)

160 *British Children's Writers, 1914-1960,* edited by Donald R. Hettinga and Gary D. Schmidt (1996)

161 *British Children's Writers Since 1960, First Series,* edited by Caroline Hunt (1996)

162 *British Short-Fiction Writers, 1915-1945,* edited by John H. Rogers (1996)

163 *British Children's Writers, 1800-1880,* edited by Meena Khorana (1996)

164 *German Baroque Writers, 1580-1660,* edited by James Hardin (1996)

165 *American Poets Since World War II, Fourth Series,* edited by Joseph Conte (1996)

166 *British Travel Writers, 1837-1875,* edited by Barbara Brothers and Julia Gergits (1996)

167 *Sixteenth-Century British Nondramatic Writers, Third Series,* edited by David A. Richardson (1996)

168 *German Baroque Writers, 1661-1730,* edited by James Hardin (1996)

169 *American Poets Since World War II, Fifth Series,* edited by Joseph Conte (1996)

170 *The British Literary Book Trade, 1475-1700,* edited by James K. Bracken and Joel Silver (1996)

171 *Twentieth-Century American Sportswriters,* edited by Richard Orodenker (1996)

172 *Sixteenth-Century British Nondramatic Writers, Fourth Series,* edited by David A. Richardson (1996)

173 *American Novelists Since World War II, Fifth Series,* edited by James R. Giles and Wanda H. Giles (1996)

174 *British Travel Writers, 1876-1909,* edited by Barbara Brothers and Julia Gergits (1997)

175 *Native American Writers of the United States,* edited by Kenneth M. Roemer (1997)

176 *Ancient Greek Authors,* edited by Ward W. Briggs (1997)

177 *Italian Novelists Since World War II, 1945-1965,* edited by Augustus Pallotta (1997)

178 *British Fantasy and Science-Fiction Writers Before World War I,* edited by Darren Harris-Fain (1997)

179 *German Writers of the Renaissance and Reformation, 1280-1580,* edited by James Hardin and Max Reinhart (1997)

180 *Japanese Fiction Writers, 1868-1945,* edited by Van C. Gessel (1997)

181 *South Slavic Writers Since World War II,* edited by Vasa D. Mihailovich (1997)

182 *Japanese Fiction Writers Since World War II,* edited by Van C. Gessel (1997)

183 *American Travel Writers, 1776-1864,* edited by James J. Schramer and Donald Ross (1997)

184 *Nineteenth-Century British Book-Collectors and Bibliographers,* edited by William Baker and Kenneth Womack (1997)

185 *American Literary Journalists, 1945-1995, First Series,* edited by Arthur J. Kaul (1998)

186 *Nineteenth-Century American Western Writers,* edited by Robert L. Gale (1998)

187 *American Book Collectors and Bibliographers, Second Series,* edited by Joseph Rosenblum (1998)

188 *American Book and Magazine Illustrators to 1920,* edited by Steven E. Smith, Catherine A. Hastedt, and Donald H. Dyal (1998)

189 *American Travel Writers, 1850-1915,* edited by Donald Ross and James J. Schramer (1998)

190 *British Reform Writers, 1832-1914,* edited by Gary Kelly and Edd Applegate (1998)

191 *British Novelists Between the Wars,* edited by George M. Johnson (1998)

192 *French Dramatists, 1789-1914,* edited by Barbara T. Cooper (1998)

193 *American Poets Since World War II, Sixth Series,* edited by Joseph Conte (1998)

194 *British Novelists Since 1960, Second Series,* edited by Merritt Moseley (1998)

195 *British Travel Writers, 1910-1939,* edited by Barbara Brothers and Julia Gergits (1998)

196 *Italian Novelists Since World War II, 1965-1995,* edited by Augustus Pallotta (1999)

197 *Late-Victorian and Edwardian British Novelists, Second Series,* edited by George M. Johnson (1999)

198 *Russian Literature in the Age of Pushkin and Gogol: Prose,* edited by Christine A. Rydel (1999)

199 *Victorian Women Poets,* edited by William B. Thesing (1999)

200 *American Women Prose Writers to 1820,* edited by Carla J. Mulford, with Angela Vietto and Amy E. Winans (1999)

201 *Twentieth-Century British Book Collectors and Bibliographers,* edited by William Baker and Kenneth Womack (1999)

202 *Nineteenth-Century American Fiction Writers,* edited by Kent P. Ljungquist (1999)

203 *Medieval Japanese Writers,* edited by Steven D. Carter (1999)

204 *British Travel Writers, 1940-1997,* edited by Barbara Brothers and Julia M. Gergits (1999)

205 *Russian Literature in the Age of Pushkin and Gogol: Poetry and Drama,* edited by Christine A. Rydel (1999)

206 *Twentieth-Century American Western Writers, First Series,* edited by Richard H. Cracroft (1999)

207 *British Novelists Since 1960, Third Series,* edited by Merritt Moseley (1999)

208 *Literature of the French and Occitan Middle Ages: Eleventh to Fifteenth Centuries,* edited by Deborah Sinnreich-Levi and Ian S. Laurie (1999)

209 *Chicano Writers, Third Series,* edited by Francisco A. Lomelí and Carl R. Shirley (1999)

210 *Ernest Hemingway: A Documentary Volume,* edited by Robert W. Trogdon (1999)

211 *Ancient Roman Writers,* edited by Ward W. Briggs (1999)

212 *Twentieth-Century American Western Writers, Second Series,* edited by Richard H. Cracroft (1999)

213 *Pre-Nineteenth-Century British Book Collectors and Bibliographers,* edited by William Baker and Kenneth Womack (1999)

214 *Twentieth-Century Danish Writers,* edited by Marianne Stecher-Hansen (1999)

215 *Twentieth-Century Eastern European Writers, First Series,* edited by Steven Serafin (1999)

216 *British Poets of the Great War: Brooke, Rosenberg, Thomas. A Documentary Volume,* edited by Patrick Quinn (2000)

217 *Nineteenth-Century French Poets,* edited by Robert Beum (2000)

218 *American Short-Story Writers Since World War II, Second Series,* edited by Patrick Meanor and Gwen Crane (2000)

219 *F. Scott Fitzgerald's* The Great Gatsby: *A Documentary Volume,* edited by Matthew J. Bruccoli (2000)

220 *Twentieth-Century Eastern European Writers, Second Series,* edited by Steven Serafin (2000)

221 *American Women Prose Writers, 1870-1920,* edited by Sharon M. Harris, with the assistance of Heidi L. M. Jacobs and Jennifer Putzi (2000)

222 *H. L. Mencken: A Documentary Volume,* edited by Richard J. Schrader (2000)

223 *The American Renaissance in New England, Second Series,* edited by Wesley T. Mott (2000)

224 *Walt Whitman: A Documentary Volume,* edited by Joel Myerson (2000)

225 *South African Writers,* edited by Paul A. Scanlon (2000)

226 *American Hard-Boiled Crime Writers,* edited by George Parker Anderson and Julie B. Anderson (2000)

227 *American Novelists Since World War II, Sixth Series,* edited by James R. Giles and Wanda H. Giles (2000)

228 *Twentieth-Century American Dramatists, Second Series,* edited by Christopher J. Wheatley (2000)

229 *Thomas Wolfe: A Documentary Volume,* edited by Ted Mitchell (2001)

230 *Australian Literature, 1788-1914,* edited by Selina Samuels (2001)

231 *British Novelists Since 1960, Fourth Series,* edited by Merritt Moseley (2001)

232 *Twentieth-Century Eastern European Writers, Third Series,* edited by Steven Serafin (2001)

233 *British and Irish Dramatists Since World War II, Second Series,* edited by John Bull (2001)

234 *American Short-Story Writers Since World War II, Third Series,* edited by Patrick Meanor and Richard E. Lee (2001)

235 *The American Renaissance in New England, Third Series,* edited by Wesley T. Mott (2001)

236 *British Rhetoricians and Logicians, 1500-1660,* edited by Edward A. Malone (2001)

237 *The Beats: A Documentary Volume,* edited by Matt Theado (2001)

238 *Russian Novelists in the Age of Tolstoy and Dostoevsky,* edited by J. Alexander Ogden and Judith E. Kalb (2001)

239 *American Women Prose Writers: 1820-1870,* edited by Amy E. Hudock and Katharine Rodier (2001)

240 *Late Nineteenth- and Early Twentieth-Century British Women Poets,* edited by William B. Thesing (2001)

241 *American Sportswriters and Writers on Sport,* edited by Richard Orodenker (2001)

242 *Twentieth-Century European Cultural Theorists, First Series,* edited by Paul Hansom (2001)

243 *The American Renaissance in New England, Fourth Series,* edited by Wesley T. Mott (2001)

244 *American Short-Story Writers Since World War II, Fourth Series,* edited by Patrick Meanor and Joseph McNicholas (2001)

245 *British and Irish Dramatists Since World War II, Third Series,* edited by John Bull (2001)

246 *Twentieth-Century American Cultural Theorists,* edited by Paul Hansom (2001)

247 *James Joyce: A Documentary Volume,* edited by A. Nicholas Fargnoli (2001)

248 *Antebellum Writers in the South, Second Series,* edited by Kent P. Ljungquist (2001)

249 *Twentieth-Century American Dramatists, Third Series,* edited by Christopher Wheatley (2002)

250 *Antebellum Writers in New York, Second Series,* edited by Kent P. Ljungquist (2002)

251 *Canadian Fantasy and Science-Fiction Writers,* edited by Douglas Ivison (2002)

Dictionary of Literary Biography Documentary Series

1 *Sherwood Anderson, Willa Cather, John Dos Passos, Theodore Dreiser, F. Scott Fitzgerald, Ernest Hemingway, Sinclair Lewis,* edited by Margaret A. Van Antwerp (1982)

2 *James Gould Cozzens, James T. Farrell, William Faulkner, John O'Hara, John Steinbeck, Thomas Wolfe, Richard Wright,* edited by Margaret A. Van Antwerp (1982)

3 *Saul Bellow, Jack Kerouac, Norman Mailer, Vladimir Nabokov, John Updike, Kurt Vonnegut,* edited by Mary Bruccoli (1983)

4 *Tennessee Williams,* edited by Margaret A. Van Antwerp and Sally Johns (1984)

5 *American Transcendentalists,* edited by Joel Myerson (1988)

6 *Hardboiled Mystery Writers: Raymond Chandler, Dashiell Hammett, Ross Macdonald,* edited by Matthew J. Bruccoli and Richard Layman (1989)

7 *Modern American Poets: James Dickey, Robert Frost, Marianne Moore,* edited by Karen L. Rood (1989)

8 *The Black Aesthetic Movement,* edited by Jeffrey Louis Decker (1991)

9 *American Writers of the Vietnam War: W. D. Ehrhart, Larry Heinemann, Tim O'Brien, Walter McDonald, John M. Del Vecchio,* edited by Ronald Baughman (1991)

10 *The Bloomsbury Group,* edited by Edward L. Bishop (1992)

11 *American Proletarian Culture: The Twenties and The Thirties,* edited by Jon Christian Suggs (1993)

12 *Southern Women Writers: Flannery O'Connor, Katherine Anne Porter, Eudora Welty,* edited by Mary Ann Wimsatt and Karen L. Rood (1994)

13 *The House of Scribner, 1846-1904,* edited by John Delaney (1996)

14 *Four Women Writers for Children, 1868-1918,* edited by Caroline C. Hunt (1996)

15 *American Expatriate Writers: Paris in the Twenties,* edited by Matthew J. Bruccoli and Robert W. Trogdon (1997)

16 *The House of Scribner, 1905-1930,* edited by John Delaney (1997)

17 *The House of Scribner, 1931-1984,* edited by John Delaney (1998)

18 *British Poets of The Great War: Sassoon, Graves, Owen,* edited by Patrick Quinn (1999)

19 *James Dickey,* edited by Judith S. Baughman (1999)

See also DLB 210, 216, 219, 222, 224, 229, 237, 247

Dictionary of Literary Biography Yearbooks

1980 edited by Karen L. Rood, Jean W. Ross, and Richard Ziegfeld (1981)

1981 edited by Karen L. Rood, Jean W. Ross, and Richard Ziegfeld (1982)

1982 edited by Richard Ziegfeld; associate editors: Jean W. Ross and Lynne C. Zeigler (1983)

1983 edited by Mary Bruccoli and Jean W. Ross; associate editor Richard Ziegfeld (1984)

1984 edited by Jean W. Ross (1985)

1985 edited by Jean W. Ross (1986)

1986 edited by J. M. Brook (1987)

1987 edited by J. M. Brook (1988)

1988 edited by J. M. Brook (1989)

1989 edited by J. M. Brook (1990)

1990 edited by James W. Hipp (1991)

1991 edited by James W. Hipp (1992)

1992 edited by James W. Hipp (1993)

1993 edited by James W. Hipp, contributing editor George Garrett (1994)

1994 edited by James W. Hipp, contributing editor George Garrett (1995)

1995 edited by James W. Hipp, contributing editor George Garrett (1996)

1996 edited by Samuel W. Bruce and L. Kay Webster, contributing editor George Garrett (1997)

1997 edited by Matthew J. Bruccoli and George Garrett, with the assistance of L. Kay Webster (1998)

1998 edited by Matthew J. Bruccoli, contributing editor George Garrett, with the assistance of D. W. Thomas (1999)

1999 edited by Matthew J. Bruccoli, contributing editor George Garrett, with the assistance of D. W. Thomas (2000)

2000 edited by Matthew J. Bruccoli, contributing editor George Garrett, with the assistance of George Parker Anderson (2001)

Concise Series

Concise Dictionary of American Literary Biography, 7 volumes (1988-1999): *The New Consciousness, 1941-1968; Colonization to the American Renaissance, 1640-1865; Realism, Naturalism, and Local Color, 1865-1917; The Twenties, 1917-1929; The Age of Maturity, 1929-1941; Broadening Views, 1968-1988; Supplement: Modern Writers, 1900-1998.*

Concise Dictionary of British Literary Biography, 8 volumes (1991-1992): *Writers of the Middle Ages and Renaissance Before 1660; Writers of the Restoration and Eighteenth Century, 1660-1789; Writers of the Romantic Period, 1789-1832; Victorian Writers, 1832-1890; Late-Victorian and Edwardian Writers, 1890-1914; Modern Writers, 1914-1945; Writers After World War II, 1945-1960; Contemporary Writers, 1960 to Present.*

Concise Dictionary of World Literary Biography, 10 volumes projected (1999-   ): *Ancient Greek and Roman Writers; German Writers; African, Caribbean, and Latin American Writers; South Slavic and Eastern European Writers.*

Dictionary of Literary Biography® • Volume Two Hundred Fifty-One

Canadian Fantasy and Science-Fiction Writers

Dictionary of Literary Biography® • Volume Two Hundred Fifty-One

Canadian Fantasy and Science-Fiction Writers

Edited by
Douglas Ivison
University of Western Ontario

A Bruccoli Clark Layman Book
The Gale Group
Detroit • San Francisco • London • Boston • Woodbridge, Conn.

Advisory Board for
DICTIONARY OF LITERARY BIOGRAPHY

John Baker
William Cagle
Patrick O'Connor
George Garrett
Trudier Harris
Alvin Kernan
Kenny J. Williams

Matthew J. Bruccoli and Richard Layman, Editorial Directors
Karen L. Rood, Senior Editor

Printed in the United States of America

The paper used in this publication meets the minimum requirements of American National Standard for Information Sciences–Permanence Paper for Printed Library Materials, ANSI Z39.48-1984.∞™

This publication is a creative work fully protected by all applicable copyright laws, as well as by misappropriation, trade secret, unfair competition, and other applicable laws. The authors and editors of this work have added value to the underlying factual material herein through one or more of the following: unique and original selection, coordination, expression, arrangement, and classification of the information.

All rights to this publication will be vigorously defended.

Copyright © 2002 by The Gale Group
27500 Drake Road
Farmington Hills, MI 48331

All rights reserved including the right of reproduction in
whole or in part in any form.

Library of Congress Cataloging-in-Publication Data

Canadian fantasy and science-fiction writers / edited by Douglas Ivison.
    p. cm.–(Dictionary of literary biography; v. 251)
"A Bruccoli Clark Layman book."
Includes bibliographical references and index.
ISBN 0-7876-4668-7 (alk. paper)
1. Fantasy fiction, Canadian–Bio-bibliography–Dictionaries. 2. Science fiction, Canadian–Bio-bibliography–Dictionaries. 3. Authors, Canadian–Biography–Dictionaries. 4. Fantasy fiction, Canadian–Dictionaries. 5. Science fiction, Canadian–Dictionaries. I. Ivison, Douglas. II. Series.

PR9192.6.F27 C36 2001
813'.087609'003–dc21
                                                                                    2001050126

For Batia

Contents

Plan of the Series xv
Introduction xvii

Jean-Pierre April (1948–) .3
   Kathleen Kellett-Betsos

Margaret Atwood (1939–) 11
   Lee Briscoe Thompson

H. Bedford-Jones (1887–1949) 22
   Peter Halasz and Don Hutchison

Lesley Choyce (1951–) 30
   Allan Weiss

Monique Corriveau (1927–1976) 36
   Jean-Louis Trudel

Denis Côté (1954–) 41
   Patti J. Kurtz

Charles de Lint (1951–) 49
   Robin Anne Reid

James De Mille (1833–1880) 61
   Douglas Ivison

Candas Jane Dorsey (1952–) 66
   Douglas Ivison

Dave Duncan (1933–) 75
   Jane Tolmie

Leslie Gadallah (1939–) 91
   Beverley Curran

William Gibson (1948–) 96
   Douglas Ivison

Phyllis Gotlieb (1926–) 108
   Douglas Barbour

Terence M. Green (1947–) 121
   Nalo Hopkinson

Tom Henighan (1934–) 127
   Batia Boe Stolar

Nalo Hopkinson (1960–) .134
   Nancy Johnston

Guy Gavriel Kay (1954–) .139
   Holly E. Ordway

Eileen Kernaghan (1939–) 149
   Clélie Rich

Crawford Kilian (1941–) .157
   Todd H. Sammons

Donald Kingsbury (1929–) 170
   Allan Weiss

Gwendolyn MacEwen (1941–1987) 175
   Dorothy Shostak

Laurence Manning (1899–1972) 180
   Everett F. Bleiler

Judith Merril (1923–1997) 185
   Elliot J. Atkins

Brian Moore (1921–1999) 197
   Darren Harris-Fain

Francine Pelletier (1959–) 207
   Amy J. Ransom

Teresa Plowright (1952–) 212
   Cristie L. March

Garfield Reeves-Stevens (1953–) 216
   Greg Beatty

Esther Rochon (1948–) 225
   Annika Hannan

Robert J. Sawyer (1960–) 237
   Austin Booth

Daniel Sernine (1955–) 246
   Jean-Louis Trudel

Sean Stewart (1965–) 258
   Alexander C. Irvine

S. M. Stirling (1954–) 263
   Christopher L. Morrow

Jean-Louis Trudel (1967–) 273
   Dan S. Paroski

A. E. van Vogt (1912–2000) 282
   J. Morton Hedrick

Élisabeth Vonarburg (1947–) 294
   Sylvie Bérard

Andrew Weiner (1949–) 309
   Mici Gold

Michelle Sagara West (1963–) 315
   Nancy Johnston

Robert Charles Wilson (1953–) 320
   Thomas March

Checklist of Further Readings 329
Contributors 331
Cumulative Index 335

Plan of the Series

... Almost the most prodigious asset of a country, and perhaps its most precious possession, is its native literary product—when that product is fine and noble and enduring.

Mark Twain*

The advisory board, the editors, and the publisher of the *Dictionary of Literary Biography* are joined in endorsing Mark Twain's declaration. The literature of a nation provides an inexhaustible resource of permanent worth. Our purpose is to make literature and its creators better understood and more accessible to students and the reading public, while satisfying the needs of teachers and researchers.

To meet these requirements, *literary biography* has been construed in terms of the author's achievement. The most important thing about a writer is his writing. Accordingly, the entries in *DLB* are career biographies, tracing the development of the author's canon and the evolution of his reputation.

The purpose of *DLB* is not only to provide reliable information in a usable format but also to place the figures in the larger perspective of literary history and to offer appraisals of their accomplishments by qualified scholars.

The publication plan for *DLB* resulted from two years of preparation. The project was proposed to Bruccoli Clark by Frederick G. Ruffner, president of the Gale Research Company, in November 1975. After specimen entries were prepared and typeset, an advisory board was formed to refine the entry format and develop the series rationale. In meetings held during 1976, the publisher, series editors, and advisory board approved the scheme for a comprehensive biographical dictionary of persons who contributed to literature. Editorial work on the first volume began in January 1977, and it was published in 1978. In order to make *DLB* more than a dictionary and to compile volumes that individually have claim to status as literary history, it was decided to organize volumes by topic, period, or genre. Each of these freestanding volumes provides a biographical-bibliographical guide and overview for a particular area of literature. We are convinced that this organization—as opposed to a single alphabet method—constitutes a valuable innovation in the presentation of reference material. The volume plan necessarily requires many decisions for the placement and treatment of authors. Certain figures will be included in separate volumes, but with different entries emphasizing the aspect of his career appropriate to each volume. Ernest Hemingway, for example, is represented in *American Writers in Paris, 1920–1939* by an entry focusing on his expatriate apprenticeship; he is also in *American Novelists, 1910–1945* with an entry surveying his entire career, as well as in *American Short-Story Writers, 1910–1945, Second Series* with an entry concentrating on his short fiction. Each volume includes a cumulative index of the subject authors and articles.

Since 1981 the series has been further augmented by the *DLB Yearbooks,* which update published entries, add new entries to keep the *DLB* current with contemporary activity, and provide articles on literary history. There have also been nineteen *DLB Documentary Series* volumes which provide illustrations, facsimiles, and biographical and critical source materials for figures, works, or groups judged to have particular interest for students. In 1999 the *Documentary Series* was incorporated into the *DLB* volume numbering system beginning with *DLB 210: Ernest Hemingway.*

We define literature as the *intellectual commerce of a nation:* not merely as belles lettres but as that ample and complex process by which ideas are generated, shaped, and transmitted. *DLB* entries are not limited to "creative writers" but extend to other figures who in their time and in their way influenced the mind of a people. Thus the series encompasses historians, journalists, publishers, book collectors, and screenwriters. By this means readers of *DLB* may be aided to perceive literature not as cult scripture in the keeping of intellectual high priests but firmly positioned at the center of a nation's life.

DLB includes the major writers appropriate to each volume and those standing in the ranks behind them. Scholarly and critical counsel has been sought in

*From an unpublished section of Mark Twain's autobiography, copyright by the Mark Twain Company

deciding which minor figures to include and how full their entries should be. Wherever possible, useful references are made to figures who do not warrant separate entries.

Each *DLB* volume has an expert volume editor responsible for planning the volume, selecting the figures for inclusion, and assigning the entries. Volume editors are also responsible for preparing, where appropriate, appendices surveying the major periodicals and literary and intellectual movements for their volumes, as well as lists of further readings. Work on the series as a whole is coordinated at the Bruccoli Clark Layman editorial center in Columbia, South Carolina, where the editorial staff is responsible for accuracy and utility of the published volumes.

One feature that distinguishes *DLB* is the illustration policy–its concern with the iconography of literature. Just as an author is influenced by his surroundings, so is the reader's understanding of the author enhanced by a knowledge of his environment. Therefore *DLB* volumes include not only drawings, paintings, and photographs of authors, often depicting them at various stages in their careers, but also illustrations of their families and places where they lived. Title pages are regularly reproduced in facsimile along with dust jackets for modern authors. The dust jackets are a special feature of *DLB* because they often document better than anything else the way in which an author's work was perceived in its own time. Specimens of the writers' manuscripts and letters are included when feasible.

Samuel Johnson rightly decreed that "The chief glory of every people arises from its authors." The purpose of the *Dictionary of Literary Biography* is to compile literary history in the surest way available to us–by accurate and comprehensive treatment of the lives and work of those who contributed to it.

The *DLB* Advisory Board

Introduction

Twenty, even ten, years ago it would have been impossible to assemble this book, for it has only been in the 1990s that Canadian science fiction and fantasy has reached the point where it could be identified as such. There have been Canadian writers of science fiction throughout the history of the modern genres, but only twenty years ago, in the first critical discussion of Canadian science fiction, pioneering critic David Ketterer was able to argue validly, in his essay "Canadian Science Fiction" in John Robert Colombo's *Other Canadas* anthology (1979), that Phyllis Gotlieb "*is* Canadian science fiction." That may have been a slight exaggeration but not really much of one. Now, at the beginning of the twenty-first century, the writing community of science fiction and fantasy, or speculative fiction (SF) as the two are often called, is vibrant and thriving in both official languages, English and French, with a whole range of domestic institutions at home and several internationally best-selling and critically acclaimed authors. Gotlieb remains an important member of the Canadian SF community, but no one could now make the claim that she *is* Canadian SF.

It might be useful to briefly define the terms and categories that underlie discussions of Canadian SF in general and that have played their part in determining the contents of this volume. "Canadian" might seem to be the simplest category to define, but the history of Canadian literature criticism shows that this task is more difficult than it might appear. Should the designation "Canadian" be reserved for those writers born in Canada? Should it include those writers who have immigrated to Canada? Writers born in Canada but living elsewhere? Writers who lived in Canada for a few years? For the purposes of this volume, "Canadian" identifies those writers who spent a significant portion of their writing careers in Canada, are generally understood to be Canadian writers, or have made significant contributions to the development of Canadian SF. These parameters mean that the American-born William Gibson is included by virtue of the fact that he has lived in Canada for his entire writing career, while a Canadian-born writer such as Gordon R. Dickson, who spent his entire adult life in the United States, is not. That is not to say that writers not included in this volume (such as Canadian-born U.K. resident Geoff Ryman or American-born Canadian resident Spider Robinson) are not Canadian; rather, they simply could not be included for logistical reasons.

The definitions of science fiction and fantasy are simultaneously self-evident and virtually impossible to determine. Both terms are artificial publishing categories, the first describing fiction dealing with technology, science, and the future, and the second describing fiction based on magic and mythology. Such definitions, however, are much too simplistic, and there is actually little real agreement on what the two terms signify. Since the introduction of the term "science fiction" into general usage in the 1930s, when it was principally associated with American pulp magazines, many editors, writers, and critics have sought to define the term. The result has been a proliferation of often contradictory definitions, and as Brian Stableford, John Clute, and Peter Nicholls write in *The Encyclopedia of Science Fiction* (1993), "there is really no good reason to expect that a workable definition of sf will ever be established. . . . And it is still not possible to describe sf as a homogeneous form of writing." In general, though, science fiction deals with the impact of science and technology on society, explores the consequences of societal change, extrapolates current conditions into the future, and speculates on alternative societies or ways of being. Furthermore, regardless of how far-fetched its imagined inventions or cosmological speculations might seem, they are grounded in natural law and rely on science and reason as legitimation and justification.

Fantasy is an often more difficult term to define satisfactorily; much of the world's literature could be described as fantasy. As John Grant and Ron Tiner write in *The Encyclopedia of Fantasy* (1997), fantasy "is a most extraordinarily porous term, and has been used to mop up vast deposits of story which this culture or that—and this era or that—deems unrealistic." Grant and Tiner go on to develop a definition of fantasy as a genre: "when set in this world, it tells a story which is impossible in the world as we perceive it; when set in an otherworld, that otherworld will be impossible, though stories set there may be possible in its terms." Essentially, then, fantasy presents its readers with a world that operates by other–apparently nonrational and supernatural–law than does the readers' world. Conventionally, fantasy has been associated with magic and the supernatural and has frequently drawn on mythological traditions and earlier historical periods for its source material. It often describes a world in which science and technology, as readers know them, are absent.

It may seem odd to pair science fiction and fantasy, but in many respects the two genres overlap, and many writers have written both science fiction and fantasy. Some writers object to the terms science fiction and fantasy, feeling that the terms have come to designate a genre ghetto, and that writing labeled as such is thus prevented from being considered serious literature. For that reason, some critics and writers have elected to use the term speculative fiction, or SF, to refer to science fiction and fantasy. This term emphasizes SF writing as an intellectual exercise, in which the writer speculates on alternative societies, futures, and ways of being, and avoids the pulpish connotations of "science fiction" and "fantasy." The term also conveniently avoids the emphasis on distinguishing between the two genres. None of these labels is wholly satisfactory, but SF can be used as a catch-all term. The writers included in this volume are generally associated with the publishing categories of science fiction and fantasy, but some writers not primarily thought of as SF writers (such as Margaret Atwood and Brian Moore) have been included because of their important contributions to the field and because they have been recognized in previous discussions of Canadian SF, such as Ketterer's seminal *Canadian Science Fiction and Fantasy* (1992).

As with science fiction and fantasy in general, the beginning of the Canadian speculative fiction tradition can be situated at various points in, or before the beginning of, Canadian literary history. The native peoples who, before the arrival of European settlers, made up the population of that part of North America that became Canada had their own longstanding traditions of fantastic oral storytelling, later translated into English or French written tales. As *The Encyclopedia of Fantasy* observes, these tales featured tricksters, shapeshifters, shamans, witches, windigos, giants, and other supernatural characters and manifestations. These native legends have been appropriated by both French and English writers, including Major John Richardson in his early Gothic romance *Wacousta* (1832), and have more recently been reappropriated by native writers such as Thomas King in *Green Grass, Running Water* (1993). Such supernatural legends and characters have also inspired writers of speculative fiction, such as Algernon Henry Blackwood in "The Wendigo" (1910) and Wayland Drew in *The Wabeno Feast* (1973), and continue to provide material for Canadian writers of fantasy and horror.

The European settlers that began in the sixteenth century to populate what is now Canada brought with them their own oral storytelling traditions, which eventually developed into regional traditions, often heavily imbued with elements of the fantastic, such as the habitant legends of Quebec, supernatural folktales of the Ottawa Valley, tall tales of western Canada, and supernatural stories about northern Canada. In some regions, such as the island of Newfoundland, for instance, these fantastic folk legends continue to survive as important markers of regional identity. Cyrano de Bergerac described the crash landing of an early astronaut in New France in *L'autre monde* (The Other World, 1657–1662), a tale with which Colombo begins *Other Canadas* and which he claims began Canadian fantastic literature; and mythical monsters, ghosts, and other supernatural creatures figured prominently in the written accounts of New France. Not until the nineteenth century, however, did Canadian fantastic fiction begin to be published.

While not strictly a work of fantasy, Richardson's most enduring novel, *Wacousta,* often cited as one of the first Canadian novels, and to a lesser extent its sequel, *The Canadian Brothers* (1840), are both set in fantastic, Gothic landscapes. These tales of the Pontiac uprising of 1763 and the War of 1812 take place along the nightmarish, dreamlike northwest frontier of southwestern Ontario and nearby American states, and they are filled with Gothic touches. Richardson, who claimed to be Canada's first professional novelist, contributes at least a sense of the fantastic possibility of Canada. Philippe-Ignace-François Aubert de Gaspé's *L'influence d'un livre* (The Influence of a Book, 1837), the first French-Canadian novel, combines the imported Gothic tradition with that of the diabolical folktale of Quebec. This work was followed two years later by the publication of a science-fictional satire on life in Lower Canada, as Quebec was then known, "Mon voyage à la lune" (My Voyage to the Moon), by Napoléon Aubin in *Le Fantasque,* a newspaper published by Aubin. Throughout the nineteenth century many French-Canadian writers, such as Joseph-Charles Taché, Louis Fréchette, and Honoré Beaugrand collected, wrote, and published, with varying sophistication, folktales and short stories that dealt with fantastic themes and topics such as witchcraft, ghosts and phantoms, werewolves, and other manifestations of the supernatural. Aurélien Boivin's *Anthologie du conte fantastique québecois au XIXe siècle* (1987) collects many of these tales.

By far the most significant work of Canadian science fiction published in the nineteenth century was James De Mille's posthumously published utopian satire *A Strange Manuscript Found in a Copper Cylinder* (1888), first published as a serial in the American magazine *Harper's Weekly* and later the same year as a book in both the United States and Britain. De Mille was a writer of boys' adventure fiction and a professor at Acadia College and Dalhousie College, and had written *A Strange Manuscript Found in a Copper Cylinder* in the late 1860s. This book, the only one of his many books that is still available at the end of the twentieth century, describes a lost world where the values are the inverse of those of Western culture. It is a complex, sophisticated work, unlike the formulaic fiction he otherwise published, and is described by Ketterer in *Canadian Science Fiction and Fantasy* as "a highly original work. It demonstrates . . . the possibility of a uniquely Canadian species of SF and fantasy that is of literary value." Ketterer argues that in writing *A Strange Manuscript Found in a Copper Cylinder* De Mille "created his own Canadian space," and suggests that De Mille's work should be assigned the seminal status that has been given to Mary Shelley's *Frankenstein* (1818) within world SF.

Appearing a few years earlier than *A Strange Manuscript Found in a Copper Cylinder* was *The Dominion in 1983* (1883), a thirty-page pamphlet published under the pseudonym Ralph Centennius. It describes a utopian Canada produced by technology and the triumph of the Anglo-Saxon, marked by a resistance to American culture and power. Like most science fiction, it fails as an accurate predictor of the future, but it is a fascinating document of the hopes and dreams of late-nineteenth-century English Canada. Jules-Paul Tardivel's *Pour la patrie: Roman du XXe siècle* (1895; translated as *For My Country*, 1975), another utopian vision of a future Canada, was the first significant French-Canadian science-fiction work. It is a vision of an independent Quebec in which Catholicism and Catholic values are dominant, and is notable as one of the first concrete expressions of the dream of Quebec separatism.

During this same period, expatriate Canadians Grant Allen and Robert Barr also published SF works. The Canadian-born Allen was a prolific British writer who published several SF works, most notably the time-travel novel *The British Barbarians* (1895). Barr, born in Glasgow but raised in Ontario, although he too lived in Britain for most of his writing career, published some SF short stories, including the science-fictional "The Doom of London" (1892) and the fantasy "The Glass-Hour" (1899), as well as one fantastic novel, *From Whose Bourne* (1893). Simon Newcomb, usually considered to be American but born and raised in Nova Scotia, also published occasional SF, including the novel *His Wisdom, the Defender* (1900), which describes how the discovery of a limitless source of energy changes the world for the better.

There were also a few other indisputably Canadian SF works published in the late nineteenth century, such as W. H. C. Lawrence's *The Storm of '92: A Grandfather's Tale Told in 1932* (1889), which describes a Canadian victory in a war between Canada and the United States in 1892; and *Tisab Ting; or, The Electrical Kiss* (1896) by Dyjan Fergus (pseudonym of Ida May Ferguson), set in late-twentieth-century Montreal.

The most famous contribution of Canadian writers of this period was the animal story, as developed by Sir Charles G. D. Roberts and Ernest Thompson Seton, which achieved considerable popularity with the publication of Seton's *Wild Animals I Have Known* (1898). Such stories are of only tangential relevance to fantasy and are intended to be realistic, though they do assign human characteristics to animals. Roberts later published one of the most significant works of Canadian SF of the early twentieth century, the prehistoric romance *In the Morning of Time* (1919). That fiction seems to have been an influence on E. J. Pratt's narrative poem "The Great Feud (A Dream of the Pliocene Armageddon)" (1926), which is set in prehistoric Australasia.

During the early twentieth century occasional minor works of SF appeared, including utopias such as Frederick Nelson's *Toronto in 1928 A.D.* (1908), H. Percy Blanchard's *After the Catastrophe: A Romance of the Age to Come* (1909), and the evangelical *Looking Forward: The Strange Experience of the Reverend Fergus McCheyne* (1913). The famous Canadian humorist and McGill University economics professor Stephen Leacock satirized the utopian tradition in *Afternoons in Utopia: Tales of the New Time* (1932), and his 1929 collection *The Iron Man and the Tin Woman with Other Such Futurities* is satirical science fiction. Also of note are the mystical fantasies of L. Adams Beck, who published much of her fiction during the last twelve years of her life, when she lived in Victoria. Blackwood briefly lived in Toronto and Muskoka, a wilderness area to the north of Toronto, and his experience in the Canadian woods provided the background for six short stories, most notably "A Haunted Island" (1906) and "The Wendigo."

The publication of French-Canadian SF in the first few decades of the century was infrequent. Ulric Barthe's *Similia similibus, ou La Guerre au Canada* (Similia similbus, or The War in Canada, 1916) is a thriller about a German invasion of Canada; Ubald Paquin's *La cité dans les fers* (City in Shackles, 1925) tells the story of a failed separatist rebellion; *Marcel Faure* (1922) is an industrial utopia by Jean-Charles Harvey; and Emmanual Desrosier's *La fin de la terre* (The End of the Earth, 1931) is a far-future story of a scientifically advanced world preparing for the apocalypse. All are of little lasting literary interest and had little impact on Quebec literature or science fiction. *Siraf: étranges révélations* (Siraf: Strange Revelations, 1934), by the French-born Alberta writer Georges Bugnet, is a philosophical fantasy that recounts the dialogue between a prairie farmer and extraterrestrial spirits.

With the launching of science fiction and fantasy pulp magazines in the United States in the 1920s, American SF began to establish itself, and what has been called the Golden Age of American SF began in 1939. Canadian writers, many of whom lived in the United States, contributed to these pulps. The most notable of these writers were H. Bedford-Jones, John L. Chapman, Leslie A. Crouch, Chester D. Cuthbert, Francis Flagg, Thomas P. Kelley, Laurence Manning, and Cyril G. Wates. Bedford-Jones was prolific, publishing more than one hundred novels and many short stories in a variety of genres, including science fiction and fantasy, under as many as fifteen pseudonyms. Kelley, a former prizefighter who called himself "King of the Canadian pulp writers," published four fantasy novels in the 1940s and one science fiction novel as a serial in *Weird Tales*. Manning achieved a significant amount of popularity in the 1930s as a result of the sixteen stories he published in the American pulp *Wonder Stories*, and he was best known for a sequence of five stories that were collected as the novel *The Man Who Awoke* (1975), described by Ketterer as the "first pulp exploration of the future of mankind." Manning was one of the more intellectually sophisticated of the pulp writers of this period.

None of these writers had any lasting impact on speculative fiction, however, with the exception of A. E. van Vogt, by far the most popular and important Canadian SF writer in the first half of the twentieth century. Although the Winnipeg-born writer moved to the United States in 1944, he had already made a significant impact in the science-fiction pulps by that time, beginning with the publication of "Black Destroyer" in the July 1939 issue of *Astounding Science-Fiction,* one of the most important American pulps. He wrote his best and most famous novel, *Slan*, first published as a serial in 1940 and later as a book in 1946, while living near Ottawa, and before moving to the United States he published approximately thirty-four short stories, which formed the basis for many of his later books. His Winnipeg-born wife, E. Mayne Hull, also published some SF, often in collaboration with van Vogt.

During World War II the importation of American and British pulp magazines was restricted, and English-Canadian magazines began to fill the void. The longest-running and most significant, *Uncanny Tales*, which published both science fiction and fantasy, appeared between November 1940 and September/October 1943. Its first six issues featured original material, but it then began to rely on reprinting stories from the American pulps, at times even plagiarizing them. Using several different pseudonyms, Kelley was a frequent contributor to *Uncanny Tales,* even writing all of the first issue. Notably, the first piece of criticism on Canadian SF appeared in the December 1942 issue: American editor and publisher Donald A. Wollheim's "Whither Canadian Fantasy?" argued that Canadian pulp SF did not exist, "it was simply an indetectable segment of American pulp writing edited and directed primarily from New York City." Despite this lack, Wollheim stated that the possibility and potential subject matter of a distinctly Canadian SF did exist but was yet to be exploited. These magazines were short-lived, however, and once the restrictions were eased there was no consistent market for English-Canadian SF until the 1980s, although some mainstream venues, such as the *Star Weekly,* the weekend supplement of the *Toronto Star,* occasionally published SF. The French-language pulp magazines that were widely available throughout Quebec from 1945 to 1970 also published occasional SF stories. The first wholly SF pulp was *Les aventures futuristes de deux savants canadiens français* (The Futuristic Adventures of Two French-Canadian Scientists), an eight-issue serial published in 1949. Similar pulp serials continued to be widely read in Quebec for the next two decades.

Beginning in the late 1930s, SF fanzines—fan-produced newsletters—appeared in Canada. The most significant of these was the Toronto-based *Canadian Fandom*, which was published from 1943 to 1958 and attempted to cover the SF scene across Canada. Ketterer describes it as "*the* fanzine of record for this period." The longest-running fanzine was *Light,* published by Leslie A. Crouch in Parry Sound, Ontario, from the late 1930s to 1961.

During this period a few significant works of Canadian SF were produced, most notably Howard O'Hagan's *Tay John* (1939), Frederick Philip Grove's *Consider Her Ways* (1947), and Yves Thériault's *Contes pour un homme seul* (Tales for a Man Alone, 1944). Not strictly fantastic, and certainly not genre fantasy, *Tay John* utilizes a Tsimshian native myth as the basis for its story, which tells of a half-breed messiah's struggles with white civilization. Tay John is a clearly mythic character, and the book is clearly mythic in structure. The German-born Grove, one of the major Canadian literary figures of the first half of the twentieth century, originally wrote *Consider Her Ways* in the 1930s and conceived of it much earlier, although it was only published near the end of his life. This description of an ant society and its march across North America serves as a complex satire on human society, and the importance of the novel within the Canadian SF tradition has been recognized by its republication in 2001 by the Canadian SF publisher Bakka Books, an imprint of Stone Fox Publishing. Thériault's book is a collection of weird and fantastic tales, which Jean-Louis Trudel cites in *The Encyclopedia of Fantasy* (1997) as marking the transition from traditional to modern fantasy in French-Canadian writing. Many of Thériault's later books, such as *La vendeur d'étoiles et autres contes* (The Seller of Stars and Other Tales, 1961), also suggest the supernatural.

Although there were several other books published during the 1940s with varying degrees of SF content, few if any of their authors could truly be considered SF writers, as they were not primarily situated within the genres of science fiction or fantasy. The most interesting of these were *The Sun and the Moon* (1944) by English-born Montreal poet P. K. Page, published under the pseudonym of Judith Cape and republished under her own name in a 1974 collection of fantastic fiction titled *The Sun and the Moon and Other Fictions;* British thriller writer, biographer, and politician John Buchan's *Sick Heart River* (1941), a metaphysical Arctic adventure that reflected the author's five-year stay in Canada as governor-general; *Erres boréales* (Boreal Wanderings, 1944) by Armand Grenier (under the pseudonym of Florent Laurin), which depicts a technologically advanced French society in the north; and Jean Berthos's *Eutopia* (1946), a vision of Quebec as a theocratic utopia. The World Science Fiction Convention, the first to be held in Canada, was held in Toronto in 1948, a notable year for Canadian SF.

During the 1950s many new American, and to a lesser extent British, SF writers were introduced, but it was a relatively bleak period for Canadian SF. The most notable works of this period include *Le Fou de L'Île* (1958; translated as *The Madman, the Kite and the Island,* 1976) by Félix Leclerc, about the arrival of a Christlike mysterious stranger on an island, his persecution, and his mysterious disappearance; and *The Pyx* (1959) by John Buell, later adapted for a 1973 motion picture. The well-known mainstream Canadian writer Hugh MacLennan published two SF stories in the 1950s: the dystopian "The Finding of the Way" (1955), which portrays a computer-controlled society, and "Remembrance Day, 2010 A.D." (1957), which describes a Russian-American battle over the moon. MacLennan later published his only SF novel, *Voices in Time* (1980), which describes a post-nuclear-holocaust Montreal. Also during the 1950s another expatriate, Dickson, who had left Canada at the age of thirteen, launched a prolific and successful career as a writer of SF. He is primarily known for his Childe Cycle, begun with the serial publication of *Dorsai!* in 1959; critics such as Ketterer have sought to identify the Canadian characteristics of his intellectually ambitious work.

Occasional works of SF interest continued to be published in the 1960s, a time when SF was gaining increased popularity with the counterculture success of books such as Robert A. Heinlein's *Stranger in a Strange Land* (1961), Frank Herbert's *Dune* (1965), and J. R. R. Tolkien's *The Lord of the Rings* (1954–1955). Speculative fiction was also becoming increasingly sophisticated and ambitious with the arrival of the British and American New Waves and such writers as J. G. Ballard, Brian W. Aldiss, Michael Moorcock, Norman Spinrad, Thomas M. Disch, Ursula K. Le Guin, and Samuel R. Delany. Yet, these dramatic changes in SF—articulated in the British magazine *New Worlds* under the editorship of Moorcock and in the *Dangerous Visions* anthology (1967) edited by the successful American SF writer Harlan Ellison—had little impact on Canadian SF. In fact, there was still no real SF scene in Canada during this time, prompting Gotlieb, a well-known and admired poet who became the foremost Canadian SF writer with the publication of *Sunburst* (1964), to describe herself in 1970 as "a Canadian poet and American science fiction writer." She published her poetry in Canada, but her science fiction in the United States. Gotlieb's first SF story, "A Grain of Manhood," was published in *Fantastic* in September 1959, and she achieved prominence with the publication of *Sunburst,* which tells the story of a group of child mutants after a nuclear accident. As in much of her fiction, telepathy is an important element. Gotlieb brought a poetic sensibility and an interest in characterization to her science fiction. She followed *Sunburst* with some well-received short fiction and novels, such as *O Master Caliban!* (1976).

Until the 1970s, Gotlieb remained the only Canadian to have an international readership as an SF writer. In 1968 Judith Merril, the American anthologist, editor, and occasional writer, moved to Toronto. She played a central role in the emergence of English-Canadian SF in the next two decades, as an editor and a promoter of Canadian SF. In addition, the collection of more than five thousand books and magazines that she brought with her to Canada formed the basis for the Spaced Out Library, initially established at Rochdale College in Toronto, where she taught, and later affiliated with the Toronto Public Library. Now known as the Merril Collection of Science Fiction, Speculation, and Fantasy, it is a valuable resource with extensive holdings of SF books and magazines; in fact, it is the largest such public library collection in the English-speaking world.

Other works of interest include Robert Green's *The Great Leap Backward* (1968), a dystopian novel set in a near-future Toronto. *Killing Ground: The Canadian Civil War* (1968), by Ellis Portal (pseudonym of Bruce Powe), is one of several SF works dealing with the potential threat of Quebec separation. Powe later published another SF work under his own name, *The Last Days of the American Empire* (1974), dealing with the threat of a rebellion by the world's underprivileged. In the 1960s W. E. Dan Ross launched a career as possibly Canada's most prolific writer, publishing 342 Gothic romances under various pseudonyms between 1963 and 1978, some of them with fantastic elements, particularly the vampire novels he published as Marilyn Ross. There were some other notable Canadian fantasies published in the 1960s: Pierre Berton, better known as a popular historian, published a children's fantasy, *The Secret World of Og,* in 1961; the medieval scholar Constance Hieatt wrote a series of children's books retelling Arthurian legends, beginning with *Sir Gawain and the Green Knight* (1967); and Ruth Nichols published the first of her epic young-adult fantasies, *A Walk out of the Wood* (1969).

French Canada could still boast no SF writers of note in the 1960s, although several writers produced books dealing with the future and/or the fantastic. Thériault, in *Si la bombe m'était contée* (If the Bomb Could Tell Me, 1962), published postdisaster stories, and Jean Tétreau wrote the post-nuclear-disaster novel *Les nomades* (The Nomads, 1967) and a collection of fantastic tales, *Volupté de l'amour et de la mort* (Delights of Love and Death, 1969). The playwright and novelist Michel Tremblay began his career as a fantastic writer, with *Contes pour buveurs attardés* (1966; translated as *Stories for Late-Night Drinkers,* 1977), a collection of Gothic tales, and the 1969 SF novel *La cité dans l'oeuf* (The City in the Egg). Jacques Ferron's *Contes* (1968) collects several short fictions influenced by Quebec folklore and featuring supernatural and fantastic elements. His novels, such as *Papa Boss* (1966) and *L'amélanchier* (1970; translated as *The Juneberry Tree,* 1975), combine fantasy with radical politics.

The late 1960s and early 1970s were a particularly important period for Canadian SF, as several writers who later became some of Canada's most popular and important SF figures immigrated to Canada then. In addition to Merril, these include Gibson, Robinson, Michael G. Coney, and Élisabeth Vonarburg, though some did not start their writing careers until later. The British-born Coney was already a published writer by the time he arrived in Canada in 1973 at the age of forty-one, eventually winning the British Science Fiction Award for *Brontomek!* (1976). One of the most prolific of Canadian SF writers, although he was not a full-time writer for much of his career as he worked as a management specialist for the British Columbia Forestry Service, he has published both science-fiction and fantasy novels. Robinson, a native of New York City, arrived in Canada the same year as Coney, moving to Nova Scotia to begin a career as a freelance writer. He quickly became a popular SF writer through the tall tales later collected in *Callahan's Crosstime Saloon* (1977) and as a result of his entertaining reviews in such SF magazines as *Galaxy* and *Analog*. He won the John W. Campbell Award for best new SF writer in 1974, and was chosen as best SF critic in 1977 by *Locus*. He has also won three Hugo Awards, winning in 1977 for "By Any Other Name," part of his first novel *Telempath* (1976), and in 1983 for "Melancholy Elephants." In 1978 "Stardance," written with his wife, Jeanne Robinson, received both the fan-selected Hugo and the writer-chosen Nebula awards. Although his later work has not received as much acclaim, he remains a popular writer and is a columnist for the national newspaper *The Globe and Mail*. His *Mindkiller* (1983) and its sequel, *Time Pressure* (1987), are partly set in Nova Scotia.

Mainstream writers published important SF books in the 1970s. Irish-born writer Brian Moore, who had spent a decade in Canada before moving to California, published a science-fiction novel dealing with a future Catholic church, *Catholics* (1972), as well as the fantastic novels *Fergus* (1970), the Governor-General's Award–winning *The Great Victorian Collection* (1975), *The Mangan Inheritance* (1979), and *Cold Heaven* (1983). The poet Gwendolyn MacEwen made distinctive contributions to SF in both poetry and prose: *The Armies of the Moon* (1972), which won the A. J. M. Smith Award, is an excellent collection of fantastic poetry, and *Noman* (1972) and its sequel, *Noman's Land* (1985), are linked collections of fantastic fables. Matt Cohen published SF-related works, including the science-fictional *The Colours of War* (1977), the Arthurian-influenced *Too Bad Galahad* (1972), and several fantasy stories. One of Canada's most important contributors to SF has been motion-picture director David Cronenberg. He began making movies, many of them with SF elements, in the late 1960s, and came to prominence in the 1970s and 1980s with SF movies such as *Rabid* (1976), *The Brood* (1979), *Scanners* (1980), and *Videodrome* (1982).

Other significant works included Drew's *The Wabeno Feast,* a powerful mix of science fiction and fantasy; H. A. Hargreaves's *North by 2000* (1975), notable primarily for being subtitled *Canadian Science Fiction;* William Weintraub's satirically dystopian take on Quebec separation, *The Underdogs* (1979); Ian Adams's near-future thriller *The Trudeau Papers* (1971); and William C. Heine's apocalyptic *The Last Canadian* (1974). Richard Rohmer, formerly a general in the Canadian military, published best-selling near-future thrillers dealing with Canadian themes and settings, beginning with *Ultimatum* (1973). American-born McGill University mathematics professor Donald Kingsbury, who had published an SF story in 1952, returned to publishing SF stories in the late 1970s, receiving Hugo nominations for "The Moon Goddess and the Sun" (1980) and the ambitious *Courtship Rite* (1982). The British-born Edward Llewellyn began publishing SF novels with the well-regarded *The Douglas Convolution* in 1979. American-born Crawford Kilian, an English professor in British Columbia, published his first novel, *The Empire of Time*, in 1978, and had earlier adapted De Mille's *A Strange Manuscript Found in a Copper Cylinder* as a radio play (1972).

British-born Monica Hughes began a prolific and successful career as a writer of SF for young adults with *Crisis on Conshelf Ten* (1975); her most famous work is her Isis trilogy, which began with *The Keeper of the Isis Light* (1980). Mordecai Richler published the best-selling children's fantasy *Jacob Two-Two Meets the Hooded Fang* (1975), later adapted as a motion picture (1979), and Margaret Laurence published the children's fantasy *Jason's Quest* (1970) and the children's time-travel story *The Olden Days Coat* (1979).

The nadir of English-Canadian SF during the 1970s was probably *The Starlost*, a television series produced for CTV, Canada's private English-language television network. Although it was created by Ellison, who had written episodes for *The Outer Limits* and *Star Trek* among other American television shows, and featured the talents of special-effects master and director Douglas Trumbull and SF writer Ben Bova, it was a disaster, lasting eighteen episodes. Ellison was so disgusted with the adaptation of his vision and scripts that he repudiated it, using the name Cordwainer Bird in the credits. Bova later wrote a hilarious novel, *The Starcrossed* (1975), based on his experiences with this project.

In the 1970s there was a dramatic increase in the amount of English-Canadian SF being published. According to Ketterer's count in *Canadian Science Fiction and Fantasy*, only 9 adult SF books were published by English-Canadian authors in the 1960s; this figure rose to 120 in the 1970s and early 1980s. Yet, despite this increase in production, there was still little sense that there was a tradition. This feeling changed with the 1979 publication of *Other Canadas*, edited by Colombo, which collected SF written by Canadians and about Canada, as well as essays on Canadian SF by Ketterer and Atwood. The anthology proves, as Colombo writes in his preface, "that there is a Canadian science fiction and fantasy, and that it is worth a serious reader's attention." In the two decades following the appearance of this work, it was no longer necessary for such a claim to be proven.

The 1970s were an important decade for French-Canadian SF as well, with, according to Ketterer, an increase from twelve adult SF books in the 1960s to fifty in the 1970s and early 1980s. Even more significant than this increase in publishing activity was the establishment by college professor Norbert Spehner of the fanzine *Requiem,* a venue for the publication of what became known as Quebec SF, or SFQ, as well as essays and reviews. It later changed its name to *Solaris* and remained, along with *imagine . . . ,* established in 1979, a central force for the development and continuing existence of the Quebec SF community. Many of the leading figures in Quebec SF have been involved with one or both of these magazines.

As in English Canada, there were many important French-Canadian SF works published during the decade, including Anne Hébert's *Les enfants du sabbat* (1975; translated as *Children of the Black Sabbath,* 1977), dealing with witchcraft and a convent. She later published a vampire novella, *Héloïse* (1980). The award-winning Acadian writer Antonine Maillet published a Governor-General's Award–winning fantasy, *Don l'Orignal* (1972; translated as *The Tale of Don l'Orignal,* 1978), that reflects her interest in Acadian folklore. Jacques Benoit followed up his surrealist novel of a primitive world, *Jos Carbone* (1967), with a parody of science fiction, *Patience et Firlipon* (1970), and a sophisticated genre fantasy set in an imaginary city, *Les princes* (1973). The well-known novelist Jacques Godbout published *L'Îsle au dragon* (1976; translated as *Dragon Island,* 1978), in which a dragon helps to save a St. Lawrence River island from an American capitalist. Jacques Brossard, a law professor and diplomat, published a sophisticated collection of political, dreamlike SF stories, *Le Métamorfaux* (The Metamorfalsis, 1974). He later published the multivolume *L'oiseau de feu* (The Firebird), the first volume of which appeared in 1989. Another writer to appear in the 1970s was Esther Rochon, who had already been publishing short fiction since the mid 1960s. Her first novel, *En hommage aux arraignées* (In Praise of Spiders), was published in 1974, and she developed into one of the most important Quebec SF writers by the mid 1980s. Louky Bersianik's *L'Euguélionne* (1976; translated as *The Euguelionne,* 1981) is a powerful feminist critique of patriarchy and the sexism of the French language, and it has received a great deal of attention by feminist scholars. Daniel Sernine (the pen name of Alain Lortie) initiated the most prolific career in Quebec SF with two collections of fantastic short stories in 1979: *Les contes de l'ombre* (Tales from the Shadows) and *Légendes du vieux manoir* (Legends from the Old Manor). A more conventional SF writer than many of his contemporaries, Sernine went on to publish more than thirty books in the next two decades. Monique Corriveau's *Compagnons du soleil* (Companions of the Sun, 1976) is an ambitious trilogy describing an apparently utopian society and the revolution that eventually attempts to transform it.

Introduction

The 1980s was the decade in which Canadian SF finally had a global impact on the SF genre; possibly even more important was that during the 1980s, the domestic institutions necessary to promote and maintain an SF community developed. *Solaris* and *imagine . . .* continued to publish many of the leading figures of Quebec SF. The Merril-edited *Tesseracts* anthology (1985) inaugurated a successful series of anthologies devoted to Canadian SF, providing an important new market for Canadian writers; to date there have been eight volumes. The success of *Tesseracts* and its sequels was followed by the establishment of an English-language SF magazine, the Edmonton-based *On Spec*. Press Porcépic began publishing the *Tesseract* anthologies in 1985, and in 1988 established the Tesseract imprint. Porcépic changed its name to Beach Holme in 1991, but continued publishing SF under the imprint Tesseract Books. In 1994 the Tesseract Books imprint was bought by a group of writers and editors led by Candas Jane Dorsey, who brought it to Edmonton to become an independent imprint of the already-existing Books Collective. Also important was the establishment of awards. The first of the Canadian Science Fiction and Fantasy Awards, known as Caspers, was given to A. E. van Vogt in 1980. Initially instituted as lifetime achievement awards, they developed into full-fledged annual, bilingual awards, and the name was eventually changed to the Aurora Award. The Prix Boréal was established the same year for Quebec SF, and the Grand Prix de la science-fiction et du fantastique québécois was established in 1984. In 1985 *L'année de la science-fiction et du fantastique québécois*, an annual review of Quebec SF, began publication. Finally, in 1989 the national, bilingual Speculative Writers Association of Canada was founded; its name was later changed to SF Canada.

All this institution building would have been wasted without talented writers. In *Canadian Science Fiction and Fantasy* Ketterer selects 1984 as the year that "everything changed," the year that Canadian SF achieved international and domestic recognition. That year American-born Vancouver writer Gibson published the spectacularly successful and influential cyberpunk novel *Neuromancer*. Gibson went on to become one of the best-known SF writers of the late twentieth century, and in addition to significant advances received a degree of attention from literary scholars that was previously unheard-of for an SF writer. Timothy Findley's fantastic retelling of the Flood, *Not Wanted on the Voyage* (1984), also received international commercial and critical success. Guy Gavriel Kay appeared on the fantasy scene with his Tolkienesque *The Fionavar Tapestry* (1984–1986) and later turned to writing interesting hybrids of fantasy and alternate history, with such critically and commercially successful books as *Tigana* (1990) and *The Lions of Al-Rassan* (1995). The Dutch-born Ottawa writer Charles de Lint began a prolific and successful career as a writer of slightly offbeat genre fantasy with two 1984 novels: *The Riddle of the Wren* and *Moonheart*. The American-born Robert Charles Wilson also achieved considerable success with *A Hidden Place* (1986) and the novels that followed throughout the 1980s and 1990s. Atwood's dystopian *The Handmaid's Tale* (1985) won major awards and became an international best-seller, and remains one of her most popular novels.

Other notable 1980s Canadian SF publications included Carleton University English professor Tom Henighan's interesting mix of Canadian setting and Viking mythology, *The Well of Time* (1988); Henighan also hosted a science-fiction program for the national television network CTV, as well as teaching courses on science fiction. Dave Duncan began a prolific career as a genre fantasy and science-fiction writer with *Shadow* (1987) and *A Rose Red City* (1987). Tanya Huff published *Child of the Grove* (1988), the first of many fantasy novels, and she later achieved renown as a writer of Toronto-set vampire novels, beginning with *Blood Price* (1991). The Alsatian-born S. M. Stirling published *Snowbrother* (1985) and went on to become a prolific writer of alternate histories and postapocalypse adventures. Tim Wynne-Jones, an already established writer, ventured into fantasy with *Fastyngange* (1988). Dorsey made a name for herself as one of the most promising Canadian SF writers with her first collection, *Machine Sex . . . and Other Stories* (1988). Terence M. Green's *The Woman Who is the Midnight Wind* (1987) collected stories he had published in major American magazines. The expatriate Canadian writer Geoff Ryman, an English resident, published his first novel, *The Warrior Who Carried Life,* in 1985. He went on to publish demanding and sophisticated SF novels such as the award-winning *The Child Garden* (1989) and *Was* (1992). Andrew Weiner, who had been producing short fiction since 1972, finally published his first novel, *Station Gehenna,* in 1987. Robertson Davies, many of whose best-selling and critically acclaimed novels have fantastic elements, won the World Fantasy Award for his collection of ghost stories, *High Spirits* (1983). W. P. Kinsella's baseball fantasy *Shoeless Joe* (1982) became one of the best-known works of Canadian speculative fiction, particularly after it was adapted as the movie *Field of Dreams* (1989).

Although Quebec SF had already begun to establish itself in the 1970s, the 1980s was also an important decade in its development, though it did not receive the same international recognition as English-Canadian SF. Most significantly, beginning in 1980 with the collection *L'oeil de la nuit* (The Eye of Night), Vonarburg has published a series of exceptional novels and stories, many of which have received recognition outside of Quebec. She has received the widest distribution of any French writer in English, as many of her stories and novels have been translated into English. In particular, *Le silence de la cité* (1981; translated as *The Silent City,* 1988), *Chroniques du Pays des Mères* (1992; translated as *In the Mother's Land,* 1992), and *Les voyageurs malgré eux* (1994; translated as *Reluctant Voyagers,* 1995) have received mass-market publication in the United States. She has also won several awards, including both the Grand Prix and the Aurora Award. Rochon solidified her reputation with award-winning novels such as *L'Épuisement du Soleil* (The Draining of the Sun, 1985) and *Coquillage* (1986; translated as *The Shell,* 1990). Both writers began to receive extensive academic attention, for SF writers at least, particularly by feminist scholars.

Jean-Pierre April was another notable new writer, first publishing a collection titled *La machine à explorer la fiction* (The Fiction Machine) in 1980. Like Philip K. Dick, with whom he is often compared, April plays with the thin line between reality and illusion, in these stories and subsequent novels. Francine Pelletier began publishing juvenile SF with *Le rendez-vous du desert* (The Desert Meeting, 1987). Michel Bélil won the Prix Boréal for his first collection of fantastic fiction, *Déménagement* (Removal, 1981), and for his first novel, *Greenwich* (1981), a horror story. René Beaulieu's collection *Légendes de Virnie* (Legends of Virnie, 1981) also won a Prix Boréal. Pierre Billon's *L'enfant du cinquième nord* (Child of the Fifth North, 1982) received the prestigious Grand Prix de la SF française, although he does not consider himself to be an SF writer.

The 1990s were a period of consolidation, with many of the writers that have already been mentioned continuing to make significant contributions to SF, and in some cases achieving increasing recognition. The early 1990s, for instance, brought the American publication of the English translations of three Vonarburg novels. The institutions—awards, magazines, and organizations—continued to develop, and interactions between French- and English-language writers and readers increased. The *Tesseracts* anthologies published some French-language writers in translation and devoted an entire volume, *Tesseracts⁹*, edited by Vonarburg and Jane Brierly (1996), to English translations of Quebec SF, allowing English-Canadian readers to become more familiar with French-language SF. As well, Canadian SF as such gained increasing exposure in the United States with the publication of the 1994 anthology *Northern Stars,* edited by American David G. Hartwell and Glenn Grant, which presented some of the best Canadian SF stories yet printed. It was followed by a 1999 sequel, *Northern Suns,* also edited by Hartwell and Grant.

Canadian SF also received increasing academic study as a worthwhile field of inquiry. While there had been important Canadian-based scholars of SF since the 1970s, most notably Darko Suvin, and the journal *Science-Fiction Studies* had been based in Montreal from 1979 to 1991, there had only been a few articles on Canadian SF until the 1990s. Concordia University English professor and well-known SF critic Ketterer published *Canadian Science Fiction and Fantasy* in 1992 and had earlier taught the first graduate seminar on the subject, at Concordia. The book is a comprehensive survey of Canadian SF from its origins in the nineteenth century. While his comments are more descriptive than analytical, Ketterer does attempt to make some generalizations about the differences between Canadian and American SF. Canadian SF, he argues, is often concerned with isolation and survival; is less optimistic about the virtues of technology; is often set against a northern, wilderness backdrop; is more interested in characterization; and is more concerned with literary quality than is American SF. Dorsey and others make similar claims in the prefaces and afterwords of the *Tesseracts* anthologies, and Dorsey's afterword to *Tesseracts³* (1990) has become a key critical statement on Canadian SF since its republication in *Northern Stars*. Grant, in his foreword to *Northern Stars,* repeats the claims that Canadian SF is more literary and that the boundaries between science fiction and fantasy, as well as genre fiction and literary fiction, are less solid for Canadian writers. Vonarburg makes similar claims in her foreword to *Tesseracts⁹*, adding that the language difference of Quebec SF writers allows them to develop "an original perspective, a voice that is their own—at the price of not making themselves heard much beyond their own borders." Quebec SF writers are privileged because they inhabit a "revolving door through which French-language and English-language science fiction writing can pass in both directions." Quebec SF thus represents the intertwining of English-language SF and French-language literary traditions.

SF has been a topic of academic discussion for Francophone scholars since at least 1979. Michel Lord, a professor at Laval University, has frequently published articles on Quebec SF in a variety of venues and cofounded the Groupe de recherche interdisciplinaire sur les littératures fantastique dans l'imaginaire québécois. Among other projects, this group has compiled an annotated bibliography of Quebec SF. Jean-Louis Trudel has been doing intensive research into the history of SF in Quebec pulp magazines. Quebec SF has been the subject of academic conference papers and even some dissertations, while there have also been academic conference papers and panels on Canadian SF at the meetings of such organizations as the Association for

Canadian and Quebec Literatures and the Modern Language Association, although there is still little real engagement by Canadian literature scholars with Canadian SF.

The first Academic Conference on Canadian Science Fiction and Fantasy was held in Toronto in 1996, and it has been followed by two more, with another conference on Canadian SF held in Ottawa in May 2001. The proceedings of the second conference have been published as *Perspectives on the Canadian Fantastic* (1998), edited by Allan Weiss, and the Spring 2001 issue of the British science-fiction journal *Foundation* focused on Canadian SF. In 1995 the National Library of Canada put together an exhibit titled "Out of This World," devoted to Canadian science fiction and fantasy. The book that accompanied the exhibit, *Out of This World* (1995), compiled by Andrea Paradis and also published in a French-language edition, includes essays by many of the most prominent Canadian SF writers of the 1990s, including Dorsey, Vonarburg, and Trudel. Edo van Belkom's *Northern Dreamers: Interviews with Famous Science Fiction, Fantasy, and Horror Writers* (1998) is another valuable resource for those interested in Canadian SF. The TVOntario show *Prisoners of Gravity*, hosted by Rick Green, was devoted to the discussion of SF and featured interviews with many SF writers, including some Canadian ones.

While the 1990s may have been a period of consolidation, some important new writers have emerged. *Golden Fleece* (1990) was the first novel by Robert J. Sawyer, who became the most successful Canadian writer within the genre. His books, such as the Nebula Award–winning *The Terminal Experiment* (1995), have been well reviewed and extremely popular throughout the world. He has won many awards and been nominated for the Hugo Award six years in a row. In addition, he was influential in beginning the Canadian branch of the Science Fiction and Fantasy Writers of America (SFWA) and has served as its president, which indicates the level of recognition he has achieved among SF writers. He has also been an active promoter of Canadian SF, contributing an entry on the subject to the second edition of *The Canadian Encyclopedia* (1988) and posting articles on the subject on his website. Nalo Hopkinson's *Brown Girl in the Ring* (1998), which combines Caribbean spirituality with a science-fictional Toronto setting, won awards and established Hopkinson as an important voice within Canadian SF. Her follow-up, *Midnight Robber* (2000), has been equally well received. British-born Anthony Swithin's medieval fantasy *Princes of Sandastre* (1990) began his *Perilous Quest for Lyonesse* series; Sean Russell's *The Initiate Brother* (1991) and Michelle Sagara West's *Into the Dark Lands* (1991) were significant novels by new writers; and Sean Stewart published several well-received fantasy and science-fiction novels, including *Nobody's Son* (1993) and *Resurrection Man* (1995). Dorsey's *Black Wine* (1997), a complex examination of gender issues, received great acclaim and won major awards. Other notable publications included Wilson's award-winning *Mysterium* (1994), Green's *Shadow of Ashland* (1996), and Nancy Baker's vampire novel *The Night Inside* (1993).

Annick Perrot-Bishop's *Les maisons de cristal* (The Crystal Houses, 1990) is an interesting collection of fantasy stories. Joël Champetier, an important promoter of Quebec SF, published the Aurora Award–winning dark fantasy *La Mémoire du lac* (The Lake's Memory, 1994). In addition to his research into the history of pulp SF in French Canada, Trudel has published many juvenile SF works as well as adult SF novels such as *Le Ressuscité de l'Atlantide* (Risen from Atlantis, 1994), which describes a French-speaking colony on Mars, and stories, including the occasional story in English. Stanley Péan uses Haitian folklore in rewriting Edgar Allan Poe in *Le tumulte de mon sang* (The Tumult of My Blood, 1991). Yves Meynard has published widely in French throughout the 1990s, with novels such as the Prix Boréal and Aurora Award–winning *La rose du désert* (The Desert Rose, 1995) and stories, as well as an English-language fantasy novel, *The Book of Knights* (1998), which received praise from Le Guin. Other significant works included Anne Legault's *Récits de Médilhaut* (Stories of Medilhaut, 1994), Alain Bergeron's *Corps machines et rêves d'anges* (Machine Bodies and Angel Dreams, 1997), Jean-Pierre Guillet's *L'Odyssée du Pénélope* (Penelope's Odyssey, 1997), and Pelletier's *Nelle de Vilvèq* (1997).

There are many authors and books that have had to be left out of this introduction, and many authors that just could not be included in this book. Whom to include in a volume such as this one, of course, is always a dilemma. That such a dilemma would have been nearly unimaginable only one or two decades ago is an exciting sign of the rapid development of Canadian SF from the occasional isolated story or novel, or sometimes writer, to a community and a tradition. When the Canadian Science Fiction and Fantasy Awards were instituted in the early 1980s, there were only enough writers to allow it to be awarded every second year; but in July 2001, two Canadian writers were on the shortlist for the Hugo Award, the most prominent SF award. While, according to some at least, Canadian SF may in general be pessimistic about the future, one can only have great expectations of the work and writers that will appear in the years to come. Canadian SF now provides an important contribution to the genres of science fiction and fantasy, and also an important component of Canadian literature, one that must be considered by Canadian literature scholars. In fact, the rapid development of Canadian SF over the past few decades is one of the most exciting developments within Canadian literature.

–Douglas Ivison

Acknowledgments

This book was produced by Bruccoli Clark Layman, Inc. Karen L. Rood is senior editor. Tracy Simmons Bitonti was the in-house editor. She was assisted by Nikki La Rocque, Bland Lawson, and Angela Shaw-Thornburg.

Production manager is Philip B. Dematteis.

Administrative support was provided by Ann M. Cheschi, Amber L. Coker, and Angi Pleasant.

Accountant is Ann-Marie Holland.

Copyediting supervisor is Sally R. Evans. The copyediting staff includes Phyllis A. Avant, Brenda Carol Blanton, Worthy B. Evans, Melissa D. Hinton, Charles Loughlin, William Tobias Mathes, Rebecca Mayo, Nancy E. Smith, and Elizabeth Jo Ann Sumner. Freelance copyeditors are Brenda Cabra and Thom Harman.

Editorial associates are Michael S. Allen, Michael S. Martin, and Pamela A. Warren.

Database manager is José A. Juarez.

Layout and graphics supervisor is Janet E. Hill. The graphics staff includes Karla Corley Brown and Zoe R. Cook.

Office manager is Kathy Lawler Merlette.

Photography supervisor is Paul Talbot. Photography editor is Scott Nemzek.

Digital photographic copy work was performed by Joseph M. Bruccoli.

The SGML staff includes Frank Graham, Linda Dalton Mullinax, Jason Paddock, and Alex Snead.

Systems manager is Marie L. Parker.

Typesetting supervisor is Kathleen M. Flanagan. The typesetting staff includes Jaime All, Patricia Marie Flanagan, Mark J. McEwan, and Pamela D. Norton. Freelance typesetter is Wanda Adams.

Walter W. Ross did library research. He was assisted by Jaime All and the following librarians at the Thomas Cooper Library of the University of South Carolina: circulation department head Tucker Taylor; reference department head Virginia W. Weathers; Brette Barclay, Marilee Birchfield, Paul Cammarata, Gary Geer, Michael Macan, Tom Marcil, Rose Marshall, and Sharon Verba; interlibrary loan department head John Brunswick; and interlibrary loan staff Robert Arndt, Hayden Battle, Barry Bull, Jo Cottingham, Marna Hostetler, Marieum McClary, Erika Peake, and Nelson Rivera.

Dictionary of Literary Biography® • Volume Two Hundred Fifty-One

Canadian Fantasy and Science-Fiction Writers

Dictionary of Literary Biography

Jean-Pierre April
(16 July 1948 –   )

Kathleen Kellett-Betsos
Ryerson Polytechnic University

BOOKS: *La Machine à explorer la fiction* (Longueuil, Quebec: Le Préambule, 1980);

TéléToTaliTé (Ville LaSalle: Hurtubise HMH, 1984);

Le Nord électrique (Longueuil, Quebec: Le Préambule, 1986);

Berlin-Bangkok (Montreal: Editions Logiques, 1989); revised edition (Paris: Editions J'ai lu, 1993);

Chocs baroques: Anthologie de nouvelles de science-fiction (Saint-Laurent: BQ, 1991);

N'ajustez pas vos hallucinettes (Montreal: Editions Québec/Amérique, 1991);

Les Voyages thanatologiques de Yan Malter (Montreal: Editions Québec/Amérique, 1995).

OTHER: "L'Avaleuse d'oiseaux," in *Dix contes et nouvelles fantastiques par dix auteurs québécois,* by April and others (Montreal: Les Quinze, 1983), pp. 13–30; republished in *Archipel,* volume 1, edited by Laurent Laplante and others (Sainte-Foy, Quebec: Editions le Griffon d'argile, 1989), pp. 1–20;

"Le Fantôme du Forum," in *Les Années-lumière,* edited by Jean-Marc Gouanvic (Montreal: VLB Editeur, 1983), pp. 31–53;

"Chronostop," in *Espaces imaginaires I,* edited by Gouanvic and Stéphane Nicot (Montreal: Les Imaginoïdes, 1983), pp. 105–125;

"Coma-123, automatexte," in *Dix nouvelles de science-fiction québécoise* (Montreal: Les Quinze, 1985), pp. 17–44;

"La Survie en rose," in *Chroniques d'amour monstre,* edited by Alain Garguir (Lille, France: Andromède, 1985), pp. 76–97; abridged version in *Secrets . . . ,* by April, Hélène Rioux, and Diane-Monique Daviau, read by Catherine Bégin, audiocassette

Jean-Pierre April

and text (Montreal: La Littérature de l'oreille, 1987), pp. 19–32;

"Impressions de Thaï Deng," in *Espaces imaginaires III,* edited by Gouanvic and Nicot (Trois-Rivières, Quebec: Les Imaginoïdes, 1985), pp. 125–159; republished in *SF: Dix années de science-fiction québécoise,* edited by Gouanvic (Montreal: Logiques, 1988), pp. 11–63;

"La Machine à explorer la fiction," in *Univers 1985* (Paris: Editions J'ai lu, 1985), pp. 50–87;

"Il pleut des astronefs," in *Univers 1986* (Paris: Editions J'ai lu, 1985), pp. 127–144;

"Mort et télévie de Jacob Miro," in *Des nouvelles du Québec* (Montreal: Valmont éditeur, 1986), pp. 19–27; republished in *Anthologie de la science-fiction québécoise contemporaine,* edited by Michel Lord (Montreal: Bibliothèque québécoise, 1988), pp. 27–38; republished in *Les Enfants d'Enéïdes* (Brussels: Phénix, 1989), pp. 129–138;

"Le Miracle de Noël," in *Nouvelles nouvelles: Fictions du Québec contemporain,* edited by Michel A. Parmentier and Jacqueline R. D'amboise (Toronto: Harcourt Brace Jovanovich, 1987), pp. 1–12;

"Coma-B², biofiction," *Univers 1988* (Paris: Editions J'ai lu, 1988), pp. 157–169;

"Angel" and "Mémère Thibodeau monte au ciel," in *Archipel,* volume 1 (Sainte-Foy, Quebec: Editions le Griffon d'argile, 1989), pp. 21–27, 29–38;

"Un amour féroce," in *Partir ou rester,* read by Nathalie Gascon, audiocassette and text (Montreal: Littérature de l'oreille, 1992), pp. 23–26;

"Rêve canadien," translation by Howard Scott of "Canadian Dream," in *Tesseracts⁴,* edited by Elisabeth Vonarburg and Jane Brierley (Edmonton, Alberta: Tesseract Books, 1996), pp. 80–98; republished in *Northern Suns: The New Anthology of Canadian Science Fiction,* edited by David G. Hartwell and Glenn Grant (New York: Tor, 1999), pp. 299–317.

SELECTED PERIODICAL PUBLICATIONS– UNCOLLECTED:

FICTION
"Emil Hitler," *Requiem,* 13 (1977): 9.

NONFICTION
"Perspectives de la science-fiction québécoise," *imagine . . .,* 2 (December 1979 – February 1980): 82–94;

"La Science-Fiction québécoise: rétrospective et prospective," *Ecriture française dans le monde,* 15–16 (1984): 3–10;

"La Science-Fiction québécoise, de l'universel au particulier," in *Les Oeuvres de création et le français au Québec, Actes du Congrès Langue et Société au Québec, Vol. III,* edited by Irène Belleau and Gilles Dorion (Quebec City: Editeur officiel du Québec, 1984), pp. 190–195;

"Lettre de Jean-Pierre April," *imagine . . .,* 54 (December 1990): 79–80;

"Post-SF: Du postmodernisme dans la science-fiction québécoise des années 80," *imagine . . .,* 61 (September 1992): 75–118;

"Sport-Fiction: Le Hockey et la science-fiction québécoise," *imagine . . .,* 77 (September 1996): 78–96.

In his 1979 essay "Perspectives de la science-fiction québécoise" ("Perspectives on Quebec Science Fiction") Jean-Pierre April wrote: "Au pays du paradoxe l'oxymoron est roi" (In the land of paradox, the oxymoron is king). This statement highlights two fundamental traits of April's writing: its grounding in Quebec, land of paradox made up of settlers and fur traders, federalists and separatists, Americanophiles and Americanophobes; and its love of oppositions, contradictions, and heterogeneity. Some critics have seized on the notion of oxymoron to characterize April's writing; others have spoken of his neobaroque style, and in "Post-SF: Du postmodernisme dans la science-fiction québécoise des années 80" (Post-SF: On Postmodernism in Quebec Science-Fiction of the 1980s, 1992) April affirmed that his work coincides with the postmodern movement in literature. Considered one of the great pioneers of Quebec science-fiction, April made his first contribution to the genre in 1977 with a short-short story titled "Emil Hitler" published in *Requiem,* one of the earliest Quebec science-fiction magazines (established in 1974 and later renamed *Solaris*). Since then, he has contributed to the field through his fiction, his essays, his teaching, his participation in science-fiction conferences in Quebec and in France, and his work from 1980 to 1990 on the editorial board of *imagine . . .,* one of the principal science-fiction magazines in Quebec. He has received several prizes, including the Prix Boréal, awarded at the annual Convention of Quebec SF, and the Prix Septième Continent, awarded by *imagine . . .* to Francophone science-fiction writers.

One of three children, Jean-Pierre April was born on 16 July 1948 in Rivière-du-Loup, a small town in eastern Quebec, to Maurice April and Rose-Alma Thibault April. Once a logger, his father worked at various jobs and was occasionally unemployed. As a child, April turned to literature and his imagination as an escape from poverty. He left Rivière-du-Loup in his late teens to pursue his studies, first at the Collège de la Pocatière, where he stayed less than a year after finding its rules rather confining, and then in Quebec, at the Collège Saint-Jean-Eudes de Québec and the Cégep de Limoilou, he graduated in 1968. He went on to study literature and linguistics at Laval University, obtaining a teacher's certificate and a degree in French. He then worked from 1971 to 1977 as a teacher in the Catholic schools of Montreal and La Pocatière. Since 1977 he has taught linguistics, literature, science fiction and fantasy, and creative writing at the Cégep de Victoriaville, a two-year college. In 1984 April and Diane Turcotte had a son named Hugo; the couple divorced in 1996.

April's first writings were not science fiction. In the early 1970s he completed a mainstream novel titled "Retour de Dat Johnson," the style of which he described in a 1996 interview in *Solaris* as realistic and close to his personal life but with certain "meta-neo-postmodern" moments. The manuscript was accepted in 1975 by the publishing house La Presse, whose literary director then was the renowned Quebec author Hubert Aquin. Two years after Aquin's suicide in 1977, however, his successor informed April that La Presse was no longer interested in the manuscript; but by that time April had shifted his attention to science fiction, being particularly influenced by English-language authors such as Philip K. Dick and J. G. Ballard. By the late 1970s April was firmly involved in the Quebec science-fiction scene, participating, for example, in the first Quebec conference on science fiction, held in Chicoutimi in 1979.

In 1980 April collected many of his short stories as well as the article "Perspectives de la science-fiction québécoise" to produce his first book, *La Machine à explorer la fiction* (The Fiction Machine), one of the first publications of the short-lived science-fiction series "Chroniques du futur" and winner of the Prix Boréal in 1981 for best science-fiction short-story collection. In the title story, a student of twentieth-century crime fiction is hired to work on a new form of telefiction projected directly into the minds of the viewers, allowing them to act on the story and to create alternate realities. As well as developing April's frequent theme of the interface between man and machine, the story demonstrates his postmodern fascination with parody—in this case, a science-fiction parody of crime fiction featuring the celebrated detective Larsan, an obvious allusion to the fictional detective Arsène Lupin.

One of the best-known stories of the collection is "Jackie, je vous aime" (Jackie, I Love You), for which April won the Prix Boréal in 1980 for best science-fiction short story. Johnny, spinner of tales and bodyguard to "Jackie Kendy" (who has been resuscitated from the dead), recounts the much-embroidered story of the American King John Kendy and his consort while he waits for his employer to finish undergoing transplants intended to prolong her life beyond her 139 years. Another tale that exploits modern myths is "King Kong III," which features a robotic King Kong about to destroy Manhattan until lured to his death by the figure of Linda Lovelace sculpted onto the Statue of Liberty. In "Le Vol de la ville" (The Flight of the City) April turns to the social myths of his own culture, portraying Montreal's Olympic Stadium as a spaceship that aliens cleverly convinced the dictator Jos Drapo Douze (an allusion to former Montreal mayor Jean Drapeau) to build. Noting in a Spring 1991 *Solaris* interview with Luc Pomerleau that the French editor of a science-fiction anthology had refused the story as "too Canadian," April insists that the propensity for megalomania and myth is characteristic of smaller nations in general. He suggests that too often what is seen as the "universal" character of science fiction is in fact predominantly American.

"Le Miracle de Noël" (The Christmas Miracle) while suggestive of the Catholic heritage of Quebec, also underscores a dominant theme in April's writing: the increased risk of sterility and of congenital deformities induced by the deteriorating condition of the environment. Characteristically, however, April treats the theme with playful humor, satirizing the human need for symbolism: should readers take hope from the fact that the new Christ child is a baby girl of mixed Caucasian and African descent?

Finally, "Coma-70" and the lengthy novella "Coma-90" introduce the character Yan Malter, a writer participating in an experiment on the afterlife. As such, his postmortem perception of a degraded, horrendously polluted future world is unique. In his introduction to April's anthology *Chocs baroques* (Baroque Shocks, 1991), Michel Lord has noted the significance of April's characteristic play on words: "Yan" suggesting "Jean"; "Malter" suggesting "Moi" and "Alter." In his article "Post-SF" April himself situates this concern with the self in the context of postmodernism: "Chose certaine, les personnages de la SF postmoderniste ne partent plus en astronefs à la découverte de l'univers; l'univers les pénètre, ils découvrent l'univers en eux-mêmes, ils sont des univers. Le Moi devient ainsi le sujet et l'objet de la post-SF" (One thing is certain: the characters of postmodern SF no longer set off in spaceships in search of the universe; the universe penetrates them, they discover the universe in themselves, they constitute universes. The Self thus becomes both the subject and the object of post-SF). In addition to its futuristic vision of a world in chaos, the "Coma" series focuses on the notion of writing itself.

The stories of *La Machine à explorer la fiction* are quite diverse but present many of April's primary themes: the power of socially constructed myths; the proliferation of alternate realities; and the human search for immortality through technology. This first collection reinforced April's standing as one of the dominant voices in Quebec science fiction, although some have criticized a certain lack of finesse in his writing style. In an interview with Sophie Beaulé, published in the August 1985 issue of *imagine . . .*, April remarks that he is more concerned with narrative and the relationship with the reader than with any institutionally approved literary style, suggesting that science fiction looks better in jeans than in a suit.

TéléToTaliTé, his second collection, published in 1984, focuses on the Aprilian theme that Claude Ecken described in the Winter 1990 issue of *Alliage* as "totalitarisme télévisuel" (televisual totalitarianism), the power of television over the collective imagination. In the title story, which won the Prix Boréal in 1981 for best science-fiction short story, the media giant Neworld has established a monopoly over "tédévision" (TD, tridimensional television) that is unexpectedly contested by a group of Inuit who have learned how to interfere with Neworld's transmissions and are offering a mystic vision to compensate for the spiritual barrenness of TD. However, the network Neworld quickly adapts, offering its own version of "tédémystique" (tédémysticism). In the same vein, "Chronostop" imagines an elderly man tracking down a missing person as a bounty hunter for the program *Télépolice*, a futuristic version of the television show *America's Most Wanted*. He ends up joining his quarry, preserved with other senior citizens in the archives of the Heritage Hospice, reduced to a disembodied consciousness happily reliving television programs from the idyllic twentieth century, including such classics as *Little House on the Prairie* and the Quebec series *Le Temps d'une paix* by Pierre Gauvreau. In "Trois Vies dans la nuit d'un sous-homme" (Three Lives in the Night of a Subhuman) the technology of Stereo-Fusion allows the prisoner Jos Zhéros to mentally live through his most violent sexual fantasies, at the same time producing the drug "septimine," which is then harvested by the prison for profit. In response to critical reactions to "Chronostop" and "Trois Vies d'un sous-homme" April admits to a particular fondness for these stories simply because they are so excessive or, to use the adjective often associated with April, so "baroque."

The two remaining stories in the collection pursue April's penchant for political satire. The novella "L'Eternel Président" (The Eternal President) recounts the kidnapping by Latin American revolutionaries of a well-loved president who turns out to be merely an easily replaced figurehead, used by the military regime as a reassuring media personality. In this story April hovers between speculative fiction and analysis of current events, since only the advanced medical technology described in this well-crafted story allows it to qualify as science fiction. April aims his political satire at his own country, its cultural and linguistic tensions, in "Canadian Dream," (only the title is in English), one of his best-known stories, translated in the English-language anthology of Quebec SF, *Tesseracts 2* (1996), under the French title "Rêve canadien." Quebec ethnologist Robert Langlois visits a mystic seer in Cameroon to examine the claim that the famed explorer Jacques Cartier had invented his voyages to Canada in order to cover up his participation in the diamond trade in Cameroon. The seer goes even further and, by the power of the spoken word, renders Canada an imaginary country. On his return home, Langlois finds that his world has been transformed: Canada is indeed a fictitious country, and "Montriall" is an Anglophone city in the United States.

Like "Le Vol de la ville," *Le Nord électrique* (The Electric North), April's first science-fiction novel, published in 1985, examines social myth from a singularly Quebecois perspective. Alluding to the James Bay hydroelectric project initiated by Quebec premier Robert Bourassa in the 1970s, April presents a new initiative: a hydroelectric project in Northern Quebec composed of 230 dams that will result in the creation of the Green Sea while flooding a considerable expanse of aboriginal lands. The great machine that is to accomplish this feat is the Multi-Max 23, which should thus prove its worth for a projected mining expedition on Mars. Although the process is largely automated, human love for symbolism dictates a driver worthy of the machine, and April draws playfully on one of the great Quebec rural novels about the colonization of the North, *Menaud, maître-draveur* (Master of the River, 1937), by Félix-Antoine Savard. The first candidate, Lucien Ménord, is electrocuted at the ceremonial launch of the Multi-Max 23 and must be replaced by his son, Serge Ménord. Cast by the media as a popular hero, romantically linked with the glamourous superstar Marik Monet-Snatch, Serge is the victim of an untimely death when the Multi-Max 23 and all its crew smash into the village of Halte-au-Hameau. Sabotage and the excessive use of "vodkola" are suspected causes. The main character, a journalist named Jean, sets out to investigate the mystery, in large part by examining the images taken of the disaster by his apparent double, Jérémie Norman. With the use of the drug "voyagel," Jean can experience the images as though he were living through them. He witnesses Serge's frantic attempt to save the Multi-Max as well as the conjuring-up of the spirit of the Wolverine by a shaman bent on sabotage. Because of April's love of ambiguity, neither Jean nor the reader can distinguish alternate realities from fiction, as the entire affair appears to have been staged by the group "Théâtre Total" in order to provide heroic images for the masses.

Although the themes of *Le Nord électrique*—such as the ambiguous potential of technology and drugs, the confusion between fiction and reality, and the human need for myth—are common to his short stories, the novel allows greater scope for April's postmodern play. This novel incorporates diverse forms of discourse, including third-person narration, journalistic writing, and quotations from learned experts on Amerindian myths of the Wolverine and on the Arien Syndrome—

that is, dangerous mental fatigue suffered by humans when technology is working too perfectly. The ludic use of intertexts is underlined by chapter titles such as "Ménord, maître-camionneur" (Ménord, master truck-driver) and "Star-Truck." In his interview with Beaulé, April noted the influence of video clips on his narrative style, and certainly the use of flashbacks, multiple narrative voices, and discursive analyses of his futuristic world impede any conventional linear reading. While noting the intended confusion of narrative voices, Lord remarked in his review in the Spring 1987 *Lettres québécoises* that the extreme baroque style of the novel is not entirely successful and that April had not yet fully made the transition from the short story to the novel, a weakness reflected in the undermining of suspense in the first few chapters.

During the 1980s April was an important part of a movement establishing links between science-fiction writing in Quebec and in France. In 1983 he collaborated with French publisher Marcel Becker to produce a special issue of the French review *Clair d'Ozone* devoted to Quebec science-fiction writers. His short stories have appeared in several anthologies published in France, including the annual *Univers* in 1985, 1986, and 1988. Since the late 1980s, April has on occasion represented Quebec at the National French Convention of science fiction; for example, the 1991 conference at Montfort-sur-Argens was summarized by April in *imagine . . .* under the title "Des Extraterrestres à Montfort-sur-Argens" (1991). He remains one of the main representatives of Quebec science fiction in France. Two of April's stories, "Les Orphelins de Hoï Tri" (The Orphans of Hoi Tri, Mille plumes, 1978) and "Les Impressions de Thaï Deng" (Impressions of Thai Deng, 1985) have also appeared in Italian translation, a fact he finds especially pleasing given his own distant Italian ancestry. And, of course, April's short stories have been widely anthologized in Quebec, ranging from the science-fiction fable "La Mort et télévie de Jacob Miro" (The Death and Telelife of Jacob Miro) in *Anthologie de la science-fiction québécoise contemporaine* (Anthology of Contemporary Quebec Science Fiction, 1988) to fantasy tales in the rural Quebec tradition such as "Mémère Thibodeau monte au ciel" (Old Lady Thibodeau Goes to Heaven) in *Archipel* (1989).

In 1989 April published a second novel, *Berlin-Bangkok,* republished in a revised version in 1993 in the science-fiction series of the mainstream French publishing house Editions J'ai lu. Envisaging a reunited Germany, April's novel was overtaken by events in Eastern Europe, and the second version includes minor modifications to conform to the actual history of the fall of the Berlin Wall. The more intimate tone and controlled style of this novel contrasts with the exuberant neoba-

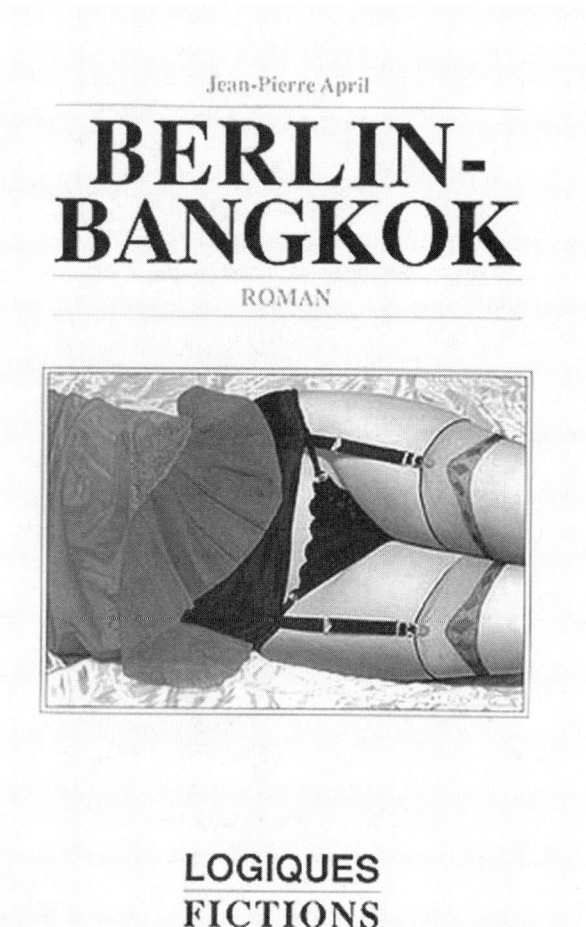

Cover for April's 1989 novel, a futuristic fable about a German whose Asian bride is the star attraction in a Thai "cyberbrothel"

roque style of *Le Nord électrique*. *Berlin-Bangkok* is a futuristic fable of the global village, examining Western exploitation of the developing world. It is also an unusual love story. A disease known as SAP, "syndrome d'accouchement prématuré" (premature birth syndrome), has struck the West, leading many Western men to choose Asian brides, supposedly exempt from SAP, to give them offspring, as opposed to using the rather unsatisfactory technology of MAMs, "matrices artificielles modulées" (modulated artificial wombs). Familiar with Thailand, and especially its drug "klong," from his work abroad for the Deutsche Drug Company, Axel Rovan consults the Berlin-Bangkok agency to find a Thai bride. He is matched with Yumi, a former prostitute of a brothel catering to German men. When Yumi disappears, he follows her to Thailand, becoming known to all as "l'Allemand-qui-cherche-sa-femme-dans-les-bordels-de-Bangkok" (the German who seeks his wife in the brothels of Bangkok). Yumi, however, has become the star research subject of experiments in cyberbrothels, generating unique sexual fantasies that clients can mentally explore by use of the machine Transphere T. Having achieved power and wealth, Yumi is able to rescue Axel from the prison-camp hell into which he has descended, rather like Eurydice revising mythology by rescuing Orpheus. The familiar science-fiction themes of man, machine, drugs, and alternate realities are merged with social analysis of potentially exploitative relationships between East and West and between men and women. While many of his earlier works deliberately focus on speculative fiction at the expense of human psychology, April moves in this novel toward greater realism, stronger characterization, and exploration of human emotion.

In 1990 April startled the Quebec science-fiction community by announcing in *imagine* . . . his decision to abandon science fiction for mainstream literature. The reasons cited include a sense of the limited ability of the genre to express his new interests, an aversion to the internal rivalries of the Quebec science-fiction scene, and especially a frustration with the limited audience for the genre. In the same letter, he also announced the imminent publication of a collection of his short stories from the 1980s. In fact, in 1991 April published two collections: *Chocs baroques* and *N'ajustez pas vos hallucinettes,* the latter directed toward adolescents.

Accompanied by an introduction by Lord, a chronology, and a bibliography, *Chocs baroques* reprises several of April's best-known stories such as "Télétotalité," "Le Vol de la ville," and "Le Fantôme du Forum" (The Phantom of the Forum). The latter story combines the theme of telekinetic powers with the Quebecois preoccupations with hockey, beer, and the great hockey player Guy Lafleur. April's love for crossing genre boundaries is evident in "La survie en rose," which won the Prix Septième Continent in 1985. It is a science-fiction love story between a woman who has decided to prolong her life by having her brain grafted onto the body of an orangutan, and the lover who follows her example, only to be abandoned for an alpha-male orangutan. In the paradoxical and autoreflexive "Coma-123, automatexte" writers no longer exist in society, but Yan Malter is dissatisfied with using an electronic fiction bank Automatex to explore his own response to works by Albert Camus, John Steinbeck, and Marie-Claire Blais. Instead he is drawn to the writings of a certain April telling the story of a certain Yan Malter.

Other stories emphasize April's deepening focus on personal relationships. In particular, April considers "Dans la forêt de mes enfances" (In the Forests of My Childhoods), which won a literary award from the Société Saint-Jean-Baptiste in 1989, a transition in his literary development away from science fiction to mainstream literature. Set in "Victorinville," the story examines the relationship between father and son, both silviculturists, although the father is part of the "Renature" movement to re-create extinct species while the son specializes in the creation of bizarre new species. Their relationship is all the more intense because the father had decided that the son be conceived from the egg of an anonymous donor, the maternal role being carried out only by a series of hired caretakers. Perhaps predictably, the son yearns to know his mother and chooses to marry, although his wife leaves him and takes their child. In his 1991 *Solaris* interview, April asserts that this story adapts the common feminist theme of generational continuity between mother and daughter to the father-son relationship.

Pursuing this examination of feminist themes, "Impressions de Thaï Deng" critically investigates the relationship between men, women, and war. In despair at losing their husbands and sons to war, a group of Thai women have established an isolated colony of pacifists, excluding all men and camouflaging their sons as girls. Having limited technological knowledge, they kidnap an electronics specialist from the city to investigate incidents of sabotage, only to find that their own sons were the saboteurs. April does not simplistically associate violence and men, but shows the propensity for violence in the women themselves and genuinely questions the possibility or wisdom of suppressing aggressive impulses. The collection thus represents the entire spectrum of April's themes new and old, with the more recent stories also demonstrating a more concise, chiseled writing style.

In publishing his short-story collection *N'ajustez pas vos hallucinettes* (1991), appearing in the series "Clip," for readers aged fourteen and older, April had his own son in mind, as he reached out to a new public. All but one of the stories were previously published for adults but are slightly modified in this collection for a younger audience, mainly through suppression of what April considers nonessential plot elements. Of special interest is "Les Orphelins de Hoï Tri," the first science-fiction story ever written by April, refused twice for publication in science-fiction magazines for not being sufficiently true to the genre. As a member of a gang of adolescents displaced by war in Asia, the young narrator can only participate in his country's return to prosperity by selling to Westerners his newborn child, whose Asian features have been made Caucasian, thanks to new medical technology. The thematic continuity between this story and *Berlin-Bangkok* is quite remarkable.

The only story in the collection expressly written for young people, "Julie Joyal appelle les étoiles," presents the diary of a young girl, conceived by artificial insemination, who would like to know about her father. Since donor anonymity had been guaranteed, various actors have been chosen to play the role of the ideal biological father of Julie and others like her. Julie's unmasking of her pseudofather is ingenious and quite hilarious. Humor is the dominant tone of the collection, notably in such Aprilian favorites as "Jackie, je vous aime" and "King Kong III." Scatological humor predominates in "Voyage au centre de la planète mer," previously published under the more descriptive title "Voyage au centre de la Digestion divine," in which the captain Noémo (a cross between the biblical Noah and Jules Verne's Captain Nemo) leads the survivors of the Flood through the digestive system of the god who will give birth to a new world. In a further blow to the human ego, the god is a young male being forced by his mother to finish his planetary soup. April's recurrent theme of individuals losing control of technology appears in "Coma-70" and "N'ajustez pas vos hallucinettes," while the inclusion of the parodic character "Doctor Sphock" in the latter story underlines the playful element of April's writing.

Despite April's written farewell to the genre in 1990, five years later he published the novel *Les Voyages thanatologiques de Yan Malter* as the culmination of almost two decades of science-fiction writing. April's fascination with Yan Malter's exploration of death and the world beyond had earlier been expressed in the four stories of the "Coma" series: "Coma-70," "Coma-90," "Coma B², biofiction," and "Coma-123, automatexte." April chose to incorporate "Coma-70," first published in 1979 as "Une nouvelle page," along with "Coma-90," into his 1995 novel. The central premise is the same: science-fiction author Yan Malter has agreed to participate in an experiment led by Doctor Ratel in which his mind will be freed to explore the afterlife. Plunged into a coma, he finds himself in a hospital in the future world of Simuli-City, having become part of a brain trust of "mindnapped" thinkers under the control of a group known as the Captors. His primary aims are to determine the true nature of Simuli-City and especially to ascertain the fate of his own fiction written before the coma. There is, however, a significant shift in focus that reflects April's growing concern with human relationships in the brave new world of technology. Whereas "Coma-90" presents a brief encounter between Yan Malter and Mira, the daughter who barely knew him, the novel begins with the daughter's search for her father. A decrepit old soul aged 106, her body composed of grafted body parts and prostheses, the daughter seeks to unlock the secret of the Memogenic box that contains her father's "mémogènes," all that remains of his consciousness. With the help of Jan Tepernic, a specialist in dead authors, Mira is able to enter her father's reality by becoming part of his fiction as his nurse and accomplice Moïra, eventually joining him in the afterlife. The novel ends with a threefold conclusion. In the epilogue, Yan Malter describes his world of the twenty-fourth century, in which the learned members of the afterlife, relieved of the tyranny of the Captors, serve as advisers to the living. However, in the first part of the "Eschatalogue" Mira reveals from her perspective of 2700 A.D. that her father's optimistic vision of a world guided by the Center of Knowledge is a sham, as she hides from him the reality of humanity's inevitable destruction. April gives a powerful description of environmental degradation: "La Terre accouchait de la mort. Toutes les eaux de la vieille mère Terre étaient imbuvables, aussi bien celles du ciel que celles de la surface que celles du sous-sol. Il pleuvait du poison. L'acide tombait du ciel. Les pluies homicides nettoyaient le globe. On ne pouvait plus que s'abreuver à la mort" (The Earth was giving birth to death. All the waters of old Mother Earth were undrinkable, whether they came from the sky or the surface or the underground. It was raining poison. Acid was falling from the sky. Homicidal rains cleansed the globe. We could only drink from death). In the final part of the Eschatalogue, situated in 2900 A.D., April gives the last word to the survivors of human destructiveness, represented by a mutant rat who has absorbed the mémogènes of Yan Malter. In fact, the mutant rats have become dependent on human mémogènes contained in edible capsules and are themselves heading toward destruction.

The bleakness of this postapocalyptic vision is undercut somewhat by April's humor, in particular, his trademark puns and neologisms carried to an extreme. Mira and Tepernic trade puns on reanimating Yan Malter: if Tepernic is "réanimateur" (reanimator) or "réanim-auteur" (reanim-author), then Mira is instead "réani-mater" (reani-mother). April underlines his own relationship with the character Yan Malter by attributing to him an earlier pseudonym: J. P. Palir, author of *La Machine à mort, Thanatotalité,* and *le Mort électrique.* J. P. Palir is in turn indistinguishable from the fictional author Janet Lapir. The distancing effect of this humor recalls April's earlier writings that subordinate human psychology to narrative and metafictional discourse. The author's concern with the future of literature and with the nature of writing in general is abundantly clear. The critical reception of this novel was not as enthusiastic as that accorded to *Berlin-Bangkok,* perhaps partly because of the predominance of abstract reflections on writing. As a testimony to the importance of his work, in 1997 April received the Arthur-Buies Award, granted to authors of distinction from Eastern Quebec.

Although he continues to publish short stories and theoretical essays on science fiction in the journal *imagine* . . . , April has indeed returned to mainstream fiction and has been completing two novels, both situated in his native region of Eastern Quebec and including some historical and autobiographical elements. He describes both works as more realistic and more personal than his science fiction, although one also incorporates some elements of fantasy fiction. The move toward general fiction appears to be a natural development, since there has always been a current of realism in April's writing from "Les Orphelins de Hoï Tri" to *Berlin-Bangkok*. As April pointed out in his article on postmodernism and science fiction, the emphasis on autoreferential writing, parody, and the blending of divergent literary genres is common to both science fiction and contemporary fiction. Furthermore, April is unlikely to abandon completely the issues that he has analyzed so strikingly in his science fiction: Canadian and international politics, ecology, intergenerational conflicts, the exploitation of the developing world, drugs, reproductive technologies, and the effects of the media. As April has Yan Malter point out: "la fiction est un mensonge qui permet de dire la vérité" (fiction is a lie that allows one to speak the truth).

Interviews:

Sophie Beaulé, "Je veux à la fois faire rire, choquer, séduire . . . ," *imagine* . . . , 29 (August 1985): 64–72;

Claude Ecken, "*Berlin-Bangkok*," *Alliage*, 6 (Winter 1990): 71–80;

François Larocque, "De la prophétie au postmodernisme," *Quebec français*, 84 (1990): 84–86;

Luc Pomerleau, "Entrevue: Jean-Pierre April," *Solaris*, 96 (Spring 1991): 26–33;

Frédérick Durand, "Entrevue avec Jean-Pierre April, l'auteur de *Berlin-Bangkok*," *imagine* . . . , 65 (September 1993): 93–96.

Bibliographies:

"Bibliographie de Jean-Pierre April," *Ecriture française dans le monde*, 6 (1984): 10–11;

"April, Jean-Pierre," in *Bibliographie analytique de la science-fiction et du fantastique québécois (1960–1985)*, edited by Aurélien Boivin and others (Quebec: Nuit blanche éditeur, 1992), pp. 32–46.

References:

Renald Bérubé, "Le fantastique, la science-fiction: 'l'inquiétante étrangeté' dans 'La légende de l'homme à la cervelle d'or' d'Alphonse Daudet' et dans 'Le fantôme du Forum' de Jean-Pierre April," in *Les Ailleurs imaginaires; les rapports entre le fantastique et la science-fiction,* edited by Aurélien Boivin and others (Quebec City: Nuit blanche éditeur, 1993), pp. 137–152;

Jean-Claude Ecken, "La Science-fiction de Jean-Pierre April," *imagine* . . . , 61 (September 1992): 119–156;

Jean-Marc Gouanvic, "Ruptures et mutations dans les conjectures romanesques rationnelles et la science-fiction du Québec de l'après-guerre (1945–1990)," in *Les Ailleurs imaginaires; les rapports entre le fantastique et la science-fiction,* edited by Aurélien Boivin and others (Quebec City: Nuit blanche éditeur, 1993), pp. 77–91;

Gouanvic, "La Science-fiction irrévérencieuse de Jean-Pierre April," *Voix et images*, 7 (Winter 1982): 421–422;

Kathleen Kellett-Betsos, "Questions de maternité/paternité dans l'oeuvre de Jean-Pierre April," *Solaris*, 133 (Spring 2000): 34–38;

Michel Lord, "Aaa! Aâh! Ha! que de belles catastrophes narratives!" *Lettres québécoises*, 45 (Spring 1987): 33–35.

Margaret Atwood
(18 November 1939 –   )

Lee Briscoe Thompson
University of Vermont

See also the Atwood entry in *DLB 53: Canadian Writers Since 1960, First Series.*

BOOKS: *Double Persephone* (Toronto: Hawkshead, 1961);
The Circle Game (Toronto: Contact, 1966);
The Animals in That Country (Toronto: Oxford University Press, 1968; Boston: Little, Brown, 1969);
The Edible Woman (Toronto: McClelland & Stewart, 1969; London: Deutsch, 1969; Boston: Little, Brown, 1969);
The Journals of Susanna Moodie (Toronto: Oxford University Press, 1970);
Procedures for Underground (Toronto: Oxford University Press, 1970; Boston: Little, Brown, 1970);
Power Politics (Toronto: Anansi, 1971; New York: Harper & Row, 1973);
Surfacing (Toronto: McClelland & Stewart, 1972; London: Deutsch, 1973; New York: Simon & Schuster, 1973);
Survival: A Thematic Guide to Canadian Literature (Toronto: Anansi, 1972);
You Are Happy (Toronto: Oxford University Press, 1974; New York: Harper & Row, 1974);
Lady Oracle (Toronto: McClelland & Stewart, 1976; New York: Simon & Schuster, 1976; London: Deutsch, 1977);
Selected Poems (Toronto: Oxford University Press, 1976; New York: Simon & Schuster, 1978);
Dancing Girls and Other Stories (Toronto: McClelland & Stewart, 1977; New York: Simon & Schuster, 1982; London: Cape, 1982);
Days of the Rebels: 1815–1840 (Toronto: Natural Science of Canada, 1977);
Two-Headed Poems (Toronto: Oxford University Press, 1978; New York: Simon & Schuster, 1980);
Up in the Tree (Toronto: McClelland & Stewart, 1978);
Life Before Man (Toronto: McClelland & Stewart, 1979; New York: Simon & Schuster, 1979; London: Cape, 1980);

Margaret Atwood (photograph by Thies Bogner, MPA; from the dust jacket for The Blind Assassin, *2000)*

Anna's Pet, with Joyce Barkhouse (Toronto: Lorimer, 1980);
True Stories (Toronto: Oxford University Press, 1981; New York: Simon & Schuster, 1981; London: Cape, 1982);
Bodily Harm (Toronto: McClelland & Stewart, 1981; New York: Simon & Schuster, 1982; London: Cape, 1982);
Second Words: Selected Critical Prose (Toronto: Anansi, 1982; Boston: Beacon, 1984);
Bluebeard's Egg (Toronto: McClelland & Stewart, 1983); republished as *Bluebeard's Egg and Other Stories* (Boston: Houghton Mifflin, 1986; London: Cape, 1987);
Murder in the Dark: Short Fictions and Prose Poems (Toronto: Coach House, 1983; London: Cape, 1984);
Interlunar (Toronto: Oxford University Press, 1984; London: Cape, 1988);

The Handmaid's Tale (Toronto: McClelland & Stewart, 1985; Boston: Houghton Mifflin, 1986; London: Cape, 1986);

Selected Poems II: Poems Selected and New, 1976–1986 (Toronto: Oxford University Press, 1986; Boston: Houghton Mifflin, 1987; London: Virago, 1992);

Selected Poems 1965–1975 (Boston: Houghton Mifflin, 1987; London: Virago, 1991);

Cat's Eye (Toronto: McClelland & Stewart, 1988; New York: Doubleday, 1989; London: Bloomsbury, 1989);

Selected Poems: 1966–1984 (Toronto: Oxford University Press, 1990);

For the Birds (Toronto: Douglas & McIntyre, 1990);

Wilderness Tips (Toronto: McClelland & Stewart, 1991; New York: Doubleday, 1991; London: Bloomsbury, 1991);

Good Bones (Toronto: Coach House, 1992; London: Bloomsbury, 1992); republished as *Good Bones and Simple Murders* (New York: Doubleday, 1994); republished as *Bones and Murder* (London: Virago, 1995);

The Robber Bride (Toronto: McClelland & Stewart, 1993; New York: Doubleday, 1993; London: Bloomsbury, 1993);

Morning in the Burned House (Toronto: McClelland & Stewart, 1995: New York: Houghton Mifflin, 1995; London: Virago, 1995);

Princess Prunella and the Purple Peanut (Toronto: Key Porter, 1995; Bristol, U.K.: Barefoot, 1995);

Strange Things: The Malevolent North in Canadian Literature (Oxford: Clarendon Press / New York: Oxford University Press, 1995);

Alias Grace (Toronto: McClelland & Stewart, 1996; New York: Doubleday, 1996; London: Bloomsbury, 1996);

Deux sollicitudes: Entretiens, by Atwood and Victor-Lévy Beaulieu (Trois Pistoles, Quebec: Editions Trois Pistoles, 1996); translated by Phyllis Aronoff and Howard Scott as *Two Solicitudes: Conversations* (Toronto: McClelland & Stewart, 1998);

In Search of 'Alias Grace': On Writing Canadian Historical Fiction (Ottawa: University of Ottawa Press, 1997);

A Quiet Game and Other Early Works, edited and annotated by Kathy Chung and Sherrill Grace (Edmonton, Alberta: Juvenilia Press, 1997);

Eating Fire: Selected Poems, 1965–1995 (London: Virago, 1998);

The Blind Assassin (Toronto: McClelland & Stewart, 2000; New York: Doubleday, 2000; London: Bloomsbury, 2000).

OTHER: "Canadian Monsters: Some Aspects of the Supernatural in Canadian Fiction," in *The Canadian Literary Imagination: Dimensions of a Literary Culture,* edited by David Staines (Cambridge, Mass.: Harvard University Press, 1977), pp. 97–122; reprinted in *Other Canadas: An Anthology of Science Fiction and Fantasy,* edited by John Robert Colombo (Toronto: McGraw-Hill Ryerson, 1979), pp. 333–351;

The New Oxford Book of Canadian Verse in English, edited by Atwood (Toronto: Oxford University Press, 1982);

The Oxford Book of Canadian Short Stories in English, edited by Atwood and Robert Weaver (Toronto: Oxford University Press, 1986); revised as *The New Oxford Book of Canadian Short Stories in English* (Toronto: Oxford University Press, 1995);

The Canlit Foodbook, edited by Atwood (Toronto: Totem, 1987);

"Freeforall," in *Tesseracts^2,* edited by Phyllis Gotlieb and Douglas Barbour (Victoria, British Columbia: Press Porcépic, 1987), pp. 130–138; reprinted in *Northern Suns: The New Anthology of Canadian Science Fiction,* edited by David G. Hartwell and Glenn Grant (New York: Tor, 1999), pp. 17–24;

The Best American Short Stories 1989, edited by Atwood and Shannon Ravenel (Boston: Houghton Mifflin, 1989);

Gwendolyn MacEwen, *The Poetry of Gwendolyn MacEwen,* 2 volumes, edited by Atwood and Barry Callaghan (Toronto: Exile, 1993, 1994).

Margaret Atwood is arguably the most prominent contemporary Canadian writer. Best known for her novels, Atwood is also admired for her accomplishments as a poet, critic, essayist, and short-story writer, and she has contributed as well to children's fiction, Canadian history, and the editing of volumes ranging from prestigious anthologies to a literary cookbook. The quantity of her output since publishing her first book in 1961 has been impressive, with more than forty books published so far, as well as book reviews and occasional writing of all sorts. In addition, she has worked in other media, including motion pictures, television, theater, cartoons, librettos, and visual art.

Margaret Eleanor Atwood was born on 18 November 1939 in Ottawa, Ontario to Margaret Dorothy (Killam) and Carl Edmund Atwood; she was the second of three children. Until her teens Atwood and her family spent much of each year in the bush country of Quebec and Ontario, where her entomologist father conducted his research, returning to Toronto for the school year. She began to write seriously at the age of sixteen. She attended Victoria College at the University of Toronto from 1957 to 1961, receiving a B.A. with honors in English. She then completed a master's degree in English at Radcliffe College, Harvard University in 1962, and later returned to begin her doctoral studies, which she never completed. Her employment has included a stint as a market researcher in Toronto and teaching positions or writer-in-residence positions at the University of British Columbia, Sir George Williams University (now Concordia University) in Montreal, the University of Alberta, York University in Toronto, the University of Toronto, the University of Alabama, and Macquarie University in Australia. She married James Polk, an American she met at Harvard, on 9 June 1967 in Boston, but they separated in the summer of 1972 and divorced in 1977. Since 1972 her companion has been novelist Graeme Gibson, with whom she has one child, Eleanor Jess, born on 17 May 1976.

Atwood's books, many of them translated into a variety of languages, are frequent selections for high school and university syllabi, and she and her writing have been the subjects of interviews, scholarly and popular articles, reviews, and graduate theses around the world. Further, her involvement with the Writers' Union of Canada and the anglophone Canadian division of PEN International (in both cases culminating in her service as president), in addition to her roles as a member of the Canadian Civil Liberties Union and the editorial board of the influential Toronto-based House of Anansi Press, and as an outspoken critic of Canadian foreign policy in matters of trade and culture, has also contributed to making her a voice of considerable importance in her native land.

The vast majority of Atwood's fictions have situated themselves firmly in the present–a highly detailed, socially recognizable, North American present day, the second half of the twentieth century–or in the historical past, a painstakingly re-created nineteenth-century Canada, usually in some stage of the Victorian era. Readers of her fiction tend to associate her with realism rather than science fiction, with telling commentary on the ways things were and are rather than the ways they might be. Her most widely known novel, however, *The Handmaid's Tale* (1985), is an obvious and striking exception; it has been described by David Ketterer in the July 1989 issue of *Science-Fiction Studies* as "the best and most successful SF novel written by a Canadian," and it won the first Arthur C. Clarke Award in 1987 for the best science-fiction novel published in a United Kingdom edition the previous year (having also won the Governor-General's Literary Award, the premier Canadian literary award, in 1985). A handful of short stories, the occasional poem, and her later novel *The Blind Assassin* (2000) supplement *The Handmaid's Tale* in demonstrating Atwood's occasional interest in fabulations of future times and in the fantastic.

Atwood herself considers technological gadgetry indispensable to her definition of science fiction, and

Watercolor portrait by Atwood of her partner, the novelist Graeme Gibson, 1974 (Thomas Fisher Rare Book Library, University of Toronto)

therefore dismisses the classification of her own work as science fiction because it lacks futuristic hardware. She is more comfortable with the term speculative fiction, which allows the sort of technological regression featured in all of her futuristic works. The term social science fiction also seems applicable to her work, in its pushing of familiar social structures into new configurations, usually dire ones.

Just as Atwood is seen more as a realist than as a science-fiction writer, so too she is not particularly widely viewed as a writer of fantastic fiction. Yet, in her poetry the blurring of the line between the imaginary and the tangible is frequent and often escalates to the point that the "real" is intimated to be an illusion, the unseen more potent and authentic than the seen. (Her poem "Daphne and Laura and So Forth," from her 1995 collection *Morning in the Burned House*, was included in Ellen Datlow and Terri Windling's ninth annual *Year's Best Fantasy and Horror* in 1996.) In her fiction, too, there are many surreal scenes, and characters sometimes move in and out of complex fantasy worlds and lives, parallel universes just a membrane apart. Atwood's inclination to the supernatural arises from her fairytale obsessions and the backwoods animism of her childhood, later compounded by her adult readings of Victorian fantasy and Canadian nature fiction. But ultimately, the reader is almost always presented with confirmations of the ascendancy of consensual reality.

The first of Atwood's occasional stories to speculate on the future or utilize the fantastic is "When It Happens," from her 1977 collection, *Dancing Girls and Other Stories;* it had previously been published in the Canadian women's magazine *Chatelaine* in 1975 and has since been anthologized in the *Penguin Book of Modern Fantasy by Women* (1995). It anticipated *The Handmaid's Tale* in its near-future, familiar setting, in its detailed attention to the gradualness of societal breakdown and yet the rapidity of its impact, and in the paradoxical combination of fearful passivity and resourcefulness with which the protagonist faces change. Mrs. Burridge moves back and forth among her present (the reader's potential near future), her near future (as this present begins to collapse), and her slightly further future (as she travels and encounters her first enemies). While virtually all of the events in the story are clearly expressed as Mrs. Burridge's worried speculations, their foundation is a social upheaval of the near future that has already begun for her (as confirmed by the new need to supplement food stocks by relearning the old art of canning). Further, disastrous developments are so fully realized, both in their vivid descriptions and in the skillful manipulation of verb tenses, that they achieve a reality and certainty of their own; as the title emphasizes, it is not a matter of "if" it happens, but "when."

"Simmering," from the 1983 collection *Murder in the Dark: Short Fictions and Prose Poems,* plays with a future marked by gender role reversal, in an entirely familiar context of barbeques, briefcases, cocktail parties, and kitchen utensils. The story, anticipating Offred's tale-telling in *The Handmaid's Tale,* is a covert narration by a woman who has been officially silenced, who dreams a decidedly female and inclusive dream (one involving both Eden and apples) of freedom, and who seeks to preserve this story by word of mouth and/or manuscript. For once with Atwood, this future is a distant one, many centuries from the present. The tyranny of gender expectations continues, but now men's way of having the upper hand is to be the guardians and repositories of cooking; and since men now do it, the baking of bread has become a profound and sacred rite. The story has considerable fun with all aspects of this rewriting of male dominance, including the transference of their stereotypical preoccupations to applications in what was once the undervalued domestic domain of females and to the sexualization of objects (such as turkey basters and carving knives) that had no such cachet in the hands of women. This future society has finally gotten women out of the kitchen, but in this recast universe that means they are still excluded from the sites of power.

The Handmaid's Tale, published in 1985, was on *The New York Times* Best Sellers list for fifteen weeks at first release, and again for eight weeks when released as a paperback in 1987, with a further four weeks in 1990 after the movie version appeared. It was a crucial crossover book for Atwood. Before that, she had been the darling of Canadian poetry lovers, fans of contemporary fiction, and women's studies specialists. But with *The Handmaid's Tale* Atwood acquired a huge popular readership and also attracted the attention of scholars in many fields outside literature. The novel began appearing in courses and articles on political science, history, sociology, philosophy, theology, environmental studies, and human biology. A large component of its initial appeal had to do with the compelling—to many readers, terrifying—vision it offered of a society of the near future, an exaggeration for (a little) better and for (the most part) worse of the reader's own, recognizable contemporary scene.

The Handmaid's Tale envisions a white, right-wing, theocratic coup having taken place in the northeast United States of the early twenty-first century. An autocratic elite, alarmed by a precipitous decline in Caucasian birth rates and by the degeneration of a "traditional" American society, has masterminded the murder of the president and a massacre in Congress, then played on public fear, ignorance, and restricted access to information and money to suspend all civil rights. A frightened, confused citizenry has hunkered down to ride out the crisis, and most have submitted meekly to the rapid imposition of many restrictions and a rigid codification of status and role in the new, dystopian state of Gilead.

Most dramatically and visibly, women are stripped of jobs and financial independence and pressed into one of eight color-coded categories: Wives of the elite (blue), young Daughters of the elite (white), Widows (black), Aunts (khaki), Handmaids (red), Marthas (dull green), Econowives (red/blue/green stripes), and Unwomen (grey). Jezebels, an unofficial group of women coerced into prostitution, are assigned a ragbag of frazzled, flashy outfits once associated with eroticism. Although virtually powerless, the group at the center of this structure is the Handmaids, fertile women forcibly recruited to try to bear children for the older, all too often sterile Commanders. All other positions, male and female, in the society revolve around the core mission of reproduction, and the myriad aspects of repression considered necessary to enforce compliance and

Atwood with her and Gibson's daughter, Eleanor Jess, 1980 (photograph by Thomas Victor)

rebuild the white population (people of color having been "relocated").

The Handmaid's Tale purports to be the transcript of one Handmaid's description of her life in the early days of the Gilead regime, in the transition generation caught between memories of life in "the time before" (the late twentieth century) and the powerful indoctrination of Gilead. Offred's tale is followed by another transcript, from a convention two hundred years later, in which academics meet to discuss the by-then defunct Gilead from the perspective of the year 2195. One arresting (and by no means reassuring) characteristic of Gilead and of the world of 2195 is that they seem so unfuturistic, in the sense that the artifacts, attitudes, customs, idiom, and actions seem quite familiar and largely unchanged from those of contemporary society. True, there is a long list of compu-items in use in Gilead (such as Compubite, Compudoc, and Compubank), but society in 1985 had already progressed to nearly that degree, and Atwood's vision of a future cashless society seems not far off. However, Gilead has regressed considerably in the realm of technology, and indeed has done so as a matter of policy, for it blames science for having contributed to the mess that necessitated a coup (artificial insemination and birth control, toxic chemicals and wastes, nuclear accidents, and so on). In consequence, women in Gilead give birth without anesthetics or surgical assistance; written language has shrunk to pictograms for all but the elite and their enforcers, the Aunts; the sexes are once again segregated and chaperoned, the women often veiled and restricted to lives without mechanical or even cosmetic aids; and televisions and other machines have only the most curtailed place in daily life. Although some phrases from the time before have lost currency, there is no Orwellian Newspeak.

Nor, in the North America of 2195 when the scholarly symposium takes place in Nunavit to study Gilead, does much appear to have changed from the reader's time. There is a little window dressing in the elevation of ethnic and female academics, but a condescending keynote speaker from England makes clear that colonialism and sexism are still firmly in place. Atwood's interest in the future appears most importantly to have to do with affirming the adage that "the more things change, the more they stay the same," and with issuing a warning that humans are not really that far from nightmarish extensions of the current world. By minimizing the number of differences between her two futures (Gilead and Nunavit) and the present, and by emphasizing that everything in Gilead has historical precedent, Atwood produces a speculative fiction that holds readers close to home and intensifies their nervousness that such things could happen. Good utopian and dystopian fiction depends on the reader's consciousness of the connection between reality and fictional future, if the vision is to have power and point. *The Handmaid's Tale* makes that connection and shows how relevant her cautionary tale is.

Like many other dystopian narratives, *The Handmaid's Tale* conjures up a future based on an extreme extrapolation of contemporary conditions. The novel furnishes standard dystopian features: lack of freedom, relentless surveillance, imposed routine, an abortive escape attempt, and an underground resistance. It has often been compared and contrasted with such dystopian classics as Aldous Huxley's *Brave New World* (1932), George Orwell's *Nineteen Eighty-Four* (1949), Evgenii Zamiatin's *We* (1924), Ray Bradbury's *Fahrenheit 451* (1953), and Anthony Burgess's *A Clockwork Orange* (1962), and the majority of assessments have ranked Atwood's novel on a par with and sometimes even superior to those classics.

The Handmaid's Tale has been extensively discussed by literary scholars. Some critics have argued that it failed as a dystopia, suggesting that the world of Gilead is utterly improbable and underdeveloped, and complaining that Atwood had sacrificed serious social criticism to romance rhetoric, mere entertainment, and/or costume Gothicism. Some felt that *The Handmaid's Tale* showed a failure of futuristic imagination, evinced in the fact that it modified in the invented future so little of the linguistic, environmental, philosophical, and social framework of the present. Yet, the majority of critics have argued that *The Handmaid's Tale* presents an effective warning against absolutist or despotic systems, using a near-future projection to show the relationship between general power structures or ideologies and the individual. Many critics took the position that Atwood had transformed the genre and produced a feminist dystopia. Ketterer speculated that the difference lay in the fact that Atwood's dystopia moves circularly, rather than linearly as was "traditional," which consequentially blunted the satire and anger with the implication that incarnations of Gilead will keep recurring. He then argued that *The Handmaid's Tale* was successful precisely because of this innovative indirection and understatement, features vilified by impatient critics expecting a more crisply efficient brand of totalitarianism than that of Gilead, a more monstrous oppressor than Commander Fred, and a less tricksterish narrator than Offred. Critics making the case of *The Handmaid's Tale* as a feminist dystopia often cited as feminist deviations from the male dystopian model the very "subversive" strategies criticized elsewhere as flaws: irrepressible humor, creativity, self-assertion, open-endedness, wordplay, Offred's fluid identity, irony, narrative evasions (including contradictory but equally valorized plotlines), overthrow of archetypes (such as light for knowledge and darkness for ignorance, disrupted by the Night chapters), and sheer survival.

For some readers the strongest alarm sounded by this novel has been environmental, a concern that links it to many other Atwood pieces. Like many conjurers of the future, Atwood fears for the planet, and her childhood experiences as the daughter of a cheerfully pessimistic entomologist, spending more than half of each year in the wilds of the Canadian Shield, have given her the ecological documentation to support those fears. In her novel the Gileadeans appear to have pulled back from the environmental abyss in time, but they now err in their extreme tampering with human nature. And, in the appended Historical Notes the dispassionate scholarly observers of Gilead two centuries later are shown to have learned little from Offred's tale. Atwood everywhere asserts humankind's capacity to destroy its surroundings and its species.

The Handmaid's Tale is by far Atwood's most influential and best-known contribution to Canadian science fiction, though she has continued to explore speculative or fantastic elements. Her next science-fiction work, the short story "Freeforall," was published in the *Toronto Star* a year after the appearance of *The Handmaid's Tale* and later anthologized in the Canadian science-fiction anthologies *Tesseracts²* (1987) and *Northern Suns* (1999). It imagines family life a few decades into the early twenty-first century. As in *The Handmaid's Tale,* Atwood envisions some of her audience's worst fears having come to pass, as society has been catastrophically damaged by virulent new forms of sexually transmitted diseases. Like Offred, Sharmayne remembers the time before, with its escalating horrors that provided the impetus for

Manuscript page for the beginning of Atwood's 1985 novel, The Handmaid's Tale *(Thomas Fisher Rare Book Library, University of Toronto)* establishing a new order. Just as Gilead was obviously centered in Cambridge, Massachusetts, the locale of "Freeforall" is a recognizable one, Toronto. Language has acquired only a few neologisms, and human nature is essentially unaltered.

As in *The Handmaid's Tale*, there is a circularity of cultural experience and a return to gender segregation and chaperoning. The new regime in "Freeforall," like Gilead, requires repression for the putative common good. Similarly, too, the reader is thrust into the middle of the action, presented with references that reveal themselves gradually, so that the reader feels a bit alien and disoriented, then with some dismay catches on. Suicide by hanging in 2026 Toronto mirrors Handmaid suicides in the same era; arranged marriages are a feature of both societies; and the dumping grounds for diseased persons in Freeforall roughly parallel the Colonies in Gilead, a lethal trash heap for the infertile and the rebellious. Sharmayne Pia Veronica Humbolt Grey may be allowed to retain her real name and exercise the power of a First Mother in the new society, but like Offred she is more than half indoctrinated, uncomfortable with her rebel thoughts. Each tale ends unresolved, with the state still in control as the women continue on to their destinies. Where the stories abruptly part company is in the status of the sexes, for Freeforall is a matriarchy, and men are primarily sperm banks to reverse the ravages of disease. The reader's surprise and perhaps amusement at the idea of a future in which husband abuse is rampant and the groom is the orange-blossomed, veiled figure at the marriage altar are as telling an exposure of enduring sexist notions as any of the traditional patriarchal oppressions found in Gilead or in Nunavit two hundred years after.

Atwood's 1992 collection *Good Bones* includes several science-fiction stories. "Homelanding," previously published in *Tesseracts³* (1990) and included in the *Norton Book of Science Fiction* (1993), also favors the intersection of futurism and feminism. The narrator, who eventually declares herself to be from another planet (Earth, making the Earthling the alien) and is discernibly Canadian, detachedly describes the bodies and sexual distinctions of her species (some have prongs while others have caverns; she is a "cavern person"); her native land, both physically and psychologically; as well as sleep, death, and human funerary customs. In the last of the six sections she names death as the common ground between the residents of her planet and the one she is visiting. She rejects the television science-fiction cliché of asking to be taken to their leader, alluding to the mechanical and technological leaders back home and announcing that she has had quite enough of them. Instead, asserting values considered feminist rather than masculinist, she asks to be taken to the abstract, the diurnal, the deeply basic components of this world: their trees, breakfasts, sunsets, bad dreams, shoes, nouns, fingers, deaths—in other words, the things that are really "worth it" in a society.

"Hardball" announces itself as a speculation on the future and proffers the notion of the future arriving like a giant, firm ball, a large dome in which living things find shelter from an otherwise sterile and empty Earth. Limited space is the governing issue, requiring a death for every birth, a rationing of food and even air (the rich, as ever, getting the most), and the banishment of cattle and fish. The only aberrations from spatial determination in this bleak scenario are a few stowaway rats. Having presented such a grim vision, the narrator acknowledges the readers' horror but reacts unsympathetically, taunting them to reject this future and order up another, implying that they are stuck with mere variations on an ineluctable future as the consequence of their relentless environmental abuses of the present.

In addition to those two science-fiction stories, there are three stories in *Good Bones* that, atypically for Atwood, do present uncompromised, complete fantasies. "Cold-Blooded" is a letter by a member of a superior insect species back to her sisters on the occasion of her voyage to the planet of Moths, a.k.a. Earth. She observes Earth witheringly through her own understandings and criteria, condescendingly pronouncing its "blood creatures" (human beings) to be primitive, stupidly inclined to prize males over females, not possessed of enough common sense to eat males after mating, unable to pupate, and horribly given to killing Earth's insects. She concludes with the satisfied observation that Earth bugs are nonetheless winning on several fronts (such as crops) and predicts, on the bright side, that when blood creatures have killed themselves through war or overpopulation (a sure thing), insects will prevail on Earth. In its overturning of the traditional order of the Great Chain of Being, "Cold-Blooded" satirically demotes humankind in general and takes an additional satiric shot at male domination. The story, while not futuristic, has premises that are marvelous: an insect letter-writer who is also an interplanetary traveler with full cerebral functioning and a penchant for prediction.

The witty "My Life as a Bat" explores another fantastic transspecies premise, matter-of-factly delivered: that the narrator has been a bat in a previous life. She speculates on the nightmares of a bat, including the mythic reversal (as in *The Handmaid's Tale*) in which dark is life and light/the sun means death. A sense of déjà vu and unusual preferences clue her in to that previous incarnation as a bat, and through bat eyes she mocks the conventions of vampire movies. A pseudo-historical rumination ensues on an alleged World War

II plot to use bats to carry bombs to the enemy, a plan rendered unnecessary by the development of the atomic bomb. In the fifth and final segment, titled "Beauty," the narrator entertains the idea that this human life, not her bat life, is the temporary phase, and that she has been sent on a mission for her true species. Longing to return to batdom, she describes its delights and prays for deliverance from evil (that is, humankind). "My Life as a Bat" sustains its fantastical premise, handles it with humor, whimsy, and passion, and incorporates into it an environmental message and implicit appeal to human beings to show compassion to other species.

As Sharon Wilson has demonstrated in *Margaret Atwood's Fairy-Tale Sexual Politics* (1993), allusions to fairy tales and mythic imagery are found throughout Atwood's short and long fiction. Nevertheless, in only one piece is the fairy-tale perspective entirely sustained. In "Unpopular Gals" from *Good Bones* the narrator identifies herself as one of the unpopular stock female figures of fairy-tale notoriety, that sorority of ugly stepsisters, wicked stepmothers, and cruel forest witches. She makes the case, however, for her centrality to the plot–that she actually is the plot, the one who gets things moving and is thus indispensable. Her soliloquy in effect gets to the heart of fairy-tale dynamics, introduces a new angle, and unmasks the core plot of many fairy tales as formulaic and sexist (although neither boring nor allegorically inaccurate). Atwood once again combines fantasy and feminism, as she has combined science fiction and feminism.

Atwood also utilizes science-fiction elements in her novel *The Blind Assassin,* published in 2000 and winner of the prestigious Booker Prize. In *The Blind Assassin* there are three intertwined narratives titled "The Blind Assassin," arranged like Chinese boxes. The outermost of these boxes is Atwood's novel as a whole, the gigantic life narrative of an elderly Ontario resident, Iris Chase Griffen, who is at pains to reveal her secrets in a complex, tantalizingly oblique way. Her deceptively linear, realistic memoir focuses particularly on her childhood and early adulthood with her sister Laura, who apparently wrote a novel published posthumously by Iris. Laura's novel is the second or middle "Blind Assassin" text, the subject of which is a forbidden romance in Depression-era Canada between a young political agitator on the lam and his upper-crust girlfriend, both unnamed. Apart from sex and wary conversations, their furtive rendezvous produce installments of the third, innermost "Blind Assassin" tale, a science-fiction concoction with which the fugitive seeks to hold his lady love's attention, rather like a male Scheherazade. This interior, incomplete, serialized novel is a study in the evolution of a science-fiction plot. The man is already a published writer of pulp science fiction, and at

Dust jacket for Atwood's Booker Prize–winning novel, which consists of a fictional memoir that includes a novel in which one of the characters tells the other a science-fiction story

nearly every tryst he presents his beloved with several narrative elements and possibilities, inviting her participation in the construction of his tale. Repeatedly the woman expresses a preference for less technological and more romantic options: deserts rather than outer space, mythological trappings over science-fiction toys such as ray guns. While she usually defers to her lover's professional experience in the genre, at several critical points she offers a dramatically different version of his scenario, a female rewriting of the male conventions of science fiction and fantasy.

This innermost "Blind Assassin" tale concerns the fantasy city of Sakiel-Norn, on the planet Zycron, ruled by tyrannical Snilfards and oppressed Ygnirods. Atwood, through her lover-storytellers, imagines backward (a world that predates this one by several millennia), and she draws direct lines between her fantasy world and this one (Zycronites being slated eventually to colonize Earth and be human forebears). Another clandestine love affair takes place: this couple, artfully parallel to the lovers in each of the two surrounding "Blind Assassin" narratives, are a sacrificial virgin, daughter of the elite (her tongue cut out to avoid any protests), and a blind hired killer, one of a cadre of enslaved children who have been blinded by their forced labors on intricate carpets and so driven to lines of work requiring manual but not visual skills: prostitution, thievery, and paid assassination by the deft and silent cutting of throats in the dark. The lovers together escape the doomed city, which is about to be crushed by invading barbarians, and then face other challenges. Finally, two conclusions—female/happy versus male/tragic—compete, as the lovers in the framing novel disagree on the proper ending for the story born of their assignations.

When the man's grim, "true to life" version of the Sakiel-Norn love affair "trumps" her sentimental one, he comes back with a different story altogether, promising to deliver the happy ending she craves. This other tale, never fleshed out or even titled, is much more standard science-fiction material: a narrative of the planet Xenor and its Lizard Men, of space fleets and star wars, of zorch-ray guns and metallic space suits, of interplanetary travel and alien forms of being, such as the luscious Peach Women. The "happy" ending he cynically offers is a claustrophobic vision of relentless and boring bliss on the Planet Aa'A, but again the woman storyteller resists; she gestures toward deconstructing the man's version by telling him that he has got it all wrong. In the end only a first installment of the innermost "Blind Assassin" is published by the activist on the run, purely to make some quick money. To his sweetheart's disappointment, it is a shoddy hybrid of the Zycron and Xenor stories, in which the pivotal love plot and the admirable blind assassin have been excised in favor of clichéd science-fiction paraphernalia. Although the woman has tried to accord the tale some great significance both as a document of their love and later as proof of her lover's survival, the man rightly dismisses this final version as "tripe," not worth a concluding installment.

Reviewers of *The Blind Assassin* have varied widely in their opinions of the quality of the innermost "Blind Assassin" tale as science fiction, the degree of success in its integration into the larger narratives of the same name, and the usefulness of that strand in Atwood's tapestry as a whole. Some reviewers have paid the science-fiction tale little or no attention, or have given peculiarly muddled and flawed little summaries almost as an aside to the dominant narratives of Iris's life and Laura's novel. The Zycron and Xenor stories, to be sure, comprise less than ten percent of the total narrative; they are included in only six of the fifteen sections of Atwood's novel. However, whether "pulp" or "literature" (it has been called both "drivel" and "masterful"), the science-fiction segments of *The Blind Assassin* play a crucial role as a structural key to the many-layered fiction into which they are folded. Further, the multidimensional blindness at the heart of the core story joins many other elements—sacrificial females, doomed lovers, vicious exploitations, all sorts of assassinations, silence and secrets, flight and freedom, death, memory, and myth—in reverberating importantly through the two "Blind Assassin" narratives that encase it (and also through Atwood's entire body of work). In *The Blind Assassin*, as in *The Handmaid's Tale*, Atwood uses and subverts science fiction to play with ideas of authorship, to dissect social and historical realities, and to present readers with a powerfully allegorical and cautionary tale.

Although only a small portion of Atwood's work can be truly classified as science fiction, *The Handmaid's Tale* and the scattering of other speculative work that she has published so far have helped to make readers aware of Canadian science fiction. Certainly, science-fiction conventions have influenced her work and provided her with another means of exploring gender politics and environmental issues, which are the two paramount concerns that inform Atwood's futurist and fantasy fiction.

Interviews:

Katherine Govier, "Q & Q Interview: Margaret Atwood," *Quill & Quire*, 51 (September 1985): 66–67;

Sue Matheson, "An Interview with Margaret Atwood," *Herizons* (January/February 1986): 20–22;

Cathy N. Davidson, "A Feminist '1984': Margaret Atwood Talks About Her Exciting New Novel," *Ms.* (February 1986): 24–26;

Beryl Donaldson Langer, "Interview with Margaret Atwood," *Australian-Canadian Studies*, 6 (1988): 125–136;

Geoff Hancock, "Tightrope-Walking over Niagara Falls," in *Margaret Atwood: Conversations*, edited by Earl G. Ingersoll (Willowdale, Ontario: Firefly, 1990), pp. 191–220.

Biographies:

Nathalie Cooke, *Margaret Atwood: A Biography* (Toronto: ECW, 1998);

Rosemary Sullivan, *The Red Shoes: Margaret Atwood Starting Out* (Toronto: HarperCollins, 1998).

References:

Raffaella Baccolini, "Breaking the Boundaries: Gender, Genre, and Dystopia," in *Par una definizione dell'utopia: Metodologie e discipline a confronto*, edited by Nadia Minerva (Ravenna, Italy: Longo, 1992), pp. 137–146;

Chinmoy Banerjee, "Alice in Disneyland: Criticism as Commodity in *The Handmaid's Tale*," *Essays on Canadian Writing*, 41 (Summer 1990): 74–92;

Frances Bartkowski, *Feminist Utopias* (Lincoln: University of Nebraska Press, 1989);

Nancy Topping Bazin, "Women and Revolution in Dystopian Fiction: Nadine Gordimer's *July's People* and Margaret Atwood's *The Handmaid's Tale*," in *Selected Essays: International Conference on Representing Revolution 1989*, edited by John Michael Crafton (Carrollton: West Georgia College, 1991), pp. 115-127;

Larry W. Caldwell, "Wells, Orwell, and Atwood: (EPI)Logic and Eu/Utopia," *Extrapolation: A Journal of Science Fiction and Fantasy*, 33 (Winter 1992): 333–345;

Glenn Deer, *Postmodern Canadian Fiction and the Rhetoric of Authority* (Montreal & Kingston, Ontario: McGill-Queen's University Press, 1994), pp. 110–129;

Chris Ferns, "The Value/s of Dystopia: *The Handmaid's Tale* and the Anti-Utopian Tradition," *Dalhousie Review*, 69 (Fall 1989): 373–382;

Peter Fitting, "The Turn from Utopia in Recent Feminist Fiction," in *Feminism, Utopia, and Narrative*, edited by Libby Falk and Sarah Webster Goodwin, Tennessee Studies in Literature 32 (Knoxville: University of Tennessee Press, 1990), pp. 141–158;

John Fitzsimmons, "'No Fate but What We Make': Complicity and Termination in Margaret Atwood's *The Handmaid's Tale*," in *Perspectives on the Canadian Fantastic*, edited by Allan Weiss (Toronto: ACCSFF, 1998), pp. 25–34;

Coral Ann Howells, *Margaret Atwood* (Basingstoke: Macmillan, 1996);

Dorothy Jones, "Not Much Balm in Gilead," *Commonwealth*, 11 (Spring 1989): 31–43;

Patricia Kane, "A Woman's Dystopia: Margaret Atwood's *The Handmaid's Tale*," *Notes on Contemporary Literature*, 185 (November 1988): 9–10;

David Ketterer, "Margaret Atwood's *The Handmaid's Tale*: A Contextual Dystopia," *Science-Fiction Studies*, 16 (July 1989): 209–217;

Martin Kuester, *Framing Truths: Parodic Structures in Contemporary English-Canadian Historical Novels* (Toronto: University of Toronto Press, 1992), pp. 124–152;

Amin Malak, "Margaret Atwood's 'The Handmaid's Tale' and the Dystopian Tradition," *Canadian Literature*, 112 (Spring 1987): 9–16;

Patrick D. Murphy, "Reducing the Dystopian Distance: Pseudo-Documentary Framing in Near-Future Fiction," *Science-Fiction Studies*, 17 (March 1990): 25–40;

Reingard M. Nischik, "Back to the Future: Margaret Atwood's Anti-Utopian Vision in *The Handmaid's Tale*," *Englische-Amerikanische Studien*, 9 (1987): 139–148;

Ken Norris, "'The University of Denay, Nunavit': The 'Historical Notes' in Margaret Atwood's *The Handmaid's Tale*," *American Review of Canadian Studies*, 20 (Autumn 1990): 357–364;

Roberta Rubenstein, "Nature and Nurture in Dystopia: *The Handmaid's Tale*," in *Margaret Atwood: Vision and Forms*, edited by Kathryn VanSpanckeren and Jan Garden Castro (Carbondale: Southern Illinois University Press, 1988), pp. 101–112;

Karen F. Stein, "Margaret Atwood's *The Handmaid's Tale*: Scheherazade in Dystopia," *University of Toronto Quarterly*, 61 (Winter 1991): 269–279;

Catharine R. Stimpson, "Atwood Woman," *Nation* (31 May 1986): 764–767;

Ruud Teeuwen "Dystopia's Point of No Return," in *Approaches to Teaching Atwood's* The Handmaid's Tale *and Other Works* (New York: Modern Language Association of America, 1996), pp. 114–121;

Lee Briscoe Thompson, *Scarlet Letters: Margaret Atwood's* The Handmaid's Tale (Toronto: ECW, 1997);

John Updike, "Expeditions to Gilead and Seegard," *New Yorker*, 135 (12 May 1986): 118–123;

Sharon Rose Wilson, *Margaret Atwood's Fairy-Tale Sexual Politics* (Jackson: University Press of Mississippi, 1993);

Diane S. Wood, "Bradbury and Atwood: Exile as Rational Decision," in *The Literature of Emigration and Exile*, edited by James Whitlark and Wendell Aycock, Studies in Comparative Literature 23 (Lubbock: Texas Tech University Press, 1992), pp. 131–142.

Papers:

Margaret Atwood's papers are held by the Thomas Fisher Rare Book Library at the University of Toronto.

H. Bedford-Jones

(29 April 1887 – 6 May 1949)

Peter Halasz and Don Hutchison

BOOKS: *The Cross and the Hammer: A Tale of the Days of the Vikings* (Elgin, Ill.: Cook, 1912);

Captain Becky's Masquerade, as Margaret Love Sanderson (Chicago: Reilly & Britton, 1912);

Captain Becky's Winter Cruise, as Sanderson (Chicago: Reilly & Britton, 1912);

Larry Borden's Redemption; or, Proving His Honesty, by Bedford-Jones and William Wallace Cook, as Emerson Baker (New York: Street & Smith, 1913);

Flamehair the Skald: A Tale of the Days of Hardrede (Chicago: McClurg, 1913);

Figs and Thistles (Long Beach, Cal.: Privately printed, 1914);

The Camp Fire Girls at Hillside, as Sanderson (Chicago: Reilly & Britton, 1914);

The Camp Fire Girls at Pinetree Camp, as Sanderson (Chicago: Reilly & Britton, 1914);

The Conquest (Elgin, Ill.: Cook, 1914);

Fruit Before Summer (Long Beach, Cal.: Privately printed, 1915);

Under Fire (New York: Howell, 1915);

Gathered Verse (Santa Barbara, Cal.: Privately printed, 1916);

The Camp Fire Girls at Top o' the World, as Sanderson (Chicago: Reilly & Britton, 1916); republished as *Mollie Wren's Promise* (Chicago: Reilly & Lee, 1936);

L'Arbre Croche Mission: A Memorable Relation Briefly Setting Forth the Historical Facts and Eschewing All Fable & Legend, as Erected by Untutored Minds, Touching upon the Justly Famed Mission of The Crooked Tree (Santa Barbara, Cal.: Privately printed, 1917);

The Myth Wawatam: Or, Alex. Henry Refuted, Being an Exposure of Certain Fictions, Hitherto Unsuspected of the Public; with which Are Also Found Some Remarks upon the Famous Old Fort Michillimackinac, All of which is Herein Written & Publish'd from the Notes of Henry McConnell, Gent. (Santa Barbara, Cal.: Privately printed, 1917);

H. Bedford-Jones

The Camp Fire Girls at Lookout Pass, as Sanderson (Chicago: Reilly & Britton, 1917); republished as *Betty at Lookout Pass* (Chicago: Reilly & Lee, 1936);

Corn Wine & Oil: Being Poems (Santa Barbara, Cal.: Privately printed, 1918);

The Story of Misión San Juan Capistrano (Santa Barbara, Cal.: Privately printed, 1918);

Bigfoot Joe and Others: Figments of Fancy (Lakeport, Mich.: Privately printed, 1919);

The Camp Fire Girls in Old Kentucky, as Sanderson (Chicago: Reilly & Britton, 1919); republished as *Jane Pellew in Kentucky* (Chicago: Reilly & Lee, 1936);

The Camp Fire Girls on a Yacht, as Sanderson (Chicago: Reilly & Lee, 1920); republished as *A Cruise of the Boojum* (Chicago: Reilly & Lee, 1936);

The Mesa Trail (Garden City, N.Y.: Doubleday, Page, 1920; Toronto: S. B. Gundy, 1920?; London: Hurst & Blackett, 1923);

The Boy Scouts of the Air in the Dismal Swamp, as Gordon Stuart (Chicago: Reilly & Lee, 1920);

The Boy Scouts of the Air at Cape Peril, as Stuart (Chicago: Reilly & Lee, 1921);

The Crazy Elk of Terrapin Swamp, as Elliott Whitney (Chicago: Reilly & Lee, 1921);

The Mardi Gras Mystery (Garden City, N.Y.: Doubleday, Page, 1921);

The Fiction Business (Denver: Student-Writer Press, 1922); revised as *This Fiction Business* (New York: Covici-Friede, 1929);

The Second Mate (Garden City, N.Y.: Garden City Publishing, 1923);

The Sheriff of Pecos (Garden City, N.Y.: Doubleday, Page, 1923);

Outlaw of Rattlesnake Gap (Garden City, N.Y.: Garden City Publishing, 1923);

The Saber-Tusk Walrus, as Whitney (Chicago: Reilly & Lee, 1923);

The Gate of Farewell, as Allan Hawkwood (London: Hurst & Blackett, 1923);

The Boss of The Big Horn, as Whitney (Chicago: Reilly & Lee, 1924);

Solomon's Quest, as Hawkwood (London: Hurst & Blackett, 1924);

Mormon Valley (Garden City, N.Y.: Garden City Publishing, 1924; London: Federation Press, 1924);

Against the Tide, as John Wycliffe (New York: Dodd, Mead, 1924);

The Star Woman (New York: Dodd, Mead, 1924; Toronto: Ryerson, 1924; London: Hurst & Blackett, 1925);

The Seal of John Solomon, as Hawkwood (London: Hurst & Blackett, 1924);

The Hazards of Smith (London: Hurst & Blackett, 1924);

The Kasbah Gate (London: Hurst & Blackett, 1924);

Splendour of the Gods (London: Hurst & Blackett, 1924?);

Blood of the Peacock (London: Hurst & Blackett, 1924);

The Gate of Farewell (London: Hurst & Blackett, 1924);

Loot!–A Novel (London: Hurst & Blackett, 1924?);

The Cruise of the Pelican (London: Hurst & Blackett, 1924?);

The Trail of the Shadow (London: Hurst & Blackett, 1924);

Viking Love, as Hawkwood (London: Hurst & Blackett, 1924);

John Solomon, Supercargo, as Hawkwood (London: Hurst & Blackett, 1924?);

John Solomon, Incognito, as Hawkwood (London: Hurst & Blackett, 1924);

Solomon's Carpet, as Hawkwood (London: Hurst & Blackett, 1925);

The Shawl of Solomon, as Hawkwood (London: Hurst & Blackett, 1925);

Gentleman Solomon, as Hawkwood (London: Hurst & Blackett, 1925);

Afoul of Destiny (London: Hurst & Blackett, 1925);

The Wilderness Trail (London: Hurst & Blackett, 1925);

Far Horizons (London: Hurst & Blackett, 1925);

A Son of the Cincinnati, as Montague Brisard (Boston: Small, Maynard, 1925);

Arizona Argonauts (New York: Garden City Press, 1925);

Rodomont: A Romance of Mont St. Michel in the Days of Louis XIV (New York: Putnam, 1926; London: Hurst & Blackett, 1926);

Saint Michael's Gold (New York: Putnam, 1926);

The Black Bull (New York: Putnam, 1927);

The Wizard of the Atlas, as Hawkwood (London: Hurst & Blackett, 1928);

D'Artagnan: The Sequel to The Three Musketeers, Augmenting and Incorporating a Fragmentary Manuscript by Alexandre Dumas (New York: Covici-Friede, 1928);

The King's Passport (New York: Putnam, 1928; London: Stanley Paul, 1928);

The Twisted Tree, by Bedford-Jones and Mary Bedford-Jones (New York: Stratford Press, 1929);

Cyrano (New York: Putnam, 1930);

The Shadow (New York: The Fiction League, 1930);

D'Artagnan's Letter, by Bedford-Jones and Mary Bedford-Jones (New York: Covici-Friede, 1931);

Drums of Dambala (New York: Covici-Friede, 1932; London: Long, 1932);

The Graduate Fictioneer (Denver: Author & Journalist Publishing, 1932);

The King's Pardon (New York: Covici-Friede, 1933);

The Mission and the Man: The Story of San Juan Capistrano (Pasadena, Cal.: San Pasqual Press, 1939);

John Barry, by Bedford-Jones, as Donald F. Bedford, and Donald Friede and Kenneth Fearing (New York: Creative Age, 1947);

West in the Saddle, as Gordon Keyne (New York: Arcadia House, 1947);

The California Trail (New York: Phoenix Press, 1948; London: Wright & Brown, 1952);

Malay Gold (Toronto: Harlequin, 1953);

The Temple of the Ten, by Bedford-Jones and W. C. Robertson (West Kingston, R.I.: Grant, 1973);

Post-Mortem: H. Bedford-Jones, edited by Michael Murphy (St. Louis: Norfolk Hall, 1980;

John Solomon, as Hawkwood (London: Hurst & Blackett, n.d.);

Kismet (London: Hurst & Blackett, n.d.).

PRODUCED SCRIPT: *Abe Lincoln's Story,* by Bedford-Jones and Carl Haverlin, radio, Mutual Broadcasting System, 2 January 1944.

TRANSLATION: Maurice de Guérin, *From Centaur to Cross: The Unpublished Correspondence & The Centaur* (New York: Covici-Friede, 1929).

SELECTED PERIODICAL PUBLICATIONS–
UNCOLLECTED: "Solomon's Submarine," *People's Magazine,* 20 (February 1916): 1–71;

"The Buddha's Elephant," as Allan Hawkwood, *All Around* (August 1916);

"Mr. Shen of Shensi," *All Story,* 74 (18 August 1917): 384–415;

"A Hand in the Game," as Hawkwood, *People's Magazine,* 28 (10 November 1918): 1–60;

"Mr. Bast's Cat," *People's Magazine* (25 November 1918);

"Khmer the Mysterious," as Hawkwood, *People's Magazine,* 29 (25 January 1919): 114–140;

"The Disembodied," *People's Magazine* (25 February 1919): 66–90;

"The Golden Woman of Khmer," as Hawkwood, *People's Magazine* (10 March 1919);

"Luck O' Louisiana," as Hawkwood, *People's Magazine* (25 May 1919);

"Fang Tung, Magician," *All Story,* 100 (2 August 1919); reprinted in *Thrills* (June 1927): 1–58;

"The Second Life of Monsieur the Devil," *Blue Book,* 32 (November 1920): 160–192;

"The Messenger," by Bedford-Jones and W. C. Robertson, *Adventure,* 27 (1 December 1920): 128–148;

"The Mysterious John Solomon," *Argosy,* 209 (25 January 1930): 602–632;

"John Solomon's Biggest Game," *Argosy,* 210 (15 February 1930): 150–167; (22 February 1930): 348–368; (1 March 1930): 516–535; (8 March 1930): 689–708; (15 March 1930): 838–855; 211 (22 March 1930): 122–139;

"Temple of the Dogs," *Argosy,* 229 (21 May 1932): 4–24;

"The Evil Eye of Bali," *Detective Fiction Weekly,* 79 (7 October 1933): 50–59;

"The Desert of Death," *Detective Fiction Weekly,* 79 (14 October 1933): 90–97;

"The Backwards Swastika," *Detective Fiction Weekly,* 79 (21 October 1933): 50–57;

"The Circles of Doom," *Detective Fiction Weekly,* 80 (28 October 1933): 68–75;

"Footsteps of Death," *Detective Fiction Weekly,* 80 (4 November 1933): 41–48;

"The Niche of Horror," *Detective Fiction Weekly,* 80 (11 November 1933): 58–67;

"Gallows Reef," *Argosy* (20 January 1934): 66–87;

"Jungle Girl," *Argosy,* 245 (10 March 1934): 2–22; (17 March 1934): 79–98; (24 March 1934): 121–139; (31 March 1934): 124–139;

"The Sleeper," *Weird Tales,* 24 (October 1934): 445–450;

"The Case of the Deathly Barque," *Argosy,* 253 (9 February 1935): 71–82;

"Spear of Gleaming Willow," *Blue Book,* 62 (February 1935): 6–17;

"The Shield of Arngrim," *Blue Book,* 63 (August 1935): 74–82;

"The Face That Launched a Thousand Ships," *Blue Book,* 65 (June 1937): 50–61;

"The Face in the Pool," as Gordon Keyne, *Blue Book,* 65 (June 1937): 86–90;

"Cleopatra's Beads," *Blue Book,* 66 (October 1937): 88–97;

"Hand of Glory," *All American Fiction* (May–June 1938);

"The Vase of Heaven and Earth," *All American Fiction,* 2 (July–August 1938): 26–36;

"The Little Black God," *Blue Book,* 67 (August 1938): 94–103;

"The Flying Dutchman," *Blue Book,* 67 (August 1938): 15–23;

"Bluebeard's Closet," *Argosy,* 285 (8 October 1938): 31–41;

"Isle of the Dead," *Argosy,* 285 (5 November 1938): 37–47;

"Cleopatra's Amulet," *Argosy,* 286 (19 November 1938): 62–71;

"The Stagnant Death," *Blue Book,* 68 (November 1938): 6–19;

"The Scythian Lamb," *Blue Book,* 68 (December 1938): 34–47;

"Wrath of the Thunderbird," *Blue Book,* 68 (January 1939): 6–19;

"The Singing Sands of Prester John," *Blue Book,* 68 (February 1939): 64–76; reprinted in *Fantastic Stories,* 12 (September 1963): 52–71;

"Amazon Woman," *Blue Book,* 68 (March 1939): 78–92;

"Five Miles to Youth," *Blue Book,* 68 (April 1939): 35–45;

"Portals of Illusion," *American Weekly* (29 May 1939 – 7 August 1939);

"Trumpets from Oblivion," *Blue Book,* 69 (May 1939): 62–73;

"The Lady and the Unicorn," *Blue Book,* 69 (June 1939): 38–51;

"Lady of the Evil Eye," *Blue Book,* 69 (July 1939): 16–29;

"The Wolf Woman," *Blue Book,* 69 (August 1939): 14–25; reprinted in *Fantastic Stories,* 12 (October 1963): 30–48;

"The Heavenly Bird," *Blue Book,* 69 (September 1939): 30–42;

"Pearls of Destiny," *All American Fiction,* 2 (September–October 1939): 67–78;

"Woman of the Sea," *Blue Book,* 69 (October 1939): 81–93;

"The Serpent People," *Blue Book,* 70 (November 1939): 18–31;

"The Hour of the Eclipse," *Short Stories* (10 March 1940): 6–41; (25 March 1940): 68–98; (10 April 1940): 56–75; (25 April 1940): 62–81;

"Mistakes Don't Pay," as Keyne, *Short Stories* (10 April 1940): 148–165;

"Sons of Kalewa," *Blue Book,* 71 (May 1940): 6–20;

"Four Men at Peace," *Blue Book,* 71 (June 1940): 40–53;

"The Artificial Honeymoon," *Weird Tales,* 35 (July 1940): 4–14;

"Emerald of Isis," *Argosy,* 302 (21 September 1940): 50–59;

"The Blind Farmer and the Strip Dancer," *Weird Tales,* 35 (September 1940): 44–55;

"The Kings Do Battle Again," as Keyne, *Weird Tales,* 35 (September 1940): 108–120;

"Ruby of France," *Argosy,* 303 (9 November 1940): 52–62;

"The Angry Amethyst," *Argosy,* 303 (30 November 1940): 35–45;

"The Wife of the Humorous Gangster," *Weird Tales,* 35 (November 1940): 42–52;

"From Out of the Dark Water," as Captain Michael Gallister, *Blue Book,* 72 (December 1940): 4–13;

"Sinister Sapphire," *Argosy,* 305 (18 January 1941): 23–27;

"Jeopardy's Jewel," *Argosy* (8 March 1941): 13–17;

"The Perilous Pearl," *Argosy,* 306 (22 March 1941): 16–22;

"The Affair of the Shuteye Medium," *Weird Tales* (March 1941): 46–57;

"The Curious Luck of the Pursuit Flyer," *Short Stories* (25 June 1941): 31–39;

"The Princess and the Prophet," as Keyne, *Blue Book,* 74 (December 1941): 2–20; (January 1942): 72–87; (February 1942): 78–95; (March 1942): 78–95;

"The Gate of Mercy," *Blue Book,* 74 (January 1942): 24–32;

"Red Moon on Flores Sea," *Blue Book,* 75 (May 1942): 64–78;

"Peace Hath Her Victories," as Keyne, *Blue Book,* 76 (January 1943): 10–19;

"The Battle for France," as Keyne, *Blue Book,* 76 (February 1943): 104–111;

"Sahara Dawn," as Keyne, *Blue Book,* 76 (March 1943): 54–62;

"Cairo Midnight," as Keyne, *Blue Book,* 76 (April 1943): 86–95;

"The Old Man of Iceland," *Short Stories* (25 April 1943): 50–60;

"Bagdad Madness," as Keyne, *Blue Book,* 77 (May 1943): 18–27;

"Tomorrow in Egypt," as Keyne, *Blue Book,* 77 (June 1943): 84–93;

"The Affair of the Drifting Face," as Keyne, *Blue Book,* 77 (July 1943): 58–67;

"His Last Appearance," *Weird Tales,* 36 (July 1943): 6–19;

"The Affair of the Two Thirteens," as Keyne, *Blue Book,* 77 (August 1943): 82–91;

"The Affair of the Unfinished Search," as Keyne, *Blue Book,* 77 (September 1943): 17–25;

"The Affair of the Beryllium Q," as Keyne, *Blue Book,* 77 (October 1943): 90–99;

"Counterclockwise," *Blue Book,* 78 (November 1943): 25–33;

"Some See, Some Do Not," *Short Stories* (10 November 1943): 49–62;

"Naples Midnight," *Blue Book,* 78 (December 1943): 26–35;

"The Past Earns the Future," as Keyne, *Blue Book,* 78 (December 1943): 42–50;

"Pharaoh Figured Wrong," *Short Stories* (10 December 1943): 51–63;

"The Fifth Freedom," *Short Stories* (25 December 1943): 55–65;

"We Who Have Fought," as Gallister, *Blue Book,* 78 (January 1944): 12–20;

"Princess of Egypt," *Blue Book,* 78 (January 1944): 40–50;

"The One-Handed Siberian," *Short Stories* (10 January 1944);

"The Architect of Samos," *Blue Book,* 78 (February 1944): 40–48;

"A Dead Man Tells," with Keyne, *Blue Book,* 78 (February 1944): 90–97;

"Ice Caves," *Short Stories* (25 February 1944): 126–139;

"The Last Macedonian," *Blue Book,* 78 (March 1944): 54–62;

"From the House of the Rat Catcher," *Weird Tales,* 37 (March 1944): 66–75;

"Gremlins Talk Japanese," *Short Stories* (10 March 1944): 58–68;

"A Matter of Routine," *Short Stories* (25 March 1944): 52–62;

"Island in the Sky," *Blue Book,* 78 (April 1944): 72–80;

"The Miraculous Buddha," *Short Stories* (10 April 1944): 88–99;

"Foxes Move Fast," *Blue Book,* 79 (May 1944): 82–90;

"Unpublished Story," *Weird Tales,* 37 (May 1944): 41–51;

"Old Man with a Staff," *Blue Book,* 79 (June 1944): 72–79;

"Aimed at Aguila," *Blue Book,* 79 (July 1944): 38–44;

"The Fabian Sword," *Blue Book,* 79 (August 1944): 12–19;

"Finding Mr. Smith," *Blue Book,* 79 (September 1944): 91–99;

"Where Freedom," *Blue Book,* 79 (October 1944): 52–60;

"The Strange Fate of Col. Clewes," as Keyne, *Blue Book,* 80 (December 1944): 58–66;

"The Gods Do Not Forget," *Blue Book,* 80 (December 1944): 97–104;

"Gimlet Eye Gunn," *Short Stories* (25 March 1945): 8–36; reprinted in *Weird Tales,* 43 (September 1951): 8–37;

"In the Beginning," *Weird Tales,* 38 (March 1945): 24–32;

"What More Can Fortune Do?," as Keyne, *Blue Book,* 80 (March 1945);

"The Case of the Final Hoard," as Keyne, *Blue Book,* 81 (July 1945): 72–95;

"Carson's Folly," *Blue Book,* 81 (July 1945): 2–13;

"The One-Legged Dancer," *Blue Book,* 81 (August 1945): 78–88;

"The Hill of Yuan," as Gallister, *Blue Book,* 81 (August 1945): 102–122;

"Grotto of the Nymphs," *Blue Book,* 81 (September 1945): 10–20;

"Wing of the Lion," *Blue Book,* 81 (October 1945): 40–50;

"The Sorcerer's Daughter," *Blue Book,* 82 (November 1945): 2–13;

"Brittany Treasure," *Blue Book,* 82 (December 1945): 40–51;

"The Pledge of Honor," *Blue Book,* 82 (January 1946): 38–49;

"Viking Loot," *Blue Book,* 82 (February 1946): 76–87;

"The Nobleman and the Ugly Barmaid," *Blue Book,* 82 (March 1946): 90–101;

"The Uranium Pomegranates," *Short Stories* (10 March 1946): 10–31; (25 March 1946): 72–93; (10 April 1946): 56–78; (25 April 1946): 92–111;

"Death-Tapped Gold," *Blue Book,* 82 (April 1946): 82–92;

"The Devil's Fire," *Blue Book,* 84 (February 1947): 46–54;

"He Who Sets a Trap," *Blue Book,* 84 (March 1947): 128–144.

H. Bedford-Jones drew a curtain of privacy about his life in a manner that has consistently frustrated would-be researchers and biographers. One of the most prolific and arguably one of the most popular authors in the first half of the twentieth century, he wrote primarily for the mass-market pulp-fiction magazines. A meaningful portion of the ninety-odd novels and the more than twelve hundred shorter works of fiction written by Bedford-Jones is either science fiction or fantasy—perhaps as much as 10 percent of his total output. Much of the rest includes significant fantastic elements. Bedford-Jones's forte, historical adventure, colored much of the science fiction and fantasy he produced. Commonly for the time, he mixed genres with abandon, paying little attention to what was crystallizing as convention. His nongenre work often included healthy doses of the fantastic, whereas his fantastic works—especially the later ones—were written prosaically, with the imaginative elements treated in a casual manner. In the nongenre material this emphasis served to inject an extra dollop of excitement, while in the genre material the understatement added an extra measure of verisimilitude.

Henry James O'Brien Bedford-Jones was born in Napanee, Ontario, on 29 April 1887, the son of a clergyman. His grandfather, Thomas Bedford Jones, brought the family to Canada from Dublin and decided to hyphenate the family surname and even to adopt a spurious coat of arms in order to impress the "colonials." Young Henry decided that the hyphenated cognomen—authentic or not—was distinctive enough to prove itself a commercial asset; he retained it as his major authorial byline. While the varied and historically accurate backgrounds of his stories reveal him to be a man of much learning, Bedford-Jones attended college for only two semesters before surrendering to the requisites of earning a livelihood. According to *The New York Times,* "he began writing professionally while studying," because, as the author himself admitted, "I found that I could only do one thing passably well—that was writing."

Two early skills that he claimed factored in his career were those of typesetting and stenography. It is not clear what year he left his native Canada, but it appears that he moved to Chicago shortly after leaving the university in order to take a job as stenographer for a railroad superintendent on the old Chicago Western. At this point his literary sales were mainly verses sold to a group of Sunday-school magazines. Bedford-Jones's versifying ability, combined with phenomenal speed on the typewriter, soon earned him enough money to quit his stenographic duties. At the age of twenty or so he moved to Conway, Michigan, where he became a reporter and jack-of-all-trades on a weekly newspaper, still doing hack work in his spare time and taking on anything that would further his ability to write engaging prose.

In Michigan the struggling young author met William Wallace Cook, one of the leading dime-novel writers of the pre–World War period, and the two became friends. Cook was a prodigious chronicler of such Street and Smith icons as Deadwood Dick, Klondike Kit, Frank Merriwell, and the redoubtable Nick Carter. Bedford-Jones became a protégé of the older author and even ghostwrote fiction for Cook. When Cook's wife died after a sudden illness, he entrusted Bedford-Jones to produce a Frank Merriwell novel for him to meet a deadline. Bedford-Jones sat down and did it for him on the spot–25,000 words in a single draft. This act of charity and skill so impressed Cook that he eventually introduced his young friend to several of his New York editors. The result was Bedford-Jones's first pulp sale–a Foreign Legion novelette to *Argosy*. He produced a longer tale for the same magazine, and an unheard-of thing happened: the issue sold out and had to be reprinted.

Bedford-Jones was in his mid twenties when he achieved success in the pulp-magazine field. As he expressed in his peculiarly titled third-person memoir, *Post-Mortem: H. Bedford-Jones* (1980), the source for most knowledge of his early life: "To his work he brought an extreme facility in typing his thoughts—not in just typing alone. He had the gift of expression. He had youth, a vigor beyond exhaustion, and an instinctive grasp on the essentials of a story. He never over-wrote—in fact, he always stressed the proper highlights and then cut the thing short."

From 1912 onward Bedford-Jones stories became a staple in such magazines as *Adventure, All-Story Weekly, Argosy, Blue Book, People's Magazine, Popular Magazine, Short Stories*, and *Top-Notch*. Because much of his work ran to novelette or novel length, his byline became a familiar sight to newsstand browsers of the period. By 1914 he was a "name" writer, and magazine publishers used that name to sell their wares. They began paying him the highest rates per word to compete for his creative services.

Possibly with the encouragement of the resulting financial security, Bedford-Jones married Helen Swing Williamson in 1914. They had three children, two daughters and a son. His firstborn, Helen Wallace Bedford-Jones, was given Cook's middle name. Following the dissolution of his marriage in 1925, Bedford-Jones wed Mary McNally Bernardin, who later collaborated on some works.

Lost cities and lost races of the East, popular prewar fantasy conceits, abound in Bedford-Jones's early work. The lost Chinese province settled by descendants of Alexander's Greeks in "The Buddha's Elephant" (1916) and the lost cities in "Khmer the Mysterious" (1919) and "The Brazen Peacock" are typical examples. The forgotten Central American settlement in the later "The Hour of the Eclipse" (1940),

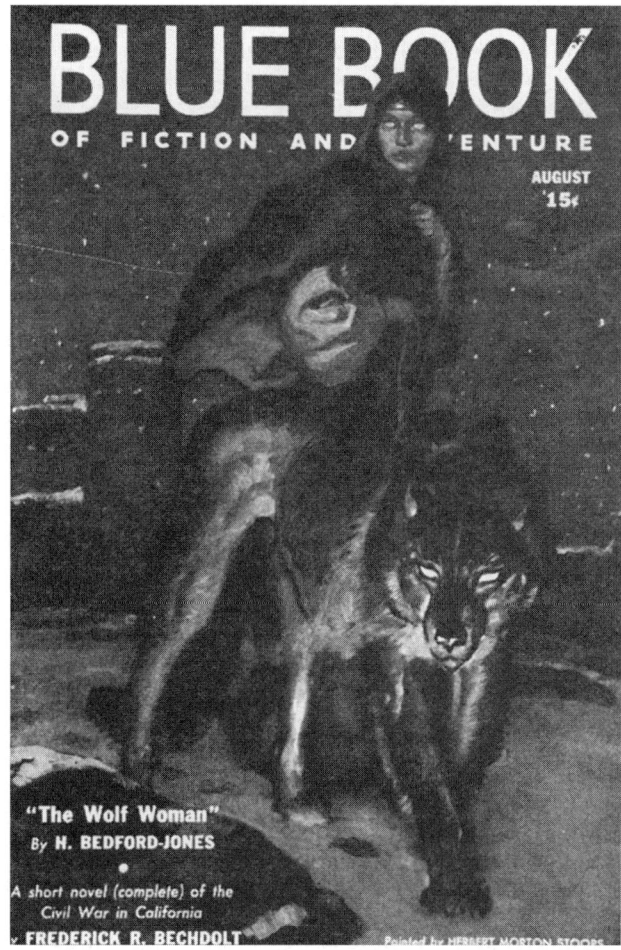

Cover for a 1939 issue of the magazine that published many of Bedford-Jones's science-fiction and fantasy stories

populated by descendants of the ancient Aztecs who had intermarried with Spanish conquistadors, brought the action closer to home.

Bedford-Jones's most popular series featured the Cockney adventurer John Solomon. This elderly, rotund clown is not the typical pulp-era hero; usually younger, more active, "surrogate" heroes were needed to move the plot along. This extended series, not all with supernatural or science-fictional plots, includes three lost-city or lost-race novels. *Solomon's Quest*, first published in the March 1915 issue of *People's Magazine*, is an adventure set partly in "Theopolis," a city surrounded by quicksand on an island in the midst of marshes. Built by Arab Christians in order to hide from the ravages of the first jihad, it also houses the stolen corpse of the prophet Mohammed–buried under a stone cross one hundred feet tall.

Solomon's Quest was immediately followed by *Gentleman Solomon* in the June 1915 issue of *People's Magazine*.

In this novel, while attempting to eradicate the "bestial" working conditions of the Belgian Congo, John Solomon stumbles across a race of white dwarves living in the caves of the White Mountains. Descended from the members of a lost Egyptian caravan led by a priest of Ma'at, this "degenerate" remnant is freed from slavery. *The Seal of John Solomon,* published in the same month in *Argosy,* returns to "Araby," a favorite haunt. In the lost city of Themoud, implausibly located in the depths of a volcano, live the descendants of Norman Crusaders guarding an age-old secret.

Both "Fang Tung, Magician" (1919) and "Mr. Shen of Shensi" (1917) feature Oriental villains inspired by Sax Rohmer's Fu Manchu. Sorcery, hypnotism, and the occult are all important plot elements. Although these stories were written during a time when the "Yellow Peril" was a racist obsession, "Fang Tung, Magician" at least demonstrates a real empathy for the Chinese people and their then-nationalist aspirations. The writing evinces a respect for and a liking of other cultures that is normally not seen in pulp literature.

This cosmopolitan attitude is evident in much of Bedford-Jones's work, perhaps because he was on the move throughout much of his life, changing his home address every year or so and traveling extensively throughout the United States and Canada. There is no clear record of his peregrinations, save that of various residences in Michigan, Ohio, Wisconsin, Indiana, and California. He acted as a part-time rector of various churches in Santa Barbara and Los Angeles in the late 1910s, suggesting a strong religious belief derived from his clergyman father. In the late 1920s he lived in Paris and London for several years, serving as foreign correspondent for the *Boston Globe.* During the 1930s his permanent residence was in Los Angeles, where he temporarily abandoned magazine publication (in 1932) in order to serve as a script doctor for 20th Century-Fox.

Although he became a United States citizen, he never forgot his Canadian roots and often used both Canadian settings and Canadian protagonists. Examples in his fantastic fiction include *The Star Woman* (1924), which is set in the territories disputed by the early fur-trading companies of the seventeenth century. In a *Weird Tales* series sardonically titled *The Adventures of a Professional Corpse* (beginning July 1940), Albertan James F. Bronson earns his living by "dying" repeatedly.

Throughout his career Bedford-Jones's writing pace was legendary, leading to many stories, some no doubt apocryphal, told by fellow writers and editors. Author and friend Vincent Starrett told of the time a friend tried to reach Bedford-Jones on the telephone. "Henry can't come to the phone," his wife is reported to have said; "He's working on a novel." The caller replied, "I'll hold on until he's finished."

A chronological examination of Bedford-Jones's output demonstrates that his early attraction to the fantastic story grew stronger with time. In later years lost races gave way to historical fantasies "framed" by a science-fictional construct. The six stories of the "Halfway House" series (beginning on 8 October 1938) both in *Argosy* and *All-American Fiction,* the thirteen stories of the "Trumpets of Oblivion" series (beginning in November 1938) in *Blue Book,* the six stories of the "Jewel" series (beginning on 21 September 1941) in *Argosy,* and finally the ten stories in the "Counterclockwise" series (beginning in November 1943) in *Blue Book* all employ various technological devices that permit the past to be seen and heard in English by present-day observers. For instance, in "The Trumpets of Oblivion," Norman Fletcher's electronic gadget depicts episodes from the past in 3-D. Each story is based on a different myth, which, upon viewing, is explained in rational terms for the skeptical and mystified members of the Inventors' Club. Similarly, the short story "In The Beginning" (March 1945) features an office safe containing a link with the philosophers, magicians, and soothsayers of past ages.

Bedford-Jones knew and understood history far better than he understood science and technology. Nevertheless, he did not hesitate to use the science-fictional devices in vogue at the time. The projectorless "movie" in "The Mysterious John Solomon" (1930); the plastic gun that shoots "tiny glass bubbles filled with highly compressed vapor" and is further described as "the most murderous weapon ever devised by man"; or more simply "the Lehigh tube" in the story "Pharaoh Figured Wrong" (1943) are typical super-scientific gadgets. Supersonic-beam weapons in "The Fifth Freedom" (1943) and the forced brain-cell growth concomitant with human brain-tissue grafts (in rats) in the Sherlockian pastiche "The Case of the Deathly Barque" (1935) are examples of the science-fictional devices he employed less often.

During World War II, Bedford-Jones's appearances in *Blue Book* eclipsed his other work. He became a de facto "house" writer, often with up to four stories per weekly issue. His wartime science-fiction and fantasy output follows two main themes—divine intervention and projections of the future.

The idea that there could be direct divine or spiritual intervention on behalf of the allies was a certain morale booster, and he made good use of it. In "Sons of Kalewa" (1940) old Finnish gods help repel the winter invader, and in "The Kings Do Battle Again" (1940) Vikings appear in wartime Norway to help at a critical juncture. Similarly, in "From Out of the Dark Water"

(1940) the "little people" are instrumental in helping to repel a Nazi incursion of Britain. "The Curious Luck of the Pursuit Flyer" (1941) features ghostly assistance to a stricken American fighter pilot in the Pacific theater. In "Red Moon on Flores Sea" (1942) the ghost of ancestor Captain Hendrik van der Broome, in his old fort, helps fight off a Japanese invasion with little more than an antique cannon.

Bedford-Jones displayed ambitious and considerably more difficult speculation in a cycle of three near-future series. The six stories of "Tomorrow's Men" (beginning in January 1943), the ten stories of "Quest Inc." (beginning in July 1943), and the seven stories of "The Strato-Shooters" (beginning in December 1943) are all set within the same immediate postwar "universe." Earthquakes have sunk half the Japanese islands under the ocean, and the allies have won the war. All of the stories are written with a pragmatic optimism seldom seen in the typical near-future cautionary scenario.

The political and economic prognostications in these stories, although not accurate blueprints, resonate eerily in hindsight. They are densely populated with fictional global institutions such as "The Coalition of the Four Freedoms," the "International Court of Justice," the "International Air Control," and the "World Refinance Organization." These prefigure the United Nations, the World Court, the IAFA, and the International Monetary Fund, respectively. Furthermore, not all countries in these series subscribe to the "Atlantic Charter," but rather actively scheme against its success, just as in the Cold War to come.

In this cycle Bedford-Jones evinces belief in the benefits of new technology without losing sight of its double-edged nature. He also writes of the benefits attendant on global commerce, as in a passage from "Gremlins Talk Japanese," published in the 10 March 1944 issue of *Short Stories:* "Air had changed everything at the war's end. It aided the tremendous economic boom that had come to the whole world as a result of reconstruction, new inventions, new ways of life and action."

After a lengthy and prolific career Henry Bedford-Jones died at the age of sixty-two, on 6 May 1949, of a heart ailment, missing confirmation of his wartime speculations by a few short years. In his introduction to Bedford-Jones's *The Graduate Fictioneer* (1932) author Erle Stanley Gardner professed his admiration and gratitude by describing his friend and mentor as "The King of the Wood Pulps." Gardner went on to become one of the best-selling authors of all time (thanks almost entirely to his Perry Mason novels), while Bedford-Jones's work rapidly disappeared from both print and popular consciousness—sharing the fate of so many once-popular pulp-fiction authors.

Neither the National Library of Canada nor the Library of Congress has complete holdings of his works; in fact, both are deficient in pulp magazines, his primary market. A handful of collectors and enthusiasts have done what they can to collect and preserve this original source material, but as yet there is no bibliography, critical study, or biography. The ephemeral nature of the medium has mitigated against longevity, and sufficient time has passed that an unknown amount of Bedford-Jones's work has doubtless been irretrievably lost. Nevertheless, a massive bibliographic project by editor and researcher Peter Ruber and collector Darrel Richardson is underway. Those who still read Bedford-Jones agree with Mike Ashley, who wrote that Bedford-Jones's "fantastic fiction had a zest which has kept it fresh over the years. It is certainly worthy of reconsideration."

References:
Lois B. Garcia, "H. Bedford-Jones: King of the Woodpulps," *Library Chronicle of The University of Texas,* 10 (1978): 73–74;
Robert Sampson, *Yesterday's Faces,* volume 6 (Bowling Green, Ohio: Bowling Green State University Popular Press, 1993).

Papers:
Although many of his manuscripts and papers have been lost, some papers are housed in the H. Bedford-Jones Collection at the Harry Ransom Humanities Research Center, University of Texas at Austin.

Lesley Choyce
(21 March 1951 –   )

Allan Weiss
York University

BOOKS: *Edible Wild Plants of Nova Scotia* (West Chezzetcook, Nova Scotia: Eastern Shore Publishing Collective, 1976);

Edible Wild Plants of the Maritimes (West Chezzetcook, Nova Scotia: Wooden Anchor Press, 1977);

Re-inventing the Wheel (Fredericton, New Brunswick: Fiddlehead Poetry Books, 1980);

Eastern Sure: Short Fiction (Halifax, Nova Scotia: Nimbus, 1980);

Fast Living (Fredericton, New Brunswick: Fiddlehead Poetry Books, 1982);

Downwind (St. John's, Newfoundland: Creative, 1984);

Billy Botzweiler's Last Dance and Other Stories (Toronto: Blewointment press, 1984);

Conventional Emotions (St. John's, Newfoundland: Creative, 1985);

The End of Ice (Fredericton, New Brunswick: Fiddlehead Poetry Books/Goose Lane, 1985);

The Dream Auditor (Charlottetown, Prince Edward Island: Ragweed Press, 1986);

The Top of the Heart (Saskatoon, Saskatchewan: Thistledown, 1986);

An Avalanche of Ocean: The Life and Times of a Nova Scotia Immigrant (Fredericton, New Brunswick: Goose Lane Editions, 1987);

Coming Up for Air (St. John's, Newfoundland: Creative, 1988);

December Six/The Halifax Solution: An Alternative to Nuclear War (Porters Lake, Nova Scotia: Pottersfield Press, 1988);

The Man Who Borrowed the Bay of Fundy, edited by Ken Hanly (Brandon, Manitoba: Dollarpoems, 1988);

The Second Season of Jonas MacPherson (Saskatoon, Saskatchewan: Thistledown Press, 1989);

Skateboard Shakedown (Halifax, Nova Scotia: Formac, 1989);

The Hungry Lizards (Don Mills, Ontario: Collier Macmillan Canada, 1990);

Skate freaks Og Graesrodder (Copenhagen: Thorup, 1990);

Wave Watch (Halifax, Nova Scotia: Formac, 1990);

Magnificent Obsessions (Kingston, Ontario: Quarry Press, 1991);

Some Kind of Hero (Don Mills, Ontario: Maxwell Macmillan Canada, 1991);

Wrong Time, Wrong Place (Halifax, Nova Scotia: Formac, 1991);

Clearcut Danger (Halifax, Nova Scotia: Formac, 1992);

The Ecstasy Conspiracy (Montreal: NuAge, 1992);

Margin of Error (Ottawa: Borealis, 1992);

Full Tilt (Don Mills, Ontario: Maxwell Macmillan Canada, 1993);

Good Idea Gone Bad (Halifax, Nova Scotia: Formac, 1993);

Transcendental Anarchy: Confessions of a Metaphysical Tourist (Kingston, Ontario: Quarry Press, 1993);

Dark End of Dream Street (Halifax, Nova Scotia: Formac, 1994);

The Republic of Nothing (Fredericton, New Brunswick: Goose Lane, 1994);

Big Burn (Saskatoon, Saskatchewan: Thistledown Press, 1995);

The Coastline of Forgetting (Lawrencetown Beach, Nova Scotia: Pottersfield Press, 1995);

Falling Through the Cracks (Halifax, Nova Scotia: Formac, 1996);

Nova Scotia: Shaped by the Sea: A Living History (Toronto: Viking, 1996);

Trapdoor to Heaven (Kingston, Ontario: Quarry Press, 1996);

Couleurs Troubles (Saint-Laurent, Quebec: Tisseyre, 1997);

Dance the Rocks Ashore: Stories New and Selected (Fredericton, New Brunswick: Goose Lane, 1997);

Go for it, Carrie (Halifax, Nova Scotia: Formac, 1997);

Famous at Last (Lawrencetown Beach, Nova Scotia: Pottersfield Press, 1998);

Beautiful Sadness (Victoria, British Columbia: Ekstasis Editions, 1998);

Carrie's Crowd (Halifax, Nova Scotia: Formac, 1998);

World Enough: A Novel (Fredericton, New Brunswick: Goose Lane, 1998);

Lesley Choyce (photograph by Jason McGroarty; from the cover for World Enough: A Novel, 1998)

Roid Rage (Madeira Park, British Columbia: Harbour, 1999);

The Summer of Apartment X (Fredericton, New Brunswick: Goose Lane, 1999);

Caution to the Wind (Victoria, British Columbia: Ekstasis Editions, 2000);

Far Enough Island (East Lawrencetown, Nova Scotia: Pottersfield Press, 2000);

Carrie's Camping Adventure (Halifax, Nova Scotia: Formac, 2001);

Cold Clear Morning (Vancouver, British Columbia: Beach Holme, 2001).

RECORDINGS: *Long Lost Planet*, by Choyce and the Surf Poets (Porters Lake, Nova Scotia: Pottersfield Press, 1996);

Sea Level, by Choyce and the Surf Poets (East Lawrencetown, Nova Scotia: Pottersfield Press, 1998).

OTHER: *Alternating Currents: A Handbook of Renewable Energy for Atlantic Canada*, edited by Choyce (Halifax, Nova Scotia: Wooden Anchor Press, 1977);

Chezzetcook: An Anthology of Contemporary Poetry and Fiction from Atlantic Canada, edited by Choyce (Halifax, Nova Scotia: Wooden Anchor Press, 1977);

The Pottersfield Portfolio, volumes 1–7, edited by Choyce (Porters Lake, Nova Scotia: Pottersfield Press, 1979–1985);

ACCESS: Atlantic Canada Community Energy Strategy Sourcebook, compiled by Choyce and Phil Thompson (Porters Lake, Nova Scotia: Pottersfield Press, 1980);

Visions from the Edge: An Anthology of Atlantic Canadian Science Fiction and Fantasy, edited by Choyce and John Bell (Porters Lake, Nova Scotia: Pottersfield Press, 1981);

The Cape Breton Collection, edited by Choyce (Porters Lake, Nova Scotia: Pottersfield Press, 1984);

Charles Bruce, *The Mulgrave Road: Selected Poems of Charles Bruce*, edited by Choyce and Andy Wainwright (Porters Lake, Nova Scotia: Pottersfield Press, 1985);

"Final Instructions," in *Tesseracts³*, edited by Candas Jane Dorsey and Gerry Truscott (Victoria, British Columbia: Tesseract Books, 1990), p. 420;

Ark of Ice: Canadian Futurefiction, edited by Choyce (Lawrencetown Beach, Nova Scotia: Pottersfield Press, 1992)–includes his "Patches," pp. 263–273;

"The Best of Both Worlds," in *Tesseracts⁴*, edited by Lorna Toolis and Michael Skeet (Victoria, British Columbia: Beach Holme, 1992), pp. 290–308;

"Writing and Publishing in the Margins: Canadian Science Fiction from the Eastern Perimeter," in *Out of This World: Canadian Science Fiction and Fantasy Literature*, compiled by Andrea Paradis (Ottawa & Kingston, Ontario: National Library of Canada/Quarry Press, 1995), pp. 204–211;

The Mi'kmaq Anthology, edited by Choyce and Rita Joe (Lawrencetown Beach, Nova Scotia: Pottersfield Press, 1997);

Atlantica: Stories from the Maritimes and Newfoundland, edited by Choyce (Fredericton, New Brunswick: Goose Lane, 2001).

SELECTED PERIODICAL PUBLICATION–UNCOLLECTED: "Kiss the Blood off My Spaceship," *Galumph* (1972).

Lesley Choyce's versatility can be seen in both his writing and his work life: he has written poetry, mainstream fiction, science fiction, surrealist fantasy, drama, and humorous essays, and he has worked as a high-school substitute teacher, television host, rehabilitation counselor, musician, and publisher, among other jobs. If anything unifies his writings, including his science fiction and fantasy, it is a pervasive concern for the environment. One major environmental issue for Choyce is the need to develop new and renewable sources of energy.

Lesley Willis Choyce was born in Riverside, New Jersey, on 21 March 1951. His father, George Choyce, was a mechanic, and his mother, Norma (née Willis), was a homemaker. He grew up in rural Cinnaminson, New Jersey, and had what he later considered an idyllic childhood; in his book of autobiographical essays, *An Avalanche of Ocean: The Life and Times of a Nova Scotia Immigrant* (1987), he describes some of his early experiences. During the late 1960s he was a songwriter and the lead guitarist for a rock band called The Wipeouts. He became an avid surfer, and surfing in all seasons has become a lifelong pursuit. After graduating from high school Choyce attended Rutgers University. Throughout this period he developed a strong social conscience, particularly regarding environmental destruction, and he became part of the counterculture movement. Among his favorite poets were Richard Brautigan and Charles Bukowski, two leading figures in that movement. He also admired Walt Whitman, Robert Frost, and Atlantic Canadian poet Alden Nowlan for their concreteness, as opposed to the more abstract poetry of T. S. Eliot and Ezra Pound.

Choyce received his B.A. from Rutgers in 1972, then enrolled as a graduate student at Montclair State College; that same year he published his first short story, a science-fiction piece called "Kiss the Blood off My Spaceship," in the Montclair student humor magazine, *Galumph.* His longtime interest in fantastic literature is also evident in the title of his master's thesis: "Fantasy and Fragmentation in the Contemporary American Novel." He obtained his M.A. in American literature from Montclair in 1974 and taught at the school for four years. He also did some substitute teaching at New Jersey high schools. He pursued further graduate work at the City University of New York (CUNY), but continued to live in New Jersey, more specifically in Morris County. From 1976 to 1978 he taught three courses at Queens College, CUNY, and two as an instructor and writing tutorial coordinator at Bloomfield College. Although he fulfilled his coursework and residency requirements, he never completed his Ph.D. On 19 August 1974 he married Terry Paul, a fellow teacher, and in 1976 they bought an old farmhouse on the Eastern Shore of Nova Scotia as a summer retreat. The Choyces have two children: Sunyata and Pamela.

In 1979 Choyce and his wife moved to Nova Scotia permanently, settling in Lawrencetown. In *An Avalanche of Ocean* he explains the move: "I became a Canadian citizen because this is a very civilized place that hasn't snapped at the seams yet with the gluttony of progress." Later in the same book he adds that the pollution, crowding, and apathy in New York drove him from the city and indeed the United States: "I couldn't help feeling that death and destruction were all around me every time I arrived in the city." As for the people, he writes, "The air was killing them. Their jobs were killing them . . . New York City, I had learned, was sustained by greed, aggression and violence and it's all buffered by an inviolate indifference that makes such a world possible." His environmental and social concerns were paramount. In fact, his first full-length published book was *Alternating Currents: A Handbook of Renewable Energy for Atlantic Canada,* which he edited in 1977. He quickly identified strongly with Nova Scotia, and the region has become a dominant presence in his work in all genres. As he told Virginia Beaton in an interview in the October 1996 issue of *Books in Canada,* "My ganglia and my senses are all tied in with the land. . . . There are certain images that burn themselves into your head."

He taught a course at St. Mary's University for one year, from 1978 to 1979, and a half course at Nova Scotia College of Art and Design during the 1981–1982 academic year. In 1981 he also joined the faculty of Dalhousie University, later becoming a full-time professor in the English department and the Transition Year Program. He has also taught creative writing for the Halifax City Continuing Education Program (1978–1982), St. Mary's University (1978–1982), and Dalhousie University (1981–1983) and was an instructor at the Dalhousie University Elderhostel (1982–1985). In addition, he has held other short-term teaching and writer-in-residence positions throughout eastern Canada and in New Jersey. In 1983 he received an M.A. in English literature from CUNY.

In 1979 Choyce founded Pottersfield Press, which publishes fiction and poetry as well as the literary periodical *Pottersfield Portfolio*. The press has brought out the work of several Nova Scotia writers, but one of its most significant publications is *Visions from the Edge: An Anthology of Atlantic Canadian Science Fiction and Fantasy*, which Choyce edited with John Bell in 1981. The book is one of the first anthologies of English-Canadian fantastic literature, following closely behind John Robert Colombo's seminal *Other Canadas*, published two years earlier. The volume collects works by well-known writers (such as Lucy Maud Montgomery, Hugh MacLennan, and Spider Robinson) and those who are obscure (such as Harold Walters and H. Percy Blanchard). For its breadth and its relatively early date, it is one of the most important publications in the history of Canadian science fiction, and its significance was appropriately recognized by reviewers such as David Ketterer, who wrote a review article for the March 1985 issue of *Science-Fiction Studies*.

Choyce's ecological concern is clearly expressed in his first novel, *Downwind,* a near-future thriller published in 1984. The world is undergoing an energy crisis even more serious than that of the 1970s, and the novel portrays the efforts of the United States to establish nuclear power plants in an environmentally sensitive—and unsafe—part of Nova Scotia. The provincial and federal governments are depicted as collaborators in the scheme; only the efforts of the main character, journalist Warren Chandler, bring the conspiracy to light and prevent mass death when a group of environmental terrorists threatens to blow up the site during the ceremony announcing the deal. The novel is somewhat melodramatic, and its characters are two-dimensional; but it is a well-researched cautionary tale about the dangers of reliance on nuclear power, particularly in the wake of the 1979 disaster at Three Mile Island in Pennsylvania. *Downwind* is at its best when it portrays the landscape and people of Nova Scotia—there are vivid descriptive passages during Warren's periodic hang-gliding excursions.

For Choyce, fantastic fiction is a means by which to explore philosophical questions through a freed imagination. He is less concerned with scientific or technological speculations per se, and more with raising political, personal, and spiritual questions. The fantastic short stories he wrote during the 1980s and collected in *The Dream Auditor* (1986) range from surrealist satires to soft science fiction. The title story, for example, depicts the possible results if the government audited dreams the way it does taxes. While playful, it nevertheless presents an Orwellian image of governmental mind control. By contrast, "Buddha at the Laundromat" is a fanciful tale relating what might happen should spiritual

Cover for Choyce's 1996 collection of fantasy and science-fiction stories, which are loosely connected by a narrative about a soul traveling through time and space

leaders return to the modern world and have to deal with the mundane realities of contemporary life. "Thanotopolis Re-visited" shows Choyce's continuing environmental interest, with its depiction of a new, cheap, abundant, and therefore—for some vested interests—threatening source of energy. The bizarre new substance that the narrator discovers, neolite, is produced through the interaction of the chemical wastes in a dump site. It does not take long for the oil companies and government to respond to the threat that neolite poses to their power. In "The Loneliness of the Long-Distance Writer," literacy makes a comeback in a McLuhanesque far future.

Some of the stories in the book suggest that Choyce has a strong interest in Eastern mysticism, or at least a desire to transcend rational and scientific approaches to the physical universe. The more surreal stories in particular challenge rationalist discourse in favor of a more holistic and intuitive vision. As he said in an interview for *Contemporary Authors* (published in 1998): "Maybe I've developed a basic mistrust of the rational, logical conclusions. I've only had the briefest glimpses beyond the surface, but I've seen enough to know that sometimes facts are not enough. There are times to make the leap, to get metaphysical, and suppose that we all live larger lives than appearances would suggest."

Choyce published widely during the 1980s while supporting himself with his teaching and other work, including the television talk show *Choyce Words* beginning in 1985. In 1989 he published *The Second Season of Jonas MacPherson,* a novel with some fantastic elements. The title character is an antisocial sixty-nine-year-old resident of Nova Scotia looking back on some of the important events in his life. Most of all, the novel is a lament for Jonas's late wife, Eleanor, and recounts his own ongoing battle with death. He regains his appreciation for life thanks to Kelly, a young female college student, and his son, Carey. The chapters of the novel are nearly separate short stories, and two portray characters in Jonas's life who possess seemingly magical powers. The title character of the chapter "What Nora Thought She Saw" may well have second sight, as she periodically has prophetic visions. Joe Allen Joe, of "Wings," is a Mi'kmaq with a strong spiritual connection to the land, and he seems to be able to make himself and others invisible. While his bond with natural spirits occasionally turns him into something of a native stereotype, he is clearly intended to represent an unsevered connection to nature that man has unfortunately lost. Jonas himself is just as strongly tied to the sea, and the sea leads to his rebirth at the end. As reviewer Dayv James-French said in *Books in Canada,* "MacPherson is something of a mystic . . . in tune with the natural rhythms of the Nova Scotia landscape" (April 1990). Overall, the novel received positive reviews, particularly by Robin Skelton in *Quill & Quire,* who called it "balanced, cunningly poised" and "a life-enhancing, life-celebrating book" (August 1989). On the other hand, Siobhan McRae in *Dalhousie Review* (1990) expressed reservations about the characterization, saying that the characters "sometimes move beyond eccentricity into the realm of the magical" but that "this treatment can be somewhat strained and stereotypical."

In 1991 Choyce engaged in his boldest formal experiment: *Magnificent Obsessions,* a work he described as a "photonovel." Each chapter consists of a photograph and then a short text that purportedly identifies the people and places in it. Byron, the narrator, describes his early years in Linden, his marriage, and his career as a photographer. Apart from being a book of lively humor, featuring imaginative interpretations of what the old photographs might depict, *Magnificent Obsessions* includes a few hints of the fantastic. As a child, Byron is inspired by newsreel footage of the *Hindenburg* to make his own zeppelin, and enlists his best friend, Frank Bodine, to help him fill it with methane. After a hearty meal of beans, they succeed in filling and launching the ship, only to see it explode spectacularly when it is shot out of the sky by paranoid dump-owner Michael C. Ovarie. Byron later invents the Primary Energy Extractor—another Choyce creation that permits unlimited energy to be drawn from widely available sources. The P.E.E. can multiply the energy output of small animals tenfold, meaning that cars could be run by insects and electrical generators by goats. Byron is not the only one in his family capable of fantastic feats: his father is able to perform magic tricks, including the unexplained levitation of a chair, and his sister Gretchen can see people's auras. Reviewer Pat Barclay in *Books in Canada* said, "Choyce's weird conjunctions of photos and text are often as much fun for the reader as they evidently were for the compiler" (March 1992). Deirdre Kelly in *Quill & Quire* (January 1991) called it "a singularly delightful book, full of originality and wit."

Choyce's Pottersfield Press continued to publish Canadian science fiction, notably publishing Terence M. Green's science fiction short-story collection *The Woman Who is the Midnight Wind* in 1987. Choyce returned to science-fiction editing with the compilation of *Ark of Ice: Canadian Futurefiction* (1992). The anthology combines new and previously published science fiction stories by Canadian writers including Green, Timothy Findley, Phyllis Gotlieb, Candas Jane Dorsey, and Margaret Atwood. In his introduction Choyce says, "My criteria for what stories would be included on this *Ark of Ice* was a simple matter of time-frame and political geography. I was looking for answers to my vague question: what might happen when tomorrow swallows up this country of Canada?" The speculations he publishes are almost universally pessimistic; as he says, "one thing that all of these stories have in common is this: they all worry about the future." Various disaster scenarios—political, environmental, nuclear, and so on—are explored in the works, and the bleak nature of the futures presented was noted by several reviewers, such as R. John Hayes in the November 1992 *Quill & Quire* and Donald Kingsbury in the Summer 1993 *Matrix.* The collection is uneven—with some pieces obviously included only for the recognition factor of their authors—but generally strong.

During the late 1980s and into the 1990s Choyce directed his energies to writing young-adult fiction as well, and won or was nominated for several awards in children's and young-adult literature.

Choyce also continued to pursue his surfing interests, even in winter, and in 1993 he became the Canadian National Surfing champion.

Choyce's occasional fantastic short stories appeared in periodicals and anthologies during the 1990s, and he collected some of them in the 1996 volume *Trapdoor to Heaven*. The stories are loosely connected by an overarching narrative about a soul traveling through time and space; the main character of this narrative is the servant, who embodies the various voices that emerge in the stories. No work by Choyce more fully exhibits the influence of Eastern philosophy, with its description of souls in free motion. Choyce seems to suggest that death may well be merely a passage to another realm rather than an end. The servant spins glass fibers that sing in different voices that insist on being heard. He is thus a force of unity out of chaos, a means by which a single soul can exist simultaneously in various states while remaining one. On the other hand, if the servant is interpreted as a symbol of the author, he may well represent the power of the writer to give new life–indeed, new lives–to his characters; he gives them all a chance to sing for the duration of the book.

The stories in *Trapdoor to Heaven*, like those in *The Dream Auditor*, are diverse in genre and theme, with some surreal fantasies such as "Rolling Down to Old Maui," science-fiction stories such as "The Big Freeze" and "The Age of Perfection," and a creation myth, "The Dreamtree." "Patches" is a story about a William Gibson–like world in which the entire population is connected physically and mentally into the Network. Some people, however, remove their patches and try to pursue a simpler, more free life. Other stories are set during the Children's Crusade ("The Density of Purpose"), ancient Rome ("The Truth"), and the Nova Scotia of the Mi'kmaqs ("Reach Out, Pull the Stars from the Sky"). Choyce's fiction continues to warn readers about the effects of reliance on technology and loss of connection to nature. Reviewers warned readers about its challenging form, and found its message overwhelming its poetry in places; Janet McNaughton said in *Quill & Quire*, "the book suffers for the bluntness of the characterization. . . . This heavy-handedness takes the shine off the book" (September 1996).

For all its diversity, Choyce's fiction expresses a unified vision of concern for the environment and a need for all people to rediscover their ties to nature. He uses the rationalist genre of science fiction, as well as surrealism, fantasy, and satire, to encourage his readers to see the world in nonscientific ways. For Choyce, humans have suffered–and made their world suffer–for their limited perspective: their utilitarian, selfish, rationalist approach. To be healthy, and to regain the health of the world, they need a more holistic vision, one that recognizes they are part of a larger human and natural universe.

Interviews:

Virginia Beaton, "Surfing the Genres," *Books in Canada*, 25 (October 1996): 11–12;

Edo van Belkom, "Lesley Choyce," in his *Northern Dreamers: Interviews with Famous Science Fiction, Fantasy, and Horror Writers* (Kingston, Ontario: Quarry Press, 1998), pp. 19–27.

Monique Corriveau
(6 September 1927 – 29 June 1976)

Jean-Louis Trudel
Université du Québec à Montréal

BOOKS: *Le Secret de Vanille* (Quebec: Pélican, 1959); revised edition (Quebec: Editions Jeunesse, 1962); revised edition (Montreal: Editions Jeunesse, 1969); revised edition (Montreal: Editions Jeunesse, 1972);

Les Jardiniers du hibou (Quebec: Editions Jeunesse, 1963);

Le Wapiti (Quebec: Editions Jeunesse, 1964); revised edition (Montreal: Cercle du Livre de France/Pierre Tisseyre, 1993); translated by J. M. L'Heureux as *The Wapiti* (Toronto: Macmillan, 1968);

Max (Quebec: Editions Jeunesse, 1965); revised edition (Montreal: Fides, 1985);

Le Maître de Messire (Quebec: Editions Jeunesse, 1965); revised edition (Montreal: Editions Jeunesse, 1971);

La Petite Fille du printemps (Quebec: Editions Jeunesse, 1966);

Cecile; Rigobert et Poncho; La Raquette (Quebec: Editions Jeunesse, 1968);

Max au rallye (Quebec: Editions Jeunesse, 1968); revised edition (Montreal: Fides, 1985);

Le Témoin (Montreal: Cercle du Livre de France, 1969);

Le Garçon au cerf-volant (Montreal: Fides, 1974); translated by David Homel as *A Perfect Day for Kites* (Vancouver: Groundwood, 1981);

Patrick et Sophie en fusée (Montreal: Héritage, 1975);

Les Saisons de la mer (Montreal: Fides, 1975); abridged and translated by Homel as *Seasons of the Sea* (Toronto: Groundwood, 1989);

Compagnon du soleil, 3 volumes (Montreal: Fides, 1976);

Ses Les Montcorbier, 2 volumes (Montreal: Fides, 1980)—comprises volume 1, *Le guerrier, 1914–1915;* and volume 2, *La mort des autres, 1916–1918;*

Max contre Macbeth (Montreal: Fides, 1985);

Max en planeur (Montreal: Fides, 1985).

OTHER: "La ronde du marché du livre," by Corriveau and Suzanne Martel, in *Création culturelle pour la jeunesse et identité québécoise*, edited by Paule Daveloy and Guy Boulizon (Montreal: Leméac, 1973), pp. 59–67.

Monique Corriveau (courtesy of Bernard Corriveau)

SELECTED PERIODICAL PUBLICATION—UNCOLLECTED: "La littérature de jeunesse de langue française," *CLA Bulletin*, 23 (September 1966): 122–124.

Monique Corriveau belonged to the first generation of French-speaking Canadian authors who could write for the young without feeling constrained by the religious and patriotic pieties that had prevailed in Quebec until 1960. Her works won the plaudits of critics and earned the highest distinctions in the field. When she turned to science fiction, she brought to the genre the respectability she had gained as well as her already considerable experience as a writer. Though she died just as French-language science fiction in Canada was gaining critical mass, she proved that science fiction for young readers could be more than fluff, and she left readers an important homegrown dystopia to ponder.

Corriveau was born Monique Chouinardon 6 September 1927 in Quebec City to François-Xavier Chouinard—a practicing lawyer and the town clerk, like his father before him—and Bernadette Chouinard, née Rouillard. Corriveau's early schooling was spent at the convent of the Ursulines in the heart of old Quebec City. She then attended the University of Toronto from 1946 to 1948, taking courses on Henri Bergson's philosophy and perfecting her grasp of English. She completed her studies at Laval University in Quebec City between 1948 and 1950, graduating with a B.A. and a B.Ph.

She was close to her only sister, Suzanne, who later became a notable writer in her own right as Suzanne Martel. The Chouinard household was full of books, and the family read avidly—Corriveau's liking for the fictional detective Sir Jerry, created by French author Mrs. H. Giraud, surfaced later in her first juveniles. Both of her grandfathers had been men of letters, writing on local history and Amerindian languages. An older cousin, Mrs. Taschereau-Fortier, was better known as a children's author under the pen name of Maxine. Naturally, both Corriveau and her sister engaged early on in the recounting of fairy tales and the writing of stories, and Corriveau decided that her goal was to write a children's book by the time she reached age twenty-one.

After attending the University of Toronto, however, she married Bernard Corriveau, a notary public, in 1951, and they went on to have ten children—five boys and five girls. As a busy mother, she wrote many of her books at the kitchen table, or in a local restaurant where she could have relative privacy.

She became active in children's literature, joining the Association des écrivains pour la jeunesse, an association for youth-fiction authors that was founded in 1948 and dissolved in 1954. She did not publish her first book until 1959, when *Le Secret de Vanille* (Vanille's Secret) appeared. Future editions of that book, like many of her others, were published by Editions Jeunesse, a publishing collective established by the Association des écrivains pour la jeunesse in 1949. When Editions Jeunesse went bankrupt in 1972 and was taken over by Fides, it left two of her novels, *Max contre Macbeth* (Max versus Macbeth) and *Max en planeur* (Max Flies a Glider) in limbo and unpublished until 1985.

Le Secret de Vanille and her second novel, *Les Jardiniers du hibou* (1963), were both well-received; both won the top award for juvenile literature from the ACELF, the national association of French-speaking teachers, with the second winning the prize in manuscript form as "Luc et ses amis" (Luc and His Friends). An historical novel set in New France, *Le Wapiti* (translated as *The Wapiti*), published in 1964, won Quebec's top literary award in the youth literature category and in 1966 was awarded the Canadian Association of Children's Librarians bronze medal as best children's book of the year. It has long been required reading in many Canadian schools.

Her first book to reveal an interest in scientific matters was not science fiction as such: *Max*, published in 1965, is a standard spy thriller featuring a young physicist from her alma mater, Laval University, who is mistakenly accused of murder and must retrieve the stolen scientific papers of his murdered colleague. She later told Louise Lemieux, in *Pleins feux sur la littérature de jeunesse au Canada français* (Spotlight on Youth Literature in French Canada, 1972), that the series of which *Max* was the first book was intended to foster in her readers an interest in science.

In the 1960s French-Canadian society was then discovering itself as part of the technological world, loosening the grip of the Catholic Church, and aspiring to the material joys of modernity. In the heady days before Expo '67, the extremely successful World's Fair held in Montreal in 1967, science and technology were seen, on the whole, as powers for good, even if evil men might misuse them for nefarious ends.

The other book Corriveau published in 1965, *Le Maître de Messire,* won Quebec's top literary award for youth literature that year. In August 1967 her children's story "Cécile," later published as part of *Cécile; Rigobert et Poncho; La Raquette* (Cécile; Rigobert and Poncho; The Snowshoe) in 1968, won a Centennial literary award. After experimenting with an adult novel, *Le Témoin* (The Witness), published in 1969, Corriveau resumed writing for young readers, though reviews had praised the sensitivity of the book and its promise of a greater talent. In 1971 she won the Michelle Le Normand award for her body of work. Five years later she received the Alvine Bélisle award from the Association pour l'Avancement des

Cover for Corriveau's 1975 novel for young adults, set on an island off the coast of Newfoundland, which received the Alvine Bélisle award from the Association pour l'Avancement des Sciences et des Techniques de la Documentation in 1976

Sciences et des Techniques de la Documentation (Association for the Advancement of the Sciences and Techniques of Documentation) for her young-adult novel *Les Saisons de la mer* (translated as *Seasons of the Sea*, 1989). The setting of that novel, a small island off the shores of Newfoundland in 1910, was as exotic as any she had tackled in a published work until then.

Corriveau did not try her hand at science fiction until the beginning of the 1970s. Her Montcorbier saga was set in a never-never-land version of India called Gotal and was first conceived in the course of childhood exchanges with her sister; but it remained unpublished until after her death, first appearing as the two-volume work *Ses Les Montcorbier* in 1980, with fifteen additional volumes still to be published. Her first published attempt at science fiction, *Patrick et Sophie en fusée* (Patrick and Sophie Take a Rocket) published in 1975, is relatively guarded in its speculation. The three young heroes, Sophie, Vincent, and Jonas, voyage aboard a time-traveling rocket back to 1380, chaperoned by Messrs. Patrick and Barthélémy. The most interesting feature is the choice of destination: the Gaspé peninsula before the coming of the Europeans. The novel can be read as reflecting the same yearning to return to a bucolic past that is seen in *Surréal 3000,* published in 1963 by her sister, in which the inhabitants of a high-tech, underground city find their way to the lush and unspoiled surface.

This last motif resurfaces with even more force in Corriveau's magnum opus, an ambitious trilogy titled *Compagnon du soleil* (Companion of the Sun), published in 1976. Though it was intended for mature readers, its plotting as a bildungsroman makes it more congenial reading for a younger audience. It is set in the future, in an unspecified part of the world, where the country of Ixanor has opted for a highly regimented way of life in order to handle its rising population. The main character, Oakim, is a Companion of the Sun, exempted from the yearly change whereby half of the population is put on a night shift and the other half resumes a day shift until the next shift change. Life in the capital city of Xantou depends on a high level of technology and an even higher level of repression. In the final book of the trilogy this life is dramatically contrasted with life in a still-undeveloped country to the south, the capital of which is called Saint-Sébastien, evoking the saint-laden toponymy of old rural Quebec. However, the choice between technological dystopia and agrarian utopia is not as clear-cut as in Martel's *Surréal 3000* or Maurice Gagnon's *Les Tours de Babylone* (The Towers of Babylon, 1972), in which the technocratic future city of Babylon is abandoned by the hero, who defects to the so-called barbarians.

The trilogy was in the works for about five years, but Corriveau appears to have hastened to finish *Compagnon du soleil* after having been diagnosed with cancer in 1974, two years before her death. The style is still relatively rough, marred by abrupt viewpoint shifts and contradictions, and the last two volumes are somewhat sketchier in execution than the first. The day before she died, her publisher, Raymonde Simard-Martin at Fides, presented her with the mock-up of the covers and box for the trilogy, but the galleys ended up being ready a day too late for the author to see them. She died on 29 June 1976.

The entire trilogy follows Oakim's progress as he moves from being part of the elite Companions to joining the clandestine Resistance to the ruling class and to deciding that Ixanor's socioeconomic system must be brought down. The revolution itself is not shown, only its preparations, and a short epilogue establishes that Oakim did succeed in overthrowing the existing hierarchy.

In the April–May 1977 issue of *Requiem* Esther Rochon suggested that the countries of Ixanor and Ditrie might correspond to France and Spain, and while other clues may point to Ixanor standing in for the Eastern bloc of the day with Ditrie as a version of impoverished Greece, this dystopia is clearly meant to hit much closer to home. The capital city of Xantou obviously refers to its builders' dream of constructing a real Xanadu, and the port city of Talas is presumably named after the Greek word for sea, *thalassa*. But Ixanor sounds like the tail end of "Amérique du Nord" or a partial twist on "North America." Given that, it is easy to interpret *Compagnon du soleil* as a rebuke of the American dream that pursues happiness so relentlessly as to risk misery in real life. For Ixanor does have a dark side: Oakim discovers that, just as an elite is allowed to enjoy daytime all of their lives, others are born to endless night. The counterparts of the Companions of the Sun are these people of the Black Moon. Indeed, Corriveau sketches as comprehensive a description of a repressive state as any known in Canadian literature, with the possible exception of the description of Manokhsor in Jacques Brossard's tetralogy, *L'Oiseau de feu* (The Firebird; 1989–1997), the first draft of which also dates back to the 1970s.

As in *Surréal 3000*, *L'Oiseau de feu*, and *Les Tours de Babylone*, the society of Ixanor is governed by a master computer, known as the Genius. Its electronic memory holds information about the entire country and each of its citizens. Every day, the building occupied by the Genius is the source of a television broadcast that sings the praises of the regime, which everyone must watch. A drug known as euforia, both relaxing and deleterious to the critical faculties, has replaced water as the common drink. Coupons are used instead of money, and most people live inside pyramidal buildings, with each dwelling built on the same standard plan, only differing in furniture, cleanliness, and quality of construction. All citizens carry an identity passbook that must be swiped through magnetic controllers wherever they go, letting the State track their every move.

Furthermore, education of the new generation of Ixanor's citizens is exclusively audiovisual, which makes it harder for the youth to ponder or criticize the contents of their courses. The imposition of a fully phonetic alphabet has also contributed to cutting them off from their culture, since the old books can no longer be read. Even imagination has been outlawed: the sober architecture of Xantou has been codified through regulation, and change has been forbidden.

No one dares to speak his or her mind, as microphones are everywhere and "social officers" are assigned to every residential building. The regular police, however, have little success in hunting down the Resistance, so Oakim's father creates covert death squads. Apart from the Resistance, the only other outlet seems to be the almost gladiatorial sports events watched by many, sometimes in huge arenas equipped with jumbo screens.

Nevertheless, Ixanor is not a dictatorship. There is no Big Brother, no cult of a supreme leader. The three Great Directors are almost anonymous. Corriveau is describing a totalitarian system, in thrall to the mandated efficiencies of the technocratic mentality. This system has no room for religion, explicitly outlawed by the State. In Ixanor, the only God still venerated, clandestinely, is mute. He is dumb in the face of his worshipers' appeals. Did the author feel that the God of her youth had fallen silent in the new and modern province of Quebec? This unspeaking God is not unlike the "unknown God" featured in Brossard's *L'Oiseau de feu*. As in that work, or Martel's *Surréal 3000*, one must flee the city to find the divine. Nature is the last refuge of the Godhead in all three works. Oakim meets the worshipers of the mute God near the collective farms outside Xantou.

However, the system has also outlawed sexism. Oakim is taught to believe in sexual equality, though he finds something almost enticing in the clearly marked sexual roles of more backward Ditrie. In a mountain fastness of Ditrie, Oakim also comes to realize that all his knowledge is useless without the means to apply it: specialization is such in Ixanor that he is a prisoner of excessively narrow training. Corriveau's critique of the division of labor in a technological society is in line with her evident nostalgia for a significant religion or an untouched natural environment. It owes much, like the works of her contemporaries, to the ideas articulated by thinkers such as Jacques Ellul and Herbert Marcuse a few years before.

Indeed, as in *Surréal 3000* or *Les Tours de Babylone*, the State is technocratic. Various sciences are practiced, such as genetics, astronomy, nuclear physics, and (somewhat improbably) astronautics. There are videotelephones, supercargo planes, tidal power stations, moving sidewalks, hovercrafts, and huge motels on wheels. Agriculture has been changed forever by collective farms arranged as linear cities, their buildings, schools, and factories stretching along a single, integrated corridor used by trains and trucks, with vast fields on each side.

Nevertheless, there are still shortages. Oakim's mother works to improve the algae-derived rations for the poor. Faced with the ever-optimistic broadcasts from the Genius, Oakim starts to question their truthfulness: if production keeps increasing, why is the country short of uranium, soap, or salt?

In her *Requiem* article Rochon noted how the trilogy was less progressive than it purported to be. Despite the officially nonsexist ideology, in Ixanor women are relegated to secondary roles; moreover, the protagonists are men. Oakim is a reluctant revolutionary, and a not a radical one at that. The trilogy is not about revolution, however, but about Oakim's learning to appraise lucidly, and critically if need be, his own society. This message remains, regardless of time and place, as subversive a message as any.

Collective dreams have always been more powerful in Quebec than in the rest of Canada. Corriveau's warning about the danger of utopias going too far, too fast, has rarely been as clearly articulated in Quebec fiction and should be read as complementing the utopian tradition launched by Jules-Paul Tardivel's *Pour la patrie* (For My Country, 1895).

The publication of *Compagnon du soleil* in a boxed set was her publisher's last homage to the best children's writer of her generation. No other science-fiction trilogy was published in French-speaking Canada until 1989, when Brossard's *L'Oiseau de feu* began to appear. Though most critics ignored Corriveau's trilogy, the most perceptive among them acknowledged her attempt to grapple with the future of technological societies, and *Compagnon de soleil* still ranks among the most ambitious works of science fiction in French-speaking Canada.

References:
Aurélien Boivin, "Hommage à Monique Corriveau," *Québec français*, 24 (December 1976): 36–37;

Agathe Dicaire, "Monique Corriveau (Profile)," *In Review*, 3 (Spring 1969): 23–25;

Louise Lemieux, "Monique Corriveau," in *Pleins feux sur la littérature de jeunesse au Canada français* (Montreal: Leméac, 1972), pp. 147–149, 209–210 ff.;

Esther Rochon, "Compagnon du soleil," *Requiem*, 3 (April–May 1977): 14–16.

Papers:
While some of Monique Corriveau's personal papers remain in private hands, a major holding of manuscripts and correspondence is in the Laval University Archives Division in Ste-Foy, Quebec.

Denis Côté
(1 January 1954 –   )

Patti J. Kurtz
Heidelberg College

BOOKS: *Hockeyeurs cybernétiques* (Montreal: Editions Paulines, 1983); translated by Jane Brierly as *Shooting for the Stars* (Windsor, Ontario: Black Moss Press, 1990); revised as *L'Arrivée des Inactifs* (Montreal: La Courte échelle, 1993);

Les Parallèles célestes (Montreal: Hurtubise HMH, 1983);

L'Invisible puissance (Montreal: Editions Paulines, 1984); translated by David Homel as *The Invisible Empire* (Windsor, Ontario: Black Moss Press, 1990); revised as *Descente aux enfers* (Montreal: La Courte échelle, 1994);

Les Géants de Blizzard (Montreal: La Courte échelle, 1985);

La Pénombre jaune (Montreal: Editions Paulines, 1986); revised edition (Saint-Laurent, Quebec: Editions Pierre Tisseyre, 1996);

Nocturnes pour Jessie (Montreal: Editions Québec/Amérique, 1987); revised as *Les Chemins de Mirlande* (Montreal: La Courte échelle, 1998);

Les Prisonniers du Zoo (Montreal: La Courte échelle, 1988);

Le Voyage dans le temps (Montreal: La Courte échelle, 1989);

L'Idole des Inactifs (Montreal: La Courte échelle, 1989);

La Vie est une bande dessinée (Saint-Laurent, Quebec: Editions Pierre Tisseyre, 1989);

La Nuit du vampire (Montreal: La Courte échelle, 1990);

La Révolte des Inactifs (Montreal: La Courte échelle, 1990);

Le Retour des Inactifs (Montreal: La Courte échelle, 1990);

Terminus cauchemar (Montreal: La Courte échelle, 1991);

Les Yeux d'emeraude (Montreal: La Courte échelle, 1991);

Je viens du futur (Saint-Laurent, Quebec: Editions Pierre Tisseyre, 1993);

Le Parc aux sortilèges (Montreal: La Courte échelle, 1994);

Aux portes de l'horreur (Montreal: La Courte échelle, 1994);

La Trahison du vampire (Montreal: La Courte échelle, 1995);

L'Ile du savant fou (Montreal: La Courte échelle, 1996);

Les Prédateurs de l'ombre (Montreal: La Courte échelle, 1997);

Les Otages de la terreur (Montreal: La Courte échelle, 1998);

Un Parfum de mystère (Montreal: La Courte échelle, 1999);

La Machine à rajeunir (Montreal: La Courte échelle, 1999);

Traque dans la neige (Paris: Albin-Michel Jeunesse, 2000);

La Machination du Scorpion Noir (Paris: Nathan, 2001).

OTHER: "Catégorie d'étrangeté numéro 7," in *Planéria: Anthologie de science-fiction,* edited by Côté (Montreal: Editions Pierre Tisseyre, 1985), pp. 11–51;

"1534," in *Dix nouvelles de science-fiction québécoise* (Montreal: Les Quinze, 1985), pp. 65–81;

"So Help Me God," in *L'Année de la science-fiction et du fantastique québécois, 1987* (Montreal: Beauport, 1988), pp. 221–237;

"La Musique du Silence," by Côté and Jean-Pierre April, in *L'Année de la science-fiction et du fantastique québécois, 1988* (Montreal: Beauport, 1989): 221–236;

"Ecrire pour la jeunesse: Mon opinion à moi," <http://home.switchboard.com/deniscote>.

SELECTED PERIODICAL PUBLICATIONS–UNCOLLECTED: "La Mort de Vincent l'usurier," *Requiem,* 13 (1976): 8;

"Le Chanteur Renaud vous parle," *imagine . . .,* 27 (1985): 123–127;

"Boîte crânienne," *imagine . . .,* 36 (1986): 23–28;

"La machine à écrire," *imagine . . .,* 36 (1986): 101–112.

Denis Côté has been called "without contest the greatest author of young people's science fiction in Quebec" by Alire, a publisher that showcases the best

Cover for Denis Côté's first published novel (1983), in which humans and robots compete against each other in hockey games

of Québécois science fiction. He is one of the most prolific, averaging two novels per year since his swift emergence on the children's writing scene in 1983 with two award-winning novels. Côté is also one of the first Québécois science-fiction writers to write novels directed primarily to young people; in part because of his influence, the market for Québécois science fiction and fantasy has expanded over the past decade. Côté distinguishes himself by addressing themes to which his young readers can relate: the quest for self-identity, the desire to escape the ugliness of reality, tolerance of difference, the ethics of drug use to improve physical prowess, the value of friendship, rock music, cults, and the UFO phenomenon. Yet, Côté brings an unusual perspective to these themes, approaching them from a philosophical rather than a scientific base; he asks metaphysical questions that force readers to examine their inner selves and contemplate man's need to create myths and legends. However, Côté does not fall prey to the temptation to instruct his young readers in morals; instead, he challenges them to think about the issues he has raised and to draw their own conclusions.

When Côté wrote *Les Parallèles célestes* (The Celestial Parallel, 1983), he did not intend it to be specifically for children but rather, as he said in an interview in *Quebec Francais* in 1989, for "a vast audience, an audience of everyone." Many of his later works show the same relevance to this universal audience. Côté continues to be concerned about the narrowness of the Québécois market for science fiction for young people; he believes that the people of Quebec remain in a state of decolonization, struggling to create forms of literature that are not parodies of foreign models. Through his own intriguing novels, which encourage readers to think about the troubling philosophical and ethical questions raised by present-day technology, Côté is participating in the work of refining a distinctly Québécois model of science fiction.

Denis Marcel Côté was born on 1 January 1954 to Paul-Emile and Fernande Côté in Quebec City. Côté's father was a civil servant, while Côté's mother devoted her time to raising Côté, his three brothers, and a sister. No doubt some of his writing has been influenced by the books he read as a child; in the 1989 *Quebec Francais* interview Côté reflected that he particularly remembers reading the Bob Morane novels by Henri Vernes. Côté attended the Université Laval in Quebec from 1973 to 1977, earning a college degree in literature, and a bachelor's degree in French studies. Côté received an M.A. in literary creation in 1984. Before becoming a professional writer in 1983, he worked as a professor of French, a civil servant, and a part-time bookseller, and he is a member of the Union of Québécois Writers.

Côté addresses the impact of technology upon human well-being and the abuse of power in his first novel, *Hockeyeurs cybernétiques* (1983; translated as *Shooting for the Stars,* 1990). While Côté wrote *Les Parallèles Célestes* first, he had some difficulty finding a publisher for this novel; thus, *Hockeyeurs cybernétiques* became his first published novel. This novel won the Grand Prize in Young People's Literature awarded by the Council of Arts of Canada and introduced Côté as a science-fiction author worthy of note. Set in 2010 against the backdrop of Lost Ark, a city divided along strict class lines, this novel features hockey star Michel Lenoir, who is unwillingly drawn into a governmental and technological power play disguised as a series of hockey games between an all-star human team and a team of humanlike robots. Watching the robot hockey players outperform his teammates—and himself—Michel questions the impact of technology upon the already impoverished "working class." Scientific advancements are often touted as "making life easier for man," but in this novel, advanced technology renders human workers virtually nonessential, resulting in widespread unemployment and concentration of wealth in the hands of a few. The hockey games between men and robots are touted as determining "the future of humanity and its place in the social fabric"; however, the publicity generated before the games are even played increases demand for the robots and relegates humanity to a nonessential role. Michel's eyes are opened to the prevalence of corruption when he discovers, with the help of journalist Virginia Lynx, that Raiders owner David Swindler is a major stockholder in both the hockey federation and the company that manufactures the robots. Michel also learns that most of the nation's businesses, including the mass media, are controlled by Swindler; TV stations have become instruments of propaganda. The power of the few to determine the fate of many is a recurring theme that concerns Côté, and in *Hockeyeurs cybernétiques* he encourages readers to think about the impact of such concentrated power. This theme and Côté's unusual treatment of it (especially his use of the hockey scenario) make this novel particularly relevant for his Québécois readers; as an ethnic minority within Canada, French Canadians may be keenly aware of the consequences and dangers of governmental abuse of power.

Côté also treats abuse of power, along with humanity's need to construct myths, in *Les Paralléles célestes*. Awarded the Grand Prize of Science Fiction and Fantasy of Quebec, *Les Paralléles célestes* reveals the power of a few to create a conspiracy of silence in a small town frequently visited by UFOs. Following a close encounter with a UFO, Andre Jacek arrives in Lambreville to find that the inhabitants are forbidden to talk about the phenomenon. Jacek's persistent quest for the truth leads him to a military base established around a strange sphere whose function and origin baffles researchers. With the help of Julian, a young American medium, Jacek succeeds in communicating with the inhabitants of the sphere, where the scientists' efforts have failed. The narrow-mindedness of the military mentality, personified in Captain Denault, is questioned, as well as the purely logical view of the scientists who are stymied by the sphere, incapable of providing an explanation to what seems to be an extraterrestrial problem. The answers lie instead within mankind, as suggested by Jacek's metaphysical explanation; the mirrored surface of the sphere suggests that man must examine his innermost self to find the answers to this phenomenon, which are embodied in the human need to create myths and the transformation of those myths in an increasingly modern society.

Côté's unusual approach to the problem and significance of the extraterrestrial encounter reflect his attempts to provide a perspective on this theme that is not what he calls a "parody" of extant North American themes and plots. In this way, Côté spurs the development of a different, Québécois brand of science fiction. Though this book was written for a wide audience, the novel was published as part of a new series of juvenile novels to take advantage of the growing popularity of Québécois young-adult science fiction in the 1980s.

Côté's preoccupation with the power wielded by cults runs through his third novel, *L'Invisible puissance* (1984; translated as *The Invisible Empire,* 1990). Following the death of rock star and pacifist John Goodman, Nicholas St. Laurent remembers reading subway graffiti labeling Goodman as an "androgyne" who must be "purified," and he suspects the Church of Balthazar of engineering Goodman's murder. Nicholas infiltrates the cult and is led to a group of cloaked and masked conspirators calling themselves "The Invisible Empire" and proclaiming their goal of "purifying" the world by systematically killing the pacifists. Through an intensive program of sleep deprivation, starvation, and brainwashing, the cult programs Nicholas to hate the pacifists; the incredible control this cult wields over the young man calls into question the ethics of power and its abuse. When Nicholas is ordered to kill a rock singer or be guillotined himself, he realizes that cults are anything but innocent. At the end of the novel, the ominous suggestion that the Church of Balthazar is growing, unchecked by governmental authority, warns about the need for constant vigilance against such concentrated power.

Allusions fill Côté's work; he admitted in the 1989 *Quebec Francais* interview that the "point of departure" for this novel was the Beatles, especially John Lennon, and that his goal was to create "a novel supported by the imagery of the Beatles." Clearly, the "Fantastic Four" of *L'Invisible puissance* bear a striking resemblance to the "Fab Four," while John Goodman's "no more war" slogan calls to mind Lennon's "give peace a chance." Goodman's wife, Soorya Oshas, mirrors Lennon's wife, Yoko Ono. Even Goodman's murder outside his hotel resonates with echoes of Lennon's death. Such allusions add a layer of meaning to the novel that may perhaps be missed by younger readers.

Peaceful resistance is offered as an alternative to abusive power and destructive weapons in *Les Géants de Blizzard* (The Giants of Blizzard, 1985). The book was a finalist for the Prize of the Canadian Council of

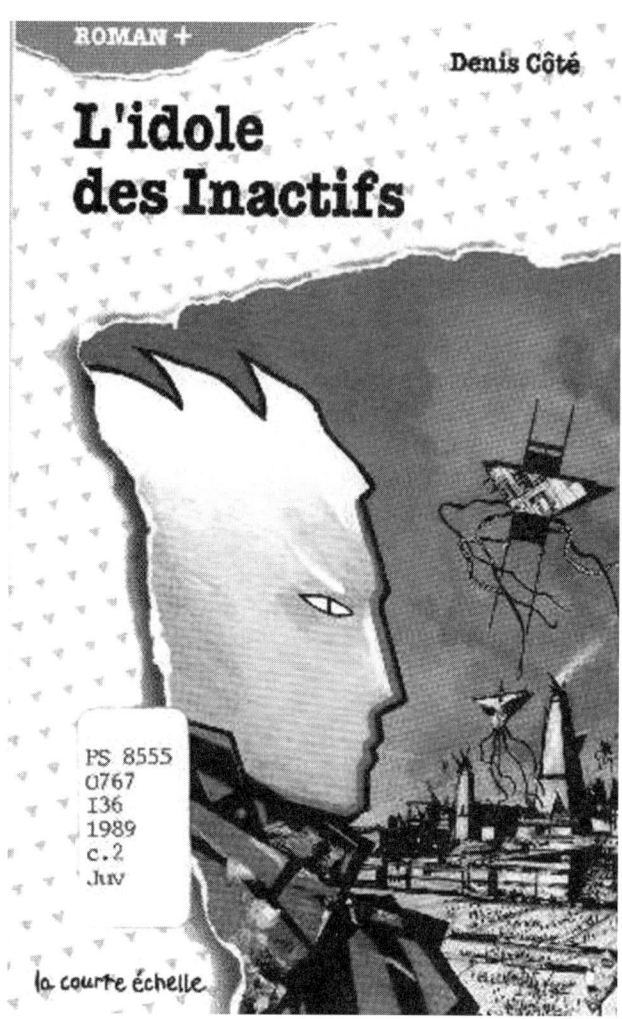

Cover for Côté's 1989 novel, the first in a trilogy about an unjust society divided into the "Actives" and "Inactives"

Arts and Literature in 1985. Two empires, the Pact and the Ghouls, struggle for dominion over the universe, their gains and losses determined not by war but through a chess game in which the stakes are control of planets. Secretly, however, the Pact is constructing powerful weapons that could destroy all life, inciting the protagonists, a group of pacifists, to travel to the planet Blizzard in an attempt to thwart this construction. The pacifism of these three travelers–Braal, Chrysalide, and Élée–is emphasized when they face life-threatening danger; they find ways to survive without injuring or killing their aggressors, and in addition, their plan to stop the Pact is a campaign of information, not aggression. Chrysalide's empathic ability to "feel" the death the patrol guards carry with them creates a more vivid illustration of the horrors of war than any narrative moralizing. The strengthening effects of interracial harmony and community are stressed as these three markedly different companions function as a group working toward a common goal. Their pacifism is stronger than the brute force of the Pact's patrols, and the trio nearly succeeds in their mission; however, only the highest level of community enjoyed by the natives of Blizzard proves powerful enough to stop the Pact's weapon construction. Such a total communal existence would end all war, but the novel suggests that although humanity may one day reach this perfect harmony, man is far from achieving such community.

In this novel, Côté's creation of a truly communal society and the connectedness of the three diverse travelers suggests the solution to the diversity of Canada itself, a diversity that is embodied, to a large extent, in the Québécois people. Côté suggests that acknowledging and celebrating such difference, rather than suppressing it, is the best course of action.

A nod to the work of Henri Vernes marks *La Pénombre jaune* (The Yellow Shadow, 1986), in which Côté asks the question: where can the line between reality and imagination be drawn? When Francine Sauve and her partner meet a man by the name of Bob Moraine, they are immediately drawn into a series of adventures reminiscent of those experienced by Vernes's fictional character Bob Morane. In addition, Moraine has deliberately fashioned his own life after that of his fictional namesake; it is never clear whether Bob Moraine is a "real" person or a fictional character. The line between fantasy and reality further blurs when Vernes enters the novel with an unpublished manuscript detailing the same adventures that are happening to the "real" Bob Moraine and his friends. Vernes theorizes that there is both a dimension of reality and a dimension of imagination, and that events imagined by writers become "real" in the latter; but Moraine's unexpected fate at the end of the novel calls Vernes's theory into question, raising the issue of whether humans can control their destinies. Presenting many layers of "reality," the novel keeps readers continually off balance, thereby ensuring that they experience the same uncertainty as the characters as to what is real and what is not.

The mirror motif and the quest for self-identity dealt with in *Les Parallèles célestes* surface again in the short story "Boîte crânienne" (The Skull, 1986), in which the narrator meets a masked stranger in a bar. Fashioned like a mirror, the mask hides the stranger's face, throwing back the narrator's reflection instead; hence the narrator is talking with "himself." This encounter enlightens the narrator, and he forgets his sorrow; intense self-examination and contemplation, then, are the means whereby man can understand and be at peace with himself. The search for identity must always begin, the story says, within one's self. Côté's

Québécois readers probably share this belief, given that their identity as Canadian speakers of French is a key element of their identity.

Nocturnes pour Jessie (Nocturnes for Jessie, 1987) ventures into the wholly marvelous. The novel, a finalist for the Governor General's Prize in 1988, centers around Jessie and Hendrix, escapees from a juvenile detention center, who seek refuge in Beyr, a city that shares with Lost Ark endemic unemployment, sharp class divisions, and violence-prone police forces. Some critics object to the adolescent violence, but in *Nocturnes pour Jessie* violence is a reflection of reality; it is neither gratuitous nor valorized. In addition, Côté describes Jessie's and Hendrix's drug addiction and subsequent withdrawal with frankness and realism; drug use is neither romanticized nor held up as a valid means of escaping the horrors of life in Beyr. The character of Ariane suggests more-valid means of escape: reading books, listening to music, and performing magic, exemplified by Ariane's search for Mirlande, a place where there is no crime, poverty, or pain. Ariane teaches Jessie to be capable of loving and allowing himself to be loved; he learns that beauty can exist, despite the surface ugliness of Beyr and of his own life. Through the juxtaposition of the ugliness of the outside world with the interior beauty of Ariane and Jessie, Côté suggests that there is an escape route from an unpleasant reality through artistic pursuits and through unselfish love.

The theme of technology and the misuse of scientific experimentation resonates throughout *Les Prisonniers du zoo* (The Prisoners of the Zoo, 1988), also a finalist for the Governor General's Prize. This novel marks the debut of Maxime, presenting for the author the challenge of telling the story through the eyes of a thirteen-year-old boy. *Les Prisonniers du zoo* also addresses a theme new to Côté: the ethics of animal experimentation. Troubled by the disappearance of a prominent zoologist, Maxime and his friend Pouce spend a night at the Zoological Gardens, where they encounter two chimpanzees, Ronald and Mikhail, who use pieces of fruit to play Queens—chesslike strategy game—while no one is watching. Their intelligence has been enhanced by experimental drugs. Afraid of reverting to their "ignorant" state, the chimps have imprisoned the zoologist to force him to manufacture more of the drug. The zoologist embodies the scientific view of experimentation for the sake of knowledge, without regard for the animals' well-being; his refusal to manufacture the intelligence-enhancing drug enables man to retain superiority over animals. Conversely, Mr. Toc, an elderly guard who works at the zoo, embodies the sympathies of the animal rights activists; his attempts to free the animals are motivated by his sympathy for their condition. In addition to presenting these opposing views, Côté allows the animals to tell their side of the story through Ronald and Mikhail, who communicate via typing on a computer keyboard. The arrest of Mr. Toc and the rescue of the zoologist suggest that the established order triumphs, but Maxime's refusal to return to the zoo at the end raises doubts as to who has truly benefited from this resolution.

In *L'Idole des Inactifs* (An Idol for the Inactives, 1989), the first in a trilogy featuring characters from *Hockeyeurs cybernétiques,* Côté returns to Lost Ark and to his themes of social inequality and rampant technology. In this novel the contrast between the "haves" and the "have-nots" is heightened through the point of view of John, a poverty-stricken Inactive on the run from the police. In this futuristic society, the Inactives are the poor and unemployed who live in a ghettolike part of the city called "Old Town." In sharp contrast are the Actives, who have jobs and social status and, appropriately, live in "New Town." Actives both fear and despise the Inactives. John's life serves as a foil to that of Michel Lenoir, who eats cereal from a crystal bowl. In Lost Ark the rapid spread of robotic technology has created such endemic unemployment that people in all sectors are rebelling; the pacifist demonstration marches of the Actives sharply contrast with the violent takeover of the Private Zone planned by the Inactives. Even among the Inactives, nonviolent resistance surfaces as an option, embodied in the intriguing telepathic Mages; the juxtaposition of the Mage Tagaras with the revolutionary jargon of Shade further enhances the contrast, indicating that pacifist resistance is preferable. In the meantime, Michel has become a demigod and a propaganda instrument for Swindler, regularly appearing on TV to extol the virtues of obedience to the leaders of Lost Ark. Michel's apparent reversal of beliefs puzzles Virginia Lynx, whose subsequent investigation makes her the target of Swindler and his robotic police. Given that the mass media have become mere propaganda instruments for the government, Virginia's quest for the truth emphasizes the importance of journalistic ethics and the dangers of absolute governmental control over information. The seeds of change and revolution are planted in *L'Idole des Inactifs;* they bear fruit in the other two novels of this trilogy.

Some of the same themes are played upon, with variations, in *Le Voyage dans le temps* (The Trip Through Time, 1989), which marks the return of thirteen-year-old Maxime. Finding a pair of old boots in his room, Maxime puts them on, thinking they are a birthday present; immediately, he and his girlfriend, Jo, are transported to Quebec in 1889. The descriptions of

Cover for Côté's 1994 novel, in which his recurring teenage hero, Maxime, and two friends are trapped in a maze of mirrors

nineteenth-century life, viewed through the eyes of two twentieth-century children, heighten the contrast between past and present; Jo and Maxime encounter townspeople who believe in sorcery, children who die of tuberculosis at an alarming rate, and an allegedly evil sorceress. The novel suggests that man has progressed phenomenally through science, at least in some ways; indeed, science is the passion of Gabrielle, the sorceress, who believes that technology will solve the social and physical problems faced by the people of 1889. However, this blind belief is gently belied by Maxime's—and the reader's—knowledge of the pervasive social ills that still plague the modern world. When Gabrielle asks Maxime to describe the future, Maxime says only that she would not survive a trip to the future, because of the shock. Thus, subtly and lyrically, the novel suggests that science and technology cannot cure all societal ills; the solutions lie elsewhere, within man himself.

Primarily a writer of novels, Côté has also written novellas, four of which are collected in *La Vie est une bande dessinée* (Life is a Comic Strip, 1989). These novellas are connected by their intertextuality and by their expression of concerns that are addressed in Côté's earlier writing. The title novella, hailed as the best of the collection, details the story of Guy, an avid collector of comic strips, who discovers a book of previously unknown Tintin comics and embarks upon a quest to learn whether the volume is real. The previous owner of the book, Ernest Beauregard, claims to be a counterfeiter who pirated the book himself, but Guy eventually learns that this claim is a lie; rather, Beauregard has created a fictitious, more adventurous life for himself than his "real" existence as an insurance salesman. Like Bob Moraine in *La Pénombre jaune*, Beauregard is not sure himself where his "real" life begins and his fictional life leaves off, and by the end of the novella, neither is Guy.

In "L'Art de créer des illusions" (The Art of Creating Illusions), Côté returns to the theme of the marvelous as Eric, a young magician, must prove his innocence of the seemingly magical theft of some computer disks. Eric uses a ploy from Sherlock Holmes's repertoire: the reenactment of the crime to demonstrate the criminal's actions. Though Eric earlier breaks a basic "rule" of magic by explaining to the audience how his disappearing trick was performed, his later reenactment retains elements of the marvelous, because he refuses to tell his sister how he entered the locked building. Filial affection is touted as vital, for Eric's sister risks arrest and danger to help her brother clear his name.

The third novella, "L'Adventure dont je suis l'heroine" (The Adventure of Which I Am the Heroine), features a strong female protagonist, Luce, as well as an intriguing variation on the popular "choose your own plot" novels. Luce wishes to join a roleplaying group whose leader does not admit women; however, Luce's determination and spunk—as well as her assault on Gilles, an obnoxious member of the group—earn her the leader's reluctant admiration and an invitation to join. In the process of her initiation, she survives a variety of trials, including kidnapping and imprisonment. Côté plays with the structure of the novella by making the reader choose his/her own path through the story; several of the choices reveal Côté's wry sense of humor, resulting in the sudden termination of the adventure or Luce's wry comments about the reader's abilities. This structure deliberately blurs the line between fantasy and reality; the first-person narration encourages the reader to identify with Luce, but "real" life does not offer the option of "trying" first one path, then another, as the novella does. Is this story "real" or a fantasy? The reader must supply the answer.

The last novella, "Ordinateur de mon coeur" (The Computer of My Heart), is imbued with intertextuality, as a young heroine falls in love with a computer programmer named Robert Charlebois, a name shared by a character from the work of Réjean Ducharme. Intrigue and technology dominate as the heroine investigates, through her computer network, a case of sabotage of Stuff Company's products, mostly food and other grocery items. The culprit turns out to be Charlebois himself, but the sabotage is accidental; Charlebois is trying to create the ultimate recyclable can, but the result is a can that dissolves on store shelves. Côté again sounds the theme of environmentalism through Charlebois's lengthy speech about the pollution that is destroying the world; technology is both cause and cure for the problem. The narrator, Song, is another strong and capable female protagonist, though her naïveté is questionable when she agrees not to turn Charlebois in because his goals are noble.

Through the visual imagery for which he is noted, Côté evokes a mood of horror in his first vampire novel, *La Nuit du vampire* (Night of the Vampire, 1990). The novel rings changes on the traditional horrific character of the vampire and echoes again Côté's theme of the importance of both diversity and tolerance. At a school music festival, Maxime and his sister, Ozzie, meet the heavy-metal group Pterodactyl and their mysterious lead guitarist, Red Lerouge. When a heavy snowstorm forces everyone to spend the night in the school, a fun evening is transformed into a frightening one; the empty and darkened school is the perfect setting for the mysterious events that follow. The clues lead Maxime to suspect that one of the musicians is a vampire, and Red Lerouge's odd behavior makes him the logical suspect; Maxime is correct, but despite Red's obvious physical differences, he and Maxime become close friends. Intolerance of diversity has striking consequences in this novel, particularly the intolerance exhibited by Etcetera, the cultural director of the school, who turns out to be the perpetrator of the mysterious incidents. His motive: he despises heavy-metal music. Such prejudice results in his appearing foolish in front of the others, while Maxime is applauded as a hero. While heavy-metal music is usually portrayed as having "evil influences" upon young people, in this case, Etcetera's hatred of that music is the evil influence that drives him to terrorize his companions. Côté again suggests that tolerance of diversity is important and necessary.

Michel Lenoir returns in *La Révolte des Inactifs* (The Revolt of the Inactives, 1990); in this novel, Virginia, escaping the Sherlocks—robots programmed to seek out and destroy enemies of the govenment—hides out in Old Town and eventually finds the "real" Michel. The Inactive revolt begins, with the goal of killing the artificially prolonged entity known as David Swindler. The story of the aftermath of the revolution is told in *Le Retour des Inactifs* (Terminus Nightmare, 1990), which brings the trilogy to its climactic close. The triumph of Michel and the Inactives over the unethical, power-hungry entity that once was known as Swindler restores the balance of social and economic power and furthers Côté's themes of social inequality.

In *Terminus cauchemar* (1991) Côté returns to the theme of technology and scientific experimentation, this time questioning the ethics of using science to create a "super-human." In focusing on the "superman" archetype, Côté raises issues that are not scientific or technical, but philosophical: how far should science go in its quest for perfection in the species of man? An even more relevant question for contemporary young people is, what are the ethics of drug use to improve performance in sports?

Can love and friendship truly exist between two people when such love involves the exclusion of everyone else? This question is asked in *Les Yeux d'emeraude* (The Eyes of Emeraude, 1991) wherein Maxime rescues a stray cat, only to discover that Emeraude is not a cat at all, but a telepathic being from another dimension. Emeraude's strange and obsessive affection for Maxime brings with it an uncharacteristic change in the behavior of Maxime's parents and his two best friends, Jo and Pouce. Emeraude is fiercely jealous of Maxime's affection for anyone except her, and when Jo lies injured in the hospital, Maxime wonders whether Emeraude has other powers besides that of telepathy. In the end, Maxime must make a difficult choice, which leads to his discovery of the truth about Emeraude and her powers. True friendship is thus portrayed as selfless and loyal; jealousy is childish and undesirable, as Maxime learns.

The need for intense self-examination runs through Côté's work, often symbolized by mirrors or other reflective surfaces. This theme predominates in *Le Parc aux sortilèges* (The Magic Park, 1994), as Maxime and his friends are trapped in a house of mirrors. Inside the mirrored maze, Maxime, Jo, and Pouce confront more terror than simply a seemingly endless labyrinth; their search for an exit becomes for each character a self-exploration. As they struggle against the terrors the maze presents them, the three friends are brought face-to-face with their inner selves and, like the narrator in "Boîte cránienne," each learns something integral about him/herself.

Red Lerouge comes back into Maxime's life in *La Trahison du vampire* (The Treason of the Vampire, 1995). In this novel the importance of trust and tolerance between friends is emphasized, for Maxime has promised Red that he will never be afraid of him. But Red mysteriously vanishes and, simultaneously, strange things happen in the city, such as the theft of blood from the Red Cross, causing Maxime to doubt his friend's abstention from vampirism. When a picture of Red appears in the newspaper as a suspect in a recent assault, Maxime feels angry and betrayed; these emotions motivate him to join Etcetera on a night expedition in search of Red. While Maxime struggles to escape the subterranean prison of the vampires after being captured, his anger at Red's apparent betrayal of his friendship grows steadily, reaching a climax when he confronts a vampire who looks like Red and who tries to kill him. Friendship and trust triumph, however, for Maxime realizes the truth when the "real" Red is willing to sacrifice his own life to save Maxime's, the ultimate mark of friendship. Red's final transformation ultimately brings him and Maxime closer than ever and reasserts the values of true friendship, which can overcome any and all difficulties.

For Denis Côté, writing is an expression of his beliefs. His themes and plots are intriguing and relevant to the readers whom he reaches in large numbers. Truly a pioneer of science fiction for younger readers, Côté seeks to break new ground and works to create a new generation of novels for the young people of Quebec. Côté's emphasis on themes of identity and diversity makes his novels particularly relevant to his Québécois readers, for whom both themes are significant. Côté also provides well-rounded protagonists who are themselves Québécois, thus setting out role models for his young audience. In addition, Côté's innovative treatment of otherwise common themes and plots of science fiction prevents his work from becoming an echo or parody of other North American science fiction. In this way he is truly breaking new ground and working toward the development of a particularly Québécois view of the world.

Interviews:

Monique Poulin, "Denis Côté, auteur," *Lurelu* 7 (1984): 22–23;

Jean-March Gouanvic and Claire LeBrun, "Lancer des débats, poser des questions, c'est le rôle de l'ecrivain de science-fiction," *Imagine,* 22 (1984): 128–135;

Claude Janelle, "Denis Côté, le révélation de l'année 83," *Solaris,* 56 (1984): 24–25;

Aurélian Boivin and Hélène Marcotte, "Denis Côté, passionné de l'ecriture," *Quebec Francais,* 75 (1989): 74–76;

Isabelle Clerc, "Denis Côté: Humaniste et auteur à succés," *Quebec Francais,* 91 (1990): 108–109;

Edith Madore, "Le côté des jeunes," *A l'affiche* (April 1992): 14–18;

Julie Martel, Interview with Denis Côté, *Vidéo-Presse,* 24 (December 1994): 22–24.

Charles de Lint
(22 December 1951 –)

Robin Anne Reid
Texas A&M University–Commerce

BOOKS: *The Oak King's Daughter: A Tale of Cerin Songweaver* (Ottawa, Ontario: Triskell Press, 1979);
The Moon is a Meadow: A Tale of Tam Tinkern (Ottawa, Ontario: Triskell Press, 1980);
A Pattern of Silver Strings: A Tale of Cerin Songweaver (Ottawa, Ontario: Triskell Press, 1981);
Glass Eyes and Cotton Strings: A Tale of Cerin Songweaver (Ottawa, Ontario: Triskell Press, 1982);
In Mask and Motley: A Tale of Cerin Songweaver (Ottawa, Ontario: Triskell Press, 1983);
The Calendar of the Trees (Ottawa, Ontario: Triskell Press, 1984);
Laughter in the Leaves: A Tale of Cerin Songweaver (Ottawa, Ontario: Triskell Press, 1984);
The Riddle of the Wren (New York: Ace, 1984);
Moonheart: A Romance (New York: Ace, 1984; London: Pan, 1990);
The Badger in the Bag: A Tale of Cerin Songweaver (Ottawa, Ontario: Triskell Press, 1985);
The Harp of the Grey Rose (Norfolk, Va.: Donning/Starblaze, 1985);
Mulengro: A Romany Tale (New York: Ace, 1985; London: Pan, 1997);
The Three Plushketeers and the Garden Slugs (Ottawa, Ontario: Triskell Press, 1985);
And the Rafters Were Ringing: A Tale of Cerin Songweaver (Ottawa, Ontario: Triskell Press, 1986);
Yarrow: An Autumn Tale (New York: Ace, 1986; London: Pan, 1992);
Ascian in Rose (Seattle, Wash.: Axolotl Press, 1987 [i.e. 1986]);
Jack, the Giant-Killer (New York: Ace, 1987);
The Lark in the Morning: A Tale of Cerin Songweaver (Ottawa, Ontario: Triskell Press, 1987);
The Drowned Man's Reel (Ottawa, Ontario: Triskell Press, 1988);
Greenmantle (New York: Ace, 1988; London: Pan, 1991);
Wolf Moon (New York: New American Library/Signet, 1988);
The Stone Drum (Ottawa, Ontario: Triskell Press, 1989);
Svaha (New York: Ace, 1989);

Charles de Lint (photograph © by Beth Gwinn)

Westlin Wind (Eugene, Ore.: Axolotl Press, 1989);
The Valley of Thunder, Philip José Farmer's *The Dungeon,* volume 3 (New York: Bantam, 1989; London: Bantam, 1990);
Berlin (Ottawa, Ontario: Fourth Avenue Press, 1989);
The Hidden City, Farmer's *The Dungeon,* volume 5 (New York: Bantam, 1990);
The Fair in Emain Macha, published together with *Ill Met in Lankhmar,* by Fritz Leiber, as Tor SF Double #19 (New York: Tor, 1990);

Drink Down the Moon (New York: Ace, 1990);

Ghostwood (Eugene, Ore.: Axolotl Press, 1990);

Angel of Darkness, as Samuel M. Key (New York: Jove, 1990);

The Dreaming Place (New York: Atheneum, 1990);

Ghosts of Wind and Shadow (Ottawa, Ontario: Triskell Press, 1990; Eugene, Ore.: Axolotl Press, 1991);

Desert Moments (Ottawa, Ontario: Triskell Press, 1991);

The Little Country (New York: Morrow, 1991; London: Pan, 1993);

Uncle Dobbin's Parrot Fair (Eugene, Ore.: Pulphouse, 1991);

Death Leaves an Echo (New York: Tor, 1991);

Our Lady of the Harbour (Eugene, Ore.: Axolotl, 1991);

Paperjack (New Castle, Va.: Cheap Street, 1992);

Merlin Dreams in the Moondream Wood (Eugene, Ore.: Pulphouse, 1992);

The Bone Woman (Ottawa, Ontario: Triskell Press, 1992);

Mr. Truepenny's Book Emporium and Gallery (New Castle, Va.: Cheap Street, 1992);

From a Whisper to a Scream, as Key (New York: Berkley, 1992);

Coyote Stories (Ottawa, Ontario: Triskell Press, 1993);

The Wishing Well (Eugene, Ore.: Axolotl Press, 1993);

Into the Green (New York: Tor, 1993);

Heartfires (Ottawa, Ontario: Triskell Press, 1994);

I'll Be Watching You, as Key (New York: Jove, 1994);

The Wild Wood (Brian Froud's Faerielands) (New York: Bantam, 1994);

Memory and Dream (New York: Tor, 1994; London: Macmillan, 1995);

Crow Girls (Ottawa, Ontario: Triskell Press, 1995);

My Life as a Bird (Ottawa, Ontario: Triskell Press, 1996);

The Fields Beyond the Fields (Ottawa, Ontario: Triskell Press, 1997);

Trader (New York: Tor, 1997; London: Macmillan, 1997);

Second Chances (Ottawa, Ontario: Triskell Press, 1998);

Someplace to Be Flying (New York: Tor, 1998; London: Macmillan, 1998);

The Buffalo Man (Burton, Mich.: Subterannean Press, 1999);

Pixel Pixies (Ottawa, Ontario: Triskell Press, 1999);

Forests of the Heart (New York: Tor, 2000);

Big City Littles (Ottawa, Ontario: Triskell Press, 2000);

The Road to Lisdoonvarna (Burton, Mich.: Subterranean Press, 2001);

The Onion Girl (New York: Tor, 2001).

Collections: *De Grijze Roos* (Antwerp, Belgium: Een Exa Uitgave, 1983);

Hedgework and Guessery (Eugene, Ore.: Pulphouse, 1991);

Spiritwalk (New York: Tor, 1992; London: Macmillan, 1994)—comprises *Merlin Dreams in the Moondream Wood, Ascian in Rose, Westlin Wind,* and *Ghostwood;*

Dreams Underfoot: The Newford Collection (New York: Tor, 1993);

The Ivory and the Horn: A Newford Collection (New York: Tor, 1995);

Jack of Kinrowan (New York: Tor, 1995)—comprises *Jack, the Giant-Killer* and *Drink Down the Moon;*

Moonlight and Vines (New York: Tor, 1999);

The Newford Stories (New York: Science Fiction Book Club, 1999)—comprises *Dreams Underfoot, The Ivory and the Horn,* and *Moonlight and Vines;*

Triskell Tales: 22 Years of Chapbooks (Burton, Mich.: Subterranean Press, 2000).

Charles de Lint is a prolific author working in a variety of genres: novels, novellas, short stories, poetry, songs, reviews, and criticism. He has won several awards for his fantasy writing, including the first annual William L. Crawford Award for Best New Fantasy Author of 1984 (presented by the International Association of the Fantastic in the Arts); the 1988 Canadian Science Fiction and Fantasy Award, or Casper, for Best Work in English for *Jack, the Giant-Killer* (1987); the 1992 Best Books for the Teen Age award from the New York Public Library for *The Little Country* (1991); the Prix Ozone 1997 for Best Foreign Fantasy Short Story; the 1998 Young Adult Library Services Association Best Books for Young Adults award for *Trader* (1997); and the 2000 World Fantasy Award for Best Collection for *Moonlight and Vines* (1999). His review columns have been published in major fantasy, science-fiction, and horror magazines; he has served as a judge on major awards committees for those genres; and he has been invited to several conferences as a guest of honor. He has published more than forty-five books (and counting), with many of his books appearing in both American and British editions, and his work has been translated into French, German, Japanese, and Spanish.

De Lint has played an important role in developing the subgenre known as "urban fantasy" or, as he prefers to call it, "mythic fiction," which he describes on his website (http://www.charlesdelint.com) as "basically mainstream writing that incorporates elements of myth and folklore, rather than secondary world fantasy." Blending fantastic elements from folktales, urban folklore, and myths with contemporary realistic settings, de Lint's work has become progressively more character-driven. He is known for his ability to create characters from marginalized social groups ("outsiders" because of their ethnicity or gender) in a genre traditionally associated with Anglo- or European-American characters.

Charles Henri Diederick Hoefsmit de Lint was born in Bussum, the Netherlands, on 22 December 1951 to Frederick Charles Hoefsmit and Gerardina Margaretha Hoefsmit-de Lint. Four months after his birth, the family moved to Canada. They lived on both sides of the Ottawa River near Ottawa, in both Ontario and Quebec; the family moved frequently because of his father's job as a surveyor, also living in Turkey and Lebanon. Ottawa remains de Lint's home and is a key presence in his earlier fiction. He was an avid reader from a young age, starting primarily with myth and folklore, then moving into fantasy with the novels of J. R. R. Tolkien and science fiction through the novels of Andre Norton. Despite his love of reading, de Lint's earliest plans were to become a musician. He loved Celtic music but could not make a living from it. He worked in music stores and played on the weekends for about fourteen years after high school, while writing songs and poetry.

De Lint began writing more seriously in the mid 1970s, writing stories for his friend John Charette to illustrate. Their work was published in small-press magazines. De Lint continued working in record stores for another half-dozen years until his novella, "The Fane of the Grey Rose," was published in the 1979 anthology *Swords Against Darkness IV*, edited by Andrew J. Offutt. That novella was later expanded into his 1985 novel *The Harp of the Grey Rose*.

In September 1980 de Lint married MaryAnn Harris, an artist, in Ottawa. De Lint credits her as an important influence, not only because she encouraged him to write but also because, as he wrote on his website, she convinced him to take his stories "out of the faerie forest and see how well they might fare on the city street." He has been a full-time writer since 1983.

Beginning in 1979, with *The Oak King's Daughter: A Tale of Cerin Songweaver*, de Lint published a series of chapbooks with his own Triskell Press, and he has continued this practice throughout his career, both with Triskell Press and with American chapbook publishers. Finally, in 1984, de Lint emerged onto the fantasy scene with two full-length novels published by the American genre publisher Ace Books. *The Riddle of the Wren* was the first to appear. The story follows Minda Sealy's attempts to escape from tormenting dreams sent by Ildran, the Dream-master. Minda finds an ally, Jan Penalurick, who gives her a talisman that lets her travel between worlds. Minda meets others who help her rescue Jan and defeat Ildran: Taneh the Loremistress; Markj'n, a tinker; and Grimbold, a wizard and talking beast. *The Riddle of the Wren* is a traditional fantasy set in a secondary world in which magical races coexist with humanity. The major themes are the conflict between good and evil and the young protagonist's search for her identity and heritage. This early novel shows de Lint drawing from Celtic mythology with its multiple gods, each one reflecting different spiritual aspects. De Lint's interest in the beings who exist between the "light" and "dark," and the female protagonist, are early signs of his efforts to expand the traditional secondary-world fantasy plot.

The Riddle of the Wren was quickly followed by the more ambitious *Moonheart: A Romance* (1984), a novel blending elements from Celtic and Native American mythology (a characteristic that de Lint develops further in later novels). The two main settings are the contemporary city of Ottawa and the spirit realms, but characters can travel to other worlds and times as well. Major characters include Sara Kendell, Kieran Foy, Thomas Hengwr, and John Tucker. Sara is the most important figure; her uncle, James Tamson or Jamie Tams, owns Tamson House, a huge house that straddles the contemporary and the spirit worlds. When Sara finds a painting of a Native American shaman and a Celtic bard, she begins a spiritual journey in which she is joined by Kieran Foy, the apprentice of Thomas Hengwr, a druid who has lived for centuries. Foy travels with Sara to the Otherworld, as the spirit realms are called, to avoid being captured by a mysterious evil force. Their enemy in Ottawa is a powerful businessman, J. Hugh Walters, who has manipulated the Canadian government into studying examples of the paranormal, especially the long-lived Thomas Hengwr. John Tucker, a special inspector for the Royal Canadian Mounted Police, provides security for the project, but begins to work against Walters. The threat in the Otherworld is an evil being named Mal'ek'a. Traveling to a different time, Sara meets the bard Taliesin, exiled from Wales by a druid named Tomasin Hengwr t'Hap (the younger Thomas). In another spirit world, Kieran meets Ha'kan'ta, a drummer and shaman. Both young protagonists are helped to discover their powers. Characters from various worlds must come to Tamson House in the Otherworld to face and defeat Mal'ek'a, who turns out to be the "evil" expelled by Thomas Hengwr after Thomas was imprisoned in stone by Taliesin's parting curse.

Rather than presenting good and evil as binary and opposing forces that try to defeat each other, the conclusion of the novel supports the belief that everyone has both good and evil in them, and part of the spiritual quest of life is learning to strengthen one's goodness. An innovative aspect of the novel is de Lint's evocation of both indigenous and European mythologies. The genocide and forced cultural assimilation of the indigenous peoples are not ignored, since some of the manitous (spirits) reveal their anger against Kieran, Sara, and the other descendants of European colonizers.

The Harp of the Grey Rose, published the next year, is a traditional fantasy set in a world that was used in *The Riddle of the Wren;* it draws on a character de Lint had created in his earlier chapbooks, Cerin Songweaver. Cerin

Dust jacket for de Lint's 1993 collection of nineteen stories set in his fictional city of Newford

meets the Grey Rose, a mysterious and beautiful woman, in the woods one day. She is fleeing from a Waster, a child of the Daketh (Dark Gods). When the Grey Rose is captured, Cerin sets out to save her; traveling with Hickathrift, a loremaster and talking beast, Cerin succeeds. However, since the Grey Rose is a child of the Tuathan (the Light Gods), her presence in the world means that her dark counterpart, Damal, can enter as well. Cerin, Hickathrift, and the Grey Rose defeat Damal, but the Grey Rose must return to her kin to preserve the Balance, the agreement between the Daketh and the Tuathan to both stay out of the middle realm, the physical world. The theme of this novel is the conflict between good and evil, expressed through a traditional fantasy plot: a young man falls in love and sets out on a quest to save his love, only to find that he must also save the world. De Lint's novel describes a harper, rather than the more usual warrior hero, and includes talking animals as companions and rescuers.

Mulengro: A Romany Tale, also published in 1985, is a novel that is much closer to horror than fantasy, and as de Lint reports, some of his readers were disturbed by the graphic violence. As a result of readers' responses to this book, de Lint adopted the open pseudonym of Samuel M. Key to identify his subsequent horror novels. As the subtitle indicates, the plot of *Mulengro* focuses on Romany (Gypsy) culture and beliefs. The two protagonists are Janfri Yayal and Ola Faher. Both are Romany (Rom) who have left their parent culture to exist, precariously, in Ottawa, in the Gaje (non-Gypsy) world. Janfri is a musician, and Ola is a writer. Both Janfri and Ola are threatened, accused of being "marhime," unclean, because of their association with non-Gypsies. When Ola is attacked by two brothers, Bob and Stan Gourlay, who intend to rape her, she kills Stan. He manifests as a *mulo,* a spirit that is capable of acting upon the world. The *drabarni* (magic worker) who is the major force of evil in the novel is called Mulengro. As a Romany child he was imprisoned in a Nazi concentration camp during World War II, as were Janfri and his family. Mulengro has come to believe Nazi propaganda that Romanies are unclean, and he is exercising his magic power to cleanse them. Janfri, Ola, and others confront Mulengro at an isolated cabin, aided by a gathering of the Rom. Ola is attacked by Stan Gourlay's *mulo,* but when she truly forgives him, the spirit loses his power. Ola and Janfri confront Mulengro and raise their own dead to oppose him. Janfri sacrifices himself by setting fire to the cabin to kill Mulengro's body, and the other Rom, led by a powerful *drabarni,* forgive the spirit of Mulengro, which prevents him from being able to act against them.

The themes of this novel are the search for identity–especially important for the two major characters, who live between and within two different cultures–and the conflict between good and evil. The fantasy elements of this novel are from Romany beliefs, which de Lint studied; *Mulengro* exemplifies de Lint's interest in researching and writing about other cultures. Since he is not native to many of the cultures he writes about, he had to address the debate over what has been called–as he writes in an essay appended to the 1985 edition of *Mulengro* and also posted on his website–"cultural appropriation, by which is usually meant: white authors mining the cultures of minorities for their own profit and gain while the voices of writers from those same minority cultures go unheard." In his essay he acknowledges the existence of the problem, but argues that the solution is not censorship or self-censorship. Instead, he says that artists who wish to explore various cultures and identities should do so with respect, based on careful research and knowledge, and that readers should read as much work by artists of many different cultures as possible.

Yarrow: An Autumn Tale, published in 1986, is the second of de Lint's novels that critics have labeled "urban fantasy." De Lint has been a major figure in this subgenre, which blends fantastic or magical elements with a mainstream or contemporary setting. In this novel, Caitlin Midhir, known as Cat, is a fantasy writer living in Ottawa. She bases her stories on her dreams of an Otherworld where she has developed friendships with fantasy creatures who share their stories. Her problem is that she has stopped dreaming for several months and cannot write. The reason for her writer's block turns out to be a centuries-old psychic vampire, Lysistratus, who lives off of dreams. Cat dreams true dreams, and Lysistratus has been preying on her dreams for months. Cat must accept the reality of her dreams in order to save herself as well as her human friends, Peter and Ben, and her Otherworld friends. In accepting the reality of her dreams, she finally accepts responsibility for her actions in the Otherworld. She ultimately defeats Lysistratus by containing his spirit within herself.

The theme of this novel is the connection between art and spirit, and the importance of both realms. Learning magic in one dimension follows a similar process as writing novels in another dimension. The protagonists participating in both processes search for truth and self-knowledge through their various spiritual journeys. *Yarrow* focuses on the conflict between good and evil but lacks a complete or easy victory since Cat does not kill Lysistratus at the end. Instead, she absorbs him and contains his spirit because part of her understands "evil" and knows how to control it.

Jack, the Giant-Killer, published in 1987, was written as part of Terri Windling's "Fairy Tale" series, in which fantasy authors write adult novels based to some extent on traditional fairy tales. De Lint's novel is based on the tradition of the "Jack," a trickster figure that appears in the folktales of various cultures. In his introduction to the book, de Lint writes that he has always been drawn to trickster figures, and that in this novel he wanted to push beyond what he had done before to bring faeries into contemporary urban settings. Jacky Rowan, a young woman living in Ottawa, learns about the presence of the Seelie and Unseelie (Faerie) Courts in her city. Helped by her best friend Kate Hazel and three faeries from the Seelie Court, Jacky goes on a quest to rescue the Laird of Kinrowan's daughter, who has been kidnapped by Wild Hunt, controlled by the Unseelie Court. Jacky's success results in a limiting of the Unseelie Court's power and in her taking the place of the *gruagagh* (wizard) Bhruic Dearg as the guardian of the Seelie Court of Kinrowan.

Jack, the Giant-Killer succeeds in its quest to create a narrative that brings faeries into an urban setting. The Celtic faeries came to Canada from Europe with the settlers, and Jacky is told that the faerie courts live in the world alongside but unseen by nonfaeries, while the native spirits have withdrawn to an Otherworld. The presence of the Jack, or trickster figure, emphasizes that the conflict between good and evil is not simply solved. As with de Lint's earlier works, a young woman is the protagonist; her friend, who helps her, is also a woman, setting the pattern for many of de Lint's later novels in which two women friends are the emotional center and focus of the narrative. The ability to create believable female characters is an issue that he addresses on his website, where he explains his process by saying that he is curious, and so he listens to what people say, tries to "immerse" himself in other people's points of view, and researches and tries to imagine what their perspectives or experiences would be like. For his female characters he says he draws on what he has observed his wife and her friends saying, as well as what he has read by women, making a "continuous and conscious effort to weed out any of the negative conditioning and stereotyping that we are all subject to."

Greenmantle, published in 1988, is a novel that sets traditional fantasy elements in a rural Canadian setting, rather than in de Lint's more typical urban settings. Tony Valenti, an enforcer for an urban criminal organization, is framed for the murder of the organization's leader. Tony escapes and hides out in a secret house he owns in the country, using the name Tony Garonne. A few years later, Frankie Treasure wins the lottery and moves with Ali, her daughter, back to her family's home, which happens to be down the road from Tony's safe house. Some distance from where Tony and the Treasures live is New Wolding, a small pagan community that has been dwindling in size for some time. The story follows two plotlines, a mundane one and an Otherworldly one. Earl Shaw, a small-time drug dealer and Frankie's former husband, plots to kidnap Ali in order to ransom her for Frankie's lottery winnings. When Shaw discovers Tony's presence, he adds assassination to his plans. The plans are disrupted by the attempts made by Lewis Datchery and Mally Meggan to draw more inhabitants to New Wolding. Both Tony and Ali are drawn to New Wolding, and Mally plans to have Ali set free the stag (a figure of power, sometimes a man, sometimes a stag, sometimes half and half) who is the focus of New Wolding worship.

Greenmantle explores the complexities of mankind's relationship with nature and the nature of belief, as well as the conflict between good and evil. The pagan villagers and their belief system are dying out, which affects the power of the deities. Certain characters are drawn to the beauty and energy of nature worship, and the power of the nature spirits then proves stronger than the urban violence attempted by several of the characters.

Wolf Moon, published the same year, is a traditional secondary-world fantasy set in an unnamed country at the Inn of the Yellow Tinker. Kern Kindregan is a werewolf pursued in his wolf form by a harper and a magic beast. Kern nearly dies but leaps from a high cliff into a

Dust jacket for de Lint's 1997 novel about a guitar maker who wakes up to find that his body has been switched with that of a confidence man

river. He ends up at the Inn, where he heals and begins to make a life for himself, and he falls in love with Ainsy, the owner of the Inn. But the harper comes to the valley, recognizes Kern, and uses his magic, focused through the harp music, to try to bring about Kern's expulsion and death. Kern, helped by Fion, who works at the Inn, finally destroys the harper's harp, kills him, and frees the valley people from the harper's malign enchantment.

Although *Wolf Moon* employs a traditional fantasy setting and characters, de Lint achieves a reversal of the traditional fantasy plot by questioning the assumption that a werewolf is "inherently" evil and by presenting a harper as evil. Kern is the major point-of-view character, which creates considerable sympathy for him. Additionally, Kern has never killed anyone until he does so to save Ainsy's uncle, Tomtim, from robbers. The harper, however, uses his music to work evil magic on innocent and vulnerable people, killing them to blame "the werewolf," and enchanting Ainsy in order to sexually force himself on her.

Svaha, published in 1989, was something of an experiment for de Lint. It makes more use of Native American culture than his other novels while incorporating cyberpunk elements, such as a dystopian corporate-controlled future, Japanese annexation of Canada, and computer hackers. Although the spiritual beliefs of Native American cultures are an important aspect of the novel, *Svaha* presents a more dystopian and more technologically focused view of a future than de Lint's other novels. In this future, corporate cultures rule the Megaplexes, where employees live well, while the unemployed barely survive among ruins in deserted cities. The highest level of technology and highest standard of living are to be found in the Enclaves, technologically protected reserves into which indigenous cultures have withdrawn. The Enclaves preserve their own self-developed technology and practice many of their traditional beliefs.

An Enclave warrior, Gahzee Animiki-Waewidum of the Turtle totem, volunteers to leave his Enclave to study why another Enclave has lost touch with the rest. Outside, he meets Lisa Bone, a "rat," or messenger, who has lost an important package that turns out to contain stolen Enclave software. Gahzee and Lisa oppose the corporate culture. Inside that corporate culture, two others, Phillip Yip and Fumiko Hirose, move from acceptance to resistance. Both couples fall in love, despite coming from different cultures or classes, and both attempt to overcome the corporate control of their lives. One couple, Phillip and Fumiko, dies in the attempt, but the other does not because Gahzee draws on different kinds of knowledge and ways of living, that of the Dreamlands (the spiritual levels of reality) and environmentalism. After Gahzee and Lisa retrieve the lost software and learn that the inhabitants of the other Enclave were murdered, Gahzee requests and gains access to that Enclave for a new project. Lisa has come into the Dreamlands with him, and he sees the possibility of creating a new tribe—consisting of humans from all cultures—expanding the spiritual and environmental message from his culture.

The environmental themes of this novel are clearly developed: the indigenous peoples do not preach some sort of return to a mythic past; instead, the message is to use technology responsibly within a noncapitalist economic system. The Megaplexes are late capitalism carried to extremes, destroying not only the natural world but also civil rights.

Drink Down the Moon, published in 1990, is a sequel to *Jack, the Giant-Killer* (both books were later collected in the 1995 omnibus edition, *Jack of Kinrowan*). It focuses on the *fiaina sidhe,* the wild faeries, allied neither with the Seelie nor the Unseelie Courts. Faeries coexist invisibly with humans, who can cross over to their world when drunk, with music, with a faerie's help, and, eventually, with practice. The human protagonist is Johnny Faw, a fiddler, whose grandfather knew the wild *sidhe*, especially Jenna, the Pook of Puxill. Jacky Rowan and Kate Hazel play important roles as well. An evil *gruagagh* moves into their area hoping to benefit from the Unseelie Court's attempted destruction of Kinrowan's Seelie Court, which was thwarted by Jacky and Kate in the earlier novel. Lacking that destruction, he attacks the *fiaina sidhe*, kills Jenna, who leads the *sidhe*, and enchants Jacky in order to get access to the Gruagagh's Tower, where Kate and Jacky have been living since the events in *Jack, the Giant-Killer*. Kate, Johnny Faw, and Jemi Pook (Jenna's half-human sister) ally to overcome the *gruagagh* and save the *fiaina sidhe*.

Drink Down the Moon explores love, friendship, and the complex nature of identity. De Lint's focus on the borderlands faeries in the characters of the *fiaina sidhe* and of Jemi—half-human, half-faerie—breaks down the binary of good versus evil in his focus on marginalized groups and outsiders. The *fiaina sidhe* are the focus, not the Seelie or Unseelie Courts, and they, like the fiddler/tinker types represented by Johnny Faw, are a marginal group.

Another novel published that year, *The Dreaming Place*, is a short novel that takes place in Newford, a fictional setting used frequently by de Lint. *The Dreaming Place* tells a story about two adolescent cousins, Nina and Ashley (Ash). The novel is split between the two cousins' perspectives; they are dual protagonists, and their relationship is the central focus of the story. Nina is having disturbing and violent dreams in which she is an animal, and she blames Ash, who has come to live with them after Ash's mother died and her father refused to have her. Ash is interested in the occult, but she is not sending the dreams. As it turns out, Nina's parents had a naming ceremony for their daughter when she was an infant and dedicated her spirit to serve the earth. Now, Ya-wau-tse, a local Kickaha earth spirit, is planning to claim Nina as a sacrifice, and she is sending Nina totem dreams. Nina's father has Kickaha ancestry, and their traditional belief is that as soon as Nina discovers her personal totem, she becomes an adult. At that point Ya-wau-tse will sacrifice her for continued life.

Ash is not aware of Nina's problems because she has her own. She skips school to spend time with Cassandra Washington, or Cassie, a fortune teller who works on the streets. Cassie introduces her to Bones, a juju man or shaman. When the police interrupt their ceremony, Bones takes them to the spirit world. There, Ash leaves her friends to travel with Lusewen, a veiled spirit. Ash learns about the threat to Nina, and Lusewen offers her a choice: Ash can go on feeling as bitter and angry as she has, or she can create a new life for herself by allowing herself to care about others, starting with her cousin. Ash decides to try to help Nina and confronts Ya-wau-tse, to offer herself in place of Nina. When her sacrifice is rejected, Ash uses Lusewen's gift of a charm bracelet (for creating) and a pomegranate, which gives Ash the power of creation rather than destruction, to bring spring instead of winter. Ash's effort also brings the totem spirits who help Ya-wau-tse complete her life cycle, which the earth spirit had unnaturally interrupted by trying to extend her life. When Nina and Ash return from the spirit world, the two have become sisters, and Ash is able to see the love her family and friends have for her.

With the focus on two young female protagonists, *The Dreaming Place* explores themes of maturing and identity. The novel emphasizes the importance of family (chosen or biological) and love/support for children (lost/alienated teenagers are important characters in some of de Lint's later work), as well as the ambiguity of good and evil. Ya-wau-tse is evil because of her desire to live forever (implying that spirits are not all immortal); this selfish desire, placing her own survival above others, is one that the protagonists face as well in their journey to maturity.

His next novel, *The Little Country* (1991), is a lengthy (more than six hundred pages) and ambitious novel set in Cornwall, England. De Lint traveled to Cornwall to research the book, since he is not comfortable writing about any place he has not experienced. It is a double novel, comprising two separate stories that are woven together in a complex narrative structure. The first story concerns Janey Little, a musician; her grandfather, Tom Little, or the Gaffer; and Felix Gavin, Janey's former lover. Janey finds a novel by William Dunthorn, an old friend of the Gaffer. This volume is being eagerly sought by members of a secret cult whose leader believes that Dunthorn's secret will give him eternal life. Nobody realizes that the "secret" is Dunthorn's book. The second story is the hidden novel, which is titled *The Little Country*. When Janey begins to read, the power of the story manifests itself, and Janey and the others eventually realize that the "story" in *The Little Country* is different for everyone. De Lint's readers get the version that Janey reads: the story of a young woman named Jodi Shepherd, who is turned into a Small (one of the mouse-sized people in stories told by the characters in Dunthorn's book) by the Widow Pender, a witch. Jodi meets Edern Gee, a piskie (the Cornish version of a pixie) whose spirit has been trapped in a mechanical man by the witch. Together, Jodi and Edern escape and defeat the Widow's attempts to kill or recapture them. The story ends with Jodi sacrificing herself to release the secret music/hidden power of the Otherworld into her own world. Jodi does not die, however, but lives on as a Small.

In the first story, John Madden, the founder and leader of the Order of the Grey Dove, and two members of the Order, Michael Bett and Lena Grant, all try to steal Dunthorn's talisman (not realizing that the talisman is the book). Janey and the Gaffer refuse to sell any of

Dunthorn's papers, and they, as well as Felix and Clare Mabley, an old friend of Janey's, are endangered by the cult's attempts to retrieve the talisman. The two stories come together at the end when Janey and the others finish reading the book, which completes the magic, and take it to the Men-an-Tol (a standing stone with a hole in it) to pass it through the hole. Dunthorn's book disappears from Janey's world but reappears in Jodi Shepherd's world, and she and her friends read a "novel" about Janey Little and her friends.

The narrative structure of *The Little Country* is similar to Celtic knotwork, interlaced designs that twist around, multiple strands woven together with no single beginning or end. The theme of the novel is the ultimate nature of magic, which is not a separate power held only by a few but an essential part of all creation and all life. "Magic" is comprehended as music, and the music that Janey and others play is a part of the universal magic. John Madden tries to control the "magic," thinking he can manipulate others; but Janey defeats him by giving him what he wants—the "magic" in its entirety. Of course, he cannot control such "power." Various characters' problems grow out of their attempts to control others, and the solution comes from love and spiritual growth, from the realization that the great "secrets" of the universe are so much simpler than people believe. Edern tells Jodi this "secret" several times, but believing in simplicity is difficult.

De Lint's next book, *Spiritwalk,* published in 1992, is a sequel of sorts to *Moonheart.* Portions of it were previously published in limited-edition chapbooks and small-press publications, and rather than a single narrative focusing on one or two major characters, as was the case with *Moonheart,* this work consists of interlocking narratives focusing on characters from the earlier work.

"Merlin Dreams in the Moondream Wood" relates Sara Kendell's childhood memories of events after she came to live in Tamson House, when she was lonely and unable to sleep at night but could nap in the garden during the day. In her dreams she meets a boy called Merlin, who lives in a tree. Eventually, she learns that he is the Merlin of legend and myth and that only love can set him free. Sara's love frees him, although she loses her power to dream for some time, until he sends it back to her.

"Ascian in Rose" is primarily about two characters who live in Tamson House. Blue, a biker, was a minor character in *Moonheart.* Blue rescues and falls in love with Emma Fenn, who has the power called "Autumnheart." This power is never clearly defined, and Emma does not use it, but the power is linked to nature. An Unseelie woodwife named Glamorgana splits Emma into two beings to gain her power. Blue finds Emma's shadow, which has been given physical form, and rescues her, calling her Button. When Glamorgana realizes Button, as Emma's soul, holds the power, she kidnaps her. Blue and Emma kill Glamorgana and rescue Button; then the two women are rejoined.

"Westlin Wind" focuses primarily on Esmerelda, Emma Fenn's childhood friend and the Westlin Wind to her Autumnheart. Esmerelda comes from England to find Emma in a coma, so she goes into the spirit world to find Emma's spirit. Emma's body is stolen from the hospital by Smoor, Glamorgana's chief gnasher, who plans to sacrifice her, but Blue and his friends save Emma's body, and Esmerelda finds Emma's spirit on the other side of the River into a spiritual reality with the help of Grandmother Toad (an aspect of a moon goddess). Emma agrees to return to her body, but both Esmerelda and Emma realize they avoid helping others: Emma by denying her powers and claiming to be weak, Esmerelda by eternally studying and never acting.

The novel-length "Ghostwood" describes what happens when Jamie Tams, who died in *Moonheart* but who lives on as a guardian spirit in Tamson House, tries to leave the House to visit Sara in the spirit worlds. Tamson House sits at a major confluence of ley lines and exists in the Otherworld as well as in contemporary Ottawa. When Jamie leaves, the house is unprotected and vulnerable. Albert Watkins, a would-be magician who wants power without having to work for it, is waiting to take over the House, and does so, drawing on the power of the First Forest (a mythic, primeval forest that is the archetype for all worldly forests) in his attempt. As a result, those living in the House are pulled into the spirit world, where the First Forest tries to reclaim the house, and the people come under attack. Albert Watkins is eventually defeated, and Tamson House is saved, but everyone experiences change. Emma Fenn learns more about her gift from Coyote, the mythic trickster spirit, and finally decides to give it up to Julianne Trelawney, a pagan inhabitant of Tamson House. Esmerelda ends up the new guardian of the house. Jamie is rescued from his fragmented state, which was caused by going into the Otherworld unprepared, and sacrifices himself by taking Albert Watkins on the Path of Souls to be reborn. Sara realizes that she has been distancing herself from Jamie; she regains her love for him and learns to support Esmerelda.

Spiritwalk is thus a collection of related narratives, with a cyclical or spiral structure embodying the Wheel of Life. The issue of responsibility is a key theme: people need to take responsibility for their own actions, and for helping others, whether human or manitou. The book has many characters who are drawn to Tamson House for many reasons, all connected to the main theme of creation.

De Lint's next book, *Dreams Underfoot,* published in 1993, is a collection of short stories, many of which had been previously published, that comprises what Windling describes in her introduction as "a cycle of urban myths and dreams." The stories are all set in Newford. De Lint had decided to set a short story in a large urban setting, making it up by drawing on elements from cities he had visited but never lived in long enough to get to know. Later, he realized that he had several stories in the same setting with a "repertory" of characters he could keep using in the future, and that city became Newford. Nineteen separate pieces make up *Dreams Underfoot;* the individual pieces have different protagonists, although there is an interlocking group of central characters, especially Jilly Coppercorn, Christy and Geordie Riddell, and Bramley Dapple. Christy is a writer; his works are mentioned in several of these stories, and the final piece, "Tallulah," is narrated in first person by Christy as he relates his brief relationship with Tally, the soul of the city of Newford.

Many of the stories show characters discovering some magical aspect that can be quite dark—verging on horror in several instances—and dealing with whether or not they wish to accept their new knowledge of the world and "reality." The "Theory of Consensual Reality," which states that things exist because people agree they exist, is an important thematic element. The various stories consist of multiple levels of storytelling, evoking both oral and written folklore traditions. Fantastic elements—such as the Skookin, a race living under the city in Old City; Bigfoot living on the streets, at least for a time; the Gemmin, who hold the memories and stories; and a mermaid who comes to shore for the love of a musician—exist alongside the gritty realities of urban life: the homeless who are trying to survive the best they can, teenagers suffering from child abuse who run away and become prostitutes, a rookie police officer shooting a young man, and a young woman committing suicide because she is afraid she will continue the cycle of abuse in her family. But the major theme of the stories is survival, with some successful rescues: a young woman, gaining courage through her music and her growing awareness of faeries, is rescued by a musician; and a lonely poet is encouraged to grow a new Tree of Tales by a conjure man. The stories almost fall into complementary pairs, darkness and light woven together. The spirit of the city may be hardening because of people's indifference to the natural world and to each other, but there are still individuals who try to take care of others.

Into the Green, published in 1993, is a secondary-world fantasy, drawing on folklore with a special focus on tinkers, reflecting de Lint's own musical interests. The novel had its genesis in short stories published in Marion Zimmer Bradley's *Sword and Sorceress* anthologies, which explains the episodic plot structure of the book. The setting is the Kingdoms of the Green Isles, and the major protagonist is Angharad, a tinker who becomes a witch and a harpist. After her husband and family die of a plague, Angharad tries to raise her dead love but is told by the spirits she communes with that she must continue living without him. Instead, she must help others with the same gifts, called the Summerblood, achieve their powers in order to keep the "music of the Middle Kingdom" (witchcraft) alive. When a nomad finds an ebony puzzle box that is a weapon against witches, Angharad reluctantly accepts the task of destroying it. She journeys in disguise and tries to find help, but too many of the Summerblood have been killed. She is finally helped by Lammond, a professional assassin; Edrie, an innkeeper; and Tom Naghatty, an alcoholic former soldier. Angharad retrieves the puzzle box, but Tom calls its darkness into himself and dies in order to destroy the evil. Lammond, angry because he cannot use the puzzle box against his enemies, tries to kill Angharad and is killed himself. At the end, Angharad travels with Veda, Lammond's companion, and begins to wonder whether people without the Summerblood could be taught to perceive the spiritual realms in order to prevent the differences between the two groups from leading to persecution of the minority.

While a traditional secondary-world fantasy, this novel ends with the idea that "witchery" is not limited to a certain group—and it carries throughout the message that a mystical talent is not a solution to all problems. Nor are those who have the power of the Summerblood able to control and manipulate others; instead, marginalized groups such as tinkers or witches are shown as being oppressed by a dominant majority who have stereotyped them in order to justify destroying them.

Memory and Dream, published in 1994, returns to Newford and focuses on the creation of visual art, paintings and drawings, as some of de Lint's earlier novels focused on music or writing. On his website, de Lint said that he took up drawing in order to get the sense of that kind of creation, and encouraged his readers to try to reclaim their various talents as well. The importance of the visual arts to this novel is clear from the start; not only are many of the main characters artists, and the plot elements focused on paintings, but descriptions of paintings created by the protagonist are also interspersed with the chapters of the novel. *Memory and Dream* is structured around a dual chronology: events that take place in the 1990s are interspersed with events that took place in the 1970s when the characters were in college at Butler University in Newford.

Isabelle is a successful artist who has buried traumatic events from her past life; but when she receives a letter from her best friend Katharine Mully, five years after the letter was written and after Kathy had died, she begins to remember her past. Then Alan Grant, a

Dust jacket, with artwork by his wife, MaryAnn Harris, for de Lint's 2000 collection of his stories originally published in chapbook editions by his Triskell Press

publisher and college friend of both Isabelle and Kathy, asks Isabelle to illustrate a collected edition of Kathy's stories, the profits from which will go toward supporting a children's foundation Kathy has created. When Isabelle returns to Newford to work on the art, she must confront all the parts of her past life there that she had tried to repress.

The traumatic events include the years when Isabelle met and became a student of Vincent Rushkin, a famous recluse. But Rushkin did not just teach her how to paint. Isabelle has the talent to create paintings of figures that can be inhabited by spirits who cross over from a nonmaterial realm, and Rushkin's teaching enabled her to bring across several beings who took the physical forms portrayed in her paintings. The embodied spirits become real in this process, although not entirely physically human, for they do not sleep, eat, or dream. Isabelle became involved romantically with John Sweetgrass, one of the embodied spirits, before she learned what her talent could achieve. Rushkin's teaching was mixed with emotional and physical abuse, however, and Isabelle finally rejected him completely, moving to the island where she grew up. When Isabelle returns to Newford, she must confront Rushkin as well as the spirits he has brought across. In the process she learns that the being she had known as Rushkin is himself an embodied spirit who came across into the human Rushkin's self-portrait. The embodied spirit killed Rushkin, and it must feed by killing other embodied spirits. This Rushkin finds and trains talented and vulnerable young women to provide him with the sustenance he needs. Isabelle and John confront the spirit Rushkin in dreamtime (which is a different level of reality, spiritual rather than physical; spirits inhabit dreamtime, but cannot dream in human form) and kill him in self-defense. Through this process of confrontation, Isabelle is able to regain her repressed memories and return to creating representational art that allows spirits who choose to do so to come across into a more material life.

One of de Lint's most powerful novels, *Memory and Dream* explores the problems of talent and the ethical issues that accompany the creative power of art, explored through the fantastic element of spirits taking the forms of figures in paintings. Evil is figured not only in the spirit form of Rushkin (who points out that the human Rushkin's self-portrait must have contained the mixture of good and evil that the spirit shows), but in the ways completely human adults abuse children, and, as a society, abuse and dispose of marginalized groups. The realistic aspects of Newford (poverty, rape and other forms of abuse, alcoholism, and drug abuse) are woven into the descriptions of the spirits who have come across, leaving an apparently immortal and nonphysical life in order to experience a material life that may be cut short at any time.

De Lint's next book, *The Ivory and the Horn*, published in 1995, is a second collection of short pieces set in Newford. This book includes fifteen stories, many of which continue the lives and stories of characters from the first collection: Maisie (Margaret), Sophie Etoile, Geordie Riddell, and Jilly Coppercorn. New characters are introduced as well, including more writers and artists, but also social workers. The fantastic elements include ghosts and spirits (some evil and some good), angels, and time travel, as well as Native American figures such as Coyote, Nokomis, and Kokopelli. Several imaginary places are presented, such as Sophie's dream city of Mabon and the mythic desert of Coyote stories. As with the first collection, the stories mix the fantastic with realistic problems such as depression, alienation, child abuse, anorexia, AIDS, cancer, and the racism experienced by people who live in Newford, from the homeless and street people to the artists and the social workers who try to help others. The characters represent the ethnic and class diversity of a large city, including African Americans, Native Americans, and Gypsies, as well as Anglo- and European-Americans.

Connecting themes include the importance of imagination and dream as part of spiritual and emotional healing, the necessity to help others survive, and the attendant problems of burnout, of giving too much and caring too much for others. The title refers to the two Gates of Greek myth: the Gate of Ivory, through which false dreams pass, and the Gate of Horn, through which true dreams pass. Neither spirituality nor mythic figures are presented as easy answers to complex social problems; instead, ambiguities and the need for self-awareness underlie most of the stories.

De Lint's next novel, *Trader*, published in 1997, is also set in Newford. Certain characters from the earlier books appear as secondary characters: Jilly Coppercorn, Geordie Riddell, Cassie, and Bones. But the protagonist is Max Trader, a guitar maker, who wakes up one morning in a different body. Somehow Trader and Johnny Devlin, a local con artist, have changed bodies, and Trader is soon homeless, trying to find a way to get back to his body. Devlin's former girlfriend, Tanya, and her roommate, Zeffy, are drawn into Trader and Devlin's conflict, as are Trader's neighbors, Lisa Fisher and her daughter, Nia. The novel is told from multiple points of view, primarily Trader's, but including Tanya, Zeffy (who begins to fall in love with "Johnny Devlin" after the transfer), and Lisa and Nia, who are having their own problems. Lisa, who has been divorced for much of Nia's life, has fallen in love with another woman, and Nia, when she sees her mother kissing a woman, believes that Lisa, as well as Trader, has been "replaced" by some sort of alien being.

The final action of the novel is set in one of the Otherworlds. Trader and Devlin are pulled into it when they first touch, and Zeffy and Nia are sent after Trader by Bones. Trader learns that his disassociation from much of life may have allowed the original trade to take place—in the Otherworld, which takes the shape of his memory of his mentor's home and workshop, he comes to terms with what has happened. Devlin manages to trade bodies yet again, this time with a bird. When the bird in Trader's body dies in an accident, Trader touches the dead body and is drawn into it. Only by committing to a strong desire for life is he able to return to Devlin's body. Zeffy, Nia, and a spirit incarnation of Bones help him return to Newford.

The central plot device of this novel, the exchange of bodies, emphasizes the important theme of self-awareness and identity. Although Trader had what he considered to be a good life, he learns that his disassociation from other human beings and his immersion in his art have left him vulnerable. He cannot hold onto his life because he has given up in important ways. As "Johnny Devlin" he talks to more people, connects to more people (and to a homeless dog he adopts) in the space of a few days than he had done in his previous life. The novel moves away from a traditional good-versus-evil structure because it lacks an easily identifiable villain who embodies that evil: Devlin is quite happy with the switch at first, but he does not know why it happened, and his mental/emotional problems prevent him from doing anything other than living off the money he can take from Trader's accounts. Evil manifests itself more in the ways people close themselves off from the natural world and each other in pursuit of a regulated, materially comfortable life.

Someplace to Be Flying, published in 1998, is de Lint's most ambitious mingling of Celtic and Native American mythologies. At the heart of the novel is the figure of Raven, who has temporarily misplaced his pot, and all the stories about Raven and the pot that also embody the Holy Grail/Cauldron myths. Around Raven are various groups of First People, spirits who can take the forms of humans and other animals. The First People were there when the medicine lands and this world were created and consist of corbae (bird people), canids (canine people), and others. They have their own conflicts carried down over the years, but only the cuckoos are truly evil. The First People have interbred with humans and animals at times over the years as well.

Someplace to Be Flying is set in contemporary Newford and focuses on humans who have some First People ancestry: Hank Walker, who drives a gypsy cab; Lily Carson, a photographer; and Kerry Madan, a young woman with a mysterious past. Raven, Jack Daw, Maida and Zia (the Crow Girls), and Ray and Coyote (called Cody in this book) are First Spirits who live alongside humans. The characters all come together on one street, specifically a boardinghouse that has become Raven's retreat. The problem is that Raven has mislaid his pot. Cody initiates the conflict by trying to find the pot to use it to correct his most recent mistake. According to Jack Daw's stories, Cody's latest "mistake" was bringing humans into being. Cody works with the cuckoos, who succeed in gaining the pot but cannot use it. Cody breaks off from the cuckoos when he learns what their goal is. Cody wants to end the world and start again, but the cuckoos want to take the corbae out of the world and dominate it. When they try, they fail. The Firstborn corbae were not "created"—they existed before. The pot/chalice is not a weapon, but sentient, and does not grant the cuckoos' wish, although the corbae are brought out of the world into the pot. Kerry is also brought into the pot to meet her missing twin, Katy. The corbae and their mixed-blood descendants meet the Grace (a goddess). The pot is just a vessel to hold the Grace in the material world (as opposed to medicine or spirit lands), not an object to be used. The protagonists are offered a choice: the world can end, or the Grace can return to the medicine lands, leaving humans to make their own grace. The pot, which breaks when the leader of the cuckoos tries to force it to destroy the corbae, is mended by Hank and Lily, and Jack Daw leads the Grace back to the medicine lands. Kerry and Katy learn they are twins. Finally, the world is restored.

The blending of creation myths from various cultures creates a thematic focus on the circular nature of creation and destruction, birth and death. Identity and change are also important aspects of this novel: humans as well as spirits need to keep growing and loving to avoid stagnation, and fear of change can hamper both humans and spirits.

Moonlight and Vines, published in 1999, is de Lint's third collection of stories set in Newford and winner of the World Fantasy Award for best collection. Of the twenty-two stories in the volume, three are new and the rest were previously published in various anthologies and chapbooks. The book opens with a poem by Wendelessen (a pseudonym that de Lint uses for some poetry) about the mingling of cultures and times in urban settings, which results in "old spirits in new skins." Continuing characters include Christy Riddell, Jilly Coppercorn, the Crow Girls from *Someplace to Be Flying,* Cassie, and Bones, but the collection has many stories with new characters as well, both humans and spirits. Several of the stories are told in interspersed first- and third-person narratives, so within each story the sense of multiple perspectives is created. Fantastic elements include Saskia, a woman who was apparently "born" in an artificial intelligence (AI) program and who decided to take human form; a vampire who wants to kill herself; one of the many Ladies of the Lake who has lost her sheath and her ability to control her shape; First Spirits; and ghosts. However, the problems of most of the characters, whether human or spirits, are shared: loneliness, the loss or lack of love, depression, illness, and death. Strongly working through all the stories are the twin themes of love and magic, with magic standing for spirituality and the sense of how limited one's perceptions of reality are. Love, in de Lint's stories, is not limited only to traditional family or heterosexual love, as several of these stories focus on lesbian characters and Newford's gay community. Instead, love is described in the broadest sense—from the sense of sympathy shared by two characters who meet and talk for the first time, through the overlooked love that characters realize is important to them, to the love of a years-long relationship and commitment between couples.

His next full-length books, both published in 2000, include the novel *Forests of the Heart* (a finalist for the 2001 Nebula Awards and the Mythopoeic Fantasy Award for Adult Literature) and the small-press collection *Triskell Tales,* which includes the stories published in chapbook editions by de Lint's Triskell Press. *The Road to Lisdoonvarna* (2001), originally written in 1985, is a departure for de Lint; he describes it on his website as "a straightforward mystery novel, as in private eye rather than the mysteries that I normally write about." The Newford novel *The Onion Girl,* appearing in October 2001, is Jilly Coppercorn's story.

As a reading of de Lint's work reveals, he is a prolific and innovative writer who is able to meld mythic elements from a variety of cultures with realistic descriptions of contemporary life. His early work drew more heavily on traditional secondary-world fantasy elements, but his later stories and novels exemplify a writer who is continually learning new elements of his craft and bringing in new ways of telling the stories that, according to de Lint, are one of the most important things about being human. He is a writer who has influenced a developing genre and who informs his readers about the other writers and musicians who have delighted him over the years. His popularity (shown by the fact that his books are continuously in print or republished soon after going out of print, and by the existence of fan-generated sites and discussion groups on the World Wide Web) may be partly attributable to the fact that he is able to deal with important social issues and characters from marginalized social groups without falling into the trap of heavy-handed preaching at his readers. While his work has not yet been studied in detail by academic critics, that should change in time. Certainly he ranks as one of the most important fantasy writers yet produced by Canada.

Interviews:

Lawrence Schimel, "An Interview with Charles de Lint," *Marion Zimmer Bradley's Fantasy Magazine,* 32 (Summer 1996): 64;

Edo van Belkom, "Charles de Lint," in his *Northern Dreamers: Interviews with Famous Science Fiction, Fantasy, and Horror Writers* (Kingston, Ontario: Quarry Press, 1998), pp. 39–49.

Reference:

Alexei Kondratiev, "Tales Newly Told," *Mythlore,* 13 (Winter 1986): 36, 54.

James De Mille

(23 August 1833 – 28 January 1880)

Douglas Ivison
University of Western Ontario

See also the De Mille entry in *DLB 99: Canadian Writers Before 1890.*

BOOKS: *John Wheeler's Two Uncles: Or, Launching into Life,* anonymous (New York: Carlton, 1860);

Andy O'Hara: Or, The Child of Promise, anonymous (New York: Carlton, 1861);

The Martyr of the Catacombs: A Tale of Ancient Rome, anonymous (New York: Carlton, 1865);

Helena's Household: A Tale of Rome in the First Century, anonymous (New York: Carter, 1867; London: Nelson, 1867); republished as *Helena's Household: An Ideal of Roman Life in the Time of Paul and Nero* (New York: Ward & Drummond, 1890);

A Week at Forestdale: Being a Summer Idyl; That Is, an Idle Tale as a Mere Trifle for an Idle Dinner Writ, as Idle Sinner (New York: Westcott, 1868);

The Dodge Club: Or, Italy in 1859 (New York: Harper, 1869);

Cord and Creese: Or, the Brandon Mystery, as the author of "The Dodge Club" (New York: Harper, 1869);

"The B.O.W.C.": A Book for Boys (Boston: Lee & Shepard, 1869);

The Boys of Grand Pré School, as the author of "The B. O. W. C." (Boston: Lothrop, 1870);

The Lady of the Ice: A Novel (New York: Appleton, 1870);

Lost in the Fog (Boston: Lee & Shepard, 1870);

The Cryptogram: A Novel (New York: Harper, 1871);

The American Baron (New York: Harper, 1871);

Among the Brigands (Boston: Lee & Shepard, 1871);

Fire in the Woods (Boston: Lee & Shepard, 1871);

A Comedy of Terrors (Boston: Osgood, 1872);

Picked Up Adrift (Boston: Lee & Shepard, 1872);

The Seven Hills (Boston: Lee & Shepard, 1872);

The Treasure of the Seas (Boston: Lee & Shepard, 1872);

A Book for Boys; Containing Stories of Boys Who Won Their Way to Honor or Wealth by Obedience, Industry and Piety (New York: Sheldon, Blakeman, 1873);

An Open Question: A Novel (New York: Appleton, 1873);

The Lily and the Cross: A Tale of Acadia (Boston: Lee & Shepard, 1874);

James De Mille (Public Archives of Nova Scotia)

The Living Link: A Novel (New York: Harper, 1874);

The Babes in the Wood: A Tragic Comedy. A Story of the Italian Revolution of 1848 (Boston: Gill, 1875);

The Early English Church: A Paper Read Before the Church of England Institute (Halifax, Nova Scotia: 1877);

The Winged Lion: Or, Stories of Venice (Boston: Lee & Shepard; New York: Dillingham, 1877);

A Castle in Spain: A Novel (New York: Harper, 1878; London: Chatto, 1884);

The Elements of Rhetoric (New York: Harper, 1878);

Old Garth: A Story of Sicily (New York: Munro, 1883);

A Strange Manuscript Found in a Copper Cylinder, anonymous (New York: Harper, 1888; London: Chatto & Windus, 1888);

Behind the Veil: A Poem (Halifax, Nova Scotia: T. C. Allen, 1893).

Editions and Collections: *James De Mille's Works,* 2 volumes (New York: Appleton/Harper, 1871–1873)–comprises volume 1, *An Open Question, The Lady of Ice,* and *A Comedy of Terrors;* volume 2, *The Cryptogram, Cord and Creese, The Dodge Club,* and *The American Baron;*

A Strange Manuscript Found in a Copper Cylinder, edited by Reginald E. Watters (Toronto: McClelland & Stewart, 1969);

A Strange Manuscript Found in a Copper Cylinder, edited by Malcolm Parks (Ottawa, Ontario: Carleton University Press, 1986).

SELECTED PERIODICAL PUBLICATIONS–UNCOLLECTED: "Acadie, and the Birth-place of Evangeline," *Putnam's Monthly* (August 1853): 140–145;

"A Voyage Long Ago," *Canadian Geographical Journal,* 11 (September 1935): 148–160.

James De Mille was one of the most successful and prolific nineteenth-century Canadian writers of popular fiction during his relatively short writing career. He is best remembered for *A Strange Manuscript Found in a Copper Cylinder* (1888), an apparently unfinished utopian novel of a lost race. Described by George L. Parker in the second edition of *The Oxford Companion to Canadian Literature* (1997) as "the most complex and philosophical nineteenth-century Canadian novel," the work has a firm position within the canon of nineteenth-century Canadian literature and an unquestioned, if minor, place within the tradition of world science fiction.

James De Mill (he later changed the spelling to "De Mille") was born on 23 August 1833 in Saint John, New Brunswick. He was the third of ten children of Nathan De Mill, a Saint John merchant, and Elizabeth De Mill. Both his parents were descendants of the Loyalists who had fled the United States after the American Revolution, the De Mills having arrived in New Netherland (now New York) in 1658. Nathan De Mill, a ruthless businessman with puritanical tendencies, frowned upon alcohol and literature and converted to the teetotaling Baptist faith as an adult. The Nova Scotia–born Elizabeth, however, appreciated literature and discussed the works of Charles Dickens and other contemporary writers with her children. The De Mill family apparently maintained a comfortable middle-class lifestyle with a large house in Saint John and a waterfront summer residence across the harbor from Saint John.

After attending the Saint John Grammar School, De Mille enrolled in the Baptist-run, nonsectarian Horton Collegiate Academy in Wolfville, Nova Scotia, in August 1847, at the age of fourteen. A year later he transferred to Acadia College, which was associated with Horton Academy, and successfully passed his first-year examinations. De Mille may have completed a second year of studies at Acadia, as well. In August 1850 he left on a trip to England with his older brother Elisha, possibly to recuperate after a lengthy illness. Arriving in England in September, they traveled throughout Britain for the next two months before venturing across the English Channel. The brothers began their tour of the Continent with two weeks in Paris and then traveled throughout France, Italy, Switzerland, Germany, and Belgium before returning to England in May 1851, finally returning home in September. Unfortunately, De Mille's journal of the trip has been lost.

In February 1852 De Mille enrolled at another Baptist university, Brown University in Providence, Rhode Island. De Mille spent the next two and a half years at Brown, graduating with an M.A. in 1854. During his time at Brown, De Mille frequented the library and was a popular member of the Philermenian Society, which met regularly to hold debates and read essays and poetry. De Mille was elected poet of the society and was a popular speaker. At Brown, De Mille developed an interest in literature, writing poetry and literary essays, some of which have survived. His first professional publication, an article titled "Acadie, and the Birth-place of Evangeline," was published in the August 1853 issue of *Putnam's Monthly.* He published a few minor poems while a student, and also published sixteen or more short stories in the final year of his studies, primarily in the Boston weekly magazine *The Flag of Our Union.* These stories were conventionally melodramatic, with, as Patricia Monk observes in *The Gilded Beaver: An Introduction to the Life and Work of James De Mille* (1991), banal plotting and weak characterization. Yet, she writes, "although they cannot be considered to have great literary value," they "are nevertheless neatly suited to their purpose of entertainment, and are by no means negligible as examples of popular-magazine fiction of their period." At his graduation on 7 September 1854 De Mille recited a poem he had composed in his capacity as class poet.

After graduation he returned to Saint John. There he took up a position as assistant editor of a weekly Baptist periodical, *The Christian Visitor,* in which capacity he may have contributed articles and stories; he held this position for about four months in 1855. De Mille returned to the United States, where he worked as a bookkeeper in Cincinnati for less than a year before coming back to Saint John in early 1856. Economic difficulties that afflicted New Brunswick in the mid 1850s had a negative impact on his father's business, with the consequence that James

De Mille was unable to depend upon his father for financial support or to join his father's business. By May 1857 De Mille had formed a partnership with Saint John businessman Hazen Fillmore to open the Colonial Book Store, a book and stationery store. The enterprise initially was a success, and they opened a second store the next year. By 1859 the business began to run into trouble. De Mille bought out his partner that year, but his financial difficulties continued, and he eventually sold the store in 1861. That same year he contributed extensively to another weekly Baptist periodical, the *Christian Watchman,* which his brother Elisha had been editing until he became ill. De Mille wrote several pieces for the paper and did much of the editorial work during his brother's illness. One of his earliest novels, *Andy O'Hara: Or, The Child of Promise* (1861), the story of a young boy who strays from his Christian faith but returns to it as an adult, was written for the *Christian Watchman.*

During this period De Mille was active as a prominent citizen of Saint John, helping to establish the Marsh Ridge Baptist Church, of which his brother Elisha became pastor in 1857. More significantly, he married his longtime fiancée, Elizabeth Anne Pryor, on 26 November 1858 in Cambridge, Massachusetts. Her father, Dr. John Pryor, was the pastor of the First Baptist Church in Cambridge and was the first president of Acadia College. De Mille probably met her while he was a student in Wolfville. Their first child, William Budd, was born in 1859, followed by a daughter, Louise Pryor, in 1865, then Ethel Maud in 1872, Alban Bertram in 1873, and Frank Wilfred in 1874.

De Mille decided to sell his bookstore after receiving an offer of a position as a professor of classics at Acadia College, and he moved to Wolfville to take up this position in the summer of 1861. He taught there for the next four years and was respected as a scholar and teacher. In August 1865, however, he resigned from Acadia in order to take a position as professor of rhetoric and history at Dalhousie College in Halifax, Nova Scotia, where he taught for fifteen years. While at Dalhousie, he offered one of the first, if not the first, college courses in Canadian history, in 1878–1879. In the mid 1860s he produced *The Martyr of the Catacombs: A Tale of Ancient Rome* (1865) and *Helena's Household: A Tale of Rome in the First Century* (1867), two anonymously published historical novels set in the Roman Empire during the early years of Christianity. The novels may have been written (and possibly even previously published) as early as the late 1850s. Despite De Mille's difficulty in getting *Helena's Household* published—he submitted it to many publishers who were not interested—the the novel met with some success, with twelve editions published by the end of the century.

In the late 1860s De Mille became a successful writer of popular fiction in various genres: boys' fiction, sensation novels, and comedies. A prolific writer of boys' fiction, he is best known in this regard for his B. O. W. C. series, which began with *"The B.O.W.C.": A Book for Boys* (1869). This book about a group of Nova Scotia boys and their secret society, the Brethren of the White Cross, is an episodic adventure tale and was followed by five sequels. These stories combined exciting action with moral, Christian-based teaching. Although conventional (but entertaining), these works are of interest for their Canadian characters and settings, which may have been loosely inspired by De Mille's own childhood experiences. The Young Dodge Club series, beginning with *Among the Brigands* (1871), told of the adventures experienced by adolescent Canadian boys touring Italy.

Capitalizing on the success of the sensation novel made popular by such authors as Wilkie Collins, De Mille published *Cord and Creese: Or, the Brandon Mystery* in 1869. A typically convoluted, melodramatic tale in which the plot is determined by coincidence, *Cord and Creese* is most notable for vivid descriptions of exotic settings and exciting action scenes. This novel was followed by other sensation novels, including *The Cryptogram: A Novel* (1870). *The Dodge Club: Or, Italy in 1859* (1869) is the first and best of De Mille's comedies, which he called his "satirical romances." This novel draws on his earlier stories of travels in Italy and satirizes both Italy and the American tourists. Of his later comedies, *The Lady of the Ice: A Novel* (1870) is notable for its Canadian setting. De Mille's popularity was such that Harpers paid him as much as $2,000 to publish his novels. His books had little enduring success, however, and were quickly forgotten. Monk observes in *The Gilded Beaver* that De Mille was aware of the ephemeral nature of his fiction; he told a family member "that he wished he could write like Mrs. Gaskell" but could not.

In 1867 his comfortable life as writer and professor was disrupted by a scandal involving his father-in-law, Dr. John Pryor, who had been minister at Granville Street Baptist Church in Halifax since 1862. Pryor was accused of immoral behavior after a late-night visit to one of his female parishioners and was dismissed from his position. Although a church tribunal cleared him of the charges, his church refused to take him back, and he was eventually forced to leave Halifax and return to the United States. During the scandal, De Mille had been one of his father-in-law's staunchest defenders, with the result that the stigma of the scandal attached to De Mille as well. Shortly after the scandal, De Mille converted to Anglicanism. De Mille's withdrawal from Halifax society during the late 1860s and early 1870s coincides with the explosion of his literary output. By the end of the 1870s, however, his literary output declined, and De Mille reemerged to give public lectures and rejoined the Institute of Science. After giving a public lecture in Saint John, he fell ill, was diagnosed with congestion of the lungs, and died on 28 Janu-

Illustration by Gilbert Gall for De Mille's posthumously published masterpiece, the utopian novel
A Strange Manuscript Found in a Copper Cylinder *(1888)*

ary 1880. Despite his success as a popular author and his position at Dalhousie, he left his affairs in financial disarray, owing as much as $20,000 upon his death.

De Mille's longest-lasting literary achievement and his greatest contribution to both Canadian literature and science fiction, *A Strange Manuscript Found in a Copper Cylinder,* was published anonymously eight years after his death. The work appears to have been mostly written during the 1860s, and whether it was actually ever completed is a matter of debate among critics of the novel. What is known is that his widow discovered the manuscript in 1887 and sent it to Harper Brothers. The work was serialized in *Harper's Weekly* in 1888 and published in book form the same year.

A Strange Manuscript Found in a Copper Cylinder is considered by critics to be the most sophisticated novel in De Mille's corpus. David Ketterer, in *Canadian Science Fiction and Fantasy Writers* (1992), claims that "there is a growing consensus that this provocative philosophical work is not only the best nineteenth-century Canadian novel but one of the best Canadian novels period."

At first glance *A Strange Manuscript Found in a Copper Cylinder* seems to be a typical adventure tale of the period, telling the story of Adam More after he is shipwrecked off Antarctica. He follows an underground river and discovers a civilization hidden behind the forbidding Antarctic ice, a place where prehistoric creatures and a strangely familiar tribe of cannibals, the Kosekin, live. He is imprisoned, experiences several life-threatening adventures, falls in love with a beautiful woman named Almah, and eventually becomes rich and powerful.

What differentiates this novel from the lost-world adventures of H. Rider Haggard, for example, is that in its portrayal of the Kosekin the novel goes beyond the simply exotic and adventurous to raise profound, if ambiguous, philosophical and cultural questions. The Kosekin society seems to be the direct opposite of late-Victorian culture. To die is the highest, even the greatest, privilege; poverty, suffering, and unrequited love are the greatest desires. To be executed and eaten is the greatest honor, of which most can only dream. Wealth, power, and realized love are deemed to be the greatest horrors, reserved only for the most abject dregs of society. Adam and Almah are only able to survive and thrive, to achieve the fantasy of wealth and power central to colonialist romances like those of Haggard, once they come to truly understand the conventions of Kosekin society and act accordingly. Only after they learn to read Kosekin society are they able to choose to become the abject in Kosekin society, and thus become its wealthy rulers. Kosekin society is not a simple inversion of late-Victorian society, however: the Kosekin are clearly a Semitic people speaking a variant of Hebrew, which suggests that their values are closer to the antimaterialistic, self-sacrificing values of Christianity than they might at first seem. The novel suggests a powerful and ambiguous critique of late-Victorian society, and of the disjunction between its ideals and its practices.

The import of *A Strange Manuscript Found in a Copper Cylinder* is further complicated by the framing structure of the novel. As the title suggests, More's manuscript is discovered floating in a cylinder. The discoverers—a wealthy yacht owner, a scientist, a doctor, and a literary critic—take turns reading the manuscript out loud, and break off for lengthy discussions of the scientific issues raised by the tale, and of the nature of More's narrative. They debate whether More's adventures are true or fictional, whether the narrative is intended to be a scientific romance or satire, and what is the object of that satire. The book ends when Lord Featherstone, the yacht owner, abruptly stops reading and declares, "That's enough for today; I'm tired, and can't read anymore. It's time for supper."

Upon first publication *A Strange Manuscript Found in a Copper Cylinder* received mixed reviews and was read as a straightforward adventure tale along the lines of Haggard's extremely popular tales being published at the same time. Some critics even went so far as anachronistically accusing the book of being a copy of—or at least heavily influenced by—Haggard, a claim that was repeated as recently as 1965 in Fred Cogswell's discussion of the novel in *The Literary History of Canada: Canadian Literature in English*, edited by Carl Klinck. The moderately successful novel was reprinted several times in the two decades following publication, but then disappeared from view. *A Strange Manuscript Found in a Copper Cylinder* was given a paragraph in J. D. Logan and Donald G. French's 1924 survey, *Highways of Canadian Literature: A Synoptic Introduction to the Literary History of Canada (English) from 1760–1924*, though they dismissed the novel as being of little importance to the Canadian literary tradition, given the absence of Canadian settings, characters, or "the Canadian national spirit." J. O. Bailey gave *A Strange Manuscript Found in a Copper Cylinder* a page in his 1947 history of science fiction, *Pilgrims Through Space and Time: Trends and Patterns in Scientific and Utopian Fiction*, though he reads the novel strictly as an adventure tale. Although R. W. Douglas recognized the allegorical or satirical insights of the book in a January 1922 article in *The Canadian Bookman*, the novel did not receive a detailed discussion until a 1955 article by A. R. Bevan in *The Dalhousie Review*.

After the novel was republished in 1969, however, *A Strange Manuscript Found in a Copper Cylinder* began to receive significant critical attention. In the early 1970s several articles were devoted to this book, which has now become a fixture in the canon of nineteenth-century Canadian literature. Developing theoretical trends such as deconstruction, postmodernism, and postcolonial theory have led to the novel being increasingly valued, as the four essays devoted to it in the Summer 1995 issue of the journal *Canadian Literature* make clear. *A Strange Manuscript Found in a Copper Cylinder* has also come to be seen as a foundational text in the history of Canadian science fiction and fantasy, demonstrating, according to Ketterer, "the possibility of a uniquely Canadian species of SF and fantasy that is of literary value." Monk's *The Gilded Beaver* is the most comprehensive study of De Mille and has contributed to the ongoing critical rediscovery of De Mille and the novel. A critical edition of *A Strange Manuscript Found in a Copper Cylinder*, edited by Malcolm Parks, was published in 1986. Although some of De Mille's other books have also been republished, *A Strange Manuscript Found in a Copper Cylinder* is possibly of even more interest to readers now than when it was first published.

References:

A. R. Bevan, "James De Mille and Archibald MacMechan," *Dalhousie Review*, 36 (Autumn 1955): 201–215;

Carole Gerson, "A Contrapuntal Reading of *A Strange Manuscript Found in a Copper Cylinder*," *Essays on Canadian Writing*, 56 (Fall 1995): 224–235;

Gwendolyn Guth, "Reading Frames of Reference: The Satire of Exegesis in James De Mille's 'A Strange Manuscript Found in a Copper Cylinder,'" *Canadian Literature*, 145 (Summer 1995): 39–59;

Maggie Kilgour, "Cannibals and Critics: An Exploration of James De Mille's *Strange Manuscript*," *Mosaic*, 30 (March 1997): 19–37;

Camille R. La Bossiere, "The Mysterious End of James De Mille's Unfinished Strange Manuscript," *Essays on Canadian Writing*, 27 (Winter 1983–1984): 41–54;

Linda Lamont-Stewart, "Rescued by Postmodernism: The Escalating Value of James De Mille's 'A Strange Manuscript Found in a Copper Cylinder,'" *Canadian Literature*, 145 (Summer 1995): 21–36;

Stephen Milnes, "Colonialist Discourse, Lord Featherstone's Yawn and the Significance of the Denouement in 'A Strange Manuscript Found in a Copper Cylinder,'" *Canadian Literature*, 145 (Summer 1995): 86–104;

Patricia Monk, *The Gilded Beaver: An Introduction to the Life and Work of James De Mille* (Toronto: ECW, 1991);

Flavio Multineddu, "A Tendentious Game with an Uncanny Riddle: 'A Strange Manuscript Found in a Copper Cylinder,'" *Canadian Literature*, 145 (Summer 1995): 62–81.

Papers:

There is a collection of James De Mille's papers in the Killam Library Archives at Dalhousie University in Halifax, Nova Scotia.

Candas Jane Dorsey
(16 November 1952 –)

Douglas Ivison
University of Western Ontario

BOOKS: *this is for you* (Vancouver, British Columbia: blewointmentpress, 1973);

Orion Rising (Vancouver, British Columbia: blewointmentpress, 1974);

Results of the Ring Toss (Vancouver, British Columbia: blewointmentpress, 1976);

A Community Study of a Non-PSS Area: The County of Mountain View (Edmonton: University of Alberta, 1980);

A Case Study of Preventive Social Service Development in Smoky River Municipal District, by Dorsey and Leslie Bella (Edmonton: University of Alberta, 1980);

A Case Study of Preventive Social Service Development in Barons-Eureka Health Unit, by Dorsey and Bella (Edmonton: University of Alberta, 1980);

A Case Study of Preventive Social Service Development in the County of Strathcona, by Dorsey and Bella (Edmonton: University of Alberta, 1980);

Hardwired Angel, by Dorsey and Nora Abercrombie (Vancouver, British Columbia: Pulp Press, 1987);

Machine Sex . . . and Other Stories (Victoria, British Columbia: Tesseract Books, 1988; London: Women's Press, 1990);

Leaving Marks (Edmonton: River Books, 1992);

Dark Earth Dreams, chapbook and CD with readings by Dorsey and music by Roger Deegan (Victoria, British Columbia: Tesseract Books/Arktos Recordings, 1994);

Black Wine (New York: Tor, 1997);

Vanilla and Other Stories (Edmonton: NeWest Publishers, 2000);

A Paradigm of Earth (New York: Tor, 2001).

OTHER: *The Nuts and Bolts of Community Economic Development*, edited by Dorsey and Ellen Ticoll (Edmonton, Alberta: Edmonton Social Planning Council, 1984);

"Afterword: Towards a Real Speculative Literature: Writer as Asymptote," in *Tesseracts³*, edited by Dorsey and Gerry Truscott (Victoria, British

Candas Jane Dorsey (photograph by Janet Duncan)

Columbia: Tesseract Books, 1990), pp. 422–427; reprinted in *Northern Stars: The Anthology of Canadian Science Fiction,* edited by David G. Hartwell and Glenn Grant (New York: Tor, 1994), pp. 370–373;

"Dvorzjak Symphony," in *Alberta ReBound,* edited by Aritha van Herk (Edmonton, Alberta: NeWest Press, 1990), pp. 275–283;

"Death of a Dream," in *Tesseracts⁴,* edited by Lorna Toolis and Michael Skeet (Victoria, British Columbia: Tesseract Books, 1992), pp. 388–414;

"Living in Cities," in *Ark of Ice: Canadian Futurefiction,* edited by Lesley Choyce (Lawrencetown Beach,

Nova Scotia: Pottersfield Press, 1992), pp. 144–159;

New Canadian Speculative Fiction, edited by Dorsey and G. N. Louise Jonasson, special issue of *Prairie Fire*, 15 (Summer 1994);

"Form=Content=Form?: Catching the Conscience of the King," in *Out of This World: Canadian Science Fiction and Fantasy Literature*, compiled by Andrea Paradis (Kingston, Ontario: Quarry Press, 1995), pp. 146–158;

"Mapping," in *Tesseracts^5*, edited by Robert Runté and Yves Meynard (Edmonton, Alberta: Tesseract Books, 1996), pp. 109–117;

"Here Be Dragons," in *Tesseracts^6*, edited by Robert J. Sawyer and Carolyn Clink (Edmonton, Alberta: Tesseract Books, 1997), pp. 213–219;

"ICE," in *Tesseracts^7*, edited by Paula Johanson and Jean-Louis Trudel (Edmonton, Alberta: Tesseract Books, 1998), pp. 197–211;

Tesseracts^8, edited by Dorsey and John Clute (Edmonton, Alberta: Tesseract Books, 1999).

SELECTED PERIODICAL PUBLICATIONS–UNCOLLECTED:

FICTION

"Turtles All the Way Down," *New York Review of Science Fiction*, 38 (October 1991): 14;

"Going Home to Baïblanca: Homage à Élisabeth Vonarburg," *Prairie Fire*, 16 (Winter 1995–1996): 88–96;

"How Many Angels Can Dance," *On Spec*, 11 (Winter 1999): 21–25.

NONFICTION

"Deconstructing Deconstructing Vietnam," *New York Review of Science Fiction*, 37 (September 1991): 12–13;

"Being One's Own Pornographer," *New York Review of Science Fiction*, 89 (January 1996): 16–18; complete version in *Paradoxa: Studies in World Literary Genres*, 2, no. 2 (1996): 191–203;

"Bathhouses for Women: A Charter Challenge for Our Time," *Prairie Fire*, 17 (Summer 1996): 34–39.

While certainly not prolific, having published only two novels and two collections of short fiction in more than two decades of writing, Candas Jane Dorsey has gained a reputation as one of Canada's most important science-fiction writers, receiving acclaim both inside and outside Canada. Her contribution to the genre extends beyond her writing; she has been one of the most important figures in the development of Canadian science fiction by virtue of her work as an editor, anthologist, critic, and publisher.

Dorsey was born in Edmonton, Alberta, on 16 November 1952, the third of three children; her father, Jack Dorsey, was an engineer and musician, and her mother, Marie Dorsey, was a registered nurse and later an historical researcher and toponymist, as well as a painter. In an interview published in Edo van Belkom's *Northern Dreamers* (1998) Dorsey described her family as a "family of book readers." She added that "in my family a book and its writer were respected. . . . They were our friends, and not discriminated against on the basis of color or creed." This youthful refusal to be limited to any specific genre as a reader clearly carried over into her career as a writer, in which she has published "mainstream" poetry, as well as more explicitly "speculative" fiction, though her fiction often blurs the lines between "literary" fiction, science fiction, and fantasy.

Dorsey began writing plays while still in high school and pursued her interest in literature and the theater at the University of Alberta, where she studied English literature and drama and worked behind the stage, receiving a B.A. in 1975. In 1973, while still a student, she started working in child care with teenage girls, which led her after four years to seek a bachelor's degree as a social worker. She returned to school and earned a Bachelor's degree in social work from the University of Calgary in 1979, becoming a registered social worker that same year. Shortly after receiving her B.S.W. and R.S.W. she shifted careers to become a freelance writer and editor, working on a variety of projects for corporations, nonprofit organizations, and governmental bodies such as the Alberta Human Rights Commission and Shaw Communications. She is a partner in Wooden Door and Associates, an Edmonton-based professional communications company.

Dorsey began her career as a published author as a poet, with a series of chapbooks published by bill bissett's notorious Vancouver-based blewointment press, which, as Frank Davey describes in *The Oxford Companion to Canadian Literature* (1983), published crudely mimeographed chapbooks on variously sized and colored paper with distinctive illustrations. The first of Dorsey's chapbooks was *this is for you*, published in 1973. It is a slight collection, only twenty pages, of unremarkable poems largely concerned with relationships and sex. It was followed the next year by the publication of *Orion Rising*, a more substantial chapbook of thirty-five pages, featuring illustrations by both Dorsey and bissett. This collection is simultaneously a bit more broad-ranging, dealing with the act of writing and spiritual issues as well as relationships and sex, and more tightly focused, centering as it does around the image of the constellation of Orion, as seen from Edmonton during the winter months. This

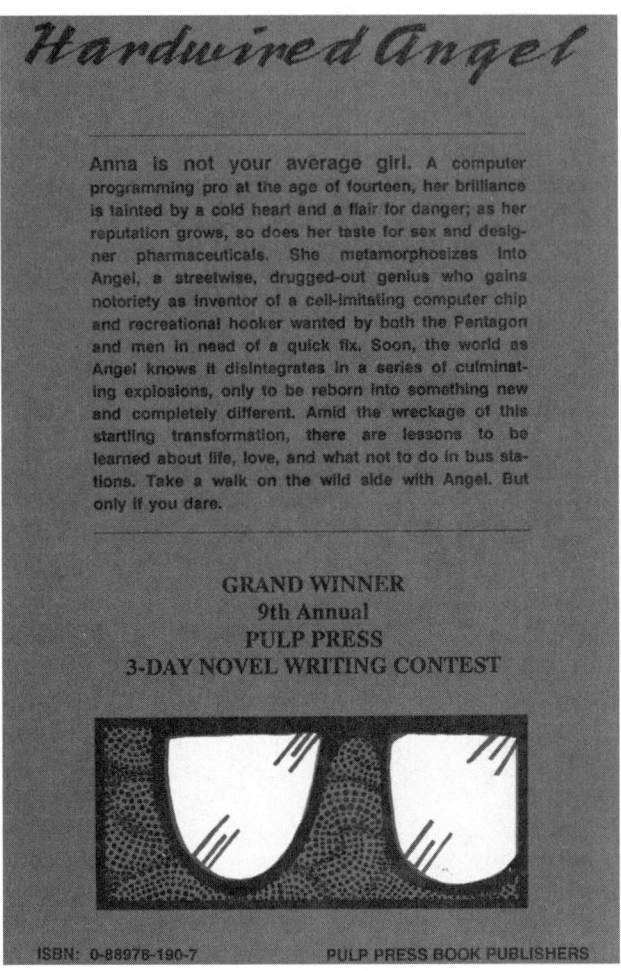

Cover for the 1987 short novel, co-authored by Dorsey, notable for making a woman the protagonist of a work in the cyberpunk genre

image, which is repeated throughout the book, anticipates her later speculative writing career: it simultaneously looks toward the stars, with all their possibilities, while remaining grounded in the specifics of place.

Results of the Ring Toss, published in 1976, was the third of her chapbooks to be published by blewointment press. Illustrated with photographs by Peter Sutherland, *Results of the Ring Toss* features Dorsey's most mature and controlled poetry, and represents a move away from the confessional, first-person poetry of her first two collections to more visual-narrative poems, often told in the third person and employing shorter, controlled lines.

Dorsey signaled a partial shift to prose, and toward speculative fiction, with the publication of the story "Columbus Hits the Shoreline Rag" in the anthology *Getting Here,* edited by Rudy Wiebe and published by NeWest Press in 1977. Her inclusion in this anthology of Alberta writers anticipated her long-time involvement in the Alberta writing scene. This story, later collected in *Machine Sex . . . and Other Stories* (1988), shows her background as a poet, as Dorsey narrates it in poetic form. Not a conventional narrative, it moves across place and time to relate the consequences of Christopher Columbus's "discovery" of America for the indigenous inhabitants, and concludes with the (imagined?) hijacking of a spaceship by a group of First Nations people, who redirect the ship into the heart of the sun in order to "claim this Fiery Ball in the name of the Indian Sovereign Nations." The story is reminiscent of the fiction produced by the so-called New Wave science-fiction writers of 1960s and 1970s—associated with the British magazine *New Worlds* and later Harlan Ellison's *Dangerous Visions* anthologies—because it combines speculative subject matter and tropes with a self-consciously literary style. It thus signaled Dorsey's refusal to allow her fiction to comfortably fit into the restrictions of the commercial science fiction being published in the American magazines. She later told van Belkom that she does not "really differentiate between mainstream and science fiction," and this refusal marks both her fiction and her criticism.

In early 1980 Dorsey made the decision to become a full-time freelance writer. "'You'll Remember Mercury'" appeared in the *NeWest Review* in 1980 and was also later collected in *Machine Sex . . . and Other Stories*. Like "Columbus Hits the Shoreline Rag," it is an experimental, poetic speculative fiction, though it represents a move toward conventional storytelling techniques, following prose rather than poetry conventions in form and structure. It is more explicitly science fictional, as it depicts human-alien first contact, one of the classic tropes of science fiction; yet, there is nothing of the space opera or science fiction adventure tale about Dorsey's story, which deals to a greater extent with relationships and isolation than with conventional science-fiction topics.

In 1983 Dorsey co-founded the Edmonton arts monthly *The Edmonton Bullet,* serving as co-editor, then editor and manager from its founding until 1988 and on its board until its dissolution in 1993. She continues to be highly involved in the Edmonton arts community, as was recognized when she was awarded a YWCA Women of Distinction Award in Arts and Culture in 1998.

"Black Dog" was published in 1984 in *blue buffalo* and later collected in *Machine Sex . . . and Other Stories* and *Dark Earth Dreams* (1994). This melancholic and elegiac story is narrated by a woman who is one of the few people who have chosen to remain on a nearly deserted Earth. But rather than developing the explanation for how this situation has come to pass, Dorsey focuses on the character of the narrator. In a review of *Dark Earth Dreams* in the Winter 1995–1996 issue of *Prairie Fire* David Annandale commented that "Dorsey gives us the bare minimum to create a world context for the characters, little hints here and there between the lines, and never lets it interfere with the pastoral tone of the story." Annandale's description of Dorsey's method in this story is an accurate description of her approach in all of her speculative fiction. She told van Belkom that "stories have within them the requirements for what must be put in and left out, and anything beyond that is gratuitous verbiage." A haunting story, "Black Dog" emphasizes the importance of one's link to place. The narrator writes, "We can't exist in a vacuum. Aware of gravity, we stand spellbound before the stars, but we don't want to get any closer. We love another force, the one that holds us together, to each other, to the ground."

In 1985 Dorsey published two more stories that were later included in *Machine Sex . . . and Other Stories:* "the white city" and "Johnny Appleseed on the New World." The former, first published in *Dinosaur Review,* is a dreamlike narrative with the bureaucratic-sounding subtitle "Report on the Expedition to Earth to Examine the After-effects of Armageddon on San Francisco." The tarotlike "reading" of the symbolism in the story, in the interpretation of the face cards provided at the conclusion, reinforces the imagism and surrealism. "Johnny Appleseed on the New World" appeared in *Tesseracts* (1985), the groundbreaking collection of Canadian science fiction edited by renowned anthologist Judith Merril. It is a story of colonization, describing the first winter experienced by seven human settlers on a new planet as they attempt to plant apple trees in their new home. The conventionality of this story is undercut, however, by the intervention of a mysterious stranger perceived only by the narrator, who seems to be responsible for their eventual success in growing apples and who is, without explanation, accepted into the group of settlers at the conclusion of the story. The significance of this story for Dorsey's career lies as much in its venue as in the story itself, for *Tesseracts* launched a market for Canadian speculative fiction and situated Dorsey within it. "Johnny Appleseed on the New World" was later included on a CD-ROM titled *Visions of Mars* (edited by the "Messenger from Earth team, which included Carl Sagan and Jon Lomberg), that was sent into space on a joint United States-Russian rocket in 1994.

In 1986 Dorsey and Nora Abercrombie won the Pulp Press International Three-Day Novel-Writing Contest with *Hardwired Angel,* published the next year by Pulp Press. Dorsey described to van Belkom the process of writing the novel: "It was silly and a great deal of fun. . . . The first day we started by going out to breakfast at Uncle Albert's Pancake House, a venerable Edmonton institution, then set up our Kaypros (tells when that was–1986) back to back on my dining room table, and our friends brought us food and sat around watching. . . . The whole thing was a bit like a hands-on workshop in novel writing." If the result was, as Dorsey described it, "a bit of fluff" created from a story she had already begun, it did bring her some publicity, and she was able to reuse the protagonist and many of the details in her most famous story, "(Learning About) Machine Sex" (1988). *Hardwired Angel* is a short (114 pages), undistinguished cyberpunk novel that tells the story of Anna, a professional computer programmer who transforms into Angel, a stereotypical cyberpunk character, streetwise and heavily involved in drugs, who invents a cell-imitating computer. This novel is most interesting as a feminist rewrite of the highly masculinist cyberpunk myth that had been developed by fellow Canadian William Gibson, most famously in *Neuromancer* (1984), and then endlessly reworked by many other writers in the next few years. Rather than being a peripheral character, as most women in cyberpunk were, Angel is the protagonist—one who, with difficulty, effectively challenges the authority of the men around her. Dorsey has been working on a screenplay adaptation of *Hardwired Angel*.

"Willows" appeared in *Tesseracts²*, edited by Phyllis Gotlieb and Douglas Barbour, in 1987. This story, which was also collected in *Machine Sex . . . and Other Stories,* relates the experiences of a space traveler (whose gender is never specified) on one of the traveler's periodic returns to Earth, during which the traveler stores up memories of being on Earth that will provide comfort during long periods of solitude in the spaceship. The traveler is accompanied by an alien who wishes to discover all he can about Earth, and there they meet a linguist and a naturalist who are also studying the planet. The latter two are collecting evidence of Earth's continuing vitality to present the government as it decides whether to allow the planet to continue to exist. Fortunately, Earth has recovered from the destructions of past centuries and is revitalized. This story is both a meditation on the importance of home and an environmentalist plea. As the naturalist tells the narrator upon discovering that lichen are now once again thriving, "If the small, delicate organisms die, the large delicate organism that is the world will die, and we would need to get it out of the way then."

Finally, in 1988 Dorsey published *Machine Sex . . . and Other Stories,* which collects six previously published stories and seven new ones. It was one of the first books published by Tesseract Books in Victoria, which began as an imprint of Press Porcépic and later, as a member of the Books Collective, became the foremost publisher of English-Canadian science fiction. *Machine Sex . . . and Other Stories,* nominated for a Canadian Science Fiction and Fantasy Award for best long-form work in English, established Dorsey as one of Canada's most important science-fiction writers and brought her work wider recognition than it had so far received. It was republished two years later in Britain by The Women's Press and received enthusiastic reviews in Canada and elsewhere. In a review in the April 1989 issue of *Locus,* Faren Miller noted that Dorsey's best stories have "that air of risk and excitement which animates the stories of Joanna Russ. This is a new writer to keep an eye on." *The Encyclopedia of Science Fiction* (1995) described the pieces in *Machine Sex . . . and Other Stories* as "terse, complex stories" that "polemically re-use and rework science fiction and fantasy tropes from a feminist perspective."

Like the previously published stories, the seven new ones vary in style and subject matter and continue Dorsey's practice of challenging the genre boundaries and practicing literary experimentation. While not all are uniformly strong, two stories—"Sleeping in a Box" and "(Learning About) Machine Sex"—are particularly noteworthy. "Sleeping in a Box" won the 1989 Canadian Science Fiction and Fantasy Award for best short-form work in English by a Canadian, the first time it had been awarded. This brief story, one of Dorsey's most conventional science-fiction works, is an evocative description of life in a colony on the moon. The inhabitants, as the title suggests, are alienated from the actual environment of the moon, confined to the box in which they live, eat, and sleep. In keeping with her usual narrative strategy, Dorsey only obliquely indicates that this moon colony is actually a penal colony of sorts, though the reader learns no more than that.

Much more substantial, and by far the most significant story in *Machine Sex . . . and Other Stories,* is "(Learning About) Machine Sex," also nominated for the Canadian Science Fiction and Fantasy Award. Angel, who had previously appeared in *Hardwired Angel,* is a computer programmer who creates a program called Machine Sex, which gives its users an orgasm. A witty commentary on the commodification of sex, "(Learning About) Machine Sex" is significant in putting a female protagonist into the role of the hacker, mythologized by many cyberpunk writers as essentially masculine. Furthermore, it is unusual in its foregrounding of Canada as an important site in the information age, displacing the Japan and America of cyberpunk writers such as Gibson.

In 1989 Dorsey was involved in the founding of the first professional association for Canadian science fiction writers, the Speculative Writers Association of Canada, later known as SF Canada. She served as its president from 1989 until 1994. That same year, she was consulted by the Copper Pig Writers Society, the founders of the Edmonton-based speculative fiction magazine *On Spec,* and served as a member of its editorial advisory board for many years.

Dorsey next published "Dvorzjak Symphony" in *Alberta ReBound* (1990), a collection of works by Alberta writers edited by well-known Alberta novelist and English professor Aritha van Herk and published by NeWest Press. A mysterious story of a night security guard at an empty barracks, and his secret lover who is hidden there, "Dvorzjak Symphony," like many of Dorsey's stories, is tantalizingly vague. The reader is only given a few hints about the broader context in which the story takes place, but it does seem to be set at some point in the future, in a strangely empty place. Ultimately, the story is about the importance of human relationships as a means of surviving the emptiness.

That same year Dorsey co-edited *Tesseracts³* with Gerry Truscott. Featuring both fiction and poetry, and writers as varied as Gibson, Margaret Atwood, Gotlieb, Charles de Lint, and Élisabeth Vonarburg, this anthology was well reviewed by science fiction critics such as Faren Miller, who noted in the July 1991 issue of *Locus* that the book is an indication of the strength of Canadian science fiction and fantasy. *Tesseracts³* is also notable for Dorsey's afterword, in which she articulates her understanding of speculative writing and attempts to situate Canadian science fiction as a boundary tradition, straddling the worlds of Canadian literature and American science fiction. Speculative writing, she suggests, is "always that asymptotic line on the graph which spends its career approaching, never arriving; always in transit between two imaginary points: take-off and destination; and therefore always beyond the binary, free to understand its fallacy." It is, she observes, a risky enterprise, one that contradicts the commercial demands of mass-market science fiction.

More important is her attempt to critically situate Canadian science fiction, the writers of which are "walking the border, the boundary if you will, as if it were a tightrope, our toes clinging to the narrow line through the special soft shoes one must wear to do tricks on the high wire." Canadian science fiction, drawing from the "mainstream" Canadian literary tradition and American science fiction—both of which, she argues, are equally interested in "speculation, alienness, exploration of frontiers in and outside self"—is therefore in a privileged position from which its practitioners can blur the boundaries imposed by genre. Canadian science fiction is "stepping as far outside the norms, the genre strictures, as we can, because the changing world, the changing world, is what matters most." Speculative fiction, then, is not about predicting the future but about shaping it, about experimenting with the future. While Miller, for one, disagrees with Dorsey's claim that Canadian science fiction is different from American science fiction in this way, the essay has gained increased significance as a critical statement about Canadian science fiction by being included in the landmark anthology *Northern Stars* (1994), which introduced Canadian science fiction, as such, to mass-market American readers.

Dorsey was appointed writer in residence at the Edmonton Public Library in 1990 and later served as writer in residence at the St. Albert, Sherwood Park,

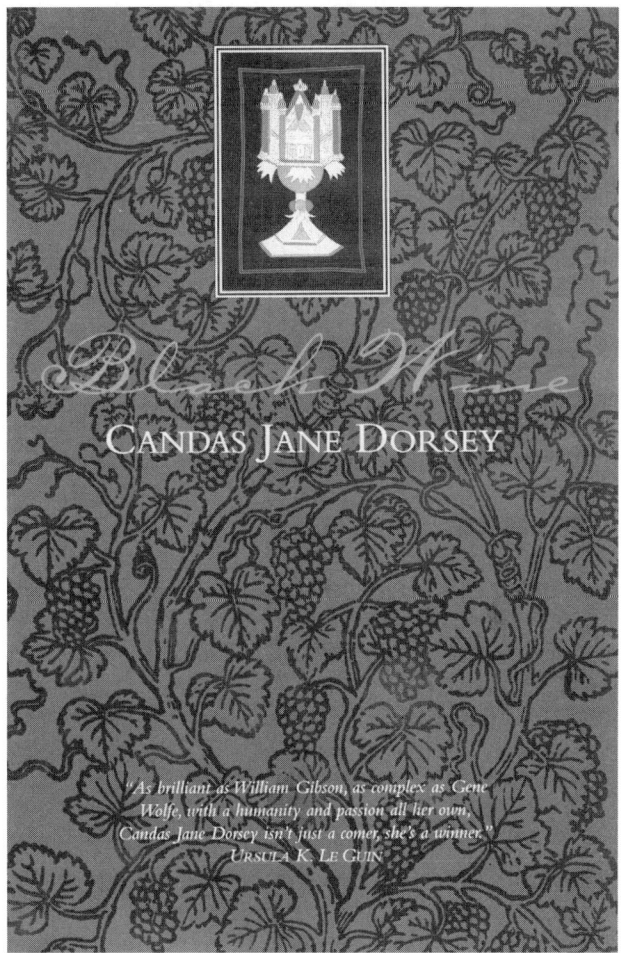

Dust jacket for Dorsey's 1997 feminist novel, about a woman's search for her mother in an oppressive future society

and Fort Saskatchewan Public Libraries in 1991, and first had a residency at the Leighton Artists Colony in 1992. She was active in the Alberta literary scene, joining the executive board of the Writers' Guild of Alberta in 1991 and serving as its president in 1993–1994. She also became a regular contributor to the *New York Review of Science Fiction*, publishing book reviews, essays, and even short fiction in its pages throughout the 1990s.

"Death of a Dream" appeared in *Tesseracts⁴*, edited by Lorna Toolis and Michael Skeet and published in 1992. It is a remarkable story that, on one level, deals with the breakdown of a marriage, child abduction, and child abuse. Dorsey extrapolates these issues into the world of virtual reality. The child in question is a dream child, one constructed over the years by the narrator and her former husband. When the joint dream of marriage disintegrates, the former husband abducts the dream child and uses her to create pornographic dreams for profit. The narrator devotes herself to tracking down her dream child, eventually joining the dream police. One of the more plot-driven of Dorsey's stories, "Death of a Dream" is nonetheless a sophisticated and chilling meditation on the consequences of virtual reality, as well as on marriage and child abuse.

That same year Dorsey contributed the less successful "Living in Cities" to Lesley Choyce's anthology of Canadian "futurefiction," *Ark of Ice*. It is a vivid portrait of a future city, presumably Edmonton, that has been preserved, and which the narrator, who owns and has restored it, is asked to show to an off-world traveler. Evocative as the story is (and it demonstrates a clear love of cities in general and Edmonton in particular), it is ultimately unfocused and confusing. Annandale complained in his Winter 1995–1996 *Prairie Fire* review of *Dark Earth Dreams*, which includes "Living in Cities," that "ellipsis has here become opacity . . . I was spending more time than I should have trying to figure out what was going on, rather than focusing on the give and take between the two protagonists."

Dorsey returned to poetry in 1992 with her first poetry collection in sixteen years, *Leaving Marks*. Categorized as erotic poetry and much more confident and effective than her earlier poetry, this collection is, as she explains in the afterword, an exploration of her interest "in ecstasy," which she sees as one of the goals of poetry and all art. Human existence, she further suggests, must consist of searching for the ecstatic, for people will save the world "by learning to love it so ecstatically that we cannot bear to ruin it or lie about it, that we must instead nurture and embrace it." The emphasis in this book on sexuality and sexual politics also anticipates a shift in Dorsey's writing. While sexuality had always been a focus of her speculative fiction, it became foregrounded in some of her work of the 1990s, particularly her novel *Black Wine* (1997). She continued to publish occasional poems in Canadian journals such as *Prairie Fire* and *Canadian Literature* throughout the 1990s.

Dorsey's important work as a publisher also began in 1992. That year she became a founding member of the Books Collective, which she described to van Belkom as "a strategic alliance of small publishers to share tasks and resources for distribution and marketing." One of the new collective's imprints was River Books, of which she was a founding editor, and which published *Leaving Marks*. Shortly after the Books Collective was founded, it purchased Tesseract Books, publisher of the *Tesseracts* anthologies and other Canadian science fiction books, and Dorsey continues to serve as the publisher of Tesseract Books. Partly as a result of her new publishing responsibilities Dorsey edited several Canadian science fiction books, most notably Heather Spears's *The Taming* (1996) and English translations of Vonarburg's *Chroniques du Pays des Mères* (1992; translated as *The Maerlande Chronicles*, 1992) for Press Porcépic and *Les Voyageurs malgré eux* (1994; translated as *Reluctant Voyagers*, 1995) for Tesseract Books.

Dorsey returned to her work as an anthologist in 1994 with a special issue of *Prairie Fire* devoted to new Canadian speculative writing. It featured fiction and poetry by a variety of writers, including Vonarburg, Spears, Teresa Plowright, and Andrew Weiner. She also released *Dark Earth Dreams,* an audio recording of her reading "Living in Cities" and "Black Dog" to musical accompaniment by noted motion-picture and modern orchestral composer Roger Deegan, packaged in a chapbook of the two stories. Dorsey and Deegan had been performing such pieces annually as part of Edmonton's First Night festivities. The discbook was released to celebrate the acquisition of Tesseract Books by the Books Collective. In his Winter 1995–1996 *Prairie Fire* review Annandale wrote that Dorsey's readings "are clear, professional, and bang-on in tone," though he finds the musical accompaniment a little too "science fiction Creepy for such gentle tales."

Dorsey received her first mass-market exposure in the United States through the inclusion of her work in three prominent anthologies published by major publishers. In 1994 "(Learning About) Machine Sex" and her afterword to *Tesseracts*[3] appeared in the groundbreaking *Northern Stars* anthology edited by David Hartwell and Glenn Grant, published by Tor Books. "(Learning About) Machine Sex" was also included in the prestigious *Norton Book of Science Fiction* (1993), edited by Ursula K. Le Guin and Brian Attebery, and *The Penguin Book of Modern Fantasy by Women* (1995), edited by A. Susan Williams and Richard Glyn Jones.

In 1995 the National Library of Canada mounted *Out of This World,* an exhibit on Canadian science fiction and fantasy. Dorsey's *Machine Sex . . . and Other Stories* was among the books displayed as part of the exhibit, and she contributed an essay, "Form=Content=Form?: Catching the Conscience of the King" to the anthology that accompanied the exhibit. In this essay, which was first an address at the W.R.I.T.E. 1994 conference, she discusses the impact of computer technology on writing and on modern society in general. Content must come first, she reminds readers, and writers must use computers as they have used all previous technologies, as a means of describing the world. In the rush to computerization, she says, society and its writers must not forget those who may be marginalized by a lack of access to computers.

"Going Home to Baïblanca" won honorable mention in a speculative-fiction writing contest sponsored by *Prairie Fire* and was published in the Winter 1995–1996 issue of that journal. Subtitled "Homage à Élisabeth Vonarburg," this story uses the name of Vonarburg's future city and echoes her distinctive mythic style in its depiction of contact between a mermaid-like Swimmer and a human Land person. A melancholy story, it reflects distrust of humankind's predatory impact upon the environment and the sea; it also carries a message against homophobia.

The same year she published "Mapping" in *Tesseracts⁵*, edited by Robert Runté and Yves Meynard. This brief story of child abuse and its impact features a male protagonist, a gay man who has been abused by his father, though he does not recall the abuse and thus suffers from a tattoolike skin disease called mapping, which has obvious echoes of AIDS and of the self-mutilations sometimes practiced by child-abuse victims. This story is one of Dorsey's less successful ones, as in this case the futuristic trappings, mainly provided by mapping, seem unnecessary and underdeveloped.

Dorsey's increasing interest in sexual politics is also evident in an essay published in 1996. "Bathhouses for Women: A Charter Challenge for Our Time" appeared in a supplement to the Summer 1996 issue of *Prairie Fire*. In this essay, which is an excerpt from a still-unpublished work in progress titled "Pornographic Culture: Some Thoughts on Sex, Gender, and the Politics of Repression" (portions of which have also appeared in *Paradoxa, The New York Review of Science Fiction,* and *Tarnations*) Dorsey complains that society prevents women from partaking in casual sex (as exemplified in gay bathhouses) and thus restricts the options available to women. She dreams of a sex-positive culture in which women could partake in casual sex, but she recognizes that her goal is still a long way off.

Dorsey participated in her sixth straight *Tesseracts* volume with the contribution of a short story titled "Here Be Dragons" to *Tesseracts⁶*, edited by Robert J. Sawyer and Carolyn Clink, in 1997. This brief and minor effort describes, somewhat obliquely, the consequences of capitalist greed for technology and narrates one character's small victory against that force. This story was overshadowed by the acclaim that her first full-length novel, *Black Wine*, received on publication that same year. In addition to enthusiastic reviews, *Black Wine* won the William L. Crawford Fantasy Award presented by the International Association for the Fantastic in the Arts to the best book-length debut of the year; the James Tiptree Jr. Award, which is given to the best science fiction book dealing with gender issues; and the Aurora Award for Best English-language Canadian science fiction novel. One of the judges of the Tiptree Award, James Patrick Kelly, lauded *Black Wine* as "an intricate, fierce and lyrical examination of gender and identity. Teeming with ideas made flesh, *Black Wine* gazes unflinching at the wonder and horror of humanity." The chair of the award committee, Terry Garey, wrote that "in *Black Wine,* Candas Dorsey took on the whole question of gender, shook it out till it suited her, cut, stitched, and fitted till she came up with a wondrous garment I had never seen before. Then she showed me it was reversible and just as wondrous on the inside, which was now the outside." Canadian speculative-fiction writer and critic Nancy Johnston described it as "an intense reading experience, layered with difficult questions about power and sexuality, the potential of community, and the possibility of transforming one's identity through language."

In a review in the January 1997 issue of *Locus* Gary K. Wolfe described *Black Wine* as "one of the most sophisticated literary SF novels of the year." Dorsey, he wrote, constructs "an elegant narrative that jumps back and forth in time shifts points of view and even styles, and offers a poet's richness of language and imagery," yet "this brilliant technique serves a plot which is positively operatic in its passions, sufferings, coincidences, and retributions." As Wolfe's comments suggest, *Black Wine* is a complicated, occasionally confusing, and challenging novel—maybe too challenging for some readers, judging by the confused customer reviews posted on the Amazon.com website. It is a poetic, highly symbolic, often dream like narrative.

Set in a fantastic far-future world of oppression, fear, and the possibility of freedom—and for the first time Dorsey conjures a fully convincing fantastic world as the backdrop to her narrative—*Black Wine* tells the story of Essa, a woman who goes in search of her mother, who abandoned the family when Essa was seven. She discovers that her mother was a princess. Eventually the victim of amnesia, Essa creates a new personality, that of Fierce-frightened, after being captured and sold as a slave in a palace where she serves the regent to whom she was once betrothed. Eventually, Essa pieces together the different pieces of her personality and reconciles with her mother.

In telling the story of Essa, Dorsey tells the often horrifying stories of many other women, and touches on themes of rape and abuse, domestic slavery, clitoridectomy, sexuality and sexual politics, freedom and desire. It is an intense novel of ideas, filled with disturbing images of violence, torture, and sexual violence, along with sexually explicit scenes depicting the complex, both oppressive and liberating, reality of sexuality. It is a novel worthy of feminist precursors such as Le Guin and Russ and is arguably one of the most accomplished works of Canadian science fiction.

Dorsey followed up *Black Wine* with "ICE" in *Tesseracts⁷*, edited by Paula Johanson and Jean-Louis Trudel and published in 1998. Inevitably disappointing, "ICE," set in twenty-first-century Hong Kong and Montreal, is a rewrite of cyberpunk; the narrator, MahLee, is partly a satire of Molly in Gibson's cyberpunk tales. While the scenes in a drowned future Montreal are quite beautiful, the rest of the story seems a little stale. MahLee reminisces about imploding drowned skyscrapers, while viewing the virtual memories of her former love LiLee (a pun on Linda Lee in Gibson's stories), a drugged-out prostitute who was sexually exploited by her boyfriend.

In January 1999 Dorsey and her partner, Timothy J. Anderson, an opera and classical singer, performer, and writer, made a Canada-wide impact when they took out an advertisement in *The Globe and Mail*, a national newspaper, asking for a patron to support their artistic endeavors. They may not have been successful, but their ad did receive a great deal of media attention, both positive and negative, and brought the issue of arts funding into the spotlight. That same year, Dorsey co-edited *Tesseracts⁸* with well-known Canadian-born speculative-fiction critic John Clute. In her brief afterword, she refines her definition of speculative fiction, which is "the creation of a metaphor that explains for us our *now*—our particular reality—by invoking not the universal but the universe." She restates her claim that there is something distinct about Canadian science fiction and insists on the importance of the local as a basis for storytelling. Dorsey published "How Many Angels Can Dance," a brief, enigmatic story, in the Winter 1999 issue of *On Spec*. In evocative, poetic prose, Dorsey describes the dancing of the angels over an unnamed, fantastic city.

Dorsey's second collection of short fiction, *Vanilla and Other Stories,* was published in May 2000 by Edmonton's NeWest Press. This book collects short stories written over the previous twenty-five years, focusing on her nongenre stories and mixing previously published and performed stories with new ones. Her second novel, *A Paradigm of Earth,* is scheduled to be published by Tor Books in October 2001, and she is co-editing an anthology of speculative fiction on prairie themes with Judy McCrosky.

As writer, editor, anthologist, publisher, fan, and activist, Dorsey has been a key figure in the development of Canadian science fiction into a mature literature, worthy of study and discussion. Certainly, her own fiction has been at the forefront of Canadian science fiction and at times of speculative fiction and Canadian literature in general. She has used the conventions and freedoms of science fiction to provocatively explore gender and sexuality.

Interview:

Edo van Belkom, "Candas Jane Dorsey," in his *Northern Dreamers: Interviews with Famous Science Fiction, Fantasy, and Horror Writers* (Kingston, Ontario: Quarry Press, 1998), pp. 51–60.

Dave Duncan
(30 June 1933 –)

Jane Tolmie
Harvard University

BOOKS: *A Rose-Red City* (New York: Ballantine, 1987; London: Legend, 1989);

Shadow (New York: Ballantine, 1987; London: Legend, 1989);

The Reluctant Swordsman: Part One of The Seventh Sword (New York: Ballantine, 1988; London: Legend, 1990);

The Coming of Wisdom: Part Two of The Seventh Sword (New York: Ballantine, 1988; London: Legend, 1990);

The Destiny of the Sword: Part Three of the Seventh Sword (New York: Ballantine, 1988; London: Legend, 1991);

West of January (New York: Ballantine, 1989);

Strings (New York: Ballantine, 1990);

Magic Casement: Part One of A Man of His Word (New York: Ballantine, 1990);

Faery Lands Forlorn: Part Two of A Man of His Word (New York: Ballantine, 1991);

Hero! (New York: Ballantine, 1991);

Perilous Seas: Part Three of A Man of His Word (New York: Ballantine, 1991);

Emperor and Clown: Part Four of A Man of His Word (New York: Ballantine, 1992);

The Cutting Edge: Part One of A Handful of Men (New York: Ballantine, 1992; London: Raven, 1994);

The Reaver Road (New York: Ballantine, 1992);

Upland Outlaws: Part Two of A Handful of Men (New York: Ballantine, 1993; London: Raven, 1995);

The Stricken Field: Part Three of a Handful of Men (New York: Ballantine, 1993);

The Living God: Part Four of A Handful of Men (New York: Ballantine, 1994);

The Cursed (New York: Ballantine, 1995);

Demon Sword: Part One of The Years of Longdirk, as Ken Hood (New York: HarperPrism, 1995);

The Hunters' Haunt (New York: Ballantine, 1995);

Past Imperative: Round One of The Great Game (New York: Avon, 1995; London: Corgi, 1997);

Present Tense: Round Two of The Great Game (New York: Avon, 1996; London: Corgi, 1997);

Dave Duncan (courtesy of the author)

Demon Rider: Part Two of The Years of Longdirk, as Hood (New York: HarperPrism, 1997);

Future Indefinite: Part Three of The Great Game (New York: Avon, 1997; London: Corgi, 1998);

Daughter of Troy: A Novel of History, Valor, and Love, as Sarah B. Franklin (New York: Avon, 1998);

Demon Knight: Part Three of The Years of Longdirk, as Hood (New York: HarperPrism, 1998);

The Gilded Chain: A Tale of the King's Blades (New York: Avon, 1998);

Sir Stalwart: A Tale of the King's Daggers (New York: Avon, 1999);

Lord of the Fire Lands: A Tale of the King's Blades (New York: Avon Eos, 1999);

The Crooked House (New York: Avon, 2000);

Sky of Swords: A Tale of the King's Blades (New York: Avon Eos, 2000);

Silvercloak (New York: Avon Eos, 2001).

Dave Duncan made a major and apparently smooth career transition at the age of fifty-three, from geological consultant to professional writer. In the course of his relatively short career he has developed an authorial voice that is intelligent and witty, and he has become one of the major Canadian fantasy and science-fiction novelists. In an unpublished e-mail interview in July 1998 Duncan commented that he "half jumped and half got pushed" into his new field.

David John Duncan was born on 30 June 1933 in Newport-on-Tay, Scotland, to Norman Duncan, a flax manufacturer, and Winifred Anderson, a homemaker with a background in domestic-science teaching. He has one brother, Michael, a retired agriculturist. After studying at Dundee High School, Duncan attended the University of St. Andrews; on his website, <http://www.daveduncan.com>, he jokes that he played "not one hole of golf all the time I was there." He received his bachelor of science degree in geology and chemistry in 1955 and immigrated to Canada that year, settling in Calgary, Alberta; he became a naturalized Canadian citizen in 1960. In 1959 he married Janet Hopwell, with whom he has one son, two daughters, and four grandchildren. At the time of his move to Canada there were no jobs for geologists in Scotland, and Canada seemed a good choice for someone wanting to work in "soft rock," meaning petroleum. In an interview with Edo van Belkom published in *Northern Dreamers* (1998), Duncan commented that "anyone who suggested in those days that Scotland would one day be a major oil exporter would have been certified daft and chained to a post." Duncan worked in Canada as a petroleum geologist from 1955 to 1976, and then established his own geological consulting business, which lasted from 1977 to 1986.

Duncan describes himself as "playing at novel writing" during these periods. Play became work in 1986 when the Del Rey imprint of Ballantine Books accepted the manuscript for Duncan's first fantasy novel, *A Rose-Red City* (1987)—two weeks into Duncan's first and only experience with unemployment, following a collapse in the Alberta oil business that put an end to his consulting career. For Duncan the transition to writing as his main occupation was made easier by his years of experience with self-employment. As he said in the unpublished 1998 interview, "the switch from science to science fiction was not actually that great—same desk, same keyboard, less drawing of maps."

Duncan says that he is "not aware of anything specifically Canadian" in his work or "anybody else's," though two of his favorite contemporary fantasy writers—Guy Gavriel Kay and Sean Russell—are both Canadian. Duncan's comment seems paradoxically rather typical of many Canadian fantasy novelists' views; it also reflects the current lack of distinction between the Canadian and American fantasy markets. Duncan has produced a large amount of work since 1987, with at least two new series in progress. He averages more than two books a year but seems wary of the label "prolific." Several broad themes are identifiable across a large body of Duncan's work: cultural alienation; the faintly reluctant, rather bumbling but predestined hero; and the workings of prophecy. Duncan does have an admirable tendency to create new worlds and/or new characters in each series or individual novel, and he often ends a given series with a degree of finality that precludes the possibility of any continuation. He thus avoids a major pitfall that afflicts much genre fantasy and science fiction, that of the Perpetual Series—rewritten and reworked but still painfully recognizable. He says he is "contemptuous of writers who, for lack of imagination or crass greed, continue to thump the same tubs forever." He writes under three names: most commonly, Dave Duncan (not to be confused with the late David Duncan, an American science-fiction and screenplay writer); Ken Hood (a play on "Do you ken whodunit?"); and Sarah B. Franklin. The three Ken Hood books are historical fantasy, while the one Sarah B. Franklin novel, *Daughter of Troy* (1998), is an historical romance.

Duncan's first novel, *A Rose-Red City,* presents a miraculous city called Mera (an abbreviation of chimera), whose immortal inhabitants are former mortals plucked from all moments of Earth's history. This land of eternal youth is governed by a mysterious Oracle, who maintains the city as a safe haven in a universe full of malignant demons. The Oracle is an active recruiter of new Meran citizens, and the action of the novel revolves around one such rescue. Jerry Howard and his charismatic companion Killer leave Mera to meet the newest recruit from Outside (in the mortal world). The new recruit turns out to be an alcoholic divorcée named Ariadne who has just kidnapped her children from her former husband. A slightly jumbled series of adventures follows: demons attack; Jerry and Ariadne develop a romance; the husband, stepmother, children, and some hired goons are all involved; the party splits up and is reassembled; and the ground shifts several times rather inexplicably. When the dust has settled, it emerges that the Oracle's original mission was misunderstood by Jerry and Killer, but there are two new Meran citizens anyway. Ariadne, in an odd quirk, turns out to be the mother of Killer, once known as Achilles in ancient Greece.

A Rose-Red City is an impressive first novel, and it displays Duncan's gift for surprising twists, but it does suffer from a bit of vagueness. The many transitions in space and time give an impression of randomness, and much of the terrain, including the city itself, would benefit from more description. There is one kind of deliberate and interesting randomness, however: the Oracle's choice of mortals to live in Mera is quite unrelated to any sense of their moral worth—it is more of a second chance than a reward. The inhabitants of Mera tend to have troubled and dubious pasts, and they undergo a kind of reformation (even exorcism, in some cases) when they decide to stay in Mera. The Oracle takes the form of a mirror and appears to each individual as a reflection of that person's true self. An interrogation of sorts follows, such that each new inhabitant must pass through a kind of fire of self-analysis. This transformative dynamic is most interesting and, as with other aspects of the novel, might benefit from more development.

Shadow, also released in 1987, brings more assurance to the technique of a sudden revelation or reversal at the end of the novel. On a planet inhabited by both humans and massive, mostly enslaved eagles, there is a hot dispute about the succession in the kingdom of Rantorra. One young skyman, Sald Harl, is unexpectedly appointed to the position of Prince Shadow—guardian to the heir apparent, Vindax. Shadow, stripped of his name and future aspirations, occupies an alienated position in the court and in his world, and is thus able to see options rather more clearly than other characters. The heir's legitimacy is called into question, and a scheming brother takes steps to remove him. Vindax, however, is crippled, not killed, and his campaign to regain the throne is largely engineered by Shadow. Unexpected help comes from the free eagles, who are revealed to be highly intelligent, but their price is freedom for the enslaved birds ridden by the skymen in Rantorra. Shadow becomes increasingly invested in the eagles' release and devises a scheme to free the Rantorran birds, while Vindax becomes increasingly obsessed with vengeance and power. Though the restoration campaign succeeds, Vindax reneges on his pledge to free the eagles and turns on Shadow. He is struck down by the eagles, who see him arrest Shadow, moments

Dust jacket for the first novel (1992) in Duncan's second tetralogy set in the magical world of Pandemia

after his accession. The two main sections of the novel are titled "Crime" (the usurpation) and "Punishment" (the restoration campaign).

In *Shadow* Duncan makes skillful use of ambiguity. Vindax is quite clearly not the king's legitimate son, a possibility raised in the reader's first view of him and substantiated throughout the novel; but his legitimate brother Jarkadon is a raping, scheming, moral vacuum. The choice becomes one between bad kings, and the eagles' intervention is a sort of inevitable punishment for crimes that it appears only Shadow can see: not just those of Vindax in his few vengeful moments on the throne, but those against the eagles as well. Vindax's treachery, madness, and death defy the more common fantasy trajectory of the triumph of rightful rule. Shadow leaves the court in the same state of alienation in which he entered it and goes home, having earned the title Friend of Eagles and played a major role in the destruction of his own kingdom.

The decision to use a displaced person as the protagonist of the novel is one of the most striking characteristics of *Shadow*. Duncan's most popular trilogy, *The*

Seventh Sword, makes use of the same technique. All three books came out in 1988 in the United States. They feature a man from Earth transported into the body of a preliterate swordsman on a world still embroiled in the Age of Legends, where gods and goddesses intervene in daily life. This world is simply called the World. Its social structure and characteristics are clearly and interestingly delineated: craftspeople, including swordsmen, can receive up to seven forehead marks designating their degree of expertise; people have parent-marks on their eyelids; and a piranha-infested River connects all the cities of the World and can move people from place to place on its own, while the piranhas act to express the pleasure or displeasure of the Goddess. Wallie Smith takes over the body of Shonsu, a swordsman of the seventh rank, and assumes the burden of a quest for the Goddess.

The first book in the series, *The Reluctant Swordsman,* covers Wallie's transition into the World and into the body of Shonsu. Wallie wakes to find himself in a large, unfamiliar body, attended by a slave girl and a priest of the Goddess. His initial assumption that he is dreaming is eroded by a brief series of uncomfortable proofs, which convince him of the existence of the gods and of the reality of his new surroundings. He acquires the long-lost seventh sword of Chioxin, said to have been given to the Goddess ages ago, and an enigmatic mission that is presented in the form of a riddle. He sets out to fulfill this quest without even understanding it, working on faith that the riddle will be solved over time. In *The Reluctant Swordsman* Wallie assembles his fellowship of the ring: seven companions, all of whom have roles to play in the fulfillment of the Goddess's quest. Wallie fulfills several of the initial requirements of his destiny, apparently quite accidentally. He is a characteristic Duncan hero: compassionate, intelligent, skilled, alienated—in this case, even divided—and a bit inept. A great deal of the entertainment value of the novel springs from its depiction of Wallie's alien perspectives on the events and customs of the World.

Book 2 in the series, *The Coming of Wisdom,* develops an antagonism between swordsmen and sorcerers that is hinted at in the first book. Wallie and his companions travel throughout the novel, mainly on the mystical River, and have several encounters during which they gradually learn more about the organization and purposes of the sorcerers. The different companions take on clearer characteristics of their own, particularly two swordsmen apprentices, brothers Nnanji and Katanji, who appear to play central roles in the Goddess's prophecy as well. Wallie commits himself to taking back the river cities that the sorcerers have occupied. He is increasingly distressed by the way events seem to unfold inexorably to fit the Goddess's riddle, and uncertain about his degree of responsibility for the ensuing bloodshed. By the end of the novel, the next step in the quest remains unclear, though the swordsmen are massing against the sorcerers. Wallie has realized what no one else has, however, which is that the sorcerers are using technological skills to build up their power base, not magic.

The final book in the trilogy, *The Destiny of the Sword,* brings the Goddess's prophecy to fruition in an unexpected and satisfying way. Wallie manages, after many mishaps and adventures, to organize a treaty between the swordsmen and the sorcerers, and then ultimately realizes that he is meant to turn over the power he has accumulated to his bloodthirsty former apprentice Nnanji. The Age of Legends has ended, and Nnanji is to be the ruler of a great Dark Age empire. Wallie's role has been to educate and prepare Nnanji for his destiny, not to assume the leading role himself. Wallie's complicated feelings about the transfer of power make the ending of the series especially effective, as he makes a series of difficult choices.

The Seventh Sword is a consistently entertaining trilogy, clearly imagined and lighthearted in tone. When in the final chapter a demigod congratulates Wallie for teaching compassion to Nnanji, Wallie retorts: "Compassion? He would kill a man as soon as eat a peanut," a remark that displays both his continual alienation from the customs of the World and his apt and amusing assessment of Nnanji's characteristics. The series has a playful feel, and though it is not the most politically or emotionally intricate Duncan series, it is a solid fantasy-adventure trilogy that displays a high quality of writing and a care for detail. Female characters fare relatively poorly in *The Seventh Sword,* being flat and rather dull, but this series marks the first sustained development of the Duncan style of heroism, which is later further explored in characters such as Rap in the two Pandemia series and Edward Exeter in *The Great Game.*

Strings and *West of January* were both released in 1989 and also feature unprepared, alienated, and resilient protagonists. *Strings* introduces a young, uneducated boy named Cedric into the political and technological war zone that is his grandmother's company, 4-I. Cedric was raised in Meadowdale, an organage—basically an organ farm where the young clones of rich folks lead healthy lives until they are summoned to be dissected. Cedric believes himself to be a clone for much of the book, but in fact he is not. His grandmother, Agnes, is the most hated woman in the world; she is a manipulative woman with an unexpected social vision that unfolds gradually throughout the text. Her company explores new worlds found on "strings," a process described using terms from superstring theory.

Most of them are uninhabitable, however, and the same rich folks who are so unwilling to age and die have the strongest interest in controlling the colonization process. Agnes, Cedric, and the psychic Princess Alya of Banzarak perform a series of complicated maneuvers that aim for both the exposure of the organage business and the establishment of diverse human populations on new, safe worlds.

Strings makes some strong plays on the language of superstring theory and gives an impression of being fast-paced and high-tech: it is full of intrigue, news coverage, and computers. While it is definitely science fiction, it has some of the characteristics of a detective novel, down to the murder mystery, though Cedric is not a hardboiled character by any means. There is a strong emphasis on environmental issues, and the novel is set in a bleak, urban wasteland that readers are clearly meant to recognize as their possible or even probable future habitat. Alya's gift is explained as a highly developed instinct for self-preservation—a sort of mutation—rather than something mystical. The peculiarities of Alya's skills make for interesting reading, as do Agnes's complex machinations and Cedric's learning experiences, but the characters themselves are not especially sympathetic. Agnes's and Alya's calculations amuse but do not attract—nor are they intended to—and Cedric is a bit of a blank slate even at the end of the novel.

Alya and Cedric have a romance that is remarkable for its coldheartedness. Alya's instinct for self-preservation fixes on Cedric as an ideal mate, and she secures him as such, quite impersonally. Cedric is thus buffeted about by the agendas of two women, and he is a weaker character as a result of a sense that he has more resilience than initiative. This impression is exactly what is said about him in the novel, however: that he is intelligent, social, unambitious, nonaggressive, and tenacious. As Agnes says, "he hangs on." At the end of the novel Cedric does achieve separation from his grandmother and her agendas, though he remains subject to Alya's. It seems from the final comments in the book that Cedric will achieve leadership despite his lack of ambition.

West of January takes the theme of the leader-in-spite-of-himself to new heights in the character of Knobil, who makes a massive leap from herdsman to god on a world called Vernier. This world has an enormously long climactic cycle—a "day" in Vernier lasts for two hundred terrestrial years, and it takes three men's lives from end to end before High Summer returns to the same spot. Knobil's adventures cover an enormous range, and he is mainly educated through adversity. He starts out as the one blond son in a family of dark-haired herdsmen and is thrust abruptly into the

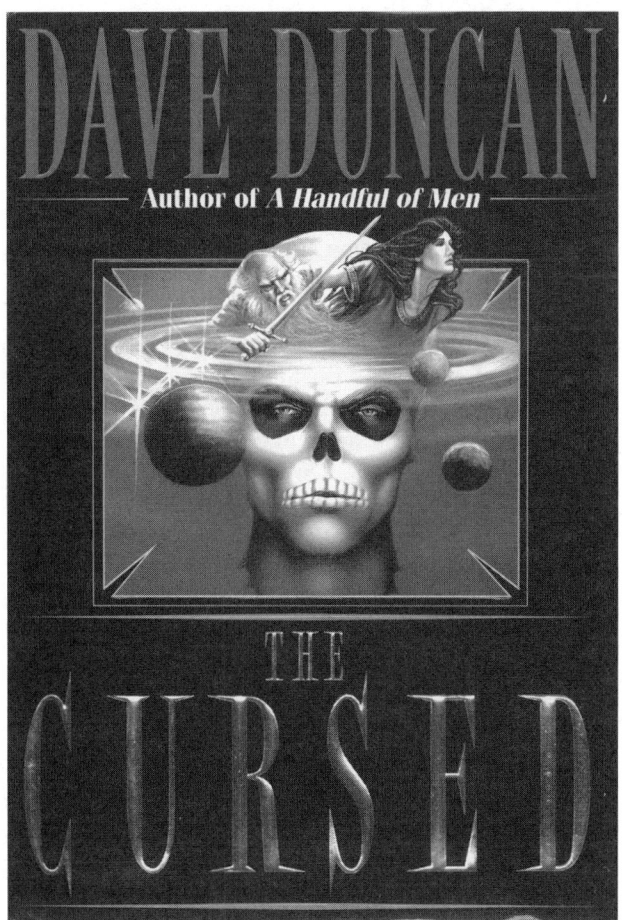

Dust jacket for Duncan's 1995 novel, in which the survivors of an epidemic of "star sickness" are left with supernormal powers that are an affliction rather than a boon

outside world when the man he believes to be his father is killed. Enigmatic human Angels travel across the land, warning of disasters to come, but the isolated peoples of Vernier pay no heed and go their separate ways. Knobil has opportunity to meet, and often to live with, representatives of almost all of the peoples of Vernier—herdfolk, seafolk, traders, miners, and so on—and to see how they react to the intervention of the Angels. His position is usually a weak and abject one. His decisions spring from necessity, and his wisdom comes from comparative and unpleasant experience. Over the course of the novel he is everything from unwilling leader to slave; he is beaten, crippled, drugged with an irreversible love potion, and even fed to worms.

As he travels, Knobil gradually accumulates a great deal of practical and theoretical savvy, as well as more knowledge about the Angels and their dwelling place, called Heaven. He eventually reaches Heaven, which contains the remnants of a planetary governing body and a Great Compact agreed on by all the first-folk, or the original settlers of Vernier. Knobil learns much about his own origins and about politics during his stay with the Angels, but when the time comes to join them, he decides instead to return to the grasslands and pursue an entirely different path, at once vengeful and visionary. He manages to unite the dispersed and isolationist herdfolk and becomes a world leader, and then a cult figure. He organizes military activities on a scale never before seen on his world, partly as vengeance for past wrongs in his own life, and partly to correct global political inadequacies of the most profound sort. *West of January* explores a possible dynamic of cultural isolationism and fragmentation, a state of simultaneous loss of unity and development of individualism on a planetary scale. In addition to being meticulously imagined, it is also politically interesting; it is an extended meditation on the idea of a colonial project that has lost all contact, over a long period of time, with the colonizing body. In 1990 Duncan won a Canadian Science Fiction and Fantasy Award from the Canadian Science Fiction and Fantasy Association for *West of January*.

Politics are similarly central to two ensuing tetralogies about a world called Pandemia, in which cultural isolationism is matched by genetic diversity—no longer miners and seafolk playing at difference, but instead imps, jotunns, fauns, djinns, gnomes, goblins, pixies, and intervening gods struggling to coexist. The first series is called *A Man of His Word* and takes its titles from the seventh stanza of John Keats's *Ode to a Nightingale* (1819): these titles are *Magic Casement* (1990), *Faery Lands Forlorn* (1991), *Perilous Seas* (1991), and *Emperor and Clown* (1992), all surprisingly apt to their subject matter. The "man of his word" is Rap, who represents a further development of the type of Duncan hero first embodied in Wallie Smith in *The Seventh Sword*. Rap is less witty and charming but even more innocent and bumbling than Wallie; while Wallie hitches up with his beautiful slave girl on his first night in the World, Rap's love for Inos—first princess and later queen of a small, strategically important, cold kingdom named Krasnegar—goes unconsummated until the end of the fourth novel while nevertheless providing thematic energy for the whole series. The first series mainly presents two stories in parallel, those of Rap and Inos, who mature and grow closer while spending most of their time apart.

In *Magic Casement* it becomes clear that Inos is heir to a small kingdom but large problems. The gods have an interest in her, and her right to rule is disputed by several powerful factions. Upon her father's death her kingdom is almost immediately overrun by foreign powers, and she has to flee through a magic casement—which displays several visual prophecies—into parts unknown. Rap, a loyal stable boy with odd gifts, leaps through afterward; the first book ends with this leap of faith. Book 2 reveals that Inos and Rap have ended up on opposite ends of the world, respectively in the land of the djinns and in Faerie, facing separate dangers. Throughout the novel the two of them become increasingly involved in a series of global political tangles and magical agendas. Rap is determined to reach Inos wherever she is, but Inos thinks that he is dead. The book ends without bringing them closer together, and Inos discards the one warning Rap manages to send.

Perilous Seas takes up the threads of their separate journeys as Inos and Rap travel furiously from place to place. Inos has come to interpret a divine warning to "trust in love" as applying to the sultan Azak, a djinn, and she agrees to marry him. After heroic efforts, Rap finally arrives in time to see Inos married to this despotic ruler, and then Rap is dragged off to be tortured to death. *Emperor and Clown* takes up this depressing situation. Inos's aunt helps Rap to escape from prison, and he recovers from terrible injuries. Meanwhile Inos's domestic situation continues to deteriorate; unable to consummate the marriage because of a curse, Azak becomes increasingly harsh and bitter. Once again Inos thinks Rap is dead. Rap has been accumulating magical abilities up to this point, and now becomes a much more significant player in the magical intrigues afoot. He finally achieves the highest possible level of magic and becomes a sorcerer, which attracts even more unwelcome attention from the ruling warlocks, all sorcerers as well. Events come to a head in the capital of the Impire, called Hub. Inos and Rap are finally in the same place at the same time. Rap defeats his main warlock enemy, Zinixo. Inos literally leaps into the fire to save Rap from a magical overload in an unprecedented way, and her unconsummated marriage to Azak is annulled according to the customs of the Impire, much to Azak's rage. This turn does not solve all problems, however. Rap and Inos are not able to marry until the problem of the magical overload is solved in a more permanent way. They finally figure out a solution, and Rap completes his transformation from stable boy to king.

Pandemia has clear and distinctive characteristics, among them the way in which magic is defined, using an idea of "words of power" that awaken and produce magical skills, and that can be accumulated and passed on, with some constraints. The different races are carefully delineated, sometimes in innovative ways (as when the inhabitants of Faerie are found to be born with the words of power that everyone else covets), as well as in the now-traditional manners (as when elves and dwarves fail to get along). Rap and Inos seem to be largely racially unaffiliated, both being products of mixed-race pairings—which have produced suspiciously human results—and they appear to look at the racial dynamics of others from a removed perspective. This view is a new twist on the cultural alienation evident in other Duncan protagonists. Inos is not a strongly textured character in this first series, and Rap comes into himself only slowly; but their romance is engaging, and the complexities of the plot are well handled. As in *A Rose-Red City,* Duncan splits his narrative more or less equally between two people on two different trajectories, one of them a female lead, and Rap fares better than Inos partly because he has more literary predecessors. *A Man of His Word* is, however, a strong and engaging series on the whole. There is a considerable wealth of imaginative detail, and the end of *Emperor and Clown* is satisfyingly plotted.

Coincident with the publication of the first Pandemia series, one stand-alone science-fiction novel, *Hero!,* came out in 1991. *Hero!* introduces Vaun, a Space Patrol officer who once became a "hero" to humans by defeating an attack by an organization called the Brotherhood, and now is called upon to do so again. The catch is that Vaun himself is a Brother, an example of *Homo factus,* an engineered improvement on *Homo sapiens*—in short, a superman. The Brotherhood is made up of genetically identical, cooperative male beings with twelve chromosomes instead of forty-six, who plant their offspring in human women in a colonizing effort. Brothers do not regard humans as people, and humans do not regard Brothers as people, a dynamic with clear didactic implications. In *Hero!* Duncan revisits the idea of the Creation turning on the Creator and focuses a lot of energy on the willful blindness of racist discourses. Vaun, caught between two conflicting sets of imperatives, looks at the arguments of both sides with a persistent skepticism and bitterness. He is not trusted by the humans but is uncomfortable with the Brothers' insistence on genetic destiny. He is unable to integrate fully into either community, and he remains an alien in both. When it comes time to make a final decision about his divided loyalties, he finds it virtually impossible to do so, since he is in the unusual position of regarding both sides as "people." He deliberately chooses the losing side, knowing that the fight will go on without him. In that moment he appears to transcend the shallower public heroism of his earlier life and achieve a state of moral resolution.

Hero! ends with the observation that the struggle between the races will go on forever. The novel is rather choppy but has many separate engaging elements, such as the aliens called "pepods," Vaun's search for acceptance, and his tormented love life. The Brotherhood is conceptually interesting but not highly convincing as a Master Race. They are meant to be frightening in their sameness and their inexorability, as many such paradigms of loss of individuality are. Vaun makes the rather obvious accusation that genetic perfection is stagnation, but the Brothers appear destined to win the genetic war in the longer run despite this hole in their logic of survival of the fittest. The Brothers represent a collective mind of a kind frequently found in science-fiction and fantasy, from the buggers in Orson Scott Card's *Ender's Game* (1985) to the Borg in *Star Trek: The Next Generation.* Vaun is an interesting choice to pit against this many-mind, as his affiliations are muddied and compromised; his opposition is a tormented one, and thus more interesting than a standard us-against-them dynamic.

The second Pandemia tetralogy, *A Handful of Men,* came out between 1992 and 1994. The guiding quotation is a verse from John Masefield's "Tomorrow" (1902), from which the book titles are taken: *The Cutting Edge* (1992), *Upland Outlaws* (1993), *The Stricken Field* (1993), and *The Living God* (1994), again, all surprisingly apt for their subject matter. This series takes up some threads from *A Man of His Word* fifteen years later. It is possible to read the two series independently, but more rewarding to read the second after the first, as it develops a sense that Rap's confrontations with the warlocks and the gods in the first series have had unforeseen and negative consequences. The millennial anxiety of the series is timely, and there are many new and engaging characters, among them the children of Rap and Inos and a range of imperial figures who have problems of their own. The character of Ylo, aide to the new imperor, Shandie, is particularly striking; he becomes great without ever recognizing or admitting it and has a fascinating connection with the imperor's wife. *A Handful of Men* is one of the few fantasy series in which a deus-ex-machina ending is not a disappointment.

The Cutting Edge sets a tone of foreboding and anxiety that endures throughout the tetralogy. The peaceful quotidian life of Krasnegar is disrupted by bleak prophecies, and the Impire as a whole is threatened at all borders. Azak, Inos's spurned former husband, is pursuing a vendetta against the Impire to salve his wounded pride, while Zinixo, Rap's old warlock enemy, has risen up again in wrath and is recruiting. Inos and Rap learn that their past actions in defusing a magical crisis have made it more likely that the millennium will bring total destruction rather than mere disorder. A god tells Rap and Inos that they will lose one of their four children—Kadie, Gath, Eva, and Holindarn—but not which one, and this threat hangs over the entire series. Rap is a much weaker sorcerer than he was, but he still answers the call to leave Krasnegar and fight the good fight. The old imperor dies at the end of the novel, and the new one, Shandie, is immediately cast into exile. This book leaves the impression that all of Rap's good intentions from the first series seem to have backfired and created hideous dilemmas in this next generation. The Protocol, an ages-old agreement controlling the activities of sorcerers, is destroyed, and a free-for-all ensues.

Book 2 catalogues Zinixo's depredations. He has amassed an army of enslaved sorcerers called the Covin, an apparently unbeatable force that actively seeks out new members and forces them into obedience. The magical resources of Pandemia are severely depleted by this activity. Rap's family is scattered across the globe, and the Impire is in chaos. The lost race of pixies resurfaces, and they appear poised to play an important role in the resolution of the prophecies made in the course of the first volume; one particular pixie, Thaile, evolves into a major character and goes through horrible rites of passage in preparation for her future. Like Rap in a previous generation, however, she is not so biddable as her superiors might want. Rap, Shandie, and a handful of men devise the idea of producing a new Protocol. Things continue to deteriorate across Pandemia throughout *Upland Outlaws,* and the novel ends with the new imperor about to be tortured to death by goblins.

The Stricken Field follows a wide range of characters during their separate tribulations: Ylo and the impress in exile; Rap hunting for aid in his quest to form a new Protocol and recruit free sorcerers; Shandie, Inos, Gath, and Kadie first among the goblins and then dispersed to follow separate paths; Thaile being groomed for a role she cannot understand; and Zinixo enthroned, disguised as the new imperor. The intrigue thickens, and loyalties are uncertain when affections can be extracted with sorcery. At the end of the novel it is still unclear what steps should be taken next to defeat the Covin, and it seems that resistance is hopeless, a feeling that is borne out in a large portion of *The Living God.* This final novel takes Zinixo right to the brink of total world domination, with only a few pockets of rebellion left. Everything goes wrong. Inos is captured by Azak, and the new Protocol remains a pipe dream. When it looks most as though Zinixo has triumphed over all opposition, Thaile and Kadie play an unexpected role in a sudden reversal of fortune, which both invokes and reverses the actions taken by Rap and Inos at the end of *A Man of His Word.* Clearly the organized obscurity of prophecy is a major theme in this series. One exchange that occurs during the education of Thaile is particularly telling. She exclaims: "I thought my return would be prophesied?" and is told, "Of course it is. So is your nonreturn." The ensuing discussion reveals a fragment of prophecy, masterfully dropped into the conversation, that she will save the College and destroy the College: a classic example of a seeming contradiction that only time can resolve.

The epilogue of *A Handful of Men* forecloses the possibility of continuation, at least with any of the characters that readers know. It is a fine exercise in understatement. People die in sentence fragments in much the same way that they die in brackets in Virginia Woolf novels. The Impire undergoes massive renovations, and Rap remains a well-meaning, self-effacing man of his word until the end; he is still the most influential character in the second series. On the whole the second Pandemia tetralogy is stronger and more assured than the first one. Rap and Inos have developed richer personalities, especially Inos, while characters such as Ylo, Shandie, Gath, Kadie, and Thaile give off strong signals of their own. In this series Duncan develops a remarkable ability to depict engaging secondary personae and plotlines.

The Reaver Road (1992) is a stand-alone novel told from the point of view of an itinerant tale-teller named Omar. It is a charming exercise based on ideas about oral tradition. Omar, called a Trader of Tales, strongly invokes ideas from Albert Bates Lord's *Singer of Tales* (1960) at many points. Omar's reliability as a narrator is questionable, a realization that must necessarily affect one's encounter with the text, in which the notions of artistic and "absolute" truth are examined and to some extent mocked. Omar's tale in this novel concerns his own brief experience as a god. The gods send him to observe the siege of a city that has never been defeated. The claim to fame of this city is the apparent intervention of a protective god in moments of danger. Omar learns that the city priests are planning to fake this moment of divine intervention, apparently in keeping with a more squalid and mundane tradition. Yet, it appears that the priests are foiled when an unexpectedly minor character becomes the embodiment of a god and saves the city. Omar is also taken for a god by the populace, by virtue of proximity, though the question of his actual origin and parentage is left shady enough that one cannot be sure that his resemblance to a particular statue in the temple is accidental; indeed, one cannot be sure of much of what he says.

The Hunters' Haunt, released in 1995, is another Omar novel, not in the least sequential but stylistically similar. Omar's tale is more intricate this time, and there is more trading of tales going on, as he is involved in a storytelling contest to save his life. During the course of a long evening of stories, a coherent picture of some past events emerges from an initial jumble of narratives. The novel is set in an inn, where Omar has been once before and is not welcome to revisit; his untimely return during a blizzard leads to a situation in which he must beat every guest's story to be allowed to stay in the inn during the storm. Organizationally the novel invokes Geoffrey Chaucer's *The Canterbury Tales* (circa 1375–1400), with a more hostile innkeeper. The innkeeper turns out to have a history that he himself is unaware of, however, and it slowly unfolds over the course of the evening, in a way that reinforces the impression that there are few coincidences around Omar.

The two Omar novels are entertaining and do not take themselves especially seriously. They are largely about the act of storytelling itself, not so much about their own individual plots; there is also a certain cult of personality revolving around the mysterious Omar, who is apparently immortal and certainly has closer connections with the gods than most people around him. The play on Homer is evident. Throughout the novel there are many extended passages and local observations about embellishment, editing, honesty, authorial license, technique, and oral cultural patterns. Each novel ends with a deliberate undermining of its own suspended disbelief, and a good laugh.

Another stand-alone novel, *The Cursed,* came out in 1995, this one featuring a female protagonist. In a world plagued with "star sickness," survivors are often worse off than the dead–they are Cursed with strange and uncontrollable abilities that alienate them from other humans, and so they are cast out to fend for themselves. The Curses include prophetic vision without the ability to speak about the future, ability to manipulate emotion without feeling any oneself, shape-shifting without volition, telepathy without constraints, and other less tangible alterations. There is a prophecy of a Renewer to come, who will unite the fragmented peoples of the world, including the Cursed, and bring about a second empire, just in time to deflect some barbarian hordes. A woman named Gwin becomes carried off on that wave of prophecy, but does not correctly understand her place in it as events unfold. When she is forced to close down her hotel after her family dies in the star sickness, she marries an older man, Bulion Tharn, in an attempt to start a new life. Her new life becomes instantly complicated when clues seem to indicate that Bulion Tharn is going to become the Renewer.

Over time, it emerges that Gwin, too, is Cursed, but the nature of her Curse remains impenetrable for a long period. Only toward the end of the novel does it emerge that Bulion is not the Renewer, and that Gwin's particular Curse gives her enormous power over other Cursed people. She becomes, rather unwillingly, a great manipulator and political leader. Though Bulion falls by the wayside, his son, also named Bulion Tharn, becomes the emperor, while Gwin is the Renewer who establishes an empire for him to inherit. Gwin occupies

Dust jacket for the first novel (1995) in Duncan's The Great Game *trilogy, in which characters move between back and forth between World War I and an alternate dimension in which they become immortal and acquire great powers*

a social space that by now is recognizable as characteristic in Duncan's work: she is an outsider looking inward, and perhaps backward over her shoulder as well. Her alienation from her own people is achieved long before she realizes she is Cursed, and it intensifies from that point, especially as her Curse is unusual even among the afflicted. She does not seem to have a complicated emotional profile, but that is not inconsistent with her position as a sort of vessel of destiny. She is strongly imagined, and her role as maker of history is convincingly developed. This book, like many Duncan novels, is invested in exploration of prophecy and its inner workings, especially in the figures of people cursed with incommunicable and problematic knowledge. Rather like the Merlins of other writers, they live backward through time. As the first Duncan heroine to be in the limelight for an entire novel, Gwin is a significant figure, and may be regarded as a sort of predecessor–in concept if not in particulars—of Briseis in *Daughter of Troy,* or of Malinda in *Sky of Swords* (2000).

Three Ken Hood fantasy-adventure novels, *The Years of Longdirk,* came out between 1995 and 1998: *Demon Sword* in 1995, *Demon Rider* in 1997, and *Demon Knight* in 1998. Duncan has not previously chosen to discuss this authorial alter ego. In tone the Ken Hood books are more swashbuckling, historically referential, and speedy than other Duncan novels, and are pleasingly zany. In a late-medieval Europe without discernible Catholicism but with the Inquisition and other such organizing bodies intact, cities are guarded by spirits called tutelaries, while demons roam free and other spirits such as hobs are generally lesser players. One Scottish hob becomes the exception to this rule when it moves into the body of Tobias Strangerson, otherwise known as Longdirk, in an unforeseen outcome of a magical experiment. Toby's possession is different from the possession enacted by a demon, since he retains his personality and eventually acquires some measure of control over the hob, but this fine distinction is not clear to everyone, particularly not the Inquisition.

Toby's hob wants to become a world traveler, and now has the means to do so, a process set in motion when Toby and his sidekick Hamish flee from Scotland hotly pursued by various enemies. *Demon Sword* sets up the uncomfortable situation in which Toby must endure throughout the series, and also establishes an opposition between Toby and the evil King Nevil, who is possessed by a demon and is appropriately called the Fiend. In this novel Toby learns a great deal about his spiritual parasite and its characteristics and learns how to function within his new and strange constraints; the hob is not evil, but is a troublemaker, often in unexpected ways, and must not be allowed to get too excited by external stimuli. Enforced celibacy is one important implication of this dynamic, as Toby learns through painful experience.

Demon Rider replaces the certainty that the hob will eventually take over Toby's entire consciousness with the idea that Toby and the hob may eventually merge into one being. Toby is hunting for exorcism if he can find it, but he gradually comes to realize that it would destroy his mind. There is a fascinating quirk to Duncan's exploration of prophecy in this series: the hob can jump backward in time when it is unhappy with a dangerous situation, and these backward leaps to second, third, or fourth chances leave residual impressions in Toby's mind, like dreams or memories—a theme that is developed throughout this text in particular. Toby and Hamish travel toward Barcelona and fall in with other travelers with peculiarities of their own. Toby becomes a sort of war leader for a small traveling band, and thus embarks on a long career of military organization and resistance to the forces of the Fiend—though he only realizes his trajectory in the last moments of the novel, when he formulates a plan to recruit an army for the defense of Italy, the next target of the Fiend's forces.

Demon Knight transforms Toby from strongman in a little ragged band to a brilliant tactician and successful rebel leader. He is so successful, in fact, that he must enchant himself in order to look unsuccessful for a while, in a complex scheme that almost backfires. Toby achieves some initial victories against the forces of the Fiend and then must increase his skills at politics. This novel explores his development as a political animal as well as a martial one. The rightful Queen of England crosses his path and must be figured into his newly politicized plans. At the end of the novel Toby wins a spectacular victory against Nevil's forces and acquires an enormous army. He becomes king of England in an odd ceremony in which he appears to marry the young Queen, but Hamish is the real bridegroom, because of Toby's enforced celibacy. It is clear at the conclusion of the novel that Toby is well on his way to becoming some kind of European ruler.

In some respects Toby is like a more troubled, and in the end more aggressive and manipulative, Wallie unleashed on the world; there is a sort of playfulness evident in both *The Seventh Sword* and *The Years of Longdirk,* but the Longdirk series is darker in tone. Toby takes up the challenge of empire that Wallie shuns. Toby is compared to figures such as El Cid and Charlemagne, in a conscious and cheeky invocation of paradigms from history and heroic literature. The end of *Demon Knight* does not conclude all or even most of the plotlines developed so far in the series. Most significantly, the chief opposition between the Fiend and Toby is intact. Other unresolved issues include the captured soul of the original king Nevil, Hamish's prediction that Toby will become king of Europe, and most tantalizingly, the total merger of hob and human—plus there is a lack of resolution in Toby's love life. Yet, Duncan is not currently working on further Ken Hood novels and has no plans to do so in the immediate future.

A trilogy called *The Great Game* was published during the same time period as the three *Demon* books: *Past Imperative* in 1995, *Present Tense* in 1996, and *Future Indefinite* in 1997. This series takes up a theme somewhat developed in the two Pandemia tetralogies: that the gods play intricate games with mortals and keep score among themselves. *The Great Game* moves back and forth between this world and a place called Nextdoor. People who visit Nextdoor become immortal there and can accumulate and work with something called *mana,* a kind of energy derived from other people, to which people from Home ("our" world, though set in the past) are more or less sensitive according to their degree of charisma. There are benign ways to acquire *mana*, through admiration or other positive emotions, and malignant ways involving fear and death. The powers conferred by *mana* are considerable and cumulative, so naturally tourists from Home can easily be taken for gods, and over time, become them. Nextdoor is involved in a religious and cultural crisis throughout the series, in tandem with the miserable events going on at Home, which is embroiled in World War I. The events of the trilogy hinge on a Nextdoor prophecy called the Filoby Testament, in which a figure known as the Liberator brings "death to Death."

A young man named Edward Exeter is the heroic, eventually messianic, figure of *The Great Game*. In *Past Imperative* (a play on the effects of prophetic speech) it becomes clear that many people who know more than Edward does about Nextdoor want to kill him. He develops a sense of self-preservation after being framed for murder and attacked several times. He takes up his dead father's affiliations with organizations called the Home Office and the Service, which are dreadfully colonial and well-intended affiliated organizations working at Home and in Nextdoor, respectively. In opposition are the Blighters and the Chamber, similarly affiliated organizations. The Blighters are responsible for World War I at Home, and the Home Office is in a much weakened position as a result. Edward wants to enlist in the war at Home but finds himself sucked into another one. He is stranded in Nextdoor by accident and starts to accumulate the *mana* and exposure necessary to prepare him to fulfill the prophecy in the Filoby Testament, without realizing what is happening. He is absent from England for three years, during which time he builds up a considerable power base Nextdoor. At the end of the novel he is seen leaving Nextdoor for England and is planning to enlist.

Present Tense takes up Edward's actual arrival, naked and babbling, in a trench at the battle of Third Ypres in 1917. Suspected of being a spy of some strange kind, he ends up incarcerated again, this time in a hospital. He is rescued by some old school friends, and more of his wide range of experiences in Nextdoor are recounted retrospectively. His friends become involved in the dispute as well, just as a whole cast of characters in Nextdoor are increasingly committed to the Liberator and his upcoming conflict with Zath, god of Death. At the end of this novel Edward and a group of friends are back in Nextdoor, where followers of Zath have been attacking the holdings and allies of the Service.

Future Indefinite moves Edward's conflict with Zath inexorably forward. The problem is that Edward's *mana* is not nearly sufficient for any confrontation with the ages-old god of Death, who is supported by the most potent forms of *mana* deriving from massive blood sacrifice. Zath has become the most powerful member of the Pentatheon, the ruling group of human gods—several of them renegade Service agents—who have been controlling Nextdoor for centuries. Edward becomes increasingly alienated by the behavior of the members of the Pentatheon and the warring human organizations, including the Service. The Service in turn is increasingly wary of his growing unorthodoxy and his opposition to their efforts to replace the Pentatheon with a more stable religion over which they have more control. Edward's final confrontation with Zath takes an interesting and, from the perspective of Nextdoor's inhabitants, shocking turn when Edward offers himself as the kind of blood sacrifice that will put his own *mana* to the best and most unexpected use. The symbiotic relationship between Home and Nextdoor is essential; Edward takes his willingness to sacrifice himself for a cause from his experiences in Flanders, watching a million men die for their beliefs. The ugliest self-sacrifice of the novel is made by an unsung hero, however: one of Edward's followers pays a terrible price to arrange for Edward's resurrection back Home while preserving his sacrifice Nextdoor. There is clearly something to be learned from the way this smaller character's actions are even more impressively selfless than those of supposedly greater souls.

The Great Game manages to balance multiple plots and counterplots: love stories, murder mysteries, simultaneous worlds and wars. There is a strong emphasis throughout the trilogy on the overtly colonial attitudes and actions of members of both the Service and the Chamber. The ugliest manifestations of this willingness to deceive and manipulate are obviously the false gods, but it takes many smaller forms, as when the Service members decide whom to kill or cure with their *mana*, or call their native servants "Carrots." Edward's turn away from loyalty to the Service is largely a product of his disillusionment with the Service's treatment of the inhabitants of Nextdoor. *The Great Game* is also critical of many aspects of organized religion, both overtly and by implication, for example in its employment of Christian mystic patterns in the Service's missionary efforts to replace the bad old gods.

In 1998 Avon Books released *Daughter of Troy,* an historical romance about the fall of Troy, under the name of Sarah B. Franklin. On his website Duncan says that the reason for the pseudonym was "because booksellers' computers become confused when a writer changes genres." *Daughter of Troy* is a lively retelling from the point of view of Briseis, Achilles's lover and former queen of Lyrnessos. This novel develops a growing tendency on Duncan's part to

Sky of Swords [Duncan] Background Information 1

	Summary	Menu
	The Trial, Day One	370.04
1.	Childhood on Ness Royal	
2.	Childhood at court	
3.	The Night of Dogs	368.01
4.	Loyal addresses; Cousin Courtney and Mr. Speaker	
5.	The King and Lord Granville	
	The Trial, Day One (continued)	
6.	Scandal with Eagle	368.03
7.	Aunt Agnes is summoned	
	The Trial, Day One (concluded)	
8.	Death of Agnes	368.04
9.	Malinda betrothed; wedding plans	368.10
10.	The wedding	369.03
11.	Malinda meets Radgar	
12.	The Blades rampage	
13.	Lord Roland takes command	
	The Trial, Day Two	
14.	Kromman talks of readings in the coach	
15.	Kromman is dead; the funeral; Roland and Courtney offer advice	
16.	The journey to Ironhall	
17.	Malinda recruits her Guard	
18.	The binding	
19.	Return to the capital, massacre in the market	
20.	Malinda's Guard settles in	
21.	The Lord Protector returns, Malinda spies on the Blades	369.04
22.	Granville threatens her	
23.	She seduces Dog	
24.	Complications of romance; second night with Dog	
25.	Interrogation, Durendal comes visiting	
26.	Journey to Ness Royal	
27.	Dog tells his story	369.04
28.	Malinda at Ness Royal	summer

Pages from what Duncan calls the "bible" for the third volume (2000) in his The King's Blades *trilogy. He uses such outlines to help him keep track of the plots of the works in his various series (Collection of Dave Duncan).*

Sky of Swords [Duncan] Background Information

Ironhall Menu

Grand Master admits, on average, one boy every two weeks, and the average stay is 5 years (roughly 14 to 19). If six per year drop out, leaving twenty, then there should be about 100 in-house at any given time. Note: If the Royal Guard averages 100 men and they serve on average 10 years, then the King must take half the graduates & assign the other half elsewhere. Second handles discipline; Prime is mother confessor among other things. A Blade thinks of his own sword as feminine.

Sopranos, beansprouts, beardless, fuzzies, seniors. Seniors bear swords.
Litany of Heroes, cat's-eye sword, the royal door,
Masters of: Rituals / Horse / Rapiers / Sabers / Archives /etc
Master Armorer

The *Hall* is Ironhall. The *hall* is where the residents eat. West House was burned in 356; GM's quarters and the flea room are in the oldest building, First House.

Fencing terminology

Ironhall technique requires knowledge of a large number of fancifully named positions, of which the following have been identified:

Attack: Cockroach, Swan, Violet, Steeple, Rainbow, Eagle
Defense: Lily, Willow, Butterfly,
Uncertain: Eggbeater, Stickleback

Night of Dogs

From *Sir Stalwart:* (Eighthmoon, 368)
The Guard had 87 men at the start of the Night of Dogs (see *Gilded Chain*).

4 died then; 12 since; Durendal was retired. Leaves	70
ADD 6 month's output	10
ADD abnormal one-year overdraft	20
TOTAL in summer of 368	100+/-

Miscellaneous

experiment with work in other genres—such as historical romance, historical fantasy, and juvenile literature. It may be possible to trace some seeds of Duncan's exploration of the character of Achilles in *Daughter of Troy* back to the character named Killer in *A Rose-Red City*. The book has not done particularly well, however, and Duncan admits responses to it have been "disappointing," adding in June 1999 that he has "no plans to write any more historicals." However, HarperCollins (successor to Avon Books) plans to bring out a mass-market edition of *Daughters of Troy* in the spring of 2002, so it may find new life.

The Gilded Chain, the first book in a fantasy trilogy titled *The King's Blades,* was released in November 1998, followed by *Lord of the Fire Lands* in October 1999 and *Sky of Swords* in October 2000. The series revolves around Ironhall, the five-year training school for the swordsmen of Ambrose, king of Chivial. His Blades are said to be the best swordsmen in the world. They are bound to loyalty and service in a ritual that involves a swordthrust to the heart, so their loyalty has an interesting artificial quality. A Blade is instantly and permanently bound to protect the person who strikes him through the heart. This person becomes the Blade's Ward, to be guarded at all times and defended to the death, regardless of his or her personal qualities or of the preferences or private sentiments of the Blade. Only the person who performs the binding can release the Blade (unless, as in *Lord of the Fire Lands,* a Blade is transformed into a firedrake), and older Blades are generally released once they are past their prime as swordsmen. The ritual binding of a Blade imparts not merely fanatical loyalty but also extra abilities: Blades are able to make do with almost no sleep, are largely without fear for their personal safety, are unable to get drunk or to deliberately ignore the welfare of their Wards, and are also endowed with impressive sexual prowess. The bond between Blade and Ward is strong enough that Blades often become dangerously unstable and/or go berserk if the Ward dies. This series does have interesting things to say about the strengths and weaknesses of a system that manufactures loyalty.

The three books of the *King's Blades* series each tell basically the same story from different perspectives. First there is the account of Sir Durendal—one of the most famous of the Blades—in *The Gilded Chain,* which offers a perspective internal to the government of Chivial. *Lord of the Fire Lands* presents the story of Radgar Æleding, who becomes king of the Baels, the chief enemies of Chivial. *Sky of Swords* is told from the perspective of Ambrose's daughter, Malinda. These novels cover the same span of time and have many common elements and characters, including Durendal, Ambrose, Radgar, and Malinda; however, the actual events of the three novels are not the same. Time itself is altered across these books, so that the events of the first and second novels are irreconcilably different, and the confusion is only resolved by a sudden shift at the end of the third novel. *Sky of Swords* is particularly well crafted, with a strong female lead, and the series as a whole is extremely solid. The shifts of perspective are smooth; the story-lines are plotted with care; and Duncan has created several interesting new professions: not just the Blades but also the Inquisitors (who can tell if people are lying) and the White Sisters (who can detect magic).

The Gilded Chain tells the life story of Durendal, a Blade who becomes King Ambrose's chancellor and a major player in contemporary politics—one who ultimately murders the king, but for a good purpose. Durendal's life trajectory is a striking one; he is not bound first to the king but to an utter loser, and the events that lead him to fame and fortune are circuitous. His initial bond to an insignificant courtier leads him into treachery and madness. When the king offers him a chance at a second binding and thus a second life, Durendal offers a comment germane to the whole series: "Binding is evil. It steals a man's soul." While the Blades are in many respects the heroes (if not always the central focus) of all three books—particularly the final book, *Sky of Swords*—they are a morally ambivalent group. In any case, the second binding ritual is successful, and Durendal's rise at court begins. He has one side-trip of particular significance, however. Together with an unpleasant and slimy Inquisitor named Kromman (a villain in all three books), Durendal travels to Samarinda at the king's orders, hoping to find the philosopher's stone. Instead he encounters a group of people who manage to live forever–in a rather grotesque manner that incidentally produces a lot of gold. These people are cannibals; by eating human flesh they rejuvenate themselves, but they must do so every day. The bones of the dead are then turned to gold. Back at court, only Kromman, Durendal, and Ambrose know of this mode of prolonging life, and for many years the matter is left alone. The king's final illness, however, leads him into temptation, and Durendal, long since released from his binding, can decide for himself about the nature of his loyalty.

Lord of the Fire Lands tracks Ambrose's life to a rather different ending: in this novel Ambrose is killed by Radgar Æleding, king of the Baels and a former student at Ironhall. Radgar's life story, like Durendal's, is full of retrospective revelations and odd quirks of fate. Radgar is raised in Chivial and trained at Ironhall despite the fact that he is the son of the late king of Baelmark–or rather, because of that fact, since he is taken to Chivial at the time of his father's murder and does not return to his homeland until he is an adult. Radgar's homeland is a peculiar place, full of what seem to be Viking raiders who nevertheless speak Old English—a land of firedrakes and necromancy, of soulless thralls and stolen brides. Among the various retrospective revelations of this novel is Chivial's extensive involvement in the murder of Radgar's father (connected, via devious routes, to anger about a bride stolen from Chivial–Radgar's mother), even though the coup is carried out by Radgar's uncle, Cynewulf (who enchants and marries Radgar's mother). Radgar becomes king of Baelmark, and declares war on Chivial–particularly on Ambrose for his past interventions in Baelish politics; the Baels harry the coastlines of Chivial for years and cause tremendous damage. Eventually the possibility arises that the war may be ended through a treaty marriage between Radgar and Ambrose's daughter, Malinda—but Radgar (in a rather unconvincing manner, considering he runs a brisk slave trade) needs to be persuaded that Malinda is a willing participant, as he apparently has personal issues about stolen brides. The decision hangs in the balance until the last scenes of the novel, but when Malinda is not sufficiently convincing, Radgar chooses the attractions of blood feud over those of matrimony.

Sky of Swords is Malinda's story, once again characterized by juxtaposition of past and present scenes. Malinda's early childhood is spent in exile from Ambrose's court with her mother, Queen Godeleva, who kills herself when told that she is being replaced by a new queen. Malinda makes her entrance at court at the age of nine—she is technically the heir to the kingdom, though ruling queens are not welcome in Chivial, and Ambrose keeps trying for a son—and, of course, there are various lurking bastards and other male relatives in the wings. Malinda's position is an awkward one, and she must struggle to make a place for herself and to establish a power base. Her adventures at court occupy the early portion of the novel; then, after Radgar's assassination of her father, Malinda really comes into her own, first as regent for a sickly baby brother and then as queen of a land torn apart by civil war and treachery. Her position becomes increasingly untenable, and during this long phase of struggle and discord, when all her remaining family turns against her, several Blades emerge as particular heroes of the novel—most notably the members of Malinda's personal guard: Audley, Dog, and Abel. Dog, an emotionally disturbed man who is also Malinda's lover, is an especially striking character; his obsession with using magic to go back in time and prevent his own birth provides the inspiration for the final events of the novel. Dog dies rescuing Malinda from captivity, but she adapts his time-altering plan to her own ends, and with the help of several Blades, manages to alter the course of history—this time around, she is sufficiently convincing as a prospective life-partner, and Radgar chooses marriage over blood-feud. Thus most of the events of the novel are retroactively disabled, and reality falls back into step with *The Gilded Chain*.

A second series, called *The King's Daggers,* also features Ironhall and is intended for younger readers. It includes *Sir Stalwart,* released as an Avon Camelot paperback original in November 1999; *The Crooked House,* which appeared in October 2000; and *Silvercloak,* released in October 2001. These are charming books, full of foiled assassination attempts, disguises, and frustrated adolescent dreams of fame at court.

The phrase "the King's Daggers" is Ambrose's joking description of two young persons who work undercover for him, investigating assassination attempts and illicit uses of sorcery: Stalwart, called Wart, a young man trained at Ironhall but employed by the government as an undercover agent and spy rather than a bound Blade; and Emerald, a young White Sister similarly employed. Wart is too young to shave, and though he is a skilled fighter, he is still able to take advantage of his extremely youthful appearance; Emerald, who like all White Sisters is able to detect magic, is also young enough to pass as a boy in the third novel of the series. The books of this series are set during the Monster Wars, a period discussed in all three of the books in the *King's Blades* series, during which the government is at odds with the elementaries (places of sorcery). During these wars, illicit uses of sorcery are constantly under investigation, and many attempts are made to assassinate King Ambrose (often involving monsters).

In *Sir Stalwart* both Wart and Emerald are publicly dismissed from their respective posts and sent off in disgrace, since disgrace provides excellent cover for secret missions. Wart and Emerald expose a nest of traitors and sorcerers in a place called Quagmarsh; these sorcerers, led by the evil Skuldigger, have been turning people into monsters and capturing White Sisters to take advantage of their skills of magic-detection. Skuldigger and his cronies plan to kill Ambrose and replace him with a regency council more friendly to the elementaries, but Wart and Emerald thwart these plans by making good use of their youth, their skills, and their assets (including barrels of garlic and a sword hidden in a lute). Further murderous plots are foiled in *The Crooked House,* where Wart and Emerald team up once again. This time the danger is doubled: one plot involves magic of a type that makes it possible to strike from a distance, and thus potentially to kill the king wherever he is; and another plot involves treachery at Ironhall–there is a student willing to die after killing King Ambrose during the ceremony of binding. This student is Wart's friend Badger, and Wart and Emerald must race against time to expose the links between the two plots, to learn something of the reasons behind them—and to thwart them both. *Silvercloak* tracks yet another murder attempt, this time an outside, professional job: a well-known assassin known as Silvercloak has been hired to kill the king and seems well able to elude all the king's finest. Silvercloak has never failed to bring down a target, and Wart and Emerald must track him—to Ironhall. Emerald goes undercover as a boy while Wart runs into some difficulties with his undercover identity, as some of his former companions from Ironhall refuse to believe that he now works for the king. But the two Daggers triumph over adversity. Silvercloak's secret is exposed, and Wart defeats him (by throwing himself off a cliff). Wart and Emerald now seem poised to enter into adult roles at court, and the king promises that he will make no more jokes about Daggers versus Blades.

The *King's Blades* series in particular has done well in the marketplace—better than *The Great Game,* probably because it effectively incorporates Wallie-like charms into darker story-lines. The series has both the cheerful appeal of Duncan's early sword-and-sorcerer books and the more textured narrative style of his later series—especially noticeable are the polished shifts in voice and the development of different timelines. The three books of the *King's Blades* deliberately tweak the reader's desire for a stable universe, not merely in the alterations of time itself but in scenes in which the same events are interpreted from many points of view (and left to the reader to sort out). In characters such as Durendal and Radgar, the Duncan hero has become more nuanced, more divided, rather less virtuous and Rap-like. Malinda is also Duncan's most compelling female lead to date, especially before she marries Radgar. The *King's Daggers* is well-positioned to attract younger readers, and more books about the Blades are planned. It should also be noted that some of Duncan's out-of-print books, such as *A Rose-Red City, Shadow, The Reaver Road,* and *The Hunters' Haunt,* have been made available in electronic format.

Duncan's writing style is clearly still evolving, and each new series showcases new developments. His explorations of the nature of heroism, the concept of prophecy, and the perspective of the outsider pervade but do not dominate his work. His willingness to imagine new situations and worlds—new diseases, loyalties, religions, forms of magic—is impressive; he is one of a relatively small number of fantasy and science-fiction novelists who have realized that the potential rewards of imaginative work are greater than the risks.

Interview:

Edo van Belkom, "Dave Duncan," in his *Northern Dreamers: Interviews with Famous Science Fiction, Fantasy, and Horror Writers* (Kingston, Ontario: Quarry Press, 1998), pp. 62–71.

Leslie Gadallah
(8 October 1939 -)

Beverley Curran
Aichi Shukutoku University

BOOKS: *Cat's Pawn* (New York: Ballantine, 1987);
The Loremasters (New York: Ballantine, 1988);
Cat's Gambit (New York: Ballantine, 1990).

OTHER: "Hanging Out in the Third World Laundromat," in *Tesseracts³*, edited by Gerry Truscott and Candas Jane Dorsey (Victoria, British Columbia: Tesseract, 1990), pp. 166–182.

SELECTED PERIODICAL PUBLICATIONS–UNCOLLECTED:

FICTION
"The Fairy Ring," *On Spec,* 1 (Fall 1989): 15–25;
"The Butterfly Effect," *On Spec,* 3 (Spring 1991): 51–64;
"The Wasp's Nest," *Senary–The Journal of Fantastic Literature* (1992): 71–78;
"Motherlove," *On Spec,* 5 (Fall 1993): 6–13;
"Dog Days," *On Spec,* 8 (Summer 1996): 76–86.

NONFICTION
"On Hard SF," *On Spec,* (Spring 1994).

Leslie Gadallah's work first appeared on science-fiction bookshelves in the late 1980s, when Canadian science-fiction writers were just beginning to make their presence known both in Canada and in the all-important American market. After a brief flurry of activity that produced three novels and some short fiction, Gadallah's creative output slowed, leaving her readers to hope that she will one day resume her promising career.

Gadallah was born Leslie Anne Payne on 8 October 1939 in a small town in southeastern Alberta. She was raised by Sydney Payne–a close relative of Gadallah's biological mother, Anna MacLauren–and his wife, Anne. Sydney and Anne Payne had two other children, William and Sharon. She attended the University of Alberta in Edmonton, receiving a bachelor of science degree in chemistry in 1960. She worked as a chemist and then as a technical editor for the Alberta Research Council, writing extensively on popular science for newspaper and radio, before (as the brief biographical notes at the back of her novels state) "abandoning the practice of science for the opportunity to write about it." Her first novel appeared in 1987, and her short fiction was published in the Edmonton-based speculative fiction magazine *On Spec* through 1996. She also served on the editorial advisory board of *On Spec* from 1989 to 1993. She lived with her husband, Fahmi, her son, daughter, and four cats on a farm in Spruce Grove, Alberta, where she worked for a family-owned research and development company in the food sciences. In 1997 she moved to Calgary, where she devotes some of her time to the study of Scots Gaelic.

Much of the appeal of Gadallah's writing is derived from her willingness to mix genres, blurring the borders of her science fiction. In her second novel, *The Loremasters* (1988), she juxtaposes past and future human history in a story where the technophobic and the technologically sophisticated form separate societies, alien to each other, and oral storytelling and speculative fiction mix in the clash of religion and technology. In her 1990 short story "Hanging Out in the Third World Laundromat" Gadallah shifts the site of the story from the mundane reality of a late-night laundromat to the landscapes of the knightly tale, the Western story, and science fiction. Her technique also reveals an interest in the endurance of story. Gadallah uses a journal as the narrative frame in her first novel; spins the narrative of *The Loremasters* into the Legend of Sarah, an oral storyteller's tale; and in the epilogue to her third novel turns the account of the heroine's quest into a bedtime story.

In all of her novels Gadallah shows her concern for the depletion of natural resources, speculating about how precious such vital commodities as water and energy will become as shortages grow more frequent as a consequence of human myopia. In her guest editorial, "On Hard SF," in the Spring 1994 issue of *On Spec,* Gadallah considers the shortsightedness that prevents humans from looking far enough into the future to ponder the significant changes that might occur as a result of modest technological inventions: "Who knew the spray can would destroy the ozone layer?" The "economics of scarcity" motivate current scientific developments, but

Cover for Leslie Gadallah's first novel (1987), set in a world populated by humans, the feline Orioni, and the insectlike Kazi

Gadallah wonders if long-term planning might also allow "something like cold fusion (or even the hot kind) . . . to become reality, giving everyone all the energy they wanted, not just in North America where that is already almost true, but also in the Delhi slums and rural Thailand, the economics of scarcity would be instantly obsolete."

In that same editorial Gadallah also states that "Being able to talk to one another is one of the most important characteristics of human society." Gadallah is extremely conscious of language and the necessity of multilingual communication in an expanded universe. The hero of her first novel, *Cat's Pawn* (1987), is a translator; in her second, accents betray the foreigner in a xenophobic society; and in her third novel, *Cat's Gambit* (1990), the ability to communicate through a range of modes, including nonaudio and mind manipulation, are examined. In her speculative fiction Gadallah retains the characteristics of Canadian speech, marking the speech of her Terran (human) characters with the occasional Canadian "eh." Her interest in multilingual and multicultural societies may mark her as a Canadian writer. Nonnative speaker error is used as a source of humor, particularly in *Cat's Gambit,* and indeed a sense of humor, especially in times of stress, is seen as peculiar to the human character.

Gadallah's writing also indicates a fascination with the cultural rites of reproduction. She believes that biological engineering, "especially genetic engineering, probably has more potential to change our immediate surroundings that anything we've done so far. . . . We are also learning to read our own genetic code, and face the possibility, and therefore the responsibility, of being able to tweak and fiddle with human heredity." In her first and third novels, the issue of reproduction is at the heart of each story, respectively, of the "egg-eating" Orioni identity and the weakening of the Kazi empire accomplished through the killing of the Broodmother, the breeding matriarch. Gadallah's imaginative universe is diverse. There are the humans, or Terrans, the Orioni, the Ledovic, the Kazi, the Roothians, Sgats, and the Rayori all rubbing "shoulders or the equivalent," as she writes in *Cat's Pawn,* in the scramble of intergalactic trade and the struggle for power. Physical appearance and modes of communication and breeding habits identify the major groups.

While Gadallah's imaginative speculations are far-reaching, and she playfully bends genres, gender roles remain predictable in her writing. Gadallah shows a fondness for the outlaw, an "irrational" loner whose motives cannot be understood by the mere use of logic. Modeled on Robin Hood (explicitly so in *Cat's Gambit*), her typical hero is a disillusioned middle-aged male who resents his father and is unwilling to become emotionally involved in a relationship. He is attracted to tough, sexy, manipulative women, but the mother of his child, who insures future progeny, is a "bovine" woman of little emotional consequence. In later works, such as her 1993 short story "Motherlove," the "outlaw" is a woman, and there is a kind of protofeminist consciousness in her resistance to social pressure.

Gadallah's first novel, *Cat's Pawn,* is the story of the relationship between Bill Anderson, a young Terran translator and one of the first humans to live among the Orioni, and Talan, an Orioni diplomat, which develops initially through their mutual interest in the game of chess. The story of Anderson and Talan is framed by a prologue and an epilogue in which Melissa Larkin, Anderson's granddaughter, eager to marry, seeks evidence of her grandfather's health by requesting Orioni medical records from Talan years after Bill Anderson and Talan's encounter. She intends to present these as evidence to the Eugenics Council in order to get their approval to have children. Melissa brings a manuscript, a journal of her grandfather, from which she hopes a psychological profile can be assessed. As Talan reads the journal, however, he is fascinated by what unfolds on the pages and, although he needs to prepare for a delicate diplomatic encounter with Kazi, he is reluctant to stop reading.

The Orioni are a feline race, whose sophisticated morality and controlled, stoic minimalism are in striking contrast to the acquisitive Kazi, a powerful and repulsive insectlike race who are the Orioni's traditional enemies. Gadallah is thorough in her imaginative investigation of the Orioni as a culture that emphasizes "the pragmatic and the provable." Their brutal breeding customs—birthing mothers must kill all but the strongest of their newborn children—are deemed necessary in order to sustain the limited resources of the desert planet for future generations, but Anderson is deeply appalled as he finally understands the Kazi name for the Orioni: "eaters of eggs." Their instincts for preservation are based on cooperation, not domination. The Orioni language is logical and unemotional, lacking the concept of loneliness or the affectionate diminution of names. Their moral code renders them vegetarians, and they have no sense of property, using space when in need of it, without any desire to own. Communications technology (the Communications/Computer Net) that ties worlds together is their chief export.

As the story unfolds, it is evident that the detached pragmatism of the Orioni is preferable to the selfishness of the Terrans or the hegemonic instincts of the Kazi. Their understanding of politic behavior is profound, unlike the Terrans, whose view of politics is jaundiced by the presence of "too many rival factions each concerned about its own power." The politics of the Orioni seem preferable to the chaos and verbosity of those from Earth, "with its teeming billions." The epilogue of *Cat's Pawn* finds Anderson gone and Talan on Earth, alive and eager to return to his home, to a place "where noise was not so all-pervasive, in a city that did not stink, in a place where solitude was respected, in a society where lies were not necessary, at least not so much."

Gadallah's second novel, *The Loremasters,* is generally considered her weakest. Writing in the *Encyclopedia of Science Fiction* (1995), John Clute described it as less impressive than Gadallah's two other novels, and David Ketterer, in *Canadian Science Fiction and Fantasy* (1992), observed that *The Loremasters* is "poorly plotted." It speculates on a future cultural schism that divides the human population, with the "technophiles" (Philes) living in enclaves within the garrison, and "technophobes" (Phobes) living a medieval lifestyle beyond the walls, fearing the Philes as witches and their highway as a "witch road" that even animals fear to cross. Life is difficult in the Phobic villages, especially in Monn, which is suffering from a prolonged dry spell and is under the threat of war from its neighbors, the Kolloans. The more comfortable lifestyle of the Philes is also threatened by a looming energy crisis. With solar and wind power unable to meet energy demands, and hydropower projects expensive and vulnerable because they must be maintained in Phobe territories, the dire demands for energy sources to maintain the Philes' enclaves for more than a generation necessitate a "treasure hunt" to uncover unknown nuclear waste disposal sites left by the Old People. Those ancestors at the end of the twentieth century (some three hundred years earlier) held considerable knowledge about nuclear energy and controlling fusion, but "energy production was a big military secret in the good old days, and you could lose your head back then for telling people how to make the world warm and comfortable for everybody." This search for resources is a dangerous one, as it forces the Philes to leave the protective walls of their enclaves and venture into the unfriendly world beyond.

Reese, a resident of the Mid-American Enclave and an anthropologist who specializes in the Phobic communities, is designated to infiltrate that community in order to investigate the existence of possible sites of usable energy. Running alongside his story is that of Sarah, a fourteen-year-old street urchin of Monn who relies on a combination of wits, charm, and theft for survival. She meets Reese and falls in love with him. Their stories bring science and magic together and explain the difference between them as "the knowing of a thing. . . . When you know a thing, it seems natural, and when you don't know, it seems magic."

Cat's Gambit is a sequel to *Cat's Pawn,* continuing the story of the Orioni begun in that novel. The heroine, Ayyah, is the granddaughter of Talan, protector and friend of Bill Anderson. At the onset of *Cat's Gambit* the desert-dwelling feline Orioni have dwindled to a desperate refugee community of about a thousand inhabitants, survivors of the brutal Kazi invasion of Orian. The Kazi empire now stretches even further than before, its strength in numbers and intricate organization: "an attack upon one cell, or even its total destruction, has minimal effect on neighboring cells. This makes the empire impossible to defeat." The Kazi behave with a powerful group loyalty that binds them through "political and cultural ties to the emperor, and . . . ties of birth and mystery to a Broodmother."

The Orioni are not the only race that resist the Kazi. Terrans, too, are under the empire's domination, but at best are reluctant subjects; among them remain outlaws such as MacDonald and Oscar Achebe, who

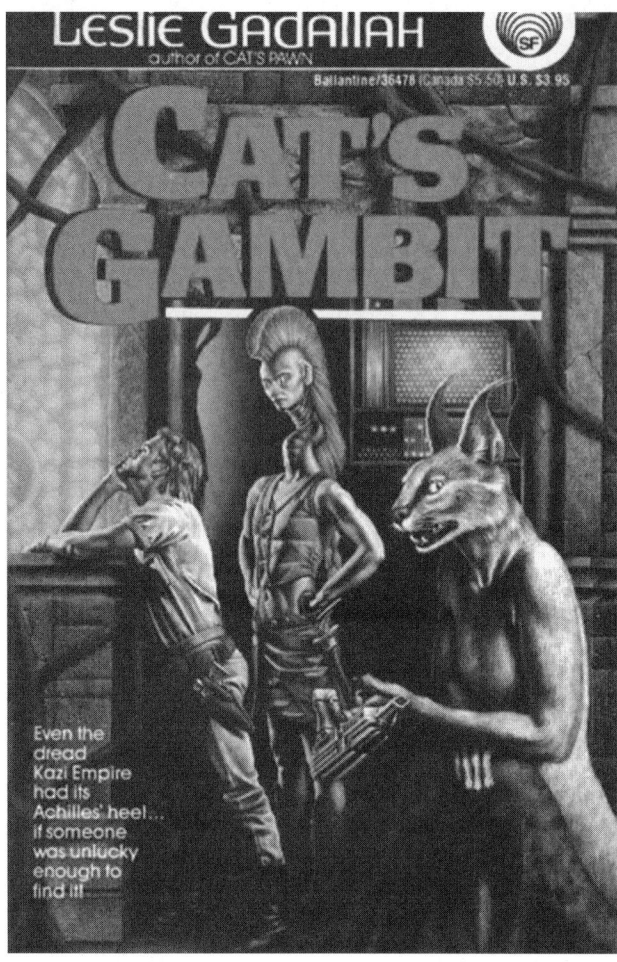

Cover for Gadallah's third novel (1990), in which characters communicate through unconventional modes such as mind manipulation

resist their foreign masters by running contraband in their unregistered vessel. This rebellious streak was much admired by Talan, who told his granddaughter to "Seek out the humans" in any attempt to do battle with the empire: "Great rebels exist among them. . . . These nonconformists become adept at finding the cracks and flaws of an organization." Again, Gadallah writes a story of shortages and need, with Ayyah and the fierce Llevici mountain warrior Delladar Oll driven to join MacDonald and Achebe in an uneasy partnership, united by their hatred of the Kazi but divided by their different cultural beliefs. The logic-loving Orioni is confused by the mutable emotions and sense of humor of the humans, and the pragmatic gunrunning of her human allies transgresses her sense of morality. While the Llevici warrior has no objections to arms trafficking, her single-minded sense of purpose is at odds with the fickle human character, but also with the need for thorough understanding and patience that marks the Orioni. Tempers flare, and friction is a constant in the intercultural interaction. Ayyah and Delladar Oll each has her own agenda, and it includes the humans only as long as they are useful. Ayyah's mission is essentially hopeless, but "primitive sentimentality" does not make her question the immorality of her manipulation of others' lives in fulfilling her plans. When their ship penetrates deep Kazi space and reaches the Broodmother, instinct overrides intellect, and Ayyah is destroyed. Delladar Oll dies too, but the "sentimental" MacDonald survives and returns Oll's sword to her village on Llevic—and so begins a cycle of storytelling that carries the tale down through the generations, surviving even the Kazi empire, until it is told to MacDonald's great-great-grandson.

Cat's Pawn and *Cat's Gambit* comprise Gadallah's most significant contributions to the field of science fiction; as Ketterer notes, they are "fast-paced and well-plotted . . . lively, mildly tragic space opera." They suggested the possibility of further volumes, which, however, have not been forthcoming.

Gadallah did make occasional contributions to Canadian science-fiction magazines and anthologies over the first half of the 1990s. "Hanging Out in the Third World Laundromat" appeared in the third volume of the pioneering *Tesseracts* anthologies, edited by fellow Alberta science-fiction writer Candas Jane Dorsey and Gerry Truscott. In this story Gadallah blurs the boundaries between genres, beginning with the grim reality of a laundromat in which Amy Thomson crosses first into the world of knights and courtly love; then into a Western saloon; and from there into space, the predictable setting for science fiction. In the first two encounters, Amy resists the leap of imagination that calls her to join the hero. In space, she is seduced by "something which seemed to have no definite boundaries . . . like sea grass waving in an ocean current" and disappears, leaving her roommate, Catherine, to search the laundromat and adjacent parking lot for clues. Everything except Amy is recovered. Gadallah is playing with the constrictions of genre that Dorsey complains about in her afterword to the anthology, "Towards a Real Speculative Literature: Writer as Asymptote." The editors likely appreciated Gadallah's effort to step outside "the genre strictures," because, as Dorsey puts it, "changing the world, the changing world, is what matters most."

Gadallah's short story "Motherlove," which appeared in the Fall 1993 issue of *On Spec,* is perhaps as much Canadian political satire as it is speculative fiction. In the contributor's notes for the issue of *On Spec* in which it appeared, Gadallah is described as "presently fighting with the county and province to protect it from the ravages of road building crews." There is a contentious tone to her narrator, an old woman who is relating her story to the police, whom she views as "part of the government"; she asserts that "Half the trouble with this world is there's too many damned rules. Too many people making up the rules. County council. Legislature. All those old guys in Ottawa, busy as freaking beavers, making up rules." Clearly Gadallah takes issue with authority, especially those government agencies that encroach on the rights and freedoms of small landowners "scratching a living out of a few acres of dry rocks." The narrator of this story seems to reflect Gadallah's own desire for autonomy; the biographical note included at the back of her novels describes her as living with her family on a small farm, "which they share with four cats, a budgie, a goat, and an uncertain number of rabbits" and where "they pursue the firm but distant goal of becoming independent of the supermarket."

The rural Canadian landscape of "Motherlove" is home to Hazel McMurty, an old woman who "Fools around a lot with cards and star-signs and stuff like that." The narrator is a friend of Hazel's, and so is her daughter, Janet, who is interested in Hazel's stories and the cards. When Barnard, Hazel's old cat, is run over, Janet is upset, and so is Hazel. As the narrator explains, "So what she gonna do? Cry some, burn these stinky herbs, bury old Bernard under the spruce in her yard, draw this star-thing on the ground. Makes her feel better, what the hell?" The probable driver of the car is a young man from the city, Howard, whom the narrator feels has been exerting too much influence over her daughter. In fact, the narrator is on bad terms with two men in the small rural community where she lives. Besides "Mr Big-City" Howard, there is a lazy local resident, George Peterson, who delivers hay two days late, and in an ensuing argument about whether or not to unload it, dumps the hay in the middle of the narrator's driveway. George and Howard are killed in an accident: ostensibly George turns the corner in his truck and hits Howard, who is crossing the street. But the details of the deaths remain murky, prompting the police to discuss the matter with the narrator, especially the significance of a tourist's eyewitness report that says there was a passenger in George's car that looked like the red tutelary plaster demons Hazel makes. Again Gadallah collapses the border between reality and fiction in her writing, leaving the reader unsure if the pragmatic, crusty narrator is playing with the police or really believes there is no such thing as magic.

A similar distrust of authority or the sincerity of bureaucratic promises is evident in "Dog Days," which was published in the Summer 1996 issue of *On Spec*. This story weaves the crime story into speculative fiction. There are the cops and robbers of the familiar crime narrative, but the landscape is a new one, where hard-drinking private investigators drink new alcohol substitutes (that still leave hangovers). Computers have caused the demise of the "city center," since "people started doing business in cyberspace," and fear and fuel rationing have emptied the streets of the nightlife that used to be at the center of the underworld. Lucrative new ventures are being sought by the kingpins of crime: "selling sin doesn't cut it the way it used to. People have got smart, or they've got scared. But something close to immortality—there's a commodity with real market value."

Louis Larouche, a private investigator, is called down to a veterinary clinic by Tracy Malone after the disappearance of some of her patients, including a special (though nameless) dog who had been released from a genetics lab when some "animal rights bozos" broke in and freed all of the experimental animals. Malone, extracting a chip from the dog's back, is able to identify him as part of a cross-genetic experiment: some of the dog's DNA was human. When Malone disappears, Larouche goes to the university to find information about the experiments, and then to Malone's house, where he finds that she is being held hostage until the dog is turned over to a criminal kingpin, Bruno Marcuso. When Larouche goes to the police to alert them that Malone is missing, they are not interested, as they are "busy putting the fear of God into a half dozen juvies and sleuthing out the reason why the doughnut shop missed the coffee break delivery." In other words, Gadallah continues to criticize the misplaced priorities that put life at risk and promise a future in disarray.

The hostage exchange results in Larouche escaping with both Malone and the dog, in exchange for giving Marcuso the gene-splicing technology. Larouche explains that the technology "should be used," and although the criminal is not his "first choice of vendors," giving him the chip is "better than it sitting in a University vault for a hundred years." He then, however, betrays Marcuso to the "data cops," the Electronic Offenses Unit. Although the technology does not fall into the hands of criminals, it seems that Gadallah agrees with her narrator when Larouche says, "Whoever works the bugs out to the point of getting approval from Health and Welfare can pretty well name his own price on the technique."

Since the publication of that story, Gadallah has not published further, although she has posted the occasional story on her website, <http://www.cadvision.com/gadalla1>. She is a prairie writer resisting regional confinement, and her work suggests that rural Alberta can be the site of speculative fiction as well as that of the realistic novel for which it is known. Cats and computers are part of both her real and imaginary worlds, and she demonstrates a marked flexibility in her ability to move between the two.

William Gibson
(17 March 1948 –)

Douglas Ivison
University of Western Ontario

BOOKS: *Neuromancer* (New York: Ace, 1984; London: Gollancz, 1984);
Burning Chrome (New York: Arbor House, 1986; London: Gollancz, 1986);
Count Zero (New York: Arbor House, 1986; London: Gollancz, 1986);
Mona Lisa Overdrive (New York: Bantam, 1988; London: Gollancz, 1988);
The Difference Engine, with Bruce Sterling (London: Gollancz, 1990; New York: Bantam, 1991);
Agrippa (A Book of the Dead), by Gibson and Dennis Ashbaugh (New York: Kevin Begos Publishing, 1992);
Virtual Light (New York: Bantam Spectra, 1993; London: Viking, 1993);
Johnny Mnemonic (New York: Ace, 1995: London: HarperCollins, 1996);
Idoru (New York: Putnam, 1996; London: Viking, 1996);
All Tomorrow's Parties (New York: Putnam, 1999; London: Viking, 1999).

PLAY PRODUCTION: *Dream Jumbo,* text by Gibson and performance art by Robert Longo, Los Angeles, UCLA Center for the Performing Arts, 1989.

PRODUCED SCRIPTS: *Johnny Mnemonic,* adapted by Gibson from his "Johnny Mnemonic," motion picture, Tristar, 1995;
"Kill Switch," by Gibson and Tom Maddox, television, *The X-Files,* Fox, 15 February 1998;
"First Person Shooter," by Gibson and Maddox, television, *The X-Files,* Fox, 5 March 2000.

OTHER: "Hippie Hat Brain Parasite," in *Semiotext(e) SF,* edited by Rudy Rucker, Peter Lamborn Wilson, and Robert Anton Wilson (New York: Semiotext(e), 1989), pp. 109–112;
"Doing Television," in *Tesseracts³,* edited by Gerry Truscott and Candas Jane Dorsey (Victoria, British Columbia: Tesseract Books, 1990), pp. 392–394;

William Gibson (photograph by Karen Moskowitz)

Ellen Datlow, ed., *Alien Sex,* foreword by Gibson (New York: Dutton, 1990);
John Shirley, *City Come A-Walking,* foreword by Gibson (Asheville, N.C.: Eyeball Books, 1996);
Samuel R. Delany, *Dhalgren,* foreword by Gibson (Hanover, N.H.: Wesleyan University Press/ University Press of New England, 1996);
Bruce Sterling, *The Artificial Kid,* introduction by Gibson (San Francisco: HardWired, 1997);

"Thirteen Views of a Cardboard City," in *Year's Best SF 3,* edited by David G. Hartwell (New York: HarperPrism, 1998), pp. 29–40.

No other Canadian speculative fiction writer, and possibly no other Canadian writer of fiction, has had as great an impact on late-twentieth-century culture as has William Gibson. Beginning with a series of short stories in science-fiction magazines in the early 1980s, and then the publication of his first novel, *Neuromancer* (1984), as a paperback original, Gibson quickly rose to the status of a cultural visionary and prophet of the information age. Winning five major science-fiction awards, *Neuromancer* went on to become a key influence on late-twentieth-century popular culture; its impact can be traced in the worlds of motion pictures, television, popular music, video games, interactive technology, and cultural theory. With its success, and that of its sequels, Gibson became a celebrity, courted by publishers, the news media, academics, art gallery curators, and Hollywood. While this quick rise to stardom may have been partially a result of the excesses of the media, no one can doubt Gibson's ability to imagine and articulate the cultural and technological changes that defined the late twentieth century. Gibson's work provided, and continues to provide, the media and society with the language with which to describe and understand these changes.

William Ford Gibson was born on 17 March 1948 in Conway, South Carolina, a small town near the coastal resort of Myrtle Beach. He was the son of William Ford Gibson, a prosperous contractor, and Otey (Williams) Gibson. The family traveled frequently, as his father went from one job to another. One of his father's contracts had a significant impact on the young Gibson: installing toilets in the Oak Ridge, Tennessee facility in which the first atomic bomb was made. Gibson grew up with stories about the intense security arrangements, and this exposure was the first intervention of a science-fictional reality into his life. As a child, he was also a consumer of science-fiction television shows and toys. His father died when Gibson was eight years old, and he and his mother moved to Wytheville, a small town in southwestern Virginia on the edge of the Appalachian Mountains, to be with her family. He described himself to Larry McCaffery in *Across the Wounded Galaxies: Interviews with Contemporary American Science Fiction Writers* (1990) as being a "bookish, geekish, can't-hit-the-baseball kind of kid" during this period. As a teenager he was a voracious reader of science fiction, increasingly drawn to the darker visions of writers such as J. G. Ballard as well as avant-garde authors such as William Seward Burroughs and Thomas Pynchon, whose visions are in many ways consonant with the grimmer science-fiction writers.

When Gibson was sixteen he went to a boarding school in Tucson, Arizona, where he was first exposed to "urban kids" and hippies. During his time in Tucson his mother died and, having been kicked out of school for smoking marijuana, he returned to Wytheville but quickly decided to leave and "spent some time bumming around," as he told McCaffery. Like many American youths during this period, Gibson headed for Canada when he was nineteen, arriving in Toronto in 1968, where he participated in the thriving hippie scene. He and his future wife, Deborah Thompson, traveled in Europe and then settled in Vancouver, British Columbia in 1972, marrying in June of that year (they went on to have two children, Graeme Ford Gibson and Claire Thompson Gibson). He enrolled in the University of British Columbia, where he received a B.A. in English in 1977.

Gibson first started writing science fiction during his time at the university, where he took a course on science fiction with the well-known scholar and critic Susan Wood. Rather than write an essay for the course, Gibson wrote a short story. After three months of work, Gibson produced "Fragments of a Hologram Rose," which was first published in the Summer 1977 issue of the Boston science-fiction fanzine *Unearth*. This brief, dense story introduces many of the elements that became identified with Gibson's later writing: a poetic evocation of the technology of what is now called virtual reality; densely referential prose; a description of a world dominated by transnational capital; and an interest in marginal spaces and characters. At the same time, this elliptical, fractured story is devoid of interesting characters and lacking in narrative drive.

After graduating from the university Gibson continued to drift, spending his time looking after his children (his wife worked as a teacher) and buying punk-rock singles, until he met John Shirley, an American science-fiction writer and punk musician, who urged him to continue writing. The result was four stories published in 1981: "Johnny Mnemonic" and "Hinterlands" appeared in the glossy science-fiction magazine *Omni;* "The Belonging Kind," a collaboration with Shirley, was published in the anthology *Shadows 4;* and, possibly most significantly for the future development of his career, "The Gernsback Continuum" was included in the anthology *Universe 11,* edited by famed science-fiction anthologist and editor Terry Carr. These four stories were the first real indication of the impact that Gibson would have on the world of science fiction.

Cover for the issue of the Boston science-fiction magazine that published Gibson's first short story

"Johnny Mnemonic," which was later made into a movie of the same title with a screenplay by Gibson, became one of the iconic and highly anthologized stories of the so-called cyberpunk movement, of which Gibson became a leading figure. Cyberpunk arose in the 1980s in seeming reaction to the progressivist ideals of mainstream science fiction, and it injected science fiction with a romanticized vision of "street culture." It combined the cynicism and tough-guy morality of the hard-boiled detective novels of Raymond Chandler and Dashiell Hammett with the bleak nihilism of punk rock and its precursors (particularly, in the case of Gibson, Lou Reed and his groundbreaking late-1960s art-rock band, The Velvet Underground), and an awareness of the dramatic ontological and epistemological changes that advances in computer technology had already begun to effect. As Gibson himself has admitted on various occasions, his writing, and that of the writers who followed him, bears the traces of a multiplicity of literary and cultural influences, from popular-culture genres such as science fiction and rock music and elite-culture figures such as Pynchon and Burroughs.

Johnny Mnemonic is a courier who has been technologically altered to allow him to carry information by storing it in his brain, and with the help of Molly Millions he is, by the end of the story, able to utilize that stored information to the benefit of himself and his friends. But the plot of the story is not what is most significant; rather, it is the setting, the underworld of the near future, a world in which the characters speak in a cynical street language and have bodies that have been technologically augmented. It is a romanticized world of drugs, despair, and random violence, in which access to technology is determined by, and determinative of, power and status. While the impact of the story has been diluted by the plethora of imitations that have appeared since its initial publication, "Johnny Mnemonic" is a remarkable work.

His other story to appear in *Omni* that year, "Hinterlands," is quite different from the cyberpunk stories with which Gibson is usually identified, but is powerful nonetheless. The unnamed narrator is a surrogate, a person who greets astronauts returning from their solo missions into the unknown. Nearly all of the astronauts come back from their missions mad or suicidal, but carrying invaluable information with them, such as a cure for cancer. It is ultimately a powerful meditation on the sublimity of the unknown and on the limits of human knowledge. Ultimately, in contrast to the explicative imperative of science fiction, nothing is explained (though Gibson is certainly not the first genre writer to write against this imperative).

"The Gernsback Continuum," which has been repeatedly anthologized since its initial publication, is a short but suggestive story in which the narrator sees "semiotic ghosts . . . bits of deep cultural imagery that have taken on a life of their own." It describes the bleeding of past visions of the future into another time, and it is a provocative meditation on popular culture and its impact on perception, recalling the short fiction of 1960s British science-fiction writer Ballard. Although cyberpunk activist (and Gibson's friend) Bruce Sterling, in the foreword to Gibson's 1986 collection *Burning Chrome,* describes "The Gernsback Continuum" as a "devastating refutation" of the simplistic "technolatry" of much science fiction, it can also be read as a less radical story, one that simply comments upon that tradition and its impact upon society.

"The Belonging Kind," written with his friend Shirley, was the first of Gibson's many collaborations. Michael Coretti, a dialectologist, encounters an intriguing woman in a bar and decides to follow her, only to discover her secret: that she physically transforms into an appropriate person as she moves from bar to bar. He discovers that there are many more like her, aliens posing as humans, and eventually becomes one himself. This story, although readable, is the least interesting and least typical of the quartet of stories Gibson published during 1981, and seems to bear more of the traces of Shirley than it does of Gibson.

Gibson's next *Omni* story, "Burning Chrome," which was published in the July 1982 issue and which was nominated for a Nebula Award, introduced the elements with which Gibson became most identified. Much of the action of the story takes place in cyberspace, or the matrix, which is "an abstract representation of the relationships between data systems." Bobby Quine, a "console cowboy" or a hacker, breaks into the computer systems of major corporations, trying to outwit the ice, or computer security systems. The narrator, Automatic Jack, builds and reconstructs computer consoles. "Burning Chrome" essentially tells the story of a high-tech bank robbery. Jack and Bobby break into a corporation's Swiss bank accounts and electronically steal the money. What is most memorable about this story, however, is its highly influential evocation of the matrix and its poetic description of the abstract space that is cyberspace. Much of the way in which cyberspace has been represented and understood is based on Gibson's description of it in this short story and on his elaboration of the concept in *Neuromancer*.

The second of his collaborations, "Red Star, Winter Orbit," was written with Sterling (with whom he later wrote *The Difference Engine*, 1990) and appeared in *Omni* in July 1983. The first man on Mars, Colonel Yuri Vasilevich Korolev, whose limbs have atrophied after years in space, is stranded on a Soviet space station after it is decommissioned and damaged in the rebellion that ensued. Korolev is preparing to die as the last man in space while the station's orbit decays, but two American squatters arrive to take possession and restore it to its orbit. Although the geopolitical speculation of the story, in which the Soviet Union is triumphant in the Cold War, now seems quaint, its libertarian identification of a site such as a space station as a resistant, autonomous place is of interest and is an idea that Gibson developed in his first novel.

By this time, something beginning to resemble a movement was beginning to coalesce around Gibson. Shirley had introduced Gibson to Sterling, a science-fiction writer from Texas who went on to enthusiastically promote both Gibson and what was soon described as the cyberpunk movement, which was canonized with the publication of Sterling's 1986 anthology, *Mirrorshades*. In October 1982 Gibson attended a science-fiction convention, ArmadilloCon, in Austin, Texas, where he read excerpts from the opening chapters of the novel he was writing. At that conference was one of the first panels on what was then being called "punk SF," and participants discussed Gibson, among other writers. In Austin he formed the writing and personal friendships that coalesced into the group of writers known as cyberpunk writers, or as the Movement. Upon leaving Austin, according to fellow science-fiction writer and friend Lewis Shiner in *Fiction 2000*, edited by George Slusser and Tom Shippey, Gibson joked, "A new axis has been formed."

Yet, charismatic as he may have been, Gibson was nervous about his ability to meet the challenge he had taken on when he had accepted Carr's commission to write a novel. He told McCaffery that "I was *terrified* once I actually sat down and started to think about what it [writing a novel] meant." When he found out that a novel was about three hundred pages long, he thought, "My God!" Despite his concerns, Gibson was up to the challenge. When *Neuromancer* appeared as a paperback original in 1984, it received an enthusiastic critical and commercial response and went on to sweep all the major science-fiction awards, winning the Philip K. Dick Award for best paperback original book, the Hugo Award (voted on by readers), the Nebula Award (voted on by members of the Science Fiction Writers of America), and other awards around the world (although it is interesting that it did not win the Canadian Science Fiction and Fantasy Award). As McCaffery put it, *Neuromancer* "burst onto the science fiction scene like a supernova." In fact, its impact was felt far beyond the genre boundaries of science fiction. McCaffery, for one, observed that "after reading *Neuromancer* for the first time, I knew I had seen the future of SF (and maybe of literature in general)." Gibson's novel has become the subject of much attention by literary, film studies, and cultural studies scholars since its publication, and it has been given a level of academic scrutiny unmatched by any other genre science-fiction novel. Famously, the influential critic of postmodernism, Fredric Jameson, noted in his 1991 book *Postmodernism, or, The Cultural Logic of Late Capitalism* that cyberpunk, exemplified by Gibson, was "the supreme *literary* expression if not of postmodernism, then of late capitalism itself."

The impact of *Neuromancer* can be seen in the acceptance of the word "cyberspace" into the modern vocabulary and in the extent to which Gibson's representation of computers, computer hackers, and the Internet has determined how they have been represented subsequently in popular culture and the news media. Gibson became the prophet of the Internet age—despite the notorious fact that he wrote the book on a typewriter, not a computer—and reading *Neuromancer* became a lifestyle statement, to an extent that few science-fiction novels have achieved before or since. In *The New York Times Book Review* of 8 September 1996 Laura Miller remembered that "in the shabby apartments of young, black-clad aficionados of punk rock and fashionable nihilism," a copy of *Neuromancer* "was *de rigeur.*"

The opening sentence of *Neuromancer* is one of the most famous in all of science fiction: "The sky above the port was the color of television, tuned to a dead channel." That sentence exemplifies what Gibson brings to science fiction: a poetic evocation of the near future, filtering scientific extrapolation through a popular-culture sensibility. The main character of *Neuromancer* is Case, a computer cowboy or hacker. After betraying one of his employers, he was punished by having his nervous system damaged, which prevented him from accessing cyberspace. Despondent, he accepts a mysterious offer from a former soldier, Armitage: he will be repaired if he agrees to do the work that Armitage requires. This agreement propels Case through the near-future world that Gibson describes, a world controlled by Japanese corporations. Case travels through the seedy underworld, meeting a wide variety of characters, memorably including space Rastafarians and some of the characters from Gibson's earlier short stories, including Molly Millions from "Johnny Mnemonic." Eventually, he penetrates the conspiracy behind Armitage's offer, only to discover an artificial intelligence at the heart of it.

Neuromancer reflects the 1980s North American fascination with and fear of Japan, which may seem slightly dated, but the book effectively limns a future not-so-alien world in which computers dominate; information is the most important currency; and bioengineering is commonplace, with the result that it becomes difficult to determine where the machine ends and the human begins. As in the 1982 motion picture *Blade Runner,* the world described in *Neuromancer* runs counter to the progressivist, pristine futures of much science fiction, substituting for it a gritty, hard-boiled sensibility. Yet, what really distinguished Gibson's first novel from much of the rest of science fiction was its sheer stylishness. Gibson was clearly as interested in the literary description of the future as in its scientific description. It is also a densely detailed, frenetically paced novel; one of the reasons for this abundance, Gibson told McCaffery, was Gibson's "terrible fear of losing the reader's attention," which motivated him to try to ensure that there was something of interest on every page.

In addition to its description of a gritty, *noir* future in which information is the basis of exchange, both legal and illegal, *Neuromancer* is possibly most notable for its description of cyberspace, or the matrix, that nonmaterial realm defined by the interaction of computer systems, which Gibson developed after watching Vancouver teenagers playing video games. He was intrigued by the fact that the video-game players were acting as if there were a real space inside the video screen. What makes Gibson's portrayal of cyberspace so effective is precisely its lack of technical limitation; cyberspace is a transcendent, dreamlike space, populated by ghosts and gods, though the degree to which Gibson's portrayal of cyberspace approaches the mystical is only hinted at in *Neuromancer,* in the artificial intelligence Wintermute, and in Wintermute's unification with its double, Neuromancer. The new entity approaches God in its representation of the entirety of cyberspace. The religious and mystical dimensions of cyberspace are further developed in the two sequels to *Neuromancer.*

Gibson followed the immense success of *Neuromancer* with the publication of two short stories, "Dogfight" and "The Winter Market." "Dogfight," written with Michael Swanwick, was published in the July 1985 issue of *Omni*. It tells the story of Deke, a petty thief and video-game shark, who is obsessed with beating all challengers in an aerial combat game. Ultimately the story serves as a commentary on the emptiness of Deke's obsession and the culture that it represents. "The Winter Market" is an unusual story in Gibson's body of work, for it incorporates what had been a remarkable absence from his fiction: Canada. It was first published in the November 1985 issue of *Vancouver* and is set in that city, his hometown. Gibson creates a portrait of Vancouver while telling a story that seems to be a meditation on the role of the artist. Casey, the narrator, is an editor of people's "psychic waveforms." He discovers and edits a new star, Lise, who becomes a media celebrity saved inside a computer, transcending her disabled physical body and achieving "cybernetic immortality." Casey's friend and confidant, Rubin, is an artist who makes art out of other people's garbage. "The Winter Market" is a moving meditation on the tension between art and commerce, on what it means to be human or machine, and on the value of place.

In 1986 Gibson published *Burning Chrome,* which collects all the short fiction he had published to date, including his three collaborations. Since the mid 1980s Gibson has published only occasional pieces of short fiction and has primarily devoted himself to writing novels and screenplays.

Count Zero, the sequel to *Neuromancer,* was also published in 1986, in hardcover (though still by a nonmainstream publisher). Bobby Newmark, the Count Zero of the title, is a computer cowboy who runs into deadly ice, or security software, on his first run, but he is saved by a cyberspace "angel." Later attacked by hit men, he is protected by a group who are loyal to the voodoo gods that exist in the matrix. Angela Mitchell, the daughter of a famous biochip developer, possesses artificially augmented intelligence and can access cyberspace without a deck, the device that all others use to enter the matrix. Controlled by gods of the matrix, Angie is the angel who had saved Bobby. Biochip technology provides the impetus for much of the plot, as Josef Virek, a multibillionaire, is trying to acquire this technology to help him achieve immortality. By the end of the novel, Angie has become a simstim or virtual-reality star, one of the celebrities of cyberspace. The plot is resolved with the help of the supernatural forces that exist in cyberspace. This supernatural or mystical element is what differentiates *Count Zero* from Gibson's earlier work. He had hinted at the supernatural at the conclusion of *Neuromancer,* but in its sequel, cyberspace is clearly dominated by supernatural presences.

The frenetic narrative and overpowering descriptive intensity that had defined *Neuromancer* are less present in *Count Zero,* which marked the beginning of Gibson's gradual shift away from the genre conventions and styles of science fiction toward a more mainstream writing style. *Count Zero* is cleanly written, still with emphasis on detailed description but with less attempt to overpower the reader with a densely realized future. Response to the novel, although enthusiastic, inevitably did not repeat the hyperbolic adulation of *Neuromancer.* Unlike its predecessor, *Count Zero* did not win any major awards, although it did place highly in the yearly readers' poll held by *Locus,* a science-fiction magazine. Science-fiction critics still praised the novel, though Gibson was obviously no longer an exciting new presence in the field; but many mainstream critics were more receptive to the less obviously pulpish, conventionally written sequel. Writing in the Summer 1989 issue of *Canadian Literature,* J. R. Wytenbroek, for instance, observed that *Count Zero* "is a better-written, better-structured novel with a more coherent and interesting plot-line, and more realistic and interesting characters than *Neuromancer.*" Science-fiction writer and critic Colin Greenland, on the other hand, suggested in the 20 June 1986 *TLS: The Times Literary Supplement* that *Count Zero* simply built on the achievements of its predecessor, adding that "*Count Zero* shows a conscientious broadening of scope and modulation of tone without any loss of brio."

After Gibson's explosion into the media landscape during 1984 and 1985, many of his short stories, as well as *Neuromancer,* were optioned by movie producers. Gibson began to get involved in the movie industry himself as the 1980s progressed; he was commissioned to write several screenplays, none of which actually were produced. The most famous of these scripts was that for *Alien³* (1992). Gibson seemed an obvious choice, since the first *Alien* movie (1979), directed by Ridley Scott, had many obvious affinities with the developing genre of cyberpunk, in both the future world that it sketched and the H. R. Giger–designed sets that combined the mechanical and the biological. Gibson's screenplay was not used in the resulting form, however, though it is widely available on the World Wide Web. His screenwriting experience was influencing his novel writing, as *Count Zero* and, to a greater extent, *Mona Lisa Overdrive* reflected.

Mona Lisa Overdrive, published in 1988, was Gibson's first book to receive hardcover publication by a major publisher, although still through its science-fiction imprint. Bobby Newmark, now a successful computer cowboy, has become the occasional boyfriend of Angie Mitchell, who is a worldwide simstim star while Bobby, in a self-imposed coma, devotes himself to the theological project of determining the shape of the matrix. The Mona Lisa of the title is a sixteen-year-old junkie who has been surgically altered to look like Angie. At the violent conclusion of the novel Angie is killed, to be replaced as a simstim star by her look-alike, Mona Lisa. But Angie and Bobby live on happily ever after in cyberspace, in a virtual heaven. Although Gibson's style may have altered, the world that he describes in *Mona Lisa Overdrive* remains essentially the same as that of its two predecessors. It is a world dominated by transnational capital, and his characters are those people who move through the margins of society living off what they can scam. The action moves between the grimy, overcrowded, polluted streets and the hideaways of the elites, with the media often serving as a point of contact between those two worlds. In fact, his increasing interest in the media world, which was further developed in his novels of the 1990s, reflected his own increasing entanglement with the media, whether as a celebrity in his own right or as a screenwriter.

With *Mona Lisa Overdrive* Gibson continued to broaden his audience, though it was becoming clear that cyberpunk, which Gibson's writing exemplified, had run its course. Certainly *Mona Lisa Overdrive,* though based in the same world as Gibson's earlier fiction and featuring many of the same characters,

Cover for the U.S. edition of Gibson's 1984 novel about a computer hacker, in which he coined the word cyberspace

including the iconic Molly Millions, was (at least stylistically) quite different from *Neuromancer,* let alone his earlier short stories. Critical reaction, while still generally positive, reflected the sense that Gibson was no longer a revolutionary presence in the field of science fiction but increasingly becoming a figure of the status quo. In a typical review Paul Kincaid observed in the 12 August 1988 *TLS* that Gibson "is showing clear and dramatic improvement as a writer, but is doing nothing fresh with this talent," and that *Count Zero* "is very much in the mainstream; it will take a fresh vision to confirm Gibson's place in the first rank." Istvan Csicery-Ronay Jr. similarly complained, in the January/February 1989 issue of *American Book Review,* that despite Gibson's "wonderfully inventive imagination and scintillating style, he has nothing new to say about the new, which is all he claims to know."

Gibson's next novel, *The Difference Engine,* collaboratively written with the Austin-based Sterling, seemed to represent a break with cyberpunk. It is an alternative-history novel set in Victorian Britain, based on the premise that the protocomputer invented by Charles Babbage but never actually built had been put into production and then transformed Victorian society, which then develops much of the technology associated with the twentieth century but based on nineteenth-century technologies such as steam power. Combining espionage and adventure with an interest in mid-Victorian geopolitics, technology, and paleontology, *The Difference Engine* is an engaging alternative history.

The Difference Engine was not so great a leap from Gibson's earlier work. Alternative history has a long tradition within science fiction, and many of Gibson and Sterling's contemporaries were also attracted to the Victorian period, writing stories and novels in what came to be called the "steampunk" subgenre. The world they described, influenced by the Victorian England of Charles Dickens, Wilkie Collins, Jekyll and Hyde, and Sherlock Holmes, was similar to that of cyberpunk fiction. As in cyberpunk, steampunk focused on the transformation of society by a technological revolution and the resulting political and economic consequences. As in cyberpunk, many steampunk writers focused on characters moving through the underworld and living at the margins of society, and on the impact of capital on everyday life. *The Difference Engine* is certainly in keeping with many of Gibson's interests, and those of Sterling, in its emphasis on the impact of technological change and its genre interest in world building—constructing a realistically extrapolated world resulting from the introduction of new technology. In addition, the novel concludes with a gesture toward the transcendent, fully in keeping with Gibson's later cyberpunk fiction. *The Difference Engine* does not represent a radical departure for Gibson, but a logical progression. Still, it did allow him to escape the limitations imposed by the expectations his earlier fiction had raised.

Gibson's next project, *Agrippa (A Book of the Dead)* (1992), was a collaboration between Gibson, visual artist Dennis Ashbaugh, and art-book publisher Kevin Begos. Released in a limited edition of fewer than five hundred copies, costing $500 for the basic edition and $1500 for the deluxe edition, *Agrippa* is composed of a series of etchings by Ashbaugh surrounding a computer disk that includes a three-thousand-word prose poem by Gibson. The disk containing the poem self-destructs after the poem is read. Gibson's poem, a semi-autobiographical meditation inspired by an old photo album that Gibson found in his family home in

Virginia, is now widely available on the World Wide Web. The novelty of the project resulted in critical attention being devoted to *Agrippa,* both in the popular media and in academic and art journals, though most of the interest was in the idea of the self-destructing book rather than in Gibson's text itself.

In 1991 Gibson had contributed to an exhibition at the San Francisco Museum of Modern Art called *Visionary San Francisco.* The result was the short story "Skinner's Room," which became a central part of his next novel, *Virtual Light* (1993). "Skinner's Room" describes life on a Golden Gate Bridge turned into a shanty town, and this vision is one of the most appealing ones in *Virtual Light* and its two sequels. True to Gibson's narrative strategy in most of his other novels, *Virtual Light* begins with apparently unrelated plot lines that gradually converge as the novel develops. Chevette Washington is a San Francisco bike messenger who lives among the homeless on the bridge. She steals what appears to be a pair of expensive yet ordinary sunglasses that turn out to be high-technology glasses called Virtual Light, which directly feed the optic nerve with electromagnetic pulses. Unknown to her, the glasses contain top-secret information: a plan to rebuild San Francisco as huge, self-sufficient towers. For that reason, she is being hunted down and has to flee. Meanwhile, Bobby Rydell, a former Los Angeles policeman who had been expelled from the LAPD for killing a man who held his family hostage, has been drifting through looking for a job. At first he is signed by a reality police television show, *Cops in Trouble,* but he is dropped when the show signs someone with a more exciting story. After that experience, he takes a job with a private security firm, IntenSecure, as a driver, but he loses that position after being sent on a fake operation as a result of misdirections received from a group of computer hackers called the Republic of Desire. Then he begins working for a private detective. In that capacity he meets Chevette, and they flee her pursuers together. Bobby eventually escapes to a trailer camp of television worshippers and then contacts the Republic of Desire, who agree to help him and Chevette. At the conclusion of the novel both Bobby and Chevette are signed by *Cops in Trouble.*

Other than Gibson's description of the shanty town on the bridge and a few other details, the world described in *Virtual Light* has less in common with the extrapolative claims of science fiction than with the critical claims of satire. The near future of *Virtual Light* seems to almost exist already, unlike that of *Neuromancer,* which seemed like audacious prophecy rather than satirical critique. For those readers who had begun to feel that Gibson's cyberpunk future had lost its novelty and had become a bit stale, the stylish prose and detailed near-present of *Virtual Light* represented a reinvigorated Gibson. Furthermore, rather than representing the failure of Gibson's imagination, *Virtual Light* simply reflects that the future that Gibson had described in his earlier fiction had nearly arrived. *Virtual Light* was Gibson's most mainstream novel to that point and certainly the most successful of his 1990s novels.

While some critics, such as Richard Ryan in the 26 August 1993 *Christian Science Monitor,* found that *Virtual Light* lacked "the same incandescence that made Gibson's *Neuromancer* and *Count Zero* so riveting," others were less distressed by its "more likable characters, a more subdued style, a less claustrophobic setting and a more upbeat ending," as Gerald Jonas wrote in the 12 September 1993 *New York Times Book Review,* for Gibson's "main interest, as always, is in creating a near-future world that can hold its own with the mind-bending reality of the present." *Virtual Light* not only confirmed Gibson's status within science fiction but also marked his increasing acceptance as a mainstream literary figure. Although the novel was published by a genre imprint (Bantam Spectra), Gibson was being marketed to the general public as a mainstream writer, as evidenced by jacket endorsements from such non-science-fiction, trendy authors as Tom Robbins and fellow Vancouverite Douglas Coupland.

Gibson's next project was his first completed movie project. Although nearly all of his fiction had been optioned at various times, and he had been commissioned to write screenplays, his first movie to actually be produced was his adaptation of "Johnny Mnemonic." He wrote the screenplay for the $38 million motion picture, which starred Keanu Reeves and was directed by his friend, artist Robert Longo. However, it was both a commercial and critical disaster, which was especially disappointing to Gibson given the extent of his involvement; not only did he write the script but also he was involved in many of the day-to-day production decisions. He vocally blamed the problems on the interference of the movie studio and made clear that he disliked the version that was released to theaters, telling Edo van Belkom in *Northern Dreamers,* for instance, that "the film that was released bears almost no resemblance to the film we shot." To coincide with the release of the movie in 1995, Gibson published *Johnny Mnemonic,* which combines the original short story and his original script and which provides a clearer indication of Gibson's vision for the movie than does the finished product. During this period Gibson also dabbled in other media, making a cameo appearance in the 1993 television miniseries *Wild Palms* (his brief dialogue is widely available on the World Wide Web), and cowriting a

Dust jacket for the U.S. edition (1991) of Gibson's co-authored alternative-history novel set in Victorian England

song, "Dog Star Girl," for pop singer Deborah Harry, who included it on her 1993 album *Debravation*.

Gibson's status at this point can be measured by the $1.4 million advance he received for his next novel, *Idoru*, which was published in 1996. An *idoru* is a virtual Japanese pop star, and the plot of *Idoru* centers around the rumors that Rez, a member of the popular rock band Lo/Rez, is about to marry an *idoru*. Chia Pet McKenzie, a Seattle teenager and member of the Lo/Rez fan club, is sent to Japan to investigate these rumors, but in doing so becomes involved in activities of the Russian mafia, as she unknowingly smuggles a nanotech assembler into Japan. Colin Laney, who is able to read patterns and nodal points in data—and can, in a sense, predict the future—is a net runner who has been hired by Lo/Rez's management to determine whether the Russian mafia is involved in Rez's upcoming marriage. As usual with Gibson, the plot of *Idoru* is of little significance; the heart of the book is in its detailed description of the media age and in its satire of contemporary society. It is also notable, however, for its creation in Chia of a believable teen-aged female protagonist, a rarity in male-written sci-

ence fiction and even more so in the often heavily masculinist world of cyberpunk. As Miller wrote in the 8 September 1996 *New York Times Book Review*, "Gibson has a remarkable insight into the minds of teen-age girls, and Chia, perhaps his most typical, is also one of his most winning creations, a Judy Blume heroine plopped down in the middle of a futuristic thriller." Despite Chia, however, Miller, like many critics, found *Idoru* to be a disappointment. In her review she wrote that although Gibson provides many interesting and provocative details and observations, these simply provide "scenery for a trip that finally doesn't seem to go anywhere . . . although *Idoru* does some unconvincing hand waving in the general direction of import, its many pleasures remain small ones." Other critics, such as Paul Quinn in the 27 September 1996 *TLS*, were more enthusiastic. Quinn wrote that "*Idoru* confirms Gibson as, virtually, a realist writer for the post-Net generation, offering us a new mimesis that opens windows on our on-screen world."

All Tomorrow's Parties, published in 1999, is the third volume in Gibson's loosely connected 1990s trilogy and, in the opinion of many, his weakest novel.

Colin Laney, now living in a cardboard box in a Tokyo subway station, is obsessed with Cody Harwood, a multibillionaire public-relations genius. Laney believes that something big is about to happen and that it will involve Harwood and the *idoru*. He sends his friend Bobby Rydell, now working as a convenience store security guard, to Los Angeles to protect the *idoru* projector. The fragmented narrative and difficult-to-summarize plot conclude with the *idoru* stepping out of every Nanofax unit in the world. *All Tomorrow's Parties* is a confusing novel that recycles many of the ideas that Gibson had introduced in its prequels and in his earlier fiction, but to less impact. The short chapters, fragmented narrative, and multiple characters prevent the reader from really engaging with the plot or any of the characters, and *All Tomorrow's Parties* received the worst reviews of Gibson's career. Michael Krantz, writing in the 6 December 1999 issue of *Time*, exemplified critical response to the novel when he wrote that "this time his teasing, multicharacter narrative leads only to an irritating headscratcher of a solution."

Despite his success and his resultant celebrity in North America, Europe, Australia, and Japan, Gibson continues to live in Vancouver, raising his family and working in his basement. A landed immigrant, Gibson has no intention of moving back to the United States, telling van Belkom that "I probably wouldn't be very comfortable, at least initially moving back to the States because it's not the place I left . . . and I've become uncomfortable living in cities where the majority of the population is armed." He is ambivalent about his identity, however, telling van Belkom that although he identifies "with the state of being Canadian" he does not quite feel that he is one.

All Tomorrow's Parties may have been a relative failure, but Gibson remains one of the highest-profile science-fiction writers and one of the few who have achieved success outside the confines of the genre. The documentary *No Maps for These Territories* (2000), directed by Mark Neale, reflects his status as a cultural visionary. The movie follows Gibson's travels across the United States by multimedia limousine as he comments on America and engages with personalities such as Sterling and members of the rock band U2. The documentary premiered at the Slamdance Film Festival in Park City, Utah, in January 2001. Although Gibson is frequently described as an American, his success has had a huge impact on the development of Canadian science fiction. His achievement, and the fact that he has remained in Canada, suggested that it was possible for science-fiction writers living in Canada to compete in the American-based science-fiction marketplace. The incredible success of *Neuromancer* signaled what David Ketterer, in *Canadian Science Fiction and Fantasy* (1992), has described as "the international arrival of Canadian science fiction." Gibson has also participated in the Canadian science-fiction community, allowing some of his fiction to be reprinted in the *Tesseracts* anthologies and participating in the founding of what is now called science-fiction Canada, the Canadian professional organization for science-fiction writers. Writing in *The Encyclopedia of Science Fiction* (1995), moreover, expatriate Canadian science-fiction critic John Clute suggests that Gibson's work exists within a pessimistic Canadian tradition that is skeptical about the possibility of transforming the world and that seeks to establish a niche, as does Canada as a whole, within the world as it exists.

Although he is often cited as a computer prophet and has been called the "poet of cyberspace," Gibson was slow to participate in the quickly expanding Internet. As recently as the mid 1990s his old Macintosh computer, which he was disappointed to discover did not live up to his idealized image of sleek high technology, did not even have a modem. That is not to say, however, that he is not interested in making use of the technology that is available. His cyberpunk trilogy is available as an electronic book, and he worked with website designers to create an elaborate William Gibson homepage (which is no longer active). Yet, his identification with "cyberspace" is both the basis of much of his success and a burden. He told Brian Johnson, in the 5 June 1995 issue of *Maclean's,* that "I know now that the word is in *The Shorter Oxford English Dictionary* and it kind of horrifies me that that's what I'll be remembered for, the thing that lasts the longest, because actually I wanted to be a novelist."

Interviews:

Timothy Leary, "High Tech High Life–William Gibson & Timothy Leary in Conversation," *Mondo 2000* (Fall 1989): 58–64;

Larry McCaffery, "An Interview with William Gibson," in *Across the Wounded Galaxies: Interviews with Contemporary American Science Fiction Writers* (Urbana: University of Illinois Press, 1990), pp. 131–150;

Daniel Fischlin, Veronica Hollinger, and Andrew Taylor, "'The Charisma Leak': A Conversation with William Gibson and Bruce Sterling," *Science-Fiction Studies,* 19 (March 1992): 1–16;

Edo van Belkom, "William Gibson," in his *Northern Dreamers: Interviews with Famous Science Fiction, Fantasy, and Horror Writers* (Kingston, Ontario: Quarry Press, 1998), pp. 83–93.

References:

Kathleen Biddick, "Humanist History and the Haunting of Virtual Worlds: Problems of Memory and Rememoration," *Genders,* 18 (Winter 1993) : 47–66;

M. Keith Booker, "Technology, History, and the Postmodern Imagination," *Arizona Quarterly,* 50 (Winter 1994): 63–87;

David Brande, "The Business of Cyberpunk: Symbolic Economy and Ideology in William Gibson," in *Virtual Realities and their Discontents,* edited by Robert Markley (Baltimore: Johns Hopkins University Press), pp. 79–106;

Thomas A. Bredehoft, "The Gibson Continuum: Cyberspace and Gibson's Mervyn Kihn Stories," *Science-Fiction Studies,* 22 (July 1995): 252–263;

Scott Bukatman, "Gibson's Typewriter," in *Flame Wars: The Discourse of Cyberculture,* edited by Mark Dery (Durham, N.C.: Duke University Press, 1994), pp. 71–89;

Bukatman, *Terminal Identity: The Virtual Subject in Postmodern Science Fiction* (Durham, N.C.: Duke University Press, 1993), pp. 146–154;

Eva Cherniavsky, "(En)gendering Cyberspace in *Neuromancer*: Postmodern Subjectivity and Virtual Motherhood," *Genders,* 18 (Winter 1993) : 32–46;

Kevin Concannon, "The Contemporary Space of the Border: Gloria Anzaldua's *Borderlands* and William Gibson's *Neuromancer*," *Textual Practice,* 12 (Winter 1998): 429–442;

Istvan Csicsery-Ronay Jr., "Antimancer: Cybernetics and Art in Gibson's *Count Zero*," *Science-Fiction Studies,* 22 (March 1995): 63–86;

Csicsery-Ronay Jr., "The Sentimental Futurist: Cybernetics and Art in William Gibson's *Neuromancer*," *Critique: Studies in Contemporary Fiction,* 33 (Spring 1992): 221–240;

Cynthia Davidson, "Riviera's Golem, Haraway's Cyborg: Reading *Neuromancer* as Baudrillard's Simulation of Crisis," *Science-Fiction Studies,* 23 (July 1996): 188–198;

Paul Delany, "'Hardly the Center of the World': Vancouver in William Gibson's 'The Winter Market,'" in *Vancouver: Representing the Postmodern City,* edited by Delany (Vancouver, British Columbia: Arsenal Pulp Press, 1994), pp. 179–192;

Tony Fabijancic, "Space and Power: 19th-Century Urban Practice and Gibson's Cyberworld," *Mosaic,* 32 (March 1999): 105–130;

Ross Farnell, "Posthuman Topologies: William Gibson's 'Architexture' in *Virtual Light* and *Idoru*," *Science-Fiction Studies,* 25 (November 1998): 459–480;

Glenn Grant, "Transcendence Through Detournement in William Gibson's *Neuromancer*," *Science-Fiction Studies,* 17 (March 1990): 41–49;

David J. Gunkel and Ann Hetzel Gunkel, "Virtual Geographies: The New Worlds of Cyberspace," *Critical Studies in Mass Communication,* 14 (June 1997): 123–137;

N. Katherine Hayles, "How Cyberspace Signifies: Taking Immortality Literally," in *Immortal Engines: Life Extension and Immortality in Science Fiction and Fantasy,* edited by George Slusser, Gary Westfahl, and Eric S. Rabkin (Athens: University of Georgia Press, 1996), pp. 111–121;

Heather J. Hicks, "'Whatever It Is That She's Since Become': Writing Bodies of Text and Bodies of Women in James Tiptree, Jr.'s 'The Girl Who Was Plugged In' and William Gibson's 'The Winter Market,'" *Contemporary Literature,* 37 (Spring 1996): 62–93;

Veronica Hollinger, "Cybernetic Deconstructions: Cyperbunk and Postmodernism," *Mosaic,* 23 (Spring 1990): 29–44;

David Ketterer, "William Gibson, *Neuromancer*, and Cyberpunk," in his *Canadian Science Fiction and Fantasy* (Bloomington: Indiana University Press, 1992), pp. 140–146;

Rob Latham, "Cyberpunk=Gibson=*Neuromancer*," *Science-Fiction Studies,* 20 (July 1993): 266–272;

Kathryne V. Lindberg, "Prosthetic Mnemonics and Prophylactic Politics: William Gibson Among the Subjectivity Mechanisms," *Boundary 2,* 23 (Summer 1996): 47–83;

Tom Maddox, "Cobra, She Said: An Interim Report on the Fiction of William Gibson," *Fantasy Review,* 9 (April 1986): 46–48;

Brian McHale, *Constructing Postmodernism* (London: Routledge, 1992), pp. 225–267;

David G. Mead, "Technological Transfiguration in William Gibson's Sprawl Novels: *Neuromancer, Count Zero,* and *Mona Lisa Overdrive*," *Extrapolation,* 32 (Winter 1991): 350–360;

Tom Moylan, "Global Economy/Local Texts: Utopian/Dystopian Tension in William Gibson's Cyberpunk Trilogy," *Minnesota Review,* 43–44 (Fall 1994/Spring 1995): 182–197;

Nicola Nixon, "Cyberpunk: Preparing the Ground for Revolution or Keeping the Boys Satisfied?" *Science-Fiction Studies,* 19 (July 1992): 219–235;

Lance Olsen, "The Shadow of Spirit in William Gibson's Matrix Trilogy," *Extrapolation,* 32 (Fall 1991): 278–289;

Olsen, "Virtual Termites: A Hypotextual Technomutant Explo(it)ration of William Gibson and the Electronic Beyond(s)," in *Cyberspace Textuality: Com-*

puter Technology and Literary Theory, edited by Marie Laure Ryan (Bloomington: Indiana University Press, 1998), pp. 224–255;

Olsen, *William Gibson* (Mercer Island, Wash.: Starmont House, 1992);

Cathy Peppers, "'I've Got You Under My Skin': Cyber(Sexed) Bodies in Cyberpunk Fictions," in *Bodily Discursions: Genders, Representations, Technologies,* edited by Deborah S. Wilson and Christine Moneera Laennac (Albany: State University of New York Press, 1997), pp. 163–185;

Ronald Schmitt, "Mythology and Technology: The Novels of William Gibson," *Extrapolation,* 34 (Spring 1993): 64–78;

Randy Schroeder, "Determinacy, Indeterminacy, and the Romantic in William Gibson," *Science-Fiction Studies,* 21 (July 1994): 155–163;

Schroeder, "Neu-Criticizing William Gibson," *Extrapolation,* 35 (Winter 1994): 330–341;

Peter Schwenger, "*Agrippa,* or, the Apocalyptic Book," in *Flame Wars: The Discourse of Cyberculture,* edited by Mark Dery (Durham, N.C.: Duke University Press, 1994), pp. 61–70;

Timo Siivonen, "Cyborgs and Generic Oxymorons: The Body and Technology in William Gibson's Cyberspace Trilogy," *Science-Fiction Studies,* 23 (July 1996): 227–244;

George Slusser and Tom Shippey, eds., *Fiction 2000: Cyberpunk and the Future of Narrative* (Athens: University of Georgia Press, 1992);

Nicholas Spencer, "Rethinking Ambivalence: Technopolitics and the Luddites in William Gibson and Bruce Sterling's *The Difference Engine,*" *Contemporary Literature,* 40 (Fall 1999): 403–429;

Claire Sponsler, "Cyberpunk and the Dilemmas of Postmodern Narrative: The Example of William Gibson," *Contemporary Literature,* 33 (Winter 1992): 625–644;

Tyler Stevens, "'Sinister Fruitiness': *Neuromancer,* Internet Sexuality and the Turing Test," *Studies in the Novel,* 28 (Fall 1996): 414–433;

Herbert Sussman, "Cyberpunk Meets Charles Babbage: *The Difference Engine* as Alternative Victorian History," *Victorian Studies,* 38 (Autumn 1994): 1–23;

Darko Suvin, "On Gibson and Cyberpunk SF," *Foundation,* 46 (Autumn 1989): 40–51;

Takayuki Tatsumi, "Comparative Metafiction: Somewhere Between Ideology and Rhetoric," *Critique: Studies in Contemporary Fiction,* 39 (Fall 1997): 2–17;

Jack G. Voller, "Neuromanticism: Cyberspace and the Sublime," *Extrapolation,* 34 (Spring 1993): 18–29;

Geoffrey Yule, "The Marginalised Short Stories of William Gibson: 'Hinterlands' and 'The Winter Market,'" *Foundation,* 58 (Summer 1993): 76–84.

Papers:

William Gibson's papers are held by the University of British Columbia, in Vancouver.

Phyllis Gotlieb
(25 May 1926 -   )

Douglas Barbour
University of Alberta

See also the Gotlieb entry in *DLB 88: Canadian Writers, 1920–1959, Second Series.*

BOOKS: *Who Knows One?* (Toronto: Hawkshead Press, 1962);
Within the Zodiac (Toronto: McClelland & Stewart, 1964);
Sunburst (Greenwich, Conn.: Fawcett, 1964; Toronto: Fitzhenry & Whiteside, 1977);
Ordinary, Moving (Toronto: Oxford University Press, 1969);
Why Should I Have All the Grief? (Toronto: Macmillan, 1969);
Doctor Umlaut's Earthly Kingdom (Toronto: Calliope Press, 1974);
O Master Caliban! (New York: Harper & Row, 1976; Toronto: McClelland & Stewart/Bantam, 1979);
The Works: Collected Poems (Toronto: Calliope Press, 1978);
A Judgment of Dragons (New York: Berkley, 1980);
Emperor, Swords, Pentacles (New York: Ace, 1982);
Son of the Morning and Other Stories (New York: Ace, 1983);
The Kingdom of the Cats (New York: Ace, 1985);
Heart of Red Iron (New York: St. Martin's Press, 1989);
Blue Apes (Edmonton, Alberta: Tesseract Books, 1995);
Flesh and Gold (New York: Tor, 1998);
Violent Stars (New York: Tor, 1999).

PRODUCED SCRIPTS: *Doctor Umlaut's Earthly Kingdom,* radio, Canadian Broadcasting Corporation, February–March 1970;
Silent Movie Days, radio, Canadian Broadcasting Corporation, 1971;
Garden Varieties, radio, Canadian Broadcasting Corporation, 3 April 1972;
The Contract, radio, Canadian Broadcasting Corporation, 1972;
God on Trial before Rabbi Ovadia, radio, Canadian Broadcasting Corporation, 18 April 1976.

Phyllis Gotlieb (courtesy of the author)

OTHER: "On Margaret Laurence," *Tamarack Review,* 52 (1969): 76–80;
"Hasidic Influences in the Work of A. M. Klein," in *The A. M. Klein Symposium,* edited by Seymour Mayne (Ottawa: University of Ottawa Press, 1974), pp. 47–64;

Tesseracts² : Canadian Science Fiction, edited by Gotlieb and Douglas Barbour (Toronto & Victoria: Press Porcépic, 1987).

According to Robert J. Sawyer, one of the most prolific and popular of the younger generation of science-fiction writers in Canada, "Phyllis Gotlieb is the grande dame of Canadian SF." Gotlieb has achieved this eminence through four decades of writing and publishing stories and novels that both celebrate and interrogate some paradigmatic science-fiction conventions. She has, from the beginning, written work that would fit into the general megatext of American science fiction, and almost all her science fiction has been published in the United States. She is best known in Canada as a poet of wide range and moral insight, and her developed style, as M. Travis Lane says in *The Oxford Companion to Canadian Literature* (1997), offers readers "musicality, colloquialism, relish for detail, and affirmation of her Jewish heritage." These qualities appear in her science fiction as well, giving it a distinctive tone.

While her imagination has traversed the galaxy, she has lived a quiet life in one city, marrying, raising children, and writing. She was born Phyllis Fay Bloom on 25 May 1926 in Toronto to Leo and Mary (Kates) Bloom, movie-theater owners. She attended Kew Beach Public School from 1931 to 1934, Withrow Avenue Public School from 1934 to 1939, Jarvis Collegiate Institute in 1939 and 1940, and Forest Hill Secondary School from 1940 to 1944. She was in high school during World War II and learned of the Nazi death camps while a senior. The Holocaust haunts her poetry, grounds the psychology of her one mainstream novel, *Why Should I Have All the Grief?* (1969), and may underlie the ethical approach to the alien in her science fiction.

She earned a B.A. in English literature in 1948 at Victoria College at the University of Toronto, where she met her future husband, Calvin Carl Gotlieb, a mathematician and computer scientist who eventually became director of the Institute of Computer Science at the University of Toronto and whose knowledge she has often utilized in her science fiction. They married on 12 June 1949, and she gained an M.A. in English literature in 1950 at University College of the University of Toronto. That same year, their son, Leo Ronald Gotlieb, was born. Daughter Margaret Susan followed in 1952, and Jane Elizabeth in 1956. By this time Gotlieb was beginning to write both poetry and science fiction. Her first small collection of poems, *Who Knows One?*, appeared as a limited-edition chapbook in 1962. Her first two published science-fiction stories, "Phantom Foot" and "A Grain of Manhood," appeared in *Amazing Science Fiction* and *Fantastic Science Fiction Stories* in 1959. Another story, "Gingerbread Boy," appeared in *IF Science Fiction* in 1961. For the next ten years she put most of her energy into poetry and novels. *Sunburst,* one of the few "classic" science-fiction novels of the period, appeared from a United States paperback publisher in 1964, and *Why Should I Have All the Grief?* came out in Canada in 1969.

Gotlieb's earliest stories are fables set in some undetermined future. According to David Ketterer in *Canadian Science Fiction and Fantasy* (1992), Gotlieb began writing science fiction "at her husband's suggestion to overcome a writer's block." Science fiction seems a perfect mode for someone who was brought up on movies, all kinds of fantastic tales, and Jewish legends, and who is also full of curiosity about scientific concepts. Her first published story, "A Grain of Manhood," includes many of the themes she has pursued throughout her career: it is about relationships, trust, maturing, and doing right by others as well as oneself. The protagonist, a young woman about to give birth, remembers the time she spent with shape-changing aliens after her ship crashed on an unknown planet. They have ESP and are able to communicate with her mind-to-mind, and apparently one of them impregnated her. Nevertheless, they let her leave, and the analogue to faeries is clear; they tell her, "If you leave we can't take you back." Eventually rescued, she returns to her husband and has her baby, and they reach a conciliation that points hopefully toward their future together. Despite its science-fiction elements, the story is almost balladlike in its representation of the aliens, who are seen only through her eyes, which perforce acknowledge the Other in culturally constructed ways. The first paragraph of the story reveals the poet at work:

> She was lying formless; the contour of her body was lost except for the white ring of pain that worked its way downward every so often like a wedding ring over a swollen knuckle. All her other miseries were encompassed by this masterpiece of nature, a force at one with lightning and thunder, the hurricane, the great reach of the four-thousand year old sequoia.

Readers of a science-fiction magazine might at first think this pain is the result of some alien invasion of the protagonist's body, only to discover that she is in childbirth (but then, as some feminist theory has argued, that is a kind of alien invasion).

Gotlieb's second published story, "Phantom Foot," a neat little puzzle story, is important for introducing the Qumedon, energy beings with a superior technology who feature in some of her later novels. Their presence sets the stage for her development of the Galactic Federation, in which most of her science

Cover for Gotlieb's first novel, published in 1964, about a group of juvenile delinquents with psychic abilities

fiction is set. In "Phantom Foot" the Qumedon are science-fiction equivalents of a malicious and powerful sorcerer, playing mind and body games with the men aboard the spaceship that was sent to try to communicate with them.

Her other early story, the sad and evocative "Gingerbread Boy," concerns a group of childlike androids created to provide children for the adults on a colonized world but being superseded by the "real" children the people are able to have now that they have left the polluted Earth behind. The question they must answer is whether or not there is a place for them in this community; some want to head for the hills in revolt, but the protagonist recognizes that their only place, however difficult, is with the people who made them and still love them in their way.

Gotlieb's first novel, *Sunburst*, immediately established her as a writer of some importance in the field, especially for its stunning exploration of ESP and psi powers and its moving representation of the protagonist's difficult adolescence as a brilliant and curious outsider. As Peter Nichols and Brian Stableford point out in *The Encyclopedia of Science Fiction* (1993), "Definitions of the term 'ESP' vary, but it may be taken to include clairvoyance, telepathy, and precognition," and they add that "ESP quickly became part of the standard repertoire of the pulp SUPERMAN." Psi powers include "psychokinesis or telekinesis (moving objects by the power of the mind); teleportation (moving oneself likewise . . .); pyrolysis (psychic fire-raising); and the ability to take control of the minds of others." The wild children of *Sunburst* have all these powers but lack ethical control. Shandy Johnson, the protagonist, has none of them; she is instead impervious to such powers, an "Imper," and on this distinction the interrogation of the superman theme turns.

An extremely well-read poet, Gotlieb uses frequent allusions in *Sunburst,* many of them explicitly attached to Shandy's wide reading, for although she is only thirteen, she is also a genius. Ketterer points out that "Gotlieb acknowledges (among a variety of literary allusions) the influence of *Odd John* (1935) by Olaf Stapledon. Shandy Johnson is an 'Odd Johnson' or, more accurately, 'Johndaughter,' and at one point she recalls an incident from Stapledon's novel." Both Ketterer and Elizabeth A. Lynn, in her introduction to the 1978 Gregg Press reprint of *Sunburst,* argue that the book appears to be a conscious interrogation of the kind of ESP superman found in such novels as A. E. van Vogt's *Slan* (1946), a figure much more often represented in science fiction than the quiet, unassuming one that Shandy discovers she may be.

Sunburst is not just Shandy's story, it is also about the other youngsters affected by the history of Sorrel Park—built in 1984 to serve an atomic power plant and isolated by the army from the rest of the world since 1994, when the plant blew up and the government immediately enforced an information blackout about the explosion. It is now 2024, and most of the "Dumplings"—so named because they are kept in "the Dump," the army's specially designed electronic prison for the forty-six psi-powered kids discovered and caught in Sorrel Park since the night in 2016 when a group of them went on a rampage but were too young and unfocused to escape the army's net—are in their late teens or early twenties. The long scene in which they discover they can combine their powers to create destruction is one of the great set pieces in the novel. Although their rampage wakens the town and brings the army running, Shandy, just three years old, sleeps through it all (the first sign of her imperviousness, not noticed by her or anyone else at the time). The import of the scene is multileveled, for in it Gotlieb uses an ancient children's rhyme to give the narrative a kind of poetic resonance; she also uses the scene to provide a bit of personal background on the older "Dumplings" and some psychological explanation for their behavior. Psychopathically delinquent, they are incapable of taking anyone else into consideration when they act, and so they run wild with no moral sense of the consequences. Only Donatus Riordan does not want to join them, but he is forced to and ends up in the Dump too. He is "a hunchback with *spina bifida* and the children called him Doydoy because of his painful stutter. . . . there was nothing wrong with his moral sense—but either the Blowup or some other freak chance had done something so terrible to the chromosome pattern that formed him and he could not help himself."

The call of the others' ESP is what drags Donatus along, even though he does have a moral sensibility. The rest become a "pack" that night:

> A single entity, and, except for the oddments, very much of a piece. The older ones had powerful shoulders, but they were all wiry and strong, the girls stringy. Their narrow faces tapered like the muzzles of wolves, shapes that marked patterns on the graphs of sociologists, along with the poverty, the hate, the heritage of crime and drunkenness, and the turbulence of movement that for once was dedicated to a single purpose.

In this case, that purpose is pure destructiveness.

Shandy is brought to the Dump because she has brought no notice upon herself, although she has skipped school and run bootleg whiskey for the family she lives with (her father and mother died when she was young). Nevertheless, she demonstrates fairly quickly that she does possess a moral sensibility, although she has not had much chance to practice it while trying to avoid notice in the town. A decided loner, she soon comes to care for Jason, the good ESPer; Marsh, the old scientist who designed "the buzzing scrambler circuit known as the Marczinek Field" that imprisons the Pack; and Dr. Urquhart, the psychiatrist who tries to work with the Dumplings or at least to understand what made them what they are. All Shandy had needed was a group of people she could admire in order to want to join the loose family they create among themselves.

There are two intertwined narratives: one a thriller having to do with the escape and recapture of the Dumplings; the other, much subtler, concerning Shandy's attempts to discover her purpose in life. Part of the pleasure of the second narrative line comes from Shandy's obsessive questioning of everybody she meets and from her surprisingly mature reason for doing so: "I am different. How do you know I haven't a purpose? Just because *I* don't know what it is doesn't mean there may not be one hidden inside me." Marsh finds this perception amusing, as does the reader, for Shandy sounds both intelligent and youthfully naive. That Gotlieb manages to catch this double aspect of her protagonist is one of the reasons the novel still reads well after more than thirty years.

The Dumplings have treated Donatus with a mixture of contempt and need during their years under the Marczinek Field: they laugh at his physical deformity but cannot function without his intelligence and memory. He is the only one to figure out how to interrupt the field for the second it takes them to escape; he then disappears, leaving them no idea of what to do. Shandy deduces his hiding place but feels he deserves to stay out of the Dump, especially if he can help the army recapture the others. Leaving a trail of destruction in their wake, the Dumplings escape to Chicago, where they attempt to take over or destroy a huge computer complex they believe controls the whole North American network. There are now three other such facilities, however; Donatus, so much more intelligent and powerful, separates and captures them. Captured by the Dumplings, the quick-witted and courageous Shandy divides them against each other, thus making Donatus's work much easier.

The other narrative, Shandy's search for her purpose in life, provides the real intellectual excitement of the novel, and with it Gotlieb contributes something new to the superman theme. Having read widely, if with little discipline, in sociology, psychology, and anthropology (her great heroine is Margaret Mead, a reminder that this novel was written in the early 1960s), Shandy is a superbly capable observer of life and people. Collating all her data, she constructs a theory that is not only intrinsically interesting but also deliberately at odds with every psi story since *Odd John* in its analysis of the meanings of fully developed psi powers in the individual. Remembering that "most normal people have vestiges of telepathy but it's stronger in babies and kids because they can't express themselves very well by talking," she suggests that

> Psychopaths have brainwaves like children. . . . *Their minds seem more primitively organized*. That's what they've got in common with all the other creatures in the world that have psi. . . . psi might be nothing but an ability that belongs to animals . . . for civilized people, just interesting garbage.

Dust jacket for Gotlieb's 1976 novel, about a robot revolt on the planet Barrazan V

In fact, although this theory might account for most of the Dumplings, it leaves out Jason and his two moral and intelligent ESPer friends. Still, its core concept, that civilization exists because of language and other technologies, stands against a lot of conventional science fiction, including perhaps Gotlieb's own later work.

If Shandy's theorizing marginalizes ESP, the logical question is Dr. Urquhart's: "Then how would you picture a supernormal who seemed reasonable in relation to Homo sapiens?" Shandy predicts a fairly ordinary-looking person, moral, intelligent, able to take care of himself, and finally "an organic part of humanity, to give his qualities to his children—if he could transmit them." Most important, "he'd watch and learn and wait." When Urquhart asks for what, her answer points to herself as the figure she has constructed: "To find out what he was." This revelation is a pure science-fiction one, although in typically understated fashion Gotlieb depicts a Shandy who realizes that she has a long way to go and that it may be a lonely road she has to follow. This novel, typically for Gotlieb, refuses absolute closure. Shandy is still thirteen, with her whole life before her; but she is also, as Lynn says, "one of the best juveniles in the SF tradition: tremendously believable, marvelously unstereotyped in a field which likes its female characters predictable. . . . She is tough, clever, and delightful. What other heroine in science fiction wonders in the midst of her adventures what Margaret Mead would have done?" This novel appeared in 1964, while Ursula K. Le Guin's first novel appeared in 1967 and Joanna Russ's in 1968. Like their work, it still stands up, and it remains perhaps Gotlieb's most important contribution to the genre.

Sunburst is sui generis, a one-of-a-kind book. During the rest of the 1960s Gotlieb mostly wrote poetry and worked on her only mainstream novel. *Why Should I Have All the Grief?* is a rather introverted, almost claustrophobic narrative. It is a character study of a young man who survived Auschwitz but cannot forgive his dead father for forcing him to experience those horrors but allowing his younger brother to escape. In one long weekend, sitting shiva for an uncle he did not even know was also in Canada, he finally begins to come to terms with his past and the way he is allowing it to destroy all present chances for happiness, including his marriage, which is on the verge of falling apart. As Gotlieb pointed out to Lynn, "People kept urging me to write a mainstream novel, and I wrote one to see if I could. It took four years, got quite a few good reviews, sold about 700 copies, and brought in $407.79. I think it was quite a good book, and it taught me a lot, but the lesson was too expensive." As well, unlike her science fiction, the novel has never been reprinted.

In 1968 "Rogue's Gambit" (later retitled "Monkey Wrench") was the first story to name the Galactic Federation (GalFed), the context for most of Gotlieb's science fiction since that time. As Stableford explains in *The Encyclopedia of Science Fiction,* "the rise and fall of a Galactic Empire" is a "central myth of GENRE SF. ('Empire' is here used with a general, almost metaphorical meaning, rather than in its politically definitive sense.) The galactic empire was a necessary invention: an imaginative framework which could accommodate any number of 'Earth-clone' worlds on which writers might deploy ordinary human characters in confrontation with any imaginable social and biological system." In her later novels and short stories Gotlieb's Galactic Federation allowed her to invent several alien sentient species and to create stories out of their inevitable conflicts and occasional resolutions. GalFed is also, perhaps, a distinctly Canadian version of the Galactic Empire.

A kind of super United Nations (UN), GalFed suffers from being poor, undermanned, and sometimes too bureaucratic for its own good, yet strives to do right for all concerned peoples. In her work Gotlieb has filled in GalFed's background, including Galactic Federation Central–the Twelveworlds of Fthel, from which GalFed tries to monitor its vast connected commonwealth. GalFed has somewhat more power than the UN to interfere on certain worlds on behalf of particular sentients, but never has enough money or resources; and the worlds connected to GalFed for trade, travel, and cultural interchange retain most of their sovereignty. GalFed's goal of including all "sentient species" allows Gotlieb the freedom to invent a wide range of aliens who nevertheless treat each other as people (or should–those who fail to do so signal their own prejudicial limitations). Gotlieb uses this standard science-fiction trope, then, in order to promote a vision of equality regarding race, gender, or even species. She has thus constructed a science-fiction ideal: to explore ethical possibilities as the fabular and the didactic mingle freely. Of course, within GalFed all "sentient species" are, by definition, "human," as that term essentially covers intelligence in whatever form. Therefore, and perhaps with the specific intention to suggest their general lack of importance in the greater scheme of things, people from the planet Earth are referred to as "Solthrees."

In addition to a few separate stories such as "Rogue's Gambit," "Mother Lode" (which first introduces the powerful ESP-using dragonlike Khagodi race and the fascinating snakelike Yefni people), and "Blue Apes" (a story about a failed colonization project by a fundamentalist sect), Gotlieb has written three series set in the GalFed universe. The first, comprising *O Master Caliban!* (1976) and *Heart of Red Iron* (1989), published more than a decade apart, concerns Dahlgren's World, its experiments in genetic engineering, and the accidental development of sentient machines, "ergs," with minds of their own. In between these two novels she published the second series, the three books of the Ungrukh Chronicles, featuring a race of large, intelligent cats. The third series consists of the thrillers *Flesh and Gold* (1998) and *Violent Stars* (1999).

O Master Caliban! (the title refers to a character in William Shakespeare's *The Tempest,* the narrative pattern of which is reversed in various ways in the novel) is both similar to and different from Gotlieb's first novel. Setting it in the GalFed universe clearly signals that it belongs to the far-future interstellar adventure mode; and despite the fascinating argument against it in *Sunburst,* ESP, especially telepathy, is seen as a necessary function of many sentient species, in order to facilitate communication among them. Then again, the need to communicate with aliens is precisely the kind of use for ESP that Shandy could not find among the humans of her near future. At any rate, like the Galactic Federation and its *lingua* or shared language, it is another "necessary invention" for genre science fiction. But Gotlieb has also chosen to explore ethical concerns in a way that much science fiction does not. Thus, *O Master Caliban!* shares with *Sunburst* an interest in the young, in moral education, and in the trials and tribulations of growing up.

The novel begins with a small ship of adolescents crash-landing in the one more-or-less habitable area of Barrazan V, otherwise known as Dahlgren's World. GalFed machines had carved this triangular space out of the surrounding jungle and erected a huge Biological Station where Edvard Dahlgren and his fellow scientists could pursue their experiments. But something went wrong, and eventually the ergs–the various robots intended to serve the scientists–revolted, killing everyone but Dahlgren and three other sentients: Sven, Dahlgren's four-armed son, genetically altered in vitro by the ergs; Esther, an intelligent, articulate, motherly gibbon; and Yigal, a large, grumpy white goat who likes to quote Michel de Montaigne. These three have been isolated at the far end of the station for nine years, not knowing if any-

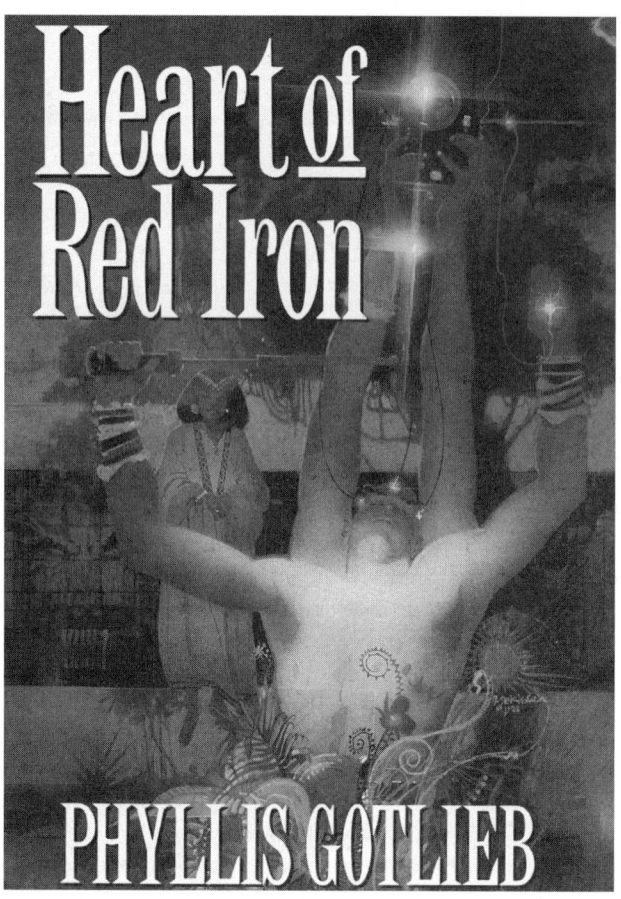

Dust jacket for Gotlieb's 1989 sequel to O Master Caliban!

one else is alive or dead, when the ship crashes nearby. The young runaways include a ten-year-old genius who can communicate with machines, but they are delinquents who have been placed in the Triskelion Order to learn how to adjust. That they have failed to do so is shown by their having stolen the small ship.

In a sense, their narrative is an educational one, as they slowly learn to work together in order to survive against the ergs. Meanwhile, Edvard Dahlgren, who failed to go mad when the ergs killed off all the other humans in the station, has to face Mod-Dahlgren, a machine that looks just like him and is now studying him to learn his behavior. He has always been a man who demonstrated little emotion, which is why his wife left him and why his son is unsure Dahlgren loves him. Dahlgren and his machine-likeness also undergo an education of sorts: both become more "human" as they realize they must work together and with the "children" (a term Gotlieb uses quite deliberately throughout the novel to suggest how immature they are) to defeat the Creator Matrix (otherwise known as the Erg-Queen), which ordered the machines to kill the people on the station and created Mod-Dahlgren.

In many ways *O Master Caliban!* is a quest narrative, with a battle against a terrible power, in this case a machine, at the end; but what sets it apart is Gotlieb's sense of detail, also found in her poetry. Esther is definitely a gibbon, even as she "mothers" Sven and the others. The youngsters' characters are defined by specifically individual traits: Joshua, a diplomat's son, prefers the jungle to the Space Academy; Koz, worshiping an idol to control his violence, finally gives his life to save them all; Mitzi, the narcissist, needs her drug sticks and the thrills she gets from freaks; Ardagh, inquisitive and tough, wants to be a doctor but faked credentials to get into college, yet she accepts and even comes to love the young stranger with four arms; and Shirvanian, ten-year-old mechanical genius and thumb-sucking, frightened little boy, can manipulate ergs and finally, with the others' help, defeat the Erg-Queen.

Gotlieb handles her complex plot with ease, shifting between the youths' quest and the two Dahlgrens' chess game; she accumulates details about the biosphere of the planet and the ergs' variety and operation always in a way that moves the action forward. Yet, the novel concentrates upon the growth of character, or the failure of such growth, in both the children and the adults, through a series of encounters and discussions that bear the ethical weight of the narrative. The kids must learn to cooperate and to properly mourn and continue on after the losses to their small community (Koz dies, and Yigal is killed). Both Dahlgrens have to learn to trust each other and achieve emotional balance. The details of these inner journeys give the novel its emotional weight.

Both of Sven's sexual experiences are presented with sharp precision: Mitzi seduces him only to say "First time I ever made it with a real freak," forcing him to look "carefully to avoid the fear and revulsion that might curdle in him later and embitter his spirit"; later he and Ardagh genuinely make love, partly because they have both seen each other clearly and liked what they saw. When Sven finally meets Dahlgren and his mechanical doppelgänger, it is a powerful moment of forgiveness and reconciliation. Gotlieb's unsentimental vision, partly clarified by the presence of animals and their lack of human hypocrisy, allows these scenes their own momentum. In the end, everyone but Yigal has gained something, even Koz, although Mitzi learns and changes the least. But they can count the cost, and it is not small.

Heart of Red Iron is both more complexly plotted and emotionally simpler than *O Master Caliban!* After writing the popular and entertaining adventures of the Ungrukh cats, Gotlieb could return to the difficult and dangerous world of Barrazan V with a greater sense of the variety of species inhabiting the Galactic Federation. The prologue to *Heart of Red Iron* describes the geological and environmental horrors of the planet: "Tectonic plates ramming together have crumpled landmasses into peaks scored with abyssal valleys. From their orbit next toward the sun asteroids crack out of the courses they ride in to bomb the surface with their alien stones." A quick reprise of the events of *O Master Caliban!* prepare the reader for the intertwined narratives to follow. These involve the crash landing of a young man running away from family and responsibility, the return of a scientific project to the Biological Station, three different sentient races—Yefni, Meshar, and Crystalloids—seeking to settle on the planet, the near destruction of a new life-form from space, and an attempt by the sentient ergs remaining there to find someone to present them as potential members to GalFed. Involved in all these events by their past associations with the place are Sven and Ardagh, now married and parents. He works for GalFed, and she has become the doctor she always wanted to be. In a sense, there is too much happening for much character development of the kind found in *O Master Caliban!*, but Gotlieb still creates several sharply observed and differentiated if somewhat stereotyped figures.

The novel begins with "the old Prima," a previously unknown nonorganic life-form that has, over the millennia, adapted to living among the asteroids. It has given birth to others like it, which now attack its ship and send it spiraling down to the surface of Barrazan V, on the edge of a volcano that might erupt and consume it at any time (though time is far slower for it than for organic life). On Fthel IV, Sir Frederik Havergal seeks Sven's aid in his attempt to recolonize the Station, but Sven does not know that Havergal's son has gone missing there. When Ardagh is called in to help a female of the Meshar, she is asked to accompany her patient back to Barrazan V. So she and Sven both return to the planet where they met fifteen years before. Mod-Dahlgren, now one of Sven's closest friends, also joins the expedition.

As the various groups try to carry out their projects, the ergs interfere, trying to find someone to represent them; a young catatonic woman who can communicate with the Crystalloids via ESP contacts the Prima's ship and insists someone save it; the Meshar woman dies, and their leader loses then regains his power; and Sven meets the brother he did not know he had (his mother, already pregnant, married Havergal after she left Dahlgren). After several complicated plot shifts, the asteroid folk are saved; Mod-Dahlgren agrees to represent the ergs to GalFed; young Havergal finally accepts responsibility for his own actions; the three species are settled in various parts of the planet; and Sven and Ardagh exorcise several ghosts from their past. Gotlieb handles her complex plotting cleanly and offers many interesting character sketches of such people as Havergal, Mod-Dahlgren, Sven and Ardagh, Prima (the crystalline intelligence with her battered ship, which turns out to be about two meters long), Han Li (the ESP interpreter for the Crystalloids), and Sandek (the Meshar who manipulates his way to lifetime leadership of his large family or tribe). Toward the end, the old erg intelligences who originally constructed the Erg-Queen finally come out of hiding in order to gain Sven and Mod-Dahlgren's confidence; comically Polonius-like in their arguing, they have much more power and, finally, more understanding of it. The narratives move so quickly toward their intertwined climaxes that the lack of the kind of maturing found in *O Master Caliban!* is hardly noticed.

Two science-fiction stories pay homage to Gotlieb's Jewish roots: "Son of the Morning" (1971) introduces the great intelligent cats who eventually filled the three volumes of the Ungrukh Chronicles; "Tauf Aleph" (1981), another of her most popular stories, concerns the difficulties of providing "one mourner/gravedigger" so that the last Jew in the galaxy "can die in peace." GalFed sends an old, refurbished robot, who has studied all the Torah, "the Writings, Prophets, and the Mishna, . . . the Talmud (Palestinian and Babylonian), . . . and Tosefta, . . . thirty-five hundred years of Commentary and Responsa," not to mention most ancient languages, in order to understand the Jewishness of Samuel Zohar ben Reuven Begelman, who is approaching his end on Tau Ceti IV. Samuel and the robot's arguments over the aboriginal species that wants to convert to honor the old man who had saved them from destruction are comically absurd and sadly elegiac at once. It is a sign of Gotlieb's capacity to create empathy for her characters that readers come to care as much for the robot as for the irascible old man.

"Son of the Morning," the second story in the GalFed universe, brings together several elements Gotlieb had been using separately—the Galactic Federation, the Qumedon (who "make their home in the Galaxy but they don't belong to GalFed. They don't need to; they have so many talents, powers and dominions"), telepathy as communication, and the politics of accommodation—and brings the clear, animal morality of the civilized Ungrukh to bear upon them. It also introduces some mysteries about their origins that are not fully resolved until the ending of the third volume:

Fortunately, GalFed was happy with the Ungrukh. (a) About a third of them were telepathic, most often the females . . . ; ESPs are rare, particularly where lan-

Pages from Gotlieb's notebooks for her 1998 novel, Flesh and Gold *(Collection of Phyllis Gotlieb)*

~~Across city~~ town
The satellite ~~city~~ was the freight sector
???

even if he had not been shielded by the helm. The prosecuting attorney blinked at him thoughtfully; the defence ~~~~ also a Solthree, went white around the mouth but did not have any~~thing~~ more to protest.

Skerow in a flash saw media people from seven worlds swarming about Khagodi, and ~~~~ any tang of corruption that might eddy about the ~~~~ moralists

"Flurry, flicker, click!
"What did ~~~~ ~~~~, why did he,

There was not much audience, ~~~~ and Skerow ~~~~ had no ~~~~ trouble getting out of court as quickly as a Khagodi is able, ~~and~~ to avoid~~ing~~ the media and the questions

The port facility was a satellite of Starry Nova, the main headquarters community of Galactic Federation on Fthel V. The name had guage is advanced, and for Galactic liaison and socio-biological sciences they are invaluable; (b) they were an evolutionary puzzle: very nearly Solthree cats with big brains, language, and a civilization only a few thousand years old and no relatives to evolve from or with on the planet.

Plunging readers into her multispecied and technologically advanced future immediately, Gotlieb also quickly underlines the animality of her two protagonists—Khreng, the tribal leader who first faced the GalFed surveyor team, and his mate, the powerful ESPer, Prandra:

> By the time Khreng and Prandra came out of deepsleep the ship was in Solthree orbit. Lights warmed around them, the deep yellow of their sun; they slipped the clasps of their webbing, leaped out snarling and yawning hugely, stretched to the limit the hinges of their fanged jaws. . . .
> They ate and got full but not satisfied; then they coupled, combed each other, and bathed.

Throughout the three books Gotlieb slips in little observations and perceptions demonstrating that the Ungrukh are still cats, albeit extremely civilized ones. In this way she keeps them from becoming mere human-substitutes while emphasizing the commonalty of all the sentient species in the GalFed universe.

The four stories in the first Ungrukh volume, *A Judgment of Dragons* (1980), include a Jewish fable, a kind of locked-room mystery, a thriller, and a tale of conflicting loyalties both human and transcendental. They argue, formally, the way in which each genre can be transformed by the science-fiction mode; and they are, therefore, science fiction more than anything. "Son of the Morning" takes the Ungrukh and their ancient ESP teacher back more than seven hundred years to a Jewish ghetto in Kostopol, where the innate goodness of the local rabbi makes it possible for what he can only think are two demons to prevent a pogrom against the Jews of the village, started by a Qumedni master of illusions. Gotlieb catches the tone of a Jewish tale even as she mixes in pure science-fiction jargon and explanation. The rabbi sees the Qumedon as Ashmedai, lord of demons; but in the end, he tells the cats: "Thank you, creatures of God." He has much to worry about, however, for the Qumedon, with darkest irony, has told him that there will be a terrible holocaust in about one hundred years, and that he has saved Kostopol only so it might be destroyed then. Knowing his prayer, "Let it be a lie," will not be answered, readers feel a profound pity.

"The King's Dogs" takes place on Sol III and involves a string of murders that are meant to frame the Ungrukh. It introduces Kinnear, the Solthree administrator whose love of the cats will involve him in many of their adventures, and carefully unravels the mystery in proper science-fiction fashion. It also introduces several other aliens, partly to demonstrate that friendship between species is possible and that any moral sentient is capable of sacrifice for the good of another. "Nebuchadnezzar" takes Khreng and Prandra to the planet of Wyaerl, home to the Yirli, where smugglers are destroying the environment. They are captured but eventually make a daring escape, outwit a dangerous hunter willing to kill fellow sentients, and help the Yirli regain control of their own world.

Finally, in "A Judgment of Dragons," Khreng and Prandra return home to begin uniting the tribes, only to discover another Qumedon trying to sell their whole race to an unknown being from another universe. There is some of the sharp irony the Ungrukh appreciate when the Qumedon they met in "Son of the Morning" appears to help them fight this new figure: "'This is our Qumedon of old acquaintance—in a new shape,' Prandra said. 'Our damned dull world is now a center of intercosmic traffic.'" The important point is the way Prandra identifies it as "our Qumedon," assuming a kind of possession over it even as it assumes a kind of godlike power over them. In the end, the Ungrukh themselves deal with the power from elsewhere, thanking it for its interest but refusing to join it in its loneliness. The Qumedni fleet, however, punishes their Qumedon by sending it to help this being. And the Ungrukh have been given a clue as to what might have created them. But there is a bitter loss, as Khreng and Prandra's son dies in the battle between the two Qumedon.

Gotlieb's next novels are intricately plotted, with so many twists and turns a reader can barely keep up. Gotlieb has called *Emperor, Swords, Pentacles* (1982), the initial letters of which spell ESP, one of her favorite novels. In chapters titled by the names of tarot cards, the narrative swings from the planet Qsaprinel, where the Emperor and his fission-brother have been fighting over the throne, to GalFed Central, where Kinnear, now a Sector Co-ordinator, takes an interest in Qsaprinel when a new Director tries to prevent him, and then to Ungruwarkh, where Khreng and Prandra are getting too old to travel but send their daughter, Emerald, and her mate, the Hillsman Raanung, to help Kinnear. There are many different players of various species in this version of the great game, including "the Locksmith," who "was a Praximif. Praximfi were the only organic shape-changing species GalFed knew of, as opposed, for instance, to Qumedon, who were energy forms." He is the only one of his mystic people to leave his home planet and deal with other members of GalFed, and much to his surprise he ends up working with the Ungrukh, the Emperor, Kinnear and his allies, and a forty-four-year-old "embryo" who is brother to the figure attempting to enslave the Qsaprinil. Emerald and Raanung are another quick-witted, sharp-tongued pair. The pace is fast, discussions sharp with idioms intimately tied to species, and the various environments believable for their inhabitants. Along the way there are plenty of surprises, and all the players get what they deserve.

Much the same can be said of *The Kingdom of the Cats* (1985), set mostly on Sol III, around the Grand Canyon. A group of Ungrukh have settled there to be studied by GalFed scientists, but suddenly most of them have been slaughtered by some unknown group. Bren, Emerald and Raanung's daughter, and big, clumsy Etrem are the only survivors, along with young twins who were away at the time. The attack sets in motion a mystery, and eventually something of a courtroom drama, but once again, the many plotlines are complicated and intertwined. Several Solthrees are involved as friends and enemies of the cats; a powerful politician with a grudge against Emerald and Raanung from *Emperor, Swords, Pentacles* is the reason for the attack but not its instigator; some Pueblo Indians aid the Ungrukh; and their Qumedon reappears. This novel finally reveals that their Qumedon more or less created the Ungrukh from Solthree leopards, "A SPLENDID TOY."

In the end a group of Ungrukh, including Emerald and Raanung, get the justice they seek from Solthree courts but refuse the revenge the Qumedon offers them. As well, in a moment out of time, as an ESP-connected single entity, they repudiate him, even knowing that he created them. And as a single force, they ask him to leave them alone. Before he goes, however, he speaks to Emerald:

> "Emerald I saw your father going out to die, and I spoke to him."
> Emerald flinched.
> "No, I did not offer him an easy death, nor give him one. I wished him the death he wanted."
> "Then, Qumedon, I thank you with all my soul."
> "At last! I have gotten a simple thanks from an Ungrukh! Then it is surely time. Good-bye, children."

In context, this exchange tells readers much about Ungrukh morality and life, and about their fierce pride. Yet, once again, Gotlieb convincingly displays the innate "humanity" of her aliens.

In one of her most complexly narrated novels, *Flesh and Gold,* she depicts this humanity for several species while providing one of her darkest glimpses of the undergrounds of various planets and species. More than the earlier works, *Flesh and Gold* mixes utopian hopes with cynically realistic awareness of how powerful the desires to degrade, use, and abuse others are in even the most civilized cultures. As the title implies, money and the power it buys interfere with ordinary people in the most basic way, by controlling their bodies. On Khagodis, the home planet of the most powerful ESP users in the galaxy, famous everywhere for their probity, a member of an undersea people later discovered to be cloned from Solthrees is murdered. When an interstellar Khagodi judge discovers one of these people on display at a licensed bordello on Fthel V, she begins an inquiry that eventually involves many different worlds.

Through the interactions of several characters from different classes and worlds, including the enigmatic Lyhhrt and various hominid species met in earlier novels, Gotlieb reveals what a complex, multispecies civilization GalFed is. That is the ideal, but when some still want to control the lives of others for their own gain, the need for laws and for the police and judges who serve them becomes clear. The telepathic judge, Skerow, discovers the amphibian woman Kobai on display at a brothel shortly after sentencing a smuggler who had bought a fellow Khagodi judge. Back at her quarters she finds him murdered and is then attacked herself. Her sense of the essential probity of her own people is severely tested as she pursues justice for Kobai and others. Meanwhile, a spy working for GalFed and infiltrating the gladiator games of an interstellar agency (which also runs the brothels) discovers other aspects of what turns out to be a huge conspiracy. Elsewhere, a former policeman goes to work at the gaming tables in the brothel where Kobai was displayed. The novel continually switches setting and focus as all these people pursue their various goals on widely separated worlds, often with the help of strangers of other species.

Flesh and Gold is a finely honed thriller, with elements of the police procedural, the spy story, the courtroom drama, and the noir adventure. All of these modes serve Gotlieb's deeply moral science-fiction vision, which drives the narrative from character to character, world to world, story to story. Eventually the various threads come together to form a bold, if bloody, tapestry.

Violent Stars, a direct sequel to *Flesh and Gold,* carries the narrative of unfinished business to several other planets. Some of the characters from the previous novel interact with new and interesting figures in their sometimes subtle, often brutal struggles with an interstellar family corporation. Most of the action takes place on Khagodis. In *Flesh and Gold* Skerow managed, with the help of GalFed operatives, to bring a galaxywide gambling and prostitution ring to trial, but now it is fighting back. Moreover, it turns out to be extremely old, tracing its beginnings back to Sol III–Earth.

Once again the interactions of several characters from various classes and various species both reveal GalFed as an intricate civilization and demonstrate that no matter how civilized a culture becomes, it can and will be corrupted by various forms of criminality. Using the warlike Ix, who have refused to join GalFed, the Zamos operation tries murder and kidnapping to prevent the trial from taking place. The Ix attack the daughter of a human diplomat whose history is far more mysterious than either she or her father realizes. Meanwhile, Skerow's former husband, who was to act as judge in the case, has been murdered. This loss is somewhat balanced by her meeting with his son, another important lawyer working on the case. Other figures from *Flesh and Gold* return to join forces in the fight against the criminal contingent.

Gotlieb remains a master at inventing a wide range of alien beings and showing them in various modes of interaction, but she makes it clear that humans are equally alien to them. There are some ironic moments when a character utterly alien to readers registers distaste or fear of human traits, and highly moving ones when they show concern and compassion for someone of another species. Like its predecessor, *Violent Stars* is a thriller, combining elements of several genres wrapped in solid science-fiction speculation. A further volume in this series, "Mindworlds," is planned for 2002.

Phyllis Gotlieb is still probably best known as the author of the classic science-fiction novel *Sunburst;* but she deserves to be evaluated for the ways in which she has consistently pursued a profoundly moral vision in all her varied works. As Lane says, "Her imagery is as magical as that of Chagall or Tchelitchew, and combines the fantastic and the mundane with Dickensian rigour. Gotlieb's primary effect is an expression of joy in the created universe."

References:

Douglas Barbour, "A Cornucopia of Poems," *Tamarack Review,* 76 (1978): 101–107;

Barbour, "Phyllis Gotlieb's Children of the Future: *Sunburst* and *Ordinary, Moving,*" *Journal of Canadian Fiction,* 3, no. 2 (1974): 72–76;

Maureen Bradbury, "'O Master Caliban!'" *Quill & Quire,* 43 (January 1972): 25;

Fred Cogswell, "Imprisoned Galaxies," *Canadian Literature,* 23 (Winter 1965): 65–67;

David Ketterer, "Phyllis Gotlieb *Is* Canadian SF?" in his *Canadian Science Fiction and Fantasy* (Bloomington & Indianapolis: Indiana University Press, 1992), pp. 67–70;

Anne Montagnes, "Gotlieb's Misery," *Saturday Night,* 84 (May 1969): 36, 38;

Janis Rapoport, "Challenging the Game" and "The Grief Is Shared," *Tamarack Review,* 54 (1970): 85–89.

Papers:

A collection of Phyllis Gotlieb's manuscripts is part of the Merril Collection at the Toronto Public Library.

Terence M. Green

(2 February 1947 -   )

Nalo Hopkinson

BOOKS: *The Woman Who is the Midnight Wind* (Porters Lake, Nova Scotia: Pottersfield Press, 1987);
Barking Dogs (New York: St. Martin's Press, 1988);
Children of the Rainbow (Toronto: McClelland & Stewart, 1992);
Shadow of Ashland (New York: Forge, 1996);
Blue Limbo (New York: Tor, 1997);
A Witness to Life (New York: Forge, 1999);
St. Patrick's Bed (New York: Forge, 2001).

OTHER: "The Night Above the Dingle Starry," in *Other Worlds,* edited by Paul Collins (St. Kilda, Australia: Void, 1978), pp. 29–48;
"Japanese Tea," in *Alien Worlds,* edited by Collins (St. Kilda, Australia: Void, 1979), pp. 241–252;
"Of Children in the Foliage," in *Aurora: New Canadian Writing, 1979,* edited by Morris Wolfe (Toronto: Doubleday Canada, 1979), pp. 102–108;
"The Woman Who is the Midnight Wind," in *Tesseracts,* edited by Judith Merril (Victoria, British Columbia: Press Porcépic, 1985), pp. 103–114; reprinted in *Northern Stars: The Anthology of Canadian Science Fiction,* edited by David Hartwell and Glenn Grant (New York: Tor, 1994), pp. 161–170;
"Ashland, Kentucky," in *Tesseracts²,* edited by Phyllis Gotlieb and Douglas Barbour (Victoria, British Columbia: Press Porcépic, 1987), pp. 88–112; reprinted in *Northern Frights,* edited by Don Hutchison (Oakville, Ontario: Mosaic Press, 1992), pp. 73–94;
"Blue Limbo," in *Ark of Ice: Canadian Futurefiction,* edited by Lesley Choyce (Lawrencetown Beach, Nova Scotia: Pottersfield Press, 1992), pp. 13–35;
"Family, Identity, and Speculative Fiction," in *Out of This World: Canadian Science Fiction and Fantasy Literature,* compiled by Andrea Paradis (Kingston, Ontario: Quarry Press, 1995), pp. 105–112;
"Barking Dogs," in *Crossing the Line: Canadian Mysteries with a Fantastic Twist,* edited by Robert J. Sawyer

Terence M. Green (photograph by Merle Casci)

and David Skene-Melvin (Lawrencetown Beach, Nova Scotia: Pottersfield Press, 1998), pp. 175–189;
"Legacy," in *Over the Edge: The Crime Writers of Canada Anthology,* edited by Peter Sellers and Sawyer (Lawrencetown Beach, Nova Scotia: Pottersfield Press, 2000), pp. 36–41.

In the April 1988 issue of *Books in Canada* Terence M. Green told fellow Canadian science-fiction writer Robert J. Sawyer that most science fiction "is just outrageous fairy tales for adults. But I've always thought the genre could produce literature. This may sound presumptuous, but I'd like to think I could help elevate it to that level." After years of struggle, by the late 1990s Green's work was widely acclaimed not only within the science-fiction genre but also increasingly by mainstream readers and critics.

In the chancy market that is Canadian science-fiction publishing, Green's writing career has had its share of peaks and valleys. As is common in the field, he began by writing short stories. They were acclaimed by readers and critics alike, who praised his quiet, deft style and his careful examination of fragile human relationships. But his stories were often published in obscure markets and could be difficult to obtain. When *The Woman Who is the Midnight Wind* (1987) collected most of his short stories into a volume, it was a critical success but was only available to a limited market. He began working on novels in the 1980s, but his success was hindered by difficulties with publishers. *Barking Dogs* (1988) was first sold to Bluejay Books, but the company went out of business before publishing the novel. *Barking Dogs* was finally published by St. Martin's Press, but that publisher then dropped its science-fiction line, leaving Green again without a publisher. His next novel, *Children of the Rainbow,* was published by McClelland and Stewart, Canada's foremost publisher, in 1992. Other Canadian science-fiction writers saw this publication as a breakthrough and hoped that large Canadian presses would begin to publish and develop local science-fiction talent. Those hopes were dashed, however, by McClelland and Stewart's failure to take future Green novels. Finally, he began publishing with the prominent New York–based science-fiction publisher Tor/Forge Books.

Despite these publishing frustrations Green has continued to develop his skills at novel writing, largely through expanding short stories into novels. He achieved significant critical success with the World Fantasy Award–nominated *Shadow of Ashland* (1996), which was described as "poignant and glowing" by prominent science-fiction critic Douglas Barbour in the 11 August 1996 *Edmonton Journal*. When asked how he continues to write despite his many setbacks, Green told Edo van Belkom in *Northern Dreamers: Interviews with Famous Science Fiction, Fantasy, and Horror Writers* (1998): "Isn't that a mystery? That's why I believe some of us are born to write and some of us are born to play the piano. . . . Well, I can write, so if I don't do it I'm wasting myself."

Terence Michael Green was born on 2 February 1947 in Toronto, Ontario, to Thomas Green, a newspaper circulation manager, and Margaret (Radey) Green, a homemaker. Green was the fourth of their five children. He attended the University of Toronto, receiving a B.A. in English in 1967, and then began a career as a high-school English teacher at the East York Collegiate Institute in Toronto in 1968. After two years he quit in order to return to school, moving to Ireland to study at University College, Dublin, from which he received an M.A. in Anglo-Irish studies in 1972. The next year he received a Bachelor of Education degree from the University of Toronto. He returned to East York Collegiate in 1972 and taught there for another two years before moving to Bayside Secondary School in rural Ontario, near the small city of Belleville. After two years there, he returned to East York Collegiate, where he stayed, with the exception of occasional leaves of absence, until his retirement from teaching in 1999. After the breakup of his first marriage, he married Merle Casci in 1994. He has two sons from his first marriage, Conor, born on 7 March 1978, and Owen, born on 16 February 1981, as well as Daniel, born on 19 November 2000 to him and Merle.

Green's first published short story, "The Night Above the Dingle Starry," appeared in a 1978 Australian anthology, *Other Worlds,* edited by Paul Collins, and it was followed the next year by "Japanese Tea" in another anthology edited by Collins, *Alien Worlds.* That same year "Of Children in the Foliage" was published in *Aurora: New Canadian Writing, 1979,* edited by Morris Wolfe. His first publication in a major science-fiction magazine was "Till Death Do Us Part," which appeared in the December 1981 issue of *The Magazine of Fantasy and Science Fiction.* Green admits that at first he was ignorant of any coherent strategy for publishing his work; he learned by doing, submitting his stories to any market that caught his fancy. He collected most of his short fiction from the previous decade in *The Woman Who is the Midnight Wind,* published by Pottersfield Press, a Nova Scotia–based small press run by fellow author Lesley Choyce. On his website (http://www.tmgreen.com) Green expresses his appreciation for the quality production this book received, particularly the cover art. Although its sales were limited by the fact that as a small-press item the collection did not receive mass distribution, *The Woman Who is the Midnight Wind* did receive positive reviews, by both mainstream and genre critics. In the Autumn 1988 issue of *Canadian Literature* Keith Wilson wrote:

> It should logically be difficult to do anything very fresh with time travel, doppelgängers, or humanoid computers, but Green does, working with situations in which emotions engage with the substitutes that science has created for the human exchanges it has helped to destroy. Whether those exchanges are between man and woman, parent and child, siblings, or teacher and taught, the stories have a wit and sympathy that push through the dutifully deployed paraphernalia of the genre.

Well-known science-fiction writer Orson Scott Card was similarly enthusiastic, writing in the May 1988 issue of *The Magazine of Fantasy and Science Fiction:* "Green is such a quiet writer that it's quite possible to overlook him for a while, possible not to realize that a string of extraordinarily good stories over the last few years have had the same byline.... I suspect Green will not significantly widen his public until his first novel appears."

Green did turn his attention to writing novels, which he described to Sawyer in the April 1988 *Books in Canada* as "the greatest commitment a writer can make, representing the greatest amount of pain, the greatest fear." For his first novel, he expanded "Barking Dogs," a short story that had initially appeared in the May 1984 issue of *The Magazine of Fantasy and Science Fiction*. His intention was to work within the conventions of popular fiction. As he told Sawyer, "For *Barking Dogs*, I studied what makes popular commercial fiction work, and I consciously set out to include those elements. Since it was a first novel, I wanted to be sure it would sell."

Barking Dogs, which finally appeared in 1988, tells the story of Mitch Helwig, a frustrated cop in a near-future Toronto, who uses his life savings to purchase a new device called a "barking dog"—an infallible lie detector that the interrogator wears hidden on his body—despite the fact that police are forbidden from using it. With the help of his "barking dog" Helwig becomes a one-man judge, jury, and executioner. In addition, he keeps his activities secret from his wife, adding more tension to a relationship that is already on the decline.

A recurring debate in Canadian literary circles is whether there are significant differences between Canadian and American science fiction. Many have argued that Canadian science-fiction heroes tend to be less individualistic and more motivated by community concerns. Similarly, some have suggested that Canadian science fiction tends to focus on the exploration of complex, delicate interactions, whether on the macro scale (planetary ecologies, international relations) or the micro (interpersonal relationships). Because his work has always explored the effects of events and systems on other people's lives, Green can be described as a quintessentially Canadian writer. *Barking Dogs*, however, with its vigilante cop plot, is in many ways a rather un-Canadian novel, leading Darlene James to describe it in the 27 June 1988 issue of *Maclean's*, a Canadian newsmagazine, as "a Canuck 'Rambo' aimed, as Green has stated, at the American market." However accurate that description may be, Green does see the novel as concerning itself with individual human lives. Helwig is trying single-handedly to address the ever-increasing levels of violence that some technologies enable, and the novel explores the impact of Helwig's actions on his emotions and on the lives of his family and friends. Because of that focus, other reviewers such as Canadian science-fiction writer Charles de Lint felt that the work had more in common with cyberpunk and director Paul Verhoeven's movie *RoboCop* (1987) than with Rambo in *First Blood* (1982). Writing in the April 1988 issue of *Locus*, Dan Chow observed that "Green makes his implacable policeman human just as Verhoeven did in *RoboCop*, and so lifts his work out of the morass." Similarly, Tom Easton enthused in the October 1988 issue of *Analog*:

> You will enjoy it. The only requirement is that you remember fondly Mickey Spillane's style of vigilantism.... But Green does not display Spillane's constant belligerence. The focus is on Helwig's interior life: his pain, his attempts to master a fate he does not understand. We are left with the question of whether ... vigilantism can possibly be a moral solution to the crime problem.

When asked by Sawyer if *Barking Dogs* is a call for urban vigilantism, Green responded, "If people read the book the way I intended it, they will see that it's not a call for anything. Rather, it presents a new situation—a world in which the cop on the beat can know beyond a shadow of a doubt whether the person he is arresting is guilty. All I'm asking is for people to think about that." *Barking Dogs* was nominated for an Aurora Award.

Green's next novel, *Children of the Rainbow*, published in 1992, was a different novel, described by Barbour in the October 1993 issue of *SF Commentary* as "an intriguing blend of history and prophecy, always an engaging read." In the twenty-first century the leader of a church that has revived Inca beliefs discovers a method of sending people back in time one hundred years. Scientist Fletcher Christian IV, a direct descendant of the *Bounty* mutineer, decides to travel to Pitcairn Island in 1972, to visit the place where his ancestor lived; but a French nuclear test in the Pacific in 1972 interferes with the time-travel technology. The scientist finds himself in chains on the Norfolk Island prison colony in 1835, in place of prisoner Bran Michael Dalton, who gets thrown to Pitcairn in 1972. Adding a Canadian element, the novel incorporates the unsuccessful 1972 attempt of Canadian David McTaggart and the ship *Greenpeace III* to prevent the French from exploding a nuclear bomb.

Children of the Rainbow was warmly received by critics, with some caveats. *Canadian Book Review Annual 1992* described it as "a glorious mix of time, space, and philosophies—a science fantasy that covers an ambitious range of topics and environments, and does so with great craftsmanship." Canadian science-fiction writer Jean-Louis Trudel, writing in the July 1997 issue of the *New York Review of Science Fiction,* was impressed by the scenes of Fletcher trying to come to terms with a nineteenth- century prison island; he said that these scenes "make for wonderful reading and they form what is by far the book's most compelling thread." He felt, however, that the parts of the book dealing with McTaggart's expedition could have been developed more thoroughly: "The thread dealing with the peace activists at sea near Mururoa may not have the intended impact on those who are too young to remember a time before the ban on atmospheric nuclear tests. It is, in part, a Canadian story and, for Canadians of that generation, it may carry the same emotional charge of Vietnam war protests for their United States counterparts," and Green "fails to make this part of the novel come alive for those who cannot be expected to share his background." Furthermore, Trudel added that another element of the book, the future story about the New Inca Church, is "peripheral to the book's main action . . . a mere *deus ex machina* serving the purposes of the author." Barbour's concerns were with the weakness of the characterization: "Green's narrative skillfully weaves the lives of his different characters together across time, but his characterizations don't always live up to their implied complexity. The closer he tries to get to their emotional hearts, the more he seems to slip toward cliché." Like Trudel, however, Barbour praised Green's description of the "psychological disruption that the time shifts create in his two central characters." Green himself, in a 1992 interview with Sawyer in *Aloud,* the newsletter of Toronto's Harbourfront Reading Series, described *Children of the Rainbow* as a story "about two people displaced in time. You don't have to be a science fiction reader to appreciate that. We're all displaced in one way or another." Like its predecessor, *Children of the Rainbow* was nominated for an Aurora Award, although the commercial success of the novel was muted by the fact that McClelland and Stewart is a Canadian publisher not associated with genre science fiction.

Green finally established himself with a prominent American genre publisher, New York's Tor Books, which had been influential in promoting Canadian science fiction to a mass audience by publishing the *Northern Stars* anthology in 1994. His next novel, *Shadow of Ashland,* was published in 1996. It was based on his earlier story "Ashland, Kentucky," which had been first published in the November 1985 issue of *Isaac Asimov's Science Fiction Magazine.* Just before dying, Leo Nolan's mother tells Leo that her brother Jack had just come to visit her, and as evidence she holds out a fresh rose, the present she claims her brother brought for her. But Jack had disappeared fifty years earlier and had not been heard from since. After Leo's mother dies, letters from Jack start to show up in the mail, dated fifty years in the past, prompting Leo to investigate. Leo traces his uncle's last known whereabouts to Ashland, Kentucky, where Jack had gone during the Great Depression in an effort to find work, and then visits Ashland to discover what became of his uncle in a search that takes him back in time.

Shadow of Ashland is the work in which Green's talents for depicting the effects of historical events on people bloomed, and it had a powerful impact. It brought Green to a wider readership and was nominated for the World Fantasy Award as well as being twice nominated for an Aurora Award (in both 1997 and 1998). It was also optioned for possible motion-picture adaptation. Both genre and mainstream critics praised Green's skill in portraying the Depression era and the people whose lives were caught up in it. In the 17 March 1996 *Ottawa Citizen* Chris Scott wrote, "In a sparse, natural way, Terence Green writes magically of the past, its allure, its artifacts and politics, its heroes and heroines. . . . This is not a 'time-warp' story, nor does Green baffle the reader with expositions of relativistic physics. Rather, this elegiac and exquisite prism of a novel refracts ordinary lives and feelings through the medium of history." Trudel was also unreservedly enthusiastic, writing in the July 1997 issue of the *New York Review of Science Fiction* that Green made "the Depression come to life, through the use as leitmotif of a few telling details. . . . He is treading Dos Passos and Steinbeck country, but the Depression no longer seems as comfortably remote, as historically distant." He called *Shadow of Ashland* "an affecting read" and suggested that its "marvelous effectiveness may owe a debt of thanks to Green's earlier novel, *Children of the Rainbow,* in the sense that authors sometimes thrash out unsuccessfully in one novel the themes that will underpin another novel's triumph." Reviewers in American publications such as *Publishers Weekly* and *The New York Times Book Review* were similarly enthusiastic.

Shadow of Ashland was an extremely personal novel for Green, inspired by his own genealogical search for a lost uncle, impelled by letters found after his mother's death. (On his website Green describes his pleasure and satisfaction that the dust jacket for the book incorporates real letters and photos from his family collection.) The missing man in the novel is named after Green's own maternal uncle, Jack Radey. Green told Gordon Morash in the 11 August 1996 *Edmonton Journal* that he was "surrounded by my

Dust jacket for Green's 1996 novel, in which a man in search of his long-lost uncle goes back in time to Depression-era Kentucky

ghosts" as he wrote *Shadow of Ashland:* "My mother did die, my dad died last year, my brother died, I had a marriage that died, I did have a baby that died, lots of stuff that happened in the past that I buried in the novel. And I exorcized a lot of demons to come to terms with these things." According to Green, the personal nature of his material was precisely what made *Shadow of Ashland* such a strong novel. As he told Sawyer in *Aloud,* "It wasn't until I started dealing with these sorts of things that my writing hit its power. Up until then, I'd been writing *stuff.* Now I incorporate painful life experience. That turned out to be my voice—the horrors of my life. A writer has to deal with what's really important, with what really moves you."

Green quickly followed the success of *Shadow of Ashland* with *Blue Limbo* (1997), a sequel to *Barking Dogs.* It was based on his Aurora-nominated short story of the same name, which had been published in Choyce's 1992 anthology, *Ark of Ice: Canadian Futurefiction.* The novel picks up Mitch Helwig's life further on its downward spiral. He has separated from his wife, who is now reluctant to let him visit his daughter, and lost his job with the Toronto Police Department. Then his only friend on the police force is killed, and the lives of his family become endangered. As in *Barking Dogs,* new technology propels the plot: Sunnybrook Hospital has developed a procedure that allows the head of a dead person to be kept aware for a few weeks after his or her death. The head can speak, but can only see a field of endless blue, and all the other senses are lost. Helwig uses Blue Limbo in his search for the people who threaten both him and his family.

Critics were generally more positive about *Blue Limbo* than they had been about Green's first novel, though much less enthusiastic than they had been about *Shadow of Ashland.* In general, reviewers suggested that Green had not achieved a balance between the action/thriller elements of the story and the moral dilemmas that it posed. Writing in the February 1997 *Quill and Quire,* Joel Yanofsky recognized Green's inventiveness but felt that he had not explored the full potential of the material: "This is the kind of imaginative leap that raises all kinds of dramatic possibilities and ethical questions—for instance, is it right to bring someone back from the dead, knowing they will die again in a short time? But Green just ends up using it as a quick and easy way for his hero to determine who is trying to kill him and his loved ones. . . . the result is a novel that proposes interesting problems but falls back on formulaic solutions." Tom Easton, in a review in the July 1997 *Analog,* suggested that the second Helwig novel had diluted the impact of the first by following the same formula, and Canadian science-fiction author Tanya Huff, writing in the 7 March 1997 *Globe and Mail,* also had mixed feelings, noting that "The Blue Limbo of the title . . . is a fascinating and well-thought-out concept, but it is used only as a plot device." She did add that the novel was "a powerful look at a man who's gone through the valley of the shadow and hasn't quite made it out the other side."

Other critics also had positive things to say. John North, in a review in the 1 March 1997 *Toronto Star,* described *Blue Limbo* as a "neat story with plenty of local color and action" and de Lint, in the April 1997

Magazine of Fantasy and Science Fiction, "liked the way Green balanced the hard-boiled action sequences with the more tender and thoughtful scenes, integrating them so that neither jars against the other." Barbour best summarizes critical reaction to *Blue Limbo* in his review in the 23 February 1997 *Edmonton Journal,* in which he argues:

> What separates Green's thrillers from conventional ones is his concern for the emotional lives of his characters. . . . Green can be sharp about the way violence works, but because he places the moments of intense violence in a context of conflicted family relationships, they have a reality too often lacking in those novels written with nothing more than Arnold Schwarzenegger or Sylvester Stallone in mind. Although it's not really in the same ballpark as the culturally rich and emotionally powerful *Shadow of Ashland, Blue Limbo* is a solid entertainment, with more than a bit of heart.

Green's next novel, *A Witness to Life* (1999), marked a return to the enthusiastic reviews that had greeted *Shadow of Ashland,* and like that novel, it was also nominated for a World Fantasy Award. It returns to the personal world of *Shadow of Ashland,* telling the story of Martin Radey (the name of Green's maternal grandfather), the father of Jack Radey, the missing man in *Shadow of Ashland*. The novel begins with Martin's death and his transformation into a starling that then travels back to review his life. In telling Martin Radey's story, *A Witness to Life* gives a detailed description of life in Toronto in the first half of the twentieth century. It is a remarkable novel, and Green's portrait of Toronto has been compared to that of James Joyce's Dublin. In the 12 June 1999 *Globe and Mail* Kevin Kennedy wrote that "Green's Joycean celebration of Toronto is worth a shelf of histories. It comes alive in a way only the best fiction can, allowing the reader to be a witness to the life of Martin Radey and the city he called home." In the September 2000 issue of *The Danforth Review,* Harold Hoefle was equally enthusiastic, noting that *A Witness to Life* "now joins the tradition of great Toronto novels." Green continues this personal story in *St. Patrick's Bed,* the sequel to *Shadow of Ashland,* appearing in September 2001.

As Barbour wrote in the 23 February 1997 *Edmonton Journal,* Green is "a writer in the tradition of Ray Bradbury and Theodore Sturgeon, a deeply humanistic student of character, and not just a creator of technophilic adventures." Given that, it is to be expected that his speculative fiction will continue to have an attraction that goes beyond the genre, through his examination of people caught up in events. His work reflects the Canadian context of a writer who can trace his family's roots in Canada back to 1849. As Green told Sawyer in the April 1988 issue of *Books in Canada,* "I think there's a place for Canadians on the world stage. . . . Canada is an interesting place. The rest of the world thinks so, even if Canadians themselves don't."

Interviews:

Robert J. Sawyer, "Interview: Terence M. Green," *Books in Canada,* 17 (April 1988): 17–18;

Sawyer, "Terence M. Green," *Aloud: The Newsletter of the Harbourfront Reading Series* (1992);

Edo van Belkom, "Terence M. Green," in his *Northern Dreamers: Interviews with Famous Science Fiction, Fantasy, and Horror Writers* (Kingston, Ontario: Quarry Press, 1998), pp. 105–114;

R. F. Briggs, interview at *Yet Another Book Review Site* (2 July 2001) <http://yetanotherbookreview.com/interview_green.htm>.

Tom Henighan
(15 October 1934 -   )

Batia Boe Stolar
Memorial University of Newfoundland

BOOKS: *Natural Space in Literature: Imagination and Environment in Nineteenth and Twentieth Century Fiction and Poetry* (Ottawa, Ontario: Golden Dog Press, 1982);

Tourists from Algol: Stories of the Unexpected (Ottawa, Ontario: Golden Dog Press, 1983);

The Well of Time (London: Collins, 1988);

Strange Attractors (Victoria, British Columbia: Beach Holme, 1991);

Home Planet: Poems (Ottawa, Ontario: Golden Dog Press, 1994);

The Presumption of Culture: Structure, Strategy, and Survival in the Canadian Cultural Landscape (Vancouver, British Columbia: Raincoast Books, 1996);

Ideas of North: A Guide to Canadian Arts and Culture (Vancouver, British Columbia: Raincoast Books, 1997);

Brian W. Aldiss (New York: Twayne, 1999);

Maclean's Companion to Canadian Arts and Culture (Vancouver, British Columbia: Raincoast Books, 2000);

Viking Quest (Vancouver, British Columbia: Beach Holme, 2001).

OTHER: *Brave New Universe: Testing the Values of Science in Society,* edited by Henighan (Ottawa: Tecumseh Press, 1980).

SELECTED PERIODICAL PUBLICATIONS–
UNCOLLECTED: "The Desirable Alien: A Source for Ford Madox Ford's *The Good Soldier,*" *Twentieth Century Literature,* 2 (April 1965): 25–29;

"Nature and Convention in *A High Wind in Jamaica,*" *Critique: Studies in Modern Fiction,* 9 (1966): 5–18;

"Tarzan and Rima: The Myth and the Message," *Riverside Quarterly,* 3 (March 1969): 256–265;

"*Green Mansions* and the Acceptance of Tragedy," *Wisconsin English Journal,* 12 (April 1970): 7–14;

"T. E. Lawrence's *Seven Pillars of Wisdom:* Vision as Pattern," *Dalhousie Review,* 51 (Spring 1971): 49–59;

"Tietjens Transformed: A Reading of *Parade's End,*" *English Literature in Transition 1880–1920,* 15 (1972): 144–154;

Tom Henighan (photograph by Marilyn Carson; from the cover for Viking Quest, *2001)*

"Shamans, Tribes, and the Sorcerer's Apprentices: Notes on the Discovery of the Primitive in Modern Poetry," *Dalhousie Review,* 59 (Winter 1979–1980): 605–620;

"Speculative Poetry: A New Anthology and Some Reflections on the Genre," *ARC: A Magazine of Poetry and Criticism,* 14 (Spring 1985): 32–46;

"The Cyclopean City: A Fantasy Image of Decadence," *Extrapolation,* 35 (Spring 1994): 68–76;

"A Short Biography," *NorthWords,* 2 (Winter 1994): 45.

Tom Henighan has produced an interesting body of work on the margins of the science-fiction genre and has also made valuable contributions to it as a teacher and critic. American-born, but a Canadian resident since 1965, Henighan has made important interventions in the culture of his adopted home as a teacher, writer, and consultant, and he has become a prominent figure in the debates over Canadian culture that have taken place in the late twentieth century.

The oldest of five children, Thomas Joseph Henighan was born on 15 October 1934 in New York City, the son of Thomas Augustine Henighan (a professional soccer player and sports writer) and Helen Patricia (Smith) Henighan, both of whom were born in Scotland. He grew up in Manhattan and the Bronx, and then in the suburbs of Westchester County, New Rochelle, and Mount Vernon, graduating from Stepinac High School in White Plains, New York, in 1952. Henighan began reading science fiction and fantasy, as well as other genres, as a child, and was a devoted listener to radio drama. Among the strongest influences on his childhood imagination were the radio dramas of Wyllis Cooper, who created two notable fantasy-supernatural radio series, *Lights Out* and *Quiet, Please*. One program in particular, titled "Northern Lights," broadcast on the *Quiet, Please* series on 30 January 1949, made a profound impact on Henighan and was one of the creative works that gave him an early and strong imaginative connection with the north. In an unpublished interview he recalled that reading the writings of astronomer James Jeans and the John W. Campbell magazine *Astounding Science Fiction*, or sitting in a candy store discussing with friends the latest theories of UFO sightings, were among "the great intellectual thrills" of his childhood and "helped open my mind to this mysterious universe we live in."

Henighan attended St. John's University in New York City, receiving a B.A. in history in 1956. He was accepted into graduate study in English literature at Columbia University, but after taking a few courses, dropped out for lack of money. He then worked as a copy boy at the United Press in New York and passed the American Foreign Service examinations, after which he was assigned for training at the Foreign Service Institute in Washington, D.C. He was appointed American vice consul in what is now Yemen in 1957, and this position initiated many years of work, travel, and study abroad; he lived for extensive periods not only in Yemen but also in Germany and England. In 1965, after working for two years as an instructor at Central Michigan University in Mount Pleasant, he moved to Canada, where he eventually became a professor of English at Carleton University in Ottawa. His higher academic degrees include an M.Litt. from Durham University in 1962 and a Ph.D. from the University of Newcastle in 1977 (by which time he was an associate professor at Carleton).

Living in the old British colony of Aden in the 1950s made a great impact on Henighan. His work allowed him to travel to the then-remote areas of Socotra, Mukalla, Ta'izz, and Baihan—all part of the present Yemen Republic. His duties included successfully investigating a sensational murder reported in *Newsweek*, rescuing American travelers, and writing economic and political reports on what was then the British colony and protectorate. He also met his future wife, Diana Collett, in the colony. They married in Bishop's Stortford, England, in 1960, and had two children: Stephen, born in Hamburg, Germany, in 1961 (he is now a professor of Hispanic studies and has published several well-regarded works of fiction), and Phoebe, born in Mount Pleasant, Michigan, in 1964. Henighan's first marriage was dissolved by divorce in 1970, and later the same year, in Newcastle upon Tyne, England, he married his former student Marilyn Carson of Brockville, Ontario. His third child, Michael, was born to them in 1979.

Henighan's serious attempts at writing began as a result of his Aden experiences. In the early 1960s he collaborated with a friend on a mystery novel called "The Jambiyah Murders," set in the colony, and when the work did not find a publisher, he wrote another mystery on his own, about an American evangelist in Britain, titled "Saved for Murder." He failed to place this work as well, but encouraged by editors such as Robert Bly and David Wagoner, he switched his efforts to poetry, and during the 1960s and 1970s he published many poems in literary magazines in both the United States and Canada. In 1976 he became associated with *Ottawa Revue*, a respected local arts magazine, of which he eventually became associate editor.

Working for *Ottawa Revue* gave him a chance to write almost daily and to establish close touch with the arts scene in Canada. He regularly covered events at the National Arts Centre in Ottawa, and also appeared as a television arts commentator. His long association with the Canada Council began at this time and led to later assignments as a speech and report writer for national Canadian arts organizations.

In the 1970s Henighan turned his attention back to science fiction. He started a course on the subject at Carleton, one of the first in Canada, and in 1976 did a series of six lectures on science-fiction classics for the CTV network, the first ever nationally broadcast in Canada. These programs offered serious critical comments on such books as H. G. Wells's *The Time Machine* (1895), Edgar Rice Burroughs's *Tarzan of the Apes* (1914), and Walter M. Miller Jr.'s *A Canticle for Leibowitz* (1960). This period culminated in the 1978 Carleton Conference on Science, Literature and Society. The results of this conference were published in *Brave New Universe: Testing the Values of Science in Society* (1980).

The overall result of Henighan's work was a cross-fertilization of artistic and scientific creativity, and this theme was extended in his final major venture as organizer, the David Bohm Conference of 1982. Henighan put together this Carleton University event to set up dialogues between Bohm, the eminent physicist and philosopher, with experts in other fields.

In 1978, with fellow English scholars Christopher Levenson and Michael Gnarowski, Henighan founded *ARC,* one of Canada's leading poetry journals. This publication was designed to combat what the founders saw as the extreme nationalistic flavor of much Canadian poetry of that era, although Henighan soon criticized Levenson's conservative editorial tastes and withdrew from the board of the magazine. Henighan's first full-length critical book, *Natural Space in Literature: Imagination and Environment in Nineteenth and Twentieth Century Fiction and Poetry,* appeared in 1982. It is a wide-ranging study of, as he writes, "the ways in which poetry and fiction since the beginning of the nineteenth century have reflected the natural environment." In this book he examines how such writers as Thomas Hardy, Wells, and D. H. Lawrence represent nature and "how their insights make a unique contribution to our knowledge of the natural environment and to human self-knowledge in that evolutionary journey now largely charted for us by the visionary explorations of modern science." Brought out by a small Ottawa publisher with a grant from the Humanities Research Council, *Natural Space in Literature* received little attention from critics and had minimal impact on literary scholarship, although it can now be seen as an anticipation of the ecocriticism that became increasingly prominent in the 1990s. Reviewers of the book tended to admire the wide-ranging argument, but at least one noted "a tendency toward generalization and superficiality" in its discussions of specific authors and works. Nonetheless, Henighan's work elicited the praise of the noted environmentalist René Dubos.

Tourists from Algol: Stories of the Unexpected (1983), a short collection of nine stories, was Henighan's first book of fiction. In keeping with the fact that Henighan does not consider himself to be strictly a science-fiction and fantasy writer but one interested in various genres and literatures, *Tourists from Algol* is difficult to categorize as genre science fiction. As the back-cover blurb states, the stories "run the gamut from adventure story to pseudo-biography, from Gothic horror and SF to fairy tale and rural comedy." The opening story, "The Explorers," combines some elements of science fiction with the supernatural, along with academic humor. Set in a near future in which civilization is on the verge of collapse and threatened by imminent nuclear war, "The Explorers" depicts a group of mountain climbers who escape from the crisis by heading off to the

Dust jacket for Henighan's 1988 historical-fantasy novel, in which Canada has been settled by Vikings and a young heroine is sent on a quest to save her village

Himalayas on a mission to search for the mythical yeti. The expedition, led by Lord Hutton, includes among its company a descendent of H. Rider Haggard, motion-picture director Sir Harry Groves, and a French mountain climber and philosopher named Foucault—amusingly pedigreed characters who evoke both the popular adventure story (Rider Haggard) and serious academic criticism (Michel Foucault). Suffering an injury, Foucault cannot join the mission and is killed while walking along the streets of Paris shouting "Revolution!" in response to the sirens announcing the impending exchange of nuclear weapons. Safe from the destruction that has afflicted the rest of the planet, but knowing of the end of the world, the other members of the expedition begin the ascent of the mountains but gradually and mysteriously disappear one by one. The last remaining explorer, Evans, eventually transcends his body and is transformed into the yeti. One of the best stories in the collection, "The Explorers" combines a typical adventure plot with mysticism, intellectual satire, and metatextual commentary.

The title story is the most clearly science-fictional piece in the collection. It tells of the establishment of a tourist resort for aliens near a small Canadian town and describes the exploitative tourist economy that develops, in which the locals are co-opted by being given jobs, or by bribes, or even by force, if necessary. The invisible tourists are made to stand for the hidden forces that Henighan seems to feel might threaten the Canadian identity, especially as a result of American economic power. A South American resistance fighter arrives in the town to recruit locals to work against the corporation and berates the Canadians for their passivity and political innocence. The story is ultimately less speculative than it is allegorical, and prefigures Henighan's strongly nationalistic views and his nonfiction books that advocate Canadian cultural survival.

The other stories fit less comfortably into genre expectations, but most of them utilize the fantastic to some degree. "Captain Flynn" is a mysterious, evocative tale that concludes in a moment of Gothic horror as an unnamed female protagonist, some kind of messenger, is threatened with a ghastly death after experiencing powerful, supernatural sexual pleasure from Captain Flynn. In "The Medium" television scientist Dr. S. experiences a moment of technological disorientation—dolphins come flying from his television monitor—while he prepares a show in Los Angeles. Ultimately, the science he relies on to explain the universe fails, and he is left without answers. "Massenet and the Disappearing Sopranos," readers are told, "takes place partially in the past, and partially in a future which meets that past only as fiction, here in the form of this story." The opera composer Jules Massenet, who died in 1912, is again composing operas for his favorite female singers. He writes an opera for Sybil Sanderson, which he begins to watch on a special television system from his home near Paris. He is admiring Sanderson's performance when a storm arises, and the television system fails. He rushes to Paris to see the rest of the show but finds that Sanderson did not perform that evening, but was replaced by Marie Heilbronn, another beautiful soprano. The composer immediately falls in love with Heilbronn and vows to write a new opera for her.

"The Borges Transfer," a meditation on marriage and communication, is a tribute to the art of Jorge Luis Borges. As the story makes clear, in this slim eighty-page volume Henighan is trying to capture the mystery and enigmatic qualities of the Borges narratives, rather than trying to write genre science-fiction and fantasy stories, and a few of the stories cannot really be classified as fantastic. The matter-of-fact story of marital discord, even murder, "At Approximately 3 P.M." is in the style of Ernest Hemingway, and its single fantastic note is the sudden arrival of a carpenter with a coffin for the distraught and alienated wife, while "Famine" is a claustrophobic story of rural despair in which a senseless quarrel leaves two brothers half-mad and their animals howling from starvation in their untended barn and sheds.

Although the overall impact of the book is reduced by its wide range of prose styles, genres, and topics, its sheer diversity reveals Henighan's varied skills as a writer. *Tourists from Algol* was a promising beginning; however, its publication by the same small publisher that had brought out *Natural Space in Literature* ensured that it had little impact on Canadian science fiction or on Canadian literature in general. It did, however, receive good reviews in prominent media such as the *Globe and Mail,* the *Toronto Star,* and the *Ottawa Citizen;* and in a March 1986 article in *Canadian Forum* Geoff Hancock, the editor of *Canadian Fiction Magazine,* cited *Tourists from Algol* as one of the important collections of Canadian metafiction of the 1980s. Writing in the Winter 1984 issue of *Canadian Literature,* Steven Lehman noted that Henighan "seems to take his inspiration from all points of the imaginative compass" and praised his ability to successfully write in different styles and forms. Well-known Canadian poet and science-fiction critic Douglas Barbour, writing in the October 1986 issue of the *NCF Guide,* was particularly enthusiastic, noting that "Henighan writes with wit, intensity and stylistic flair . . . *Tourists from Algol* is a shockingly good introduction to an imagination both weirdly lit and extraordinarily expansive."

In 1988 Henighan published his most significant work of fiction, *The Well of Time,* an historical fantasy set in an imaginary medieval Canada crisscrossed with Viking kingdoms. The novel, framed by the narration of the poet Skallgrim, tells the story of Ingrid, a Viking girl who lives in the frontier village of Wayland, located in the area of Manitoba historically populated by Icelandic settlers, and in Henighan's alternative history, a place at the fringes of the Viking settlement. As the story begins the villagers are suffering from repeated harassment by the undead Grey Folk. An old wanderer (the god Odin in mortal form) arrives to tell Einar, the town healer, that Ingrid, one of his daughters, must go on a quest to Iceland in order to find a sacred elixir and save the village. Along the way she encounters various mysterious beings drawn from Norse, Celtic, and Native mythology and is herself transformed into the ravenous Windigo, the cannibal monster of Ojibway and Cree legend. Her journey involves both her sexual and spiritual initiation, and at the end she confronts and defeats the patriarchal Odin, returning to the Viking kingdom to save her village and to help make peace between her people and the Skraelings, the native inhabitants of northern Canada.

Henighan's gloomy depiction of the northern landscape, and mindscape, is evocative, and the world he describes is fully realized. Furthermore, in Ingrid he has created a memorable heroine, one who is an appealing corrective to the masculinist tendencies of much heroic fantasy. *The Well of Time* benefits from the breadth of Henighan's historical and mythological expertise, particularly in the way that it utilizes not only Norse but also Arthurian, Christian, goddess, and native lore. The mythological underpinnings of his fantasy are indeed complex and give Ingrid's journey a depth and significance they might otherwise lack. *The Well of Time* can be considered one of the best Canadian fantasies of the 1980s, and it is one of the best fantasy attempts to create a mythology of the Canadian north.

The Well of Time, although completed in 1986, proved a difficult book for Henighan to market in Canada. It had been solicited by General Publishing in Toronto, but when the interested editor resigned, Henighan decided to withdraw the manuscript. He then submitted it to McClelland and Stewart, probably the leading Canadian publisher of the time, and it was considered for their Seal Books contest. Although it was a runner-up, it was not accepted for publication. Meanwhile, Henighan had sent it to a New York agent, who had no luck placing it there. A chance meeting with a colleague led to the placing of the book with an agent in London, England, and a sale to Collins followed. The book appeared in hardcover around the world, but received little promotional support and thus received little attention from critics and had disappointing initial sales.

Nonetheless, a professor of Norse Studies at the University of Toronto reviewed the book favorably in the *Ottawa Citizen,* and a reviewer for the *Kingston Whig-Standard* (25 February 1989) wrote: "Henighan successfully incorporates diverse old world tales into this magnificent saga, while at the same time addressing a topic which can still hold the attention of the modern world: the quest of women for recognition." In *The Encyclopedia of Fantasy* (1997) John Clute called the book "impressive," although Douglas Hill, writing in the March 1989 *Books in Canada,* was more equivocal, admiring the "compelling atmosphere" of the book and the power of Henighan's prose but complaining that "the last third of the novel runs out of steam somewhat: characterization, description, psychology all seem to go slack."

Henighan had wanted to write a sequel to the Viking novel, but the lack of sales success mitigated against his doing so. Collins urged him to try another "heroinic" fantasy, and after many months of research, he wrote several hundred pages of a novel about Dido, queen and founder of Carthage. This tale, however, aroused no interest at Collins, and Henighan turned his attention back to short stories and poetry.

In 1991 his second collection of short fiction, *Strange Attractors,* appeared. It was published by Tesseract Books,

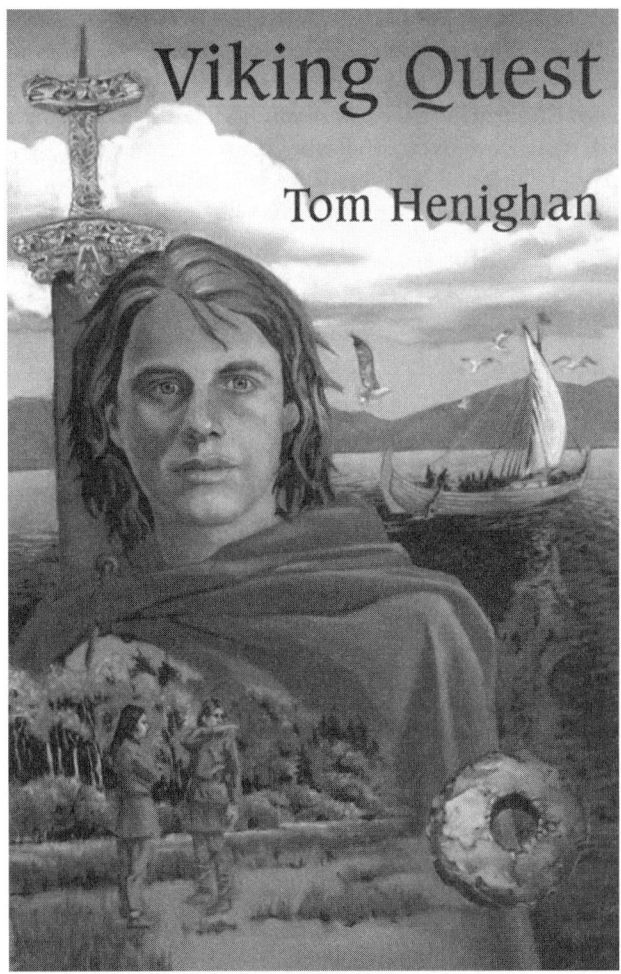

Cover for Henighan's second novel, a work for young readers about the son of the Viking leader Leif Eriksson

then a genre imprint of Beach Holme Publishing (formerly Press Porcépic). Possibly as a result, *Strange Attractors* is more specifically addressed to a science-fiction audience than was Henighan's first collection. All nine stories, including "Tourists from Algol," which is reprinted, have some fantastic or scientific element and are classifiable as genre fantasy and specifically as science fiction. The most substantial story in the collection, certainly in terms of length, is the seventy-five-page novella "Book of Tobit." Based on a biblical story (which is itself based on an ancient folktale), Henighan's narrative features a post-apocalypse setting, somewhat reminiscent of the *Mad Max* movies of the late 1970s and early 1980s. Some unspecified catastrophe has destroyed civilization, and Toby Johnson and his father, Talby, live under constant threat from roving gangs of bikers. When Talby is attacked and brutally blinded, the old man realizes that to live he must send Toby to collect some money owed him by a relative. A passing black stranger, Jim White, offers to accompany Toby on his journey. With Toby's dog, they travel through a devastated landscape of scrapped cars and polluted rivers, and Toby learns from Jim about the ravages wrought by the demon warrior Azmud, who has taken over the farmstead they are bound for, killed Talby's relative, and bewitched Sarah, the relative's beautiful daughter. The boy confronts the albinolike Azmud, and at Jim's urging escapes with the girl while his companion battles the demon to the death. On the homeward passage, Toby's final stage of initiation takes place: he makes love with Sarah, and when one of the bikers responsible for blinding Talby kills himself in a foolish game, Toby charitably buries him. Arriving home, Toby finds to his amazement that his father can now see. Talby tells him how an angel appeared to him in a dream and cured his blindness. When Talby admits that the angel in his dream was a black man, the boy realizes that Jim White has survived and worked a miracle. He leads Sarah up to their cabin in joy.

The other stories in *Strange Attractors* are less optimistic. "Dark Christmas" is a gloomy fable in which a boy wakes up on Christmas Eve to find that everything has changed for the worse. Only by drinking a magic potion given him by a talking rat can he temporarily forget the bleakness of life and return to the illusion of a merry Christmas. The story seems to urge readers to remember the less fortunate and not to be rendered insensitive by such seasons of phony good cheer. "Perfect Place" describes a future civilization of women only, as represented by the crew of the *Inanna,* an interstellar spaceship searching the stars for the unknown. After a malfunction they land on a planet that could be Earth, where they discover a statue of a beautiful woman or goddess, whom they joyfully claim as a sister. But then they find other statues, representing the vanished gender, "the leering half-humans with the hairy faces and the brawny arms, who, as the artists with infinite pride showed, had seized and grasped and penetrated their ancient human sisters." In "The Trophy," set off the coast of Nova Scotia in a future ice age, protagonist Valders destroys himself and his most valuable trophy, a frozen ancient "ice man," before imperious South American traders can wrest it from him. "Visiting Mother" describes a world in which children are born in artificial wombs and breeding factories, but the illusion of family is maintained by assigning to everyone his or her own robotic mother. In this comic story the protagonist caves in to the same kind of sentimental adulation of "mom" so prominent in some of the contemporary marketing of Mother's Day.

Strange Attractors is a competent, readable collection of stories. More consistent in approach than *Tourists from Algol,* it works better as a book, although the individual stories do not seem as ambitious as those of the earlier volume. Writing in *The Encyclopedia of Fantasy,* Clute observes that *Strange Attractors,* like *The Well of Time,* "finds mythic echoes in the natural spaces of the great Canadian wilderness." This statement is true of some, but not all, of the stories and possibly represents the most significant achievement of this collection. *Strange Attractors* received somewhat mixed reviews from Dave Panchyk in the *Edmonton Journal* and from John Degen in *Books in Canada,* although it was also praised by Sheldon Wiebe in the *Calgary Herald* and by Barbour in the *Canadian Forum* of July-August 1991.

Despite his three books of fiction, by the early 1990s some reviewers were treating Henighan as primarily a poet working in the vein of science fiction and fantasy. In 1994 he did publish a volume of poetry, *Home Planet,* and he had published an essay on speculative poetry in the Spring 1985 issue of *ARC.* Ostensibly a review of Robert Frazier's 1984 anthology *Burning with a Vision: Poetry of Science and the Fantastic,* Henighan's article provides a definition of speculative poetry. Arguing that poetry has a long history of engagement with both the fantastic and science, Henighan suggests that speculative poetry has an important role to play in the scientific age: "Its function," he argues, "is to mediate between the implicit grandeur of the scientific cosmos and the everyday terror experienced by many in the face of scientific and technological change." Speculative poetry is becoming more prominent, he suggests, because it reflects people's ambivalence toward science: "on the one hand expressing awe . . . on the other, registering and defining ultimate kinds of alienation, dehumanizations, the spectre of apocalypse." Speculative poetry also, he notes, reflects the postmodern blurring of boundaries between elite and popular cultures, and "also carries on its language games at many of the points of intellectual, stylistic and psychical dislocation emphasized by" postmodernism.

Henighan had previously published two speculative poems, "Bonsai Man" and "Visitation," in the 1987 Canadian science-fiction anthology *Tesseracts[2],* edited by Barbour and Phyllis Gotlieb. "Bonsai Man" is a fantastic poem in which a two-foot-tall Bonsai man gradually constructs his environment and even his family. "Visitation" is a moving poem of alien abduction that reveals the sense of longing and despair at the heart of the alien abduction phenomenon. "Paolo to Francesca," a cosmological poem first published in the July/August 1988 issue of *Star Line,* was nominated for a Rhysling Award, which is given by the American-based Science Fiction Poetry Association. In 1990 "She announces . . ." another speculative poem, appeared in *Tesseracts[3],* edited by Gerry Truscott and Candas Jane Dorsey. Employing scientific and cosmological imagery, it describes a voice issuing from a radio studio, flying out into deep space where it wakes "spirals of quiet time/curved lightly/as delicate ears." The following year Henighan published three speculative poems in *Tesseracts[4],* edited by Lorna Toolis and Michael Skeet. "Clark Kent in

Old Age," as the title suggests, is the dramatic monologue of an elderly Superman, and more generally, a meditation on the effects of aging. "The Great Comedians" combines an evocation of the performing styles of great comedians with cosmological speculation, and "Pointing North" is a free adaptation of a piece of nonsense verse by the Swiss poet Christian Morgenstern, with allusions to Canada and to the vocation of the poet.

Home Planet reprints all of the *Tesseracts* poems, plus many new ones. Not all of the poems are speculative, and they deal with a wide range of subjects, some of them quite mundane, such as the self-explanatory "Opening the Cottage." Conventional poems about marriage and children mix with ones such as "First Contact," which describes a wife's infidelity with an alien being. The collection features various kinds of poetry, from the brief near-haikus in the second section to the cycle titled "Ghost Stones," which, reminiscent of *The Well of Time*, employs Celtic mythology and takes as an organizing principle the idea that North America was colonized by the Celts.

Although a little uneven, *Home Planet* makes clear that Henighan is an interesting and worthwhile, if not particularly original, poet and one of Canada's best speculative poets. Writing in the Autumn 1997 issue of *Canadian Literature*, Stefan Haag applauded Henighan's "fine ability to detect ironies in our attitudes towards technology and science fiction themes." Haag also noted Henighan's use of ritual and myth, commenting that "while at times the expression of this liking becomes formulaic, in some instances it adds to the richness of this poet's vision."

Henighan put his years of experience as an arts reporter and consultant to work in his next book. *The Presumption of Culture: Structure, Strategy and Survival in the Canadian Cultural Landscape*, published in 1996, was a timely intervention in the cultural debates of the 1990s. In it Henighan pointed to the crisis in Canadian culture caused by government cutbacks in funding and other factors and proposed some solutions. The book was controversial and by no means universally praised, but received far more attention than Henighan's previous books and established him as an expert on Canadian cultural issues. He followed *The Presumption of Culture* with *Ideas of North: A Guide to Canadian Arts and Culture* (1997), the first general survey of the subject. Henighan's third book on the subject, *MacLean's Companion to Canadian Arts and Culture*, published in 2000, carried over the idea of including lists of artists and institutions and provided an overview of the Canadian arts situation at the beginning of the twenty-first century. These books have led to Henighan's appearances on national radio and television. They have also aroused the wrath of some critics, notably poet Frank Davey, whose scathing review of the first two books was published in the June 1988 issue of *English Studies in Canada*, an attack Henighan answered in the December 1998 issue of the same magazine.

In 1999 Henighan published a book that showed he had not lost his interest in science fiction. *Brian W. Aldiss* surveys the work of the British science-fiction writer, one of whose short stories has been made into the Steven Spielberg film *A. I.* (2001). Published in the Twayne English Author Series, this critical discussion covers the whole of Aldiss's work, both his genre and mainstream fiction, and incidentally ventures the opinion that science fiction has lost much ground to fantasy on both bookstore shelves and in the consciousness of young readers.

In 2001 Henighan's second novel, *Viking Quest*, appeared. This young-adult novel is set in Newfoundland around the year 1000, and focuses on the coming of age of Leif Eriksson's fifteen-year-old son Rigg. An historical novel and not a fantasy, the book once again shows Henighan's ability to evoke the northern landscape, and it establishes an appropriate set of mythical reference points in the leading characters' minds. As Andrea Deakin wrote in her syndicated column "Off the Shelf," Henighan's tale, although a "gripping story of adventure," is "much more, for it projects a real sense of how the Vikings understood the world."

Henighan has written other stories for young readers. One of these, "Tunnel Down to Moonrise," a time-travel story about Stonehenge, completed in 1997, elicited a contract from Somerville Press in Toronto, although he later withdrew the manuscript from the publisher. As of 2001 he has two more young-adult books with northern settings in the planning stage, one of them a sequel to *Viking Quest*. He also continues to write poetry, and achieved honorable mention for a sequence on Tarzan in a chapbook competition held by the Cranberry Press of Windsor, Ontario, in March 1999. A second volume of poems, with virtually no science-fiction or fantasy content, is complete. He also has finished a volume of mainstream stories, and has contributed essays to the first two travel volumes in the *Literary Trips: Following in the Footsteps of Fame* series, published in both Canada and the United States. His main literary focus of the moment is on his long Yemen memoir, in which his affinity for the desert landscape should finally be expressed.

In an interview with the noted columnist and author Charles Gordon in the *Ottawa Citizen* (14 April 1997), Henighan expressed the opinion that for writers "versatility is a curse." As Gordon wryly commented: "but it doesn't seem to bother him all that much." Henighan's activity in other fields has not prevented him from making some notable contributions to Canadian science-fiction and fantasy writing and teaching. While he seems to have no plans to continue his work in this field, a suitable opportunity—and his enduring fascination with the genre—may draw him back to it in the future.

Nalo Hopkinson
(20 December 1960 –   )

Nancy Johnston
University of New Brunswick Saint John

Nalo Hopkinson (photograph by David Findlay)

BOOKS: *Brown Girl in the Ring* (New York: Warner, 1998);
Midnight Robber (New York: Warner, 2000);
Skin Folk (New York: Warner, 2001).

PRODUCED SCRIPTS: "Indicator Species," radio, *Outlook,* CBC, 2000.

OTHER: "Money Tree," in *Tesseracts6,* edited by Robert J. Sawyer and Carolyn Clink (Edmonton, Alberta: Tesseract Books, 1997), pp. 149–160;
"Riding the Red," in *Black Swan, White Raven,* edited by Ellen Datlow and Terri Windling (New York: Avon/Nova, 1997), pp. 56–60;
"A Habit of Waste," in *Northern Suns: The New Anthology of Canadian Science Fiction,* edited by David G. Hartwell and Glenn Grant (New York: Tor, 1999), pp. 153–166; reprinted in *Women of Other Worlds: Excursions through Science Fiction and Feminism,* edited by Helen Merrick and Tess Williams (Perth, Australia: University of Western Australia Press, 1999), pp. 262–276;
"Precious," in *Silver Birch, Blood Moon,* edited by Datlow and Windling (New York: Avon Eos, 1999), pp. 93–99;
"Slow Cold Chick," in *Northern Frights 5,* edited by Don Hutchison (Oakville, Ontario: Mosaic, 1999), pp. 69–79;
"Greedy Choke Puppy" and "Ganger," in *Dark Matter: Anthology of Science Fiction, Fantasy and Speculative Fiction by Black Writers,* edited by Sheree Thomas (New York: Warner, 2000), pp. 103–112, 135–152; "Greedy Choke Puppy" reprinted in *Year's Best Fantasy and Horror,* edited by Datlow and Windling (New York: St. Martin's Press, 2001); and in *Year's Best Fantasy,* edited by Hartwell (New York: HarperCollins, 2001);
Whispers from the Cotton Tree Root: Caribbean Fabulist Fiction, edited by Hopkinson (Montpelier, Vt.: Invisible Cities Press, 2000)–includes her "Glass Bottle Trick."

SELECTED PERIODICAL PUBLICATIONS–UNCOLLECTED: "Delany's *Mad Man:* the Dark Side of Human Desire," *WORD: Toronto's Black Culture Magazine* (27 October – 9 November 1994): 10;
"Griffonne," excerpt, *Obsidian III: Literature in the African Diaspora* 2, no. 2 (Fall/Winter 2000–2001).

Nalo Hopkinson's impressive debut novel, *Brown Girl in the Ring* (1998), won her immediate attention and the prestigious 1999 John W. Campbell Award for best new science-fiction writer. In this novel Hopkinson presents a powerful tale about a near-future Toronto in the grips of urban decay, set against fantastical images derived from Caribbean poetry, traditional song, and folklore. *Midnight Robber* (2000), her second novel, is a rich character-driven work about exile and cultural estrangement and has garnered Hopkinson nominations for both Hugo and Sunburst Awards. Her success confirms Hopkinson's place as an inventive and intelligent new voice in contemporary science fiction.

Noelle Nalo Hopkinson was born on 20 December 1960 in Kingston, Jamaica, to Freda and Muhammed Abdur-Rahman Slade Hopkinson, who were both involved in the arts. She has one brother, Keïta. Hopkinson spent her childhood in Jamaica, Trinidad, Guyana, and briefly in the United States while her father was studying theater at Yale University. Her parents fostered her early interest in the arts by taking her to plays, movies, dance performances, and readings. Her father, who died in 1993 and to whom she dedicated her first novel, was a playwright, poet, and actor in Derek Walcott's influential Trinidad Theatre Workshop. From her father's bookshelves, she read fantastical literature, from Greek mythology and Homer's *Odyssey* to Caribbean folklore and European "classics" such as *Gulliver's Travels* (1726). When Hopkinson was eleven or twelve, her mother, a library clerk, let her use an adult library card. At the Kingston Public Library, Hopkinson found the adult science-fiction section, where she discovered science-fiction New Wave writers such as Harlan Ellison. After her family moved to Toronto, Ontario, in 1977, when she was sixteen, Hopkinson completed high school and then enrolled at Toronto's York University, studying French and Russian language and literature and receiving a Bachelor of Arts (Honours) degree in 1982. In Toronto, where she still lives, she has held various positions as library supervisor and arts administrator. Between 1992 and 1996 she was also a freelance writer of nonfiction articles for local Toronto papers, including an interview with noted author Samuel R. Delany, published in the 27 October – 9 November 1994 issue of *WORD: Toronto's Black Culture Magazine.*

While working at a public library in North York (then a suburb of Toronto and now part of the city), Hopkinson sought out and read the work of black science-fiction writers such as Delany, Octavia Butler, Charles Saunders, Steve Barnes, and Virginia Hamilton. She was exhilarated that black writers were writing science fiction, as she told Gregory E. Rutledge in the Winter 1999 issue of *African American Review:* "Some time in my 20s I saw a photograph of Chip Delany, with whose work I'd fallen in love on first encountering it, and realized that he was black. I'd never heard of such a thing before. I wept. It felt as though my universe had doubled in size."

In 1993 Hopkinson launched her science-fiction career by attending writing workshops, joining a writers' group, and sending her fiction to genre magazines. "A Habit of Waste," her first completed science-fiction short story, was published in the Spring 1996 issue of the feminist literary journal *Fireweed*. It presents the emotional conflict of a female protagonist at odds with her cultural heritage. The title alludes to a line from Slade Hopkinson's poem "The Madwoman of Papine: Two Cartoons with Captions" (1976), which presents the complex layers of internalized racism inherited by the "ex-colonized" people. Like the poem, Hopkinson's story explores some of the aftermath of colonization. The main character, a young Afro-Caribbean woman living in Canada, experiences extreme body hatred and self-alienation in a future where, for a price, technology can allow people to make a "body switch" into a ready-made model. The story opens as the protagonist, now wearing a white female body, is able to view "herself" from the outside when she sees her handsome black body worn by a stranger.

In 1995 Hopkinson attended the Clarion Science Fiction and Fantasy Writers Workshop at Michigan State University and studied with writers-in-residence Joe Haldeman, Nancy Kress, Pat Murphy, Karen Joy Fowler, Tim Powers, and Delany. The Clarion story "Riding the Red" was her first sale in the professional science-fiction market, published in the 1997 anthology *Black Swan, White Raven,* edited by Ellen Datlow and Terri Windling. It retells the story of Little Red Riding Hood from the perspective of the grandmother, who insinuates that "riding the red" is a female mystery, perhaps a sexual rite of passage for young and older women. Another story written at Clarion, "Precious," was also sold to Datlow and Windling and published in their 1999 anthology *Silver Birch, Blood Moon*. Since Clarion, Hopkinson has continued to use folkloric material in her novels and short fiction. Much of her inspiration comes from her extensive research into Afro-Caribbean folklore and culture. For instance, Hopkinson's "Money Tree," published in the 1997 anthology *Tesseracts^6,* edited by Robert J. Sawyer and Carolyn Clink, is derived from the Jamaican legend of the Golden Table.

Her first novel, *Brown Girl in the Ring,* began as six manuscript pages submitted to a writing course taught by famed science-fiction author and editor Judith Merril, who had a huge impact on the Toronto science-fiction community. While researching health risks in immigrant Caribbean communities, Hopkinson had developed her initial ideas about a young woman who grapples with prophetic visions. After extensive

Cover for Hopkinson's first book (1998), a novel about a young Afro-Caribbean woman who has prophetic visions in a dystopian future Toronto

research into Orisha worship, Hopkinson entered the Warner Aspect First Novel contest with only ten thousand words of the novel written. Once complete, the highly original finished novel received the Warner Aspect First Novel award, as a result of which Warner Books published it in 1998. *Brown Girl in the Ring* also received the *Locus* First Novel Award and was on the preliminary ballot for the Nebula Award. In 1999 she was honored with the prestigious John W. Campbell Award for Best New Writer and the Ontario Arts Council Foundation Award for Emerging Writers.

Brown Girl in the Ring begins in the "Burn," the now-abandoned city core of a future Toronto, which has been barricaded after the core economic base has collapsed and government authority has crumbled. L. Timmel Duchamp, in an August 1998 review posted on the World Wide Web (http://ltimmel.home.mindspring.com/ring.html), compares the Burn to Delany's 1975 novel *Dhalgren,* but it also resembles another hybrid community, the San Francisco "Bridge" community in William Gibson's *Virtual Light* (1993). Twelve years after the Riots, the hybrid community of the inner city has pockets of resistance even to the Posse, a gang run by Rudy, a figure who is more of an allegorical representation of evil than a fully realized character. He is a "shadow-catcher," a character not unlike Doro in Butler's *The Pattern Master* (1976), who controls the living through the dead and enthralls weaker souls in his "duppy bowl." The frame story begins with a deal struck between Rudy and a government official to harvest a living heart out of the Burn and to deliver it to the ailing Ontario premier.

The protagonist is Ti-Jeanne, a young Afro-Caribbean woman who can "see with more than sight" and whose visions make her fearful for her sanity. As the visions grow more powerful, she becomes estranged from her grandmother, Mami Gros-Jeanne, a healer and spiritual leader, who represents the spiritual world that Ti-Jeanne rejects. Ti-Jeanne is torn by personal demons: her fear of inheriting the "madness" of her mother, Mi-Jeanne; her own lover's decline into an addiction to Buff, which the author defines as a (fictional) street drug, derived from the bufo toad; and her self-alienation from her heritage. Of all the characters in the novel, Gros-Jeanne is the most compelling. Gros-Jeanne is adept in Orisha traditions: "I don't work the dead, I serve the spirits and I heal the living." She is the one who tries to teach Ti-Jeanne to control her "gift" and who helps her to enlist the spirits and defeat Rudy.

Brown Girl in the Ring resonates with images from Hopkinson's research into Caribbean literature, poetry, traditional song, and folklore. As in her short story "A Habit of Waste," Hopkinson prefaces a chapter with lines from her father's poem "The Madwoman of Papine" to introduce themes of self-alienation and cultural estrangement. The three women in the novel are also closely linked by name to three fictional brothers who confront the devil in famed Saint Lucian writer Walcott's play *Ti-Jean and His Brothers* (1957).

The climax of the novel is foreshadowed in the title. The phrase "brown girl in the ring," Hopkinson observes in a 1999 online interview with Craig E. Engler (http://cyberhaven.com/books/sciencefiction/hopkins.html), comes from an English-Caribbean ring game song played by girls and is "a metaphor for experience" for Ti-Jeanne: "In my novel, the protagonist is a young woman facing the challenge of discovering and demonstrating her own survival skills, quickly, as her life becomes increasingly endangered." When Gros-Jeanne is murdered for her heart, Ti-Jeanne musters her strength in a ceremony that calls on the aid of her Eshu, an Afro-Caribbean deity; Papa Legbara; and her spiritual ancestors to fight Rudy and free herself and her mother's soul.

Hopkinson uses Trinidadian and Caribbean vernacular speech in her dialogue and adds a distinctive rhythm to the narrative. While Ti-Jeanne may deny her cultural and spiritual heritage for much of the novel, her dreams are represented in a vivid first-person vernacular narrative. As Hopkinson suggests to Rutledge, the Caribbean characters survive and adapt in the Burn because they "learn to code-switch, to jump back and forth between various language usages as needed."

Hopkinson's second novel, *Midnight Robber* (2000), also engages the material of Caribbean folklore. The novel was originally conceived as her first published story, "Midnight Robber," published in *Exile Magazine* in 1995, and as she writes on her website (http://www.sff.net/people/nalo/), it "was inspired by legends of the Jamaican folk hero/villain Three-Finger Jack." Two of the three folk tales that structure the narrative were first published as the short stories "Tan-Tan and the Rolling Calf" and "Tan-Tan and Dry Bone" in the Summer 1997 and Spring–Summer 1999 issues of *Lady Churchill's Rosebud Wristlet*. Tan-Tan's story is told in the first-person voice of a storyteller who is eager to recount the trickster tale of "the midnight robber." Unlike her previous novel, the narrative does not shift between standard English and vernacular dialogue. Instead, Hopkinson presents a distinctly original Creole, a multiethnic and multicultural tongue, in which rhythm and cadence are important to the tale and the telling. In a 2000 interview with Betsy Mitchell (http:www.twbookmark.com/authors/84/1272/interviews9676.html), Hopkinson insists that language "shapes not only the names for the technology we create, but the type of technology we create. I wondered what technologies a largely African diasporic culture might build, what stories its people might tell itself about technology. So a communication device that sees and hears becomes a 'four-eye;' literally, a seer." In this context, the central themes in the novel–a girl's exile and disempowerment–are expressed through the protagonist's efforts to give voice to her strange world.

At the beginning of the novel, Tan-Tan, the protagonist, is a young girl who lives on a pan-Caribbean planet, Toussaint. On this world, a computer named Granny-Nanny is a sentient intelligence, much like the AI in Ursula K. Le Guin's *Always Coming Home* (1985), who is programmed to perform benign surveillance of the human inhabitants in exchange for a life in which most material needs are met and physical labor is no longer necessary. Tan-Tan's childhood and her utopian life on Toussaint are disrupted forever when her father commits a murder and kidnaps his daughter to share in his exile on "a dub version of Toussaint" called New Half Way Tree. As Tan-Tan grows up without the protection of the AI, the love of her mother, Ione, or the

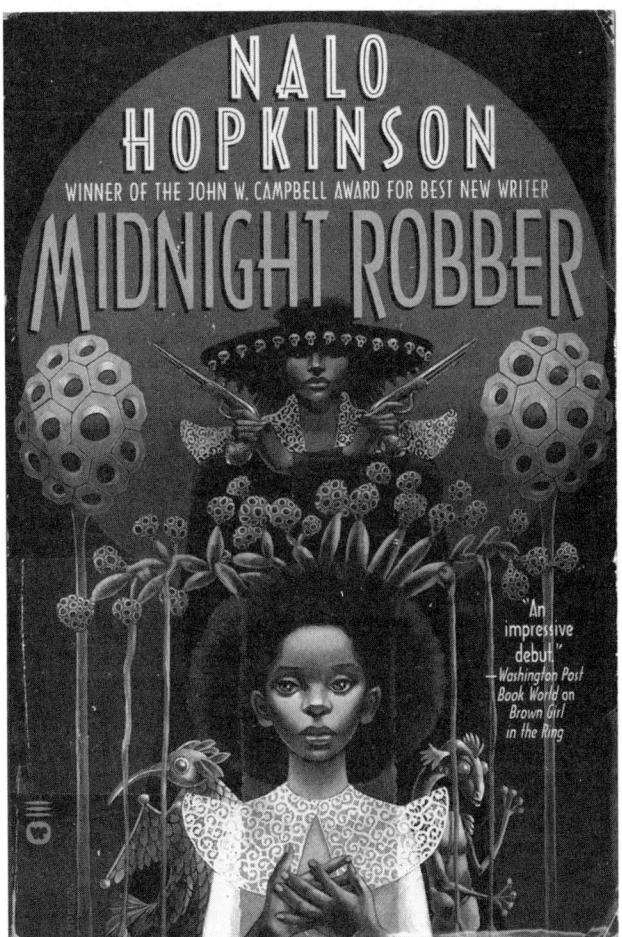

Cover for Hopkinson's 2000 novel about a girl who kills her sexually abusive father

security of Toussaint, she becomes vulnerable to her father's sexual abuse. The characterization of this daughter-father relationship is compelling in its psychological complexity. When Tan-Tan kills her father in self-defense, she goes on an archetypal journey that shares many of the elements of European and Afro-Caribbean folk tales: a journey into a strange land, a trickster who slips the yoke of the law, a jealous and revengeful stepmother, encounters with strange and shape-shifting creatures, the unmasking of evil through wit rather than brawn, and a final confrontation with personal demons. In Hopkinson's hands, the folkloric elements bring a multidimensional and feminist slant to a young woman's quest.

One of the key folkloric elements in the story involves Tan-Tan's identification with "the midnight robber," a Trinidadian carnival figure who appears in elaborate bandit costume to regale his audience with outlandish tales of his capture and escape in a speech of "stream of consciousness fabulation," as Hopkinson describes it on her website, that has echoes of "the Caribbean history of the African slave trade." Like the midnight robber, Tan-Tan is an exile estranged from her once-powerful father, Mayor Antonio. On New Half Way Tree, Tan-Tan's consciousness divides when she cannot reveal her father's escalating violence; at the same time, she finds it increasingly difficult to separate her own experiences from the oral tales about the trickster midnight robber. Not until the final carnival scene when Tan-Tan takes up her role as the midnight robber can she confront her own fears and face her nemesis Janisette, her stepmother. Their dispute over her father's death is a symbolic ritual conflict or high-noon showdown. The role of the audience in the scene is well conceived; like some readers, they are restless and even shocked by Tan-Tan's "crudeness" and language. There are those who heckle Tan-Tan, those who cheer her, those who are stunned by their own culpability, and those who refuse to understand her rhymes about her father's abuse.

Midnight Robber, like its predecessor, was enthusiastically received and confirmed that Hopkinson is a rising star in speculative fiction in Canada, the United States, and beyond (her first novel has been translated into French and Polish). *Midnight Robber* was shortlisted for the James R. Tiptree Jr. Award, the Nebula, the Hugo Award, and the Sunburst Award. The lack of sentimentality and the remarkable hopefulness of her fictional characters are evidence of her mature writing style. *Skin Folk* (2001) is a collection of her short stories, and she is at work on another novel, "Griffonne," which she describes on her website: "Among many other focii, it deals with women's sex magic and diasporic African history in a variety of places and times." She is also establishing herself as a voice in the critical and political debates of speculative fiction, feminism, and Afro-futurism. In her essay "Dark Ink: Science Fiction Writers of Colour," posted on her website, Hopkinson confirms that science fiction offers her a potentially subversive discourse: "Speculative fiction has reinvented itself repeatedly at the hands of the new wave, feminist, cyberpunk and queer writers. Perhaps idealistically, I believe that it will also open up to fantastical expressions from communities of colour."

Interviews:

Gregory E. Rutledge, "Speaking in Tongues: An Interview with Science Fiction Writer Nalo Hopkinson," *African American Review,* 33 (Winter 1999): 589–601;

Craig E. Engler, "Nalo Hopkinson Subverts Science Fiction," *Cyberhaven.com* (1999) <http://www.cyberhaven.com/books/sciencefiction/hopkinson.html>;

Betsy Mitchell, "Interview with Nalo Hopkinson," *TimeWarnerBookmark.com* (2000) <http://twbookmark.com/authors/84/1272/interview9676.html>.

References:

Jennifer Burwell and Nancy Johnston, "A Dialogue on SF and Utopian Fiction, between Nalo Hopkinson and Élisabeth Vonarburg," *Foundation: The International Review of Science Fiction,* 81 (Spring 2001): 40–47;

Gregory E. Rutledge, "The Urban Jungle and Nalo Hopkinson's Speculative Fiction: How Capitalism Underdeveloped the Black Americas and Left a Brown Girl in the Ring," *Foundation: The International Review of Science Fiction,* 81 (Spring 2001): 22–39.

Guy Gavriel Kay
(7 November 1954 -)

Holly E. Ordway
University of Massachusetts Amherst

BOOKS: *The Summer Tree* (Toronto: McClelland & Stewart, 1984; New York: Arbor House, 1985; London: Allen & Unwin, 1985);

The Wandering Fire (Toronto: HarperCollins, 1986; New York: Arbor House, 1986; London: Allen & Unwin, 1986);

The Darkest Road (Toronto: HarperCollins, 1986; New York: Arbor House, 1986; London: Unwin Hyman, 1987);

Tigana (Toronto: Viking, 1990; New York: Viking, 1990; London: Viking, 1990);

A Song for Arbonne (Toronto: Viking, 1992; New York: Crown, 1993; London: HarperCollins, 1992);

The Lions of Al-Rassan (Toronto: Viking, 1995; New York: HarperPrism, 1995; London: HarperCollins, 1995);

Sailing to Sarantium (Toronto: Viking, 1998; New York: HarperPrism, 1998; London: Earthlight, 1998);

Lord of Emperors (Toronto: Viking, 2000; New York: HarperPrism, 2000; London: Earthlight, 2000).

Now an established figure in the field of fantasy literature, Guy Gavriel Kay achieved prominence with his acclaimed high-fantasy trilogy *The Fionavar Tapestry*, consisting of *The Summer Tree* (1984), *The Wandering Fire* (1986), and *The Darkest Road* (1986). Following that success, Kay has carved out a distinctive place in the genre with his subsequent carefully crafted stand-alone novels of "history with a twist," as he calls it. Settings reminiscent of medieval France, Renaissance Italy, and early medieval Spain allow Kay to examine the possibilities of what is, what might have been, and what could be, while challenging the traditional limits of what modern fantasy can do. Kay's novels are characterized by lyrical language and a strong sense of place, influenced by his tendency to research and write while abroad. Although he uses the conventions of fantasy, he is never restricted by them.

Kay was born in Weyburn, Saskatchewan, on 7 November 1954 to parents Samuel Kay, a surgeon, and Sybil (Birstein) Kay, an artist. His brothers Jeffrey and Rex are, respectively, a lawyer and a psychiatrist.

Guy Gavriel Kay *(photograph © by Beth Gwinn; from the dust jacket for* Lord of Emperors, *2000)*

Kay also trained to be a lawyer; after earning a B.A. in philosophy from the University of Manitoba in 1975, he completed his LL.B. from the University of Toronto in 1978. However, since 1982 he has earned his living as a writer.

Kay's early love of literature was encouraged by his parents, who read to him regularly; Greek mythology and the tales of the Brothers Grimm caught his imagination the most, despite (or perhaps because of) not being typical "children's stories." Kay's introduction to the fantasy genre came through reading seminal authors such as J. R. R. Tolkien, E. R. Eddison,

Lord Dunsany, and Fritz Leiber. His reading interests continued to develop over the years; as an adult, he is an avid reader of nonfiction as well as fiction. Among fiction writers, Kay particularly admires Gabriel García Márquez, Milan Kundera, Thomas Flanagan, Shirley Hazzard, and Cormac McCarthy, as well as the earlier works of Dorothy Dunnett, John Updike's "Rabbit" novels, and George Garrett's Elizabethan historical fiction.

As a teenager Kay had at least three quite distinct career aspirations: to play right wing for the Toronto Maple Leafs hockey team; to become a lawyer, emulating Clarence Darrow; and to become a best-selling author. A critical occurrence in his achievement of the third goal came when he was a student at the University of Manitoba. Kay knew Christopher Tolkien, J. R. R. Tolkien's son, through Christopher's second wife's family. Christopher Tolkien was named literary executor after his father died, and he invited Kay to Oxford to assist him in editing Tolkien's fragmentary and uncompleted *The Silmarillion*. Kay accepted, having already a strong interest in fantasy, folklore, and mythology; as he said in an unpublished 1998 interview, "Who in their right mind would NOT have been interested in the project?" Kay worked on *The Silmarillion* for a year, from 1974 to 1975, while he finished his B.A. Although the casual reader would not know of his contribution to the work, the tremendous success of *The Silmarillion* when it was published in 1977–it sold a million copies in the first four months alone–undoubtedly led the publishing industry to look favorably on Kay when the time came for his own writing to be submitted for publication.

His work on the Tolkien project reinforced Kay's interest in writing, but he also recognized that it was not a profession that someone young and inexperienced could rely upon for income. He thus returned to Canada and earned his law degree. He was still drawn to writing, however: after finishing his degree, he went abroad to write his first, unpublished, novel.

Kay took his call to the Bar but never practiced law. He turned to writing again, this time in a different medium. He had become friends with prominent criminal lawyer Edward Greenspan, who was also the host of the popular Canadian Broadcasting Corporation (CBC) radio and television series *The Scales of Justice,* which dramatizes real Canadian legal cases. This friendship led to Kay's becoming a writer and producer in the CBC drama department and later serving as the principal writer and associate producer for *The Scales of Justice* radio program. His writing was successful–he won an award from the Canadian Law Reform Commission in 1985 for best media treatment of a legal issue–and he worked on the series until 1989. Kay continues to write for television occasionally as a change of pace between novels.

On 15 July 1984 Kay married Laura Beth Cohen, a marketing consultant; they have two sons. Also in 1984 his first novel, *The Summer Tree,* the first volume of *The Fionavar Tapestry,* was published by prominent Canadian publisher McClelland & Stewart. *The Fionavar Tapestry* is best considered as a single work since its three parts are not self-contained, and Kay produced them in fairly rapid succession over the span of two years.

The first volume of the trilogy tells how five college students from present-day Toronto are transported to the magical world of Fionavar, where they are needed to take part in an epic war against evil that threatens not only Fionavar but also all the worlds that, like this world, are reflections of it. In the second volume, *The Wandering Fire,* Fionavar suffers from an unnaturally prolonged winter brought about by a traitorous mage working for Rakoth Maugrim, the enemy. Returning to Fionavar after a brief stint in their own world, the five Torontonians help to summon the spirit of King Arthur to assist in the war against Rakoth. As became his habit, Kay did much of his writing abroad: *The Wandering Fire* was written while he was staying at a friend's farm in New Zealand. While the earlier book also ended on a cliff-hanging note, *The Wandering Fire* is even less self-contained than *The Summer Tree,* and the action picks right up again in *The Darkest Road*. In the final book events move toward a climactic battle of the forces of good and evil, with the ultimate destruction of Rakoth coming through the half-mortal child that was the product of his rape of Jennifer, one of the Toronto students.

Kay told Andrew A. Adams in a 1995 interview that with *The Fionavar Tapestry* he consciously chose "to work squarely in the Tolkien tradition while trying to allow room for character development and plausibility that I tended to find missing in most post-Tolkien high fantasy. In a way it was a challenge to the debasing of the genre." The world of Fionavar clearly shows the effects of Kay's immersion in Middle-earth during the year he spent working on the manuscript of *The Silmarillion*. The gray-bearded mage Loren Silvercloak, who gathers the five characters from this world, is modeled on the figure of Gandalf. Similarly, the villain, Rakoth Maugrim the Unraveller, suggests Tolkien's Sauron in his motivation of the plot, though for other aspects of Rakoth's character Kay draws heavily on Norse mythology.

A larger Tolkienesque element than the figures of Silvercloak and Rakoth is the Fionavar version of elves: the music-loving lios alfar, who live in the magic-hidden forest of the Shadowland. Brendel, the first lios alfar to appear in the novels, is a "silver-haired figure" with an "ethereal, flame-like quality." Later, Brendel explains more about his people, showing that they share many of the noble and mysterious qualities that distinguished Tolkien's elves from their folktale ancestors: "We live very long, and age will not kill us, but we do die . . . by sword or fire, or grief of heart. And weariness will lead us to sail to our song, though that is a different thing. . . . Westward lies a place not found on any map. A world shaped by the Weaver for the lios alfar alone, and there we go when we leave Fionavar, unless Fionavar has killed us first."

 The dwarves in Kay's novels likewise show a Tolkien influence; mountain-dwelling, they love good workmanship and are at least in part implicated in the raising of an ancient evil, in this case Rakoth. One of the first Fionavar characters to be introduced, Matt Sören, is a dwarf who provides the energy for Loren's magic. Later in the trilogy he is revealed to be the king of the dwarves, who gave up his kingship forty years earlier to wander with Loren; and in *The Darkest Road* he returns to the mountain home of his people to reclaim his crown, as Thorin does in *The Hobbit* (1937).

 Kay also works with traditional elements from the genre of fantasy in general, starting with the choice to write *The Fionavar Tapestry* as a trilogy. But the most noteworthy of the traditional devices that Kay uses is that of transporting characters from the contemporary world to a magical one. Probably the most famous use of this device is in C. S. Lewis's *Chronicles of Narnia* (1950–1956); a later example is Stephen Donaldson's six-book *Chronicles of Thomas Covenant*, which began in 1977. During the 1980s there was a host of variations on the theme, often involving college students; the first volume of one of these, Joel Rosenberg's *Guardians of the Flame* series, was published the year before *The Summer Tree* appeared.

 These echoes of the work of Tolkien and others situate Kay's trilogy clearly in the context of the tradition of high-fantasy literature. What makes *The Fionavar Tapestry* successful on its own terms as a story, however, is Kay's ability to show the influence of other works without being limited by it. From various elements of the fantasy tradition, Kay constructs a backdrop for what he draws from his own imagination. The plot of his trilogy shows plenty of originality in its playing out of the struggle of good and evil; Kay avoids the traditional "quest" plot and instead weaves a many-stranded story of the various ways in which the people of Fionavar and this world pull

Cover for the second volume (1986) of Kay's trilogy in which five Toronto college students are transported to a magical world that bears strong similarities to J. R. R. Tolkien's Middle Earth

together their defenses against Rakoth. Kay also introduces his own elements into the world that he has created, such as an intriguing system of magic in which a mage must draw his power from the life energy of a "source" to whom he is bonded for life.

 Kay's five real-world characters are more than just tools to introduce the reader to Fionavar through their eyes: his interest in the characters leads him to develop them fully as individuals. He thus succeeds in emphasizing, as he intended, the importance of strong characterization in a story. More so than in many high-fantasy novels, Kay's characters act in ways consonant with their histories and their personalities, and not just as their roles require them to act. A common theme running through Kay's handling of characters in the three novels is that of responsibility and free will. All the Toronto characters must choose whether, and how, to participate in the fight against evil; this choice is a painful one, forcing them to come to terms with themselves and with others, and often to suffer or make great sacrifices. In the end, all the characters are profoundly, and realistically, changed by their experiences in Fionavar. Kay's emphasis on the Toronto characters does not, however, lead him to neglect the native Fionavar characters. Figures such as the playboy prince Diarmuid, the chieftain Ivor (who is like a father to his people), the lovely and fierce princess Sharra, the cold priestess Jaelle, and the seer Ysanne are rounded out and shown to have realistic loves, fears, and motives.

Furthermore, Kay's fascination with comparative mythology, in particular the works of Joseph Campbell and Robert Graves, leads him to make extensive use of real-world myths and legends, which he handles in his own way. *The Summer Tree* in particular shows a dominant Norse influence in its mythological elements. The most significant of these is the Yggdrasil-like tree that provides the title of the novel. In times of great need, the king would sacrifice himself to the god by hanging for three days and nights to die on the tree. This conception of the king and the sacred tree draws on James Frazer's famous description of the King in the Wood, as presented in *The Golden Bough* (1890–1915). The King in the Wood is both a sacrificial victim and an intercessor between god and man, used to gain a boon such as rain for the crops. Both of these conceptions—the king as intercessor with the god for good weather, and the king as sacrificial victim—come into play in *The Summer Tree*. When it becomes clear that only extreme actions will break a terrible drought that is devastating the land, Paul, one of the Toronto characters, volunteers to go in the High King's place to hang on the Summer Tree and die. Through his suffering, Paul experiences a transcendent union with the god; he is permitted to live and is granted new powers to use in the fight against Rakoth. His self-sacrifice and its results reenact the ordeal of Odin on Yggdrasil, the World Tree, to gain the runic knowledge.

Another noteworthy Norse element in *The Fionavar Tapestry* is the characterization of the antagonist, Rakoth Maugrim, who bears a strong resemblance to the Norse Loki. Like Loki, he is a malevolent god bound beneath a mountain; the action of the plot revolves around his successfully breaking his restraints and attempting to bring about his own version of Ragnarök. Similarly, another antagonist, Galadan the Wolflord, draws heavily on the figure of the Fenris Wolf.

Kay does not limit himself to working with only Norse mythology. Celtic mythology is evident in the naming of Macha and Nemain as twin goddesses of war, the stag-horned forest god Cernan, a cauldron that brings the dead to life, and the existence of the Wild Hunt. Elements of pre-Indo-European religion are also evident in the existence of Dana, the mother goddess: blood and fertility rites performed by her priestesses occur throughout the trilogy. This mixing of what seem to be disparate mythological elements with Kay's own invention is justified by the nature of the world of Fionavar. As Loren explains in *The Summer Tree*, "There are many worlds . . . caught in the loops and whorls of time. Seldom do they intersect, and so for the most part they are unknown to each other." Fionavar is "the prime creation, which all the others imperfectly reflect." Such a conception of the multiple reflections of one world suggests an influence from Roger Zelazny's Amber novels. In *Nine Princes in Amber* (1970) and its sequels, the world of Amber is revealed as the one true world, of which all the others are merely shadows or reflections.

Kay also makes extensive use of the Arthurian legends in the last two volumes of the trilogy. Arthur is summoned to help fight Rakoth, only to discover that one of the Toronto characters is the reincarnated Guinevere. When Lancelot is woken from a magical sleep to aid them in their struggle, the famous love triangle is complete. Kay does not introduce these archetypal characters until the second book of the trilogy, however, suggesting a possible influence from Robert Holdstock's fantasy novel *Mythago Wood* (1984). Holdstock's premise is that legendary figures can come to life in certain places where potent images and desires from the human unconscious interact with the natural environment: an Arthur or a Robin Hood might spring up where people desperately need a hero. Similarly, Kay's Arthur is revived again and again in different worlds when he is needed to fight against evil. Kay's explanation is that Arthur is performing expiation for having ordered the death of innocent children to be sure of killing his incestuous son Mordred.

The Fionavar Tapestry has enjoyed popularity with readers as well as praise from critics. Critical reception of the first volume, *The Summer Tree*, was favorable on the whole. Reviewers praised the detailed world and Kay's capable handling of the Tolkien influence, despite noting a tendency toward heavy-handed prose and a sometimes disconcertingly fragmentary narrative style. In the 1986 Locus Poll Awards, *The Summer Tree* was ranked fourth for best first novel and seventh for best fantasy novel overall. Since *Locus Magazine* has a readership consisting of a mix of fantasy and science-fiction readers, professional writers, and aspiring writers, this annual poll provides a good middle ground of judgment between fans and fellow writers. *The Summer Tree* was also a runner-up for the Book of the Year award from the Science Fiction Book Club, coming in behind Anne McCaffrey's *Killashandra* and the next runner-up, Orson Scott Card's *Ender's Game*.

Kay's prose flowed more smoothly as the series proceeded, though it was still not as polished as it became in his later, stand-alone volumes. The use of a frequently shifting point of view remained constant: Neil Randall shows in the Summer 1991 issue of *Canadian Literature* that "One typical chapter in *The Wandering Fire*, for example, Chapter 8, shifts the focalization [point of view] four times. . . . Only three chapters in the entire trilogy are focalized through just one character, and one chapter, the eighth of *The Summer Tree*, shifts focalization twenty-one times." The effect of this technique on narrative and plot structure may have alienated some reviewers and readers. Writing in the Autumn/Winter 1989 issue of *Canadian Literature*, J. R. Wytenbroek, who found the trilogy to be a powerful work of fiction overall, captured the general concern with his statement that "the wealth of characters and multiplicity of situations become a little confusing. Kay constantly cuts characters off before they explain something important, or simply informs the reader that one character is telling another something important, without divulging what it is. He seems to take for granted that a reader will remember that hint, that partial conversation later when the author fills the gaps." Kay's use of the shifting point of view improved with practice, however, and his later novels make a more moderate and effective use of this technique.

Kay earned substantially more attention with the concluding volumes of *The Fionavar Tapestry* than he did with the opening volume. *The Wandering Fire* won the 1987 Casper Award for the best work of Canadian speculative fiction; the award is roughly equivalent in prestige and voting procedures to the Hugo Award. *The Wandering Fire* was also a Science Fiction Book Club main selection. *The Darkest Road* was ranked twelfth in the 1987 Locus Poll and was nominated for the 1988 Casper Award; it was defeated by Charles de Lint's *Jack the Giant Killer*.

Kay's Fionavar trilogy seems to have purged his system of all that he had to say in high fantasy, for his subsequent novels have taken up an entirely different and little-used thread of fantasy literature. And despite the success of *The Fionavar Tapestry*, his stand-alone novels have made the greatest impact in the fantasy genre. The first of these novels is *Tigana* (1990). In a world strongly reminiscent of Renaissance Italy, a group of patriots struggle to overthrow a conquering sorcerer-king who punished the people of

Dust jacket for the U.S. edition (1993) of Kay's 1992 novel, a historical fantasy set in a world based on medieval France

one province—Tigana—for the death of his son in battle by creating an enchantment that prevents any non-Tiganan from remembering even the name of that province, let alone its achievements in art and culture. The detailed, authentic feel of the world is partly the result of the fact that it was written in Tuscany, as Kay continued his practice of writing his books while abroad. The novel shows careful research; some of the influences that Kay acknowledges in the final product are Carlo Ginzburg's *Night Battles* (1966) and the work of Kundera, Gene Brucker, Jacob Burckhardt, Joseph Huizinga, Lauro Martines, and Iris Origo.

While the setting is modeled on fifteenth-century Italian geography, politics, and culture, the themes that Kay works with are clearly of the twentieth century. One of these is the nature and importance of cultural identity and the effects of the cultural obliteration often practiced by conquerors, as in the old Soviet Union, Ireland, China, and in Native American reservations. Another major theme of *Tigana* is how oppression is not merely political but affects all aspects of personal interactions, including sexual relationships. Kay's inspiration to develop this idea came from his reading of Kundera's *Laughable Loves* (1974).

Kay's attention to character development in *Tigana* is to good effect; "Memorable characters" was one of the merits cited by the *Library Journal* when it reviewed *Tigana* as "Highly recommended" in its August 1990 issue. Among these complex characters are Brandin, the conqueror, and Dianora, his Tiganan concubine. Despite Dianora's original intention to assassinate Brandin, the man who threatens to destroy even the memory of her homeland, she comes to love him. Brandin's flaw, however, may actually lie in his capacity for love: his grief at his son's death is what starts the train of events leading to his downfall. The cast of characters is smaller and more manageable than in the Fionavar novels, yet the plot is more complex, since Kay has freed himself from trying to produce another version of the typical epic good-versus-evil conflict.

Some loose ends remain in the finished product, such as the "Night Walkers," whose dream-battles occupy a significant portion of the narrative near the center of the novel but who have no apparent function in the plot overall. Their presence may be an attempt to push the reader to see the world of *Tigana* as a real world in which not everything is part of a story. This effect is certainly the intention of the conclusion of the novel, in which three important characters see a riselka, a magical selkie-like woman whose appearance foretells that one of the three will be blessed, one will die, and one will have his life changed. Rather than being an indication of an upcoming sequel, this open ending indicates that for these characters, as for real people, life goes on beyond the bounds of the story that has been told in the novel.

Tigana received wide critical attention. It won the 1991 Aurora Award (as the Caspers were then known) and earned the third ranking in the Locus Poll, behind Ursula K. Le Guin's *Tehanu* and Terry Pratchett and Neil Gaiman's *Good Omens*. Additionally, the novel was nominated for the prestigious World Fantasy Award and for the Mythopoeic Award.

During the same year *Tigana* was published, Kay's father passed away; Kay stopped writing for a while, fearing that his grief would have too great an impact on his next book. But the birth of Kay's first son a few months later brought a different emotional effect, and his next novel is tinged with both sadness and hope.

In *A Song for Arbonne* (1992) Kay continued to work with history in crafting a fantasy world. Written during two visits to Provence, the novel is set in a world that clearly reflects medieval France. Provence itself becomes Arbonne, a beautiful country of troubadours and courtly love, in which women hold positions of respect and power and a goddess and a god are worshipped equally. Arbonne is divided within itself, however, by a feud between noblemen based on a decades-past tragedy of love, and so it is vulnerable to a threat from the north. Northern France, the origin of the brutal Albigensian Crusade that devastated Provence in real history, is represented in the novel by the northern land of Gorhaut, a patriarchal warrior culture unsettled by a peace treaty that dispossessed many of its people. This treaty turns out to be but one move in a complex series of political maneuvers that ends with Blaise, the self-exiled son of a Gorhautian nobleman, defending the southern kingdom of Arbonne against an invading army from Gorhaut.

Kay typically spends about a year researching a new novel and a year writing it, and he is never hesitant about acknowledging the sources of his fiction. The research done for *A Song for Arbonne* is evident in the richly detailed medieval setting and in the sources Kay credits: the French historians Georges Duby, Phillippe Aries, and Emmanuel Le Roy Ladurie; the work of Urban Tigner Holmes, Frances and Joseph Gies, and Friedrich Heer; and, for knowledge of the history and the work of the troubadours, Frederick Golden, Paul Blackburn, Alan Press, and Meg Bogin. However, the depth of Kay's involvement with the historical background of his novel does not mean that he feels obliged to stick to the path of historical events. The novel relates a version of the real Albigensian Crusade, but because *A Song for Arbonne* is fantasy, Kay can keep the reader in suspense as to the outcome: he is not tied to the historical ending of the crusade for his novel. What Kay does, in effect, with the ending of *A Song for Arbonne* is produce an alternate history: a turn of events that could have happened in this world but did not.

In the novel, the Gorhautian Blaise comes to realize, almost in spite of himself, that Arbonne is not the decadent and corrupt culture his fanatical father would have him believe but is a valuable and beautiful culture strengthened, not weakened, by the contribution of women. His bold and ultimately successful strike for the crown of Gorhaut, combined with the ability of the feuding noblemen of Arbonne to come together in their country's hour of need, allows a resolution of the conflict that leaves both realms whole and stable.

The fact that the worlds of Arbonne and Tigana both have two moons suggests, along with a few other clues, that *A Song for Arbonne* is set in the

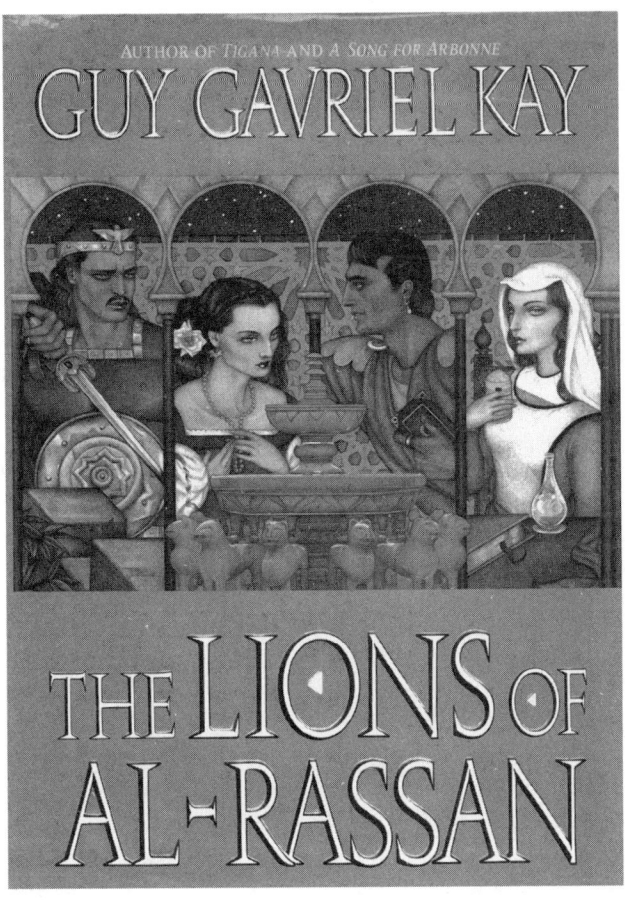

Dust jacket for the U.S. edition of Kay's 1995 novel, which uses historical events as a basis for a story set in an alternate Iberian peninsula

same world as *Tigana,* and the same universe as Fionavar. However, Kay makes clear that these hints are metaphorical, not literal. Arbonne is, in fact, distinguished from Tigana not just in the different setting but also in the role that magic plays in the novel. While magic plays a crucial role in the plot of *Tigana,* it is almost incidental in *A Song for Arbonne.* The high priestess of the goddess catches occasional glimpses of otherworldly insight, but these are fragmentary and fleeting. The action of the story is almost entirely political and psychological, with the main fantastic element simply the alternate-world setting. The reduced presence of magic, and the silent god and almost-silent goddess, provide a counterpart to the Gorhautian priests' perception of Arbonne as a land where witchcraft runs rampant. Even what seems like a direct intercession from the goddess in the final battle is ambiguous: it is actually staged by an ordinary mortal, but on the inspiration of the high priestess's vision.

A Song for Arbonne has not received the attention that *Tigana* has, despite showing the same complexity and displaying a more tightly crafted plot. While in 1998 *A Song for Arbonne* made the Internet Top 100 SF/Fantasy List, which is compiled through reader votes, it had the lowest ranking, at 78, while at number 6 *Tigana* had the highest spot of any of Kay's novels. It may be that Kay's readers were taken aback at the shift away from magic, after the thoroughly fantastic Fionavar books and *Tigana;* in fact, a prepublication notice in the 1 September 1992 *Library Journal* claimed that "Fantasy fiction writer Kay here changes pace with a historical novel" and mistook Arbonne for a city located in Provence. Nonetheless, the novel did receive a nomination for the 1993 Aurora Award for Canadian speculative fiction.

The Lions of Al-Rassan (1995) continues the trend away from magic and toward the use of real historical events. The story takes place in an alternate Iberian peninsula, with a disunited Esperaña composed of Jaddite kingdoms in the north, which are opposed in the south by Al-Rassan, a land of small Asharite kingdoms slowly coming under the sway of one powerful king. Living precariously in Al-Rassan are the Kindath, hated by the Jaddites and only tolerated by the Asharites. The Jaddites, Asharites, and Kindath are alternate versions of the medieval Christians, Moors, and Jews, respectively; Kay accurately portrays the complex interrelations of the different groups on both the religious and the political level, and the factions that struggle for power within the Jaddite and Asharite camps. For the background information and inspiration for *The Lions of Al-Rassan,* Kay particularly notes the work of Richard Fletcher, David Wasserstein, T. F. Glick, Nancy G. Siraisi, S. D. Goitein, Bernard Reilly, Pierre Riché, Rheinhart Dozy, and the writings of Manfred Ullman on medicine.

The plot of *The Lions of Al-Rassan* combines the history of the reconquest of Spain with the story of the Spanish national hero the Cid as it is told in the epic poem *Poema del Cid* and in historical records. Rodrigo Belmonte, Kay's version of the Cid, is the best warrior of one of the Jaddite kingdoms, but through an altercation with an enemy in the court he is forced to accept exile. This situation leads him south to the kingdoms of Al-Rassan, where he encounters the similarly exiled Asharite Ammar ibn Khairan. Their fates, and that of the female physician Jehane, become linked as the peninsula moves inevitably toward a war of conquest that is nominally a holy war.

Kay never loses sight of the complexity of this situation. One way in which he presents this complexity is to use Jehane as a main viewpoint character; her people, the Kindath, suffer abuses and restrictions under Asharite rule but stand to lose everything with a Jaddite victory. As in his other novels, Kay uses the technique of shifting viewpoints to give different perspectives on the situation: apart from Jehane, the reader sees through the eyes of Rodrigo; Ammar; Alvar, a young Jaddite soldier; the Kindath chancellor to an Asharite king; the leader of a fundamentalist Asharite group in the southern deserts; Rodrigo's young son Diego; and an outlaw. At a few points in the novel the author's manipulation of the viewpoints to prolong the suspense of important scenes is evident, but this flaw is mainly noticeable in contrast to the deft handling of the viewpoints overall.

Characterization continues to be an important element in Kay's writing. *The Lions of Al-Rassan* does not rely on clichéd heroes and villains; the characters are real people with various loyalties, sometimes divided and always believable. The character of Rodrigo is heavily based on that of Rodrigo Díaz de Bivar, the Cid, but it is far more rounded than the straightforward warrior of the *Poema del Cid.* As might be expected in a novel dealing mainly with the reconquest of Spain, a greater proportion of the characters are male than in *A Song for Arbonne,* but Kay manages to include several interesting women. Besides the primary character of Jehane, notable secondary female characters include Queen Ines of Valledo and Rodrigo's wife, Miranda. Jehane was actually the first creative spark of the book; her character was inspired by a picture of a female physician in a book about medieval medicine.

More than his previous novels, *The Lions of Al-Rassan* exhibits a tension between the historical and the fantastic. In one sense it is Kay's most realistic and historical novel. Magic has almost no role in the story; the only element of the fantastic is a visionary talent that one of Rodrigo's sons has. The novel is also strongly grounded in historical reality, portraying the situation in medieval Iberia with fidelity.

Yet, in another way, *The Lions of Al-Rassan* is much more dependent on the characteristics of the fantasy genre than *A Song for Arbonne.* The nature of this dependency can best be seen in reviewer Robert Killheffer's comment on the character of Jehane, in his lengthy discussion of the novel in the December 1995 *Magazine of Fantasy & Science Fiction*. He explains why she "might have bothered me in a purely historical novel":

> she brings a very modern attitude to bear in most of her dealings—she's fiercely independent, uncowed in the presence of male power, free to travel nearly alone from city to city, and so on. Not an impossibility in the 11th or 12th century, but it would take a lot more work to make her convincing in an historical context. Here, in Al-Rassan, I'm more willing to suspend my disbelief, give Kay the benefit of the doubt, go with the flow.

The fantasy genre gives Kay the leeway to work his concerns with modern issues into the historically based setting.

The primary focus of the novel is on how ideologies, both political and religious, harden toward conflict and what that does to the ability of individuals to communicate and relate freely: as Kay states, a twentieth-century theme. The concern of the novel with issues of cultural conflict and the response of human beings to acts of brutality is also highly relevant to modern readers. Kay takes pains to show the reality of war and its consequences, as in a gruesome raid on a village that Rodrigo's men are too late to stop, and in a surprise attack of Asharite warriors on Rodrigo's camp that nearly kills his son. Kay's attitude toward violence is expressed not just in the narrative but also through the eyes of his characters, including the Jaddite soldiers Rodrigo and Alvar; the latter eventually abandons his profession as a soldier to become a physician. Since the culture that Kay uses as his source viewed war as a glorious and honorable occupation, the ambivalence that Rodrigo and Alvar display toward warfare makes them, like Jehanc, far more modern than medieval.

Kay's decision to highlight modern issues through his characters makes the story more accessible; however, it also means that the novel cannot provide an avenue for a reader to understand the mindset of an alien culture. The consequences of Kay's choice can be seen in his handling of his source material, as shown in an early scene in which Rodrigo confronts Garcia de Rada, a fellow vassal of the king, who has made an unauthorized and brutal raid on a village. The sense that de Rada has been shamed by Rodrigo in this encounter is important to understanding the motivation for his later actions. In the historical account of this incident, the Cid pulls out part of his enemy's beard before setting him free; however, while such an action was perceived as humiliating at the time of the Cid, it would mean little to a modern reader unfamiliar with the different values of that culture. Kay therefore introduces a subtle change: Rodrigo, instead of pulling de Rada's beard, scars his face with a whip. With this change, Kay offers his readers a more understandable motivation for de Rada's hatred of Rodrigo.

In addition to allowing Kay to work with modern themes in a medieval setting, the fantasy nature of *The Lions of Al-Rassan* gives him the freedom to reshape history to fit his story. As he showed in *A Song for Arbonne,* Kay is comfortable with producing alternate history when it will best serve his story, so he is able to maintain suspense while retelling historical events. The readers of *The Lions of Al-Rassan* can hope for a peaceful, or at least less destructive, resolution. While Kay's conclusion does not stray far from historical reality, he does compress hundreds of years of the reconquest of Spain into a single lifetime, ending the novel with a complete Jaddite conquest of the peninsula. If Kay had used the strict historical ending to the Cid's wars, the conclusion would have been one without resolution; the Asharites would have lost ground without being defeated, only to be slowly pushed out of Esperaña city by city over the next three hundred years. The compressed timespan that Kay chooses has the distinct artistic advantage of allowing Kay to show the complexities of the reconquest through the eyes of characters from both sides of the conflict. Despite its brutalities, Al-Rassan has been portrayed as a place where culture and learning reached heights unknown in the Jaddite north, and the news of the final extinction of the Asharite culture in the peninsula is as bittersweet to the reader as it is to many of the characters.

The Lions of Al-Rassan gained its share of critical attention, being nominated for the 1996 Aurora Award and ranking fourth among fantasy novels in the 1996 Locus Poll. Its popularity with readers can be gauged by its eighth-place ranking in the 1998 Internet Top 100 SF/Fantasy List, only two slots below his most widely acclaimed novel, *Tigana.*

Kay's next project was a return to the multivolume works with which he began his career. *The Sarantine Mosaic,* comprising two volumes—*Sailing to Sarantium* (1998) and *Lord of Emperors* (2000)—is, like *The Fionavar Tapestry,* essentially a unified work divided into separate volumes for publishing convenience. Following the pattern of his previous novels, Kay utilizes late antiquity as the foundation for his story. Sarantium is based on sixth-century Byzantium, as well as the myths and stories that have developed around it, notably including William Butler Yeats's poetic imagining of it. In "On Writing *Sailing to Sarantium,*" an essay posted on the authorized website devoted to Kay (http://www.brightweavings.com), the author discusses why Byzantium appealed to him as source material: "In Byzantium—which became my own alchemical Sarantium—I found magic and mysteries, sexuality, dazzling art, chariot racing in the magnificent Hippodrome (with partisan brawling in the streets before and after), warfare, political intrigue, and the ageless clashes between east and west, secular and pious, artist and soldier, walled city and open countryside." In the first volume, Crispin, a mosaic artist, travels to Sarantium, the imperial capital, at the request of the emperor, in order to begin work on a new sanctuary there. Crispin's travels and adventures on his way to Sarantium and then his adventures within the capital city provide readers with a detailed view of that world. In *Lord of Emperors* the political intrigue becomes more complex as readers are drawn deeper into Sarantine society.

Kay's enthusiastic readers frequently compare his work to Tolkien's, but the comparison is not particularly useful in understanding Kay's writing. Tolkien is the single most important influence on modern fantasy, a debt that Kay acknowledges in his Fionavar books; yet, Kay's stand-alone novels are notable in part because they contribute to a branch of fantasy literature that is not dependent on or directly descended from Tolkien. Kay's novels of "fantastic history" owe a debt, conscious or unconscious, to the work of Lord Dunsany at the first quarter of this century. Dunsany is best known for his classic novel *The King of Elfland's Daughter* (1924), which fits into the Tolkienesque tradition of fantasy. However, Dunsany also wrote two noteworthy but lesser-known novels set in an undefined, fantastic Golden Age of Spain: *Don Rodríguez:*

Chronicles of Shadow Valley (1922) and *The Charwoman's Shadow* (1926). As Kay did more than sixty years later, Dunsany draws on a real setting and culture as inspiration for novels that are clearly fantasy in their themes and occurrences. Most novels in the Tolkien tradition strive to completely immerse the reader in the secondary world, an effect that Dunsany does not commit himself to sustaining. Particularly in *Don Rodríguez,* Dunsany shows an awareness of the disjunction between the times he writes of and the present day, which he uses to evoke in the reader a dreamy nostalgia for the Golden Age. In his novels, and especially in *The Lions of Al-Rassan,* Kay shows a similar awareness of the contrast between the setting of the novel and the world of the reader, which he uses to introduce into the narrative modern issues that he can assume will interest his reader.

Kay's stand-alone novels are doubly original: first, by the simple fact of existing outside the powerful Tolkien tradition, and second, by innovating within the slender tradition of alternate history. Kay's novels stand on a base of history and culture from this world, but by casting that base in an entirely new world—Tigana, Arbonne, Esperaña and Al-Rassan, Sarantium—he has the freedom to work with historical events and situations to say something new about them and speculate on what might have been and what could be.

Kay appears committed to innovation. After expanding the borders first of high fantasy in particular and then fantasy in general, he is striving to stretch his work to overlap what is typically called "mainstream fiction." As he told Henry Mietkiewicz in the 14 November 1992 *Toronto Star,* his aim is "to reach adult readers who wouldn't normally buy fantasy, but love the big historicals by James Clavell or epics like *The Name of the Rose.*" If fantasy literature does move out of the shadows and into mainstream popularity and critical acceptance, Kay—who can now claim to be one of the most critically praised and best-selling Canadian writers around the world—will undeniably have played a key role.

Interviews:

Andrew A. Adams, "Interview with Guy Gavriel Kay" (January 1995) <http://www-theory.dcs.st-and.ac.uk/~aaa/GGK.html>;

Edo van Belkom, "Guy Gavriel Kay," in his *Northern Dreamers: Interviews with Famous Science-Fiction, Fantasy, and Horror Writers* (Kingston, Ontario: Quarry Press, 1999), pp. 149–157.

References:

James Allard, "'The Unacknowledged Legislators of the World': Songs and Poetry in Guy Gavriel Kay's *A Song for Arbonne,*" in *Perspectives on the Canadian Fantastic,* edited by Allan Weiss (Toronto: Academic Conference on Canadian Science Fiction and Fantasy, 1998), pp. 9–14;

Neil Randall, "Shifting Focalization and the Strategy of Delay: The Narrative Weaving of 'The Fionavar Tapestry,'" *Canadian Literature,* 129 (Summer 1991): 40–54.

Eileen Kernaghan
(6 January 1939 -   )

Clélie Rich

BOOKS: *The Upper Left-Hand Corner: A Writer's Guide for the Northwest,* by Kernaghan, Edith Surridge, and Patrick Kernaghan (Vancouver, British Columbia: J. J. Douglas / Seattle: Madrona, 1975);
Journey to Aprilioth (New York: Ace, 1980);
Songs from The Drowned Lands (New York: Ace, 1983);
The Sarsen Witch (New York: Ace, 1989);
Walking After Midnight, by Kernaghan and Jonathon Kay (New York: Berkley, 1990);
Dance of the Snow Dragon (Saskatoon, Saskatchewan: Thistledown Press, 1995);
The Dark Gardens of the Zodiac (Vancouver, British Columbia: Neville Books, 1999);
The Snow Queen (Saskatoon, Saskatchewan: Thistledown Press, 2000).

OTHER: "The Devil We Know," in *WomanSpace,* edited by Claudia Lamparti (Lebanon, N.H.: New Victoria Publishers, 1981), pp. 59–74;
"Letter from Mars-Dome #1," in *Tesseracts,* edited by Judith Merril (Victoria, British Columbia: Press Porcépic, 1985), pp. 62–63;
"The Sorcerer's Child," in *The Window of Dreams: New Canadian Writing for Children,* edited by Mary Alice Downie, Elisabeth Greene, and M. A. Thompson (Toronto: Methuen, 1986), pp. 82–93;
Poems, in *Light Like a Summons,* edited by J. Michael Yates (Vancouver, British Columbia: Cacanadadada, 1989);
"Tales from the Holograph Woods," in *Tesseracts³,* edited by Candas Jane Dorsey and Gerry Truscott (Victoria, British Columbia: Tesseract Books, 1990), p. 61;
"Carpe Diem," in *Tesseracts³,* edited by Dorsey and Truscott (Victoria, British Columbia: Press Porcépic, 1990), pp. 197–206; reprinted in *Northern Stars: The Anthology of Canadian Science Fiction,* edited by David G. Hartwell and Glenn Grant (New York: Tor, 1994), pp. 275–281; reprinted in *On Spec: The First Five Years,* edited by the *On Spec* Collective (Edmonton, Alberta: Tesseract

Eileen Kernaghan (photograph by Diane Jarvis Jones)

Books, 1995), pp. 16–24; reprinted in *Aurora Awards: Anthology of Prize-Winning Science Fiction and Fantasy,* edited by Edo van Belkom (Kingston, Ontario: Quarry Press, 1999), pp. 18–25;
"The Tulpa," in *The Blue Jean Collection,* edited by Peter Carver (Saskatoon, Saskatchewan: Thistledown Press, 1992), pp. 206–223;
"The Weighmaster of Flood," in *Ark of Ice: Canadian Futurefiction,* edited by Lesley Choyce (Lawrence-

town Beach, Nova Scotia: Pottersfield Press, 1992), pp. 170–180;

"Couples," in *Tesseracts⁴*, edited by Lorna Toolis and Michael Skeet (Victoria, British Columbia: Beach Holme, 1992), pp. 159–179;

"Circle Dance," in *The 1994 Rhysling Anthology* (Moscow, Idaho: Science Fiction Poetry Association, 1994), p. 22; reprinted in *On Spec: The First Five Years*, edited by the *On Spec* Collective (Edmonton, Alberta: Tesseract Books, 1995), pp. 107–109;

"Dragon-Rain," in *Magic: A Collection of the Fantastical*, edited by David C. and Morgan L. Kopaska-Merkel (Tuscaloosa, Ala.: Stone Lightning Press, 1995), pp. 149–172; reprinted in *The Year's Best Fantasy and Horror Ninth Annual Collection*, edited by Ellen Datlow and Terri Windling (New York: St. Martin's Press, 1996), pp. 183–197;

"Tourists," in *Notes Across the Aisle*, edited by Peter Carver (Saskatoon, Saskatchewan: Thistledown Press, 1995), pp. 170–182;

"Through the Window of the Garden Shed" and "Chiaroscuro," in *Tesseracts⁵*, edited by Robert Runté and Yves Meynard (Edmonton, Alberta: Tesseract Books, 1996), pp. 235, 305;

Poems, in *Quintet: Themes & Variations* (Victoria, British Columbia: Ekstasis Editions, 1998);

"The Road to Shambhala," in *What If . . . ? Amazing Stories*, edited by Monica Hughes (Toronto: Tundra Books, 1998), pp. 90–102;

"Seven Things I Know About Green" and "Zero Visibility," in *Tesseracts⁷*, edited by Paula Johanson and Jean-Louis Trudel (Edmonton, Alberta: Tesseract Books, 1998), pp. 27, 280;

"Dinner with H.P.B.," in *Crime Through Time*, edited by Miriam Grace Monfredo and Sharan Newman (New York: Berkley, 1999), pp. 222–240;

"Avebury," in *TransVersions: An Anthology of New Fantastic Literature*, edited by Marcel Gagné and Sally Tomasevic (Mississauga, Ontario: Paper Orchid Press, 2000), p. 103.

An award-winning novelist, poet, bookseller, workshop leader, part-time teacher, and mentor, Eileen Kernaghan is as well-known a presence at West Coast science-fiction conventions as she is at literary events and festivals. Over the thirty years that she has been writing, fantasy has gone from being considered a subliterary genre to having a place in the ranks of respectable literature. When her first novel, *Journey to Aprilioth*, was published in 1980, fantasy was still the domain of genre writers. Reviewers in mainstream literary periodicals such as *Books in Canada* complained that they did not like "books about elves" (though Kernaghan has never written about elves). Nine years later, however, when *The Sarsen Witch*, the third book in the Grey Isles Trilogy, was published, fantasy was being taken more seriously. In a review in *The Reader* (June 1989) fellow Canadian science-fiction writer Michael Coney stated, "Kernaghan writes the way people ought to write; her prose has a smooth, poetic flow that draws you irresistibly into her world of horse-tribes and clan-chiefs and Stonehenge, and the story of Naeri the witch."

Kernaghan's preferred brand of magic is the magic of the shaman, which lies dormant inside all humans until they learn to unlock its power. It is a world of magic closely linked to the worlds of religion and spirituality. Kernaghan's specialty is historical fantasy, whether it is the prehistory of the Bronze Age, some four thousand years ago—in Europe or in the Indus Valley—or the atmospheres of eighteenth-century Bhutan or nineteenth-century Scandinavia. Kernaghan's research is meticulous, and as a result her novels resonate with details and descriptions that instantly place the modern reader inside the story, however distant and unfamiliar the culture may be.

Kernaghan was born Eileen Shirley Monk on 6 January 1939 in Enderby Hospital, in the interior of British Columbia. She was the first of two children born to Belinda Maude (née Pritchard) and William Alfred Monk, and she had an isolated rural upbringing on their dairy farm in the village of Grinrod. A solitary child, she had an insatiable appetite for books. Her mother taught her to read before she went to school, and from the age of five she read fairy tales, ghost stories, Greek myths, pulp magazines, and an entire collection of *Weird Tales* from her uncle's general store. Later, her tastes grew to include the work of Thomas Hardy, Jane Austen, and Charles Dickens.

Her interest in writing developed early. In grade three she wrote a pastiche of *Alice's Adventures in Wonderland* (1865), which she called "Molly in Mouseland." When she was twelve, she made her first sale: her story "Wolverine," about a boy trapper in the north woods, was published by *The Vancouver Sun*. She received $12.65. While in junior high school, she became a stringer for the *Enderby Commoner* newspaper, responsible for covering the social events of her area. She proved to be so shy, however, that her mother had to research the social events for the column on her behalf.

She considered becoming a journalist, but that plan was discouraged by one of her teachers, who said that journalism was a poor career choice for a woman. After graduating from high school, Kernaghan attended the University of British Columbia in Vancouver, where she studied English, history, and anthropology. In her first year at the university she met Patrick Walter Kernaghan, a fellow student, and in 1958 she returned to Sicamous, in the interior of British Columbia, where she taught elementary school for three years. In August 1959 she and Patrick Kernaghan married. They have three children: Michael William, born in 1961; Susan Heather, born in 1962; and Gavin Walter, born in 1964. In 1962 the Kernaghans moved back to Vancouver, and a year later to Burnaby, a neighboring suburb. Kernaghan worked first as a substitute elementary teacher and later became coordinator for the Burnaby Arts Council. As the 1960s progressed, Kernaghan became involved in the writing community in and around Burnaby. In 1967 she co-founded the Burnaby Writers' Society. One of the oldest writers' groups in Canada, the society has for more than thirty years produced a monthly newsletter, consisting almost exclusively of market news and suggestions for aspiring writers, compiled by Kernaghan. She also co-wrote a writer's handbook, *The Upper Left-Hand Corner: A Writer's Guide for the Northwest*. Originally privately printed by the society, it was so successful that it was published as a book in 1975; two revised editions have since appeared.

Kernaghan returned to writing when her youngest son was in kindergarten. After a few forays into the world of short fiction, she realized that she needed the breadth and expanse of full-length works to express her ideas, so she turned to novels. Writing two pages every morning, she produced her first novel, *Journey to Aprilioth*, the first volume of her Grey Isles Trilogy of prehistoric fantasy novels. In this trilogy Kernaghan painstakingly describes the west of England and the area around Stonehenge in the Bronze Age, circa 2000 B.C. Although the people of the Grey Isles Trilogy predate the Celts by some two thousand years, Kernaghan successfully demonstrates the connection between traditional fantasy characters and early historical Celtic characters.

A major element in each of Kernaghan's novels is the journey, whether inner or outer, and in most cases both are present. *Journey to Aprilioth* centers on the travels of Nhiall, a novice priest, in a time when the few remaining priests are losing their influence over the people of the Westland, even as they are losing the knowledge of sorcery from their ancestors, the Great Ones. The Old Gods, whom the Great Ones had vanquished, had begun to stir again. The Great Ones had begun to build a huge circle of stones in order to bind the Old Gods once more, but before the circle was completed, the sea had risen up and swallowed the land. Now, years later, only a handful of men have preserved the knowledge of the Great Ones, and only a few know that the Old Gods are once more restless. Nhiall's people have moved so far away from their memories of wisdom that when a chieftain dies, his family opens up an ancient grave in order to bury him in the manner of the Great Ones. In an effort to prevent this desecration of the grave, Nhiall accidentally kills the dead chief's brother.

Cover for the final volume (1989) in Kernaghan's Grey Isles Trilogy, about a prehistoric witch's coming of age

Nhiall flees in the night. Assisted by one of his superiors in the priesthood, he is taken to a place of shelter, and there given his mission by his fellow priests. He is to leave the Westlands and travel south in search of the fabled city of Aprilioth, to which some of the Great Ones had traveled before the coming of the sea. Armed with a crystal, a vision, and an axe from the tomb of a Great One, Nhiall sets out on a journey that leads him from his home and relative safety in the Westland through the length and breadth of Bronze-Age Europe until he reaches Aprilioth, the fabled city on the Mediterranean. At the beginning of the novel Nhiall is an innocent young acolyte, concerned only with which branch of knowledge he wishes to explore. His journey is not of his own choosing, but is thrust upon him by his circumstances. Few of Kernaghan's protagonists choose their journeys, and Nhiall is the first in a series of young people who are torn from their homes and sent away to gain knowledge.

Journey to Aprilioth received good reviews. A critic for *The Vancouver Sun* (26 June 1981) said, "Kernaghan's prose is crafted with care, her plot plausible and her narrative well-balanced. Meticulous attention to geographic and historical detail imbue the fantasy with a rich depth of field, a quality frequently lacking in the genre." Another critic for *The West Coast Review of Books* (July 1981) wrote that Kernaghan "handles her material deftly" and "spins a captivating tale," and the journal gave Kernaghan a silver Porgy award for original paperback fantasy. As *The Vancouver Sun* reviewer suggested, the success of *Journey to Aprilioth* is at least partly attributable to the careful research that became characteristic of Kernaghan's work.

Kernaghan has said that she is not sure whether she writes to write, or whether she writes to research, and she explores the background of each novel as thoroughly as possible. When she was partway through the writing of *Journey to Aprilioth*, after the research was completed, a new method of archeological dating based on the detection of carbon emissions from excavated objects indicated that Stonehenge and other similar European sites were significantly older than many similar Mediterranean monoliths. As this new finding seemed to imply that cultural influences moved to eastern Europe from western Europe, rather than the other way, Kernaghan immediately revisited much of her previous research into the background of the novel in order to avoid embarrassing errors.

The second book in the trilogy, *Songs from The Drowned Lands* (1983), is a prequel to *Journey to Aprilioth*. A collection of linked short stories, it explores the time when the Great Ones perceived that there was a tear in the pattern of order, which would inevitably allow the Old Gods to break through. Included are the stories of Thieras, the hawk-maid who has visions of the land being swallowed by the water; Eirech of the Golden Eyes, who turns away from order toward chaos and trades his silver voice for the gift of immortality from the Faerie; Dhan the sailor, who builds a great ship and sails away to the south and the city of Aprilioth; Siod'h, who builds the great circle of stones to mend the break in the pattern; and Ainn, the oldest and wisest voice in the book, who has built a tower by the sea and watches for the coming of the water.

According to Kernaghan in an unpublished 1999 interview, *Songs from The Drowned Lands* "mirrors our fear of the world suddenly coming to a cataclysmic end" and shows "how different people react in unique ways." In her comment on the inside cover of the book, fantasy writer Jane Yolen praised the book because it "has the strength and purity of the old Irish tales fleshed out with a modern storyteller's eye to characterization." Writing in *Kinesis* (July/August 1988) Melanie Conn said:

> Kernaghan has an exceptional ability to ground her stories in the details of everyday life. Even for a reader who is unfamiliar with the conventions of fantasy, the use of magic in the book seems to emerge as a natural tool to understand and cope with significant events.... In Kernaghan's hands, as in Joanna Russ and Elizabeth Lynn, women appear alongside men as women complete in themselves, protagonists and heroines in control of their own destinies.

Songs from The Drowned Lands won the Canadian Science Fiction and Fantasy Award in 1985.

The final book in the trilogy, *The Sarsen Witch*, was published in 1989. Its main character, Naeri, is born of witchfolk but has been captured by Ricca, the chieftain of the horselords. Naeri's gift is the art of geomancy, the ability to read the patterns of power in the earth. At the hands of her cousin Daui the minstrel, she begins to learn her abilities; from her kinsman Nhiall, she learns the knowledge of Aprilioth; and through her awakening love for Gwi the smith, she learns to be an individual. Ricca takes Naeri as his fourth wife and makes use of her powers to fulfill his dream of raising a sun temple in his own honor. Naeri convinces him that the best place for his temple is on the site of the ancient sun temple of power stones that lie at the heart of his lands. Naeri's presence as Ricca's wife fosters an alliance between the horselords and the witchfolk, and the two groups unite not only in the rebuilding of the great temple but also in war against Ricca's enemies. The treaty is betrayed, however, and Naeri and Gwi flee from Ricca's camp to the Summer Country, where ultimately Ricca finds them. Writing in *Canadian Science Fiction and Fantasy* (1992), David Ketterer praised *The Sarsen Witch* for its "thorough research" and "the poetic flow of Kernaghan's prose and believable characterization," calling it "a superior historical fantasy."

The Sarsen Witch was short-listed for the 1990 Casper, or Canadian Science Fiction and Fantasy Award, for best long-form work in English, losing to Dave Duncan's *West of January* (1989). Kernaghan did win a Casper that year–her second–when "Carpe Diem," published in the Fall 1989 issue of *On Spec*, won for best short-form work in English. "Carpe Diem" has been Kernaghan's most successful short story, reprinted many times. Atypical for Kernaghan, this story is science fiction. It describes the experiences of a group of older women staying in a hospital ward in order to receive Assessment. They are tested for diseases and medical conditions in order to determine whether they can be treated or should be Reassigned.

Dance of the Snow Dragon

"Accursed one," said Jatsang, in a voice so soft that Sangay could barely make out the words, "What have you done with our tea?"

The tulpa rose and strolled to the edge of the precipice. Gleefully, he pointed into the yawning gulf below. An awful silence followed. Sangay held his breath, waiting to see what would happen next. Jatsang's face was white with fury, but all she said to the tulpa, in a curiously flat, indifferent voice, was "I am sick of the sight of you, tulpa. Go sleep behind those rocks, where we do not have to look at you."

Instead of obeying, the tulpa deliberately moved closer to the fire. Jatsang ignored him, and Sangay knew that the decision had been made. From now on, she would simply bide her time. After a while, like a bored child, the tulpa began to scoop up handfuls of small stones and toss them into the air. Tiring of that game, he threw one at Jatsang, hard enough to sting, and barely missed her head.

"Go away," said Jatsang sharply. "You are banished from this world. I have no more need of you."

The tulpa got heavily to its feet. What a clumsy, shambling creature it had become, thought Sangay -- when once it had been a thing of grace and dignity. Where now was the noble friend, the brave protector who had snatched him from the Serpent's jaws? Heartsick and without hope, Sangay offered up one final plea. "Maybe we do not need him now, Lady, but think of the journey that lies ahead...."

Corrected typescript page for Kernaghan's 1995 historical fantasy novel for young adults, set in eighteenth-century Bhutan (Collection of Eileen Kernaghan)

As the reader discovers when one of the women is Reassigned, this designation means death for the patient and distribution of her healthy organs. An effective and understated extrapolation of the consequences of organ transplant technology, "Carpe Diem" is also a moving meditation on aging and death.

Although best known as a writer of fiction, Kernaghan is also an accomplished poet, with publications in a variety of magazines and anthologies. She describes her poetry as "slip-stream," or the category of poetry that bridges the huge gulf between genre and literary magazines. Two of her poems, "Tales from the Holograph Woods" and "Circle Dance," have been nominated for the prestigious Rhysling Award, given by the Science Fiction Poetry Association, in 1988 and 1994, respectively.

Kernaghan contributed sixteen poems to *Light Like a Summons* (1989), edited by J. Michael Yates, which collected the work of five British Columbia women poets. Her poems in this volume mostly reflect her interest in Celtic themes, arising principally from the research she had been doing for her novels. *Light Like a Summons* received favorable reviews, with critics singling out Kernaghan for praise. Writing in the Spring 1996 issue of *Canadian Literature,* A. M. Forbes wrote that "Eileen Kernaghan is perhaps the most consciously intertextual of the poets in *Light Like a Summons*. The voices of many writers—Blake, Yeats, Thomas, Stevens and Plath—are echoed in her poems, as are the mythologies and philosophies to which she turns in her search for meaning not confined to the corners of the present time and space."

Although not a formal part of the Grey Isles Trilogy, Kernaghan's next novel, the unpublished "Winter on the Plain of Ghosts," was set in the same era, but in the ancient Indus Valley city of Mohenjo-Daro. Again it features a young protagonist, torn from his family and sent on a great journey. Unusually for Kernaghan's work, it was written in the first person, from the vantage point of old age, looking back on the main character's life.

Kernaghan turned next to young-adult fiction. Her interest was drawn to reincarnation, which could perhaps be considered the greatest journey of all. Vancouver moviemaker Jonathon Kay's documentary *Walking After Midnight* (1988) featured interviews with several celebrities on their beliefs in reincarnation and past lives, and Kernaghan worked with Kay on a companion book to the movie, which was published in 1990. Editing an interview with the Dalai Lama on the Buddhist concept of reincarnation renewed Kernaghan's interest in northern Tibetan Buddhism. That prompted her to begin further research, which eventually formed the background of her first young-adult novel, *Dance of the Snow Dragon* (1995), set in eighteenth-century Bhutan.

Sangay Tensing is an eight-year-old yak-herder who has been chosen by the lamas to become a monk in the White Leopard monastery. Sangay leaves his home and family and travels with the monks to the White Leopard Dzong, where he will commence his studies as a novice. But Sangay has always dreamed of dancing, and when he meets Wanjur, a monk who is a temple dancer, Sangay begins to consider that he might also have a destiny as a temple dancer. However, after a few days at the Dzong, he begins his new life as an apprentice monk. The studies and the lifestyle are hard, but gradually he adapts.

When Sangay is fourteen, he is a gangly youth with little control or gracefulness, but he is finally allowed to commence the study of the dance. He has no aptitude for it whatsoever, although in his imagination "he danced as though his limbs were wind and fire and water. He danced, in waking dreams, as the gods were said to dance in the heavenly kingdom Guru Rimpoche." In practice, however, he turns from dance to the study of archery, where he begins to excel, but he also begins to depart from the tenets of the Middle Way and starts to get into trouble with his superiors. Finally, he is sent to a hermitage to consider whether he wishes to continue to be a monk, or to return to the outside world. There, for one hundred days of darkness, he meditates upon his alternatives. But in his dreams and thoughts, only one thing comes to him: his true journey must be toward the mythical city of Shambhala. He returns to the Dzong, where he is granted permission to leave and follow his destiny. He encounters the sorceress Jatsang, and together they proceed toward the holy city of Sangay's quest. Up to this point in the book, Kernaghan has so carefully built up a realistic world in which demons and sorcerers are as real as the butter-lamps and bronze gongs that when Jatsang and Sangay begin to move into the realms of magic, the reader easily accepts it. Central to this book is the Buddhist concept that magic is not a thing apart from life but a basic fact of everyday life. Sangay's search for Shambhala is an archetypal spiritual quest, which perfectly matches the physical journeys at the heart of Kernaghan's work and which is a metaphor for the inward journeys.

Dance of the Snow Dragon exemplifies Kernaghan's use of the themes of journey and change to introduce the reader to extremely unusual worlds. Just as the protagonist, who is usually young and curious about life, leaves his or her comfortable environment and is forced to take a look at a broader world, the readers simultaneously learn about a world that may exist by different rules from theirs. For example, in *Dance of the Snow*

Dragon the reader is introduced to the many deities and beings of the land of the Druk-yul as the young Sangay is being shown the wonders of the three temples of the first monastery he has ever seen.

Dance of the Snow Dragon met with approval from its reviewers. A critic for *The Vancouver Sun* (26 August 1998) called it "one of the best fantasies for young people that I have read for some time." A reviewer for *Quill & Quire* (June 1995) said, "the audience for this book will be readers of high fantasy of all ages, but should not be so limited. . . . The old Tibet is gone forever, but strong echoes of its feudal theocracy and enveloping mysticism emit from this work of fiction."

During the 1980s and 1990s Kernaghan and her husband ran a used-book store, Neville Books, which specialized in science fiction, fantasy, and military history and which became a home for readings and meetings of the writing community. In the 1990s she continued her involvement in that community, co-founding another writers' association, the Lonely Cry, a loose collection of British Columbia science-fiction writers that promotes their work on the association website, in the occasional newsletter, or through appearances at local science-fiction conventions.

During the mid 1990s Kernaghan was one of five women poets working together to write poems on specific themes. The work of this group evolved into *Quintet: Themes & Variations,* published in 1998. Although Kernaghan continues to work with her favorite themes, her contributions in this collection also explore the aging process, Buddhism, reincarnation, music, and color. Some of her most startling poems open pleasantly but turn into something quite violent and unexpected with the closing lines. *Quintet: Themes & Variations* received favorable reviews. In the Fall 1998 issue of *A Room of One's Own* Virginia Aulin wrote that "though each single poem is strong enough to stand on its own, when the disparate lyrics are woven together, they produce a provocative melody." Reviewing the collection on the Amazon.com website, J. Michael Yates called it "the best anthology I have read in ten years, perhaps closer to twenty," and then went on to say that "*Quintet,* given both themes and variations, is perhaps closer to western Baroque music than the original concept of renga."

The next year, Kernaghan published her first solo collection of poetry, a chapbook titled *The Dark Gardens of the Zodiac* (1999). It presents a personal selection of her poetry, which can perhaps be classified more as science fiction or science poetry than fantasy. Scientific topics such as matter and anti-matter and holographs are combined with such purely poetic forms as ghazals and gloses.

Cover for Kernaghan's 2000 novel for young adults, a retelling of the Hans Christian Andersen tale of a girl's adventures on her quest to rescue her friend from an evil queen

With Kernaghan's next novel, another young-adult tale, she moved into slightly more modern times than in her previous novels. *The Snow Queen* (2000) retells the Hans Christian Andersen story in the setting of 1840s Scandinavia. In a town in southern Denmark, Gerda and Kai are next-door neighbors who have grown up together. When the Baroness Aurore–young, elegant, and a woman of great learning–arrives in town, Kai is entranced by her. She invites him to return to her estate in Sweden to become her student and assistant. Kai accepts, and they depart. Months go by without word from Kai, and Gerda becomes increasingly worried. She decides that she will find him and embarks upon what appears to be a short journey into Sweden. When she arrives at the baroness's estate, however, she discovers that the baroness has departed to Saamiland for the summer. Undaunted, and with some help from various kindhearted women, Gerda heads north.

She is waylaid, however, in the north of Sweden by a robber-chieftain who takes her back to his camp, where Gerda is made captive by Ritva, the chieftain's daughter, who adopts Gerda as her new pet. Ritva herself is on a journey. Her mother is a Lapp-Saami shaman, and Ritva's own shamanic powers are beginning to develop. Ritva, illiterate and savage, is the antithesis of the well-raised Gerda. However, they become allies, and eventually friends. When Gerda becomes ill, Ritva uses her powers to see if she can discover where Kai is. Her spirit goes on a dream-journey and sees Kai captive in an ice palace at the end of the world. Along with Ritva's old reindeer, Ba, the two young women set out to find this place.

The relationship between Gerda and Ritva is characteristic of Kernaghan's fiction, in which, as was common in societies in earlier times, she uses mentors as another way for her young protagonists to mature. In both of Kernaghan's young-adult novels her protagonists acquire mentors—Jatsang in *Dance of the Snow Dragon* and Ritva in *The Snow Queen*—who have knowledge of the worlds beyond the physical.

Gerda's great gift is that she attracts people who willingly help her. In the course of their journey, the girls receive enough assistance to learn that the baroness is the Snow Queen, known to Ritva's people as a terrible enchantress. A Danish captain agrees to take them to Spitzbergen Island, but the ship is blown off course and is trapped in the ice. Gerda, Ritva, and Ba eventually continue across the ice. Finally, they pass through the Cave of Winds and come to a bleak, icy palace in the middle of a frozen lake; there, Kai is trying to solve the Snow Queen's ice puzzle, believing that if he solves it, she will give him the key to all knowledge. Gerda and Ritva confront the Snow Queen and demand Kai's release. The queen sets them three impossible tasks: to capture the cold light of a star in a box; to catch a giant silver pike with neither hook nor net; and to embroider a cover for a chest with neither needle nor embroidery silks. Using a combination of Ritva's powers and Gerda's scientific knowledge, they complete all three tasks. However, they cannot agree to a fourth and final task, sacrificing Ba, and instead they plan to escape from the palace, taking Kai with them.

When the Snow Queen pursues them, they defeat her through sorcery and escape with Kai. The answer to the ice puzzle is revealed. Ritva continues on her journey with Ba, and Gerda takes Kai back to southern Denmark.

Several journeys are described in *The Snow Queen*: Gerda's outward journey in pursuit of Kai, Ritva's inward journey to accept her shamanic powers as being of value and use, and Gerda's inward journey to reach maturity. Like all of Kernaghan's women, Gerda exemplifies the personal power women can develop when they choose to break out of the roles that their societies have assigned to them.

Atypically, in *The Snow Queen* Kernaghan introduces a companion animal, in the form of Ba, the aging and endearing reindeer. Ba has no magical powers, and in some ways he is more of a hindrance than a help, but in other ways his presence, and the need to keep him alive, helps Ritva and Gerda make decisions necessary to continue their journey.

Science-fiction and fantasy reviewers praised *The Snow Queen*. In *Locus* (July 2000) Carolyn Cushman wrote: "The Hans Christian Andersen story is mixed with elements from the Kalevala and Saami shamanism in this intelligent, magical young adult fantasy about a Danish girl who ventures into the far north to rescue the boy she loves." Terri Windling called the work "deceptively gentle, lyrically written by a long underrated Canadian fantasist" on her website (http://www.endicott-studio.com/remdats.html). *The Snow Queen* was one of the ten novels short-listed for the Children's Book of the Year Award from the Canadian Library Association, and it won the 2001 Aurora (as the Canadian Science Fiction and Fantasy Awards are now called) for the best long-form work in English. This award recognized Kernaghan's continuing importance in Canadian science fiction, twenty years after her first novel was published.

Whether Kernaghan returns to the world of adult fiction or continues with young-adult fantasies, her books, poems, and short fiction will continue to reach a wide audience of readers who have come to value well-crafted writing and stories that maintain a curiosity about the world and its wonders.

Crawford Kilian

(7 February 1941 -   )

Todd H. Sammons
University of Hawai'i at Mānoa

BOOKS: *Wonders, Inc.* (Berkeley, Cal.: Parnassus, 1968);
The Last Vikings (Toronto, Ontario: Clarke, Irwin, 1974);
Go Do Some Great Thing: The Black Pioneers of British Columbia (Vancouver, British Columbia: Douglas & McIntyre, 1978; Seattle: University of Washington Press, 1978);
The Empire of Time (New York: Ballantine, 1978; London: Legend, 1988);
Icequake (Vancouver, British Columbia: Douglas & McIntyre, 1979; London: Sidgewick & Jackson, 1979; New York: Bantam, 1980);
Eyas (Toronto, Ontario: McClelland & Stewart, 1982; New York: Bantam, 1982);
Exploring British Columbia's Past (Vancouver, British Columbia: Douglas & McIntyre, 1983);
Tsunami (Vancouver, British Columbia: Douglas & McIntyre, 1983; Toronto, Ontario & New York: Bantam, 1984);
Brother Jonathan (New York: Berkley, 1985; Victoria, British Columbia: Beach Holme, 1995);
School Wars: The Assault on B. C. Education (Vancouver, British Columbia: New Star Books, 1985);
Lifter (New York: Berkley, 1986); revised edition (Victoria, British Columbia: Beach Holme, 1992);
The Fall of the Republic: A Novel of the Chronoplane Wars (New York: Ballantine, 1987; London: Legend, 1988);
Rogue Emperor: A Novel of the Chronoplane Wars (New York: Ballantine, 1988);
Gryphon (New York: Ballantine, 1989);
Greenmagic (New York: Ballantine, 1992);
Redmagic (New York: Ballantine, 1995);
2020 Visions: The Futures of Canadian Education (Vancouver, British Columbia: Arsenal Pulp Press, 1995);
The Communications Book: Writing for the Workplace, by Kilian, Leslie Savage, Azza Sedky, and Martin Wittman (Scarborough, Ontario: Prentice Hall / Allyn & Bacon Canada, 1997);

Crawford Kilian (courtesy of the author)

Writing Science Fiction and Fantasy (Bellingham, Wash. & North Vancouver, British Columbia: International Self-Counsel Press, 1998);
Writing for the Web (Bellingham, Wash. & North Vancouver, British Columbia: International Self-Counsel Press, 1999); revised and expanded as *Writing for the Web: Geeks' Edition* (Bellingham,

Wash. & North Vancouver, British Columbia: International Self-Counsel Press, 2000).

PRODUCED SCRIPTS: *A Strange Manuscript Found in a Copper Cylinder,* adapted from James De Mille's novel, radio, Canadian Broadcasting Corporation, 1972;

Little Legion, radio, Canadian Broadcasting Corporation, 1972;

Generals Die in Bed, adapted from Charles Yale Harrison's novel, radio, Canadian Broadcasting Corporation, 1973;

Wonders, Inc., radio, Canadian Broadcasting Corporation, 1973;

Senator Connor's Big Comeback, radio, Canadian Broadcasting Corporation, 1974;

The Mob Has Got the Bomb, radio, Canadian Broadcasting Corporation, 1975.

SELECTED PERIODICAL PUBLICATIONS–UNCOLLECTED: "The Cheerful Inferno of James De Mille," *Journal of Canadian Fiction,* 1 (Summer 1972): 61–67;

"In Defence of Esther Summerson," *Dalhousie Review,* 54 (Summer 1974): 318–328.

On his website (http://www.capcollege.bc.ca/magic/cmns/crofpers.html), Crawford Kilian offers this self-characterization: "I'm a teacher and writer in Vancouver, BC, Canada, with interests in fiction, journalism, Webwriting, education, the environment, and social issues in general–especially the society of the Internet." Despite the demands of his full-time teaching job and his prolific journalistic output, he has produced more than twelve volumes of science fiction and fantasy. Unlike other science-fiction writers who have immigrated to Canada, however, Kilian has not inaugurated any revolutions in the genre, though he has rung changes on several time-honored generic conventions; most of these changes are explainable in terms of his liberal politics.

Crawford Kilian was born in New York City on 7 February 1941 to Victor William Cosgrove Kilian, a writer and engineer, and Verne Debney Kilian, a teacher. Six months after his birth the family moved to Los Angeles, California, where they stayed until 1950. Then they moved to Mexico City, where Kilian attended English-language private schools until the family returned to Los Angeles in 1954. Kilian graduated from Santa Monica High School in 1958. After a theatrical interlude for a season in upstate New York, Kilian matriculated at Columbia University, majoring in English and graduating in 1962. He spent a year doing freelance writing, then served from 1963 to 1965 in the U.S. Army. From 1965 to 1967 Kilian worked in Berkeley, California, at the Lawrence Berkeley Laboratory, first as a librarian, then as a technical writer-editor. Kilian married Alice Hayes Fairfax on 8 April 1966. Shortly after, in 1967, the Kilians immigrated to Vancouver, British Columbia.

After a year as an instructor at Vancouver Community College, in 1968 Kilian joined the faculty of the newly formed two-year Capilano College in North Vancouver, where he continues to teach communications and writing courses. In 1972 Kilian received an M.A. in English from Simon Fraser University in Burnaby, British Columbia (a suburb of Vancouver), writing a thesis titled "The Great War and the Canadian Novel, 1915–1926." In May 1973 Kilian became a naturalized Canadian citizen. He was elected in 1980 to serve a two-year term as a school trustee for North Vancouver. After losing a reelection bid in 1982, Kilian became the regular education columnist for the Vancouver *Province,* writing the column until 1994. From 1983 to 1984, Kilian and his wife taught English at the Guangzhou Institute of Foreign Languages in Guangzhou, People's Republic of China. They have two daughters, Anna Catherine and Margaret Cathleen.

By the time Kilian published his first science-fiction novel, he had already published two children's books and written radio scripts for the Canadian Broadcasting Corporation, as well as academic and other articles. Although Kilian's first science-fiction novel, *The Empire of Time,* published in 1978, is also the first novel of a series called *The Chronoplane Wars,* it was probably written as a singleton: it is self-contained; one protagonist dies at the end, and the other permanently "retires"; and Kilian wrote five other science-fiction novels before returning to the series nearly a decade later with *The Fall of the Republic* (1987) and *Rogue Emperor* (1988).

All three novels share the same basic situation. In the later part of the twentieth century, chaos is being held off by Trainables, young people capable of absorbing, processing, and remembering prodigious amounts of data: under optimum conditions, the best Trainables can learn in four hours what an unTrainable would take two or three years to learn. The pressure on the world's resources, however, is unexpectedly relieved by Richard Ishizawa's discovery in 1998 of chronoplanes–eleven slightly different versions of Earth, all of which are "downstream" or "downtime." These eleven Earths range from Beulah in 1787 A.D. to Tharmas in 70,787 B.C.; all are being colonized (thus relieving population pressure) by sending people to them through I-Screens (named after Ishizawa). Soon discovered are two Earths "uptime": Ulro (2222 A.D.) and Urizen (3571 A.D.). They are not being colonized for the simple reason that, in both, Earth has been rendered uninhabitable by a catastrophic event, called Doomsday, that will take place on 22 April 2089. Thus, the International Federation (IF) is created; its main tasks are to discover exactly how the biosphere of the 2089 Earth will be destroyed and to figure out what must be done to prevent that disaster.

Probably the most important arm of the IF is the Agency for Intertemporal Development (AID), whose permanent deputy of operations is Eric Wigner; Jerry Pierce, the protagonist of all three novels in the series, is Wigner's best field operative. One of the primary tasks of the AID is to scour the Earths downtime for "endos" (short for endochronics, the indigenous people of a downtime Earth) capable of being Trained, to aid in the massive effort of thwarting Doomsday. Another task is to make sure that the various governments of the four historical worlds downtime—the rest are prehistoric—allow their endos to emigrate to Wigner's Earth; the political maneuvering involved frequently changes the course of history on the downtime Earth. Thus, *The Chronoplane Wars* mixes four science-fiction subgenres: superman stories, time-travel stories, end-of-the-world stories, and alternate-history stories.

Each novel of the series, however, also has its own individuality. In *The Empire of Time*, Wigner sends Pierce to Orc (12,165 B.C.) to investigate supposed sabotage at the Weapons Development Site of the IF, near present-day Santa Monica, California. The novel takes place over the course of just five kaleidoscopically crowded days (7–12 February 2015), perhaps to allow its readers a taste of what it is like to be Jerry Pierce, Alpha-class Trainable. All three novels in *The Chronoplane Wars* series are reminiscent of Jack Williamson, with his late-1930s *Legion of Time* series (in which agents race around in time trying to save their world from extinction), and *The Empire of Time* in particular is influenced by Ian Fleming. Expert marksmanship; skill at personal combat; fluency in several languages (including ancient Greek); unusual knowledge of various arcane subjects; confidence; decisiveness; a gorgeous and smart female sidekick; success against overwhelming odds (including escape from seemingly impossible situations); respect for worthy opponents; and a license to kill, with the killer instinct to go along with it: these are all the James Bond–like characteristics of Jerry Pierce.

Unlike many science-fiction protagonists, however, Pierce changes over the course of this novel. As an AID assassin, essentially—of individuals, of endo tribes, even of whole governments—Pierce has done some truly horrible things, so horrible that the Agency has to Block his memory of them or he would not be able to function. When those Blocks are removed—by Anita !Kosi, a Trainable endo from Luvah (the next chronoplane downtime from Orc)—Pierce is forced to remember just how ruthless he has been. His worst memory is that he had recommended the use of an artificially designed virus to exterminate an endo tribe near a resort settlement on Luvah; the virus mutated and killed everyone in the settlement, including Pierce's mother, who had migrated to Luvah. By the end of the novel, Pierce has become a happy, popular teacher at a university on Tharmas, the Earth farthest downtime. When Beulah's William Blake (Blake's mythology provides the names for all of the chronoplane Earths) tries to recruit Pierce to help form the Intertemporal League, an attempt to give the chronoplanes some strength in dealing with Earth, and to forestall war between the chronoplanes. Pierce refuses, claiming that humanity "can't rely on heroes any more."

The novel indicates Kilian's dislike for two American agencies that during the 1950s and 1960s spread into various developing countries throughout the world. Wigner's AID resembles the real Agency for International Development (including the striking similarity in the abbreviations) in openly offering assistance to governments sympathetic to American interests, but it also resembles the Central Intelligence Agency (CIA) in covertly destabilizing countries that oppose those interests. Before he figures out what is truly going on at the Orcian weapons facility, Pierce had believed in Wigner's realpolitik, deterministic, and CIA-like credo: that in order to save Earth from Doomsday, they must—and will—do whatever is necessary, no matter what the cost. But when Pierce figures out that Doomsday is easily avoided, he is brought up short by Wigner's refusal to act on this discovery. Since solving the Doomsday puzzle obviates the need for AID, and since Wigner has a controlling personality that cannot imagine being powerless, Wigner would rather lie than disturb the status quo. Two final and decisive measures of Pierce's development beyond Wignerian determinism: Pierce not only ensures Wigner's death but also glories in the freedom restored to the human race on all the chronoplane Earths.

Kilian's second science-fiction novel, *Icequake*, published in 1979, forms a doublet with *Tsunami* (1983). Set in 1985, just a few years after their dates of publication, the two novels are Kilian's contribution to the world-catastrophe science-fiction subgenre. His worldwide catastrophe has two causes. First, the Earth's magnetic field disappears, resulting in too much ultraviolet light reaching the surface of the planet. Crops die; and livestock, blind and crazed with pain, must be destroyed. With no grain available for feed, no more livestock can be raised. And since the base of the marine food chain is also disrupted, the fishing industry is soon defunct. Second, an enormous Antarctic "icequake" pushes tons of the iceshelf off the continent and into the oceans, heralding–after tsunamis (icequake-generated tidal waves) kill hundreds of millions–a new Ice Age.

Icequake focuses on the effects of the catastrophe on a small group of people: the twenty-seven scientists, technicians, and support staff members of New Shackleton Station, the Antarctic locus of the Commonwealth Antarctic Research Programme (CARP). The station, nicknamed Shacktown, houses citizens from all the major Commonwealth countries: Australia, Britain, Canada, Ireland, New Zealand, and Scotland, as well as a token black from Jamaica and a few people from the United States. (During the course of the novel, these twenty-seven are joined by three Russians and three more Americans.) Although the point of view shifts among several of the characters–including station leader Hugh Adams, an Irishman transplanted to New Zealand; Al Neal, the American chief pilot; and Katerina Varenkov, the Russian exchange physician–readers experience most of the novel through the eyes of Penny Constable, an American staff writer for a science magazine.

The themes of the novel stem directly from its setting in Antarctica. It describes the beautiful and awe-inspiring topography of the place, its glaciers, nunataks (mountains surrounded by glacial ice), crevasse fields, seracs (ice thrusts), pressure ridges, mountain ranges, volcanoes, sastrugi ("wind-carved ice sculptures"); the various indignities that Antarctica inflicts on the human body, ranging from frozen snot (particularly irksome to the moustache-less Penny) to amputation and even death; the insignificance of human beings when measured against the tremendous power of nature, and a concomitant despondency or fear; and, conversely, the resiliency and indomitability of the human spirit, such as when Penny says to a crevasse from which a friend has just been rescued, "You'll never kill us." It also expresses nostalgia for the early explorers of the continent–both imaginative exploration, in the case of the Canadian author James De Mille, to whom Kilian dedicates the book, and actual exploration, in the case of the Englishman Sir Ernest Shackleton, after whom New Shackleton Station is named. As well, the novel concerns the desire to measure up to these early explorers.

But *Icequake* is also a science-fiction novel of the "hardest" kind, as its depiction of the effects of the catastrophes is worked out rigorously. The scientists of Shacktown specialize in the scientific disciplines of climatology, geology, geophysics, glaciology, meteorology, and seismology, and Kilian allows them all a turn on center stage to explain what has been happening from the perspective of their expertise. Kilian's scientists, however, are also human beings with human problems. Ben Whitcumb, the American seismologist, has a crush on Penny and allows himself to be terrorized by Gordon Ellerslee, the Canadian engineer who is interested in Jeanne Taylor. She is a student glaciologist, sleeping with her mentor but pregnant as a result of a liaison with a school chum before she reached Shacktown. Steve Kennard, a Canadian seismologist, drives Penny out of his bed, although they eventually reconcile.

The novel thus has its soap-operatic moments. But it is also a rousing adventure story, with scores of dangers overcome, including a helicopter crash, a reconnaissance flight through an erupting volcano, a daring rescue of three Russians (including Katerina's husband), the passage of their almost-too-thick ice island over an undersea mountain ridge, a fire that nearly destroys Shacktown, and a desperate traverse over hundreds of kilometers of treacherous ice. Finally, it is a mark of Kilian's maturity as a writer that even in just his second novel, he does not opt for a comforting conclusion. When the Shackletonians fly into Christchurch, New Zealand, they discover that a lot has changed in a few months: the whole country is under martial law; everything is rationed (food, beer, phone calls); curfew is at 7:00 P.M., lights out at 11:00 P.M.; newspapers are just a few pages long and censored so as not to depress their readers any more than they already are; and, comparatively speaking, New Zealand is in good shape.

Most of Kilian's next novel, *Eyas,* published in 1982 and his longest to date, reads like a typical fantasy novel. Including the maps reminiscent of the North American continent–especially the Pacific Northwest and New Orleans–that are de rigueur in all fantasies, *Eyas* presents a fully realized secondary world, called Alland, complete with a large cast of characters and cultures (including the brutes, an intelligent but not human species); a vast terrain populated by both familiar and unfamiliar flora and fauna; a sky devoid of stars, but not of a large object called Skyland; a supernatural creature (a telepathic whale called the Goddess); two dangerous creatures (walking trees and the Hell-spawned Messengers); magic (including farhearing and windinvoking, the latter particularly useful for the People, the seagoing society who raise Eyas, the eponymous hero); and a conflict that leads to a war for control of this entire world. *Eyas* also seems to share with other fantasies certain romance elements: dreams; a pauper-hero endowed by the Goddess with powers that eventually turn him into a prince, including the ability to understand, help, or inspire every creature–animal, brute, or human–he comes into contact with; the theme of good versus evil; and a quest that eventually saves the world from Armageddon.

Toward the end, however, readers realize that *Eyas* is actually a far-future science-fiction novel, for all of the fantasy elements are eventually given a rational scientific basis. Because the setting is 10,000,000 years in Earth's future, the maps are not just reminiscent of the North American continent but represent that continent as it might actually appear that far in the future. The brutes have been genetically engineered from various species alive today, and most of the odd flora and fauna are derived from plants and animals that also can be seen on Earth today. Skyland turns out to be an enormous artificial satellite. The stars reappear when a Shield enclosing the sun and inner planets is destroyed. The Goddess is a "cetohuman," able to genetically alter baby Eyas in order to give him his comprehensively empathic abilities. Hell is a literal place, where the dead are managing the living in order to "harvest" (feed on) them when they die. Finally, magic stems from latent human abilities.

Kilian has said that he wrote *Eyas* to record the anxieties and hopes that he and his wife were experiencing about raising their two daughters. One of these anxieties is about having enough personal energy to devote to children: the "nuclear" family among the People consists of four spouses—two husbands and two wives—so each child has four parents, not two. Second, the novel reflects anxiety about engendering healthy attitudes toward sex and gender roles: the People rarely wear clothes; consensual and monogamous sex are the norm, so rape and adultery are aberrations punishable usually by banishment; and gender roles are clearly defined. Another anxiety is about protecting children from violence, including sexual predation: Eyas learns that the person he most idolizes, Brightspear, has raped and killed their sister (and other young women). Brightspear also makes Eyas watch as in the opening stages of the war Brightspear slaughters Eyas's wives and children, while burning their village to the ground.

Kilian masters these anxieties, and hope triumphs: Eyas and his allies win the war, defeating Brightspear and all the awful things he represents. In the epilogue Eyas lies dying from a senseless accident; but the human race has joined forces with the other species to remake Earth, and the stars are now within their reach.

Fritz Leiber's classic science-fiction disaster novel *The Wanderer* (1964) established the narrative pattern for many novels of the same type: Leiber represented the wide scope of the disaster by shifting the point of view among different sets of characters all over the world. With *Tsunami*, reluctantly written at the request of the publisher as the sequel to *Icequake*, Kilian has both adopted and adapted this pattern for his pair of world-catastrophe novels. While *Icequake* focuses on a small group of people in a bleak place, *Tsunami* depicts several groups of people in much more densely populated areas, primarily the Bay Area in northern California and the Monterey peninsula and Carmel Valley farther down the California coast.

In a way, then, Kilian's two novels form a diptych about the same event: one side representing the origin of the catastrophe, the Antarctic icequake; the other side representing the consequences of the catastrophe. Further evidence that the novels are diptychal rather than sequential includes the fact that both start at nearly the same time (7 February 1985 for *Icequake*; a day later for *Tsunami*). Certain events rivet the two novels together, such as a military coup in the United States that topples the president from power. Two of the main protagonists are related, not just by blood but also by profession: Steve Kennard, one of the seismologists in *Icequake*, is the younger brother of Don Kennard, a physical oceanographer in *Tsunami*. And both novels end about the same time (early August) and on the same note: the new Ice Age is coming, so people had better get ready for it. In another way, however, the two novels are sequential. Survival is the grand theme of both, but survival in *Icequake* means simply getting from Shacktown to civilization, whereas survival in *Tsunami* means learning how to cope with the aftermath of the disaster. Looked at this way, then, *Icequake* ends where *Tsunami* begins.

Kilian's imagination reprises the political paradox that is California, a state that in the north has Berkeley, hotbed of left-wing politics, and in the south Carmel, home of the arch-conservative John Birch Society. The military, furthermore, permeates all regions of the state. Kilian makes the most of these settings. The academics Don, his wife, Kirstie (a climatologist), and their friends Sam Steinberg (an astrophysicist) and Einar Bjarnason (Sam's graduate student) eventually ally themselves with the Berkeley "local," a form of community governance based on cooperation and negotiation that has spontaneously appeared in the aftermath of the disaster. The Hollywood types, led by Robert Anthony Allison, a movie producer, and his wife, Hollywood sex goddess Shauna Dawn McGuire, set up a near-feudal fiefdom in the hills above Carmel; they govern by intimidation and force. The novel works out this ideological split in both small and large ways. Sam, for instance, hates Allison's latest movie, *Gunship*, calling it "the pornography of violence." While the Berkeley local repels a military takeover, Allison becomes the civilian "commander-in-chief" of an army that eventually controls a large part of the state.

Kilian, however, is not dispassionately imagining the various ways human beings cope with catastrophe. The Berkeley local plans to meet its energy needs with methane, a renewable source of power, while Allison has no plans to solve his energy problem except to salvage gasoline, a notoriously nonrenewable energy source, from a tanker sunk off the Carmel coast. Blacks from the housing project above Hunter's Point help the Berkeley local defeat the attempted military takeover of San Francisco; blacks in Allison's army help institute a reign of terror throughout Carmel and Monterey. Finally, most of Don's academic group survive; the one exception—Sam—dies a *Les Misérables*–like hero's death on the barricades at the Battle of Shattuck Square. But most of Allison's group dies or deserts: his wife succumbs to malignant melanoma; his best friend eventually takes off for Los Angeles; his survivalist nemesis finally catches up to Allison and kills him, after which his military commander, seeing the writing on the wall, cheerfully heads north. So Kilian clearly favors the way liberals cope. Like its predecessor, *Tsunami* is ultimately optimistic—or at least hopeful—about humanity's chances of surviving these catastrophes.

Brother Jonathan, published in 1985, another singleton, is a near-future extrapolation; the book was revised and republished by Beach Holme in 1995. Set in the mid twenty-first century, the novel presents a recognizable future in which the media is all-important and most people are reduced to nonproductive consumers. Corporations have usurped almost all the functions of nations, although surprisingly little has really changed. Wars have become takeovers. The United Nations is now the Consortium. Class hierarchies have been redefined in corporate terms: from the top down, there are corporation shareholders, executives, professionals, technicians, patrons (whose only "job" is to consume what the corporation produces), and nonstats (short for "nonstatus"). The nonstats are wholly owned by the corporation and include the turings (self-aware artificial intelligences), variously brain-damaged human beings, and animals used for research purposes. The future in this novel is reminiscent of that in C. M. Kornbluth and Frederik Pohl's 1953 classic *The Space Merchants.* Although the protagonist of that novel is a high-status advertising executive brought so low that he experiences his society from underneath, whereas in *Brother Jonathan* the nonstat protagonists eventually wind up completely changing their society, both novels rigidly separate the producing few from the consuming many—an idea also used in Kornbluth's 1951 short story "The Marching Morons."

The protagonists of *Brother Jonathan* are brain-damaged human beings Gretchen Hoffman and Jonathan Trumball. They, along with an artificially blind-and-deaf German shepherd and two artificially half-paralyzed chimpanzees, are experimental subjects for a research project that will save the Intertel Corporation, which is trying to fight off a takeover bid. Dr. Perkin, head of the project, implants "polydendronic computers" into his animal and human subjects, resulting in nearly miraculous recoveries for both. At stake is more than just Intertel: the computer assault programs of its attacker, the Flanders Corporation, are so good that Flanders could wind up taking over all corporations, essentially ruling the world. The novel thus warns that if the logic of rampant corporatism goes on, eventually the entire world will be owned by only one corporation.

Unusual among Kilian's novels, *Brother Jonathan* takes place almost entirely indoors—in Perkin's research institute, a couple of hospitals, an underground mall, various apartments, and various offices. About the only outdoor space is a park visited by allies of the protagonists, although not by the protagonists themselves. The indoor settings thus do thematic work, since the novel poises the protagonist's physical and social constraints against their desire, eventually achieved, for freedom.

Kilian's liberalism is particularly obvious in this novel: the desire for and achievement of freedom; unfettered choice as a necessary corollary to achieving freedom; the value of diversity; blurring or obliteration of boundaries; an openness to new ideas and experiences; curiosity as a good thing; an openness to change; the importance of sharing and cooperation; the damage that indifference among caregivers can cause; and the damage that prejudice can cause. Finally, the corporations' treatment of their animal, human, and turing nonstats can be read as an allegory of race relations in North America.

In *Lifter,* published in 1986 and revised in 1992, another singleton, Kilian grafts a well-known formula for writing a science-fiction novel onto a popular genre—the young-adult novel. The result is an interesting variation on the science-fiction juvenile genre made famous by Robert A. Heinlein. The well-known formula is H. G. Wells's: the best way to write science fiction is to change only one thing about the "real" world and then trace the consequences of that change. Kilian wastes no time introducing the change: on the first page of *Lifter,* sixteen-year-old Rick Stevenson wakes up floating six feet above his bedroom floor. He has somehow "lifted"; eventually, he learns how to lift so well that he is mistaken by the nearby air force base radar for a UFO.

Lifter has all the familiar trappings of a young-adult novel set at a contemporary California high school, including jocks, cheerleaders, nerds, and hoods; several bad teachers; one exceptionally good teacher (who is also a superb football coach); a principal doing his best; and a troubled but redeemable teenage protagonist. Before the novel begins, Rick, a computer genius, has hacked his way into various Canadian banks, not to enrich himself but as a prank. Caught, Rick has been placed on a two-year probation with the condition that he not even touch a computer during that time. The high-school principal has put Rick into a science class for the "severely gifted," where Rick finally meets interesting classmates (they call themselves the Awkward Squad) and a teacher that he can respect: Mr. Gibbs. The day after Rick lifts for the first time, he meets the new girl in school, Pat Llewellyn, also the newest member of the Awkward Squad. Pat has not had an easy life: a congenital hip problem makes walking painful and slow; her mother is dead; her stepmother hates her so much that her father abandoned her at age thirteen to a series of foster homes and various high schools; and she is now living in a group foster home. Naturally, Rick and Pat, semi-misfits both, fall in love, to the delight of Rick's architect mother, Melinda.

An important purpose of many science-fiction juveniles, including Heinlein's, is to teach their adolescent readers the methods, goals, and values of science in order to inspire their readers to grow up to be scientists. An important purpose of many young-adult novels is to pose ethical problems in order to help socialize their adolescent readers. *Lifter* coalesces these two purposes. As a student deeply influenced by Gibbs's trust in the scientific method, Rick feels that he must keep lifting a secret at least until he can learn how to control it and teach it to others. Rick's ethical problem, however, is that he is not sure that he should ever reveal his discovery. He worries about what would happen to Pat and Melinda. He fears the worldwide changes that this discovery would inevitably cause. He suspects that the military might co-opt lifting (and him) for its own nefarious purposes. And, in his darkest moments, he just knows that some crazy person will kill him.

It is difficult not to see additional similarities between Heinlein's juveniles and *Lifter*. Heinlein's juveniles are all written in the first-person, as is *Lifter*, unusual in Kilian's work. Heinlein's young protagonists are frequently isolated and somewhat smart-alecky geniuses with hidden resources who are forced into making adult decisions; this description fits Rick fairly well. Heinlein's young protagonists are also not one-dimensional; perhaps the most interesting development in *Lifter* is Rick's metamorphosis from nerd to football hero, courtesy of lifting. Gibbs, both as Rick's science teacher and his football coach, can easily be seen as the mature Heinlein individual mentoring a likely youngster into competency, although Kilian, true to his liberalism, makes more of Gibbs's blackness than Heinlein might. Like many Heinlein females, Melinda

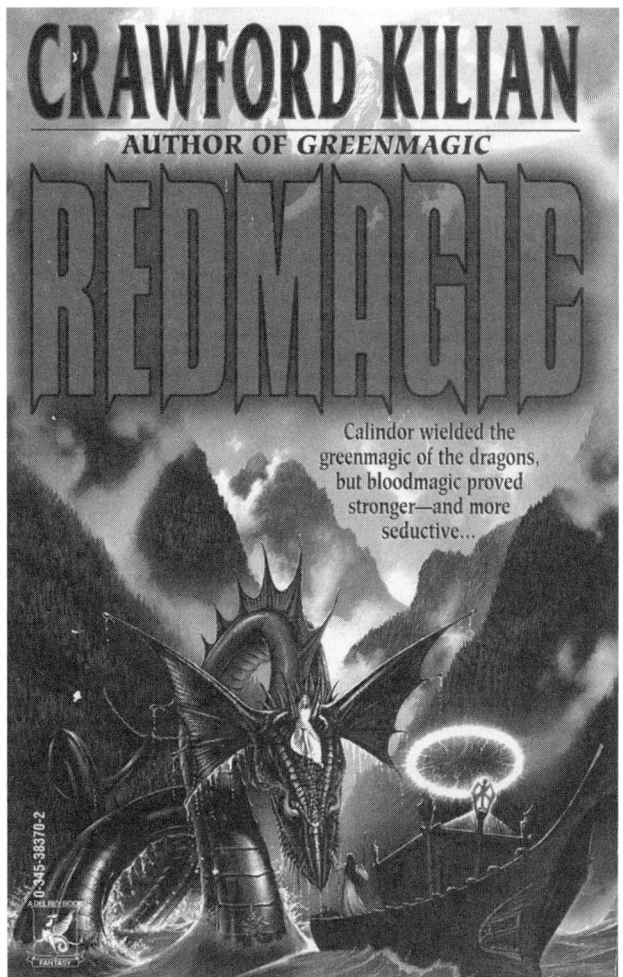

Cover for Kilian's 1995 sequel to his 1992 fantasy novel
Greenmagic, *in both of which the magician
Calindor defeats evil forces*

and Pat are both quite independent. And in what he thinks is a clever ploy to solicit Gibbs's advice about his ethical problem, Rick makes up a science-fiction story with a plot close to an early Heinlein story, "'Let There Be Light'" (1940).

But Kilian is not simply consciously or unconsciously aping Heinlein: the way Kilian resolves Rick's ethical dilemma points up a fundamental ideological difference between the two authors. Heinlein and Rick are libertarian, radical conservatives; Kilian and Pat are liberals. Rick fears what would happen if everyone could lift—he wants lifting restricted to the competent few (maybe even only to himself) so that it will not be abused by various fools. Pat has more trust in human nature—most people, she feels, will not abuse lifting, and the good generated by lifting will far outweigh the evil. (In this belief she is a bit self-serving, since if she is allowed to lift in public, she will never have to wear her leg brace or use a cane again.) In the end Pat wins; Rick acknowledges his error; and the secret is out.

The Fall of the Republic, published in 1987, is the second novel in *The Chronoplane Wars* series. While *The Empire of Time* introduces the two protagonists—Eric Wigner and Jerry Pierce—at the end of their secret-agent careers, *The Fall of the Republic* depicts the beginning of those careers, circa 1999. The series came about at the eagerly accepted request of Kilian's editor at Del Rey, Owen Lock. Thus, readers learn about Pierce's days as a newly minted (he is all of seventeen years old) T-Colonel ("T" for "Trainable") in charge of the 23rd Military District (Idaho and eastern Oregon). Readers learn next about Wigner's first job as a researcher for the CIA—and how Wigner recruits Pierce into a plan to pick up the pieces after the coming breakdown of government in the United States. Included in the plan is the importance—obvious to both men but painfully opaque to their unTrainable superiors—of exploring the ruins of Ulro, one of the chronoplane Earths "uptime," in order to gather intelligence on what the future will bring. Finally, readers watch all of the moves and countermoves involved in Wigner's Machiavellian plan. Eventually, the plan succeeds: Wigner winds up controlling the operations arm of the Agency for Intertemporal Development (AID), while Pierce embarks on his first mission in a long career as an AID field agent—at the end of *The Fall of the Republic,* Pierce is on prehistoric Luvah (22,249 B.C.), recruiting indigenous adolescents for Trainability testing.

If *The Empire of Time* balances all four main themes of the series—time travel, alternate history, superman, and end-of-the-world—*The Fall of the Republic* focuses mainly on the latter two of those themes. Because Trainability is a genetic predisposition in only one out of every six or seven human beings, unTrainables react to Trainables the way Homo sapiens in science-fiction novels usually react to Homo superior: with fear and loathing, and even, in this novel, with anti-Trainable riots. Conversely, Trainables—most of whom are young (Wigner is just four years older than Pierce)—are impatient at best and dismissive at worst with unTrainables. The end-of-the-world theme is somewhat modified in *The Fall of the Republic,* as the title indicates, into "the end of a political system." What dies in this novel are the quasi-military Civil Emergency Agency and its Executive Committee, de facto rulers of the United States; what rises in their place is the International Federation (IF), a super-United Nations and the parent of Wigner and Pierce's AID.

Much of *The Fall of the Republic* takes place in New York City, including all of the Ulro "radioactive wasteland" scenes. One of the biographical in-jokes in the novel occurs in chapter fourteen, when Wigner tells the orange-juice-loving Senator Diane Cooledge that a blight endangering the California orange crop will be cured by the work of a geneticist from Zhongshan University in Guangzhou, China; Zhongshan was the cross-town rival of the Chinese institute where Kilian taught in 1983–1984. Kilian's presentation of the Wabbies, who precipitate the crisis that brings down the government of the United States, is connected to his nonfiction about the dangers of the neo-Nazi movement. "Wabbie" is short for the White American Brotherhood, a "radical hick" (Kilian's term) group— lower-class, survivalist, sexist, anti-education, fundamentalist Christian crazies. But probably the most important connection between Kilian's novel and his life is what he does with the conflict between young and old: the young protagonists (plus Jasmine Jones, a beautiful Trainable who eventually joins them) versus their elders (primarily Jonathan Clement, Wigner's boss, who loves and is loved by Jasmine). Kilian became a young adult during the 1960s. So, the young triumph in *The Fall of the Republic,* but at a huge cost, signaled most clearly by the near-catatonic fugues that Pierce experiences twice in the novel.

Rogue Emperor, published the next year and the third novel in *The Chronoplane Wars* series, takes place in the autumn of 2005, about six years after *The Fall of the Republic* and about a decade before *The Empire of Time,* its temporal locus on Pierce's Earth. On the chronoplane Earth called Ahania, where most of the action of the novel occurs, it is 22 May 100 A.D.

Much is the same as in the other two novels in the series. The AID is still recruiting indigenous adolescents for Training in order to help stave off Doomsday, the calamity threatening Earth in the late twenty-first century. The Briefing and Conditioning that enables Trainable agents to function effectively in the past exacts a price, the least of which is migraine-like headaches. The agents' weapon of choice is the Mallory .15, capable at its highest power setting of slicing trees in half. There is a lot of James Bond–like cloak-and-dagger, including the typical Bondian dichotomy between the bad girl (Maria Donovan, one of the inner circle of the villain) and the good girl (Sabina, a gladiatrix).

Rogue Emperor, however, also differs from its two predecessors in several noticeable ways. First, the novel focuses on only one of the two series protagonists: Jerry Pierce. Indeed, the other series protagonist, Wigner, never appears in person. Instead—and not often—Pierce talks to Wigner via phone or imagines what Wigner might say about something Pierce has just done or not done. Second, *Rogue Emperor* includes more sex than the other two series novels: Pierce winds up letting Maria seduce him, and he eventually sleeps with Sabina too.

Third, the novel develops material in *The Fall of the Republic* about the White American Brotherhood (Wabbies) into a full-blown critique of the dangers of the present-day Christian Right. After their putsch fails, the surviving Wabbies, led by "Dear Michael" (Michael Martel), regroup as the Church Militant and grow into a force that the AID must deal with (by exiling them to Albion in 8127 B.C.). They eventually infiltrate Ahanian Rome, where they kill Emperor Domitian and try to install Martel as emperor, long before Rome was Christianized on "our" Earth. In other words, the Church Militant records the liberal Kilian's worst fears about the contemporary Christian Right: that they will grow into a neo-fascist political force strong enough to wrest government from "idolaters."

The most noticeable difference between *Rogue Emperor* and the two previous novels in the series is that Kilian mutes three of the main themes of the series (superman, end-of-the-world, and time travel) in favor of the fourth: alternate history. Kilian depicts first-century Rome in great detail: its customs, including the desire for bloodshed, satisfied by the carnage in the Flavian Amphitheater (the Colosseum); its values, such as piety (that is, reverence toward father and fatherland); its politics, such as the importance of the consuls; its class structure—Pierce's Trainable guide is Gaius, scion of a senatorial family, but Pierce also meets many people of lower status; its architecture on both grand and humble scales, whether Domitian's palace or a one-room flat; its transportation, including the famous Roman roads; its military, including organization, officers, weapons, armor, tactics, and camp layout; and its literature, as Pierce meets, befriends, and exchanges quotations with the poet Juvenal and the essayist Pliny the Younger.

It will be interesting to see if Kilian continues the series. He easily could, since he has at least three historical chronoplanes left: late eighteenth-century Beulah, twelfth-century Eden, and tenth-century B.C. Los.

If *Lifter* pays homage to H. G. Wells's "minimalist" theory of how to write a science-fiction novel, then Kilian's 1989 singleton, *Gryphon,* which grew out of Owen Lock's suggestion that Kilian write a space opera. *Gryphon* has all the trappings of a Smithian space opera, including a planet capable of much-faster-than-light travel, an alien species intent on subjugating humanity, and humans who wield extraordinary powers, including a kind of telepathy. Like Smith before him, Kilian loads every page with all manner of technological wonders: force fields, gravity and antigravity generators, molecular machines (molmacs), and robots galore, as well as ideas such as dermographs (programmable whole-body tattoos) and meteorography (weather artistry on a continental scale).

The novel takes place in 2396, several centuries after an event that completely changed the course of human history: Contact, "on a Sunday in 2030," when the Pirid or Brith (nicknamed "trolls" because of their appearance) suddenly showed up on every television set in the world and taught humans how to access the Database, a three-million-year-old compilation of the wisdom of the galaxy. Contact, however, so exacerbates Earth's political instability that within fifty years the planetary population has shrunk from billions to just twenty million. By the time *Gryphon* opens, those twenty million people, each one a near-immortal who controls virtually limitless resources, have developed a culture valuing personal autonomy so highly that physical proximity to another human being is avoided as unpleasant. Child-bearing is also almost unheard-of, as is child-raising. Both activities are ceded to machines; neither activity is seen as important. So while individuals lead long and interesting lives—often centered on sex (many gain well-deserved reputations as sexual geniuses) and violence (wars and duels are common and are sometimes even fought to the death, although molmacs can resurrect participants)—the human race itself is moribund.

Protagonist Alexander (Alex) Macintosh, named after a Canadian hero of the War of 1812, achieves citizenship and therefore full autonomy on his twenty-fifth birthday; the date also marks contact with the Chaiar-controlled planet Habrakha. The Chaiar—humanoids that are nicknamed "gryphons" because they resemble the legendary lion-eagle—are interstellar missionaries who have come to offer human beings the opportunity to join them in the Pattern, a quasi-religious community organism that proves attractive to many humans. The Chaiar ruthlessly exterminate those who resist joining the Pattern, including Alex's father. Indeed, at first Alex and several of the people who were at his birthday party succumb to the Chaiar (the Pattern propagates via alien molmacs), but in a plot twist reminiscent of Heinlein's *The Puppet Masters* (1951), Alex and his friends—aided by wild terrestrial molmacs and by a gryphon named Victor, whom Alex's father had "grown" from a Chaiar genome in the Database as a birthday present for Alex—escape from the Pattern and embark on a Grand Tour of the Solar System, drumming up resistance to the Chaiar wherever they go. Eventually, of course, they are captured. But in space opera, evil never prospers, so in a clever ending that bears comparison to Wells's *The War of the Worlds* (1898), good triumphs—and Alex returns to Earth prepared to give up inconsequential sex and violence in favor of the much more worthwhile work of repairing a planet ravaged by Chaiar anger against the few humans who were able to stand up against them, including Alex's mother.

Gryphon is thus a dual-level bildungsroman. On the personal level, Alex becomes a full-fledged adult. On the species level, the human race also grows up, turning from infantile pleasure-seeking to more-adult concerns—not just fixing Earth's damaged ecology but also thinking about exploring the rest of the universe. The main theme of the novel, then, is a liberal compromise between competing ideologies. *Gryphon* urges readers to realize that what is best for the human race is neither unbridled individuality bordering on anarchy (post-Contact culture clearly parodies Heinleinian libertarianism) nor nearly mindless communitarianism (like the Wabbies in *Rogue Emperor,* the Chaiar are the scariest kind of totalitarians—they have the power to impose their will on almost anyone and to kill those who resist) but rather a culture that balances the needs of the individual and the community.

In his next novels, *Greenmagic* (1992) and *Redmagic* (1995), Kilian returns to fantasy, a genre he flirted with in his much-earlier *Eyas*. But if *Eyas* is fantasy manqué—because the fantastic elements are eventually given a scientific basis—*Greenmagic* and *Redmagic* are full-blown nontechnological fantasies. To all of the fantasy elements from *Eyas,* Kilian has added two mainstays of the genre: magic and feudalism. The protagonist of these two novels, Dheribi (later given his "true name," Calindor), is at the center of both additions. Dheribi's mother and biological father are magicians, so, naturally, he grows up to be a magician even more powerful than they. And since Dheribi's stepfather, Albohar, is the Aryo (king) of Aishadan, one of the Five Kingdoms of Cantarea, Dheribi also has been brought up familiar with all of the reciprocal obligations owed between a feudal lord and his retainers. *Redmagic* starts just two years after *Greenmagic* ends and shares many of its characters. Finally, the two novels are thematic mirror images. In *Greenmagic* Dheribi, serving the good goddess Callia, eventually faces and defeats Mekhpur, a man turned evil god; in *Redmagic* Calindor, nearly seduced by an evil magic, eventually faces and helps defeat the Exteca, a race intent on conquering Calindor's people in order to feed the Exteca's True Gods.

Traces of Kilian's values and life are not hard to find in the two novels. A central theme of *Greenmagic* is the clash between the Menmannar, Dheribi's mountain tribe, and the Badakhar, the plains people ruled by Albohar. The Menmennar are dark-eyed, dark-haired, and dark-skinned, while the Badakhar are blue-eyed, blond-haired, and fair-skinned; and many Menmannar are Badakhi slaves. Kilian's criticism of the evil of slavery is obvious. The central event in *Redmagic* is the Extecan invasion of Cantarea. Extecan society is highly stratified: emperor (the Tecutli Itzlac), nobility (pipiltin), priests, warriors (teteuctin), commoners (maeceuali), and slaves. The Extecan capital is Tola, home to a gigantic pyramid housing on its various faces chapels to several of the True Gods, whose anger must be constantly placated by human sacrifice, including the offering of the victim's heart. The status system, taboos, honorifics, and cannibalism are meant to remind readers of the Aztecs; Kilian dedicates the book to Michael Butler and Christopher Trumbo, "who listened to the first stories long ago in Mexico," where Kilian lived from 1950 to 1954.

More important than these biographical traces, however, is the fact that these two fantasy novels restate almost all of the major themes of Kilian's science-fiction novels: education, liberal activism, environmentalism, and computers. The science-fiction novels as a group deal variously with education. In the novels of *The Chronoplane Wars* Kilian imagines Trainables, young people with truly amazing learning skills. In *Brother Jonathan* and *Lifter* the protagonists are all high-school age. In *Icequake* and *Tsunami* many of the protagonists have at least college degrees; several have doctorates. The human beings in *Gryphon* know even more than Trainables. And the human beings in *Eyas* learn "organically"—not in school but in the home or as apprentices. Spanning *Greenmagic* and *Redmagic* is not just a similar "organic" concept of education (no schools—and no Department of Education—to be found anywhere in Cantarea) but also a thirst for knowledge on the part of magicians that has a downside: spending too much time pursuing magical knowledge usually means a concomitant ignorance of what motivates human beings.

Kilian's science-fiction novels also present his liberal activism, most generally expressed as the valuing of change, even if that change is seemingly disastrous. Things are definitely smashed in *The Chronoplane Wars* (nationalism is defunct; Earth awaits its Doomsday), in *Eyas* (a personal vendetta nearly destroys civilization), in *Icequake* and *Tsunami* (the new Ice Age is on its way), and in *Gryphon* (Earth has been devastated by an alien invasion). And things definitely are about to change in *Brother Jonathan* (the corporate society is about to be re-formed) and in *Lifter* (humans are about to learn how to fly). But underlying all of the disasters, real and potential, is Kilian's guarded optimism about the human ability not just to survive but, with a lot of work, even to prosper. *Greenmagic* and *Redmagic* present the same dynamic: in *Greenmagic,* and after a war, feudalism yields to a form of democracy; in *Redmagic,* and after a near-war, theism yields to atheism, to everyone's benefit.

Chapter One

May 23, 1935

We seem to be on the brink of a ~~second~~ World War. Chancellor Kreutzer ~~Luxemburg~~ has ~~rejected~~ demanded France~~'s demand that she~~ withdraw ~~her~~ troops from ~~East Anglia~~ Sussex and ~~Yorkshire~~ Kent. This morning's telegram from the Pentagon reports skirmishes between Volksarmee units and the French Foreign Legion regiment stationed near Oxford. If it turns into serious fighting, we will certainly ~~have to honor our commitment~~ almost be dragged into it on France~~~~'s side.

As a ~~career~~ Marine, I suppose I ought to rejoice at the prospect: great fleets ~~again~~ steaming across the Atlantic ~~and Pacific~~, amphibious assaults, and a war of dramatic movement in the air as well as on land and sea. It will make the career of many an officer, and many a future politician as well. ~~After all, where would President Crayton be today if he hadn't led the assault on Marseilles in '21?~~

~~But 1919-21 was a just war against the reactionary French and the greedy Japanese, and our casualties were slight. (I take some pride in my own contributions to saving Marines' lives at Marseilles and in the whole Mediterranean theater.)~~ ~~In theory Germany should be unable to fight~~ This time we will be going up against revolutionary Germany, an industrial giant with a highly trained army and a fanatic communist government. Rosa Luxemburg may inspire dirty jokes among my colleagues, but Boadicea humbled the Romans.

But after ~~seeing how Germany and Russia destroyed one another, I can't believe the comm~~

A year ago no one would have imagined this. The Kaiser had won a Pyrrhic victory over the Russians, only to be overthrown by the Communists. Surely they would be incapable of fighting again for a generation. Instead, they've rebuilt their market federation and even drawn in the Dutch and Austro-Hungarians. Now they want Southern England back, even if it means fighting the French Federation... and us.

Corrected typescript page for Kilian's alternate-history novel "To the Ruins of London," a work-in-progress (Collection of Crawford Kilian)

Kilian expresses his third major theme, environmentalism, positively in the many descriptions of pristine nature scattered throughout the science-fiction novels and present also in the two fantasy novels, and negatively by his horror of environmental mismanagement. That mismanagement in the science-fiction novels is natural (*Icequake* and *Tsunami*), man-made (Doomsday in *The Chronoplane Wars* is caused by a scientific experiment gone awry, and similarly problematic science causes most of the environmental problems in *Eyas*), or alien (*Gryphon*). Even novels set so much "indoors" as *Brother Jonathan* and *Lifter* bespeak Kilian's awareness of the value of the unspoiled outdoors. In *Greenmagic* Aishadan ("Burning Stone"), Albohar's capital and the seat of the evil god Mekhpur, is an environmental nightmare—overcrowded and filthy. Dheribi's parents' village, Tanshadabela ("Two Stream Village"), on the other hand, is an environmental paradise—just the right size, clean, and bestrewn with pleasant-smelling flowers. The goddess Callia so despises what Mekhpur and his followers have done to Cantarea that at the end of the novel she unleashes a cataclysm that scours the land clean. In *Redmagic* the Exteca are presented, almost literally, as a blight that will besmirch Cantarea almost as badly as Mekhpur did.

Kilian's science fiction also makes frequent use of computers. In *Icequake* and *Tsunami*, set in contemporary times, computers are present, but only as a minor element, congruent with the place of computers in the late 1970s and early 1980s. In *The Empire of Time* and *Rogue Emperor*, set slightly later, computers are more obvious, but still in the background. In all the rest of Kilian's science fiction, however, computers are foregrounded. In *Eyas*, a sentient computer named the Archivist runs Skyland; artificial intelligences are also characters in *Brother Jonathan* and *Gryphon*. The protagonist of *Lifter* is a computer nerd. And a computer network and a computer virus figure prominently in *The Fall of the Republic*. At first it would seem impossible for the computer theme to appear in the two fantasy novels characterized as nontechnological, and nothing even remotely resembling a computer shows up in *Greenmagic* or *Redmagic*. Still, Kilian makes magic into a "technology." For example, "focusing" allows the magician to perceive telescopically and microscopically. Greenmagic and redmagic both, in different ways, are able to affect nature—making infertile land blossom or bringing water to a desert. Finally, the Open Dream (where one's ancestors exist after their death, guiding their descendants) can be perceived, and is even presented this way in the two novels as a vast information-retrieval system.

Kilian has not attracted a great deal of attention from science-fiction critics, with a few brief exceptions. David Ketterer in his *Canadian Science Fiction and Fantasy* (1992) devotes a lengthy, but mainly descriptive, paragraph to Kilian, and Kilian merits an entry by John Clute in *The Encyclopedia of Science Fiction* (1993), edited by Clute and Peter Nicholls, although that entry is finally dismissive: "Kilian slips too often into generic dogpaddling." George Kelley has also written an entry on Kilian for *Twentieth-Century Science-Fiction Writers*, in the second (1986) and succeeding editions. The only sustained examination of his work, however, is a short piece by John Boardman in a semi-professional fanzine, *Niekas*.

All of Kilian's first five science-fiction novels—from *The Empire of Time* through *Brother Jonathan*—were reviewed in general-interest periodicals such as *Publishers Weekly* as well as in science-fiction magazines such as *Analog*. The next four novels—*Lifter* through *Gryphon*—were not reviewed at all in the general-interest periodicals and attracted only moderate attention in the science-fiction magazines. Only with the two fantasies (*Greenmagic* and *Redmagic*) has Kilian made it back into the reviewing columns of both kinds of magazines.

According to most critics, Kilian's strength is fast-paced plotting; even the two fantasies, which are both longer than any of the science-fiction novels except *Eyas*, are full of incident. Critics also seem to agree that his weakness is character development. The best that the reviewers can do is call his characterization "standard." More typically, Kilian's characters are described as "cardboard," "not accomplished," "weak," or even "dull and wooden." The truth about Kilian's characters, therefore, is probably somewhere in the middle: they are neither unpleasantly cardboard nor fully rounded.

The question of Kilian's "Canadianness" is a vexed one. First, in academia today at least, the idea of a national literature (that is, a body of works sharing common characteristics because produced in the same geopolitical region) has gone the way of the comparative literature paradigm that most obviously supports such a notion—into oblivion. Second, Kilian himself is an immigrant to Canada, arriving in his mid twenties and therefore, perhaps, immune, or at least not as susceptible as a native would be, to Canadian "influences." Third, people are just beginning to figure out what "Canadian literature" is, so they may not be all that close to figuring out what "Canadian science fiction" is, despite Ketterer's book.

Still, Canada does make its way into Kilian's work in several ways. Kilian sets many of his novels in Canada or in the Pacific Northwest near Canada, even his two fantasy novels: turning the map at the beginning of *Redmagic* upside down, one recognizes the western part of the North American continent, with the somewhat utopian Dragon Lands roughly where Vancouver is. Kilian also sprinkles references to "things Canadian" throughout his novels, such as the Canadian banks in *Lifter,* that Rick Stevenson hacks into from California. Kilian occasionally indulges in some Canadian anti-Americanism. In *Gryphon,* for instance, Alex recalls "ancient history"–that "the American Decline" began after the assassination of President John F. Kennedy.

In *Survival: A Thematic Guide to Canadian Literature* (1972), Margaret Atwood argues that survival is the most important Canadian literary theme. Survival does figure largely in all of Kilian's work, from the attempt to stave off Doomsday in *The Chronoplane Wars* to Calindor's fight to save his people in *Redmagic.* Canadian writers are also interested in immigration. Again, this theme appears throughout Kilian's work, although most notably in *The Chronoplane Wars* with the forced emigration of people from "our" Earth to the various Earths "downtime." The third major Canadian theme that Kilian uses is federalism, the idea that the best way for disparate political entities to join together is in a loose association, with local prerogatives jealously guarded against encroachment by a regional or national authority. Canadian federalism becomes in Kilian's work a distinct preference for the tribe over the nation, and a concomitant valuing of personal loyalties over patriotism. The best example is *Eyas,* in which the eponymous protagonist forges a federally organized "army" out of human and brute tribes, only to disband it after their great triumph over Brightspear, who wants to turn Alland into one big nation.

Kilian continues to write, having finished but not yet published "Stone," a crime thriller with a slight science-fiction element. He is also hard at work on "Deserter," a mainstream novel; and he has plans for a science-fiction alternate history novel, as yet untitled. One suspects that these novels will be of a piece with his work to date: based on, but not limited by, tried and true generic conventions; exploring Kilian's lifelong interests; and imbued with his basically optimistic liberalism.

Reference:

John Boardman, "Crowded Future: Nihil Humanum," *Niekas,* 39 (1989): 5, 52.

Donald Kingsbury

(12 February 1929 –)

Allan Weiss
York University

BOOKS: *Courtship Rite* (New York: Timescape Books, 1982); republished as *Geta* (London: Panther, 1984);

The Moon Goddess and the Son (New York: Baen, 1986; London: Grafton, 1988);

Psychohistorical Crisis (New York: Tor, 2001).

OTHER: "Shipwright," in *The Best Science Fiction Novellas of the Year #1*, edited by Terry Carr (New York: Ballantine, 1979), pp. 110–152;

"To Bring in the Steel," in *The Best Science Fiction of the Year #8*, edited by Carr (New York: Ballantine, 1979), pp. 89–135;

"The Moon Goddess and the Son," in *The Best Science Fiction Novellas of the Year #2*, edited by Carr (New York: Ballantine, 1980), pp. 69–129;

"The Survivor," in *Man-Kzin Wars IV*, edited by Larry Niven (New York: Baen, 1991), pp. 1–244;

"The Heroic Myth of Lieutenant Nora Argamentine," in *Man-Kzin Wars VI*, edited by Niven (New York: Baen, 1994), pp. 3–254;

"The Cauldron," in *Northern Stars: The Anthology of Canadian Science Fiction*, edited by David G. Hartwell and Glenn Grant (New York: Tor, 1994), pp. 236–253;

"Historical Crisis," in *Far Futures*, edited by Gregory Benford (New York: Tor, 1995), pp. 149–241.

SELECTED PERIODICAL PUBLICATIONS–UNCOLLECTED: "Ghost Town," *Astounding Science Fiction*, 49 (June 1952): 58–81;

"The Right to Breed," *Astounding Science Fiction* (April 1955);

"The Janus-Headed Arrow of Time," *Analog Science Fact & Fiction* (February 1995).

Donald Kingsbury's works can be classified as "hard science fiction"; they feature speculations in such hard sciences as physics and aeronautics and demonstrate a solid grounding in scientific fact and principles. Yet, his focus is generally on the psychological and social effects of technological developments. He explores new definitions of "human" by tracing the development of vastly different cultures in alien conditions. As he said in an interview that appeared in *Contemporary Authors* (2000), "Designing new kinds of humans, new governments, and odd cultures is my favorite sport."

Donald MacDonald Kingsbury was born on 12 February 1929 in San Francisco. His father was Hector MacDonald Kingsbury, a mining engineer, and his mother was Laura Kingsbury (née Barker). In 1930 his father was hired to assist in the development of the gold mines in New Guinea. The only means of traveling to and from their new home was by plane, and Kingsbury spent his early years becoming as familiar with airplanes and air travel as other children might become with cars. The result of these experiences was a lifelong interest in aeronautics, one that is reflected in many of his works. His childhood was somewhat isolated; he and his two sisters were the only children in their small mining town, so that most of his interaction was with adults, including the twenty servants who worked for his parents. He also met many pilots, including a future astronaut.

When Kingsbury was six, his family moved back to California in order to provide him with a proper education. En route to California they traveled around the Far East and Hawaii, and Kingsbury has credited those experiences with prompting a tendency in his fiction to traverse the galaxy. While he was in the sixth grade his family moved to Tyrone, New Mexico, a silver-mining town, and the landscape around it was later the inspiration for his planet Geta. Around this time, Kingsbury discovered science fiction through the *Brick Bradford* comic strip, which appeared in the local newspaper. His introduction to literary science fiction came through his mother's readings of H. G. Wells's *The Invisible Man* (1897) and his own reading, at the age of ten, of a collection of Wells's works. While helping out with wartime paper drives, he encountered the pulp magazines, particularly *Astounding Science Fiction*. He was especially impressed by the works of A. E. van Vogt, Isaac Asimov, and Murray Leinster. He had long been

Dust jacket for Donald Kingsbury's 1986 novel, about a woman obsessed with going to the moon

interested in becoming a writer and tried his hand at fiction, adhering to a schedule of writing two pages each day.

His father's work took the family to Hanover, New Hampshire, where Kingsbury attended high school. Then, in 1948, Hector Kingsbury was asked to develop zinc mines in Quebec. Donald Kingsbury entered McGill University to study mathematics. In 1950 he married Mireille Fortier, with whom he had two children, Dani and Joel, before divorcing in 1960. Throughout this period he pursued his writing interests, and his first sale was the short story "Ghost Town" to *Astounding Science Fiction* in 1952. The story concerns the City of Citadel, a military base on the moon that is threatened with being shut down and completely evacuated; because peace has come after a brief war between the United States and the Soviet Union, the army no longer wishes to pay for the upkeep of the base. The story portrays various reactions to the impending evacuation–most inhabitants share the feelings of Abe Srenco, head of Seven Miles Per Second Transport Corporation, who does not want to leave his home. Colonel Hans D. "Handy" Tool arrives in a military spaceship to begin the evacuation, but Srenco convinces him that it would be far more expensive to refit the freighters and other base ships for evacuation than to keep the base operating. Most noteworthy about the story is the character of Diana, a little girl who was born on the moon and identifies with it so strongly that she fears moving to the Earth. She is clearly a precursor of the protagonist of Kingsbury's novel *The Moon Goddess and the Son* (1986).

His early attempts to write novels–first for a contest at *Galaxy* magazine, then a mainstream novel on the advice of his agent–failed, and he largely abandoned the science-fiction field. He wrote an article for the April 1955 issue of *Astounding Science Fiction*, "The Right to Breed," which generated great controversy over its somewhat cold-blooded view of the possible benefits of nuclear war for the human race. The article exhibits a strain of Social Darwinism later expressed in his markedly libertarian fiction, though Kingsbury had deliberately made this piece "hard-line" and "ruthless" at the request of editor John W. Campbell.

In 1955 Kingsbury became a naturalized Canadian citizen. He obtained his B.Sc. in 1956 and became a professor of mathematics at McGill, where he remained until his retirement in 1986. In 1960 he earned his M.Sc., but he never pursued his Ph.D. While he did not publish any science fiction during this period, he did publish controversial newspaper articles in the *McGill Daily,* including one that argued in favor of group marriages. The articles often attracted hostile reactions, but his radical speculations later gained a more accommodating response when couched in fictional terms.

In the 1970s, wanting to return to science fiction, Kingsbury attended science-fiction conventions in order to make contacts. After hearing Ben Bova–the editor of *Analog,* the successor of *Astounding Science Fiction*–speak at panels, Kingsbury wrote and sold a science article to Bova. Soon afterward he sold "Shipwright," his first science-fiction story publication in more than twenty-five years.

"Shipwright" appeared in the April 1978 issue of *Analog.* It concerns Jotar Plaek, an engineer from the planet Lager, where members of that profession are part of a quasi-clerical elite. Engineers are not allowed to marry, but Plaek falls in love with Misubisi Kasumi, a woman he meets first at a bar and again when she arrives as a delegate from the planet Akira. Plaek needs Akiran support for a new faster-than-light drive; he has also been anxious to pass down his legacy of technical knowledge. Owing to "kalmakovian" (anti-Einsteinian) effects, different parts of the generation ship he designs move through time at different speeds–while Plaek flies his ship to Akira, entire generations come and go among the students in the university he founds. The novella introduces a prominent theme in Kingsbury's fiction: parenthood, especially the absence of parents. Plaek abandons Kasumi and the child he has with her, then later takes them both on his starship but never quite fulfills his role as father. He manipulates "his" people on board the ship so that the society he creates is as purely scientific as possible. Plaek becomes a god of sorts to the Misubisi clan–a father in the most distant sense of the word. Like many of Kingsbury's characters, Plaek lacks strong human bonds and buries himself in his scientific work.

In Kingsbury's next novella, "To Bring in the Steel," first published in the July 1978 issue of *Analog SF,* Meddrick Kell is a solitary miner on a democratic vessel operating in the asteroid belt. After the suicide of his former wife, he declares that he wants their daughter, Celia–whom he has never seen–to live with him. His crew will not allow him to bring her aboard their ship, the *Pittsburgh,* unless he hires a governess, since they see him as incapable of taking proper care of the child, who is seven years old. In revenge he hires a high-priced call girl, Lisa Maria Sorenti, to fill the role, counting on her to disrupt the marriages of his crew members. When she arrives with Celia, the three form an odd but stable family. Although Kell is considerably older than Lisa, they become lovers, and she learns enough from him to save his life at the end. The novella portrays their relationship as mainly sexual, and their conversation is based far more on witty banter than tender expressions–common features of male-female relationships in Kingsbury's work.

His first published novel, *Courtship Rite,* appeared in 1982. It is about a human colony on the planet Geta. The society that develops has lost its memories of its origins and worships as a god the starship that had seeded the colony and continues to orbit the planet. The harsh environment of Geta is not conducive to much life, and because there is so little that is edible, people engage in ritual cannibalism during famines and at funerals. The novel is similar to Frank Herbert's *Dune* (1965) in its examination of the cultural and psychological effects of the environment on populations. But Kingsbury dismisses the idea that a planet will have one uniform set of conditions, or that its inhabitants will be all alike. Thus, Geta is divided into clans, some of which perform certain planet-wide functions, such as porters, mathematicians, and predictors. The starship is seen as a god but is nothing more than a comatose artificial intelligence that was stripped to its "bones" by the colonists when its interstellar motors failed. The colonization process was lethal, and much knowledge was lost; but bits and pieces are recovered from the shambles of the original settlements, notably a crystal containing the entire human genetic code and a history of war that ends at the twentieth century.

Marriages on the planet involve groups (with a maximum of six people), not couples, and the plot focuses on the quest for a third wife to join husbands Gaet, Hoemei, and Joesai and their wives Teenae and Noe. In this way Kingsbury can explore the concept of group marriages without, as he said in a 1986 interview with David Homel, "bringing in a whole set of social baggage that would normally be attached in a mainstream novel." The Prime Predictor of the planet, Tae ran-Kaiel, dies, and his successor, Aesoe, forbids the group to marry their first choice, Kathein, as he wants her for himself. They are obliged for political reasons to marry Oelita the Clanless One, proponent of a heresy that says the "moon" of the planet is an artificial object. The five spouses subject Oelita to a "Death Rite"–a series of dangerous tests that she is able to pass. She obtains a computer chip containing distressing information on human–and her planet's–history, and is traumatized by what she learns. The five spouses triumph over their political and even military foes and end up marrying both Kathein and Oelita, forming the first-ever seven-person marriage.

The novel received wide critical acclaim, with reviewers citing in particular its complex and plausible world-building and its characterization. Most reviewers–with the exception of Amelia A. Rutledge in *Science Fiction and Fantasy Book Review* (September 1982)–compared it favorably to *Dune,* praising Kingsbury for creating a more credible planet with harsh conditions, along with the variety of cultures that such conditions would produce. Above all, reviewers such as John Clute in *Fantasy and Science Fiction* (December 1982) and Faren Miller in *Locus* (June 1982) recognized Kingsbury's bold thought experiment in designing a world in which cannibalism and group marriages are the norm; Clute referred to it as "a considerable accomplishment." On the other hand, there was almost universal dislike for the role of Humility, a Liethe (member of a powerful clan of females who reproduce mainly by cloning) who acts as a sort of deus ex machina, and some reviewers questioned whether a society as primitive as the one on Geta could develop its more advanced forms of technology. In 1983 *Courtship Rite* won the Crompton Crook and *Locus* Awards for best first novel and was nominated for the Hugo Award.

Kingsbury's next novel, *The Moon Goddess and the Son*, although not published in book form until 1986, was actually published in a different form before *Courtship Rite*; it first appeared as a novella in the December 1979 issue of *Analog*. The novella version focuses on Diana Osborne (later Grove) and her efforts to escape her abusive father and go to the moon, where she is inexorably drawn. She is conscious of being the namesake of the Roman goddess of the moon, hunting, and virginity, and as a way of giving shape to her rootless life she emulates the goddess's various attributes. She becomes obsessed with Byron McDougall, a famous air force and shuttle pilot who represents an ideal as well as a means of escape. Diana's determination to reach the moon provides the main narrative drive to the work, and McDougall's technical problem-solving skills showcase Kingsbury's own scientific knowledge. "The Moon Goddess and the Son" was nominated for the 1980 Hugo Award for best novella.

The structural cohesion of the novella breaks down in the novel version, in which other narrative lines are pursued. Kingsbury pays greater attention to the character of McDougall and also introduces other characters such as Joseph Synmann, Limon Barnes, and Peter Kaissel, who are engaged in a game simulation designed to explore the Russian mind and therefore, they hope, reveal ways to prevent nuclear war. The novel jumps abruptly not only in terms of place and point of view but also in time; the episodes are not presented in strict chronological order, so the reader must be particularly attentive. Like Diana, Byron is a product of an abusive father—a military man who "trains" him as a young boy—and he passes on that legacy of macho ideals to his own son, Charlie. Diana pursues and even has an affair with Byron, but it is clear that her real romantic counterpart is Charlie, who is only drawn to the moon because of his attraction to her (as well as pressure from his father to follow in his footsteps).

Lengthy passages concerning the simulation subplot demonstrate Kingsbury's interest in the role of cultural

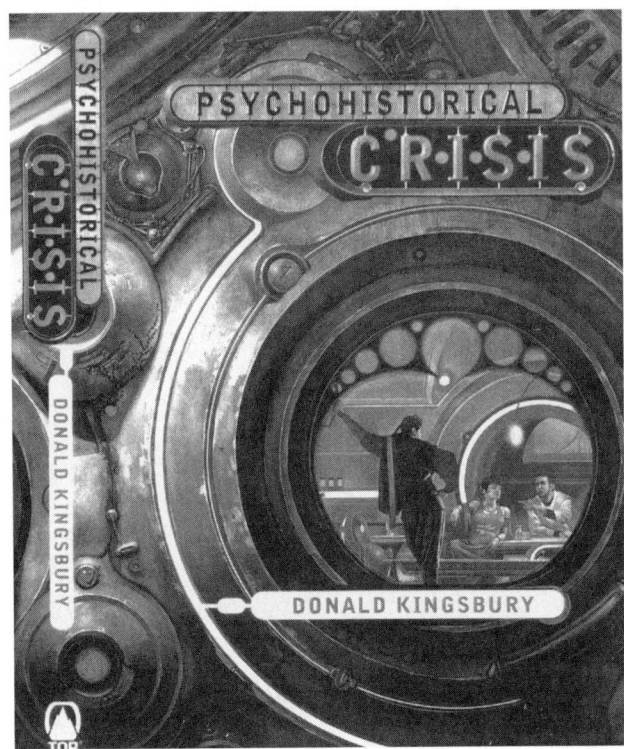

Cover for Kingsbury's 2001 novel, set in the capital of the Milky Way in the 761st century, in which people depend on digital augmentation of their brains to carry out the simplest tasks

psychology in human behavior, although at the expense of the narrative drive. Kingsbury provides his reader with a detailed account of Russian history as it might have shaped Russian thinking, but Barnes and Kaissel's efforts fail to prevent an "accidental" war from breaking out after an Afghani guerrilla air attack on the Kremlin and the Russian embassy in Ottawa. On the other hand, the war does not escalate, and Barnes is able to convince the new Soviet leaders to follow a different, less dangerous path. Kingsbury has often said in interviews that his purpose in portraying future conflicts is not to predict them, but rather to warn his readers of dangerous possibilities so that these futures will not come true.

One of the ways Barnes and the others manipulate the Soviets is through computers. Those working in the thinktank (which is humorously dubbed the "Cathedral of Saint-Marx the Benevolent") use false news reports and a computer game to steer Soviet psychology in a more Western direction. As was the case in *Courtship Rite*, computer technology thus represents the major technological means by which human change will occur. Another similarity between *The Moon Goddess and the Son* and earlier works is the handling of male-female relationships. Because these relationships are so often portrayed in primarily sexual terms, and because the men and women engage in Kingsbury's familiar witty repartee, the characters often seem too much alike. Kingsbury succeeds in distinguishing his characters through their personal or professional obsessions, but character depth is often sacrificed to thematic concerns.

Reviewers generally liked the novel, although its complex narrative structure led *Locus* reviewer Miller (November 1986) to call it "frustrating" and to note that "there are moments when literary jet lag sets in, and some scenes are bewildering." Both Miller and Don D'Ammassa, in *Science Fiction Chronicle* (March 1987), praised Kingsbury's characterization and formal experimentation.

In all these works Kingsbury aims for plausibility, taking nothing for granted in his technical and psychological details. But perhaps the most important connection between them is that they are all set in a single future history, as part of what he has referred to as the Finger Pointing Solward series. In this approach, Kingsbury is clearly influenced by his reading of Asimov, particularly the Foundation series. Like Asimov, Kingsbury portrays humanity on a vast canvas spanning time and space; *The Moon Goddess and the Son* presents a near-future when humans have barely colonized the moon, while *Courtship Rite* is set much farther forward in time and outward in space. Also like Asimov, Kingsbury wishes to trace the broader psychological implications of living in alien environments and what the results of such galactic expansion might be for human social, cultural, and to some extent physical evolution. Kingsbury has been working for some time on another novel set in his universe, a sequel to *Courtship Rite* called "The Finger Pointing Solward," and a portion of that work appeared in *Northern Stars: The Anthology of Canadian Science Fiction* (1994) as "The Cauldron." The excerpt concerns Tuagi, a soldier in training who is the product of years of genetic manipulation; he is obsessed with becoming a good warrior and, perhaps even more, with learning who his "senior mother"—the one who supplied the bulk of his genetic material—was. As elsewhere, the theme of parenthood, especially lost parents, is quite prominent.

In addition, Kingsbury has contributed to the science-fiction practice of writing novels and shorter works set in other authors' universes. In 1995 he published "Historical Crisis" in the anthology *Far Futures,* which is set in an alternate version of Asimov's Foundation universe. But most of his work in this category has been in Larry Niven's universe, with two short novels in the Man-Kzin Wars series. Both "The Survivor" in *Man-Kzin Wars IV* (1991) and "The Heroic Myth of Lieutenant Nora Argamentine" in *Man-Kzin Wars VI* (1994) concern a human military hero who is captured by the catlike Kzin. Nora is subjected to genetic alteration and brain surgery to erase her memories and make her more like a nonsentient Kzin female. The first novel focuses on a somewhat cowardly Kzin who, through a series of accidents and "lucky" breaks, becomes a soldier and then hero of the Kzin Patriarchy. Short-Son undergoes a series of name and identity changes as he matures and finds his calling; he is one of Kingsbury's most engaging characters. The second novel is about the rescue of Nora by her cousin, Yankee Clandeboye. His mission is complicated by internecine strife among the humans and by the fact that Nora is more Kzin than human now, and even has a child who is genetically human but trained as a Kzin. Her human identity may never be fully recovered, but Yankee decides to use her story to stir up humanity's now-dormant fighting spirit. It has been many years since the last Man-Kzin War, and he is convinced that a new and more dangerous Kzin offensive will come soon. To save humanity from its own pacifist ways, he begins to turn Nora into a myth, one that will inspire Earth's fighters when the battle turns rough.

What is most important about these works for an understanding of Kingsbury is their libertarian nature. Like much libertarian science fiction, Kingsbury's Man-Kzin stories take a Darwinist approach to interspecies relationships and emphasize military adventure over character (though the characterization of the Kzin "Trainer-of-Slaves" was praised in reviews). Particularly in "The Heroic Myth of Nora Argamentine" there are fairly stock Kingsbury characters, notably the young and attractive girl (in this case Chloe Blumenhandler) who falls in love with a considerably older man, usually a hero (Yankee). Kingsbury is adept at bringing the Kzin world to life, exhibiting once again his interest in alien cultures and psychology.

Kingbury's next novel, *Psychohistorical Crisis* (2001) is an expansion of "Historical Crisis." It takes place 1500 years after a millennia-long interregnum during which psychohistorian mathematicians take over and run the galactic Empire. They encounter their share of troubles in doing so, falling prey to the old Chinese curse "May you get what you want."

When Kingsbury focuses on culture rather than technology, as in *Courtship Rite,* he succeeds best in engaging his reader at more than an intellectual level. Throughout his fiction Kingsbury stresses the necessity for human beings to be tested—by harsh environments, by cultural misunderstandings, and above all by war—in order to evolve and therefore survive.

Interviews:
Robert J. Sawyer, *Books in Canada,* 12 (February 1983): 29–30;
Sawyer, "Interview: Donald Kingsbury," *Science Fiction Review,* 51 (Summer 1984): 9–15;
David Homel, "Kingsbury: Time Travel without Baggage," *Quill & Quire,* 52 (December 1986): 4;
Keith Soltys, "Donald Kingsbury: An Interview," *Torus,* 3 (April 1988): 15–19.

Gwendolyn MacEwen
(1 September 1941 – 30 November 1987)

Dorothy Shostak
Dalhousie University

See also the MacEwen entry in *DLB 53: Canadian Writers Since 1960, First Series.*

BOOKS: *Selah* (Toronto: Aleph, 1961);
The Drunken Clock: Poems (Toronto: Aleph, 1961);
The Rising Fire: Poems (Toronto: Contact, 1963);
Julian the Magician (Toronto: Macmillan, 1963; New York: Corinth, 1963);
A Breakfast for Barbarians: Poems (Toronto: Ryerson, 1966);
The Shadow-Maker (Toronto: Macmillan, 1969);
King of Egypt, King of Dreams: A Novel (Toronto: Macmillan, 1971);
The Armies of the Moon (Toronto: Macmillan, 1972);
Noman (Ottawa: Oberon, 1972);
Magic Animals: Selected Poems Old and New (Toronto: Macmillan, 1974); revised as *Magic Animals: Selected Poems of Gwendolyn MacEwen* (Don Mills, Ontario: Stoddart, 1984);
Terror and Erebus: A Verse Play for Radio (Toronto: Tamarack Review, 1974);
The Fire-Eaters (Ottawa: Oberon, 1976);
Mermaids and Ikons: A Greek Summer (Toronto: Anansi, 1978);
The Trojan Women: A Play (Toronto: Playwrights Co-op, 1979);
The Chocolate Moose (Toronto: New Canada Press, 1981);
The T. E. Lawrence Poems (Oakville, Ontario: Mosaic, 1982);
Earth-light: Selected Poetry of Gwendolyn MacEwen, 1963–1982 (Toronto: General Publishing, 1982);
The Honey Drum: Seven Tales from Arab Lands, (Oakville, Ontario: Mosaic, 1983);
Noman's Land: Stories (Toronto: Coach House, 1985);
Afterworlds (Toronto: McClelland and Stewart, 1987);
Dragon Sandwiches (Windsor, Ontario: Black Moss, 1987);
The Shadowmaker: Four Pieces for Baritone and Orchestra, 1977/78, libretto by MacEwen, music by Rudi Martinus van Dijk (Amsterdam: Doremus, 1991);

Gwendolyn MacEwen

The Birds: A Modern Adaptation of Aristophanes' Comedy (Toronto: Exile Editions, 1993).

Collection: *The Poetry of Gwendolyn MacEwen,* edited by Margaret Atwood and Barry Callaghan, 2 volumes (Toronto: Exile Editions, 1993, 1994)—comprises volume 1, *The Early Years,* and volume 2, *The Later Years.*

PLAY PRODUCTIONS: *The Shadowmaker: Four Pieces for Baritone and Orchestra,* libretto by MacEwen, music by Rudi Martinus van Dijk, Toronto, 24 October 1978;

The Trojan Women: A New Version, Toronto, St. Lawrence Centre, 22 November 1978;

Arcana, libretto by MacEwen, music by Christos Hatzis, Toronto Dance Theatre, 28 October 1983.

PRODUCED SCRIPTS: *Terror and Erebus: A Verse Play for Radio,* radio, Canadian Broadcasting Corporation Radio, 10 January 1965;

Tesla, radio, CBC Radio, 14 March 1967;

The Celebration of Evil, radio, *Ideas* series, CBC Radio, 9 May 1967;

The World of Neshiah, radio, CBC Radio, 3 October 1967; revised production, CBC Radio, 10 December 1967;

Gwendolyn MacEwen Introduces series, radio, *Anthology* series, CBC Radio, 5, 12, 19, 26 April 1969;

Carneval, radio, libretto by MacEwen, music by Ron Collier, CBC Radio, 4 March 1973.

OTHER: Yannis Ritsos, "Helen" and "Orestes," translated by MacEwen and Nikos Tsingos in their *Trojan Women* (Toronto: Exile Editions, 1981).

SELECTED PERIODICAL PUBLICATION–UNCOLLECTED: "A Poet's Journey into the Interior," *Cross-Canada Writers' Quarterly,* 8 (1986): 19.

Gwendolyn MacEwen was one of Canada's best-known mythopoeic writers in the 1960s, 1970s, and 1980s. Her startling themes of myth, magic, alchemy, and dream, as well as the setting of many works in exotic lands and cultures and her incantatory, invocatory language, earned praise as her work fascinated and challenged her readers to rethink the boundaries of Canadian literature. She wrote in a wide variety of genres and won several awards for her writing. Science fiction and fantasy comprise only a small portion of her work, but provided her short lyric poems, especially, with themes and imagery throughout her career.

Gwendolyn Margaret McEwen was born in Toronto, Ontario, on 1 September 1941, the second daughter of Alick and Elsie (Mitchell) McEwen, and attended public schools in Toronto and Winnipeg, Manitoba. Her interest in science fiction and magic began in childhood: she loved superhero comic books and at age twelve invented a number game in an attempt to magically control reality. Her need for a sense of control may have stemmed from the disruptions to family life caused by her mother's mental illness and, later, her father's alcoholism. When as a teen she read that the Macs were the ancient Scottish bards, and having already decided to become a writer, she changed her name from "McEwen" to "MacEwen."

In her high-school writings she created magicians and scientists whose professional pursuits always brought them up against the unexpected mysteries of the universe. She published her first poem at seventeen, and a year later she left Western Technical-Commercial School in Toronto to devote her life to full-time writing. She lived most of her adult life in Toronto.

MacEwen began to write science fiction early in her career. An unpublished drama titled "The Lady and the Robot" dates from the early 1960s. An unpolished sketch about the allure of artificial intelligence, "The Lady and the Robot" is told as a dialogue between a woman named Leslie and a robot named Carl, whom she wants to seduce: "I came to you because you are beautiful because of your reason. Your decisions are sharp; you are a razor, Carl, and a knife also. You are a blade." The machine responds with delightful irony: "YES, I UNDERSTAND YOUR METAPHORS; YOU ARE SAYING THAT I AM CLEAN AND SHARP. YES, THAT IS SO. PLEASE GO ON." Leslie discovers that reciprocal passion is impossible between a human and a robot.

MacEwen was fascinated by the occult, and in 1959 studied Hebrew at a heder in order to be able to read the Cabala. MacEwen's first two chapbooks, *Selah* (1961) and *The Drunken Clock: Poems* (1961), are both strongly influenced by Western mysticism and metaphysics. The latter collection includes "In Defence of Magic," one of MacEwen's first poems about magic as it relates to alchemy and faith, and "Wristwatch and Nile Time," an early meditation on the nature of time and time travel. As a rising young poet, she married the well-known poet Milton Acorn, eighteen years her senior, in 1962, but the marriage lasted only a few months. She began to live with the flamboyant, self-styled magician Bob Mallory and published a new poetry collection, *The Rising Fire* (1963), which introduced several of her favorite themes in science fiction and fantasy. "Universe And: The Electric Garden" contemplates the nature of the physical universe; "Inquiry Into Time" further explores the nature of time and time travel; and "Nikolayev and Popovich: The Cosmic Brothers" presents human perception of the "outer" world as being intimately connected to the psyche, as one of the astronauts

> finds at the end of the universe
> not walls, but mirrors
> reflecting the question mark
> of his own face back in
> to study it ironically,
> like brothers, amazed
> at their own similarity.

MacEwen was also reading the traditional texts of Western alchemy at this time, and the collection includes "The Magician: Three Themes" and several poems using alchemical imagery.

MacEwen saw magic and poetry as intimately related. She wrote in her essay "A Poet's Journey into the Interior," published in *Cross-Canada Writers' Quarterly* in 1986: "For me, language has enormous, almost magical power, and I tend to regard poetry in much the same way as the ancients regarded the chants or hymns used in holy festivals—as a means of invoking the mysterious forces which move the world, inform our deepest and most secret thoughts, and often visit us in sleep." MacEwen saw the role of the poet to be shamanistic, reminding humanity about the mystical realms of the spirit and the paths to cultivate it. In the same essay she claimed that poetry "travels between the 'inner' world of the *psyche* and the 'outer' world of things, and between Past and Future. In a way the poet resembles a magician or time-traveller."

This view influenced not only her poetry, but also her fiction. MacEwen's first novel, *Julian the Magician* (1963), takes as its theme the inability of the real world to understand the authentic magician. In nineteenth-century Europe, Julian performs sleight of hand as a livelihood, but also studies "the work," the mystical transformation of human consciousness into divinity, as taught in the traditions of the Cabala and Jacob Boehme. Julian is not a typical hero of the fantasy genre: his enemy is human ignorance, not evil, and his life parallels Christ's life and death. Despite an occasional clumsiness of language, the novel was well received, although some critics disapproved of its structure, finding the journal entries "completely unreadable," according to Dave Godfrey in *The Tamarack Review* (1964), or "too coy," according to Elizabeth Barrett in *Evidence* (1964). In retrospect, *Julian the Magician* is an early postmodern novel whose self-reflexivity and fragmentary narrative are meant to convey something of the paradox of the conscious mind attempting to know what is outside of itself.

MacEwen began to live with an Egyptian man (known only as "Salah") in 1965, and she taught herself Arabic. In 1966 she received a grant to travel to Cairo to conduct research for an historical novel based on the life of Pharaoh Akhenaton. That summer she wrote *King of Egypt, King of Dreams: A Novel*, which was not published until 1971. She had hoped that the novel would produce enough income to enable her to concentrate on writing poetry, but sales were disappointing.

In the mid 1960s MacEwen also wrote several radio plays for the Canadian Broadcasting Corporation (CBC) and created her most fully realized work of science fiction, her radio play *The World of Neshiah*. Never published, this play was first broadcast by CBC Radio on 3 October 1967 as part of the *Introducing* series; a slightly revised version was broadcast on 10 December 1967 as part of the *CBC Stage* series. *The World of Neshiah* explores ideas about cultural relativity, memory, and time. The play is set on Neshiah, the fifth of seven earths. Neshiah, which is also the word for "forgetting" in the natives' fictional language, is a world where the inhabitants have no memory of past time, but can "remember" the future. Edward E. Equinox, the first visitor from Earth, is an ambassador who visits Neshiah ostensibly to study its culture. The time perception of the inhabitants of Neshiah shocks him: he sees the people of Neshiah as deficient or abnormal, their lack of memory of the past as a handicap. The plot of the drama revolves around the king of Neshiah's "memory" of his own murder on the coming day. Equinox urges him to try to prevent it, but the king only reluctantly agrees, because it is arrogant, barbaric, and "not in good taste" to try to prevent the calamities of the future.

The strength of the play is in MacEwen's wry exposure of the reciprocity of paternalistic and imperialistic attitudes in such a meeting of cultures. However, the play is not entirely satisfactory in its exploration of time and memory: many paradoxes and inconsistencies appear in the way that memory functions on Neshiah. Moreover, the narrative is unclear as to whether Neshiah is another planet or an alternate reality: the people of Neshiah speak English, eat porridge, and have court jesters. Although the portrayal of King Christopher is entertaining, Christopher and his culture come across as childish, inept, and inane. MacEwen does use irony effectively to inject the play with humor: Christopher adopts Equinox's quotation from A. A. Milne as his motto or mantra, then converts it into scrambled "words of wisdom." Despite the flaws, MacEwen revised the play for television and as a short story, although neither revision was used.

MacEwen continued to write poetry that repeats the themes and imagery explored in her science fiction and fantasy, although often they are used metaphorically, as in "The Astronauts," "Thesis," "The Magician," "Manzini: Escape Artist," and "Black Alchemy," from *A Breakfast for Barbarians: Poems* (1966). MacEwen's fame as a poet increased with the publication of *The Shadow-Maker* (1969), for which she received a Governor-General's Literary Award for poetry. This work continues her interest in magic and alchemy in poems such as "Invocations" and "The Taming of the Dragon."

In 1969 MacEwen met Greek folksinger Nikos Tsingos. They were married in a traditional ceremony in Greece in October 1971 and then returned to Toronto. MacEwen had been working for several years on a tale

Cover for MacEwen's final poetry collection (1987), in which she returned to her interest in science and magic. The book was awarded the Governor-General's Award after her death on 30 November 1987.

MacEwen uses science-fiction elements in her next collection of poems, *The Armies of the Moon* (1972), winner of the 1973 A. J. M. Smith Award. The title poem posits a future in which humans, unaware of the invisible inhabitants of the moon, begin to exploit the resources of the moon, only to be defeated in a great battle in the Lake of Death: "men will be powder, they will go down under / the swords of the unseen silver armies, / become one with the gorgeous anonymous moon." In this collection, images from scientific and science-fiction discourses continue to provide MacEwen with metaphors for the human consciousness striving to evolve.

Despite her literary success, MacEwen and her husband sought a more stable income and in the summer of 1973 opened The Trojan Horse, a Greek café in Toronto. Although popular, the café made little money, and they were forced to sell it about a year later. Their marriage became troubled, and after a second trip to Greece, during which they hoped to resolve their marital problems, MacEwen and Tsingos separated in 1976. That year MacEwen published *The Fire-Eaters,* in which many poems deal with pain–physical, emotional, and spiritual–encountered in daily life. Only one poem in this volume, "Carnival," takes up MacEwen's old theme of magic, but in this poem the magician seems lonely and stuck: "I dance alone, I asked to dance alone . . . / I can't move at all." MacEwen received the Queen's Silver Jubilee Medal in 1978, but at this point in her career she stopped writing either poetry or science fiction and fantasy for a time, producing instead a travel memoir, a translation of a classic drama by Euripides, and a children's book, before publishing new poems in 1982.

During the late 1970s and early 1980s MacEwen's financial crisis deepened. MacEwen, who had possibly inherited her father's constitutional susceptibility to alcoholism, had begun drinking during the breakdown of her marriage to Tsingos. She was hospitalized several times when she tried to conquer the addiction on her own. After she and Tsingos filed for divorce in 1983, MacEwen traveled in late spring of 1984 to London and Scotland to meet her relatives. When she returned to Canada, she was appointed writer in residence at the University of Western Ontario in 1984 and at the University of Toronto in 1986. During this period, MacEwen published a second collection of fables, *Noman's Land: Stories* (1985), that mixed the mundane and the magical in creating a mythological Canada.

MacEwen died on 30 November 1987 as a result of alcohol-related health problems. She won a posthumous Governor-General's Award for her final collection of new poems, *Afterworlds* (1987), in which she returned to her interest in science and magic. The poem

in which Julian the magician reappears. In the short story "The Second Coming of Julian the Magician," published in her 1972 collection *Noman,* Julian again encounters problems with his audience and has to work in burlesque houses and summer carnivals in Canada during the 1970s. Bookings are rare, and he ends up as night watchman in an electrical generation plant, finally pitting the power of his magic against that of "the Machine." He dreams he grows to fill the entire universe, and, like Nikolayev and Popovich, at the edge sees his own reflection: "a shimmering silver form at the end. At the moment I realized it was *myself,* I awoke." In *Canadian Science Fiction and Fantasy* (1992), David Ketterer describes *Noman* as a collection of "highly evocative fables," in which the boundaries between the magical and the mundane are blurred.

"Past and Future Ghosts" revisits the nature of time and memory, and "The Tao of Physics" meditates on the nature of the physical universe, the role of the poet and the creative process, the inextricability of the "light" and "dark" sides of human experience, and the inevitability of death:

> Here where events have a tendency to occur
> My chair and all its myriad inner worlds
> Whirl around in the carousel of space; I hurl
> Breathless poems against my lord Death, send these
> Words, these words,
> Careening into the beautiful darkness.

MacEwen's work in the genres of science fiction and fantasy will probably remain on the margins. The ideas she explores in her poetry are not as well-developed in her fiction and drama. However, because of the suggestiveness she achieves in the medium of poetry, her mystical, cosmic vision will likely continue to be popular.

Interviews:

Bev Daurio and Mike Zizis, "An Inner View of Gwendolyn MacEwen," *Intrinsic*, 5-6 (1978): 56-65;

Patricia Keeney Smith, "WQ Interview with Gwendolyn MacEwen," *Cross-Canada Writers' Quarterly*, 5 (1983): 114-117;

Bruce Meyer and Brian O'Riordan, "The Magic of Language," in *In Their Words: Interviews with Fourteen Canadian Writers* (Toronto: Anansi, 1984), pp. 96-105.

Biography:

Rosemary Sullivan, *Shadow Maker: The Life of Gwendolyn MacEwen* (Toronto: HarperCollins, 1995).

References:

Margaret Atwood, "Canadian Monsters: Some Aspects of the Supernatural in Canadian Fiction," in *The Canadian Imagination: Dimensions of a Literary Culture*, edited by David Staines (Cambridge, Mass.: Harvard University Press, 1977), pp. 97-122;

Atwood, "MacEwen's Muse," *Canadian Literature*, 45 (1970): 24-32;

Jan Bartley, *Invocations: The Poetry and Prose of Gwendolyn MacEwen* (Vancouver: University of British Columbia Press, 1983);

Frank Davey, *From There to Here: A Guide to English-Canadian Literature Since 1960* (Erin, Ontario: Press Porcépic, 1974), pp. 177-181;

Davey, "Gwendolyn MacEwen: The Secret of Alchemy," *Open Letter*, second series 4 (1973): 5-23;

Thomas M. F. Gerry, "'Green Yet Free of Seasons': Gwendolyn MacEwen and the Mystical Tradition of Canadian Poetry," *Studies in Canadian Literature / Etudes en littérature canadienne*, 16 (1991): 147-161;

E. B. Gose, "They Shall Have Arcana," *Canadian Literature*, 21 (1964): 36-45;

R. F. Gillian Harding, "Iconic Mythopoeia in MacEwen's *The T. E. Lawrence Poems*," *Studies in Canadian Literature / Etudes en littérature canadienne*, 9 (1984): 95-107;

R. F. Gillian Harding-Russell, "Gwendolyn MacEwen's 'The Nine Arcana of the Kings' as Creative Myth and Paradigm," *English Studies in Canada*, 14 (June 1988): 204-217;

Clement Moisan, "Ecriture et errance dans les poesies de Gwendolyn MacEwen et Nicole Brossard," *Canadian Review of Comparative Literature / Revue canadienne de littérature comparée*, 2 (1975): 72-92;

Liza Potvin, "Gwendolyn MacEwen and Female Spiritual Desire," *Canadian Poetry*, 28 (Spring-Summer 1991): 18-39;

Ellen Warwick, "To Seek a Single Symmetry," *Canadian Literature*, 71 (Winter 1976): 21-34.

Papers:

Gwendolyn MacEwen's papers are held in the Thomas Fisher Rare Book Library at the University of Toronto.

Laurence Manning

(1899 – 10 April 1972)

Everett F. Bleiler

BOOKS: *The How and Why of Better Gardening* (New York: Van Nostrand, 1951);
The Man Who Awoke (New York: Ballantine, 1975; London: Sphere, 1977).

OTHER: "The Living Galaxy," in *The Science Fiction Galaxy,* edited by Groff Conklin (New York: Perma Books, 1950), pp. 227–242;
"Good-bye, Ilha!" in *Beyond Human Ken,* edited by Judith Merril (New York: Random House, 1952);
"The City of the Living Dead," by Manning and Fletcher Pratt, in *The Second Avon Fantasy Reader,* edited by Donald A. Wollheim and George Ernsberger (New York: Avon, 1969), pp. 136–161.

SELECTED PERIODICAL PUBLICATIONS–UNCOLLECTED: "The Voyage of the *Asteroid,*" *Wonder Stories Quarterly* (Summer 1932);
"The Wreck of the *Asteroid,*" *Wonder Stories* (December 1932–February 1933);
"The Call of the Mech-Men," *Wonder Stories* (November 1933);
"Caverns of Horror," *Wonder Stories* (March 1934);
"Voice of Atlantis," *Wonder Stories* (July 1934);
"The Living Galaxy," *Wonder Stories* (September 1934);
"The Moth Message," *Wonder Stories* (December 1934);
"The Prophetic Voice," *Wonder Stories* (April 1935);
"Seeds from Space," *Wonder Stories* (June 1935);
"World of the Mist," *Wonder Stories* (September–October 1935);
"Expedition to Pluto," by Manning and Fletcher Pratt, *Planet Stories* (Winter 1939);
"Men on Mars," *Fantastic Story Magazine* (Spring 1952);
"Mr. Mottle Goes Poof," *Fantasy Fiction* (August 1953).

Of the several Canadian-born authors who wrote science fiction for the American pulp magazines during the early years of the 1920s and 1930s, Laurence Manning was the most significant both for his mastery of fictional techniques and for his anticipation of later modes of thought.

Lawrence Edward Manning, who wrote as Laurence Manning, was born in St. John, New Brunswick, in 1899. After attending local schools, he matriculated at the University of King's College School of Law–then in Windsor, Nova Scotia–where he received a bachelor's degree in civil law in 1919. Manning is said to have served in the Royal Canadian Air Force as a second lieutenant during the latter part of World War I, although judging from his college attendance during that period, Manning probably did not see active service. After a brief period of work on a Halifax newspaper, in 1920 Manning came to the United States, where he is said to have acquired citizenship. In 1928 he married his wife, Edith, with whom he had two daughters and one son. He worked as a writer for *Florists Exchange,* a Philadelphia trade magazine for nurseries and florists that he later edited. Still later, in New York City, he became manager and in 1938 owner of the Kelsey Nursery Service, a mail-order organization selling garden materials. In connection with this work in horticulture Manning prepared a gardening manual, *The How and Why of Better Gardening* (1951).

During the 1930s Manning took an active part in rocket experimentation. He was one of the founding members of the American Interplanetary Society (later known as the American Rocket Society) in April 1930 and served as president of the organization in 1934. He participated in 1932 in early experiments that included high-gravity tests with guinea pigs and liquid-fuel rockets in 1933 and 1934; he also edited the journal of the society. The work of the American Rocket Society (which in 1963 merged with The Institute of Aerospace Sciences to become The American Institute of Aeronautics and Astronautics) has been described by Frank H. Winter in *Prelude to the Space Age: The Rocket Societies, 1924–1940* (1983) as historically important in the development of high-altitude rockets.

Manning began to write science fiction in about late 1929 or early 1930 when he collaborated with Fletcher Pratt on the short story "The City of the Living Dead," published in the May 1930 issue of *Science*

Wonder Stories. Set in an indeterminate future, the story is concerned with virtual-reality machines so perfected that people can spend their entire lives and eventually die in the fantasy worlds the machines produce. The idea was not new, having been first significantly introduced by A. Merritt in his 1923 story "The Face in the Abyss" and further developed in G. Peyton Wertenbaker's 1929 story "The Chamber of Life," with both of which stories Manning and Pratt were almost certainly acquainted. Manning and Pratt, however, stressed social implications of the basic concept more than did their predecessors. The story, which is probably Pratt's in writing and development, is inferior to Manning's solo use of the dream machine concept in *The Man Who Awoke* series.

Manning did not publish any more fiction until two years later, when his short novel "The Voyage of the *Asteroid*" appeared in the Summer 1932 issue of *Wonder Stories Quarterly*. A low-key, circumstantial description of the first interplanetary voyage, technologically based on the work of the American Rocket Society, the story involves a large, liquid-fueled step rocket, the *Asteroid*, which makes a successful trip to Venus. The rocketry is realistic, but Manning followed pulp literary convention in his description of Venus as a water-covered planet similar to Earth and with life forms comparable to those of the dinosaur past of Earth.

A serialized sequel, "The Wreck of the *Asteroid*," appeared in *Wonder Stories* from December 1932 to February 1933. The misleadingly titled story (the *Asteroid* is not wrecked) tells of the exploration of Mars. The *Asteroid* remains on Phobos, one of the moons of Mars, while an exploratory capsule lands on the planet. The explorers discover that the canals are actually deep rifts with atmosphere and food resources at the bottom adequate for human survival. The rifts, however, are inhabited by enormous, ferocious, seasonal insects against which the explorers have little or no defense. In the description of Martian fauna and flora, Manning's interest in biology and ecology is manifest. His interpretation of the geography of Mars—as of Venus—was scientifically inaccurate according to then-current knowledge, but was fictionally acceptable in its day.

The works that made Manning's reputation, however, were not based on rocket research but were built around social and ecological factors in future cultures and told as experience stories. In *The Man Who Awoke* series, Norman Winters, a wealthy retired banker who is obsessed with the future, constructs an underground vault equipped with automatic survival devices and takes a drug that places him in suspended animation. A small clock powered by an artificial stream will awaken him at a programmed time. In later episodes, when Winters encounters superior science, his retreat

Cover, with illustration by Frank R. Paul, for a 1934 issue of a pulp magazine that includes Laurence Manning's tale of a psychologist who gains the ability to communicate telepathically with the inhabitants of Atlantis

becomes vastly more sophisticated and reliable. As the series continues, Winters awakens at five-thousand-year intervals to experience the culture of that time and then returns to his vault. Such time-hopping was not unknown in early science fiction and writings about utopias, but most of the serious earlier fiction stressed political economics, particularly varieties of socialism.

"The Man Who Awoke," the first story in the series, was published in the March 1933 issue of *Wonder Stories*. In this first episode, set around A.D. 5000, selfishness is the theme, as Winters awakens to a world that might be considered an ecological extremist's ideal. The inhabitants of North America have developed a forest culture in some ways reminiscent of such earlier utopias as William Henry Hudson's *A Crystal Age* (1887) and William Morris's *News from Nowhere* (1890), although Manning's culture maintains a better balance between nature and advanced technology than did those predecessors, which did not accommodate to material progress. Field agriculture no longer exists; food and raw materials are obtained from specially bred trees or fungi grown on felled trees. Cities no longer exist; humankind lives in small settlements of controlled size within the forests. When the population within a settlement reaches a certain size, a new community is founded elsewhere. Individual settlements are more or less autonomous and have peaceful relations with each other. In this episode Manning's concept of future land treatment contrasts strongly with the ideas of his contemporaries. In Otfrid van Hanstein's "The Hidden Colony" (1935), for example, whole landscapes are razed and leveled, and field crops are produced by totally automated machinery.

Winters emerges from his cell during a crisis in a nearby village. There is discord between age groups because a new settlement is planned, and the younger people resent that food trees will have to be destroyed. Winters, who does not fully understand the situation, is manipulated by one faction. In the violence that breaks out, Winters is fortunate to escape back to his vault, which friendly scientists have improved for him. During his stay in the forest culture, his friends complain bitterly about the waste of resources and destruction of environment that had taken place during Winters's era.

Winters's second awakening, described in "Master of the Brain" (April 1933), occurs five thousand years later to a markedly different world. Whereas the previous culture was semi-anarchistic and nature-centered, the culture of 10,000 A.D. is machine-controlled: all humankind's activities, down to each individual person and piece of machinery, are planned, structured, maintained, and ruled by a supercomputer called the Brain.

The Brain–similar to the global computer in Lionel Britton's 1930 expressionist *Brain: A Play of the Whole Earth*–provides a materialistic eutopia. There is no want or crime; all necessities of life are furnished; and work is limited to approximately an easy hour a day. Access to pleasure cities resembling a Victorian preacher's idea of Sodom and Gomorrah is offered as a reward for good behavior. In exchange, the Brain demands total assimilation and will not tolerate independent individuals. Outsiders who are captured, as Winters is, either join the Brain or are put to death.

Most members of the society accept the Brain's rule, although a small underground recognizes that humanity is degenerating under the Brain's control and must regain freedom, even at the cost of losing the Brain's technology and eutopia. Winters, as an alien able to reach the Brain's circuits, is responsible for its destruction.

Winters's third awakening, in A.D. 15,000, as imperfectly foreshadowed in "The City of Sleep"(May 1933), is into the world sketchily developed in "The City of the Living Dead." The cultural pattern is an evasion of life. In a global scientific culture, humanity is concentrated in enormous, futuristic cities, with nothing but wilderness existing elsewhere. Material wants are fulfilled by atomic synthesis machines. Virtually all of the human race is permanently connected to virtual-reality dream machines. These sleepers are grudgingly cared for by a tiny group of technicians in each city. The lure of the machine is overpowering. As one character, Jalna, points out, why should she suffer the dissatisfactions of life when, by entering a dream machine, she can enjoy the illusion of a blissful married life with her lover Eric? The human race is at the edge of extinction, but Winters precipitates a tiny secession that will create a new mankind, without the dream machines.

The most interesting of Winters's awakenings is described in "The Individualists" (June 1933). The culture of A.D. 20,000 is based on an extreme, different sort of egotism–total individualism. Scientists, poets, and musicians–incredible geniuses by present-day standards–live in total isolation, jealously guarding their knowledge or creations and conducting murderous scientific warfare against their peers. In this richly detailed story Winters escapes a monomaniacal biologist intent on vivisecting Winters and using his cells for research.

Winters's last awakening, parallel to the awakening of the human race, is described in "The Elixir" (August 1933). In A.D. 25,000 conflict and tension between the individual and the group have been resolved by an evolved altruism; old age and death have been removed by cellular regeneration; interstellar travel is feasible; and galactic humanity has arrived. A rejuvenated Winters sets out to explore the universe. His exploration is not wholly a physical matter, for the future culture is concerned with absolute Meaning, and Winters's quest is both philosophical and religious. Groups around the universe are attempting to derive an understanding of existence in what amounts to a diluted mystical quest. This quest for ideals seems to be an innate development in Manning's thought, perhaps influenced by Olaf Stapledon's *Last and First Men: A Story of the Near and Far Future* (1930). The individual stories of *The Man Who Awoke* were collected and published in 1975, three years after Manning's death.

Connected with *The Man Who Awoke* series is "The Living Galaxy" (September 1934), set in the same universe as the series hundreds of millions of years in the future. With the three great discoveries of *The Man Who Awoke* (atomic energy, atomic synthesis, and immortality) humanity has spread to the stars, even to "space" outside the universe. A peril threatens the inhabited stellar systems: a life form composed of a small galaxy is destroying stars and must be removed.

It is unfortunate that Manning did not develop this story into a longer work. A second series of five stories, *Tales of the Stranger Club,* invokes the tradition of

British club stories: members describe past or present experiences of an incredible or outlandish sort. Possibly Manning had in mind as models the Jorkens stories of Edward John Moreton Drax Plunkett, the eighteenth baron Dunsany, or certain of G. K. Chesterton's works. Manning's tales are entertaining but usually lack the depth of *The Man Who Awoke*.

"The Call of the Mech-Men" (November 1933) opens the series with peppery old Colonel Marsh, who believes that there is something odd about the north magnetic pole. He is right; his expedition discovers that the pole is a beacon set up by stranded intelligent machine beings from space. Marsh and his companion are captured and put into a zoo. The story is said to have been written as a parody of interplanetary invasion stories. "Caverns of Horror" (March 1934) describes a peculiar, horrendous underworld beneath an area of Long Island. The solution to the puzzle presented by the story—where can one find the most dangerous beasts near New York City?—is given by the title supplied by the magazine editors. "The Moth Message" (December 1934) focuses on an interesting analogy: the patterns on the wings of certain moths not only resemble writing, but are actually messages bred into them by a tiny colony of Atlanteans stranded in the Southwest.

Manning's deftly and amusingly treated world-saver story, "Seeds from Space" (June 1935), centers on Blenkins, a playboy on vacation on the Maine coast. Blenkins chances to retrieve three seeds from a shower that flies past him into the ocean. Planted in his Manhattan apartment, the seeds sprout into superintelligent trees that not only have ancestral memory but also master human sciences in hours. The trees are not malevolent, but as superior life forms will take over Earth. Who can stop them? Not a scientist, not a military man, but the alcoholic Blenkins, who recognizes when the trees become drunk on manure and are vulnerable. "Seeds from Space" parodies stories of the day that concerned the salvation of the world.

The most significant of the *Tales of the Stranger Club* stories is "Voice of Atlantis" (July 1934). The story combines a fascinating narrative with Manning's serious thought on modern civilization. The psychologist Volking, working on a device to measure brain electricity, accidentally constructs a thought helmet that connects him with the Atlantean center for telepathic communication with the future. The priest scientist whom Volking contacts is most interested when Volking tells him of the destruction of Atlantis, for the Atlanteans have no knowledge of what happened to their land, and cultures far in the future with whom Atlanteans are in communication have lost the legend of Atlantis. The priest scientist takes Volking on a mental walk through Atlantis to meet the kings, who decide

Cover for the June 1935 issue of the pulp, with a Paul illustration for Manning's satirical story about superintelligent trees that threaten to take over the world

that Volking's knowledge is too dangerous to be revealed. He is forced to return to his present time and destroy his apparatus.

The story is neatly handled, but more interesting than the events is a long discussion between Volking and the Atlantean priest on the nature of civilization, the conservation of resources, the role of knowledge, and similar topics. Atlantis is a sacred society with a superficially barbaric culture based on physical slave labor. But in the persons of a small learned class, Atlantean culture is far beyond humans scientifically. The Atlantean priest regards modern, wasteful, noisy civilization, as described by Volking, with scorn and horror, the work of clever monkeys.

"Voice of Atlantis" affords a paradox: Manning, a pioneer in one of the most visionary areas of technology, rocket research, also embraces a weltanschauung that is essentially antimodern, opposed to the use of machines, and verges on a nonrational concept of history. The same mode of thought is apparent in "The Elixir" and in his later short novel "World of the Mist" (1935).

An independent story, "The Prophetic Voice," published in the April 1935 issue of *Wonder Stories,* sets up a parabolic puzzle situation based on the limitations of knowledge. Several hundred years from the present, telepathic communication with the future is possible. A strange message arrives from the future: in two years there will be no humanity on Earth unless precautions are taken. The future voice does not know what happened but urges, offering techniques, that humankind enter suspended animation for a few decades. Eighty years later humankind emerges to find the world unchanged. Renewed communication with the future reveals ignorance of the message. The message could not have been a hoax by a contemporary because the science involved was far superior to that of the recipients. Where did the message originate? Was it from space, a ruse to clear the Earth for alien exploration? Since there is no way of identifying future thought transmitters, will humanity soon be exterminated by the beings who sent the message? The story provides no answers to the questions it raises.

Further movement away from mechanistic science fiction into somewhat mystical science fiction is visible in Manning's serialized short novel "World of the Mist," published in the September and October 1935 issues of *Wonder Stories*. Although the narrative employs a rocket journey involving the latest technology, the interest lies in the access to a mystical experience provided by the rocket rather than in its technology. Three friends, each of whom is suffering from emotional distress or pain, decide to explore the potential for changing space-time with the hypothetical substance "neutronium." After building a spaceship, the three friends set out hoping to find a neutronium asteroid, which they unexpectedly do. Through a chain of circumstances they are forced to fly through a neutronium ring, whereupon they find themselves in an otherworld that is a reversal of reality. What is solid in this world is empty in the otherworld. The empty area of the otherworld is inhabited by a red mist that seems to have personality and intelligence. In what may be an attempt to communicate, the mist displays panoramas of terrestrial forms and causes strange dreams. The explorers are forced to leave with their questions unresolved, since there is a chemical reaction between the mist and the metal of their ship. The survivors plan to return to the world of the mist to try to understand it. *Wonder Stories* was discontinued before "Maze of Creation"–a sequel announced in February 1936 that was presumably to explain the alien entity–could be published, and no manuscript of the work has been discovered. Manning wrote at least two other unpublished novels: "Grogue's Doom," known only by title and presumably lost, and an almost surrealistic untitled novel about adaptation to ocean life, probably written in the late 1960s.

Manning received little attention for his work beyond the 1930s. A novelette in collaboration with Pratt, "Expedition to Pluto," published in the Winter 1939 issue of *Planet Stories* but perhaps written considerably earlier, is a routine space opera. Three slight stories from the early 1950s–"Men on Mars"(1952), "Good-bye, Ilha!"(1952), and "Mr. Mottle Goes Poof"(1953)–possibly indicate that Manning attempted to resume writing fiction. Manning retired from his mail-order business in 1962. He died in Highlands, New Jersey, on 10 April 1972.

Today Laurence Manning is almost forgotten. He never achieved the reputation that certain of his less-skilled fellow writers had, and he stopped writing before new trends in science fiction emerged. His work was side-trail science fiction in its day, written with mainstream care, concerned neither with novelties of science and technology nor with raw thrills and perils. In his better stories his concern is with ideas about ecology, the relation between humanity and the environment, cycles of history, and ultimates of existence, concepts that are now seen as modern. Setting aside the elements of dated science, Manning's stories can be seen as more modern today than they were in the 1930s.

Reference:

Everett F. Bleiler, ed., *Science-Fiction: The Gernsback Years* (Kent, Ohio: Kent State University Press, 1998), pp. 271–278.

Judith Merril
(21 January 1923 - 12 September 1997)

Elliot J. Atkins
University of Liverpool

BOOKS: *Shadow on the Hearth* (Garden City, N.Y.: Doubleday, 1950; London: Sidgwick & Jackson, 1953); revised edition (London: Roberts & Vinter, 1966);

Outpost Mars, by Merril and C. M. Kornbluth, as Cyril Judd (New York: Abelard, 1952; London: New English Library, 1966); republished as *Sin in Space* (New York: Beacon, 1961);

Gunner Cade, by Merril and Kornbluth, as Judd (New York: Simon & Schuster, 1952; London: Gollancz, 1964);

Out of Bounds: Seven Stories (New York: Pyramid, 1960);

The Tomorrow People (New York: Pyramid, 1960);

Daughters of Earth (London: Gollancz, 1968; Garden City, N.Y.: Doubleday, 1969); republished as *Daughters of Earth and Other Stories* (Toronto: McClelland & Stewart, 1985);

Survival Ship and Other Stories (Toronto: Kakabeka, 1973);

The Best of Judith Merril (New York: Warner, 1976).

RECORDING: *Survival Ship and The Shrine of Temptation,* read by Merril, New York, Caedmon, 1978.

OTHER: *Shot in the Dark,* edited by Merril (New York: Bantam, 1950);

"Barrier of Dread," in *Journey to Infinity,* edited by Martin H. Greenberg (New York: Gnome Press, 1951);

"Survival Ship," in *Tomorrow, the Stars,* edited by Robert A. Heinlein (New York: Doubleday, 1951); reprinted in *Transformations,* edited by Daniel Roselle (New York: Fawcett, 1973); reprinted in *Anthropology Through Science Fiction,* edited by Carol Mason, Greenberg, and Patricia Warrick (New York: St. Martin's Press, 1974), pp. 185–195;

"That Only a Mother," in *World of Wonder,* edited by Fletcher Pratt (New York: Twayne, 1951), pp. 347–357; reprinted in *Science Fiction Hall of Fame Volume 1,* edited by Robert Silverberg (New York: Doubleday, 1970); reprinted in *Women of Wonder,*

Judith Merril (from the dust jacket for The 9th Annual of the Year's Best SF, *1964)*

edited by Pamela Sargent (New York: Vintage, 1975); reprinted in *Science Fiction of the '40's,* edited by Frederik Pohl, Greenberg, and Joseph D. Olander (New York: Avon, 1978); reprinted in *The Road to Science Fiction #3,* edited by James E. Gunn (New York: Mentor, 1979);

Beyond Human Ken, edited by Merril (New York: Random House, 1952); abridged as *Selections from Beyond Human Ken* (New York: Pennant, 1954);

"Daughters of Earth," in *The Petrified Planet* (New York: Twayne, 1952);

"Death Is the Penalty," in *Beyond the End of Time,* edited by Pohl (New York: Permabooks, 1952);

"So Proudly We Hail," in *Star Science Fiction Stories,* edited by Pohl (New York: Ballantine, 1953);

Beyond the Barriers of Space and Time, edited by Merril (New York: Random House, 1954; London: Sidgwick & Jackson, 1955);

Human?, edited by Merril (New York: Lion, 1954);

Galaxy of Ghouls, edited by Merril (New York: Lion, 1955); republished as *Off the Beaten Orbit* (New York: Pyramid, 1959);

SF: '56: The Year's Greatest Science Fiction and Fantasy, edited by Merril (New York: Gnome Press, 1956);

SF: '57: The Year's Greatest Science Fiction and Fantasy, edited by Merril (New York: Gnome Press, 1957);

SF: '58: The Year's Greatest Science Fiction and Fantasy, edited by Merril (New York: Gnome Press, 1958);

SF: '59: The Year's Greatest Science Fiction and Fantasy, edited by Merril (New York: Gnome Press, 1959);

"Dead Center," in *A Treasury of Great Science Fiction, Vol. 2,* edited by Anthony Boucher (New York: Doubleday, 1959);

The 5th Annual of the Year's Best SF, edited by Merril (New York: Simon & Schuster, 1960); republished as *The Best of Sci-Fi 5* (London: Mayflower-Bell, 1966);

"Exile from Space," in *The Fantastic Universe Omnibus,* edited by Hans Stefan Santesson (New York: Prentice Hall, 1960), pp. 114–156;

"Project Nursemaid," in *Six Great Short Science Fiction Novels* (New York: Dell, 1960), pp. 51–150;

The 6th Annual of the Year's Best SF, edited by Merril (New York: Simon & Schuster, 1961); republished as *The Best of Sci-Fi* (London: Mayflower-Bell, 1963);

The 7th Annual of the Year's Best SF, edited by Merril (New York: Simon & Schuster, 1962); republished as *The Best of Sci-Fi–Two* (London: Mayflower-Bell, 1964);

The 8th Annual of the Year's Best SF, edited by Merril (New York: Simon & Schuster, 1963); republished as *The Best of Sci-Fi No. 4* (London: Mayflower-Bell, 1965);

"A Big Man with the Girls," with James MacCreigh, in *Escape to Earth,* edited by Ivan Howard (New York: Belmont Books, 1963);

The 9th Annual of the Year's Best SF, edited by Merril (New York: Delacorte Press, 1964); republished as *9th Annual S-F* (London: Mayflower-Bell, 1967);

"The Deep Down Dragon," in *The Seventh Galaxy Reader,* edited by Pohl (New York: Doubleday, 1964);

10th Annual Edition of The Year's Best SF, edited by Merril (New York: Delacorte, 1965); republished as *10th Annual S-F* (London: Mayflower-Bell, 1967);

11th Annual Edition of The Year's Best SF, edited by Merril (New York: Delacorte Press, 1966);

Path Into the Unknown: The Best of Soviet Science Fiction, edited by Merril (Bristol, England: MacGibbon & Kee, 1966; New York: Delacorte Press, 1968);

SF: The Best of the Best, edited by Merril (New York: Delacorte Press, 1967; London: Hart-Davis, 1968);

"Death Cannot Wither," by Merril and A. J. Budrys, in *Rod Serling's Devils and Demons,* edited by Rod Serling (New York: Bantam, 1967), pp. 40–60;

"The Shrine of Temptation," in *Gods for Tomorrow,* edited by Roger Elwood (New York: Award, 1967); reprinted in *The Devil His Due,* edited by Douglas Hill (London: Hart-Davis, 1967);

England Swings SF: Stories of Speculative Fiction, edited by Merril (Garden City, N.Y.: Doubleday, 1968); republished as *The Space-Time Journal* (London: Panther, 1972);

SF 12, edited by Merril (New York: Delacorte Press, 1968); republished as *The Best of Sci-Fi 12* (London: Mayflower-Bell, 1970);

"Rain Check," in *Crime Prevention in the 30th Century,* edited by Hans Stefan Santesson (New York: Walker, 1969), pp. 116–134;

"The Lady Was a Tramp," as Rose Sharon, in *The Venus Factor,* edited by Vic Ghidalia and Elwood (New York: MacFadden-Bartell, 1972), pp. 142–161;

"Peeping Tom," in *The 7 Deadly Sins of Science Fiction,* edited by Isaac Asimov, Greenberg, and Charles G. Waugh (New York: Fawcett, 1980);

Tesseracts, edited by Merril (Victoria, British Columbia: Press Porcépic, 1985); Merril's introduction, "We Have Met the Alien (And It Is Us)," reprinted in *Northern Stars: The Anthology of Canadian Science Fiction* (New York: Tor, 1994), pp. 15–23;

"In the Land of the Unblind," in *Tesseracts³,* edited by Candas Jane Dorsey and Gerry Truscott (Victoria, British Columbia: Press Porcépic, 1990), pp. 327–330;

Lesley Choyce, ed., *Ark of Ice: Canadian Futurefiction,* afterword by Merril (East Lawrencetown, Nova Scotia: Pottersfield Press, 1992);

Andrea Paradis, comp., *Out of This World: Canadian Science Fiction and Fantasy Literature,* foreword by Merril (Kingston, Ontario: Quarry Press, 1995), pp. 9–11.

SELECTED PERIODICAL PUBLICATIONS–
UNCOLLECTED: "What Do You Mean–Science? Fiction?," *Extrapolation,* 7 (May 1966): 30–46; and 8 (December 1966): 2–19; reprinted in *The Other Side of Realism: Essays on Modern Fantasy and Science Fiction,* edited by Thomas D. Clareson (Bowling Green, Ohio: Bowling Green State University Popular Press, 1971), pp. 53–95;

"Better to Have Loved: From a Memoir in Progress," *New York Review of Science Fiction,* 59 (July 1993): 7–14.

Although Judith Merril was born in Manhattan and wrote the vast majority of her science fiction in the United States during the 1950s, her contribution to the sphere of Canadian science fiction between 1969 (when she moved permanently to Toronto) and her death in 1997 was both profound and manifold. On 10 August 1970 she established—via the donation of her book collection to the Toronto Public Library—what became the Merril Collection of Science Fiction, Speculation, and Fantasy, the biggest publicly housed science-fiction collection in the world. She was actively involved with the Writers Union of Canada, as well as with forming the Toronto-based science-fiction writers' group Hydra North. Moreover, she edited *Tesseracts* (1985), the first in a series of groundbreaking Canadian science-fiction anthologies. She was also responsible, albeit indirectly, for the initiation of the annual Canadian science-fiction conference Cancon. Given these details it is not difficult to see why, in his speech given at the 1992 tribute "Judith Merril, Woman of the Future," fellow Canadian resident and science-fiction writer Spider Robinson called Merril "the honest-to-God Mother of Canadian Science Fiction."

As far as the development of the science-fiction genre is concerned, Merril's modest fictional output—fewer than thirty short stories and only two novels (not including her collaborative works)—is of unquestionable significance. Chris Morgan has correctly pointed out that "thematically most of her stories fall into a fairly small number of categories," a phenomenon that can be attributed to their close proximity of composition. With the exception of the science-fiction poem "Auction Pit" (1973) and the experimental short story "In the Land of the Unblind" (1990), Merril wrote all of her science fiction between 1948 and 1963. She was one of the first women writing for the pulps to see the potential of science fiction as a medium for articulating feminist concerns, and she manipulated the male-dominated genre accordingly. In doing so, she paved the way for many female writers who have, in the years since then, completely reinvented science fiction.

Although Merril's role as a practitioner of feminist science fiction is significant, her position as an anthologist and critic is what has secured her reputation worldwide. She was an intelligent commentator on the field, and her reviews and journalism helped shape the face of the genre during the 1950s and 1960s. Ultimately, Merril insisted on the plurality of the acronym "SF," refusing to see it as a ghetto circumscribed by narrow genre conventions but rather as the space in which

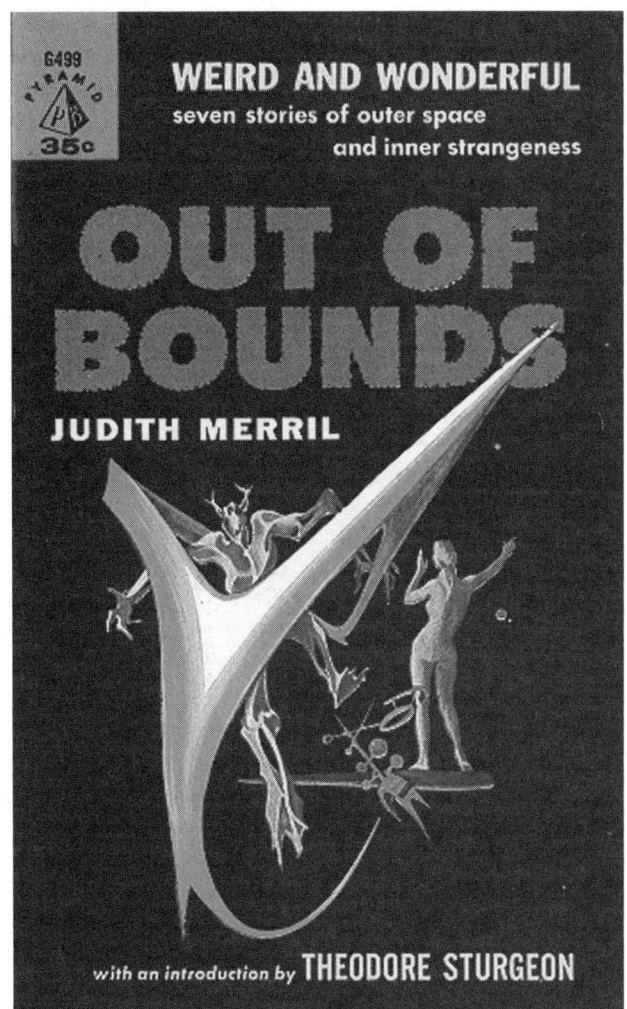

Cover for Merril's 1960 collection of science-fiction stories (courtesy of John B. Ower Science Fiction Collection, Rare Books and Special Collections, Thomas Cooper Library, University of South Carolina)

to create a new hybrid literature capable of successfully reflecting the myriad concerns of the late twentieth century. J. G. Ballard, in his article "The Widest Windows onto the New: A Tribute to Judith Merril," published in *Interzone* in April 1996, summed up Merril as "strong-willed and combative, sensitive and astute, quick to quarrel and forgive, the shrewdest judge of fiction, fearless exposer of humbug and pretension and capable of surprising shifts into a positively feline femininity that could be quite disorientating."

Only a handful of critical articles have been published on Merril's science fiction, the majority of them taking the form of entries in science-fiction encyclopedias. Although critics have tended to approach her writing from a similar perspective—examining it in relation to its historical moment, feminist thinking, and the conventions that typified contemporaneous genre science fiction—they are in no way unified in their attitudes to it. While commentators such as Elizabeth Cummins view Merril as an often-great writer whose work is an expression of feminist radicalism necessarily tempered by the constraints of the period in which it was written, Lisa Tuttle states in her entry for *The Encyclopedia of Science Fiction* (1993), "Women SF Writers," that Merril's fiction deals with "acceptable feminine concerns" in a sentimental fashion. Morgan, in his essay in *Science Fiction Writers* (1982), criticizes Merril for producing what he calls "kitchen-sink science fiction," practically devoid of character and pitched at "a perpetual emotional screech." Personal preferences and political orientation aside, there is a key reason that can be cited for the divergent opinions of these critics. Merril's best work reflects the suspicion of fixed ideological systems experienced by many intellectuals after World War II, thus denying the kind of unified reading that would allow her exact intentions to be pinpointed. The dilemma inherent in distinguishing between subjective and objective truths is a ubiquitous theme in her writing.

Merril was born Josephine Juliet Grossman on 21 January 1923, into a family of Jewish intellectuals in New York City. She became Judith Grossman unofficially soon after her birth, as a result of her grandmother's belated insistence that her parents should not name her after her famous grandfather, Rabbi Joseph Grossman. Her mother, Ethel Hurwitch, was a suffragette and a founder of Hadassah, the Women's Zionist Organization of America. Her father, Samuel Grossman, was involved with the group that founded the Yiddish Art Theatre and was also a writer in the Jewish educational field. Crippled physically by illness, emotionally by the death of his young son, and economically by the Great Depression, Samuel Grossman committed suicide when Judith was still a child. Merril's friend and agent, Virginia Kidd, has written in her introduction to *The Best of Judith Merril* (1976) that Merril found it extremely difficult to come to terms with his death. Kidd goes on to state that Merril's "handsome, creative father was not only the person for whom she was searching, but also—inevitably—the model she was striving to emulate." The absent father is a key image in Merril's fiction.

In 1936, when Judith was thirteen, she moved with her mother back to New York and, while attending the City College there, became involved with the Young People's Socialist League (YPSL), an involvement that led to her publishing articles in a Trotskyist periodical, *Challenge of Youth*. Her Jewish origins were an important influence on her formative years. In the text of his tribute speech, posted on a memorial website (http://www.chtorr.com/judithmerril.htm), Robinson quotes her: "I was born a Zionist in those golden days of socialist Zionism, and until I was in my early teens at least, knew that my future was in a kibbutz: I was preparing for it, and studied Hebrew until I was about fifteen, by which time I had progressed from social Zionism to socialism to the YPSLs, and no longer knew that my future was in a kibbutz." Merril's growing distance from her mother's religious beliefs coincided with her discovery that her mother wanted her to become a writer and "Certified Intellectual," and Merril claimed that as a rebellious consequence of this fact, she stopped writing at fifteen and "didn't start again until after I had a baby and I was in San Francisco and my mother was in New York."

In 1940 Judith Grossman, who was still in her teens, married Danny Zissman (a friend from the YPSL) and moved to Philadelphia. During this period, Zissman encouraged her to read his copies of *Astounding Science-Fiction,* but she declined. According to Robinson, Merril's search for reading matter in an attempt to divert herself from a simultaneous bout of toothache and grippe was what finally made her turn to her husband's magazines. After reading installments of Robert A. Heinlein's *Methuselah's Children* (1941) and L. Sprague de Camp's *The Stolen Dormouse* (1941), she was hooked, and upon regaining her health she immediately set out to acquire more science fiction. In 1941 the Zissmans returned to New York, and the following year their daughter, Merril, was born—although Judith Zissman initially borrowed her daughter's first name as her nom de plume, she acquired it legally after becoming a Canadian citizen.

By 1943 Danny Zissman was in the U.S. Navy, and Merril was, as she wrote in the July 1993 *New York Review of Science Fiction,* a "camp-following sailor's wife" living in San Francisco and writing again for the first time since her teens. Later in the same year, her husband overseas, she returned once again to New York and moved to Greenwich Village, where she engaged in an "experiment in communal living" with Kidd and their two children. She became involved with a science-fiction fan group called the Futurian Society of New York, a body of would-be writers who, to a large extent, shared Merril's left-wing views. Some members were openly communists. Because the majority of the Futurians were involved in the war effort, Merril's best friends during this period were those members not eligible for military service, namely Johnny Michel, Donald Wollheim, and Robert A. W. Lowndes. In 1945 she was divorced from Zissman.

While in New York, Merril worked as a file clerk and a waitress and published two "middling bad detective pulps" in such periodicals as *Crack Detective Magazine* before becoming an editor at Bantam Books in 1948. In the same year, after much encouragement from her new acquaintance Theodore Sturgeon, Merril published her first science-fiction short story, "That Only a Mother," which appeared to some acclaim in the then-prestigious *Astounding Science-Fiction*. The story has been anthologized many times since. Merril declared in an interview with David Seeds (1997) that "I did not think that I was good enough to write SF, and stated that opinion until Ted Sturgeon pounded on my head and said 'yes you are, yes you can, do it now.'" Sturgeon has given his own account of his early relationship with Merril in his introduction to her *Out of Bounds: Seven Stories* (1960).

In Merril's most important work of criticism, the 1966 *Extrapolation* article "What Do You Mean—Science? Fiction?," she writes that in the late 1930s *Astounding Science-Fiction* editor John W. Campbell aided the maturation of American genre science fiction greatly by insisting that his stable of writers produce work that dealt with the human impact of technology rather than simply with futuristic gadgetry. She goes on to lament, however, that Campbell's own technophilic personal interests led to his failure to maintain this sociological editorial directive. Much of Merril's fiction can be seen as a manifestation of Campbell's revolutionary vision. "That Only a Mother" and her first and best novel, *Shadow on the Hearth* (1950), for instance, are both concerned with the perils of nuclear technology; but instead of discussing the science underpinning that field, Merril concentrates on the lives of the ordinary people brought into contact with it. More unorthodox still, as far as male-oriented late-1940s science fiction is concerned, is that these people are wives and mothers. David G. Hartwell has stated, in the introduction to a 1978 reprint of Thomas M. Disch's *The Genocides* (1965), that "up to the early 1960s" American science fiction "stood for rationality, for the validity of the scientific method and the usefulness of scientific knowledge to solve problems." In "That Only a Mother" and *Shadow on the Hearth* female emotions—rather than any ratiocinative process—drive the respective narratives. This engagement with emotions rather than machines has led Brian Stableford to state, in *Survey of Science Fiction Literature* (1979), that Merril's work is "characterized by the ability to make science fiction themes individually significant to the reader."

"That Only a Mother" is set during a near-future war and deals with the experiences of Maggie, a young woman who gives birth while her nuclear-technician husband is away from home serving with the military. Although Maggie's letters to her spouse, throughout the narrative, reassure him that their offspring is completely normal—having escaped the mutations inflicting many newborn babies in the United States—it ultimately transpires that the child has no arms or legs, and that Maggie either has been intentionally deluding her-

Dust jacket for a volume of the science-fiction anthology that Merril began in 1956 and edited, under various titles, until 1968

self or is in fact psychotic. The story is mediated in two ways: in the form of edited extracts from her various correspondences and via Maggie's perception of events related in the third person. This structure denies the reader access to the young woman's internal motivations, and as such not only makes her actions extremely unsettling but also makes problematic the extent to which they can be positioned politically. If Maggie is understood to have been driven insane by the stress of bearing a mutated child, then the pejorative image of feeble femininity so common in traditional genre science fiction and Western culture is perpetuated. If, however, she is perceived to have taken the decision to disregard the societal norms that govern her world and live by rules of her own devising, then the story can be seen to have a more-radical edge.

Given the fact that much of Merril's later, less politically ambiguous science fiction takes the form of social critique, it seems reasonable to read "That Only a Mother" in the same way, and to view Maggie's actions as a repudiation of the world that surrounds her—a world that is significantly similar to late-1940s America. Merril makes clear the symbolic parallels between the near-future world of her story (set in 1953) and her contemporaneous reality: she incorporates no futuristic trappings beyond a few labor-saving domestic devices, already beginning to proliferate in the United States at that time; she bases her narrative on the Cold War anxieties that were building at the time it was published; and she refers to "Oak Ridge," an actual nuclear research facility. Several examples of what Merril refers to in her *Extrapolation* article as a "Preaching Story," one that condemns the dawn of the nuclear age, appeared in the West from the 1940s onward. However, Merril's work is atypical of this kind, suggesting that in addition to the threat of radioactivity, the U.S. population is also in danger from the country itself. The text makes no mention of what country the United States is supposed to be in conflict with, an omission made all the more significant by the implicit suggestion that the American media, if not fabricating the war completely, may be at least falsifying reports of it—*"Now Maggie, don't get started on that. No accidents. No hits. Take the nice newspaper's word for it."* Furthermore, despite statements to the contrary from the American medical body, the radiation that has mutated Maggie's child possibly originates from her husband, Hank, as a consequence of his time working at Oak Ridge. This situation is made darker by the implication that Hank may well murder his child because of its deformity, despite the fact that the child appears to possess a highly precocious intelligence.

The 1950s were a hugely productive and successful period for Merril. She had married Frederik Pohl, another prominent science-fiction writer, in 1949, after meeting him at the 1947 Worldcon in Philadelphia. On 25 September 1950 she gave birth to their daughter, Ann. In the same year, Pohl and Lester del Rey formed a science-fiction writers' group, the Hydra Club, with Merril among its initial nine members, and Merril published *Shadow on the Hearth*. The work was critically well received—*The New York Times* dedicated an entire daily column to it—and was eventually made into *Atomic Attack*, a 1950 television presentation that starred Phyllis Thaxter and Walter Matthau.

There are several parallels between "That Only a Mother" and *Shadow on the Hearth*. Both works encompass an antinuclear agenda and are mediated through the eyes of a woman, stressing that the domestic space and the battlefield, which were such separate entities for the American population during World War II, would become horribly conflated in the event of a nuclear war. The works differ, however, in their presentation of the mundane. While Maggie's equivocal mental state and the possibility of a murderous mate give "That Only a Mother" a Gothic sensibility, *Shadow on the Hearth* is far more rooted in the everyday, and the admonitory power of the work is therefore more potent. The novel details the attempts made by a timorous American housewife, Gladys Mitchell, to maintain some semblance of domestic normality despite the fact that her husband, Jon, is missing in the radioactive diaspora surrounding Manhattan Island, which has been devastated by an atomic bomb. To make matters worse, Gladys also has to contend with the facts that her daughters, Ginny and Barbara, may have been contaminated by radioactive rain; her son, Tom, a technical student, has been "mobilized into the Army"; and a fugitive, Dr. Levy, is using her house as a hideout because he is wanted by the authorities. Almost all of the action in the novel takes place in the Mitchells' home, with the horrors of the "poisoned wasteland" permeating this sphere only through radio bulletins and the reports of the antiradiation-suited militia (the hospital scenes and the brief glimpses of Jon's apocalyptic surroundings are the only exceptions).

This image of the home as claustrophobic prison has a dual agenda. On the one hand, it is central to the antinuclear aspect of the novel—stressing that atomic weapons have rendered obsolete any notion of the home as sanctuary. On the other hand, it frames the feminist theme of the novel. Gladys's entrapment within the domestic environment during the nuclear war is ultimately an extreme version of her everyday position as housewife. Yet, within this hostile space she is able to acquire a sense of self, which is not dependent on her husband. Initially Gladys is barely able to function without Jon's presence, pitifully pleading for him to return when she first confronts the disheveled fugitive, Dr. Levy. But as the work continues, she secures more independence, and the point at which she removes Jon's symbolic woolen robe represents the beginnings of a new, stronger Gladys, capable of repelling intruders from her home, be they looters or sexual predators such as the lubricious neighbor-turned-official, Mr. Turner.

For all her triumphs, however, Gladys's story does not end happily. Merril sold the novel to the Family Book Club, who for commercial reasons replaced the original ending—in which Jon Mitchell is shot dead by a military patrol as he approaches his own house—with one in which he successfully completes his grueling journey. Despite these editorial changes, the work nevertheless concludes on a grim note: Gladys's declaration that "the war's *over*" belies the fact that her family's nightmare may just be beginning, given the genetic mutations that followed the attacks on Hiroshima and Nagasaki, which were becoming common knowledge at the end of the 1940s. In 1966, while in the United Kingdom, Merril partially restored her original text for an edition published by Roberts and Vinter.

Similarly to "That Only a Mother," there is an implicit suggestion in *Shadow on the Hearth* that the United States population is threatened by a variety of internal rather than external forces: the trigger-happy troops enforcing martial law (and intentionally interrogating pedestrians past curfew so that they can be immediately re-arrested); the media, whose untrustworthy reports make the motive of the controlling U.S. military body as sinister as it is unclear; the looters who are repelled by the Mitchell household's frying-pan fusillade; or the government investigators whose racism seems to be their key motivation for arresting Gladys's maid, Veda Klopak, on suspicion of sabotage. Although the latter's name appears to be of East European origin, her dialect has traces of black English, implicitly stressing that the demonization of difference in 1950s America is not restricted to the Russians and Chinese. Moreover, it is a telling comment on the nature of a society that was gripped at the time by McCarthyism that Dr. Levy is wanted for his attempts at educating the American public about the horrors of nuclear catastrophe. This dystopian picture of a paranoid United States disseminating misinformation, killing its own, and manipulating the threat of external enemies as a means of societal control at home is one that prefigures the themes of much American science fiction written during the 1950s. Moreover, the depiction of the political aspects of the wartorn country highlights another key aspect of Merril's work, science fiction as social criticism.

During this period Merril was also involved with several collaborative projects. She wrote *Outpost Mars* (1952), *Gunner Cade* (1952), and "Sea-Change" (1953) with Pohl's good friend Cyril (C. M.) Kornbluth, under the joint pseudonym Cyril Judd, as well as writing "A Big Man with the Girls" (1963) with Pohl (writing as James MacCreigh) and "Death Cannot Wither" (1967) with A. J. Budrys. In 1957 she also published two stories, "A Woman of the World" and "The Lady Was a Tramp," under the pseudonym Rose Sharon, for fear that their risqué themes would be unfavorably received. Merril and Pohl divorced in 1953.

In an article she wrote for *The New York Review of Science Fiction* in July 1993, Merril states her belief that "art is by nature revolutionary" and that "a vital function of the artist" is "to produce and publish 'virtual realities' of social change." Given her pacifistic, left-wing political beliefs and the illiberal, nationalistic bent of 1950s American society, Merril's radicalism is unsurprising. Throughout her body of fiction she continually presents sociological paradigms that are diametrically opposed to the social conventions prevalent in her native country. The least ambiguous of the works featuring such models are the novels she wrote with Kornbluth, *Outpost Mars* and *Gunner Cade*.

Both these texts have been ignored by critics or dismissed as routine, but they are significant for the politically unorthodox themes underpinning them. Kornbluth's political beliefs were to the Left, similar to Merril's, and he too made it clear that he saw science fiction as a potentially subversive medium, in his essay "The Failure of Science Fiction as Social Criticism." *Outpost Mars*—originally serialized in *Galaxy* as "Mars Child" between May and July 1951—is a relatively unambiguous critique of the social and ecological ramifications of both a capitalist economy and the media that maintains its naturalized status. In the novel Mars has become a hellish, industrialized extension of a resource-exhausted Earth, where male workers become addicted to the narcotic they manufacture, and women prostitute themselves. Overseeing this seamy state of affairs is the corrupt governor of the planet, Hamilton Bell, who also looks after the interests of Mars's most powerful and avaricious businessman, Brenner. In opposition to the activities of these two men are the heroes of the work, a multiracial Martian colony that is run along socialist lines, the nucleus of which is the wise and kindly Dr. Tony Hellman. The colonists wish to break free from their economic and technological reliance on both Earth and the Martian industrialists, but are hampered by several factors. They are wrongly accused by Bell of stealing a consignment of Brenner's drug "marcaine" and must find it before they are shut down; a notoriety-hungry writer on Earth, Douglas Graham, publishes spurious defamatory reports about the colony; and Brenner attempts to bribe the colonists into leaving Mars so that he can acquire their laboratories and increase his pharmaceutical production. The colony eventually vanquishes the evil industrialists, proves its innocence, and becomes self-sufficient.

Merril wrote in her *Extrapolation* article that "science fiction was, for a time, virtually the only vehicle of political dissent" in the United States, and this point is amply demonstrated by *Outpost Mars*. The work not only condemned free enterprise at the height of the Joseph McCarthy witchhunts but also featured generously delineated characters who are, as one of their antagonists makes clear, "communists." In addition to its political unconventionality the work is also heterodox in genre terms. The novel is a breakaway from the science-centric science fiction of the 1950s and a move toward speculative fiction, which Merril championed in her capacity as an anthologist. Broadly speaking, speculative fiction is concerned with societal rather than technological extrapolation: the detailing of an egalitarian interaction between sexual and racial

Dust jacket for the U.S. edition (1969) of Merril's collection that includes, in addition to the title work, Project Nursemaid and Homecalling

The recurrent engagement with the militaristic in Merril's fiction can be seen as part of a more overarching theme in her work, which Cummins describes in the Fall 1992 issue of *Extrapolation* as an examination of "the relationship of self and other." In "Whoever You Are"–published in the December 1952 issue of *Startling Stories*–this theme overlays a narrative dealing with the response of Earth's military to a group of extraterrestrials who have been caught attempting to breach the protective force field that encompasses the solar system. Investigators who are sent onto the tranquilized interlopers' ship find contradictory evidence as to their intentions. A message from a human astronaut, whose ship the aliens are flying, states that the aliens are a loving, telepathic race who want only to exchange knowledge with humanity. A hidden journal written by the captain of the mission shortly before he killed himself, however, declares that the aliens have his crew "under some form of hypnotic control" and must not be trusted. The ambiguity as to the captain's state of mind and the real motives of the aliens make it impossible for the "Staff of Solar Defense" or the reader to determine the truth of the situation. This uncertainty leads to the former group destroying the alien ship, killing an American astronaut in the process.

As with all of Merril's best work, the metaphorical dimensions of this story are manifold. On one level, it can be seen as a plaintive admission that the paranoia engendered by the Cold War demonization of "the other" has made the epistemological dilemmas of life even more pronounced for the American population. In such a distrustful climate, love and hate become indistinguishable. The work also intimates, through the image of the impenetrable shield hermetically sealing in American bodies, that the creation of "iron curtains" is a practice not restricted to the communist sphere–the American ban on the free interchange of scientific information after 1949 was implicitly criticized in many stories published in the science-fiction magazines in the 1950s. On another level, the presence of a character called "Gentile" and the destruction of aliens who are dark-skinned and human in form suggest that the work is also a comment on the racist mentality that divided 1950s America.

In the story "Daughters of Earth" (1952) the interaction of alien races is once again broached, this time within another favorite science-fiction frame of Merril's, the colonization of space. The narrative takes the form of journal entries written by successive generations of women pioneers, whose interstellar expeditions take them ever farther away from Earth. The central narrative within this fragmented collection details how a human colony splits into two ideological factions when its first contact with an alien life form, the

groups is far more important to its authors than any discussion of hard science.

As well as criticizing American demonization of "non-American" political views, Merril also condemned her country's use of militarism against alternative political systems. Merril and Kornbluth's other collaborative novel, *Gunner Cade*–originally published in *Astounding Science-Fiction* between March and May 1952–deals with a venal, totalitarian government that draws attention away from its own corruption by orchestrating wars, which are followed by the media in the same way as if they were sporting events. Through the course of the narrative, an elite soldier, Cade, slowly comes to realize that the pseudo-religious creeds that justify his participation in these wars are without foundation. By pointing out the mutability of ideological systems, the novel forces readers to consider the worth of their own beliefs and the validity of the political system that governs their own lives.

Ullerns, results in the death of a colonist. While one group wants to exterminate the Ullerns immediately, the other believes, correctly, that the fatality was accidental and wishes to understand and communicate with the aliens. The story ends with the liberal group, the unquestionable heroes of the piece, venturing into space as technologically advanced partners with the Ullerns. The inclusion in the work of the term "gooks," the reference to a "28th Parallel"–a term evocative of the 38th Parallel, which divided North and South Korea–and the presence of unsympathetic and bellicose Americans attempting to exterminate a culture that they do not understand all indicate that to some degree the story is a comment on American encounters with the "communist other" in the Korean War, which was contemporary with the writing of the story.

The motif of self and other in "Daughters of Earth" also engages with another dominant theme in Merril's work: feminism. Just as the narrative implies a need for interracial understanding, it also clearly posits the need for more understanding between the sexes. By describing a future society in which women are free to live in whatever fashion they choose–roaming the galaxy if they so wish–the work throws into stark relief the lack of options available to women in 1950s American society. Furthermore, the fact that the story takes the form of a women-authored journal detailing alternative female experiences suggests that women must take issue with the unequal stereotypes prevalent in patriarchal society and present new, positive images of femininity. Like many of Merril's works, the short story "Stormy Weather," published in the Summer 1954 issue of *Startling Stories,* includes such an image. The narrative deals with female astronaut and telepath Catherine Andauer, who single-handedly pilots a space station in Earth's orbit–a job she has acquired because women are more suited to it than men of the same age. Despite being preoccupied with concerns over her relationship–her boyfriend has not been in psychic contact for three days–Catherine nevertheless nonchalantly saves the world by destroying a "parti-cloud," a deadly "mass of fragmentary rocks and pebbles," which is on course for Earth. The story is not only engaged in celebrating female equality/superiority, it is also a subversion of the space-suited-damsel-in-distress role assigned to so many women characters in 1950s science-fiction motion pictures, fiction, and illustrations. This sense of genre play is enhanced by the hybridity of the work: half "hard" science fiction–full of details of the technological minutia necessary to maintain life on board the station–and half women's romance tale.

Another key feminist work by Merril is "Dead Center," first published in the November 1954 issue of *The Magazine of Fantasy and Science Fiction.* Stableford describes it as "one of the most emotionally powerful science fiction stories ever written," and it was reprinted in *Best American Short Stories 1955.* The story is an example of the way in which Merril uses prejudice, in this case about gender roles, for didactic ends. It deals with the plight of Ruth Kruger, the wife of Jock Kruger, the first astronaut to land on the moon; she is the co-designer of the rocket that takes him there. After a mistake on his part, possibly brought about by his worries over his wife's unidentifiable misgivings about the mission, he is marooned on the moon, and Ruth is assigned the task of designing the rescue ship. Her distraction during this project leads to her neglecting her young son, Toby; erroneously believing that his mother is planning to leave Earth on the retrieval rocket, Toby stows away on board, causing it to crash and kill him. Because of this incident Ruth commits suicide, and Jock starves to death before help can arrive.

The complexity of the work rests, to a large degree, in the way in which it manipulates the reader's assumptions about the role of women. The delineation of a female scientist (a rare thing in 1950s science fiction) who fails in her professional capacity and in her roles as wife and mother could be seen as a reactionary avocation of female domesticity. However, close reading of the work reveals that the limiting cultural mores inherent in Ruth's world, rather than Ruth's behavior per se, are what lead to her family's downfall. There is an implicit suggestion, for instance, that Jock's fatal doubts arise from his knowledge that the designer of his ship is a woman. Moreover, Toby's emotional turmoil as a consequence of being inculcated with the belief that he, as a male, should look after his mother, is a key factor in his fatal actions. Ultimately, the story suggests that revolutionary cultural changes must take place if women are to be able to function alongside men as equals in the workplace.

Although Merril attacks sexual inequality and pejorative cultural stereotypes, she does not, as Cummins points out in the Fall 1992 *Extrapolation,* question the extent to which gender itself may be a cultural construct, nor does she contest "the underlying hierarchical pattern of patriarchy." Cummins, taking her theoretical lead from feminist writer Sarah Lefanu, describes this variety of sexual politics as "feminised" rather than "feminist." Cummins goes on to state that Merril's employment of female characters who are innately superior to men in certain regards–being more suited to space travel, for instance–also intimates that she did not contest the biological essentialist view that the sexes are intrinsically different. Cummins does not dismiss Merril's feminism; she simply highlights how its limitations are a product of the thinking that defined Merril's historical moment.

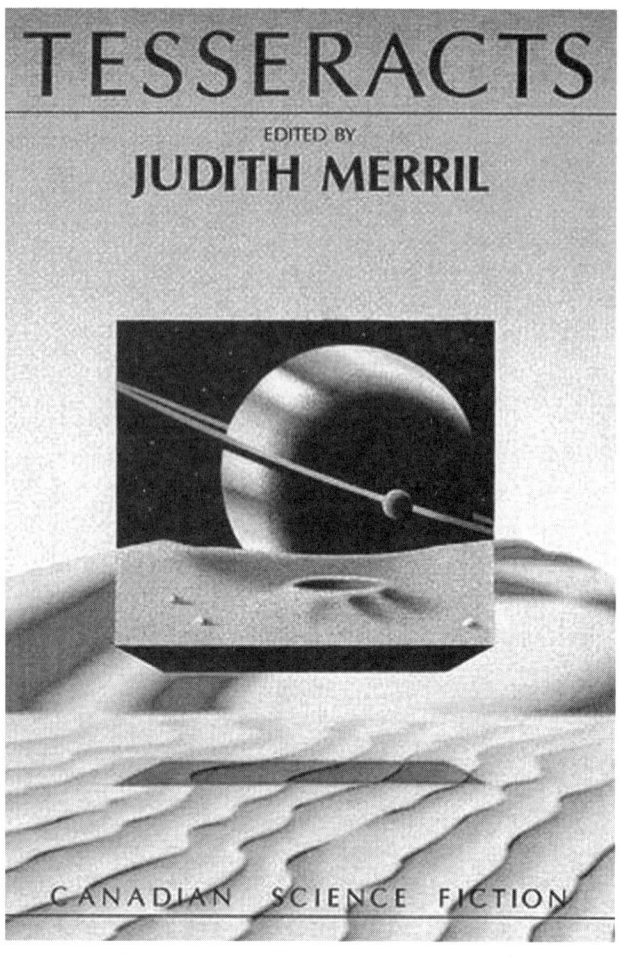

Cover for the 1985 volume, edited by Merril, that began the series of ground-breaking Canadian science-fiction anthologies

Merril's feminism can also be seen to have influenced her choice of science-fiction motifs. While she usually shunned the masculine realm of technological exposition, she embraced other aspects of 1950s genre science fiction more appropriate to her concerns. Extrasensory perception (ESP), for instance, generally taking the form of either telepathy or a heightened empathic understanding of others' feelings, plays a central role in many of her stories. The fact that John W. Campbell's interest in the paranormal initiated a "psi-boom" in 1950s science fiction makes it tempting to see this trend as being economically motivated. However, the way in which Merril uses the motif to enhance the humanistic preoccupations in her work undermines this suggestion somewhat. Anna's capacity for receiving and understanding the emotions of her fellow colonists in *Outpost Mars,* for instance, underlines the anticapitalist agenda of the work. Her empathic abilities, which are portrayed as a kind of enhanced "female sensitivity," are a warm, antiscientific foil to the coldly rational minds of her group's antagonists. In "Connection Completed," first published in the November 1954 issue of *Universe,* Merril uses the motif as means of plaintively highlighting the emotional turmoil endured by alienated city dwellers by making it ambiguous as to whether a desperately lonely man is in telepathic contact with a woman he sees in a cafeteria or is merely imagining it. In *The Tomorrow People* (1960) a Martian organism, rather than using its telepathic powers to enslave humanity—a stock theme in much genre science fiction—instead shows its willingness for contact by broadcasting messages of love.

The significance of Merril's second and last novel, *The Tomorrow People,* lies in the extent to which it is an extreme expression of her dissatisfaction with the clichéd conventions of traditional science fiction—which, although being established during the 1930s and 1940s, still held powerful sway over the genre at the beginning of the 1960s, particularly in the realm of science-fiction cinema. The novel details the decline of protagonist Johnny Wendt, an astronaut who has become a violent alcoholic after returning from Earth's second Mars shot without his colleague, Doug Laughlin. Fueling Wendt's dissolution are his failings as a lover with his partner Lisa Trovi, the knowledge that he has been diagnosed as having experienced homosexual desire for Doug, and his fear of space flight. Clearly, such a protagonist is a radical break from the masculine heroes of space opera, and Merril overtly indicates that her novel is in dialogue with the pulp science-fiction magazines that featured such figures. At one point in the work it is stated that "If it was a magazine story . . . little Mars-bugs would turn out to be secret-super-intelligences with invincible powers, from Betelgeuse. . . . Pretty soon they'd take the whole world over, too—except for The Hero, who'd dash in and save everyone just in time." Wendt is anything but a hero, flawed by his humanity like so many of the characters in the story.

By positioning her work in opposition to hackneyed, preconceived notions of what science fiction should be, Merril prefigures the thinking behind much of the so-called New Wave writings. In addition to its author's favorite motifs—telepathy, planetary colonization, and the magnanimous alien—*The Tomorrow People* encompasses themes that became central to the revolutionary mid-1960s development of science fiction: the mad astronaut, a preoccupation with sexual relations and psychological motivation, and the employment of alien landscapes that metaphorically represent psychological states. Just as moribund Mars symbolizes the barren heart of capitalist endeavor in *Outpost Mars,* in *The Tomorrow People* the arid slopes of the planet represent Wendt's mental dislocation.

Merril's reputation as a pioneering anthologist was established in the 1950s. She edited five science-fiction collections between 1950 and 1955 before initiating her famous *Year's Best* series, which ran from 1956 until 1968. Cummins has suggested, in the Spring 1994 issue of *Extrapolation,* that the impact of the series on the development of science fiction makes Merril the most influential science-fiction anthologist ever to have worked in the field. Whether this claim is true or not, as John Clute pointed out in 25 September 1997 issue of *The Guardian,* Merril's skill at "scouring non-SF journals for SF stories published for reason of commercial camouflage without the label" ensured that her collections continually pushed the boundaries of the genre, and in doing so gathered praise and criticism in roughly equal measure. In Merril's anthologies experimental fiction by such authors as Jorge Luis Borges appeared alongside works by more traditional science-fiction names, such as Isaac Asimov. In the same year that the initiatory *Year's Best* collection appeared, Merril, along with Damon Knight and James Blish, also organized the first Milford Science Fiction Writers Conference, an institution she directed until 1961 that still survives in a British incarnation.

During the 1960s Merril's standing as a science-fiction commentator eclipsed her role as an author. After the publication of *The Tomorrow People* she published only three science-fiction short stories, all of which, Stableford points out, were "commissioned to accompany cover illustrations." Nevertheless, Merril's job as book reviewer for the esteemed magazine *Fantasy and Science Fiction* and her annual state-of-science-fiction editorials in the *Year's Best* series ensured that she remained a prominent figure within fandom. During this period Merril is perhaps most famous for her involvement with what became known as the New Wave. However, despite championing the work of the writers and editors who made up this "movement" after attending the World SF Convention in England in 1964, and editing the experimental anthology *England Swings SF: Stories of Speculative Fiction* (1968), she did not coin the term *New Wave,* as has been claimed, and later came "to regret its use." Cummins, in the Fall 1995 issue of *Extrapolation,* has examined Merril's relation to this literary phenomena and shown that it was far more balanced and less didactic than has previously been suggested, a fact testified to by Merril's two-part essay "What Do You Mean—Science? Fiction?" and various articles for *Fantasy and Science Fiction* written between May 1965 and May 1969. Merril championed the radical moves away from genre convention, but she in no way considered the New Wave as the terminus of the evolution of science fiction. During the 1960s Merril also got married for the last time, to merchant mariner and union organizer Daniel Sugrue; they divorced in 1975.

In 1966 Merril, by then the science-fiction editor of *Playboy,* went on a material-gathering trip to England, a visit that ultimately resulted in her permanently leaving the United States. She stated, in an interview published in *The Best of Judith Merril,* that during her stay in the U.K. she was shocked by reports of the Vietnam conflict in "the foreign press instead of the American press," and this realization, along with the hostility she faced from foreign nationals angry at the continuation of the war, led to her resolving to return to the United States to "*do something about it.*" In the spring of 1967 she did return home, but was as unable to sanction the actions of revolutionaries as she was those of the Lyndon Johnson administration. Although Merril organized the famous "for and against the war" article in the June 1968 edition of *Galaxy* and campaigned against the draft, she finally left the United States after her first-hand experience of the violent suppression of an anti-war demonstration at the Democratic National Convention in Chicago in August 1968.

Upon her arrival in Toronto in 1969 Merril moved into Rochdale College, where she embraced the countercultural bent of the place, aiding draft dodgers and deserters and acting as guru to the hippie populace. When the college closed in 1970, her collection of five thousand books, which had originally been donated to the institution, was moved to the Toronto Public Library, where it became "The Spaced Out Library" and then, despite Merril's protests, "The Merril Collection." Her move away from the United States did nothing to lift the writer's block that had prevented her from writing new science fiction for years, but as always, she continued her involvement with the field while also working for the Canadian Broadcasting Corporation orchestrating documentaries. Merril was also engaged in a variety of other science-fiction-related endeavors in her new home country. She worked to establish a place for Canadian science fiction in school curricula; she toured the country giving readings and lectures and running writing workshops; and she introduced TVOntario's broadcasts of *Dr. Who* between 1978 and 1981. She also was involved with SeCon, the Secondary Universe 4 Conference, which took place in Toronto in 1971 and which encouraged the study of science fiction by Canadian academics. Moreover, she also received several Canadian arts-council grants to write her memoirs. Although only a fragment of her autobiographical writings was published in her lifetime (in the July 1993 edition of *The New York Review of Science Fiction*), a box of unpublished papers was discovered in Merril's apartment after her death from heart failure on 12 September 1997.

Merril's status in the country in which she eventually became a citizen is made clear by the mass of tributes from fellow science-fiction writers, colleagues, and fans after her demise, and by the two lifetime achievement Casper Awards, the Canadian Science Fiction awards, that she received—one in 1983 for contributions to the field, and one in 1986 for achievements in editing. As David Ketterer has noted in *Canadian Science Fiction and Fantasy* (1992), Merril "played a major role in enlivening and promoting Canadian SF," as an editor, as a promoter of Canadian science fiction and of science fiction in Canada, and as a mentor. Canadian science fiction did not really exist before Merril's arrival in Canada, and it was an undeniable fact by the time of her death. Certainly, she was not solely responsible for the remarkable development of Canadian science fiction in the last decades of the twentieth century, but few have made as significant a contribution to it as she did.

Interviews:

David Seed, "One of Postwar SF's Formative Figures," *Interzone* (December 1997): 13–26;

Mark Rich, "Remembering Cyril: An Interview with Judith Merril," *New York Review Science Fiction*, 12 (September 1999): 1, 4–6.

References:

Paul Brians, "Nuclear Family/Nuclear War," *Papers on Language and Literature*, 26 (Winter 1990): 134–142;

Elizabeth Cummins, "Short Fiction by Judith Merril," *Extrapolation*, 33 (Fall 1992): 202–214;

Cummins, "Judith Merril: Scouting SF," *Extrapolation*, 35 (Spring 1994): 5–14;

Cummins, "Judith Merril: A Link with the New Wave– Then and Now," *Extrapolation*, 36 (Fall 1995): 198–209;

Samuel R. Delany, "A Tribute to Judith Merril," *New York Review of Science Fiction*, 10 (November 1997): 1, 9;

Terence Holt, "The Bomb and the Baby Boom," *Tri-Quarterly*, 80 (Winter 1990–1991): 206–220;

Richard Law, "Science Fiction Women: Victims, Rebels, Heroes," in *Proceedings of the Second Annual Conference of EAPSCU,* edited by Malcolm Hayward (English Association of the Pennsylvania State Colleges and Universities, 1983), pp. 53–58;

Chris Morgan, "Judith Merril," in *Science Fiction Writers: Critical Studies of the Major Authors from the Early Nineteenth Century to the Present Day,* edited by Everett Franklin Bleiler (New York: Scribner, 1982), pp. 433–439;

Catherine Podojil, "Sisters, Daughters, and Aliens," in *Critical Encounters: Writers and Themes in Science Fiction,* edited by Dick Riley (New York: Ungar, 1978), pp. 70–86;

Brian Stableford, "The Short Fiction of Judith Merril," in *Survey of Science Fiction Literature,* volume 4, edited by Frank N. Magill (New Jersey: Salem Press, 1979).

Brian Moore
(25 August 1921 – 11 January 1999)

Darren Harris-Fain
Shawnee State University

BOOKS: *Wreath for a Redhead* (Toronto: Harlequin, 1951); republished as *Sailor's Leave* (New York: Pyramid, 1953);

The Executioners (Toronto: Harlequin, 1951);

French for Murder, as Bernard Mara (New York: Fawcett, 1954);

A Bullet for My Lady, as Mara (New York: Fawcett, 1954);

Judith Hearne (London: Deutsch, 1955; Toronto: Collins, 1955); republished as *The Lonely Passion of Judith Hearne* (Boston: Little, Brown, 1956); republished as *The Lonely Passion of Miss Judith Hearne* (Harmondsworth, U.K.: Penguin, 1959);

This Gun for Gloria, as Mara (New York: Fawcett, 1956);

Intent to Kill, as Michael Bryan (London: Eyre & Spottiswoode, 1956; New York: Dell, 1956);

The Feast of Lupercal (Boston: Little, Brown, 1957; London: Deutsch, 1958); republished as *A Moment of Love* (London: Panther, 1965);

Murder in Majorca, as Bryan (New York: Dell, 1957; London: Eyre & Spottiswoode, 1958);

The Luck of Ginger Coffey (Boston: Little, Brown, 1960; London: Deutsch, 1960);

An Answer from Limbo (Boston: Little, Brown, 1962; London: Deutsch, 1963);

Canada, with the editors of *Life* (New York: Time, 1963);

The Emperor of Ice-Cream (Toronto: McClelland & Stewart, 1965; New York: Viking, 1965; London: Deutsch, 1966);

I Am Mary Dunne (Toronto: McClelland & Stewart, 1968; New York: Viking, 1968; London: Cape, 1968);

Fergus (Toronto: McClelland & Stewart, 1970; New York: Holt, Rinehart & Winston, 1970; London: Cape, 1971);

The Revolution Script (Toronto: McClelland & Stewart, 1971; New York: Holt, Rinehart & Winston, 1971; London: Cape, 1972);

Brian Moore (photograph by Miriam Berkley; from the dust jacket for The Magician's Wife, *1998)*

Catholics (Toronto: McClelland & Stewart, 1972; London: Cape, 1972; New York: Holt, Rinehart & Winston, 1973);

The Great Victorian Collection (Toronto: McClelland & Stewart, 1975; New York: Farrar, Straus & Giroux, 1975; London: Cape, 1975);

The Doctor's Wife (Toronto: McClelland & Stewart, 1976; New York: Farrar, Straus & Giroux, 1976; London: Cape, 1976);

Two Stories (Northridge, Cal.: Santa Susana Press, 1978);

Family Album (New York: Farrar, Straus & Giroux, 1979); republished as *The Mangan Inheritance* (Toronto: McClelland & Stewart, 1979; London: Cape, 1979);

The Temptation of Eileen Hughes (Toronto: McClelland & Stewart, 1981; New York: Farrar, Straus & Giroux, 1981; London: Cape, 1981);

Cold Heaven (Toronto: McClelland & Stewart, 1983; New York: Holt, Rinehart & Winston, 1983; London: Cape, 1983);

Black Robe (Toronto: McClelland & Stewart, 1985; New York: Dutton, 1985; London: Cape, 1985);

The Color of Blood (Toronto: McClelland & Stewart, 1987; New York: Dutton, 1987; London: Cape, 1987);

Lies of Silence (New York: Doubleday, 1990; London: Bloomsbury, 1990);

No Other Life (New York: N. A. Talese, 1993; London: Bloomsbury, 1993);

The Statement (London: Bloomsbury, 1995; New York: Dutton, 1996);

The Magician's Wife (London: Bloomsbury, 1997; New York: Dutton, 1998).

PLAY PRODUCTION: *Catholics*, ACT: A Contemporary Theatre, Seattle, May 1980.

PRODUCED SCRIPTS: *The Luck of Ginger Coffey*, motion picture, Continental, 1964;

Torn Curtain, motion picture, Universal, 1966;

Catholics, television, CBS, November 1973;

Le Sang des autres (The Blood of Others), television, Antenne-2, 1984;

Black Robe, motion picture, Alliance, 1991.

OTHER: "A Vocation," in *The Irish Genius*, edited by Devin A. Garritty (New York: New American Library, 1960), pp. 125–128;

"Grieve for the Dear Departed," in *Pick of Today's Short Stories*, no. 12, edited by John Pudney (London: Putnam, 1961), pp. 179–188;

"Off the Track," in *Ten for Wednesday Night*, edited by Robert Weaver (Toronto: McClelland & Stewart, 1961), pp. 159–167; republished in *Modern Canadian Stories*, edited by Giose Rimanelli and Roberto Ruberto (Toronto: Ryerson, 1966), pp. 239–246;

"Lion of the Afternoon," in *A Book of Canadian Stories*, edited by Desmond Pacey (Toronto: Ryerson, 1962), pp. 283–293;

"Preliminary Pages for a Work of Revenge," in *The Dolmen: Miscellany of Irish Writing*, edited by John Montague and Thomas Kinsella (Dublin: Dolmen, 1962), pp. 1–7; republished in *Canadian Writing Today*, edited by Mordecai Richler (Harmondsworth, U.K.: Penguin, 1970), pp. 135–145;

"The Sight," in *Irish Ghost Stories*, edited by Joseph Hone (London: Hamilton, 1977), pp. 100–119.

SELECTED PERIODICAL PUBLICATIONS–UNCOLLECTED: "The Expatriate Writer," *Antigonish Review*, 17 (Spring 1974): 27–30;

"The Writer as Exile," *Canadian Journal of Irish Studies*, 2 (December 1976): 5–17;

"The State of Fiction," *New Review*, 5 (Summer 1978): 52–53;

"Going Home," *New York Times Book Review*, 7 February 1999, pp. 7, 27.

Brian Moore is often discussed as one of the last modern practitioners of fiction in the realist mode, and indeed realist is an apt description of most of his novels. In a handful of his works, however, he abandons the strictly mimetic in favor of the fantastic, with impressive results. Though he was thus not a writer of genre fantasy by any means, such excursions into another mode of fiction were hardly unusual for Moore, who throughout his career straddled the border between "popular" and "serious" fiction.

The straddling of borders, in fact, could be taken as a metaphor for Moore's life and career. Although he spent most of his life in North America, he wrote frequently about his native Northern Ireland. Much of his fiction is set in Canada, where he lived for eleven years, but he also wrote a fair amount about the United States, where he lived from 1959 until his death in 1999. Moore began his career as a novelist writing mostly pseudonymous crime thrillers published in the popular paperback format, but at the same time he was working on serious, realistic novels such as *Judith Hearne* (1955) and *The Luck of Ginger Coffey* (1960). Moore also crossed borders by adapting certain ones of his novels for theater, cinema, and television productions.

In a way, Moore is a throwback to the fiction writers of the late-Victorian and Edwardian periods. Like many British writers in the late nineteenth and early twentieth centuries, he was prolific and extremely diverse, with an audience both diffuse and difficult to characterize. He was equally comfortable writing realistic fiction or fantasy about the past or the present. His work is well crafted, yet the craft is practically invisible. As Bruce Stovel observes in speaking of Moore's writing, "realism is not a matter of content, nor a credo, but a formal term describing a certain kind of story told in a certain way." In this sense, even Moore's fantasies can be called realistic.

Brian (pronounced BREE-an) Moore was born on 25 August 1921 in Belfast, Northern Ireland, one of nine children of James Bernard Moore, a surgeon and university lecturer, and Eileen McFadden Moore. His family's highest values were education and their Roman Catholic faith. Even in childhood Moore chafed under the strictures of organized religion, and eventually he abandoned Catholicism altogether. Nor did he entirely fulfill his parents' expectations for his education. He attended Catholic schools in Belfast, but he left St. Malachy's College in 1938. The experience was typically nightmarish, as is revealed in his fictional depictions of Irish Catholic education in the 1930s. Even though Moore began taking classes in Belfast offered through the University of London in 1938, the start of World War II the following year effectively terminated his formal studies. Moore was thus largely self-educated.

In 1940 Moore volunteered for Belfast's Air Raid Precautions Unit and National Fire Service, and in April 1941 he experienced the German air attacks on the city. He became a port official with the British Ministry of War Transport in 1943, and over the next two years he followed Allied occupation forces into France, Italy, and northern Africa. In Poland, toward the end of the war, he visited the liberated Nazi concentration camp in Auschwitz and witnessed the advance of Russian troops. After the war Moore remained in Poland as an official with the United Nations Relief and Rehabilitation Administration, which oversaw the reconstruction of Warsaw; he then traveled as a freelance journalist through the Scandinavian countries.

Moore returned to England in 1947, but he did not stay long. Early in 1948 he immigrated to Canada, following a lover. Their relationship did not last, but he remained in Canada, becoming a citizen in 1953. During most of his first year in Canada he worked as a clerk in a construction camp in Thessalon, Ontario. After a brief stay in Toronto, Moore next moved to Montreal, where he gained employment with the English-language *Montreal Gazette*–first as a proofreader, then as a reporter. He stayed with the newspaper from 1949 to 1955, and during this period he also began writing and publishing pulp-style stories in *Weekend Magazine*. At the same time, he was also beginning to write "serious" stories. The first of these to be published, "Sassenach," appeared in the *Northern Review* in 1951. That same year Moore published two pulp-style paperback novels, *Wreath for a Redhead* and *The Executioners*. Also in 1951, he married his first wife, Jacqueline Scully Sirois, and in 1954 they had a son, Michael Moore.

Moore's next two works of pulp fiction, *French for Murder* (1954) and *A Bullet for My Lady* (1954), came out under the pseudonym Bernard Mara. A novel published under his own name in 1955, *Judith Hearne,* established his reputation. Moore's first "serious" novel, it concerns a middle-aged woman in Belfast who attempts to come to terms with who she is and where she is going. Like several of Moore's realistic novels set in Northern Ireland, it

Dust jacket for Moore's semi-autobiographical 1970 fantasy novel, about a screenwriter who is visited by ghosts from his past–including his own younger self

deals both with characters facing personal crises and failures and with the way Irish society often oppresses or represses such characters. *Judith Hearne* received the Authors' Club of Great Britain Annual First Novel Award, although *Judith Hearne* was actually Moore's fifth novel. The success of the book enabled him to leave his reporting job to focus on his writing full time.

Despite Moore's entrance into literary respectability, he continued to write pulp novels using pseudonyms, as well as more mainstream works under his own name, for the remainder of the 1950s. An example of the latter is *The Feast of Lupercal* (1957), a novel about a middle-aged man in Belfast who both desires and fears romantic attachment. It received the Quebec Literary Prize for that year.

Moore's increasing literary success led to greater opportunities for travel and exposure to fellow writers. In 1958, for instance, Granville Hicks invited him to be a guest at Yaddo, an artists' colony near Saratoga Springs, New York. The following year Moore received a

Guggenheim Fellowship, which took him to New York City for a time.

Throughout the 1960s Moore continued to consolidate his growing reputation and popularity with a series of novels. Among them were *The Luck of Ginger Coffey*, a 1960 novel about an Irishman who moves his family to Montreal, which received the Governor General's Award in fiction; *An Answer from Limbo* (1962), another family narrative about the clash of Irish and North American culture; *The Emperor of Ice-Cream* (1965), an autobiographical novel drawing on Moore's adolescence in Belfast; and *I Am Mary Dunne* (1968), a study of a thrice-married woman coming to terms with her life in Canada and the United States. Moore also collaborated with the editors of *Life* magazine to create a coffee-table book on Canada in 1963.

Moore became increasingly involved in other projects, especially for the stage and screen. He was consulted for a 1961 stage adaptation of *Judith Hearne*, directed by Daniel Petrie and Jose Quintano, and an operatic version of *The Luck of Ginger Coffey* produced at the O'Keefe Centre in Toronto two years later. In 1964 Moore wrote a screen adaptation of *The Luck of Ginger Coffey;* the following year he moved to Malibu, California, to work as a screenwriter for Alfred Hitchcock's movie *Torn Curtain* (1966). After this project, though Moore remained a Canadian citizen and, in his later years, spent his summers in Nova Scotia, southern California was his home. He occasionally taught as an adjunct professor at the University of California, Los Angeles.

The 1960s were eventful for Moore personally as well as professionally. In 1961 a Canada Council Award allowed him to travel to London to work on a novel; that same year he received a grant from the National Institute of Arts and Letters in the United States. Amid all the honors and travels, however, Moore's first marriage ended. In 1967 he wed his second wife, Jean Denney.

Moore's first fantasy novel, *Fergus* (1970), is also one of his most autobiographical works. Many of the protagonist's relatives are based on actual members of Moore's family. In *Brian Moore: The Chameleon Novelist* (1998) Denis Sampson calls *Fergus* "the novel that examines most directly Moore's familial inheritance"—and there are more than a few similarities between the main character, Fergus Fadden, and Moore himself. For instance, Fergus is an Irish American novelist working in Hollywood as a screenwriter, much as Moore had worked with Hitchcock on *Torn Curtain*.

Set in southern California in the late 1960s, the novel concerns a day in Fergus's life. He has come to California not only to work on a screenplay but also to escape his past, in particular his estranged wife. He finds, however, that the past is not so easily shaken. Now in his forties, Fergus is attempting to build a new life for himself; he is also experiencing a classic midlife crisis. Though living with an attractive redhead in her twenties, he worries about the physical changes wrought by middle age and about his memory, which seems to him to be failing. The fantastic events of the day, however, enable him to come to terms with his life as he grapples with ghosts from his past, dredged up from his memories.

Although the ontological status of the ghosts that populate *Fergus* is ambiguous, to Fergus they are certainly more than metaphors or memories—and here the fantastic element of the novel enters in. Throughout the day he has one encounter after another with a variety of figures from his past: parents, siblings, aunts, teachers, priests, friends, and lovers. To Fergus they seem as real as life, and in fact they can be touched (a characteristic that Moore uses to comic effect when Fergus finds he can fondle a neighbor woman he lusted after in his youth). At times these apparitions appear to him when other people are in the room, but he is the only one who sees or hears them, much like William Shakespeare's Hamlet, who sees and hears his father's spirit while confronting his mother, who cannot perceive the ghost. Nor do all the phantoms Fergus interacts with seem to be ghosts in the conventional sense. Besides their apparent corporeality—they sometimes vanish when he turns his back on them, but just as often they walk off into the distance after he opens the patio door for them—not all of the figures are spirits of the dead. In many cases Fergus converses not with one of the departed but with a spirit version of someone in his past who is still living. Sometimes this spirit is a contemporary manifestation of a person not present, such as his wife or daughter; at other times it is a younger form of a now older person in his past, such as one of his siblings. Most remarkably, at times Fergus is even visited by a ghostly version of his younger self.

Fergus responds to these visitations with amazement and doubts about his sanity but also with a sense of wonder as he strives to understand his personal history. For instance, he comes to a greater understanding about his family members and his relationships with them through his conversations with their ghosts. Similarly, he gains a broader perspective on his friendships and romantic involvements. Fergus looks at and listens to his younger self and is embarrassed by how foolish he was—as well as how foolish he still is. He also is able to live out a few youthful fantasies, such as beating a sadistic schoolmaster and having his way with a neighbor's wife whom he coveted as an adolescent.

Fergus also reacts at times with fear. The apparitions are rarely threatening, but there are two key scenes in which he finds himself attacked, verbally and physically, for his sins. One occurs immediately after he fondles the neighbor's wife, at which point a host of figures from his native Limerick put him on trial. The other occurs near the end of the novel, when he cannot recall the identity of a woman from his past who appears to him, and the same gang from Limerick again threatens him. While Fergus castigates himself for his youthful foolishness, he also realizes how much of his present life is still foolish and vain.

Complicating the situation is Fergus's rejection of the Roman Catholic faith in which he was raised—a matter of some controversy as he converses with his pious parents and other members of his family, as well as with representatives from the church. He wonders, if the ghosts are in any sense real, whether there is indeed an afterlife. He never learns a satisfactory answer, leaving the reader to wonder whether Fergus was visited by actual apparitions or simply his own imaginings. As he comes to a sense of reconciliation with these figures from the past, however, it appears that they have achieved what they were sent for and are now released, and that Fergus will wake to a new day and resume the rest of his life as usual.

Ultimately, the reason for all of these experiences appears to be to teach Fergus a lesson about who he is and how he came to be that way, as well as to show him how significant all the relationships of his life have actually been and continue to be. The novel, however, is not simply a contemporary updating of Charles Dickens's *A Christmas Carol* (1843), in which the moral lesson threatens to overshadow the story itself. Indeed, what makes *Fergus* noteworthy is that, despite the fantastic nature of the plot, which is by turns comic and poignant, it works quite well as a realistic depiction of the protagonist's life. Moore convincingly portrays a wide variety of characters, both real and ghostly, through description and dialogue. He does the same for the setting, from the fashions of the time to the furniture. The novel is not only interesting to read for the supernatural events, which are effectively worked into an otherwise mundane day in the life of a writer, but it is also effective on the level of characterization and environment.

Nonetheless, *Fergus* did not achieve the same level of critical response as Moore's better-known books. Though it was respectfully reviewed in Ireland and England, the critical reception in the United States was poor, a response that baffled and frustrated Moore, who desired to connect with a readership in his adopted country. Later critics, however, have since considered *Fergus* an important contribution to his body of work.

After the publication of *Fergus*, Moore continued to write novels at a steady rate, among them *The Revolution Script* (1971) and *Catholics* (1972), recipient of the W. H. Smith Prize. *Catholics* is a work of speculative fiction, if not science fiction, set in a near future in which the Catholic Church, expanding on the reforms of the Second Vatican Council (1962–1965), has done away with the confessional and the Latin mass and has embraced a fully inclusive ecumenism.

The plot of *Catholics* concerns a group of isolated Irish monks who persist in the old ways. When hundreds of devout, traditional Catholics flock there, an American representative from the church makes his way to their island abbey from Amsterdam to deliver the church's order to conform to their newly adopted ecumenism. The first portion of the novel focuses on a young church representative, James Kinsella. He has fully absorbed the new spirit of the church, which focuses more on social than theological issues of the day and more on what the various branches of Christianity have in common than on what historically made the Roman Catholic Church unique. As Stovel points out in "Brian Moore: The Realist's Progress" (1981), the title of the novel is a pun: "all the world is about to become Catholic, since the word has regained its original meaning, all-embracing." Yet the novel also concentrates on specific, traditional issues in the Catholic faith.

The conflict embodied in the pun of the title emerges in the clash between Kinsella and the abbot of the Irish monastery he visits. At first this conflict is presented from the young man's perspective, but in the last third of the novel the perspective switches to the abbot as he ponders the future of the church in this brave new world. What makes his defense of the values of traditional Catholicism all the more striking in the context of the novel and its futuristic setting is the deepness of his own spiritual doubts. As is typically the case in Moore's fantastic fiction, ideas about the supernatural point to questions about its existence, in particular about the possibility of religious truth. In the end, readers, like the characters in his fantastic novels, are left with no definitive answers, only with questions.

In 1973, a year after the publication of *Catholics*, Moore adapted the novel for television. It aired on CBS in November, with Trevor Howard as the abbot and Martin Sheen as Kinsella. In his review Leonard Maltin calls the adaptation verbose yet affecting. (It was released on videotape in 1991 as *The Conflict*.) Toward the end of the 1970s Moore adapted the novel as a play. It ran briefly in Seattle in 1980; a revised version had short runs in Edmonton, Alberta, and Stamford, Connecticut, the following year.

In 1975 Moore published his next work of fantasy and perhaps the best-known of his fantastic novels, *The Great Victorian Collection*. The book earned him his second Governor General's Award in fiction, as well as the James Tait Black Memorial Award. Like *Fergus*, the novel has a contemporary California setting and effectively combines the fantastic with the realistic. Even more than *Fergus*, *The Great Victorian Collection* supports the claims

Dust jacket for Moore's 1975 novel, about a Canadian scholar who becomes the curator of a collection of Victorian objects that magically appears in a California motel parking lot

that more than one critic has made concerning the impact of Moore's adopted California on his work. In the Summer 1976 issue of *Critical Quarterly* Kerry McSweeney notes that Canada, important as it was in Moore's development, "has not stimulated his imagination in the way America has done." As Paul Binding remarks in *Books and Bookmen* (February 1980), "It is America, with its vigorous non-realistic, especially Gothic literary tradition, which would seem to have supplied Brian Moore with the fictional forms that he needed, that can express—with their violent epiphanies and their distortions and eruptions of the irrational—the anguishes of the uprooted and spiritually homeless, and the baffling diversities of Western society which can contain both puritan, taboo-ridden, pleasure-fearing Belfast and hedonistic, lost, restless California."

Binding's assessment applies strongly to *The Great Victorian Collection*. Moore painstakingly details the assorted items in a fantastic collection of Victoriana that miraculously appears in a motel parking lot in Carmel, California. Moore was influenced in this direction by one of the most antirealist of writers, the Argentinian Jorge Luis Borges: "The idea of writing *The Great Victorian Collection* didn't come from Borges," Moore explained in a 1977 interview with Hubert de Santana, "but reading him gave me the courage to try." Equally impressive is Moore's depiction of 1970s California—its culture, conversation, clothing, climate, and characters.

The protagonist of the novel, a young Canadian scholar of Victorian history named Anthony Maloney, visits northern California for a seminar and rents a car to see the Big Sur region. He stays in Carmel at a motel, where he has an amazing dream: he finds himself in London, where he is led by a mysterious stranger through a door that leads him to his motel room. Then, looking out the window onto an empty lot, he sees a "most astonishing collection of Victorian artifacts, *objets d'art*, furniture, household appliances, paintings, jewelry, scientific instruments, toys, tapestries, sculpture, handicrafts, woolen and linen samples, industrial machinery, ceramics, silverware, books, furs, men's and women's clothing, musical instruments, a huge telescope mounted on a pedestal, a railway locomotive, marine equipment, small arms, looms, bric-a-brac, and curiosa." Maloney wakes from the dream, looks out his motel window, and sees the collection, as though it had materialized from his dream.

Afraid he is still dreaming, Maloney tries to determine whether the objects are, indeed, real and, if so, whether they are authentic. He later experiments with the possibility of relocating the collection, but when he tries to do so with a toy, he sees that it now displays on its underside the words "Made in Japan." Fearing that the entire collection will turn ersatz if he continues, Maloney rents the lot from the motel, provides for guards, and calls the newspapers to have the collection verified and photographed.

What follows is a circus of chaos. The media is skeptical but willing to exploit the story. The police doubt Maloney's story and threaten to charge him with theft, while scholars called in to corroborate the authenticity of the items cast doubt on the matter and bicker among themselves. What is more, when photographed, handled, and examined over time, items in the collection appear to Maloney to lose something of their authenticity, even though their authentic status is almost consistently validated throughout the novel. Moreover, once word of the collection has spread, hordes of people come to see it, although they are kept away.

In the process Moore does an excellent job of exploring the consequences that such an event might produce were it actually to happen, made all the more effective by Maloney's own skepticism: "Maloney did not believe in God. . . . Nor did he believe in evil spirits, extrasensory perception, or creatures from another planet. Even now, looking out at the Collection, he did not for a moment entertain the notion that some mystical Presence had willed this to come to pass. Nor could he believe it was a hoax: the Collection was too astonishing, too valuable to be anyone's prank." Through the use of realistic details and the various responses of the characters, Moore enables readers to experience a willing suspension of disbelief.

At the same time, Moore also does a careful job of describing not only contemporary culture but also the Victorian era. Through the collection, Victorian life is portrayed nostalgically but not sentimentally. Maloney points out—perhaps having read Steven Marcus's landmark study *The Other Victorians: A Study of Sexuality and Pornography in Mid-Nineteenth-Century England* (1966)—that "The Victorians had many secrets," and parts of the collection reveal in particular their sexual obsessions. In general, the more hidden aspects of Victorian culture represented by certain parts of the collection have a larger symbolic import, as one of the central themes of the novel is the difference between appearance and reality, fantasy and truth. Just as the Victorians were not always what they seemed, Maloney, now seeing himself in the public eye, realizes that how he appears to others is not how he appears to himself. As always in Moore's fantasy work, the macrocosm points to the microcosm; at the center of all the supernatural doings stands a real human being.

Indeed, the true focus of *The Great Victorian Collection* is not the fabulous collection itself, but rather its all too human curator. Understandably, Maloney's life is changed by the experience, but for the worse. Continuing to stay in his motel room adjacent to the collection that he maintains by day and dreams of by night, he loses his university position, his already-deteriorating marriage falls apart, and other relationships in his life are frustrated. As with most of Moore's fiction, then, ranging from realistic novels such as *Judith Hearne* to fantastic ones such as *Fergus*, this book, despite the fantastic quality of the story, is essentially a study of character.

Ultimately, the wonderful collection brings about Maloney's destruction. His initial dream of touring the collection on foot is replaced by a maddening one in which he monitors it all night on a black-and-white closed-circuit television screen. Determined not to repeat the experience and desperate for a momentary escape, he travels to Los Angeles with Fred Vaterman, the local reporter who broke the story, and Mary Ann, Fred's girlfriend and Maloney's assistant. Hoping to dream something different, Maloney instead finds himself unable to sleep at all. His attraction to Mary Ann promises to develop into a relationship as they grow closer and Fred leaves in disgust at Maloney's inability to sleep and dream. The relationship with Mary Ann, however, is also frustrated—a significant loss since she has been the collection's greatest admirer and believer after Maloney, and now even she gives up on him. He tries taking her to Toronto, but, again, nothing happens. When he returns to Carmel, he finds the collection has continued to fade, and even a repeat of the television-monitor dream fails to halt its decline into a state of disrepair. Eventually, Maloney's physical deterioration mirrors that of the collection, and what began as a marvelous dream ultimately brings about his end. The collection, much diminished in charm, survives him as a cheap tourist attraction.

As with much fantasy, *The Great Victorian Collection* is loaded with metaphorical implications. In addition to dealing with such larger questions as the nature of reality and truth, the novel touches on issues such as how one's dreams can be helpful or hurtful, how the importance of one's dreams may not be readily apparent to others, and how an obsession with the past can prevent one from living in the present. The novel, however, is not at all like a parable. As with his other fantasy works, Moore avoids simple answers to big questions, and the story is always foremost rather than some deeper meaning or interpretation.

Moreover, *The Great Victorian Collection* stands as a lesson of the perils facing the creative artist, a claim argued by Sampson in *Brian Moore: The Chameleon Novelist* and supported by a detailed statement Moore made to interviewer Robert Sullivan in the December 1976/January 1977 issue of *London Magazine*:

> *The Great Victorian Collection* was something I was led into, because I have never wanted to repeat myself. . . . *The Great Victorian Collection* seemed to be the metaphor I wanted. I love the idea of the past on our door-step, unchangeable, irrevocable, the feeling that we can't walk away from it. Of course, at the same time the book is a paradigm of artistic creation. In a way, I have my own "Collection" to escape from; if I had not changed and written these new novels I would be very much like the hero in *The Great Victorian Collection*, caught, trapped, forced to dream the same dream, to repeat versions of *Judith Hearne*, to write those Belfast novels over and over again.

From this perspective, one could claim that Moore's fantastic fiction, rather than standing as aberrations in the career of an otherwise realistic novelist, constituted an important means for the author to reinvent himself.

Another way in which Moore sought to expand his reach as a writer in the mid-to-late 1970s was to return to the short story, a form he rarely wrote in and had not attempted in more than a decade. "The Sight," his contribution to a 1977 collection titled *Irish Ghost Stories*, is really less a ghost story per se and more a melding of the realistic and the supernatural typical of his fantastic fiction.

Dust jacket for Moore's final fantasy novel (1983), in which a woman discovers that her husband has returned from the dead

The protagonist is an affluent Irish attorney in New York; his problem is at first rather mundane, involving a growth on his back. It is probably benign, but the man comes to fear that it may be more serious, and his anxiety is treated somewhat comically. The fantastic twist in the story comes when the reader learns that the lawyer's housekeeper, a traditional old woman from Ireland, possesses the ability to predict the approach of death from the expressions on a person's face. What she sees in his face is another matter.

After three more realistic novels–*The Doctor's Wife* (1976), *The Mangan Inheritance* (1979), and *The Temptation of Eileen Hughes* (1981)–Moore published his fourth and last work of fantasy, *Cold Heaven* (1983). Like *Fergus* and *The Great Victorian Collection*, this novel is also at heart a study of character. Again, the setting is contemporary– primarily California, with some scenes set in the French Riviera and Manhattan. Despite the intrusion of the supernatural into the natural world, the real significance is how the events impact the life of the protagonist, Marie Davenport. She sees her husband, Alex, die in a boating accident in France (an event similar to one that, nearly three decades earlier, incapacitated Moore for three days while he was writing *Judith Hearne*). Alex's body is recovered, but on the following day it is no longer in the hospital where it was taken. Rather than lingering on this mysterious event and her husband's seeming resurrection, however, Moore concentrates on Marie's response–a combination of confusion, panic, and guilt.

Two factors are prominent in *Cold Heaven*. The first is Marie's religious doubts, which are challenged by these unusual events. Despite Moore's agnosticism, or perhaps because of it, religion is a key element in almost all of his fiction, as he explores such issues as how faith shapes people and how they perceive the world, what the loss of faith does to a person, whether there might in fact be religious truth, and whether such truth, if it exists, can be known. Marie struggles to reconcile her husband's miraculous disappearance in death and later his apparent reappearance in life with her religious attitudes, which were formed in rebellion against her Catholic upbringing. Her unbelief is further challenged by her encounters with the elderly Mother St. Jude, who carries a sense of the mystic about her. Complicating matters is another major factor in Marie's response, her guilt over the fact that she was unfaithful to her husband. During their trip to Nice, France, she had planned to tell Alex that she was leaving him, but his sudden death and the subsequent events throw her plans into chaos.

Marie believes, despite the doctors' protestations that her husband is truly dead, that he revived in the morgue and walked out of the hospital. Her belief is confirmed by the fact that his belongings are no longer there when she returns to their room. Apparently, she thinks, Alex wants to return to their temporary home in New York without letting her or anyone else know. Narrowly missing him there (she finds evidence that he had recently been in the apartment) and in a state of panic, she calls her lover in California. Her husband, however, finds her lover's message and heads to the motel near Carmel where Marie and her lover began their affair. She has no choice, it seems, but to follow.

As the setting shifts from France to New York and then to California, the viewpoint remains Marie's. Therefore, the reader is as puzzled as she is about what exactly happened to her husband. When the couple finally meets in the California motel, Marie learns more, but neither she nor the reader is ever given a complete explanation for her husband's situation. As a physician, Alex treats his condition clinically, but his findings are incompatible with medical science. Apparently, he was, indeed, dead in the hospital in Nice and then revived. Moreover, he has died a few more times, if death is understood to be the cessation of breathing and a heartbeat. In between these deaths, monitoring his vital signs, Alex finds that both his pulse and his temperature are abnormally low—too low to sustain life. As it turns out, his uncanny resurrections are short-lived, and he finally dies for good.

Before his final death Alex explains to Marie that he has been disoriented and, in his more lucid moments, was afraid that he would be exploited as a medical freak. The reader sees little of her husband, but through such scenes and Marie's memories the reader sees her husband as selfish and unsympathetic. In contrast, Marie's lover, Daniel, is caring and supportive. These facts, however, do little to reduce her feelings of guilt, and throughout she feels she is being punished.

The reader learns that this feeling is connected not only to her affair but also to her feelings about religion, combined in her self-description as an "unbelieving adulteress." Marie has rejected her religious upbringing, but the events of the novel cast doubt on her skepticism. She gradually comes to feel that she is being harassed by some external force: "They have done this to Alex to punish me. They did not kill me in that accident because they still plan to use me." Who "they" are and what plan "they" might have for her, however, are uncertain through much of the novel. As a priest points out at the end of the book, "God doesn't reveal himself to us in an unmistakable way." Alex's mysterious resurrections, however, are not the only supernatural elements in Marie's life. She also has a vision of her namesake, the Virgin Mary.

This vision, which occurs at Carmel, is hazy, but it includes a request to tell the local priests so that the location may become a place of pilgrimage. Marie's reluctance to have anything to do with the Catholic Church or its representatives then becomes part of her cycle of guilt. She wonders whether she is being punished for this as well. Eventually, her vision is confirmed by a young nun at the local convent, although Marie has doubts—as does the monsignor who accompanies them, much like the abbot in *Catholics* who agonizes over his loss of faith.

Eventually, Marie withstands the threat posed by "these unreal events . . . happening in this real, reassuringly ordinary world," successfully combating "the defeat of my will" and returning in the end to her doubts and to her comfortable, if mundane and imperfect, existence. Her complacency, however, has been shattered. In the place of complete skepticism there is now a lingering sense that mysteries have been unfolded, even if not completely revealed. If there is a God, the book suggests, this being is beyond comprehension; if there is a heaven, it might well be cold to human endeavor. People's behavior is often inscrutable, Moore tells readers, and even more so any realm beyond their own.

Although Moore published several noteworthy books after *Cold Heaven*, among them the historical novel *Black Robe* (1985), about the efforts of a seventeenth-century Jesuit to convert Canadian Indians, none of these incorporates fantasy; thus, his fantastic fiction represents only a small part of a prolific career. Nonetheless, his fantasy novels—unlike his early paperback thrillers, which have been largely ignored by critics—are hardly a negligible portion of his work, and most critics of Moore's fiction have rightly included them in their studies of the author.

Moore's fantastic fiction is interesting not only because of his skill at blending the supernatural with the realistic and the inventiveness of his imagination, though these are certainly significant. Also important is the way he uses fantasy. Though Moore effectively conveys a sense of wonder in these works, the fantasy in them is never employed for its own sake or for escapism. Rather, like many talented fantasists, he draws on the supernatural both to reveal certain aspects of his protagonists' personalities and to illustrate a moral point. While marvelous, the fantastic events in these works are inevitably unsettling, often leading the characters who experience them to personal insights they would rather have avoided.

Moore's novels of the fantastic, though few, are an important part of a respectable literary career. His work was nominated for the prestigious Booker Prize more than once. He was a Fellow of the Royal Society of Literature and received honorary degrees from Queens University in Belfast and the National University of Ireland in Dublin. Moore's writing has been the focus of several critical studies. By the time of his death at his Malibu home on 11 January 1999, he had built a solid reputation as one of the best writers of Canadian citizenship, even if he did not achieve the same level of fame accorded such writers as Margaret Atwood and Robertson Davies. As Christopher Lehmann-Haupt, a book reviewer for *The New York Times*, wrote, "He was one of the best-known obscure writers alive."

Bibliographies:

Richard Studing, "A Brian Moore Bibliography," *Eire-Ireland: A Journal of Irish Studies*, 10 (Autumn 1975): 89–105;

Robert J. Stanton, *A Bibliography of Modern British Novelists*, volume 1 (New York: Whitston, 1978), pp. 535–567;

Marlys Chevrefils, ed., *The Brian Moore Papers: First Accession and Second Accession–An Inventory of the Archive at the University of Calgary Libraries* (Calgary: University of Calgary Press, 1987);

Brian McIlroy, "A Brian Moore Bibliography: 1974–1987," *Irish University Review*, 18 (Spring 1988): 106–133.

Interviews:

Robert Fulford, "Robert Fulford Interviews Brian Moore," *Tamarack Review*, 23 (Spring 1962): 5–18;

Hallvard Dahlie, "Brian Moore: An Interview," *Tamarack Review*, 46 (Winter 1968): 7–29;

Richard B. Sale, "An Interview in London with Brian Moore," *Studies in the Novel*, 1 (Spring 1969): 67–80;

Donald Cameron, "Brian Moore," in his *Conversations with Canadian Novelists*, volume 2 (Toronto: Macmillan, 1973), pp. 64–85;

John Graham, "Brian Moore," in *The Writer's Voice*, edited by George Garrett (New York: Morrow, 1973), pp. 51–74;

Richard T. Bray, "A Conversation with Brian Moore," *Critic: A Catholic Review of Books and the Arts*, 35 (Fall 1976): 42–48;

Robert Sullivan, "Brian Moore: A Clinging Climate," *London Magazine* (December 1976/January 1977): 63–71;

Hubert de Santana, "Interview with Brian Moore," *Maclean's* (11 July 1977): 4–7;

Bruce Meyer and Brian O'Riordan, *In Their Words: Interviews with Fourteen Canadian Writers* (Toronto: Anansi, 1984), pp. 168–183.

References:

Hallvard Dahlie, *Brian Moore* (Boston: Twayne, 1981);

Jeanne Flood, *Brian Moore* (Lewisburg, Pa.: Bucknell University Press / London: Associated University Presses, 1974);

Kerry McSweeney, "Brian Moore: Past and Present," *Critical Quarterly*, 18 (Summer 1976): 53–66;

McSweeney, "Brian Moore's Grammars of the Emotions," in his *Four Contemporary Novelists: Angus Wilson, Brian Moore, John Fowles, V. S. Naipaul* (Kingston & Montreal: McGill-Queen's University Press / London: Scolar, 1983), pp. 55–99;

Christopher Murray, ed., *Irish University Review*, 18 (Spring 1988)–special issue on Moore;

Jo O'Donoghue, *Brian Moore: A Critical Study* (Dublin: Gill & Macmillan, 1990);

Raymond J. Porter, "Miracle, Mystery, and Faith in Brian Moore's *Catholics*," *Eire-Ireland: A Journal of Irish Studies*, 10, no. 3 (1975): 79–88;

Denis Sampson, *Brian Moore: The Chameleon Novelist* (Dublin: Marino, 1998);

Bruce Stovel, "Brian Moore: The Realist's Progress," *English Studies in Canada*, 7 (Summer 1981): 183–200;

Robert Sullivan, *A Matter of Faith: The Fiction of Brian Moore* (Westport, Conn.: Greenwood Press, 1996);

Eamonn Wall, "'Even Better Than the Real Thing': Brian Moore's *The Great Victorian Collection*," *Colby Quarterly*, 34 (December 1998): 303–314.

Papers:

A large collection of Brian Moore's papers is located in the Special Collections Division, University of Calgary Libraries, Alberta, Canada.

Francine Pelletier
(25 April 1959 -   )

Amy J. Ransom
Anna Maria College

BOOKS: *Le Temps des migrations* (Longeuil, Quebec: Le Préambule, 1987);
Le Rendez-vous du désert (Montreal: Editions Paulines, 1987);
Jardins de lumière (Boucherville, Quebec: Graficor, 1988);
Mort sur le Redan (Montreal: Editions Paulines, 1988);
Le Crime de l'Enchanteresse (Montreal: Editions Paulines, 1989);
Monsieur Bizarre (Montreal: Editions Paulines, 1990);
Des Vacances bizarres (Montreal: Editions Paulines, 1991);
La Forêt de métal (La Salle, Quebec: Hurtubise HMH, 1991);
Le Septième écran (Montreal: Editions Paulines, 1992);
La Saison de l'exil (Montreal: Editions Paulines, 1992);
La Bizarre aventure (Montreal: Editions Paulines, 1993);
La Planète du mensonge (Montreal: Editions Paulines, 1993);
Le Cadavre dans la glissoire (Montreal: Editions Paulines, 1994);
Une Nuit bizarre (Montreal: Médiaspaul, 1994);
Le Fantôme de l'opérateur (Montreal: Médiaspaul, 1996);
Cher ancêtre (Montreal: Médiaspaul, 1996);
Damien mort ou vif (Montreal: Médiaspaul, 1997);
Nelle de Vilvèq—Le Sable et l'acier 1 (Quebec: Editions Alire, 1997);
Samiva de Frée—Le Sable et l'acier 2 (Quebec: Editions Alire, 1998);
Issabel de Qohosaten—Le Sable et l'acier 3 (Quebec: Editions Alire, 1998);
Télé-rencontre (Montreal: Hurtubise HMH, 1999);
Les Eaux de Jade (Montreal: Médiaspaul, 2000);
Le Crime de Culdéric (Montreal: Médiaspaul, 2001).

OTHER: "Instant," in *Dix nouvelles de science-fiction québécoise*, edited by André Carpentier (Montreal: Editions Quinze, 1985), pp. 109–123;
Par chemins inventés, edited by Pelletier (Montreal: Editions Québec/Amérique, 1992);

Francine Pelletier

"Écrire des histoires de filles dans un univers masculin," in *Visions d'autres mondes: La littérature fantastique et de science-fiction canadienne,* edited by Andrea Paradis (Montreal: Editions RD, 1995), pp. 186–193;
"Cloche vaine," in *Escales sur Solaris,* edited by Joël Champetier and Yves Meynard (Hull, Quebec: Editions Vents d'Ouest, 1995), pp. 53–66; translated by Howard Scott as "Empty Ring" in *Tesseracts⁵,* edited by Meynard and Robert Runté (Edmonton, Alberta: Tesseract Books, 1996), pp. 28–39;

"La Migratrice," translated by Wendy Green as "The Mother Migrator," in *Tesseracts², edited by Élisabeth Vonarburg and Jane Brierly (Edmonton, Alberta: Tesseract Books, 1996), pp. 64–79.

SELECTED PERIODICAL PUBLICATIONS–UNCOLLECTED: "Le retour des gueux," *Pour ta belle gueule d'ahuri,* 6 (1983): 41–42;
"La traversée d'Algir," *imagine . . . ,* 20 (January 1984): 11–15;
"La volière," *imagine . . . ,* 24 (October 1984): 19–31;
"Le milieu plutôt que l'âge," *Nuit Blanche,* 20 (October–November 1985): 49–50;
"Cher ancêtre," *imagine . . . ,* 39 (April 1987): 63–73;
"En bout de ligne," *Solaris,* 73 (May–June 1987): 22–26;
"La Petite," *imagine . . . ,* 46 (December 1988): 105–120; translated by Jane Brierly as "Guinea Pig" in *Tesseracts³,* edited by Candas Jane Dorsey and Gerry Truscott (Victoria, British Columbia: Tesseract Books, 1990), pp. 413–424;
"1988: L'anneé de tous les clichés?" *Solaris,* 84 (April 1989): 5;
"Eaux mortes, eaux vives," *Solaris,* 87 (October 1989): 5–10.

After Élisabeth Vonarburg and Esther Rochon, Francine Pelletier is one of the most active and best-known woman writers in Quebec science fiction. Though she is often forced by a limited market to publish for an adolescent audience, her trilogy for adults, *Le Sable et l'acier* (Sand and Steel, 1997–1998), marks a turning point in her career. While classical American science fiction inspired her antecedents in Quebec, Pelletier represents the first generation of science-fiction writers in her province to claim a primarily local influence on her work. Although she has read (in translation) anglophone authors ranging from Isaac Asimov to Ursula K. Le Guin, Pelletier's first exposure to the genre came from the pages of the Quebec review *Solaris,* and its contributors–such as Vonarburg, Jean-Pierre April, and Daniel Sernine–were the main influences that prompted her to write science fiction.

Francine Pelletier was born on 25 April 1959 in Laval, Quebec, a Montreal suburb, to archivist Laure Gauthier and Claude E. Pelletier, genealogist for the Association of the Pelletier Families. Her family already included two sisters, Johanne (1954–1983) and Luce (born in 1956), and a brother, Claude Jacques (born in 1962), would soon become the final addition to the family. As a teenager she had an active imagination and a taste for reading that developed into a consuming desire to write. She submitted her first work to publishers at the age of sixteen and subsequently received her first rejection. Advised by her parents that earning a living as a writer would be highly unlikely in Quebec–a reality that Pelletier still struggles with–she obtained a degree in French education from the Université du Québec à Montréal in 1981.

Although she was first published in 1977, in a student journal, she did not become active in the Quebec science-fiction movement as a means of realizing her goal of becoming a professional writer until the early 1980s. Her own tastes first leaned toward the detective novel, and she resisted her brother's attempts to interest her in science fiction. Finally, discouraged by several rejections, she took his advice and attended the writing workshops of Vonarburg, a pioneer of Quebec science fiction, who became a mentor to Pelletier. Winning the Boréal Conference prize for impromptu writing in 1981 and 1983 respectively, her stories "Le retour des gueux" (The Beggars' Return, 1983) and "La traversée d'Algir" (Algir's Crossing, 1984) opened the doors of the publication world, and her work soon began to appear on a regular basis in the Quebec science-fiction journals *Solaris* and *imagine . . . ,* and occasionally in mainstream literary magazines.

With a growing reputation, Pelletier published four stories in 1984 and became a member of the editorial board of *Solaris*. "La volière" (The Aviary), published in the October 1984 issue of *imagine . . . ,* introduces one of Pelletier's imaginary worlds while demonstrating the sophistication of her narrative ability. Through a frame and flashbacks, it vividly describes emotional states that the protagonist, a moviemaker named Iris, wishes to record in her *cinéma de l'émotion* (emotion films). Dramatizing Iris's struggle to visit the planet Arkadie to film its birdlife in the wild, the story examines the power of art over science. Denied permission by a forbidding scientist, Iris can make her movie only in the aviary on Asterman, Earth's relay station to its space colonies. Relying on an artificial situation to complete her project, Iris triumphs as her art succeeds in transmitting the encounter with alien birds as an intense emotional experience for her movie audience.

Asterman and the planet Arkadie became the setting for subsequent works, including the 1985 story "Instant," as well as Pelletier's first collection, *Le Temps des migrations* (The Time of the Migrations, 1987), winner of the Prix Boréal for best book in 1988. Its related stories blend realist detail from the contemporary world with the author's projections of technological and sociological developments of the future. "La Migratrice" (translated as "The Mother Migrator" and published in *Tesseracts²* in 1996) deals with space colonization and genetic experimentation; "Ceux qui restent" (Those Who Remain) opposes colonists against a government that prefers to harvest space resources with exploited guest workers. "Là-bas, la mer" (Down There, the Sea)

Cover for Pelletier's 1989 novel for young adults, one of a series featuring her ecological-warrior heroine, Arialde Henke

and "La Petite fille du silence" (Daughter of Silence), for which Pelletier received a Grand Prix de la science-fiction et du fantastique québécois in 1988, center around problems of sexual relationships, fertility, and the family of the future. On the Asterman space station and the Earth it orbits, nearly all humans have become sterile, and sexual relations outside of marriage are much freer; as a result, "normal" sexual reproduction becomes an aberration in a world in which babies come from genetic factories. "Les Merles rouges" (The Redbirds) proposes the development of a new race of hybrid humans adapted to survive on the planet Arkadie. As a result of these experiments, Arialde Henke faces the discrimination that accompanies difference.

Like many other writers of science fiction in Quebec, Pelletier envisions society as a repressive force that suffocates protagonists with its excessive control, while it mystifies them about their own identity by creating legends or simply withholding information. The narrative often results from the efforts of the hero or—as in Pelletier's work—the heroine to obtain freedom and knowledge. Parallels quickly appear between the monolithic administration that runs Pelletier's fictional Asterman and the Canadian federal capital of Ottawa, or between the Arkadians, a hybrid race of humans adapted to a new land, and the Québécois people who have preserved and adapted an isolated francophone culture in the far north of America. While supporting the separatist movement as a means of preserving francophone culture in Quebec, Pelletier denies any particular political significance to her work, or to Quebec science fiction in general. Yet, these cultural resonances in the colonization of a planet named Arkadie (Acadia), "Cette soi-disant Nouvelle Terre" (this so-called New World), which Pelletier imagines in *Le temps des migrations,* cannot go unremarked.

Perhaps this cultural identification explains Pelletier's fondness for Arialde Henke, the heroine of "Les Merles rouges," whom she later featured in an entire series of adolescent space mysteries, including *Mort sur le Redan* (Death on the Redan, 1988), *Le Crime de l'Enchanteresse* (The Sorceress's Crime, 1989), *Le Septième écran* (The Seventh Screen, 1992), *La Saison de l'exil* (The Season of Exile, 1992), and *La Planète du mensonge* (The Planet of Lies, 1993). In these works the author creates an intelligent, independent young woman determined to protect the fauna of her home planet against the economic exploitation of outsiders. Doing so without didacticism, Pelletier explains that the goal of her adolescent fiction is simply to encourage young people to read by entertaining them.

Teaching French as a second language in Laurenval from 1985 to 1990, Pelletier soon learned to combine her interest in writing with her training in pedagogy through the growing market of juvenile fiction. She made her debut in this market in 1987 with two stories, including the fantastic "Cher ancêtre" (Dear Ancestor), published in the April 1987 issue of *imagine . . .* and later the basis for two teen novels; its heroine, the daughter of a librarian and a genealogist, closely mirrors Pelletier. That year she also published her first adolescent novel, *Le Rendez-vous du désert* (The Desert Meeting), which begins to develop another vision of the future that recurs in her work: a post-apocalyptic Earth that has become a massive desert. This coming-of-age story addresses themes that appear in Pelletier's writing for adults, such as the environment, reproduction, and the struggle for identity of a female protagonist, but in a manner appropriate to its target age group. In *Le Rendez-vous du désert* the teenage heroine, Coril, with the help of a strong female mentor, makes a dangerous desert crossing to find her own path to identity. Rejecting the safe role of farmer's apprentice that social forces want her to accept, Coril chooses the more adventurous life of a *coursière*, a messenger between the cities and farms isolated by the extensive desertification. The biographical inspiration of the narrative appears transparent, reflecting the author's conflict as a young woman caught between her parents' recommendations to pursue a "safe" career in education and her own desire for the riskier path of a writer.

Throughout the late 1980s Pelletier remained highly active, publishing stories and short novels for adolescents. She represented Quebec at a science-fiction and fantasy conference in Roanne, France, in 1989, delivering a paper on Quebec writing workshops in the genre. That same year, in the *Solaris* article "1988: L'Anneé de tous les clichés?" (1988: The Year of All the Clichés?), she defended the high literary quality of science fiction in her province, rallying the close-knit community that had formed around the specialized journals with the battle cry: "il faut crier très fort que la SFQ, *c'est bon–et: c'est nous!*" (We must shout out loud that Quebec science fiction *is good–and: it's us!*). At the same time, she expressed concern over a trend toward facile plot lines and poorly developed characters in certain works; however, the hectic pace of her own activity may have allowed her space opera tales "En Bout de ligne" (At the End of the Line), published in the May–June 1987 issue of *Solaris,* and "Eaux mortes, eaux vives" (Dead Waters, Living Waters), published in the October 1989 issue of *Solaris,* to display similar problems.

In 1990 an appointment to the Directing Committee of the Quebec Administrative Council for Youth Communication allowed Pelletier to give up teaching. While organizing workshops in creative writing for young people, she also served as a freelance *correctrice* for the Quebec Ministry of Education. Still unable to support herself exclusively as a writer, from 1993 to 1999 she worked as an editorial secretary at Médiaspaul (formerly Editions Paulines), the Montreal press that has published the bulk of her novels for adolescents since 1990. During this decade, in addition to more stories for teens, Pelletier produced for an adult audience one novella, eight short stories, two poems, two opinion pieces, and her most ambitious work so far, the trilogy *Le Sable et l'acier.*

Nelle de Vilvèq, the first work in this trilogy, published in 1997, in some ways resembles Pelletier's earlier juvenile fiction; she admits that it represents a transitional work, as she shifted from writing children's to adult novels. Told through the personal journal of the title character, the novel recounts the experiences of a young woman who is quickly thrown into adulthood living on the streets of Vilvèq. Recalling Margaret Atwood's *The Handmaid's Tale* (1985), the novel depicts a society controlled by a firm-handed bourgeoisie, which dictates reproduction and family life through La Genète, a genetic factory. In Vilvèq, which represents a future Quebec, children grow up collectively until the age of apprenticeship, at which time they join a middle-class family. All the children are kept in ignorance about the workings of the world around them; food and goods arrive via a mysterious, fatally caustic river, along whose banks live the underclass of dockworkers, prostitutes, and a genetically engineered race of slaves called *éfans.* Willful and curious, Nelle rejects all control; her overriding desire for liberty and for answers to her questions leads her away from the privileged Upper City into the heart of the underworld. As the novel closes, she begins to find answers to her questions only by bargaining her way onto a trade ship as mistress of its legendary captain, the Voyageur. A cliffhanger ending leaves readers hoping that their own questions will be answered in the remainder of the trilogy.

Samiva de Frée, the second volume of *Le Sable et l'acier,* published in 1998, recounts the adventures of its eponymous heroine, who lives on the planet that provides Nelle's Earth with its resources. A member of the military police that protect the alien Terriens from potentially hostile Sarionites, Samiva has rejected her past on the poverty-stricken island of Frée. Intertwining the mystery of Samiva's origins with her unauthorized investigation of the murder of another officer, Pelletier strays somewhat from the mission of her trilogy. Although the novel demonstrates her narrative sophistication, Pelletier's emphasis of the murder mystery reveals her continued penchant for her first love: detective fiction. It may leave the science-fiction reader unsatisfied, wanting more development of the relationship between the fascinating worlds of Nelle and Samiva. In the final volume of the trilogy, *Issabel de Qohosaten* (1998), the heroine, Issabel, joins Nelle and Samiva to liberate those oppressed in and around Vilvèq. The book also reveals that Nelle's ancestors originated on Earth but left the planet after the "Grand Catastrophe," which resulted in toxic and desert-like conditions. The conclusion satisfies the reader's questions and makes a statement about united for change.

Pelletier has received consistent praise and support from the Quebec science-fiction community, but *Nelle de Vilvèq* was Pelletier's first work to gain the attention of the general Quebec press. Overall, it earned favorable reviews, with a few readers commenting on the excessive reliance on a mystery plot, or on a lack of depth to some characters. Apart from brief mentions in the rare articles published on Quebec science fiction, no critical study of any of Pelletier's works has appeared–not even commentary on the feminist perspective. A preface in *Nelle de Vilvèq* claims that the purpose of the trilogy is to tell "l'histoire de femmes ordinaires" (the story of ordinary women). And while Nelle and Samiva turn out to be far from ordinary, throughout *Le Sable et l'acier* Pelletier develops an imaginary universe, enriched with cultural and geographical detail, in which strong female characters play out their own destinies and fulfill their own desires for knowledge in spite of strong forces of social repression.

These strong heroines provide the basis for much of Pelletier's work. The author readily admits the important influence that being a woman exerts on her writing, particularly as she works in a genre dominated by men; only a handful of women currently write French-language science fiction. Her opinion piece "Ecrire des histoires de filles dans un univers masculin" (Writing Girls' Stories in a Masculine Universe, 1995), first published in *Visions d'autres mondes: La littérature fantastique et de science-fiction canadienne* in 1995, points out the lack of female readership for the genre and argues that part of the problem remains the prejudice of women and girls against literature that they perceive as unemotional and too technical. Pelletier works against these stereotypes, providing characters with whom a female readership can identify, as well as expressing her own frustrations as a minority with characters such as Samiva de Frée–an army officer, both a foreigner and female–who repeatedly overcome the obnoxious reactions of men to a woman's presence in what they perceive as their own domain.

Pelletier does not, however, wish to write a distinctly feminine brand of science fiction, and she admits that the early feminist anthologies bored her. In an unpublished interview dated 22 June 1998, Pelletier said, "la SF est moins science que fiction" (science fiction is less science than fiction), and although she has projected some clever technological innovations into her future landscape (such as the art of *envir*–interior decorating through holographic projection), telling a story clearly comes first. She also expresses a preference for the speculative aspects of the genre, "jouer avec des hypothèses et des 'si'; projeter dans le futur les craintes et les inquiétudes suscitées par le présent" (playing with hypotheses and "ifs"; projecting into the future the fears and anxieties raised by the present). Early short stories and certain aspects of the adult novels demonstrate her skill in this area, though in interviews Pelletier constantly sidesteps political issues and theoretical debates. This reluctance to dig too deeply into topics that are nonetheless of apparent importance to her appears reflected in her fiction, in which feminist, environmentalist, and sovereignists social analysis remains all too often at the surface only.

Pelletier has attained a level of success that permits her to live exclusively by writing. She still shares her talent in writers' workshops. She can now focus more energy on developing her career as an author of adult science fiction, with another novel for Editions Alire in progress. She also hopes to break into the difficult French market, as well as to publish an English translation of *Nelle de Vilvèq*. Although her potential as a writer cannot be denied, it remains to be seen where Pelletier's career will go. She could continue to produce entertaining, if somewhat formulaic works, one step above her adolescent novels. But if she can develop some of the stronger, original social commentary found in speculative works such as "La Petite," published in the December 1988 issue of *imagine* . . . and published in English translation as "Guinea Pig" in *Tesseracts*² (1990), which takes a hard look at the ramifications of organ transplants and donors, she could rival her mentor, Vonarburg, as the "first lady" of Quebec science fiction.

Interviews:

Littérature et la vie au collégial, edited by Anne Marie Alonzo (Mont-Royal, Quebec: Modulo, 1991), pp. 66–69;

Maurice Alarie, "Francine Pelletier, écrivaine en science-fiction pour la jeunesse," *Le journal de Sainte-Dorothée* (9 November 1997): 8;

Christine Fortier, "Francine Pelletier: La passion d'écrire," *Filles d'aujourd'hui,* 18 (July 1998): 64–65.

Reference:

Andrea Paradis, ed., *Visions d'autres mondes: La littérature fantastique et de science-fiction canadienne* (Montreal: Editions RD, 1995).

Teresa Plowright

(4 November 1952 –)

Cristie L. March
University of Virginia

BOOK: *Dreams of an Unseen Planet* (New York: Arbor House, 1986; London: Grafton House, 1990); revised edition (Victoria, British Columbia: Press Porcépic, 1989).

OTHER: "Making History," in *Howe Sounds: Facts, Fiction and Fantasy from the Writers of Bowen Island,* edited by Richard Littlemore (Bowen Island, British Columbia: Bowen Island Arts Council, 1994), pp. 89–103;
"The Wheel of Life," in *Tesseracts⁷,* edited by Paula Johanson and Jean-Louis Trudel (Edmonton, Alberta: Tesseract Books, 1998), pp. 218–219.

SELECTED PERIODICAL PUBLICATION–UNCOLLECTED: "Out the Other Side," *Prairie Fire,* 15 (Summer 1994): 76–81.

Teresa Plowright is one of a growing number of Canadian women science-fiction and fantasy writers who use the genre as a means not only of exploring futuristic or otherworldly possibilities but also of addressing larger issues within present social and cultural structures. In an unpublished 21 July 1998 interview she said, "I think many writers are drawn to speculative fiction because it allows you to deal with big themes."

Teresa Irene Plowright was born on 4 November 1952 in South Burnaby, a suburb of Vancouver, British Columbia, to Kenneth and Ingrid (née Wennberg) Plowright. Her father owned a small printing business, where Plowright worked sometimes during her youth. Her mother worked in the "cash cage" at the *Vancouver Sun* newspaper when Plowright was young, then later attended to the bookkeeping in the family print shop. Plowright was educated in a Catholic primary school in Burnaby and a Catholic girls' school in New Westminster, although she attended public school for tenth and eleventh grades. An only child, Plowright spent a great deal of time reading. While she wrote poetry when younger, she stopped writing entirely during her adolescence and did not begin again until she finished college.

Teresa Plowright (courtesy of the author)

Plowright began attending the University of British Columbia in 1970 and studied literature and languages. She initially majored in French but took several Spanish and English literature courses as well. While comparative literature studies interested her, the university offered no major in the subject. After her third year at the university, Plowright spent a year traveling in Europe with her husband, Brian Higgins (they married in 1971), and returned for a fourth year, during which she switched majors to honors English. The switch was prompted by the increased freedom for comparative literature that honors English offered and by her admiration for one of her teachers, the well-known American feminist literary critic Annette Kolodny (with whom she has maintained a correspondence). After earning her B.A., Plowright took an extra qualifying year in communications theory at Simon Fraser University, where she also became interested in computers; her project involved the computer analysis of French sonnets.

At this point her first marriage ended. "We were just very young–high school sweethearts," Plowright explained in an unpublished 16 July 1998 interview. A year later, while in California, she met Russel Wills, a psychologist. They moved to Ottawa and Montreal and married in 1977, and Plowright began a two-year masters program in communications at McGill University. During her coursework she became interested in telecommunications policy and pursued a job in that field upon receiving her master's degree.

By this time the urge to write, long suppressed, reemerged. Plowright arranged a leave of absence for a few months and traveled with her husband to Corfu, Greece, where she started work on her novel *Dreams of an Unseen Planet* (1986). Upon their return, she continued her government job for another year, but her desire to write prompted the couple's move back to Vancouver. She then worked with a telecommunications consulting company but found that writing part-time was not allowing her to concentrate enough on the novel. She quit her consulting job and began writing full-time, finally completing the novel in 1986.

Dreams of an Unseen Planet relates the story of an American space colony, Ventura, on the planet Gaea, and the struggle of its inhabitants to reconcile the demands of the planet with their need for survival. The narrative focuses on one woman, Miera, and her reactions to (and role in) the circumstances and events that have enveloped the colony. Ventura, cut off from communication with Earth by atmospheric and geomagnetic interference from Gaea, transforms from a healthy site of scientific exploration and progressive development into a paranoid and fragmented population guided in Big-Brother fashion by the government of the Center. The most pressing concern is the colonists' sterility. The colonists' inability to successfully conceive and bear children, coupled with the incomprehensible yet oppressive presence of the planet, are instrumental in the devolution of the community, resulting in histrionic, quasi-orgiastic Estros periods ostensibly aimed at alleviating the fertility problem. Finally, the Center sends Miera and Daphne, her rival for the affections of her former lover Michael, on a reconnaissance mission to Earth in preparation for the colonists' return.

As the novel progresses, Miera comes to recognize the futility of returning to Earth, which is still engaged in the world conflict that first inspired the colonists' journey to Gaea and now is ravaged and socially fragmented by man-made diseases, or "pandemics." She also realizes the colonists' need to attune themselves to Gaea, which has proven to be a living, sentient entity and the means by which the colony can overcome its paralyzing sterility–both literally and figuratively. In the process, Miera overcomes her own feelings of isolation and begins to understand her relationship not only with Gaea, which has responded to her, but also with her fellow colonists, particularly Michael, from whom she has become estranged.

In her 1995 essay "Consider Her Way: Canadian Science Fiction and Fantasy by Women," Christine L. Kulyk speculates that *Dreams of an Unseen Planet*–in which the planet itself is a conscious and communicative entity, in fact "a character in the book"–is "fundamentally related to the Canadian experience of trying to manage a country with a population relatively thinly spread out from sea to sea to sea." David Ketterer, in *Canadian Science Fiction and Fantasy* (1992), also sees the novel as deeply concerned with people's "harmonious psychic relationship to the environment."

Certainly Miera's shuttle flight back to Earth and her subsequent choice to return to Gaea point to an increased awareness of, and symbiosis with, the environment. Her shuttle companion, Daphne, describes the citizens of Earth as being afraid of the landscape outside of the self-contained cities, safe under their transparent domes. When Daphne dies from a vaccination against the pandemics, Miera, realizing the disturbing environmental claustrophobia that has gripped the communities of Earth, decides that the inhabitants of Gaea have the opportunity to create a properly communicative relationship with the planet. On returning to Gaea, she finds that the colonists have begun to understand and engage with the planet, resulting in the birth of twelve children who have a telepathic relationship with Gaea and the colonists. In the 21 July 1998 interview Plowright noted that "many people crave nature in a spiritual way" as a means of fulfillment: "I agree with Salman Rushdie that we have a 'god-hole' that needs to be filled," she explained, but when people "can't fill that hole with an organized religion (as many in the West can't) where does one turn?" *Dreams of an Unseen Planet* provides an exploration of that troubled relationship between individuals and communities, and their environment.

The novel also explores concerns and problems specifically related to women. While Plowright maintains that all relationships are complicated and multifaceted, *Dreams of an Unseen Planet* focuses on Miera and charts her reconciliation with conflicting images of herself. Miera is plagued by doubt about her professional

Dust jacket for Plowright's 1986 novel, about a colony of earthlings on a sentient planet

and personal relationships and her increasing fascination with Gaea itself. Thirty-seven and retiring in nature, she questions her desirability both as a scientist and as a lover, and throughout most of the novel she reveals an inability to approach others. As a result, she cannot recognize the positive relationships offered to her by her colleagues. Plowright commented in the 21 July 1998 interview that a friend "told me that I tend to have female characters who get overwhelmed by the complications in their situations. I was surprised to hear this; but I guess it's true." For a large part of the novel, Miera remains trapped in her situation. Yet, ultimately she does come to understand her relationship with Gaea, and this understanding empowers her to react and respond in definitive ways to the events that surround her. She leaves Earth and convinces the colonists that return is impossible in the near future, committing them to an "adapt or perish" approach to Gaea. Miera also recognizes her own self-worth and her role in the colony, and finally reconciles herself with Michael.

Two years after the publication of *Dreams of an Unseen Planet*, Plowright's first son, Rustin, was born on 19 February 1988. The following year, Plowright and her family moved to Bowen Island off the coast of Vancouver. Rustin was followed by his brothers: Devan, born on 1 February 1990, and Reed, born on 4 March 1993.

Plowright's writing career has slowed since the birth of her children; she decided early in their childhood to devote a great deal of time to them. While she has embraced this choice, she does regret the effect her time limitations has on her writing. "The solitary thinking that precedes a book, the ruminations on an idea or an image, the half-dreamy considerations . . . just don't happen," she said in the 21 July 1998 interview; "There's no place or time." Yet, despite these family demands, Plowright has continued her writing, although many "writer-mothers," she noted in the 16 July 1998 interview, have "to wait decades to really get back to writing" with any sort of frequency. "There've been times I wished I could just forget about writing altogether, for this phase of life," she explained in the 21 July 1998 interview, "But it does seem to be an urge that simply will not go away and must be expressed."

As a result, Plowright has turned to shorter works, including three published short stories. "Out the Other Side," which appeared in the Summer 1994 volume of *Prairie Fire*, focuses on Sol, a young woman who lives in the disintegrating and relatively abandoned remains of London in the wake of extraterrestrial "invasion." Large objects like "seeds" or "eggs" have fallen on the city and lain dormant, while the government and wealthy and middle-class citizens have fled, leaving the city to squatters and the occasional groups of well-to-do people whose sons are bussed in to use the athletic fields. The narrative refers often to the ordered nature of the life before, a thought on which the story ends as Sol struggles to escape pursuit—and, the story implies, rape and murder—by the boys who have followed her home.

As with *Dreams of an Unseen Planet*, Plowright negatively depicts cityscapes and the agoraphobia of people hiding inside to avoid the horrors of the environment that surrounds them. Sol's entrapment in an uncontrollable situation mirrors that of Miera, although Miera manages to regain control and shape events in her life, while Sol's story reveals no such escape. Both "Out the Other Side" and *Dreams of an Unseen Planet* also center on the inscrutable and mysterious nature of the alien "other," but again, the endings of the two works differ drastically. Gaea gradually becomes a knowable entity—the children born at the end of the novel are intimately intertwined with it—but the alien objects that destroy

London lie menacingly in the streets, their purpose unresolved at the end of the story.

"Making History," a short story that appeared in the anthology *Howe Sounds: Facts, Fiction and Fantasy from the Writers of Bowen Island* (1994), concerns another futuristic scenario in which the human population cannot come to terms with the Earth's environment. Serious overcrowding inspires an intellectual group's plan to terraform a small planet, but they cannot receive the funding for such an operation without the approval of an influential cult leader's cloned descendants. The government, fearful of these two clones' potentially subversive power, has placed them under house arrest, thus requiring Wakefield, the intellectuals' spokesperson, to use an intermediary in order to communicate with either of the clones. His role is complicated by the fact that he must choose one of the clones to make the terraforming journey with them. Finally, he devises a test to determine which of the clones is the better person, but the intermediary, eager to influence the legacy of such a decision, changes the result. As with Sol and Miera, Wakefield becomes mired in a situation over which he has no control. Like Miera, he acts to remedy this situation, but as with Sol, events block his actions.

Plowright's story "The Wheel of Life," published in *Tesseracts*[7] in 1998, addresses the ways people respond to aging. In this futuristic story three types of life cycles are available: the Naturalists age "normally," the Renewers replace their skins and are cremated when they reach one hundred years of age, and the Journeybackers age to fifty, then revert to childhood over the subsequent fifty years, finally dying as infants. When Edward changes his mind about Journeybacking and instead chooses Renewal, his mother, Molly, feels secure in knowing that while the rest of his family regresses, he will stand, beaconlike, protecting them. The story, though quite short, presents some complex issues. It subtly draws parallels between the care required by the elderly and the care required by infants, but it directs the reader's attention to the privileging that society places on the young at the expense of the old. Claire, Molly's Naturalist mother, frightens her grandchildren and makes Molly uneasy, yet Edward looks forward to caring for his Journeybacker wife, Victoria, when she is as helpless as Claire was at ninety-two. By calling the reader's attention to the way children in this world invariably aid their parents, whatever the route to death, Plowright questions the privileging of youthful appearance in the face of social reality.

Several of Plowright's finished works remain unpublished. Her second novel, originally titled "Into That Good Night," was completed and sold to Beach Holme in 1991, but as a result of publication problems the contract fell through. Involvement on the part of the Writers Union of Canada prompted Beach Holme to pay the original contracted advance and revert the rights back to Plowright, who redrafted the novel in 1997 and retitled it "Some Natural Tears." In the 21 July 1998 interview she explained that the novel explores "how science is changing the boundaries of life and death." In 1997 she also completed a screenplay titled "Boy Genius." Teresa Plowright has been working on texts for children's books and a young-adult science-fiction trilogy.

Reference:

Christine L. Kulyk, "Consider Her Way: Canadian Science Fiction and Fantasy by Women," in *Out of This World: Canadian Science Fiction & Fantasy Literature,* compiled by Andrea Paradis (Kingston, Ontario: Quarry Press, 1995), pp. 159–169.

Garfield Reeves-Stevens
(1953 –)

Greg Beatty

Garfield Reeves-Stevens (photograph © 1988 by Paul Till; from the dust jacket for Nighteyes, *1989)*

BOOKS: *Bloodshift* (Toronto: Virgo Press, 1981; New York: Warner, 1990; London: Pan, 1992);

Dreamland (Toronto: McClelland & Stewart/Bantam, 1986 [1985]; New York: Warner, 1991);

Children of the Shroud (Toronto: Doubleday Canada, 1987; New York: Warner, 1990);

Star Trek: Memory Prime, by Reeves-Stevens and Judith Reeves-Stevens (New York: Pocket Books, 1988; London: Titan, 1988);

Nighteyes (New York: Doubleday, 1989);

Energy: How Do They Move It? by Reeves-Stevens and Judith Reeves-Stevens (Agincourt, Ontario: Gage Educational, 1990 [1989]);

Energy: What Makes the Colours? by Reeves-Stevens and Judith Reeves-Stevens (Agincourt, Ontario: Gage Educational, 1990 [1989]);

Energy: Which Way is North? by Reeves-Stevens and Judith Reeves-Stevens (Agincourt, Ontario: Gage Educational, 1990 [1989]);

Life: How Are They the Same? by Reeves-Stevens and Judith Reeves-Stevens (Agincourt, Ontario: Gage Educational, 1990 [1989]);

Life: Where Did They Go? by Reeves-Stevens and Judith Reeves-Stevens (Agincourt, Ontario: Gage Educational, 1990 [1989]);

Life: Where Does It Come From? by Reeves-Stevens and Judith Reeves-Stevens (Agincourt, Ontario: Gage Educational, 1990 [1989]);

Matter: How Does It Clean? by Reeves-Stevens and Judith Reeves-Stevens (Agincourt, Ontario: Gage Educational, 1990 [1989]);

Matter: Why Does It Break? by Reeves-Stevens and Judith Reeves-Stevens (Agincourt, Ontario: Gage Educational, 1990 [1989]);

Matter: Why Does It Float? by Reeves-Stevens and Judith Reeves-Stevens (Agincourt, Ontario: Gage Educational, 1990 [1989]);

Science Around Me: An Introduction to Science and Technology, Level One, Series B. Teacher's Resource Book, by Reeves-Stevens and Judith Reeves-Stevens (Agincourt, Ontario: Gage Educational, 1990 [1989]);

Science Around Me: An Introduction to Science and Technology, Level Two, Series B. Teacher's Resource Book, by Reeves-Stevens and Judith Reeves-Stevens (Agincourt, Ontario: Gage Educational, 1990 [1989]);

Science Around Me: An Introduction to Science and Technology, Level Three, Series B. Teacher's Resource Book, by Reeves-Stevens and Judith Reeves-Stevens (Agincourt, Ontario: Gage Educational, 1990 [1989]);

Space: How Much Do They Need? by Reeves-Stevens and Judith Reeves-Stevens (Agincourt, Ontario: Gage Educational, 1990 [1989]);

Space: What Makes It Look Closer? by Reeves-Stevens and Judith Reeves-Stevens (Agincourt, Ontario: Gage Educational, 1990 [1989]);

Space: Where is It? by Reeves-Stevens and Judith Reeves-Stevens (Agincourt, Ontario: Gage Educational, 1990 [1989]);

Time: How Old Is It? by Reeves-Stevens and Judith Reeves-Stevens (Agincourt, Ontario: Gage Educational, 1990 [1989]);

Time: What Happens First? by Reeves-Stevens and Judith Reeves-Stevens (Agincourt, Ontario: Gage Educational, 1990 [1989]);

Time: When Will They Come and Go? by Reeves-Stevens and Judith Reeves-Stevens (Agincourt, Ontario: Gage Educational, 1990 [1989]);

Dark Matter (New York: Doubleday, 1990; London: Pan, 1992);

Shifter: The Chronicles of Galen Sword #1, by Reeves-Stevens and Judith Reeves-Stevens (New York: Penguin, 1990; London: ROC, 1991);

Star Trek: Prime Directive, by Reeves-Stevens and Judith Reeves-Stevens (New York: Pocket Books, 1990; London: Simon & Schuster, 1991);

Nightfeeder: The Chronicles of Galen Sword #2, by Reeves-Stevens and Judith Reeves-Stevens (New York: ROC, 1991; London: ROC, 1992);

Alien Nation #1: The Day of Descent, by Reeves-Stevens and Judith Reeves-Stevens (New York: Pocket Books, 1993);

Star Trek: Federation, by Reeves-Stevens and Judith Reeves-Stevens (New York & London: Pocket Books, 1994);

The Making of Star Trek: Deep Space Nine, by Reeves-Stevens and Judith Reeves-Stevens (New York: Pocket Books, 1994);

The Art of Star Trek, by Reeves-Stevens and Judith Reeves-Stevens (New York: Pocket Books, 1995);

Star Trek: The Ashes of Eden, by Reeves-Stevens, Judith Reeves-Stevens, and William Shatner (New York: Pocket Books, 1995); reprinted in *Star Trek: Odyssey* (New York: Pocket Books, 1998);

Star Trek: The Return, by Reeves-Stevens, Judith Reeves-Stevens, and Shatner (New York: Pocket Books, 1996: London: Pocket Books, 1997); reprinted in *Star Trek: Odyssey* (New York: Pocket Books, 1998);

Star Trek: Avenger, by Reeves-Stevens, Judith Reeves-Stevens, and Shatner (New York: Pocket Books, 1997); reprinted in *Star Trek: Odyssey* (New York: Pocket Books, 1998);

Star Trek, The Next Generation: The Continuing Mission: A Tenth Anniversary Tribute, by Reeves-Stevens and Judith Reeves-Stevens (New York: Pocket Books, 1997);

Star Trek Phase II: The Lost Series, by Reeves-Stevens and Judith Reeves-Stevens (New York: Pocket Books, 1997);

Star Trek: Odyssey, by Reeves-Stevens, Judith Reeves-Stevens, and Shatner (New York: Pocket Books, 1998);

Star Trek: Spectre, by Reeves-Stevens, Judith Reeves-Stevens, and Shatner (New York: Pocket Books, 1998);

Icefire, by Reeves-Stevens and Judith Reeves-Stevens (New York: Pocket Books, 1998);

Quicksilver, by Reeves-Stevens and Judith Reeves-Stevens (New York: Pocket Books, 1999);

Star Trek: Dark Victory, by Reeves-Stevens, Judith Reeves-Stevens, and Shatner (New York: Pocket Books, 1999);

Star Trek: Deep Space Nine: Millennium, Book 1: The Fall of Terok Nor, by Reeves-Stevens and Judith Reeves-Stevens (New York: Pocket Books, 2000);

Star Trek: Deep Space Nine: Millennium, Book 2: The War of the Prophets, by Reeves-Stevens and Judith Reeves-Stevens (New York: Pocket Books, 2000);

Star Trek: Deep Space Nine: Millennium, Book 3: Inferno, by Reeves-Stevens and Judith Reeves-Stevens (New York: Pocket Books, 2000);

Star Trek: Preserver, by Reeves-Stevens, Judith Reeves-Stevens, and Shatner (New York: Pocket Books, 2000);

The Return of Galen Sword, by Reeves-Stevens and Judith Reeves-Stevens (Los Angeles: Babbage Press, 2000);

Going to Mars: The Untold Story of Mars Pathfinder and NASA's Bold New Missions for the 21st Century, by Reeves-Stevens, Judith Reeves-Stevens, and Brian Muirhead (New York: Pocket Books, 2001).

OTHER: *Kids' Stuff: The Game Grown-ups Just Can't Win,* compiled by Reeves-Stevens, Campbell Kingsburgh, and Steve Heaslip (Markham, Ontario & Harmondsworth, U.K.: Penguin, 1984);

Popular Music: From Tin Pan Alley to Michael Jackson, compiled by Reeves-Stevens and Paul Till (Markham, Ontario & Harmondsworth, U.K.: Penguin, 1984);

For Women's Eyes Only: Trivia for 51% of the Population, compiled by Reeves-Stevens and Judith Reeves-Stevens (Markham, Ontario & Harmondsworth, U.K.: Penguin, 1984);

Television: From Uncle Miltie to The A-Team, compiled by Reeves-Stevens (Markham, Ontario & Harmondsworth, U.K.: Penguin, 1984);

"August," in *Shivers: An Anthology of Canadian Ghost Stories,* edited by Greg Ioannou and Lynne Missen

(Toronto: McClelland-Bantam, 1990 [1989]), pp. 14–20;
"CHIPS," by Reeves-Stevens and Judith Reeves-Stevens, in *Shivers: An Anthology of Canadian Ghost Stories,* edited by Ioannou and Missen (Toronto: McClelland-Bantam, 1990 [1989]), pp. 133–150;
"Masks," in *The Further Adventures of the Joker,* edited by Martin H. Greenberg (New York: Bantam, 1990), pp. 291–308;
"Blueblood," by Reeves-Stevens and Judith Reeves-Stevens, in *Chilled to the Bone,* edited by Robert T. Garcia (East Rutherford, N.J.: Mayfair Games, 1991), pp. 181–208;
"Part Five," in *The Ultimate Frankenstein,* edited by Byron Preiss, David Keller, Megan Miller, and John Gregory Betancourt (New York: Dell, 1991), pp. 249–270;
"Outport," in *Ark of Ice: Canadian Futurefiction,* edited by Lesley Choyce (Lawrencetown Beach, Nova Scotia: Pottersfield Press, 1992), pp. 197–208; reprinted in *Northern Stars: The Anthology of Canadian Science Fiction,* edited by David G. Hartwell and Glenn Grant (New York: Tor, 1994), pp. 308–317;
"Tear Down," in *Northern Frights,* edited by Don Hutchison (Oakville, Ontario: Mosaic, 1992), pp. 5–14;
"The Warrior of the Final Dawn," in *The Further Adventures of Superman,* edited by Greenberg (New York: Bantam Spectra, 1993);
"The Eddies," in *Northern Frights 2,* edited by Hutchison (Oakville, Ontario: Mosaic, 1994), pp. 31–56;
"One Last Night in The Mos Eisley Cantina: The Tale of the Wolfman and the Lamproid," by Reeves-Stevens and Judith Reeves-Stevens, in *Star Wars: Tales from the Mos Eisley Cantina,* edited by Kevin J. Anderson (New York: Bantam Spectra, 1995), pp. 362–380;
"A Bad Feeling: The Tale of EV-9D9," by Reeves-Stevens and Judith Reeves-Stevens, in *Star Wars: Tales from Jabba's Palace,* edited by Anderson (New York: Bantam Spectra, 1996), pp. 268–294;
"'Second star to the right and straight on 'til morning,'" by Reeves-Stevens and Judith Reeves-Stevens, in *Star Trek: The Lives of Dax,* edited by Marco Palmieri (New York: Pocket Books, 1999).

Garfield Reeves-Stevens is a prolific writer who has received more attention from the reading public and other writers than from critics or awards committees within the science-fiction and fantasy communities. This difference may be caused by the ease with which he has moved among a range of genres and forms, both in his independently written work and in the many works he has co-authored with his wife, Judith. Individual novels can be classified as horror, science fiction, mainstream thriller, fantasy, or the kind of simple adventure that might have been found in the magazine pulps from the Golden Age of genre fiction. In addition to their books and short fiction, the Reeves-Stevenses have written scripts for a wide range of animated television series, comic books, and movies.

Francis Garfield Reeves-Stevens was born in 1953 in Oakville, Ontario and grew up in nearby Toronto. His father worked in various industries and was also an inventor, often building his prototypes at home. His mother had been a fan of science fiction as a young girl, and reading and the imagination were highly prized within the Reeves-Stevens family. Unlike many American science-fiction writers who spent their formative years participating in formal and informal activities related to the genre (such as fandom), Reeves-Stevens began his early work unaware of any sort of Canadian community of writers. He said in an unpublished interview that this sort of social and creative isolation—and developing the internal resources to deal with it—might be a hallmark of Canadian science fiction. This self-directed nature may contribute to the ease with which many Canadian writers move among genres.

Several themes shape the apparently disparate works written by Reeves-Stevens (and his wife) into a unified whole. First among these unifying themes is a deep belief in the power of stories (usually origin stories). To learn something that is not known, in any arena, will change the world in Reeves-Stevens's fiction. His world is a place where the stories circulated by organized authorities are wrong. Sometimes they are simply out of date, passed on because of social ossification. More often, they are designed to serve vested interests, so that exposing hidden truths is always liberating. A powerful strain of anti-authoritarianism runs through these works. In novels written with his wife, this trait often leads to the creation of genuine heroes. In his independent work Reeves-Stevens creates figures that he has said he sees more as survivors than as heroes, figures he sees as therefore more Canadian than a hero who wins outright. British Canada, according to Reeves-Stevens, is marked by consensus and acceptance. In exposing the truth of a situation, the protagonist discovers a situation to which he must adapt, rather than one he can simply conquer. In novels where the hero does conquer, it is at great cost, which is itself transformative.

Another repeated trope that defines the Reeves-Stevenses' work as Canadian is open suspicion of the amoral hubris of the American government. Rather than praising secrecy or loss of innocent life as necessary in a realm of realpolitik, as do thriller writers such as Tom Clancy (with whom they have been compared), the Reeves-Stevenses repeat a specific pattern of characterization throughout their work. The reasoning of those in power is carefully delineated; readers always see the necessities driving individual choices. The reader is allowed to sympathize with even the darkest villains, but the plot

Dust jacket for Reeves-Stevens's 1990 novel, about a scientific genius who is a serial killer

mechanism always punishes these figures. Finally, an enthusiasm for existing fictional and mythic structures repeatedly emerges. Creatures, heroes, and plotlines are adopted for reuse, and several of the couple's fictions openly draw inspiration from older works.

All of these tropes can be seen in Reeves-Stevens's first three novels, which can be more properly categorized as thrillers than as science fiction or fantasy per se, though each of them includes elements of both technological advance and the supernatural. His first novel, *Bloodshift*, published in 1981, treats vampirism as a disease. The plot is complex, tracing centuries-old conspiracies hidden deep within the Society of the Jesuits and the Catholic Church as a whole. This secret society is dedicated to obliterating the vampires, who are ruled by their own dark Conclave. Seeking to drive things in a third direction—the preservation of the human species rather than good or the evil of predation—is a multilayered American intelligence agency. This agency is tracking the phenomenon commonly known as cancer and killing scientists who discover that cancer is actually a worldwide mutation that will kill off humanity unless people somehow learn the reason that yber (vampires) are immune from cancer.

Two relative innocents shaped by circumstances are caught between these competing forces—Granger Helman, a human assassin, and St. Claire, a vampire made so by accident. Granger is supremely competent but is little more than a pawn in the hands of such forces. He is nevertheless the only survivor of all the viewpoint characters; the novel ends with Granger transformed into a vampire and in sole possession of knowledge of the impending biological tragedy. The action in *Bloodshift* takes place at a breakneck pace. Plot twists are thrown off every few pages. As a result, characterization is strikingly underdeveloped; even the hero is little more than a placeholder. At the close of the book Granger's entire previous life has been wiped away, but there is almost no sense of what this change means to him or to readers.

Reeves-Stevens's next novel, *Dreamland*, published in 1986, develops a different kind of scenario and addresses some of the weaknesses of its predecessor. *Dreamland* is set in the world's greatest amusement park, only days away from its grand opening. This creative and commercial triumph faces a set of challenges. Some of them are the now-familiar conspiracies, in which criminal elements among the upper echelon of the park plot to steal computer technology; some are personal, as park employees are given a more fully realized array of life challenges. The largest threat, however, comes from the Presence: a malign supernatural entity that had been confined for decades to the land on which the park was built, but which now has access to the world at large by directly influencing the machinery and programming of Dreamland. The cutting-edge technology that has been applied to creating illusions for fun is exposed to be a hairbreadth away from horror. The presence of malign forces, whether they are supernatural, such as the Presence, or human, such as the criminal plotting that leads to assassinations in the corporate structure of Dreamland, is all that is needed to transform an amusement park into a realm of horror.

Children of the Shroud, published in 1987, has the same strengths and weaknesses as Reeves-Stevens's debut. The plot is bold: miracles and magic are afoot in the world because the cellular remnants clinging to the Shroud of Turin have been cloned, producing a host of young men with variations on Christlike powers. However, this new age of miracles is not matched by even an attempt at addressing the spiritual dimensions of great power or the profound character of a scriptural Christ. It is intriguing to unhinge Christlike powers from their context, but it removes the great charge; these young men might as well have personal access to nuclear weapons for all the meaning these powers carry. As with the choice to portray vampirism as a disease or mutation, the result in *Children of the Shroud* is an action-filled thriller with little weight and no memorable characters. Both this novel and *Bloodshift* attempt to interweave multiple plot strands, but without full control of the structure, so that timing is off.

Reeves-Stevens's writing career entered a new stage in the late 1980s as a result of two interconnected decisions. First, he started collaborating with his wife, Judith, with the result that all his novels published after 1990 are collaborative. Second, the Reeves-Stevenses began writing *Star Trek* novels, which brought them onto the best-seller lists but did little for their critical standing, and began working in the media of movies and television.

Reeves-Stevens met his wife when they were both working for a publishing house, Collier-Macmillan Canada, in Toronto; he was a math production editor, and she was a developmental editor in English as a second language. Judith came from a background similar to Reeves-Stevens's: her mother had been a science-fiction reader as a young girl, and her father was a university professor. She was born in Provost, Alberta and grew up in the provincial capital of Edmonton. She attended the University of Alberta in Edmonton, receiving a B.A. in modern languages and classics, followed by a master's degree in education. The Reeves-Stevenses wrote a series of science and technology textbooks—dealing with topics such as time, matter, energy, space, and life—for first- through third-graders, published in Canada by Gage Educational. While completing fifteen textbooks, they had learned that they enjoyed writing together and decided to try writing a collaborative science-fiction novel. Since they were both highly familiar with the *Star Trek* universe, they chose it for their first shared work of fiction.

The couple submitted five premises to Pocket Books, the publisher of *Star Trek* books, and Pocket selected the premise that became *Star Trek: Memory Prime* (1988). The *Star Trek* television show, only moderately successful in its first run in the 1960s, has become a marker of mainstream cultural acceptance of science fiction. At times scorned by genre purists, the original series has spawned several movies, a later direct sequel (*Star Trek: The Next Generation*), spin-offs (*Star Trek: Deep Space Nine* and *Star Trek: Voyager*), and a highly successful series of books that began with novelizations of the original series and then progressed to original, though formulaic, novels using *Star Trek* characters and situations. More than one hundred original novels have been set in the *Star Trek* universe, many of them written by well-known science-fiction writers.

Star Trek: Memory Prime was number 42 in the original *Star Trek* series. It is built around a complex plot involving Vulcan assassins who are adepts of the society of T'Pel, a cultural residue from the time before the planet's transition to a base of logic. The assassins are responding to action initiated by a small number of artificial intelligences (AIs). A convention of the Federation's greatest scientists serves as innocent bystanders and camouflage for a larger struggle. The now-familiar crew from the original starship *Enterprise* solves all of the challenges in a technically inventive fashion that still manages to stay within the bounds mandated by the publisher. Specifically, basing the threat in a secret society and physically contained AIs allows Captain Kirk, Mr. Spock, and the rest of the crew to serve as fixers in a highly dramatic situation that at no time threatens previously existing plot structures established by the show.

Themes from Reeves-Stevens's earlier independent work emerge in this novel. The existing bureaucratic structure built to contain the AIs is corrupt, and few members of it can be trusted unless vouched for in terms of emotion and commitment. The necessity of quickly signaling casual readers that these are in fact the characters known from television, however, produces dialogue and characterization that are little more than a collection of clichés and speech tags. Action is laboriously described, as if attempting to transcribe familiar actions from the show itself. The four weeks that *Star Trek: Memory Prime* spent on *The New York Times* paperback best-seller list can be attributed primarily to the *Star Trek* franchise.

Reeves-Stevens's next two solo novels represent his greatest achievement. Both are examples of the "what if?" school of science fiction, and strikingly, both are also books in which distortions of romantic love are major forces motivating key character action. He wrote *Nighteyes,* published in 1989, in direct response to the success of Whitley Strieber's purportedly nonfictional accounts of UFO experiences, *Communion* (1987) and *Transformation* (1988). *Nighteyes* picks up the details of the myriad alien abduction accounts and extrapolates them into a striking and coherent future. The novel depicts a world in which the United States government has been covering up evidence of UFO sightings for years and is still actively involved in both investigating such sightings and explaining them away. All the tabloid claims—of abduction, of biological sampling, of having children with a range of misshapen but humanoid aliens—prove to be accurate leakages of an extensive program to save the human race. The aliens prove to be human time-travelers, their appearance the result of an unexplained holocaust and millions of years of evolution. They are trying to introduce the genetic vigor of early humanity to a race that has evolved in almost unrecognizable directions. They accomplish this goal by manipulating many individual humans, abducting them for years, and causing them to fall in love and breed both humans of a particular strain and human-"alien" half-breeds.

The main characters in the book are competent, intelligent professionals, all of whom have greater control of their personal destiny than most of the race. When the abductions are exposed and their pace accelerates, each of these characters must deal with a rapid and repeated restructuring of his or her world. Their reactions, from severe anxiety in the case of FBI agent Vincent, to peevish anger in the case of Steven Gilmore, to calm acceptance in the case of his daughter Sarah, give *Nighteyes* poignancy. Characters face a situation almost mystical in nature and intensity. Throughout the novel the themes of transformative knowledge, and of the individual discovering his or her role in a larger whole, are explored. Time travel and neurological manipulation of the emotions give new life to age-old questions of free will and self-determination. These philosophical quandaries are faced directly only late in *Nighteyes,* when the mystery is fully exposed. Readers are caught up in the most architecturally complex plot Reeves-Stevens has thus far shaped. Independent story lines involving the Gilmores, the Federal Bureau of Investigation (FBI), professional UFO investigators, and an improvised task force of mental health professionals and physicists are all tracked in meticulous detail, and all come together into a single unified whole. Explanations for abduction memories move smoothly from speculative physics to pop psychology mechanisms such as recovered memories and to original evocations of the experience of being trapped by aliens.

Reeves-Stevens and his wife and frequent co-author, Judith (photograph by Thompson Geo-survey/Roland Gunner; from the dust jacket for Quicksilver, *1999)*

Nighteyes treats abduction accounts with such respect that the novel gained a great deal of notoriety in UFO circles when it was linked to the 1989 Linda Cortile abduction case. Skeptical investigators saw strong similarities between the fictional events of *Nighteyes* and supposedly true events reported by UFO investigator Budd Hopkins, who detailed his investigation of the Cortile case in his book *Witnessed: The True Story of the Brooklyn Bridge UFO Abductions* (1996). UFO enthusiasts still read *Nighteyes* voraciously and closely follow Reeves-Stevens's career.

In 1990 Reeves-Stevens published *Dark Matter,* which plumbed the depths of another and far more terrifying fascination, the serial killer. In the eyes of some theorists, serial murder is the distinguishing crime of the late twentieth century, symptomatic of an alienated society and fragmented selves. Journalists, novelists, and theorists strive to understand the serial killer and vie to control his image in the mass mind. One defining characteristic of the serial killer in popular mythology is that the killer is driven by a personal vision in which killing other people in a ritualized fashion is a path to transcendence. *Dark Matter* was written in direct response to Thomas Harris's novel *Red Dragon* (1981), which featured Hannibal Lecter and inspired the movie *Manhunter* (1986). *Dark Matter* asks: What would the world be like if there were a killer who transcended himself every time he killed?

At once horror novel and tale of detection, *Dark Matter* is Reeves-Stevens's best work of science fiction. The novel begins with a brutal torture scene in which an unnamed figure removes the skull from a woman who is still alive and aware of what is going on. He is looking into her brain so he can understand the mystery of how she thinks, and by doing so, understand the mysteries of the universe. The woman dies, but the process lifts her killer to a new level of understanding. The next chapter introduces Dr. Charis Neale, a physicist who is late for the Nobel Prize ceremony in Stockholm where three of her coworkers—all male—share the prize for physics. Once there, she meets her colleagues Adam Weinstein and Lee Kwong; all three await the entrance of Anthony Cross. Each of these characters is an outsider in his or her own way. Neale is a brilliant physicist in her own right but is kept a perennial outsider in a chauvinistic field because of her gender, youth, and beauty. Weinstein is an aging Jew, accustomed to abusing power by sexually harassing young women; Kwong is homosexual, and there also are rumors of his sexually harassing young men.

But none are as fully the outsider as Anthony Cross. His is the most brilliant mind physics has seen since Albert Einstein, perhaps the greatest ever. However, as the reader learns, Cross is also a visionary who can see his scientific discoveries long before he can demonstrate them, and a product of a dysfunctional home where he was repeatedly beaten and abused. Any one of these factors would have left him in permanent isolation. Taken together, they fuse to shape a mad scientist whose psyche is both splintered and nearly divine in its capacity. Like Victor Frankenstein, Cross moves into forbidden realms of knowledge at a terrible price; like Frankenstein, he carries a host of innocents with him to destruction. He also carries Neale, Weinstein, and Kwong with him, all of whom are hypnotized by his genius, but none of whom are in any way innocent. Early in Cross's career each of them learns about the terrible fusion of death and creation in Cross; each becomes bound to keeping Cross's killing secret, so that his discoveries can continue and they can continue to profit from them. After the Nobel Prize ceremony, the U.S. government is also involved. Via a thinly disguised dummy organization, it funds Cross's research to gain an edge in the weapons race; the government considers a few lives lost along the way to be an acceptable bargain.

Los Angeles police detective Kate Duvall becomes involved when Cross tortures someone to death in her city. Black and female in a department that welcomes those in neither category, she is a workaholic isolated by her devotion to her job. Her mind is no match for Cross's, but her compassion and sense of justice carry her on despite that. Duvall's investigation comes at a time when Cross is on the threshold of both his greatest breakthrough and personal disintegration. As Cross points out, the two inquiries—one into criminal matters, the other into physics—move in an eerie parallel. It is never clear which discovery causes which in the book, nor whom the reader's allegiances should follow. Anthony Cross is a multiple murderer, but he was also savagely abused as a child, and he is a profound genius; *Dark Matter* asks readers to consider whether either factor excuses his crimes. One of Reeves-Stevens's greatest achievements in this book is to make the rationalizations that those around Cross go through understandable, even appealing. In doing so, Reeves-Stevens fuses a theme that defines the serial killer novel—that acting beyond the realm of human morality causes one's mind to surpass the limits of human understanding—with the long-standing science-fiction element of worship of the scientist. *Dark Matter* asks one of the core questions of science fiction: How far is too far in the quest for knowledge?

Cross's final invention gives him a way to call upon the latent energy of the universe, bound up in what scientists call dark matter, by use of his will alone. It allows him to travel through space and eventually time, seeking the answers to all the mysteries of the universe and of his own being. The two questions are shown to be intricately interwoven. Cross's isolation from the human universe is finally made literal, as Cross and Neale leave this universe to start a new one, a universe in which they would never be alone and never doubt the reality of love. Duvall is the only major character still alive and functioning at the close of the book. Her particular blend of ethics and compassion is allowed to pass a final judgment on Cross's world, telling readers that some levels of power and knowledge cannot be accessed without destruction, and that people are better off for that. This ending is a highly original one, in a novel that began as a conscious attempt to answer previous works in the genre. In 1994 *Dark Matter* won France's Grand Prix de l'imaginaire, that country's highest award for speculative fiction.

In 1989 the Reeves-Stevenses moved to Los Angeles to pursue their interest in writing scripts for both television and movies, while continuing to write collaborative fiction. In 1990, the year that *Dark Matter* was published, the Reeves-Stevenses also published *Star Trek: Prime Directive,* another competent variation on *Star Trek* characters and situations.

More notably, that year the couple published their first original collaborative work, the first volume of their fantasy series *The Chronicles of Galen Sword*. The series rests on a premise long familiar in fantasy literature. There are two overlapping realities: the everyday world, which is known as the Second World, and the First World, which is the source of all things magical and arcane. Most of the Second World legends have a base in First World beings (vampires, werewolves, fairies), and the Reeves-Stevenses produce an impressive array of new creatures as well as showing previously unknown sides to existing entities. The core narrative follows the efforts of Galen Sword, amnesiac exile from the First World, to discover his past and regain his inheritance. Each volume within the series has a plot built around specific First World entities. The first volume, *Shifter,* selected as one of the Best Fantasy Novels of 1990 by *Science Fiction Chronicle,* follows Sword's attempts to capture a werewolf. The were—or shifter—Martin, turns out be half-shifter, half-human, and just as caught between worlds as Sword is. Initially a captive, Martin joins Sword and his intriguing band of investigators. Martin is Tarzan-simple about some things, but emotionally and ethically pure. Sword, originally a fairly immature character, must prove himself worthy of Martin's trust in *Shifter* and *Nightfeeder,* its 1991 sequel, built around an extended interaction with a humane and impressive vampire. A third volume, *Dark Hunter,* was written shortly after *Nightfeeder* but not published until 2000 as part of a special omnibus volume, *The Return of Galen Sword,* which includes slightly updated versions of the first two volumes and information about the related 1991 short story "Blueblood." Additional volumes are planned.

Galen Sword's character is far more intriguing than that of the protagonists in Reeves-Stevens's early independent novels. His predicament evokes heroes from classical mythology who had to uncover their parentage in order to find their destiny. His magically induced amnesia binds him, producing an intensely personal frustration that echoes the ignorance of human society regarding the First World. Sword's personal suffering equips him to deal with the metaphysical challenges of a magical reality and motivates him to become a hero worthy of this challenge. The fact that he must find his destiny by cooperating with a highly diverse band of investigators (each of whom is as isolated in his or her own way as Sword is) brings a social element to his character that is comparatively rare in speculative fiction. His growing ability to mediate disputes among disparate team members, as much as magic and bravery, make Galen Sword a hero worthy of critical examination.

After the Reeves-Stevenses moved to Los Angeles, they quickly achieved success in television. One of their first scripts to be produced after their arrival in Los Angeles was *Maggie's Secret,* a CBS Schoolbreak Special, of which they were cowriters. It received both the 1990 Scott Newman Drug Abuse Prevention Award and a Daytime Emmy nomination in the category of Outstanding Writing for a Children's Special.

Maggie's Secret is relatively unusual because it falls outside the fantastic genres in which the Reeves-Stevens usually work. The large majority of their script work in the years since has been in those genres. They have been active in fleshing out concepts and characters created by others, often from works considered popular classics in their respective genres, usually works with a central and clearly defined hero at the center. During 1992 and 1993 they wrote seven episodes of the animated series *The Legend of Prince Valiant* and three episodes of *Batman: The Ani-*

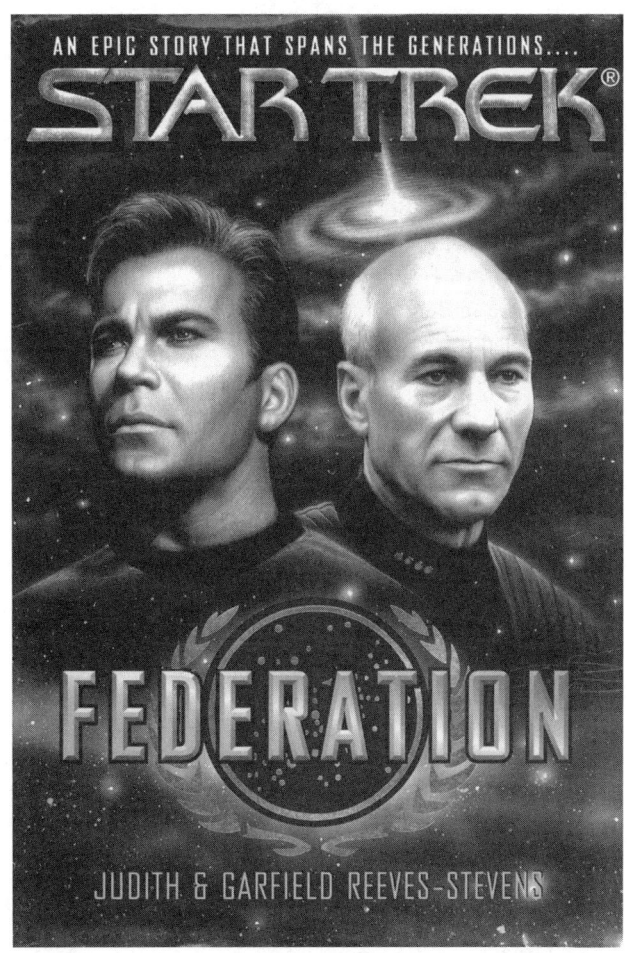

Dust jacket for the 1994 novel by the Reeves-Stevenses, featuring characters from the television series Star Trek *and* Star Trek: The Next Generation

mated Series, receiving an Emmy Certificate for Outstanding Writing in Animation for the latter.

As the 1990s progressed, the Reeves-Stevenses became further involved in television. In addition to writing the pilot for the animated series *Phantom 2040* and writing the scripts for nine of the episodes that ran between 1994 and 1996, they served as executive story editors for thirty-two episodes. They took on similar responsibilities for the animated *Flash Gordon,* writing the pilot and five episodes between 1996 and 1998 and serving as executive story editors for twenty-six episodes. This work has been praised by writers in the popular press. *Wired,* for example, singled out *Phantom 2040* for being hip and clever, and specifically praised the intricate story line and intelligent dialogue as being rare among animated series.

They returned to the world of *Star Trek* in 1994 with the publication of *Star Trek: Federation.* In this book the crew of the original *Enterprise* and characters from the *Enterprise* of *Star Trek: The Next Generation* come together in a particularly inventive fashion. They exchange discreetly coded messages while traveling through the gravity well of a black hole after the two ships are exposed to the two halves of a mystery that spans centuries. *Star Trek: Federation* quickly became one of the best-selling *Star Trek* novels ever published. The Reeves-Stevenses followed that success with a series of *Star Trek* novels written with William Shatner (whose name is exclusively featured on the front cover, with the Reeves-Stevenses only being identified as co-authors on the inside of the book), who had starred as Captain Kirk in the original series and the first seven movies. As a result these novels focus on Kirk at the end of his Star Fleet career and beyond, and derive both their strengths and weaknesses from that focus. Kirk's history is examined in ways that are often quite deep, so that his character actually develops in the books. At points throughout the sequence—*The Ashes of Eden* (1995), *The Return* (1996), *Avenger* (1997), *Spectre* (1998), *Dark Victory* (1999), and *Preserver* (2000)—but especially in *Avenger,* readers can glimpse a character who rises out of the flat writing and acting found in the original series to embody the archetypal power that his fans have long claimed for him. However, because the novels were written with Shatner and focus so tightly on Kirk, they dissolve repeatedly into narcissism. The smallest details of Kirk's character receive far more attention than they deserve, and his abilities are praised in an extended fashion. The plots collapse at least once in each book as a result of the necessity of having Kirk carry the day when it would not be appropriate or credible for him to win.

The Reeves-Stevenses have also had several opportunities to write about television (Reeves-Stevens had already published *Television: From Uncle Miltie to* The A-Team in 1984). Their editor at Pocket Books approached them in regard to writing "behind the scenes" accounts of the *Star Trek* series. This initial inquiry has produced a series of nonfiction works that promote the iconography of popular science fiction or that popularize science in ways that echo the Golden Age. Most of these works extend themes common throughout their fiction. In 1994 the first of these nonfiction volumes, *The Making of Star Trek: Deep Space Nine,* appeared. In this book the Reeves-Stevens' appreciation of the work of others, their enthusiasm for popular forms, and their love of detailed background emerge as they recount the workaday world of television production in a way that demystifies the processes involved but retains the magic of the final product.

The Art of Star Trek, published in 1995, is a blend of fannish excess and cool commercialism, but their two other nonfiction *Star Trek* books deserve at least brief comment. *Star Trek Phase II: The Lost Series,* published in 1997, was written to tell an untold story, as the introduction explains. It functions as an homage to lost opportunities and gives the reader the sense that the Reeves-Stevenses can appreciate the potential grandeur of the original *Star Trek* series in a way that network executives and producers could not. Likewise, *Star Trek, The Next Generation: The Continuing Mission: A Tenth Anniversary Tribute,* published the same year, takes the disparate energies that made individual episodes of *Star Trek: The Next Generation* so uneven and reworks them into a coherent history. Continuing their nonfiction work, the Reeves-Stevenses have also ventured into the world of popular science with *Going to Mars: The Untold Story of Mars Pathfinder and NASA's Bold New Missions for the 21st Century* (2001), written with Brian Muirhead, the flight systems manager for the Mars Pathfinder mission.

The Reeves-Stevenses published their first non-*Star Trek* novel in seven years with *Icefire,* published in 1998. *Icefire* and its 1999 follow-up, *Quicksilver,* marked a shift into the world of the techno-thriller exemplified by Clancy. *Icefire,* partially based on research the authors conducted on a trip to Antarctica, combines the disaster novel and the techno-thriller in a fast-paced action story. Rogue Chinese army generals have planted nuclear bombs under the Antarctic permafrost in order to create a gigantic wave that will cause destruction throughout the Pacific Ocean and all along the Pacific coast. Captain Mitch Weber, a Navy SEAL, and Corry Rey, an oceanographer, are a bickering couple who come up with the technological solution that will save the day. In keeping with the genre, the emphasis of the book is on fast-paced action and technological detail rather than character analysis, but most critics agreed that it was an exciting read. *Quicksilver* is another fast-paced techno-thriller, in which terrorists take control of the Pentagon. As most critics observed, both books seemed designed as the template for blockbuster movie adaptations.

John Clute wrote in *The Encyclopedia of Fantasy* (1997) that "frustratingly," Garfield Reeves-Stevens "seems to lack the ambition his skill demands." Certainly, at his (or their) best, as in *Nighteyes, Dark Matter,* and *The Chronicles of Galen Sword*, Reeves-Stevens and his wife are able to take formulaic genre fiction and expand its limitations in provocative or interesting new directions. Frequently, however, and especially since their move to Los Angeles, the Reeves-Stevenses seem content to flesh out the formula they are working with in an entertaining and readable fashion.

Esther Rochon
(27 June 1948 -   )

Annika Hannan
University of Toronto

BOOKS: *En hommage aux araignées* (Montreal: L'Actuelle, 1974); republished as *L'Etranger sous la ville* (Montreal: Editions Paulines, 1986);

Der Träumer in der Zitadelle, German translation by Otto Martin (Munich: Heyne Verlag, 1977);

L'Epuisement du soleil (Longueuil: Le Préambule, 1985); expanded and republished in two volumes as *Le Rêveur dans la citadelle* (Quebec: Editions Alire, 1998) and *L'Archipel Noir* (Quebec: Editions Alire, 1999);

Coquillage (Montreal: Editions de la Pleine Lune, 1985); translated by David Lobdell as *The Shell* (Ottawa: Oberon, 1990);

Le Traversier (Montreal: Editions de la Pleine Lune, 1987);

L'Espace du diamant (Montreal: Editions de la Pleine Lune, 1990);

Le Piège à souvenirs (Lachine, Quebec: Editions de la Pleine Lune, 1991);

L'Ombre et le cheval (Montreal: Editions Paulines, 1992);

Lame (Montreal: Québec/Amérique, 1995);

Aboli (Beauport: Editions Alire, 1996);

Ouverture (Beauport: Editions Alire, 1997);

Secrets (Quebec: Editions Alire, 1998);

Or (Quebec: Editions Alire, 1999);

Sorbier (Quebec: Editions Alire, 2000).

OTHER: "The Starfish," translated by Alexandre Amprimoz, in *Magic Realism,* edited by Geoff Hancock (Toronto: Aya Press, 1980), pp. 149–154;

"Xils," translated by Lucille Nelson, in *Northern Stars: The Anthology of Canadian Science Fiction,* edited by David G. Hartwell and Glenn Grant (New York: Tor, 1994), pp. 282–285.

SELECTED PERIODICAL PUBLICATIONS–UNCOLLECTED:
FICTION
"Petite ballade orwélienne," *Le Devoir,* cahier 5 (17 November 1984): xv;

Esther Rochon

"L'Initiateur et les étrangers," as Esther Blackburn, *imagine . . . ,* 38 (February 1987): 102–109;

"Par-dessus la tête," *imagine . . . ,* 39 (April 1987): 19–28;

"L'Ivresse de la chute," *XYZ,* 28 (1991): 58;

"Le Chat blanc," *Vidéo-Presse,* 23, no. 3 (1993);

"L'attrait du bleu," *Solaris,* 113 (Spring 1995): 14–15.

NONFICTION
"Sur Lovecraft," *Requiem,* 8 (1976): 5;

"Sur Jean Ray," *Requiem,* 11 (1976): 17;

"Ursula Le Guin," *Requiem,* 14 (1977): 15;

"Lovecraft et Québec," *Requiem,* 18 (1977): 8–10;

"Notes sur *L'Epuisement du soleil,*" *imagine . . . ,* 3 (March 1980): 24–38;

"Alien," *imagine . . .*, 4 (June 1980): 39–40;

"Films et livres de SF: Une appréciation de *The Dark Crystal* et de *Return of the Jedi*," *imagine . . .*, 19 (October–November 1983): 35–46;

"Les femmes dans *1984*," *imagine . . .*, 25 (1984): 17–33;

"Oser actualiser l'utopie," *Canadian Woman Studies,* 6, no. 2 (1985): 66–68;

"Two Early Readings of Lovecraft and Their Consequences," *Lovecraft Studies,* 35 (Fall 1986): 1–8;

"Notes on *Coquillage*," translated by Steven Lehman, *Science-Fiction Studies,* 19 (1992): 20–31.

Esther Rochon is considered a major figure in Quebec science-fiction and fantasy writing. Her involvement in the promotion of this literature and the originality of her literary productions have made for a strong and continually growing presence within Quebec. Despite translations of some of her work into German, Dutch, and English, and the availability of her work in France, Rochon has yet to receive substantial international attention. Many critics attribute Rochon's mainly local success to the paucity of English translations of her work, and some also argue that Rochon is underrated even within Quebec.

Rochon's ancestors are of Scottish, Irish, and Quebecois origins. She was born Esther Blackburn in Quebec City on 27 June 1948. She spent a few of her early years in Ottawa; then in 1956 she moved to Montreal and has lived there since. Her parents, Maurice and Marthe Blackburn, had met in Quebec City within the musical circles of the day. Rochon's father completed extensive music training, focusing on the piano and composition, and studied in Boston with Igor Stravinsky during World War II. He and his wife later collaborated on operas. They both took positions at the National Film Board, Rochon's mother as a scriptwriter and her father as a composer of operas and scores. Through her parents' involvement in artistic and intellectual circles, Rochon was exposed at a young age to science fiction (primarily through the French magazine *Planète*) and to creative expression.

Between 1956 and 1964 Rochon was enrolled in "cours classiques"–secondary education leading to postsecondary studies–at the Collège Marie de France in Montreal. She mentions (for example, in "Two Early Readings of Lovecraft and Their Consequences," 1986) that she read H. P. Lovecraft and other writers such as Ray Bradbury and Isaac Asimov partly in reaction to the obligatory, tiresome literature taught at school; she paid 50¢ each for her first novels by H. G. Wells and Asimov at a local drugstore. Her sense of the subversive potential of literature began to form at this point.

Rochon indicates in "Two Early Readings of Lovecraft and Their Consequences" that even as a four- or five-year-old she was given to inventing stories. In her teenage years she began to write down her imaginative visions in order to share them with others. At age sixteen she tied with Michel Tremblay for the Premier Prix, section Contes, du concours des Jeunes Auteurs de Radio-Canada; her story was a science-fiction entry titled "L'Initiateur et les étrangers" (The Initiator and the Strangers). This maturely written piece tells of extraterrestrials in human form that destroy much of the earth by means of fire but fail to compromise the integrity of the survivor, Ludwig. The tone, as Rochon describes it, is initially intellectual but becomes emotional, and the story concludes on an optimistic note. During the award ceremonies, part of "L'Initiateur et les étrangers" was read on television.

While both of her parents encouraged her to write, Rochon attributes to her father an especially good eye for the "strange" and remembers being strongly affected by the Lovecraft stories he gave her to read. In an article for the Fall 1986 issue of *Lovecraft Studies* Rochon admits that while other teenage girls had crushes on movie stars and singers, she was taken with the imagination and sensitivity of Lovecraft; to her, his works exhibited intelligence, deep but subdued emotion, a sense of poetry, and a reflection on the nature of reality. At the same time, she adds, she was learning through her parents about colonialism and its relation to Quebec, and about the challenge by intellectuals and artists such as her parents to "the old Jansenist values of Quebec's strict Catholicism."

Rochon went on to study mathematics at the Université de Montréal, obtaining a bachelor's degree in 1968 and a master's degree in algebra in 1969. One of her only formal jobs was working as a teaching assistant marking exams. She dated Jean-François Rochon, a telecommunications analyst, for three years, and the couple married in 1970. Though beginning a doctorate in mathematics, Rochon soon felt the strain of raising two children (her daughter, Viviane, and son, Olivier, were born in 1973 and 1975, respectively) while trying to study full time and to write fiction; she consequently abandoned her degree having completed all requirements except the dissertation.

Rochon's intense interest in both mathematics and creative writing might suggest two widely different trains of thought. For the writer, however, these areas are complementary: both, she says, involve a language, have certain rules, and carry an allusive dimension. But fiction soon dominated her interests, largely because of the influence of Lovecraft; to him Rochon attributes her decision to become a writer as well as her use of "the pleasures of dream and writing as an antidote to difficult situations." She was particularly influenced by Lovecraft's idea, expressed in his story "Through the Gates of the Silver Key" (1932), that life consists of mental images which may derive from reality or from dreams, the two sources being equally valid; such concerns foreshadow Rochon's later interest in Tibetan Buddhist philosophy. Other influences on her work include science-fiction or fantasy writers Selma Lagerlöf, Frank Herbert, Robert Heinlein, and Jean Ray; she admits to being particularly stimulated by those writers who balance evocative imagery with philosophical and theoretical concerns. Many critics link her work with that of Ursula K. Le Guin (about whose work Rochon has written a critical article), seeing a relationship between Rochon's *En hommage aux araignées* (In Praise of Spiders, 1974) and Le Guin's *The Tombs of Atuan* (1971). While Rochon acknowledges their mutual interest in Eastern philosophies and credits Le Guin with clearing a path for women's writing, she denies being profoundly influenced by the American writer, since Rochon had begun to write before she had read Le Guin's work.

Rochon's writing is diverse, ranging from articles on literature and cinema to a script for a documentary on the genocide of the Armenians (a project that was never realized because it lacked sufficient funding). She has also evaluated movie scripts and projects for Téléfilm Canada and has written technical manuals for the Société de téléinformatique. Her fictional works are eclectic as well. In an interview with Michel Lord in *Lettres québécoises* (Winter 1985–1986) Rochon says that while she has written poems and short stories, she is particularly comfortable with the novel form because it allows her not only to create a setting but also to explore theories. In particular, science fiction and fantasy allow her a range of images and symbols with which she can explore human emotions, anxieties, and desires. Reading the science-fiction journal *Analog* in the 1960s, Rochon was struck by the play of ideas, the startling images, and the well-crafted stories, and took such works as her model. By translating such stories she also taught herself English.

Rochon was one of the first Quebecois writers to contribute to the science-fiction journal *Requiem* (which later became *Solaris*). Moreover, with an eye to developing Quebec science fiction and supporting the work of new writers, Rochon helped to establish the journal *imagine . . .* in 1979. She acted as co-editor between 1979 and 1981, leaving the post because she felt uneasy in that position of authority. The journal opened itself to different types of science fiction, ranging from hard science to more speculative or avant-garde types; this open-minded approach to the genre appears to harmonize with Rochon's own work, which many critics see

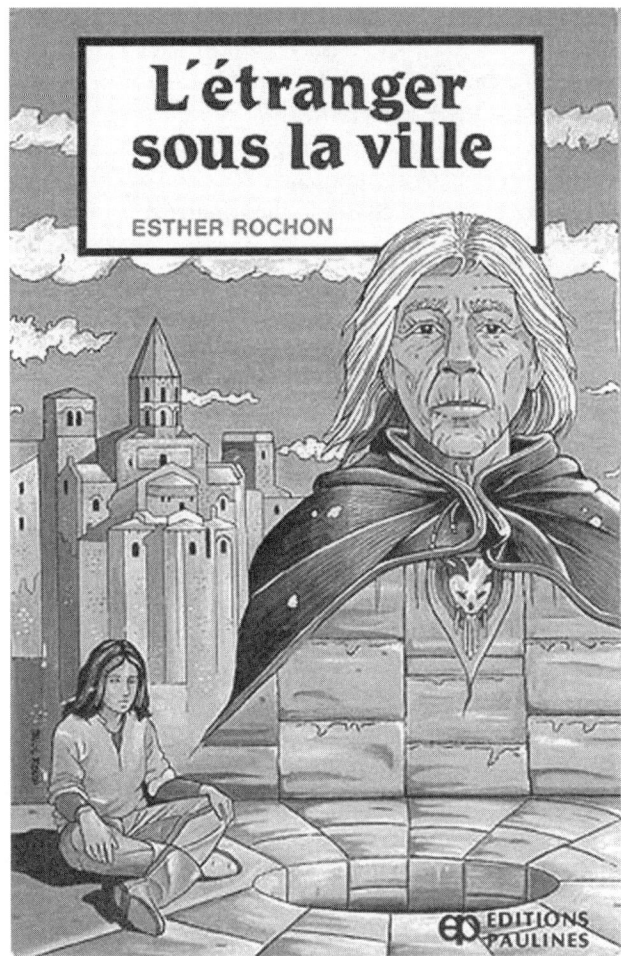

Cover for the 1986 children's version of Rochon's first novel, En hommage aux araignées (1974), about a professor who tries to inspire hope in an apathetic northern people

as poised somewhere between science fiction and fantasy. What also characterizes Rochon's works, and what consequently earned them the label "magic realist," is their strong connection to the quotidian and to a familiar Earth; several of her short stories blatantly evoke Montreal, and her novels often allegorically point to this location. Rochon insists that science-fiction and fantasy writing is not about the future or about distant places, but about the "here and now."

From the start, Rochon's texts have garnered favorable criticism. Her first novel, *En hommage aux araignées,* launched the Vrénalik trilogy, a series that was twenty-seven years in the making. This early novel was widely praised for its quality. Jacques Pelletier commented in *Livres et auteurs québécois* (1974) on the subtle and engaging style of the novel, comparing it to the sober, spare prose of Jacques Benoît. Vital Gadbois judged it a remarkable story written in a clear, controlled manner. Reginald Martel wrote in *La Presse* (21 December 1974) that "Dès son premier roman, Esther

Rochon s'impose en effet par la rigueur et la précision de son style, par la cohérence de l'organisation de la matière romanesque.... Il faut dire qu'elle a tout de suite renoncé au traditionnel premier roman biographique, pour plonger directement dans l'imaginaire" (From her first novel, Rochon commands attention by the rigor and precision of her style and the coherence and organization of the material.... Significantly, she has bypassed the traditional biographical first novel to plunge directly into the imaginary). Tightly structured—perhaps a carryover of Rochon's mathematical logic—the novel is also highly imaginative. As Pelletier pointed out, *En hommage aux araignées* runs counter to many of the Quebecois novels of its time, being neither a realist nor an experimental novel but instead "ouvr[ant] toutes grandes les portes de l'imaginaire" (opening widely the doors of the imagination). Republished in a children's version as *L'Etranger sous la ville* (The Stranger Under the City, 1986), the novel received a special mention in the Conseil des Arts children's literature awards.

En hommage aux araignées is filtered through the narrator Anar Vranengal, a female witch once in love with Professor Jouskilliant Green and now given to a retrospective look at their time together in Frulken, capital city of the Vrénalik Archipelago, home of the Asven people. Hailing from the abundant and progressive south, Green is a figure of renewal in the frozen archipelago of the north; though initially unclear of his purpose in Frulken, he is urged by the leader of the city, Fékril Candanad, to attempt to inspire hope in the people after four hundred years of sickness and disasters. But the apathetic Asven, convinced that they are subject to a curse and must simply await their release, eventually discourage Green in his efforts. The male witch Ivendra, who succeeds the aging Skaad and who will in turn tutor Anar, is the only eager student of Green's philosophies.

A key aspect of the novel is Green's descent, in frustration and defeat, to the abandoned vaults lying just below the citadel of the city, where he lives in isolation for seventeen years. Anar, intrigued by the mystery of Green, brings him to the surface. Both characters (though to a lesser degree, in Anar's case) come to recognize their desire for self-knowledge and inner strength; within the murky depths of the vaults, and perhaps of the unconscious, each thus undergoes certain trials. The novel is largely focused on the themes of knowledge and perception, as Anar and Green help one another to heighten their awareness of the beauty and mystery of life. The eponymous spiders in the vaults symbolize Green's visionary capacities—the spiders are blind but highly perceptive creatures—and his darker, unpredictable side; the kind of ambiguity evident in his position is a familiar (and positive) component of Rochon's works.

The novel has been seen in a biblical light, with Green as a messiah figure. One can also detect a sociopolitical element relating to Quebec's history—four hundred years—of struggle and change; or more accurately, the novel foregrounds a lack of change: Vrénalik is a "pays perdu" (lost country, or colloquially, boondocks) that fails to act to ensure its own survival. As in many of Rochon's works, the personal has a strong impact on the public, and vice versa; the individual is often considered in relation to the society from which she or he emerges and which she or he has the potential to alter. In Rochon's view, the text should motivate the reader to take action or at least to think differently about the world.

The exploration of dualities of darkness and light or reason and intuition in *En hommage aux araignées* suggests that Rochon had been thinking and writing along Buddhist lines even before she began frequenting the Dharmadhatu, a Buddhist meditation center in Montreal, in 1977. She joined the center in 1980, and her engagement with Buddhism seems to have strengthened her burgeoning ideas about personal fulfillment vis-à-vis the external world. The philosophy helped her to find a spiritual means of dealing with important changes in her life, such as the birth of her children; it also, she says, allows her to imagine a more harmonious and just interaction between people.

Rochon also links her philosophy with feminist concerns, often basing her fictions on strong or potentially strong female characters who discover how to meet their needs and to lead others in the same direction. Women characters are central to Rochon's utopian vision of an equitable, even androgynous, society; the leveling of conventional gender binaries, whether within a society or a single character, is presented with a humanist, progressive thrust. Annick Chapdelaine, in a 1995 essay, sets Rochon's works in the context of contemporary science fiction by women that aims to destroy female stereotypes; she notes how Rochon both challenges the prevalent notion that women lack the capacity to write science fiction and expands the genre to include her own sociological and metaphysical concerns.

One of the most important of Rochon's Buddhist mentors is a woman: Yeshe Tsogyel, a queen who lived in Tibet in the eighth century and who played a key role in the expansion of Buddhism in that country. In her essay "Oser actualiser l'utopie" (1985) Rochon praises Tsogyel's poetic and mythical style of writing, commending in particular her cultivation of the heart and spirit as opposed to the intellect. In this article Rochon takes aim at the North American self-involvement and indolence that prevent people from acting for the greater good. Yet, she also sees the possibility for a utopia in the here and now through self-development (as opposed to self-involvement) and an active social engagement. As Rochon puts it in this essay, "la réalisation d'une vision de société heureuse commence par le travail sur soi en vue d'aider tout le monde" (the creation of a healthy society begins with a self-development aimed at the benefit of all). Women, in her utopian vision, have an important role to play as they share positions of authority and responsibility with men but also develop their own interests. Asked by Hélène Colas whether she creates different roles for her female and male characters, Rochon says that her female characters are more down-to-earth and more resourceful than the male characters, the latter often appearing arrogant or powerless. However, the potential for both sexes to learn and change is always present in the writer's works.

For three months in 1983 Rochon and her children participated in Buddhist study and meditation programs in Pennsylvania; such programs continue to draw her interest, and she often visits a meditation center in Vermont. During the early 1980s she also wrote many of the stories assembled in her two collections, *Le Traversier* (The Ferry, 1987) and *Le Piège à souvenirs* (The Trap of Memories, 1991). In 1984 she wrote the story "La Ville aux animaux, la montagne aux fantômes" for a short-story contest organized by Radio-Canada.

The Vrénalik cycle continues with *L'Epuisement du soleil* (The Draining of the Sun, 1985), a novel about the interaction between the Vrénalik Archipelago and the regions lying to the south of it. This work was originally published in sections in the journal *imagine . . . .* Rochon indicates that she began to formulate ideas for the novel as early as 1963, when she consciously decided to create a beautiful, well-crafted story in order to make her life useful. Her ideas came from two dreams she had concerning the characters of the prospective novel and their discovery of a statue. In fact, all of the writer's novels and a third of her short stories depict one or several of her dreams.

In *L'Épuisement du soleil* Rochon again focuses on knowledge and change in both self and society as she portrays the Asven before and after their decline. *L'Epuisement du soleil* expands upon the earlier *En hommage aux araignées* by moving beyond the bounds of individual success to consider that of the community at large. The prosperity characterizing Vrénalik four hundred years earlier–of ambiguous character since based upon conformity and even tyranny–comes to ruin under the power-hungry, materialist leader of the Asven, Skern Strénid. The events of this earlier time constitute a novel within the novel, titled *Le Rêveur dans la citadelle* (The Dreamer in the Citadel); this section was initially a self-contained novel written in French but published first in German as *Der Träumer in der Zitadelle* (1977). In 1998 *Le Rêveur dans la citadelle* appeared in a version independent of *L'Epuisement du soleil* (where it had its first publication in French in 1985) and with two additional chapters, making it the first complete version of the story.

Within *L'Epuisement du soleil*, "Le Rêveur dans la citadelle" is the manuscript of Jouskilliant Green, who in *En hommage aux araignées* had translated into his own language the books of Asven legends he discovered in the vaults. Under Skern's orders, the male witch Shaskath becomes the Dreamer, exploiting a drug-induced dream power to command the winds and thereby protect Vrénalik's shipping trade. With one of Skern's many wives, Inalga de Bérilis, the Dreamer eventually rebels against Skern's tyranny and, despite an initial impulse to save Vrénalik, launches the deadly curse of the neglected ocean god, Haztlén. Taïm Sutherland's experiences add a bildungsroman effect: eventually rejecting both the materialism of his southern roots and the passivity of the Asven, he embarks on a journey to locate the missing statue of Haztlén. Anar and her witch mentor, Ivendra, both of whom wish to end the perpetual "winter" of the Archipelago, are Sutherland's guiding forces. The cycle thus traces Anar's maturation from curious but still inhibited youth to visionary, confident adult, as well as the Archipelago's emergence from darkness into light.

This novel, like the first of the series, has been read in the context of Quebec's social and political history, and Rochon confirms that 1970s politics in particular are at issue. The opposition between the Archipelago and the south corresponds to that between Quebec and the colonizing countries that threaten it, such as English Canada, the United States, France, and Europe in general. Rochon even compares Quebec's position to that of Native Canadians vis-à-vis the white population, but emphasizes the Quebec/colonizer relationship. Skern Strénid, a technocrat motivated by economic interests to the detriment of cultural concerns, could be seen as an allegory for Premier Robert Bourassa. The author acknowledges the influence of writers such as Gaston Miron, Jean-Guy Pilon, and Fernand Ouellette on her approach to the novel, referring to their sense of cultural malaise vis-à-vis Catholicism and national identity; in her interview with Jean Royer (1987) she admits to channeling "une sorte d'angoisse québécoise caractéristique" (a typical Quebecois anxiety) into the composition of the novel.

But the Archipelago is not simply a victim within Rochon's fictions; the author speaks metaphorically about the Archipelago as an adolescent who under-

Cover for Rochon's 1985 novel about the sexual and emotional interaction of five people with a sea monster

stands oppression but who lacks the maturity or autonomy to act against it, thereby remaining passive and powerless. Sutherland, she commented in her interview with Lord, essentially carries the marks of doubt that pervaded Quebec as it "se rendait compte des limites de son mythe du pays" (realized the limits of its myth of nationhood). Rochon tells how she used to listen to her fellow Quebecois on Radio-Canada phone-in shows to get a sense of how her characters could serve as links between the individual and the collective; as she told Royer, "Une des choses qu'on adore [au Québec], c'est d'essayer de savoir ce qu'on est collectivement et comment certains individus le réalisent plus que d'autres" (One of the things we love here [in Quebec] is to try to understand who we are as a people and how certain individuals comprehend this better than others). She advocates a concerted effort on the part of the Quebecois to maintain their language and distinct cultural identity.

In a more personal sense, the novel links intimately with Rochon's worldview at the time she was shaping the story line; the text deals only briefly with marriage and children because Rochon had neither married nor had children yet when she began to plan it. She acknowledges that the Archipelago symbolizes her center of being, an imaginative place through which she could address her own frustrations and questions about the meaning of life. Lovecraft's *The Dream Quest of Unknown Kadath* (1943), particularly its attention to dreams, was a possible influence on the composition of the novel.

The use of color is an important part of Rochon's evocation of place and also of mindset; the grays, blacks, and browns of the Archipelago landscape highlight the melancholy and repression of the people and correspond to the Gaspé peninsula of Quebec. Some of the writer's attraction to color stems from her interest in Buddhist legends, in which the characters' appearances and clothing are described in great detail, as are their actions. Rochon connects each character in *L'Epuisement du soleil* with colors corresponding to their personalities; black, for example, conveys death, wisdom and folly, and solitude, while white symbolizes anger and knowledge. The number three plays a highly symbolic role in the novel; Rochon's detailed explanatory notes ("Notes sur *L'Épuisement du soleil*," published in *imagine . . .* in 1980) tell how she worked cosmological concepts of the yin and yang into trigrams that structure the text.

In her reading of the novel Élisabeth Vonarburg refers to the center—so crucial to Rochon's work—as both a milieu where the world and the individual interpenetrate, and a goal pursued by the individual; both situations gravitate toward an inner peace attainable through the "spontaneity of reality" or acceptance of contradictory forces as complementary. As Vonarburg writes in her "Notes sur Esther Rochon" (1985), "La circonférence du monde chez Rochon (sa limite) n'est 'nulle part,' parce que tout est (par)tout: l'horrible et le beau, la mort et la vie" (The circumference of Rochon's fictional world [its limit] is "nowhere," because everything is everywhere: the horrible and the beautiful, death and life). Vonarburg's interest in Rochon's work extended to a suggestion that Rochon contribute to an anthology of erotic works by women; the project never came to fruition, but the proposal led to the publication of the novel *Coquillage* (The Shell, 1985), an extract from which was Rochon's planned contribution.

Fabien Ménard commented that Rochon's more extensive novels, those dealing with the history of a people (as with the Vrénalik cycle), lack the sensuality of an intimate text such as *Coquillage* but display a richness of story and storytelling. Estelle Dansereau, however, faulted *L'Epuisement du soleil* for its misleading structure and impalpable characters. Royer, writing in *Le Devoir* in May 1986, called both *L'Epuisement du soleil* and *Coquillage* breathtaking novels, the first because of its epic nature and the second because of its poetic aspects.

Coquillage is not part of the Vrénalik cycle but does use an island setting to explore the sexual and emotional interaction between five adults and an androgynous, telepathic, centuries-old monster/nautilus. In 1987 Rochon won the prestigious Grand Prix de la science-fiction et du fantastique québecois for *Coquillage*. "Dans la fôret de vitrail" and "La Nappe de velours rose." *L'Epuisement du soleil* had earned Rochon the same prize in 1986, an interesting outcome considering that *L'Epuisement du soleil* had enormous difficulty getting published. The jury selected Rochon for the 1987 prize because of the quality of her writing, the imaginativeness of her stories, and her ability to portray the social climate. *Coquillage* also won the Prix Boréal (as did *L'Epuisement du soleil*) and was a finalist for the Jean Béraud Molson Prize. Ménard argued that because of its sensuality, strangeness, and poetic quality, *Coquillage* constitutes one of the key moments of Quebecois fantasy writing.

The story line of *Coquillage* originated in a dream Rochon had when she was pregnant with her daughter. The dream involved the enormous shell that both the nautilus and the human characters occupy, as well as the nautilus's emergence from its home in a deadly gush of foam. Rochon indicates in her 1992 "Notes on *Coquillage*" (which include helpful chronologies of the events of the novel) that these dream aspects were incorporated faithfully into an early version of *Coquillage*–a short story titled "Mourir une fois pour toutes" (written in 1976)–but were altered in the novel itself. Rochon notes that the story carries the marks of a difficult period in mid-1970s Quebec: an economic crisis and the closure of several publishing houses, including the publisher (L'Actuelle) of her first novel. Linked to this atmosphere were her ambivalent feelings about writing. The novel version reflects a greater optimism, revolving not around death but life, and paying greater attention to the possible harmony between men and women. Substituting Xunmil (a female character) for Xehinn (a male character), furthermore, Rochon was able to invest her own thoughts and feelings as a woman; she thus created a more realistic and ironic portrayal of that character.

Coquillage is framed by conversations between Doctor François Drexel and his former secretary (and now deathbed nurse), Xunmil, as they remember their days at the shell. The text shifts between the present, in which Xunmil attempts to keep François from a death linked to his repressed love for the monster, and a past in which François's father, Thrassl, learns to indulge his own erotic love for the sea creature. As Thrassl gradually gives himself emotionally and physically to the monster–consequently strengthening his ties with François's mother, Irène Drexel, and Irène's husband, Vincent Pralitt, and accessing his deepest desires–the novel explores the human potential for growth via the knowledge and acceptance of sexual needs and wants. The individual is seen to be particularly enriched through his or her engagement with the external "other," whether in a positive or negative sense; the monster is both entirely selfless and loving (as François says, it is "tout l'amour au monde," all the love in the world), and a drain on Thrassl's energy and health. Indeed, as David Ketterer writes in "*The Shell,* An Exquisite Monstrosity" (1992), the monster "would seem to embody all that is wonderful and all that is most hideous and disgusting about the human condition, particularly love, sex and death."

The enriching and destructive aspects of the monster and of life are necessary to a full existence; the novel reflects Buddhist concepts of the spontaneity of reality. Rochon acknowledges that the novel is intimately related to her Buddhist interests: just before beginning to write *Coquillage* in 1980, she met Chogyam Trungpa Rinpoche, a Buddhist master who visited the Dharmadhatu in Montreal, and this encounter gave her the confidence to pursue her writing according to her own visions. The meeting with Rinpoche also prompted Rochon to affirm her faith by taking two Buddhist vows; in order to afford the required trip, Rochon, acting on a friend's advice, decided to write a "best-seller." Understanding the appeal of eroticism to readers, she embarked upon *Coquillage*.

Ketterer praises *Coquillage* as a "superbly realized, poetic, carefully structured, temporally scrambled narrative" and indicates that it was the first of Rochon's novels to gain mainstream attention. He does not explain why this novel attracted readers beyond the realm of science fiction or fantasy, but one can speculate that the bizarre eroticism and accessible story line–not to mention the English translation–were attractive to a variety of readers. The novel stands apart from Rochon's other works because of its highly sensual content and style; the dialogue between characters is both spare and weighty, laden with symbolic import and charged with emotion. The author deems the novel an intimate work lacking social dimensions; yet, it is difficult not to see the harmony within the shell as socially significant, particularly as this atmosphere contrasts the cold, concrete city of Clindis (probably a metaphor for Montreal) nearby.

The novel might also have raised interest as a rewriting of Mary Shelley's *Frankenstein; or, The Modern Prometheus* (1818). To borrow Ketterer's line of thought, both *Coquillage* and *Frankenstein* originated in dreams of pregnancy, birth, and death, and both feature sympathetic "monsters" who speak directly to the reader. Moreover, both monsters wish to mate, Rochon's nautilus even seeking to reproduce itself; hundreds of years pass before it eventually finds a suitable carrier for its children in Thrassl, the novel thus overturning human biological limitations. The monsters also share the status of social outcast, as *Coquillage*, like *Frankenstein*, questions notions of normality and authority.

But Rochon adds a specifically Quebecois dimension to the novel by way of its geographical correspondence to the St. Lawrence region; the nautilus's island is modeled on Clamrock Island, in the bay of Kamouraska (the North Shore of the St. Lawrence is the setting for the fictional Vrénalik). Ketterer places *Coquillage* in the tradition of Quebecois "fantastique" novels with river settings, such as Jacques Godbout's *L'Isle au dragon* (1976), Félix Leclerc's *Le Fou de l'île* (1958), and Antonine Maillet's *Don L'Orignal* (1972).

The 1987 collection *Le Traversier* brings together nine imaginative, thought-provoking science-fiction stories that were published between 1975 and 1986 in various Quebecois, English Canadian, and French journals. The writing often carries the dreamlike quality and air of simplicity conveyed in *Coquillage*. Deeply rooted in Rochon's Buddhist philosophy, the stories focus on the different means by which characters from various planets search for and locate the center, that place of harmony, love, and contact between worlds. The recurrent image of the labyrinth is an especially potent metaphor for the psychological, spiritual, and emotional twists and turns of the journey toward the center; other means of reaching the center, such as via ferry and train rides, or the transformation from human to dragonfly or starfish, are conveyed in stunning images. Several stories feature female protagonists who undertake such quests amid the distractions or temptations of romance, family responsibilities, and careers.

Jean Pettigrew insisted in *Nuit blanche* (White Night, October–November 1987) that there is a particular "ton Esther Rochon, un style Esther Rochon" and argues that *Le Traversier* displays both of these elements; that tone, he maintains, is passive, and the style, sober. Mark Benson finds the emphasis on inner harmony a perfect antidote to the nuclear menace haunting daily life. Lord considered certain stories marred by abstraction linked to their philosophical basis but praised the range of approaches to the quest motif and its transformative power. The collection was nominated for an Aurora Award in the category of Best Long-Form Work in French (1987–1988).

Rochon has remained actively involved with the Quebecois literary community since her work on *imagine . . .* in the late 1970s and early 1980s. In 1985 she became a member of the Union des écrivains québécois (UNEQ). In 1988 she served on the jury and the administrative council for the designation of the Grand Prix Logidisque. And from 1988 to 1990 she was on the editorial board of the Quebecois short-story journal *XYZ*.

The last novel in the Vrénalik cycle, *L'Espace du diamant* (The Space of the Diamond, 1990), is considered the best of the series and possibly Rochon's best work. The novel received a nomination for an Aurora Award for Best Long-Form Work in French (1989–1990) and earned Rochon the Grand Prix de la science-fiction et du fantastique québécois in 1991. A blend of narrative voices telling their stories, and of different narrative forms (prose, poetry, and ballad), this complex, challenging work treats the development of a utopian Asven society. While Skern Strénid and Taïm Sutherland explore the south in search of a meaning to their lives (a requisite period of isolation in the quests that often mark Rochon's fictions), the people of the north embark on an age of discovery; the latter, however, also face the threat of industrial exploitation. Sutherland, savior of the Asven in *L'Epuisement du soleil*, becomes the key to a new society when he agrees to work for the Emperor Othoum in Serling-Catadial. As a "jayènn" (or person possessed of certain ancient powers), Sutherland is hired to seduce la Dragonne, a she-dragon creature with planet-wide influence who is the guardian of the power of Catadial, and channel her force into the city. By doing so, Sutherland will earn for the Asven the construction of their own ideal city, La Ville Rouge, in Catadial.

Queen Suzanne—sorcerer, founder of cities, and protector of orphans—is an inspirational force for Skern throughout the novel; his dream of making love to her accords him a new and secret power. Similarly, Sutherland's passion for the sorcerer-queen Solune brings him the happiness and peace he has sought; the force and beauty of the couple's lovemaking is conveyed in dazzling images: "Enflammé, il souffrait; bleue comme saphir, elle ne savait pas flamboyer. Ils échangèrent flamme et saphir" (Impassioned, he suffered; blue as sapphire, she could not burn the same way. They exchanged flame and sapphire). Gabrielle Pascal identifies a feminist spiritual moral in *Coquillage* and *L'Espace du diamant*, arguing that the transgression introduced in both works by means of the marvelous (principally the nautilus and the sorcerers) is a liberating device on a grand scale. She adds that Rochon gives equal weight to her heroines' magical and quotidian actions in an effort to free her female characters from the demands imposed by success and stereotypical images of women.

The title of the novel refers to a mythical, utopian space at the confluence of an outer void and an inner human richness. The Vrénalik trilogy does indeed cul-

Cover for the second volume (1996) in Rochon's "Chroniques Infernales" series about a multitude of hells

minate an ideal society, for Catadial (and its offshoot, La Ville Rouge) is a realm of open minds, balanced work and recreation, social support programs, harmony, justice, and creativity. Rochon thus succeeds in her effort to portray a state of affairs that amplifies the more personal orientation of *Coquillage* and the emphasis of *L'Epuisement du soleil* on social discord as opposed to social improvement. *L'Espace du diamant* foregrounds the hallmarks of Rochon's fiction, what Lord calls a democracy of thought and privileging of difference and transformation. Rochon points out that the novel is heavily influenced by Shambhala and Buddhist teachings; she describes Shambhala as a secular spiritual path that is utopian in vision and socially (as opposed to personally) oriented. So keen was her interest in the approach that she helped to revise the tranlation of Chogyam Trungpa Rinpoche's book *Shambhala* (1990) from English to French. For Rochon, Buddhism and Shambhala accord with science fiction in their mutual interest in communicating values. Rochon also signals the importance in *L'Espace du diamant* of marginality, suggesting that the Asven could be thought of as an allegory for the Quebecois, the Native Americans, or even of artists alienated by society. She rejects the idea that magic per se informs the novel, preferring to see a marvelous and imaginative dimension; if there is magic, she concedes, it lies in a Shambhala-informed discovery of the innate wisdom of the world, rather than a magic power over the world. That the novel is multilayered and demands much of its reader is, in the writer's estimation, a highly desirable result of her efforts.

Ménard took exception to the utopian element of the novel in his article "Les Pièges de l'utopie" (The Traps of Utopia, in *Solaris,* January–February 1991). Arguing that "le danger avec l'utopie, c'est précisément de verser dans une extrémité, puis d'en oublier l'autre face" (the danger with utopias lies in emphasizing one extreme to the neglect of the other), Ménard faulted Rochon for failing to take an ironic position with respect to her perfect society and thus ignoring the void that inescapably underlies the apparent perfection. He credited the writer with undertaking an ambitious project, but lamented the focus of the novel on certain narrative voices to the exclusion of others. By contrast, Pascal praised the rich tone created by the plurality of voices. Pettigrew considered *L'Espace du diamant* to be not only Rochon's best novel, but also a major work within Quebecois literature; he commented on its remarkable characters and wise teachings (seeing, in fact, a viable dystopian utopia) and also on Rochon's mastery of tone and rhythm. Similarly, Lord maintained in "Magie et perversion" (in the Spring 1991 *Lettres québécoises*) that *L'Espace du diamant* "possède ce souffle et cet densité que l'on ne retrouve que dans les grandes oeuvres" (possesses that vigor and depth found only in the great works) and compared the author to a goldsmith refining her piece for twenty years with a consummate art.

Le Piège à souvenirs assembles nine science-fictional and fantastic short stories that deal with different aspects of memory, whether of a negative nature—as in the painful and violent memories of failed relationships in "La Roseraie"—or of a more positive kind, as with the museum that displays artistry, music, and literature in the otherwise alienating world of "Le Musée de Psal" (The Psal Museum, first written for radio in a series produced by André Major and broadcast on Radio-Canada in the summer of 1988). Memory, as with most elements in Rochon's fiction, can be both liberating and educational or restrictive and deadening; but whatever its nature, the act of remembering is a crucial element of the present and future for both the individual and the community. "La Roseraie," for example, reveals the harmful effects of the burden of memory, as the narrator unleashes her aggression and despair through vivid dreams of murder and a bizarre self-projection into imaginary realms. In "L'Ange et le pont" (The Angel and the Bridge), the almost animate statue of an angel commemorates executed Quebec patriots of the 1837 rebellion; the sensitive narrator recognizes the statue as a tribute to a past idealism, wisdom, and spirit of sacrifice. The theme of the city as a sterile concrete jungle, one premised upon "progress" to the neglect of a proper homage to the past, shapes this story. In a similar vein, the title story allegorizes the loss of Quebec's cultural memory through characters forced to leave their homeland and literally vacuum up their history. The abuses of a partly robotic, partly human (male) being, whose television-screen eyes feature scenes of violence, prompt the narrator of the story "Canadoule" (Canada?) to remember what the world ought to look like: imaginatively boundless but still human and intimate.

Technology, when used to dominate and exploit, manifests itself in highly negative terms in Rochon's work. The biological element is extremely important to Rochon's vision of a utopian society; texts such as "Canadoule" emphasize the necessity of human exchange and contact to a progressive world. Many of the stories in *Le Piège à souvenirs* feature female protagonists who challenge the banalities, limits, and patriarchal abuses of everyday life: such figures explore the vastness of human thought, of death (always potentially enriching in Rochon's work), and of the universe.

Critical reception of these nine diverse and engaging stories has been mixed. In his 29 February 1992 review in *Le Devoir*, Louis Cornellier took Rochon to task for the confusing plotlines, uncertain style, and lack of dramatic progression. Lord's review of the collection in *Lettres québécoises* disputed Cornellier's analysis and emphasized the beauty of Rochon's work, acknowledging her status as one of Quebec's best writers. Lord praised the ostensibly simple yet translucent writing in *Le Piège à souvenirs*, even as he recognized Rochon's difficulties with the short-story form; Rochon, Lord suggested, seems more at ease with the novel because it allows her to develop her imagination more fully. In her review of the collection for *Nuit blanche*, Angèle Laferrière credited the stories with the excellence marking the author's previous publications.

L'Ombre et le cheval (The Shadow and the Horse, 1992) is Rochon's second novel for adolescents and was a finalist for both the Governor General's Award for children's literature (1992) and the Prix 12–17 (1992). Sixteen-year-old Ella is faced with the leadership of her desert village after her grandfather Anskad disappears and her great-uncle Sim becomes seriously ill. A key aspect of her responsibilities is the management of the village's livelihood, which is also her own inherited artistic talent: the projection of luminous horses onto the night sky by means of colored gases. Ella, like other female protagonists in Rochon's works, attempts to reconcile her duty to her fellow citizens with her struggle to define herself as a woman; the latter aspect involves overcoming social expectations that would impose a false sense of self. Though targeting issues of concern to young adults—including first love, sexuality, maturity, relationships with parents, and self-esteem—*L'Ombre et le cheval* is written with the same elegance of phrase and profundity of ideas as Rochon's adult-oriented works. The novel is replete with images: water becomes a gift from the earth, and the sun is a necessary and fecund wound in the sky. Jean Levasseur referred to this text as a novel-poem and compared its lyricism to that found in the works of Jacques Poulin, Anne Hébert, Tahar Ben Jelloun, or Antoine de Saint-Exupéry. *L'Ombre et le cheval* also engages a sophisticated argument on the importance of art to cultural and spiritual survival, especially in the face of an encroaching mechanization (represented by the city and its appropriation of the horse images). In a gesture toward the idealism often found in Rochon's work, the people of the village face an uncertain future but meet it with a will toward action and a respect for life.

Rochon's focus shifts somewhat with *Lame* (1995), the first novel in her "Chroniques Infernales" series detailing distant, numerous hells populated by human and nonhuman characters alike. Mysterious judges send Lame to the soft hell (where the body becomes increasingly grotesque and immobile) for failing to love herself or to liberate herself from the burden of past tribulations. Themes of justice and loyalty emerge in Lame's rescue of Vaste–the man who saves her from hell but who abuses her after they marry–from his own condemnation in the hot hell. An important mentor figure is the "bonne âme" (good soul) Roxanne, who aids Lame (a play on "l'âme" or "soul") in her search for self-confidence. The hermaphroditic prince of hells, Rel, faces his own battles with justice as he challenges his father's reign of brutality. Both Roxanne and Rel (who eventually becomes Lame's husband) learn from Lame as she performs acts of love and compassion in order to overcome torment and isolation.

Despite the dark nature of the subject matter–the tortures of hell often graphically realized–the novel indulges comic moments linked to Lame's transformation or Roxanne's past. Rochon confirms the presence of autobiographical elements in the novel and admits that she wrote *Lame* at a point when she felt a humorous distance from her life. Such humor also counteracts the horror of the underworld as Rochon adds, in typical fashion, a sense of balance and hope.

In a review for the Autumn 1995 *Lettres québécoises* Claude Janelle pointed out that Rochon is the first Quebecois writer to dare to portray hell–a surprising fact, he noted, given the Catholic-based morality that gripped the province until the 1960s. Janelle praised Rochon for creating a personal but not moralistic vision of damnation, one in which suffering gives rise to beauty and redemption; as he said, "C'est la grande réussite d'Esther Rochon que de dégager de cette violence omniprésente un espoir de salut" (Rochon's triumph lies in postulating the hope of salvation amidst omnipresent violence). Yet, as with Dansereau's assessment of *L'Epuisement du soleil,* Janelle found fault with the rigid style of writing in *Lame.* Francine Bordeleau, writing for *Spirale,* lamented the lack of direction and imagination in the novel. By contrast, Simon Dupuis, writing for *Solaris,* deemed the work an absolute success because of its polished air and poetic allegory of self-discovery.

Aboli (Abolished, 1996) is the second volume in the "Chroniques Infernales" series and depicts the territory that hosts the cold hell when it moves from its original setting, the now-ancient hells. The move is part of the reforms that Rel enacts in an effort to regenerate the ancient hells through the cessation of violence and the teaching of positive values. While the inhabitants of the ancient hells are largely willing to re-educate themselves, the native inhabitants of the new hell scorn the incoming damned. Séril Daha, an autochthonous painter, is inspired by Lame to bring about a greater harmony between the indigenous inhabitants and the damned. His struggle ends brutally when his fellow citizens assassinate him. Again the themes of justice, love, and the role of art or artists dominate Rochon's fiction, as do those of transformation and sexuality; the hermaphroditic Rel, whose gender corresponds to his duties and desires, exemplifies Rochon's interest in a supple sexual and social identity.

Jean-Louis Trudel considered *Aboli* a more successful novel than *Lame* because the latter is flawed by unnecessary repetitions and lengthy passages. He suggested that the originality and fascination of Rochon's work lies not in its style but in its lucidity and honesty; human faults and passions, he contended, are openly exposed and criticized.

The series continues with *Ouverture* (Opening, 1997), a novel that explores the seven other new hells, among which are the "poisoned hell," the "cutting hell," and the "rapid hell." Lame's reluctant exposure to these locales raises her awareness of the work yet to be done to bring about new and vibrant societies; as the novel states, and as Rochon's work testifies, "un autre monde est toujours possible" (a different world is always possible). Rel attempts to convince the "sbires" or administrators of justice that the future of the various hells is intimately linked with acts of compassion. Marital problems interweave with more general questions of devotion and peace; as with other texts by Rochon, tenderness and sensuality function as energizing, restorative forces on both a personal and social level. Séril Daha continues to play an important role by way of the oracular canvas he gave Lame before he died. After an intense study of the painting, Lame realizes that its central sphere and leafy border depict her own situation: the center symbolizes the life and death she must confront and accept, while the leaves represent the childhood intuition she has lost. Similarly, Rel attempts a nostalgic reconnection with the realm behind the green door, a passage to wisdom and growth like the green statue of Haztlén in the Vrénalik series.

Rochon's subsequent endeavors include a revised and expanded edition of *L'Epuisement du soleil* in a two-volume format (*Le Rêveur dans la citadelle*, 1998, and *L'Archipel Nor*, 1999), and the fourth volume in the "Chroniques Infernales" series, *Secrets* (1998). This latter work details Rel's early experiences behind the green door and his imminent departure for Vrénalik. The Vrénalik series and the "Chroniques Infernales" series thus merge, with Rel representing Haztlén and the "juste" (or just/fair person) Fax realizing that he was Taïm Sutherland in an earlier life. In the spring of 1998 Rochon published an article in *Lovecraft Studies* on Lovecraft's relation to Buddhism, evidently still drawn to her early mentor's writing and thought.

The "Chroniques Infernales" and Vrénalik series continue in *Or* (1999) and *Sorbier* (2000). *Or* includes a hidden dedication to Rochon's son, Olivier, who died in 1998: his initials comprise the title. Rochon's essay on the genesis of the "Chroniques Infernales" appears on the publisher's website (http://www.alire.com).

As Rochon continues to produce highly imaginative fiction she stands to gain increasing critical acclaim. Using magic, science, and fantasy to question traditional social codes, Rochon also channels them into moving and inspiring acts of compassion, justice, peace, and love. Such human qualities remain at the heart of her vision.

Interviews:

Hélène Colas, "Entrevue avec Esther Rochon, auteure de *L'Epuisement du soleil*," *imagine . . .*, 28 (June 1985): 69–77;

René Beaulieu, "Entretien avec Esther Rochon," *Solaris*, 63 (September–October 1985): 11–18;

Michel Lord, "Esther Rochon," *Lettres québécoises*, 40 (Winter 1985-1986): 36–39;

Jean Royer, "Esther Rochon: Le Défi de l'imaginaire," in *Ecrivains contemporains: Entretiens 4 (1981–1986)* (Montreal: L'Hexagone, 1987), pp. 255–260;

Colas, "Les Voies d'une utopie: Entrevue avec Esther Rochon," *imagine . . .*, 58 (December 1991): 69–81.

References:

Annick Chapdelaine, "Inner and Outer Space in Esther Rochon," in *International Women's Writing: New Landscapes of Identity*, edited by Anne E. Brown and Marjanne E. Goozé (Westport, Conn.: Greenwood Press, 1995), pp. 126–136;

David Ketterer, "*The Shell*, An Exquisite Monstrosity," *Science Fiction Studies*, 19 (1992): 17–19;

Gabrielle Pascal, "Esther Rochon: merveilleux et transgression," in *Le Roman québécois au féminin, 1980-1995*, edited by Pascal (Montreal: Triptyque, 1995), pp. 47–56;

Élisabeth Vonarburg, "Notes sur Esther Rochon," *Solaris*, 63 (September–October 1985): 19–23.

Robert J. Sawyer
(29 April 1960 -)

Austin Booth
State University of New York at Buffalo

BOOKS: *Golden Fleece* (New York: Warner, 1990; revised edition, New York: Tor, 1999);

Far-Seer (New York: Ace, 1992; London: New English Library, 1995);

Fossil Hunter (New York: Ace, 1993; London: New English Library, 1995);

Foreigner (New York: Ace, 1994; London: New English Library, 1995);

End of an Era (New York: Ace, 1994; London: New English Library, 1994);

The Terminal Experiment (New York: HarperPrism, 1995; London: New English Library, 1995);

Starplex (New York: Ace, 1996);

Frameshift (New York: Tor, 1997; London: HarperCollins, 1999);

Illegal Alien (New York: Ace, 1997; London: HarperCollins, 1998);

Factoring Humanity (New York: Tor, 1998; London: HarperCollins, 1999);

Flashforward (New York: Tor, 1999);

Calculating God (New York: Tor, 2000).

OTHER: "The Contest," in *100 Great Fantasy Short Short Stories,* edited by Isaac Asimov, Terry Carr, and Martin H. Greenberg (Garden City, N.Y.: Doubleday, 1984), pp. 43–44;

"Where the Heart Is," in *Ark of Ice: Canadian Futurefiction,* edited by Lesley Choyce (East Lawrencetown, Nova Scotia: Pottersfield Press, 1992), pp. 216–234;

"Just Like Old Times," in *Dinosaur Fantastic,* edited by Mike Resnick and Greenberg (New York: DAW, 1993), pp. 13–26; reprinted in *Northern Stars: The Anthology of Canadian Science Fiction,* edited by David G. Hartwell and Glenn Grant (New York: Tor, 1994), pp. 318–328; reprinted in *On Spec: The First Five Years,* edited by the *On Spec* Editorial Collective (Edmonton, Alberta: Tesseract Books, 1995), pp. 39–51; reprinted in *Aurora Awards: An Anthology of Prize-Winning Science Fiction and Fantasy,* edited

Robert J. Sawyer (photograph by Carolyn Clink; from the dust jacket for Illegal Alien, *1997)*

by Edo van Belkom (Kingston, Ontario: Quarry Press, 1999), pp. 113–125;

"You See But You Do Not Observe," in *Sherlock Holmes in Orbit,* edited by Resnick and Greenberg (New York: DAW, 1995), pp. 344–360; reprinted in *Nebula Awards 31,* edited by Pamela Sargent (New York: Harcourt Brace, 1997), pp. 188–205; reprinted in *Time Machine: The Greatest Time Travel Stories Ever Written,* edited by Bill Adler Jr. (New York: Carroll & Graf, 1997), pp. 191–206;

"Lost in the Mail," in *TransVersions,* 1, edited by Dale L. Sprovie and Sally McBride (1995): 16–24;

"Above it All," in *Dante's Disciples,* edited by Peter Crowther and Edward E. Kramer (Clarkston, Ga.: White Wolf, 1996), pp. 281–292;

"Peking Man," in *Dark Destiny III: Children of Dracula,* edited by Kramer (Clarkston, Ga.: White Wolf, 1996), pp. 18–29; reprinted in *Aurora Awards: An Anthology of Prize-Winning Science Fiction and Fantasy,* edited by van Belkom (Kingston, Ontario: Quarry Press, 1999), pp. 179–188;

"Forever," in *Return of the Dinosaurs,* edited by Resnick and Greenberg (New York: DAW, 1997), pp. 194–203;

"Gator," in *Urban Nightmares,* edited by Josepha Sherman and Keith R. A. DeCandido (Riverdale, N.Y.: Baen, 1997), pp. 3–14;

"The Hand You're Dealt," in *Free Space,* edited by Kramer and Brad Linaweaver (New York: Tor, 1997), pp. 221–240;

Tesseracts⁶, edited by Sawyer and Carolyn Clink (Edmonton, Alberta: Tesseract Books, 1997);

van Belkom, *Death Drives a Semi,* introduction by Sawyer (Kingston, Ontario: Quarry Press, 1998);

Crossing the Line: Canadian Mysteries with a Fantastic Twist, edited by Sawyer and Skene-Melvin (East Lawrencetown, Nova Scotia: Pottersfield Press, 1998);

Over the Edge: The Crime Writers of Canada Anthology, edited by Sawyer and Peter Sellers (East Lawrencetown, Nova Scotia: Pottersfield Press, 1999);

"Stream of Consciousness," in *Packing Fraction and Other Tales of Science and Imagination,* edited by Julie E. Czerneda (Toronto: Trifolium, 1999), pp. 53–76;

"Iterations," in *TransVersions: An Anthology of New Fantastic Literature,* edited by Marcel Gagné and Sally Tomasevic (Mississauga, Ontario: Paper Orchid Press, 2000), pp. 6–14;

"The Shoulders of Giants," in *Star Colonies,* edited by Greenberg and John Helfers (New York: DAW, 2000), pp. 1–22;

"Star Light, Star Bright," in *Far Frontiers,* edited by Greenberg and Larry Segriff (New York: DAW, 2000), pp. 51–69.

Robert J. Sawyer has taken an active role within the science-fiction community both in Canada and around the world, and he has worked to promote international awareness of Canadian science fiction. He is the author of twelve novels (with more planned) as well as many pieces of short fiction, and he has served as president of the Science Fiction and Fantasy Writers of America, founded the Canadian division of that organization, and won several national and international awards. In addition to his fiction, Sawyer wrote a column, "On Writing," for the Canadian science-fiction magazine *On Spec* from Spring 1995 to Winter 1997. He has taught science-fiction writing at Ryerson Polytechnic University, the University of Toronto, and various writers' workshops and has co-edited three anthologies of Canadian fiction. Sawyer is also a significant historian of the genre, contributing the entry on "science fiction" to *The Canadian Encyclopedia,* the second and subsequent editions. Sawyer's website (http://www.sfwriter.com) includes full texts of several short stories and sample chapters from novels as well as full-length articles, interviews, and reviews, as well as many links to sites discussing Canadian science fiction, and science fiction in general. Furthermore, Sawyer is a common presence on Canadian television and radio as a commentator on science fiction and science.

Sawyer is a hard-science-fiction writer whose work is influenced by the novels of Arthur C. Clarke and the character-driven stories of Frederik Pohl. His fiction documents conflicts between science and superstition; in Sawyer's world, science is singularly able to explain or reveal truth—the mechanisms of this apparently chaotic and random universe are revealed to the reader through well-explained scientific fact. While Sawyer's work is traditional hard science fiction in the sense that its origin lies in extrapolative science and technology, it differs from common conceptions of science fiction in two ways. First, Sawyer's focus, even in his "dinosaur" trilogy, is the moral struggles humans face in the present. The setting for Sawyer's works is frequently earth in the not-too-distant future, a future that turns out to resemble the present in remarkable ways. The genre of science fiction thus allows Sawyer to illuminate current ethical dilemmas, rather than merely displaying a series of technological predictions and predilections. Second, Sawyer's stories cross genre boundaries—his work includes mysteries, adventures, courtroom dramas, space operas, medical thrillers, even love stories—with an ease that contributes to their wide appeal. Sawyer is also a vocal champion of Canada and Canadian science fiction, and his writing includes many references to Canada.

Robert James Sawyer was born in Ottawa, Ontario, on 29 April 1960 to John Arthur and Virginia Kivley (Peterson) Sawyer, the second of three sons. His father was an economics professor, his mother a statistician. He grew up in Toronto, where his father taught, and Sawyer began reading science fiction when he was ten. As he recalled in a 1996 online interview in *Delos SF,* "When my father discovered I was watching science-fiction programs on television [the British-made puppet show *Fireball XL5*], rather than trying to discourage me from that, he instead went out and bought some science fiction books for me. He didn't read SF himself, but he knew the name Isaac Asimov from Asimov's non-fiction

Dust jacket for Sawyer's 1997 novel, a medical thriller involving cloning, telepathy, insurance fraud, and neo-Nazis

work, and so that's who he started me with." Sawyer moved from Asimov to Clarke and Pohl. While he thought about writing science fiction, his primary interest was dinosaurs. He spent hours at the Royal Ontario Museum in Toronto, as he said in the March 1993 issue of *Books in Canada*, "staring at the dinosaur skeletons, wondering about them. They were just so big, so ancient, so mysterious." Throughout high school, Sawyer's goal remained becoming a paleontologist, until upon graduation it hit him that he "didn't want to spend the next ten years in school pursuing a Ph.D. so that I could make $17,000 a year sifting dirt. I wanted to do something exciting *now*." Deciding to become a professional writer, he enrolled in the Ryerson Polytechnical Institute (now Ryerson Polytechnic University) to study radio and television arts, and he graduated with a bachelor of applied arts degree in 1982.

After graduating, Sawyer became a freelance writer, publishing more than two hundred feature articles for Canadian and American magazines. He married Carolyn Clink, a Canadian poet, on 22 December 1984.

During the 1980s Sawyer also sold several short stories to *The Village Voice, Leisure Ways,* and *Amazing Stories*. One of his first stories, "Motive," written when he was nineteen, became part of a starshow trilogy at the Strasenburgh Planetarium in Rochester, New York, the result of a science-fiction writing contest judged by Asimov. Although "Motive" was never published, it did show glimpses of Sawyer's future work: it introduced the dinosaurs of the Quintaglio trilogy; it was concerned with the potential dangers of artificial intelligence; and it was set on a spaceship named *Starplex,* later featured in Sawyer's 1996 novel of the same name. Sawyer's second short-fiction publication, "If I'm Here, Imagine Where They Sent My Luggage," published in the 14 January 1981 issue of *The Village Voice,* also won a writing contest, a competition for short-short science-fiction stories (which had to be exactly 250 words in length, excluding the title) sponsored by *The Village Voice*. (The full text of the story now appears on the back of Sawyer's business card.) By 1990 Sawyer and Clink had saved enough money so that with the publication that year of his first novel, *Golden Fleece,* he could become a full-time science-fiction writer. Although Sawyer achieved success as a novelist with *Golden Fleece,* he has continued to publish many other pieces of award-winning short fiction in both magazines and anthologies. "Just Like Old Times," first published in the Summer 1993 issue of *On Spec,* won the Aurora Award for short fiction in 1994 as well as the 1993 Arthur Ellis Award, presented by the Crime Writers of Canada, for best short story; "You See But You Do Not Observe," from the 1995 anthology *Sherlock Holmes in Orbit,* won the 1995 fan-voted Homer Award for best short story and the 1996 Grand Prix de l'imaginaire for best foreign short story; "Above it All," from the 1996 anthology *Dante's Disciples,* won the 1996 Homer for best short story; "Peking Man," from the 1996 anthology *Dark Destiny III: Children of Dracula,* won the 1997 Aurora for short fiction; "The Hand You're Dealt," from the 1997 anthology *Free Space,* won the *Science Fiction Chronicle* Reader Award for best short story; and "Stream of Consciousness," from the 1999 anthology *Packing Fraction and Other Tales of Science and Imagination,* won the 2000 Aurora Award for best short story.

Golden Fleece, winner of an Aurora Award for best novel and a Homer Award for best first novel, is a murder mystery set on a starship named *Argo*. Sawyer frequently combines the conventions of science fiction and mystery in his fiction. Inspired by Arthur C. Clarke and Stanley Kubrick's *2001: A Space Odyssey* (1968), *Golden Fleece* is narrated by a computer named JASON who murders a crew member whom he decides is jeopardizing the mission of the ship. Like many of Sawyer's works, the novel presents hard science—artificial intelligence and interstellar travel—within a story rich in theme and character. *Golden Fleece* concerns a common anxiety about artificial intelligence: the computer, which people have made as human as possible, becomes a threat when it behaves too much like a human by asserting its independence. The novel explores the relationship between computers and humans through the presentation of two similar characters: Aaron, the captain of the ship, and JASON, the computer that runs the ship. Like Aaron, JASON is intellectually advanced but emotionally immature; indeed, JASON comes to represent Aaron's own narcissistic desire for complete knowledge and power. If what is frightening about JASON is his ability to see without emotion or empathy, what is frightening about Aaron is his similar lack of emotion. Aaron's ability to cover up his feelings, however, is precisely what makes him unreadable to JASON; in other words, Aaron is so repressed that JASON cannot read his behavior. Further, JASON's inability to read Aaron is what makes the computer the most human. In short, *Golden Fleece* is both about the dangers of artificial intelligence—that is, that fundamental controls are not yet in place—and about what it means to be human.

With Sawyer's next novels, the Quintaglio series, he returned to his first love: dinosaurs. According to Sawyer, dinosaurs are a natural subject for science-fiction writing; dinosaurs, like aliens, are a species about which people know little but with which they are fascinated, and thinking about dinosaurs helps people to think about the earth and their place in its history. As Sawyer writes on his website, "dinosaurs were a truly alien form of life, and we learn about them solely through logic and deduction and science. Well, my novels have a real fascination with aliens, too, and, of course, my books revel in the scientific process, and in the kind of puzzle-solving paleontologists have to do all the time." In the series Sawyer creates a faraway planet inhabited by Quintaglios, intelligent dinosaurs who possess both an advanced civilization and consciousness. With the Quintaglio series, Sawyer does more than simply perform creative paleontology; he fabricates an entire world complete with government, history, religion, and an evolving science. Sawyer also takes on intellectual history itself—the stories of *Far-Seer* (1992), *Fossil Hunter* (1993), and *Foreigner* (1994) treat three great revolutions of thought: Galileo's vision of an astronomy that does not focus on earth, Charles Darwin's theory of evolution, and Sigmund Freud's notion of the unconscious.

The dinosaur protagonist of the Homer Award–winning *Far-Seer* is Afsan, an apprentice to the court astrologer. On a pilgrimage he discovers (with the aid of his far-seer, or telescope) that the Quintaglio world is not the center of the universe as he thought. He discovers that the world is round; that planets revolve around the sun; that his planet is at varying distances from other planets, stars, and moons; and, most dramatically, that the planet the Quintaglios inhabit is a moon that is about to break up into a ring around the planet it orbits. The description of Afsan's attempts to convince the other dinosaurs of his discovery is a tale of the conflicting visions of religion and science, faith and fact.

In *Fossil Hunter*, also a recipient of the Homer Award, Sawyer continues the story of the Quintaglios through the tale of Toroca, the son of Afsan, who follows in his father's footsteps. During his search for the mineral needed for the Quintaglios' space-flight evacuation from their world, Toroca discovers their fossil record. Toroca, like Darwin, comes to conclusions that are unpopular with his fellow Quintaglios—namely, that the Quintaglios were transplanted onto their moon from somewhere else. Toroca is able to trace the evolution of the species and discovers their origin is the Nanotyrannus, a dwarf dinosaur. As in *Far-Seer*, the science in *Fossil Hunter* is clear and factual; the simple-curve increase in the ratio of brain to body size that the Quintaglios discover, for example, is a well-founded scientific observation.

The last volume in the Quintaglio trilogy, *Foreigner*, describes the Quintaglios' race to escape from their moon before it disintegrates. In this novel a female dinosaur, Mokleb, modeled after Freud, explores the territoriality and aggressive drives that create problems for the Quintaglios' cooperation, necessary if they are to emigrate. Taken together, the three novels in the series cover a great span of intellectual history; the collapsing of this history into a mere three generations only creates a greater sense of the wonder of scientific discovery.

Sawyer's next novel, *End of an Era* (1994), winner of both the Homer Award and the Japanese Seiun Award, also pays attention to dinosaurs. It is the story of two paleontologists traveling back in time to discover the cause of the dinosaurs' extinction. In both *End of an Era* and *Fossil Hunter* Sawyer tackles potential reasons for the dinosaurs' extinction, but he comes up with contradictory, equally plausible answers. While *Fossil Hunter* basically argues that life is an accident, *End of an Era* argues that the universe created life in order to document itself, in order to maintain knowledgeable observers. Sawyer plays with several different principles of theoretical physics and allows readers to consider the ways in which different theories of the universe influence the ways in which they understand their position within that universe.

With *The Terminal Experiment*, serialized in *Analog* as "Hobson's Choice" from mid December 1994 to March 1995 and published as a book in 1995, Sawyer turned away from dinosaurs to the near future, a setting he has used for most of the rest of his novels to date, but without abandoning his attention to large issues. The main

Caricature of Sawyer by Y. Komri (Collection of Robert J. Sawyer)

theme of the novel is the search for scientific proof of the existence of the human soul. An intellectual thriller, *The Terminal Experiment* won the Nebula, Aurora, and Homer Awards for best novel and was nominated for the Hugo Award. *The Terminal Experiment* is typical of Sawyer's cross-genre writing; the novel is both hard science fiction and a murder mystery. As he stated in the *Delos SF* interview, science fiction is "often about technology or neat tricks of science, but not about anything human. Well, *The Terminal Experiment* is a very human novel, and it is, quite literally, about the human heart—or soul—in conflict with itself; the main character of the novel ends up face-to-face with an artificial-intelligence simulation of his own all-too-fallible human soul."

The Terminal Experiment is set in Toronto in the near future and tells the story of Peter Hobson, a medical student who begins to question the boundary between life and death when a motorcycle-accident victim whose organs are being harvested shows a pulse. After graduating as a biomedical engineer, Hobson works on the development of a highly sensitive EEG to determine the actual instant of death. As part of his research, Hobson and a colleague, Sarkar Muhammed, perfect the creation of a neural scan of the brain. Using this procedure, they create three copies of Hobson's brain, stored in computers: the first Hobson copy, with all fear of aging and dying removed, simulates immortality; the second has all memory of physical existence edited out and thus simulates life after death; and the third is the control. The story also involves several interwoven subplots including Hobson's wife's affair, Hobson's father-in-law's death from an adverse reaction to medicine, and a police investigation of Hobson for the murder of his wife's lover and father.

Despite his publishers' anxieties, Sawyer refused to shy away from the highly charged issues raised by *The Terminal Experiment,* especially the question of when the soul arrives and thus the legitimacy of abortion. While the novel positions itself somewhere between pro-choice and pro-life stances, its exploration of moral and political ambivalence is what makes it a powerful and realistic novel. In *The Terminal Experiment* Sawyer invokes the world of the postmodern, the world of the artificial simulated self. The inviolable self has become a multiple, distributed system. Reality has been transferred into computer-generated images. At the same time, the novel does not dismantle the equation of the natural with the real. Just as the novel explores a complex ethical middle ground, it maintains a philosophical middle ground as well—even as it supports postmodern assumptions that simulacra are signs without referents, it also posits a real moral truth in the soul of Hobson. That is to say, unlike much cyberpunk fiction, the artificial is bounded by a presence outside the artificial; people are grounded in the real, and their motives and impulses are not mere manufactured responses but are, in some way, the truth. In other words, *The Terminal Experiment* does not result in the pessimism that readers have come to expect of postmodern works in general and cyberpunk in particular.

With *Starplex,* published in 1996 and winner of the Aurora and Homer Awards, Sawyer returns to a familiar science-fiction genre: space adventure. The tale ranges over ten billion years and over six billion light years. *Starplex* tells the story of Keith Lansing, the commander of *Starplex,* a giant spaceship. The crew of *Starplex* is made up of four species: humans, dolphins, Ibs, and the Waldahudin. A global village, *Starplex* redefines national and species identity; images and information are communicated across species as well as ethnic, cultural, and linguistic boundaries. As with the Quintaglio cycle, Sawyer creates aliens that are not only interesting in their own right but also do much to reveal humans to themselves. The Ibs' death ritual, for example, illuminates humans' (lesser) sense of duty to their species, as well as the place of shame and guilt within their culture. Similarly, the social difficulties of the Waldahudin are parables of human egotism and aggression.

The various subplots of *Starplex* intersect: the search for a missing dark-matter alien infant and the Ibs' shocking death ritual emphasize the need to understand and respect other cultures. In addition, like many of Sawyer's works, *Starplex* is about epistemology, or the ways in which people acquire knowledge and understanding. Through exploring the ways in which various species come to know (such as memory, physical sense, time, emotion, identification, and sound), the novel reveals why different species understand their positions in the universe differently. The hard science in *Starplex* is clearly set forth; the novel tackles many of the great puzzles of quantum physics and cosmology, including dark matter, galaxy formation, and the origin and fate of the universe. The crew's discovery of dark-matter aliens the size of planets is not only one of the most dramatic sections of the novel but also a good explanation for the behavior of dark matter. The crew also learns that this universe is the result of aliens' aesthetic arrangement of the galaxies into pleasing shapes. The precocity or whimsy of the arrangement of the universe does not create a sense of danger, however, but rather a sense of being part of something much larger than human egos usually entertain. Similarly, the revelation of the beings who are responsible for the "shortcuts" through space that Lansing and his crew use to navigate star systems raises questions not merely of time travel and space, but of man's position in a larger universe. Through one of the shortcuts, Lansing encounters his future (immortal) self, in some of the most fascinating passages in the novel. While *The Terminal Experiment* explored immortality within the context of the mind as a set of neurological events that can be imitated or stored in computer networks, in *Starplex* immortality is examined within the context of parables of resurrection and survival. Again, Sawyer reminds readers of the importance of understanding other cultures (even, in this case, their own culture in the future) through establishing points of commonality such as a shared sense of self. As his future self explains to Lansing, the future (and the world of Sawyer's science fiction as well) has to be presented in recognizable ways because some realities—metaphysical, physical, and symbolic—must be shared in order to communicate.

His next novel, *Frameshift,* published in 1997, was a return to the medical thriller genre. Like *The Terminal Experiment,* this novel investigates boundaries and their disruption by technological progress. *Frameshift* is also concerned with epistemology, with questions of knowledge and resisting knowledge. Pierre Tardivel, a French Canadian scientist who suffers from Huntington's disease, works on the Human Genome Project, mankind's attempt to map a complete sequencing of all the DNA that makes up a person. Pierre's wife, Molly Bond, is a psychology professor who is telepathic. After Pierre and Molly are attacked by a neo-Nazi, they discover that there have been a rash of murders of people with soon-to-develop genetic diseases. Later they learn that Pierre's insurance company holds policies on a large number of the murder victims. Finally, the insurance company is linked to a neo-Nazi attempt to kill off people with genetic diseases both because they are seen as unfit and in order to avoid the large payments the company will be forced to make should the victims live. The novel also has several significant interwoven subplots: the first is Pierre's discovery that the source of Molly's telepathic abilities is a genetic "frameshift." Pierre's search for the genetic difference that explains Molly's gift leads him to the realization that their daughter, Amanda, is cloned from the DNA of Hapless Hannah, a Neanderthal. The second significant subplot is a story beginning with a devastating scene of the Treblinka concentration camp and leading to the career of Avi Meyer, a survivor's son who dedicates his life to the hunt for Nazi war criminals. Meyer was involved in the conviction (later overturned) of John Demjanjuk as Ivan the Terrible—in a novel concerned with what makes up individual identity, this case of mistaken identity becomes important.

Frameshift is one of Sawyer's best and most complex works, linking Huntington's disease, telepathy, junk DNA, cloning, Neanderthals, Nazis, and insurance fraud. The major concern of the novel is genetic destiny, for both individuals and the species. Pierre's work concerns the discovery of a second level of coded information in human DNA. At this point scientists do not know the purpose of 90 percent of human DNA; hence the name junk DNA. Pierre discovers the possibility that junk DNA contains the gene for certain diseases such as Huntington's. (Sawyer avoids the facile ending of letting his hero discover a cure in time to save himself, however.) Junk DNA shows not only human genetic destiny, but genetic possibilities—the novel argues that humans' genetic future as a species, the next evolutionary shift, could be a shift from speech to telepathy. Pierre discovers that Molly has evolved to this next stage of the species through a genetic mutation. In one family, then, Sawyer presents the evolution of the human species from Neanderthals to telepaths, from Amanda to Molly.

Pierre's story is both a story of the personal effects of a genetic disorder (Huntington's), and a story of the human race's past (Hannah) and future (telepathy). That is to say, the novel explores genetics on both the large, species scale and the small, quotidian scale. If *The Terminal Experiment* is about the beginning and future of each individual, and *Starplex* is about the beginning and future of the universe, then *Frameshift* falls somewhere in between, because it is about the beginning and the future of the human race. While *Frameshift* is a story of genetic possibility, it is also a story of genetic programming, of Pierre's inescapable fate. Furthermore, the novel is an investigation of where genetic research can lead: on the one hand, a project such as the Human Genome Project (a real project) might one day result in the eradication of diseases such as Huntington's, but, on the other hand, such a project could be an extremely powerful discriminatory weapon. The genetic mapping of complex diseases and traits, when combined with the ability of computers to map the correlations between particular genetic markers and complex traits or behaviors, will create difficult ethical questions.

Frameshift is about epistemology as well as ethics. The questions of how one knows and whether knowledge can be responsibly handled or rejected are investigated through several of the plots: Molly's telepathy usually prevents her from having relationships precisely because she knows what others are thinking; the knowledge that genetic testing provides is demonstrated to be a potentially dangerous power; and Pierre, like many children of parents with Huntington's, did not want to know whether he was likely to develop the disease. (Sawyer also makes a strong case for socialized medicine along the way; in Canada, Pierre would not have had to undergo genetic testing in order to receive medical insurance.) *Frameshift* is undoubtedly one of Sawyer's best works and is an example of the potential of extrapolative fiction to profoundly influence ethical and technological decision making. *Frameshift* won the Seiun Award of Japan for best foreign novel in 2000.

In Sawyer's next novel he returns to a classic science-fiction scenario–an encounter with aliens. *Illegal Alien*, published in 1997, is a legal thriller with plenty of courtroom dramatics; it tells the story of eight aliens who left Alpha Centauri 210 years before the novel takes place. Upon entry into this solar system, the alien ship is damaged by a meteorite from the Kuiper belt, and the aliens, the Tosoks, need help from humans to rebuild their ship. Soon after their arrival, one of the aliens, Hask, is arrested for the murder of Cletus Calhoun, one of the first humans to make contact. Again, *Illegal Alien* explores how the creation of knowledge is determined by cultural circumstances; in this case, how knowledge is created within a culture defined by the Tosoks' quadrilateral anatomy and a trinary star system. Sawyer shows readers how the Tosoks' anatomy, astronomy, and religion create systems of meaning; how the Tosok culture feels to those who inhabit it; and how it makes them think.

The Tosoks' understanding of themselves as creatures of an evolutionary process is what finally explains Cletus's murder. In addition to its exciting, fast-paced plot, *Illegal Alien* explores how a species sees itself within the context of a religious understanding of creation rather than an understanding based on the evolutionary process. Sawyer is less concerned with "proving" evolution than in examining the profound effect of evolutionary theory on how people see themselves and others. Believing in a creation myth that posits one as chosen can be destructive; as Hask points out, if one does not believe one is a member of the only chosen species, one is less likely to destroy others to preserve oneself:

> We used to think we were the divinely created children of God–and that, of course, would be sufficient to give us the right to do whatever we deemed necessary; if God did not want us to do it, after all, she would thwart our attempt. But when we discovered that that is not true, that we are merely products of evolution, well, then, the question of having the right to do something no longer enters into it. . . . If we can advantage our species, then we have the right and the obligation to do so.

In other words, if a species believes it is the only chosen race, it has the right to destroy other worlds in order to exist. Sawyer is also careful to show readers, however, that evolutionary curiosity may also be destructive–in *Illegal Alien*, for example, such curiosity leads to murder. Again, through the aliens' self-examination, readers come to examine themselves and to interrogate the notion that they are the "chosen ones." As Sawyer claims on his website, "At the heart of science fiction is the human desire to find ourselves. A seeking of the self through reaching others." The play of the title, *Illegal Alien*, raises interesting comparisons between the Tosoks' experience and other forms of alienation within modern culture. The courtroom scenes, in fact, resemble other trials in which race and racism have played a large role; as with many court cases, the effects and results of the case have as much to do with power and how the participants feel about and interact with each other, as with actual legal facts.

Despite Sawyer's success around the world, he has remained committed to Canada and Canadian science fiction. Canadian characters, settings, and cultural references pepper his novels to various extents. He further demonstrated his commitment to the genre by editing, with his wife, the sixth installment of the *Tesseracts* anthology series, published in 1997. He edited another Canadian science-fiction anthology, this time with David Skene-Melvin, *Crossing the Line: Canadian Mysteries with a Fantastic Twist* (1998), which further demonstrated Sawyer's interest in mixing mystery and science fiction.

A short version of Sawyer's next novel, *Factoring Humanity* (1998), won the Premio UPC de Ciencia Ficción, awarded by the Universitat Politècnica de Catalunya in Spain, for best novella. *Factoring Humanity* links disparate themes of alien contact, artificial intelligence, and memory in a plot about the status and marketing of knowledge. Heather Davis, a psychology professor at the

University of Toronto in the year 2017, deciphers a series of radio messages received from inhabitants of a planet orbiting Alpha Centauri, the nearest star system. The messages tell her how to build a machine that transports her not into outer space, but into other people's memories, a giant network of connections. Her husband, Kyle, is an artificial intelligence expert who is trying to create a machine to think like a human while also thinking faster than any human or machine. When Kyle and Heather's daughter, Becky, accuses Kyle of sexual molestation, the family is thrown into chaos. Heather is able to use her machine to show that Becky's memories are false, and the specter of false memory is linked to the ominous corporate forces that are trying to buy Kyle's knowledge of artificial intelligence.

Like cyberpunk, *Factoring Humanity* describes a world in which the focus of narrative is not on story but on memory. When Heather crawls into the machine, she experiences not only information recovery—that is, other people's stories—but also information overload. Through a complex set of metaphors, the alien machine comes to resemble not only Kyle's ideal artificial intelligence but also the human brain itself. Heather's entry into the metamemory machine is described as an entry into the self, as if individual psychology exists as a miniature mirror of the universe. In fact, the machine the aliens have instructed her to build resembles the human brain, which has hundreds of billions of intricate, interrelated cells. Both Heather's machine and the human brain have a much greater storage density than Kyle's computer. Like William Gibson's cyberspace, the alien machine in *Factoring Humanity* is a dense matrix of networks that allows intimacy between an individual mind and the matrix. Human information circuits come to resemble (and perhaps be indistinguishable from) the nonhuman networks that Kyle has devoted his life to studying. As in many of Sawyer's works, understanding of the other brings one to a closer understanding of oneself; in this case, the aliens have literally enabled humans to understand themselves and each other. Whether man is ready for such knowledge is another question. *Factoring Humanity* implies that if memory is something that can exist in something resembling ROM storage—that is, if memories can be maintained elsewhere (or in Becky's case, be someone else's)—then human identity itself must be redefined.

Flashforward, published in 1999, also won the Premio UPC de Ciencia Ficción, as well as the Aurora Award. In this novel, a team of physicists, led by Lloyd Simcoe and Theo Procopides, is conducting a high-energy experiment, which accidentally induces a global consciousness shift. Everyone on Earth is temporarily shifted twenty-one years into the future, and experiences several minutes of that future. *Flashforward* describes the efforts to understand what happened, and more signifi-

Dust jacket for Sawyer's 1998 novel, about a machine that allows the user to tap into other people's memories

cantly, the consequences of knowing one's future, both on the personal level and for society as a whole. Like its predecessors, *Flashforward* explores provocative ideas in an accessible manner.

Through the 1970s, many Canadian science-fiction writers were more influenced by their American counterparts than by previous and current Canadian writers. Since the mid 1970s, however, Canadian science-fiction writers have started to include more Canadian references and settings in their works. Rejecting American definitions of the genre, these writers are creating new visions of a Canadian future. The typical features of Canadian fiction—the Canadian as exile or immigrant, the harshness of a settlement culture, the encounter with unmapped territory—are standard features of Sawyer's work as well. Several of his works support Margaret Atwood's notion that the central theme of Canadian literature is struggle against a murderous landscape. Canada, in Sawyer's hands, seems predisposed toward science fiction. After all, as he told *Science Fiction Chronicle* in September 1993, "Canada was drawn together not by war or rebellion, but by a giant, almost-impossible engineering project—the building of the Canadian Pacific Railway. The story of Canada's history reads like a good *Analog* serial."

Sawyer is known for his excellent character development, rare in the hard-science-fiction world—his characters are neither simply good nor simply evil but rather complex characters whose lives describe the murky area of individual subjectivity. Even in Sawyer's first novel, *Golden Fleece*, it is difficult to determine who is more evil, JASON (the computer) or Aaron (the captain).

Sawyer's characterization skill stems from his understanding of hard science fiction as a genre that, while exploring technology, concentrates on what it is like to be human in the face of technological possibilities. Technology functions as a character in Sawyer's works, even in those works where there is not an actual named artificial intelligence. For Sawyer, technology is a tool for the imagination, a means of discovering new territories of experience and image. His works are structured by the conflict between an understanding of technology as a means toward freedom from the necessities of work and daily life, and an understanding of technology (particularly artificial intelligence and virtual reality) as tools of war and commerce. Sawyer's works uniformly explore the ethical and social implications of new technologies. Attempts to discover and describe aspects of human intelligence that can be simulated by machines is a theme common to many of his works; investigating artificial or machine intelligence not only offers the opportunity to explore a true "other"—a disembodied mentality that does not function like humans'—but also offers the possibility of defining the nature of knowledge itself.

Sawyer's works include a mixture of serious science and irony typical of much postmodern fiction—his plots frequently undermine themselves, and his characters make moral statements at the same time as they question the ability of these statements to have an effect. Finally, his work produces neither a utopia nor a dystopia but a way of surpassing or transcending the opposition between them. As such, Sawyer's writing is part of a contemporary movement in science fiction that seeks to go beyond simplistic choices between the absolute good and the absolute bad. At the same time, Sawyer's work is meant to make a moral impact. As he said in the September 1993 *Science Fiction Chronicle*, "If I lived in a different time or place, I might have been a polemicist or essayist, rather than a fiction writer. But today, nobody wants to stand still to listen to a well-reasoned argument. So by using the metaphoric devices of aliens and time travel and future worlds, I get to talk about issues without people bringing their natural resistance or their preconceptions to the table." Sawyer writes not merely to entertain or to present scientific theories, but to deliver a message, or at least posit difficult ethical questions. The "future" that Sawyer invokes is a comment on the present—a means of working through fears, anxieties, and desires about contemporary culture.

Despite Sawyer's ability to write novels that could easily be marketed as mainstream thrillers, he has remained loyal to science fiction as the genre that allows him the greatest freedom to communicate his perspective. He says on his website:

> I write science fiction not just because I love the genre—I do—but also because I think it's an important form of communication. SF lets us talk about really fundamental issues: whether or not God exists, what it means to be human, and so on; it's a laboratory for thought experiments about the human condition. Of course I want to entertain my readers, but I also love the fact that SF also lets me help them to think about new things, or about old things in new ways.

According to Sawyer, science fiction allows readers to see themselves as they are through creating circumstances that provide unusual viewpoints (including those of computers, dinosaurs, and aliens). As he said in the *Books in Canada* interview: "We're living in a world in which people are undergoing all kinds of experiences that our parents never dreamed of, a world of biotechnology and surrogate children, of global communications nets and virtual reality, of whole new realms of human interaction. In a world that's changing so incredibly rapidly, people really need to spend a little time saying 'gee, where are these trends taking us?' Science fiction helps us think about ourselves and our world, about what it means to be human."

Interviews:

Andrew Weiner, "Profile: Getting Respect," *Books in Canada* (March 1993): 22–25;

T. Jackson King, "*SFC* Interview: Robert J. Sawyer," *Science Fiction Chronicle* (September 1993): 5, 30–31;

Luigi Pachì, "Views: An Interview with Robert J. Sawyer," *Delos SF*, 1996 <http://www.fantascienza.com/delos/ie/sawyer.html>;

Edo van Belkom, "Robert J. Sawyer," in his *Northern Dreamers: Interviews with Famous Canadian Science Fiction, Fantasy and Horror Writers* (Kingston, Ontario: Quarry Press, 1998), pp. 197–209;

James Schellenberg and David M. Switzer, "Interview with Robert J. Sawyer," *Challenging Destiny*, 5 (January 1999): 32–44;

David Mathew, "Beyond Humanity," *Interzone*, 149 (November 1999): 27–31.

Daniel Sernine
(7 November 1955 –   )

Jean-Louis Trudel
Université du Québec à Montréal

BOOKS: *Les Contes de l'ombre* (Montreal: Sélect, 1979);

Légendes du vieux manoir (Montreal: Sélect, 1979);

Organisation Argus (Montreal: Editions Paulines, 1979); translated by David Homel as *Those Who Watch Over the Earth* (Windsor, Ontario: Black Moss, 1990);

Le Trésor du "Scorpion" (Montreal: Editions Paulines, 1980); translated by Frances Morgan as *Scorpion's Treasure* (Windsor, Ontario: Black Moss, 1990);

Le Vieil Homme et l'espace (Longueuil, Quebec: Le Préambule, 1981);

L'Epée Arhapal (Montreal: Editions Paulines, 1981); translated by Morgan as *The Sword of Arhapal* (Windsor, Ontario: Black Moss, 1990);

La Cité inconnue (Montreal: Editions Paulines, 1982);

Les Méandres du temps (Longueuil, Quebec: Le Préambule, 1983);

Argus intervient (Montreal: Editions Paulines, 1983); translated by Ray Chamberlain as *Argus Steps In* (Windsor, Ontario: Black Moss, 1990);

Ludovic (Montreal: Pierre Tisseyre, 1983); revised edition (Saint-Lambert, Quebec: Héritage, 1992);

Quand vient la nuit (Longueuil, Quebec: Le Préambule, 1983);

Le Cercle violet (Montreal: Pierre Tisseyre, 1984); revised edition (Montreal: Pierre Tisseyre, 1993);

Les Envoûtements (Montreal: Editions Paulines, 1985);

Argus: Mission mille (Montreal: Editions Paulines, 1988);

Jardins sous la pluie (Boucherville, Quebec: Graficor, 1988);

La Nef dans les nuages (Montreal: Editions Paulines, 1989);

Nuits blêmes (Montreal: XYZ, 1990);

Quatre destins (Montreal: Editions Paulines, 1990);

Boulevard des étoiles, 2 volumes (Montreal: Ianus, 1991); revised edition (Amiens, France: Encrage, 1998);

Le Cercle de Khaleb (Saint-Lambert, Quebec: Héritage, 1991);

Les Rêves d'Argus (Montreal: Editions Paulines, 1991);

La Fresque aux trois démons (LaSalle, Quebec: Hurtubise HMH, 1991);

Daniel Sernine (photograph by Julie Martel)

La Magicienne Bleue (Montreal: Pierre Tisseyre, 1991);

Chronoreg (Montreal: Québec/Amérique, 1992); revised edition (Beauport, Québec: Alire, 1999);

La Couleur nouvelle (Montreal: Québec/Amérique, 1993);

Les Portes mystérieuses (Saint-Lambert, Quebec: Héritage, 1993);

Manuscrit trouvé dans un secrétaire (Saint-Laurent, Quebec: Pierre Tisseyre, 1994);

Sur la scène des siècles (Montreal: Ianus, 1995);

La Traversée de l'apprenti-sorcier (Montreal: Médiaspaul, 1995);

L'arc-en-cercle (Saint-Lambert, Quebec: Héritage, 1995);

Petites fugues en lettres mineures (Saint-Lambert, Quebec: Dominique, 1997).

OTHER: *Aurores boréales 2,* edited by Sernine (Longueuil, Quebec: Le Préambule, 1985);

"Monsieur Olier devient ministre," in *SF: Dix années de science-fiction québécoise,* edited by Jean-Marc Gouanvic (Montreal: Logiques, 1988), pp. 214–268;

"Sa Fleur de Lune," in *Sous des Soleils étrangers,* edited by Yves Meynard and Claude J. Pelletier (Laval, Quebec: Ianus, 1989), pp. 55–70;

"Science-fiction et fantastique pour jeunes, un survol de la planète," in *Visions d'autres mondes: La littérature fantastique et de science-fiction canadienne,* compiled by Andrea Paradis (Montreal: Editions RD, 1995), pp. 102–110; translated as "Science Fiction and Fantasy for the Young, an Overview of the Planet," in *Out of This World: Canadian Science Fiction and Fantasy Literature,* compiled by Paradis (Kingston, Ontario: Quarry Press, 1995), pp. 96–104;

Concerto pour six voix, edited by Sernine (Montreal: Médiaspaul, 1997).

SELECTED PERIODICAL PUBLICATIONS– UNCOLLECTED:

FICTION

"Loin des vertes prairies," *Solaris,* 8, no. 6 (November–December 1982): 21–30;

"Une journée dans la vie de Clara Niowecki," *Pandore,* 1 (April 1985): 15–19;

"Métal qui songe," *imagine . . . ,* 10 (February 1989): 9–21;

"Des nouvelles de la planète," *XYZ, la revue de la nouvelle,* 5 (May–Summer 1989): 8–12;

"Pluies amères," *Solaris,* 17, no. 4 (Spring 1992): 27–33;

"Ailleurs," *Québec Science,* 33, no. 4 (December 1994 – January 1995): 42–46.

NONFICTION

"La science-fiction pour jeunes au Québec (1)," as Alain Lortie, *Requiem,* 3, no. 4 (June–July 1977): 14–16;

"La science-fiction pour jeunes au Québec (2)," as Lortie, *Requiem,* 3, no. 5 (September–October 1977): 6–8;

"La science-fiction pour jeunes au Québec (3)," as Lortie, *Requiem,* 4, no. 1 (January 1978): 16–19;

"Fantastique: DeWarren, Merritt, Hodgson," as Lortie, *Solaris,* 5, no. 5 (October–November 1979): 12–16;

"Les archives du fantastique," as Lortie, *Solaris,* 6, no. 3 (June 1980): 12–16;

"La SF pour adolescents," as Lortie, *Québec français,* 42 (May 1981): 77–79;

"L'année 1983–1984 en science-fiction québécoise," *Lurelu,* 7, no. 3 (Winter 1985): 33–35;

"Écrire pour les jeunes," *Nuit blanche* (October–November 1985): 50–51;

"SF québécoise et SF canadienne: trajectoires convergentes?" *Solaris,* 13, no. 3 (September–October 1987): 38–39;

"Historique de la SFQ," *Solaris,* 14, no. 1 (May–June 1988): 41–47;

"Le point sur le Grand Prix de la Science-Fiction et du Fantastique québécoise," *Courrier SF* (November 1990): 28–33;

"SF québécoise et SF canadienne: trajectoires parallèles?" *Solaris,* 16, no. 3 (November–December 1990): 16.

It would be easier to account for the absence of a vibrant and distinctive body of science-fiction works in French-speaking Canada than it is to explain its existence. Few countries have spawned an autonomous science-fiction tradition able to stand the comparison with American imports. However, there is a francophone school of Canadian science fiction, and Daniel Sernine is one of the reasons that it exists. As an early witness to its evolution, as a writer who has devoted himself from the first to writing unabashed science fiction and fantasy, and as an editor who has nurtured a generation of younger writers, he has shaped the field as it exists today in French-speaking Canada.

Daniel Sernine was born Alain Lortie on 7 November 1955 in Montreal, Quebec, where he has spent his entire life, never straying for long from the western quarter of the city. His father, Paul-Émile Lortie, worked as a building inspector for the forerunner of the Canadian Housing and Mortgage Corporation, and his mother, Marcelle Lortie (née Lelièvre), completed high school and stopped working after her marriage. He was the younger of two sons, his brother having been born two years earlier.

He attended a series of Catholic private schools, including the prestigious Collège Notre-Dame, where he soon evinced an undoubted precocity as a student and as a writer. He was twelve when he started his first story, a science-fiction adventure distantly inspired by the original *Star Trek* series, though he never completed it. He entered Collège Jean-de-Brébeuf at the age of fourteen, although most entering students were two or three years older. At the age of fifteen, he spent part of his summer vacation in the family basement, finishing his first short story, this time a fantastical tale inspired by authors he still cites as influences: Guy de Maupassant, Claude Seignolle, H. P. Lovecraft, Abraham Mer-

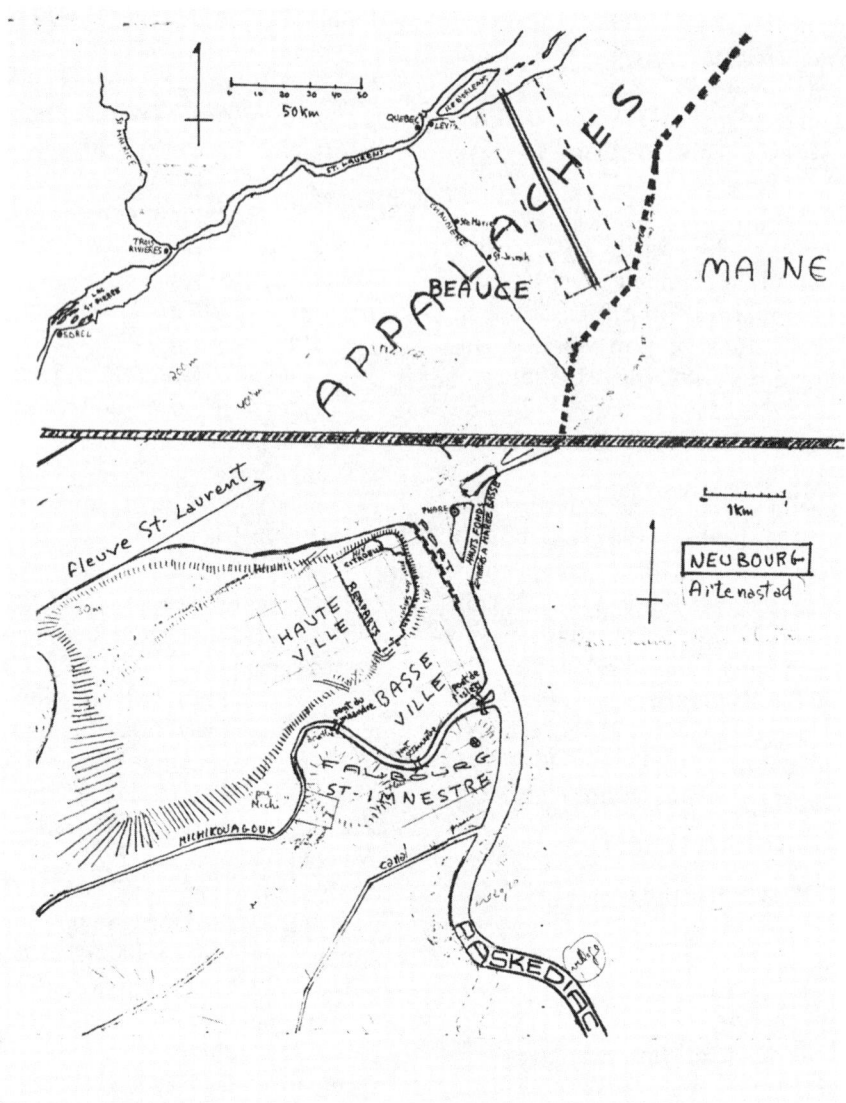

Sernine's earliest map of the fictional Paskédiac Valley, part of a reimagined Quebec, the setting for many of his works (Collection of Jean-Louis Trudel)

ritt, Edgar Allan Poe, Algernon Blackwood, William Hope Hodgson, and Arthur Machen. His science-fiction universe was conceived almost simultaneously, starting with a story written for a French course in 1971 or so, which chronicled the history of colonists on a distant planet.

At the age of sixteen, after completing his college studies, Lortie entered the nearby Université de Montréal. He graduated with a bachelor's degree in history in 1975 and then earned a Master of Library Sciences in 1977, often working as a tutor to students who were his own age. In 1972 he had begun working on what was published in 1984 as *Le Cercle violet* (The Purple Circle).

He was still finishing his undergraduate studies when he published his first stories in 1975 in the fifth issue of the newly established *Requiem,* the first periodical devoted to genre science fiction and fantasy in French-speaking Canada. He wrote under the name Daniel Sernine, after one of his favorite fictional characters, Arsène Lupin, who used Sernine as an alias. Although a typesetting error mangled the second story, Sernine overlooked this less than auspicious beginning and went on to make a name for his alter ego as an author of efficient though fairly standard tales of fantasy. The only pieces of writing that he has ever published under his own name are reviews of French-Canadian fiction for young readers, published in *Requiem* and *Solaris,* and a few other critical articles.

Over the next few years, Sernine laid the basis for a writing career, publishing several science-fiction and fantasy short stories that drew favorable comment from the nascent community of readers and writers. In 1976 an early science-fiction story, "Agonie en trois exemplaires" (Three Iterations of Agony), appeared in *Requiem* 11. The next year, his science-fiction novelette "Exode 5" (Exodus 5) won the first Prix Dagon (which is now known as the Prix Solaris) in a writing contest organized by *Requiem*.

That year, he was faced with sharply divergent career choices. He could pursue writing as a full-time vocation, which entailed huge financial uncertainty and little hope of any pay-off in the context of French-speaking Canada; or he could hunt for a secure job in the field of library science. Though he took on a couple of short-term jobs at the Bibliothèque nationale du Québec over the following year, he opted to concentrate on a writing career. The first step was to move from the less than lucrative magazine field into publishing books. Yet, given his choice of subject matter, gaining a toehold in the Quebec publishing industry was far from easy in the late 1970s.

At a time when magical realism was in its ascendance in world literature and the fantastical was being handled in new and powerful ways by writers such as Anne Hébert, Sernine chose to explore a brand of fantasy that was essentially Gothic in its relentless pursuit of the eerie and uncanny. His early stories, clearly influenced by the classic tales of such authors as Jean Ray and Ann Radcliffe, were gathered in the collections *Les Contes de l'ombre* (Tales from the Shadow, 1978) and *Légendes du vieux manoir* (Legends from the Old Manor, 1979).

Fifteen years later, the same stories were repackaged as parts of collections for younger readers, such as *Les Portes mystérieuses* (Mysterious Doors) and *La Couleur nouvelle* (A New Color), both published in 1993, at the height of the vogue for children's horror fiction. It is no longer possible for modern readers, who are in isolation, to fully appreciate the stories of inescapable destinies and vengeful powers dwelling just beyond their ken. The world in which Gothic horror could scare or chill readers no longer exists; it vanished with industrialization and the pervasive cult of material consumption. This development was true even in the late 1970s, and Sernine therefore proceeded to build a world in which his tales of fear and unease would make sense. In so doing, he embarked upon the writing of the longest sustained series of Quebec dark fantasy.

In 1979 he started composing "Adeline," a novel of Gothic horror for adults, while simultaneously working on what became *Le Trésor du "Scorpion"* (1980; translated as *Scorpion's Treasure*). Both stories were set in a reimagined part of Quebec, revolving around the fictional fishing village of Cap-Fantôme and the equally fictional Paskédiac Valley, dotted with the town of Neubourg, the village of Chandeleur, and the manor of Granverger. Over five centuries, the fates of the Michay and Davard families are intertwined with the manifestations of unearthly powers. The Bertin and Vignal families serve as two lesser dynasties and provide several key characters. A total of seventeen books are closely tied to these settings and to the centuries-long clash of good and evil, and several more of Sernine's books are linked to the main saga, though more distantly. Although "Adeline" did not appear in print until 1994, as part of *Manuscrit trouvé dans un secrétaire* (Manuscript Found in a Secretary), the other story was Sernine's second young-adult novel to be published by Editions Paulines under its Jeunesse-Pop imprint.

His first young-adult novel, *Organisation Argus* (translated as *Those Who Watch Over the Earth*), published by Editions Paulines in 1979, was science fiction and part of a future history that includes "Exode 5." In Sernine's science-fictional universe, the Earth is watched over by human overseers, part of a secret organization based on an asteroid called Erymede. Gifted with advanced technology by benevolent aliens, the Erymeans, as they are known, keep an eye on Earth affairs in the hope of saving humanity from itself. The devotion of the Erymeans to the cause of peace and to the thwarting of the Great Powers is not unlike that of the fictional Unipax organization in a series of young-adult books written by French-Canadian author Maurice Gagnon between 1965 and 1968.

Whereas horror is often intimate and always immediate in Sernine's fantasy, usually focusing on the frailties of the human body and mind, his science-fiction stories draw on aspects of the real world as the sources of similar fears. Nuclear war, overpopulation, and ecological devastation are the three horsemen of Sernine's early apocalyptic visions. A measure of the author's pessimism is the fact that the Erymeans are in no sense all-powerful: they are unable to remedy the problems caused by the overpopulation and overexploitation of the planet, though they stand ready to try to cut short any nuclear exchange.

The anxieties that culminated during the early years of Ronald Reagan's U.S. presidency are evident in Sernine's first science-fiction collection, *Le Vieil Homme et l'espace* (The Old Man and Space), published in 1981. In "La planète malade d'humanité" (A Planet Sick with Humankind) the protagonist, an Erymean agent driven insane by the ills caused by pollution and overpopulation, envisions a cleansing catastrophe to bring about the cure of Earth by eliminating most of humanity; it turns out that the Erymeans have planned such an intervention. In "Boulevard des Etoiles" (Stardust Boulevard) the survivors of an unspecified catas-

Cover for Sernine's first young-adult novel (1979), in which Earth is watched over from an asteroid by a secret society of humans who have been given advanced technology by benevolent aliens

trophe cavort aimlessly among the carnival attractions of a city rebuilt with the help of the Erymeans. In "Fin de règne" (Kingdom's End) a far-future Earth is occupied by a handful of humans, the only ones who stayed behind after the rest of humanity mutated and achieved a form of immaterial transcendence. The remaining humans can only hope for the return of the Erymeans, who left aboard the spaceships of the Exodus.

The radical anomie of the characters in such fin-de-siècle stories as "Boulevard des Etoiles" and the later "Les amis de Monsieur Soon" (The Friends of Mr. Soon, 1983) and "La tête de Walt Umfrey" (Umfrey's Head, 1984) seems prescient in retrospect, anticipating the rootless heroes of the novels of Bret Easton Ellis and Jay McInerney a few years later. Even the indignant pessimism of Gil Behrer in "La planète malade d'humanité" rings truer than some rosier contemporary scenarios—even if the Earth of 1995 turned out to be less of a decaying cesspit than Sernine had forecast.

Sernine's antiheroic stance is even clearer in "Loin des vertes prairies" (A Long Way From the Green Fields), published in the November–December 1982 issue of *Solaris* (the former *Requiem*). The Heinleinian echo of the title (recalling *The Green Hills of Earth*, 1951) adds emphasis to the depiction of Garfield Francke, a highly competent member of a cadre of space pilots charged with defending the solar system against an unspecified alien enemy. Yet, this basic situation reminiscent of space-opera plots going back to Edmond Hamilton's "Crashing Suns" (1928) is subverted to show the trauma suffered by Francke and force the reader to understand his flight in the face of the enemy. The absurdity of war is a recurring theme in Sernine's fiction, already as clearly delineated in this story as in future efforts such as *Chronoreg* (1992).

Two young-adult novels, *L'Epée Arhapal* (translated as *The Sword of Arhapal*) published in 1981, and *La Cité inconnue* (The Unknown City), published the following year, built on the foundation laid by *Le Trésor du "Scorpion."* The Neubourg and Granverger cycle, as it is known, was taking form, melding many of the classical motifs of European fantasy with New World settings. However, the works published in 1983 best illustrate the various directions explored by Sernine. A new collection of fantastic tales, *Quand vient la nuit* (When Night Comes), was published by Le Préambule, the same publishing house that also put out, at the same time, Sernine's full-fledged science-fiction novel *Les Méandres du temps* (The Meanders of Time).

Composed in two stages, in March 1981 and September 1983, the narrative frame of *Quand vient la nuit* showcases Sernine's writing at its best, illustrating how his prose had improved since the first story published in *Requiem*. The stories themselves were written between August 1979 and the first half of 1983. Compared to the sometimes painfully obvious tales of the 1979 collections, such stories as "Petit démon" (Little Demon, 1983) and "Hécate à la gueule sanglante" (Bloody Jawed Hecate, 1981) demonstrate maturity of tone, deftness in the handling of multiple characters, and stylistic lushness.

As in earlier works, Sernine remained indebted to past masters for key components of his fiction, and he acknowledged many of his inspirations in the epigraphs of *Quand vient la nuit*. A Catholic influence may be perceived in his sense of the body's vulnerability not only to pain but to its appetites. Evil is often a tangible presence, manifesting as outright demons, as in "Petit démon," or as supernatural creatures whose lusts are unrestrained by either reason or morality, as in "Isangma" (1983). An old Catholic distrust of pagan rituals may also be revealed in Sernine's portrayal of the natives as pawns of malevolent spirits, all too willing to placate them with human sacrifices. Sernine's early schooling no doubt included the requisite tales of pious Catholic missionaries tortured by Amerindian "savages." Though some of Sernine's settings have shallow roots in Quebec, the monsters depicted in his fiction have much deeper ones, harking back to the old French-Canadian storytelling tradition, with its werewolves, lascivious demons, and pitiable ghosts.

In French-Canadian letters a related fantastical strain flourished for several decades in the latter half of the nineteenth century, bracketed by the bracing Enlightenment skepticism of Aubert de Gaspé Sr. and by the mocking disbelief of thoroughly modern Louis Fréchette. Many of the stories published in that span were literary adaptations of contemporary folktales. Sernine's dark fantasy is uncomfortably poised between the often deeply religious horror of this traditional folklore, the stylish evocations of the supernatural by the European masters, and the modern recognition of the sexuality encoded and repressed within the fantastical context of earlier Gothic fiction. In Quebec, Hébert's *Les Enfants du Sabbat* (1975; translated by Carol Dunlop-Hébert as *Children of the Black Sabbath,* 1977) attempted to lay bare the underpinnings of traditional horror, but by then it already felt anachronistic. Perhaps the only way to retain the full flavor of the traditional *fantastique* tale and its gory denizens while delving into its inarticulate sexual fears was to go back in time, like Sernine, and fashion a more congenial version of historical reality. The end result has been at times highly effective, as in the teasingly nostalgic "Ses dents" (His Teeth, 1983), but it has also felt forced and artificial, as in "Le masque" (The Mask, 1981) or "L'icône de Kiev" (The Icon from Kiev, 1983).

Les Méandres du temps reworked many of the themes already present in *Organisation Argus* and "Loin des vertes prairies." Since the novel was intended for a more mature audience than the Jeunesse-Pop readership, Sernine was able to deepen and broaden his critique of secretive governments maneuvering in the waning years of the Cold War. The story also articulates Sernine's antimilitary viewpoint clearly. While the Erymeans watch over the Earth to prevent full-scale war from breaking out, Nicolas Dérec is a young telepath taking part in experiments funded by the Canadian Ministry of Defence. His fate becomes intertwined with that of the Erymean telepath Karilian, who has been sent back to Earth after a premonitory vision leads him to fear the outbreak of nuclear Armageddon. Nevertheless, the choice of a sixteen-year-old as one of the protagonists did not let *Les Méandres du temps* stand entirely apart from Sernine's works for younger readers. Dérec's juvenile indignation seems excessively trenchant and simplistic at times, even if there is more understanding shown for the scientists pressured to work for the military than in *Organisation Argus*.

A juvenile science-fiction novel, *Argus intervient* (translated as *Argus Steps In*), also appeared in 1983, published by Editions Paulines, while *Ludovic,* a fantasy novel for a slightly older audience, was released by another publisher, Pierre Tisseyre. Nevertheless, to supplement his income, Sernine accepted work as a first reader for Editions Paulines that year and wrote a nonfiction piece for the magazine *Lurelu,* which covers French-language youth fiction in Canada. This last sale marked the start of an ongoing involvement with *Lurelu:* he joined the editorial staff in 1987 and became editor in 1991.

While *Argus intervient* was the next installment in Sernine's science-fiction series and basically a quick action romp, *Ludovic* was a more substantial novel. Acknowledging the influence of J. R. R. Tolkien's *The Lord of the Rings* (1954–1955), the story follows the adventures of Ludovic Bertin as he twice makes his way into the fortress of the Necromancer, in an imaginary kingdom, to save its inhabitants from a growing evil. Ludovic comes from Chandeleur in the Paskédiac Valley and crosses over into this magic world, but the link with the Granverger cycle only serves as a bridging device; the novel focuses more on the responsibilities of the young nobles that Ludovic befriends.

By this time Sernine felt at ease with taking a more active role in the distinct fields of Quebec science fiction and Quebec youth fiction. In 1983 he joined the editorial team of *Solaris*. Two years later he became a member of the board of directors of Communication-Jeunesse, the nonprofit advocacy group for youth fiction in French-speaking Canada, and he eventually served as vice president from 1989 to 1993.

In 1985 he edited the second installment of the *Aurores boréales* (Northern Lights) anthologies, a sign of the confidence that imprint editor and *Requiem* founder Norbert Spehner placed in him. The stature Sernine had acquired by then was confirmed when, later that year, he became the editor of the Jeunesse-Pop imprint for the Editions Paulines publishing house. The following year, he joined the board of the Grand Prix de la science-fiction et du fantastique québécois, which administers the award of the same name. He served as president of the board from 1989 to 1993, when he resigned. Finally, in 1988, he joined the board of SFSF Boréal Inc., the nonprofit society in charge of the annual Boréal science-fiction conventions, serving first as vice president and then as president from 1991 to 1996.

Despite all these other activities, Sernine's literary output was not immediately affected. Given the standard he had just set, 1984 might have ranked as a fal-

Cover for Sernine's 1983 collection of stories, in some of which evil takes the bodily form of a demon

low year if the lone book he published that year, *Le Cercle violet,* had not been a keystone of the Granverger cycle. It earned its author wider literary recognition than he had previously achieved; and, aimed at the same audience on the verge of adulthood as *Ludovic,* it won the Canada Council prize for young-adult literature in French.

The opening scenes are a clear homage to Alain-Fournier's *Le Grand Meaulnes* (1913; translated by Françoise Delisle as *The Wanderer,* 1953) as the protagonist visits an unknown mansion in the woods and glimpses, in the midst of a costume ball, a young girl he will never forget: she becomes his lover later in life. Yet, young Pierre Michay must first survive an assassination attempt and learn of his family curse before starting to look for her. The family feud with the Davards has resulted in the Michay men dying in mysterious circumstances, always in autumn. Elements of the basic situation point to the influence exerted on Sernine by *Le bracelet de vermeil* (1937), a young-adult novel by French author Serge Dalens.

Adorned with Sernine's own illustrations and maps, the book was a pivotal one in the Granverger cycle. Set in 1899, it marked the reconciliation of the two families and the banishment of the demon called into this world by the Davard sorcerers. The demon-haunted nineteenth century gives way to a new century, and it becomes clear that the Granverger cycle is its own metaphor, trading the depths of adult fiction for a clear parallel between the gradual beating back of magic and the mutation of youthful enthusiasm into adult experience.

In French literature, adolescence became a land of lost content shortly after the turn of the twentieth century, identified as an age all its own by studies such as Pierre Mendousse's *L'Âme de l'adolescent* (1909) and novels such as Louis Pergaud's *La Guerre des boutons* (War of the Buttons, 1912). Yet, Sernine does not idealize adolescence. The Paskédiac Valley is hardly a lost Eden one might long to find again, and *Le Cercle violet* is hardly pervaded by regret for vanished innocence. Instead, Pierre Michay's one glimpse of beauty and purity is needed to support him through the harsh and lonely years of his childhood.

Magic is dark in Sernine's world. At best, it tells his characters things they would rather not have heard, or it compels them to fight battles that will avail them precious little. But the uncertainties of fantasy force readers to focus on the ephemera of everyday life, on the details of what so soon passes away and loses importance as people age. Magic, once banished, is what is missed when memory dwells on the past. It was to be expected, then, that Pierre Michay would leave the Paskédiac Valley after the demon Abaldurth is exiled for good and after he has finally met his beloved. Pierre takes his thirst for justice and his yearning for the romance of life to Europe. The closing scene of *Le Cercle violet* betrays again the influence of *Le Grand Meaulnes,* with the hero returning from his travels to learn that his beloved has died while giving birth to their child. *Le Cercle violet* went through three printings, and a slightly revised edition was published in 1993, making it probably Sernine's most popular work.

Over the next five years, Sernine's involvement with the field in various capacities resulted in a lessening of his frantic writing pace. His work for *Lurelu* and as writer-editor for Editions Paulines took its toll, and he was no longer able to write full time. However, as an editor, he recruited a new generation of authors to write for the Jeunesse-Pop imprint. Esther Rochon and Philippe Gauthier contributed a couple of titles, while Francine Pelletier, starting in 1987, soon became a mainstay of the imprint. Johanne Massé, starting in 1985, and

Joël Champetier, with a first book in 1990, also helped to turn the imprint into one that places its major emphasis on science fiction and fantasy.

Nevertheless, Sernine continued to publish. Another Granverger book, *Les envoûtements* (Bewitchments), was published in 1985 by Editions Paulines and intended for readers younger than fifteen; it was the last of his early juveniles to go through more than one printing as of 1998. Another installment in his science-fiction series, *Argus: Mission mille* (Argus: Mission 1000), published in 1988, added little to his portrait of the mysterious Erymeans. A children's book, *Jardins sous la pluie* (Gardens under the Rain), published that same year, set a story of budding love between a sixteen-year-old boy and a twelve-year-old girl in a near future mostly characterized by new movies and musical technologies.

The young-adult novel *La Nef dans les nuages* (The Ship in the Clouds), published in 1989, featured an intersection of Sernine's two main series: the ancestors of the Erymeans from his future history show up in the Paskédiac Valley, his favored pseudo-historical setting. The nineteenth century lends itself well to this crossing of genre boundaries, but the transgression underlines one of his main themes: the progressive disenchantment of the world. While Sernine originally constructed an enchanted world wherein his tales of the fantastic could be set, the main narrative, spanning five hundred years of the Paskédiac Valley's history, is a story of disenchantment. In *La Nef dans les nuages* the powers of the Vignal family, which had been perceived as supernatural a century before, start to be interpreted as possibly rational. After all, the Erymean stories include characters with extrasensory powers and perceptions, such as Nicolas Dérec in *Les Méandres du temps* or Denis Blackburn in *Chronoreg;* the former can glimpse the future and the latter can travel back in time. A possible ancestor of Nicolas Dérec appears in "Le sorcier d'Aïtétivché" (The Sorcerer of Aitetivche, 1979), hinting at an early connection between the two universes.

Before bringing the Granverger cycle to a close, however, Sernine again illustrated his range as a fantasy author. While *Quatre destins* (Four Destinies), published in 1990, collected the revised versions of four fantastical tales set in Neubourg or Granverger, adapted for the younger readers of the Jeunesse-Pop imprint, the other collection published that year, *Nuits blêmes* (Pale Nights), was intended for a more sophisticated audience. The tales of *Nuits blêmes* are urban fantasy, with a modern edge entirely different from the Gothic ambiance of many of the Granverger stories. That same year, four of his young-adult novels were translated into English for Black Moss Press but failed to make a significant impact. Reviews in English-speaking Canada were few and mixed. The *Nuits blêmes* stories, however, did impress reviewers and critics in French-speaking Canada. The Montreal settings and the reliance on more subtle disruptions of consensual reality established that Sernine could move beyond the traditional fantasy of the Granverger tales and laid the groundwork for the renewal of his writing in the 1990s.

At the time, the French-language science-fiction field was in a profound state of crisis. In France the venerable *Fiction* magazine had folded. In Quebec two specialized publishers had essentially run out of steam: Editions Le Préambule had stopped publishing science fiction in 1987, while the "Autres mers, autres mondes" (Other Seas, Other Worlds) imprint of Editions Logiques ceased publishing in 1991. The Boréal conventions, beset by financial troubles, went into a prolonged hiatus after the one in Ottawa in 1989. With a small group, Sernine worked hard to keep the Prix Boréal going, preparing a renaissance that took shape around 1995.

Despite these problems facing the genre, in 1991 Sernine published six books. Both *Les Rêves d'Argus* (The Dreams of Argus) and *La Magicienne Bleue* (The Blue Magician) feature children enjoying short escapades into dreamworlds of their own. In *Les Rêves d'Argus* the Erymeans have developed a form of virtual reality for those wishing to abscond from their humdrum lives, however briefly. In *La Magicienne Bleue,* a children's book with no overt science-fiction or fantasy elements, the young heroes are treated to stories of a delightful never-never land by a neighbor.

Another children's book, *La Fresque aux trois démons* (The Three-Demon Fresco), was a reworking of another of Sernine's early fantastical tales set in Neubourg. Along with the publication of *Quatre destins,* it confirmed that these fantastical tales, originally written for a general readership, now mainly appealed to a younger generation reared on a steady diet of horror fiction.

Le Cercle de Khaleb (The Khaleb Circle), however, was written for older teenagers, and it was a significant addition to the Granverger cycle. Composed as a coda to *Le Cercle violet,* it firmly anchors the Paskédiac Valley in official Quebec history, since the young hero's mother is arrested for opposing conscription during World War II, which leads Maxime Michay-Argenson to spend the remainder of the war with his relatives in the old manor Granverger. During his stay Maxime and his distant cousin Virgile discover and settle unfinished business from fifty years before.

Boulevard des Étoiles gathered in two volumes several science-fiction stories dating back to the early stories. It also included new material in the form of two novellas, "Hôtel Carnivalia" (Hotel Carnivalia) and "À la recherche de Monsieur Goodtheim" (Looking for Mr. Goodheim). Sernine's fondness for the 1960s and 1970s is most obvious in a story such as "Hôtel Carnivalia," which features a character named Morry Jimmison, an obvious reference to Jim Morrison. In this story readers finally learn that most of the population of Earth was wiped out, not by the Erymeans, as "Boulevard des Étoiles" had hinted, but by a powerful race of aliens known as the Alii. Bereft of their original idealism (not unlike the utopians of the 1960s stranded in the late 1980s), both the Terran survivors and the Erymeans are reduced to more ignoble pursuits, as is made clear in "À la recherche de Monsieur Goodtheim," which mirrors the disillusioned heroes and flashy settings of cyberpunk.

The two-volume *Boulevard des Étoiles* earned the Prix Boréal for best book, as selected by readers, while "À la recherche de Monsieur Goodtheim" from the second volume won the Prix Boréal for best short story. The young-adult novel *Le Cercle de Khaleb* won the Prix 12/17 de la Foire du Livre et du Salon du Livre de Montréal, awarded by the twin book fairs of Montreal and Brive, France, for best young-adult book of the year. Capping the list, the Grand Prix de la science-fiction et du fantastique québécois was awarded for both works and *Les Rêves d'Argus*, thereby recognizing Sernine's achievement in producing the best body of work, in speculative fiction, in French-speaking Canada in 1991.

Despite its critical success, *Boulevard des Étoiles* had been published only by a small press, a sign of the lack of outlets for French-language science fiction at the time. Indeed, the Jeunesse-Pop imprint was becoming the only option for both well-known and upcoming authors. This situation seemed on the verge of changing when the Sextant imprint was created by the Québec/Amérique publishing house in 1994, but it proved short-lived. As a result, Sernine continued to exert a significant influence on the publication of science fiction and fantasy in French-speaking Canada. Whether he diverted his stable of authors from writing for a broader audience or effectively encouraged them to stick it out through the lean years remains to be seen.

The publication *Québec Amérique,* by a major publisher, of *Chronoreg* in 1992 was another milestone in Sernine's career. The novel maintains a furious pace as it detours through drug-fueled time loops. In this time line Mikhail Gorbachev was assassinated shortly after his accession to power, which resolves the inconsistency between Sernine's future history and current events. Thus, in this alternate version of the world, the Soviet Union and the United States are still playing Cold War games, and a new front has been created by Quebec's independence and its resultant bid for control of Labrador. A brush war between Quebec and Canadian soldiers is raging in the wilds of Labrador, complicated by the presence of Quebec irregulars who operate outside the laws of war. The Soviet Union and the United States have discreetly taken sides, with the Soviets helping Quebec.

Denis Blackburn, a Quebec soldier in this war, has a limited telepathic ability that is amplified by drugs. He discovers on a trip to Mexico to rescue a friend, Sébastien, who has fallen in with rural insurgents, that excessive doses of an illegal drug called chronoreg will enable him to "chronoregress." But Sébastien, who never grasped that Denis loved him, dies in a minor battle between the army and the rebels. Blackburn's first trip back in time is a failure, so he seeks more of the drug in order to return before Sébastien's final firefight. By the time he gets enough chronoreg, however, Sébastien's death has receded too far into the past to be changed. Back in Quebec, Blackburn's missions grow increasingly important, until he is sent to tackle the Irregulars, who are preventing a peace accord between Quebec and Canada. Commanding the Irregulars is Jac Marin, Blackburn's first lover. Blackburn starts to use chronoreg again, mostly to avoid being killed, and he manages to infiltrate the base of the Irregulars, but not before they explode an atomic bomb, putting an end to peace negotiations and provoking a retaliatory strike that results in the death of the young Chicoutimi boy Jodi, a prostitute whom Blackburn had grown to love. Thus, Blackburn goes back in time, overdosing on chronoreg and risking his sanity. He succeeds in part, preventing the nuclear explosion, but when he wakes up, his brain is irreversibly damaged. The epilogue takes place in a dreamland where the ending bifurcates, with Blackburn's lover, a fantasized mix of Sébastien and Jodi, either evaporating away or waiting for him.

Chronoreg is a complete creation, combining science-fiction tropes such as psi-drugs, time travel and paradoxes, ecological extrapolation, alternate history, and the unavoidable Erymeans. And, like the rest of Sernine's works, it is unflinchingly political. Blackburn deals with the dirt stirred by human passions, and he pays more than once the price exacted by war, with his flesh and his soul. He tackles love and death, and eventually is forced to choose between his old love for Jac Marin and his newfound affection for Jodi, and perhaps he loses both in the end—or perhaps not.

As intensively visual as it is intensely moral, *Chronoreg* represents a serious attempt to raise the writing of action science fiction to new heights in Quebec. A fully adult work, it offers the most gripping narrative in French-Canadian science fiction since Agnès Guitard's *Les Corps communiants* (1981). It earned Sernine the 1994 Aurora Award for the best Canadian speculative-fiction work in French.

Blackburn is no doubt one of Sernine's most deeply human characters, torn between multiple loves and loyalties. Sernine's homosexuality seems to lend a particular poignancy to the relationships between young men and paternal surrogates in many of his works. Gil Behrer and Karilian are early instances of such father figures, the first choosing to kill a surrogate son and the second killing himself to avoid having to execute his illegitimate son, Nicolas Dérec. In *Chronoreg* Blackburn does progress beyond such destructiveness, since he fights to save the two young men he has loved. Yet, both die in the end, nonetheless, victims of a war whose absurdity is tellingly expressed by the opening sentence of the second chapter: "Ce pourrait être l'enfer: l'homme, pressé de tout connaître, a inventé la guerre pour en avoir un avant-goût" (This could be Hell itself: Man, driven to know everything, invented war to get a foretaste).

In that one sentence Sernine conflates the Faustian urge of Western civilization to *know*, beyond good and evil, and the poisoned fruit of this same thrust. Yet, he is far from a systematic enemy of reason or applied science. His jaundiced view of technology is subordinated to his bleak opinion of humanity: the same petty fears, unreasoning passions, and enduring flaws surface both in his fantasy and in his science fiction.

In 1993 Sernine collected even more of his earlier fantastical tales to make up two new books for young readers, *La Couleur nouvelle* and *Les Portes mystérieuses*. Besides the reworked reprints, the two collections included a handful of original stories illustrating his continuing turn toward a less traditional version of fantasy.

The next year, he delivered another fully adult novel, *Manuscrit trouvé dans un secrétaire*. A work of dark fantasy, it delved once more into the history of the Davard-Michay feud, but it was set outside the confines of the Paskédiac Valley, in late-twentieth-century Cap-Fantôme. The main character is a writer whose experiences reflect Sernine's years in the literary milieu of Quebec. While the novel is something

Cover for Sernine's 1994 novel, a ghost story in which the protagonist is a writer who seems to be losing his grip on reality

of a traditional ghost story, the fantastic intrudes in the form of inexplicable interludes, as if the protagonist is losing his grip on reality—a technique that recurs in *L'arc-en-cercle* (The Raincircle, 1995). In *Manuscrit trouvé dans un secrétaire* Sernine's balancing act did not attain the equilibrium demonstrated in *Quand vient la nuit* or *Le Cercle violet*. The wildly Gothic story of Adeline within the main story clashed with the measured tonalities of the older writer's palette. Nevertheless, by treating Adeline's story as a fiction, Sernine was able to reconcile its grotesque flourishes with his finely detailed portrait of an unsuccessful writer on the edge of paranoia. The novel won the 1994 Prix Boréal for best book.

In 1995 Sernine brought the Granverger cycle to a close with two works capping the saga at both ends in time. Set in the far past of 1595, *La Traversée de l'apprenti-sorcier* (The Sorcerer's Apprentice's Crossing) follows young Alexandre Davard from France to Canada, where he explores the future settings of Neubourg, Chandeleur, and Granverger. At the other end of the temporal span, *L'arc-en-cercle* tells the story of young Etienne Vignal while he was at a summer camp near Chandeleur. The action is set in 1995 to end the Granverger cycle on the same date that was previously established in "La planète malade d'humanité" for the devastation of Earth, marking the real start of Sernine's future history.

With the end of the Granverger cycle it became clear that, whatever Sernine's early literary ambitions had been, the main theme of the overarching narrative was perfectly suited to its embedding in a series of books for children and teenagers. The slow disenchantment of the world, as demons are banished (in *Le Cercle violet*) and magic wish-fulfillment trinkets are discarded (in *Le Cercle de Khaleb* and *L'Arc-en-cercle*), matches the growing-up process of the young protagonists.

There is something lucid about Sernine's identification of a world ruled by dark magics and of the most irrational age of Man, in thrall to a continuous "becoming" driven by the body's imperatives. Pierre Michay's renouncing of the love of his childhood after his triumph over supernatural powers is perhaps the most heavily freighted decision in the Sernine opus.

In *La Relève du matin* (The Morning's Changing of the Guard, 1920), Henry de Montherlant lamented that Hermes, who was the God of Adolescence, was also the God of Twilight: for him, youth was the only time when one had any sense of beauty or any desire for virtue. However, Sernine's adolescents are not content with letting beautiful mysteries lie: the secrets of the Paskédiac are rarely less than portentous, and therein lies their charm, no doubt, compared to the paltry mysteries of childhood. In the final analysis the clearest distinction between Sernine's science fiction and his children's fantasy is that his young characters have the will and the means to change the world, while his adult characters grapple with a much more obdurate world.

However, his third publication in 1995 showed him to be moving beyond this dichotomy: the collection *Sur la scène des siècles* (And the Centuries for a Stage) was an even more convincing demonstration that Sernine could write a different brand of the fantastical. Drawing on his interest in history, the author set his tales in Ancient Egypt, Babylon, Aleppo, Palestine, and an historical cross-section of Europe. The refined cruelty, sensitivity, and delicacy of the stories were remarked upon by critics. The three 1995 books together earned Sernine his second Grand Prix de la science-fiction et du fantastique québécois.

Sernine's next collection for young readers, *Petites fugues en lettres mineures* (Little Fugues in Letters Minor, 1997), is more of a mix than the previous ones, encompassing reprints of early fantastical tales as well as a couple of newer science-fiction efforts. With its publication, most of the author's early fantasy works are back in print, with a few exceptions.

As with the efforts of Isaac Asimov late in his writing life, there is an almost obsessive component to Sernine's meticulous enfolding of as many of his stories as possible within the same fictional construct. This determination to preserve consistency at all costs has led Sernine to alter his future history along the way. In "Des nouvelles de la planète" (News from the Planet), published in the May–Summer 1989 issue of *XYZ*, the protagonist of "La planète malade d'humanité," Gil Behrer, is shown to be delusional. In *Chronoreg* Sernine altered history drastically by killing off Gorbachev before his reforms got under way, which means the entire Erymean time line can now be read as an alternate history.

Daniel Sernine describes his brand of pessimism as lucidity. Yet, though he has been more often cited for his prolific output than for his actual works, his works have been read by most of the new generation of Quebec science-fiction and fantasy writers. Several of his children's books have been reprinted, and his short fiction has also enjoyed multiple incarnations. Since 1975 he has put together a dark fantasy saga whose fascination can only be gauged by reading it in its entirety. The quest for closure, in all senses of the word, of Sernine's characters results in an ever more perfect circularity.

Interviews:

Jean-Pierre Moumon and Martine Blond, "Rencontre avec l'auteur: Daniel Sernine," *Antarès*, 1 (March 1981): 130–140;

Norbert Spehner, "Entrevue: Daniel Sernine," *Solaris*, 9, no. 3 (June–July 1983): 21–24;

Pierre D. Lacroix, "Interview avec Daniel Sernine," *Carfax*, 1 (Fall 1984): 16–19;

Michel Lord, "Entrevue avec Daniel Sernine," *Québec français*, 64 (December 1986): 28–30;

Yves-Daniel Mercier, "Entretien avec Daniel Sernine," *Færie*, 1 (February 1987): 27–33;

Luc Pomerleau, "Entrevue: Daniel Sernine," *Solaris*, 13, no. 3 (September–October 1987): 18–23;

Lacroix, "Entrevue," *Courrier SF*, 1 (Summer 1988): 11–17;

Francine Pelletier, "Du fantastique et de la SF," *XYZ*, 29 (Spring 1992): 73–84;

Fabien Ménard, "De l'écriture, de la violence et du temps," *Solaris,* 18, no. 4 (Spring 1993): 30–43;

Mel Yoken, "Entretien avec Daniel Sernine," *French Review,* 69 (May 1997): 873–886;

André-François Ruaud, "Entretien avec Daniel Sernine," in *Boulevard des Étoiles* by Sernine (Amiens, France: Encrage, 1998), pp. 241–248.

Bibliographies:

Aurélien Boivin, "Biographie et bibliographie," *Québec français,* 64 (December 1986): 38;

Pierre D. Lacroix, "Bibliographie exhaustive," *Carfax,* 3 (December 1986): 86–98;

Daniel Sernine, "Bibliographie," in his *Boulevard des Étoiles 2: À la Recherche de Monsieur Goodtheim* (Montreal: Ianus, 1991), pp. 181–221.

References:

Roger Bozzetto, "Daniel Sernine, auteur de science-fiction et de fantastique," *Canadian Children's Literature/Littérature canadienne pour la jeunesse,* 41 (1986): 44–54;

Daniel Coulombe, "Femme engagées et poètes enseignés dans *Le Cercle de Khaleb*," *Solaris,* 20, no. 4 (Spring 1995): 22–23;

Coulombe and Marie-Claude Maltais, "Les Abénaquis dans l'oeuvre de Sernine," *Temps Tôt,* 5 (January 1994): 28–30;

Simon Dallaire, "*Les Méandres du temps:* une analyse structuraliste," *Solaris,* 14, no. 6 (April 1989): 35–39;

Simon Dupuis, "Le cycle de Sernine," *Lurelu,* 14, no. 3 (Winter 1992): 7–9;

Christiane Gauthier, "Sernine: un monde fantastique," *Des Livres et des Jeunes,* 34 (Fall 1989): 2–5;

Alain Jacques, "Ludovic, Sernine et Tolkien," *Cirth de Gandalf* (January 1992): 10–14;

Michel Lamontagne, "Chronoreg ou le spectacle du sang," *Solaris,* 17, no. 4 (Spring 1992): 63–65;

Lamontagne, "Repérer les humains parmi les automates," *Solaris,* 16, no. 5 (January–February 1990): 28–30;

Claire Lebrun, "Un point tournant dans l'oeuvre de Daniel Sernine," *Canadian Children's Literature/Littérature canadienne pour la jeunesse,* 63 (1991): 95–97;

Lebrun, "Un univers souterrain," *Des Livres et des Jeunes,* 21 (Summer 1985): 17–21;

Michel Lord, "Entre l'espoir et le désespoir: un univers de sensations," *Québec français,* 64 (December 1986): 31–35;

Ursula Rapp, "Traditions et intertextualité dans <<Belphéron>> de Daniel Sernine," in *Les Voies du fantastique québécois,* edited by Maurice Émond (Quebec: Nuit Blanche, 1990), pp. 203–222;

Jean-Louis Trudel, "Fantastique: Daniel Sernine," *KWS,* 19 (May 1996): 21–24;

Sylvie Vincent, "L'aventure et ses limites: les Amérindiens dans l'oeuvre fantastique pour la jeunesse de Daniel Sernine," *Recherches amérindiennes au Québec,* 17 (Fall 1987): 79–94;

Élisabeth Vonarburg, "Daniel Sernine entre deux mondes," *imagine . . . ,* 5 (June 1984): 53–68;

Vonarburg, "La reproduction du corps dans l'espace, ou Naissance et renaissance dans l'espace," in *Les Ailleurs imaginaires: Les rapports entre le fantastiqe et la science-fiction,* edited by Boivin, Emond & Lord (Quebec: Nuit Blanche, 1993), pp. 205–233;

Vonarburg, "The Reproduction of the Body in Space," in *State of the Fantastic: Selected Essays from the Eleventh Conference on the Fantastic in the Arts,* edited by Nicholas Ruddick (Westport, Conn.: Greenwood Press, 1992), pp. 59–72.

Sean Stewart
(2 June 1965 -   )

Alexander C. Irvine
University of Denver

BOOKS: *Passion Play* (Victoria, British Columbia: Tesseract Books, 1992; New York: Ace, 1993);
Nobody's Son (Don Mills, Ontario: Maxwell Macmillan Canada, 1993; New York: Ace, 1995);
Resurrection Man (New York: Ace, 1995);
Clouds End (New York: Ace, 1995);
The Night Watch (New York: Ace, 1997);
Mockingbird (New York: Ace, 1998);
Galveston (New York: Ace, 2000).

Sean Stewart is a member of the new generation of Canadian science-fiction writers following the trail to American readership blazed by Charles de Lint and American expatriates such as William Gibson and Spider Robinson. Stewart is winning acclaim both within the science-fiction community and from the Canadian and American press: each of his first two books received the Aurora Award for best novel, and his third, *Resurrection Man* (1995), was cited by *The New York Times* as a 1995 Notable Book. His fellow writers speak of him in superlatives, and popular reviews compare him to the best of those contemporaries: Margaret Atwood, Ursula K. Le Guin, and even J. R. R. Tolkien.

Stewart was born Michael Sean Irwin on 2 June 1965 in Lubbock, Texas, to Kay Lanette (née Thornton) Irwin, an English professor, and Louis Irwin, a biochemist. His parents divorced when Sean was quite young. His mother soon remarried, and his stepfather, Joe Stewart, adopted Sean before the age of three, when the family moved to Alberta. One result of this upheaval was that Stewart spent his childhood and adolescence shuttling between two different worlds: he spent the school year in his parents' Edmonton university culture and summers in the heat of his grandparents' Texas fundamentalism. The differences, both physical and psychological, between the two landscapes impressed themselves on him; in an interview with Paula Simons in the March 1996 issue of *Saturday Night* he speaks of being "transfixed between cultures." This phrase applies to Stewart's position in the literary landscape as well. His novels work closely with time-tested set pieces of fantasy literature but combine them with the concerns of individual morality and right action that twentieth-century readers have grown accustomed to seeing in the context of strict psychological realism. Asked in a 1995 *Holland SF* interview if there is any difference between Canadian and American science fiction, or between science fiction and literature, Stewart replied, "I'm a bit skeptical." This skepticism of borders and boundaries permeates—and in one sense defines—the writer's work.

Stewart set his sights on a writing career while still in elementary school, and he has never held another job for any significant length of time. After graduating with honors from the University of Alberta in 1986, he married his high-school sweetheart, Christine Beck, on 20 June 1987. For the first several years of their marriage, the couple—and the first of their two daughters, Caitlin (born in 1990)—subsisted on Beck's scholarship money as she pursued a doctorate in psychobiology. Another daughter, Rowan, was born in 1994, by which time Stewart's writing had begun to bring in enough money that they were no longer a single-income family. After living in Vancouver for several years and then spending three years in Houston, Texas, the family moved to Monterey, California. From Monterey the family moved to Davis, California.

Passion Play (1992), Stewart's first published novel and the fifth he had completed, won Canada's highest awards for both speculative fiction and first mystery novel. It tells the story of Diane Fletcher, a "shaper"—a sort of forensic psychic who works by divining patterns in apparently chaotic sequences of events—working with the police to solve the murder of a prominent actor during a televised production of Christopher Marlowe's *Doctor Faustus* (1594). *Passion Play* is set in a near-future fundamentalist ("Redemptionist" in the novel) America that has been its own trope in the genre at least since Thomas M. Disch's *On Wings of Song* (1979) or Atwood's *The Handmaid's Tale* (1985)—which Stewart professes never to have read. Within that setting, however, surprising events collide in ways that shed light not just on

258

Sean Stewart (photograph by Biko; from the dust jacket for Galveston, 2000)

the narrative, but on the reader's generic expectations. Diane Fletcher struggles with being a female psychic working for an aggressively masculinist police force that, among other things, represents a society that hounds and rejects shapers. She is a post-Expressionist, cripplingly self-aware Sam Spade, and the title of the novel could well refer to her own last days before the solution of the crime brings her to a point of psychological collapse.

Much of the impact of *Passion Play* derives from its textual interplay with *Doctor Faustus,* and as with any overtly intertextual novel, *Passion Play* becomes intensely self-reflexive. The novel begins: "When I try to write it down it dies: I find myself speaking with my father's polished, thoughtful voice." This first sentence of Stewart's first published novel thus sounds two notes that echo throughout his subsequent books: from the beginning of his literary career, his attention has continually returned to both the question of writing and the problematic presence of the father.

The next two books Stewart wrote, *Clouds End* (1995) and *Nobody's Son* (1993), were both completed before *Resurrection Man,* which in order of publication falls between them. *Clouds End,* Stewart said in an unpublished 9 July 1998 interview, is his "homage to Tolkien, certainly the most important writer in my life over the long haul," and, without being a pastiche or knockoff, it displays this indebtedness on every page. The eponymous island of the book is home to an isolated tribe of fisherpeople who bear representative names such as Brook, Rope, and Foam. When the young heroine, Brook, runs afoul of a "haunt," a spirit from the Mist that borders the world, she is "twinned"; the spirit assumes her shape, which in the folk traditions of Clouds End inevitably means that the twinned person will be killed so the haunt can escape the Mist. But the haunt, Jo, warns the inhabitants of Clouds End that the near-mythical Forest People are advancing on Delta, the Sea People's closest settlement to the mainland. A quest ensues, with Brook, Rope, and others from their village going off to assist the people of Delta; along the way, they encounter Heroes of Legend, travel all the way to the Forest People's home of Arbor, and return after the war between the people of sea and forest has ended with the collapse of the Forest People's monarchy back in Arbor.

Although superficially a traditional quest story, *Clouds End* is set in a landscape so rigidly partitioned and oriented into binaries of land and sea, city and country, that the reader is unable to take anything about the setting at face value. Like the tension created by the collision of science-fiction and mystery genres in *Passion Play*, this juxtaposition of comfortable fantasy tropes with meticulously overdetermined names and landscapes forces the reader to compare the story of *Clouds End* to all the other stories similar to *Clouds End* that he or she might have read before. The characters' continual concern with their own stories and the stories of the people they know redoubles the reader's impression of *Clouds End* as a meditation on the possibilities and limitations of quest fantasy. The Heroes of Legend seek revenge that the narrative exposes to be simple murder; the war between the Deltans and the Forest People is conducted by means of fire and poison; back in Arbor, the Emperor murders his own son and then commits suicide; in general, wherever traditional quest fantasy finds heroism, *Clouds End* instead offers the more sordid elements of Jacobean drama.

Characters in the book are given to saying that big stories always become small stories, and like so many of the truisms that Stewart's characters apply to themselves, this one applies equally to the narrative itself. What heroism there is in the book revolves around family rather than great battles. Brook's parents have drowned long ago, and when she and Rope have twins, the birth is, in some measure, solace for the psychic wounds they still carry from their experiences of the war at Delta. But the novel is ambiguous even on this point, as Jo (the only character not named for a thing), growing more desperate to secure her existence in the world outside the Mist, reaches a crisis point in her conflict between self-preservation and a genuine love for the human she has twinned. The inevitable lethal conflict between human and doppelgänger occurs offstage during the last two pages of the book; whether the reader believes that Brook or a masquerading Jo returns to the twin children, enough uncertainty remains to question seriously not only the most important event of the story but also the reader's impulse for direct and explicit closure.

During the writing of *Clouds End* in 1989 and 1990, Stewart's wife was pregnant with their first child. The couple had also recently moved from Edmonton to Vancouver, where they lived until 1995, and the starkly drawn personal and cultural clashes in the novel resonate with the anxieties and discontinuities of Stewart's life at the time. Imminent fatherhood may also have spurred him into the careful consideration of the aftershocks of fatherhood that drives the narrative of *Nobody's Son*.

In the 9 July 1998 interview Stewart characterized *Nobody's Son* as "an attempt to consolidate what I had learned in *Clouds End*," and the two novels are concerned with the same core issues. *Nobody's Son*, like *Clouds End*, is set in a partitioned landscape and takes a hard look at the real actions that go into what people call heroism. The low-born—and fatherless—protagonist of the story, Shielder's Mark, braves the Ghostwood and breaks the spell hanging over the Red Keep, succeeding where generations of heroes have failed. Then he goes to court to announce his deeds and claim his reward from the king.

Nobody's Son thus unfolds along fairly typical lines, even given the gloomy atmosphere of the early chapters and the hero's near-obsessive ruminations on his quest and the others who have attempted it before him. From the beginning, the novel is quest fantasy with what might be termed a contemporary sensibility—the characters speak inarticulately and swear constantly in a variety of dialects, while Mark completes the quest by ambushing some of the denizens of the Keep and cheating the others. He is a hero more in the mold of Frodo Baggins than of Roland. He is also, in a book peopled with men who make it a point to quote their lineages to anyone who will listen, Nobody's Son, both because his father was a common blacksmith and because his father is gone.

There is another hero who survived by his wits and went by the name of Nobody, and *Nobody's Son* can be read as an attempt on Stewart's part to offer a lineage of heroism and heroic fantasy in which the progenitor is quick-witted Odysseus rather than lumbering, plate-mailed Lancelot. In this light, Mark might fruitfully be seen as a sort of obverse of Telemachus: common, homeless, searching for great deeds not because his father's exploits demand it but because the banality and cowardice of his father's actions demand redress.

Plunged into the unfamiliar world of court intrigues (not to mention marriage to the king's youngest daughter, Gail), Mark finds himself overwhelmed. Returning to the Red Keep, he finds that the curse is not completely lifted; the parricide that caused it must be exorcised somehow. In the final confrontation of the novel, the ghosts of the Red Keep, and more importantly, Mark's ghosts, are dispelled by his realization that "there's other things than ashes" between fathers and sons. At this moment, Mark discovers his ability to accommodate grief and go on, rather than making the facts of grief and loss central to his existence. Once again, the big story of quests and castles and kings becomes the small story of people—husbands rather than heroes, wives instead of princesses, the search for faith replacing the blind pursuit of history.

Stewart's next novel, *Resurrection Man*, appears to be quite a change of pace. It was contracted for at the time he sold *Passion Play* to the Ace imprint of Berkley in the United States, and some of the trappings of the earlier novel appear on the periphery of *Resurrection Man*;

but this new novel became something different, pursuing the questions raised in *Nobody's Son* rather than those intrinsic to his first novel. *Resurrection Man* also signaled Stewart's arrival on the mainstream quadrant of the literary horizon, as it garnered excellent reviews from *The New York Times, The Washington Post,* and the *Toronto Globe and Mail.*

In the arresting first scene of *Resurrection Man* a young man named Dante Ratkay is confronting the unlikely appearance of his own dead body in his own bed. Along with his sister, Sarah, and half brother, Jet, he takes the body down to the family's boathouse to perform an autopsy in the hope of preventing whatever killed this mysterious double from actually killing Dante. Unfolding from there, the story involves Dante's struggle to save himself from the darker manifestations of the magic that has begun seeping back into an ambiguous 1990s United States. But behind that is a story of sibling rivalry and of a family struggling with the overbearing presence of a father.

The father in *Resurrection Man* is an unusual one for a Stewart novel, because he is present and benign—save for his incarnations in Dante's dreams, in which he is bending over his son with a scalpel, much as Dante bends over himself at the beginning of the book. Dr. Ratkay smokes a pipe, has witty opinions, and continually spouts quotations from classical authors. In a strange turn of the narrative, those quotations begin to appear as epigraphs to each chapter. It is as if Diane Fletcher's fear expressed in the first sentence of *Passion Play* has come true: as the book is written down, it comes out in the father's voice. As if to further this impression, the epilogue, written in Jet's voice, is framed by the kind of self-reflexive phrase that begins *Passion Play:* "As I write this," Jet begins, and he looks across the whole of the landscape that defines his childhood, coming to rest on the tree whose roots entangle his dead father. Most explicitly, similar to *Passion Play* but continuing a vein from each of Stewart's novels, the epilogue to *Resurrection Man* weaves together the questions of writing, fathers, and absence.

The Night Watch (1997), Stewart's next novel, was the last to be written in Vancouver, and its elegiac tone befits this circumstance. The magic that in *Resurrection Man* had just consolidated its hold on the world is now on the wane, and the old arrangement between the two halves of Vancouver that kept magic to the north of the river and technology operational on the Southside is collapsing. Winter, the strongman in charge of the Southside, enters into an agreement with the citizens of Vancouver's Chinatown to protect them from the deformed monsters that leap the barriers from Downtown with increasing frequency. As with all political arrangements in Stewart novels, the stationing of armed

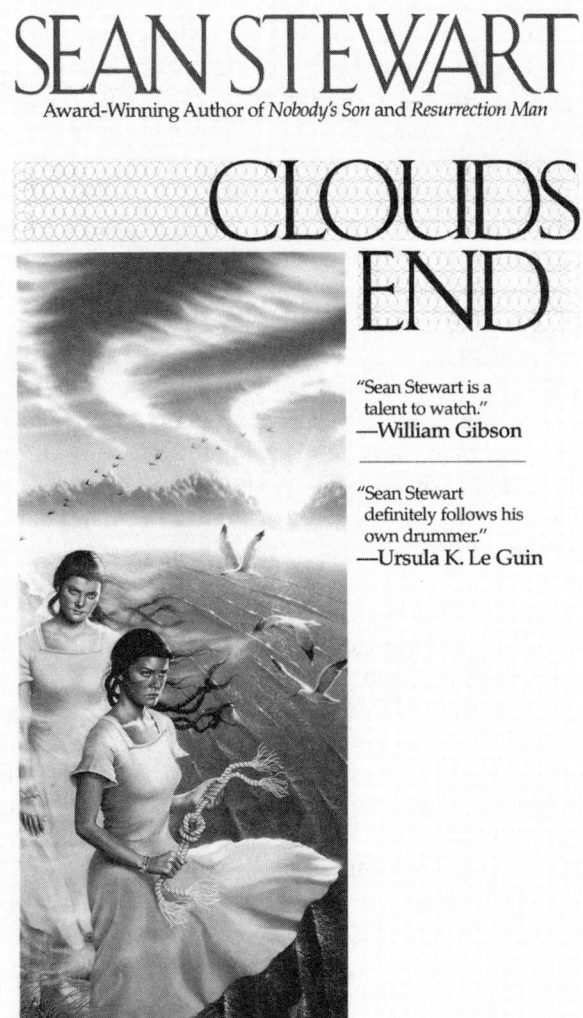

Dust jacket for Stewart's 1995 novel, a quest narrative that he calls his homage to J. R. R. Tolkien

and cybernetically enhanced "Snows" in Chinatown—which, rather than segregating magic, has attempted to live in some sort of balance with it by enshrining various Powers and allowing technology to evaporate—becomes a quagmire, especially after Vancouver's ambassador to the Southside dies under mysterious circumstances.

Attempting to navigate this labyrinth of dangers are three families, each fractured in some way having to do with the fathers. Winter's granddaughter Emily, appalled at the lengths to which her grandfather has gone to preserve technology in the Southside, flees to Vancouver; Nick, the divorced father of Raining and Lark, dies helping them escape back to Vancouver after the ambassador's death; and, in the city, the Chinatown minister Water Spider must arrive at a rapprochement with his father, Floating Ant, while saving himself from a power struggle in the Chinatown hierarchy. Stewart was heavily involved in theater during and after college, and his novels often display a consciousness of dramatic principles even when these are not as explicit as in *Passion Play*. *The Night Watch* recalls the patterns of Renaissance drama—one of its structural sources is in fact *Romeo and Juliet*—in its attention to political matters as an excuse to focus on family relationships, in its loosely parallel panoply of dysfunctional families, and finally in the unlikely political marriage that prevents war between Chinatown and the Southside of Vancouver.

While in Houston, Stewart published *Clouds End* and began working on his next novel, *Mockingbird* (1998). A surprising book not least because of its determined departure from everything a reader might expect from Stewart, *Mockingbird* is nonetheless a story of a child—Toni Beauchamp—adjusting to a parent's shadow, and, in this case, to the bizarre pantheon of household godlings who sporadically possess Toni as they did her mother, Elena. Its differences from previous Stewart novels, though, are striking. The symbolic, binary landscapes of *Clouds End* and *The Night Watch* are replaced by a nearly verisimilitudinous Houston; the parent causing all of the posthumous trouble, Elena, is female; and the recognizable, quotidian world of the reader aggressively intrudes in the form of commodities speculation, unsuccessful dates, and a sustained metaphoric use of baseball. Concerns of writing and reflexivity remain, however. The first-person narrative of *Mockingbird* begins with Toni Beauchamp telling readers that "this is the story of how I became a mother," and it ends with her valediction: "We are all singers, in this family, and we are also songs." The novel was short-listed for the 1999 World Fantasy Award. Stewart completed the cycle begun by *Resurrection Man* and *The Night Watch* with *Galveston* (2000), winner of the inaugural Sun Burst Award for Canadian Literature of the Fantastic, in 2001.

Stewart operates in a different idiom from that of Canada's two premier genre fantasists, Charles de Lint and Guy Gavriel Kay. His work, even when saturated with magic or set in imaginary landscapes, concerns itself much more intimately with the emotional lives of its characters rather than with the typical fantasy tropes. He brings a nineteenth-century sensibility to the contemporary mode of magic realism and is in many ways a writer's writer, acutely aware of his influences and predecessors; his works abound with references to such writers as Dante Alighieri, William Shakespeare, and T. S. Eliot, and his dialogue owes much to Jane Austen. Canadian literature's closest parallels to Stewart can be found in writers—such as Atwood—who like him work fruitfully between genre traditions and the conventions of literary realism.

Interviews:

"Sean Stewart: Holland SF Interview," 29 December 1995, <http://www.redshift.com/~sstewart/hsf_interview.html>;

Paula Simons, "Forming New Hobbits," *Saturday Night* (March 1996): 73–75.

S. M. Stirling

(30 September 1954 –   )

Christopher L. Morrow
Texas A & M University

BOOKS: *Snowbrother* (New York & Scarborough, Ontario: New American Library, 1985; revised and enlarged edition, Riverdale, N.Y.: Baen, 1992);

The Sharpest Edge, by Stirling and Shirley Meier (New York & Scarborough, Ontario: New American Library, 1986); revised and enlarged as *Saber and Shadow* (Riverdale, N.Y.: Baen, 1992);

Marching through Georgia (New York: Baen, 1988);

The Cage, by Stirling and Meier (New York: Baen, 1989);

Under the Yoke (Riverdale, N.Y.: Baen, 1989);

The Stone Dogs (New York: Baen, 1990);

The Children's Hour, by Stirling and Jerry Pournelle (Riverdale, N.Y.: Baen, 1991);

The Forge, by Stirling and David Drake (New York: Baen, 1991);

Go Tell the Spartans, by Stirling and Pournelle (Riverdale, N.Y.: Baen, 1991);

Shadow's Son, by Stirling and Meier and Karen Wehrstein (Riverdale, N.Y.: Baen, 1991);

The Hammer, by Stirling and Drake (Riverdale, N.Y.: Baen, 1992);

The Anvil, by Stirling and Drake (Riverdale, N.Y.: Baen, 1993);

Blood Feuds: A Novel of War World, by Stirling and Judith Tarr, Susan Shwartz, and Harry Turtledove (Riverdale, N.Y.: Baen, 1993);

The City Who Fought, by Stirling and Anne McCaffrey (New York: Baen, 1993);

Prince of Sparta, by Stirling and Pournelle (Riverdale, N.Y.: Baen, 1993);

The Steel, by Stirling and Drake (Riverdale, N.Y.: Baen, 1993);

Blood Vengeance: A Novel of War World, by Stirling and Tarr, Shwartz, and Turtledove (Riverdale, N.Y.: Baen, 1994);

The Rose Sea, by Stirling and Holly Lisle (Riverdale, N.Y.: Baen, 1994);

The Sword, by Stirling and Drake (Riverdale, N.Y.: Baen, 1995);

Babylon 5: Betrayals (New York: Dell, 1996);

The Chosen, by Stirling and Drake (Riverdale, N.Y.: Baen, 1996);

Drakon (Riverdale, N.Y.: Baen, 1996);

The Rising, by Stirling and James Doohan (Riverdale, N.Y.: Baen, 1996);

The Ship Avenged (Riverdale, N.Y.: Baen, 1997);

Island in the Sea of Time (New York: Penguin, 1998);

Against the Tide of Years (New York: Roc, 1999);

The Privateer, by Stirling and Doohan (Riverdale, N.Y.: Baen, 1999);

The Reformer, by Stirling and Drake (Riverdale, N.Y.: Baen, 1999);

The Independent Command, by Stirling and Doohan (Riverdale, N.Y.: Baen, 2000);

On the Oceans of Eternity (New York: Roc/Penguin Putnam, 2000);

T2: Infiltrator (New York: HarperEntertainment, 2001);

The Peshawar Lancers (Roc/New American Library, 2002).

Collection: *The Domination* (Riverdale, N.Y.: Buen, 1999)–comprises *Marching through Georgia, Under the Yoke,* and *The Stone Dogs.*

OTHER: "Necessity," in *The Burning Eye,* War World, no. 1, edited by Jerry Pournelle (Riverdale, N.Y.: Baen, 1988);

"The Woman Warrior," in *New Destinies,* volume 4, edited by Jim Baen (Riverdale, N.Y.: Baen, 1988);

"The Children's Hour," by Stirling and Pournelle, in *Man-Kzin Wars II,* edited by Larry Niven (Riverdale, N.Y.: Baen, 1989);

"Roachstompers," in *New Destinies,* volume 8, edited by Baen (Riverdale, N.Y.: Baen, 1989);

"The Asteroid Queen," by Stirling and Pournelle, in *Man-Kzin Wars III,* edited by Niven (Riverdale, N.Y.: Baen, 1990);

The Fantastic World War II: The War That Wasn't, edited by Stirling, Frank D. McSherry Jr., Charles G. Waugh, and Martin Harry Greenberg, with an introduction by Stirling (New York: Baen, 1990);

Cover for the second novel (1989) in S. M. Stirling's alternate-history series about the Domination of Draka, a militaristic, slaveholding empire founded in Africa by fleeing American Tories during the Revolutionary War

"Fusion," in *New Destinies,* volume 9, edited by Baen (Riverdale, N.Y.: Baen, 1990);

The Fantastic Civil War, edited by McSherry, with an introduction by Stirling (Riverdale, N.Y.: Baen, 1991);

"The Man Who Would Be Kzin," by Stirling and Greg Bear, in *Man-Kzin Wars IV,* edited by Niven (Riverdale, N.Y.: Baen, 1991);

Power, edited by Stirling (Riverdale, N.Y.: Baen, 1991);

"Shame and Honor," in *Sauron Dominion,* War World, no. 3, edited by Pournelle (Riverdale, N.Y.: Baen, 1991);

"In the Hall of the Mountain King," by Stirling and Pournelle, in *Man-Kzin Wars V,* edited by Niven (Riverdale, N.Y.: Baen, 1992);

"Kings Who Would Die," in *Invasion,* War World, no. 4, edited by Pournelle (Riverdale, N.Y.: Baen, 1994);

"A Whiff of Grapeshot," in *More Than Honor* (Riverdale, N.Y.: Baen, 1998);

Drakas! edited by Stirling (Riverdale, N.Y.: Baen, 2000).

Since his first novel was published in 1985, S. M. Stirling has established himself as an author adept at writing along the broad generic spectrum that includes science fiction and fantasy. With significant works in fantasy, military science fiction, and alternate history, Stirling creates vividly detailed and well-developed worlds, ranging from a post-apocalyptic barbarian culture that wields magic to a technologically advanced alternate universe in which different species of humans have been created through genetic engineering. In addition to his versatility in genre and setting, Stirling presents well-developed (and developing) characters who, in addition to futuristic external conflicts, face internal battles relevant to life today. One of the masters of the battle scene, he has sometimes been criticized for being too graphically violent. While these realistic descriptions of violence, occasionally accompanied by equally realistic descriptions of sex, are intended for a mature audience, they are secondary to the characters and themes.

Though highly popular with avid science-fiction and fantasy readers, Stirling has not yet garnered much academic attention, receiving instead only brief mention in major science-fiction reference works. Despite this lack of scholarly interest in his work, Stirling has proven himself a popular and accomplished author of military science fiction and fantasy who, in addition to writing his own novels and series, has collaborated with other science-fiction authors such as Shirley Meier, David Drake, and Anne McCaffrey to create more intriguing and diverse worlds and characters.

Born on 30 September 1954 in Metz, France, Stephen Michael Stirling is the son of Alfred Bruce Stirling and Marjorie Totterdale Stirling. His father, a wing commander in the Royal Canadian Air Force, most likely bestowed on his son the love of military strategy and history that has emerged prominently in Stirling's writing. Over the course of his life Stirling has lived in Europe, North America, and various parts of Africa. He also speaks English and French and possesses partial knowledge of Swahili and Afrikaans. Educated in Canada, Stirling received his B.A. with honors from Carleton University in Ottawa and his LL.B. (bachelor of laws) at Osgoode Hall, York University, in Toronto. In 1988 he married Janet Cathryn Moore and became a full-time writer. Described by David Ketterer in *Canadian Science Fiction and Fantasy* (1992) as a "lawyer, historian, and novelist," Stirling now resides in Santa Fe, New Mexico, and vacations every year in Nantucket, Massachusetts.

Stirling has explored a variety of themes in his fictional worlds. These themes range from the difficulties of finding a unique identity to questions of humanity and the conflicts that surround the interaction of different cultures. In many of his works he explores the boundaries of evil and the often ambiguous nature of the characters living in morally bankrupt cultures and societies. Several of Stirling's reviewers have commented negatively on what they see as a positive portrayal of this malignancy. Indeed, he does not condemn characters for the beliefs they hold as a result of the influence of society. Rather, he tries to create a point of identification between a character and readers that forces the latter to interrogate notions of evil and humanity. Tied up with these questions of evil and humanity is Stirling's continuing interest in what factors lead to overcoming internal and external conflicts, including, of course, military conquest. Though the keys to success differ from novel to novel, he avoids reducing the issue to one of good versus evil.

Stirling presents many of his recurring and evolving themes in his first series, the Fifth Millennium. The first novel in this fantasy series, *Snowbrother* (1985; revised, 1992), thematically depicts the subordination of the good/evil dichotomy to questions of power and might while also exploring the growth and conflict that arises from the interaction of two cultures. Moreover, the growth of the protagonist, Shkai'ra, continues to be a theme throughout the series as she moves away from her individualist nature to become not only a lover and friend but also a mother. The series also examines the interaction between cultures not only through Shkai'ra's adventures but also through the adoption of children from a different culture; the themes of fellowship, love, divided loyalties, and the problems of identity that surround adoption between cultures are interspersed throughout.

First published three years before Stirling became a full-time author, *Snowbrother* was written while he was attending law school, an experience to which he later attributed the "savage and bloodthirsty" tone of the novel. Seven years after the book came out, Stirling published a revised and enlarged edition in which the plot remains the same but a prologue is added that explains more about the Kommanz culture and Shkai'ra's motivation through the novel. Set almost five thousand years in the post-apocalyptic future, the novel centers on the Kommanz, a brutal, warlike, and individualistic people who live on the plains of Central Almerkun. In the epigraph that opens the prologue, Stirling, with characteristic wry wit, provides a clue about the origin of these people. They have descended from the Ztrateke ahkomman, which, as Fred Runk points out in *Fantasy Review* (May 1985), bears a strong phonetic resemblance to "Strategic Air Command."

The Kommanz raiding party, led by Shkai'ra, the first of many strong female characters in Stirling's novels, raids the peaceful nearby Minztan village of Newstead. Through this raid Stirling explores the interaction of two quite distinct cultures and the way this interaction changes both the characters involved and their respective societies. Living in the forests, the Minztans are peaceful, family-oriented environmentalists, the complete opposite of the Kommanza. Rather than presenting only Shkai'ra's perspective, Stirling splits the narrative to include Maihu, a captured Minztan.

At this point, one would expect *Snowbrother* to represent the classic struggle between good and evil. Stirling sets his work apart, however, by refusing to descend to those binaries. Violating the tradition of letting the "good guys" win, he shows that in the Fifth Millennium—and, later, in many of his other fictional worlds—questions of "good" and "evil" are often secondary to questions of power and might. Focusing more on the influences that the Kommanza and Minztan cultures have on one another, Stirling refuses to provide moral commentary on their interaction. This realistic approach allows him to depict the Minztan going against their beliefs by forming a special group to combat the raiders. Similarly, Shkai'ra surpasses her personal and cultural biases by giving Maihu, a fledgling magician, the warrior's honor of being cremated.

The Sharpest Edge (1986), written by Stirling and Meier, is the first of the collaborative novels in the Fifth Millennium series. Afer meeting at a convention in 1983, Stirling and Meier began their collaboration by wondering what would happen if characters from their previously published works met each other. In 1985 Stirling introduced Meier to Karen Wehrstein, later another Fifth Millennium collaborator, and founded, with four other writers, a Toronto-based group known as the "Bunch of Seven." Later, this group expanded to become the "Bunch of Nine," consisting of Stirling, Meier, Wehrstein, Tanya Huff, Marie Hughes, Louise Hypher, Terri Neal, Fiona Pattan, and Mike Wallis.

Like Stirling's first novel, *The Sharpest Edge* was also later revised and enlarged, appearing in 1992 as *Saber and Shadow*. In addition to the changes to the text, this later edition includes three appendices: a glossary, domestic and cultural information on the major societies depicted in the Fifth Millennium series, and a short explanation of the formation of the series that illuminates the usually obscure collaborative techniques of the authors. Maintaining creative control of certain characters, the two (later three, when Wehrstein joined them) authors collaborated closely, resulting in novels that do not lose their stylistic continuity or consistency. This collaborative series is also noteworthy because the cultures and characters initially appeared in works written singly by the writers. The result, as they realize, is a world that has a dissonance and discontinuity in the cultures that appropriately reflects reality.

The novel presents Shkai'ra exiled from her homeland and working as a mercenary on the eastern coast of North America. She meets Megan Whitlock, a character from Meier's earlier works. The discontinuity or clash between cultures becomes apparent again as Megan and Shkai'ra, both outsiders in the Fehinnan city of Illizbuah, become firmly entangled in a local power struggle. The characters are outsiders to each other as well, each coming from different sides of the Lannic (Atlantic) Ocean. Having come into the possession of a letter wanted by three separate factions in the city (the military, a religious group, and merchants), Shkai'ra and Megan spend almost the entire novel fending off attackers and trying to sell the letter to the highest bidder. This nonstop action may account for the dissatisfaction of some reviewers with the plot clarity in the novel. Though Meier and Stirling do not always fully explain the machinations occurring in the city, these omissions only serve to foreground the main subject of their book: the relationship between Shkai'ra and Megan. Described on the cover of the revised edition as "a novel of fellowship," the work portrays the profound growth of the individualist Shkai'ra of *Snowbrother*. Readers can see Shkai'ra becoming more social, as well as more gentle and understanding, as she and Megan move from friendship to romance.

Stirling's next novel in the Fifth Millennium series, *The Cage* (1989), is also the product of collaboration with Meier. Having successfully escaped the factions of Illizbuah, Shkai'ra and Megan return to Megan's homeland of F'talezon. There they must face Habiku Smoothtongue, the man who usurped Megan's merchant house by selling her into slavery. On the river journey to F'talezon the two women undergo a series of adventures, including a challenge that leaves Shkai'ra with the prize of two Thanish children, Sova and Francosz.

Though the main theme of *The Cage* concerns Megan's external quest for (and internal conflict with) vengeance, the theme of Shkai'ra's development is still present. Whereas in *Saber and Shadow* she overcomes her individualistic upbringing to grow close to Megan, now she must tackle the difficulties of becoming a mother figure. In addition, she still has to adapt to the foreign cultures she encounters. Though a need for vengeance drives both Megan and, later, Shkai'ra (whose adopted son, Francosz, is killed as a result of Habiku's orders), that need is mediated by Stirling's attention to Shkai'ra's broader character development, thereby keeping the theme of vengeance from dominating the novel.

For the final novel of the Fifth Millennium series, *Shadow's Son* (1991) Stirling and Meier were joined by Wehrstein. Once Megan's merchant house has been restored, she and Shkai'ra set off in search of Megan's son, Lixand, who was sold into slavery when he was a toddler. When Megan receives a report that locates her son in Arkos, capital of the Arkan empire, she and Shkai'ra join the invading Yeoli army, under the command of Chevenga, the Yeoli king and a character from Wehrstein's earlier works; joining this force represents their best opportunity to reach the city. While the army invades deeper into the Arkan empire, Shkai'ra's Kommanz background enables her to advance through the ranks. As a subplot to the novel, an Arkan spy, Matthas Bennas, learns of Megan's plans to find her son and uses this information to try to blackmail her into killing the Yeoli king. Also on the expedition is Sova, now the adopted daughter of both Shkai'ra and Megan. Though initially left behind, Sova sneaks away and catches up with the army as they travel toward Arkos.

Running throughout *Shadow's Son* is the theme of divided loyalties and the internal struggles they create. In order to avoid killing Chevenga, Megan sends Shkai'ra to rescue Lixand, thus making Matthas's ploy ineffective. Shkai'ra demonstrates the depth of her growth by choosing to sneak away from the army rather than stay and accumulate honor through battle. This course of action clearly violates her honor-driven upbringing. For Shkai'ra, choosing between the divided loyalties is easy; her lover and spouse, Megan, comes first. The novel also explores the problems of identity for adopted children. Sova, "won" by Shkai'ra, has trouble reconciling her former life and parents with her current ones. This instability only exacerbates Sova's struggle for identity. Ultimately, she is able to overcome the division of having been born a Thane and raised by a Kommanza through the realization that she is free to choose her own identity. *Shadow's Son* aptly explores the issues of identity and loyalty in an unstable world. Though filled with graphically detailed descriptions of violence, the novel provides an insightful examination of the characters and their struggles.

Stiling's next major series, the Domination of Draka, is a mix of military science fiction and alternate history. Throughout the series, he again illustrates that good does not always conquer evil. Developing this theme in the first novel, *Marching through Georgia* (1988), Stirling also highlights the difficulty in separating a character from–or condemning him because of–the society in which he lives. Throughout the first three books of the series, the evil Draka conquer the world with overwhelming power and might. Not until the last novel in the series, *Drakon* (1996), are the "good guys" able to succeed in stopping the Draka. In this victory the factors for success shift from raw power to ingenuity and exploitation of the enemy's weakness. The third novel, *The Stone Dogs* (1990), explores the themes of vengeance, grief, and divided loyalties that also inform the Fifth Millennium series.

Rather than beginning at the time period in which the history becomes alternate, as many authors do, Stirling begins *Marching through Georgia* during World War II in 1942, more than 150 years after the historical event. In this alternate world war, three superpowers battle for control over the world: the United States, Nazi Germany, and the Domination of Draka. Founded in South Africa by American Loyalists fleeing America during the Revolutionary War, the Domination of Draka (named after Sir Francis Drake) opened its arms to dissidents, including Confederate families after the American Civil War. Ruled by self-exiled, aristocratic dissidents, Draka is based on "racist feudalism" and imposes a strict system of slavery on most of its inhabitants. The Draka are also cruel, militaristic, and intent on taking over the world, enslaving native populations as they go. Trained as soldiers from childhood, the Draka are faster, stronger, and more able on the battlefield than other armed forces. Yet, rather than dwelling solely on the national and global machinations of the Draka, Stirling concentrates on the human level. Rather than tracing one character's development over the course of several novels, the series follows a single family, with each ensuing novel featuring a protagonist from the next generation of the family.

Marching through Georgia, which occurs in Soviet Georgia, shares its title with an American Civil War song, chronicles the adventures of a Draka centurion, Erik von Shrakenberg, and an American reporter, William Dreiser. The centurion and his unit are responsible for holding a mountain pass in Soviet Georgia against the larger German Wehrmacht units. Dreiser accompanies the Draka army as a result of an unlikely alliance between the Draka and the United States against Germany. The plot is relatively simple but, importantly, allows the reader a chance to learn about the Draka without being explicitly told about them. As is characteristic of Stirling's writing, the novel includes a great amount of military detail, strategy, and graphic descriptions of war. Though a few reviewers have criticized Dreiser's sporadic running commentary, his presence serves mainly to deepen the depiction of the Draka rather than to make him a major character.

Unlike Dreiser, and again to the dissatisfaction of some reviewers, Stirling refuses to pass moral judgment on his characters. Indeed, this initial novel of the series has

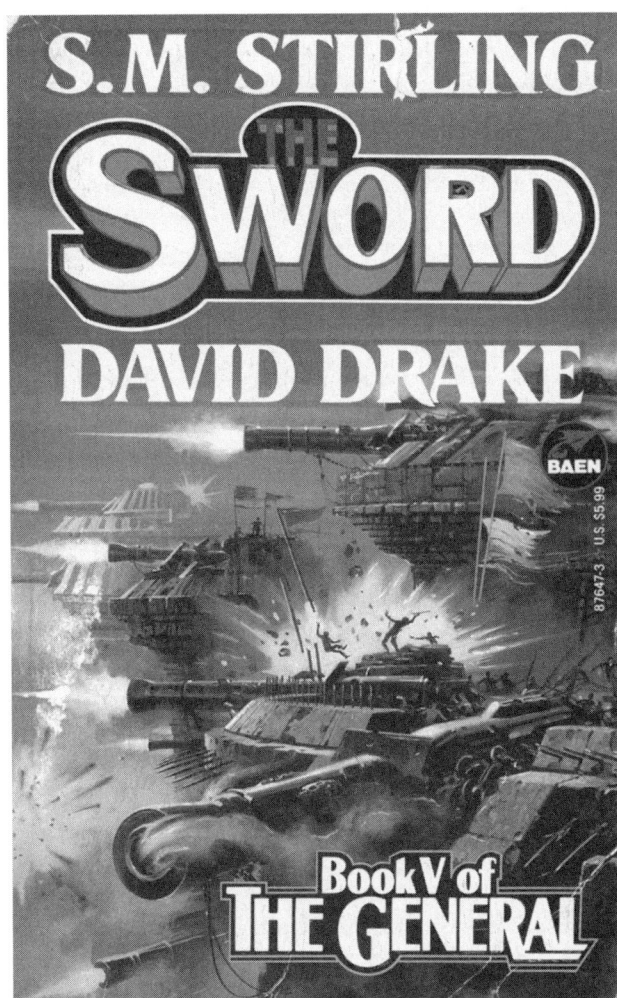

Cover for the final novel (1995) in Stirling and David Drake's series about the adventures of General Raj Whitehall on the planet Bellevue

garnered him the most critical attention, earning him both acclaim and notoriety. Stirling returns to the theme of the difficulties of condemning an entire people based on their society. Von Shrakenberg possesses a great deal of honor, self-respect, and loyalty. In fact, this sympathetic protagonist sometimes doubts the morality of his society. Ultimately, these doubts are counteracted by a stronger sense of loyalty and love for his country, which, despite the nature of the Domination of Draka, are admirable qualities. As Fred Lerner writes in his review for *VOYA* (December 1988), "Stirling skillfully manages to portray the Domination as the repulsively evil regime that it is while kindling the reader's identification with its men and women on the front lines." Other reviewers have criticized *Marching through Georgia* for not taking a stronger position against the Domination of Draka. John Clute, in the *Encyclopedia of Science Fiction* (1995), even suggests that Stirling presents the Domination "with affection." On the other hand, Algis Budrys, writing in *The Magazine of Science Fiction and Fantasy* (October 1988), expresses dissatisfaction because Stirling gives no indication of how von Shrakenberg's doubts will "eventually lead to a democratic enlightenment in his culture." Budrys goes on to say that the Draka basically represent the Western perception of South Africa. Perhaps this is Stirling's point. In his introduction to *The Fantastic World War II: The War That Wasn't* (1990), Stirling writes that alternate histories are "the most useful way of throwing a unique light on the present by the shadow of *what might have been.*" Certainly this claim applies to the Draka.

This shadow of the present continues in the next novel in the series, *Under the Yoke* (1989), as a Cold War emerges between the United States and the Domination of Draka rather than between the United States and the Soviet Union. Having conquered the Germans in World War II, the Draka were left in control of Europe, Asia (minus Japan, Indonesia, and India), and Africa. With less military violence than in *Marching through Georgia,* the sequel moves the focus from Erik to his cousin Tanya von Shrakenberg. Having participated in the war, she and her husband build their plantation estate in what was formerly France. On the other side of the split narrative, Stirling presents Frederick Kustaa, an American secret agent who infiltrates Finland to equip resistance fighters. Having completed the first part of his mission, Kustaa also tries to smuggle Ernst Oerbach, a scientist who could unlock the secrets of the fusion bomb, out of Finland. Stirling's separate plotlines merge when Kustaa's contact is Marya Sokolowska, a captured Polish nun who is also a recently purchased chattel of Tanya.

One of the main themes and subplots of the novel concerns the adaptation of native populations to Domination control. Stirling critically examines three slaves on Tanya's plantation, Marya, Chantal, and Solange, each of whom deals with her new status in different ways. Having been a slave the longest, Solange has accepted and even enjoys her place in life as a favored slave. Chantal, on the other hand, cannot tolerate her status as property, especially when her new master uses her sexually, as is his right in the Domination. Though she cannot actively resist, she shows the most dissatisfaction of the three with her enslavement. Ultimately, Chantal begins to withdraw in an attempt to cope with her situation. As a nun Marya also struggles with her status. Yet, she struggles inwardly and as a result gains the trust of her masters, which eventually enables her to aid Kustaa. Chantal's inability to cope rationally with her situation causes her to compromise Marya and Kustaa's attempt to extract Oerbach. As a result Marya and Kustaa sacrifice themselves so that Chantal, pregnant with her master's child, can escape to America. Shifting the tone slightly from the first novel in the series, Stirling portrays the Draka as increasingly evil by allowing more identification and sympathy to fall to the American cause. Because it has not received the same amount of critical attention as *Marching through Georgia, Under the Yoke,* despite its exploration of how people deal with being enslaved, has often been relegated to the status of a less distinguished sequel.

Like *Under the Yoke,* the third book in the Domination of Draka series, *The Stone Dogs* (1990), has received little critical attention. In this novel Stirling maintains a split narrative between two Americans, Frederick and Marya Lefarge (Chantal's twin children), and Yolande Ingolfsson, daughter of Erik's sister, Johanna. *The Stone Dogs* deviates from the previous two novels in that it takes place over a large number of years, spanning almost all of Yolande's life. The plot traces the continuation of the Cold War up to the Final War, when the American-led Alliance escapes in a colonization spaceship to a distant star. Stirling again shows that being morally in the right does not guarantee victory. The Domination of Draka wins its struggle to conquer the world and its surrounding space. Throughout her life, Yolande takes part in this victory as she moves from being a fighter pilot in the conquest of India, where she purchases Marya, to commanding a task force of warships in space and, eventually, a planet.

Themes of vengeance, grief, and confused loyalties are explored in *The Stone Dogs.* In the conquest of India, Yolande loses her lover, Myfwany. Unable to deal with the loss, she mercilessly tortures Marya, whom she sees as responsible for her lover's death. Unlike Megan from the Fifth Millennium series, Yolande's grief and her pursuit of vengeance consume her. This grief, which is intimately linked with her need for vengeance, is masterfully portrayed by Stirling. Though it does not excuse Yolande's actions, it does allow the reader to sympathize with her. She eventually stops torturing Marya, but, as one last cruel act, she makes the captured American serve as a breeder for Myfwany's clone, whom Yolande will raise as her own daughter. Adding to the problems of adaptation that Marya faces is a newborn child, Gwendolyn Infolgsson. Because a breeder not only carries and delivers a child but also serves as its wet nurse and nanny, a strong bond develops between mother and child that throws a human element into the binaries of "good" and "evil."

These binaries become clearer in the fourth novel in the Draka series, *Drakon.* The Draka have been trying for four hundred years to reach Samothrace (the planetary home of the exiled Alliance) and finish off their rivals. Up to this point, the extreme distance between the Earth and the planet has rendered this goal virtually impossible. Gwendolyn, from *The Stone Dogs,* is still alive, courtesy of Draka bioengineering technology. Researching technology that might allow the Domination to reach their enemy on Samothrace, an accident sends her four hundred years into the past, not only to a different time but also into a parallel plane. It soon becomes clear that Stirling's alternate world is no longer alternate. Landing in what appears to be present-day America, Gwendolyn begins plans to take over the world and install herself as a planetary governor. Unwilling to let her prey upon the helpless planet, the United States of Samothrace sends Agent Kenneth Lefarge, most likely a distant descendant of the Lefarges from previous books, to destroy her before she can take over the planet. He teams up with a New York detective, Henry Carmaggio, to stop Gwendolyn from opening a molehole through time, space, and dimensional planes that will allow the Draka army to complete the conquest of Earth.

Thematically, *Drakon* seems to be a diversion from previous novels in the series. In this case, good does defeat evil. Stirling makes it clear, however, that the heroes do not succeed because of their inherent goodness. Instead, Henry and Kenneth use plasma guns built from the latter's equipment and a little ingenuity to play to Gwendolyn's weakness. Though morals still matter little in the Drakon world, intellect overcomes power and might. Linked to the theme of ingenuity is that of blind ambition. Gwendolyn is overconfident in her abilities as a Draka. As a result, Henry and other volunteers are able to distract her through battle long enough for Kenneth to destroy the beacon she was using to contact the Draka. Both Kenneth and Gwendolyn die in an apparent victory for the "good guys." Yet, the novel does not end with a complete resolution of the conflict. Gwendolyn's cloned infant is still alive and in the care of her human recruits. Stirling does not preclude the possibility of a sequel, thus leaving the suggestion of more Domination in the future.

Stirling's second military science-fiction series, The General, also tells a story of world domination. In these novels Stirling and coauthor Drake make it clear that the dominators are the "good guys." Set on the planet Bellevue, the five books in the series focus on a military officer, Raj Whitehall. Like the protagonists from the Draka series, he must use ingenuity in order to lead his army to victory against larger, more powerful armies. The first novel, *The Forge* (1991), is set many years after an apocalyptic war resulted in a technological collapse eliminating space travel and computers on Bellevue. Adventuring in ancient catacombs under the capital city, Raj encounters a sentient computer that selects him to reunite the world under his guidance. With the computer presenting mind's-eye depictions of the possible outcomes of crucial decisions, Raj sets out to accomplish his mission.

In each of the subsequent novels in the series—*The Hammer* (1992), *The Anvil* (1993), *The Steel* (1993), and *The Sword* (1995)—Raj works to conquer the Southern Territories, the Brigade, and the Colony. In addition to the external armies, he also faces an increasingly jealous and paranoid ruler, Barholm Clerett, who fears his military power and threatens to execute him. After Raj reunites the planet, the computer, named Center, decides that it is time to overthrow Clerett and install Raj's candidate, Thom Poplanich. Since the plot takes place over the course of the five books, the General is more like a serial novel than a series of novels. Yet, Drake and Stirling keep each novel fast paced by avoiding the repetition of strategies and tactics, thus making each military campaign distinct. The characters captivate the imagination and supplement what can be at times a predictable plot. In spite of the lack of originality in the plot, most reviewers, in light of the superb battle scenes as well as the highly detailed presentation of military tactics, say that this series will appeal to military-science buffs.

The Hammer includes a one-page note explaining the collaboration between Stirling and Drake for the General series. Researching and outlining the series, Drake based Raj on the sixth-century Byzantine general Belisarius. In Drake's words, Stirling translated Raj from the outline "into life and vibrancy." In a review of *The Forge* in *Booklist* (January 1991) Roland Green picks up on this translation and also echoes other critics' appraisal of Stirling's worlds, describing Bellevue as "a full-blown world with a lived-in quality."

Bringing Drake's research to life, Stirling explores several themes throughout this series, including the triumph of ingenuity over brawn. As a result of Clerett's paranoia, Raj's army is continually understaffed, thus forcing him to outsmart rather than overpower his opponents. Another theme of the series concerns the boundaries and responsibilities of love. Raj's wife, Suzette, sleeps with politically powerful men in order to obtain information that will aid her husband's missions. Throughout the series Raj's staff debates Suzette's behavior; ultimately, the novels make clear that her actions reflect depth rather than insincerity in her love.

Finally, in a more pronounced way, Stirling and Drake explore the theme of leadership and ambition. The General novels support a "lead from the front" style of leadership. Raj consistently risks his life by placing himself in the thick of the action. As a result of putting himself in the same danger that his army faces, he commands not only the respect but also the loyalty of his armies. With each successive victory Raj's army develops more faith and belief in him, as well as more reverence. In several places throughout the series the soldiers call for Raj to take the governorship himself. These calls begin to affect him, and he must struggle internally with his own ambition. Indeed, he might have assumed the mantle of governor had it not been for Center's presentation of the probable results of such an act. Thus, a secondary theme to that of ambition is that those who lead in peace should not be the same people who led in war. In the last novel of the series,

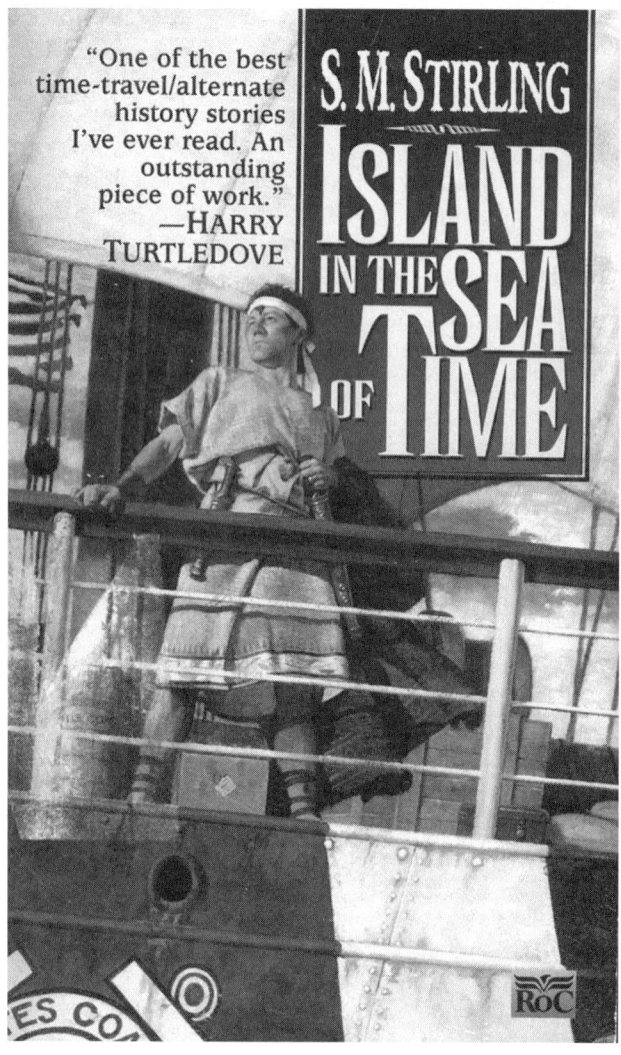

Cover for Stirling's 1998 novel, in which Nantucket Island and the surrounding waters are transported back in time to 1250 B.C.

The Sword, Center shows Raj glimpses of the future illustrating that his efforts to save his planet from descending into barbarity have succeeded.

Though not in the General series, Drake and Stirling's next collaborative novel, *The Chosen* (1996), is a sort of sequel, continuing the story of Center's quest to reunite humanity. Raj, now a disembodied personality inside the computer, and Center contact two young adopted brothers on the planet Visager. The boys, John Hosten and Jeffrey Farr, must work to keep the planet from coming under the power of a nation known as the Land of the Chosen that bears a strong resemblance to the Domination of Draka. Throughout the novel the Chosen, a nation that grants citizenship only to the physically and mentally superior, attack and conquer weaker countries. John and Jeffrey, with Center and Raj's help, serve in these countries to help them resist the invading Chosen armies.

The Chosen presents villains who are defeated as a direct result of their own actions. John and Jeffrey are able to stop their foes from rolling over their country, the Republic of Santander, because the Chosen overextend themselves. The Chosen are also brought down by an uprising of their lower classes, which they have kept in strict subjugation. The Chosen relegate people to the service classes for physical defects. Thus, the novel also illustrates the danger of underestimating someone based on a handicap. John was actually born to a Chosen officer but was denied citizenship because of his clubfoot. For this reason his mother took him to the Republic of Santander, where such prejudices do not exist. John becomes successful in life both physically and intellectually, and he is instrumental in the defeat of the Chosen. Though his high-ranking biological father commits suicide before John can reach him, he wanted to teach his father this same lesson. Though reviewers have found the descriptions of armaments in *The Chosen* to be as tiring, they have also praised the novel for its character development and well-paced, action-filled plot.

The theme of disabled humans and their usefulness is reiterated with the character of Simeon in Stirling and McCaffrey's collaborative novel, *The City Who Fought* (1993). The authors delve further into this theme by raising the question of what it means to be human, specifically in relation to love and parenting. Not wholly abandoning the theme of strategic victory, Stirling and McCaffrey have their protagonists use sheer intellect to defeat might and become victorious. In addition to continuing to examine questions of humanity, *The Ship Avenged* (1997), a sequel written by Stirling alone, also illustrates the benefits of collaboration, showing that while individualism is sometimes a good trait, it is often not enough.

The City Who Fought begins as the Kolnari pirates attack the planet of Bethel; Amos ben Sierra Nueva is forced to flee with his people. Arriving at space station SSS-900, they inform the crew that they are being chased. As a way of deflecting the attention of the Central World's navy, the Kolnari always remove the evidence of their crimes. This practice leads them to chase the Bethelites and find the virtually defenseless space station. The station is controlled by a "shellperson" named Simeon, who is, in effect, the space station itself. Not merely an artificial-intelligence unit, Simeon is actually a deformed human who has been placed in a "shell" that can be put into spaceships and space stations. In addition, every shellperson has a partner known as his brawn, who serves as his mobile representative. On SSS-900 the brawn is Channa Hap, who, to Simeon's displeasure, is not only new but also female. Playing to the pirates' greed, Simeon, who studies military history in his spare time, devises a plan to lure the pirates, who are led by Belazir, into looting the station long enough to let the Central World navy arrive. Also on the station is a small girl, who is adept at computers and electronics, named Joat (an acronym for "jack-of-all-trades"), who lives in the ventilation shafts and maintenance passageways. Having escaped slavery after being sold by her uncle, Joat has no wish for further contact with humans. Early in the novel Simeon and Channa describe her aptly as a "feral child."

The City Who Fought also features a return to themes from the Fifth Millennium series concerning parenting and love. After discovering Joat, Channa convinces Simeon that they should adopt the small girl. Their first task is to convince Joat that Simeon is indeed human; then they must convince the authorities. Though Simeon's fitness as a parent is explored only briefly at the beginning of the novel, the theme of his humanity continues through his relationship with Channa. Though they get off to a rocky start, by the end of the novel they are clearly in love. However, as a shellperson, Simeon has limits to the ways he can express his love. He shows the sincerity of his feelings by overcoming his own selfishness and jealousy and facilitating the relationship between Channa and her other love, Amos. The cruelty of the Kolnari pirates who occupy the station for a short time serves as a contrast to Simeon's humanity. Though *The City Who Fought* has received mixed reviews, most critics agree that the action in the book compensates for its shortcomings.

The events in *The Ship Avenged* take place ten years after the battle for space station SSS-900. In this novel Channa and Simeon serve only as background characters to their adopted daughter, Joat. Joat, now captain of her own merchant ship, *Wyal* (an acronym for "while you ain't looking"), becomes entangled in a Kolnari plot to destroy Bethel. Having developed a virus that causes disorientation and memory loss in its victims, Belazir captures Amos and makes him an immune carrier of the disease. Joat is then hired to deliver Amos back to his planet. After subduing the virus with the help of a scientist, she returns to Belazir's ship to rescue her love interest, Central Worlds Security agent Bros Sperin, who has been held as insurance.

The Ship Avenged illustrates that while independence is an admirable quality, it is not always enough. Joat's adventures are resolved, but not through her efforts alone. Though she reaches Bros, they are discovered and must rely on the Yeoned family, who is also attacking the pirates, to save them. Afterward, because of a fine earlier in the novel, Joat loses her ship and must scrape together enough money to try to repurchase it at auction. Though she asks Simeon for a loan, she does not tell her powerful adopted father why she needs it, nor does she ask for his personal help. In the meantime, Bros buys the *Wyal* for Joat; knowing her independence, he does not reveal that he used his retirement money for the purchase.

Another theme continued from *The City Who Fought* is the exploration of what it means to be human. In a subplot of *The Ship Avenged*, Soamosa, Amos's cousin, is captured by the Kolnari and falls in love with Belazir's son, Karak, who is clearly unfit to be a pirate. Stirling does not devote a great deal of space to this love story, thus leaving reviewers the opportunity to criticize the subplot as unconvincing and unbelievable. Still, the subplot serves to further the theme of humanity as treated in the previous novel. After escaping Belazir, Soamosa and Karak are reunited with Amos on Joat's ship. Declaring her love for the pirate, Soamosa sparks a debate between Amos and his head of security, Joseph, about the humanity of Karak and whether or not an individual can be separated from the culture in which he was raised.

Stirling's next three novels reiterate some of the themes he has previously explored and introduces some new ones. *The Rose Sea* (1994) returns to the theme of evil defeating evil but also probes the relationship between predestination and free will. *The Rising* (1996) features a character who becomes disabled late in life and must learn to cope with his tragedy. The novel also underscores the benefits of friendship and support during hard times. This theme is also present in *Island in the Sea of Time* (1998), in which friendship and support play a major role in the survival of the island that is the setting of the story. In this novel Stirling examines the interaction of different cultures and the dangers of assuming one "knows" a culture.

The Rose Sea, written with Holly Lisle, marks a return to the fantasy genre for Stirling. In the magically rich world of this novel, Bren Morkaarin, a minor military officer, and Karah Grenlaarin, a horse rancher's daughter, become entangled in a conflict between two rival nations, emperors, and religions. Like Megan and Shkai'ra in their combat with evil in the Fifth Millennium series, Karah and Bren (along with Amourgin Thurdhad) are the only ones who can save their nation from the evil Darkist, ruler of Tarin Tseld. Helped significantly by different gods, these three characters, part of the XIXth Imperial Regiment of Foot, quest not only against Darkist but also against their own equally evil commander, Grand Constable Willek Tornsaarin. Told from many different perspectives, the novel has an intricate plot complemented by several subplots that keep the reader in suspense.

This suspense in *The Rose Sea* serves to bear out many of the themes in the novel, such as destiny. Karah appears to be simply a rancher's daughter, but the reader learns by the end of the novel that she is actually "fateborn" and thus the only one with the power to cross the Rose Sea and retrieve the Theophone of the Gods, which will enable them to defeat the evil forces. Her spiritual guide, however, reminds her that being fateborn does not guarantee success. She must still prove herself worthy; thus, Stirling and Lisle confront the tension between fate and free will. Karah survives the trials and, with Bren, is able to defeat Darkist and Willek. This victory restores Bren, the rightful heir previously thought to be a bastard, to the throne of the Tykissian Empire.

In Stirling's previous novels the protagonists achieve success through their power or intelligence. In *The Rose Sea* the main characters succeed not only as a result of their own efforts but also because they have approval of the gods. Another prominent factor in their victory is the way evil brings about its own destruction. Darkist dies at the hands of a monster of his own creation, while Konzin, a thief, dies as a result of his own attempts at deception.

Two years after *The Rose Sea* was published, Stirling returned to science fiction with *The Rising*. Written with James Doohan, the actor who played Montgomery "Scotty" Scott on the television series *Star Trek* (1966–1969), *The Rising* is the first volume of the Flight Engineer series. After suffering a battle wound that leaves him with a prosthetic hand, the former fighter pilot Peter Raeder is retrained as a flight engineer and assigned to duty on the newly commissioned light carrier *Invincible*. In addition to being responsible for the maintenance of the fighter aircraft on the spaceship, he is assigned the task of finding the saboteur who has been plaguing the warship. Raeder's nation is in the midst of a war over antihydrogen fuel with a group of religious fanatics known as the Mollies. The light carrier uses a significantly lower amount of fuel but is still in the experimental stage. In order to prevent the light-carrier program from being terminated, Raeder must find the saboteur while the spaceship is an active participant in the war. Rescuing a freighter from raiders, finding a way to destroy a battle cruiser, and saving a five-month supply of antihydrogen stolen from the Mollies, he shows an initiative that consistently puts his life and career in jeopardy. The novel ends with the capture of the saboteur but with the war effort far from over, opening the way for the next two novels in the Flight Engineer series, *The Privateer* (1999) and *The Independent Command* (2000). Complementing Raeder's internal development is the growth of his lieutenant, Cynthia Robbins. Because of her dour disposition and lack of personal skills, most of the crew of the ship believes that she is the saboteur. Not only does Raeder find the real culprit and clear Robbins's name, he also treats her as a friend and strives to help her become more sociable. Robbins grows and shows the promise of breaking free from her self-imposed shell.

The theme of fellowship and support also appears in *Island in the Sea of Time*. In this alternate-history novel of time travel, a temporal anomaly takes the Massachusetts island of Nantucket and the surrounding waters back in time to the year 1250 B.C. Included in these waters and thus also transported back in time is the *Eagle*, a three-masted Coast Guard windjammer kept around for training purposes. *Island in the Sea of Time* features a medley of diverse characters, each with his own stories and development. After the initial confusion of the time shift, the islanders set up a purely democratic system of government headed by a former law-enforcement officer, Jared Cofflin. Leading the sea contingent and impromptu navy of Nantucket is Marion Alston, an African American woman. Cofflin and Alston must not only deal with the islanders who are not stable enough to cope with the time shift but also must solve problems such as providing enough food for everyone. With no power plant and a finite supply of fuel for generators, the islanders soon find that most of their technology is inoperable. They are forced to work together to produce by hand many of the necessities of life. After the islanders trade trinkets for food with the tribes then inhabiting England, the plot is stimulated by the defection of William Walker, a power-hungry sailor, and Pamela Lisketter, an overzealous environmentalist who takes the islanders' newly built boats and their firearms. Lisketter heads south to harm the Olmecs (ancestors of the Aztecs), taking Cofflin's wife as a hostage, while Walker travels to England to build his empire.

As Stirling's most complex novel, *Island in the Sea of Time* tackles many issues. In one sense the novel is about adaptation and mutual support. The islanders are able to survive because of their ingenuity, ability to adapt, and reliance upon one another. Stirling also illustrates the dangers of assuming that one understands a culture. The Olmecs, who see the environmentalists as intruders only, attack them in spite of their altruistic intentions. Embedded in this turn of events is the folly of romanticizing a lost culture: the islanders have to rescue the environmentalists from becoming human sacrifices. At a deeper level *Island in the Sea of Time* is a novel of second chances. Not only do the islanders get a second chance with their treatment of the environment and indigenous peoples, but also most of the characters in the novel receive personal second chances in both love and life. The novel ends with a good sense of closure but allows the possibility of sequels, which Stirling has promised will appear.

Though reviewers have often criticized Stirling for his graphic depictions of sex and violence accompanied by exhaustive technical and strategic details, these qualities lend a well-developed and realistic aspect to both his characters and his worlds. As the author of fantasy, military science fiction, and alternate history novels, S. M. Stirling has proven himself able to write across the genre of science fiction and fantasy exploring themes and motifs of human behavior relevant to life today.

Reference:

David Ketterer, *Canadian Science Fiction and Fantasy* (Bloomington: Indiana University Press, 1992).

Jean-Louis Trudel
(10 July 1967 –)

Dan S. Paroski
University of Ottawa

BOOKS: *Aller simple pour Saguenal* (Montreal: Paulines, 1994);
Pour des soleils froids (Paris: Fleuve Noir, 1994);
Le Ressuscité de l'Atlantide (Paris: Fleuve Noir, 1994);
Un trésor sur Serendib (Montreal: Médiaspaul, 1994);
Les Voleurs de mémoire (Montreal: Médiaspaul, 1995);
Les Rescapés de Serendib (Montreal: Médiaspaul, 1995);
Le Prisonnier de Serendib (Montreal: Médiaspaul, 1995);
Les Princes de Serendib (Montreal: Médiaspaul, 1996);
Des Colons pour Serendib (Montreal: Médiaspaul, 1996);
Fièvres sur Serendib (Montreal: Médiaspaul, 1996);
Un printemps à Nigelle (Montreal: Médiaspaul, 1997);
Un été à Nigelle (Montreal: Médiaspaul, 1997);
Un hiver à Nigelle (Montreal: Médiaspaul, 1997);
Un automne à Nigelle (Montreal: Médiaspaul, 1998);
Les Bannis de Bételgeuse (Montreal: Médiaspaul, 1998);
13,5 km sous Montréal (Montreal: Marie-France, 1998);
Les Contrebandiers de Cañaveral (Montreal: Médiaspaul, 1999);
Demain, les étoiles (Saint-Laurent: Pierre Tisseyre, 2000);
Guerre pour un harmonica (Montreal: Médiaspaul, 2000);
Nigelle par tous les temps (Montreal: Médiaspaul, 2000);
Les Transfigurés du Centaure (Montreal: Médiaspaul, 2001).

OTHER: "Les Proscrits de Géhenna," in *Les Enfants d'Enéïdes* (Brussels: Phénix, 1989), pp. 75–94; translated by John Greene as "Proscripts of Gehenna," in *Tesseracts³*, edited by Candas Jane Dorsey and Gerry Truscott (Victoria, British Columbia: Tesseract Books, 1990), pp. 372–391;
"Les Protocoles du désir," as Laurent McAllister, with Yves Meynard, in *L'Année de la Science-Fiction et du Fantastique Québécois, 1988*, edited by Claude Janelle and Jean Pettigrew (Quebec: Le Passeur, 1989), pp. 207–220;
"La Douzième vie des copies," in *Au nord de Nulle-Part: Une Anthologie Francophone,* Collection Variana, no. 3, edited by Dominique Warfa and others (Liège, Belgium: Groupe Phi, 1992), pp. 11–22;

Jean-Louis Trudel (Studio Jostens Photo)

"The Falafel is Better in Ottawa," in *Ark of Ice: Canadian Futurefiction,* edited by Lesley Choyce (Lawrencetown Beach, Nova Scotia: Pottersfield Press, 1992), pp. 85–94;
"Remember, the Dead Say," in *Tesseracts⁴,* edited by Lorna Toolis and Michael Skeet (Victoria: Beach Holme, 1992), pp. 368–387; republished in *Northern Stars: The Anthology of Canadian Science Fiction,*

edited by David G. Hartwell and Glenn Grant (New York: Tor, 1994), pp. 101–113;

"Eléments de la chaleur et de la froideur," in *Persistance de la Vision: Programme* (Yverdon-les Bains, 27–30 April 1995), pp. 26–29;

"Le Pierrot diffracté," as McAllister, with Meynard, in *Escales sur Solaris: Anthologie de Science-Fiction et de Fantastique*, edited by Meynard and Joël Champetier (Hull: Vents d'Ouest, 1995), pp. 115–155;

"Sang froid," as McAllister, with Meynard, in *Sang Froid: Sang pour Sang Québec*, Hugues Morin (Saint-Hyacinthe: Ashem Fictions, 1995), pp. 16–22;

"La Science-fiction d'expression française au Canada (1839–1989)," in *Visions d'autres mondes: La littérature fantastique et de science-fiction canadienne*, compiled by Andrea Paradis (Montreal: Editions RD, 1995); translated by Trudel as "Science Fiction in Francophone Canada (1839–1989)," in *Out of This World: Canadian Science Fiction & Fantasy Literature*, compiled by Paradis (Kingston, Ontario: Quarry Press, 1995);

"Contamination," translated by Donald McGrath, in *Tesseracts^Q* (Edmonton, Alberta: Tesseract Books, 1996), pp. 26–46;

"Lamente-toi, Sagesse!" in *Genèse* (Paris: J'ai Lu, 1996), pp. 253–284;

"The Paradigm Machine," in *Tesseracts^5*, edited by Robert Runté and Meynard (Edmonton, Alberta: Tesseract Books, 1996), pp. 93–108;

"Canada: 2. French," in *The Encyclopedia of Fantasy*, edited by John Clute and John Grant (London: Orbit, 1997), pp. 162–163;

"Les Codes de l'honneur," in *Concerto pour six voix* (Montreal: Médiaspaul, 1997), pp. 113–136;

"Where Angels Fall," translated by Trudel in *Tesseracts^6*, edited by Robert J. Sawyer and Carolyn Clink (Edmonton, Alberta: Tesseract Books, 1997): 179–180;

"The Case of the Serial *De Québec à la Lune*, by Veritatus," as McAllister, with Meynard, translated by Trudel and Meynard in *Arrowdreams: An Anthology of Alternate Canadas*, edited by Mark Shainblum and John Dupois (Winnipeg: Nuage, 1998), pp. 173–191;

"Le Deuxième carnet de Villard," in *SF98: Les Meilleurs récits de l'année* (Luisant: Bélial/Orion, 1998), pp. 65–78;

"Scorpion dans le cercle du temps," in *Escales sur l'horizon* (Paris: Fleuve Noir, 1998), pp. 387–469;

"Zwicky, Fritz," in *American National Biography*, edited by John Garraty (New York: Oxford University Press, 1998);

"L'Arche de tous les temps," in *Escales 2000* (Paris: Fleuve Noir, 1999), pp. 253–292;

"Holes in the Night," in *Tesseracts^8*, edited by John Clute and Candas Jane Dorsey (Edmonton, Alberta: Tesseract Books, 1999), p. 57;

"Les Derniers lecteurs," in *Escales 2001* (Paris: Fleuve Noir, 2000), pp. 93–140.

TRANSLATIONS: John Park, "La Peste logicielle," *Solaris*, no. 94 (1990): 7–13;

Park, "Printemps–Coucher de soleil," *Solaris*, no. 98 (1990): 24;

Park, "La Baleine d'Andor," *Yellow Submarine*, no. 109 (1994): 38–55;

Jean-Claude Dunyach, "The Dead Eye of the Camera," in *Full Spectrum*, volume 5 (New York: Bantam, 1995), pp. 268–274;

Michel Martin, "Tortoise on the Sidewalk," translated by Trudel and Yves Meynard, in *Tesseracts^5*, edited by Robert Runté and Meynard (Edmonton, Alberta: Tesseract Books, 1996), pp. 135–151;

Daniel Sernine, "The Travels of Nica Marcopol," in *Tesseracts^5*, edited by Runté and Meynard (Edmonton, Alberta: Tesseract Books, 1996), pp. 263–272;

Sylvie Bédard, "A Wall," in *Tesseracts^6*, edited by Robert J. Sawyer and Carolyn Clink (Edmonton, Alberta: Tesseract Books, 1997): 45–48.

SELECTED PERIODICAL PUBLICATIONS–UNCOLLECTED: "Œuvre de paix," *imagine . . .* , no. 24 (1984): 11–17;

"Le Maire," *imagine . . .* , no. 27 (1985): 63–68;

"Le Ressuscité de l'Atlantide," *imagine . . .* (1985–1987), no. 29: 49–59, no. 30: 77–101, no. 32: 171–189, no. 35: 89–101, no. 36: 91–101, no. 37: 107–122, no. 40: 77–94, no. 41: 87–93;

"Flash," *Samizdat*, nos. 5–6 (1986): 34–47;

"Demain l'espoir," *L'Apropos*, 5, no. 2 (1987): 30–39;

"Jonction," *Samizdat*, no. 9 (1987): 25–27;

"Lucas 19," *imagine . . .* , no. 39 (1987): 115–125;

"Monde retapé: A vendre," *Samizdat*, nos. 11–12 (1987): 37–43;

"Les Murs," *La Rotonde*, 55 (1 March 1988): 14;

"L'Envers des étoiles," *imagine . . .* , no. 46 (1989): 69–84;

"Hier, j'ai été la multitude," *CSF*, 7 (1989): 16–20;

"Satan aussi a ses miracles," *CSF*, 9 (1990): 30–38;

"Les Jeux de la paix et de la guerre," *imagine . . .* , no. 55 (1991): 31–68;

"Report 323: A Quebecois Infiltration Attempt," *CSF*, 10 (1991): 23–26; translated by Mikhaila Kretova as "Delo 323," *Zatsaritsinskii Vestnik*, 36 [160] (1993): 2; translated by Trudel as "Report 323: A

Quebecois Infiltration Attempt," *Prairie Fire* (1994): 20–26;

"Pour des soleils froids," *Temps tôt* (1991–1992), no. 11: 7–17, no. 12: 33–43, nos. 13–14: 7–8, no. 15: 19–30, no. 16: 13–24, no. 17: 7–18, no. 18: 7–17, no. 19: 9–26, no. 20: 7–22, no. 22: 7–23;

"Deti Solntsa," translated by S. Mikheeva, *L'zya*, 28 (1992): 11; republished as "Enfants du soleil," *Magie Rouge*, nos. 38–39 (1993): 60;

"L'Homme qui n'avait plus de remords," *Samizdat*, no. 22 (1992): 4–9;

"Les Instincteurs de cruauté," *Solaris*, no. 102 (1992): 7–14;

"The Eclipsing Binary EG Serpentis," with J. D. Fernie and Stefan Mochnacki, *Astronomical Journal*, 105 (June 1993): 2291–2298;

"La Coagulation des vouivres," as Laurent McAllister, with Yves Meynard, *Temps tôt*, no. 22 (1993): 31;

"Un papillon à Mashak," *Solaris*, no. 105 (1993): 5–15;

"Les Ponts du temps," *Solaris*, no. 107 (1993): 36–46;

"Procruste," *Samizdat*, no. 24 (1993): 7–13; translated by Miruna Secu as "Procust," *Helion*, 4 (1994): 47–53;

"L'Arbre qui plantait des hommes," as McAllister, with Meynard, *imagine . . .*, special "Décollage" edition (1994): 26–31;

"Entre la nuit et l'illusion," *imagine . . .*, special "Décollage" edition (1994): 80–85;

"Savez-vous?" *Horrifique*, no. 12 (1994): 13–18;

"Stella Nova," *On Spec*, no. 16 (1994): 31–43;

"Les Chaînes de saint Léonard," *Temps tôt*, no. 35 (1995): 7–28;

"Le Peuple de Protée," *Solaris*, no. 115 (1995): 5–12;

"Les touristes," *Miniature*, 24 (1995): 15–23;

"Les Escrocs," *Solaris*, no. 117 (1996): 7–14;

"Un message du serveur finlandais," *Art le Sabord*, no. 43 (1996): 22–24;

"L'Obsession," *Ozone*, no. 4 (1996): 55–58;

"L'Œil de Dieu–'L'Œil de Dieu dans l'herbe' (Mahani)," *Temps tôt*, no. 40 (1996): 7–14;

"Des anges sont tombés," *Le Portique de Soleil*, 26 / *Miniature*, 30 (1997): 32–33; translated by L. Fominoi as "Padayoushchié Angeli," *Nepoceda*, 3 [60] (1998): 16;

"Le Berger de comètes," *Les Débrouillards*, no. 163 (1997): ii–xv;

"Le Cas du plastique électrique," *Les Débrouillards*, no. 166 (1997): ii–xv;

"Le Choix du lion, le festin des chacals," *Etoiles vives*, 1 (1997): 123–155;

"Le Club des Branchés," *Les Débrouillards*, no. 166 (1997): ii–xiv;

"Fictions et fantascience," *Solaris*, no. 122 (1997): 4–9;

"Les Jardiniers," *Eloizes*, 24 (1997): 58–61;

Cover for Trudel's first book (1994), in which the teenage protagonist and his woman companion defend the environment of the planet Nou-Québec against those who would exploit and pollute it

"Terre de liberté," *Yellow Submarine*, no. 125 (1998): 41–51;

"Waiting Till the Stars Scream," with Phyllis Gotlieb, *TransVersions*, nos. 8–9 (1998): 110–117;

"Les Sculpteurs de Mars," *Les Débrouillards*, no. 176 (1998): ii–xv;

"Fausse balle au Stade!" *Les Débrouillards*, no. 178 (1998): ii–xv;

"Passions étouffées sous la pierre cendreuse," *Solaris*, no. 130 (1999): 19–29.

Jean-Louis Trudel, writer, critic, translator, and teacher of physics and astronomy, is an ardent promoter of French-Canadian science fiction and a member of various literary organizations and associations, including *SF Canada*, for which he served as president from 1994 to 1996. Perhaps best known for his science-fiction novels for adolescents in the "Jeunesse-pop" series published by Médiaspaul, Trudel has also written mystery novels for adolescents as well as several science-fiction novels for adults published in France. He is also a distinguished, award-winning short-story writer and a regular contributor to the science-fiction magazines *Solaris* and *imagine . . .*, both published in Quebec. A finalist in several writing contests, Trudel won the first-place *Solaris* prize for "Les Instincteurs de cruauté" (The Cruelty Instinctors, 1992) and the 1997 Prix Aurora for "Lamente-toi, sagesse!" (Weep, O Wisdom!, 1996). The latter prize is awarded to the best science-fiction or fantasy short story in Canada.

Trudel was born on 10 July 1967 in the English-language-dominated city of Toronto. His father, Hubert Louis Trudel, was a native of the French-speaking community of Saint-Boniface, Manitoba, and was a financial analyst until his retirement. Trudel's mother, Annick Mérant, is from Saint-Nazaire, France. In 1969 the family moved to Sudbury, in northern Ontario, where Trudel's sister, Sylvie, his only sibling, was born that same year.

In 1972 the family moved to the Ottawa Valley region, where Trudel, from a quite early age, became an avid reader of popular comics such as *Tintin* and *Spirou* and, simultaneously, discovered his love and passion for writing and drawing. At the age of eleven Trudel won his first writing prize for a short story about a flight around the world in an airplane. An enthusiastic admirer of Antoine de Saint-Exupéry, a French aviator and author, and all subjects pertaining to aviation history, Trudel was already showing signs of interest in science and technology that later came to dominate his writing career.

For the next few years Trudel's interest in science was intensified by his reading of science-fiction novels by such well-known writers as Isaac Asimov, and he became a devoted fan of the hit movie *Star Wars* (1977). During this period Trudel subscribed to *imagine . . .*, a science-fiction magazine in which his first published short story, "Œuvre de paix" (Peace Work, 1984), appeared. During his last year of high school he wrote a 180-page novel that, while it was never published, laid the basis for the first two novels of *Les Mystères de Serendib* (Mysteries of Serendib, 1995–1996), a science-fiction series for adolescents. Upon completion of his education at the University of Ottawa, where he obtained a B.Sc. in physics (1990), Trudel moved to Toronto, where he obtained an M.Sc. in astronomy (1991). In 1993 he returned to writing; over the course of the next two years alone, he published five novels, as well as several short stories.

Trudel's first published work, "Œuvre de paix," is about a group of rival "Bosses" who, following a nuclear world war that devastated Earth and drove all of humanity into anarchy and the underground, gather together to pledge allegiance to the ruling world government, thus hoping to avert further conflict and bloodshed. One "Boss" and his followers, however, opt not to sign the treaty, which would have taken away their right to self-determination, and are ordered destroyed by the central government as a means of preserving peace. The commander who is assigned the task of annihilating the so-called renegades does so without questioning either the motives or the morality of his superiors, to the dismay of his subordinates. The story challenges the legitimacy of organized institutions that would give themselves the authority to deny a people the right to self-government and self-determination. Cultural autonomy and self-determination are, in fact, recurrent themes in many of Trudel's works.

Another notable theme often found in Trudel's works is the accentuation of the French language and its pertinence to the continuation of the cultural identity of Quebeckers. An early example is "Report 323: A Quebecois Infiltration Attempt" (1991), a bilingual short story of political significance that recounts the conversation of two characters, one speaking English and the other French. Set in Ottawa, the story centers on a French-speaking, unemployed man from Hull in Quebec, which is depicted as a sovereign nation. He is interrogated by an English-speaking character who attempts to intimidate him into signing a confession stating that he is a French spy who has entered Canada with the sole purpose of stealing national secrets. The protagonist, who is actually a bilingual Franco-Ontarian, is nonetheless not permitted to speak English, while his tormentor, who was originally French-speaking, refuses to talk in French. Coerced into signing his confession, the exhausted hero reveals to the reader that he is not a French spy from Quebec and that he simply wanted to inquire about the identity of the new occupants of his Ottawa childhood home. Ironic, innovative, and astringently humorous, the story effectively repudiates those who would reject or belittle the existence of an ambiguous cultural identity that is neither French nor English but Canadian.

Many of Trudel's works focus on the malignity of human nature and the marginalization of those who are weak and different. In the award-winning short story "Les Instincteurs de cruauté" he presents the adventures of a young, genetically altered clone, created for the purpose of waging war, who is found to be somewhat deficient during routine tests performed on troops riding in spaceships on their way to the war zone. Marked with a sign that identifies him as flawed and to be killed at first sight, his only salvation is to kill his antagonists, thus proving his worth and proper functioning. His very uniqueness permits him to prevail as he discovers that to be human is also to have an undauntable will to survive. At the end of the story, however, he is rehabilitated and becomes a perfect automaton, stripped of all his memories, his identity, and his individuality.

Trudel's first novel, *Aller simple pour Saguenal* (One-Way Ticket to Saguenal, 1994), is a science-fiction mystery for adolescents. The hero, Sylvain, is a fourteen-year-old boy who, upon his arrival on the planet Nou-Québec, must unravel the mysterious disappearance of his parents, ecologists sent to the planet to investigate the cause of the near extinction of a newly introduced species of genetically altered salmon. Characterized by an abundance of intriguing scientific devices and instruments that attest to Trudel's extensive scientific knowledge, this fast-moving novel explores the ecological aspects of a planet and its wildlife in danger of extinction because of pollution.

Aided by Paladia, a young woman several years older than he, Sylvain must outwit avaricious adults bent on exploiting the planet's natural resources. The antagonists in the story are all those in a position of power and authority at large commercial enterprises or in government posts, including the mayor of the small town of Saguenal, who is also the heroine's father.

While warning of the dangers of the exploitation of natural resources and its consequences (in this case, the release of heavy metals into a river), Trudel demonstrates how the marginalized and weak can sometimes overcome a much stronger opponent. While the young heroes succeed in saving the neosalmon from extinction, the true instigators of the crime nevertheless remain at large and are beyond the reach of the law. Another noteworthy aspect of *Aller simple pour Saguenal* is the attention that Trudel pays to details of racial, ethnic, and religious heterogeneity, thus accentuating his own cultural uniqueness as a Franco-Ontarian. Nou-Québec, initially introduced in this novel, later served as a key setting for many space-traveling Quebecois in Trudel's subsequent works.

Following *Pour des soleils froids* (Cold Suns, 1994), a science-fiction novel for adults based on his short story "Les Jeux de la paix et de la guerre" (Games of Peace and War, 1991), which relies extensively on scientific detail, Trudel published *Un trésor sur Serendib* (Treasure on Serendib, 1994), an imaginative novel for adolescents that introduces Serendib, a planet with an environment based on the tropical landscape and climate of Sri Lanka. Trudel subsequently used the planet as the setting for the *Mystères de Serendib* series.

In *Un trésor sur Serendib* the hero, Samuel, is a seventeen-year-old boy from Nou-Québec who finds himself involved in a murder mystery on Serendib, where, upon his arrival, he witnesses the interrogation

Cover for Trudel's 1994 novel about a seventeen-year-old boy who must race the villains to find a hidden treasure on the tropical planet Serendib

and subsequent murder of a scientific explorer who is reputed to have discovered a hidden treasure. The young hero must find the hidden treasure before the villains, but, unable to obtain any help from the local authorities or even from his parents (who, he knows, would not understand him), he must rely on the help of a younger boy and the latter's alien friends called the Glogs, a space-exploring race. The Glogs are usually mistrusted by humans because of their physical and cultural heterogeneity. With Serendib, Trudel creates a setting where a technologically advanced world is juxtaposed with ancient traditional French-Canadian customs accentuating the important role tradition plays in the continuity of a culture.

Le Ressuscité de l'Atlantide (Risen from Atlantis, 1994) is a science-fiction mystery novel for adults set in Chicago two hundred years in the future, following the rebuilding of civilization in the wake of a devastating nuclear world war that plunged humanity into anarchy. The hero is a cryogenically preserved adult human who is revived, only to find himself deeply involved in the criminal activities of powerful and socially prominent but corrupt characters bent on profiting from the slave trade of revived humans. This trade is a profitable business facilitated by the fact that the slaves have limited intelligence as a result of brain damage sustained during the yet-to-be-perfected cryogenic process.

The focal point of the novel is the internal turmoil of the hero. He is himself a victim of the slavers, who, in an effort to eliminate all traces of his past, have had his already deficient memory erased and replaced by the memories of two different individuals, one real and the other fictional. This corollary dual identity is marked by ambivalence and is comparable to that of the French minority living outside of the province of Quebec: their identity is dichotomous, made up of their shared French ancestry and of the influence of the English-speaking majority in their communities. The only way out of this dangerous world, in which the hero is misunderstood, is to escape to a new, French-speaking colony on Mars where old traditional values are still practiced and where one's identity can be found through a common history. As in Trudel's previous novels, the greed-driven evil culprits are individuals and organizations in high places who remain largely unpunished for their crimes.

In 1995, having just obtained an M.A. in the history and philosophy of science and technology from the University of Toronto, Trudel published *Les Voleurs de mémoire* (The Memory Thieves), a mystery novel for adolescents based on several themes already developed in *Le Ressuscité de l'Atlantide*. The setting of the novel is Montreal in the distant future, following a devastating nuclear war that forced much of the population into underground shelter, where, in sharp contrast to the lives of the rich, who lead a comfortable existence on the surface, the poor must struggle to survive in drug-infested ghettos. The heroine, a young girl who awakes to find herself in an underground shelter following the unexplainable loss of her memory, embarks on a quest to uncover her mysterious past with the help of two unlikely characters: Emil, a young orphan, and Henryk, a revived cryogenically preserved scientist characterized by his underdeveloped, childlike body. The heroine's search for her past leads her to a meeting with her parents, rich surface dwellers; this encounter convinces her that she is much happier living in the desolate underground in the company of her new friends. She also discovers that her memory loss was not caused by a drug overdose, as she previously believed, but instead resulted from an illegal surgical procedure intended to prevent her from disclosing the cloning experiments of a rich scientist intent on prolonging life. In *Les Voleurs de mémoire* Trudel accentuates the sharp contrast between the lives of the poor and the rich, who exploit the poor by stealing their memory, hence their very individuality and identity. Appalled by her own past behavior as a rich surface-dweller, the heroine and her companions opt to form a new colony on the planet Nou-Québec, where they will embrace the French language and culture and be allowed to prosper without the encumbrance of outside influences.

The *Mystères de Serendib* series comprises five novels set on Serendib in which humans, Glogs, and natives who resemble the people of Sri Lanka coexist in an uneasy amalgamation of ancient and modern ways of life. The first, *Les Rescapés de Serendib* (Serendib Castaways, 1995), is a well-written novel set 750 years following the time period of *Un trésor sur Serendib*. Following the crash of their spaceship, the young protagonists, Mikkkilo and Anne, a Glog prince and the daughter of the governor of Serendib, must overcome old prejudices and put aside their misgivings in order to survive in the treacherous jungles and deserts of the outback of Serendib. The novel examines the prejudices that can arise from stereotyping based on differences in skin color, language, and religion. While adults and those in power are antipathetic to new ideas and are reluctant to abandon old values and prejudices, the younger generation seems more apt to form lasting interracial friendships, despite physical and cultural differences. Unfortunately, those in the right are the weak (adolescents and cultural minorities shunned for their physical appearance or religion) and find it difficult to overcome the opposition fueled by the greed, mistrust, and religious dogmatism of those who hold the reins of power.

Le Prisonnier de Serendib (The Prisoner of Serendib, 1995) builds further on the themes developed in *Les Rescapés de Serendib*, but in this case the main characters are two girls and a boy. Despite the opposition of adults, the three must combine all their resources to help Glog prince Mikkkilo escape from his human captors, who have imprisoned him for a crime he did not commit. His escape is of the utmost importance, as only his personal intervention can prevent an imminent war between humans and Glogs. Personal development and friendship are central to the novel as the protagonists struggle to overcome the prejudice of those in power, whose stubbornness is at the root of wars and suffering. More than in his previous novels, Trudel advocates tolerance and global acceptance of differences, without regard to race, religion, or caste.

Friendship is also the fundamental theme of *Les Princes de Serendib* (The Princes of Serendib, 1996), in which the young Glog prince who was rescued by his human friends in *Le Prisonnier de Serendib* must in turn rescue them from a group of insurgent radical Glogs, who, adhering to old myths, beliefs, and fears, have condemned their captives to death. Advocating friendship, tolerance, and peace, the prince mounts a daring rescue attempt in the belief that it is better to live as a tolerated minority than to risk provoking global war. The story ends with a general meeting of all races intended to form a global government with an assembly of representatives which would, for the first time, give a voice to all of the minorities on Serendib. The harmonious and combined effort of all of the peoples on the planet will be necessary to combat the dangers of global warning, which threaten the life of their planet.

In *Des Colons pour Serendib* (Settlers for Serendib, 1996) the young protagonists stow away on a spaceship and travel to an asteroid that has been transformed into a giant space vessel. On their journey they visit a planet that has been ravaged by mining and the subsequent pollution of a giant corporation. Upon their arrival on the asteroid spaceship, the main characters are confronted once again by the old prejudices and misgivings of the inhabitants, Glogs who have left their home planet many centuries ago in search of a new, less polluted home. The heroes must use their combined efforts to save not only the Glogs living on the asteroid ship but also their own planet. Only by amalgamating all their resources, including the technical knowledge of the Glogs and a moon created by the humans, are the Glogs and the humans able to reverse the axial shifting of Serendib, thereby preventing global warming and volatile weather patterns that soon would have caused the planet to become uninhabitable.

Fièvres sur Serendib (Serendib Fevers, 1996), the last novel in the *Mystères de Serendib* series, is a humorous story about an overzealous religious character who undertakes a long and treacherous journey from Nou-Québec in the company of a young heroine whose faith, in contrast to that of her companion, is founded on scientific facts. Upon landing in a small native village on Serendib that reflects the culture and lifestyle of a Sri Lankan village, the unlikely pair meets a young adolescent who informs them that a deadly fever is being spread unwittingly by foreigners in a spaceship and that it has infected and killed nearly all of the inhabitants of his native village. After several adventures, the trio finally finds the foreigners, including the heroine's father, who are employees of a large commercial pharmaceutical organization searching for plants intended for the development of new drugs. Having bypassed normal safety protocols intended to protect native inhabitants from contamination and in an attempt to save time and money, the scientists have inadvertently introduced a virus to Serendib that, while harmless to humans, is deadly to the natives

Cover for Trudel's 1994 novel in which a cryogenically preserved hero battles slave traders in post-nuclear-holocaust Chicago

of the planet, not unlike the introduction of European diseases to North America and the devastating consequences it had on Native Americans.

The *Saisons à Nigelle* series for adolescents comprises four novels: *Un printemps à Nigelle* (One Spring in Nigelle, 1997), *Un été à Nigelle* (One Summer in Nigelle, 1997), *Un hiver à Nigelle* (One Winter in Nigelle, 1997), and *Un automne à Nigelle* (One Autumn in Nigelle, 1998). Set in the present, *Un printemps à Nigelle* is a mystery novel in which the two main characters, a fourteen-year-old boy and his resourceful older sister, both visitors from North America, follow the trail of a mysterious young man whom they have witnessed stealing a briefcase from a German tourist while on a visit to the ruins of an ancient castle in Nigelle, France. The protagonists undergo many adventures in secret underground tunnels while unearthing historical facts about the German occupation of France during

J.-L. Trudel/Transfigurés du Centaure/Version 1

— Mais non! Je n'ai jamais songé à mentir. Seulement, je me suis dit que nous nous ressemblons tellement, entre clones, que je pourrais remplacer Tim. Sauf que...

Il se mordit la lèvre, incapable de prononcer un autre mot. Samuel se lança à nouveau:

— Tu as peur qu'ils ne t'aiment pas?

— Je ne sais pas! protesta-t-il, une fêlure dans la voix. C'est pour ça que je te le demande. Mais s'ils m'aimaient, est-ce que je serais capable de les aimer?

— J'en suis sûr.

— Mais comment le savoir?

— Le jour où tu souffrirais de savoir qu'ils s'en font pour toi, tu saurais que tu les aimes.

— Tu es sûr?

— Tu ne me fais pas confiance?

Tam eut l'air sceptique. Son expérience des galeries de Dante lui avait avant tout enseigné à coincer sans tarder les gens qui s'en faisaient pour lui, pour leur extorquer une faveur ou quelques stellars.

Pendant ce temps, Onofrio Bone les avait menés dans une avenue latérale, moins grande que le boulevard principal mais encore monumentale. Comme les seules ouvertures dans les murs de chaque côté étaient des portes anonymes ouvrant sur les hangars de l'astroport, les urbanistes avaient accroché la verdure nanotech aux murs eux-mêmes. Ainsi, les portes étaient entourées de roses trémières et les murs étaient bordés de pelouse presque bleue, juste assez larges pour que des paons y fissent la roue. Les queues déployées des oiseaux nanotech affichaient des motifs bien différents des œillades abstraites des paons de la Terre: paysages d'autres mondes, portraits de célébrités et logos des compagnies de Nu-America qui les avaient fabriqués.

L'AgnoSophiste s'arrêta devant une porte.

— Ici, c'est l'astronef marchand *Phersu*. (Il regarda à gauche et à droite.) Je me demande si ça vaudrait la peine de jouer à cette porte un petit air d'harmonica...

Le visage de Renkun se ferma, mais le clone n'eut pas le temps de répondre.

La porte du hangar voisin coulissa bruyamment. En face, une autre porte claqua en s'ouvrant. Des hommes en uniformes de synthosoie pare-laser en débouchèrent. Ils se rangèrent en demi-cercle, pistolasers braqués sur Samuel et ses compagnons.

— Pas un geste! commanda leur chef.

Au bout de la rue, d'autres hommes apparurent, leurs armes en bandoulière.

Une escouade au complet venait d'envahir l'avenue, déserte un instant plus tôt. Des larmes de dépit gonflèrent les yeux de Samuel. Ils n'avaient pas prévu que l'astronef qu'ils

51

Corrected typescript page for the draft of a novel Trudel published in 2001 (Collection of Jean-Louis Trudel)

World War II. They also hear a tale about a hidden treasure that they prove really exists; upon discovering the treasure, they decide to donate it to the victims of the war and its survivors. Departing somewhat from his earlier themes of racial discrimination and the preservation of cultural identity, Trudel, who has traveled extensively throughout Europe from an early age, portrays a delightful picture of the countryside of France.

In *Un été à Nigelle* several young characters visit eleventh-century Nigelle by means of a virtual-reality machine that permits them to become avatars in a computer-designed plot simulation. Upon learning that a friend is trapped in a computer simulation in which he believes himself to be an eleventh-century character condemned to be killed for the murder of his brother, the protagonists must find a means of rescuing him before his avatar is decapitated. The death of the avatar could cause irreparable brain damage to their friend if, as they suspect, the simulation safeguards are malfunctioning. Discovering that the malfunction is caused by a computer virus, they are unable to obtain the aid of adults and must rely on each other to save the life of their friend. While warning of the dangers of technology should it fall into the wrong hands, as well as advocating the importance of friendship, Trudel takes the reader on a detailed journey to medieval France that is laced with mystery and the unexpected.

Un hiver à Nigelle, the third novel in the *Saisons à Nigelle* series, is a mystery set in France three years before the beginning of World War II. The protagonists, Léon and Bébert, two thirteen-year-old boys, must outwit an evil old woman who has stolen the memory of a beautiful young girl. Having discovered that the old woman is actually the mythical Gorgon, who survives by imprisoning souls and thereby robbing her victims of their memory and their will to live, the main characters, who are themselves about to suffer the same fate, are saved in turn by the young girl whom they have rescued. Unable to communicate with adults because of a hex that the Gorgon has put on them, thus preventing them from revealing the truth, they can rely only on their friendship to combat the primordial evil that threatens to steal their memory and will. The loss of memory, and thus of one's identity, constitutes the loss of existence. Stepping into the realm of witchcraft and the supernatural, Trudel examines the unemployment and the economic crises that helped to pave the way for Adolf Hitler's rise in Germany and to catapult Europe into world war.

Les Bannis de Bételgeuse (Betelgeuse Outcasts, 1998) is a rather technical science-fiction novel for adolescents that reprises many of the original Nou-Québécois characters from *Un trésor sur Serendib,* including Cristofine, the semi-intelligent navigator computer of the spaceship *Christophe.* Following this novel Trudel published *13,5 km sous Montréal* (13.5 km beneath Montreal, 1998), in which the protagonists are a twelve-year-old girl, Starie, and a twenty-four-year-old man, Axel. After the rebuilding of Montreal following a devastating nuclear world war that has left the poor living underground, the two main characters undertake a long journey through the abandoned tunnels of the Montreal subway system in search of the Biosphere, where they hope to obtain a rose for an unemployed friend who wishes to give a flower to the woman he loves. Their quest leads them to underground tunnels, where they witness poverty-stricken people forced to sell their blood in order to survive. They also visit the surface, where, in sharp contrast to the underground, people live in beautiful, big houses, and roses are abundant. Starie, who at the beginning of the novel has difficulty choosing a career, decides to pursue studies in botany. The main themes in this fast-moving novel are the injustice of caste distinction and the importance of education in the lives of young people.

Trudel continues to develop his characters and themes. *Contrebandiers de Cañaveral* (The Smugglers of Cañaveral, 1999) focuses on individual freedom. Commander Nikto of the Nouvel Empire threatens the life of Ferrale Filon because of her attempts to gain freedom. The hero, Samuel from *Un trésor sur Serendib,* must rescue her from certain death. Set in France, *Nigelle par tous les temps* (Nigelle at All Times, 2000), like *Un hiver à Nigelle,* involves mythical, supernatural beings. In this novel Michel Paradis falls in love with a mysterious young girl whom he must rescue from an evil supernatural force. *Guerre pour un harmonic* (War for a Harmonica, 2000) is a fast-moving novel in which Samuel and Ferrale must race against time to solve the mystery of a strange harmonica that causes death to all who dare to play it. Unlocking its secret is the only way to avert war.

Trudel, who resides in Montreal, is working on several new novels and short stories. As for his future plans, he stated in an unpublished June 1999 interview that "I'd like to partly wrap up this phase of my career and concentrate hereafter on writing novels for the general readership. . . . Still, there are no guarantees in this business, and I may veer toward writing in English more for the American market, or keep writing books for the YA [young adult] market. We'll have to see."

Interviews:

"Entrevue: Jean-Louis Trudel," *Solaris,* no. 110 (1994): 20–26;

"Entrevue avec Jean-Louis Trudel," *Vidéo-Presse,* 4 (May 1995): 22–24;

Claude Janelle, "Pour une science-fiction *savante,*" *Lettres québécoises,* 78 (Summer 1995): 35–36;

"Lettres ontariennes," FM Radio-Canada, 23 August 1996.

A. E. van Vogt

(26 April 1912 – 26 January 2000)

J. Morton Hendrick

See also the van Vogt entry in *DLB 8: Twentieth-Century American Science-Fiction Writers.*

BOOKS: *Slan* (Sauk City, Wis.: Arkham, 1946; London: Weidenfeld & Nicolson, 1953);

The Weapon Makers (Providence, R.I.: Hadley, 1947; revised edition, New York: Greenberg, 1952; London: Weidenfeld & Nicolson, 1954); republished as *One Against Eternity* (New York: Ace, 1955);

The Book of Ptath (Reading, Pa.: Fantasy Press, 1947; London: Panther, 1969); republished as *Two Hundred Million A.D.* (New York: Paperback Library, 1964);

The World of Ā (New York: Simon & Schuster, 1948); republished as *The World of Null-Ā* (New York: Ace, 1953; London: Dobson, 1969);

Out of the Unknown, by van Vogt and E. Mayne Hull (Los Angeles: Fantasy, 1948); republished as *The Sea Thing and Other Stories* (London: Sidgwick & Jackson, 1970);

The Voyage of the Space Beagle (New York: Simon & Schuster, 1950; London: Grayson, 1951); republished as *Mission: Interplanetary* (New York: New American Library, 1952);

Masters of Time, with *The Changeling* (Reading, Pa.: Fantasy Press, 1950); *Masters of Time* republished as *Earth's Last Fortress* (New York: Ace, 1960); *The Changeling* revised and enlarged as *The Beast* (Garden City, N.Y.: Doubleday, 1963); *The Beast* republished as *The Moonbeast* (London: Panther, 1969);

The House That Stood Still (New York: Greenberg, 1950; London: Weidenfeld & Nicolson, 1953); republished as *The Mating Cry* (New York: Galaxy, 1960); republished as *The Undercover Aliens* (St. Albans, U.K.: Panther, 1976);

Triad: Three Complete Science Fiction Novels by A. E. van Vogt (New York: Simon & Schuster, 1951)—comprises *Slan, The World of Ā,* and *The Voyage of the Space Beagle;*

A. E. van Vogt (courtesy of the Ashley Grayson Literary Agency)

The Weapon Shops of Isher (New York: Greenberg, 1951; London: Weidenfeld & Nicolson, 1952);

Away and Beyond (New York: Pellegrini & Cudahy, 1952; London: Panther, 1963);

Destination: Universe! (New York: Pellegrini & Cudahy, 1952; London: Eyre & Spottiswoode, 1953);

The Mixed Men (New York: Gnome Press, 1952); republished as *Mission to the Stars* (New York: Berkley, 1955; London: Brown, Watson, 1960);

The Universe Maker (New York: Ace, 1953); republished in *The Universe Maker and The Proxy Intelligence: Science Fiction* (London: Sidgwick & Jackson, 1976);

Planets for Sale, by van Vogt and Hull (New York: Frederick Fell, 1954; St. Albans, U.K.: Panther, 1978);

The Pawns of Null-A (New York: Ace, 1956); republished as *The Players of Null-A* (New York: Berkley, 1966; London: Dobson, 1970);

The Hypnotism Handbook, by van Vogt and Charles E. Cooke (Los Angeles: Griffin, 1956);

Empire of the Atom (Chicago: Shasta, 1957; London: New English Library, 1978);

The Mind Cage (New York: Simon & Schuster, 1957; Hertfordshire, U.K.: Panther, 1960);

Siege of the Unseen (New York: Ace, 1959); republished as *Three Eyes of Evil* in *Three Eyes of Evil and Earth's Last Fortress: Two Science Fiction Novels* (London: Sidgwick & Jackson, 1973);

The War Against the Rull (New York: Ace, 1959; London: Panther, 1961);

The Violent Man (New York: Farrar, Straus & Cudahy, 1962);

The Wizard of Linn (New York: Ace, 1962; London: New English Library, 1975);

The Twisted Men (New York: Ace, 1964); republished as *The Rogue Ship* (Garden City: Doubleday, 1965; London: Dobson, 1967);

Monsters (New York: Paperback Library, 1965); republished as *Science Fiction Monsters* (New York: Paperback Library, 1967); republished as *The Blal* (New York: Kensington, 1976);

The Winged Man, by van Vogt and Hull (Garden City, N.Y.: Doubleday, 1966; London: Sidgwick & Jackson, 1967);

A Van Vogt Omnibus: Planets for Sale, The Beast, The Book of Ptath (London: Sidgwick & Jackson, 1967);

The Far-Out Worlds of A. E. van Vogt (New York: Ace, 1968; London: Sidgwick & Jackson, 1973); enlarged as *The Worlds of A. E. van Vogt* (New York: Ace, 1974);

The Silkie (New York: Ace, 1969; London: New English Library, 1973);

Quest for the Future (New York: Ace, 1970; London: Sidgwick & Jackson, 1971);

Children of Tomorrow (New York: Ace, 1970; London: Sidgwick & Jackson, 1972);

The Battle of Forever (New York: Ace, 1971; London: New English Library, 1973);

M-33 in Andromeda (New York: Paperback Library, 1971);

Van Vogt Omnibus 2 (London: Sidgwick & Jackson, 1971)—comprises *The Mind Cage, The Winged Man,* and *Slan;*

More Than Superhuman (New York: Dell, 1971; London: New English Library, 1975);

The Proxy Intelligence and Other Mind Benders (New York: Paperback Library, 1971); *The Proxy Intelligence* republished in *The Universe Maker and The Proxy Intelligence: Science Fiction;*

The Book of van Vogt (New York: DAW, 1972); republished as *Lost: Fifty Suns* (New York: DAW, 1977; London: New English Library, 1980);

The Darkness on Diamondia (New York: Ace, 1972; London: Sidgwick & Jackson, 1974);

The Money Personality (West Nyack, N.Y.: Parker, 1972; Wellingborough, U.K.: Thorsons, 1975);

Future Glitter (New York: Ace, 1973; London: Sidgwick & Jackson, 1976); republished as *Tyranopolis* (London: Sphere, 1977);

The Secret Galactics (Englewood Cliffs, N.J.: Prentice-Hall, 1974; London: Sidgwick & Jackson, 1975); republished as *Earth Factor X* (New York: DAW, 1976);

The Man with a Thousand Names (New York: DAW, 1974; London: Sidgwick & Jackson, 1975);

The Best of A. E. van Vogt, edited by Angus Wells (London: Sidgwick & Jackson, 1974)—comprises "Vault of the Beast," "The Weapon Shop," "The Storm," "Juggernaut," "Hand of the Gods," "The Cataaaaa," "The Monster," "Dear Pen Pal," "The Green Forest," "War of Nerves," "The Expendables," "Silkies in Space," and "The Proxy Intelligence";

Reflections of A. E. van Vogt: The Autobiography of a Science Fiction Giant, with a Complete Bibliography (Lakemont, Ga.: Fictioneer Books, 1975);

The Best of A. E. van Vogt, introduction by Barry Malzberg (New York: Pocket Books, 1976)—comprises "Don't Hold Your Breath," "All We Have on this Planet," "War of Nerves," "The Rull," "The Semantics of Twenty-first Century Science," "Future Perfect," "Being an Examination of the Ponsian and Holmesian Secret Deductive Systems," "Home of the Gods," "The Violent Male," "Prologue to 'The Silkie,'" and "The Proxy Intelligence";

The Gryb (New York: Zebra, 1976; London: New English Library, 1980);

Supermind (New York: DAW, 1977; London: Sidgwick & Jackson, 1978);

The Anarchistic Colossus (New York: Ace, 1977; London: Sidgwick & Jackson, 1978);

Pendulum (New York: DAW, 1978; London: New English Library, 1982);

The Enchanted Village (Dearborn Heights, Mich.: Misfit Press, 1979);

Renaissance (New York: Pocket Books, 1979);

The Cosmic Encounter (Garden City: Doubleday, 1980; London: New English Library, 1981);

Computerworld (New York: DAW, 1983; London: New English Library, 1986); republished as *Computer*

Eye (Beverly Hills, Cal.: Morrison Raven Hill, 1985);

Null-A Three (New York: DAW, 1985; London: Sphere, 1985);

The Weapon Shops of Isher and The Weapon Makers (London: New English Library, 1988); republished as *Empire of Isher* (New York: Orb, 2000);

A Report on the Violent Male (Los Angeles: N.p., n.d.; Nottingham, U.K.: Paupers' Press, 1992);

Futures Past: The Best Short Fiction of A. E. van Vogt (San Francisco: Tachyon, 1999).

SELECTED PERIODICAL PUBLICATION–UNCOLLECTED: "The Development of a Science Fiction Writer: III," *Foundation*, 3 (March 1973): 26–30.

Without doubt, A. E. van Vogt was the first great Canadian science-fiction writer. In his heyday he was one of the most popular science-fiction authors in the world and is considered to belong to the so-called golden age of writers in the genre, along with such masters as Robert A. Heinlein, Isaac Asimov, and Arthur C. Clarke. Certainly, until the explosion of Canadian science fiction in the 1980s no Canadian had as high a profile as van Vogt within the genre. Although his prominence in Canadian science fiction has now been eclipsed as a result of the success of such writers as William Gibson, Guy Gavriel Kay, and Robert J. Sawyer, and his work is no longer as widely read, van Vogt's early fiction represents one of the greatest achievements in Canadian science fiction and has had a lasting, if underappreciated, impact on the genre.

Alfred Elton Vogt was born on 26 April 1912 to Heinrich (later Henry) and Agnes Buhr Vogt on his grandparents' farm just outside of Gretna, Manitoba, Canada. Although biographical accounts of van Vogt have stated that he was born into a Dutch Canadian family, his parents were in fact German-speaking Mennonites, as were many of the inhabitants of rural Manitoba, and German was the language of the household in the author's early years. The family added "van" to their surname in order to make it sound Dutch, presumably in response to the anti-German sentiments common in Canada in the late 1930s. They first lived in Neville, a small, rural town in the neighboring province of Saskatchewan, where van Vogt's father and uncles were partners in a general store. At this time his father was studying law by correspondence and soon received his law degree. The family moved to Swift Current, Saskatchewan, and then Morden, Manitoba, before finally moving to the fast-growing city of Winnipeg, Manitoba, then the most important city on Canada's prairies, where his father took a position as the western Canadian agent for the Holland-American Shipping Lines.

Van Vogt, aged fourteen at the time of the move to Winnipeg, found the transition from small-town to big-city life traumatic. He was behind in school and had to repeat the tenth grade. Earlier an outgoing child, he became increasingly introverted and struggled with social insecurity for the rest of his life. Lonely, van Vogt found refuge in the pages of Hugo Gernsback's science-fiction magazine *Amazing Stories,* which he began reading with the November 1926 issue. Like many of his generation, van Vogt found that reading science fiction provided him with a sense of wonder and excitement that was missing from his life. "Reading science fiction," he later wrote in *The Best of A. E. van Vogt,* "lifted me out of the do-be-and-have world and gave me glimpses backward and forward into the time and space distances of the universe. . . ." This reading provided him with "the pleasure and excitement of contemplating the beginning and end of existence." He continued to read *Amazing Stories* regularly until 1930, when he became disenchanted by the conservative direction the magazine took under a new editor, T. O'Conor Sloane.

Van Vogt's final year of high school coincided with the beginning of the Great Depression, which caused his father to lose his position with Holland-American. This financial setback made it impossible for van Vogt to go on to college, as had been intended. He spent the next few months doing odd jobs and spending a great deal of time in his bedroom reading pulp fiction (though not science fiction), serious literature, history, psychology, and science. In particular he was intrigued by the mathematician and philosopher Alfred North Whitehead's *Science and the Modern World.* (1925). From Whitehead, van Vogt came away with an insight, described by Alexei and Cory Panshin in *The World Beyond the Hill: Science Fiction and the Quest for Transcendence* (1989) as a "vision of an organic and interconnected universe evolving through creativeness and cooperation." This vision is reflected in much of the science fiction van Vogt later wrote.

In early 1931 van Vogt took a civil service examination and was offered a job in Ottawa as a census clerk. While living in Ottawa he took a correspondence course in writing from the Palmer Institute of Authorship. After completing his work in Ottawa he returned to Winnipeg, where he continued to study writing, taking various writing manuals out of the Winnipeg library. Most influential on his developing craft were the books of John Gallishaw, who taught that every sentence should convey emotion, imagery, or suspense and that a story should be broken down into short scenes, each of which should have a clear purpose. Van Vogt's unique style can be attributed to his strict adherence to these guidelines throughout his writing career. For example, he religiously observed a rule of stringing together scenes of about eight hundred words in his novels and short stories.

Van Vogt decided to put his learning to work and write a short story to enter into a contest held by the confession magazine *True Story*. The resulting story, about a girl made homeless by the Depression, did not win a prize, but he did sell it to the magazine for $110. Encouraged by that success, he wrote many more such stories, including one that won a $1,000 prize in another confession-magazine contest, until he grew tired of writing fiction that he did not like. Van Vogt then turned to writing for trade papers, newspaper supplements, and pulp magazines. He also wrote short radio plays for the Canadian Broadcasting Corporation, receiving a total of $600 for fifty plays. At the same time, he worked for the Maclean Publishing Company as their western Canadian representative.

In 1938 van Vogt rediscovered his love for science fiction after buying the August issue of *Astounding Science-Fiction* at a Winnipeg drugstore. He was particularly impressed by a story credited to Don A. Stuart, "Who Goes There?" Van Vogt wrote to the editor of the magazine, the highly influential John W. Campbell Jr., the actual author of the story, and offered to write a similar piece. Campbell responded encouragingly, and van Vogt wrote his first science-fiction story, "Vault of the Beast" (1940). Campbell eventually accepted the story after requesting revisions and, as it turned out, after van Vogt had already become one of the biggest stars in *Astounding Science-Fiction*.

Eventually published in the August 1940 issue of *Astounding Science-Fiction*, "Vault of the Beast," like "Who Goes There?," is a story about a space monster, a shape-shifting, telepathic android. The creature has been sent to Earth by its alien masters to pose as a human and find a mathematician with the ability to free one of their fellow aliens, who has been trapped for millennia in a vault on Mars. The trapped alien knows how to shift from one dimension to another, information the other aliens intend to use in order to rule the universe. The android is successful in finding the mathematician, and thus the aliens are able to open the vault on Mars, but only by painfully transforming the android into a key to the lock of the vault. Just before the vault is opened, the mathematician, Jim Brender, discovers that opening it will kill the prisoner and foil the aliens' plans. The telepathic android discovers this information but, in a moment of self-sacrifice, decides not to reveal it to the aliens. The android is destroyed, but so is the prisoner. Thus, the android chooses to protect humanity rather than save its own life by following the goals of its masters.

Cover for the July 1939 magazine issue, featuring van Vogt's story of a spaceship crew's encounter with a monster, that has been called the inaugural publication of the golden age of science fiction

Although "Vault of the Beast," like much of van Vogt's fiction, has many logical flaws and inconsistencies, it is remarkably powerful, possessing "the inexorable pace of a fevered dream," as the Panshins write in *The World Beyond the Hill: Science Fiction and the Quest for Transcendence*: "Writing as relentless as this had never been seen in the SF pulp magazines." The most original aspect of the story, however, is that much of it is told from the perspective of the android. As the Panshins suggest, "Nobody [in pulp science fiction] had ever dared before to write from inside the psyche of so different and monstrous a being."

Spurred on by Campbell's enthusiastic initial response to "Vault of the Beast," van Vogt set to work on a new story, "Black Destroyer" (1939). This tale of interstellar exploration describes an encounter between a survey ship from a galaxy-spanning human civilization and the monstrous inhabitant of an isolated planet. Members of the crew land on the planet and explore a destroyed city, where they encounter the survivor of a long-dead civilization. Coeurl is an ancient, powerful, catlike being who at first seems to be omnipotent. He

Dust jacket for the book publication (1946) of van Vogt's first novel, about a race of mutants who are discriminated against by humans but ultimately supplant them as the dominant species. The work was first published in serial form in Astounding Science-Fiction in 1940 and established van Vogt as a major science-fiction author.

responds to the arrival of the humans with murderous rage and then takes control of the spaceship. Ultimately, however, the powerful yet primitive Coeurl is defeated by the humans' superior scientific and technological knowledge. "Black Destroyer," a fantasy of human power and dominance, emphasized the importance of scientific and technical knowledge and thus accurately reflected the values Campbell wished to set forth in the pages of *Astounding Science-Fiction*. It is little wonder, then, that he enthusiastically accepted the story. It was published as the cover story in the July 1939 issue, an issue that has often been cited as the inaugural publication of the golden age of science fiction. "Black Destroyer" was later incorporated into van Vogt's novel *The Voyage of the Space Beagle* (1950). Campbell encouraged him to submit more fiction to both *Astounding Science-Fiction* and its fantasy-oriented companion publication, *Unknown* (later renamed *Unknown Worlds*). Even though he was only able to write part-time, van Vogt quickly set to work to meet Campbell's request, publishing a fantasy story,

"The Sea Thing," in the January 1940 issue of *Unknown*; "Discord in Scarlet," a sequel to "Black Destroyer," in the December 1939 issue of *Astounding Science-Fiction*; and "Repetition" in the April 1940 issue of the same magazine.

Van Vogt married Edna Mayne Hull, originally from Brandon, Manitoba, on 9 May 1939. He had met Hull, a freelance author in her own right, at the Winnipeg Writers Club. After marrying van Vogt, she worked as his typist and also published several stories of her own, as well as others written in collaboration with her husband. When World War II broke out in September 1939, the civil service of Canada offered van Vogt a position as a clerk in the Department of National Defence, so he headed to Ottawa, and his wife followed shortly afterward. Although he did not really want to take the new job, he did so because he felt he needed to serve his country in wartime, and he could not join the army because of his poor eyesight.

Van Vogt had started work on his first novel while still in Winnipeg, and, although his new job in Ottawa left him little time for writing, he doggedly continued working on it. In fact, he now needed the additional income from his writing, as the civil-service job barely paid the rent in the wartime boomtown that was Ottawa. After coming home from work, van Vogt would work on his novel until retiring for the night, leaving a longhand draft for his wife to type up the next day. It took six months, but he finally completed the novel in the spring of 1940 and sent it off to Campbell. *Slan*, which went on to become possibly his best-known novel, was serialized in *Astounding Science-Fiction* from September to December 1940.

Slans are long-lived, telepathic mutants with two hearts and with golden tendrils on their heads. They are intellectually and physically superior to normal humans, who persecute them and attempt to exterminate them. As the beginning of the novel two slans, Jommy Cross and his mother, are desperately trying to escape from pursuing normal humans; Jommy escapes, but his mother is killed. This opening was inspired by van Vogt's reading of Canadian animal-story writer Ernest Thompson Seton's *The Biography of a Grizzly* (1900), which opens similarly, with a young cub whose mother is killed and then has to grow up on its own. Jommy grows up and assumes his powers; he then becomes involved with various plots and intrigues related to some tendrilless slans he discovers who can pass as human. Ultimately, he discovers that the world dictator, Keir Gray, whom his mother had implored him to kill, is actually a slan, and that the slan girl with whom he fell in love is Gray's daughter. In actuality, the planet is being run by a secret cabal of slans, and one day Jommy will take his rightful place as a leader.

Rather than an unfortunate mutation, the slans in fact represent the future of humanity.

Slan was immensely successful and was voted the most popular story of the year by readers of *Astounding Science-Fiction*. The wish-fulfillment fantasy that a group of social outcasts is in reality superior to the rest of society, and that such a group ultimately comes to take control, strongly resonated with the science-fiction fan community, or fandom, that had developed in the 1930s. In fact, the slogan "fans are slans" echoed through the halls of science-fiction conventions for years to come. In *Canadian Science Fiction and Fantasy* (1992) David Ketterer suggests that this wish-fullfilment fantasy might at least partially be attributed to van Vogt's sense of inferiority in relation to the Canadians of British heritage who formed the elite of the country, as well as to the inferiority complex that Canada had in regard to Europe and the United States. "Van Vogt's use of the superman theme," Ketterer writes, "might plausibly be viewed as a particularly Canadian manifestation of a superiority complex masking an inferiority complex."

Already a major figure in the world of pulp science fiction as a result of the handful of stories he had so far published, van Vogt was elevated to the status of a major author in the genre by the success of *Slan*. Certainly, as Sam Moskowitz observes in *Seekers of Tomorrow: Masters of Modern Science Fiction* (1966), "There was no ignoring *Slan*. By any standard it was a milestone in science fiction." The novel was published in book form in 1946. Although van Vogt continued to be a quite popular author for the rest of the 1940s and beyond, in many ways *Slan* was the high-water mark of his career, and he was only rarely able to return to such heights in status and popularity.

Exciting and exhilarating as the action-packed *Slan* is, the novel has, like nearly all of van Vogt's fiction, too many implausibilities, inconsistencies, anachronisms, and holes in the plot to stand up to careful scrutiny. *Slan* simply does not make logical sense. As the Panshins point out, "In *Slan,* things operate according to the dictates of dream logic. . . . In this story, coincidences, unlikelihoods and radical transitions abound–but as within a dream, this just seems the way that things naturally ought to happen." Judged by the conventions of realist, scientifically plausible science fiction, this dreamlike quality in van Vogt's writing may be his biggest weakness, but it is also what provides works such as *Slan* with their hallucinatory power. As Charles Platt observes in *Dream Makers: The Uncommon People Who Write Science Fiction* (1980), van Vogt's stories are "eerie, powerful journeys into symbolic depths of the psyche. When you open one of his novels, you open the subconscious. He writes dreams." This aspect of van Vogt's writing later influenced more-substantial science-fiction writers, such as Philip K. Dick.

The dreamlike nature of van Vogt's fiction was partly the result of his unique approach to writing. Rarely did he have a clear outline of a story or novel when he started; rather, he simply followed his muse as the story developed. Furthermore, he actually developed plots out of his dreams. As he told Platt, "when I was working on a story, I would waken myself every hour and a half, through the night–force myself to wake up, think of the story, try to solve it, and even as I was thinking about it I would fall back asleep. And in the morning, there would be a solution for that particular story problem. Now, that's penetrating the subconscious, in my opinion."

Van Vogt was unable immediately to follow up the success of *Slan* as a result of his increasing workload at the Department of National Defence, publishing only two stories in *Astounding Science-Fiction* in the fourteen months after *Slan* had finished its run. "The Seesaw," which was published in the July 1941 issue, was a significant addition to his body of work, as it initiated one of his better-known series of stories. Inspired by Campbell's assertion that Heinlein's stories were linked to form a common vision of the future, van Vogt began to search for a common thread in his fiction. In a March 1977 letter to the members of the Science Fiction Writers of America, which is quoted by the Panshins, he discussed his realization that his stories were bound together by the premise that "in every rock, in every grain of sand, in every cell there is a 'memory' of ancient origins, and of the history of that cell going back to the beginning of things. If we could but read the signals that these bits of matter are showing us, we would have the answers we seek." In "The Seesaw" he consciously attempted to articulate this premise.

"The Seesaw" begins with the mysterious appearance of a building on a city street. It turns out to be a weapon shop from the future, with a sign saying that the "right to buy weapons is the right to be free." C. J. McAllister, a newspaper reporter, enters the store to investigate after a policeman had been refused entrance. Once in the store, he learns that he has entered a different reality, in which the weapon shop and its sister stores are in conflict with the empire of Isher. Thus begin McAllister's adventures as he shifts through time, alternately farther into the past and future; his temporal movements are linked to those of a powerful Isher machine. McAllister and the Isher machine are the opposite ends of a cosmic seesaw. Ultimately, his movements, he realizes, will result in the formation of the planets. The story thus presents a cosmological vision of the beginning and, presumably, the end of the universe. It also provides a political commentary on the

Dust jacket for the 1948 book version of van Vogt's complex and controversial novel, first serialized in Astounding Science-Fiction in 1945, that was inspired by the theories of the Polish logician Alfred Korzybski. It was republished in 1953 as The World of Null-A.

relationship between the libertarian forces of the weapon shops and the authoritarian imperial forces of Isher: neither could exist without the other. "The Seesaw" was later incorporated with other stories into van Vogt's 1951 "fix-up" novel, *The Weapon Shops of Isher*. (*Fix-up* is a term van Vogt coined to describe novels assembled out of previously written, related stories; it has since become a widely used term in science fiction.)

Frustrated by the increasing demands of his job, which was preventing him from doing the writing he needed in order to support himself and his wife, van Vogt resigned from his position in 1941. He and Edna moved to a cottage along the Gatineau River, just north of Ottawa, and he began working full-time on his writing. He was encouraged in his efforts that September, when he received a letter from Campbell informing him that since Heinlein was planning to retire he was in need of many submissions from writers of the caliber of van Vogt. Campbell was willing to accept twenty thousand to twenty-five thousand words of fiction a month from van Vogt for his two magazines. Van Vogt rose to the challenge, beginning an exhausting regimen of writing from the time he got up in the morning until eleven in the evening, seven days a week, a practice he was to continue to follow for years to come.

In the fall of 1941 the van Vogts moved to Toronto, where van Vogt continued diligently working to meet the demand for his stories. Beginning with the February 1942 issue, van Vogt was nearly a constant presence in *Astounding Science-Fiction* over the course of the next three years; this period of peak productivity resulted in some of his best work. "Co-operate—or Else!," published in the April 1942 issue of the magazine, was the first of van Vogt's Rull stories, which he later assembled as a fix-up novel, *The War Against the Rull* (1959). "Co-operate—or Else!" is set in a future in which humanity has ventured out into the stars and formed an alliance with thousands of alien races. Trevor Jamieson is taking an ezwal, a newly encountered species that he has discovered to be sentient, to Earth when their spaceship is attacked by the violent and warlike Rull, who have declared interstellar war against humans and their alliance. After the two crashland on a primitive planet, Jamieson is able to convince the ezwal that they must cooperate in order to survive the dangers of the planet and withstand the threat of the Rull. The idea of cooperation, which certainly must have reflected the imperatives of the ongoing war effort, was an element of much of van Vogt's fiction during this period and was central to his vision of the future of humanity.

The May 1942 issue of *Astounding Science-Fiction* featured a story that van Vogt himself has described as his best: "Asylum." In a crime-free future a journalist, William Leigh, investigates a series of murders in which the victims were drained of blood and static electricity. In his investigations he comes across two space vampires, or Dreeghs, who are intellectually and physically superior to humans. As a result of a tragic accident in the distant past, these two Dreeghs require frequent transfusions of blood and human life force in order to survive. Jeel and Merla, the two Dreeghs that Leigh encounters, fled their ordered extermination (because of their condition) and in their wanderings came to Earth, which, because it is at a primitive level of development, promises to be an easy source of blood and life force.

Rather than being the home of intelligent life, then, Earth is a relatively young colony, which the Galactic empire studiously avoids until it has reached the necessary level of development to be included in Galactic civilization. In order to keep an eye on things, a Galactic Observer–a Klugg, relatively inferior to the two Dreeghs–has been assigned to the solar system, and the Dreeghs need to eliminate him in order to continue using the Earth for their purposes. The Dreeghs take control of Leigh, discover the identity of the Galactic Observer, and send Leigh to the Observer's meteorite near Jupiter in order to pierce the defenses of the meteorite. He does so, and then Merla, the female Dreegh, takes him in order to suck out his blood and life force. To her surprise, Leigh sucks energy from her, rather than the other way around, and Leigh is revealed to be in reality a Great Galactic, with an IQ of 1200, who has disguised himself as Leigh in order to foil the Dreeghs' plot. Earth is saved. More significantly, the story represents an attempt by van Vogt to imagine and articulate what such an all-powerful, all-knowing creature would be like. In "Asylum" he makes a provocative gesture toward the transcendent.

"The Weapon Shop," published in the December 1942 issue of *Astounding Science-Fiction,* is set in the same fictional universe as "The Seesaw" and was later incorporated into *The Weapon Shops of Isher*. In this story van Vogt provides a more detailed description of the purpose and history of the weapon shops. Fara Clark is a typical motor repairman and loyal supporter of the Isher empire. When his business is ruined, he enters the weapon shop in his village in order to purchase a gun with which to kill himself. Instead of being sold a gun, however, he is taken to another location, where he is told that the bank and corporation that put him out of business are in fact secretly owned by the empress of Isher. Clark is recompensed for his losses, but more importantly, he is told about the weapon shops. He learns that the guns sold by the shops can be used only to defend their owners from the injustices of the empire, not for purposes of aggression. The guns, then, as the signs on the stores claim, give their owners the right to be free. Clark then returns home with the power to reestablish himself.

Although Campbell accepted and published "The Weapon Shop" with enthusiasm, his acceptance letter expressed reservations illustrating the singularity of van Vogt's storytelling. The Panshins quote Campbell's response: "'Weapon Shop' was, like much of your material, good without any detectable reason for being interesting. Technically, it doesn't have plot, it starts nowhere in particular, wanders about, and comes out in another completely indeterminate place. But, like a park path, it's a nice little walk." The problem, for Campbell and critics of van Vogt's work, is that in "The Weapon Shop" and other van Vogt stories, little actually happens, with the characters often jumping more or less randomly from one situation to another for no apparent reason. As the Panshins aptly describe it, "In a van Vogt story, things didn't seem to *happen* so much as they just *were*."

"The Weapon Shop" was followed by van Vogt's "The Search," published in the January 1943 issue of *Astounding Science-Fiction*. Ralph Drake, apparently a traveling salesman suffering from amnesia, undergoes a series of adventures before discovering a group of time travelers, called Possessors, who range through time in order to fix problems and guide humanity in the right direction. Drake discovers he is one of the Possessors, who are all marked by the reversed position of their internal organs, and is able to prevent another Possessor from destroying all the Possessors and their good works. The concept of a powerful force outside the flow of time with the ability to guide and protect humanity is one that echoed throughout the science fiction of the next few decades. Like *Slan,* "The Search" is a wish-fulfillment fantasy in which the unexceptional protagonist is revealed to be exceptional and a member of a hidden group who secretly controls things, a fantasy that can be seen as congruent with the mythology of science-fiction fandom and van Vogt's own self-perception.

Van Vogt's second novel, *The Weapon Makers,* was serialized in *Astounding Science-Fiction* from February to April 1943. Essentially a sequel to the stories that were later assembled as *The Weapon Shops of Isher,* the novel further develops the fictional universe introduced in "The Seesaw." Robert Hedrock is an agent of the weapon shops who has become a captain of the empress's guard and her lover. He is much more than that, however, being an immortal who has had many different identities through the millennia. Hedrock was both the first Isher emperor and the founder of the weapon shops, and at various times since he has been a leader of the weapon shops or husband of an Isher empress. Dan Neelan is a typical van Vogtian ordinary character, an asteroid miner investigating the fate of his scientist brother, who was involved in the invention of an infinity drive that would allow interstellar travel. Neelan becomes caught up in the intrigues of the empress. He eventually escapes and heads into space in search of his brother. He encounters spiderlike, immortal aliens who are intrigued by his devotion to his brother and set out to study him. The aliens are impressed by the self-sacrifice exhibited by Neelan and others, including Empress Innelda Isher. Because the aliens lack the ability to engage in self-sacrifice, they judge humanity to be their superior. As they conclude, "here is the race that shall rule the sevagram." Van Vogt's use of the word *sevagram* is indicative of his writing strategies: he uses it for effect, regardless of what it might mean. As John Clute writes in *The Encyclopedia of Science Fiction* (1993), in the placement of the word, "which seems to open universes to the reader's gaze,

Van Vogt, circa 1950

and in its resonant mysteriousness, for its precise meaning is unclear, this use of the word 'sevagram' may well stand as the best working demonstration in the whole of genre sf of how to impart a sense of wonder." Although *The Weapon Makers* did not receive as enthusiastic a response as *Slan,* it remains one of van Vogt's better novels. As Moskowitz observes, "the complexity of time and spatial lore that van Vogt embroidered into the story was staggering to the imagination," and this complexity compensates for weaknesses in the novel. *The Weapon Makers* was published in book form in 1947.

Van Vogt's next novel, *The Book of Ptath,* was his only fantasy novel. It was published in the October 1943 issue of *Unknown Worlds,* as Campbell's fantasy magazine was now named. Ptath is a god who has temporarily given up his godhood and taken on the personae of various humans in order to rediscover humanity. Like many of van Vogt's heroes he struggles to rediscover his real identity. He wakes as an amnesiac and gradually comes to an awareness of his godhood. In the process of doing so he battles an evil goddess, Ineznia, and saves Earth. In general, van Vogt's few fantasy stories are less successful than his science-fiction stories; they are little more than rewrites of his science fiction in fantasy dress. *The Book of Ptath* is no exception. Although it is fast-paced and exciting, the novel is often confusing and awkward, without the transcendent rewards of van Vogt's best science fiction. *The Book of Ptath* was republished as a book in 1947.

Van Vogt's "Far Centaurus," published in the January 1944 issue of *Astounding Science-Fiction,* was another well-received story. A spaceship sets out on a five-hundred-year voyage to another star system, with the crew in suspended animation. When the ship arrives, the crew discovers that it is already inhabited by humans; other, later spaceships were able to make the journey in much shorter time as a result of technological advances. Their voyage rendered pointless, the crew members dive into a star that sends them back to the time period in which the journey began. An intriguing comment on the concept of space exploration employing suspended animation, "Far Centaurus" nevertheless suffers from a careless consideration of time travel, as Colin Wilson points out in an essay in *Science Fiction Writers: Critical Studies of the Major Authors from the Early Nineteenth Century to the Present Day* (1982).

In 1944 the van Vogts left Canada and moved to Los Angeles, where they spent the rest of their lives, eventually becoming American citizens. Although in some respects van Vogt's greatest successes still lay ahead of him (he only started publishing in book form after arriving in Los Angeles, for example), and he continued to publish new work until the mid 1980s, it is probably safe to say that his reputation rests largely on the work that he produced from 1938 to 1944, the period when he was writing science fiction in Canada. As Ketterer notes, the "approximately thirty-four SF stories that he wrote while in Canada formed the bulk of eleven books published later." That period in van Vogt's writing marks one of the greatest achievements in Canadian science-fiction history, and if he had never written another word after leaving Canada, he would still be considered one of the greats of the era.

Although van Vogt's move to Los Angeles eventually had significant, unexpected consequences for his life and career, at first he continued to write and publish without interruption. His next novel, *The World of Ā,* serialized in *Astounding Science-Fiction* from August to October 1945, was his most controversial, eliciting both great enthusiasm and total confusion in readers. While still in Canada, van Vogt had become intrigued by the Polish thinker Alfred Korzybski's theory of general semantics. In *Science and Sanity: An Introduction to Non-Aristotelian Systems and General Semantics* (1933) Korzybski argued that the problems of humanity stemmed from an adherence to Aristotelian logic, with its reliance on binary oppositions (good/bad, either/or, and so forth), and that humanity needed to develop a more complex, non-Aristotelian (Ā, or null-A) logic. Doing so, he argued, would facilitate better communication among people and thus resolve many of the problems facing humanity. Korzybski's ideas had been circulating in science-fiction circles for a few years. Notably, van Vogt's editor, Campbell, had expressed an interest in them, and Heinlein had based a short novel, *If This Goes On–* (1940) on Korzybski's theories. Van Vogt joined the International Society for General Semantics and decided to write a novel dramatizing some of Korzybski's ideas.

The World of Ā is set in the year 2560 in an egalitarian society based on null-A thinking. The protagonist, Gilbert Gosseyn (pronounced "go sane"), arrives in the big city to be tested by the Games Machine, which will determine his future position in society, only to discover that everything he thought he knew about himself is false and that he has no idea who he really is. The novel presents Gosseyn's adventures as he moves through various selves and attempts to discover his identity. In typical van Vogt fashion, he turns out to be a clone of the immortal superman who originally established the null-A civilization. The convoluted plot, which is virtually impossible to summarize adequately, is quite confusing, even in comparison to van Vogt's other works, and the relationship of the action to Korzybski's ideas is not always clear. This confusion is compounded by the fact that the novel is, as Moskowitz notes, "carelessly and choppily written." *Astounding Science-Fiction* received several letters from readers complaining that the story made no sense. Damon Knight complained in a scathing 1945 article, revised and collected in his *In Search of Wonder: Essays on Modern Science Fiction* (1956), that the novel "is one of the worst allegedly-adult science fiction stories ever published. . . . *The World of Ā* abounds in contradictions, misleading clues and irrelevant action." Van Vogt must have taken such criticisms to heart, for he made substantial revisions and added more detailed explications when preparing the novel for book publication in 1948; unfortunately, in doing so he diluted the hectic pace of the serialized version. He also wrote a sequel, *The Pawns of Null-A*, published in 1956.

Still, for many other readers, *The World of Ā* was one of van Vogt's best works. Wilson says that the novel "is as original and exciting as anything he ever wrote" and "is among his best books because it combines physical and intellectual excitement with an indefinable sense of the presence of another dimension of meaning." The editors of *A Reader's Guide to Science Fiction* (1979) included *The World of Ā* in their basic science-fiction library (it was the only van Vogt novel selected for inclusion). The impact of the novel resulted in an increase in sales of Korzybski's book, as van Vogt's readers tried to make sense of the concept of null-A. Even now there are sites on the World Wide Web devoted to discussions of the relationship between general semantics and *The World of Ā*.

Around this time van Vogt started using Van as his first name socially. His recently widowed sister, Edna, joined the van Vogts in Los Angeles, and his wife began to go by her middle name, Mayne, in order to avoid confusion. In 1946 van Vogt and his wife were the guests of honor at the fourth World Science Fiction Convention. That same year *Slan* was republished; it was van Vogt's first book publication. Over the next decade and a half he reworked and republished much of his other work from *Astounding Science-Fiction* and *Unknown Worlds* in book form.

"A Son is Born," published in the May 1946 issue of *Astounding Science-Fiction,* was the first of a series of stories set in a future society based on the Roman Empire and clearly inspired by Robert Graves's historical novel *I, Claudius* (1934). In this series, scientists are the priests and the atom is their object of worship. Clane Linn, the protagonist, is another van Vogt mutant character with exceptional intelligence. "A Son is Born" and the following stories in the series were collected in 1957 as the fix-up *Empire of the Atom*.

In the latter half of the 1940s van Vogt's fiction began to appear less regularly in the pages of *Astounding Science-Fiction,* in part because he had begun publishing in other magazines, but also, perhaps, because more of his time was devoted to preparing his earlier material for book publication. Still, in 1947 readers of *Astounding Science-Fiction* voted van Vogt their favorite science-fiction writer, and in this period some of his best stories were published, including a new Rull story, "The Rull," that appeared in the May 1948 issue of the magazine. "The Rull" provides a more sympathetic and detailed portrait of the Rull instead of depicting them strictly as an external threat to humanity and other species. Barry Malzberg, in his introduction to the 1976 Pocket Books collection titled *The Best of A. E. van Vogt,* describes "The Rull" as van Vogt's best short story. "The Monster," published in the August 1948 issue of *Astounding Science-Fiction,* is described by Arthur Jean Coax in *DLB 8: Twentieth-Century American Science-Fiction Writers* (1981) as "quintessential van Vogt." It is an intensely written story about the arrival of an alien race on an Earth on which all human life has ended and their attempts to resurrect representative men from different eras. Four men are brought back to life, each more powerful than his predecessor; the fourth man brings humanity back to life, making everyone immortal. "Enchanted Village," published in the July 1950 issue of *Other Worlds,* is an evocative tale in

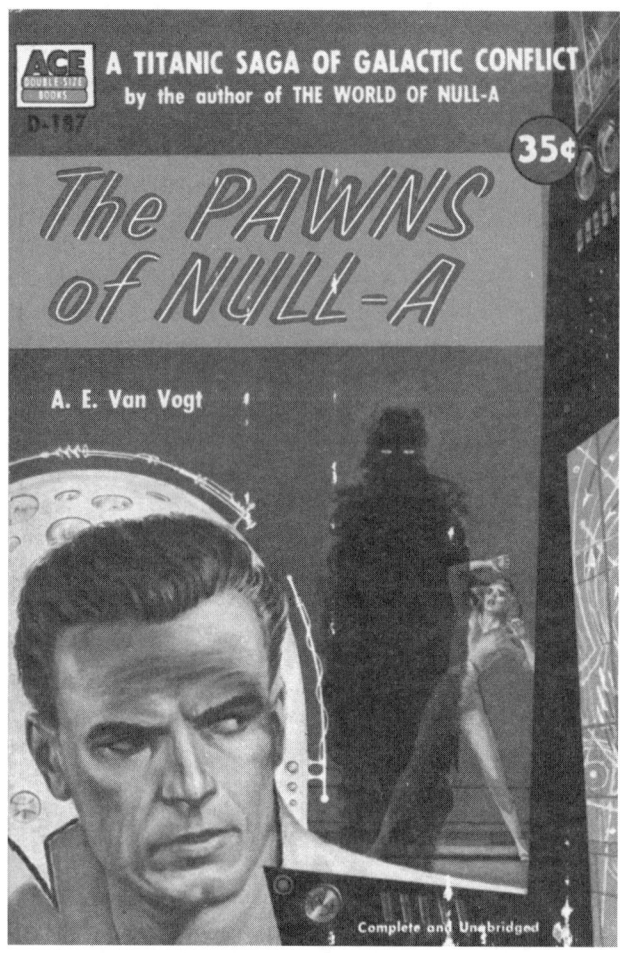

Cover for van Vogt's 1956 sequel to The World of Ā

which a space explorer stranded on Mars physically transforms himself into a Martian in order to survive.

The Voyage of the Space Beagle, published in 1950, is a fix-up novel in which van Vogt incorporated "Black Destroyer" and other early stories into a narrative about the voyages of a spaceship. In the novel van Vogt added a new character, Elliot Grosvenor, who is a Nexialist. The practitioners of Nexialism are psychologically trained to be able to synthesize vast amounts of knowledge, providing a vision of the whole rather than simply parts of reality. The use of Nexialism, as Clute suggests, is another example of van Vogt's continuing interest in pseudoscientific disciplines that promised to foster physical or mental superiority.

The use of Nexialism in *The Voyage of the Space Beagle* is indicative of van Vogt's increasing interest in and involvement with L. Ron Hubbard's theory of Dianetics. In an article in the May 1950 issue of *Astounding Science-Fiction,* Hubbard, a prolific pulp writer, had introduced this pseudopsychological self-help treatment, and there was a great deal of interest in the topic in science-fiction circles. Van Vogt was attracted to Dianetics because it promised a scientific, rather than a mystical, approach to achieving self-knowledge and fulfillment. Quickly, van Vogt was recruited by Hubbard to head up the Dianetics office in California. Van Vogt and his wife both became Dianetics auditors, those who facilitated the treatment, and van Vogt was involved with the practice for the rest of his life. He rejected Hubbard's later development of Dianetics into the Church of Scientology, however, as he could not accept its mysticism and religiosity.

Van Vogt's increasing involvement with Dianetics resulted in a drastic decline in his output as a writer. Although his fiction was not absent from bookstores in the 1950s, since he was publishing many fix-up novels and short-story collections drawn from earlier material, his work did not appear in science-fiction magazines, and he published little new fiction for more than a decade. The one exception was his novel *The Mind Cage* (1957), which van Vogt described as an effort to psychoanalyze himself and discover why he was attracted to the concept of supermen.

Van Vogt's next new work was his only non-science-fiction novel, *The Violent Man* (1962). In it he explored a concept he had been developing, which he called the theory of the Right Man. A Right Man is someone who cannot accept being wrong and will react with violence if his authority is questioned. Examples of Right Men include such figures as Adolf Hitler, Joseph Stalin, and Mao Tse-Tung. In *The Violent Man* van Vogt illustrates this theory through discussions between a captured American and the Communist Chinese instructor who is attempting to brainwash him. Van Vogt had expected that the novel would be a best-seller, but it failed to have the impact he had hoped for, and he never again wrote a book aimed at a general audience.

Van Vogt returned to science fiction with "The Expendables," a story about a duel between a spaceship and an alien civilization that was published in the September 1963 issue of *If.* He followed that work with more stories and novels, but he was never able to recapture the success and status he had achieved in the 1940s. *The Silkie,* published as a series of stories in *If* from 1964 to 1967 and as a complete novel in 1969, is an engaging reworking of the myth of the merman. *The Battle of Forever* (1971), often cited as the best novel of van Vogt's second period of writing, tells the story of Modyun, who has survived the extermination of humanity; he undergoes a series of adventures and eventually achieves his rightful superman status. Van Vogt's fiction of the 1970s and

1980s met with increasing indifference because his style and themes seemed increasingly outdated as science fiction developed in new directions. His last novel, *Null-A Three* (1985), was a second sequel to *The World of Ā.*

Van Vogt's wife, Mayne, died on 20 January 1975; he married Lydia Brayman, a linguist and court interpreter, on 6 October 1979. Essentially retired from writing after *Null-A Three,* he lived the rest of his life in Los Angeles. In his last years he suffered from Alzheimer's disease, and he died from pneumonia on 26 January 2000.

Van Vogt no longer has the central place in the science-fiction pantheon that he once did, but he has certainly made a unique and powerful contribution to the genre with his powerful and dreamlike imaginings of transcendence and supermen. Although works by later writers have shown his influence, no one has ever written quite like van Vogt, and his voice remains unique. His achievements were recognized in 1980 with a Casper award for lifetime achievement from the Canadian Science Fiction and Fantasy Association. In 1996 he was named Grand Master, the highest honor given by the Science Fiction and Fantasy Writers of America; was given a special award for lifetime achievement at the World Science Fiction Convention; and was elected as one of the first four inductees into the Science Fiction and Fantasy Hall of Fame.

Ultimately, what was so powerful about van Vogt's fiction was its vision that humanity was and should be at the center of the universe. As he wrote in the postscript to his short-story collection *Destination: Universe!* (1952), his fiction "glorifies man and his future." Van Vogt, as Donald A. Wollheim writes in *The Universe Makers: Science Fiction Today* (1971), "has an instinctual belief in humanity, he believes in the invincibility of humanity, he refuses to accept boundaries of time and space." Van Vogt's readers have shared, and continue to share, this vision with him.

Interview:

Jeffrey Elliot, "Interview: A. E. van Vogt," *Science Fiction Review,* 23 (November 1977): 19–23.

References:

Boris Eizykman, *Science-fiction et capitalisme: critique de la position de désir de la science* (Paris: Mame, 1973), pp. 201–205;

Jeffrey M. Elliot, "A. E. van Vogt: A Writer with a Winning Formula," *Science Fiction Voices,* 2 (1979): 30–40;

Scott Ellis, "Surrational Dreams: A. E. van Vogt and Mennonite Science Fiction," *Prairie Fire,* 15 (Summer 1994): 204–219;

Damon Knight, "Cosmic Jerrybuilder: A. E. van Vogt," in his *In Search of Wonder: Essays on Modern Science Fiction* (Chicago: Advent, 1956), pp. 36–50;

Sam Moskowitz, *Seekers of Tomorrow: Masters of Modern Science Fiction* (Westport, Conn.: Hyperion, 1966), pp. 213–228;

Alexei and Cory Panshin, *The World Beyond the Hill: Science Fiction and the Quest for Transcendence* (Los Angeles: Tarcher, 1989), pp. 447–520, 582–587, 624–629;

Charles Platt, *Dream Makers: The Uncommon People Who Write Science Fiction* (New York: Berkley, 1980), pp. 133–144;

Colin Wilson, "A. E. van Vogt," in *Science Fiction Writers: Critical Studies of the Major Authors from the Early Nineteenth Century to the Present Day,* edited by E. F. Bleiler (New York: Scribners, 1982), pp. 209–217;

Donald A. Wollheim, *The Universe Makers: Science Fiction Today* (New York: Harper & Row, 1971), pp. 45–49.

Élisabeth Vonarburg

(5 August 1947 –)

Sylvie Bérard

BOOKS: *L'Oeil de la nuit* (Longueuil, Quebec: Le Préambule, 1980);

Le Silence de la cité (Paris: Denoël, 1981); translated by Jane Brierley as *The Silent City* (Victoria, British Columbia: Press Porcépic, 1988; London: Women's Press, 1990; New York: Bantam, 1992); revised edition (Beauport, Quebec: Alire, 1998);

Janus (Paris: Denoël, 1984);

Comment écrire des histoires: Guide de l'explorateur (Beloeil, Quebec: La Lignée, 1986);

Histoire de la princesse et du dragon (Montreal: Québec/Amérique, 1990);

Ailleurs et au Japon (Montreal: Québec/Amérique, 1991);

Chroniques du Pays des Mères (Montreal: Québec/Amérique, 1992); translated by Brierley as *In the Mother's Land* (New York: Bantam, 1992); republished as *The Maerlande Chronicles* (Victoria, British Columbia: Beach Holme, 1992; revised edition, Beauport, Quebec: Alire, 1999);

Les Contes de la Chatte Rouge (Montreal: Québec/Amérique, 1993);

Les Voyageurs malgré eux (Montreal: Québec/Amérique, 1994); translated by Brierley as *Reluctant Voyagers* (Edmonton, Alberta: Tesseract Books, 1995; New York: Bantam, 1995);

Contes de Tyranaël (Montreal: Québec/Amérique, 1994);

Chanson pour une sirène, by Vonarburg and Yves Meynard (Hull, Quebec: Vents d'Ouest, 1995);

Les Rêves de la Mer: Tyranaël 1 (Beauport, Quebec: Alire, 1996);

Le Jeu de la Perfection: Tyranaël 2 (Beauport, Quebec: Alire, 1996);

Mon frère l'ombre: Tyranaël 3 (Beauport, Quebec: Alire, 1997);

L'Autre Rivage: Tyranaël 4 (Beauport, Quebec: Alire, 1997);

La Mer allée avec le soleil: Tyranaël 5 (Beauport, Quebec: Alire, 1997);

Le Lever du récit: Poésie (Montreal: Les Herbes rouges, 1999);

Élisabeth Vonarburg (courtesy of the author)

La Maison au bord de la mer (Beauport, Quebec: Alire, 2000);

Slow Engines of Time, translated by Vonarburg and others (Edmonton, Alberta: Tesseract Books, 2000).

TRANSLATIONS: Tanith Lee, *La Tombe de naissance* (Verviers, France: Marabout SF, 1976);

Chelsea Quinn Yarbro, *Fausse Aurore,* translated as Catherine Vonarburg (Paris: Denoël, 1979);

James Tiptree Jr., *Par-delà les murs du monde* (Paris: Denoël, 1979);

Jayge Carr, *L'Abîme de Léviathan* (Paris: Albin-Michel, 1982);

Lee, *Le Jour, la nuit* (Paris: Albin-Michel, 1982);

Jack Chalker, *Le Diable vous emportera* (Paris: Albin-Michel, 1983);

R. A. Lafferty, *Le Livre d'or de Lafferty* (Paris: Presses Pocket, 1984);

Jack Williamson, *Le Livre d'or de Jack Williamson* (Paris: Presses Pocket, 1988);

Anne McCaffrey, *La Dame de la tour: Le Livre d'or d'Anne McCaffrey*, edited and translated by Vonarburg (Paris: Presses Pocket, 1993);

Marion Zimmer Bradley, *Le Livre d'or de Marion Zimmer Bradley* (Paris: Presses Pocket, 1994);

Guy Gavriel Kay, *La Tapisserie de Fionavar: Tome I: L'Arbre de l'été* (Montreal: Québec/Amérique, 1994);

Gerald Nicosia, *Memory Babe, une biographie critique de Jack Kerouac* (Montreal: Québec/Amérique, 1994);

Kay, *La Tapisserie de Fionavar: Tome II: Le Feu vagabond* (Montreal: Québec/Amérique, 1995);

Kay, *La Tapisserie de Fionavar: Tome III: La Route obscure* (Montreal: Québec/Amérique, 1995);

Bradley, *La Chute d'Atlantis* (Paris: Presses Pocket, 1996);

Bradley and Holly Isle, *En Glenravenne* (Brussels: Lefrancq, 1998);

Kay, *Les Lions d'Al-Rassan* (Quebec: Alire, 1999);

Kay, *La Mosaïque de Sarance* (Paris: Buchet/Chastel, 2001).

OTHER: "Marée haute," *Requiem*, 19 (January 1978): 8–11; translated by Maxim Jakubowski as "High Tide," in *Twenty Houses of the Zodiac*, edited by Jakubowski (London: New English Library, 1979); republished as "Marée haute," in *Les Vingt Maisons du Zodiaque* (Paris: Denoël, 1979), pp. 75–85;

"Voyage au bout de la nuit ordinaire," in *Traces* (Jonquière, Quebec: Editions Sagamie/Québec, 1984), pp. 159–168;

"La Maison au bord de la mer," in *Dix Nouvelles de science-fiction québécoise*, edited by André Carpentier (Montreal: Les Quinze, 1985), pp. 213–237; translated as "Home by the Sea," in *Tesseracts*, edited by Judith Merril (Victoria, British Columbia: Press Porcépic, 1985), pp. 4–20; republished in *Northern Stars*, edited by David G. Hartwell and Glenn Grant (New York: Tor Books, 1994), pp. 68–81;

"Le Jeu des coquilles de nautilus," in *Aurores Boréales II*, edited by Daniel Sernine (Longueuil, Quebec: Le Préambule, 1986), pp. 253–290; translated as "Chambered Nautilus," in *Tesseracts⁴*, edited by Lorna Toolis and Michael Skeet (Victoria, British Columbia: Beach Holme, 1992), pp. 227–262;

"Mané, Thékel, Pharès," as Sabine Verreault, in *Espaces imaginaires IV* (Trois-Rivières, Quebec: Les Imaginoïdes, 1986), pp. 105–168;

"Les Femmes et la science-fiction," in *Les Oeuvres de création et le français au Québec: Tome III* (Québec: Editeur officiel, 1986), pp. 185–189;

"Gehenna," translation of "Géhenne," in *Per Ardua Ad Astra 2* (Toronto: Ad Astra, 1987): 9–27;

"Cold Bridge," translation of "Le pont du froid," in *Invisible Fiction: Contemporary Stories from Québec* (Toronto: Anansi, 1987): 267–297;

"In the Pit," translation of "Dans la fosse," in *Tesseracts²*, edited by Phyllis Gotlieb and Douglas Barbour (Victoria, British Columbia: Press Porcépic, 1987), pp. 25–43;

"Mourir, un peu," as Sabine Verreault and Élisabeth Vonarburg, in *Sous des soleils étrangers* (Laval, Quebec: Ianus, 1989), pp. 91–115;

"La machine lente du temps," in *La Frontière éclatée* (Paris: Le Livre de Poche, 1989), pp. 374–442;

Denys Chabot, *L'Eldorado dans les glaces*, introduction by Vonarburg (Montreal: HMH, 1989), pp. 7–14;

"Cogito," translation, in *Tesseracts³*, edited by Candas Jane Dorsey and Gerry Truscott (Victoria, British Columbia: Press Porcépic, 1991), pp. 62–82;

"Le Premier Accroc ne compte pas," in *La Première Fois*, edited by Charles Montpetit (Montreal: Québec/Amérique, 1991), pp. 59–80;

"La Littérature et la vie au collégial," in *La Littérature et la vie au collégial* (Montreal: Modulo, 1991), pp. 102–106;

"La Science-fiction et le fantastique au collégial," in *Actes du Colloque: La Littérature et la vie au collégial* (Jonquière, Quebec: Collège de Jonquière, 1991), pp. 173–175;

"Mettre la main à la pâte: Les Ateliers d'écriture," in *Actes du Colloque: La Littérature et la vie au collégial* (Jonquière, Quebec: Collège de Jonquière, 1991), pp. 203–208;

"The Reproduction of the Body in Space," in *State of the Fantastic, Selected Essays from the Eleventh Conference on the Fantastic in the Arts* (Westport, Conn.: Greenwood Press, 1992), pp. 59–72; revised as "La Reproduction du corps dans l'espace ou naissance et renaissance dans l'espace," in *Les Ailleurs imaginaires: Les rapports entre le fantastique et la science-fiction* (Quebec: Nuit blanche éditeur, 1993), pp. 205–229;

"Un bruit de pluie," in *1991: L'Année de la science-fiction et du fantastique québécois*, edited by Claude Janelle (Montreal: Logiques/Le Passeur, 1993), pp. 251–281;

"L'Hiver, c'est mon pays," in *Un lac, un fjord* (Chicoutimi, Quebec: Éditions JCL, 1994), pp. 93–95;

"La Louïne," in *Le Bal des ombres* (Montreal: Québec/Amérique Jeunesse, 1994), pp. 93-129;

Philip K. Dick, *Omnibus: Tome III*, preface by Vonarburg and others (Paris: Presses de la Cité, 1994), pp. 1353-1357;

"Le Langage de la nuit," in *La Nuit* (Quebec/Montreal: Musée de la Culture et de la Civilisation/XYZ éditeur, 1995), pp. 109-123;

"Le Pays où l'on arrive toujours," in *Un lac, un fjord 2: Lieux mythiques* (Chicoutimi, Quebec: Editions JCL, 1995), pp. 7-13;

"Les Femmes et la science-fiction," in *Visions d'autres monde: La Littérature fantastique et de science-fiction canadienne*, compiled by Andrea Paradis (Montreal: Editions RD, 1995), pp. 194-205; translated as "Women and Science Fiction," in *Out of this World: Canadian Science Fiction and Fantasy*, compiled by Paradis (Kingston, Ontario: Quarry Press, 1995), pp. 177-187;

Tesseracts⁹, edited by Vonarburg and Jane Brierley (Edmonton, Alberta: Tesseract Books, 1996);

"Vous êtes ICI," in *Un lac, un fjord 3: La Ville* (Chicoutimi, Quebec: Editions JCL, 1996), pp. 129-133;

"*La Plaie*, un roman flamboyant de Nathalie Henneberg," in *Le Feu aux Etoiles*, edited by Gilles Dumay (Le Plessis-Brion: Destination Crépuscule/La SF Entreprise, 1996), pp. 28-42;

"La Révélation," by Vonarburg and Paul Roux, in *Images d'ailleurs* (Laval: Editions Mille Iles, 1996), pp. 7-24;

"Le Début du cercle," in *Genèses* (Paris: J'ai Lu, 1996), pp. 15-98;

"The Sleeper in the Crystal," translation by Howard Scott of "Le Dormeur dans le cristal," as Sabine Verreault, in *Tesseracts⁶*, edited by Robert J. Sawyer and Carolyn Clink (Edmonton, Alberta: Tesseract Books, 1997), pp. 243-254;

"Le Musée de l'impermanence," in *Effet de lieu* (Granby, Quebec: 3e Impérial, 1998), pp. 2-21;

"Celles qui vivent au-dessus des nuages," in *SF98: Les Meilleurs Récits de l'année* (Morets/Loing-Le-Plessis-Brion: Bifrost/Etoiles vives, 1998), pp. 201-217.

SELECTED PERIODICAL PUBLICATIONS—UNCOLLECTED:

POETRY

"Poèmes," *Solaris*, 102 (Summer 1992): 5, 72, 75, 77;

Poems, *Estuaire*, 74 (Fall 1994): 55-60.

FICTION

"Paradise Glossed," by Vonarburg and Jean-Joël Vonarburg, *Requiem*, 13 (December 1976-January 1977): 8;

"La Femme à rebours," by Vonarburg and Jean-Joël Vonarburg, *Requiem*, 14 (February-March 1977): 10;

"Conte de pierre haute," by Vonarburg and Jean-Joël Vonarburg, *Requiem*, 20 (March 1978): 14;

"L'Or, l'encens et la myrrhe," *La Nouvelle Barre du jour: Science-fiction*, 79-80 (June 1979): 119-131;

"Retour au Pays des Mères," *Pour ta belle gueule d'ahuri*, 6 (1983): 10-14;

"Oneïros," *imagine . . .*, 21 (April 1984): 97-115;

"Retour sur Colonie," by Vonarburg and Joël Champetier, *Solaris*, 75 (September-October 1987): 6-13;

"Transhumance," *Arcade: Au-delà du réel*, 18 (October 1989): 21-24;

"Pupa," *XYZ: La Revue de la nouvelle: Poupées*, 20 (November 1989): 51-55;

"Ici, des Tigres," *Le Sabord: Métamorphoses*, 25 (Spring-Summer 1990): 16;

"La Mer allée . . . ," *Solaris*, 94 (Fall 1990): 7-14;

"Suspends ton vol," *Solaris*, 99 (Winter 1991-1992): 21-26;

"L'Aile," *Temps Tôt*, 9 (1991): 52-53;

"Initiatiques," *Liberté*, 34 (August 1992): 4-14;

"The Knot," translation of "Le Nœud," *Amazing Stories*, 67 (March 1993): 9-13;

"Bande Ohne Ende," English translation, *Tomorrow Speculative Fiction*, 2 (June 1994);

"Paguyn and Kithulai," *Prairie Fire*, 15 (Summer 1994): 96-104; republished as "Povesta lui Paguyn si a lui Kitulai," in *Helion*, 2 (August 1995): 43-51;

"Les Poligloti," *Le Progrès du Saguenay/Lac St-Jean: Cahier littéraire* (2 April 1995): 8; translated as "The Poli-Gloti," *Communiqué* (1996);

"Amber Rain," translation of "Celles qui vivent au-dessus des nuages," in *Tomorrow Speculative Fiction*, 3 (April 1995): 24-30;

"L'Ombre de l'arbre," *Stop*, 143 (July-August-September 1995): 39-50;

"Janus," English translation, *Tomorrow Speculative Fiction*, 3 (December 1995): 42-56;

"R.V.," *Le Sabord*, 43 (Spring-Summer 1996): 10.

NONFICTION

"La Science-fiction au Québec?" *Requiem*, 15 (April-May 1977): 12-13;

"Les Femmes et la SF," *Requiem*, 17 (November 1977): 10-15;

"Les Créateurs d'univers," *Requiem*, 18 (December 1977): 12-14;

"La Science-fiction, pédagogie de l'avenir," *Réseau*, 6 (1977);

"Réflexions sur la SF et l'écriture," *Requiem*, 20 (March 1978): 22-27; translated in *Astralia Speculative Fiction* (1980);

"La Nourriture du futur," *Réseau*, 7 (1978);

"*L'Heroic Fantasy*," *Requiem*, 25 (November 1979): 18-21; 27 (January–February 1980): 8-12; *Solaris*, 28 (March–April 1980): 11-14;

"Science Fiction in Québec, A Survey," by Vonarburg and Norbert Spehner, *Science Fiction Studies*, 7 (March 1980): 191-199;

"Ecrire (de la SF)," 10 parts, *Solaris*, 32-43 (November/December 1980–December 1984/January 1985); translated in *Quasar* (December 1984–January 1985);

"Un atelier d'écriture sur la science-fiction," in *Québec français: Spécial science-fiction*, 42 (May 1981): 82-83;

"Automatisation et désautomatisation dans les machines conjecturales ou 'Jusqu'où peut-on aller ailleurs?'," *Protée*, 10 (Spring 1982): 59-68;

"L'Imaginaire au pouvoir," *Réseau*, 14 (1982);

"Science-fiction, fantastique, création et enseignement," *Arcade: Actes du colloque Création et enseignement*, 4-5 (September 1983): 57-63;

"La Science-fiction ou le mythes modernes," *Critère: Le Nouveau Paysage mythique*, 36 (Fall 1983): 57-64;

"La Fantasy: en guise d'introduction," *Solaris*, 51 (January–February 1984): 16-18;

"Daniel Sernine entre deux mondes," *imagine . . . : Actes du Congrès Boréal V*, 22 (May 1984): 53-68;

"Ludovic sur le divan, essai d'approche psychocritique du roman de Daniel Sernine," *Solaris*, 54 (July 1984): 25-27;

"Voyage au pays de Sernine, suite et fin provisoire," *Solaris*, 57 (September–October 1984): 13-15;

"SF: savoir-fiction," *Protée*, 13 (Spring 1985): 113-120;

"Notes sur l'oeuvre d'Esther Rochon," *Solaris*, 63 (September–October 1985): 19-23;

"Les Critères de choix littéraires," *Solaris*, 70 (November–December 1986): 15-20;

"La SF québécoise," *Proxima Spécial*, 1, (1986): 55-69;

"Instantané de la SF québécoise," *Cahiers pour la littérature populaire*, 8-9 (1987): 85-97;

"La Fantaisie ou le retour aux sources," *Europe: "Le Fantastique américain,"* 707 (March 1988): 105-113;

"De l'U.S.A.ge de motifs SF en littérature non-SF ou Pas assez c'est déjà trop," *Solaris*, 86 (September 1989): 33-36;

"Des sexes, de la parole, des noms et du pouvoir, des colloques universitaires, de la mercantilisation, de la rigueur morale et de la fine pointe du progrès, ou: Quelques réflexions vaseuses, émotives, subjectives, confuses et pour tout dire bien féminines sur le colloque 1991 de l'International Conference on the Fantastic in the Arts, ou: Linéaires et non linéaires, et le compte à rebours continue," *Solaris*, 98 (Fall 1991): 38-43;

"Le Rapport au réel dans la SF, la littérature générale et la poésie," *Solaris*, 102 (Summer 1992): 59-66;

"So Many Children," *Aloud*, 2 (October 1992);

"Littérature au carré, littérature au cube: la SF," as Isabel Gavra-Bourthes, *Nous les Martiens*, 22 (1992);

"So You Want to be a Science Fiction Writer?" *New York Review of Science-Fiction*, 57 (May 1993): 1, 3-5;

"Retour au *Matin des magiciens* de Louis Pauwels et Jacques Bergier," *Solaris*, 109 (Spring 1994): 53-55;

"La Science-fiction et les héroïnes de la modernité," *Philosophiques: Actes du Colloque: Les femmes et la société nouvelle*, 21 (Fall 1994): 453-457;

"Suzy McKee Charnas," *Solaris*, 113 (Spring 1995): 24-33.

Writer, translator, essayist, editor, and critic, Élisabeth Vonarburg is a key figure in the science-fiction field in Quebec, and one of the most acclaimed science-fiction authors in Canada. She has published more than fifteen books, several essays and reviews, and many short stories, for which she has received multiple awards and invitations to science-fiction conventions. Many of her texts have been translated in several languages and distributed in the United States and England as well as in distant countries such as Italy, Romania, and Japan. Joan Gordon's appreciation of *Le Silence de la cité* (1981; translated as *The Silent City*, 1988) and *Chroniques du Pays des Mères* (1992; translated as *In the Mother's Land*, 1992) in a review in the January 1994 issue of *The New York Review of Science Fiction* may apply to every one of Vonarburg's writings: all "are significant contributions to the body of feminist sf, making equal partners of politics, style, and storytelling."

Vonarburg was born Élisabeth Ferron-Wehrlin-Morché on 5 August 1947 in a hospital in the sixteenth *arrondissement* of Paris. Her mother, Jeanne Morché, had been born in Phnom Penh in 1913. After her divorce from her first husband Morché had traveled in the French colonies, obtained her degree, and then worked as a head pharmacist for the occupational armies in Germany in the early 1940s. At the time Élisabeth was born, Morché was running her own pharmacy in Blanc-Mesnil, in the Parisian suburb. René Ferron-Wehrlin, Élisabeth's father, was born in 1897. He had been enrolled in the French army as a professional soldier and became a colonel in the Engineers Corps; in the 1930s he had worked on the Maginot Line. He had also been married previously and already had three daughters and a son. He had met Morché while he was working in Indochina. The Ferron-Wehrlins lived in greater Paris until 1954 and then moved to Sergines, a small town in the Yonne department. The young Élisabeth attended the municipal school there until entering the Lycée classique de jeunes filles and later, the Lycée Mallarmé in the city of Sens.

Cover for Vonarburg's second novel (1981), translated as The Silent City *in 1988, about a mutant girl who learns to defy a male authority figure*

Vonarburg had her first contact with fantasy and science fiction at the age of sixteen when she read *Le Matin des magiciens* by Louis Pauwels and Jacques Bergier (1960; translated as *The Dawn of Magic*, 1974). Long before this experience, however, she had been an avid reader of comic books such as the French monthly *Spirou*, with its outlandish characters. As she often says of herself, she was "born to life in 1947 (France), to reading in 1952 (myths, fairy tales, comics, adventure), to writing in 1958 (poetry) and to science-fiction in 1964 (at last!)." Upon registering at the Université de Dijon, Vonarburg chose to study in a language and literature program. In 1969 she received her B.A., and she then began to amalgamate her personal interests and her scholarly work by submitting an M.A. thesis on the topic of "Fantastique et science-fiction: Évolution de quelques thèmes littéraires classiques dans les littératures conjecturales" (Science Fiction and the Fantastic: The Evolution of a Few Classical Literary Themes in Conjectural Literatures).

On 15 December 1969 she married Swiss-born Jean-Joël Vonarburg. This event was of great importance in her life, not only because he remained her literary accomplice until 1982 but also because she inherited a new home base and a nom de plume that remained with her after their official divorce in 1990. In 1972, with a Certificat d'aptitude professionnelle à l'enseignement secondaire and an Agrégation de lettres modernes in hand, she was prepared to become a lycée teacher of French. Nevertheless, in 1973 her husband was assigned to Chicoutimi, Quebec, for his obligatory military service; and she has lived there ever since. She has written about her northern experience and about her ability to create a home for herself wherever she lives, so long as she lives in French far away from the cities. These texts were published in the first three annual books of *Un lac, un fjord* (A Lake, A Fjord, 1994–1996), which was produced by a local publisher. She became a Canadian citizen in 1976, but kept her French and Swiss citizenships.

Soon after arriving in her new hometown, Vonarburg was hired as a part-time teacher in the department of arts and literature at the Université du Québec à Chicoutimi. She later taught at the Cégep (college of general and vocational education) of Chicoutimi (1977), at the Université du Québec à Rimouski (1983), and at the Université Laval in Sainte-Foy, Quebec (1990). She taught various courses, including seminars on fantastic literatures, science fiction, and creative writing. She took part in various symposia on education and published some essays on the teaching of literature and science fiction, beginning with "La Science-fiction, pédagogie de l'avenir" (Science Fiction: Educational Method for the Future), published in *Réseau* in 1978.

Once in Chicoutimi, Vonarburg also began to pursue a semiprofessional career as a singer. She had been singing and composing her own songs ever since she was a teenager, and her parents had given her a Spanish guitar. After meeting her husband she began to work more seriously on her songwriting. She took part in some festivals in the late 1970s and sang in nightclubs and on the radio (on Radio-Canada). In 1978 she won the Grand Prix du Festival de la Chanson du Saguenay/Lac-Saint-Jean.

As early as 1974, while teaching part-time, Vonarburg embarked on a career as a critic and essayist for the science-fiction magazine *Requiem*–now known as *Solaris*–for which she became literary editor in 1979. She organized and chaired the first Congrès québécois sur la science-fiction et le fantastique (Quebec Conference on Science Fiction and the Fantastic), known as

Boréal I, which was held in July 1979 at the Université du Québec à Chicoutimi. Though she had been writing for more than ten years, her first science-fiction short story was not published until 1976. She started to write in cooperation with her husband, and together they published short-short stories in *Requiem:* "Paradise Glossed" (December 1976–January 1977); "La femme à rebours" (February–March 1977); and "Conte de pierre haute" (March 1978). Vonarburg's first solo short story, "Marée haute," published in the January 1978 issue of *Requiem,* was her first significant success. In 1979 it became her first fiction piece to be translated, under the title of "High Tide," for publication in Maxim Jakubowski's international anthology *Twenty Houses of the Zodiac.* It was also published in its original version in the French edition of the same anthology (*Les Vingt Maisons du Zodiaque,* 1979), and was translated into German, Swedish, and Japanese as well.

"Marée haute" seems to be the first published text linked to the story Vonarburg already had in mind (and in her notebooks) and that she developed on a larger scale in her *Tyranaël* books nearly twenty years later. The main character of "Marée haute" is the young Aärne, who does not approve of the way his people, the Mathaü, invade a planet and transform it so it becomes a mirror of their home world. Despite the prohibition of his elders, Aärne sets off to explore the new world to which he has been brought. He studies its wildlife and plants and encounters the half-bird, half-fly "olfits." One night, these strange creatures communicate with him and warn him of imminent danger. The Mathaü will not listen to him, so he escapes alone. After his departure, a gigantic tidal wave destroys the colony. "Marée haute" presents many of the major paradigms Vonarburg developed in her subsequent publications: the Self and the alien, nature and culture, the individual and the collective, the familiar and the Great Unknown.

In 1976 Vonarburg also began working as a translator. Her first translation was Tanith Lee's *Birthgrave* (1975; translated as *La tombe de naissance,* 1976). She kept on avidly reading both French- and English-language science fiction. James Tiptree Jr. (pseudonym of Alice B. Sheldon), one of the best female science-fiction writers of the 1970s, was among her favorite authors, and Vonarburg particularly admired Tiptree's ability to maintain the secret of her female identity. Consequently, in 1979 she asked Denoël editor Élisabeth Gille to let her translate Tiptree's 1978 novel *Up the Walls of the World.* The same year, Vonarburg translated Chelsea Quinn Yarbro's *False Dawn* (1978). Working as a part-time translator since then, she has had the opportunity to translate American and Canadian authors such as Anne McCaffrey, Marion Zimmer Bradley, and Guy Gavriel Kay for various French and Québécois publishers.

L'Oeil de la nuit, published in Longueuil, Quebec in 1980, was Vonarburg's first book. It was composed of six short stories that may be considered as six specific points of entry into the author's universes. "L'Oeil de la nuit" won the Prix Dagon in 1978. This story of a *rêveur* (dreamer) who can foresee the tragic destiny of strange people and see them appearing later in his own reality is incorporated into the last volume of the *Tyranaël* series. "Le Pont du froid" (published as "Cold Bridge" in *Invisible Fiction: Contemporary Stories from Québec,* 1987) and "Le Nœud" (translated as "The Knot" in the March 1993 issue of *Amazing Stories*) depict the recurring "Pont" (Bridge), a time/space travel device used by Vonarburg in subsequent stories and ultimately explained in the novel *Les Voyageurs malgré eux* (1994; translated as *Reluctant Voyagers,* 1995). "Janus," later translated and republished in *Tomorrow Speculative Fiction* (December 1995) throws some light on the matter of the "biosculpture"–a topos from which the author extrapolates in other work, notably for the *ommachs* (androids built with organic material) of *Le Silence de la cité.* "Géhenne" was translated as "Gehenna" and published in *Per Ardua Ad Astra 2* (1987); with its snowy landscapes and immense park evocative of the huge Parc des Laurentides that stretches between the Saguenay region and southern Quebec, this story is apparently connected to the author's adopted country. The story of a heterosexual couple who meets an amnesiac young woman, it can also be associated with other Vonarburg stories based on triangular familial and/or amorous relationships. While the last short story in *L'Oeil de la nuit,* "Éon," may not be explicitly related to the author's cosmogony, it still reflects her preoccupation with gender, sex, and identity. Throughout her work these issues are linked to her feminist commitment, for all her fictions deal with a revision of generally accepted ideas.

Regardless of the differences between individual stories, *L'Oeil de la nuit* deals with recurring themes, including the relation between history and actual time. All the characters have to live with a ponderous past and identities that they either recall vividly or have forgotten after suffering some form of cruel treatment and must recover in some way. Although its genre is science fiction and not fantasy, Vonarburg's fiction concentrates more on biological and humanistic issues than on hard science. With *L'Oeil de la nuit,* which won the 1981 Prix de la Centrale des bibliothèques de prêt du Saguenay/Lac-Saint-Jean (Saguenay/Lac-Saint-Jean Central Library Award), Vonarburg imprinted her mark on a burgeoning contemporary science-fiction movement in Quebec and set the tone for her whole fictional world.

Cover for Vonarburg's 1986 guide to creative writing

From July 1980 to June 1981 Vonarburg worked on *Le Silence de la cité,* released in 1981 by the French publisher Denoël. This novel about sexual identity and father(ish)-daughter(ish) relationships combines various science-fictional and utopian themes such as the postcataclysmic world, the underground city, androids, Amazons, and mutants. It features Elisa, a mutant who lives in a bunker as big as a city. She has the ability to shift her physical identity, but has been conditioned to modify her appearance only when she is ordered to do so by a masculine figure who has authority over her. Elisa gradually learns to exert her free will. She eventually tries to preserve the memory of her civilization but does not attempt to play god and save the world as her acting father had tried to do.

The difference between Québécois and French press runs is significant: three thousand copies for the Quebec-published *L'Oeil de la nuit,* as compared to twelve thousand for *Le Silence de la cité.* Moreover, six thousand additional copies of the latter were reprinted. The book was well received and reviewed in newspapers and periodicals of various importance, such as *Le Lac St-Jean, Le Soleil,* and *Nuit blanche* (Quebec); *Fiction* (France); and *La Liberté* (Switzerland). It also won various science-fiction awards, including the Grand Prix de la Science-fiction française for Best Novel; the Prix Rosny Aîné for Best Novel; and the Prix Boréal. It was translated into English by Jane Brierley; Vonarburg said in an interview for the September 1991 issue of *Locus* that "I like the voice of my translator, Jane Brierley. What the American reader will get is some kind of third personality made up of Jane and I." The translation was published as *The Silent City* in Canada (1988), Great Britain (1990), and the United States (1992); in 1998 the novel was also published in German translation. The English version was reviewed as extensively as the original one, in newspapers such the *Toronto Star* (4 May 1989) and in science-fiction magazines such as *Foundation* (Spring 1991) and *Asimov's Science Fiction* (Mid December 1992). *The Silent City* was short-listed for the 1989 Casper (later known as Aurora) Awards, for best English-language novel.

For the next few years Vonarburg published only a small number of short stories in magazines. In 1982 she edited the Spring special issue of *Protée* on *Science-fiction et fantastique,* in which she also published an article: "Automatisation et désautomatisation dans les machines conjecturales ou 'Jusqu'où peut-on aller ailleurs?'"(Automation and De-Automation in Conjectural Machines, or, "How Far Can We Go Elsewhere?"). The same year she organized and chaired the Troisième congrès international francophone sur la SF et le fantastique/Boréal et Cie (Third International Francophone Congress on SF and the Fantastic/Boréal and Company), the proceedings of which appeared in the Fall 1982 issue of *Protée.* As she relates in the January 1998 issue of *Sol Rising,* dedicated to Judith Merril, Vonarburg ingenuously invited Merril to the convention, "And she came. And we met, face to face. And that's it. Almost." This event was fundamental in the young writer's life, for Vonarburg has frequently said that Merril's fiction, and Merril herself, taught her that there could be female heroines.

Vonarburg and her husband split up while she was working on her second book, *Janus* (1984), comprising eight short stories completed between 1976 and 1982. As with Vonarburg's first novel, *Janus* was published in France by Denoël. Two of the short stories in the book, "Éon" and "Janus," were already part of *L'Oeil de la nuit.* This collection is more organic than the previous one: the stories are intrinsically linked to each other and share similar use of science-fiction strategies. Claude Janelle, in the 1984 edition of *L'Année de la science-fiction et du fantastique québécois,* asserts that "*Janus* permet de dégager une structure d'ensemble qui se met en place dans l'Oeuvre exigeante d'Élisabeth Vonarburg" (one can detect in *Janus* the development of a comprehensive structure in Élisabeth Vonarburg's complex work). The collection deals in an original and informed fashion with the common but manifold and ambivalent issues evoked by the title story.

The stories collected in this book also show how the author was gradually charting a territory, a universe that has multifarious ramifications in subsequent work. The characters, or rather the names of characters (Talitha, Egon), technological devices (the "Pont"), and fictive sites (Baïblanca) all serve to provide links between these short pieces of fiction and evoke elements from one tale to the next in a process that transcends the borders of a given collection or a singular short story. For example, the *métames* (protean creatures) motif, which is at the heart of the novel *Le Silence de la cité*, appears only in "Dans la fosse" and "Bande Ohne Ende." However, in each of these stories, the city name "Baïblanca" seems a constant, appearing also in short stories included in the "cycle du Pont" (Bridge cycle). Likewise, the short story "L'Oiseau de cendres" does not specifically feature mutants, but the "station Lagrange" (Lagrange Station), the place where they are conditioned, is mentioned. The author's mastery of thematic complexity, her lyricism, and her storytelling skills earned her the 1985 Saguenay/Lac-Saint-Jean Troph'Art en Littérature. The book was also a finalist for the 1985 Grand Prix de la SF et du Fantastique Québécois.

Vonarburg had become well known in science-fiction circles in Quebec as well as in the literary field. By the time of the 1984 publication of *Janus*, she had obtained several creative-writing grants from the Canada Council for the Arts and from Quebec's Ministry of Cultural Affairs. She had also led many creative workshops and served on several literary juries, as she has continued to do throughout her career. Despite this involvement, in a personal guide to creative writing she published in 1986 (reprinted in 1990 and 1995), *Comment écrire des histoires: Guide de l'explorateur* (How to Write Stories: the Explorer's Guide), Vonarburg claims that she has no authority to teach creative writing, only the will to share her experience. This acclaimed guide has two main parts: the first focuses on narrative structures and the second on narrative problems. Some writing exercises are proposed by the author in a section that separates the two. She concludes with an appendix in which she divulges that the short story "L'Oiseau de cendres," included in *Janus*, was initiated during a creative-writing workshop, and she describes her writing process and some of her creative strategies in relation to this text. The same year that this creative-writing guide was published, Vonarburg also worked for the *Chronique hebdomadaire sur les livres SF,* on Radio-Canada-CBJ, from January to May 1986.

While Vonarburg could be considered by this time a skillful and widely published author, she still encountered some obstacles, even within Québécois science-fiction circles. Her work had not been published often in the other Quebec science-fiction magazine, *imagine . . . ,* because its editor, Jean-Marc Gouanvic, felt that her stories were too "oniriques" (dreamlike). As a matter of fact, "Onéiros" was until then her only published work in the magazine, commissioned by artistic director Catherine Saouter Caya for its April 1984 special issue, for which Caya had asked authors to create a text inspired by a drawing. Vonarburg had previously tried several times to submit her short stories to *imagine . . . ,* but had always been told that they were unpublishable. She then conceived one of the most famous hoaxes in Quebec science-fiction history, submitting a story to Gouanvic as Sabine Verreault, purportedly a young, unpublished author. Gouanvic wasted no time in accepting "Le Dormeur dans le cristal" for the February 1986 issue. The reading committee of the magazine subsequently accepted two other texts from the same author, including "Mané, Tékel, Pharès," published in the anthology *Espaces imaginaires IV* (1986), in which Gouanvic speaks highly of the so-called obscure author, writing that "sa qualité majeure est un style d'une rare justesse" (her major quality is an uncommonly accurate style). Vonarburg eventually revealed her hoax in a private meeting with the editor and even published a short story, "Mourir, un peu" (in *Sous des soleils étrangers,* 1989), in collaboration with Sabine Verreault. In the preface to the first edition of this story she suggests that Élisabeth and Sabine are the same person: "Cette nouvelle est une grande première pour Sabine et pour moi: nous n'éprouvons plus le besoin de nous cacher l'une derrière l'autre et réciproquement. Nous savons maintenant mieux qui nous sommes—et que nous nous complétons assez bien, ma foi" (This short story is a great premiere for Sabine and for myself: we do not feel the need to hide behind each other any longer. We now know who we are—and, well, we complement one another fairly well). Of course, as Vonarburg stated in *Solaris* (September–October 1987), this entire situation may not have helped restore friendly relationships between *imagine . . .* and *Solaris,* as she was still the editor of the latter.

Scholarship remained one of Vonarburg's interests. In particular, she was interested in some of the epistemological aspects of science fiction, such as the way science-fiction narratives construct their fictive knowledge and how they are read. In May 1985 she led a conference on *Approche des littératures conjecturales,* on what she calls "conjectural fiction," which took place as

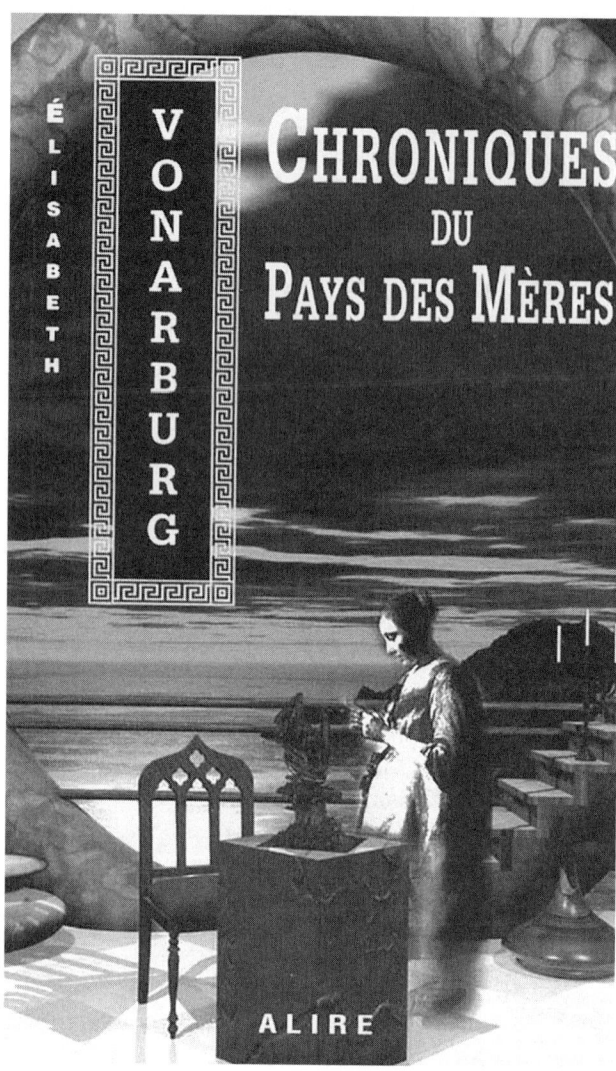

Cover for Vonarburg's 1992 novel, set in a future feminist utopia

part of the Congrès de l'ACFAS (French Canadian Association for the Promotion of Science), an annual multidisciplinary conference of Quebec academics held at the Université du Québec à Chicoutimi; in June 1988 she organized, at the same university, the first Colloque international sur la SF et le fantastique québécois (International Colloquium on Quebec SF and the Fantastic) along with the tenth Congrès Boréal.

Since 1986 she has been a member of the Groupe de recherche interdisciplinaire sur les littératures fantastiques dans l'imaginaire québécois (Interdisciplinary Research Group on Fantastic Literatures in the Quebec Imagination), or GRILFIQ, at the Université Laval. In 1987 she defended her dissertation, "La Seconde Naissance: Entre la Même et l'Autre" (The Second Birth: Between the Self and the Other), and received a Ph.D. in French from the Université Laval. The thesis actually takes the form of a creative (fictive) dissertation in which a hypothetical female narrator studies the work of Vonarburg, as the author explained in an interview in the September–October 1987 issue of *Solaris*:

> Le travail que j'ai fait pour ma thèse se situe en 2037 et la narratrice, qui étudie Vonarburg, se pose des questions car certaines des choses mentionnées dans ses fictions ne se sont pas encore produites; elle replace l'Oeuvre dans la mentalité de l'époque et dit qu'à cette époque c'était de la SF "parce que ça n'existait pas." (The work I have done for my thesis is set in 2037, and the female narrator, who is analyzing Vonarburg's work, is puzzled because some of the facts mentioned in the fiction pieces have yet to happen; she reinstates the work in its historical cultural context and says that at this time it was deemed to be SF "because these things did not yet exist.")

The narrator's (and Vonarburg's) conclusion is that most of the science-fiction content lies in the reader's head.

Vonarburg has developed ideas about such concepts as Same/Other, reality/fantasy, and identity/otherness and continues to do so in papers published in various learned periodicals. For instance, in "SF: Savoir-fiction" (SF: Knowledge-Fiction), published in the Spring 1985 issue of *Protée*, she argues that the main structural movement in science fiction is the appropriation of scientific information by the imagination, which links science fiction to dreams, fantasies, and myths. In "Le Rapport au réel dans la SF, la littérature générale et la poésie" (SF, Mainstream Literature, Poetry, and How They Relate to the Real World), a paper published in the Summer 1992 issue of *Solaris*, she maintains that even though one wants to believe in the objective reality of the world, the main "carburant" (fuel) at work in science fiction (and in reality) is dream.

As a scholar and as a writer, Vonarburg is also intensely concerned by feminist issues in science fiction. She has delivered several papers on this topic, and on women science-fiction writers, at various conferences such as the Congrès Boréal (Chicoutimi, 1979), EUROCON (Stresa, 1980), and the Congrès francophone sur la SF et le fantastique (Trois-Rivières, 1982). She continues to publish papers on women and science fiction as well as on female writers. For example, in "Les femmes et la science-fiction," published in two parts in the Spring 1985 issue of *Les Cahiers de la femme* and in *Les Oeuvres de création et le français au Québec: Tome III* (1986), she presents a survey of women writers of science fiction and concludes by maintaining that the best way to get rid of cultural determiners is to identify, understand, and use them, instead of being used by them. Among these (pre)determinations, she points out reproduction and seeks to discern whether men and women writers use it in a similar manner.

Between 1988 and 1990 Vonarburg carried out postdoctoral research on the motif of reproduction in science-fiction works written by women. She outlined some of her conclusions in a paper first published as "Birth and Rebirth in Space" in *Foundation* (Spring 1991), then revised as "The Reproduction of the Body in Space," published in *State of the Fantastic, Selected Essays from the Eleventh Conference on the Fantastic in the Arts* (1992) and as "La Reproduction du corps dans l'espace ou naissance et renaissance dans l'espace," published in *Les Ailleurs imaginaires: Les Rapports entre le fantastique et la science-fiction* (1993). She maintains that "Our society *is* a patriarchal one, where for men (*and* women), it requires less energy to identify with the Father's image/world than with the Mother's image/world. The male Self who tries to win the Mother back may be trying to have it all, to exist more (by having more . . .); the female Self may be trying merely to *exist*."

In 1987 Vonarburg won the Casper Award for Best Short Story in French; "La Carte du Tendre," which was then part of an anthology featuring several types of love stories, *Aimer*, edited by André Carpentier, was later included in Vonarburg's third short-story collection, *Ailleurs et au Japon* (1991). At this time she started to receive invitations to various writers' meetings, giving talks to the Guilde des écrivains de la Saskatchewan (Saskatchewan Writers' Guild), Ottawa Independent Writers Association, the Association des auteurs des Cantons de l'est (The Eastern Townships Authors' Association), and the Société des écrivains de Toronto (Toronto Writers' Society). In 1990 she won the Casper Award once again for "Cogito," published in *imagine . . .* in December 1988. This story, translated by Brierley for *Tesseracts³* (1991) and later published in the June 1996 issue of *Tomorrow Speculative Fiction,* relates the story of young Nathany, who lives in Cyblande, a planet where all senses are replaced with a cyborganic device. The little girl ultimately disconnects all her perceptions, just to see what it is like. This short story may be considered an attempt to deconstruct the Cartesian "I think, therefore I am," but it also has the tone of a fable in which the author seems to speak directly to the reader. Like Vonarburg's other child protagonists, Nathany is a solitary young girl fighting to be a free-thinking individual.

In 1991 Vonarburg won the same award again, now known as the Aurora Award, for Best Science Fiction or Fantasy Short Story in French, for "Ici, des Tigres," published in the Spring–Summer 1990 issue of *Le Sabord* (a Québécois literary periodical). Again, this story is about female transformation, but it is also one of the author's most atypical stories (Dr. Jekyll and Mr. Hyde retold), dealing with a fantastic and overworked subject matter (including the title) in a fresh fashion.

That same year, Vonarburg won yet another Aurora Award for Best Science Fiction or Fantasy Book in French for *Histoire de la princesse et du dragon* (1990), a fantasy story for young readers. She won the Aurora again in 1992 for *Ailleurs et au Japon,* a collection for which she was also a finalist for the 1992 Grands Prix Culturels du Saguenay/Lac-Saint-Jean, and for which she earned the 1992 Grand Prix Logidec de la Science Fiction et du Fantastique Québécois. This book includes some selected pieces from the author's publications, including "Cogito," the eponymous story "Ailleurs et au Japon" (previously released under the identity of Sabine Verreault), and "Mourir, un peu." In "Le Matin du Magicien," initially published in the 1986 edition of *L'Année de la science-fiction et du fantastique québécois,* Vonarburg seemingly exorcised her archaic readings and her first influence. She sets the narrative in the Notre-Dame-de-Paris district and uses a style of pure fantastic inspiration, though the fantastic object is not a fictive book but a drawing. A notice in the 1987 issue of *L'Année de la science-fiction et du fantastique québécois* praised the story, mentioning "une écriture très travaillée qui contribue à une atmosphère insolite et troublante et à la qualité impressionnante de la nouvelle" (a very polished style contributing to the peculiar and troubling atmosphere and impressive quality of this short story).

With *Chroniques du Pays des Mères* Vonarburg explores yet another subgenre. With this feminist novel of an (almost) all-women utopia, published simultaneously in 1992 in Quebec, in English-speaking Canada (as *The Maerlande Chronicles*), and in the United States (as *In the Mother's Land*), the writer penetrated the North American market as well as the mainstream market. The book was highly praised in several countries and earned many prizes. It was reviewed in some of the major science-fiction periodicals, including *Science Fiction Eye* (December 1992), *SFRA Review* (March/April 1993), and *The New York Review of Science Fiction* (January 1994). In Canada it won the 1993 Aurora Award for Best Science Fiction and Fantasy Book in French and, in Quebec, the Grand Prix Logidec de la SF québécoise and the Prix Boréal for Best Novel, as well as the Prix Création du Gala du Salon du livre du Saguenay/Lac-Saint-Jean for Best Novel. The same year, in the United States, it won the Philip K. Dick Special Jury Award and was a finalist for the James Tiptree Jr. Award. In Europe it was short-listed both for the 1993 Prix Rosny Aîné for Best Novel and for the 1996 Dublin International Award. The book was also translated into German as *Die Maerlande Chroniken* (1997).

Vonarburg had been preparing this book for a long time. She already had the story in mind in 1980,

Cover for Vonarburg's semi-autobiographical 1994 novel, about a young literature teacher who embarks on a journey of self-discovery

feminine encompasses the masculine. For this reason, this work may not translate well; Karen Hellekson, in the March/April 1993 issue of *SFRA Review,* said of *In the Mother's Land* that it "is definitely a translated novel: English, . . . with its lack of gender, doesn't do it justice." However, as Vonarburg pointed out (in the Fall 1993 issue of *Solaris*), most critics nevertheless praised the quality of the style and the accuracy of the feminization, both in the original version and in the translation.

From 1993 to 1997 Vonarburg worked as a science-fiction columnist for *Demain la veille,* a program on contemporary trends broadcasted on Radio-Canada-CBF. Also, publishing house Québec/Amérique launched a new Québécois science-fiction line, and editor Jean Pettigrew asked Vonarburg for a novel to initiate this line. *Les Voyageurs malgré eux* was published in January 1994 as number one of the "Sextant" series. The author promoted her own book as well as the entire series in various interviews on radio and television, and in newspapers. A year later the English translation was released by the American publisher Bantam Spectra, and it was republished in 1996 by the Canadian publisher Tesseract Books.

This complex literary project is a good illustration of Vonarburg's versatility, as it combines four novels in one: begun as a uchrony (a utopia set in a parallel world), the story continues as a mystery novel, then as an initiatory narrative; and its ending is almost mystical. Vonarburg constructs the fictional world of *Les Voyageurs malgré eux* around what initially appears to be an alternate Québécois present time. It is her most Québécois novel and the one that is most influenced by her life in the Saguenay region. It could also be considered her most autobiographical narrative, as it tells the story of a young literature teacher of French extraction living in Montreal, who discovers who she is and what her world is about as she goes farther north to the "Pays des Sags" (Land of the Sags). Vonarburg introduces fugitive visions of potential here-and-now and outlandish worlds in the fragmented imagination of her heroine, Catherine Rhymer. The author also injects some significant allusions to her past work, excerpting segments from some of her short stories, mostly from the "Cycle du Pont"—as she herself points out in an introductory note to the novel. For example, "La Machine lente du temps" (The Slow Engines of Time) and "Le Jeu des coquilles de nautilus" (Chambered Nautilus) are intimately linked to *Les Voyageurs malgré eux:* the same figures, or at least characters bearing the same names, are involved; the fictional space is similar; and the "Pont" is a recurrent motif.

In the Summer 1994 issue of *Lettres québécoises* Claude Janelle argued that this novel may be too autoreferential to gain the interest of new readers:

when she had begun writing her previous novel. However, what might have remained a small episode in an eventual Mother's Land trilogy had turned into a full-fledged novel, *Le Silence de la cité,* and eleven more years passed before *Chroniques du Pays des Mères* was released. The action of this later work is set in the far future of *Le Silence de la cité,* when all has been forgotten about ancient technology, and where 90 percent of society is female. Lisbeï, the main character, tries to expose the past as well as reconcile herself with her own destiny and identity. Both novels, with other Vonarburg short stories, belong to the "cycle de Baïblanca" (Baïblanca cycle), although the style and structure of *Chroniques du Pays des Mères* are much more complex, dealing with a fictive epistolary form and (at least) a triple discursive temporality. This women's fictive world is also supported by an all-feminine grammar according to which, contrary to contemporary French usage, the

> Je n'arrive pas à me défaire de l'impression que *Les Voyageurs malgré eux* cherche trop à faire la synthèse de tout ce que l'auteure a publié jusqu'à ce jour. . . . J'ose à peine imaginer l'état de confusion du lecteur qui aborderait l'Oeuvre d'Élisabeth Vonarburg par l'entremise de ces *Voyageurs malgré eux* (I just cannot let go of the feeling that *Les Voyageurs malgré eux* is a contrived attempt to achieve a synthesis of everything the author has published to date. . . . I hardly dare imagine the state of confusion of a reader being introduced to the work of Élisabeth Vonarburg through this book).

In the February 1996 issue of *The New York Review of Science Fiction,* however, Kathleen Ann Goonan maintained that *Reluctant Voyagers* "is not a book to hurry through. Although it is structured as a mystery, it is best not to be impatient for answers, for they come gradually, and often seem to contradict one another. . . . The book lives in its details, slowly; richly." The novel, which was short-listed for the 1995 Philip K. Dick Award and won the 1996 Aurora Award for Best Novel in French, remains a prime example of the author's creative skills and her global literary project. It shows her mastery of various subgenres and her ability to propose a unified novel based on such diverse styles. Such intertextual strategies also draw on veiled references to Vonarburg's cosmogonic and autobiographical world: the main character evokes all the Catherines/Kathryns interspersed in her work and refers directly to the name she gave to the heroine of her autobiographical juvenile story "Le Premier Accroc ne compte pas" published in *La Première Fois* (1991). The French translation of Yarbro's *False Dawn* (*Fausse Aurore,* 1979) also was published under the name of "Catherine Vonarburg," although, by the author's admission, this circumstance was because of a typo.

Vonarburg never stopped working as a translator. She translated some well-known authors for the French publisher Presses Pocket for its series of the best science-fiction and fantasy short stories. Between 1994 and 1995 she translated Kay's three-volume series *The Fionavar Tapestry* (1984–1986).

In 1995 Vonarburg was short-listed for the French Prix St-Exupéry valeurs jeunesse for *Les Contes de la Chatte Rouge* (Tales of the Red Cat, 1993), another collection for young readers that reveals the author's love for cats. That same year, she published a book as co-author with Yves Meynard, *Chanson pour une sirène* (1993), a novelette that has since been translated as "Song for a Siren" and made available on the web page of *Tomorrow Speculative Fiction.* A year later Vonarburg published another book of juvenile literature, *Contes de Tyranaël* (Tales of Tyranaël, 1994), which was a finalist for the 1995 Prix Brives-Montréal. Even though it was produced for young readers, this collection of fictive legends remains of great importance, for it introduces the mythological background of the *Tyranaël* series.

For a long time Vonarburg had been thinking about writing a major science-fiction saga with a planet as its main character. She started working on some episodes of this series in 1966, and thirty years later her notebooks included approximately two thousand rough pages of material. Several of her previous short stories are set in the same universe or in similar worlds: "L'Oeil de la nuit" (1978), "Thalassa" (1984), and "Paguyn and Kithulai" (1994) are obvious examples. The *Tyranaël* series had already been promised to Pettigrew, the "Sextant" editor; but when Québec/Amérique decided to terminate the series and Pettigrew started his own publishing company, Les Editions Alire, Vonarburg followed him. The young publisher needed a major series to launch his imprint; and Vonarburg agreed that it would be convenient to release the whole story within a short period of time—an opportunity she might not have obtained from a mainstream publisher such as Québec/Amérique. *Tyranaël* comprises more than two thousand pages and is made up of five novels published between August 1996 and November 1997.

The series relates the story of the colonization of the planet Tyranaël, from which native inhabitants have mysteriously vanished more than three centuries before the arrival of Terrans. Nobody knows why they left or where they went, even though all their buildings still remain on the planet. *Les Rêves de la Mer* (1996) presents two narrative tenses: the time of the main character, Eïlai, on Tyranaël, and the colonization era on the newly named Virginia, in which the real hero is the planet itself. Eïlai (who, like some of her people, can see into the future, the past, and other presents) has dreamed that intruders on Tyranaël will drastically change her planet in her own future or in the future of a parallel time. Consequently, her people drift from Tyranaël to escape such a future before it happens. The temporal complexity is amplified by the presence, in the narrative, of Tyranaël legends (some of which can be found in *Contes de Tyranaël*). *Les Rêves de la Mer* establishes a link with the following part of the cycle via the appearance of young Simon Rossem, who, through his successive resurrections, remains an important character throughout the pentalogy. This novel also introduces an enigma that is partially solved at the end of the cycle: the mystery of a strange Sea that covers the real sea during half the Tyranaëlian year and absorbs all energy and living matter.

Le Jeu de la Perfection (1996) is set a few decades later. Simon is the main character, acting more or less successfully as a deus ex machina. The title of this novel is important, for it stresses the relation between the game called Jeu de la Perfection (Perfection Game)

Cover for Vonarburg's 1997 novel, the fifth and final volume in her series about the colonization of the planet Tyranaël

that the ancient Tyranaël inhabitants used to play–a game in which winning is more hazardous than losing–and the way Simon plays with the future of his own planet and with the lives of vulnerable individuals. At the end of the novel, the history of Virginia has yet to be written, and one can only guess what will happen to a human species undergoing a mutation that gives people extrasensory abilities.

Readers can follow Mathieu's escape 160 years later from a concentration camp-like system in *Mon Frère l'ombre* (1997) set 160 years later. Mathieu shows no extrasensory power in a world where everyone can at least sense or be sensed by other people; he had been kept prisoner in order to be "débloqué" (unjammed–in order to awake his latent abilities). With a little help from Simon, he gradually learns to trust other people. He takes part in a voluntary experiment in order to unjam his extrasensory capabilities. Led by a unicorn, he makes a fascinating discovery: his own powers are revealed to him, and he crosses the mysterious Sea to find a new world–the world to which the ancient inhabitants of Tyranaël have fled.

L'Autre Rivage (1997), the fourth novel of the series, is comprised of two parallel narratives. The first one starts on the alternative planet where the Ranao–the original inhabitants of Tyranaël–have been moved by the Sea; protagonist Lian (Liam), grandson of an illustrious human "Passeur" (someone able to cross the sea without being dissolved), has grown up in a society that rejects him because everyone is afraid of what he represents–the disappearance of extrasensory powers and the exile from their home world, Tyranaël. The other narrative appears later in the book and relates the story of Alicia (Alice), who grew up in the Lagrange satellite flying away from a devastated Earth and has lived a virtual Virginian existence to which, for political reasons, she has been dedicated. She has to travel to the planet to research an ancient propulsion system. On Virginia, Lian does not find as wonderful a world as he was expecting and discovers the occult system of the planet, whereby all destinies are governed by powerful mutants. Alice also gets a taste of Virginian treachery, but, above all, her own human faculties disappoint her. The two characters eventually meet each other and find some serenity.

The last volume of the series, *La Mer allée avec le soleil* (1997), tells the story of Taïriel, granddaughter of a renowned "Passeur," who, once again, does not experience the same psi powers as her compatriots. Deaf, blind, and invisible in a world where everybody is at least sensitive, she dreams of flying away with the departing Lagrange station. Her meeting with the enigmatic Samuel changes her plans and makes the two of them uncover the occult history of Tyranaël.

The whole saga is rich and complex. Each novel has its own set of themes and autonomous plot. For example, while *Les Rêves de la Mer* gives major cues about Tyranaël's story and relates the first decades of the new colony named Virginia, *Le Jeu de la Perfection* concentrates on Simon's obsessive quest. However, even though every volume can be read independently, all five novels have complex ramifications within the entire cycle. For instance, one of the characters found in all of the books, Simon, conveys an essential viewpoint on reality and history, which is depicted in the novels not as a progression marked by courage and glory but as a condition subjected to the chaotic relation between cause and consequence. Many of Vonarburg's characters also share a common status: as outsiders, they benefit from a differing perspective. Consequently, though it can be enjoyable to read the first two novels before reading the third, *Mon Frère l'ombre,* it is possible to grasp the plot and reconstruct the entire Virginian world by assembling the fundamental data disseminated throughout the narrative and reaching beyond one's own prejudices—which is the course followed by the main character, Mathieu. Likewise, in *L'Autre Rivage,* Lian-Liam and Alicia-Alice, because of their hybrid origin, have access to a double point of view. This perspective can be associated not only with the author's own emigrant status ("I'm a world unto myself," Vonarburg confessed in the September 1991 issue of *Locus)* but also within the identifying framework she has been developing in her fiction as well as her essays for more than twenty-five years. The fifth volume of the *Tyranaël* series, *La Mer allée avec le soleil,* closes on a new beginning and the ingression of another extraterrestrial culture that will multiply perceptual potentialities.

Simon is in some ways a paternal figure in the cycle. Several fathers are represented in the whole cycle and in other works by Vonarburg; they are always imperfect, their children constantly trying to escape from them symbolically. The *Tyranaël* cycle also represents the apotheosis of one of Vonarburg's most flourishing leitmotivs: "la mer" (the sea), which can also be related to "la mère" (the mother). The "mer" motif, combined or not with its homonym, can be found in various texts, especially in the titles of many of the author's short stories. For example, "La Maison au bord de la mer" (Home by the Sea) features an artificial daughter (an android) who goes back to her metaphorical mother's house by the sea. In the same manner, in "Le Premier Accroc ne compte pas" Catherine, Vonarburg's fictive alter ego, experiences the beginning of the end of her childhood when she meets a boy on holiday by the sea. In "Le Jeu des coquilles de nautilus" the main character, Talitha, encounters a doppelgänger named Tilitha who lives under the sea. And of course, the Sea may be considered as the main (really living) character of *Tyranaël.*

The series has sold well since its first release in August 1996. *Les Rêves de la Mer* has already been reprinted, which means that more than the initial three thousand copies have been sold—quite a large run in the Quebec context. The series is part of the top ten bestsellers' list of *Le Soleil* (Quebec), and each volume has been abundantly reviewed in such periodicals as *La Presse, Nuit blanche, Proxima, Lettres québécoises,* and *Solaris.* The first volume won the 1997 Prix Boréal. The same year, Vonarburg won the Grand Prix de la SF et du Fantastique Québécois, both for the first three volumes of *Tyranaël* and for "Le Début du cercle," a short story published in France in the anthology *Genèse* (1996)—this story also won the 1997 Prix Boréal for Best Short

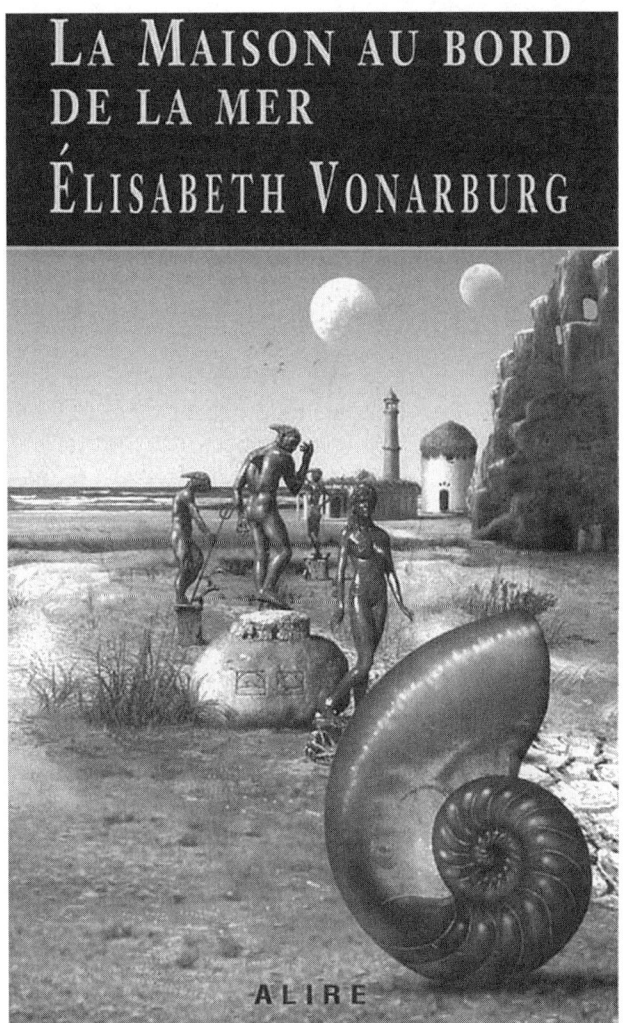

Cover for Vonarburg's 2000 collection, in which the title story concerns an android who returns to her "mother's" home by the sea

Story. The first novels of the series were awarded the 1997 Prix Gala du Livre Saguenay/Lac-Saint-Jean and, in France, the 1997 Babet d'or of the Foire du Livre de Saint-Etienne.

From 1997 to 2000, Vonarburg served as the chairperson for her local professional writers' association in the Saguenay region; since 1999, she has also been president of the Québécois Société de fantastique et de science-fiction Boréal. Her most recent award is the Prix du Conseil québécois de la Femme en littérature, a one-time literary prize given in 1998 by the Québécois Council for Women's Affairs on its twentieth anniversary. Two of her earliest novels have been republished by Alire: *Le Silence de la cité* in 1998. In 2000, she published a collection of her most recent short stories, *Le Jeu des coquilles de nautilus. Chroniques du Pays des Mères* and *The Slow Engines of Time* in 1999, a collection of eight translated stories (half of them translated by the author) was also released in 2000 by Tesseracts Books.

Vonarburg is the most prominent science-fiction writer in Quebec and is known to readers far beyond the borders of the province, in many languages. She has been the subject of several academic papers, even dissertations, and has achieved wide respect as a leading feminist figure. She is among the writers who have done the most to put Quebec science fiction on the map for readers around the world.

Interviews:

Luc Pomerleau, "Entrevue Élisabeth Vonarburg," *Solaris,* 75 (September–October 1987): 42–48;

"Élisabeth Vonarburg: A World Apart," *Locus,* 368 (September 1991): 5, 77;

Louise Alain, "Entre Mères et Monde," *Femmes d'action,* 22 (February–March 1993): 27–30;

Alain, Joël Champetier, and Daniel Sernine, "Élisabeth Vonarburg," *Solaris,* 106 (Fall 1993): 39–50;

Marie-Pierre Lockwell, "Elisabeth Vonarburg: Chronique du Pays des Simulacres," *Nuit blanche,* 58 (December 1994–January/February 1995): 25–29;

Sernine, "Elisabeth Vonarburg," *Vidéo-presse,* 24 (June 1995): 22–24;

Alain Deglise, "Élisabeth Vonarburg: 'Je vis entourée d'extraterrestres,'" *Dernière heure* (21 February 1998): 22–23;

Edo van Belkom, "Élisabeth Vonarburg," in his *Northern Dreamers: Interviews with Famous Science Fiction, Fantasy, and Horror Writers* (Kingston, Ontario: Quarry Press, 1998), pp. 211–234;

Sylvie Bérard, "Dialogue sur l'utopie, le féminisme et autres sujets connexes: Élisabeth Vonarburg interviewée par Sylvie Bérard," *Tessera,* 26 (Summer 1999): 95–104;

Bérard, "Venues, vues, vécues: Entre le sujet science-fictionnel et l'auteure science-fictive," *Dalhousie French Studies,* 47 (Fall 1999): 115–132.

Bibliography:

Aurélien Boivin, Maurice Emond, and Michel Lord, *Bibliographie analytique de la science-fiction et du fantastique québécois* (Quebec: Nuit blanche, 1992), pp. 539–547.

References:

Sylvie Bérard, "Éclatement," in "Je pense or je suis: Discours et identité dans la SF côté femmes: Entre la new wave et le cyberpunk," dissertation, Université du Québec à Montréal, 1997, pp. 212–273;

Bérard, "En mer miroir," *Solaris,* 123 (Fall 1997): 35–38;

Bérard, "Fictional Arborescence and Allusive Coherence in Élisabeth Vonarburg's Universe," in *Proceedings of the Academic Conference on Canadian Science Fiction & Fantasy,* edited by Allan Weiss (Toronto, 1998), pp. 35–49;

Bérard, "Les nouvelles d'Élisabeth Vonarburg ou la nouvelle au-delà du recueil," *XYZ: La revue de la nouvelle,* 43 (Fall 1995): 65–80;

Janice-Marie Bogstad, "Gender, Power and Reversal in Contemporary Anglo-American and French Feminist Science Fiction," dissertation, University of Wisconsin, 1992;

Madeleine Borgomano, "Science-fiction: Du merveilleux au fantastique à travers *La Mémoire double* et 'La Machine lente du temps,'" in *Les Ailleurs imaginaires: Les Rapports entre le fantastique et la science-fiction,* edited by Aurélien Boivin, Maurice Émond, and Michel Lord (Quebec: Nuit blanche, 1993), pp. 153–165;

Guy Bouchard, "L'inversion des rôles masculins et féminins dans *Chroniques du pays des mères* d'Elisabeth Vonarburg," *Solaris,* 112 (Winter 1994): 29–32;

Lynda Giroux, "Elisabeth, la fantastique . . . réapparaît avec *Les contes de la chatte rouge,*" *Des livres et des jeunes,* 47 (Summer 1994): 2–5;

Michel Lord, "Les arthitectures de l'imaginaire," in *Panorama de la littérature québécoise contemporaine,* edited by Réginald Hamel (Montréal: Guérin, 1997), pp. 264–268;

A. F. Ruaud, "Dossier Vonarburg: Critique et entretien," *Bifrost,* 3 (November 1996): 99–104;

Pamela Sargent, "New Threads in the Tapestry," *Amazing Stories,* 67 (November 1992): 52–56;

Suzanne Vanina, "Élisabeth Vonarburg, écrivaine," *Magie Rouge,* 15 (1988): 10–19.

Andrew Weiner

(17 June 1949 –)

Mici Gold

BOOKS: *Stay Slim for Good,* by Weiner, Zalman Amit, and E. Ann Sutherland (New York: Walker, 1976; Toronto: Fitzhenry & Whiteside, 1976);

Stop Smoking for Good, by Weiner, Amit, and Sutherland (New York: Walker, 1976);

Guide to Intelligent Drinking, by Weiner, Amit, and Sutherland (New York: Walker, 1977; Toronto: Fitzhenry & Whiteside, 1977);

Phobia Free: How to Fight Your Fears, by Weiner, Amit, and Sutherland (New York: Stein & Day, 1977);

Effective Time Management (Willowdale, Ontario: Hume, 1983);

P.A.T., the First Fifty Years: Building the Human Resource Management Function (Toronto: Personnel Association of Toronto, 1986);

The Financial Post Moneywise Magazine Dictionary of Personal Finance (Toronto: Random House, 1987);

Station Gehenna (New York: Congdon & Weed, 1987; Toronto: Worldwide, 1988);

Distant Signals and Other Stories (Victoria, British Columbia: Press Porcépic, 1989);

Envahisseurs! (Le Pressis-Brion, France: Bifrost/Etoiles Vives, 1998);

This is the Year Zero (East Lawrencetown, Nova Scotia: Pottersfield Press, 1998);

Signaux Lointains (Le Pressis-Brion, France: Bifrost/Etoiles Vives, 1999);

En approachant de la fin (Le Pressis-Brion, France: Bifrost/Etoiles Vives, 2000).

OTHER: "The Band from the Planet Zoom," in *Why I Left Harry's All-Night Hamburgers and Other Stories from Isaac Asimov's Science Fiction Magazine,* edited by Sheila Williams and Charles Ardai (New York: Delacorte, 1990), pp. 183–198;

"Changes," in *In Dreams,* edited by Paul J. McCauley and Kim Newman (London: Gollancz, 1992), pp. 319–342;

"Eternity, Baby," in *Tesseracts⁴,* edited by Lorna Toolis and Michael Skeet (Edmonton, Alberta: Tesseract Books, 1992), pp. 263–289;

"The Letter," in *Ark of Ice: Canadian Futurefiction,* edited by Lesley Choyce (East Lawrencetown, Nova Scotia: Pottersfield Press, 1992), pp. 36–48;

"Bootlegger," in *Tesseracts⁶,* edited by Robert J. Sawyer and Carolyn Clink (Edmonton, Alberta: Tesseract Books, 1997), pp. 67–80;

"The Slow," in *Tesseracts⁷,* edited by Paula Johanson and Jean-Louis Trudel (Edmonton, Alberta: Tesseract Books, 1998), pp. 48–60;

"Crossing," in *Northern Frights 5,* edited by Don Hutchison (Oakville, Ontario: Mosaic, 1999), pp. 107–123.

SELECTED PERIODICAL PUBLICATIONS–UNCOLLECTED:

FICTION

"The Deed," *Magazine of Fantasy and Science Fiction,* 54 (May 1978): 39–70;

"The Comedians," *Magazine of Fantasy and Science Fiction,* 56 (February 1979): 114–123;

"Lost Alaskan Terminal Retreat Blues," *Quarry,* 30 (Summer 1981): 5–15;

"Station Gehenna," *Magazine of Fantasy and Science Fiction,* 62 (April 1982): 92–123;

"The Third Test," *Interzone,* 1 (Summer 1982): 16–20;

"The Housing Problem," *Leisureways* (November 1982): 16–18;

"On the Ship," *Magazine of Fantasy and Science Fiction,* 64 (May 1983): 85–98;

"Takeover Bid," *Rod Serling's The Twilight Zone Magazine,* 3 (June 1983): 77–81;

"Invaders," *Isaac Asimov's Science Fiction Magazine,* 7 (October 1983): 60–75;

"The Alien Station," *Isaac Asimov's Science Fiction Magazine,* 8 (October 1984): 89–93;

"The Investigation," *Border Land,* 1 (Spring 1986): 25–26;

"This Year Next Year," *Rod Serling's The Twilight Zone Magazine,* 6 (August 1986): 64–70;

Andrew Weiner (photograph by Nathaniel-Moses Weiner)

"Twenty-two Steps to the Apocalypse," by Weiner and Terence M. Green, *Isaac Asimov's Science Fiction Magazine*, 12 (January 1988): 118–129;

"The Grandfather Problem," *Isaac Asimov's Science Fiction Magazine*, 12 (August 1988): 108–111;

"The Egg," *Amazing Stories*, 63 (September 1988): 120–127;

"Seeing," *Magazine of Fantasy and Science Fiction*, 83 (September 1992): 103–158;

"Wavelength," by Weiner and Green, *Canadian Fiction Magazine* (July 2000): 97–98.

NONFICTION

Reply to Yoshiyuki Tanaka, *Psypherboria*, no. 13 (Summer 1989): 48–56;

"Realism in SF," *Quantum*, no. 38 (Fall 1990/Winter 1991);

"SF–Not!" *New York Review of Science Fiction*, no. 57 (May 1993): 20–22.

Like many Canadian science-fiction writers, Andrew Weiner was born elsewhere and came to Canada as an adult. Although he has published one novel, four collections, and more than fifty short stories, he is possibly better known as a writer of nonfiction. One of Canada's most prolific short-story writers, Weiner has published in prestigious periodicals and anthologies in several countries and has received nominations for awards in both the United Kingdom and Canada. His stories have been reprinted frequently, some in other languages, and three have been filmed for television.

Andrew Simon Weiner was born on 17 June 1949 in London, England, to Joseph Weiner, a Russian-born cabinetmaker who came to England at the age of five, and Rachel Papier, a native of the United Kingdom. Weiner has an older sister, Anne. Weiner received his basic education in England, where he also earned a B.A. in social psychology in 1970 and an M.S. in social psychology in 1973 from the London School of Economics. There he also met his future wife, Barbara Moses, a Canadian. They married the year he graduated, and then came to Canada in 1974. At first they lived in Montreal, but moved to Toronto in 1977 so Barbara could complete her Ph.D. at the University of Toronto. They live there with their son, Nathaniel, and Weiner helps his wife run her consulting firm.

Weiner does not usually set his tales in outer space or in the far future; instead, he prefers modern settings and events that are apocalyptic or transformative. When he does include aliens, they are obvious metaphors for humankind. His characters, human or alien, often wrestle with madness, uncertain identities, and ambiguous events. The music industry, finance, and the arts are frequent subjects, drawn from his years of freelancing, but in Weiner's hands these and other mundane topics become truly speculative. His writing characteristically hovers between mainstream and science fiction or science fantasy.

Influenced by avant-garde science-fiction writers such as J. G. Ballard and William Seward Burroughs, as well as by mainstream writers, Weiner began writing in his late teens. Initially, the stories were experimental, in the form of Ballard's "The Assassination Weapon" (1967) and other British New Wave writing; but when he submitted them to the English magazine *New Worlds,* the magazine most associated with the British New Wave, editor Michael Moorcock rejected them. His first sale, however, involved just such a story, "Empire of the Sun." He had submitted it to an American editor at *New Worlds,* James Sallis, but instead the story found its way to Harlan Ellison, who accepted it for the prestigious New Wave science-fiction anthology *Again, Dangerous Visions* (1972). In this debut story, later collected in an altered version, in Weiner's *Distant Signals and Other Stories* (1989), Kaheris, "the unknown astronaut, existential hero," goes insane after some sort of encounter with aliens while in orbit. As a result, he winds up as an employable mental patient in a 1990s London devastated by war with Mars. He experiences what might be hallucinations about humanity being at war with Martians, and he expects the sun to go supernova at any time. Because the story is told entirely from the psychotic's perspective, however, the nature and reality of the events are unclear. In an unpublished July 1998 interview Weiner said that "Empire of the Sun" is "a teenager's version of J. G. Ballard." And in a 1989 letter to Japanese fan Yoshiyuki Tanaka, later published in the Summer 1989 issue of *Psypherboria,* Weiner writes, "I was 18 when I wrote it, and it shows." Regardless, his achievement inspired him to continue.

After this initial success, Weiner's next story, "The Deed," did not appear until six years later, when it was published in the May 1978 issue of *The Magazine of Fantasy and Science Fiction.* During that time he honed his writing skills while working as an advertising copywriter and a rock music critic, completed his master's degree, and moved to Canada. Psychosis is again an important factor in "The Deed," although in this story Weiner follows a conventional narrative format. The viewpoint character is psychiatrist Seymour Stern, one of seven crew members aboard the first ship to travel to another star through "null space." The effect of null space on humans is an unknown quantity, although Stern suspects it may affect the crew strongly. Almost immediately after entering null space, the crew does fall victim to the "nothingness" beyond the hull. Several of them progress from neurotic to psychotic; one commits suicide; and another is killed while attacking his crewmates. When the ship finally reaches Alpha Centauri, the religiously minded Captain Webb precipitates a disastrous first encounter, with theological overtones. In his letter to Tanaka, Weiner says that "The Deed" is "based in Freud's theories of the 'primal horde.' There is really no scientific basis for this theory, but it's a wonderful myth, one which sheds considerable light on the workings of leadership, social hierarchy and patriarchal culture."

Weiner next sold "The Comedians" to *The Magazine of Fantasy and Science Fiction* for its February 1979 issue. This story is the first of several humorous pieces and one of the few to draw from his Jewish background. In this story Murray Fogel, a jaded comedian in his forties, gets his brother-in-law Mintz to send him back in time to undergo analysis by the great Sigmund Freud himself. As Fogel discovers when he gets there, however, Mintz has sent him to an alternate universe, one in which Freud did not continue his medical career but began a new career as a comedian named Ziggy Freed. When Murray fails to return to his own time at the prescribed moment, he is faced with a career change of his own. "I'm by no means a pure Freudian," Weiner writes in his letter to Tanaka, "but I do enjoy playing around with his ideas."

In 1981 Weiner sold two stories, "Getting Near the End" and "Lost Alaskan Terminal Retreat Blues." The first of these, published in the 1981 anthology *Proteus* and later collected in *Distant Signals and Other Stories,* is the more significant of the two because Weiner later wrote two additional stories with the same characters and has drafted a novel about them. "Getting Near the End" introduces readers to Martha Nova, her music, and the millennial future that she sings about. It is written in an experimental form similar to that of "Empire of the Sun": the events are somewhat disjointed; several characters are battling madness in some form; and the world is about to end or change. As the story opens, Martha is preparing to sing what will be her final concert, while civilization appears to be collapsing. With her are a man identified only as "the dancer," and her son, Daniel, the child of an astronaut. This astronaut, Jake Denning, is starting to go insane. Martha's former personal manager, Levett, has already received treatment for madness caused when he comprehended Martha's prescience. Now the government wants Levett to get close to Martha and find out what she really knows.

Weiner's science-fiction career took off in 1982 when five of his stories were published, including "Station Gehenna," which appeared in the April 1982 issue of *The Magazine of Fantasy and Science Fiction* and was expanded into a novel five years later. Additional stories have appeared almost every year since, though he claims in an interview with Edo van Belkom in *Northern Dreamers: Interviews with Famous Science Fiction, Fantasy, and Horror Writers* (1998) that he has been "blocked" for a few years after giving up smoking.

His best-known story is "Distant Signals," which first appeared in the May/June 1984 issue of *Rod Serling's The Twilight Zone Magazine* and has been reprinted many times, including in the prestigious *Norton Book of Science Fiction,* edited by Ursula K. Le Guin and Brian Attebery (1993). The story was filmed as an episode of the syndicated American television series *Tales from the Darkside* in the mid 1980s. In his notes for *Signaux Lointains,* a 1999 collection in French, Weiner says his inspiration for the story came from Walter Tevis's novel *The Man Who Fell to Earth* (1963). "Distant Signals" concerns a strangely dressed young man named "Smith" who arrives in Hollywood with a briefcase of gold and the intention of re-creating a bad television Western canceled twenty years earlier after only one season. Bill Hurn, the original writer, has moved on to less embarrassing projects, and Vance Maccoby, the brooding star, has become an overweight alcoholic. Accepting no obstacles, Smith is determined that another full season of the show shall be made, to reveal the identities of the amnesiac gunslinger, Cooper, and the mysterious drifter, Loomis, who shadows him. Throughout the production Smith evades questions about where the show will be broadcast. In the interview with van Belkom, Weiner said that he envisioned the alien as an obsessive fan, "the dead hand of the past, squeezing the life out of the present," though a fellow science-fiction writer thought that the story was about "the enduring power of art." In his story notes for *Signaux Lointains* Weiner relates that the story originally had a different ending, one in which the alien returns to his home planet, but Weiner revised it at the urging of Ted Klein, editor of *The Twilight Zone Magazine.*

Two other Weiner stories have also been adapted for television: "Going Native," first published in the Winter 1985 issue of *Night Cry* and collected in *Distant Signals and Other Stories,* and "The News from D Street," first published in the September 1986 issue of *Isaac Asimov's Science Fiction Magazine* and also collected in *Distant Signals and Other Stories.* In his notes for *Signaux Lointains* Weiner says that "Going Native" was also inspired by *The Man Who Fell to Earth,* and he suspects that the producers of *Tales from the Darkside* changed the gender of the protagonist to avoid comparisons with the 1976 movie version (starring David Bowie) of Tevis's novel. In this story an alien sent to Earth to observe humanity decides to join a therapy group. Unexpectedly, he finds himself drawn into their ways of thinking and feeling and their loneliness, until he and the reader both wonder if he is really an alien or just delusional. In an interview with Terence M. Green in the October 1987 issue of *Books in Canada* Weiner said that aliens are metaphors, and he expanded on this idea in the interview with van Belkom: "I have no interest in aliens other than as projections of our own minds. Which is, of course, exactly what they are. . . . The alien is by definition the other, and therefore unimaginable."

"The News from D Street" was filmed as an episode of the Canadian-produced series *Welcome to Paradox,* which premiered in August 1998 on Showcase in Canada and the Sci-Fi Channel in the United States. As the story opens, it appears to be a straightforward mystery in which an "inquiry agent" named Joseph Kay is hired to look for a missing person. The mysterious graffiti he sees everywhere suggests something of vast importance is going on or is imminent, but he cannot quite remember what he should do about it. This story is one of Weiner's few works to consider artificial intelligence, though the concept does not actually drive the story.

The other well-known story from Weiner's early career is "Klein's Machine," first published in the April 1985 issue of *Isaac Asimov's Science Fiction Magazine* and collected in *Distant Signals and Other Stories.* Philip Herbert Klein, a twenty-three-year-old resident of New York City, is found on a bus in Mt. Vernon, Ohio, with no idea how he got there. He is in a distressed mental state and says only that he has been traveling a long way. Dr. Lawrence Segal, the psychiatrist social worker, tries to understand the "boy" who believes he has been "traveling in time." Though the events in the story are equivocal, the reader sees that Klein really did travel in time. A humorous part of this story is the opportunity it gives Weiner, by means of the psychiatrist's report, to make deprecating remarks about science fiction as literature and about its readers. It is, Weiner admits in his notes for *Signaux Lointains,* "one of the stories I'm proudest of."

Weiner's first novel, *Station Gehenna,* was published in 1987 in response to Isaac Asimov's request for material for his "Isaac Asimov Presents" series. Editor Judith Merril had earlier asked Weiner to shorten the novelette "Station Gehenna" for inclusion in an anthology of Canadian science fiction, but he thought the story was, if anything, too short, as certain issues in the plot were not really resolved. So he took the opportunity to expand it into a novel, completing the longer version in about three months.

The plot for both story and novel are almost identical, differing mainly in the ending and in details about the motivation for colonizing such an unlikely planet. *Station Gehenna* also reflects what Weiner feels to be a limited Canadian influence, as it deals with the issue of survival in an "overwhelming and merciless" environment (a quotation from Freud used in the book). "That's sometimes what I felt in Montreal," he told Green in *Books in Canada;* "Montreal is not the Far North–it's not all that cold–but it's a shock when you're not used to that." The novel also addresses the concept that conquering the universe is an archetypally male approach: "The book is about technology, about the program of technology. I guess you could say that's a male program," he explained in *Books in Canada.* Less obviously, *Station Gehenna* also presents the female perspective on that program. Overall, though, the book is a mystery story, "but an intellectual mystery," he insisted in *Books in Canada,* describing the plot as "*Ten Little Indians* set on the planet

Solaris," referring to the influence of Stanislaw Lem's work.

The book opens with the main character, Victor Lewin (called Jake in the short story), looking down on the planet Gehenna from the spaceship that has brought him there. He has come to Gehenna to analyze the morale of the small crew running the terraforming station on the planet, because one of them recently committed suicide. He soon discovers that whatever affected deceased Leisure Officer Arthur Duggan is still affecting the crew, especially the male members, including himself. Tech Person Norm Remus suggests to him that Duggan was killed. In his quest to discover the truth, Lewin interacts with Duggan's widow, Science Officer Valerie Theron; Nutrition Officer Charlotte McKinley; Administrator Franz Muller; and Medical Officer Greta Vichevski. As he is compelled to eliminate the more obvious explanations for what is happening, Lewin confronts the idea that there might be some sort of alien sentience on the planet.

Though the novel includes many interesting philosophical ideas, it suffers from a weakness in characterization. Characters that work well as archetypes in a short story seem cold and unsympathetic in a long work that does not develop sensory detail or emotional nuance. For example, Weiner does not explore Lewin's relationship with Theron, to whom he is obviously attracted. Still, the book did well, earning back its advance and being reprinted in paperback.

Two years after *Station Gehenna* appeared, Weiner published his first collection of short fiction under the title of his best-known story, *Distant Signals and Other Stories*. This collection of twelve pieces includes several of Weiner's favorites and best-known stories, as well as two new ones, "Leaving the Planet" and "Inspiration." The first of these resembles "Getting Near the End," as it features a female musician, Louise D'Arcy, with a transformative vision. The difference is that her vision is not her own. This story is another of Weiner's works to involve sentient artificial intelligence. "Inspiration" is a more interesting story, as it addresses the question of where artistic vision comes from. Weiner's colleague and friend, best-selling science-fiction writer Robert J. Sawyer, suggested in a personal communication that "Inspiration" is the story that best describes Weiner's attitude toward talent: that talent is something that "rides your back that you'd like to be able to take off from time to time." In an August 1998 personal e-mail Weiner confided that "I always saw this as a story about creativity, and the lengths to which people will go to achieve it—the characters aren't 'driven' by their talent, but rather by their lack of it."

One of the best stories in the collection is undoubtedly "Waves," first published in *Isaac Asimov's Science Fic-*

Dust jacket for Weiner's first science-fiction novel (1987), about a mysterious force attacking the male colonists on a desolate planet

tion Magazine in March 1987. It resembles mainstream writing, because science has little to do with the story. It takes place in an artist colony—or a seaside town where the residents fancy themselves artists, at any rate—during a period of economic depression called "The Pause." The main character is Ken Vale, the man who predicted the Pause but who is taking a respite from the academic world to staff a bookstore that rarely breaks even and to make "synthvids" (computer-generated entertainment videos) in his spare time. The colony receives a visit from Marianne Reiss, a former astronaut and physicist who has become a singer and a collector of brain holograms. Both Ken and Marianne are interested in waves—economic waves or brain waves—but Marianne is playing for higher stakes. The imagery of waves permeates the piece, from the oceanic tides on the beach to the electromagnetic radiation of distant space.

Although this collection attracted some critical praise, it apparently did not reach the wider science-fiction reading audience. This lack of circulation is partly attributable to the fact that it was produced as a trade paperback by a small Canadian publisher that has since gone out of business (though many of its titles are carried by Tesseract Books of Edmonton). It is also partly a reflection of what the market for science fiction is like. The unimaginative cover does not bear the words "science fiction" or garish aliens or spaceships, although "a spaceship would have been an improvement," Weiner said in an August 1998 personal communication. In fact, some readers have doubted whether it really is science fiction, as he explains in "SF–Not!" in the May 1993 issue of *The New York Review of Science Fiction*.

Weiner's second collection of stories appeared in 1998 in a volume named for one of his more-experimental but lesser-known stories, *This is the Year Zero*. Although the collection includes one story from 1983 ("One More Time," first published in the *Chrysalis 10* anthology), and a couple from 1987 ("Going to Meet the Alien," first published in the August 1987 issue of *The Magazine of Fantasy and Science Fiction*, and "The Alien in the Lake," first published in the September 1987 *Isaac Asimov's Science Fiction Magazine*), the rest of the thirteen stories were written in the 1990s. Nine of the stories involve aliens and reiterate Weiner's belief that humans can never understand aliens, their purposes, or their motives. Transformative music appears in three stories, psychosis in five, and one is a humorous "feminist" story. The volume also includes two stories not printed elsewhere: "The New Frequencies" and "The Disappearance Artist."

In "The New Frequencies" the main character is a rock music critic who is never named and is asked by Marge Daley of COPCAME (Committee of Parents Concerned About Musical Embedding) to write about how rock music transmits messages intended to disrupt society. The Committee's primary concern is a group called Plan Ten, about whom nothing is known except that they have produced their first CD of unusual music with a strange beat. When the rock music critic is contacted by the professed manager of the group, he jumps at the chance to meet the musicians and announce their next release. The story gives Weiner an opportunity to comment on pop music when the main character meets with the creator of Plan Ten and says "But this isn't just music. . . . It actually alters consciousness." To which the creator responds: "Of course it does. . . . That's what music *does,* if it's any good at all."

"The Disappearance Artist" is one of Weiner's best stories. It is a delightfully modern fantasy story exploring how artists maintain their equanimity and sustain their vision. The disappearance artist is Richard Ducharme, a second-rate academic and poet looking for inspiration until he chances upon a carnival in Mexico and convinces the artist there to divulge the techniques of disappearing–literally. He happens to sit next to a television publicist on the jet home, and she helps him launch his career. Not surprisingly, his fame increases dramatically, and his ego with it; and soon he is pushing himself beyond his limits. When his art starts to go wrong, he has to reinvent himself, and then do it again.

This is the Year Zero, like Weiner's first collection, received some favorable critical attention, especially for the two new stories. Its commercial success has again been hampered by its publication by a small Canadian publisher, rather than the major American genre publisher that Weiner needs in order to reach a wider audience.

Weiner has produced dozens of professional articles on many subjects, including some extensive commentary about science fiction. Though his essays have mostly appeared in small-press magazines and fanzines, most were reprinted in *Alouette*, a now-defunct newsletter of the Canadian regional division of the Science Fiction and Fantasy Writers of America. These articles reveal that Weiner is widely read and well versed in the genre, and furthermore, that he brings his background in psychology to understanding the archetypes and themes of the literature. One of his most interesting pieces of commentary is "Realism in SF," which first appeared in *Quantum* in 1991. In this essay he discusses the differences between science fiction and fantasy while showing that both are fantasy. The distinction is that science fiction is inspired by science. "'Hard' SF writers apply the Protestant work ethic to their dreaming," Weiner writes; "They have to work up a sweat to give themselves permission to dream at all. . . . High fantasy writers, on the other hand, let their dreams run amuck, conjuring up whole new worlds at the flick of a magical amulet." Writers on the border zones between the two forms combine a bit of both. What Andrew Weiner looks for in a story is strangeness, but strangeness containing an "element of psychological truth"–which is exactly how someone might describe Weiner's own writing.

Interviews:

Terence M. Green, "Andrew Weiner," *Books in Canada* (October 1987): 38–40;

André François Ruaud, "Entretien avec Andrew Weiner," *Yellow Submarine,* 125 (March 1998): 26–31;

Edo van Belkom, "Andrew Weiner," in his *Northern Dreamers: Interviews with Famous Science Fiction, Fantasy, and Horror Writers* (Kingston, Ontario: Quarry Press, 1998), pp. 225–233.

Michelle Sagara West
(5 May 1963 -   )

Nancy Johnston
University of New Brunswick Saint John

BOOKS: *Into the Dark Land,* as Michelle Sagara (New York: Ballantine, 1991);
Children of the Blood, as Sagara (New York: Ballantine, 1992);
Lady of Mercy, as Sagara (New York: Ballantine, 1993);
Chains of Darkness, Chains of Light, as Sagara (New York: Ballantine, 1994);
Hunter's Oath, as Michelle West (New York: DAW, 1995);
Hunter's Death, as West (New York: DAW, 1996);
The Broken Crown, as West (New York: DAW, 1997);
The Uncrowned King, as West (New York: DAW, 1998);
The Shining Court, as West (New York: DAW, 1999);
Sea of Sorrows, as West (New York: DAW, 2001).

OTHER: "Birthnight," as Michelle Sagara, in *Christmas Bestiary,* edited by Rosalind M. Greenberg and Martin H. Greenberg (New York: DAW, 1992), pp. 199-218;
"Shadow of a Change," in *Dinosaur Fantastic,* edited by Mike Resnick and Martin H. Greenberg (New York: DAW, 1993), pp. 145-159; reprinted in *Dinosaurs!* edited by Martin H. Greenberg (New York: Penguin/Donald I. Fine Books, 1996), pp. 63-78;
"For Love of God," in *Alternate Warriors,* edited by Resnick (New York: Tor, 1993), pp. 278-291;
"Hunger," in *Christmas Ghosts,* edited by Resnick and Martin H. Greenberg (New York: DAW, 1993), pp. 15-26;
"Four Attempts at a Letter," in *By Any Other Fame,* edited by Resnick and Martin H. Greenberg (New York: DAW, 1994), pp. 49-56;
"Winter," in *Deals with the Devil,* edited by Resnick, Martin H. Greenberg, and Loren D. Estleman (New York: DAW, 1994), pp. 30-43;
"What She Won't Remember," in *Alternate Outlaws,* edited by Resnick (New York: Tor, 1994), pp. 278-291;

Michelle Sagara West (photograph by Tom Robe)

"The Hidden Grove," in *Witch Fantastic,* edited by Resnick and Martin H. Greenberg (New York: DAW, 1995), pp. 307-319;
"When a Child Cries," in *Phantoms of the Night,* edited by Richard Gilliam and Martin H. Greenberg (New York: DAW, 1996), pp. 33-46;

"Choice," as Michelle West, in *Sword of Ice,* edited by Mercedes Lackey (New York: DAW, 1997), pp. 143–169;

"The Law of Man," as West, in *Elf Fantastic,* edited by Martin H. Greenberg (New York: DAW, 1997), pp. 24–48;

"The Sword in the Stone," as West, in *Alternate Tyrants,* edited by Resnick (New York: Tor, 1997), pp. 284–304;

"Turn of the Card," as Michelle Sagara West, in *Tarot Fantastic,* edited by Martin H. Greenberg and Lawrence Schimel (New York: DAW, 1997), pp. 197–226;

"Under the Skin," as West, in *Elf Magic,* edited by Martin H. Greenberg (New York: DAW, 1997), pp. 11–30;

"The Vision of Men," as Sagara West, in *The Fortune Teller,* edited by Schimel and Martin H. Greenberg (New York: DAW, 1997), pp. 293–308; reprinted in *Things Invisible to See,* edited by Schimel (Boston: Circlet Press, 1998), pp. 187–212;

"Kin," as West, in *Olympus,* edited by Martin H. Greenberg and Brian D. Arthurs (New York: DAW, 1998), pp. 282–299.

SELECTED PERIODICAL PUBLICATION– UNCOLLECTED: "Guilty Pleasures," *Magazine of Fantasy and Science Fiction,* 90 (May 1996): 40–43.

Michelle Sagara West is a prolific fantasy writer, the author of ten novels and nearly twenty short stories. Although she has yet to garner academic attention, she has received two John W. Campbell Award nominations for her first novels, *Into the Dark Lands* (1991) and *Children of the Blood* (1992). She has also achieved critical recognition in the science-fiction press for her high-fantasy series *The Sacred Hunt* (*The Hunter's Oath,* 1995, and *The Hunter's Death,* 1996) and has been praised for her development of complex characters and unusual cultures. In an interview with Edo van Belkom (1998) West affirms that high fantasy, for her, is best defined by its "use of archetypes and is almost always informed by the concept of justice, of a just outcome to a situation; in its barest sense its about coming of age, about struggling for justice, about how the one and the other are interconnected." In keeping with her own definition, her short fiction and fantasy novels explore the conflicts between individual desire, social responsibility, morality, and power.

The eldest of four children, Michelle Michiko Sagara was born on 5 May 1963 in East York, a municipality of Toronto, Ontario, where she still resides. In at least one story, "Under the Skin" (1997), the wooded urban parks of East York form the background for a revelation of hidden magic. From earliest childhood, Sagara's parents encouraged a love of reading, which guaranteed her a sanctioned escape and privacy. Elaborating on her childhood reading in her column "Guilty Pleasures" (1996), she writes: "I started reading before I was seven; cut my teeth on Enid Blyton (about whom I will say nothing in these more enlightened times) and Nancy Drew, and moved on to the more fondly remembered Burroughs, Alcott, Lewis, Garner and Tolkien." In a 1996 article by Scott Colbourne for *Quill & Quire* she further asserted that J. R. R. Tolkien remains one of the "imaginative pillars" for her writing. After attending local public schools, Sagara "diverged from the regular course" and went to the Alternative Independent Study Program (AISP) for high school. She studied physics at the University of Toronto after graduating from the ISP, but she soon changed her major to English literature. With the intention of pursuing her writing career, Sagara left the university a few credits short of receiving a degree. In 1989 she married Tom West, with whom she has two children.

Since 1986 West has worked at Bakka Books in Toronto, the oldest science-fiction bookstore in Canada. At Bakka, she expanded her impressive knowledge about the genre, which informs her often humorous review column for *The Magazine of Science Fiction and Fantasy.* Perhaps as important, she gained valuable experience about the retail book business. Understanding the industry, she says, has allowed her to retain some pragmatism about book publishing and to preserve the sense of stability and sanity necessary to keep writing. In the late 1980s West worked with then store manager Tanya Huff, a local writer who was beginning to receive popular attention for her fantasy fiction. West credits Huff with helping to bring her work to the attention of the Del Rey imprint of Ballantine Books. Her first book-length manuscript, initially conceived as a short story, was completed in November of 1987 and submitted to Del Rey in 1988. After extensive rewrites at the direction of Veronica Chapman and Lester del Rey, West reshaped the manuscript into the two fantasy novels that begin *The Book of the Sundered* tetralogy: *Into the Dark Lands* and *Children of the Blood.*

In *The Sundered* series West introduces motifs familiar to high fantasy: an epic battle of Light and Dark and the struggle of a human protagonist to reconcile an attraction to both. Erin of Elliath, one of many dynamic female characters in West's fiction, is both a military leader and a healer to the descendants of the Bright Heart. When Erin is captured by the forces of Darkness, she finds that she and her captor, the Dark Lord Stephanos, share a mutual fascination. The remaining novels chronicle Erin's emotional struggle to accept the betrayal by her lover, her efforts to vindicate her people, and a fated uniting of the twin forces of Light and Dark. The series is dominated by a somber mood and intense character-driven scenes. A self-described organic writer, West insists that she dislikes strict plot outlines and begins with the emotional structure of her novels. Thus, she places more emphasis on the psychological growth of her characters than on the expression of an intellectual structure. Although these novels are punctuated by moving emotional crises and rousing battles, the pacing is often slow and the plot drawn out. West admits that shipping numbers were disappointing for the final two books. In the interview with van Belkom she has indicated that when the third volume, *The Lady of Mercy* (1993), went out of print at Del Rey three months after its publication and before the appearance of the fourth and final novel, *Chains of Darkness, Chains of Light* (1994), she feared the series would languish. Although quite happy with her editorial relationships at Del Rey, she states in the same interview that she was motivated by the birth of her first child to seek the security of a publisher who would keep her backlist in print.

The Sacred Hunt, her next high-fantasy series, was purchased from Del Rey by West's new publisher, DAW. In the Colbourne article West suggests that her aim in *The Hunter's Oath* and *The Hunter's Death* was to embody "honour, ethics, a sense of duty, things upon which worlds can be saved or new worlds can be built." Crisis in *The Sacred Hunt* hinges on individual decisions to either refuse or assume responsibility for shaping the future. The protagonists are two young men committed to an annual ritual hunt, a pact with their god that ensures the prosperity of the Breodanir community and may lead to the deaths of the human participants. The huntbrother, Stephen, and his hunter lord, Gillam, are called upon by a mysterious seer, Evayne, to take up a quest that may prevent the Lord of Hell, Allasakar, from reestablishing his reign in the mortal city of Averalaan. The cast of characters for both novels is large and includes several powerful women, including Evayne; the Breodanir ladies; the Terafin, the head of a great House of Averalaan; and Jewel, the leader of a den of street youths. West has suggested that the most psychologically complex figures in her fiction are often female characters thrown into positions of authority; they are characters who view power as a moral responsibility often undertaken at the expense of idealism and individual desires.

Stylistically, *The Sacred Hunt* is more mature and assured than her previous series. Many high-fantasy motifs and images recur to original effect in these two volumes: sacred weapons, an oath between brothers, psychic bonds between humans and animals, enchanted mazes, shape-shifting demons, warring mages, and a journey through human and magic realms. The viewpoint of the story shifts between principal characters such as Stephen, Jewel, and Gillam as well as between minor but well-developed characters such as Gillam's mother. This multiplicity adds a complex layering of emotional perspectives to key events. An interesting innovation is the periodic reappearance and viewpoint shift to Evayne, a time-shifting seer with only partial knowledge of the present and future. This character is poignantly out of sequence with the other characters in the novel; sometimes she appears to them as a vulnerable young woman and elsewhere as a magician grown powerful with age. In a review for *Locus* (September 1995) Carolyn Cushman compared West's character favorably to T. H. White's Merlyn, who ages backward in *The Once and Future King* (1958).

West's next series, *The Sun Sword,* takes place about fifteen years after the events of *The Sacred Hunt.* The books in this series are *The Broken Crown* (1997), *The Uncrowned King* (1998), *The Shining Court* (1999), and *Sea of Sorrows* (2001). These books, well received by her readers, are challenging for readers not familiar with epic fantasy, particularly since some of the volumes top seven hundred pages. Once again, the dark lord Allasakar, defeated temporarily by the hunter lords, may rise again as the political machinations and social tensions within the Dominion of Annagar escalate. In the first novel, conflicts between clans and intrigues within the segregated women's quarters add psychological interest. The heart of *The Broken Crown,* West says, is the exploration of polarized cultures. Much of this novel juxtaposes the internal politics of this patriarchal world with the actions of principal characters such as the gifted Diora Maria di'Marano, the power-hungry General Alesso, and Valedan, the only surviving heir to the Sun Sword of the Dominion. West is an admirer of Canadian fantasy author Guy Gavriel Kay, as she stated in the interview with van Belkom, and she respects high-fantasy writers who can "stitch the world into its people." In this respect, she is most proud of the complex world-building of this novel and how it shapes the emotional reactions of her characters.

The second novel of the series, *The Uncrowned King,* does answer some of her concerns, expressed in the van Belkom interview, that readers will be challenged by the "opacity of the culture." Perhaps because the cultural context has been carefully established, the second book has a narrower focus and develops the emotional growth of familiar characters: Jewel, a character from *The Sacred Hunt;* Kiril, a

Cover for the first novel (1995) in West's two-part high-fantasy series The Sacred Hunt, in which two huntsmen must prevent the Lord of Hell from reestablishing his reign in the city of Averalaan

half-mortal daughter of Allasakar; and the uncrowned king, Valedan. West says that "my favourite character, the person I feel most conveys something essential about myself," is Jewel; this character "came out of nowhere and took over in a way that can't be explained rationally." The series, which closes with the forthcoming *The Sun Sword,* continues to be popular with her fans.

While West frequently argues that she prefers a larger canvas for her fantasies, she is also a talented writer of short fiction. Her short stories explore her principal themes and demonstrate her stylistic experimentation with viewpoint and structure. In a 1994 interview with Mici Gold, West has suggested that short stories allow "a lot more room to experiment with style and with texture." Although she declares herself a novice at short fiction, she has been writing stories since the late 1980s. When her first two short stories were rejected by genre magazines, she turned more exclusively to her fantasy novels. Since then, all of West's short stories have been commissioned pieces in themed anthologies, including several alternate-history anthologies edited by Mike Resnick. She admits that the extensive research necessary to write these stories is especially demanding. Success depends, she says, on the reader's understanding of the extrapolated historical events as well as the author's writing skills.

Among her alternate histories, "Four Attempts at a Letter" (1994) and "What She Won't Remember" (1994) are particularly noteworthy. In "Four Attempts at a Letter," like many of her fantasy novels, West considers the personal consequences faced by a woman assuming a position of power. The focus is on Golda Meir's state of mind before the vital proclamation that established the State of Israel. In an alternate 1948, David Ben-Gurion, Zionist leader and the first and longest-serving prime minister of Israel, is martyred. Meir–who, in real life, played a more diplomatic role as appointed chief of the Histadrut's political section–must assume the military leadership of Israel. What makes this story stylistically successful and emotionally poignant is West's use of four personal letter drafts written to an American correspondent to tell the story. These letters illustrate and, with each redrafting, gradually disguise Meir's fear of failure, her idealism and political resolve, as well as grief for her family. A quite different story, "What She Won't Remember," offers an alternate view of the development of a writer's literary and moral consciousness. Taking Agatha Christie's eleven-day disappearance and apparent amnesiac episode in December 1926 as an historical starting point, West follows Christie through a passionate sexual liaison with a man discovered to be a sociopathic killer.

The comic "Shadow of a Change" in *Dinosaur Fantastic* (1993) is surprising among West's stories. She has an animated sense of humor, which comes through in personal interviews and her review columns but less frequently in her novels. This story features April Stephens, a flustered typist working in an office typing pool. Her life is meticulously organized to keep her from losing a precarious sense of control. As the story begins, April believes disaster is looming since she has missed the downtown bus for work. Gradually she begins to feel unlike herself; when she starts "looking a little green," everyone is too polite to admit the change. Her repressed sensual desires become translated quite literally into carnivorous urges. By the end of the story, April has transformed from repressed typist to a scaled monster poised to devour the unsuspecting meter man.

As in her fantasy novels, West's stories often explore the complexities of relationships and the meaning of love. In "Winter" (1994) Michael, a human character, is pursued by a demon in search of souls. West offers an interesting twist on the demon-lover story as Michael gives up his soul for the demon's promise that he will love him. The consequences of human fear and prejudice is an important theme in this story. Michael's lover, for instance, is comfortable with the rejection and homophobia of Michael's family since he is, after all, a demon of hell. The focus is less on the politics of the couple's same-sex relationship than on the process by which the two characters learn to love each other. Similarly, "The Vision of Men," in *The Fortune Teller* (1997), treats themes of fear, trust, and commitment. Jonathon Seaton has the ability to foretell the future, the deaths of his closest family members, and the inevitable pattern of his own relationships. Like many of West's psychic characters, he finds foresight a curse and burden. Jonathon is emotionally stunted and isolated by his fear to begin any future when he knows "there won't be one." Jonathon, who is gay, is closeted by his foresight rather than his sexuality. His lover ultimately advises him to ignore the "shadows," in particular his fear that he may foretell his lover's death, and to have faith in the process of love represented in the present. Jonathon's dilemma with his foretelling also has literary connotations. Foresight and vision represent the act of imagination. Just as West emphasizes her own organic writing process, Jonathon discovers that "until he set foot on a path, until he'd written the prologue to the story and sometimes the first chapter, the crystal would not reveal anything to him at all."

In an unpublished October 1999 interview, West insists that she begins her writing from a "purely intellectual," even clinical, standpoint, she does not end the process there: "It's only when the words hit the page . . . that those characters become, in the literary sense of the word, living, breathing and thinking entities—when, in fact, I realize that they would not follow the neat and tidy grid that I've called 'story' when I've made my first plan of battle." West's central and even her minor characters are deftly created; she succeeds in both short and long fiction as a writer of highly realized characters.

Interviews:
Mici Gold, "Michelle Sagara: Motherhood and the Writing Muse," *Sol Rising,* 10 (May 1994): 6–7;
Edo van Belkom, "Michelle Sagara West," in his *Northern Dreamers: Interviews with Famous Science Fiction, Fantasy, and Horror Writers* (Kingston, Ontario: Quarry Press, 1998), pp. 235–244.

References:
Scott Colbourne, "God in All Worlds: Entire Lands Spring from the Mind of SF Writer Michelle Sagara, But Her Inspiration Draws from Earth," *Quill & Quire,* 62 (August 1996): 1, 25;
Kristine Kathryn Rusch, Editorial, *Magazine of Fantasy & Science Fiction,* 90 (May 1996): 5–7.

Robert Charles Wilson
(1953 -)

Thomas March
New York University

BOOKS: *A Hidden Place* (New York: Bantam, 1986; London: Orbit, 1990);

Memory Wire (New York: Bantam, 1987; London: Orbit, 1990);

Gypsies (New York: Doubleday, 1989; London: Orbit, 1990);

The Divide (New York: Doubleday, 1990; London: Orbit, 1990);

A Bridge of Years (New York: Doubleday, 1991; London: New English Library, 1994);

The Harvest (New York: Bantam, 1992; London: New English Library, 1993);

Mysterium (New York: Bantam, 1994; London: New English Library, 1995);

Darwinia (New York: Tor, 1998; London: Millennium, 1999);

Bios (New York: Tor, 1999; London: Millennium, 2000);

The Perseids and Other Stories (New York: Tor, 2000);

The Chronoliths (New York: Tor, 2001).

OTHER: "State of the Art," in *The Best from Fantasy and Science Fiction: A 40th Anniversary Anthology,* edited by Edward L. Ferman (New York: St. Martin's Press, 1989), pp. 312–321;

"Extras," in *Tesseracts⁴,* edited by Lorna Toolis and Michael Skeet (Victoria: Beach Holme, 1992), pp. 59–86;

"Ballads in ¾ Time," in *Northern Stars: The Anthology of Canadian Science Fiction,* edited by David G. Hartwell and Glenn Grant (New York: Tor, 1994), pp. 343–353;

"The Perseids," in *Northern Frights 3,* edited by Don Hutchison (Oakville, Ontario: Mosaic, 1995), pp. 123–150; republished in *Aurora Awards: An Anthology of Prize-Winning Science Fiction & Fantasy,* edited by Edo van Belkom (Kingston, Ontario: Quarry, 1999), pp. 150–178;

"The Inner Inner City," in *Northern Frights 4,* edited by Hutchison (Oakville, Ontario: Mosaic, 1997), pp. 151–176;

Robert Charles Wilson (photograph by Robert Di Maio; from the dust jacket for The Perseids and Other Stories, *2000)*

"Protocols of Consumption," in *Tesseracts⁶: Canadian Speculative Fiction,* edited by Robert J. Sawyer and Carolyn Clink (Edmonton: Tesseract, 1997); pp. 267–290;

"The Observer," in *The UFO Files,* edited by Ed Gorman and Martin H. Greenberg (New York: DAW, 1998), pp. 16–36;

"Divided by Infinity," in *Starlight,* volume 2, edited by Patrick Nielsen Hayden (New York: Tor, 1998), pp. 13–43;

"Plato's Mirror," in *Northern Frights 5,* edited by Hutchison (Oakville, Ontario: Mosaic, 1999), pp. 241–259;

"The Dryad's Wedding," in *Star Colonies,* edited by Greenberg and John Helfers (New York: Daw, 2000), pp. 95–124;

"The Great Goodbye," *Nature,* 407, no. 6802 (21 September 2000).

Robert Charles Wilson has won or been nominated for several of the most prestigious awards in science fiction, including the Philip K. Dick Award and the Aurora Award, for *Darwinia;* his penetration of the psychological depths of his characters has provoked comparisons to the science-fiction writer Theodore Sturgeon. In addition to his novels, Wilson has published several short stories in such publications as *The Magazine of Fantasy and Science Fiction, Isaac Asimov's Science Fiction Magazine,* and *Northern Frights*. One of his short stories, "The Perseids" (1995), won the Aurora Award and was nominated for the Nebula Award.

Wilson was born in Whittier, California, in 1953. At the age of nine he moved with his family to Canada, where he has lived ever since. He grew up in Toronto and then moved to Nanaimo, British Columbia. As an adult, he moved to Vancouver before returning to Toronto, where he currently lives with his second wife, Sharry. Before becoming a full-time writer, Wilson worked for the Ontario Human Rights Commission as a transcriptionist and as an extra in the movie industry. His other interests include repairing vacuum-tube electronics, a hobby from the technological past that he pursues even as he postulates many possible scientific futures.

Known for the way they merge technological fantasy with the psychological and metaphysical, Wilson's novels embody both the hopes and fears that constitute humanity's relationship with scientific possibility. His narratives often revolve around the experience of one isolated or alienated individual; in *Canadian Science Fiction and Fantasy* (1992) David Ketterer refers to such characters as "Wilson's divided, alienated personalities." The development of Wilson's narratives often hinges on a character's coming to terms with or overcoming his isolation. These protagonists, however, resist such a classification, just as they often resist or struggle with their past and present connections with other human beings. Because they are not always comfortable with their isolation or even likable, correct, or confident in what they must do, Wilson's protagonists ring true and allow him to present a fantastical world in terms of what are enduringly human qualities.

Nominated for the Philip K. Dick Award, the Aurora Award, and the Locus Magazine Award in 1987, *A Hidden Place* (1986), Wilson's first novel, follows the emotional adventure of two small-town outcasts, Travis Fisher and Nancy Wilcox, who befriend Anna Blaise, a mysterious girl from another world. Travis, the son of a prostitute, loved his mother in spite of the derision heaped upon her by her sister and brother-in-law, with whom Travis has come to live following his mother's death. Nancy, a fiercely independent advocate of free love, is equally unsuited to the small-town milieu. As Travis and Anna recoil from the conventional relationships around them, yearning for more from each other and from others, Wilson depicts, in a second narrative interwoven throughout the text, the story of two other souls struggling to find one another in a world not their own. Combining fantasy with the tangible pathos of young alienation, *A Hidden Place* is an allegory of love, human connection, and, perhaps, the impossibility of each.

The second narrative in the novel follows a hobo named Bone, who comes from the same planet as Anna and is traveling with two companions, Deacon and Archie. Bone's enormous size provides Deacon with the security he needs to indulge his psychotic criminal impulses. After Deacon wounds Bone and murders Archie, Bone escapes to finish his journey toward the mysterious girl befriended by Travis and Nancy. Only at the moment of this reunion with Anna does the contrast between Bone and his former companions become most effective. The earthly vulgarity and barbarism of Deacon and Archie have been integral to Bone's experience of humanity, just as Anna's experience of love and friendship has been integral to hers. The cruelty and animalistic self-indulgence of Bone's former companions foster an appreciation for his wonder and innocence, in spite of his inability to articulate them.

On the world from which Bone and Anna come, *male* and *female* do not mean the same thing as they do on Earth. Whereas humans can be said to partake of the qualities of either sex, just as they arise from the union of the two sexes, in Anna's and Bone's world, males and females are two distinct species. In an echo of the Platonic myth of the origin of the sexes, they unite, however, as one being. Anna and Bone are two halves of one such being, separated as they traveled from their world to Earth. In order to return to their world, they must find each other and unite again. Only when they are reunited does the reader realize that the novel is actually about their quest for union and not that of Travis and Nancy, whose frustrations and intrigues merely help to create interest in Anna and set the stage for the revelation of her otherworldly nature.

Anna and Bone function as mirrors, both figuratively and literally. Anna reveals to people what they want to believe, their fondest hopes and dreams, while Bone reveals to people what they really are. Each, however, is equally frightening, as Nancy and Travis learn. Wilson's use of two interwoven narratives accentuates the disconnection that the final union of Anna and

Dust jacket for Wilson's 1989 novel, about three siblings who inherit from their space-alien parents the ability to open doors to alternate universes

Bone resolves. The most profound statement of the significance of Anna's and Bone's journeys lies in the contrast between the perfection of their union and the alienation experienced by those around them. Travis's aunt lives in fear of his uncle, who has become bored with his wife and seeks sexual comfort elsewhere. The relationship between Travis and Nancy seems ideal by comparison, in spite of the occasional discrepancies between what each of them wants from the other. Ultimately, only the relationship between Anna and Bone reaches perfection as they unite to form a whole, a state constantly aspired to but unattainable for the human couples depicted in the novel. By suggesting that a complete, enduring love is achievable only in terms of such fantastic otherworldliness, Wilson reinforces the desirability of this love at the same time that he asserts the impossibility of attaining it. Each of the narratives in the novel, however, revolves around an isolated, alienated protagonist, a typical Wilson character type, here serving as a counterpoint to the fantasy of connection that infects the text as a whole.

Memory Wire (1987) marks Wilson's movement into a more distinctly science-fiction mode. It is the story of a twenty-first-century world that has been altered by the discovery of a giant stone (or fragments of it) in a Brazilian rain forest. The stone is a memory device from an ancient civilization. Scientists have discovered that it contains encoded information that they can access—history and technological information from an alien race. Just a touch from one of the stone fragments, which are sold on the black market and have all but replaced traditional narcotics, enables a user to retrieve memories otherwise lost or indistinct in order to escape from the realities of the present. The closer these fragments, called "oneiroliths," are found to the core of the impact crater made by the original, as yet undiscovered, core stone, the stronger they are. As people have acquired the ability to duplicate them in labs, a subculture has sprung up around their use, and churches have been founded to celebrate their metaphysical properties.

The South American territory where the stones are mined, Pau Seco, is an internationally ruled slave-labor camp. The inhabitants toil for overlords, scrambling for oneiroliths and never escaping the desperation of the poverty that has led them to this place. It is a lawless area, combining elements of the old American West with the diamond-mining culture of parts of twentieth-century Africa. Cruz Wexler, a mystical figure resembling the psychedelic-drug guru Timothy Leary, finances a secret expedition to the heart of Pau Seco in an attempt to secure a piece of the core stone for himself. What follows is a combination of a quest narrative and a morality play lamenting not the emptiness of contemporary drug culture but the social malaise precipitated by war, of which the yearning for personal oblivion, usually through drugs, is both cause and effect.

Wexler's band of pharmacological and military spies includes Ray Keller, Byron Ostler, and Teresa Rafael. Ray, the protagonist of *Memory Wire,* formerly served with the Angels, an elite force of military documentarians implanted with a device that records every sight and sound they perceive. He has reentered the Angel service in order to accompany his friend Byron, another former Angel, on his expedition to Pau Seco. Both men are in love with Teresa, though Ray, under the influence of his Angel implant, is unable to articulate or even acknowledge these feelings. The implant supersedes all human emotion, the better to enable a wearer to encounter and record the horrors of war without flinching. Thus, embedded in this narrative about the mercenary underbelly of spiritual yearning is a critique of technology and its potential for dehumanization.

The mission of Wexler's band is complicated by the presence of Stephen Oberg, a deviant member of the Agency in charge of the Angel elite. Oberg is frightened by the oneiroliths and is on a mission to destroy the one that Ray, Byron, and Teresa have managed to steal from the Pau Seco mine. During the war in which Ray served as an Angel, Oberg was what was known as a "monster," part of an elite platoon comprised of men made more aggressive by their genetic makeup, men who could kill without remorse. Oberg must overcome his past of pillaging and indiscriminate murder; his one contact with an oneirolith has forced him to face this past. He represents not only an impediment to Wexler's goal of possessing a deep-core oneirolith but also the human aversion to past and memory that the oneiroliths have been put on Earth to obliterate.

Teresa, perhaps the most psychologically damaged of all the characters, represents the possibility of purity, harmony with the past, and hope for the future. The product of an abusive, poverty-stricken home, she once turned to drugs in order to escape painful memories of the past. With the oneiroliths she has found an escape from the present that brings her into contact with the past on her own time and her own terms. Memory is a choice. It is through Teresa that the final mystery of the stones is revealed. Once in possession of the deep-core fragment stolen from Pau Seco, she discovers that such fragments have the strongest ability to interface with humans. She comes into contact with the beings from whom the stone comes, humanlike winged people who are much more interested in communication and memory than the people of Earth are. Teresa is exposed to a world in which memory is not repressed but kept available for instant recollection. The oneiroliths are the gift of the winged people, containing their entire history and capable of bringing humans into closer contact with their own history, painful as it may be. Oberg's defeat comes, appropriately, at the hands of Teresa and one of the oneiroliths; as she touches him with it, a return of a painful memory throws him off balance and sends him falling to his death.

Wilson's subsequent novels rarely put the achievement of such a divine state in a straightforwardly positive light. In these books he explores more deeply the complexity and untenability of the conditions of alienation and connection. In *Gypsies* (1989) he departs somewhat from his exploration of individual alienation. After their biological parents are violently murdered, three children, Laura, Karen, and Tim, are raised by stepparents who are frightened of the powers the three share. The children are capable, individually and together, of opening doors into other worlds, alternate universes. A figure they often encounter in these worlds is the Gray Man, later known as Walker, who stalks the children, watching over them as a tempting angel. The narrative begins after the children have reached adulthood and gone their separate ways. Tim has disappeared, Laura and Karen are in contact only infrequently, and Karen's son, Michael, is beginning to manifest the same strange ability shared by his mother and her siblings.

When Karen decides to visit Laura after a long period without contact, Michael's powers begin to manifest themselves more strongly, leading the siblings to face a past they had ignored and a future that, because of their abilities, promises great danger to them all. Spending time with Laura causes Karen to begin remembering her powers again, after having repressed them in search of a "normal" life. It turns out that their biological parents were refugees from another world, an alternate Earth known as the "Novus Ordo," where they had been engineered to possess this capacity for interdimensional travel. Walker, who has been following the children throughout their lives, was the third

Cover for the 1992 paperback edition of Wilson's 1991 novel, about successive owners of a secluded house that is a node in a network of time machines

product of this experiment and was bred with a malevolent devotion to his creators. The murderer of the parents, he is now on a quest to bring the children back to his home world. He also intends to bring back Michael, who has a "pure," more powerful form of the special ability, one that the researchers on the home world have been anticipating for generations.

Once Walker has trapped Laura, Karen, and Michael in the Novus Ordo with the aid of Tim, who has turned traitor, a battle begins for their freedom as well as for their souls. In the Novus Ordo, America is under the thrall of a theocratic government obsessed with the intersection of quantum physics and the supernatural. Carl Neumann, leader of the Plenum Project, which created Walker and the biological parents of Laura, Karen, and Tim, wants to use their abilities to transport armies into enemy territory. In a thinly veiled criticism of the Catholic Church, Wilson creates the character of Cardinal Palestrina, a Machiavellian figure who allies himself with the Plenum Project, turning a blind eye to its heresy, in order to use its advances to crush the armies of the infidels.

In *Gypsies* Wilson presents the failure of an unreflecting individualism and the triumph of familial connection. The only alienated characters in the novel, Walker and Tim, are isolated and independent only in their own minds and are constantly at the mercy of their scientific masters. They thus become pitiful figures, in spite of the fear they evoke. When the family escapes, the breach of familial connection that existed at the beginning is overcome, as it is only together that they have been able to come to terms with their shared past and shared powers. *Gypsies* also marks the first appearance of the alternate universe and pagan religious elements that Wilson employed later in *Mysterium* (1994).

The Divide (1990) combines Wilson's concerns with biotechnology, the frailty of human interrelationships, and man's alienation not only from others but from himself. John Shaw is the product of a secret government experiment in genetically engineered intelligence. Designed to be the perfect man, he is now the victim of the increased cortical function that scientists gave him years ago. Maxim Kyriakides, the lead scientist on the project, was like a father to John, until a decrease in funding forced the project to a close, sending the boy into the home of adoptive parents who did not understand his prodigious intelligence. To compensate for his feelings of awkwardness and failure to belong, John created Benjamin, an alternative personality of mediocre intelligence and ambitions. The novel follows Benjamin's struggle with the reemergence of John and the duel the two fight over who is to have dominance over the body and life that they share.

Like the classic Frankenstein story upon which it is modeled, *The Divide* is a meditation on fatherhood and the nature of the father-child bond. Kyriakides' interest in John/Benjamin stems from guilt over his role in the experiment and a renewed sense of paternal obligation. Susan Christopher, a student of Kyriakides who falls in love with John, has also been drawn to the scientist as a father figure, following the death of her own father from cancer. At the close of the novel both Benjamin and John have left a legacy–Benjamin has impregnated his girlfriend, Amelie, and John has left behind the only legacy he can, an intellectual one. It is a scheme, left on a computer disk for Susan, for curing the metastasis of cancer.

The resistance to connection often seen in Wilson's protagonists is remarkably heightened in John/Benjamin. Each resists the dominance of the other as strongly as they both resist coming to terms with the painful past that has created this schism. Their fusion comes about, however, through a gesture of connection with another human being, Amelie. As they rescue her from an attack by her abusive brother Roch, John and Benjamin finally merge. Nevertheless, connection, when it comes, is painful and also presents an occasion for more loss: Amelie leaves Benjamin rather than stay and accept the financial help of Kyriakides. Her gesture represents the ultimate triumph of independence as she breaks the chain of connection to the failed father Kyriakides, refusing to submit herself or her child to that kind of dependence, in spite of the hardship and loneliness that may face them.

Echoing *Memory Wire* and continuing Wilson's critique of biotechnology, *A Bridge of Years* (1991), which was nominated for a Philip K. Dick Award in 1992, presents the prospect not only of a terrible future in which human beings engage in vicious combat over petty matters but also the prospect of another, later future in which they—or their evolutionary descendants—have risen above this combat. The novel takes place in the Pacific Northwest in the late 1980s and in New York City in the mid twentieth century. The primary locus of the narrative is a secluded house, a node in a gigantic network of time machines, called time tunnels, that run between past and future. Shifting between these two temporal locations, the structure of the novel embodies the fluidity and fractured essence of time that the story line itself suggests.

The tunnels were constructed by human descendants in the distant future for use in anthropological and historical research. The guardians of the tunnels, the time travelers, have been recruited at various stages in history to protect the network from intruders. Ben Collier, the owner of the secluded house, is one of these guardians. As the novel opens, he is murdered by Billy Gargullo, a soldier from a nearer future in which combat fighters wear a protective armor that merges with their bodies, insulates them from pain and emotion—like the Angel implant in *Memory Wire*—and becomes an addiction, an aspect of their personality that not only enables them but also compels them to kill without compunction.

After Ben's death the house passes through several owners who ultimately discover the secrets that it harbors. Tom Winter, the first owner after Ben, learns that the house is overrun by tiny cybernetic devices, ranging from microscopic to insect sized, which constantly work to maintain the home—cleaning up spills, fixing machinery, and, eventually, repairing Ben. After Tom discovers the time tunnel, he disappears into it and begins a new life in New York City decades earlier, unaware that Gargullo has also landed there. Catherine Simmons, who occupies the house after Tom's disappearance, uncovers the secrets of the place more completely, learning that Ben has never abandoned it. His body has been reconstructed by the cybernetic devices; he and Catherine, along with Tom's friend Doug Archer, rescue Tom from the past and prepare to battle Gargullo, an aberration from the future who should never have accessed the tunnels in the first place.

A Bridge of Years embodies a couple of Wilson's typical concerns: the horror of technological intervention in human physiology and, as in Wilson's next novel, *The Harvest* (1992), a vision of nanotechnology in which tiny mechanisms can enter the bloodstream and change human physiology relatively innocuously. The nanotechnological devices are products not of an alien civilization but of the human future, a better future that can be reached only by persevering through a nearer future, more dreadful than the historical past. These two futures are only implied, however. The novel depicts only the present and the past to which the characters travel. The future is left to be discovered and remains malleable; the characters themselves realize in the end that, although they have seen a terrible future, they can work against its inevitability. The path toward this better world begins with the pitting of one technology against another when Ben designs a cybernetic nanomechanism that can disrupt and destroy Gargullo's body armor. Thus, technology in the right hands can undo the harm inflicted upon the world by technology misused. As in other Wilson novels, the despair is presented honestly, and the hope that remains is, as a result, more believable.

All the main characters in *The Harvest* are isolated and alienated in some way from their communities—that is, until a mysterious phenomenon appears on Earth, dividing humanity between those who accept immortality and those who resist it. Also set in the Pacific Northwest, *The Harvest* depicts a world in which alien beings have infiltrated humans via microscopic nanomachines that alter the genetic makeup of people, rendering them not only immortal but also part of a greater communal consciousness. Matthew Wheeler, a doctor, has returned to his hometown of Buchanan, Oregon, out of a sense of community, but he is unable to pursue a serious relationship because of his lingering love for his dead wife. Tom Kindle lives alone in the mountains, having rejected contemporary society. Joey Commoner and his girlfriend, Beth Porter, are typical teenage outcasts, each suffering from a sense of worthlessness (Joey has a tattoo of the word *Worthless* on his shoulder) and suspicion of the world around them.

This unlikely band of allies comes together in resistance to the alien presence, which they see as having enslaved the rest of the world. In cities and towns across the globe, "Helpers," enigmatic conical struc-

Dust jacket for Wilson's 1992 novel, in which humans are offered immortality by alien beings–but at a price that some are not willing to pay

tures that respond to questions but have no apparent life of their own, have been directing the transformation of all who have accepted the invitation to immortality. This is the crux of the dilemma Wheeler and his colleagues face–those who have come under the thrall of the alien species have done so by choice, accepting the invitation of immortality offered at the moment of the microbes' invasion. With this immortality comes an inability–as with the oneiroliths in *Memory Wire*–to forget one's past or deny one's former mistakes. For some, like Colonel John Tyler, this prospect is too painful to face, while others simply do not want to alter what it means to be human. Still, only one in ten thousand refuses the offer of immortality.

As most of the world prepares to "die" and be subsumed by the "Artifact"–a traveling world–that the aliens are creating for them, Wheeler and his cohorts try to determine how, and where, they will survive in a world where the climate is now unpredictable and the infrastructure will eventually deteriorate without enough people to maintain it. Tyler, on his own solitary quest, attempts to resist the alien influence by taking up arms against it, only to learn that he is facing an enemy that does not fight back because its regenerative properties make defense unnecessary. Wheeler loses all of his friends and family to the aliens' offer of immortality, as have the rest of his colleagues. They strike out across the country, hoping to avoid the climactic upheavals of the coast, and eventually meet up with Tyler, who is en route to the safe haven in Ohio promised to them by the aliens themselves.

Along the way, however, Tyler becomes a tyrant, wresting control of the group from Wheeler and establishing a fascist military regime in miniature, in which his word is law, by penalty of death. Tyler's eventual demise comes through his inability to relinquish any of his authority for the greater good of the many. Wheeler counteracts this inflexible individualism; he makes a deal with the aliens, and the Artifact splits in two, one half roaming the universe, the other half staying around Earth to help and guide those who refused the offer of immortality. In exchange Wheeler agrees to allow himself and Beth, the only two remaining in their group, to be infected by the neocytes again, but it is up to them, at death, to decide whether to accept the aliens' offer of immortality. These characters have been united only by virtue of their refusal to join. Their communality is a function of their determined independence, although in the end this independence is contingent on and appreciative of the needs of others.

Mysterium, for which Wilson won the Philip K. Dick Award in 1995, opens with the mysterious transportation of the town of Two Rivers into another dimension, one in which the history of the Western world changed in favor of Gnostic Christianity, rather than Roman Christianity, and in which the United States is now jointly ruled by civilian and religious governments. The critique of theocracy echoes *Memory Wire,* just as the cause of the transportation of the town–scientific experimentation on an alien device that alters space and time–marks a return to Wilson's favorite themes of healthy scientific skepticism, multidimensionality, and alien intervention. Alan Stern, a brilliant physicist recruited by the United States government to lead the project, is presumed to have died in an explosion or reaction at the research facility outside of Two Rivers; this event has caused the displacement of the town. Howard Poole, Stern's scientist nephew, was away at the time of the reaction and survives to become part of the resistance movement established after religious fascists in the alternate universe take over the town and subject it to martial law.

The arrival of the Proctors from Le Bureau de la Convenance Religeuse, led by Simeon Demarch, seems benevolent at first; the military exercises that they oversee appear to be simply a form of caution rather than aggression. They employ historians and ethnographers, among them Linneth Stone, to gather material on Two Rivers and develop an historical database of the things found there. It becomes clear as time wears on, however, that the intention of the Bureau is to destroy the town, aided by the nuclear technology that they discover in scientific materials taken from Two Rivers.

Dexter Graham, a misfit local history teacher, leads a resistance movement in Two Rivers with the aim not of overthrowing the Proctors but of merely surviving. Haunted by guilt over his possible complicity in the deaths of his wife and son in a fire years ago, Graham relishes his isolation, barely able to care when his lover, Evelyn Woodward, begins an affair with Demarch. Graham is mobilized, however, by the threat of annihilation and by his growing love for Linneth, herself an outcast of sorts, her position in the Proctors' society tenuous owing to the religious heresy of her parents. Together, and with the help of Poole, they unlock the secrets of the displacement of Two Rivers.

The three are unable, however, to prevent the Proctors from visiting a nuclear holocaust on the town. This defeat, lending futility to their struggle, makes their effort all the more valiant. Poole has suspected all along that Stern, his uncle, has somehow remained alive in the strange radioactive wasteland of the research facility. Poole tests his theory in the end by entering the facility, exposing himself to the radiation and certain death, and finds his uncle next to the mysterious alien object, which his uncle's notes have characterized as a "wormhole boat" that allows its possessor to create a universe according to his or her own laws. When Graham and Linneth, along with other escapees, enter the facility just as the nuclear explosion begins in town, they learn that Poole and his uncle have created a portal to another world, one more benevolent and not ruled by a theocracy like the one Stern inadvertently brought about through his fascination with Gnosticism. Only by transcending their skepticism and alienation, though these traits at first brought them together, do Dexter and Linneth survive. Wilson leaves the true origin of the alien object unknown, its mystery a matter of faith and its nature, like the worlds it creates, a matter open for interpretation.

Wilson's 1995 short story "The Perseids" is narrated by a divorced, bitter, aging bookstore clerk whose interest in astronomy leads him into an affair with Robin Slattery, a telescope salesperson. Their relationship is complicated by the continuing presence in their lives of a mystic artist named Roger, whose theory of existence is that life is the colonizer of domains, which it makes into ecologies, expanding outward into newer domains, ad infinitum. Human beings, in this model, are simply colonies with intellect, into which alien cultures insinuate themselves. The narrator is unimpressed with this cosmology, and he eventually loses Robin to Roger. While the themes of alienation and failed con-

Dust jacket for Wilson's collection of short fiction set in Toronto. The title story, originally published in 1995, won the Aurora Award and was nominated for the Nebula Award.

nection do not differentiate "The Perseids" from the rest of Wilson's works, the story is an important precursor to his next novel, in which traces of the concept of domains are retained and expanded into his first articulation of a full-fledged cosmology.

Darwinia (1998), set in 1912, depicts a displacement similar to that of the town of Two Rivers in *Mysterium*. A phenomenon divides the earth into two halves, one in which all remains as it has been, the other in which all history has been erased, with Europe apparently returned to a primeval, uninhabited state. The protagonist, Guilford Law, signs on as the photographer for an expedition that travels to this new/old continent, Darwinia. Leaving his wife and daughter behind, Law joins the Finch expedition to Darwinia and ends up as one of the only survivors of the group, along with a man named Tom Compton. Fearing Law is dead, his family moves to Australia without him, and he begins a new life in Italy once the continent has been tamed. He is plagued throughout his life by a vision of himself as a young soldier who claims to have been killed in a war that never happened, at least not in the world as he knows it.

In interludes in the narrative Wilson informs the reader that what has occurred is the result of a celestial battle between superhuman intelligences who have created an intragalactic archive and those who seek to destroy it. The archive has been invaded by a demonic force called psilife, which, like a computer virus, has infected the archive and begun altering all that is recorded there. The archive was created by the forces of intelligence, noospheres, which acted as storage houses for all that has ever existed in sentient form. They created the archive at the end of time in order to give everlasting form to the intelligence that has existed in the galaxy. The psilife, or demons, have never had temporal, material form and are trying to gain it by entering the archive and taking form there. An extension of the theme of an advanced alien influence present in *The Harvest* and *A Bridge of Years,* the notion of the archive establishes a metaphysical basis for all that occurs in the novel. Because of the different lives of the protagonists—one originally archived in the natural course of history, one the result of the universal alteration of worlds that results from the psilife invasions—the concept of the archive raises questions about the nature of reality itself.

Law and Compton are typical Wilson characters, cut off from the world—even when, as in Law's case, leading a seemingly normal life. They are united by their shared experience of visions of these "other selves," who are actually their true selves sent to rescue them—and the world—from the invasion of the psilife into the archive. All of the action in the novel, in fact, takes place in the archive. The Earth has been gone for eons. Law is actually a storage unit, though a sentient one. His ghost remains and returns, as the ghosts of others have done, to encourage them to win the battle against the psilife. The psilife have their own scions on this artificial Earth, such as Elias Vale, a clairvoyant to the wealthy, who becomes, as many others do, a material vessel for the psilife, eventually taking monstrous form to fight Law and Compton and those like them. In *Darwinia* Wilson postulates a complete cosmology that the earlier novels fall short of constructing. This cosmology has a breadth of scope that promises further consideration of the metaphysics, as well as the possible physics, of science fiction.

Wilson's next novel, *Bios* (1999), is set in the twenty-second century, where humanity has discovered extraterrestrial life on the planet Isis. This life, however, is deadly to humans. The novel tells the story of Zoe Fisher, a cloned and genetically engineered woman who has been bred to be resistant to the biology of Isis so that she can explore the planet. Her explorations reveal the secrets of Isis, as well as the secrets within her. *The Perseids and Other Stories* (2000) is a remarkable collection of short fiction set in the city of Toronto. The stories insert the fantastic and supernatural into a loving portrait of life in Wilson's hometown.

Interviews:

Edo van Belkom, *Northern Dreamers: Interviews with Famous Science Fiction, Fantasy, and Horror Writers* (Kingston: Quarry, 1998), pp. 245–253;

Allan Weiss, "Robert Charles Wilson," *Science Fiction Chronicle* (February–March 1999): 8, 38–42.

Reference:

Thomas P. Linkfield, "The Evil in Michigan's Northern Forests," *Midwestern Miscellany,* 11 (1983): 40–48.

Checklist of Further Readings

Bell, John and Lesley Choyce, eds. *Visions from the Edge: An Anthology of Atlantic Canadian Science Fiction and Fantasy.* Porters Lake, Nova Scotia: Pottersfield Press, 1981.

Benson, Eugene and William Toye, eds. *The Oxford Companion to Canadian Literature,* second edition. Toronto: Oxford University Press, 1997.

Boivin, Aurélien, ed. *Le conte fantastique québécois au XIXe siècle.* Montréal: Fides, 1987.

Boivin, Maurice Emond and Michel Lord. *Bibliographie analytique de la science-fiction et du fantastique québécois (1960–1985).* Québec: Nuit blanche, 1991.

Boivin, et al. *Les ailleurs imaginaires: les rapports entre le fantastique et la science-fiction.* Québec: Nuit blanche, 1993.

Burwell, Jennifer and Nancy Johnston, eds. *Foundation,* 81 (2001).

Clute, John and Peter Nicholls, eds. *Encyclopedia of Science Fiction,* revised edition. New York: St. Martin's Press, 1995.

Clute and John Grant, eds. *Encyclopedia of Fantasy.* New York: St. Martin's Press, 1997.

Colombo, John Robert, ed. *Other Canadas: An Anthology of Science Fiction and Fantasy.* Toronto: McGraw-Hill Ryerson, 1979.

Colombo, et al. *CDN SF & F: A Bibliography of Canadian Science Fiction and Fantasy.* Toronto: Hounslow Press, 1979.

Emond, Maurice, ed. *Anthologie de la nouvelle et du conte fantastique québécois au XXe siècle.* Montréal: Fides, 1987.

Emond, ed. *Les voies du fantastique québécois.* Québec: Nuit blanche, 1991.

Hartwell, David G. and Glenn Grant, eds. *Northern Stars: The Anthology of Canadian Science Fiction.* New York: Tor, 1994.

Hartwell. *Northern Suns: The New Anthology of Canadian Science Fiction.* New York: Tor, 1999.

Ketterer, David. *Canadian Science Fiction and Fantasy.* Bloomington & Indianapolis: Indiana University Press, 1992.

Moskowitz, Sam. "Canada's Pioneer Science-Fantasy Magazine," *Science-Fiction Studies,* 17 (March 1990): 84–92.

On Spec Editorial Collective. *On Spec: The First Five Years.* Edmonton: Tesseract Books, 1995.

Paradis, Andrea, comp. *Out of This World: Canadian Science Fiction and Fantasy Literature.* Kingston, Ontario & Ottawa, Ontario: Quarry Press & National Library of Canada, 1995.

Sernine, Daniel. "Historique de la SFQ," *Solaris,* 79 (May–June 1988): 41–47.

van Belkom, Edo. *Northern Dreamers: Interviews with Famous Science Fiction, Fantasy, and Horror Writers*. Kingston, Ontario: Quarry Press, 1998.

van Belkom, ed. *Aurora Awards: An Anthology of Prize-Winning Science Fiction and Fantasy*. Kingston, Ontario: Quarry Press, 1999.

Vonarburg, Élisabeth and Norbert Spehner. "SF in Québec: A Survey," *Science-Fiction Studies*, 7 (July 1980): 191–199.

Weiss, Allan, ed. *Perspectives on the Canadian Fantastic: Proceedings of the 1997 Academic Conference on Canadian Science Fiction and Fantasy*. Toronto: ACCSFF, 1998.

Wollheim, Donald A. "Whither Canadian Fantasy?" *Uncanny Tales*, 2 (December 1942): 115–119; reprinted in *Friendly Aliens: Thirteen Stories of the Fantastic Set in Canada by Foreign Authors*, edited by John Robert Colombo. Toronto: Hounslow Press, 1981, pp. 175–179.

Contributors

Elliot J. Atkins . . . . *University of Liverpool*
Douglas Barbour . . . . *University of Alberta*
Greg Beatty . . . . *Bellingham, Washington*
Sylvie Bérard . . . . *Montreal, Quebec*
Everett F. Bleiler . . . . *Interlaken, New York*
Austin Booth . . . . *State University of New York at Buffalo*
Beverley Curran . . . . *Aichi Shukutoku University*
Mici Gold . . . . *Toronto, Ontario*
Peter Halasz . . . . *Mississauga, Ontario*
Annika Hannan . . . . *University of Toronto*
Darren Harris-Fain . . . . *Shawnee State University*
J. Morton Hendrick . . . . *London, Ontario*
Nalo Hopkinson . . . . *Toronto, Ontario*
Don Hutchison . . . . *Toronto, Ontario*
Alexander C. Irvine . . . . *University of Denver*
Douglas Ivison . . . . *University of Western Ontario*
Nancy Johnston . . . . *University of New Brunswick Saint John*
Kathleen Kellett-Betsos . . . . *Ryerson Polytechnic University*
Patti J. Kurtz . . . . *Heidelberg College*
Cristie L. March . . . . *University of Virginia*
Thomas March . . . . *New York University*
Christopher L. Morrow . . . . *Texas A&M University*
Holly E. Ordway . . . . *University of Massachusetts Amherst*
Dan S. Paroski . . . . *University of Ottawa*
Amy J. Ransom . . . . *Anna Maria College*
Robin Anne Reid . . . . *Texas A&M University–Commerce*
Clélie Rich . . . . *Vancouver, British Columbia*
Todd H. Sammons . . . . *University of Hawai'i at Mānoa*
Dorothy Shostak . . . . *Dalhousie University*
Batia Boe Stolar . . . . *Memorial University of Newfoundland*
Lee Briscoe Thompson . . . . *University of Vermont*
Jane Tolmie . . . . *Harvard University*
Jean-Louis Trudel . . . . *Université du Québec à Montréal*
Allan Weiss . . . . *York University*

Cumulative Index

Dictionary of Literary Biography, Volumes 1-251
Dictionary of Literary Biography Yearbook, 1980-2000
Dictionary of Literary Biography Documentary Series, Volumes 1-19
Concise Dictionary of American Literary Biography, Volumes 1-7
Concise Dictionary of British Literary Biography, Volumes 1-8
Concise Dictionary of World Literary Biography, Volumes 1-4

Cumulative Index

DLB before number: *Dictionary of Literary Biography,* Volumes 1-251
Y before number: *Dictionary of Literary Biography Yearbook,* 1980-2000
DS before number: *Dictionary of Literary Biography Documentary Series,* Volumes 1-19
CDALB before number: *Concise Dictionary of American Literary Biography,* Volumes 1-7
CDBLB before number: *Concise Dictionary of British Literary Biography,* Volumes 1-8
CDWLB before number: *Concise Dictionary of World Literary Biography,* Volumes 1-4

A

Aakjær, Jeppe 1866-1930 . . . . DLB-214
Abbey, Edwin Austin 1852-1911 . . . . DLB-188
Abbey, Maj. J. R. 1894-1969 . . . . DLB-201
Abbey Press DLB-49
The Abbey Theatre and Irish Drama, 1900-1945 . . . . DLB-10
Abbot, Willis J. 1863-1934 . . . . DLB-29
Abbott, Jacob 1803-1879 . . . . DLB-1, 243
Abbott, Lee K. 1947- DLB-130
Abbott, Lyman 1835-1922 . . . . DLB-79
Abbott, Robert S. 1868-1940 . . . . DLB-29, 91
Abe Kōbō 1924-1993 . . . . DLB-182
Abelard, Peter circa 1079-1142? DLB-115, 208
Abelard-Schuman DLB-46
Abell, Arunah S. 1806-1888 . . . . DLB-43
Abell, Kjeld 1901-1961 . . . . DLB-214
Abercrombie, Lascelles 1881-1938 . . . . DLB-19
Aberdeen University Press Limited DLB-106
Abish, Walter 1931- DLB-130, 227
Ablesimov, Aleksandr Onisimovich 1742-1783 . . . . DLB-150
Abraham à Sancta Clara 1644-1709 . . . . . . DLB-168
Abrahams, Peter 1919- DLB-117, 225; CDWLB-3
Abrams, M. H. 1912- DLB-67
Abramson, Jesse 1904-1979 . . . . DLB-241
Abrogans circa 790-800 . . . . DLB-148
Abschatz, Hans Aßmann von 1646-1699 . . . . DLB-168
Abse, Dannie 1923- DLB-27, 245
Abutsu-ni 1221-1283 . . . . DLB-203
Academy Chicago Publishers DLB-46
Accius circa 170 B.C.-circa 80 B.C. DLB-211
Accrocca, Elio Filippo 1923- DLB-128
Ace Books DLB-46
Achebe, Chinua 1930- DLB-117; CDWLB-3
Achtenberg, Herbert 1938- DLB-124
Ackerman, Diane 1948- DLB-120
Ackroyd, Peter 1949- DLB-155, 231
Acorn, Milton 1923-1986 . . . . DLB-53

Acosta, Oscar Zeta 1935?- DLB-82
Acosta Torres, José 1925- DLB-209
Actors Theatre of Louisville DLB-7
Adair, Gilbert 1944- DLB-194
Adair, James 1709?-1783? DLB-30
Adam, Graeme Mercer 1839-1912 . . . . DLB-99
Adam, Robert Borthwick II 1863-1940 . . . DLB-187
Adame, Leonard 1947- DLB-82
Adameşteanu, Gabriel 1942- DLB-232
Adamic, Louis 1898-1951 . . . . DLB-9
Adams, Abigail 1744-1818 . . . . DLB-200
Adams, Alice 1926-1999 . . . . DLB-234, Y-86
Adams, Bertha Leith (Mrs. Leith Adams, Mrs. R. S. de Courcy Laffan) 1837?-1912 . . . . DLB-240
Adams, Brooks 1848-1927 . . . . DLB-47
Adams, Charles Francis, Jr. 1835-1915 . . . . DLB-47
Adams, Douglas 1952- Y-83
Adams, Franklin P. 1881-1960 . . . . DLB-29
Adams, Hannah 1755-1832 . . . . DLB-200
Adams, Henry 1838-1918 . . . . . . DLB-12, 47, 189
Adams, Herbert Baxter 1850-1901 . . . . DLB-47
Adams, J. S. and C. [publishing house] DLB-49
Adams, James Truslow 1878-1949 . . . . DLB-17; DS-17
Adams, John 1735-1826 . . . . DLB-31, 183
Adams, John 1735-1826 and Adams, Abigail 1744-1818 . . . . DLB-183
Adams, John Quincy 1767-1848 . . . . DLB-37
Adams, Léonie 1899-1988 . . . . DLB-48
Adams, Levi 1802-1832 . . . . DLB-99
Adams, Samuel 1722-1803 . . . . DLB-31, 43
Adams, Sarah Fuller Flower 1805-1848 . . . . DLB-199
Adams, Thomas 1582 or 1583-1652 . . . . . . DLB-151
Adams, William Taylor 1822-1897 . . . . DLB-42
Adamson, Sir John 1867-1950 . . . . DLB-98
Adcock, Arthur St. John 1864-1930 . . . . . . DLB-135
Adcock, Betty 1938- DLB-105
"Certain Gifts" DLB-105
Adcock, Fleur 1934- DLB-40
Addison, Joseph 1672-1719 . . . DLB-101; CDBLB-2

Ade, George 1866-1944 . . . . DLB-11, 25
Adeler, Max (see Clark, Charles Heber)
Adonias Filho 1915-1990 . . . . DLB-145
Adorno, Theodor W. 1903-1969 . . . . DLB-242
Advance Publishing Company DLB-49
Ady, Endre 1877-1919 . . . . . . DLB-215; CDWLB-4
AE 1867-1935 . . . . DLB-19; CDBLB-5
Ælfric circa 955-circa 1010 . . . . DLB-146
Aeschines circa 390 B.C.-circa 320 B.C. DLB-176
Aeschylus 525-524 B.C.-456-455 B.C. DLB-176; CDWLB-1
Afro-American Literary Critics: An Introduction DLB-33
After Dinner Opera Company Y-92
Agassiz, Elizabeth Cary 1822-1907 . . . . . . DLB-189
Agassiz, Louis 1807-1873 . . . . DLB-1, 235
Agee, James 1909-1955 . . . . DLB-2, 26, 152; CDALB-1
The Agee Legacy: A Conference at the University of Tennessee at Knoxville Y-89
Aguilera Malta, Demetrio 1909-1981 . . . . DLB-145
Ai 1947- DLB-120
Aichinger, Ilse 1921- DLB-85
Aidoo, Ama Ata 1942- DLB-117; CDWLB-3
Aiken, Conrad 1889-1973 . . . . DLB-9, 45, 102; CDALB-5
Aiken, Joan 1924- DLB-161
Aikin, Lucy 1781-1864 . . . . DLB-144, 163
Ainsworth, William Harrison 1805-1882 . . DLB-21
Aistis, Jonas 1904-1973 . . . . . DLB-220; CDWLB-4
Aitken, George A. 1860-1917 . . . . DLB-149
Aitken, Robert [publishing house] DLB-49
Akenside, Mark 1721-1770 . . . . DLB-109
Akins, Zoë 1886-1958 . . . . DLB-26
Aksakov, Sergei Timofeevich 1791-1859 . . . . DLB-198
Akutagawa, Ryūnosuke 1892-1927 . . . . . . DLB-180
Alabaster, William 1568-1640 . . . . DLB-132
Alain de Lille circa 1116-1202/1203 . . . . . DLB-208
Alain-Fournier 1886-1914 . . . . DLB-65
Alanus de Insulis (see Alain de Lille)
Alarcón, Francisco X. 1954- DLB-122

335

Cumulative Index

Alarcón, Justo S. 1930- DLB-209
Alba, Nanina 1915-1968 .... DLB-41
Albee, Edward 1928- DLB-7; CDALB-1
Albert the Great circa 1200-1280 ...... DLB-115
Albert, Octavia 1853-ca. 1889 .... DLB-221
Alberti, Rafael 1902-1999 .... DLB-108
Albertinus, Aegidius circa 1560-1620 .... DLB-164
Alcaeus born circa 620 B.C. DLB-176
Alcott, Bronson 1799-1888 .... DLB-1, 223
Alcott, Louisa May 1832-1888
  ... DLB-1, 42, 79, 223, 239; DS-14; CDALB-3
Alcott, William Andrus 1798-1859 .... DLB-1, 243
Alcuin circa 732-804 .... DLB-148
Alden, Beardsley and Company DLB-49
Alden, Henry Mills 1836-1919 .... DLB-79
Alden, Isabella 1841-1930 .... DLB-42
Alden, John B. [publishing house] DLB-49
Aldington, Richard
  1892-1962 .... DLB-20, 36, 100, 149
Aldis, Dorothy 1896-1966 .... DLB-22
Aldis, H. G. 1863-1919 .... DLB-184
Aldiss, Brian W. 1925- DLB-14
Aldrich, Thomas Bailey
  1836-1907 .... DLB-42, 71, 74, 79
Alegría, Ciro 1909-1967 .... DLB-113
Alegría, Claribel 1924- DLB-145
Aleixandre, Vicente 1898-1984 .... DLB-108
Aleksandravičius, Jonas (see Aistis, Jonas)
Aleksandrov, Aleksandr Andreevich
  (see Durova, Nadezhda Andreevna)
Aleramo, Sibilla 1876-1960 .... DLB-114
Alexander, Cecil Frances 1818-1895 ..... DLB-199
Alexander, Charles 1868-1923 .... DLB-91
Alexander, Charles Wesley
  [publishing house] DLB-49
Alexander, James 1691-1756 .... DLB-24
Alexander, Lloyd 1924- DLB-52
Alexander, Sir William, Earl of Stirling
  1577?-1640 .... DLB-121
Alexie, Sherman 1966- DLB-175, 206
Alexis, Willibald 1798-1871 .... DLB-133
Alfred, King 849-899 .... DLB-146
Alger, Horatio, Jr. 1832-1899 .... DLB-42
Algonquin Books of Chapel Hill DLB-46
Algren, Nelson
  1909-1981 ..... DLB-9; Y-81, Y-82; CDALB-1
Nelson Algren: An International
  Symposium Y-00
Allan, Andrew 1907-1974 .... DLB-88
Allan, Ted 1916- DLB-68
Allbeury, Ted 1917- DLB-87
Alldritt, Keith 1935- DLB-14
Allen, Ethan 1738-1789 .... DLB-31
Allen, Frederick Lewis 1890-1954 ...... DLB-137
Allen, Gay Wilson 1903-1995 .... DLB-103; Y-95
Allen, George 1808-1876 .... DLB-59
Allen, George [publishing house] DLB-106

Allen, George, and Unwin Limited DLB-112
Allen, Grant 1848-1899 .... DLB-70, 92, 178
Allen, Henry W. 1912- Y-85
Allen, Hervey 1889-1949 .... DLB-9, 45
Allen, James 1739-1808 .... DLB-31
Allen, James Lane 1849-1925 .... DLB-71
Allen, Jay Presson 1922- DLB-26
Allen, John, and Company DLB-49
Allen, Paula Gunn 1939- DLB-175
Allen, Samuel W. 1917- DLB-41
Allen, Woody 1935- DLB-44
Allende, Isabel 1942- DLB-145; CDWLB-3
Alline, Henry 1748-1784 .... DLB-99
Allingham, Margery 1904-1966 .... DLB-77
Allingham, William 1824-1889 .... DLB-35
Allison, W. L. [publishing house] DLB-49
The *Alliterative Morte Arthure and the Stanzaic
  Morte Arthur* circa 1350-1400 .... DLB-146
Allott, Kenneth 1912-1973 .... DLB-20
Allston, Washington 1779-1843 ...... DLB-1, 235
Almon, John [publishing house] DLB-154
Alonzo, Dámaso 1898-1990 .... DLB-108
Alsop, George 1636-post 1673 .... DLB-24
Alsop, Richard 1761-1815 .... DLB-37
Altemus, Henry, and Company DLB-49
Altenberg, Peter 1885-1919 .... DLB-81
Althusser, Louis 1918-1990 .... DLB-242
Altolaguirre, Manuel 1905-1959 .... DLB-108
Aluko, T. M. 1918- DLB-117
Alurista 1947- DLB-82
Alvarez, A. 1929- DLB-14, 40
Alver, Betti 1906-1989 ..... DLB-220; CDWLB-4
Amadi, Elechi 1934- DLB-117
Amado, Jorge 1912- DLB-113
Ambler, Eric 1909-1998 .... DLB-77
American Conservatory Theatre DLB-7
American Fiction and the 1930s DLB-9
American Humor: A Historical Survey
  East and Northeast
  South and Southwest
  Midwest
  West DLB-11
The American Library in Paris Y-93
American News Company DLB-49
The American Poets' Corner: The First
  Three Years (1983-1986) Y-86
American Publishing Company DLB-49
American Stationers' Company DLB-49
American Sunday-School Union DLB-49
American Temperance Union DLB-49
American Tract Society DLB-49
The American Trust for the
  British Library Y-96
The American Writers Congress
  (9-12 October 1981) Y-81
The American Writers Congress: A Report
  on Continuing Business Y-81

Ames, Fisher 1758-1808 .... DLB-37
Ames, Mary Clemmer 1831-1884 .... DLB-23
Amiel, Henri-Frédéric 1821-1881 ...... DLB-217
Amini, Johari M. 1935- DLB-41
Amis, Kingsley 1922-1995
  ...... DLB-15, 27, 100, 139, Y-96; CDBLB-7
Amis, Martin 1949- DLB-194
Ammianus Marcellinus
  circa A.D. 330-A.D. 395 .... DLB-211
Ammons, A. R. 1926- DLB-5, 165
Amory, Thomas 1691?-1788 .... DLB-39
Anania, Michael 1939- DLB-193
Anaya, Rudolfo A. 1937- DLB-82, 206
Ancrene Riwle circa 1200-1225 .... DLB-146
Andersch, Alfred 1914-1980 .... DLB-69
Andersen, Benny 1929- DLB-214
Anderson, Alexander 1775-1870 .... DLB-188
Anderson, David 1929- DLB-241
Anderson, Frederick Irving 1877-1947 ... DLB-202
Anderson, Margaret 1886-1973 .... DLB-4, 91
Anderson, Maxwell 1888-1959 .... DLB-7, 228
Anderson, Patrick 1915-1979 .... DLB-68
Anderson, Paul Y. 1893-1938 .... DLB-29
Anderson, Poul 1926- DLB-8
Anderson, Robert 1750-1830 .... DLB-142
Anderson, Robert 1917- DLB-7
Anderson, Sherwood
  1876-1941 ..... DLB-4, 9, 86; DS-1; CDALB-4
Andreae, Johann Valentin 1586-1654 ... DLB-164
Andreas Capellanus
  flourished circa 1185 .... DLB-208
Andreas-Salomé, Lou 1861-1937 .... DLB-66
Andres, Stefan 1906-1970 .... DLB-69
Andreu, Blanca 1959- DLB-134
Andrewes, Lancelot 1555-1626 ..... DLB-151, 172
Andrews, Charles M. 1863-1943 .... DLB-17
Andrews, Miles Peter ?-1814 .... DLB-89
Andrews, Stephan Pearl 1812-1886 ..... DLB-250
Andrian, Leopold von 1875-1951 ...... DLB-81
Andrić, Ivo 1892-1975 ...... DLB-147; CDWLB-4
Andrieux, Louis (see Aragon, Louis)
Andrus, Silas, and Son DLB-49
Andrzejewski, Jerzy 1909-1983 .... DLB-215
Angell, James Burrill 1829-1916 .... DLB-64
Angell, Roger 1920- DLB-171, 185
Angelou, Maya 1928- DLB-38; CDALB-7
Anger, Jane flourished 1589 .... DLB-136
Angers, Félicité (see Conan, Laure)
Anglo-Norman Literature in the Development
  of Middle English Literature DLB-146
The *Anglo-Saxon Chronicle* circa 890-1154 .. DLB-146
The "Angry Young Men" DLB-15
Angus and Robertson (UK) Limited DLB-112
Anhalt, Edward 1914-2000 .... DLB-26
Anners, Henry F. [publishing house] DLB-49
Annolied between 1077 and 1081 .... DLB-148

Annual Awards for *Dictionary of Literary Biography*
    Editors and Contributors Y-98, Y-99, Y-00

Anselm of Canterbury 1033-1109 . . . . . . .DLB-115

Anstey, F. 1856-1934 . . . . DLB-141, 178

Anthony, Michael 1932- DLB-125

Anthony, Piers 1934- DLB-8

Anthony, Susanna 1726-1791. . . . . .DLB-200

Antin, David 1932- DLB-169

Antin, Mary 1881-1949 . . . . DLB-221; Y-84

Anton Ulrich, Duke of Brunswick-Lüneburg
    1633-1714 .DLB-168

Antschel, Paul (see Celan, Paul)

Anyidoho, Kofi 1947- DLB-157

Anzaldúa, Gloria 1942- DLB-122

Anzengruber, Ludwig 1839-1889 . . . . . . .DLB-129

Apess, William 1798-1839 . . . . DLB-175, 243

Apodaca, Rudy S. 1939- DLB-82

Apollonius Rhodius third century B.C. . . . DLB-176

Apple, Max 1941- DLB-130

Appleton, D., and Company DLB-49

Appleton-Century-Crofts. DLB-46

Applewhite, James 1935- DLB-105

Applewood Books DLB-46

April, Jean-Pierre 1948- DLB-251

Apuleius circa A.D. 125-post A.D. 164
    . . . . .DLB-211; CDWLB-1

Aquin, Hubert 1929-1977 . . . . .DLB-53

Aquinas, Thomas 1224 or 1225-1274 . . . . DLB-115

Aragon, Louis 1897-1982. . . . . .DLB-72

Aralica, Ivan 1930- DLB-181

Aratus of Soli
    circa 315 B.C.-circa 239 B.C. DLB-176

Arbasino, Alberto 1930- DLB-196

Arbor House Publishing Company DLB-46

Arbuthnot, John 1667-1735 . . . . .DLB-101

Arcadia House .DLB-46

Arce, Julio G. (see Ulica, Jorge)

Archer, William 1856-1924 . . . . .DLB-10

Archilochhus
    mid seventh century B.C.E. DLB-176

The Archpoet circa 1130?-? DLB-148

Archpriest Avvakum (Petrovich)
    1620?-1682 . . . . .DLB-150

Arden, John 1930- DLB-13, 245

Arden of Faversham. DLB-62

Ardis Publishers. Y-89

Ardizzone, Edward 1900-1979 . . . . .DLB-160

Arellano, Juan Estevan 1947- DLB-122

The Arena Publishing Company DLB-49

Arena Stage DLB-7

Arenas, Reinaldo 1943-1990 . . . . .DLB-145

Arendt, Hannah 1906-1975 . . . . .DLB-242

Arensberg, Ann 1937- Y-82

Arghezi, Tudor 1880-1967. . . DLB-220; CDWLB-4

Arguedas, José María 1911-1969 . . . . . . .DLB-113

Argueta, Manilio 1936- DLB-145

Arias, Ron 1941- DLB-82

Arishima, Takeo 1878-1923. . . . . .DLB-180

Aristophanes circa 446 B.C.-circa 386 B.C.
    . . . . .DLB-176; CDWLB-1

Aristotle 384 B.C.-322 B.C.
    . . . . .DLB-176; CDWLB-1

Ariyoshi Sawako 1931-1984 . . . . .DLB-182

Arland, Marcel 1899-1986. . . . . .DLB-72

Arlen, Michael 1895-1956 . . . . DLB-36, 77, 162

Armah, Ayi Kwei 1939- DLB-117; CDWLB-3

Armantrout, Rae 1947- DLB-193

Der arme Hartmann ?-after 1150. . . . . . . .DLB-148

Armed Services Editions DLB-46

Armstrong, Martin Donisthorpe
    1882-1974 .DLB-197

Armstrong, Richard 1903- DLB-160

Arndt, Ernst Moritz 1769-1860 . . . . .DLB-90

Arnim, Achim von 1781-1831 . . . . .DLB-90

Arnim, Bettina von 1785-1859 . . . . .DLB-90

Arnim, Elizabeth von (Countess Mary
    Annette Beauchamp Russell)
    1866-1941 .DLB-197

Arno Press DLB-46

Arnold, Edward [publishing house]. DLB-112

Arnold, Edwin 1832-1904 . . . . .DLB-35

Arnold, Edwin L. 1857-1935 . . . . .DLB-178

Arnold, Matthew
    1822-1888 . . . . DLB-32, 57; CDBLB-4

Preface to *Poems* (1853) DLB-32

Arnold, Thomas 1795-1842. . . . . .DLB-55

Arnott, Peter 1962- DLB-233

Arnow, Harriette Simpson 1908-1986 . . . . .DLB-6

Arp, Bill (see Smith, Charles Henry)

Arpino, Giovanni 1927-1987 . . . . .DLB-177

Arreola, Juan José 1918- DLB-113

Arrian circa 89-circa 155 . . . . .DLB-176

Arrowsmith, J. W. [publishing house] DLB-106

The Art and Mystery of Publishing:
    Interviews Y-97

Arthur, T. S.
    1809-1885 . . . . DLB-3, 42, 79, 250; DS-13

The Arthurian Tradition and
    Its European Context DLB-138

Artmann, H. C. 1921-2000 . . . . .DLB-85

Arvin, Newton 1900-1963 . . . . .DLB-103

Asch, Nathan 1902-1964 . . . . DLB-4, 28

Ascham, Roger 1515 or 1516-1568 . . . . . .DLB-236

Ash, John 1948- DLB-40

Ashbery, John 1927- DLB-5, 165; Y-81

Ashbridge, Elizabeth 1713-1755 . . . . .DLB-200

Ashburnham, Bertram Lord
    1797-1878. .DLB-184

Ashendene Press DLB-112

Asher, Sandy 1942- Y-83

Ashton, Winifred (see Dane, Clemence)

Asimov, Isaac 1920-1992. . . . . .DLB-8; Y-92

Askew, Anne circa 1521-1546 . . . . .DLB-136

Aspazija 1865-1943 . . . . DLB-220; CDWLB-4

Asselin, Olivar 1874-1937 . . . . .DLB-92

The Association of American Publishers Y-99

The Association for Documentary Editing . . . Y-00

Astley, William (see Warung, Price)

Asturias, Miguel Angel
    1899-1974 . . . . DLB-113; CDWLB-3

At Home with Albert Erskine Y-00

Atheneum Publishers. DLB-46

Atherton, Gertrude 1857-1948. . . . . DLB-9, 78, 186

Athlone Press. .DLB-112

Atkins, Josiah circa 1755-1781 . . . . .DLB-31

Atkins, Russell 1926- DLB-41

Atkinson, Louisa 1834-1872 . . . . .DLB-230

The Atlantic Monthly Press. DLB-46

Attaway, William 1911-1986 . . . . .DLB-76

Atwood, Margaret 1939- DLB-53, 251

Aubert, Alvin 1930- DLB-41

Aubert de Gaspé, Phillipe-Ignace-François
    1814-1841 . . . . .DLB-99

Aubert de Gaspé, Phillipe-Joseph
    1786-1871 . . . . .DLB-99

Aubin, Napoléon 1812-1890 . . . . .DLB-99

Aubin, Penelope
    1685-circa 1731 . . . . .DLB-39

Preface to *The Life of Charlotta
    du Pont* (1723) DLB-39

Aubrey-Fletcher, Henry Lancelot (see Wade, Henry)

Auchincloss, Louis 1917- DLB-2, 244; Y-80

Auden, W. H. 1907-1973 . . .DLB-10, 20; CDBLB-6

Audio Art in America: A Personal Memoir . . . Y-85

Audubon, John James 1785-1851 . . . . . . .DLB-248

Audubon, John Woodhouse
    1812-1862 .DLB-183

Auerbach, Berthold 1812-1882 . . . . .DLB-133

Auernheimer, Raoul 1876-1948. . . . . .DLB-81

Augier, Emile 1820-1889 . . . . .DLB-192

Augustine 354-430. . . . . .DLB-115

Responses to Ken Auletta Y-97

Aulus Cellius
    circa A.D. 125-circa A.D. 180? DLB-211

Austen, Jane
    1775-1817 . . . . .DLB-116; CDBLB-3

Auster, Paul 1947- DLB-227

Austin, Alfred 1835-1913. . . . . .DLB-35

Austin, Jane Goodwin 1831-1894 . . . . . . .DLB-202

Austin, Mary 1868-1934 . . . . . DLB-9, 78, 206, 221

Austin, William 1778-1841. . . . . .DLB-74

Australie (Emily Manning)
    1845-1890 .DLB-230

Author-Printers, 1476–1599. . . . . .DLB-167

Author Websites Y-97

Authors and Newspapers Association DLB-46

Authors' Publishing Company DLB-49

Avallone, Michael 1924-1999. . . . . Y-99

Avalon Books. DLB-46

Avancini, Nicolaus 1611-1686 . . . . .DLB-164

Avendaño, Fausto 1941- DLB-82
Averroëö 1126-1198 .... DLB-115
Avery, Gillian 1926- DLB-161
Avicenna 980-1037 .... DLB-115
Avison, Margaret 1918- DLB-53
Avon Books DLB-46
Avyžius, Jonas 1922-1999 .... DLB-220
Awdry, Wilbert Vere 1911-1997 .... DLB-160
Awoonor, Kofi 1935- DLB-117
Ayckbourn, Alan 1939- DLB-13, 245
Aymé, Marcel 1902-1967 .... DLB-72
Aytoun, Sir Robert 1570-1638 .... DLB-121
Aytoun, William Edmondstoune
   1813-1865 .... DLB-32, 159

B

B. V. (see Thomson, James)
Babbitt, Irving 1865-1933 .... DLB-63
Babbitt, Natalie 1932- DLB-52
Babcock, John [publishing house] DLB-49
Babits, Mihály 1883-1941 ... DLB-215; CDWLB-4
Babrius circa 150-200 .... DLB-176
Baca, Jimmy Santiago 1952- DLB-122
Bache, Benjamin Franklin 1769-1798 .... DLB-43
Bacheller, Irving 1859-1950 .... DLB-202
Bachmann, Ingeborg 1926-1973 .... DLB-85
Bačinskaitė-Bučienė, Salomėja (see Nėris, Salomėja)
Bacon, Delia 1811-1859 .... DLB-1, 243
Bacon, Francis
   1561-1626 .... DLB-151, 236; CDBLB-1
Bacon, Sir Nicholas circa 1510-1579 .... DLB-132
Bacon, Roger circa 1214/1220-1292 .... DLB-115
Bacon, Thomas circa 1700-1768 .... DLB-31
Bacovia, George
   1881-1957 .... DLB-220; CDWLB-4
Badger, Richard G., and Company DLB-49
Bagaduce Music Lending Library Y-00
Bage, Robert 1728-1801 .... DLB-39
Bagehot, Walter 1826-1877 .... DLB-55
Bagley, Desmond 1923-1983 .... DLB-87
Bagley, Sarah G. 1806-1848 .... DLB-239
Bagnold, Enid 1889-1981 ... DLB-13, 160, 191, 245
Bagryana, Elisaveta
   1893-1991 .... DLB-147; CDWLB-4
Bahr, Hermann 1863-1934 .... DLB-81, 118
Bailey, Abigail Abbot 1746-1815 .... DLB-200
Bailey, Alfred Goldsworthy 1905- DLB-68
Bailey, Francis [publishing house] DLB-49
Bailey, H. C. 1878-1961 .... DLB-77
Bailey, Jacob 1731-1808 .... DLB-99
Bailey, Paul 1937- DLB-14
Bailey, Philip James 1816-1902 .... DLB-32
Baillargeon, Pierre 1916-1967 .... DLB-88
Baillie, Hugh 1890-1966 .... DLB-29
Baillie, Joanna 1762-1851 .... DLB-93

Bailyn, Bernard 1922- DLB-17
Bainbridge, Beryl 1933- DLB-14, 231
Baird, Irene 1901-1981 .... DLB-68
Baker, Augustine 1575-1641 .... DLB-151
Baker, Carlos 1909-1987 .... DLB-103
Baker, David 1954- DLB-120
Baker, Herschel C. 1914-1990 .... DLB-111
Baker, Houston A., Jr. 1943- DLB-67
Baker, Nicholson 1957- DLB-227
Baker, Samuel White 1821-1893 ...... DLB-166
Baker, Thomas 1656-1740 .... DLB-213
Baker, Walter H., Company
   ("Baker's Plays") DLB-49
The Baker and Taylor Company DLB-49
Bakhtin, Mikhail Mikhailovich
   1895-1975 .... DLB-242
Balaban, John 1943- DLB-120
Bald, Wambly 1902- DLB-4
Balde, Jacob 1604-1668 .... DLB-164
Balderston, John 1889-1954 .... DLB-26
Baldwin, James 1924-1987
   .... DLB-2, 7, 33, 249; Y-87; CDALB-1
Baldwin, Joseph Glover
   1815-1864 .... DLB-3, 11, 248
Baldwin, Louisa (Mrs. Alfred Baldwin)
   1845-1925 .... DLB-240
Baldwin, Richard and Anne
   [publishing house] DLB-170
Baldwin, William circa 1515-1563 ..... DLB-132
Bale, John 1495-1563 .... DLB-132
Balestrini, Nanni 1935- DLB-128, 196
Balfour, Sir Andrew 1630-1694 .... DLB-213
Balfour, Arthur James 1848-1930 ..... DLB-190
Balfour, Sir James 1600-1657 .... DLB-213
Ballantine Books DLB-46
Ballantyne, R. M. 1825-1894 .... DLB-163
Ballard, J. G. 1930- DLB-14, 207
Ballard, Martha Moore 1735-1812 .... DLB-200
Ballerini, Luigi 1940- DLB-128
Ballou, Maturin Murray
   1820-1895 .... DLB-79, 189
Ballou, Robert O. [publishing house] DLB-46
Balzac, Honoré de 1799-1855 .... DLB-119
Bambara, Toni Cade
   1939- DLB-38, 218; CDALB-7
Bamford, Samuel 1788-1872 .... DLB-190
Bancroft, A. L., and Company DLB-49
Bancroft, George 1800-1891 ... DLB-1, 30, 59, 243
Bancroft, Hubert Howe 1832-1918 ... DLB-47, 140
Bandelier, Adolph F. 1840-1914 ...... DLB-186
Bangs, John Kendrick 1862-1922 ..... DLB-11, 79
Banim, John 1798-1842 .... DLB-116, 158, 159
Banim, Michael 1796-1874 .... DLB-158, 159
Banks, Iain 1954- DLB-194
Banks, John circa 1653-1706 .... DLB-80
Banks, Russell 1940- DLB-130
Bannerman, Helen 1862-1946 .... DLB-141

Bantam Books DLB-46
Banti, Anna 1895-1985 .... DLB-177
Banville, John 1945- DLB-14
Banville, Théodore de 1823-1891 ...... DLB-217
Baraka, Amiri
   1934- DLB-5, 7, 16, 38; DS-8; CDALB-1
Barańczak, Stanisław 1946- DLB-232
Baratynsky, Evgenii Abramovich
   1800-1844 .... DLB-205
Barbauld, Anna Laetitia
   1743-1825 .... DLB-107, 109, 142, 158
Barbeau, Marius 1883-1969 .... DLB-92
Barber, John Warner 1798-1885 .... DLB-30
Bàrberi Squarotti, Giorgio 1929- DLB-128
Barbey d'Aurevilly, Jules-Amédée
   1808-1889 .... DLB-119
Barbier, Auguste 1805-1882 .... DLB-217
Barbilian, Dan (see Barbu, Ion)
Barbour, John circa 1316-1395 .... DLB-146
Barbour, Ralph Henry 1870-1944 ..... DLB-22
Barbu, Ion 1895-1961 .... DLB-220; CDWLB-4
Barbusse, Henri 1873-1935 .... DLB-65
Barclay, Alexander circa 1475-1552 ... DLB-132
Barclay, E. E., and Company DLB-49
Bardeen, C. W. [publishing house] DLB-49
Barham, Richard Harris 1788-1845 .... DLB-159
Barich, Bill 1943- DLB-185
Baring, Maurice 1874-1945 .... DLB-34
Baring-Gould, Sabine
   1834-1924 .... DLB-156, 190
Barker, A. L. 1918- DLB-14, 139
Barker, Arthur, Limited DLB-112
Barker, George 1913-1991 .... DLB-20
Barker, Harley Granville 1877-1946 ..... DLB-10
Barker, Howard 1946- DLB-13, 233
Barker, James Nelson 1784-1858 ...... DLB-37
Barker, Jane 1652-1727 .... DLB-39, 131
Barker, Lady Mary Anne 1831-1911 ... DLB-166
Barker, William circa 1520-after 1576 ... DLB-132
Barkov, Ivan Semenovich 1732-1768 ... DLB-150
Barks, Coleman 1937- DLB-5
Barlach, Ernst 1870-1938 .... DLB-56, 118
Barlow, Joel 1754-1812 .... DLB-37
The Prospect of Peace (1778) DLB-37
Barnard, John 1681-1770 .... DLB-24
Barne, Kitty (Mary Catherine Barne)
   1883-1957 .... DLB-160
Barnes, A. S., and Company DLB-49
Barnes, Barnabe 1571-1609 .... DLB-132
Barnes, Djuna 1892-1982 .... DLB-4, 9, 45
Barnes, Jim 1933- DLB-175
Barnes, Julian 1946- DLB-194; Y-93
Barnes, Margaret Ayer 1886-1967 .... DLB-9
Barnes, Peter 1931- DLB-13, 233
Barnes, William 1801-1886 .... DLB-32
Barnes and Noble Books DLB-46

Barnet, Miguel 1940- DLB-145	Baum, L. Frank 1856-1919 .... DLB-22	Beer, Johann 1655-1700 .... DLB-168
Barney, Natalie 1876-1972 .... DLB-4	Baum, Vicki 1888-1960 .... DLB-85	Beer, Patricia 1919-1999 .... DLB-40
Barnfield, Richard 1574-1627 .... DLB-172	Baumbach, Jonathan 1933- Y-80	Beerbohm, Max 1872-1956 .... DLB-34, 100
Baron, Richard W., Publishing Company DLB-46	Bausch, Richard 1945- DLB-130	Beer-Hofmann, Richard 1866-1945 .... DLB-81
	Bausch, Robert 1945- DLB-218	Beers, Henry A. 1847-1926 .... DLB-71
Barr, Amelia Edith Huddleston 1831-1919 .... DLB-202, 221	Bawden, Nina 1925- DLB-14, 161, 207	Beeton, S. O. [publishing house] DLB-106
Barr, Robert 1850-1912 .... DLB-70, 92	Bax, Clifford 1886-1962 .... DLB-10, 100	Bégon, Elisabeth 1696-1755 .... DLB-99
Barral, Carlos 1928-1989 .... DLB-134	Baxter, Charles 1947- DLB-130	Behan, Brendan 1923-1964 .... DLB-13, 233; CDBLB-7
Barrax, Gerald William 1933- DLB-41, 120	Bayer, Eleanor (see Perry, Eleanor)	
Barrès, Maurice 1862-1923 .... DLB-123	Bayer, Konrad 1932-1964 .... DLB-85	Behn, Aphra 1640?-1689 .... DLB-39, 80, 131
Barrett, Eaton Stannard 1786-1820 ...... DLB-116	Baynes, Pauline 1922- DLB-160	Behn, Harry 1898-1973 .... DLB-61
Barrie, J. M. 1860-1937 ...... DLB-10, 141, 156; CDBLB-5	Baynton, Barbara 1857-1929 .... DLB-230	Behrman, S. N. 1893-1973 .... DLB-7, 44
	Bazin, Hervé 1911-1996 .... DLB-83	Belaney, Archibald Stansfeld (see Grey Owl)
Barrie and Jenkins DLB-112	Beach, Sylvia 1887-1962 .... DLB-4; DS-15	Belasco, David 1853-1931 .... DLB-7
Barrio, Raymond 1921- DLB-82	Beacon Press DLB-49	Belford, Clarke and Company DLB-49
Barrios, Gregg 1945- DLB-122	Beadle and Adams DLB-49	Belinksy, Vissarion Grigor'evich 1811-1848 .... DLB-198
Barry, Philip 1896-1949 .... DLB-7, 228	Beagle, Peter S. 1939- Y-80	
Barry, Robertine (see Françoise)	Beal, M. F. 1937- Y-81	Belitt, Ben 1911- DLB-5
Barry, Sebastian 1955- DLB-245	Beale, Howard K. 1899-1959 .... DLB-17	Belknap, Jeremy 1744-1798 .... DLB-30, 37
Barse and Hopkins DLB-46	Beard, Charles A. 1874-1948 .... DLB-17	Bell, Adrian 1901-1980 .... DLB-191
Barstow, Stan 1928- DLB-14, 139	A Beat Chronology: The First Twenty-five Years, 1944-1969 .... DLB-16	Bell, Clive 1881-1964 .... DS-10
Barth, John 1930- DLB-2, 227		Bell, Daniel 1919- DLB-246
Barthelme, Donald 1931-1989 .... DLB-2, 234; Y-80, Y-89	Periodicals of the Beat Generation DLB-16	Bell, George, and Sons DLB-106
	The Beats in New York City DLB-237	Bell, Gertrude Margaret Lowthian 1868-1926 .... DLB-174
Barthelme, Frederick 1943- DLB-244; Y-85	The Beats in the West DLB-237	
Bartholomew, Frank 1898-1985 .... DLB-127	Beattie, Ann 1947- DLB-218; Y-82	Bell, James Madison 1826-1902 .... DLB-50
Bartlett, John 1820-1905 .... DLB-1, 235	Beattie, James 1735-1803 .... DLB-109	Bell, Madison Smartt 1957- DLB-218
Bartol, Cyrus Augustus 1813-1900 .... DLB-1, 235	Beatty, Chester 1875-1968 .... DLB-201	Bell, Marvin 1937- DLB-5
Barton, Bernard 1784-1849 .... DLB-96	Beauchemin, Nérée 1850-1931 .... DLB-92	Bell, Millicent 1919- DLB-111
Barton, John ca. 1610-1675 .... DLB-236	Beauchemin, Yves 1941- DLB-60	Bell, Quentin 1910-1996 .... DLB-155
Barton, Thomas Pennant 1803-1869 ..... DLB-140	Beaugrand, Honoré 1848-1906 .... DLB-99	Bell, Robert [publishing house] DLB-49
Bartram, John 1699-1777 .... DLB-31	Beaulieu, Victor-Lévy 1945- DLB-53	Bell, Vanessa 1879-1961 .... DS-10
Bartram, William 1739-1823 .... DLB-37	Beaumont, Francis circa 1584-1616 and Fletcher, John 1579-1625 .... DLB-58; CDBLB-1	Bellamy, Edward 1850-1898 .... DLB-12
Basic Books DLB-46		Bellamy, John [publishing house] DLB-170
Basille, Theodore (see Becon, Thomas)		Bellamy, Joseph 1719-1790 .... DLB-31
Bass, Rick 1958- DLB-212	Beaumont, Sir John 1583?-1627 .... DLB-121	La Belle Assemblée 1806-1837 .... DLB-110
Bass, T. J. 1932- Y-81	Beaumont, Joseph 1616-1699 .... DLB-126	Bellezza, Dario 1944-1996 .... DLB-128
Bassani, Giorgio 1916- DLB-128, 177	Beauvoir, Simone de 1908-1986 .... DLB-72; Y-86	Belloc, Hilaire 1870-1953 .... DLB-19, 100, 141, 174
Basse, William circa 1583-1653 .... DLB-121	Becher, Ulrich 1910- DLB-69	Belloc, Madame (see Parkes, Bessie Rayner)
Bassett, John Spencer 1867-1928 .... DLB-17	Becker, Carl 1873-1945 .... DLB-17	Bellonci, Maria 1902-1986 .... DLB-196
Bassler, Thomas Joseph (see Bass, T. J.)	Becker, Jurek 1937-1997 .... DLB-75	Bellow, Saul 1915- DLB-2, 28; Y-82; DS-3; CDALB-1
Bate, Walter Jackson 1918-1999 ..... DLB-67, 103	Becker, Jurgen 1932- DLB-75	
Bateman, Christopher [publishing house] DLB-170	Beckett, Samuel 1906-1989 .... DLB-13, 15, 233; Y-90; CDBLB-7	Belmont Productions DLB-46
		Bels, Alberts 1938- DLB-232
Bateman, Stephen circa 1510-1584 ...... DLB-136	Beckford, William 1760-1844 .... DLB-39	Belševica, Vizma 1931- DLB-232; CDWLB-4
Bates, H. E. 1905-1974 .... DLB-162, 191	Beckham, Barry 1944- DLB-33	Bemelmans, Ludwig 1898-1962 .... DLB-22
Bates, Katharine Lee 1859-1929 .... DLB-71	Becon, Thomas circa 1512-1567 .... DLB-136	Bemis, Samuel Flagg 1891-1973 .... DLB-17
Batiushkov, Konstantin Nikolaevich 1787-1855 .... DLB-205	Becque, Henry 1837-1899 .... DLB-192	Bemrose, William [publishing house] DLB-106
	Beddoes, Thomas 1760-1808 .... DLB-158	Ben no Naishi 1228?-1271? DLB-203
Batsford, B. T. [publishing house] DLB-106	Beddoes, Thomas Lovell 1803-1849 ...... DLB-96	Benchley, Robert 1889-1945 .... DLB-11
Battiscombe, Georgina 1905- DLB-155	Bede circa 673-735 .... DLB-146	Bencúr, Matej (see Kukučin, Martin)
The Battle of Maldon circa 1000 .... DLB-146	Bedford-Jones, H. 1887-1949 .... DLB-251	Benedetti, Mario 1920- DLB-113
Baudelaire, Charles 1821-1867 .... DLB-217	Beecher, Catharine Esther 1800-1878 .. DLB-1, 243	Benedict, Pinckney 1964- DLB-244
Bauer, Bruno 1809-1882 .... DLB-133	Beecher, Henry Ward 1813-1887 .... DLB-3, 43, 250	Benedict, Ruth 1887-1948 .... DLB-246
Bauer, Wolfgang 1941- DLB-124		Benedictus, David 1938- DLB-14
	Beer, George L. 1872-1920 .... DLB-47	

Cumulative Index

Benedikt, Michael 1935- DLB-5

Benediktov, Vladimir Grigor'evich 1807-1873 .... DLB-205

Benét, Stephen Vincent 1898-1943 .... DLB-4, 48, 102, 249

Benét, William Rose 1886-1950 .... DLB-45

Benford, Gregory 1941- Y-82

Benjamin, Park 1809-1864 .... DLB-3, 59, 73, 250

Benjamin, S. G. W. 1837-1914 .... DLB-189

Benjamin, Walter 1892-1940 .... DLB-242

Benlowes, Edward 1602-1676 .... DLB-126

Benn Brothers Limited DLB-106

Benn, Gottfried 1886-1956 .... DLB-56

Bennett, Arnold 1867-1931 .... DLB-10, 34, 98, 135; CDBLB-5

Bennett, Charles 1899-1995 .... DLB-44

Bennett, Emerson 1822-1905 .... DLB-202

Bennett, Gwendolyn 1902- DLB-51

Bennett, Hal 1930- DLB-33

Bennett, James Gordon 1795-1872 .... DLB-43

Bennett, James Gordon, Jr. 1841-1918 .... DLB-23

Bennett, John 1865-1956 .... DLB-42

Bennett, Louise 1919- DLB-117; CDWLB-3

Benni, Stefano 1947- DLB-196

Benoit, Jacques 1941- DLB-60

Benson, A. C. 1862-1925 .... DLB-98

Benson, E. F. 1867-1940 .... DLB-135, 153

Benson, Jackson J. 1930- DLB-111

Benson, Robert Hugh 1871-1914 .... DLB-153

Benson, Stella 1892-1933 .... DLB-36, 162

Bent, James Theodore 1852-1897 ......DLB-174

Bent, Mabel Virginia Anna ?-? DLB-174

Bentham, Jeremy 1748-1832 ....DLB-107, 158

Bentley, E. C. 1875-1956 .... DLB-70

Bentley, Phyllis 1894-1977 .... DLB-191

Bentley, Richard [publishing house] DLB-106

Benton, Robert 1932- and Newman, David 1937- DLB-44

Benziger Brothers DLB-49

Beowulf circa 900-1000 or 790-825 .... DLB-146; CDBLB-1

Berent, Wacław 1873-1940 .... DLB-215

Beresford, Anne 1929- DLB-40

Beresford, John Davys 1873-1947 ....DLB-162, 178, 197

"Experiment in the Novel" (1929) DLB-36

Beresford-Howe, Constance 1922- DLB-88

Berford, R. G., Company DLB-49

Berg, Stephen 1934- DLB-5

Bergengruen, Werner 1892-1964 .... DLB-56

Berger, John 1926- DLB-14, 207

Berger, Meyer 1898-1959 .... DLB-29

Berger, Thomas 1924- DLB-2; Y-80

Berkeley, Anthony 1893-1971 .... DLB-77

Berkeley, George 1685-1753 ..... DLB-31, 101

The Berkley Publishing Corporation DLB-46

Berlin, Lucia 1936- DLB-130

Berman, Marshall 1940- DLB-246

Bernal, Vicente J. 1888-1915 .... DLB-82

Bernanos, Georges 1888-1948 .... DLB-72

Bernard, Harry 1898-1979 .... DLB-92

Bernard, John 1756-1828 .... DLB-37

Bernard of Chartres circa 1060-1124? ... DLB-115

Bernard of Clairvaux 1090-1153 .... DLB-208

The Bernard Malamud Archive at the Harry Ransom Humanities Research Center. Y-00

Bernard Silvestris flourished circa 1130-1160 .... DLB-208

Bernari, Carlo 1909-1992 ....DLB-177

Bernhard, Thomas 1931-1989 ....DLB-85, 124; CDWLB-2

Bernstein, Charles 1950- DLB-169

Berriault, Gina 1926-1999 .... DLB-130

Berrigan, Daniel 1921- DLB-5

Berrigan, Ted 1934-1983 .... DLB-5, 169

Berry, Wendell 1934- DLB-5, 6, 234

Berryman, John 1914-1972 .... DLB-48; CDALB-1

Bersianik, Louky 1930- DLB-60

Berthelet, Thomas [publishing house] DLB-170

Berto, Giuseppe 1914-1978 ....DLB-177

Bertolucci, Attilio 1911- DLB-128

Berton, Pierre 1920- DLB-68

Bertrand, Louis "Aloysius" 1807-1841 .... DLB-217

Besant, Sir Walter 1836-1901 ...... DLB-135, 190

Bessette, Gerard 1920- DLB-53

Bessie, Alvah 1904-1985 .... DLB-26

Bester, Alfred 1913-1987 .... DLB-8

Besterman, Theodore 1904-1976 .... DLB-201

The Bestseller Lists: An Assessment Y-84

Bestuzhev, Aleksandr Aleksandrovich (Marlinsky) 1797-1837 .... DLB-198

Bestuzhev, Nikolai Aleksandrovich 1791-1855 .... DLB-198

Betham-Edwards, Matilda Barbara (see Edwards, Matilda Barbara Betham-)

Betjeman, John 1906-1984 .... DLB-20; Y-84; CDBLB-7

Betocchi, Carlo 1899-1986 .... DLB-128

Bettarini, Mariella 1942- DLB-128

Betts, Doris 1932- DLB-218; Y-82

Beùkoviù, Matija 1939- DLB-181

Beveridge, Albert J. 1862-1927 .... DLB-17

Beverley, Robert circa 1673-1722 ..... DLB-24, 30

Bevilacqua, Alberto 1934- DLB-196

Bevington, Louisa Sarah 1845-1895..... DLB-199

Beyle, Marie-Henri (see Stendhal)

Białoszewski, Miron 1922-1983 .... DLB-232

Bianco, Margery Williams 1881-1944 ... DLB-160

Bibaud, Adèle 1854-1941 .... DLB-92

Bibaud, Michel 1782-1857 .... DLB-99

Bibliographical and Textual Scholarship Since World War II.................. Y-89

Bichsel, Peter 1935- DLB-75

Bickerstaff, Isaac John 1733-circa 1808.... DLB-89

Biddle, Drexel [publishing house]........ DLB-49

Bidermann, Jacob 1577 or 1578-1639 .... DLB-164

Bidwell, Walter Hilliard 1798-1881 ...... DLB-79

Bienek, Horst 1930- DLB-75

Bierbaum, Otto Julius 1865-1910 .... DLB-66

Bierce, Ambrose 1842-1914? DLB-11, 12, 23, 71, 74, 186; CDALB-3

Bigelow, William F. 1879-1966.......... DLB-91

Biggle, Lloyd, Jr. 1923- DLB-8

Bigiaretti, Libero 1905-1993 ....DLB-177

Bigland, Eileen 1898-1970 .... DLB-195

Biglow, Hosea (see Lowell, James Russell)

Bigongiari, Piero 1914- DLB-128

Billinger, Richard 1890-1965 .... DLB-124

Billings, Hammatt 1818-1874 .... DLB-188

Billings, John Shaw 1898-1975 ....DLB-137

Billings, Josh (see Shaw, Henry Wheeler)

Binding, Rudolf G. 1867-1938 .... DLB-66

Bingay, Malcolm 1884-1953............ DLB-241

Bingham, Caleb 1757-1817 .... DLB-42

Bingham, George Barry 1906-1988 ......DLB-127

Bingham, Sallie 1937- DLB-234

Bingley, William [publishing house]..... DLB-154

Binyon, Laurence 1869-1943 .... DLB-19

Biographia Brittanica DLB-142

Biographical Documents I Y-84

Biographical Documents II.................. Y-85

Bioren, John [publishing house] DLB-49

Bioy Casares, Adolfo 1914- DLB-113

Bird, Isabella Lucy 1831-1904 .... DLB-166

Bird, Robert Montgomery 1806-1854 ... DLB-202

Bird, William 1888-1963 .... DLB-4; DS-15

Birken, Sigmund von 1626-1681 .... DLB-164

Birney, Earle 1904- DLB-88

Birrell, Augustine 1850-1933 .... DLB-98

Bisher, Furman 1918- DLB-171

Bishop, Elizabeth 1911-1979 .... DLB-5, 169; CDALB-6

Bishop, John Peale 1892-1944 ...... DLB-4, 9, 45

Bismarck, Otto von 1815-1898 .... DLB-129

Bisset, Robert 1759-1805 .... DLB-142

Bissett, Bill 1939- DLB-53

Bitzius, Albert (see Gotthelf, Jeremias)

Bjørnvig, Thorkild 1918- DLB-214

Black, David (D. M.) 1941- DLB-40

Black, Walter J. [publishing house]....... DLB-46

Black, Winifred 1863-1936............ DLB-25

The Black Aesthetic: Background DS-8

Black Theaters and Theater Organizations in America, 1961-1982: A Research List DLB-38

Black Theatre: A Forum [excerpts] DLB-38

Blackamore, Arthur 1679-? DLB-24, 39

Blackburn, Alexander L. 1929- Y-85

Blackburn, Paul 1926-1971 . . . . . . .DLB-16; Y-81

Blackburn, Thomas 1916-1977 . . . . .DLB-27

Blackmore, R. D. 1825-1900 . . . . .DLB-18

Blackmore, Sir Richard 1654-1729. . . . . . .DLB-131

Blackmur, R. P. 1904-1965 . . . . .DLB-63

Blackwell, Basil, Publisher DLB-106

Blackwood, Algernon Henry
 1869-1951 . . . . DLB-153, 156, 178

Blackwood, Caroline 1931-1996 . . . . .DLB-14, 207

Blackwood, William, and Sons, Ltd. DLB-154

Blackwood's Edinburgh Magazine
 1817-1980 . . . . .DLB-110

Blades, William 1824-1890 . . . . .DLB-184

Blaga, Lucian 1895-1961 . . . . .DLB-220

Blagden, Isabella 1817?-1873 . . . . .DLB-199

Blair, Eric Arthur (see Orwell, George)

Blair, Francis Preston 1791-1876 . . . . .DLB-43

Blair, James circa 1655-1743. . . . . .DLB-24

Blair, John Durburrow 1759-1823 . . . . . . .DLB-37

Blais, Marie-Claire 1939- DLB-53

Blaise, Clark 1940- DLB-53

Blake, George 1893-1961. . . . . .DLB-191

Blake, Lillie Devereux 1833-1913 . . .DLB-202, 221

Blake, Nicholas 1904-1972. . . . . .DLB-77
 (see Day Lewis, C.)

Blake, William
 1757-1827. . . . . . . .DLB-93, 154, 163; CDBLB-3

The Blakiston Company DLB-49

Blandiana, Ana 1942- DLB-232; CDWLB-4

Blanchot, Maurice 1907- DLB-72

Blanckenburg, Christian Friedrich von
 1744-1796. . . . . .DLB-94

Blaser, Robin 1925- DLB-165

Blaumanis, Rūdolfs 1863-1908 . . . . .DLB-220

Bleasdale, Alan 1946- DLB-245

Bledsoe, Albert Taylor 1809-1877 . .DLB-3, 79, 248

Bleecker, Ann Eliza 1752-1783 . . . . .DLB-200

Blelock and Company DLB-49

Blennerhassett, Margaret Agnew
 1773-1842 . . . . .DLB-99

Bles, Geoffrey [publishing house]. DLB-112

Blessington, Marguerite, Countess of
 1789-1849 . . . . .DLB-166

The Blickling Homilies circa 971 . . . . . . .DLB-146

Blind, Mathilde 1841-1896 . . . . .DLB-199

Blish, James 1921-1975. . . . . .DLB-8

Bliss, E., and E. White
 [publishing house] DLB-49

Bliven, Bruce 1889-1977 . . . . .DLB-137

Blixen, Karen 1885-1962 . . . . .DLB-214

Bloch, Robert 1917-1994 . . . . .DLB-44

Block, Lawrence 1938- DLB-226

Block, Rudolph (see Lessing, Bruno)

Blondal, Patricia 1926-1959 . . . . .DLB-88

Bloom, Harold 1930- DLB-67

Bloomer, Amelia 1818-1894 . . . . .DLB-79

Bloomfield, Robert 1766-1823 . . . . .DLB-93

Bloomsbury Group DS-10

Blotner, Joseph 1923- DLB-111

Blount, Thomas 1618?-1679 . . . . .DLB-236

Bloy, Léon 1846-1917 . . . . .DLB-123

Blume, Judy 1938- DLB-52

Blunck, Hans Friedrich 1888-1961 . . . . . .DLB-66

Blunden, Edmund 1896-1974 . . .DLB-20, 100, 155

Blundeville, Thomas 1522?-1606 . . . . . . .DLB-236

Blunt, Lady Anne Isabella Noel
 1837-1917 . . . . .DLB-174

Blunt, Wilfrid Scawen 1840-1922 . . . .DLB-19, 174

Bly, Nellie (see Cochrane, Elizabeth)

Bly, Robert 1926- .DLB-5

Blyton, Enid 1897-1968 . . . . .DLB-160

Boaden, James 1762-1839 . . . . .DLB-89

Boas, Frederick S. 1862-1957. . . . . .DLB-149

The Bobbs-Merrill Archive at the
 Lilly Library, Indiana University Y-90

Boborykin, Petr Dmitrievich 1836-1921 . .DLB-238

The Bobbs-Merrill Company DLB-46

Bobrov, Semen Sergeevich
 1763?-1810 .DLB-150

Bobrowski, Johannes 1917-1965 . . . . .DLB-75

The Elmer Holmes Bobst Awards in Arts
 and Letters Y-87

Bodenheim, Maxwell 1892-1954. . . . . . .DLB-9, 45

Bodenstedt, Friedrich von 1819-1892 . . . .DLB-129

Bodini, Vittorio 1914-1970. . . . . .DLB-128

Bodkin, M. McDonnell 1850-1933 . . . . . . .DLB-70

Bodley, Sir Thomas 1545-1613 . . . . .DLB-213

Bodley Head DLB-112

Bodmer, Johann Jakob 1698-1783 . . . . . . .DLB-97

Bodmershof, Imma von 1895-1982 . . . . . .DLB-85

Bodsworth, Fred 1918- DLB-68

Boehm, Sydney 1908- DLB-44

Boer, Charles 1939- DLB-5

Boethius circa 480-circa 524 . . . . .DLB-115

Boethius of Dacia circa 1240-? DLB-115

Bogan, Louise 1897-1970 . . . . .DLB-45, 169

Bogarde, Dirk 1921- DLB-14

Bogdanovich, Ippolit Fedorovich
 circa 1743-1803 . . . . .DLB-150

Bogue, David [publishing house] DLB-106

Böhme, Jakob 1575-1624 . . . . .DLB-164

Bohn, H. G. [publishing house] DLB-106

Bohse, August 1661-1742. . . . . .DLB-168

Boie, Heinrich Christian 1744-1806. . . . . .DLB-94

Bok, Edward W. 1863-1930 . . . . . .DLB-91; DS-16

Boland, Eavan 1944- DLB-40

Boldrewood, Rolf (Thomas Alexander Browne)
 1826?-1915 . . . . .DLB-230

Bolingbroke, Henry St. John, Viscount
 1678-1751 . . . . .DLB-101

Böll, Heinrich
 1917-1985 . . . . DLB-69; Y-85; CDWLB-2

Bolling, Robert 1738-1775 . . . . .DLB-31

Bolotov, Andrei Timofeevich
 1738-1833 . . . . .DLB-150

Bolt, Carol 1941- DLB-60

Bolt, Robert 1924-1995 . . . . .DLB-13, 233

Bolton, Herbert E. 1870-1953 . . . . .DLB-17

Bonaventura DLB-90

Bonaventure circa 1217-1274 . . . . .DLB-115

Bonaviri, Giuseppe 1924- DLB-177

Bond, Edward 1934- DLB-13

Bond, Michael 1926- DLB-161

Boni, Albert and Charles
 [publishing house] DLB-46

Boni and Liveright. DLB-46

Bonner, Marita 1899-1971 . . . . .DLB-228

Bonner, Paul Hyde 1893-1968. . . . . DS-17

Bonner, Sherwood (see McDowell, Katharine
 Sherwood Bonner)

Robert Bonner's Sons DLB-49

Bonnin, Gertrude Simmons (see Zitkala-Ša)

Bonsanti, Alessandro 1904-1984 . . . . . . .DLB-177

Bontempi, Arna 1902-1973 . . . . .DLB-48, 51

The Book Arts Press at the University
 of Virginia. Y-96

The Book League of America DLB-46

Book Publishing Accounting: Some Basic
 Concepts Y-98

Book Reviewing in America: I. Y-87

Book Reviewing in America: II Y-88

Book Reviewing in America: III Y-89

Book Reviewing in America: IV Y-90

Book Reviewing in America: V Y-91

Book Reviewing in America: VI Y-92

Book Reviewing in America: VII Y-93

Book Reviewing in America: VIII. Y-94

Book Reviewing in America and the
 Literary Scene Y-95

Book Reviewing and the
 Literary Scene Y-96, Y-97

Book Supply Company DLB-49

The Book Trade History Group Y-93

The Book Trade and the Internet Y-00

The Booker Prize. Y-96

Address by Anthony Thwaite,
 Chairman of the Booker Prize Judges
 Comments from Former Booker
 Prize Winners Y-86

The Books of George V. Higgins:
 A Checklist of Editions and Printings Y-00

Boorde, Andrew circa 1490-1549 . . . . . .DLB-136

Boorstin, Daniel J. 1914- DLB-17

Booth, Franklin 1874-1948. . . . . .DLB-188

Booth, Mary L. 1831-1889 . . . . .DLB-79

Booth, Philip 1925- Y-82

Booth, Wayne C. 1921- DLB-67

Booth, William 1829-1912. . . . . .DLB-190

Borchardt, Rudolf 1877-1945 .... DLB-66
Borchert, Wolfgang 1921-1947 ...... DLB-69, 124
Borel, Pétrus 1809-1859 .... DLB-119
Borges, Jorge Luis
 1899-1986 .... DLB-113; Y-86; CDWLB-3
Börne, Ludwig 1786-1837 .... DLB-90
Bornstein, Miriam 1950- DLB-209
Borowski, Tadeusz
 1922-1951 .... DLB-215; CDWLB-4
Borrow, George 1803-1881 ..... DLB-21, 55, 166
Bosch, Juan 1909- DLB-145
Bosco, Henri 1888-1976 .... DLB-72
Bosco, Monique 1927- DLB-53
Bosman, Herman Charles 1905-1951.... DLB-225
Bostic, Joe 1908-1988 .... DLB-241
Boston, Lucy M. 1892-1990 .... DLB-161
Boswell, James
 1740-1795 .... DLB-104, 142; CDBLB-2
Boswell, Robert 1953- DLB-234
Bote, Hermann
 circa 1460-circa 1520 .... DLB-179
Botev, Khristo 1847-1876 .... DLB-147
Botta, Anne C. Lynch 1815-1891 ..... DLB-3, 250
Botto, Ján (see Krasko, Ivan)
Bottome, Phyllis 1882-1963 .... DLB-197
Bottomley, Gordon 1874-1948 .... DLB-10
Bottoms, David 1949- DLB-120; Y-83
Bottrall, Ronald 1906- DLB-20
Bouchardy, Joseph 1810-1870 .... DLB-192
Boucher, Anthony 1911-1968 .... DLB-8
Boucher, Jonathan 1738-1804 .... DLB-31
Boucher de Boucherville, George
 1814-1894 .... DLB-99
Boudreau, Daniel (see Coste, Donat)
Bourassa, Napoléon 1827-1916 .... DLB-99
Bourget, Paul 1852-1935 .... DLB-123
Bourinot, John George 1837-1902 .... DLB-99
Bourjaily, Vance 1922- DLB-2, 143
Bourne, Edward Gaylord
 1860-1908 .... DLB-47
Bourne, Randolph 1886-1918 .... DLB-63
Bousoño, Carlos 1923- DLB-108
Bousquet, Joë 1897-1950 .... DLB-72
Bova, Ben 1932- Y-81
Bovard, Oliver K. 1872-1945 .... DLB-25
Bove, Emmanuel 1898-1945 .... DLB-72
Bowen, Elizabeth
 1899-1973 .... DLB-15, 162; CDBLB-7
Bowen, Francis 1811-1890 .... DLB-1, 59, 235
Bowen, John 1924- DLB-13
Bowen, Marjorie 1886-1952 .... DLB-153
Bowen-Merrill Company DLB-49
Bowering, George 1935- DLB-53
Bowers, Bathsheba 1671-1718 .... DLB-200
Bowers, Claude G. 1878-1958 .... DLB-17
Bowers, Edgar 1924-2000 .... DLB-5

Bowers, Fredson Thayer
 1905-1991 ....DLB-140; Y-80, 91
Bowles, Paul 1910-1999 ......DLB-5, 6, 218; Y-99
Bowles, Samuel III 1826-1878 .... DLB-43
Bowles, William Lisles 1762-1850 ...... DLB-93
Bowman, Louise Morey 1882-1944 ...... DLB-68
Boyd, James 1888-1944 .... DLB-9; DS-16
Boyd, John 1919- DLB-8
Boyd, Thomas 1898-1935 .... DLB-9; DS-16
Boyd, William 1952- DLB-231
Boyesen, Hjalmar Hjorth
 1848-1895 ....DLB-12, 71; DS-13
Boyle, Kay 1902-1992 .....DLB-4, 9, 48, 86; Y-93
Boyle, Roger, Earl of Orrery 1621-1679... DLB-80
Boyle, T. Coraghessan 1948- DLB-218; Y-86
Božić, Mirko 1919- DLB-181
Brackenbury, Alison 1953- DLB-40
Brackenridge, Hugh Henry
 1748-1816.................... DLB-11, 37
Brackett, Charles 1892-1969............ DLB-26
Brackett, Leigh 1915-1978 .... DLB-8, 26
Bradburn, John [publishing house] DLB-49
Bradbury, Malcolm 1932-2000 ....DLB-14, 207
Bradbury, Ray 1920- DLB-2, 8; CDALB-6
Bradbury and Evans DLB-106
Braddon, Mary Elizabeth
 1835-1915 ....DLB-18, 70, 156
Bradford, Andrew 1686-1742 .... DLB-43, 73
Bradford, Gamaliel 1863-1932 .... DLB-17
Bradford, John 1749-1830 .... DLB-43
Bradford, Roark 1896-1948 .... DLB-86
Bradford, William 1590-1657 .... DLB-24, 30
Bradford, William III 1719-1791 ..... DLB-43, 73
Bradlaugh, Charles 1833-1891 .... DLB-57
Bradley, David 1950- DLB-33
Bradley, Ira, and Company DLB-49
Bradley, J. W., and Company DLB-49
Bradley, Katherine Harris (see Field, Michael)
Bradley, Marion Zimmer 1930-1999 ...... DLB-8
Bradley, William Aspenwall 1878-1939 .... DLB-4
Bradshaw, Henry 1831-1886 .... DLB-184
Bradstreet, Anne
 1612 or 1613-1672 .... DLB-24; CDABL-2
Bradūnas, Kazys 1917- DLB-220
Bradwardine, Thomas circa
 1295-1349 .... DLB-115
Brady, Frank 1924-1986 .... DLB-111
Brady, Frederic A. [publishing house] DLB-49
Bragg, Melvyn 1939- DLB-14
Brainard, Charles H. [publishing house] .. DLB-49
Braine, John 1922-1986 . DLB-15; Y-86; CDBLB-7
Braithwait, Richard 1588-1673 .... DLB-151
Braithwaite, William Stanley
 1878-1962..................... DLB-50, 54
Braker, Ulrich 1735-1798 .... DLB-94
Bramah, Ernest 1868-1942 .... DLB-70

Branagan, Thomas 1774-1843 .... DLB-37
Branch, William Blackwell 1927- DLB-76
Branden Press....................... DLB-46
Branner, H.C. 1903-1966................ DLB-214
Brant, Sebastian 1457-1521............DLB-179
Brassey, Lady Annie (Allnutt)
 1839-1887 .... DLB-166
Brathwaite, Edward Kamau
 1930- DLB-125; CDWLB-3
Brault, Jacques 1933- DLB-53
Braun, Matt 1932- DLB-212
Braun, Volker 1939- DLB-75
Brautigan, Richard
 1935-1984 .... DLB-2, 5, 206; Y-80, Y-84
Braxton, Joanne M. 1950- DLB-41
Bray, Anne Eliza 1790-1883 .... DLB-116
Bray, Thomas 1656-1730 .... DLB-24
Brazdžionis, Bernardas 1907- DLB-220
Braziller, George [publishing house] DLB-46
The Bread Loaf Writers' Conference 1983 ... Y-84
Breasted, James Henry 1865-1935 .... DLB-47
Brecht, Bertolt
 1898-1956 ....DLB-56, 124; CDWLB-2
Bredel, Willi 1901-1964 .... DLB-56
Bregendahl, Marie 1867-1940.......... DLB-214
Breitinger, Johann Jakob 1701-1776 ..... DLB-97
Bremser, Bonnie 1939- DLB-16
Bremser, Ray 1934- DLB-16
Brennan, Christopher 1870-1932 .... DLB-230
Brentano, Bernard von 1901-1964....... DLB-56
Brentano, Clemens 1778-1842 .... DLB-90
Brentano's DLB-49
Brenton, Howard 1942- DLB-13
Breslin, Jimmy 1929-1996 .... DLB-185
Breton, André 1896-1966 .... DLB-65
Breton, Nicholas circa 1555-circa 1626... DLB-136
The Breton Lays
 1300-early fifteenth century DLB-146
Brewer, Luther A. 1858-1933...........DLB-187
Brewer, Warren and Putnam DLB-46
Brewster, Elizabeth 1922- DLB-60
Breytenbach, Breyten 1939- DLB-225
Bridge, Ann (Lady Mary Dolling Sanders
 O'Malley) 1889-1974 .... DLB-191
Bridge, Horatio 1806-1893............. DLB-183
Bridgers, Sue Ellen 1942- DLB-52
Bridges, Robert
 1844-1930 .... DLB-19, 98; CDBLB-5
The Bridgewater Library DLB-213
Bridie, James 1888-1951................ DLB-10
Brieux, Eugene 1858-1932 .... DLB-192
Brigadere, Anna 1861-1933 .... DLB-220
Briggs, Charles Frederick
 1804-1877..................... DLB-3, 250
Bright, Mary Chavelita Dunne (see Egerton, George)
Brimmer, B. J., Company............. DLB-46
Brines, Francisco 1932- DLB-134

Brink, André 1935- DLB-225

Brinley, George, Jr. 1817-1875 ....DLB-140

Brinnin, John Malcolm 1916-1998........DLB-48

Brisbane, Albert 1809-1890 ....DLB-3, 250

Brisbane, Arthur 1864-1936.............DLB-25

British Academy.....................DLB-112

The British Critic 1793-1843 ....DLB-110

The British Library and the Regular Readers' Group......................Y-91

British Literary Prizes Y-98

The British Review and London Critical Journal 1811-1825.................DLB-110

British Travel Writing, 1940-1997........DLB-204

Brito, Aristeo 1942- DLB-122

Brittain, Vera 1893-1970 ....DLB-191

Brizeux, Auguste 1803-1858 ....DLB-217

Broadway Publishing Company DLB-46

Broch, Hermann 1886-1951.........DLB-85, 124; CDWLB-2

Brochu, André 1942- DLB-53

Brock, Edwin 1927- DLB-40

Brockes, Barthold Heinrich 1680-1747....DLB-168

Brod, Max 1884-1968 ....DLB-81

Brodber, Erna 1940- DLB-157

Brodhead, John R. 1814-1873 ....DLB-30

Brodkey, Harold 1930-1996 ....DLB-130

Brodsky, Joseph 1940-1996 ....Y-87

Brodsky, Michael 1948- DLB-244

Broeg, Bob 1918- DLB-171

Brøgger, Suzanne 1944- DLB-214

Brome, Richard circa 1590-1652 ....DLB-58

Brome, Vincent 1910- DLB-155

Bromfield, Louis 1896-1956..........DLB-4, 9, 86

Bromige, David 1933- DLB-193

Broner, E. M. 1930- DLB-28

Bronk, William 1918-1999..............DLB-165

Bronnen, Arnolt 1895-1959............DLB-124

Brontë, Anne 1820-1849 ....DLB-21, 199

Brontë, Charlotte 1816-1855 ......DLB-21, 159, 199; CDBLB-4

Brontë, Emily 1818-1848 ......DLB-21, 32, 199; CDBLB-4

Brook, Stephen 1947- DLB-204

Brook Farm 1841-1847 ....DLB-223

Brooke, Frances 1724-1789..........DLB-39, 99

Brooke, Henry 1703?-1783...............DLB-39

Brooke, L. Leslie 1862-1940 ....DLB-141

Brooke, Margaret, Ranee of Sarawak 1849-1936 ....DLB-174

Brooke, Rupert 1887-1915 ....DLB-19, 216; CDBLB-6

Brooker, Bertram 1888-1955............DLB-88

Brooke-Rose, Christine 1923- DLB-14, 231

Brookner, Anita 1928- DLB-194; Y-87

Brooks, Charles Timothy 1813-1883...DLB-1, 243

Brooks, Cleanth 1906-1994........DLB-63; Y-94

Brooks, Gwendolyn 1917-2000 ....DLB-5, 76, 165; CDALB-1

Brooks, Jeremy 1926- DLB-14

Brooks, Mel 1926- DLB-26

Brooks, Noah 1830-1903.........DLB-42; DS-13

Brooks, Richard 1912-1992..............DLB-44

Brooks, Van Wyck 1886-1963...........DLB-45, 63, 103

Brophy, Brigid 1929-1995 ....DLB-14

Brophy, John 1899-1965 ....DLB-191

Brossard, Chandler 1922-1993 ....DLB-16

Brossard, Nicole 1943- DLB-53

Broster, Dorothy Kathleen 1877-1950 ....DLB-160

Brother Antoninus (see Everson, William)

Brotherton, Lord 1856-1930 ....DLB-184

Brougham and Vaux, Henry Peter Brougham, Baron 1778-1868 ....DLB-110, 158

Brougham, John 1810-1880..............DLB-11

Broughton, James 1913-1999.............DLB-5

Broughton, Rhoda 1840-1920 ....DLB-18

Broun, Heywood 1888-1939 ....DLB-29, 171

Brown, Alice 1856-1948.................DLB-78

Brown, Bob 1886-1959 ....DLB-4, 45

Brown, Cecil 1943- DLB-33

Brown, Charles Brockden 1771-1810 ....DLB-37, 59, 73; CDALB-2

Brown, Christy 1932-1981 ....DLB-14

Brown, Dee 1908- Y-80

Brown, Frank London 1927-1962 ....DLB-76

Brown, Fredric 1906-1972 ....DLB-8

Brown, George Mackay 1921-1996 ....DLB-14, 27, 139

Brown, Harry 1917-1986 ....DLB-26

Brown, Larry 1951- DLB-234

Brown, Marcia 1918- DLB-61

Brown, Margaret Wise 1910-1952.........DLB-22

Brown, Morna Doris (see Ferrars, Elizabeth)

Brown, Oliver Madox 1855-1874 ....DLB-21

Brown, Sterling 1901-1989 ....DLB-48, 51, 63

Brown, T. E. 1830-1897 ....DLB-35

Brown, Thomas Alexander (see Boldrewood, Rolf)

Brown, Warren 1894-1978 ....DLB-241

Brown, William Hill 1765-1793 ....DLB-37

Brown, William Wells 1815-1884 ....DLB-3, 50, 183, 248

Browne, Charles Farrar 1834-1867 ....DLB-11

Browne, Frances 1816-1879 ....DLB-199

Browne, Francis Fisher 1843-1913........DLB-79

Browne, Howard 1908-1999 ....DLB-226

Browne, J. Ross 1821-1875 ....DLB-202

Browne, Michael Dennis 1940- DLB-40

Browne, Sir Thomas 1605-1682 ....DLB-151

Browne, William, of Tavistock 1590-1645 ....DLB-121

Browne, Wynyard 1911-1964 ......DLB-13, 233

Browne and Nolan....................DLB-106

Brownell, W. C. 1851-1928..............DLB-71

Browning, Elizabeth Barrett 1806-1861 ....DLB-32, 199; CDBLB-4

Browning, Robert 1812-1889 ....DLB-32, 163; CDBLB-4

Introductory Essay: *Letters of Percy Bysshe Shelley* (1852) DLB-32

Brownjohn, Allan 1931- DLB-40

Brownson, Orestes Augustus 1803-1876 ....DLB-1, 59, 73, 243

Bruccoli, Matthew J. 1931- DLB-103

Bruce, Charles 1906-1971 ....DLB-68

John Edward Bruce: Three Documents....DLB-50

Bruce, Leo 1903-1979 ....DLB-77

Bruce, Mary Grant 1878-1958..........DLB-230

Bruce, Philip Alexander 1856-1933.......DLB-47

Bruce Humphries [publishing house] DLB-46

Bruce-Novoa, Juan 1944- DLB-82

Bruckman, Clyde 1894-1955 ....DLB-26

Bruckner, Ferdinand 1891-1958 ....DLB-118

Brundage, John Herbert (see Herbert, John)

Brutus, Dennis 1924- DLB-117, 225; CDWLB-3

Bryan, C. D. B. 1936- DLB-185

Bryant, Arthur 1899-1985.............DLB-149

Bryant, William Cullen 1794-1878 ....DLB-3, 43, 59, 189, 250; CDALB-2

Bryce Echenique, Alfredo 1939- DLB-145; CDWLB-3

Bryce, James 1838-1922...........DLB-166, 190

Bryden, Bill 1942- DLB-233

Brydges, Sir Samuel Egerton 1762-1837 ..DLB-107

Bryskett, Lodowick 1546?-1612 ....DLB-167

Buchan, John 1875-1940 ....DLB-34, 70, 156

Buchanan, George 1506-1582 ....DLB-132

Buchanan, Robert 1841-1901 ....DLB-18, 35

"The Fleshly School of Poetry and Other Phenomena of the Day" (1872), by Robert Buchanan DLB-35

"The Fleshly School of Poetry: Mr. D. G. Rossetti" (1871), by Thomas Maitland (Robert Buchanan) DLB-35

Buchman, Sidney 1902-1975 ....DLB-26

Buchner, Augustus 1591-1661..........DLB-164

Büchner, Georg 1813-1837 ..DLB-133; CDWLB-2

Bucholtz, Andreas Heinrich 1607-1671 ...DLB-168

Buck, Pearl S. 1892-1973 ...DLB-9, 102; CDALB-7

Bucke, Charles 1781-1846 ....DLB-110

Bucke, Richard Maurice 1837-1902........DLB-99

Buckingham, Joseph Tinker 1779-1861 and Buckingham, Edwin 1810-1833 ....DLB-73

Buckler, Ernest 1908-1984................DLB-68

Buckley, William F., Jr. 1925- DLB-137; Y-80

Buckminster, Joseph Stevens 1784-1812 ....DLB-37

Buckner, Robert 1906- DLB-26

Budd, Thomas ?-1698 ....DLB-24

Budrys, A. J. 1931- DLB-8

Cumulative Index

Buechner, Frederick 1926- Y-80
Buell, John 1927- DLB-53
Bufalino, Gesualdo 1920-1996 .... DLB-196
Buffum, Job [publishing house].......... DLB-49
Bugnet, Georges 1879-1981 .... DLB-92
Buies, Arthur 1840-1901............... DLB-99
Building the New British Library
 at St Pancras...................... Y-94
Bukowski, Charles 1920-1994 ... DLB-5, 130, 169
Bulatović, Miodrag
 1930-1991 .... DLB-181; CDWLB-4
Bulgarin, Faddei Venediktovich
 1789-1859..................... DLB-198
Bulger, Bozeman 1877-1932 ....DLB-171
Bullein, William
 between 1520 and 1530-1576....... DLB-167
Bullins, Ed 1935- DLB-7, 38, 249
Bulwer, John 1606-1656............... DLB-236
Bulwer-Lytton, Edward (also Edward Bulwer)
 1803-1873...................... DLB-21
"On Art in Fiction" (1838) DLB-21
Bumpus, Jerry 1937- Y-81
Bunce and Brother DLB-49
Bunner, H. C. 1855-1896............DLB-78, 79
Bunting, Basil 1900-1985 .... DLB-20
Buntline, Ned (Edward Zane Carroll Judson)
 1821-1886 .... DLB-186
Bunyan, John 1628-1688 ..... DLB-39; CDBLB-2
Burch, Robert 1925- DLB-52
Burciaga, José Antonio 1940- DLB-82
Bürger, Gottfried August 1747-1794 ..... DLB-94
Burgess, Anthony
 1917-1993......... DLB-14, 194; CDBLB-8
The Anthony Burgess Archive at
 the Harry Ransom Humanities
 Research Center................... Y-98
Anthony Burgess's 99 Novels:
 An Opinion Poll..................... Y-84
Burgess, Gelett 1866-1951 .... DLB-11
Burgess, John W. 1844-1931 .... DLB-47
Burgess, Thornton W. 1874-1965 .... DLB-22
Burgess, Stringer and Company DLB-49
Burick, Si 1909-1986..................DLB-171
Burk, John Daly circa 1772-1808 .... DLB-37
Burk, Ronnie 1955- DLB-209
Burke, Edmund 1729?-1797 .... DLB-104
Burke, James Lee 1936- DLB-226
Burke, Kenneth 1897-1993 .... DLB-45, 63
Burke, Thomas 1886-1945........... DLB-197
Burley, Dan 1907-1962 .... DLB-241
Burlingame, Edward Livermore
 1848-1922 .... DLB-79
Burnet, Gilbert 1643-1715............ DLB-101
Burnett, Frances Hodgson
 1849-1924 .... DLB-42, 141; DS-13, 14
Burnett, W. R. 1899-1982 .... DLB-9, 226
Burnett, Whit 1899-1973 and
 Martha Foley 1897-1977......... DLB-137

Burney, Fanny 1752-1840.............. DLB-39
Dedication, *The Wanderer* (1814)......... DLB-39
Preface to *Evelina* (1778) DLB-39
Burns, Alan 1929- DLB-14, 194
Burns, John Horne 1916-1953 .... Y-85
Burns, Robert 1759-1796 .... DLB-109; CDBLB-3
Burns and Oates.................... DLB-106
Burnshaw, Stanley 1906- DLB-48
Burr, C. Chauncey 1815?-1883 .... DLB-79
Burr, Esther Edwards 1732-1758 .... DLB-200
Burroughs, Edgar Rice 1875-1950 .... DLB-8
Burroughs, John 1837-1921 .... DLB-64
Burroughs, Margaret T. G. 1917- DLB-41
Burroughs, William S., Jr. 1947-1981 ..... DLB-16
Burroughs, William Seward 1914-1997
 .... DLB-2, 8, 16, 152, 237; Y-81, Y-97
Burroway, Janet 1936- DLB-6
Burt, Maxwell Struthers
 1882-1954 .... DLB-86; DS-16
Burt, A. L., and Company DLB-49
Burton, Hester 1913- DLB-161
Burton, Isabel Arundell 1831-1896...... DLB-166
Burton, Miles (see Rhode, John)
Burton, Richard Francis
 1821-1890 .... DLB-55, 166, 184
Burton, Robert 1577-1640............. DLB-151
Burton, Virginia Lee 1909-1968......... DLB-22
Burton, William Evans 1804-1860 ...... DLB-73
Burwell, Adam Hood 1790-1849 .... DLB-99
Bury, Lady Charlotte 1775-1861 .... DLB-116
Busch, Frederick 1941- DLB-6, 218
Busch, Niven 1903-1991............... DLB-44
Bushnell, Horace 1802-1876.............DS-13
Bussieres, Arthur de 1877-1913......... DLB-92
Butler, Charles ca. 1560-1647.......... DLB-236
Butler, Guy 1918- DLB-225
Butler, E. H., and Company........... DLB-49
Butler, Josephine Elizabeth 1828-1906 ... DLB-190
Butler, Juan 1942-1981............... DLB-53
Butler, Judith 1956- DLB-246
Butler, Octavia E. 1947- DLB-33
Butler, Pierce 1884-1953............ DLB-187
Butler, Robert Olen 1945- DLB-173
Butler, Samuel 1613-1680......... DLB-101, 126
Butler, Samuel 1835-1902......... DLB-18, 57, 174
Butler, William Francis 1838-1910...... DLB-166
Butor, Michel 1926- DLB-83
Butter, Nathaniel [publishing house].....DLB-170
Butterworth, Hezekiah 1839-1905 .... DLB-42
Buttitta, Ignazio 1899- DLB-114
Butts, Mary 1890-1937............... DLB-240
Buzzati, Dino 1906-1972...............DLB-177
Byars, Betsy 1928- DLB-52
Byatt, A. S. 1936- DLB-14, 194
Byles, Mather 1707-1788 .... DLB-24

Bynneman, Henry
 [publishing house] DLB-170
Bynner, Witter 1881-1968 .... DLB-54
Byrd, William circa 1543-1623.........DLB-172
Byrd, William II 1674-1744 .... DLB-24, 140
Byrne, John Keyes (see Leonard, Hugh)
Byron, George Gordon, Lord
 1788-1824.......... DLB-96, 110; CDBLB-3
Byron, Robert 1905-1941............. DLB-195

C

Caballero Bonald, José Manuel
 1926- DLB-108
Cabañero, Eladio 1930- DLB-134
Cabell, James Branch 1879-1958 ....DLB-9, 78
Cabeza de Baca, Manuel 1853-1915..... DLB-122
Cabeza de Baca Gilbert, Fabiola
 1898- DLB-122
Cable, George Washington
 1844-1925 ....DLB-12, 74; DS-13
Cable, Mildred 1878-1952 .... DLB-195
Cabrera, Lydia 1900-1991 .... DLB-145
Cabrera Infante, Guillermo
 1929- DLB-113; CDWLB-3
Cadell [publishing house]............. DLB-154
Cady, Edwin H. 1917- DLB-103
Caedmon flourished 658-680.......... DLB-146
Caedmon School circa 660-899 .... DLB-146
Cafés, Brasseries, and Bistros.............DS-15
Cage, John 1912-1992 .... DLB-193
Cahan, Abraham 1860-1951 ...... DLB-9, 25, 28
Cain, George 1943- DLB-33
Cain, James M. 1892-1977 .... DLB-226
Caird, Mona 1854-1932 ....DLB-197
Čaks, Aleksandrs
 1901-1950 .... DLB-220; CDWLB-4
Caldecott, Randolph 1846-1886......... DLB-163
Calder, John (Publishers), Limited DLB-112
Calderón de la Barca, Fanny
 1804-1882 .... DLB-183
Caldwell, Ben 1937- DLB-38
Caldwell, Erskine 1903-1987 .... DLB-9, 86
Caldwell, H. M., Company DLB-49
Caldwell, Taylor 1900-1985.............DS-17
Calhoun, John C. 1782-1850 .... DLB-3, 248
Călinescu, George 1899-1965 .... DLB-220
Calisher, Hortense 1911- DLB-2, 218
A Call to Letters and an Invitation
 to the Electric Chair,
 by Siegfried Mandel............... DLB-75
Callaghan, Mary Rose 1944- DLB-207
Callaghan, Morley 1903-1990 .... DLB-68
Callahan, S. Alice 1868-1894 ....DLB-175, 221
Calloo Y-87
Callimachus circa 305 B.C.-240 B.C......DLB-176
Calmer, Edgar 1907- DLB-4
Calverley, C. S. 1831-1884............ DLB-35

Calvert, George Henry
1803-1889 . . . . .DLB-1, 64, 248

Calvino, Italo 1923-1985 . . . . .DLB-196

Cambridge, Ada 1844-1926. . . . . .DLB-230

Cambridge Press DLB-49

Cambridge Songs (Carmina Cantabrigensia)
circa 1050 . . . . .DLB-148

Cambridge University Press DLB-170

Camden, William 1551-1623. . . . . .DLB-172

Camden House: An Interview with
James Hardin. Y-92

Cameron, Eleanor 1912- DLB-52

Cameron, George Frederick
1854-1885 . . . . .DLB-99

Cameron, Lucy Lyttelton 1781-1858. . . . .DLB-163

Cameron, Peter 1959- DLB-234

Cameron, William Bleasdell 1862-1951 . . .DLB-99

Camm, John 1718-1778 . . . . .DLB-31

Camon, Ferdinando 1935- DLB-196

Camp, Walter 1859-1925 . . . . .DLB-241

Campana, Dino 1885-1932 . . . . .DLB-114

Campbell, Bebe Moore 1950- DLB-227

Campbell, Gabrielle Margaret Vere
(see Shearing, Joseph, and Bowen, Marjorie)

Campbell, James Dykes 1838-1895 . . . . . .DLB-144

Campbell, James Edwin 1867-1896 . . . . . .DLB-50

Campbell, John 1653-1728. . . . . .DLB-43

Campbell, John W., Jr. 1910-1971 . . . . .DLB-8

Campbell, Roy 1901-1957 . . . . .DLB-20, 225

Campbell, Thomas 1777-1844 . . . . . .DLB-93, 144

Campbell, William Wilfred 1858-1918 . . . .DLB-92

Campion, Edmund 1539-1581. . . . . .DLB-167

Campion, Thomas
1567-1620 . . . . .DLB-58, 172; CDBLB-1

Campton, David 1924- DLB-245

Camus, Albert 1913-1960 . . . . .DLB-72

The Canadian Publishers' Records
Database Y-96

Canby, Henry Seidel 1878-1961 . . . . .DLB-91

Candelaria, Cordelia 1943- DLB-82

Candelaria, Nash 1928- DLB-82

Canetti, Elias
1905-1994 . . . . .DLB-85, 124; CDWLB-2

Canham, Erwin Dain 1904-1982. . . . . . . .DLB-127

Canitz, Friedrich Rudolph Ludwig von
1654-1699 . . . . .DLB-168

Cankar, Ivan 1876-1918. . . . . DLB-147; CDWLB-4

Cannan, Gilbert 1884-1955 . . . . .DLB-10, 197

Cannan, Joanna 1896-1961 . . . . .DLB-191

Cannell, Kathleen 1891-1974. . . . . .DLB-4

Cannell, Skipwith 1887-1957 . . . . .DLB-45

Canning, George 1770-1827. . . . . .DLB-158

Cannon, Jimmy 1910-1973 . . . . .DLB-171

Cano, Daniel 1947- DLB-209

Cantú, Norma Elia 1947- DLB-209

Cantwell, Robert 1908-1978 . . . . .DLB-9

Cape, Jonathan, and Harrison Smith
[publishing house] DLB-46

Cape, Jonathan, Limited DLB-112

Čapek, Karel 1890-1938 . . . .DLB-215; CDWLB-4

Capen, Joseph 1658-1725. . . . . .DLB-24

Capes, Bernard 1854-1918. . . . . .DLB-156

Capote, Truman 1924-1984
. . . . DLB-2, 185, 227; Y-80, Y-84; CDALB-1

Caproni, Giorgio 1912-1990 . . . . .DLB-128

Caragiale, Mateiu Ioan 1885-1936. . . . . . .DLB-220

Cardarelli, Vincenzo 1887-1959. . . . . . . .DLB-114

Cárdenas, Reyes 1948- DLB-122

Cardinal, Marie 1929- DLB-83

Carew, Jan 1920- DLB-157

Carew, Thomas 1594 or 1595-1640. . . . .DLB-126

Carey, Henry circa 1687-1689-1743. . . . . . .DLB-84

Carey, M., and Company DLB-49

Carey, Mathew 1760-1839. . . . . .DLB-37, 73

Carey and Hart DLB-49

Carlell, Lodowick 1602-1675. . . . . .DLB-58

Carleton, William 1794-1869. . . . . .DLB-159

Carleton, G. W. [publishing house]. DLB-49

Carlile, Richard 1790-1843 . . . . .DLB-110, 158

Carlson, Ron 1947- DLB-244

Carlyle, Jane Welsh 1801-1866 . . . . .DLB-55

Carlyle, Thomas
1795-1881 . . . . .DLB-55, 144; CDBLB-3

"The Hero as Man of Letters: Johnson,
Rousseau, Burns" (1841) [excerpt] DLB-57

The Hero as Poet. Dante;
Shakspeare (1841) DLB-32

Carman, Bliss 1861-1929. . . . . .DLB-92

Carmina Burana circa 1230 . . . . .DLB-138

Carnero, Guillermo 1947- DLB-108

Carossa, Hans 1878-1956 . . . . .DLB-66

Carpenter, Humphrey
1946- DLB-155; Y-84, Y-99

The Practice of Biography III: An Interview
with Humphrey Carpenter Y-84

Carpenter, Stephen Cullen ?-1820?. DLB-73

Carpentier, Alejo
1904-1980 . . . . .DLB-113; CDWLB-3

Carr, Marina 1964- DLB-245

Carrier, Roch 1937- DLB-53

Carrillo, Adolfo 1855-1926 . . . . .DLB-122

Carroll, Gladys Hasty 1904- DLB-9

Carroll, John 1735-1815. . . . . .DLB-37

Carroll, John 1809-1884 . . . . .DLB-99

Carroll, Lewis
1832-1898 . . . . . .DLB-18, 163, 178; CDBLB-4

The Lewis Carroll Centenary Y-98

Carroll, Paul 1927- DLB-16

Carroll, Paul Vincent 1900-1968. . . . . .DLB-10

Carroll and Graf Publishers DLB-46

Carruth, Hayden 1921- DLB-5, 165

Carryl, Charles E. 1841-1920 . . . . .DLB-42

Carson, Anne 1950- DLB-193

Carswell, Catherine 1879-1946 . . . . .DLB-36

Cărtărescu, Mirea 1956- DLB-232

Carter, Angela 1940-1992 . . . . .DLB-14, 207

Carter, Elizabeth 1717-1806 . . . . .DLB-109

Carter, Henry (see Leslie, Frank)

Carter, Hodding, Jr. 1907-1972 . . . . .DLB-127

Carter, John 1905-1975 . . . . .DLB-201

Carter, Landon 1710-1778 . . . . .DLB-31

Carter, Lin 1930- Y-81

Carter, Martin 1927-1997. . . . DLB-117; CDWLB-3

Carter, Robert, and Brothers. DLB-49

Carter and Hendee DLB-49

Cartwright, Jim 1958- DLB-245

Cartwright, John 1740-1824. . . . . .DLB-158

Cartwright, William circa 1611-1643 . . . .DLB-126

Caruthers, William Alexander
1802-1846 . . . . .DLB-3, 248

Carver, Jonathan 1710-1780. . . . . .DLB-31

Carver, Raymond
1938-1988 . . . . DLB-130; Y-83, Y-88

First Strauss "Livings" Awarded to Cynthia
Ozick and Raymond Carver
An Interview with Raymond Carver Y-83

Cary, Alice 1820-1871 . . . . .DLB-202

Cary, Joyce 1888-1957. . . .DLB-15, 100; CDBLB-6

Cary, Patrick 1623?-1657 . . . . .DLB-131

Casey, Juanita 1925- DLB-14

Casey, Michael 1947- DLB-5

Cassady, Carolyn 1923- DLB-16

Cassady, Neal 1926-1968 . . . . .DLB-16, 237

Cassell and Company DLB-106

Cassell Publishing Company. DLB-49

Cassill, R. V. 1919- DLB-6, 218

Cassity, Turner 1929- DLB-105

Cassius Dio circa 155/164-post 229. . . . . .DLB-176

Cassola, Carlo 1917-1987. . . . . .DLB-177

The Castle of Perseverance circa 1400-1425 . .DLB-146

Castellano, Olivia 1944- DLB-122

Castellanos, Rosario
1925-1974 . . . . .DLB-113; CDWLB-3

Castillo, Ana 1953- DLB-122, 227

Castillo, Rafael C. 1950- DLB-209

Castlemon, Harry (see Fosdick, Charles Austin)

Čašule, Kole 1921- DLB-181

Caswall, Edward 1814-1878 . . . . .DLB-32

Catacalos, Rosemary 1944- DLB-122

Cather, Willa
1873-1947 . . . .DLB-9, 54, 78; DS-1; CDALB-3

Catherine II (Ekaterina Alekseevna), "The Great,"
Empress of Russia 1729-1796 . . . . . . .DLB-150

Catherwood, Mary Hartwell 1847-1902 . . .DLB-78

Catledge, Turner 1901-1983 . . . . .DLB-127

Catlin, George 1796-1872. . . . . .DLB-186, 189

Cato the Elder 234 B.C.-149 B.C. DLB-211

Cattafi, Bartolo 1922-1979 . . . . .DLB-128

Catton, Bruce 1899-1978 . . . . .DLB-17

Cumulative Index

Catullus circa 84 B.C.-54 B.C. DLB-211; CDWLB-1
Causley, Charles 1917- DLB-27
Caute, David 1936- DLB-14, 231
Cavendish, Duchess of Newcastle, Margaret Lucas 1623-1673 .... DLB-131
Cawein, Madison 1865-1914 .... DLB-54
Caxton, William [publishing house] DLB-170
The Caxton Printers, Limited DLB-46
Caylor, O. P. 1849-1897 .... DLB-241
Cayrol, Jean 1911- DLB-83
Cecil, Lord David 1902-1986 .... DLB-155
Cela, Camilo José 1916- Y-89
Celan, Paul 1920-1970 ...... DLB-69; CDWLB-2
Celati, Gianni 1937- DLB-196
Celaya, Gabriel 1911-1991 .... DLB-108
A Celebration of Literary Biography Y-98
Céline, Louis-Ferdinand 1894-1961 ...... DLB-72
The Celtic Background to Medieval English Literature DLB-146
Celtis, Conrad 1459-1508 .... DLB-179
Center for Bibliographical Studies and Research at the University of California, Riverside Y-91
The Center for the Book in the Library of Congress Y-93
Center for the Book Research Y-84
Centlivre, Susanna 1669?-1723 .... DLB-84
The Centre for Writing, Publishing and Printing History at the University of Reading Y-00
The Century Company DLB-49
Cernuda, Luis 1902-1963 .... DLB-134
Cervantes, Lorna Dee 1954- DLB-82
Ch., T. (see Marchenko, Anastasiia Iakovlevna)
Chaadaev, Petr Iakovlevich 1794-1856 .... DLB-198
Chacel, Rosa 1898- DLB-134
Chacón, Eusebio 1869-1948 .... DLB-82
Chacón, Felipe Maximiliano 1873-? DLB-82
Chadwick, Henry 1824-1908 .... DLB-241
Chadwyck-Healey's Full-Text Literary Databases: Editing Commercial Databases of Primary Literary Texts Y-95
Challans, Eileen Mary (see Renault, Mary)
Chalmers, George 1742-1825 .... DLB-30
Chaloner, Sir Thomas 1520-1565 .... DLB-167
Chamberlain, Samuel S. 1851-1916 ..... DLB-25
Chamberland, Paul 1939- DLB-60
Chamberlin, William Henry 1897-1969 ... DLB-29
Chambers, Charles Haddon 1860-1921 ... DLB-10
Chambers, María Cristina (see Mena, María Cristina)
Chambers, Robert W. 1865-1933 .... DLB-202
Chambers, W. and R. [publishing house] DLB-106
Chamisso, Albert von 1781-1838 .... DLB-90
Champfleury 1821-1889 .... DLB-119
Chandler, Harry 1864-1944 .... DLB-29

Chandler, Norman 1899-1973 .... DLB-127
Chandler, Otis 1927- DLB-127
Chandler, Raymond 1888-1959 .... DLB-226; DS-6; CDALB-5
Raymond Chandler Centenary Tributes from Michael Avallone, James Ellroy, Joe Gores, and William F. Nolan Y-88
Channing, Edward 1856-1931 .... DLB-17
Channing, Edward Tyrrell 1790-1856 .... DLB-1, 59, 235
Channing, William Ellery 1780-1842 .... DLB-1, 59, 235
Channing, William Ellery II 1817-1901 .... DLB-1, 223
Channing, William Henry 1810-1884 .... DLB-1, 59, 243
Chaplin, Charlie 1889-1977 .... DLB-44
Chapman, George 1559 or 1560-1634 .... DLB-62, 121
Chapman, John DLB-106
Chapman, Olive Murray 1892-1977 ..... DLB-195
Chapman, R. W. 1881-1960 .... DLB-201
Chapman, William 1850-1917 .... DLB-99
Chapman and Hall DLB-106
Chappell, Fred 1936- DLB-6, 105
"A Detail in a Poem" DLB-105
Chappell, William 1582-1649 .... DLB-236
Charbonneau, Jean 1875-1960 .... DLB-92
Charbonneau, Robert 1911-1967 .... DLB-68
Charles, Gerda 1914- DLB-14
Charles, William [publishing house] DLB-49
Charles d'Orléans 1394-1465 .... DLB-208
Charley (see Mann, Charles)
Charteris, Leslie 1907-1993 .... DLB-77
Chartier, Alain circa 1385-1430 .... DLB-208
Charyn, Jerome 1937- Y-83
Chase, Borden 1900-1971 .... DLB-26
Chase, Edna Woolman 1877-1957 .... DLB-91
Chase, Mary Coyle 1907-1981 .... DLB-228
Chase-Riboud, Barbara 1936- DLB-33
Chateaubriand, François-René de 1768-1848 .... DLB-119
Chatterton, Thomas 1752-1770 .... DLB-109
Essay on Chatterton (1842), by Robert Browning DLB-32
Chatto and Windus DLB-106
Chatwin, Bruce 1940-1989 .... DLB-194, 204
Chaucer, Geoffrey 1340?-1400 .... DLB-146; CDBLB-1
Chauncy, Charles 1705-1787 .... DLB-24
Chauveau, Pierre-Joseph-Olivier 1820-1890 .... DLB-99
Chávez, Denise 1948- DLB-122
Chávez, Fray Angélico 1910- DLB-82
Chayefsky, Paddy 1923-1981 ..... DLB-7, 44; Y-81
Cheesman, Evelyn 1881-1969 .... DLB-195
Cheever, Ezekiel 1615-1708 .... DLB-24
Cheever, George Barrell 1807-1890 ...... DLB-59

Cheever, John 1912-1982 ...... DLB-2, 102, 227; Y-80, Y-82; CDALB-1
Cheever, Susan 1943- Y-82
Cheke, Sir John 1514-1557 .... DLB-132
Chelsea House DLB-46
Chênedollé, Charles de 1769-1833 .... DLB-217
Cheney, Ednah Dow 1824-1904 ..... DLB-1, 223
Cheney, Harriet Vaughn 1796-1889 ...... DLB-99
Chénier, Marie-Joseph 1764-1811 .... DLB-192
Chernyshevsky, Nikolai Gavrilovich 1828-1889 .... DLB-238
Cherry, Kelly 1940- Y-83
Cherryh, C. J. 1942- Y-80
Chesebro', Caroline 1825-1873 .... DLB-202
Chesney, Sir George Tomkyns 1830-1895 .... DLB-190
Chesnut, Mary Boykin 1823-1886 ...... DLB-239
Chesnutt, Charles Waddell 1858-1932 .... DLB-12, 50, 78
Chesson, Mrs. Nora (see Hopper, Nora)
Chester, Alfred 1928-1971 .... DLB-130
Chester, George Randolph 1869-1924 ... DLB-78
The Chester Plays circa 1505-1532; revisions until 1575 .... DLB-146
Chesterfield, Philip Dormer Stanhope, Fourth Earl of 1694-1773 .... DLB-104
Chesterton, G. K. 1874-1936 ... DLB-10, 19, 34, 70, 98, 149, 178; CDBLB-6
Chettle, Henry circa 1560-circa 1607 .... DLB-136
Cheuse, Alan 1940- DLB-244
Chew, Ada Nield 1870-1945 .... DLB-135
Cheyney, Edward P. 1861-1947 .... DLB-47
Chiara, Piero 1913-1986 .... DLB-177
Chicano History DLB-82
Chicano Language DLB-82
Child, Francis James 1825-1896 ... DLB-1, 64, 235
Child, Lydia Maria 1802-1880 ..... DLB-1, 74, 243
Child, Philip 1898-1978 .... DLB-68
Childers, Erskine 1870-1922 .... DLB-70
Children's Book Awards and Prizes DLB-61
Children's Illustrators, 1800-1880 ...... DLB-163
Childress, Alice 1916-1994 .... DLB-7, 38, 249
Childs, George W. 1829-1894 .... DLB-23
Chilton Book Company DLB-46
Chin, Frank 1940- DLB-206
Chinweizu 1943- DLB-157
Chitham, Edward 1932- DLB-155
Chittenden, Hiram Martin 1858-1917 .... DLB-47
Chivers, Thomas Holley 1809-1858 .. DLB-3, 248
Cholmondeley, Mary 1859-1925 .... DLB-197
Chomsky, Noam 1928- DLB-246
Chopin, Kate 1850-1904 ... DLB-12, 78; CDALB-3
Chopin, Rene 1885-1953 .... DLB-92
Choquette, Adrienne 1915-1973 .... DLB-68
Choquette, Robert 1905- DLB-68
Choyce, Lesley 1951- DLB-251

Chrétien de Troyes circa 1140-circa 1190..............DLB-208

Christensen, Inger 1935- DLB-214

The Christian Publishing Company DLB-49

Christie, Agatha 1890-1976 .... DLB-13, 77, 245; CDBLB-6

Christine de Pizan circa 1365-circa 1431..............DLB-208

Christus und die Samariterin circa 950 ......DLB-148

Christy, Howard Chandler 1873-1952 ...DLB-188

Chulkov, Mikhail Dmitrievich 1743?-1792..................DLB-150

Church, Benjamin 1734-1778............DLB-31

Church, Francis Pharcellus 1839-1906 ....DLB-79

Church, Peggy Pond 1903-1986 ....DLB-212

Church, Richard 1893-1972............DLB-191

Church, William Conant 1836-1917 ......DLB-79

Churchill, Caryl 1938- DLB-13

Churchill, Charles 1731-1764...........DLB-109

Churchill, Winston 1871-1947..........DLB-202

Churchill, Sir Winston 1874-1965 ....DLB-100; DS-16; CDBLB-5

Churchyard, Thomas 1520?-1604.......DLB-132

Churton, E., and Company............DLB-106

Chute, Marchette 1909-1994...........DLB-103

Ciardi, John 1916-1986 ....DLB-5; Y-86

Cibber, Colley 1671-1757..............DLB-84

Cicero 106 B.C.-43 B.C.........DLB-211, CDWLB-1

Cima, Annalisa 1941- DLB-128

Čingo, Živko 1935-1987 ....DLB-181

Cioran, E. M. 1911-1995..............DLB-220

Čipkus, Alfonsas (see Nyka-Niliūnas, Alfonsas)

Cirese, Eugenio 1884-1955 ....DLB-114

Cīrulis, Jānis (see Bels, Alberts)

Cisneros, Sandra 1954- DLB-122, 152

City Lights Books DLB-46

Cixous, Hélène 1937- DLB-83, 242

Clampitt, Amy 1920-1994 ....DLB-105

Clancy, Tom 1947- DLB-227

Clapper, Raymond 1892-1944...........DLB-29

Clare, John 1793-1864 ....DLB-55, 96

Clarendon, Edward Hyde, Earl of 1609-1674 ....DLB-101

Clark, Alfred Alexander Gordon (see Hare, Cyril)

Clark, Ann Nolan 1896- DLB-52

Clark, C. E. Frazer Jr. 1925- DLB-187

Clark, C. M., Publishing Company.......DLB-46

Clark, Catherine Anthony 1892-1977 .....DLB-68

Clark, Charles Heber 1841-1915.........DLB-11

Clark, Davis Wasgatt 1812-1871 ....DLB-79

Clark, Eleanor 1913- DLB-6

Clark, J. P. 1935- DLB-117; CDWLB-3

Clark, Lewis Gaylord 1808?-1873 ....DLB-3, 64, 73, 250

Clark, Walter Van Tilburg 1909-1971 ....DLB-9, 206

Clark, William (see Lewis, Meriwether)

Clark, William Andrews Jr. 1877-1934 ...DLB-187

Clarke, Austin 1896-1974.............DLB-10, 20

Clarke, Austin C. 1934- DLB-53, 125

Clarke, Gillian 1937- DLB-40

Clarke, James Freeman 1810-1888 ....DLB-1, 59, 235

Clarke, Lindsay 1939- DLB-231

Clarke, Marcus 1846-1881 ....DLB-230

Clarke, Pauline 1921- DLB-161

Clarke, Rebecca Sophia 1833-1906 ......DLB-42

Clarke, Robert, and Company DLB-49

Clarkson, Thomas 1760-1846 ....DLB-158

Claudel, Paul 1868-1955 ....DLB-192

Claudius, Matthias 1740-1815 ....DLB-97

Clausen, Andy 1943- DLB-16

Clawson, John L. 1865-1933 ....DLB-187

Claxton, Remsen and Haffelfinger DLB-49

Clay, Cassius Marcellus 1810-1903.......DLB-43

Cleage, Pearl 1948- DLB-228

Cleary, Beverly 1916- DLB-52

Cleary, Kate McPhelim 1863-1905 ......DLB-221

Cleaver, Vera 1919- and Cleaver, Bill 1920-1981..............DLB-52

Cleland, John 1710-1789 ....DLB-39

Clemens, Samuel Langhorne (Mark Twain) 1835-1910 ....DLB-11, 12, 23, 64, 74, 186, 189; CDALB-3

Mark Twain on Perpetual Copyright Y-92

Clement, Hal 1922- DLB-8

Clemo, Jack 1916- DLB-27

Clephane, Elizabeth Cecilia 1830-1869 ....DLB-199

Cleveland, John 1613-1658 ....DLB-126

Cliff, Michelle 1946- DLB-157; CDWLB-3

Clifford, Lady Anne 1590-1676.........DLB-151

Clifford, James L. 1901-1978 ....DLB-103

Clifford, Lucy 1853?-1929..... DLB-135, 141, 197

Clifton, Lucille 1936- DLB-5, 41

Clines, Francis X. 1938- DLB-185

Clive, Caroline (V) 1801-1873..........DLB-199

Clode, Edward J. [publishing house] DLB-46

Clough, Arthur Hugh 1819-1861 ....DLB-32

Cloutier, Cécile 1930- DLB-60

Clouts, Sidney 1926-1982 ....DLB-225

Clutton-Brock, Arthur 1868-1924 ....DLB-98

Coates, Robert M. 1897-1973........DLB-4, 9, 102

Coatsworth, Elizabeth 1893- DLB-22

Cobb, Charles E., Jr. 1943- DLB-41

Cobb, Frank I. 1869-1923 ....DLB-25

Cobb, Irvin S. 1876-1944.........DLB-11, 25, 86

Cobbe, Frances Power 1822-1904 ....DLB-190

Cobbett, William 1763-1835 .... DLB-43, 107

Cobbledick, Gordon 1898-1969 ....DLB-171

Cochran, Thomas C. 1902- DLB-17

Cochrane, Elizabeth 1867-1922 ......DLB-25, 189

Cockerell, Sir Sydney 1867-1962........DLB-201

Cockerill, John A. 1845-1896 ....DLB-23

Cocteau, Jean 1889-1963...............DLB-65

Coderre, Emile (see Jean Narrache)

Coe, Jonathan 1961- DLB-231

Coetzee, J. M. 1940- DLB-225

Coffee, Lenore J. 1900?-1984 ....DLB-44

Coffin, Robert P. Tristram 1892-1955.....DLB-45

Coghill, Mrs. Harry (see Walker, Anna Louisa)

Cogswell, Fred 1917- DLB-60

Cogswell, Mason Fitch 1761-1830........DLB-37

Cohan, George M. 1878-1942 ....DLB-249

Cohen, Arthur A. 1928-1986............DLB-28

Cohen, Leonard 1934- DLB-53

Cohen, Matt 1942- DLB-53

Colbeck, Norman 1903-1987...........DLB-201

Colden, Cadwallader 1688-1776 ......DLB-24, 30

Colden, Jane 1724-1766 ....DLB-200

Cole, Barry 1936- DLB-14

Cole, George Watson 1850-1939 ....DLB-140

Colegate, Isabel 1931- DLB-14, 231

Coleman, Emily Holmes 1899-1974 ....DLB-4

Coleman, Wanda 1946- DLB-130

Coleridge, Hartley 1796-1849 ....DLB-96

Coleridge, Mary 1861-1907..........DLB-19, 98

Coleridge, Samuel Taylor 1772-1834 ....DLB-93, 107; CDBLB-3

Coleridge, Sara 1802-1852..............DLB-199

Colet, John 1467-1519 ....DLB-132

Colette 1873-1954 ....DLB-65

Colette, Sidonie Gabrielle (see Colette)

Colinas, Antonio 1946- DLB-134

Coll, Joseph Clement 1881-1921 ....DLB-188

Collier, John 1901-1980................DLB-77

Collier, John Payne 1789-1883 ....DLB-184

Collier, Mary 1690-1762 ....DLB-95

Collier, P. F. [publishing house]..........DLB-49

Collier, Robert J. 1876-1918.............DLB-91

Collin and Small DLB-49

Collingwood, W. G. 1854-1932 ....DLB-149

Collins, An floruit circa 1653............DLB-131

Collins, Isaac [publishing house] DLB-49

Collins, Merle 1950- DLB-157

Collins, Mortimer 1827-1876 ....DLB-21, 35

Collins, Tom (see Furphy, Joseph)

Collins, Wilkie 1824-1889 ....DLB-18, 70, 159; CDBLB-4

Collins, William 1721-1759 ....DLB-109

Collins, William, Sons and Company DLB-154

Collis, Maurice 1889-1973.............DLB-195

Collyer, Mary 1716?-1763? DLB-39

Colman, Benjamin 1673-1747 ....DLB-24

Colman, George, the Elder 1732-1794.....DLB-89

Colman, George, the Younger 1762-1836 ....DLB-89

Colman, S. [publishing house] DLB-49	A Contemporary Flourescence of Chicano Literature Y-84	Coppée, François 1842-1908 . . . . .DLB-217
Colombo, John Robert 1936- DLB-53		Coppel, Alfred 1921- Y-83
Colquhoun, Patrick 1745-1820 . . . . DLB-158	Continental European Rhetoricians, 1400-1600. . . . . DLB-236	Coppola, Francis Ford 1939- DLB-44
Colter, Cyrus 1910- DLB-33	The Continental Publishing Company. . . . DLB-49	Copway, George (Kah-ge-ga-gah-bowh) 1818-1869 . . . . .DLB-175, 183
Colum, Padraic 1881-1972 . . . . DLB-19	Conversations with Editors Y-95	
Columella fl. first century A.D. DLB-211	Conversations with Publishers I: An Interview with Patrick O'Connor Y-84	Corazzini, Sergio 1886-1907 . . . . DLB-114
Colvin, Sir Sidney 1845-1927 . . . . DLB-149		Corbett, Richard 1582-1635 . . . . DLB-121
Colwin, Laurie 1944-1992 . . . . . . .DLB-218; Y-80	Conversations with Publishers II: An Interview with Charles Scribner III Y-94	Corbière, Tristan 1845-1875 . . . . .DLB-217
Comden, Betty 1919- and Green, Adolph 1918- DLB-44		Corcoran, Barbara 1911- DLB-52
	Conversations with Publishers III: An Interview with Donald Lamm Y-95	Cordelli, Franco 1943- DLB-196
Come to Papa Y-99		Corelli, Marie 1855-1924 . . . . DLB-34, 156
Comi, Girolamo 1890-1968 . . . . DLB-114	Conversations with Publishers IV: An Interview with James Laughlin. Y-96	Corle, Edwin 1906-1956. . . . . Y-85
The Comic Tradition Continued [in the British Novel] DLB-15		Corman, Cid 1924- DLB-5, 193
	Conversations with Rare Book Dealers I: An Interview with Glenn Horowitz Y-90	Cormier, Robert 1925-2000 . . . DLB-52; CDALB-6
Commager, Henry Steele 1902-1998 . . . . . DLB-17	Conversations with Rare Book Dealers II: An Interview with Ralph Sipper Y-94	Corn, Alfred 1943- DLB-120; Y-80
The Commercialization of the Image of Revolt, by Kenneth Rexroth DLB-16		Cornford, Frances 1886-1960. . . . . DLB-240
Community and Commentators: Black Theatre and Its Critics DLB-38	Conversations with Rare Book Dealers (Publishers) III: An Interview with Otto Penzler. Y-96	Cornish, Sam 1935- DLB-41
		Cornish, William circa 1465-circa 1524 . . DLB-132
Commynes, Philippe de circa 1447-1511. . . . . DLB-208	The Conversion of an Unpolitical Man, by W. H. Bruford DLB-66	Cornwall, Barry (see Procter, Bryan Waller)
		Cornwallis, Sir William, the Younger circa 1579-1614 . . . . DLB-151
Compton-Burnett, Ivy 1884?-1969 . . . . . . DLB-36	Conway, Moncure Daniel 1832-1907. DLB-1, 223	
Conan, Laure 1845-1924 . . . . DLB-99		Cornwell, David John Moore (see le Carré, John)
Concord History and Life DLB-223	Cook, David C., Publishing Company DLB-49	Corpi, Lucha 1945- DLB-82
Concord Literary History of a Town DLB-223	Cook, Ebenezer circa 1667-circa 1732. . . . . DLB-24	Corrington, John William 1932-1988 . . . . DLB-6, 244
Conde, Carmen 1901- DLB-108	Cook, Edward Tyas 1857-1919 . . . . DLB-149	
Conference on Modern Biography Y-85	Cook, Eliza 1818-1889 . . . . DLB-199	Corriveau, Monique 1927-1976 . . . . DLB-251
Congreve, William 1670-1729 . . . . DLB-39, 84; CDBLB-2	Cook, Michael 1933- DLB-53	Corrothers, James D. 1869-1917 . . . . DLB-50
	Cooke, George Willis 1848-1923 . . . . DLB-71	Corso, Gregory 1930- DLB-5, 16, 237
Preface to Incognita (1692) DLB-39	Cooke, Increase, and Company DLB-49	Cortázar, Julio 1914-1984. . . .DLB-113; CDWLB-3
Conkey, W. B., Company DLB-49	Cooke, John Esten 1830-1886 . . . . DLB-3, 248	Cortéz, Carlos 1923- DLB-209
Conn, Stewart 1936- DLB-233	Cooke, Philip Pendleton 1816-1850 . . . . DLB-3, 59, 248	Cortez, Jayne 1936- DLB-41
Connell, Evan S., Jr. 1924- DLB-2; Y-81		Corvinus, Gottlieb Siegmund 1677-1746 . . . . DLB-168
Connelly, Marc 1890-1980 . . . . DLB-7; Y-80	Cooke, Rose Terry 1827-1892 . . . . . . .DLB-12, 74	
Connolly, Cyril 1903-1974 . . . . DLB-98	Cook-Lynn, Elizabeth 1930- DLB-175	Corvo, Baron (see Rolfe, Frederick William)
Connolly, James B. 1868-1957 . . . . DLB-78	Coolbrith, Ina 1841-1928 . . . . DLB-54, 186	Cory, Annie Sophie (see Cross, Victoria)
Connor, Ralph 1860-1937 . . . . DLB-92	Cooley, Peter 1940- DLB-105	Cory, William Johnson 1823-1892 . . . . DLB-35
Connor, Tony 1930- DLB-40	"Into the Mirror" DLB-105	Coryate, Thomas 1577?-1617 . . . . . . .DLB-151, 172
Conquest, Robert 1917- DLB-27	Coolidge, Clark 1939- DLB-193	Ćosić, Dobrica 1921- DLB-181; CDWLB-4
Conrad, John, and Company DLB-49	Coolidge, George [publishing house] DLB-49	Cosin, John 1595-1672 . . . . DLB-151, 213
Conrad, Joseph 1857-1924 . . . . DLB-10, 34, 98, 156; CDBLB-5	Coolidge, Susan (see Woolsey, Sarah Chauncy)	Cosmopolitan Book Corporation DLB-46
	Cooper, Anna Julia 1858-1964 . . . . DLB-221	Costain, Thomas B. 1885-1965 . . . . DLB-9
Conroy, Jack 1899-1990 . . . . Y-81	Cooper, Edith Emma (see Field, Michael)	Coste, Donat 1912-1957 . . . . DLB-88
Conroy, Pat 1945- DLB-6	Cooper, Giles 1918-1966 . . . . DLB-13	Costello, Louisa Stuart 1799-1870 . . . . DLB-166
Considine, Bob 1906-1975 . . . . DLB-241	Cooper, J. California 19??- DLB-212	Cota-Cárdenas, Margarita 1941- DLB-122
The Consolidation of Opinion: Critical Responses to the Modernists DLB-36	Cooper, James Fenimore 1789-1851 . . . . . . DLB-3, 183, 250; CDALB-2	Côté, Denis 1954- DLB-251
Consolo, Vincenzo 1933- DLB-196		Cotten, Bruce 1873-1954 . . . . .DLB-187
Constable, Archibald, and Company DLB-154	Cooper, Kent 1880-1965 . . . . DLB-29	Cotter, Joseph Seamon, Sr. 1861-1949 . . . . DLB-50
Constable, Henry 1562-1613 . . . . DLB-136	Cooper, Susan 1935- DLB-161	Cotter, Joseph Seamon, Jr. 1895-1919 . . . . DLB-50
Constable and Company Limited DLB-112	Cooper, Susan Fenimore 1813-1894 . . . . . DLB-239	Cottle, Joseph [publishing house] DLB-154
Constant, Benjamin 1767-1830 . . . . DLB-119	Cooper, William [publishing house] DLB-170	Cotton, Charles 1630-1687 . . . . DLB-131
Constant de Rebecque, Henri-Benjamin de (see Constant, Benjamin)	Coote, J. [publishing house] DLB-154	Cotton, John 1584-1652 . . . . DLB-24
	Coover, Robert 1932- DLB-2, 227; Y-81	Cotton, Sir Robert Bruce 1571-1631 . . . . . DLB-213
Constantine, David 1944- DLB-40	Copeland and Day DLB-49	Coulter, John 1888-1980 . . . . DLB-68
Constantin-Weyer, Maurice 1881-1964 . . . DLB-92	Ćopić, Branko 1915-1984 . . . . DLB-181	Cournos, John 1881-1966 . . . . DLB-54
Contempo Caravan: Kites in a Windstorm . . . Y-85	Copland, Robert 1470?-1548 . . . . DLB-136	
	Coppard, A. E. 1878-1957 . . . . DLB-162	Courteline, Georges 1858-1929 . . . . DLB-192

Cousins, Margaret 1905-1996 ....DLB-137
Cousins, Norman 1915-1990..........DLB-137
Couvreur, Jessie (see Tasma)
Coventry, Francis 1725-1754 ....DLB-39
Dedication, *The History of Pompey the Little* (1751) DLB-39
Coverdale, Miles 1487 or 1488-1569.....DLB-167
Coverly, N. [publishing house] DLB-49
Covici-Friede DLB-46
Coward, Noel 1899-1973 ....DLB-10, 245; CDBLB-6
Coward, McCann and Geoghegan DLB-46
Cowles, Gardner 1861-1946 ....DLB-29
Cowles, Gardner "Mike" Jr. 1903-1985 .... DLB-127, 137
Cowley, Abraham 1618-1667 ......DLB-131, 151
Cowley, Hannah 1743-1809 ....DLB-89
Cowley, Malcolm 1898-1989 .... DLB-4, 48; Y-81, Y-89
Cowper, William 1731-1800 ......DLB-104, 109
Cox, A. B. (see Berkeley, Anthony)
Cox, James McMahon 1903-1974 ....DLB-127
Cox, James Middleton 1870-1957 ....DLB-127
Cox, Leonard ca. 1495-ca. 1550 ....DLB-236
Cox, Palmer 1840-1924................DLB-42
Coxe, Louis 1918-1993 ....DLB-5
Coxe, Tench 1755-1824................DLB-37
Cozzens, Frederick S. 1818-1869 ....DLB-202
Cozzens, James Gould 1903-1978 .....DLB-9; Y-84; DS-2; CDALB-1
James Gould Cozzens—A View from Afar Y-97
James Gould Cozzens Case Re-opened Y-97
James Gould Cozzens: How to Read Him.... Y-97
Cozzens's *Michael Scarlett* Y-97
James Gould Cozzens Symposium and Exhibition at the University of South Carolina, Columbia Y-00
Crabbe, George 1754-1832 ....DLB-93
Crace, Jim 1946- DLB-231
Crackanthorpe, Hubert 1870-1896 ......DLB-135
Craddock, Charles Egbert (see Murfree, Mary N.)
Cradock, Thomas 1718-1770 ....DLB-31
Craig, Daniel H. 1811-1895.............DLB-43
Craik, Dinah Maria 1826-1887 ......DLB-35, 136
Cramer, Richard Ben 1950- DLB-185
Cranch, Christopher Pearse 1813-1892 ....DLB-1, 42, 243
Crane, Hart 1899-1932 .....DLB-4, 48; CDALB-4
Crane, R. S. 1886-1967 ....DLB-63
Crane, Stephen 1871-1900 ....DLB-12, 54, 78; CDALB-3
Crane, Walter 1845-1915 ....DLB-163
Cranmer, Thomas 1489-1556 .....DLB-132, 213
Crapsey, Adelaide 1878-1914...........DLB-54
Crashaw, Richard 1612 or 1613-1649....DLB-126
Craven, Avery 1885-1980 ....DLB-17
Crawford, Charles 1752-circa 1815 ......DLB-31

Crawford, F. Marion 1854-1909 ....DLB-71
Crawford, Isabel Valancy 1850-1887......DLB-92
Crawley, Alan 1887-1975...............DLB-68
Crayon, Geoffrey (see Irving, Washington)
Crayon, Porte (see Strother, David Hunter)
Creamer, Robert W. 1922- DLB-171
Creasey, John 1908-1973 ....DLB-77
Creative Age Press....................DLB-46
Creech, William [publishing house]......DLB-154
Creede, Thomas [publishing house] DLB-170
Creel, George 1876-1953 ....DLB-25
Creeley, Robert 1926- ... DLB-5, 16, 169; DS-17
Creelman, James 1859-1915 ....DLB-23
Cregan, David 1931- DLB-13
Creighton, Donald Grant 1902-1979......DLB-88
Cremazie, Octave 1827-1879 ....DLB-99
Crémer, Victoriano 1909?- DLB-108
Crescas, Hasdai circa 1340-1412? DLB-115
Crespo, Angel 1926- DLB-134
Cresset Press DLB-112
Cresswell, Helen 1934- DLB-161
Crèvecoeur, Michel Guillaume Jean de 1735-1813 ....DLB-37
Crewe, Candida 1964- DLB-207
Crews, Harry 1935- DLB-6, 143, 185
Crichton, Michael 1942- Y-81
A Crisis of Culture: The Changing Role of Religion in the New Republic......DLB-37
Crispin, Edmund 1921-1978 ....DLB-87
Cristofer, Michael 1946- DLB-7
Crnjanski, Miloš 1893-1977 .... DLB-147; CDWLB-4
Crocker, Hannah Mather 1752-1829.....DLB-200
Crockett, David (Davy) 1786-1836 .... DLB-3, 11, 183, 248
Croft-Cooke, Rupert (see Bruce, Leo)
Crofts, Freeman Wills 1879-1957.........DLB-77
Croker, John Wilson 1780-1857 ....DLB-110
Croly, George 1780-1860...............DLB-159
Croly, Herbert 1869-1930 ....DLB-91
Croly, Jane Cunningham 1829-1901 ......DLB-23
Crompton, Richmal 1890-1969 ....DLB-160
Cronin, A. J. 1896-1981................DLB-191
Cros, Charles 1842-1888................DLB-217
Crosby, Caresse 1892-1970 ....DLB-48
Crosby, Caresse 1892-1970 and Crosby, Harry 1898-1929 ....DLB-4; DS-15
Crosby, Harry 1898-1929 ....DLB-48
Crosland, Camilla Toulmin (Mrs. Newton Crosland) 1812-1895 ....DLB-240
Cross, Gillian 1945- DLB-161
Cross, Victoria 1868-1952 ....DLB-135, 197
Crossley-Holland, Kevin 1941- DLB-40, 161
Crothers, Rachel 1878-1958..............DLB-7
Crowell, Thomas Y., Company DLB-49

Crowley, John 1942- Y-82
Crowley, Mart 1935- DLB-7
Crown Publishers DLB-46
Crowne, John 1641-1712................DLB-80
Crowninshield, Edward Augustus 1817-1859 ....DLB-140
Crowninshield, Frank 1872-1947.........DLB-91
Croy, Homer 1883-1965 ....DLB-4
Crumley, James 1939- DLB-226; Y-84
Cruse, Mary Anne 1825?-1910 ....DLB-239
Cruz, Migdalia 1958- DLB-249
Cruz, Victor Hernández 1949- DLB-41
Csokor, Franz Theodor 1885-1969 ....DLB-81
Csoóri, Sándor 1930- DLB-232; CDWLB-4
Cuala Press DLB-112
Cullen, Countee 1903-1946 ....DLB-4, 48, 51; CDALB-4
Culler, Jonathan D. 1944- DLB-67, 246
Cullinan, Elizabeth 1933- DLB-234
The Cult of Biography Excerpts from the Second Folio Debate: "Biographies are generally a disease of English Literature" – Germaine Greer, Victoria Glendinning, Auberon Waugh, and Richard Holmes.................. Y-86
Cumberland, Richard 1732-1811.........DLB-89
Cummings, Constance Gordon 1837-1924 ....DLB-174
Cummings, E. E. 1894-1962.............DLB-4, 48; CDALB-5
Cummings, Ray 1887-1957 ....DLB-8
Cummings and Hilliard................DLB-49
Cummins, Maria Susanna 1827-1866 ....DLB-42
Cumpián, Carlos 1953- DLB-209
Cunard, Nancy 1896-1965 ....DLB-240
Cundall, Joseph [publishing house] DLB-106
Cuney, Waring 1906-1976...............DLB-51
Cuney-Hare, Maude 1874-1936..........DLB-52
Cunningham, Allan 1784-1842 .....DLB-116, 144
Cunningham, J. V. 1911- DLB-5
Cunningham, Peter F. [publishing house].................DLB-49
Cunquiero, Alvaro 1911-1981.........DLB-134
Cuomo, George 1929- Y-80
Cupples, Upham and Company DLB-49
Cupples and Leon DLB-46
Cuppy, Will 1884-1949................DLB-11
Curiel, Barbara Brinson 1956- DLB-209
Curll, Edmund [publishing house].......DLB-154
Currie, James 1756-1805 ....DLB-142
Currie, Mary Montgomerie Lamb Singleton, Lady Currie (see Fane, Violet)
Cursor Mundi circa 1300 ....DLB-146
Curti, Merle E. 1897- DLB-17
Curtis, Anthony 1926- DLB-155
Curtis, Cyrus H. K. 1850-1933 ....DLB-91

Curtis, George William
1824-1892 .... DLB-1, 43, 223

Curzon, Robert 1810-1873 .... DLB-166

Curzon, Sarah Anne 1833-1898 .... DLB-99

Cushing, Harvey 1869-1939 .... DLB-187

Custance, Olive (Lady Alfred Douglas)
1874-1944 .... DLB-240

Cynewulf circa 770-840 .... DLB-146

Czepko, Daniel 1605-1660 .... DLB-164

Czerniawski, Adam 1934- DLB-232

D

Dabit, Eugène 1898-1936 .... DLB-65

Daborne, Robert circa 1580-1628 .... DLB-58

Dąbrowska, Maria
1889-1965 .... DLB-215; CDWLB-4

Dacey, Philip 1939- DLB-105

"Eyes Across Centuries: Contemporary
Poetry and 'That Vision Thing,'".... DLB-105

Dach, Simon 1605-1659 .... DLB-164

Daggett, Rollin M. 1831-1901 .... DLB-79

D'Aguiar, Fred 1960- DLB-157

Dahl, Roald 1916-1990 .... DLB-139

Dahlberg, Edward 1900-1977 .... DLB-48

Dahn, Felix 1834-1912 .... DLB-129

Dal', Vladimir Ivanovich (Kazak Vladimir
Lugansky) 1801-1872 .... DLB-198

Dale, Peter 1938- DLB-40

Daley, Arthur 1904-1974 .... DLB-171

Dall, Caroline Healey 1822-1912 ..... DLB-1, 235

Dallas, E. S. 1828-1879 .... DLB-55

From *The Gay Science* (1866) DLB-21

The Dallas Theater Center DLB-7

D'Alton, Louis 1900-1951 .... DLB-10

Daly, Carroll John 1889-1958 .... DLB-226

Daly, T. A. 1871-1948 .... DLB-11

Damon, S. Foster 1893-1971 .... DLB-45

Damrell, William S. [publishing house] ... DLB-49

Dana, Charles A. 1819-1897 ...... DLB-3, 23, 250

Dana, Richard Henry, Jr.
1815-1882 .... DLB-1, 183, 235

Dandridge, Ray Garfield DLB-51

Dane, Clemence 1887-1965 .... DLB-10, 197

Danforth, John 1660-1730 .... DLB-24

Danforth, Samuel, I 1626-1674 .... DLB-24

Danforth, Samuel, II 1666-1727 .... DLB-24

Dangerous Years: London Theater,
1939-1945 .... DLB-10

Daniel, John M. 1825-1865 .... DLB-43

Daniel, Samuel 1562 or 1563-1619 ...... DLB-62

Daniel Press DLB-106

Daniells, Roy 1902-1979 .... DLB-68

Daniels, Jim 1956- DLB-120

Daniels, Jonathan 1902-1981 .... DLB-127

Daniels, Josephus 1862-1948 .... DLB-29

Daniels, Sarah 1957- DLB-245

Danilevsky, Grigorii Petrovich
1829-1890 .... DLB-238

Dannay, Frederic 1905-1982 and
Manfred B. Lee 1905-1971 .... DLB-137

Danner, Margaret Esse 1915- DLB-41

Danter, John [publishing house] DLB-170

Dantin, Louis 1865-1945 .... DLB-92

Danzig, Allison 1898-1987 .... DLB-171

D'Arcy, Ella circa 1857-1937 .... DLB-135

Darke, Nick 1948- DLB-233

Darley, Felix Octavious Carr 1822-1888 . DLB-188

Darley, George 1795-1846 .... DLB-96

Darmesteter, Madame James
(see Robinson, A. Mary F.)

Darwin, Charles 1809-1882 .... DLB-57, 166

Darwin, Erasmus 1731-1802 .... DLB-93

Daryush, Elizabeth 1887-1977 .... DLB-20

Dashkova, Ekaterina Romanovna
(née Vorontsova) 1743-1810 ...... DLB-150

Dashwood, Edmée Elizabeth Monica de la Pasture
(see Delafield, E. M.)

Daudet, Alphonse 1840-1897 .... DLB-123

d'Aulaire, Edgar Parin 1898- and
d'Aulaire, Ingri 1904- DLB-22

Davenant, Sir William 1606-1668 ... DLB-58, 126

Davenport, Guy 1927- DLB-130

Davenport, Marcia 1903-1996 .... DS-17

Davenport, Robert ?-? DLB-58

Daves, Delmer 1904-1977 .... DLB-26

Davey, Frank 1940- DLB-53

Davidson, Avram 1923-1993 .... DLB-8

Davidson, Donald 1893-1968 .... DLB-45

Davidson, John 1857-1909 .... DLB-19

Davidson, Lionel 1922- DLB-14

Davidson, Robyn 1950- DLB-204

Davidson, Sara 1943- DLB-185

Davie, Donald 1922- DLB-27

Davie, Elspeth 1919- DLB-139

Davies, Sir John 1569-1626 .... DLB-172

Davies, John, of Hereford 1565?-1618 ... DLB-121

Davies, Peter, Limited DLB-112

Davies, Rhys 1901-1978 .... DLB-139, 191

Davies, Robertson 1913- DLB-68

Davies, Samuel 1723-1761 .... DLB-31

Davies, Thomas 1712?-1785 .... DLB-142, 154

Davies, W. H. 1871-1940 .... DLB-19, 174

Daviot, Gordon 1896?-1952 .... DLB-10
(see also Tey, Josephine)

Davis, Arthur Hoey (see Rudd, Steele)

Davis, Charles A. 1795-1867 .... DLB-11

Davis, Clyde Brion 1894-1962 .... DLB-9

Davis, Dick 1945- DLB-40

Davis, Frank Marshall 1905-? DLB-51

Davis, H. L. 1894-1960 .... DLB-9, 206

Davis, John 1774-1854 .... DLB-37

Davis, Lydia 1947- DLB-130

Davis, Margaret Thomson 1926- DLB-14

Davis, Ossie 1917- DLB-7, 38, 249

Davis, Owen 1874-1956 .... DLB-249

Davis, Paxton 1925-1994 .... Y-89

Davis, Rebecca Harding 1831-1910 ... DLB-74, 239

Davis, Richard Harding 1864-1916
.... DLB-12, 23, 78, 79, 189; DS-13

Davis, Samuel Cole 1764-1809 .... DLB-37

Davis, Samuel Post 1850-1918 .... DLB-202

Davison, Peter 1928- DLB-5

Davydov, Denis Vasil'evich
1784-1839 .... DLB-205

Davys, Mary 1674-1732 .... DLB-39

Preface to *The Works of
Mrs. Davys* (1725) DLB-39

DAW Books DLB-46

Dawson, Ernest 1882-1947 .... DLB-140

Dawson, Fielding 1930- DLB-130

Dawson, Sarah Morgan 1842-1909 ..... DLB-239

Dawson, William 1704-1752 .... DLB-31

Day, Angel flourished 1583-1599 .... DLB-167, 236

Day, Benjamin Henry 1810-1889 .... DLB-43

Day, Clarence 1874-1935 .... DLB-11

Day, Dorothy 1897-1980 .... DLB-29

Day, Frank Parker 1881-1950 .... DLB-92

Day, John circa 1574-circa 1640 .... DLB-62

Day, John [publishing house] DLB-170

Day, The John, Company DLB-46

Day Lewis, C. 1904-1972 .... DLB-15, 20
(see also Blake, Nicholas)

Day, Mahlon [publishing house] DLB-49

Day, Thomas 1748-1789 .... DLB-39

Dazai Osamu 1909-1948 .... DLB-182

Deacon, William Arthur 1890-1977 ...... DLB-68

Deal, Borden 1922-1985 .... DLB-6

de Angeli, Marguerite 1889-1987 .... DLB-22

De Angelis, Milo 1951- DLB-128

De Bow, J. D. B.
1820-1867 .... DLB-3, 79, 248

de Bruyn, Günter 1926- DLB-75

de Camp, L. Sprague 1907-2000 .... DLB-8

De Carlo, Andrea 1952- DLB-196

De Casas, Celso A. 1944- DLB-209

Dechert, Robert 1895-1975 .... DLB-187

Dee, John 1527-1608 or 1609 ...... DLB-136, 213

Deeping, George Warwick 1877-1950 ... DLB 153

Defoe, Daniel
1660-1731 .... DLB-39, 95, 101; CDBLB-2

Preface to *Colonel Jack* (1722) DLB-39

Preface to *The Farther Adventures of
Robinson Crusoe* (1719) DLB-39

Preface to *Moll Flanders* (1722) DLB-39

Preface to *Robinson Crusoe* (1719) DLB-39

Preface to *Roxana* (1724) DLB-39

de Fontaine, Felix Gregory 1834-1896 .... DLB-43

De Forest, John William 1826-1906 .. DLB-12, 189

DeFrees, Madeline 1919- DLB-105

"The Poet's Kaleidoscope: The Element of Surprise in the Making of the Poem" DLB-105

DeGolyer, Everette Lee 1886-1956 ...... DLB-187

de Graff, Robert 1895-1981 .... Y-81

de Graft, Joe 1924-1978 .... DLB-117

De Heinrico circa 980? DLB-148

Deighton, Len 1929- DLB-87; CDBLB-8

DeJong, Meindert 1906-1991 .... DLB-52

Dekker, Thomas circa 1572-1632 ...... DLB-62, 172; CDBLB-1

Delacorte, Jr., George T. 1894-1991 ...... DLB-91

Delafield, E. M. 1890-1943 .... DLB-34

Delahaye, Guy 1888-1969 .... DLB-92

de la Mare, Walter 1873-1956 ...... DLB-19, 153, 162; CDBLB-6

Deland, Margaret 1857-1945 .... DLB-78

Delaney, Shelagh 1939- DLB-13; CDBLB-8

Delano, Amasa 1763-1823 .... DLB-183

Delany, Martin Robinson 1812-1885 ..... DLB-50

Delany, Samuel R. 1942- DLB-8, 33

de la Roche, Mazo 1879-1961 .... DLB-68

Delavigne, Jean François Casimir 1793-1843 .... DLB-192

Delbanco, Nicholas 1942- DLB-6, 234

Del Castillo, Ramón 1949- DLB-209

De León, Nephtal 1945- DLB-82

Delgado, Abelardo Barrientos 1931- DLB-82

Del Giudice, Daniele 1949- DLB-196

De Libero, Libero 1906-1981 .... DLB-114

DeLillo, Don 1936- DLB-6, 173

de Lint, Charles 1951- DLB-251

de Lisser H. G. 1878-1944 .... DLB-117

Dell, Floyd 1887-1969 .... DLB-9

Dell Publishing Company DLB-46

delle Grazie, Marie Eugene 1864-1931 .... DLB-81

Deloney, Thomas died 1600 .... DLB-167

Deloria, Ella C. 1889-1971 .... DLB-175

Deloria, Vine, Jr. 1933- DLB-175

del Rey, Lester 1915-1993 .... DLB-8

Del Vecchio, John M. 1947- DS-9

Del'vig, Anton Antonovich 1798-1831 .... DLB-205

de Man, Paul 1919-1983 .... DLB-67

DeMarinis, Rick 1934- DLB-218

Demby, William 1922- DLB-33

De Mille, James 1833-1880 .... DLB-251

Deming, Philander 1829-1915 .... DLB-74

Deml, Jakub 1878-1961 .... DLB-215

Demorest, William Jennings 1822-1895 .... DLB-79

De Morgan, William 1839-1917 .... DLB-153

Demosthenes 384 B.C.-322 B.C. DLB-176

Denham, Henry [publishing house] DLB-170

Denham, Sir John 1615-1669 .... DLB-58, 126

Denison, Merrill 1893-1975 .... DLB-92

Denison, T. S., and Company DLB-49

Dennery, Adolphe Philippe 1811-1899 ... DLB-192

Dennie, Joseph 1768-1812 ..... DLB-37, 43, 59, 73

Dennis, John 1658-1734 .... DLB-101

Dennis, Nigel 1912-1989 .... DLB-13, 15, 233

Denslow, W. W. 1856-1915 .... DLB-188

Dent, J. M., and Sons DLB-112

Dent, Tom 1932-1998 .... DLB-38

Denton, Daniel circa 1626-1703 .... DLB-24

DePaola, Tomie 1934- DLB-61

Department of Library, Archives, and Institutional Research, American Bible Society Y-97

De Quille, Dan 1829-1898 .... DLB-186

De Quincey, Thomas 1785-1859 .... DLB-110, 144; CDBLB-3

"Rhetoric" (1828; revised, 1859) [excerpt] DLB-57

Derby, George Horatio 1823-1861 .... DLB-11

Derby, J. C., and Company DLB-49

Derby and Miller DLB-49

De Ricci, Seymour 1881-1942 .... DLB-201

Derleth, August 1909-1971 .... DLB-9; DS-17

Derrida, Jacques 1930- DLB-242

The Derrydale Press DLB-46

Derzhavin, Gavriil Romanovich 1743-1816 .... DLB-150

Desaulniers, Gonsalve 1863-1934 .... DLB-92

Desbordes-Valmore, Marceline 1786-1859 .... DLB-217

Deschamps, Emile 1791-1871 .... DLB-217

Deschamps, Eustache 1340?-1404 ...... DLB-208

Desbiens, Jean-Paul 1927- DLB-53

des Forêts, Louis-Rene 1918- DLB-83

Desiato, Luca 1941- DLB-196

Desnica, Vladan 1905-1967 .... DLB-181

DesRochers, Alfred 1901-1978 .... DLB-68

Desrosiers, Léo-Paul 1896-1967 .... DLB-68

Dessì, Giuseppe 1909-1977 .... DLB-177

Destouches, Louis-Ferdinand (see Céline, Louis-Ferdinand)

De Tabley, Lord 1835-1895 .... DLB-35

Deutsch, André, Limited DLB-112

Deutsch, Babette 1895-1982 .... DLB-45

Deutsch, Niklaus Manuel (see Manuel, Niklaus)

Deveaux, Alexis 1948- DLB-38

The Development of the Author's Copyright in Britain DLB-154

The Development of Lighting in the Staging of Drama, 1900-1945 .... DLB-10

"The Development of Meiji Japan" DLB-180

De Vere, Aubrey 1814-1902 .... DLB-35

Devereux, second Earl of Essex, Robert 1565-1601 .... DLB-136

The Devin-Adair Company DLB-46

De Vinne, Theodore Low 1828-1914 .... DLB-187

Devlin, Anne 1951- DLB-245

De Voto, Bernard 1897-1955 .... DLB-9

De Vries, Peter 1910-1993 .... DLB-6; Y-82

Dewdney, Christopher 1951- DLB-60

Dewdney, Selwyn 1909-1979 .... DLB-68

Dewey, John 1859-1952 .... DLB-246

Dewey, Orville 1794-1882 .... DLB-243

Dewey, Thomas B. 1915-1981 .... DLB-226

DeWitt, Robert M., Publisher DLB-49

DeWolfe, Fiske and Company DLB-49

Dexter, Colin 1930- DLB-87

de Young, M. H. 1849-1925 .... DLB-25

Dhlomo, H. I. E. 1903-1956 .... DLB-157, 225

Dhuoda circa 803-after 843 .... DLB-148

The Dial 1840-1844 .... DLB-223

The Dial Press DLB-46

Diamond, I. A. L. 1920-1988 .... DLB-26

Dibble, L. Grace 1902-1998 .... DLB-204

Dibdin, Thomas Frognall 1776-1847 ..... DLB-184

Di Cicco, Pier Giorgio 1949- DLB-60

Dick, Philip K. 1928-1982 .... DLB-8

Dick and Fitzgerald DLB-49

Dickens, Charles 1812-1870 .... DLB-21, 55, 70, 159, 166; CDBLB-4

Dickey, James 1923-1997 .... DLB-5, 193; Y-82, Y-93, Y-96; DS-7, DS-19; CDALB-6

James Dickey Tributes Y-97

The Life of James Dickey: A Lecture to the Friends of the Emory Libraries, by Henry Hart Y-98

Dickey, William 1928-1994 .... DLB-5

Dickinson, Emily 1830-1886 .... DLB-1, 243; CDWLB-3

Dickinson, John 1732-1808 .... DLB-31

Dickinson, Jonathan 1688-1747 .... DLB-24

Dickinson, Patric 1914- DLB-27

Dickinson, Peter 1927- DLB-87, 161

Dicks, John [publishing house] DLB-106

Dickson, Gordon R. 1923- DLB-8

Dictionary of Literary Biography Yearbook Awards Y-92, Y-93, Y-97, Y-98, Y-99, Y-00

The Dictionary of National Biography DLB-144

Didion, Joan 1934- DLB-2, 173, 185; Y-81, Y-86; CDALB-6

Di Donato, Pietro 1911- DLB-9

Die Fürstliche Bibliothek Corvey Y-96

Diego, Gerardo 1896-1987 .... DLB-134

Digges, Thomas circa 1546-1595 .... DLB-136

The Digital Millennium Copyright Act: Expanding Copyright Protection in Cyberspace and Beyond Y-98

Dillard, Annie 1945- Y-80

Dillard, R. H. W. 1937- DLB-5, 244

Dillingham, Charles T., Company DLB-49

The Dillingham, G. W., Company DLB-49

Dilly, Edward and Charles [publishing house] DLB-154

Dilthey, Wilhelm 1833-1911 .... DLB-129

Dimitrova, Blaga 1922- ... DLB-181; CDWLB-4

Dimov, Dimitr 1909-1966 .... DLB-181

Cumulative Index

Dimsdale, Thomas J. 1831?-1866....... DLB-186
Dinescu, Mircea 1950- DLB-232
Dinesen, Isak (see Blixen, Karen)
Dingelstedt, Franz von 1814-1881 ...... DLB-133
Dintenfass, Mark 1941- Y-84
Diogenes, Jr. (see Brougham, John)
Diogenes Laertius circa 200 ....DLB-176
DiPrima, Diane 1934- DLB-5, 16
Disch, Thomas M. 1940- DLB-8
Disney, Walt 1901-1966............... DLB-22
Disraeli, Benjamin 1804-1881........ DLB-21, 55
D'Israeli, Isaac 1766-1848............. DLB-107
Ditlevsen, Tove 1917-1976 .... DLB-214
Ditzen, Rudolf (see Fallada, Hans)
Dix, Dorothea Lynde 1802-1887 ..... DLB-1, 235
Dix, Dorothy (see Gilmer, Elizabeth Meriwether)
Dix, Edwards and Company DLB-49
Dix, Gertrude circa 1874-? DLB-197
Dixie, Florence Douglas 1857-1905.......DLB-174
Dixon, Ella Hepworth
  1855 or 1857-1932 .... DLB-197
Dixon, Paige (see Corcoran, Barbara)
Dixon, Richard Watson 1833-1900 ...... DLB-19
Dixon, Stephen 1936- DLB-130
Dmitriev, Ivan Ivanovich 1760-1837..... DLB-150
Dobell, Bertram 1842-1914............ DLB-184
Dobell, Sydney 1824-1874 .... DLB-32
Dobie, J. Frank 1888-1964 .... DLB-212
Döblin, Alfred 1878-1957 .... DLB-66; CDWLB-2
Dobson, Austin 1840-1921 .... DLB-35, 144
Doctorow, E. L.
  1931- DLB-2, 28, 173; Y-80; CDALB-6
Documents on Sixteenth-Century
  Literature DLB-167, 172
Dodd, Anne [publishing house] DLB-154
Dodd, Mead and Company DLB-49
Dodd, Susan M. 1946- DLB-244
Dodd, William E. 1869-1940 .... DLB-17
Doderer, Heimito von 1896-1968........ DLB-85
Dodge, B. W., and Company.......... DLB-46
Dodge, Mary Abigail 1833-1896 ...... DLB-221
Dodge, Mary Mapes
  1831?-1905............ DLB-42, 79; DS-13
Dodge Publishing Company........... DLB-49
Dodgson, Charles Lutwidge (see Carroll, Lewis)
Dodsley, R. [publishing house]......... DLB-154
Dodsley, Robert 1703-1764.............. DLB-95
Dodson, Owen 1914-1983 .... DLB-76
Dodwell, Christina 1951- DLB-204
Doesticks, Q. K. Philander, P. B.
  (see Thomson, Mortimer)
Doheny, Carrie Estelle 1875-1958 ...... DLB-140
Doherty, John 1798?-1854 .... DLB-190
Doig, Ivan 1939- DLB-206
Doinaş, Ştefan Augustin 1922- DLB-232
Domínguez, Sylvia Maida 1935- DLB-122

Donahoe, Patrick [publishing house] DLB-49
Donald, David H. 1920- DLB-17
The Practice of Biography VI: An
  Interview with David Herbert Donald.... Y-87
Donaldson, Scott 1928- DLB-111
Doni, Rodolfo 1919- DLB-177
Donleavy, J. P. 1926- DLB-6, 173
Donnadieu, Marguerite (see Duras, Marguerite)
Donne, John
  1572-1631......... DLB-121, 151; CDBLB-1
Donnelley, R. R., and Sons Company DLB-49
Donnelly, Ignatius 1831-1901.......... DLB-12
Donohue and Henneberry DLB-49
Donoso, José 1924-1996.....DLB-113; CDWLB-3
Doolady, M. [publishing house] DLB-49
Dooley, Ebon (see Ebon)
Doolittle, Hilda 1886-1961 .... DLB-4, 45
Doplicher, Fabio 1938- DLB-128
Dor, Milo 1923- DLB-85
Doran, George H., Company.......... DLB-46
Dorgelès, Roland 1886-1973 .... DLB-65
Dorn, Edward 1929-1999............... DLB-5
Dorr, Rheta Childe 1866-1948 .... DLB-25
Dorris, Michael 1945-1997 ....DLB-175
Dorset and Middlesex, Charles Sackville,
  Lord Buckhurst, Earl of 1643-1706....DLB-131
Dorsey, Candas Jane 1952- DLB-251
Dorst, Tankred 1925- DLB-75, 124
Dos Passos, John 1896-1970
  .... DLB-4, 9; DS-1, DS-15; CDALB-5
John Dos Passos: Artist Y-99
John Dos Passos: A Centennial
  Commemoration Y-96
Dostoevsky, Fyodor 1821-1881 .... DLB-238
Doubleday and Company DLB-49
Dougall, Lily 1858-1923................ DLB-92
Doughty, Charles M.
  1843-1926 .... DLB-19, 57, 174
Douglas, Lady Alfred (see Custance, Olive)
Douglas, Gavin 1476-1522 .... DLB-132
Douglas, Keith 1920-1944 .... DLB-27
Douglas, Norman 1868-1952 .... DLB-34, 195
Douglass, Frederick 1818-1895
  .... DLB-1, 43, 50, 79, 243; CDALB-2
Douglass, William circa 1691-1752....... DLB-24
Dourado, Autran 1926- DLB-145
Dove, Arthur G. 1880-1946 .... DLB-188
Dove, Rita 1952- DLB-120; CDALB-7
Dover Publications DLB-46
Doves Press DLB-112
Dowden, Edward 1843-1913 .... DLB-35, 149
Dowell, Coleman 1925-1985 .... DLB-130
Dowland, John 1563-1626 ....DLB-172
Downes, Gwladys 1915- DLB-88
Downing, J., Major (see Davis, Charles A.)
Downing, Major Jack (see Smith, Seba)

Dowriche, Anne
  before 1560-after 1613.............DLB-172
Dowson, Ernest 1867-1900......... DLB-19, 135
Doxey, William [publishing house] DLB-49
Doyle, Sir Arthur Conan
  1859-1930 ...DLB-18, 70, 156, 178; CDBLB-5
Doyle, Kirby 1932- DLB-16
Doyle, Roddy 1958- DLB-194
Drabble, Margaret
  1939- DLB-14, 155, 231; CDBLB-8
Drach, Albert 1902- DLB-85
Dragojević, Danijel 1934- DLB-181
Drake, Samuel Gardner 1798-1875.......DLB-187
The Dramatic Publishing Company...... DLB-49
Dramatists Play Service DLB-46
Drant, Thomas early 1540s?-1578 ...... DLB-167
Draper, John W. 1811-1882............ DLB-30
Draper, Lyman C. 1815-1891 .... DLB-30
Drayton, Michael 1563-1631 .... DLB-121
Dreiser, Theodore 1871-1945
  ....DLB-9, 12, 102, 137; DS-1; CDALB-3
Dresser, Davis 1904-1977.............. DLB-226
Drewitz, Ingeborg 1923-1986........... DLB-75
Drieu La Rochelle, Pierre 1893-1945 ..... DLB-72
Drinker, Elizabeth 1735-1807 .... DLB-200
Drinkwater, John
  1882-1937 ....DLB-10, 19, 149
Droste-Hülshoff, Annette von
  1797-1848 ....DLB-133; CDWLB-2
The Drue Heinz Literature Prize
  Excerpt from "Excerpts from a Report
  of the Commission," in David
  Bosworth's *The Death of Descartes*
  An Interview with David Bosworth....... Y-82
Drummond, William, of Hawthornden
  1585-1649 .... DLB-121, 213
Drummond, William Henry
  1854-1907 .... DLB-92
Druzhinin, Aleksandr Vasil'evich
  1824-1864 .... DLB-238
Dryden, Charles 1860?-1931 ....DLB-171
Dryden, John
  1631-1700...... DLB-80, 101, 131; CDBLB-2
Držić, Marin
  circa 1508-1567 ....DLB-147; CDWLB-4
Duane, William 1760-1835............. DLB-43
Dubé, Marcel 1930- DLB-53
Dubé, Rodolphe (see Hertel, François)
Dubie, Norman 1945- DLB-120
Dubois, Silvia 1788 or 1789?-1889 ...... DLB-239
Du Bois, W. E. B.
  1868-1963 ....DLB-47, 50, 91, 246; CDALB-3
Du Bois, William Pène 1916-1993 ...... DLB-61
Dubrovina, Ekaterina Oskarovna
  1846-1913 .... DLB-238
Dubus, Andre 1936-1999 .... DLB-130
Ducange, Victor 1783-1833 .... DLB-192
Du Chaillu, Paul Belloni 1831?-1903 .... DLB-189
Ducharme, Réjean 1941- DLB-60
Dučić, Jovan 1871-1943 .....DLB-147; CDWLB-4

Duck, Stephen 1705?-1756 . . . . .DLB-95
Duckworth, Gerald, and Company
    Limited DLB-112
Duclaux, Madame Mary (see Robinson, A. Mary F.)
Dudek, Louis 1918- DLB-88
Duell, Sloan and Pearce DLB-46
Duerer, Albrecht 1471-1528. . . . . DLB-179
Duff Gordon, Lucie 1821-1869 . . . . DLB-166
Dufferin, Helen Lady, Countess of Gifford
    1807-1867 . . . . DLB-199
Duffield and Green DLB-46
Duffy, Maureen 1933- DLB-14
Dufief, Nicholas Gouin 1776-1834. . . . . DLB-187
Dugan, Alan 1923- DLB-5
Dugard, William [publishing house] DLB-170
Dugas, Marcel 1883-1947 . . . . .DLB-92
Dugdale, William [publishing house]. DLB-106
Duhamel, Georges 1884-1966 . . . . .DLB-65
Dujardin, Edouard 1861-1949 . . . . DLB-123
Dukes, Ashley 1885-1959 . . . . .DLB-10
Dumas, Alexandre *père* 1802-1870. . . . . DLB-119, 192
Dumas, Alexandre *fils* 1824-1895. . . . . . . DLB-192
Dumas, Henry 1934-1968 . . . . .DLB-41
du Maurier, Daphne 1907-1989 . . . . DLB-191
Du Maurier, George 1834-1896. . . . . DLB-153, 178
Dunbar, Paul Laurence
    1872-1906 . . . . .DLB-50, 54, 78; CDALB-3
Dunbar, William
    circa 1460-circa 1522. . . . . .DLB-132, 146
Duncan, Dave 1933- DLB-251
Duncan, Norman 1871-1916 . . . . .DLB-92
Duncan, Quince 1940- DLB-145
Duncan, Robert 1919-1988 . . . . . . .DLB-5, 16, 193
Duncan, Ronald 1914-1982 . . . . .DLB-13
Duncan, Sara Jeannette 1861-1922 . . . . .DLB-92
Dunigan, Edward, and Brother DLB-49
Dunlap, John 1747-1812. . . . . .DLB-43
Dunlap, William 1766-1839. . . . . . . DLB-30, 37, 59
Dunn, Douglas 1942- DLB-40
Dunn, Harvey Thomas 1884-1952 . . . . . .DLB-188
Dunn, Stephen 1939- DLB-105
"The Good, The Not So Good" DLB-105
Dunne, Finley Peter 1867-1936 . . . . . . .DLB-11, 23
Dunne, John Gregory 1932- Y-80
Dunne, Philip 1908-1992. . . . . .DLB-26
Dunning, Ralph Cheever 1878-1930 . . . . . . .DLB-4
Dunning, William A. 1857-1922 . . . . .DLB-17
Dunsany, Lord (Edward John Moreton
    Drax Plunkett, Baron Dunsany)
    1878-1957 . . . . DLB-10, 77, 153, 156
Duns Scotus, John circa 1266-1308 . . . . . . DLB-115
Dunton, John [publishing house] DLB-170
Dunton, W. Herbert 1878-1936. . . . . DLB-188
Dupin, Amantine-Aurore-Lucile (see Sand, George)
Dupuy, Eliza Ann 1814-1880. . . . . DLB-248
Durand, Lucile (see Bersianik, Louky)

Duranti, Francesca 1935- DLB-196
Duranty, Walter 1884-1957. . . . . .DLB-29
Duras, Marguerite 1914-1996 . . . . .DLB-83
Durfey, Thomas 1653-1723 . . . . .DLB-80
Durova, Nadezhda Andreevna
    (Aleksandr Andreevich Aleksandrov)
    1783-1866 . . . . DLB-198
Durrell, Lawrence 1912-1990
    . . . . DLB-15, 27, 204; Y-90; CDBLB-7
Durrell, William [publishing house]. DLB-49
Dürrenmatt, Friedrich
    1921-1990 . . . . .DLB-69, 124; CDWLB-2
Duston, Hannah 1657-1737 . . . . DLB-200
Dutt, Toru 1856-1877 . . . . DLB-240
Dutton, E. P., and Company DLB-49
Duvoisin, Roger 1904-1980 . . . . .DLB-61
Duyckinck, Evert A.
    1816-1878 . . . . .DLB-3, 64, 250
Duyckinck, George L. 1823-1863 . . . . . DLB-3, 250
Duyckinck and Company DLB-49
Dwight, John Sullivan 1813-1893 . . . . . DLB-1, 235
Dwight, Timothy 1752-1817 . . . . .DLB-37
Dybek, Stuart 1942- DLB-130
Dyer, Charles 1928- DLB-13
Dyer, Sir Edward 1543-1607 . . . . DLB-136
Dyer, George 1755-1841 . . . . .DLB-93
Dyer, John 1699-1757 . . . . .DLB-95
Dyk, Viktor 1877-1931. . . . . DLB-215
Dylan, Bob 1941- DLB-16

E

Eager, Edward 1911-1964 . . . . .DLB-22
Eagleton, Terry 1943- DLB-242
Eames, Wilberforce 1855-1937 . . . . DLB-140
Earle, Alice Morse 1853-1911 . . . . DLB-221
Earle, James H., and Company DLB-49
Earle, John 1600 or 1601-1665 . . . . DLB-151
Early American Book Illustration,
    by Sinclair Hamilton DLB-49
Eastlake, William 1917-1997 . . . . .DLB-6, 206
Eastman, Carol ?- DLB-44
Eastman, Charles A. (Ohiyesa)
    1858-1939 . . . . DLB-175
Eastman, Max 1883-1969 . . . . .DLB-91
Eaton, Daniel Isaac 1753-1814 . . . . DLB-158
Eaton, Edith Maude 1865-1914. . . . . DLB-221
Eaton, Winnifred 1875-1954 . . . . DLB-221
Eberhart, Richard 1904- DLB-48; CDALB-1
Ebner, Jeannie 1918- DLB-85
Ebner-Eschenbach, Marie von
    1830-1916 . . . . .DLB-81
Ebon 1942- DLB-41
E-Books Turn the Corner Y-98
Ecbasis Captivi circa 1045 . . . . DLB-148
Ecco Press DLB-46
Eckhart, Meister circa 1260-circa 1328 . . . DLB-115
The Eclectic Review 1805-1868 . . . . DLB-110

Eco, Umberto 1932- DLB-196, 242
Edel, Leon 1907-1997. . . . . DLB-103
Edes, Benjamin 1732-1803. . . . . .DLB-43
Edgar, David 1948- DLB-13, 233
Edgeworth, Maria
    1768-1849 . . . . .DLB-116, 159, 163
The Edinburgh Review 1802-1929. . . . . DLB-110
Edinburgh University Press. DLB-112
The Editor Publishing Company. DLB-49
Editorial Institute at Boston University Y-00
Editorial Statements. DLB-137
Edmonds, Randolph 1900- DLB-51
Edmonds, Walter D. 1903-1998 . . . . .DLB-9
Edschmid, Kasimir 1890-1966. . . . . .DLB-56
Edson, Russell 1935- DLB-244
Edwards, Amelia Anne Blandford
    1831-1892 . . . . DLB-174
Edwards, Dic 1953- DLB-245
Edwards, Edward 1812-1886. . . . . DLB-184
Edwards, James [publishing house] DLB-154
Edwards, Jonathan 1703-1758 . . . . .DLB-24
Edwards, Jonathan, Jr. 1745-1801 . . . . .DLB-37
Edwards, Junius 1929- DLB-33
Edwards, Matilda Barbara Betham
    1836-1919 . . . . DLB-174
Edwards, Richard 1524-1566 . . . . .DLB-62
Edwards, Sarah Pierpont 1710-1758. . . . . . DLB-200
Effinger, George Alec 1947- DLB-8
Egerton, George 1859-1945. . . . . DLB-135
Eggleston, Edward 1837-1902 . . . . .DLB-12
Eggleston, Wilfred 1901-1986 . . . . .DLB-92
Eglītis, Anšlavs 1906-1993. . . . . DLB-220
Ehrenreich, Barbara 1941- DLB-246
Ehrenstein, Albert 1886-1950 . . . . .DLB-81
Ehrhart, W. D. 1948- DS-9
Ehrlich, Gretel 1946- DLB-212
Eich, Günter 1907-1972 . . . . DLB-69, 124
Eichendorff, Joseph Freiherr von
    1788-1857 . . . . .DLB-90
Eifukumon'in 1271-1342 . . . . DLB-203
1873 Publishers' Catalogues DLB-49
Eighteenth-Century Aesthetic
    Theories DLB-31
Eighteenth-Century Philosophical
    Background. DLB-31
Eigner, Larry 1926-1996 . . . . .DLB-5, 193
Eikon Basilike 1649 . . . . DLB-151
Eilhart von Oberge
    circa 1140-circa 1195. . . . . DLB-148
Einhard circa 770-840 . . . . DLB-148
Eiseley, Loren 1907-1977 . . . . DS-17
Eisenberg, Deborah 1945- DLB-244
Eisenreich, Herbert 1925-1986 . . . . .DLB-85
Eisner, Kurt 1867-1919 . . . . .DLB-66
Eklund, Gordon 1945- Y-83
Ekwensi, Cyprian
    1921- DLB-117; CDWLB-3

Elaw, Zilpha circa 1790-? DLB-239

Eld, George [publishing house] DLB-170

Elder, Lonne III 1931- DLB-7, 38, 44

Elder, Paul, and Company DLB-49

The Electronic Text Center and the Electronic Archive of Early American Fiction at the University of Virginia Library Y-98

Eliade, Mircea 1907-1986 . . . DLB-220; CDWLB-4

Elie, Robert 1915-1973 . . . . DLB-88

Elin Pelin 1877-1949 . . . . DLB-147; CDWLB-4

Eliot, George 1819-1880 . . . . DLB-21, 35, 55; CDBLB-4

Eliot, John 1604-1690 . . . . DLB-24

Eliot, T. S. 1888-1965
. . . . DLB-7, 10, 45, 63, 245; CDALB-5

T. S. Eliot Centennial Y-88

Eliot's Court Press DLB-170

Elizabeth I 1533-1603 . . . . DLB-136

Elizabeth of Nassau-Saarbrücken after 1393-1456 . . . . DLB-179

Elizondo, Salvador 1932- DLB-145

Elizondo, Sergio 1930- DLB-82

Elkin, Stanley 1930-1995 . . . . DLB-2, 28, 218; Y-80

Elles, Dora Amy (see Wentworth, Patricia)

Ellet, Elizabeth F. 1818?-1877 . . . . DLB-30

Elliot, Ebenezer 1781-1849 . . . . DLB-96, 190

Elliot, Frances Minto (Dickinson) 1820-1898 . . . . DLB-166

Elliott, Charlotte 1789-1871 . . . . DLB-199

Elliott, George 1923- DLB-68

Elliott, George P. 1918-1980 . . . . DLB-244

Elliott, Janice 1931- DLB-14

Elliott, Sarah Barnwell 1848-1928 . . . . . . DLB-221

Elliott, Thomes and Talbot DLB-49

Elliott, William III 1788-1863 . . . . DLB-3, 248

Ellis, Alice Thomas (Anna Margaret Haycraft) 1932- DLB-194

Ellis, Edward S. 1840-1916 . . . . DLB-42

Ellis, Frederick Staridge [publishing house] DLB-106

The George H. Ellis Company DLB-49

Ellis, Havelock 1859-1939 . . . . DLB-190

Ellison, Harlan 1934- DLB-8

Ellison, Ralph 1914-1994 . . . . DLB-2, 76, 227; Y-94; CDALB-1

Ellmann, Richard 1918-1987 . . . . . . DLB-103; Y-87

Ellroy, James 1948- DLB-226; Y-91

Elyot, Thomas 1490?-1546 . . . . DLB-136

Emanuel, James Andrew 1921- DLB-41

Emecheta, Buchi 1944- DLB-117; CDWLB-3

Emendations for *Look Homeward, Angel* Y-00

The Emergence of Black Women Writers DS-8

Emerson, Ralph Waldo 1803-1882
. . . . DLB-1, 59, 73, 183, 223; CDALB-2

Ralph Waldo Emerson in 1982 . . . . Y-82

Emerson, William 1769-1811 . . . . DLB-37

Emerson, William 1923-1997 . . . . Y-97

Emin, Fedor Aleksandrovich circa 1735-1770 . . . . DLB-150

Empedocles fifth century B.C. DLB-176

Empson, William 1906-1984 . . . . DLB-20

Enchi Fumiko 1905-1986 . . . . DLB-182

"Encounter with the West" DLB-180

The End of English Stage Censorship, 1945-1968 . . . . DLB-13

Ende, Michael 1929-1995 . . . . DLB-75

Endō Shūsaku 1923-1996 . . . . DLB-182

Engel, Marian 1933-1985 . . . . DLB-53

Engels, Friedrich 1820-1895 . . . . DLB-129

Engle, Paul 1908- DLB-48

English, Thomas Dunn 1819-1902 . . . . . . DLB-202

English Composition and Rhetoric (1866), by Alexander Bain [excerpt] DLB-57

The English Language: 410 to 1500 . . . . . DLB-146

Ennius 239 B.C.-169 B.C. DLB-211

Enright, D. J. 1920- DLB-27

Enright, Elizabeth 1909-1968 . . . . DLB-22

Epic and Beast Epic DLB-208

Epictetus circa 55-circa 125-130 . . . . DLB-176

Epicurus 342/341 B.C.-271/270 B.C. DLB-176

Epps, Bernard 1936- DLB-53

Epstein, Julius 1909- and Epstein, Philip 1909-1952 . . . . DLB-26

Equiano, Olaudah circa 1745-1797 . . . . DLB-37, 50; DWLB-3

Olaudah Equiano and Unfinished Journeys: The Slave-Narrative Tradition and Twentieth-Century Continuities, by Paul Edwards and Pauline T. Wangman DLB-117

The E-Researcher: Possibilities and Pitfalls . . . Y-00

Eragny Press DLB-112

Erasmus, Desiderius 1467-1536 . . . . DLB-136

Erba, Luciano 1922- DLB-128

Erdrich, Louise 1954- DLB-152, 175, 206; CDALB-7

Erichsen-Brown, Gwethalyn Graham (see Graham, Gwethalyn)

Eriugena, John Scottus circa 810-877 . . . . DLB-115

Ernst, Paul 1866-1933 . . . . DLB-66, 118

Ershov, Petr Pavlovich 1815-1869 . . . . DLB-205

Erskine, Albert 1911-1993 . . . . Y-93

Erskine, John 1879-1951 . . . . DLB-9, 102

Erskine, Mrs. Steuart ?-1948 . . . . DLB-195

Ertel', Aleksandr Ivanovich 1855-1908 . . . . DLB-238

Ervine, St. John Greer 1883-1971 . . . . DLB-10

Eschenburg, Johann Joachim 1743-1820 . . . DLB-97

Escoto, Julio 1944- DLB-145

Esdaile, Arundell 1880-1956 . . . . DLB-201

Eshleman, Clayton 1935- DLB-5

Espriu, Salvador 1913-1985 . . . . DLB-134

Ess Ess Publishing Company DLB-49

Essex House Press DLB-112

Essop, Ahmed 1931- DLB-225

Esterházy, Péter 1950- DLB-232; CDWLB-4

Estes, Eleanor 1906-1988 . . . . DLB-22

Estes and Lauriat DLB-49

Estleman, Loren D. 1952- DLB-226

Eszterhas, Joe 1944- DLB-185

Etherege, George 1636-circa 1692 . . . . . . DLB-80

Ethridge, Mark, Sr. 1896-1981 . . . . DLB-127

Ets, Marie Hall 1893- DLB-22

Etter, David 1928- DLB-105

Ettner, Johann Christoph 1654-1724 . . . . DLB-168

Eupolemius flourished circa 1095 . . . . . . DLB-148

Euripides circa 484 B.C.-407/406 B.C.
. . . . DLB-176; CDWLB-1

Evans, Augusta Jane 1835-1909 . . . . DLB-239

Evans, Caradoc 1878-1945 . . . . DLB-162

Evans, Charles 1850-1935 . . . . DLB-187

Evans, Donald 1884-1921 . . . . DLB-54

Evans, George Henry 1805-1856 . . . . DLB-43

Evans, Hubert 1892-1986 . . . . DLB-92

Evans, M., and Company DLB-46

Evans, Mari 1923- DLB-41

Evans, Mary Ann (see Eliot, George)

Evans, Nathaniel 1742-1767 . . . . DLB-31

Evans, Sebastian 1830-1909 . . . . DLB-35

Evaristi, Marcella 1953- DLB-233

Everett, Alexander Hill 1790-1847 . . . . . . DLB-59

Everett, Edward 1794-1865 . . . . . . DLB-1, 59, 235

Everson, R. G. 1903- DLB-88

Everson, William 1912-1994 . . . . . DLB-5, 16, 212

Ewart, Gavin 1916-1995 . . . . DLB-40

Ewing, Juliana Horatia 1841-1885 . . . DLB-21, 163

The Examiner 1808-1881 . . . . DLB-110

Exley, Frederick 1929-1992 . . . . DLB-143; Y-81

von Eyb, Albrecht 1420-1475 . . . . DLB-179

Eyre and Spottiswoode DLB-106

Ezera, Regīna 1930- DLB-232

Ezzo ?-after 1065 . . . . DLB-148

F

Faber, Frederick William 1814-1863 . . . . . DLB-32

Faber and Faber Limited DLB-112

Faccio, Rena (see Aleramo, Sibilla)

Fagundo, Ana María 1938- DLB-134

Fair, Ronald L. 1932- DLB-33

Fairfax, Beatrice (see Manning, Marie)

Fairlie, Gerard 1899-1983 . . . . DLB-77

Fallada, Hans 1893-1947 . . . . DLB-56

Fancher, Betsy 1928- Y-83

Fane, Violet 1843-1905 . . . . DLB-35

Fanfrolico Press DLB-112

Fanning, Katherine 1927 . . . . DLB-127

Fanshawe, Sir Richard 1608-1666 . . . . . . DLB-126

Fantasy Press Publishers DLB-46

Fante, John 1909-1983 . . . . DLB-130; Y-83
Al-Farabi circa 870-950. . . . . DLB-115
Farabough, Laura 1949- DLB-228
Farah, Nuruddin 1945- . . . DLB-125; CDWLB-3
Farber, Norma 1909-1984 . . . . DLB-61
Farigoule, Louis (see Romains, Jules)
Farjeon, Eleanor 1881-1965 . . . . DLB-160
Farley, Harriet 1812-1907 . . . . DLB-239
Farley, Walter 1920-1989 . . . . DLB-22
Farmborough, Florence 1887-1978 . . . . . . DLB-204
Farmer, Penelope 1939- DLB-161
Farmer, Philip José 1918- DLB-8
Farnaby, Thomas 1575?-1647 . . . . DLB-236
Farningham, Marianne (see Hearn, Mary Anne)
Farquhar, George circa 1677-1707 . . . . DLB-84
Farquharson, Martha (see Finley, Martha)
Farrar, Frederic William 1831-1903 . . . . . . DLB-163
Farrar and Rinehart DLB-46
Farrar, Straus and Giroux DLB-46
Farrell, J. G. 1935-1979 . . . . DLB-14
Farrell, James T. 1904-1979 . . . . DLB-4, 9, 86; DS-2
Fast, Howard 1914- DLB-9
Faulkner, George [publishing house] DLB-154
Faulkner, William 1897-1962
 . . . DLB-9, 11, 44, 102; DS-2; Y-86; CDALB-5
William Faulkner Centenary Y-97
"Faulkner 100–Celebrating the Work,"
 University of South Carolina, Columbia . Y-97
Impressions of William Faulkner Y-97
Faulkner and Yoknapatawpha Conference,
 Oxford, Mississippi Y-97
Faulks, Sebastian 1953- DLB-207
Fauset, Jessie Redmon 1882-1961 . . . . DLB-51
Faust, Irvin 1924- DLB-2, 28, 218; Y-80
Fawcett, Edgar 1847-1904 . . . . DLB-202
Fawcett, Millicent Garrett 1847-1929 . . . . . DLB-190
Fawcett Books DLB-46
Fay, Theodore Sedgwick 1807-1898 . . . . . DLB-202
Fearing, Kenneth 1902-1961 . . . . DLB-9
Federal Writers' Project DLB-46
Federman, Raymond 1928- Y-80
Fedorov, Innokentii Vasil'evich
 (see Omulevsky, Innokentii Vasil'evich)
Feiffer, Jules 1929- DLB-7, 44
Feinberg, Charles E. 1899-1988 . . . . DLB-187; Y-88
Feind, Barthold 1678-1721 . . . . DLB-168
Feinstein, Elaine 1930- DLB-14, 40
Feiss, Paul Louis 1875-1952 . . . . DLB-187
Feldman, Irving 1928- DLB-169
Felipe, Léon 1884-1968 . . . . DLB-108
Fell, Frederick, Publishers DLB-46
Felltham, Owen 1602?-1668 . . . . DLB-126, 151
Felman, Soshana 1942- DLB-246
Fels, Ludwig 1946- DLB-75
Felton, Cornelius Conway 1807-1862 . . DLB-1, 235

Fenn, Harry 1837-1911 . . . . DLB-188
Fennario, David 1947- DLB-60
Fenner, Dudley 1558?-1587? DLB-236
Fenno, Jenny 1765?-1803 . . . . DLB-200
Fenno, John 1751-1798 . . . . DLB-43
Fenno, R. F., and Company DLB-49
Fenoglio, Beppe 1922-1963 . . . . DLB-177
Fenton, Geoffrey 1539?-1608 . . . . DLB-136
Fenton, James 1949- DLB-40
Ferber, Edna 1885-1968 . . . . DLB-9, 28, 86
Ferdinand, Vallery III (see Salaam, Kalamu ya)
Ferguson, Sir Samuel 1810-1886 . . . . DLB-32
Ferguson, William Scott 1875-1954 . . . . . . DLB-47
Fergusson, Robert 1750-1774 . . . . DLB-109
Ferland, Albert 1872-1943 . . . . DLB-92
Ferlinghetti, Lawrence
 1919- DLB-5, 16; CDALB-1
Fermor, Patrick Leigh 1915- DLB-204
Fern, Fanny (see Parton, Sara Payson Willis)
Ferrars, Elizabeth 1907- DLB-87
Ferré, Rosario 1942- DLB-145
Ferret, E., and Company DLB-49
Ferrier, Susan 1782-1854 . . . . DLB-116
Ferril, Thomas Hornsby 1896-1988 . . . . . DLB-206
Ferrini, Vincent 1913- DLB-48
Ferron, Jacques 1921-1985 . . . . DLB-60
Ferron, Madeleine 1922- DLB-53
Ferrucci, Franco 1936- DLB-196
Fetridge and Company DLB-49
Feuchtersleben, Ernst Freiherr von
 1806-1849 . . . . DLB-133
Feuchtwanger, Lion 1884-1958 . . . . DLB-66
Feuerbach, Ludwig 1804-1872 . . . . DLB-133
Feuillet, Octave 1821-1890 . . . . DLB-192
Feydeau, Georges 1862-1921 . . . . DLB-192
Fichte, Johann Gottlieb 1762-1814 . . . . DLB-90
Ficke, Arthur Davison 1883-1945 . . . . DLB-54
Fiction Best-Sellers, 1910-1945 . . . . DLB-9
Fiction into Film, 1928-1975: A List of Movies
 Based on the Works of Authors in
 British Novelists, 1930-1959 . . . . DLB-15
Fiedler, Leslie A. 1917- DLB-28, 67
Field, Barron 1789-1846 . . . . DLB-230
Field, Edward 1924- DLB-105
Field, Joseph M. 1810-1856 . . . . DLB-248
Field, Michael
 (Katherine Harris Bradley [1846-1914]
 and Edith Emma Cooper
 [1862-1913]) DLB-240
"The Poetry File" DLB-105
Field, Eugene
 1850-1895 . . . . DLB-23, 42, 140; DS-13
Field, John 1545?-1588 . . . . DLB-167
Field, Marshall, III 1893-1956 . . . . DLB-127
Field, Marshall, IV 1916-1965 . . . . DLB-127
Field, Marshall, V 1941- DLB-127
Field, Nathan 1587-1619 or 1620 . . . . DLB-58

Field, Rachel 1894-1942 . . . . DLB-9, 22
A Field Guide to Recent Schools of American
 Poetry Y-86
Fielding, Helen 1958- DLB-231
Fielding, Henry
 1707-1754 . . . . . . DLB-39, 84, 101; CDBLB-2
"Defense of Amelia" (1752) DLB-39
From The History of the Adventures of
 Joseph Andrews (1742) DLB-39
Preface to Joseph Andrews (1742) DLB-39
Preface to Sarah Fielding's The Adventures
 of David Simple (1744) DLB-39
Preface to Sarah Fielding's Familiar Letters
 (1747) [excerpt] DLB-39
Fielding, Sarah 1710-1768 . . . . DLB-39
Preface to The Cry (1754) DLB-39
Fields, Annie Adams 1834-1915 . . . . DLB-221
Fields, James T. 1817-1881 . . . . DLB-1, 235
Fields, Julia 1938- DLB-41
Fields, Osgood and Company DLB-49
Fields, W. C. 1880-1946 . . . . DLB-44
Fifty Penguin Years Y-85
Figes, Eva 1932- DLB-14
Figuera, Angela 1902-1984 . . . . DLB-108
Filmer, Sir Robert 1586-1653 . . . . DLB-151
Filson, John circa 1753-1788 . . . . DLB-37
Finch, Anne, Countess of Winchilsea
 1661-1720 . . . . DLB-95
Finch, Robert 1900- DLB-88
Findley, Timothy 1930- DLB-53
Finlay, Ian Hamilton 1925- DLB-40
Finley, Martha 1828-1909 . . . . DLB-42
Finn, Elizabeth Anne (McCaul)
 1825-1921 . . . . DLB-166
Finnegan, Seamus 1949- DLB-245
Finney, Jack 1911-1995 . . . . DLB-8
Finney, Walter Braden (see Finney, Jack)
Firbank, Ronald 1886-1926 . . . . DLB-36
Firmin, Giles 1615-1697 . . . . DLB-24
First Edition Library/Collectors'
 Reprints, Inc. Y-91
Fischart, Johann
 1546 or 1547-1590 or 1591 . . . . DLB-179
Fischer, Karoline Auguste Fernandine
 1764-1842 . . . . DLB-94
Fischer, Tibor 1959- DLB-231
Fish, Stanley 1938- DLB-67
Fishacre, Richard 1205-1248 . . . . DLB-115
Fisher, Clay (see Allen, Henry W.)
Fisher, Dorothy Canfield 1879-1958 . . . DLB-9, 102
Fisher, Leonard Everett 1924- DLB-61
Fisher, Roy 1930- DLB-40
Fisher, Rudolph 1897-1934 . . . . DLB-51, 102
Fisher, Steve 1913-1980 . . . . DLB-226
Fisher, Sydney George 1856-1927 . . . . DLB-47
Fisher, Vardis 1895-1968 . . . . DLB-9, 206
Fiske, John 1608-1677 . . . . DLB-24

Fiske, John 1842-1901 . . . . DLB-47, 64	Follen, Charles 1796-1840 . . . . DLB-235	Foster, Michael 1904-1956 . . . . DLB-9
Fitch, Thomas circa 1700-1774 . . . . DLB-31	Follen, Eliza Lee (Cabot) 1787-1860 . . . DLB-1, 235	Foster, Myles Birket 1825-1899 . . . . DLB-184
Fitch, William Clyde 1865-1909 . . . . DLB-7	Follett, Ken 1949- DLB-87; Y-81	Foucault, Michel 1926-1984 . . . . DLB-242
FitzGerald, Edward 1809-1883 . . . . DLB-32	Follett Publishing Company DLB-46	Foulis, Robert and Andrew / R. and A. [publishing house] DLB-154
Fitzgerald, F. Scott 1896-1940 . . . . DLB-4, 9, 86, 219; Y-81, Y-92; DS-1, 15, 16; CDALB-4	Folsom, John West [publishing house] DLB-49	
	Folz, Hans between 1435 and 1440-1513 . . . . DLB-179	Fouqué, Caroline de la Motte 1774-1831 . . . . DLB-90
F. Scott Fitzgerald Centenary Celebrations Y-96	Fontane, Theodor 1819-1898 . . . . DLB-129; CDWLB-2	Fouqué, Friedrich de la Motte 1777-1843 . . . . DLB-90
F. Scott Fitzgerald Inducted into the American Poets' Corner at St. John the Divine; Ezra Pound Banned Y-99	Fontes, Montserrat 1940- DLB-209	Four Seas Company DLB-46
	Fonvisin, Denis Ivanovich 1744 or 1745-1792 . . . . DLB-150	Four Winds Press DLB-46
"F. Scott Fitzgerald: St. Paul's Native Son and Distinguished American Writer": University of Minnesota Conference, 29-31 October 1982 . . . . Y-82	Foote, Horton 1916- DLB-26	Fournier, Henri Alban (see Alain-Fournier)
	Foote, Mary Hallock 1847-1938 . . . . DLB-186, 188, 202, 221	Fowler and Wells Company DLB-49
		Fowles, John 1926- DLB-14, 139, 207; CDBLB-8
First International F. Scott Fitzgerald Conference Y-92	Foote, Samuel 1721-1777 . . . . DLB-89	Fox, John 1939- DLB-245
Fitzgerald, Penelope 1916- DLB-14, 194	Foote, Shelby 1916- DLB-2, 17	Fox, John, Jr. 1862 or 1863-1919 . . . DLB-9; DS-13
Fitzgerald, Robert 1910-1985 . . . . Y-80	Forbes, Calvin 1945- DLB-41	Fox, Paula 1923- DLB-52
Fitzgerald, Thomas 1819-1891 . . . . DLB-23	Forbes, Ester 1891-1967 . . . . DLB-22	Fox, Richard K. [publishing house] DLB-49
Fitzgerald, Zelda Sayre 1900-1948 . . . . Y-84	Forbes, Rosita 1893?-1967 . . . . DLB-195	Fox, Richard Kyle 1846-1922 . . . . DLB-79
Fitzhugh, Louise 1928-1974 . . . . DLB-52	Forbes and Company DLB-49	Fox, William Price 1926- DLB-2; Y-81
Fitzhugh, William circa 1651-1701 . . . . . . DLB-24	Force, Peter 1790-1868 . . . . DLB-30	Foxe, John 1517-1587 . . . . DLB-132
Flagg, James Montgomery 1877-1960 . . . . DLB-188	Forché, Carolyn 1950- DLB-5, 193	Fraenkel, Michael 1896-1957 . . . . DLB-4
Flanagan, Thomas 1923- Y-80	Ford, Charles Henri 1913- DLB-4, 48	France, Anatole 1844-1924 . . . . DLB-123
Flanner, Hildegarde 1899-1987 . . . . DLB-48	Ford, Corey 1902-1969 . . . . DLB-11	France, Richard 1938- DLB-7
Flanner, Janet 1892-1978 . . . . DLB-4	Ford, Ford Madox 1873-1939 . . . . . . DLB-34, 98, 162; CDBLB-6	Francis, C. S. [publishing house] DLB-49
Flannery, Peter 1951- DLB-233		Francis, Convers 1795-1863 . . . . DLB-1, 235
Flaubert, Gustave 1821-1880 . . . . DLB-119	Ford, J. B., and Company DLB-49	Francis, Dick 1920- DLB-87
Flavin, Martin 1883-1967 . . . . DLB-9	Ford, Jesse Hill 1928-1996 . . . . DLB-6	Francis, Sir Frank 1901-1988 . . . . DLB-201
Fleck, Konrad (flourished circa 1220) DLB-138	Ford, John 1586-? DLB-58; CDBLB-1	Francis, Jeffrey, Lord 1773-1850 . . . . DLB-107
	Ford, R. A. D. 1915- DLB-88	François 1863-1910 . . . . DLB-92
Flecker, James Elroy 1884-1915 . . . . . . DLB-10, 19	Ford, Richard 1944- DLB-227	François, Louise von 1817-1893 . . . . DLB-129
Fleeson, Doris 1901-1970 . . . . DLB-29	Ford, Worthington C. 1858-1941 . . . . DLB-47	Franck, Sebastian 1499-1542 . . . . DLB-179
Fleißer, Marieluise 1901-1974 . . . . . . DLB-56, 124	Fords, Howard, and Hulbert DLB-49	Francke, Kuno 1855-1930 . . . . DLB-71
Fleischer, Nat 1887-1972 . . . . DLB-241	Foreman, Carl 1914-1984 . . . . DLB-26	Frank, Bruno 1887-1945 . . . . DLB-118
Fleming, Abraham 1552?-1607 . . . . DLB-236	Forester, C. S. 1899-1966 . . . . DLB-191	Frank, Leonhard 1882-1961 . . . . DLB-56, 118
Fleming, Ian 1908-1964 . . DLB-87, 201; CDBLB-7	Forester, Frank (see Herbert, Henry William)	Frank, Melvin (see Panama, Norman)
Fleming, Paul 1609-1640 . . . . DLB-164	Forman, Harry Buxton 1842-1917 . . . . . . DLB-184	Frank, Waldo 1889-1967 . . . . DLB-9, 63
Fleming, Peter 1907-1971 . . . . DLB-195	Fornés, María Irene 1930- DLB-7	Franken, Rose 1895?-1988 . . . . . . DLB-228, Y-84
Fletcher, Giles, the Elder 1546-1611 . . . . . DLB-136	Forrest, Leon 1937-1997 . . . . DLB-33	Franklin, Benjamin 1706-1790 . . . . DLB-24, 43, 73, 183; CDALB-2
Fletcher, Giles, the Younger 1585 or 1586-1623 . . . . DLB-121	Forster, E. M. 1879-1970 . . . . DLB-34, 98, 162, 178, 195; DS-10; CDBLB-6	
Fletcher, J. S. 1863-1935 . . . . DLB-70		Franklin, James 1697-1735 . . . . DLB-43
Fletcher, John (see Beaumont, Francis)	Forster, Georg 1754-1794 . . . . DLB-94	Franklin, Miles 1879-1954 . . . . DLB-230
Fletcher, John Gould 1886-1950 . . . . . . DLB-4, 45	Forster, John 1812-1876 . . . . DLB-144	Franklin Library DLB-46
Fletcher, Phineas 1582-1650 . . . . DLB-121	Forster, Margaret 1938- DLB-155	Frantz, Ralph Jules 1902-1979 . . . . DLB-4
Flieg, Helmut (see Heym, Stefan)	Forsyth, Frederick 1938- DLB-87	Franzos, Karl Emil 1848-1904 . . . . DLB-129
Flint, F. S. 1885-1960 . . . . DLB-19	Forten, Charlotte L. 1837-1914 . . . . . . DLB-50, 239	Fraser, G. S. 1915-1980 . . . . DLB-27
Flint, Timothy 1780-1840 . . . . DLB-73, 186	Charlotte Forten: Pages from her Diary DLB-50	Fraser, Kathleen 1935- DLB-169
Flores-Williams, Jason 1969- DLB-209		Frattini, Alberto 1922- DLB-128
Florio, John 1553?-1625 . . . . DLB-172	Fortini, Franco 1917- DLB-128	Frau Ava ?-1127 . . . . DLB-148
Fo, Dario 1926- Y-97	Fortune, Mary ca. 1833-ca. 1910 . . . . DLB-230	Fraunce, Abraham 1558?-1592 or 1593 . . DLB-236
Foix, J. V. 1893-1987 . . . . DLB-134	Fortune, T. Thomas 1856-1928 . . . . DLB-23	Frayn, Michael 1933- DLB-13, 14, 194, 245
Foley, Martha (see Burnett, Whit, and Martha Foley)	Fosdick, Charles Austin 1842-1915 . . . . . . DLB-42	Frederic, Harold 1856-1898 . . . . DLB-12, 23; DS-13
Folger, Henry Clay 1857-1930 . . . . DLB-140	Foster, Genevieve 1893-1979 . . . . DLB-61	
Folio Society DLB-112	Foster, Hannah Webster 1758-1840 . . . DLB-37, 200	Freeling, Nicolas 1927- DLB-87
	Foster, John 1648-1681 . . . . DLB-24	

Freeman, Douglas Southall 1886-1953 .... DLB-17; DS-17
Freeman, Legh Richmond 1842-1915 .....DLB-23
Freeman, Mary E. Wilkins 1852-1930 .... DLB-12, 78, 221
Freeman, R. Austin 1862-1943 ....DLB-70
Freidank circa 1170-circa 1233.........DLB-138
Freiligrath, Ferdinand 1810-1876 ....DLB-133
Frémont, John Charles 1813-1890 ....DLB-186
Frémont, John Charles 1813-1890 and Frémont, Jessie Benton 1834-1902 ...DLB-183
French, Alice 1850-1934 .... DLB-74; DS-13
French Arthurian Literature............DLB-208
French, David 1939- DLB-53
French, Evangeline 1869-1960..........DLB-195
French, Francesca 1871-1960 ....DLB-195
French, James [publishing house].........DLB-49
French, Samuel [publishing house].......DLB-49
Samuel French, Limited................DLB-106
Freneau, Philip 1752-1832 ...... DLB-37, 43
Freni, Melo 1934- DLB-128
Freshfield, Douglas W. 1845-1934........DLB-174
Freytag, Gustav 1816-1895 ....DLB-129
Fried, Erich 1921-1988..................DLB-85
Friedan, Betty 1921- DLB-246
Friedman, Bruce Jay 1930- DLB-2, 28, 244
Friedrich von Hausen circa 1171-1190....DLB-138
Friel, Brian 1929- DLB-13
Friend, Krebs 1895?-1967? DLB-4
Fries, Fritz Rudolf 1935- DLB-75
Fringe and Alternative Theater in Great Britain DLB-13
Frisch, Max 1911-1991 .... DLB-69, 124; CDWLB-2
Frischlin, Nicodemus 1547-1590 .... DLB-179
Frischmuth, Barbara 1941- DLB-85
Fritz, Jean 1915- DLB-52
Froissart, Jean circa 1337-circa 1404......DLB-208
Fromentin, Eugene 1820-1876 ....DLB-123
Frontinus circa A.D. 35-A.D. 103/104 ....DLB-211
Frost, A. B. 1851-1928.......... DLB-188; DS-13
Frost, Robert 1874-1963 ....DLB-54; DS-7; CDALB-4
Frothingham, Octavius Brooks 1822-1895 ....DLB-1, 243
Froude, James Anthony 1818-1894 .... DLB-18, 57, 144
Fruitlands 1843-1844...................DLB-223
Fry, Christopher 1907- DLB-13
Fry, Roger 1866-1934 ....DS-10
Fry, Stephen 1957- DLB-207
Frye, Northrop 1912-1991....... DLB-67, 68, 246
Fuchs, Daniel 1909-1993 ..... DLB-9, 26, 28; Y-93
Fuentes, Carlos 1928- DLB-113; CDWLB-3
Fuertes, Gloria 1918- DLB-108
Fugard, Athol 1932- DLB-225

The Fugitives and the Agrarians: The First Exhibition Y-85
Fujiwara no Shunzei 1114-1204.........DLB-203
Fujiwara no Tameaki 1230s?-1290s?.....DLB-203
Fujiwara no Tameie 1198-1275 ....DLB-203
Fujiwara no Teika 1162-1241 ....DLB-203
Fulbecke, William 1560-1603? DLB-172
Fuller, Charles H., Jr. 1939- DLB-38
Fuller, Henry Blake 1857-1929 ....DLB-12
Fuller, John 1937- DLB-40
Fuller, Margaret (see Fuller, Sarah)
Fuller, Roy 1912-1991 ....DLB-15, 20
Fuller, Samuel 1912- DLB-26
Fuller, Sarah 1810-1850 ..... DLB-1, 59, 73, 183, 223, 239; CDALB-2
Fuller, Thomas 1608-1661.............DLB-151
Fullerton, Hugh 1873-1945 ....DLB-171
Fullwood, William flourished 1568......DLB-236
Fulton, Alice 1952- DLB-193
Fulton, Len 1934- Y-86
Fulton, Robin 1937- DLB-40
Furbank, P. N. 1920- DLB-155
Furman, Laura 1945- Y-86
Furness, Horace Howard 1833-1912 ....DLB-64
Furness, William Henry 1802-1896 ....DLB-1, 235
Furnivall, Frederick James 1825-1910 ....DLB-184
Furphy, Joseph (Tom Collins) 1843-1912 ....DLB-230
Furthman, Jules 1888-1966 ....DLB-26
Furui Yoshikichi 1937- DLB-182
Fushimi, Emperor 1265-1317...........DLB-203
Futabatei, Shimei (Hasegawa Tatsunosuke) 1864-1909 ....DLB-180
The Future of the Novel (1899), by Henry James DLB-18
Fyleman, Rose 1877-1957..............DLB-160

G

Gadallah, Leslie 1939- DLB-251
Gadda, Carlo Emilio 1893-1973 ....DLB-177
Gaddis, William 1922-1998......... DLB-2, Y-99
Gág, Wanda 1893-1946.................DLB-22
Gagarin, Ivan Sergeevich 1814-1882 .....DLB-198
Gagnon, Madeleine 1938- DLB-60
Gaine, Hugh 1726-1807................DLB-43
Gaine, Hugh [publishing house] DLB-49
Gaines, Ernest J. 1933- DLB-2, 33, 152; Y-80; CDALB-6
Gaiser, Gerd 1908-1976................DLB-69
Gaitskill, Mary 1954- DLB-244
Galarza, Ernesto 1905-1984............DLB-122
Galaxy Science Fiction Novels..........DLB-46
Gale, Zona 1874-1938 .... DLB-9, 228, 78

Galen of Pergamon 129-after 210 .... DLB-176
Gales, Winifred Marshall 1761-1839 .....DLB-200
Gall, Louise von 1815-1855..............DLB-133
Gallagher, Tess 1943- DLB-120, 212, 244
Gallagher, Wes 1911- DLB-127
Gallagher, William Davis 1808-1894.......DLB-73
Gallant, Mavis 1922- DLB-53
Gallegos, María Magdalena 1935- DLB-209
Gallico, Paul 1897-1976 ....DLB-9, 171
Gallop, Jane 1952- DLB-246
Galloway, Grace Growden 1727-1782 ....DLB-200
Gallup, Donald 1913- DLB-187
Galsworthy, John 1867-1933 ...... DLB-10, 34, 98, 162; DS-16; CDBLB-5
Galt, John 1779-1839 ....DLB-99, 116
Galton, Sir Francis 1822-1911 ....DLB-166
Galvin, Brendan 1938- DLB-5
Gambit..............................DLB-46
Gamboa, Reymundo 1948- DLB-122
Gammer Gurton's Needle DLB-62
Gan, Elena Andreevna (Zeneida R-va) 1814-1842 ....DLB-198
Gannett, Frank E. 1876-1957 ....DLB-29
Gao Xingjian 1940- Y-00
Gaos, Vicente 1919-1980................DLB-134
García, Andrew 1854?-1943............DLB-209
García, Lionel G. 1935- DLB-82
García, Richard 1941- DLB-209
García-Camarillo, Cecilio 1943- DLB-209
García Lorca, Federico 1898-1936........DLB-108
García Márquez, Gabriel 1928- DLB-113; Y-82; CDWLB-3
Gardam, Jane 1928- DLB-14, 161, 231
Garden, Alexander circa 1685-1756........DLB-31
Gardiner, John Rolfe 1936- DLB-244
Gardiner, Margaret Power Farmer (see Blessington, Marguerite, Countess of)
Gardner, John 1933-1982.......... DLB-2; Y-82; CDALB-7
Garfield, Leon 1921-1996 ....DLB-161
Garis, Howard R. 1873-1962...........DLB-22
Garland, Hamlin 1860-1940 .. DLB-12, 71, 78, 186
Garneau, Francis-Xavier 1809-1866 .....DLB-99
Garneau, Hector de Saint-Denys 1912-1943 ....DLB-88
Garneau, Michel 1939- DLB-53
Garner, Alan 1934- DLB-161
Garner, Hugh 1913-1979................DLB-68
Garnett, David 1892-1981...............DLB-34
Garnett, Eve 1900-1991................DLB-160
Garnett, Richard 1835-1906 ....DLB-184
Garrard, Lewis H. 1829-1887 ....DLB-186
Garraty, John A. 1920- DLB-17
Garrett, George 1929- DLB-2, 5, 130, 152; Y-83
Fellowship of Southern Writers........... Y-98

Garrett, John Work 1872-1942 . . . . DLB-187

Garrick, David 1717-1779 . . . . DLB-84, 213

Garrison, William Lloyd
1805-1879 . . . . DLB-1, 43, 235; CDALB-2

Garro, Elena 1920-1998 . . . . DLB-145

Garth, Samuel 1661-1719 . . . . DLB-95

Garve, Andrew 1908- DLB-87

Gary, Romain 1914-1980 . . . . DLB-83

Gascoigne, George 1539?-1577 . . . . DLB-136

Gascoyne, David 1916- DLB-20

Gaskell, Elizabeth Cleghorn
1810-1865 . . . . . . DLB-21, 144, 159; CDBLB-4

Gaspey, Thomas 1788-1871 . . . . DLB-116

Gass, William H. 1924- DLB-2, 227

Gates, Doris 1901- DLB-22

Gates, Henry Louis, Jr. 1950- DLB-67

Gates, Lewis E. 1860-1924 . . . . DLB-71

Gatto, Alfonso 1909-1976 . . . . DLB-114

Gault, William Campbell 1910-1995 . . . . DLB-226

Gaunt, Mary 1861-1942 . . . . DLB-174, 230

Gautier, Théophile 1811-1872 . . . . DLB-119

Gauvreau, Claude 1925-1971 . . . . DLB-88

The *Gawain*-Poet
flourished circa 1350-1400 . . . . DLB-146

Gay, Ebenezer 1696-1787 . . . . DLB-24

Gay, John 1685-1732 . . . . DLB-84, 95

Gayarré, Charles E. A. 1805-1895 . . . . DLB-30

Gaylord, Charles [publishing house] DLB-49

Gaylord, Edward King 1873-1974 . . . . . . DLB-127

Gaylord, Edward Lewis 1919- DLB-127

Geda, Sigitas 1943- DLB-232

Geddes, Gary 1940- DLB-60

Geddes, Virgil 1897- DLB-4

Gedeon (Georgii Andreevich Krinovsky)
circa 1730-1763 . . . . DLB-150

Gee, Maggie 1948- DLB-207

Gee, Shirley 1932- DLB-245

Geßner, Salomon 1730-1788 . . . . DLB-97

Geibel, Emanuel 1815-1884 . . . . DLB-129

Geiogamah, Hanay 1945- DLB-175

Geis, Bernard, Associates DLB-46

Geisel, Theodor Seuss 1904-1991 . . . DLB-61; Y-91

Gelb, Arthur 1924- DLB-103

Gelb, Barbara 1926- DLB-103

Gelber, Jack 1932- DLB-7, 228

Gelinas, Gratien 1909- DLB-88

Gellert, Christian Fürchtegott
1715-1769 . . . . DLB-97

Gellhorn, Martha 1908-1998 . . . . Y-82, Y-98

Gems, Pam 1925- DLB-13

Genet, Jean 1910-1986 . . . . DLB-72; Y-86

Genette, Gérard 1930- DLB-242

Genevoix, Maurice 1890-1980 . . . . DLB-65

Genovese, Eugene D. 1930- DLB-17

Gent, Peter 1942- Y-82

Geoffrey of Monmouth
circa 1100-1155 . . . . DLB-146

George, Henry 1839-1897 . . . . DLB-23

George, Jean Craighead 1919- DLB-52

George, W. L. 1882-1926 . . . . DLB-197

George III, King of Great Britain and Ireland
1738-1820 . . . . DLB-213

George V. Higgins to Julian Symons Y-99

Georgslied 896? DLB-148

Gerber, Merrill Joan 1938- DLB-218

Gerhardie, William 1895-1977 . . . . DLB-36

Gerhardt, Paul 1607-1676 . . . . DLB-164

Gérin, Winifred 1901-1981 . . . . DLB-155

Gérin-Lajoie, Antoine 1824-1882 . . . . DLB-99

German Drama 800-1280 . . . . DLB-138

German Drama from Naturalism
to Fascism: 1889-1933 . . . . DLB-118

German Literature and Culture from Charlemagne
to the Early Courtly Period
. . . . DLB-148; CDWLB-2

German Radio Play, The DLB-124

German Transformation from the Baroque
to the Enlightenment, The DLB-97

The Germanic Epic and Old English
Heroic Poetry: *Widsith, Waldere,*
and *The Fight at Finnsburg* DLB-146

Germanophilism, by Hans Kohn DLB-66

Gernsback, Hugo 1884-1967 . . . . DLB-8, 137

Gerould, Katharine Fullerton
1879-1944 . . . . DLB-78

Gerrish, Samuel [publishing house] DLB-49

Gerrold, David 1944- DLB-8

The Ira Gershwin Centenary Y-96

Gerson, Jean 1363-1429 . . . . DLB-208

Gersonides 1288-1344 . . . . DLB-115

Gerstäcker, Friedrich 1816-1872 . . . . DLB-129

Gerstenberg, Heinrich Wilhelm von
1737-1823 . . . . DLB-97

Gervinus, Georg Gottfried
1805-1871 . . . . DLB-133

Geston, Mark S. 1946- DLB-8

Al-Ghazali 1058-1111 . . . . DLB-115

Gibbings, Robert 1889-1958 . . . . DLB-195

Gibbon, Edward 1737-1794 . . . . DLB-104

Gibbon, John Murray 1875-1952 . . . . DLB-92

Gibbon, Lewis Grassic (see Mitchell, James Leslie)

Gibbons, Floyd 1887-1939 . . . . DLB-25

Gibbons, Reginald 1947- DLB-120

Gibbons, William ?-? DLB-73

Gibson, Charles Dana
1867-1944 . . . . DLB-188; DS-13

Gibson, Graeme 1934- DLB-53

Gibson, Margaret 1944- DLB-120

Gibson, Margaret Dunlop 1843-1920 . . . . DLB-174

Gibson, Wilfrid 1878-1962 . . . . DLB-19

Gibson, William 1914- DLB-7

Gibson, William 1948- DLB-251

Gide, André 1869-1951 . . . . DLB-65

Giguère, Diane 1937- DLB-53

Giguère, Roland 1929- DLB-60

Gil de Biedma, Jaime 1929-1990 . . . . . . DLB-108

Gil-Albert, Juan 1906- DLB-134

Gilbert, Anthony 1899-1973 . . . . DLB-77

Gilbert, Sir Humphrey 1537-1583 . . . . . DLB-136

Gilbert, Michael 1912- DLB-87

Gilbert, Sandra M. 1936- DLB-120, 246

Gilchrist, Alexander 1828-1861 . . . . DLB-144

Gilchrist, Ellen 1935- DLB-130

Gilder, Jeannette L. 1849-1916 . . . . DLB-79

Gilder, Richard Watson 1844-1909 . . . . DLB-64, 79

Gildersleeve, Basil 1831-1924 . . . . DLB-71

Giles of Rome circa 1243-1316 . . . . DLB-115

Giles, Henry 1809-1882 . . . . DLB-64

Gilfillan, George 1813-1878 . . . . DLB-144

Gill, Eric 1882-1940 . . . . DLB-98

Gill, Sarah Prince 1728-1771 . . . . DLB-200

Gill, William F., Company DLB-49

Gillespie, A. Lincoln, Jr. 1895-1950 . . . . . . DLB-4

Gilliam, Florence ?-? DLB-4

Gilliatt, Penelope 1932-1993 . . . . DLB-14

Gillott, Jacky 1939-1980 . . . . DLB-14

Gilman, Caroline H. 1794-1888 . . . . . . DLB-3, 73

Gilman, Charlotte Perkins 1860-1935 . . . DLB-221

Gilman, W. and J. [publishing house] DLB-49

Gilmer, Elizabeth Meriwether 1861-1951 . . DLB-29

Gilmer, Francis Walker 1790-1826 . . . . . . DLB-37

Gilroy, Frank D. 1925- DLB-7

Gimferrer, Pere (Pedro) 1945- DLB-134

Gingrich, Arnold 1903-1976 . . . . DLB-137

Ginsberg, Allen
1926-1997 . . . . DLB-5, 16, 169, 237; CDALB-1

Ginzburg, Natalia 1916-1991 . . . . DLB-177

Ginzkey, Franz Karl 1871-1963 . . . . DLB-81

Gioia, Dana 1950- DLB-120

Giono, Jean 1895-1970 . . . . DLB-72

Giotti, Virgilio 1885-1957 . . . . DLB-114

Giovanni, Nikki 1943- DLB-5, 41; CDALB-7

Gipson, Lawrence Henry 1880-1971 . . . . DLB-17

Girard, Rodolphe 1879-1956 . . . . DLB-92

Giraudoux, Jean 1882-1944 . . . . DLB-65

Gissing, George 1857-1903 . . . . . . DLB-18, 135, 184

The Place of Realism in Fiction (1895) DLB-18

Giudici, Giovanni 1924- DLB-128

Giuliani, Alfredo 1924- DLB-128

Glackens, William J. 1870-1938 . . . . DLB-188

Gladstone, William Ewart
1809-1898 . . . . DLB-57, 184

Glaeser, Ernst 1902-1963 . . . . DLB-69

Glancy, Diane 1941- DLB-175

Glanville, Brian 1931- DLB-15, 139

Glapthorne, Henry 1610-1643? DLB-58

Glasgow, Ellen 1873-1945 . . . . DLB-9, 12

Glasier, Katharine Bruce 1867-1950 . . . . . DLB-190

Glaspell, Susan 1876-1948 . . . . . . DLB-7, 9, 78, 228
Glass, Montague 1877-1934 . . . . DLB-11
Glassco, John 1909-1981 . . . . DLB-68
Glauser, Friedrich 1896-1938 . . . . DLB-56
F. Gleason's Publishing Hall DLB-49
Gleim, Johann Wilhelm Ludwig
   1719-1803 . . . . DLB-97
Glendinning, Victoria 1937- DLB-155
The Cult of Biography
   Excerpts from the Second Folio Debate:
   "Biographies are generally a disease of
   English Literature" Y-86
Glinka, Fedor Nikolaevich 1786-1880 . . . . DLB-205
Glover, Keith 1966- DLB-249
Glover, Richard 1712-1785 . . . . DLB-95
Glück, Louise 1943- DLB-5
Glyn, Elinor 1864-1943 . . . . DLB-153
Gnedich, Nikolai Ivanovich 1784-1833 . . . DLB-205
Gobineau, Joseph-Arthur de
   1816-1882 . . . . DLB-123
Godber, John 1956- DLB-233
Godbout, Jacques 1933- DLB-53
Goddard, Morrill 1865-1937 . . . . DLB-25
Goddard, William 1740-1817 . . . . DLB-43
Godden, Rumer 1907-1998 . . . . DLB-161
Godey, Louis A. 1804-1878 . . . . DLB-73
Godey and McMichael DLB-49
Godfrey, Dave 1938- DLB-60
Godfrey, Thomas 1736-1763 . . . . DLB-31
Godine, David R., Publisher DLB-46
Godkin, E. L. 1831-1902 . . . . DLB-79
Godolphin, Sidney 1610-1643 . . . . DLB-126
Godwin, Gail 1937- DLB-6, 234
Godwin, M. J., and Company DLB-154
Godwin, Mary Jane Clairmont
   1766-1841 . . . . DLB-163
Godwin, Parke 1816-1904 . . . . . . DLB-3, 64, 250
Godwin, William 1756-1836
   . . . . . . DLB-39, 104, 142, 158, 163; CDBLB-3
Preface to *St. Leon* (1799) DLB-39
Goering, Reinhard 1887-1936 . . . . DLB-118
Goes, Albrecht 1908- DLB-69
Goethe, Johann Wolfgang von
   1749-1832 . . . . DLB-94; CDWLB-2
Goetz, Curt 1888-1960 . . . . DLB-124
Goffe, Thomas circa 1592-1629 . . . . DLB-58
Goffstein, M. B. 1940- DLB-61
Gogarty, Oliver St. John 1878-1957 . . . . DLB-15, 19
Gogol, Nikolai Vasil'evich 1809-1852 . . . . DLB-198
Goines, Donald 1937-1974 . . . . DLB-33
Gold, Herbert 1924- DLB-2; Y-81
Gold, Michael 1893-1967 . . . . DLB-9, 28
Goldbarth, Albert 1948- DLB-120
Goldberg, Dick 1947- DLB-7
Golden Cockerel Press DLB-112
Golding, Arthur 1536-1606 . . . . DLB-136
Golding, Louis 1895-1958 . . . . DLB-195

Golding, William
   1911-1993 . . . . . DLB-15, 100; Y-83; CDBLB-7
Goldman, Emma 1869-1940 . . . . DLB-221
Goldman, William 1931- DLB-44
Goldring, Douglas 1887-1960 . . . . DLB-197
Goldsmith, Oliver 1730?-1774
   . . . . . . DLB-39, 89, 104, 109, 142; CDBLB-2
Goldsmith, Oliver 1794-1861 . . . . DLB-99
Goldsmith Publishing Company DLB-46
Goldstein, Richard 1944- DLB-185
Gollancz, Sir Israel 1864-1930 . . . . DLB-201
Gollancz, Victor, Limited DLB-112
Gombrowicz, Witold
   1904-1969 . . . . DLB-215; CDWLB-4
Gómez-Quiñones, Juan 1942- DLB-122
Gomme, Laurence James
   [publishing house] DLB-46
Goncharov, Ivan Aleksandrovich
   1812-1891 . . . . DLB-238
Goncourt, Edmond de 1822-1896 . . . . . . DLB-123
Goncourt, Jules de 1830-1870 . . . . DLB-123
Gonzales, Rodolfo "Corky" 1928- DLB-122
González, Angel 1925- DLB-108
Gonzalez, Genaro 1949- DLB-122
Gonzalez, Ray 1952- DLB-122
Gonzales-Berry, Erlinda 1942- DLB-209
   "Chicano Language" DLB-82
González de Mireles, Jovita
   1899-1983 . . . . DLB-122
González-T., César A. 1931- DLB-82
Goodbye, Gutenberg? A Lecture at the
   New York Public Library,
   18 April 1995, by Donald Lamm Y-95
Goodis, David 1917-1967 . . . . DLB-226
Goodison, Lorna 1947- DLB-157
Goodman, Allegra 1967- DLB-244
Goodman, Paul 1911-1972 . . . . DLB-130, 246
The Goodman Theatre DLB-7
Goodrich, Frances 1891-1984 and
   Hackett, Albert 1900-1995 . . . . DLB-26
Goodrich, Samuel Griswold
   1793-1860 . . . . DLB-1, 42, 73, 243
Goodrich, S. G. [publishing house] DLB-49
Goodspeed, C. E., and Company DLB-49
Goodwin, Stephen 1943- Y-82
Googe, Barnabe 1540-1594 . . . . DLB-132
Gookin, Daniel 1612-1687 . . . . DLB-24
Goran, Lester 1928- DLB-244
Gordimer, Nadine 1923- DLB-225; Y-91
Gordon, Adam Lindsay 1833-1870 . . . . . DLB-230
Gordon, Caroline
   1895-1981 . . . . . . DLB-4, 9, 102; DS-17; Y-81
Gordon, Giles 1940- DLB-14, 139, 207
Gordon, Helen Cameron, Lady Russell
   1867-1949 . . . . DLB-195
Gordon, Lyndall 1941- DLB-155
Gordon, Mary 1949- DLB-6; Y-81
Gordone, Charles 1925-1995 . . . . DLB-7

Gore, Catherine 1800-1861 . . . . DLB-116
Gore-Booth, Eva 1870-1926 . . . . DLB-240
Gores, Joe 1931- DLB-226
Gorey, Edward 1925-2000 . . . . DLB-61
Gorgias of Leontini
   circa 485 B.C.-376 B.C. DLB-176
Görres, Joseph 1776-1848 . . . . DLB-90
Gosse, Edmund 1849-1928 . . . . . DLB-57, 144, 184
Gosson, Stephen 1554-1624 . . . . DLB-172
The Schoole of Abuse (1579) DLB-172
Gotlieb, Phyllis 1926- DLB-88, 251
Go-Toba 1180-1239 . . . . DLB-203
Gottfried von Straßburg
   died before 1230 . . . . DLB-138; CDWLB-2
Gotthelf, Jeremias 1797-1854 . . . . DLB-133
Gottschalk circa 804/808-869 . . . . DLB-148
Gottsched, Johann Christoph
   1700-1766 . . . . DLB-97
Götz, Johann Nikolaus 1721-1781 . . . . DLB-97
Goudge, Elizabeth 1900-1984 . . . . DLB-191
Gough, John B. 1817-1886 . . . . DLB-243
Gould, Wallace 1882-1940 . . . . DLB-54
Govoni, Corrado 1884-1965 . . . . DLB-114
Gower, John circa 1330-1408 . . . . DLB-146
Goyen, William 1915-1983 . . . . . DLB-2, 218; Y-83
Goytisolo, José Augustín 1928- DLB-134
Gozzano, Guido 1883-1916 . . . . DLB-114
Grabbe, Christian Dietrich 1801-1836 . . . . DLB-133
Gracq, Julien 1910- DLB-83
Grady, Henry W. 1850-1889 . . . . DLB-23
Graf, Oskar Maria 1894-1967 . . . . DLB-56
Graf Rudolf
   between circa 1170 and circa 1185 . . . DLB-148
Graff, Gerald 1937- DLB-246
Grafton, Richard [publishing house] DLB-170
Grafton, Sue 1940- DLB-226
Graham, Frank 1893-1965 . . . . DLB-241
Graham, George Rex 1813-1894 . . . . DLB-73
Graham, Gwethalyn 1913-1965 . . . . DLB-88
Graham, Jorie 1951- DLB-120
Graham, Katharine 1917- DLB-127
Graham, Lorenz 1902-1989 . . . . DLB-76
Graham, Philip 1915-1963 . . . . DLB-127
Graham, R. B. Cunninghame
   1852-1936 . . . . DLB-98, 135, 174
Graham, Shirley 1896-1977 . . . . DLB-76
Graham, Stephen 1884-1975 . . . . DLB-195
Graham, W. S. 1918- DLB-20
Graham, William H. [publishing house] . . . DLB-49
Graham, Winston 1910- DLB-77
Grahame, Kenneth
   1859-1932 . . . . DLB-34, 141, 178
Grainger, Martin Allerdale 1874-1941 . . . . DLB-92
Gramatky, Hardie 1907-1979 . . . . DLB-22
Grand, Sarah 1854-1943 . . . . DLB-135, 197
Grandbois, Alain 1900-1975 . . . . DLB-92

Grandson, Oton de circa 1345-1397..... DLB-208

Grange, John circa 1556-?............. DLB-136

Granich, Irwin (see Gold, Michael)

Granovsky, Timofei Nikolaevich
   1813-1855..................... DLB-198

Grant, Anne MacVicar 1755-1838 ...... DLB-200

Grant, Duncan 1885-1978................DS-10

Grant, George 1918-1988............... DLB-88

Grant, George Monro 1835-1902....... DLB-99

Grant, Harry J. 1881-1963 .... DLB-29

Grant, James Edward 1905-1966 .... DLB-26

Grass, Günter 1927- ...DLB-75, 124; CDWLB-2

Grasty, Charles H. 1863-1924 .... DLB-25

Grau, Shirley Ann 1929- DLB-2, 218

Graves, John 1920- Y-83

Graves, Richard 1715-1804............ DLB-39

Graves, Robert 1895-1985
   ....DLB-20, 100, 191; DS-18; Y-85; CDBLB-6

Gray, Alasdair 1934- DLB-194

Gray, Asa 1810-1888 .... DLB-1, 235

Gray, David 1838-1861 .... DLB-32

Gray, Simon 1936- DLB-13

Gray, Thomas 1716-1771 .... DLB-109; CDBLB-2

Grayson, Richard 1951- DLB-234

Grayson, William J. 1788-1863.... DLB-3, 64, 248

The Great Bibliographers Series........... Y-93

The Great Modern Library Scam.......... Y-98

The Great War and the Theater, 1914-1918
   [Great Britain] DLB-10

The Great War Exhibition and Symposium at
   the University of South Carolina........ Y-97

Grech, Nikolai Ivanovich 1787-1867 ..... DLB-198

Greeley, Horace 1811-1872 .. DLB-3, 43, 189, 250

Green, Adolph (see Comden, Betty)

Green, Anna Katharine
   1846-1935 .... DLB-202, 221

Green, Duff 1791-1875 .... DLB-43

Green, Elizabeth Shippen 1871-1954 .... DLB-188

Green, Gerald 1922- DLB-28

Green, Henry 1905-1973 .... DLB-15

Green, Jonas 1712-1767................ DLB-31

Green, Joseph 1706-1780............... DLB-31

Green, Julien 1900-1998............ DLB-4, 72

Green, Paul 1894-1981........DLB-7, 9, 249; Y-81

Green, T. and S. [publishing house] DLB-49

Green, Terence M. 1947- DLB-251

Green, Thomas Hill 1836-1882 .... DLB-190

Green, Timothy [publishing house] DLB-49

Greenaway, Kate 1846-1901.......... DLB-141

Greenberg: Publisher DLB-46

Green Tiger Press................. DLB-46

Greene, Asa 1789-1838................ DLB-11

Greene, Belle da Costa 1883-1950 ...... DLB-187

Greene, Benjamin H.
   [publishing house] DLB-49

Greene, Graham 1904-1991
   ....DLB-13, 15, 77, 100, 162, 201, 204;
               Y-85, Y-91; CDBLB-7

Greene, Robert 1558-1592 .... DLB-62, 167

Greene, Robert Bernard (Bob) Jr.
   1947- DLB-185

Greenfield, George 1917-2000 .... Y-00

Greenhow, Robert 1800-1854 .... DLB-30

Greenlee, William B. 1872-1953........ DLB-187

Greenough, Horatio 1805-1852 ...... DLB-1, 235

Greenwell, Dora 1821-1882 .... DLB-35, 199

Greenwillow Books DLB-46

Greenwood, Grace (see Lippincott, Sara Jane Clarke)

Greenwood, Walter 1903-1974...... DLB-10, 191

Greer, Ben 1948- DLB-6

Greflinger, Georg 1620?-1677.......... DLB-164

Greg, W. R. 1809-1881 .... DLB-55

Greg, W. W. 1875-1959 .... DLB-201

Gregg, Josiah 1806-1850......... DLB-183, 186

Gregg Press..................... DLB-46

Gregory, Isabella Augusta Persse, Lady
   1852-1932 .... DLB-10

Gregory, Horace 1898-1982........... DLB-48

Gregory of Rimini circa 1300-1358 ..... DLB-115

Gregynog Press DLB-112

Greiffenberg, Catharina Regina von
   1633-1694 .... DLB-168

Greig, Noël 1944- DLB-245

Grenfell, Wilfred Thomason
   1865-1940..................... DLB-92

Gress, Elsa 1919-1988 .... DLB-214

Greve, Felix Paul (see Grove, Frederick Philip)

Greville, Fulke, First Lord Brooke
   1554-1628 ....DLB-62, 172

Grey, Sir George, K.C.B. 1812-1898 .... DLB-184

Grey, Lady Jane 1537-1554 .... DLB-132

Grey Owl 1888-1938 .... DLB-92; DS-17

Grey, Zane 1872-1939 .... DLB-9, 212

Grey Walls Press DLB-112

Griboedov, Aleksandr Sergeevich
   1795?-1829..................... DLB-205

Grier, Eldon 1917- DLB-88

Grieve, C. M. (see MacDiarmid, Hugh)

Griffin, Bartholomew flourished 1596 ....DLB-172

Griffin, Gerald 1803-1840 .... DLB-159

The Griffin Poetry Prize.................. Y-00

Griffith, Elizabeth 1727?-1793........ DLB-39, 89

   Preface to *The Delicate Distress* (1769) DLB-39

Griffith, George 1857-1906............DLB-178

Griffiths, Ralph [publishing house]...... DLB-154

Griffiths, Trevor 1935- DLB-13, 245

Griggs, S. C., and Company.......... DLB-49

Griggs, Sutton Elbert 1872-1930 .... DLB-50

Grignon, Claude-Henri 1894-1976 ..... DLB-68

Grigorovich, Dmitrii Vasil'evich
   1822-1899 .... DLB-238

Grigson, Geoffrey 1905- DLB-27

Grillparzer, Franz
   1791-1872 ....DLB-133; CDWLB-2

Grimald, Nicholas
   circa 1519-circa 1562 .... DLB-136

Grimké, Angelina Weld 1880-1958 ... DLB-50, 54

Grimké, Sarah Moore 1792-1873 .... DLB-239

Grimm, Hans 1875-1959 .... DLB-66

Grimm, Jacob 1785-1863 .... DLB-90

Grimm, Wilhelm
   1786-1859............. DLB-90; CDWLB-2

Grimmelshausen, Johann Jacob Christoffel von
   1621 or 1622-1676......DLB-168; CDWLB-2

Grimshaw, Beatrice Ethel 1871-1953 .....DLB-174

Grindal, Edmund 1519 or 1520-1583 ... DLB-132

Griswold, Rufus W.
   1815-1857.................. DLB-3, 59, 250

Grosart, Alexander Balloch 1827-1899... DLB-184

Gross, Milt 1895-1953 .... DLB-11

Grosset and Dunlap DLB-49

Grossman, Allen 1932- DLB-193

Grossman Publishers DLB-46

Grosseteste, Robert circa 1160-1253..... DLB-115

Grosvenor, Gilbert H. 1875-1966........ DLB-91

Groth, Klaus 1819-1899 .... DLB-129

Groulx, Lionel 1878-1967 .... DLB-68

Grove, Frederick Philip 1879-1949....... DLB-92

Grove Press DLB-46

Grubb, Davis 1919-1980 .... DLB-6

Gruelle, Johnny 1880-1938............ DLB-22

von Grumbach, Argula
   1492-after 1563? DLB-179

Grymeston, Elizabeth
   before 1563-before 1604 .... DLB-136

Gryphius, Andreas
   1616-1664 ....DLB-164; CDWLB-2

Gryphius, Christian 1649-1706......... DLB-168

Guare, John 1938- DLB-7, 249

Guerra, Tonino 1920- DLB-128

Guest, Barbara 1920- DLB-5, 193

Guèvremont, Germaine 1893-1968 ...... DLB-68

Guidacci, Margherita 1921-1992 ...... DLB-128

Guide to the Archives of Publishers, Journals,
   and Literary Agents in North American
   Libraries..................... Y-93

Guillén, Jorge 1893-1984 .... DLB-108

Guilloux, Louis 1899-1980............. DLB-72

Guilpin, Everard
   circa 1572-after 1608? DLB-136

Guiney, Louise Imogen 1861-1920 ...... DLB-54

Guiterman, Arthur 1871-1943 .... DLB-11

Günderrode, Caroline von
   1780-1806..................... DLB-90

Gundulić, Ivan
   1589-1638 ....DLB-147; CDWLB-4

Gunn, Bill 1934-1989 .... DLB-38

Gunn, James E. 1923- DLB-8

Gunn, Neil M. 1891-1973 .... DLB-15

Gunn, Thom 1929- DLB-27; CDBLB-8

Gunnars, Kristjana 1948- DLB-60

Günther, Johann Christian 1695-1723 ....DLB-168

Gurik, Robert 1932- DLB-60

Gustafson, Ralph 1909- DLB-88

Gütersloh, Albert Paris 1887-1973 ....DLB-81

Guthrie, A. B., Jr. 1901-1991.........DLB-6, 212

Guthrie, Ramon 1896-1973 ....DLB-4

The Guthrie Theater DLB-7

Guthrie, Thomas Anstey (see Anstey, FC)

Gutzkow, Karl 1811-1878 ....DLB-133

Guy, Ray 1939- DLB-60

Guy, Rosa 1925- DLB-33

Guyot, Arnold 1807-1884 .... DS-13

Gwynne, Erskine 1898-1948 ....DLB-4

Gyles, John 1680-1755 ....DLB-99

Gysin, Brion 1916- DLB-16

H

H.D. (see Doolittle, Hilda)

Habermas, Jürgen 1929- DLB-242

Habington, William 1605-1654 ....DLB-126

Hacker, Marilyn 1942- DLB-120

Hackett, Albert (see Goodrich, Frances)

Hacks, Peter 1928- DLB-124

Hadas, Rachel 1948- DLB-120

Hadden, Briton 1898-1929 ....DLB-91

Hagedorn, Friedrich von 1708-1754......DLB-168

Hagelstange, Rudolf 1912-1984 ....DLB-69

Haggard, H. Rider 1856-1925 ....DLB-70, 156, 174, 178

Haggard, William 1907-1993 .... Y-93

Hagy, Alyson 1960- DLB-244

Hahn-Hahn, Ida Gräfin von 1805-1880 ....DLB-133

Haig-Brown, Roderick 1908-1976 ....DLB-88

Haight, Gordon S. 1901-1985 ....DLB-103

Hailey, Arthur 1920- DLB-88; Y-82

Haines, John 1924- DLB-5, 212

Hake, Edward flourished 1566-1604.....DLB-136

Hake, Thomas Gordon 1809-1895 ....DLB-32

Hakluyt, Richard 1552?-1616 ....DLB-136

Halas, František 1901-1949 ....DLB-215

Halbe, Max 1865-1944 ....DLB-118

Halberstam, David 1934- DLB-241

Haldane, J. B. S. 1892-1964..........DLB-160

Haldeman, Joe 1943- DLB-8

Haldeman-Julius Company DLB-46

Haldone, Charlotte 1894-1969 ....DLB-191

Hale, E. J., and Son DLB-49

Hale, Edward Everett 1822-1909 ....DLB-1, 42, 74, 235

Hale, Janet Campbell 1946- DLB-175

Hale, Kathleen 1898- DLB-160

Hale, Leo Thomas (see Ebon)

Hale, Lucretia Peabody 1820-1900 ....DLB-42

Hale, Nancy 1908-1988 .... DLB-86; DS-17; Y-80, Y-88

Hale, Sarah Josepha (Buell) 1788-1879 ....DLB-1, 42, 73, 243

Hale, Susan 1833-1910 ....DLB-221

Hales, John 1584-1656...............DLB-151

Halévy, Ludovic 1834-1908 ....DLB-192

Haley, Alex 1921-1992 ....DLB-38; CDALB-7

Haliburton, Thomas Chandler 1796-1865 ....DLB-11, 99

Hall, Anna Maria 1800-1881 ....DLB-159

Hall, Donald 1928- DLB-5

Hall, Edward 1497-1547..............DLB-132

Hall, Halsey 1898-1977 ....DLB-241

Hall, James 1793-1868 .... DLB-73, 74

Hall, Joseph 1574-1656 ....DLB-121, 151

Hall, Radclyffe 1880-1943 ....DLB-191

Hall, Samuel [publishing house]..........DLB-49

Hall, Sarah Ewing 1761-1830..........DLB-200

Hall, Stuart 1932- DLB-242

Hallam, Arthur Henry 1811-1833 ....DLB-32

On Some of the Characteristics of Modern Poetry and On the Lyrical Poems of Alfred Tennyson (1831) DLB-32

Halleck, Fitz-Greene 1790-1867 ....DLB-3, 250

Haller, Albrecht von 1708-1777 ....DLB-168

Halliday, Brett (see Dresser, Davis)

Halliwell-Phillipps, James Orchard 1820-1889 ....DLB-184

Hallmann, Johann Christian 1640-1704 or 1716? DLB-168

Hallmark Editions DLB-46

Halper, Albert 1904-1984 ....DLB-9

Halperin, John William 1941- DLB-111

Halstead, Murat 1829-1908............DLB-23

Hamann, Johann Georg 1730-1788 ....DLB-97

Hamburger, Michael 1924- DLB-27

Hamilton, Alexander 1712-1756.........DLB-31

Hamilton, Alexander 1755?-1804 ....DLB-37

Hamilton, Cicely 1872-1952 .... DLB-10, 197

Hamilton, Edmond 1904-1977............DLB-8

Hamilton, Elizabeth 1758-1816 .....DLB-116, 158

Hamilton, Gail (see Corcoran, Barbara)

Hamilton, Gail (see Dodge, Mary Abigail)

Hamilton, Hamish, Limited............DLB-112

Hamilton, Ian 1938- DLB-40, 155

Hamilton, Janet 1795-1873............DLB-199

Hamilton, Mary Agnes 1884-1962 ......DLB-197

Hamilton, Patrick 1904-1962........DLB-10, 191

Hamilton, Virginia 1936- DLB-33, 52

Hammett, Dashiell 1894-1961 ....DLB-226; DS-6; CDALB-5

The Glass Key and Other Dashiell Hammett Mysteries Y-96

Dashiell Hammett: An Appeal in TAC Y-91

Hammon, Jupiter 1711-died between 1790 and 1806................DLB-31, 50

Hammond, John ?-1663................DLB-24

Hamner, Earl 1923- DLB-6

Hampson, John 1901-1955 ....DLB-191

Hampton, Christopher 1946- DLB-13

Handel-Mazzetti, Enrica von 1871-1955 ...DLB-81

Handke, Peter 1942- DLB-85, 124

Handlin, Oscar 1915- DLB-17

Hankin, St. John 1869-1909............DLB-10

Hanley, Clifford 1922- DLB-14

Hanley, James 1901-1985 ....DLB-191

Hannah, Barry 1942- DLB-6, 234

Hannay, James 1827-1873 ....DLB-21

Hano, Arnold 1922- DLB-241

Hansberry, Lorraine 1930-1965 .... DLB-7, 38; CDALB-1

Hansen, Martin A. 1909-1955 ....DLB-214

Hansen, Thorkild 1927-1989 ....DLB-214

Hanson, Elizabeth 1684-1737 ....DLB-200

Hapgood, Norman 1868-1937..........DLB-91

Happel, Eberhard Werner 1647-1690 ....DLB-168

The Harbinger 1845-1849 ....DLB-223

Harcourt Brace Jovanovich DLB-46

Hardenberg, Friedrich von (see Novalis)

Harding, Walter 1917- DLB-111

Hardwick, Elizabeth 1916- DLB-6

Hardy, Thomas 1840-1928 ....DLB-18, 19, 135; CDBLB-5

"Candour in English Fiction" (1890)......DLB-18

Hare, Cyril 1900-1958...............DLB-77

Hare, David 1947- DLB-13

Hargrove, Marion 1919- DLB-11

Häring, Georg Wilhelm Heinrich (see Alexis, Willibald)

Harington, Donald 1935- DLB-152

Harington, Sir John 1560-1612 ....DLB-136

Harjo, Joy 1951- DLB-120, 175

Harkness, Margaret (John Law) 1854-1923....................DLB-197

Harley, Edward, second Earl of Oxford 1689-1741 ....DLB-213

Harley, Robert, first Earl of Oxford 1661-1724 ....DLB-213

Harlow, Robert 1923- DLB-60

Harman, Thomas flourished 1566-1573 ..DLB-136

Harness, Charles L. 1915- DLB-8

Harnett, Cynthia 1893-1981 ....DLB-161

Harper, Edith Alice Mary (see Wickham, Anna)

Harper, Fletcher 1806-1877 ....DLB-79

Harper, Frances Ellen Watkins 1825-1911....................DLB-50, 221

Harper, Michael S. 1938- DLB-41

Harper and Brothers DLB-49

Harpur, Charles 1813-1868 ....DLB-230

Harraden, Beatrice 1864-1943 ....DLB-153

Harrap, George G., and Company Limited............................DLB-112	Harvey, Gabriel 1550?-1631...DLB-167, 213, 236	Haywood, Eliza 1693?-1756............DLB-39
Harriot, Thomas 1560-1621............DLB-136	Harvey, Jean-Charles 1891-1967........DLB-88	From the Dedication, *Lasselia* (1723)......DLB-39
Harris, Alexander 1805-1874...........DLB-230	Harvill Press Limited................DLB-112	From *The Tea-Table*..................*DLB-39*
Harris, Benjamin ?-circa 1720........DLB-42, 43	Harwood, Lee 1939-...................DLB-40	From the Preface to *The Disguis'd Prince* (1723)......................DLB-39
Harris, Christie 1907-.................DLB-88	Harwood, Ronald 1934-................DLB-13	Hazard, Willis P. [publishing house].....DLB-49
Harris, Frank 1856-1931.............DLB-156, 197	Hašek, Jaroslav 1883-1923..DLB-215; CDWLB-4	Hazlitt, William 1778-1830.........DLB-110, 158
Harris, George Washington 1814-1869..................DLB-3, 11, 248	Haskins, Charles Homer 1870-1937......DLB-47	Hazzard, Shirley 1931-..................Y-82
Harris, Joel Chandler 1848-1908............DLB-11, 23, 42, 78, 91	Haslam, Gerald 1937-.................DLB-212	Head, Bessie 1937-1986.........DLB-117, 225; CDWLB-3
Harris, Mark 1922-...............DLB-2; Y-80	Hass, Robert 1941-...............DLB-105, 206	Headley, Joel T. 1813-1897...DLB-30, 183; DS-13
Harris, Wilson 1921-........DLB-117; CDWLB-3	Hastings, Michael 1938-................DLB-233	Heaney, Seamus 1939-............DLB-40; Y-95; CDBLB-8
Harrison, Mrs. Burton (see Harrison, Constance Cary)	Hatar, Győző 1914-..................DLB-215	Heard, Nathan C. 1936-................DLB-33
Harrison, Charles Yale 1898-1954.......DLB-68	The Hatch-Billops Collection...........DLB-76	Hearn, Lafcadio 1850-1904......DLB-12, 78, 189
Harrison, Constance Cary 1843-1920...DLB-221	Hathaway, William 1944-..............DLB-120	Hearn, Mary Anne (Marianne Farningham, Eva Hope) 1834-1909.............DLB-240
Harrison, Frederic 1831-1923.........DLB-57, 190	Hauff, Wilhelm 1802-1827..............DLB-90	Hearne, John 1926-....................DLB-117
"On Style in English Prose" (1898)......DLB-57	A Haughty and Proud Generation (1922), by Ford Madox Hueffer.............DLB-36	Hearne, Samuel 1745-1792.............DLB-99
Harrison, Harry 1925-..................DLB-8	Haugwitz, August Adolph von 1647-1706.....................DLB-168	Hearne, Thomas 1678?-1735...........DLB-213
Harrison, James P., Company..........DLB-49	Hauptmann, Carl 1858-1921........DLB-66, 118	Hearst, William Randolph 1863-1951....DLB-25
Harrison, Jim 1937-....................Y-82	Hauptmann, Gerhart 1862-1946..........DLB-66, 118; CDWLB-2	Hearst, William Randolph, Jr. 1908-1993.....................DLB-127
Harrison, Mary St. Leger Kingsley (see Malet, Lucas)	Hauser, Marianne 1910-.................Y-83	Heartman, Charles Frederick 1883-1953.....................DLB-187
Harrison, Paul Carter 1936-............DLB-38	Havel, Václav 1936-.......DLB-232; CDWLB-4	Heath, Catherine 1924-................DLB-14
Harrison, Susan Frances 1859-1935......DLB-99	Haven, Alice B. Neal 1827-1863........DLB-250	Heath, James Ewell 1792-1862..........DLB-248
Harrison, Tony 1937-.............DLB-40, 245	Havergal, Frances Ridley 1836-1879....DLB-199	Heath, Roy A. K. 1926-................DLB-117
Harrison, William 1535-1593..........DLB-136	Hawes, Stephen 1475?-before 1529.....DLB-132	Heath-Stubbs, John 1918-..............DLB-27
Harrison, William 1933-..............DLB-234	Hawker, Robert Stephen 1803-1875......DLB-32	Heavysege, Charles 1816-1876..........DLB-99
Harrisse, Henry 1829-1910.............DLB-47	Hawkes, John 1925-1998.........DLB-2, 7, 227; Y-80, Y-98	Hebbel, Friedrich 1813-1863...............DLB-129; CDWLB-2
The Harry Ransom Humanities Research Center at the University of Texas at Austin..................Y-00	John Hawkes: A Tribute.................Y-98	Hebel, Johann Peter 1760-1826..........DLB-90
Harryman, Carla 1952-................DLB-193	Hawkesworth, John 1720-1773.........DLB-142	Heber, Richard 1774-1833.............DLB-184
Harsdörffer, Georg Philipp 1607-1658...DLB-164	Hawkins, Sir Anthony Hope (see Hope, Anthony)	Hébert, Anne 1916-2000...............DLB-68
Harsent, David 1942-..................DLB-40	Hawkins, Sir John 1719-1789......DLB-104, 142	Hébert, Jacques 1923-.................DLB-53
Hart, Albert Bushnell 1854-1943........DLB-17	Hawkins, Walter Everette 1883-?........DLB-50	Hecht, Anthony 1923-.............DLB-5, 169
Hart, Anne 1768-1834.................DLB-200	Hawthorne, Nathaniel 1804-1864...DLB-1, 74, 183, 223; CDALB-2	Hecht, Ben 1894-1964....DLB-7, 9, 25, 26, 28, 86
Hart, Elizabeth 1771-1833.............DLB-200	Hawthorne, Nathaniel 1804-1864 and Hawthorne, Sophia Peabody 1809-1871......................DLB-183	Hecker, Isaac Thomas 1819-1888.....DLB-1, 243
Hart, Julia Catherine 1796-1867.........DLB-99		Hedge, Frederic Henry 1805-1890..................DLB-1, 59, 243
The Lorenz Hart Centenary..............Y-95	Hawthorne, Sophia Peabody 1809-1871...............DLB-183, 239	Hefner, Hugh M. 1926-...............DLB-137
Hart, Moss 1904-1961...................DLB-7	Hay, John 1835-1905..........DLB-12, 47, 189	Hegel, Georg Wilhelm Friedrich 1770-1831......................DLB-90
Hart, Oliver 1723-1795.................DLB-31	Hayashi, Fumiko 1903-1951............DLB-180	Heide, Robert 1939-..................DLB-249
Hart-Davis, Rupert, Limited...........DLB-112	Haycox, Ernest 1899-1950..............DLB-206	Heidish, Marcy 1947-...................Y-82
Harte, Bret 1836-1902 ....DLB-12, 64, 74, 79, 186; CDALB-3	Haycraft, Anna Margaret (see Ellis, Alice Thomas)	Heißenbüttel, Helmut 1921-1996........DLB-75
Harte, Edward Holmead 1922-..........DLB-127	Hayden, Robert 1913-1980..........DLB-5, 76; CDALB-1	Heike monogatari....................DLB-203
Harte, Houston Harriman 1927-........DLB-127	Haydon, Benjamin Robert 1786-1846.....................DLB-110	Hein, Christoph 1944-....DLB-124; CDWLB-2
Hartlaub, Felix 1913-1945..............DLB-56	Hayes, John Michael 1919-.............DLB-26	Hein, Piet 1905-1996..................DLB-214
Hartlebon, Otto Erich 1864-1905........DLB-118	Hayley, William 1745-1820..........DLB-93, 142	Heine, Heinrich 1797-1856...DLB-90; CDWLB-2
Hartley, L. P. 1895-1972............DLB-15, 139	Haym, Rudolf 1821-1901..............DLB-129	Heinemann, Larry 1944-..................DS-9
Hartley, Marsden 1877-1943............DLB-54	Hayman, Robert 1575-1629.............DLB-99	Heinemann, William, Limited.........DLB-112
Hartling, Peter 1933-...................DLB-75	Hayman, Ronald 1932-................DLB-155	Heinesen, William 1900-1991..........DLB-214
Hartman, Geoffrey H. 1929-............DLB-67	Hayne, Paul Hamilton 1830-1886................DLB-3, 64, 79, 248	Heinlein, Robert A. 1907-1988...........DLB-8
Hartmann, Sadakichi 1867-1944.........DLB-54	Hays, Mary 1760-1843............DLB-142, 158	Heinrich Julius of Brunswick 1564-1613.....................DLB-164
Hartmann von Aue circa 1160-circa 1205...DLB-138; CDWLB-2	Hayward, John 1905-1965..............DLB-201	

Heinrich von dem Türlîn
 flourished circa 1230 . . . . DLB-138

Heinrich von Melk
 flourished after 1160 . . . . DLB-148

Heinrich von Veldeke
 circa 1145-circa 1190 . . . . DLB-138

Heinrich, Willi 1920- DLB-75

Heinse, Wilhelm 1746-1803 . . . . DLB-94

Heinz, W. C. 1915- DLB-171

Heiskell, John 1872-1972 . . . . DLB-127

Hejinian, Lyn 1941- DLB-165

Heliand circa 850 . . . . DLB-148

Heller, Joseph
 1923-1999 . . . . . . DLB-2, 28, 227; Y-80, Y-99

Heller, Michael 1937- DLB-165

Hellman, Lillian 1906-1984 . . . . . DLB-7, 228; Y-84

Hellwig, Johann 1609-1674 . . . . DLB-164

Helprin, Mark 1947- Y-85; CDALB-7

Helwig, David 1938- DLB-60

Hemans, Felicia 1793-1835 . . . . DLB-96

Hemenway, Abby Maria 1828-1890 . . . . . DLB-243

Hemingway, Ernest 1899-1961
 . . . . . DLB-4, 9, 102, 210; Y-81, Y-87, Y-99;
 DS-1, DS-15, DS-16; CDALB-4

The Hemingway Centenary Celebration at the
 JFK Library Y-99

Ernest Hemingway: A Centennial
 Celebration Y-99

The Ernest Hemingway Collection at the
 John F. Kennedy Library Y-99

Ernest Hemingway's Reaction to James Gould
 Cozzens Y-98

Ernest Hemingway's Toronto Journalism
 Revisited: With Three Previously
 Unrecorded Stories Y-92

Falsifying Hemingway Y-96

Hemingway: Twenty-Five Years Later Y-85

Not Immediately Discernible . . . but Eventually
 Quite Clear: The *First Light* and *Final Years*
 of Hemingway's Centenary Y-99

Hemingway Salesmen's Dummies Y-00

Second International Hemingway Colloquium:
 Cuba Y-98

Hémon, Louis 1880-1913 . . . . DLB-92

Hempel, Amy 1951- DLB-218

Hemphill, Paul 1936- Y-87

Hénault, Gilles 1920- DLB-88

Henchman, Daniel 1689-1761 . . . . DLB-24

Henderson, Alice Corbin 1881-1949 . . . . . . DLB-54

Henderson, Archibald 1877-1963 . . . . DLB-103

Henderson, David 1942- DLB-41

Henderson, George Wylie 1904- DLB-51

Henderson, Zenna 1917-1983 . . . . DLB-8

Henighan, Tom 1934- DLB-251

Henisch, Peter 1943- DLB-85

Henley, Beth 1952- Y-86

Henley, William Ernest 1849-1903 . . . . DLB-19

Henning, Rachel 1826-1914 . . . . DLB-230

Henningsen, Agnes 1868-1962 . . . . DLB-214

Henniker, Florence 1855-1923 . . . . DLB-135

Henry, Alexander 1739-1824 . . . . DLB-99

Henry, Buck 1930- DLB-26

Henry VIII of England 1491-1547 . . . . . . DLB-132

Henry of Ghent
 circa 1217-1229 - 1293 . . . . DLB-115

Henry, Marguerite 1902-1997 . . . . DLB-22

Henry, O. (see Porter, William Sydney)

Henry, Robert Selph 1889-1970 . . . . DLB-17

Henry, Will (see Allen, Henry W.)

Henryson, Robert
 1420s or 1430s-circa 1505 . . . . DLB-146

Henschke, Alfred (see Klabund)

Hensley, Sophie Almon 1866-1946 . . . . DLB-99

Henson, Lance 1944- DLB-175

Henty, G. A. 1832?-1902 . . . . DLB-18, 141

Hentz, Caroline Lee 1800-1856 . . . . DLB-3, 248

Heraclitus
 flourished circa 500 B.C. DLB-176

Herbert, Agnes circa 1880-1960 . . . . DLB-174

Herbert, Alan Patrick 1890-1971 . . . . . DLB-10, 191

Herbert, Edward, Lord, of Cherbury
 1582-1648 . . . . DLB-121, 151

Herbert, Frank 1920-1986 . . . . . . DLB-8; CDALB-7

Herbert, George 1593-1633 . . . DLB-126; CDBLB-1

Herbert, Henry William 1807-1858 . . . . . DLB-3, 73

Herbert, John 1926- DLB-53

Herbert, Mary Sidney, Countess of Pembroke
 (see Sidney, Mary)

Herbert, Zbigniew
 1924-1998 . . . . DLB-232; CDWLB-4

Herbst, Josephine 1892-1969 . . . . DLB-9

Herburger, Gunter 1932- DLB-75, 124

Hercules, Frank E. M. 1917-1996 . . . . DLB-33

Herder, Johann Gottfried 1744-1803 . . . . . . DLB-97

Herder, B., Book Company DLB-49

Heredia, José-María de 1842-1905 . . . . DLB-217

Herford, Charles Harold 1853-1931 . . . . . DLB-149

Hergesheimer, Joseph 1880-1954 . . . . . . DLB-9, 102

Heritage Press DLB-46

Hermann the Lame 1013-1054 . . . . DLB-148

Hermes, Johann Timotheus
 1738-1821 . . . . DLB-97

Hermlin, Stephan 1915-1997 . . . . DLB-69

Hernández, Alfonso C. 1938- DLB-122

Hernández, Inés 1947- DLB-122

Hernández, Miguel 1910-1942 . . . . DLB-134

Hernton, Calvin C. 1932- DLB-38

Herodotus circa 484 B.C.-circa 420 B.C.
 . . . . DLB-176; CDWLB-1

Heron, Robert 1764-1807 . . . . DLB-142

Herr, Michael 1940- DLB-185

Herrera, Juan Felipe 1948- DLB-122

Herrick, E. R., and Company DLB-49

Herrick, Robert 1591-1674 . . . . DLB-126

Herrick, Robert 1868-1938 . . . . DLB-9, 12, 78

Herrick, William 1915- Y-83

Herrmann, John 1900-1959 . . . . DLB-4

Hersey, John 1914-1993 . . . DLB-6, 185; CDALB-7

Hertel, François 1905-1985 . . . . DLB-68

Hervé-Bazin, Jean Pierre Marie (see Bazin, Hervé)

Hervey, John, Lord 1696-1743 . . . . DLB-101

Herwig, Georg 1817-1875 . . . . DLB-133

Herzog, Émile Salomon Wilhelm
 (see Maurois, André)

Hesiod eighth century B.C. DLB-176

Hesse, Hermann
 1877-1962 . . . . DLB-66; CDWLB-2

Hessus, Helius Eobanus 1488-1540 . . . . . . DLB-179

Hewat, Alexander circa 1743-circa 1824 . . . DLB-30

Hewitt, John 1907- DLB-27

Hewlett, Maurice 1861-1923 . . . . DLB-34, 156

Heyen, William 1940- DLB-5

Heyer, Georgette 1902-1974 . . . . DLB-77, 191

Heym, Stefan 1913- DLB-69

Heyse, Paul 1830-1914 . . . . DLB-129

Heytesbury, William
 circa 1310-1372 or 1373 . . . . DLB-115

Heyward, Dorothy 1890-1961 . . . . DLB-7, 249

Heyward, DuBose 1885-1940 . . . DLB-7, 9, 45, 249

Heywood, John 1497?-1580? DLB-136

Heywood, Thomas
 1573 or 1574-1641 . . . . DLB-62

Hibbs, Ben 1901-1975 . . . . DLB-137

Hichens, Robert S. 1864-1950 . . . . DLB-153

Hickey, Emily 1845-1924 . . . . DLB-199

Hickman, William Albert 1877-1957 . . . . . . DLB-92

Hicks, Granville 1901-1982 . . . . DLB-246

Hidalgo, José Luis 1919-1947 . . . . DLB-108

Hiebert, Paul 1892-1987 . . . . DLB-68

Hieng, Andrej 1925- DLB-181

Hierro, José 1922- DLB-108

Higgins, Aidan 1927- DLB-14

Higgins, Colin 1941-1988 . . . . DLB-26

Higgins, George V.
 1939-1999 . . . . DLB-2; Y-81, Y-98, Y-99

George V. Higgins to Julian Symons Y-99

Higginson, Thomas Wentworth
 1823-1911 . . . . DLB-1, 64, 243

Highwater, Jamake 1942?- DLB-52; Y-85

Hijuelos, Oscar 1951- DLB-145

Hildegard von Bingen 1098-1179 . . . . DLB-148

Das Hildesbrandslied
 circa 820 . . . . DLB-148; CDWLB-2

Hildesheimer, Wolfgang
 1916-1991 . . . . DLB-69, 124

Hildreth, Richard 1807-1865 . . . DLB-1, 30, 59, 235

Hill, Aaron 1685-1750 . . . . DLB-84

Hill, Geoffrey 1932- DLB-40; CDBLB-8

Hill, George M., Company DLB-49

Hill, "Sir" John 1714?-1775 . . . . DLB-39

Hill, Lawrence, and Company,
 Publishers DLB-46

Hill, Leslie 1880-1960 . . . . DLB-51

Hill, Susan 1942- DLB-14, 139	Hoffman, William 1925- DLB-234	Hölty, Ludwig Christoph Heinrich 1748-1776 .... DLB-94
Hill, Walter 1942- DLB-44	Hoffmanswaldau, Christian Hoffman von 1616-1679 .... DLB-168	Holub, Miroslav 1923-1998 .... DLB-232; CDWLB-4
Hill and Wang DLB-46	Hofmann, Michael 1957- DLB-40	Holz, Arno 1863-1929 .... DLB-118
Hillberry, Conrad 1928- DLB-120	Hofmannsthal, Hugo von 1874-1929 .... DLB-81, 118; CDWLB-2	Home, Henry, Lord Kames (see Kames, Henry Home, Lord)
Hillerman, Tony 1925- DLB-206	Hofstadter, Richard 1916-1970 .... DLB-17, 246	Home, John 1722-1808 .... DLB-84
Hilliard, Gray and Company DLB-49	Hogan, Desmond 1950- DLB-14	Home, William Douglas 1912- DLB-13
Hills, Lee 1906- DLB-127	Hogan, Linda 1947- DLB-175	Home Publishing Company DLB-49
Hillyer, Robert 1895-1961 .... DLB-54	Hogan and Thompson DLB-49	Homer circa eighth-seventh centuries B.C. DLB-176; CDWLB-1
Hilton, James 1900-1954 .... DLB-34, 77	Hogarth Press DLB-112	Homer, Winslow 1836-1910 .... DLB-188
Hilton, Walter died 1396 .... DLB-146	Hogg, James 1770-1835 .... DLB-93, 116, 159	Homes, Geoffrey (see Mainwaring, Daniel)
Hilton and Company DLB-49	Hohberg, Wolfgang Helmhard Freiherr von 1612-1688 .... DLB-168	Honan, Park 1928- DLB-111
Himes, Chester 1909-1984 .... DLB-2, 76, 143, 226	von Hohenheim, Philippus Aureolus Theophrastus Bombastus (see Paracelsus)	Hone, William 1780-1842 .... DLB-110, 158
Hindmarsh, Joseph [publishing house] DLB-170	Hohl, Ludwig 1904-1980 .... DLB-56	Hongo, Garrett Kaoru 1951- DLB-120
Hine, Daryl 1936- DLB-60	Holbrook, David 1923- DLB-14, 40	Honig, Edwin 1919- DLB-5
Hingley, Ronald 1920- DLB-155	Holcroft, Thomas 1745-1809 .... DLB-39, 89, 158	Hood, Hugh 1928- DLB-53
Hinojosa-Smith, Rolando 1929- DLB-82	Preface to *Alwyn* (1780) DLB-39	Hood, Mary 1946- DLB-234
Hinton, S. E. 1948- CDALB-7	Holden, Jonathan 1941- DLB-105	Hood, Thomas 1799-1845 .... DLB-96
Hippel, Theodor Gottlieb von 1741-1796 .... DLB-97	"Contemporary Verse Story-telling" DLB-105	Hook, Theodore 1788-1841 .... DLB-116
Hippocrates of Cos flourished circa 425 B.C. DLB-176; CDWLB-1	Holden, Molly 1927-1981 .... DLB-40	Hooker, Jeremy 1941- DLB-40
Hirabayashi, Taiko 1905-1972 .... DLB-180	Hölderlin, Friedrich 1770-1843 DLB-90; CDWLB-2	Hooker, Richard 1554-1600 .... DLB-132
Hirsch, E. D., Jr. 1928- DLB-67	Holiday House DLB-46	Hooker, Thomas 1586-1647 .... DLB-24
Hirsch, Edward 1950- DLB-120	Holinshed, Raphael died 1580 .... DLB-167	hooks, bell 1952- DLB-246
Hoagland, Edward 1932- DLB-6	Holland, J. G. 1819-1881 .... DS-13	Hooper, Johnson Jones 1815-1862 .... DLB-3, 11, 248
Hoagland, Everett H., III 1942- DLB-41	Holland, Norman N. 1927- DLB-67	Hope, Anthony 1863-1933 .... DLB-153, 156
Hoban, Russell 1925- DLB-52; Y-90	Hollander, John 1929- DLB-5	Hope, Christopher 1944- DLB-225
Hobbes, Thomas 1588-1679 .... DLB-151	Holley, Marietta 1836-1926 .... DLB-11	Hope, Eva (see Hearn, Mary Anne)
Hobby, Oveta 1905- DLB-127	Hollinghurst, Alan 1954- DLB-207	Hope, Laurence (Adela Florence Cory Nicolson) 1865-1904 .... DLB-240
Hobby, William 1878-1964 .... DLB-127	Hollingsworth, Margaret 1940- DLB-60	Hopkins, Ellice 1836-1904 .... DLB-190
Hobsbaum, Philip 1932- DLB-40	Hollo, Anselm 1934- DLB-40	Hopkins, Gerard Manley 1844-1889 .... DLB-35, 57; CDBLB-5
Hobson, Laura Z. 1900- DLB-28	Holloway, Emory 1885-1977 .... DLB-103	Hopkins, John (see Sternhold, Thomas)
Hobson, Sarah 1947- DLB-204	Holloway, John 1920- DLB-27	Hopkins, John H., and Son DLB-46
Hoby, Thomas 1530-1566 .... DLB-132	Holloway House Publishing Company ... DLB-46	Hopkins, Lemuel 1750-1801 .... DLB-37
Hoccleve, Thomas circa 1368-circa 1437 .... DLB-146	Holme, Constance 1880-1955 .... DLB-34	Hopkins, Pauline Elizabeth 1859-1930 .... DLB-50
Hochhuth, Rolf 1931- DLB-124	Holmes, Abraham S. 1821?-1908 .... DLB-99	Hopkins, Samuel 1721-1803 .... DLB-31
Hochman, Sandra 1936- DLB-5	Holmes, John Clellon 1926-1988 ..... DLB-16, 237	Hopkinson, Francis 1737-1791 .... DLB-31
Hocken, Thomas Morland 1836-1910 .... DLB-184	"Four Essays on the Beat Generation" DLB-16	Hopkinson, Nalo 1960- DLB-251
Hodder and Stoughton, Limited DLB-106	Holmes, Mary Jane 1825-1907 ..... DLB-202, 221	Hopper, Nora (Mrs. Nora Chesson) 1871-1906 .... DLB-240
Hodgins, Jack 1938- DLB-60	Holmes, Oliver Wendell 1809-1894 ...... DLB-1, 189, 235; CDALB-2	Hoppin, Augustus 1828-1896 .... DLB-188
Hodgman, Helen 1945- DLB-14	Holmes, Richard 1945- DLB-155	Hora, Josef 1891-1945 .... DLB-215; CDWLB-4
Hodgskin, Thomas 1787-1869 .... DLB-158	The Cult of Biography Excerpts from the Second Folio Debate: "Biographies are generally a disease of English Literature" Y-86	Horace 65 B.C.-8 B.C. DLB-211; CDWLB-1
Hodgson, Ralph 1871-1962 .... DLB-19		Horgan, Paul 1903-1995 ...... DLB-102, 212; Y-85
Hodgson, William Hope 1877-1918 .... DLB-70, 153, 156, 178	Holmes, Thomas James 1874-1959 ...... DLB-187	Horizon Press DLB-46
Hoe, Robert III 1839-1909 .... DLB-187	Holroyd, Michael 1935- DLB-155; Y-99	Hornby, C. H. St. John 1867-1946 ..... DLB-201
Hoeg, Peter 1957- DLB-214	Holst, Hermann E. von 1841-1904 ...... DLB-47	Hornby, Nick 1957- DLB-207
Højholt, Per 1928- DLB-214	Holt, Henry, and Company DLB-49	Horne, Frank 1899-1974 .... DLB-51
Hoffenstein, Samuel 1890-1947 .... DLB-11	Holt, John 1721-1784 .... DLB-43	Horne, Richard Henry (Hengist) 1802 or 1803-1884 .... DLB-32
Hoffman, Charles Fenno 1806-1884 ... DLB-3, 250	Holt, Rinehart and Winston DLB-46	
Hoffman, Daniel 1923- DLB-5	Holtby, Winifred 1898-1935 .... DLB-191	Horney, Karen 1885-1952 .... DLB-246
Hoffmann, E. T. A. 1776-1822 .... DLB-90; CDWLB-2	Holthusen, Hans Egon 1913- DLB-69	Hornung, E. W. 1866-1921 .... DLB-70
Hoffman, Frank B. 1888-1958 .... DLB-188		

Horovitz, Israel 1939- DLB-7
Horton, George Moses 1797?-1883? DLB-50
Horváth, Ödön von 1901-1938 ......DLB-85, 124
Horwood, Harold 1923- DLB-60
Hosford, E. and E. [publishing house].....DLB-49
Hoskens, Jane Fenn 1693-1770?.........DLB-200
Hoskyns, John 1566-1638 ....DLB-121
Hosokawa Yūsai 1535-1610............DLB-203
Hostovský, Egon 1908-1973 ....DLB-215
Hotchkiss and Company...............DLB-49
Hough, Emerson 1857-1923.........DLB-9, 212
Houghton, Stanley 1881-1913 ....DLB-10
Houghton Mifflin Company DLB-49
Household, Geoffrey 1900-1988 ....DLB-87
Housman, A. E. 1859-1936 ... DLB-19; CDBLB-5
Housman, Laurence 1865-1959..........DLB-10
Houston, Pam 1962- DLB-244
Houwald, Ernst von 1778-1845 ....DLB-90
Hovey, Richard 1864-1900 ....DLB-54
Howard, Donald R. 1927-1987 ....DLB-111
Howard, Maureen 1930- Y-83
Howard, Richard 1929- DLB-5
Howard, Roy W. 1883-1964...........DLB-29
Howard, Sidney 1891-1939....... DLB-7, 26, 249
Howard, Thomas, second Earl of Arundel 1585-1646.....................DLB-213
Howe, E. W. 1853-1937 ....DLB-12, 25
Howe, Henry 1816-1893 ....DLB-30
Howe, Irving 1920-1993 ....DLB-67
Howe, Joseph 1804-1873 ....DLB-99
Howe, Julia Ward 1819-1910 ....DLB-1, 189, 235
Howe, Percival Presland 1886-1944 .....DLB-149
Howe, Susan 1937- DLB-120
Howell, Clark, Sr. 1863-1936 ....DLB-25
Howell, Evan P. 1839-1905 ....DLB-23
Howell, James 1594?-1666.............DLB-151
Howell, Soskin and Company..........DLB-46
Howell, Warren Richardson 1912-1984 ....DLB-140
Howells, William Dean 1837-1920 .... DLB-12, 64, 74, 79, 189; CDALB-3
Introduction to Paul Laurence Dunbar, Lyrics of Lowly Life (1896)..........DLB-50
Howitt, Mary 1799-1888 ....DLB-110, 199
Howitt, William 1792-1879 and Howitt, Mary 1799-1888..........DLB-110
Hoyem, Andrew 1935- DLB-5
Hoyers, Anna Ovena 1584-1655 ....DLB-164
Hoyos, Angela de 1940- DLB-82
Hoyt, Henry [publishing house] DLB-49
Hoyt, Palmer 1897-1979...............DLB-127
Hrabal, Bohumil 1914-1997............DLB-232
Hrabanus Maurus 776?-856...........DLB-148
Hronský, Josef Cíger 1896-1960 .....DLB-215
Hrotsvit of Gandersheim circa 935-circa 1000................DLB-148

Hubbard, Elbert 1856-1915.............DLB-91
Hubbard, Kin 1868-1930................DLB-11
Hubbard, William circa 1621-1704 ....DLB-24
Huber, Therese 1764-1829 ....DLB-90
Huch, Friedrich 1873-1913 ....DLB-66
Huch, Ricarda 1864-1947 ....DLB-66
Huck at 100: How Old Is Huckleberry Finn? Y-85
Huddle, David 1942- DLB-130
Hudgins, Andrew 1951- DLB-120
Hudson, Henry Norman 1814-1886 ......DLB-64
Hudson, Stephen 1868?-1944 ....DLB-197
Hudson, W. H. 1841-1922 ..... DLB-98, 153, 174
Hudson and Goodwin..................DLB-49
Huebsch, B. W. [publishing house] DLB-46
Oral History: B. W. Huebsch Y-99
Hueffer, Oliver Madox 1876-1931........DLB-197
Hugh of St. Victor circa 1096-1141 .,....DLB-208
Hughes, David 1930- DLB-14
Hughes, Dusty 1947- DLB-233
Hughes, Hatcher 1881-1945 ....DLB-249
Hughes, John 1677-1720................DLB-84
Hughes, Langston 1902-1967 .... DLB-4, 7, 48, 51, 86, 228; CDALB-5
Hughes, Richard 1900-1976..........DLB-15, 161
Hughes, Ted 1930-1998 ....DLB-40, 161
Hughes, Thomas 1822-1896 .... DLB-18, 163
Hugo, Richard 1923-1982 ....DLB-5, 206
Hugo, Victor 1802-1885 ...... DLB-119, 192, 217
Hugo Awards and Nebula Awards DLB-8
Hull, Richard 1896-1973 ....DLB-77
Hulme, T. E. 1883-1917 ....DLB-19
Hulton, Anne ?-1779? DLB-200
Humboldt, Alexander von 1769-1859 .....DLB-90
Humboldt, Wilhelm von 1767-1835.......DLB-90
Hume, David 1711-1776................DLB-104
Hume, Fergus 1859-1932................DLB-70
Hume, Sophia 1702-1774 ....DLB-200
Hume-Rothery, Mary Catherine 1824-1885.....................DLB-240
Humishuma (see Mourning Dove)
Hummer, T. R. 1950- DLB-120
Humorous Book Illustration DLB-11
Humphrey, Duke of Gloucester 1391-1447.....................DLB-213
Humphrey, William 1924-1997...DLB-6, 212, 234
Humphreys, David 1752-1818...........DLB-37
Humphreys, Emyr 1919- DLB-15
Huncke, Herbert 1915-1996 ....DLB-16
Huneker, James Gibbons 1857-1921 .....DLB-71
Hunold, Christian Friedrich 1681-1721 ...DLB-168
Hunt, Irene 1907- DLB-52
Hunt, Leigh 1784-1859 .... DLB-96, 110, 144
Hunt, Violet 1862-1942............ DLB-162, 197
Hunt, William Gibbes 1791-1833 ....DLB-73

Hunter, Evan 1926- Y-82
Hunter, Jim 1939- DLB-14
Hunter, Kristin 1931- DLB-33
Hunter, Mollie 1922- DLB-161
Hunter, N. C. 1908-1971..............DLB-10
Hunter-Duvar, John 1821-1899 ....DLB-99
Huntington, Henry E. 1850-1927 ......DLB-140
Huntington, Susan Mansfield 1791-1823 ....DLB-200
Hurd and Houghton DLB-49
Hurst, Fannie 1889-1968 ....DLB-86
Hurst and Blackett....................DLB-106
Hurst and Company DLB-49
Hurston, Zora Neale 1901?-1960 ....DLB-51, 86; CDALB-7
Husson, Jules-François-Félix (see Champfleury)
Huston, John 1906-1987 ....DLB-26
Hutcheson, Francis 1694-1746..........DLB-31
Hutchinson, Ron 1947- DLB-245
Hutchinson, R. C. 1907-1975..........DLB-191
Hutchinson, Thomas 1711-1780 ....DLB-30, 31
Hutchinson and Company (Publishers) Limited DLB-112
Hutton, Richard Holt 1826-1897.........DLB-57
von Hutton, Ulrich 1488-1523 ....DLB-179
Huxley, Aldous 1894-1963 .... DLB-36, 100, 162, 195; CDBLB-6
Huxley, Elspeth Josceline 1907-1997 .... DLB-77, 204
Huxley, T. H. 1825-1895 ....DLB-57
Huyghue, Douglas Smith 1816-1891......DLB-99
Huysmans, Joris-Karl 1848-1907 ....DLB-123
Hwang, David Henry 1957- DLB-212, 228
Hyde, Donald 1909-1966 and Hyde, Mary 1912- DLB-187
Hyman, Trina Schart 1939- DLB-61

I

Iavorsky, Stefan 1658-1722 ....DLB-150
Iazykov, Nikolai Mikhailovich 1803-1846.....................DLB-205
Ibáñez, Armando P. 1949- DLB-209
Ibn Bajja circa 1077-1138 ....DLB-115
Ibn Gabirol, Solomon circa 1021-circa 1058................DLB-115
Ibuse, Masuji 1898-1993 ....DLB-180
Ichijō Kanera (see Ichijō Kaneyoshi)
Ichijō Kaneyoshi (Ichijō Kanera) 1402-1481.....................DLB-203
The Iconography of Science-Fiction Art DLB-8
Iffland, August Wilhelm 1759-1814.......DLB-94
Ignatow, David 1914-1997...............DLB-5
Ike, Chukwuemeka 1931- DLB-157
Ikkyū Sōjun 1394-1481 ....DLB-203
Iles, Francis (see Berkeley, Anthony)

Cumulative Index DLB 251

Illich, Ivan 1926- DLB-242	Holroyd, Michael Y-99	Iser, Wolfgang 1926- DLB-242
The Illustration of Early German Literar Manuscripts, circa 1150-circa 1300 .. DLB-148	Horowitz, Glen......................... Y-90	Isherwood, Christopher 1904-1986 .... DLB-15, 195; Y-86
Illyés, Gyula 1902-1983 .... DLB-215; CDWLB-4	Jakes, John Y-83	The Christopher Isherwood Archive, The Huntington Library Y-99
Imbs, Bravig 1904-1946 .... DLB-4	Jenkinson, Edward B..................... Y-82	Ishiguro, Kazuo 1954- DLB-194
Imbuga, Francis D. 1947- DLB-157	Jenks, Tom Y-86	Ishikawa Jun 1899-1987 .... DLB-182
Immermann, Karl 1796-1840 .... DLB-133	Kaplan, Justin Y-86	The Island Trees Case: A Symposium on School Library Censorship An Interview with Judith Krug An Interview with Phyllis Schlafly An Interview with Edward B. Jenkinson An Interview with Lamarr Mooneyham An Interview with Harriet Bernstein Y-82
Inchbald, Elizabeth 1753-1821 .... DLB-39, 89	King, Florence Y-85	
Inge, William 1913-1973... DLB-7, 249; CDALB-1	Klopfer, Donald S....................... Y-97	
Ingelow, Jean 1820-1897.......... DLB-35, 163	Krug, Judith Y-82	
Ingersoll, Ralph 1900-1985............ DLB-127	Lamm, Donald Y-95	
The Ingersoll Prizes Y-84	Laughlin, James Y-96	
Ingoldsby, Thomas (see Barham, Richard Harris)	Lindsay, Jack Y-84	Islas, Arturo 1938-1991 .... DLB-122
Ingraham, Joseph Holt 1809-1860 .... DLB-3, 248	Mailer, Norman Y-97	Issit, Debbie 1966- DLB-233
Inman, John 1805-1850 .... DLB-73	Manchester, William Y-85	Ivanišević, Drago 1907-1981 .... DLB-181
Innerhofer, Franz 1944- DLB-85	McCormack, Thomas Y-98	
Innis, Harold Adams 1894-1952......... DLB-88	McNamara, Katherine Y-97	Ivaska, Astrīde 1926- DLB-232
Innis, Mary Quayle 1899-1972.......... DLB-88	Mellen, Joan Y-94	Ivers, M. J., and Company............ DLB-49
Inō Sōgi 1421-1502................... DLB-203	Menaher, Daniel........................ Y-97	Iwaniuk, Wacław 1915- DLB-215
Inoue Yasushi 1907-1991 .... DLB-181	Mooneyham, Lamarr Y-82	Iwano, Hōmei 1873-1920 .... DLB-180
International Publishers Company DLB-46	Nosworth, David Y-82	Iwaszkiewicz, Jarosław 1894-1980....... DLB-215
Interviews:	O'Connor, Patrick Y-84, Y-99	Iyayi, Festus 1947- DLB-157
Anastas, Benjamin Y-98	Ozick, Cynthia Y-83	Izumi, Kyōka 1873-1939............. DLB-180
Baker, Nicholson Y-00	Penner, Jonathan Y-83	
Bank, Melissa Y-98	Pennington, Lee Y-82	

J

Bernstein, Harriet Y-82	Penzler, Otto........................... Y-96
Betts, Doris Y-82	Plimpton, George Y-99
Bosworth, David....................... Y-82	Potok, Chaim Y-84	Jackmon, Marvin E. (see Marvin X)
Bottoms, David........................ Y-83	Prescott, Peter S........................ Y-86	Jacks, L. P. 1860-1955 .... DLB-135
Bowers, Fredson....................... Y-80	Rabe, David Y-91	Jackson, Angela 1951- DLB-41
Burnshaw, Stanley Y-97	Rallyson, Carl.......................... Y-97	Jackson, Charles 1903-1968 .... DLB-234
Carpenter, Humphrey Y-84, Y-99	Rechy, John Y-82	Jackson, Helen Hunt 1830-1885 .... DLB-42, 47, 186, 189
Carr, Virginia Spencer Y-00	Reid, B. L. Y-83	
Carver, Raymond...................... Y-83	Reynolds, Michael Y-95, Y-99	Jackson, Holbrook 1874-1948.......... DLB-98
Cherry, Kelly Y-83	Schlafly, Phyllis........................ Y-82	Jackson, Laura Riding 1901-1991........ DLB-48
Coppel, Alfred Y-83	Schroeder, Patricia Y-99	Jackson, Shirley 1916-1965 .... DLB-6, 234; CDALB-1
Cowley, Malcolm...................... Y-81	Schulberg, Budd Y-81	
Davis, Paxton Y-89	Scribner, Charles III.................... Y-94	Jacob, Naomi 1884?-1964............. DLB-191
De Vries, Peter Y-82	Sipper, Ralph Y-94	Jacob, Piers Anthony Dillingham (see Anthony, Piers)
Dickey, James Y-82	Staley, Thomas F....................... Y-00	
Donald, David Herbert.................. Y-87	Styron, William Y-80	Jacob, Violet 1863-1946 .... DLB-240
Ellroy, James Y-91	Toth, Susan Allen....................... Y-86	Jacobi, Friedrich Heinrich 1743-1819 ..... DLB-94
Fancher, Betsy Y-83	Tyler, Anne Y-82	Jacobi, Johann Georg 1740-1841........ DLB-97
Faust, Irvin Y-00	Vaughan, Samuel Y-97	Jacobs, George W., and Company....... DLB-49
Fulton, Len Y-86	Von Ogtrop, Kristin Y-92	Jacobs, Harriet 1813-1897............. DLB-239
Garrett, George........................ Y-83	Wallenstein, Barry Y-92	Jacobs, Joseph 1854-1916 .... DLB-141
Greenfield, George Y-91	Weintraub, Stanley..................... Y-82	Jacobs, W. W. 1863-1943............. DLB-135
Griffin, Bryan Y-81	Williams, J. Chamberlain Y-84	Jacobsen, Jørgen-Frantz 1900-1938...... DLB-214
Guilds, John Caldwell.................. Y-92	Editors, Conversations with Y-95	Jacobsen, Josephine 1908- DLB-244
Hardin, James......................... Y-92	Interviews on E-Publishing.............. Y-00	Jacobson, Dan 1929- DLB-14, 207, 225
Harrison, Jim Y-82	Irving, John 1942- DLB-6; Y-82	Jacobson, Howard 1942- DLB-207
Hazzard, Shirley Y-82	Irving, Washington 1783-1859 .... DLB-3, 11, 30, 59, 73, 74, 183, 186, 250; CDALB-2	Jacques de Vitry circa 1160/1170-1240... DLB-208
Higgins, George V..................... Y-98		Jæger, Frank 1926-1977............... DLB-214
Hoban, Russell Y-90	Irwin, Grace 1907- DLB-68	Jaggard, William [publishing house]......DLB-170
	Irwin, Will 1873-1948................. DLB-25	Jahier, Piero 1884-1966 .... DLB-114
		Jahnn, Hans Henny 1894-1959 ..... DLB-56, 124

Jakes, John 1932- Y-83	Jensen, Thit 1876-1957 .... DLB-214	Johnson, Owen 1878-1952 .... Y-87
Jakobson, Roman 1896-1982 .... DLB-242	Jephson, Robert 1736-1803 .... DLB-89	Johnson, Pamela Hansford 1912- DLB-15
James, Alice 1848-1892 .... DLB-221	Jerome, Jerome K. 1859-1927 .... DLB-10, 34, 135	Johnson, Pauline 1861-1913 .... DLB-92
James, C. L. R. 1901-1989 .... DLB-125	Jerome, Judson 1927-1991 .... DLB-105	Johnson, Ronald 1935-1998 .... DLB-169
James, George P. R. 1801-1860 .... DLB-116	Jerrold, Douglas 1803-1857 .... DLB-158, 159	Johnson, Samuel 1696-1772 .... DLB-24; CDBLB-2
James, Henry 1843-1916 ...... DLB-12, 71, 74, 189; DS-13; CDALB-3	Jessc, F. Tennyson 1888-1958 .... DLB-77	Johnson, Samuel 1709-1784 .... DLB-39, 95, 104, 142, 213
James, John circa 1633-1729 .... DLB-24	Jewel, John 1522-1571 .... DLB-236	Johnson, Samuel 1822-1882 .... DLB-1, 243
James, M. R. 1862-1936 .... DLB-156, 201	Jewett, John P., and Company DLB-49	Johnson, Susanna 1730-1810 .... DLB-200
James, Naomi 1949- DLB-204	Jewett, Sarah Orne 1849-1909 .... DLB-12, 74, 221	Johnson, Terry 1955- DLB-233
James, P. D. 1920- ...DLB-87; DS-17; CDBLB-8	The Jewish Publication Society DLB-49	Johnson, Uwe 1934-1984 ..... DLB-75; CDWLB-2
James VI of Scotland, I of England 1566-1625 .... DLB-151, 172	Jewitt, John Rodgers 1783-1821 .... DLB-99	Johnston, Annie Fellows 1863-1931 .... DLB-42
Ane Schort Treatise Conteining Some Revlis and Cautelis to Be Obseruit and Eschewit in Scottis Poesi (1584) DLB-172	Jewsbury, Geraldine 1812-1880 .... DLB-21	Johnston, Basil H. 1929- DLB-60
	Jewsbury, Maria Jane 1800-1833 .... DLB-199	Johnston, David Claypole 1798?-1865 .... DLB-188
	Jhabvala, Ruth Prawer 1927- DLB-139, 194	Johnston, Denis 1901-1984 .... DLB-10
James, Thomas 1572?-1629 .... DLB-213	Jiménez, Juan Ramón 1881-1958 .... DLB-134	Johnston, Ellen 1835-1873 .... DLB-199
James, U. P. [publishing house] DLB-49	Jin, Ha 1956- DLB-244	Johnston, George 1913- DLB-88
James, Will 1892-1942 .... DS-16	Joans, Ted 1928- DLB-16, 41	Johnston, Sir Harry 1858-1927 .... DLB-174
Jameson, Anna 1794-1860 .... DLB-99, 166	Jōha 1525-1602 .... DLB-203	Johnston, Jennifer 1930- DLB-14
Jameson, Fredric 1934- DLB-67	Johannis de Garlandia (see John of Garland)	Johnston, Mary 1870-1936 .... DLB-9
Jameson, J. Franklin 1859-1937 .... DLB-17	John, Errol 1924-1988 .... DLB-233	Johnston, Richard Malcolm 1822-1898 .... DLB-74
Jameson, Storm 1891-1986 .... DLB-36	John, Eugenie (see Marlitt, E.)	Johnstone, Charles 1719?-1800? DLB-39
Jančar, Drago 1948- DLB-181	John of Dumbleton circa 1310-circa 1349 .... DLB-115	Johst, Hanns 1890-1978 .... DLB-124
Janés, Clara 1940- DLB-134	John of Garland (Jean de Garlande, Johannis de Garlandia) circa 1195-circa 1272 ..... DLB-208	Jolas, Eugene 1894-1952 .... DLB-4, 45
Janevski, Slavko 1920- DLB-181; CDWLB-4		Jones, Alice C. 1853-1933 .... DLB-92
Janvier, Thomas 1849-1913 .... DLB-202	Johns, Captain W. E. 1893-1968 .... DLB-160	Jones, Charles C., Jr. 1831-1893 .... DLB-30
Jaramillo, Cleofas M. 1878-1956 .... DLB-122	Johnson, Mrs. A. E. ca. 1858-1922 ...... DLB-221	Jones, D. G. 1929- DLB-53
Jarman, Mark 1952- DLB-120	Johnson, Amelia (see Johnson, Mrs. A. E.)	Jones, David 1895-1974 ...DLB-20, 100; CDBLB-7
Jarrell, Randall 1914-1965 ..DLB-48, 52; CDALB-1	Johnson, B. S. 1933-1973 .... DLB-14, 40	Jones, Diana Wynne 1934- DLB-161
Jarrold and Sons DLB-106	Johnson, Benjamin [publishing house] DLB-49	Jones, Ebenezer 1820-1860 .... DLB-32
Jarry, Alfred 1873-1907 .... DLB-192	Johnson, Benjamin, Jacob, and Robert [publishing house] DLB-49	Jones, Ernest 1819-1868 .... DLB-32
Jarves, James Jackson 1818-1888 .... DLB-189		Jones, Gayl 1949- DLB-33
Jasmin, Claude 1930- DLB-60	Johnson, Charles 1679-1748 .... DLB-84	Jones, George 1800-1870 .... DLB-183
Jaunsudrabiņš, Jānis 1877-1962 .... DLB-220	Johnson, Charles R. 1948- DLB-33	Jones, Glyn 1905- DLB-15
Jay, John 1745-1829 .... DLB-31	Johnson, Charles S. 1893-1956 .... DLB-51, 91	Jones, Gwyn 1907- DLB-15, 139
Jean de Garlande (see John of Garland)	Johnson, Denis 1949- DLB-120	Jones, Henry Arthur 1851-1929 .... DLB-10
Jefferies, Richard 1848-1887 .... DLB-98, 141	Johnson, Diane 1934- Y-80	Jones, Hugh circa 1692-1760 .... DLB-24
Jeffers, Lance 1919-1985 .... DLB-41	Johnson, Dorothy M. 1905–1984 .... DLB-206	Jones, James 1921-1977 .... DLB-2, 143; DS-17
Jeffers, Robinson 1887-1962 .... DLB-45, 212; CDALB-4	Johnson, E. Pauline (Tekahionwake) 1861-1913 .... DLB-175	James Jones Papers in the Handy Writers' Colony Collection at the University of Illinois at Springfield Y-98
Jefferson, Thomas 1743-1826 .... DLB-31, 183; CDALB-2	Johnson, Edgar 1901-1995 .... DLB-103	
	Johnson, Edward 1598-1672 .... DLB-24	The James Jones Society Y-92
Jégé 1866-1940 .... DLB-215	Johnson, Fenton 1888-1958 .... DLB-45, 50	Jones, Jenkin Lloyd 1911- DLB-127
Jelinek, Elfriede 1946- DLB-85	Johnson, Georgia Douglas 1877?-1966 .... DLB-51, 249	Jones, John Beauchamp 1810-1866 ...... DLB-202
Jellicoe, Ann 1927- DLB-13, 233		Jones, LeRoi (see Baraka, Amiri)
Jemison, Mary circa 1742-1833 .... DLB-239	Johnson, Gerald W. 1890-1980 .... DLB-29	Jones, Lewis 1897-1939 .... DLB-15
Jenkins, Dan 1929- DLB-241	Johnson, Greg 1953- DLB-234	Jones, Madison 1925- DLB-152
Jenkins, Elizabeth 1905- DLB-155	Johnson, Helene 1907-1995 .... DLB-51	Jones, Major Joseph (see Thompson, William Tappan)
Jenkins, Robin 1912- DLB-14	Johnson, Jacob, and Company DLB-49	
Jenkins, William Fitzgerald (see Leinster, Murray)	Johnson, James Weldon 1871-1938 .... DLB-51; CDALB-4	Jones, Marie 1955- DLB-233
Jenkins, Herbert, Limited DLB-112		Jones, Preston 1936-1979 .... DLB-7
Jennings, Elizabeth 1926- DLB-27	Johnson, John H. 1918- DLB-137	Jones, Rodney 1950- DLB-120
Jens, Walter 1923- DLB-69	Johnson, Joseph [publishing house] DLB-154	Jones, Thom 1945- DLB-244
Jensen, Johannes V. 1873-1950 .... DLB-214	Johnson, Linton Kwesi 1952- DLB-157	Jones, Sir William 1746-1794 .... DLB-109
Jensen, Merrill 1905-1980 .... DLB-17	Johnson, Lionel 1867-1902 .... DLB-19	Jones, William Alfred 1817-1900 .... DLB-59
	Johnson, Nunnally 1897-1977 .... DLB-26	

Jones's Publishing House DLB-49

Jong, Erica 1942- DLB-2, 5, 28, 152

Jonke, Gert F. 1946- DLB-85

Jonson, Ben
1572?-1637 . . . . DLB-62, 121; CDBLB-1

Jordan, June 1936- DLB-38

Joseph and George Y-99

Joseph, Jenny 1932- DLB-40

Joseph, Michael, Limited DLB-112

Josephson, Matthew 1899-1978 . . . . DLB-4

Josephus, Flavius 37-100 . . . . DLB-176

Josiah Allen's Wife (see Holley, Marietta)

Josipovici, Gabriel 1940- DLB-14

Josselyn, John ?-1675 . . . . DLB-24

Joudry, Patricia 1921- DLB-88

Jovine, Giuseppe 1922- DLB-128

Joyaux, Philippe (see Sollers, Philippe)

Joyce, Adrien (see Eastman, Carol)

Joyce, James 1882-1941
 . . . . DLB-10, 19, 36, 162, 247; CDBLB-6

James Joyce Centenary: Dublin, 1982 . . . . Y-82

James Joyce Conference Y-85

A Joyce (Con)Text: Danis Rose and the
Remaking of *Ulysses* Y-97

The New *Ulysses* Y-84

Jozsef, Attila 1905-1937 . . . . . DLB-215; CDWLB-4

Judd, Orange, Publishing Company DLB-49

Judd, Sylvester 1813-1853 . . . . DLB-1, 243

Judith circa 930 . . . . DLB-146

Julian of Norwich
1342-circa 1420 . . . . DLB-1146

Julius Caesar
100 B.C.-44 B.C. DLB-211; CDWLB-1

June, Jennie
(see Croly, Jane Cunningham)

Jung, Franz 1888-1963 . . . . DLB-118

Jünger, Ernst 1895- DLB-56; CDWLB-2

Der jüngere Titurel circa 1275 . . . . DLB-138

Jung-Stilling, Johann Heinrich
1740-1817 . . . . DLB-94

Justice, Donald 1925- Y-83

Juvenal circa A.D. 60-circa A.D. 130
 . . . . DLB-211; CDWLB-1

The Juvenile Library
(see Godwin, M. J., and Company)

K

Kacew, Romain (see Gary, Romain)

Kafka, Franz 1883-1924 . . . . . DLB-81; CDWLB-2

Kahn, Roger 1927- DLB-171

Kaikō Takeshi 1939-1989 . . . . DLB-182

Kaiser, Georg 1878-1945 . . . . DLB-124; CDWLB-2

Kaiserchronik circca 1147 . . . . DLB-148

Kaleb, Vjekoslav 1905- DLB-181

Kalechofsky, Roberta 1931- DLB-28

Kaler, James Otis 1848-1912 . . . . DLB-12

Kames, Henry Home, Lord
1696-1782 . . . . DLB-31, 104

Kamo no Chōmei (Kamo no Nagaakira)
1153 or 1155-1216 . . . . DLB-203

Kamo no Nagaakira (see Kamo no Chōmei)

Kampmann, Christian 1939-1988 . . . . DLB-214

Kandel, Lenore 1932- DLB-16

Kanin, Garson 1912-1999 . . . . DLB-7

Kant, Hermann 1926- DLB-75

Kant, Immanuel 1724-1804 . . . . DLB-94

Kantemir, Antiokh Dmitrievich
1708-1744 . . . . DLB-150

Kantor, MacKinlay 1904-1977 . . . . DLB-9, 102

Kanze Kōjirō Nobumitsu 1435-1516 . . . . DLB-203

Kanze Motokiyo (see Zeimi)

Kaplan, Fred 1937- DLB-111

Kaplan, Johanna 1942- DLB-28

Kaplan, Justin 1925- DLB-111; Y-86

The Practice of Biography V:
An Interview with Justin Kaplan Y-86

Kaplinski, Jaan 1941- DLB-232

Kapnist, Vasilii Vasilevich 1758?-1823 . . . DLB-150

Karadžić, Vuk Stefanović
1787-1864 . . . . DLB-147; CDWLB-4

Karamzin, Nikolai Mikhailovich
1766-1826 . . . . DLB-150

Karinthy, Frigyes 1887-1938 . . . . DLB-215

Karsch, Anna Louisa 1722-1791 . . . . DLB-97

Kasack, Hermann 1896-1966 . . . . DLB-69

Kasai, Zenzō 1887-1927 . . . . DLB-180

Kaschnitz, Marie Luise 1901-1974 . . . . DLB-69

Kassák, Lajos 1887-1967 . . . . DLB-215

Kaštelan, Jure 1919-1990 . . . . DLB-147

Kästner, Erich 1899-1974 . . . . DLB-56

Katenin, Pavel Aleksandrovich
1792-1853 . . . . DLB-205

Kattan, Naim 1928- DLB-53

Katz, Steve 1935- Y-83

Kauffman, Janet 1945- DLB-218; Y-86

Kauffmann, Samuel 1898-1971 . . . . DLB-127

Kaufman, Bob 1925- DLB-16, 41

Kaufman, George S. 1889-1961 . . . . DLB-7

Kavanagh, P. J. 1931- DLB-40

Kavanagh, Patrick 1904-1967 . . . . DLB-15, 20

Kawabata, Yasunari 1899-1972 . . . . DLB-180

Kay, Guy Gavriel 1954- DLB-251

Kaye-Smith, Sheila 1887-1956 . . . . DLB-36

Kazin, Alfred 1915-1998 . . . . DLB-67

Keane, John B. 1928- DLB-13

Keary, Annie 1825-1879 . . . . DLB-163

Keary, Eliza 1827-1918 . . . . DLB-240

Keating, H. R. F. 1926- DLB-87

Keatley, Charlotte 1960- DLB-245

Keats, Ezra Jack 1916-1983 . . . . DLB-61

Keats, John 1795-1821 . . . DLB-96, 110; CDBLB-3

Keble, John 1792-1866 . . . . DLB-32, 55

Keckley, Elizabeth 1818?-1907 . . . . DLB-239

Keeble, John 1944- Y-83

Keeffe, Barrie 1945- DLB-13, 245

Keeley, James 1867-1934 . . . . DLB-25

W. B. Keen, Cooke and Company DLB-49

Keillor, Garrison 1942- Y-87

Keith, Marian 1874?-1961 . . . . DLB-92

Keller, Gary D. 1943- DLB-82

Keller, Gottfried
1819-1890 . . . . DLB-129; CDWLB-2

Kelley, Edith Summers 1884-1956 . . . . DLB-9

Kelley, Emma Dunham ?-? DLB-221

Kelley, William Melvin 1937- DLB-33

Kellogg, Ansel Nash 1832-1886 . . . . DLB-23

Kellogg, Steven 1941- DLB-61

Kelly, George E. 1887-1974 . . . . DLB-7, 249

Kelly, Hugh 1739-1777 . . . . DLB-89

Kelly, Piet and Company DLB-49

Kelly, Robert 1935- DLB-5, 130, 165

Kelman, James 1946- DLB-194

Kelmscott Press DLB-112

Kemble, E. W. 1861-1933 . . . . DLB-188

Kemble, Fanny 1809-1893 . . . . DLB-32

Kemelman, Harry 1908- DLB-28

Kempe, Margery circa 1373-1438 . . . . DLB-146

Kempner, Friederike 1836-1904 . . . . DLB-129

Kempowski, Walter 1929- DLB-75

Kendall, Claude [publishing company] DLB-46

Kendall, Henry 1839-1882 . . . . DLB-230

Kendall, May 1861-1943 . . . . DLB-240

Kendell, George 1809-1867 . . . . DLB-43

Kenedy, P. J., and Sons DLB-49

Kenkō circa 1283-circa 1352 . . . . DLB-203

Kennan, George 1845-1924 . . . . DLB-189

Kennedy, Adrienne 1931- DLB-38

Kennedy, John Pendleton 1795-1870 . . DLB-3, 248

Kennedy, Leo 1907- DLB-88

Kennedy, Margaret 1896-1967 . . . . DLB-36

Kennedy, Patrick 1801-1873 . . . . DLB-159

Kennedy, Richard S. 1920- DLB-111

Kennedy, William 1928- DLB-143; Y-85

Kennedy, X. J. 1929- DLB-5

Kennelly, Brendan 1936- DLB-40

Kenner, Hugh 1923- DLB-67

Kennerley, Mitchell [publishing house] . . . DLB-46

Kenny, Maurice 1929- DLB-175

Kent, Frank R. 1877-1958 . . . . DLB-29

Kenyon, Jane 1947-1995 . . . . DLB-120

Keough, Hugh Edmund 1864-1912 . . . . . DLB-171

Keppler and Schwartzmann DLB-49

Ker, John, third Duke of Roxburghe
1740-1804 . . . . DLB-213

Ker, N. R. 1908-1982 . . . . DLB-201

Kerlan, Irvin 1912-1963 . . . . DLB-187

Kermode, Frank 1919- DLB-242

Kern, Jerome 1885-1945 . . . . DLB-187

Kernaghan, Eileen 1939- DLB-251

Kerner, Justinus 1776-1862 . . . . DLB-90

Kerouac, Jack 1922-1969 . . . DLB-2, 16, 237; DS-3; CDALB-1

The Jack Kerouac Revival Y-95

"Re-meeting of Old Friends": The Jack Kerouac Conference Y-82

Kerouac, Jan 1952-1996 . . . . DLB-16

Kerr, Charles H., and Company DLB-49

Kerr, Orpheus C. (see Newell, Robert Henry)

Kesey, Ken 1935- DLB-2, 16, 206; CDALB-6

Kessel, Joseph 1898-1979 . . . . DLB-72

Kessel, Martin 1901- DLB-56

Kesten, Hermann 1900- DLB-56

Keun, Irmgard 1905-1982 . . . . DLB-69

Key and Biddle DLB-49

Keynes, Sir Geoffrey 1887-1982 . . . . DLB-201

Keynes, John Maynard 1883-1946 . . . . DS-10

Keyserling, Eduard von 1855-1918 . . . . . . DLB-66

Khan, Ismith 1925- DLB-125

Khaytov, Nikolay 1919- DLB-181

Khemnitser, Ivan Ivanovich 1745-1784 . . . . DLB-150

Kheraskov, Mikhail Matveevich 1733-1807 . . . . DLB-150

Khomiakov, Aleksei Stepanovich 1804-1860 . . . . DLB-205

Khristov, Boris 1945- DLB-181

Khvoshchinskaia, Nadezhda Dmitrievna 1824-1889 . . . . DLB-238

Khvostov, Dmitrii Ivanovich 1757-1835 . . . . DLB-150

Kidd, Adam 1802?-1831 . . . . DLB-99

Kidd, William [publishing house] DLB-106

Kidder, Tracy 1945- DLB-185

Kiely, Benedict 1919- DLB-15

Kieran, John 1892-1981 . . . . DLB-171

Kiggins and Kellogg DLB-49

Kiley, Jed 1889-1962 . . . . DLB-4

Kilgore, Bernard 1908-1967 . . . . DLB-127

Kilian, Crawford 1941- DLB-251

Killens, John Oliver 1916- DLB-33

Killigrew, Anne 1660-1685 . . . . DLB-131

Killigrew, Thomas 1612-1683 . . . . DLB-58

Kilmer, Joyce 1886-1918 . . . . DLB-45

Kilroy, Thomas 1934- DLB-233

Kilwardby, Robert circa 1215-1279 . . . . . DLB-115

Kimball, Richard Burleigh 1816-1892 . . . . DLB-202

Kincaid, Jamaica 1949- DLB-157, 227; CDALB-7; CDWLB-3

King, Charles 1844-1933 . . . . DLB-186

King, Clarence 1842-1901 . . . . DLB-12

King, Florence 1936 . . . . Y-85

King, Francis 1923- DLB-15, 139

King, Grace 1852-1932 . . . . DLB-12, 78

King, Harriet Hamilton 1840-1920 . . . . . DLB-199

King, Henry 1592-1669 . . . . DLB-126

King, Solomon [publishing house] DLB-49

King, Stephen 1947- DLB-143; Y-80

King, Susan Petigru 1824-1875 . . . . DLB-239

King, Thomas 1943- DLB-175

King, Woodie, Jr. 1937- DLB-38

Kinglake, Alexander William 1809-1891 . . . . DLB-55, 166

Kingsbury, Donald 1929- DLB-251

Kingsley, Charles 1819-1875 . . . . DLB-21, 32, 163, 178, 190

Kingsley, Henry 1830-1876 . . . . DLB-21, 230

Kingsley, Mary Henrietta 1862-1900 . . . . . DLB-174

Kingsley, Sidney 1906- DLB-7

Kingsmill, Hugh 1889-1949 . . . . DLB-149

Kingsolver, Barbara 1955- DLB-206; CDALB-7

Kingston, Maxine Hong 1940- DLB-173, 212; Y-80; CDALB-7

Kingston, William Henry Giles 1814-1880 . . . . DLB-163

Kinnan, Mary Lewis 1763-1848 . . . . DLB-200

Kinnell, Galway 1927- DLB-5; Y-87

Kinsella, Thomas 1928- DLB-27

Kipling, Rudyard 1865-1936 . . . . DLB-19, 34, 141, 156; CDBLB-5

Kipphardt, Heinar 1922-1982 . . . . DLB-124

Kirby, William 1817-1906 . . . . DLB-99

Kircher, Athanasius 1602-1680 . . . . DLB-164

Kireevsky, Ivan Vasil'evich 1806-1856 . . . DLB-198

Kireevsky, Petr Vasil'evich 1808-1856 . . . DLB-205

Kirk, Hans 1898-1962 . . . . DLB-214

Kirk, John Foster 1824-1904 . . . . DLB-79

Kirkconnell, Watson 1895-1977 . . . . DLB-68

Kirkland, Caroline M. 1801-1864 . . . . . . DLB-3, 73, 74, 250; DS-13

Kirkland, Joseph 1830-1893 . . . . DLB-12

Kirkman, Francis [publishing house] DLB-170

Kirkpatrick, Clayton 1915- DLB-127

Kirkup, James 1918- DLB-27

Kirouac, Conrad (see Marie-Victorin, Frère)

Kirsch, Sarah 1935- DLB-75

Kirst, Hans Hellmut 1914-1989 . . . . DLB-69

Kiš, Danilo 1935-1989 . . . . . . DLB-181; CDWLB-4

Kita Morio 1927- DLB-182

Kitcat, Mabel Greenhow 1859-1922 . . . . . DLB-135

Kitchin, C. H. B. 1895-1967 . . . . DLB-77

Kittredge, William 1932- DLB-212, 244

Kiukhel'beker, Vil'gel'm Karlovich 1797-1846 . . . . DLB-205

Kizer, Carolyn 1925- DLB-5, 169

Klabund 1890-1928 . . . . DLB-66

Klaj, Johann 1616-1656 . . . . DLB-164

Klappert, Peter 1942- DLB-5

Klass, Philip (see Tenn, William)

Klein, A. M. 1909-1972 . . . . DLB-68

Kleist, Ewald von 1715-1759 . . . . DLB-97

Kleist, Heinrich von 1777-1811 . . . . DLB-90; CDWLB-2

Klinger, Friedrich Maximilian 1752-1831 . . . . DLB-94

Klíma, Ivan 1931- DLB-232; CDWLB-4

Kliushnikov, Viktor Petrovich 1841-1892 . . . . DLB-238

Oral History Interview with Donald S. Klopfer Y-97

Klopstock, Friedrich Gottlieb 1724-1803 . . . . DLB-97

Klopstock, Meta 1728-1758 . . . . DLB-97

Kluge, Alexander 1932- DLB-75

Knapp, Joseph Palmer 1864-1951 . . . . DLB-91

Knapp, Samuel Lorenzo 1783-1838 . . . . . . DLB-59

Knapton, J. J. and P. [publishing house] DLB-154

Kniazhnin, Iakov Borisovich 1740-1791 . . . . DLB-150

Knickerbocker, Diedrich (see Irving, Washington)

Knigge, Adolph Franz Friedrich Ludwig, Freiherr von 1752-1796 . . . . DLB-94

Knight, Charles, and Company DLB-106

Knight, Damon 1922- DLB-8

Knight, Etheridge 1931-1992 . . . . DLB-41

Knight, John S. 1894-1981 . . . . DLB-29

Knight, Sarah Kemble 1666-1727 . . . . DLB-24, 200

Knight-Bruce, G. W. H. 1852-1896 . . . . . DLB-174

Knister, Raymond 1899-1932 . . . . DLB-68

Knoblock, Edward 1874-1945 . . . . DLB-10

Knopf, Alfred A. 1892-1984 . . . . Y-84

Knopf, Alfred A. [publishing house] DLB-46

Knopf to Hammett: The Editoral Correspondence Y-00

Knorr von Rosenroth, Christian 1636-1689 . . . . DLB-168

"Knots into Webs: Some Autobiographical Sources," by Dabney Stuart DLB-105

Knowles, John 1926- DLB-6; CDALB-6

Knox, Frank 1874-1944 . . . . DLB-29

Knox, John circa 1514-1572 . . . . DLB-132

Knox, John Armoy 1850-1906 . . . . DLB-23

Knox, Lucy 1845-1884 . . . . DLB-240

Knox, Ronald Arbuthnott 1888-1957 . . . . . DLB-77

Knox, Thomas Wallace 1835-1896 . . . . . . DLB-189

Kobayashi Takiji 1903-1933 . . . . DLB-180

Kober, Arthur 1900-1975 . . . . DLB-11

Kobiakova, Aleksandra Petrovna 1823-1892 . . . . DLB-238

Kocbek, Edvard 1904-1981 . . . DLB-147; CDWB-4

Koch, Howard 1902- DLB-26

Koch, Kenneth 1925- DLB-5

Kōda, Rohan 1867-1947 . . . . DLB-180

Koenigsberg, Moses 1879-1945 . . . . DLB-25

Koeppen, Wolfgang 1906-1996 . . . . DLB-69

Koertge, Ronald 1940- DLB-105

Koestler, Arthur 1905-1983 . . . . . . Y-83; CDBLB-7

Kohn, John S. Van E. 1906-1976 and Papantonio, Michael 1907-1978 ..... DLB-187

Kokoschka, Oskar 1886-1980 .... DLB-124

Kolb, Annette 1870-1967 .... DLB-66

Kolbenheyer, Erwin Guido 1878-1962 .... DLB-66, 124

Kolleritsch, Alfred 1931- DLB-85

Kolodny, Annette 1941- DLB-67

Kol'tsov, Aleksei Vasil'evich 1809-1842 .... DLB-205

Komarov, Matvei circa 1730-1812 ...... DLB-150

Komroff, Manuel 1890-1974 .... DLB-4

Komunyakaa, Yusef 1947- DLB-120

Koneski, Blaže 1921-1993 ... DLB-181; CDWLB-4

Konigsburg, E. L. 1930- DLB-52

Konparu Zenchiku 1405-1468? DLB-203

Konrád, György 1933- DLB-232; CDWLB-4

Konrad von Würzburg circa 1230-1287 .... DLB-138

Konstantinov, Aleko 1863-1897 .... DLB-147

Konwicki, Tadeusz 1926- DLB-232

Kooser, Ted 1939- DLB-105

Kopit, Arthur 1937- DLB-7

Kops, Bernard 1926?- DLB-13

Kornbluth, C. M. 1923-1958 .... DLB-8

Körner, Theodor 1791-1813 .... DLB-90

Kornfeld, Paul 1889-1942 .... DLB-118

Kosinski, Jerzy 1933-1991 .... DLB-2; Y-82

Kosmač, Ciril 1910-1980 .... DLB-181

Kosovel, Srečko 1904-1926 .... DLB-147

Kostrov, Ermil Ivanovich 1755-1796 ..... DLB-150

Kotzebue, August von 1761-1819 .... DLB-94

Kotzwinkle, William 1938- DLB-173

Kovačić, Ante 1854-1889 .... DLB-147

Kovič, Kajetan 1931- DLB-181

Kozlov, Ivan Ivanovich 1779-1840 ...... DLB-205

Kraf, Elaine 1946- Y-81

Kramer, Jane 1938- DLB-185

Kramer, Larry 1935- DLB-249

Kramer, Mark 1944- DLB-185

Kranjčević, Silvije Strahimir 1865-1908 .... DLB-147

Krasko, Ivan 1876-1958 .... DLB-215

Krasna, Norman 1909-1984 .... DLB-26

Kraus, Hans Peter 1907-1988 .... DLB-187

Kraus, Karl 1874-1936 .... DLB-118

Krauss, Ruth 1911-1993 .... DLB-52

Kreisel, Henry 1922- DLB-88

Krestovsky V. (see Khvoshchinskaia, Nadezhda Dmitrievna)

Krestovsky, Vsevolod Vladimirovich 1839-1895 .... DLB-238

Kreuder, Ernst 1903-1972 .... DLB-69

Krėvė-Mickevičius, Vincas 1882-1954 ... DLB-220

Kreymborg, Alfred 1883-1966 ...... DLB-4, 54

Krieger, Murray 1923- DLB-67

Krim, Seymour 1922-1989 .... DLB-16

Kristensen, Tom 1893-1974 .... DLB-214

Kristeva, Julia 1941- DLB-242

Krleža, Miroslav 1893-1981 ..DLB-147; CDWLB-4

Krock, Arthur 1886-1974 .... DLB-29

Kroetsch, Robert 1927- DLB-53

Kross, Jaan 1920- DLB-232

Krúdy, Gyula 1878-1933 .... DLB-215

Krutch, Joseph Wood 1893-1970 .... DLB-63, 206

Krylov, Ivan Andreevich 1769-1844 .... DLB-150

Kubin, Alfred 1877-1959 .... DLB-81

Kubrick, Stanley 1928-1999 .... DLB-26

Kudrun circa 1230-1240 .... DLB-138

Kuffstein, Hans Ludwig von 1582-1656 .... DLB-164

Kuhlmann, Quirinus 1651-1689 .... DLB-168

Kuhnau, Johann 1660-1722 .... DLB-168

Kukol'nik, Nestor Vasil'evich 1809-1868 .... DLB-205

Kukučín, Martin 1860-1928 .... DLB-215; CDWLB-4

Kumin, Maxine 1925- DLB-5

Kuncewicz, Maria 1895-1989 .... DLB-215

Kundera, Milan 1929- DLB-232; CDWLB-4

Kunene, Mazisi 1930- DLB-117

Kunikida, Doppo 1869-1908 .... DLB-180

Kunitz, Stanley 1905- DLB-48

Kunjufu, Johari M. (see Amini, Johari M.)

Kunnert, Gunter 1929- DLB-75

Kunze, Reiner 1933- DLB-75

Kupferberg, Tuli 1923- DLB-16

Kurahashi Yumiko 1935- DLB-182

Kureishi, Hanif 1954- DLB-194, 245

Kürnberger, Ferdinand 1821-1879 ..... DLB-129

Kurz, Isolde 1853-1944 .... DLB-66

Kusenberg, Kurt 1904-1983 .... DLB-69

Kushchevsky, Ivan Afanas'evich 1847-1876 .... DLB-238

Kushner, Tony 1956- DLB-228

Kuttner, Henry 1915-1958 .... DLB-8

Kyd, Thomas 1558-1594 .... DLB-62

Kyffin, Maurice circa 1560?-1598 ...... DLB-136

Kyger, Joanne 1934- DLB-16

Kyne, Peter B. 1880-1957 .... DLB-78

Kyōgoku Tamekane 1254-1332 .... DLB-203

L

L. E. L. (see Landon, Letitia Elizabeth)

Laberge, Albert 1871-1960 .... DLB-68

Laberge, Marie 1950- DLB-60

Labiche, Eugène 1815-1888 .... DLB-192

Labrunie, Gerard (see Nerval, Gerard de)

La Capria, Raffaele 1922- DLB-196

Lacombe, Patrice (see Trullier-Lacombe, Joseph Patrice)

Lacretelle, Jacques de 1888-1985 .... DLB-65

Lacy, Ed 1911-1968 .... DLB-226

Lacy, Sam 1903- DLB-171

Ladd, Joseph Brown 1764-1786 .... DLB-37

La Farge, Oliver 1901-1963 .... DLB-9

Laffan, Mrs. R. S. de Courcy (see Adams, Bertha Leith)

Lafferty, R. A. 1914- DLB-8

La Flesche, Francis 1857-1932 ....DLB-175

Laforge, Jules 1860-1887 ....DLB-217

Lagorio, Gina 1922- DLB-196

La Guma, Alex 1925-1985 .... DLB-117, 225; CDWLB-3

Lahaise, Guillaume (see Delahaye, Guy)

Lahontan, Louis-Armand de Lom d'Arce, Baron de 1666-1715? DLB-99

Laing, Kojo 1946- DLB-157

Laird, Carobeth 1895- Y-82

Laird and Lee DLB-49

Lalić, Ivan V. 1931-1996 .... DLB-181

Lalić, Mihailo 1914-1992 .... DLB-181

Lalonde, Michèle 1937- DLB-60

Lamantia, Philip 1927- DLB-16

Lamartine, Alphonse de 1790-1869 ......DLB-217

Lamb, Lady Caroline 1785-1828 .... DLB-116

Lamb, Charles 1775-1834 .... DLB-93, 107, 163; CDBLB-3

Lamb, Mary 1764-1874 .... DLB-163

Lambert, Betty 1933-1983 .... DLB-60

Lamming, George 1927- ...DLB-125; CDWLB-3

L'Amour, Louis 1908-1988 ....DLB-206; Y-80

Lampman, Archibald 1861-1899 .... DLB-92

Lamson, Wolffe and Company DLB-49

Lancer Books DLB-46

Landesman, Jay 1919- and Landesman, Fran 1927- DLB-16

Landolfi, Tommaso 1908-1979 ....DLB-177

Landon, Letitia Elizabeth 1802-1838 ..... DLB-96

Landor, Walter Savage 1775-1864 ....DLB-93, 107

Landry, Napoléon-P. 1884-1956 .... DLB-92

Lane, Charles 1800-1870 .... DLB-1, 223

Lane, F. C. 1885-1984 .... DLB-241

Lane, John, Company DLB-49

Lane, Laurence W. 1890-1967 .... DLB-91

Lane, M. Travis 1934- DLB-60

Lane, Patrick 1939- DLB-53

Lane, Pinkie Gordon 1923- DLB-41

Laney, Al 1896-1988 ....DLB-4, 171

Lang, Andrew 1844-1912 ......DLB-98, 141, 184

Langevin, André 1927- DLB-60

Langgässer, Elisabeth 1899-1950 .... DLB-69

Langhorne, John 1735-1779 .... DLB-109

Langland, William circa 1330-circa 1400 .... DLB-146

Langton, Anna 1804-1893 . . . . DLB-99	Lawrence, D. H. 1885-1930 . . . . . DLB-10, 19, 36, 98, 162, 195; CDBLB-6	Lee, Li-Young 1957- DLB-165
Lanham, Edwin 1904-1979 . . . . .DLB-4	Lawrence, David 1888-1973 . . . . DLB-29	Lee, Manfred B. (see Dannay, Frederic, and Manfred B. Lee)
Lanier, Sidney 1842-1881 . . . . .DLB-64; DS-13	Lawrence, Jerome 1915- and Lee, Robert E. 1918-1994 . . . . .DLB-228	Lee, Nathaniel circa 1645-1692 . . . . .DLB-80
Lanyer, Aemilia 1569-1645 . . . . DLB-121	Lawrence, Seymour 1926-1994 . . . . Y-94	Lee, Sir Sidney 1859-1926 . . . . DLB-149, 184
Lapointe, Gatien 1931-1983. . . . . .DLB-88	Lawrence, T. E. 1888-1935 . . . . .DLB-195	Lee, Sir Sidney, "Principles of Biography," in *Elizabethan and Other Essays* DLB-149
Lapointe, Paul-Marie 1929- DLB-88	Lawson, George 1598-1678 . . . . DLB-213	Lee, Vernon 1856-1935 . . . . DLB-57, 153, 156, 174, 178
Larcom, Lucy 1824-1893. . . . . .DLB-221, 243	Lawson, Henry 1867-1922. . . . . DLB-230	
Lardner, John 1912-1960. . . . . DLB-171	Lawson, John ?-1711 . . . . .DLB-24	Lee and Shepard DLB-49
Lardner, Ring 1885-1933 . . . . . . DLB-11, 25, 86, 171; DS-16; CDALB-4	Lawson, John Howard 1894-1977 . . . . . . .DLB-228	Le Fanu, Joseph Sheridan 1814-1873 . . . . DLB-21, 70, 159, 178
Lardner 100: Ring Lardner Centennial Symposium Y-85	Lawson, Louisa Albury 1848-1920 . . . . . . .DLB-230	Leffland, Ella 1931- Y-84
	Lawson, Robert 1892-1957 . . . . .DLB-22	le Fort, Gertrud von 1876-1971 . . . . DLB-66
Lardner, Ring, Jr. 1915-2000 . . . . DLB-26, Y-00	Lawson, Victor F. 1850-1925. . . . . .DLB-25	Le Gallienne, Richard 1866-1947 . . . . DLB-4
Larkin, Philip 1922-1985 . . . . . .DLB-27; CDBLB-8	Layard, Sir Austen Henry 1817-1894 . . . . .DLB-166	Legaré, Hugh Swinton 1797-1843. . . . . DLB-3, 59, 73, 248
La Roche, Sophie von 1730-1807. . . . . DLB-94		
La Rocque, Gilbert 1943-1984. . . . . DLB-60	Layton, Irving 1912- DLB-88	Legaré, James Mathewes 1823-1859 . . . DLB-3, 248
Laroque de Roquebrune, Robert (see Roquebrune, Robert de)	LaZamon flourished circa 1200 . . . . .DLB-146	The Legends of the Saints and a Medieval Christian Worldview DLB-148
	Lazarević, Laza K. 1851-1890 . . . . .DLB-147	
Larrick, Nancy 1910- DLB-61	Lazarus, George 1904-1997 . . . . .DLB-201	Léger, Antoine-J. 1880-1950 . . . . .DLB-88
Larsen, Nella 1893-1964 . . . . .DLB-51	Lazhechnikov, Ivan Ivanovich 1792-1869 . . . . .DLB-198	Leggett, William 1801-1839. . . . . .DLB-250
La Sale, Antoine de circa 1386-1460/1467 . . . . DLB-208		Le Guin, Ursula K. 1929- DLB-8, 52; CDALB-6
	Lea, Henry Charles 1825-1909 . . . . .DLB-47	
Lasch, Christopher 1932-1994. . . . . .DLB-246	Lea, Sydney 1942- DLB-120	Lehman, Ernest 1920- DLB-44
Lasker-Schüler, Else 1869-1945 . . . . . .DLB-66, 124	Lea, Tom 1907- DLB-6	Lehmann, John 1907- DLB-27, 100
Lasnier, Rina 1915- DLB-88	Leacock, John 1729-1802 . . . . DLB-31	Lehmann, John, Limited DLB-112
Lassalle, Ferdinand 1825-1864. . . . . .DLB-129	Leacock, Stephen 1869-1944 . . . . .DLB-92	Lehmann, Rosamond 1901-1990. . . . . . . .DLB-15
Latham, Robert 1912-1995 . . . . .DLB-201	Lead, Jane Ward 1623-1704. . . . . .DLB-131	Lehmann, Wilhelm 1882-1968 . . . . .DLB-56
Lathrop, Dorothy P. 1891-1980. . . . . .DLB-22	Leadenhall Press DLB-106	Leiber, Fritz 1910-1992 . . . . .DLB-8
Lathrop, George Parsons 1851-1898 . . . . . . DLB-71	Leakey, Caroline Woolmer 1827-1881 . . .DLB-230	Leibniz, Gottfried Wilhelm 1646-1716. . . . DLB-168
Lathrop, John, Jr. 1772-1820 . . . . .DLB-37	Leapor, Mary 1722-1746 . . . . DLB-109	Leicester University Press DLB-112
Latimer, Hugh 1492?-1555 . . . . .DLB-136	Lear, Edward 1812-1888 . . . . . . .DLB-32, 163, 166	Leigh, W. R. 1866-1955 . . . . .DLB-188
Latimore, Jewel Christine McLawler (see Amini, Johari M.)	Leary, Timothy 1920-1996 . . . . .DLB-16	Leinster, Murray 1896-1975 . . . . DLB-8
	Leary, W. A., and Company DLB-49	Leiser, Bill 1898-1965 . . . . .DLB-241
Latymer, William 1498-1583 . . . . .DLB-132	Léautaud, Paul 1872-1956 . . . . .DLB-65	Leisewitz, Johann Anton 1752-1806. . . . . . . DLB-94
Laube, Heinrich 1806-1884 . . . . .DLB-133	Leavis, F. R. 1895-1978 . . . . .DLB-242	Leitch, Maurice 1933- DLB-14
Laud, William 1573-1645 . . . . .DLB-213	Leavitt, David 1961- DLB-130	Leithauser, Brad 1943- DLB-120
Laughlin, James 1914-1997 . . . . DLB-48; Y-96	Leavitt and Allen DLB-49	Leland, Charles G. 1824-1903 . . . . .DLB-11
James Laughlin Tributes Y-97	Le Blond, Mrs. Aubrey 1861-1934 . . . . . . DLB-174	
Conversations with Publishers IV: An Interview with James Laughlin Y-96	le Carré, John 1931- DLB-87; CDBLB-8	Leland, John 1503?-1552. . . . . .DLB-136
		Lemay, Pamphile 1837-1918 . . . . .DLB-99
Laumer, Keith 1925- DLB-8	Lécavelé, Roland (see Dorgeles, Roland)	Lemelin, Roger 1919- DLB-88
Lauremberg, Johann 1590-1658. . . . . .DLB-164	Lechlitner, Ruth 1901- DLB-48	Lemercier, Louis-Jean-Népomucène 1771-1840 . . . . .DLB-192
Laurence, Margaret 1926-1987 . . . . .DLB-53	Leclerc, Félix 1914- DLB-60	
Laurentius von Schnüffis 1633-1702 . . . . .DLB-168	Le Clézio, J. M. G. 1940- DLB-83	Le Moine, James MacPherson 1825-1912. . . . . .DLB-99
Laurents, Arthur 1918- DLB-26	*Lectures on Rhetoric and Belles Lettres* (1783), by Hugh Blair [excerpts] DLB-31	
Laurie, Annie (see Black, Winifred)		Lemon, Mark 1809-1870 . . . . .DLB-163
Laut, Agnes Christiana 1871-1936 . . . . . . .DLB-92	Leder, Rudolf (see Hermlin, Stephan)	Le Moyne, Jean 1913- DLB-88
Lauterbach, Ann 1942- DLB-193	Lederer, Charles 1910-1976. . . . . .DLB-26	Lemperly, Paul 1858-1939. . . . . .DLB-187
Lautreamont, Isidore Lucien Ducasse, Comte de 1846-1870 . . . . DLB-217	Ledwidge, Francis 1887-1917 . . . . .DLB-20	L'Engle, Madeleine 1918- DLB-52
	Lee, Dennis 1939- DLB-53	Lennart, Isobel 1915-1971 . . . . .DLB-44
Lavater, Johann Kaspar 1741-1801 . . . . . . .DLB-97	Lee, Don L. (see Madhubuti, Haki R.)	Lennox, Charlotte 1729 or 1730-1804. . . . . .DLB-39
Lavin, Mary 1912-1996 . . . . .DLB-15	Lee, George W. 1894-1976 . . . . .DLB-51	
Law, John (see Harkness, Margaret)	Lee, Harper 1926- DLB-6; CDALB-1	Lenox, James 1800-1880 . . . . .DLB-140
Lawes, Henry 1596-1662. . . . . .DLB-126	Lee, Harriet (1757-1851) and Lee, Sophia (1750-1824) DLB-39	Lenski, Lois 1893-1974 . . . . .DLB-22
Lawless, Anthony (see MacDonald, Philip)		Lentricchia, Frank 1940- DLB-246
Lawless, Emily (The Hon. Emily Lawless) 1845-1913 DLB-240	Lee, Laurie 1914-1997 . . . . .DLB-27	Lenz, Hermann 1913-1998 . . . . .DLB-69

371

Cumulative Index DLB 251

Lenz, J. M. R. 1751-1792 .... DLB-94
Lenz, Siegfried 1926- DLB-75
Leonard, Elmore 1925- DLB-173, 226
Leonard, Hugh 1926- DLB-13
Leonard, William Ellery 1876-1944 ...... DLB-54
Leonowens, Anna 1834-1914 .... DLB-99, 166
LePan, Douglas 1914- DLB-88
Lepik, Kalju 1920-1999 .... DLB-232
Leprohon, Rosanna Eleanor 1829-1879 ... DLB-99
Le Queux, William 1864-1927 .... DLB-70
Lermontov, Mikhail Iur'evich
   1814-1841 .... DLB-205
Lerner, Max 1902-1992 .... DLB-29
Lernet-Holenia, Alexander 1897-1976 ..... DLB-85
Le Rossignol, James 1866-1969 .... DLB-92
Lescarbot, Marc circa 1570-1642 .... DLB-99
LeSeur, William Dawson 1840-1917 ..... DLB-92
LeSieg, Theo. (see Geisel, Theodor Seuss)
Leskov, Nikolai Semenovich 1831-1895 .. DLB-238
Leslie, Doris before 1902-1982 .... DLB-191
Leslie, Eliza 1787-1858 .... DLB-202
Leslie, Frank 1821-1880 .... DLB-43, 79
Leslie, Frank, Publishing House DLB-49
Leśmian, Bolesław 1878-1937 .... DLB-215
Lesperance, John 1835?-1891 .... DLB-99
Lessing, Bruno 1870-1940 .... DLB-28
Lessing, Doris
   1919- DLB-15, 139; Y-85; CDBLB-8
Lessing, Gotthold Ephraim
   1729-1781 .... DLB-97; CDWLB-2
Lettau, Reinhard 1929- DLB-75
Letter from Japan Y-94, Y-98
Letter from London Y-96
Letter to [Samuel] Richardson on *Clarissa*
   (1748), by Henry Fielding DLB-39
A Letter to the Editor of *The Irish Times* Y-97
Lever, Charles 1806-1872 .... DLB-21
Lever, Ralph ca. 1527-1585 .... DLB-236
Leverson, Ada 1862-1933 .... DLB-153
Levertov, Denise
   1923-1997 .... DLB-5, 165; CDALB-7
Levi, Peter 1931- DLB-40
Levi, Primo 1919-1987 .... DLB-177
Lévi-Strauss, Claude 1908- DLB-242
Levien, Sonya 1888-1960 .... DLB-44
Levin, Meyer 1905-1981 .... DLB-9, 28; Y-81
Levine, Norman 1923- DLB-88
Levine, Philip 1928- DLB-5
Levis, Larry 1946- DLB-120
Levy, Amy 1861-1889 .... DLB-156, 240
Levy, Benn Wolfe 1900-1973 .... DLB-13; Y-81
Lewald, Fanny 1811-1889 .... DLB-129
Lewes, George Henry 1817-1878 .... DLB-55, 144
"Criticism In Relation To
   Novels" (1863) DLB-21

The Principles of Success in Literature
   (1865) [excerpt] DLB-57
Lewis, Agnes Smith 1843-1926 .... DLB-174
Lewis, Alfred H. 1857-1914 .... DLB-25, 186
Lewis, Alun 1915-1944 .... DLB-20, 162
Lewis, C. Day (see Day Lewis, C.)
Lewis, C. S.
   1898-1963 ..... DLB-15, 100, 160; CDBLB-7
Lewis, Charles B. 1842-1924 .... DLB-11
Lewis, Henry Clay 1825-1850 .... DLB-3, 248
Lewis, Janet 1899-1999 .... Y-87
Lewis, Matthew Gregory
   1775-1818 .... DLB-39, 158, 178
Lewis, Meriwether 1774-1809 and
   Clark, William 1770-1838 ..... DLB-183, 186
Lewis, Norman 1908- DLB-204
Lewis, R. W. B. 1917- DLB-111
Lewis, Richard circa 1700-1734 .... DLB-24
Lewis, Sinclair
   1885-1951 ..... DLB-9, 102; DS-1; CDALB-4
Sinclair Lewis Centennial Conference Y-85
Lewis, Wilmarth Sheldon 1895-1979 .... DLB-140
Lewis, Wyndham 1882-1957 .... DLB-15
Lewisohn, Ludwig 1882-1955 ...DLB-4, 9, 28, 102
Leyendecker, J. C. 1874-1951 .... DLB-188
Lezama Lima, José 1910-1976 .... DLB-113
L'Heureux, John 1934- DLB-244
Libbey, Laura Jean 1862-1924 .... DLB-221
The Library of America DLB-46
The Licensing Act of 1737 .... DLB-84
Lichfield, Leonard I [publishing house] ...DLB-170
Lichtenberg, Georg Christoph 1742-1799 .. DLB-94
The Liddle Collection Y-97
Lieb, Fred 1888-1980 ....DLB-171
Liebling, A. J. 1904-1963 ....DLB-4, 171
Lieutenant Murray (see Ballou, Maturin Murray)
Lighthall, William Douw 1857-1954 ...... DLB-92
Lilar, Françoise (see Mallet-Joris, Françoise)
Lili'uokalani, Queen 1838-1917 .... DLB-221
Lillo, George 1691-1739 .... DLB-84
Lilly, J. K., Jr. 1893-1966 .... DLB-140
Lilly, Wait and Company DLB-49
Lily, William circa 1468-1522 .... DLB-132
Limited Editions Club DLB-46
Limón, Graciela 1938- DLB-209
Lincoln and Edmands DLB-49
Lindesay, Ethel Forence
   (see Richardson, Henry Handel)
Lindsay, Alexander William, Twenty-fifth Earl
   of Crawford 1812-1880 .... DLB-184
Lindsay, Sir David circa 1485-1555 ..... DLB-132
Lindsay, Jack 1900- Y-84
Lindsay, Lady (Caroline Blanche Elizabeth Fitzroy
   Lindsay) 1844-1912 .... DLB-199
Lindsay, Vachel 1879-1931 .... DLB-54; CDALB-3
Linebarger, Paul Myron Anthony
   (see Smith, Cordwainer)

Link, Arthur S. 1920-1998 .... DLB-17
Linn, Ed 1922-2000 .... DLB-241
Linn, John Blair 1777-1804 .... DLB-37
Lins, Osman 1924-1978 .... DLB-145
Linton, Eliza Lynn 1822-1898 .... DLB-18
Linton, William James 1812-1897 .... DLB-32
Lintot, Barnaby Bernard
   [publishing house] DLB-170
Lion Books DLB-46
Lionni, Leo 1910-1999 .... DLB-61
Lippard, George 1822-1854 .... DLB-202
Lippincott, J. B., Company DLB-49
Lippincott, Sara Jane Clarke 1823-1904 ... DLB-43
Lippmann, Walter 1889-1974 .... DLB-29
Lipton, Lawrence 1898-1975 .... DLB-16
Liscow, Christian Ludwig 1701-1760 ..... DLB-97
Lish, Gordon 1934- DLB-130
Lisle, Charles-Marie-René Leconte de
   1818-1894 ....DLB-217
Lispector, Clarice
   1925-1977 ....DLB-113; CDWLB-3
A Literary Archaeologist Digs On: A Brief
   Interview with Michael Reynolds by
   Michael Rogers Y-99
The Literary Chronicle and Weekly Review
   1819-1828 .... DLB-110
Literary Documents: William Faulkner
   and the People-to-People Program....... Y-86
Literary Documents II: *Library Journal*
   Statements and Questionnaires from
   First Novelists Y-87
Literary Effects of World War II
   [British novel] DLB-15
Literary Prizes Y-00
Literary Prizes [British] DLB-15
Literary Research Archives: The Humanities
   Research Center, University of Texas..... Y-82
Literary Research Archives II: Berg Collection
   of English and American Literature of
   the New York Public Library........... Y-83
Literary Research Archives III:
   The Lilly Library Y-84
Literary Research Archives IV:
   The John Carter Brown Library Y-85
Literary Research Archives V:
   Kent State Special Collections Y-86
Literary Research Archives VI: The Modern
   Literary Manuscripts Collection in the
   Special Collections of the Washington
   University Libraries Y-87
Literary Research Archives VII:
   The University of Virginia Libraries Y-91
Literary Research Archives VIII:
   The Henry E. Huntington Library Y-92
Literary Research Archives IX:
   Special Collections at Boston University .. Y-99
The Literary Scene and Situation and ... Who
   (Besides Oprah) Really Runs American
   Literature? Y-99
Literary Societies Y-98, Y-99, Y-00
"Literary Style" (1857), by William
   Forsyth [excerpt] DLB-57

Literatura Chicanesca: The View From
  Without........................DLB-82
Literature at Nurse, or Circulating Morals (1885),
  by George Moore DLB-18
Littell, Eliakim 1797-1870 ....DLB-79
Littell, Robert S. 1831-1896............DLB-79
Little, Brown and Company DLB-49
Little Magazines and Newspapers DS-15
The Little Review 1914-1929 .... DS-15
Littlewood, Joan 1914- DLB-13
Lively, Penelope 1933- DLB-14, 161, 207
Liverpool University Press DLB-112
The Lives of the Poets....................DLB-142
Livesay, Dorothy 1909- DLB-68
Livesay, Florence Randal 1874-1953 ......DLB-92
"Living in Ruin," by Gerald Stern.......DLB-105
Livings, Henry 1929-1998.............DLB-13
Livingston, Anne Howe 1763-1841 ... DLB-37, 200
Livingston, Myra Cohn 1926-1996.......DLB-61
Livingston, William 1723-1790 ....DLB-31
Livingstone, David 1813-1873 ....DLB-166
Livingstone, Douglas 1932-1996 ....DLB-225
Livy 59 B.C.-A.D. 17 ....DLB-211; CDWLB-1
Liyong, Taban lo (see Taban lo Liyong)
Lizárraga, Sylvia S. 1925- DLB-82
Llewellyn, Richard 1906-1983...........DLB-15
Lloyd, Edward [publishing house].......DLB-106
Lobel, Arnold 1933- DLB-61
Lochridge, Betsy Hopkins (see Fancher, Betsy)
Locke, David Ross 1833-1888........DLB-11, 23
Locke, John 1632-1704.........DLB-31, 101, 213
Locke, Richard Adams 1800-1871 ....DLB-43
Locker-Lampson, Frederick
  1821-1895 ....DLB-35, 184
Lockhart, John Gibson
  1794-1854 .... DLB-110, 116, 144
Lockridge, Ross, Jr. 1914-1948 .... DLB-143; Y-80
Locrine and Selimus.....................DLB-62
Lodge, David 1935- DLB-14, 194
Lodge, George Cabot 1873-1909.........DLB-54
Lodge, Henry Cabot 1850-1924 ....DLB-47
Lodge, Thomas 1558-1625 ....DLB-172
From *Defence of Poetry* (1579) DLB-172
Loeb, Harold 1891-1974 ....DLB-4
Loeb, William 1905-1981 ....DLB-127
Lofting, Hugh 1886-1947..............DLB-160
Logan, Deborah Norris 1761-1839 ......DLB-200
Logan, James 1674-1751............DLB-24, 140
Logan, John 1923- DLB-5
Logan, Martha Daniell 1704?-1779 ......DLB-200
Logan, William 1950- DLB-120
Logau, Friedrich von 1605-1655 ....DLB-164
Logue, Christopher 1926- DLB-27
Lohenstein, Daniel Casper von
  1635-1683 ....DLB-168

Lomonosov, Mikhail Vasil'evich
  1711-1765........................DLB-150
London, Jack
  1876-1916 ..... DLB-8, 12, 78, 212; CDALB-3
The London Magazine 1820-1829 ....DLB-110
Long, David 1948- DLB-244
Long, H., and Brother DLB-49
Long, Haniel 1888-1956 ....DLB-45
Long, Ray 1878-1935..................DLB-137
Longfellow, Henry Wadsworth
  1807-1882 ....DLB-1, 59, 235; CDALB-2
Longfellow, Samuel 1819-1892 ....DLB-1
Longford, Elizabeth 1906- DLB-155
Longinus circa first century DLB-176
Longley, Michael 1939- DLB-40
Longman, T. [publishing house] DLB-154
Longmans, Green and Company DLB-49
Longmore, George 1793?-1867 ....DLB-99
Longstreet, Augustus Baldwin
  1790-1870 .... DLB-3, 11, 74, 248
Longworth, D. [publishing house].......DLB-49
Lonsdale, Frederick 1881-1954 ....DLB-10
A Look at the Contemporary Black Theatre
  Movement.....................DLB-38
Loos, Anita 1893-1981..... DLB-11, 26, 228; Y-81
Lopate, Phillip 1943- Y-80
López, Diana
  (see Isabella, Ríos)
López, Josefina 1969- DLB-209
Loranger, Jean-Aubert 1896-1942 ....DLB-92
Lorca, Federico García 1898-1936.......DLB-108
Lord, John Keast 1818-1872 ....DLB-99
The Lord Chamberlain's Office and Stage
  Censorship in England DLB-10
Lorde, Audre 1934-1992 ....DLB-41
Lorimer, George Horace 1867-1939 ......DLB-91
Loring, A. K. [publishing house] DLB-49
Loring and Mussey DLB-46
Lorris, Guillaume de (see *Roman de la Rose*)
Lossing, Benson J. 1813-1891 ....DLB-30
Lothar, Ernst 1890-1974 ....DLB-81
Lothrop, D., and Company............DLB-49
Lothrop, Harriet M. 1844-1924..........DLB-42
Loti, Pierre 1850-1923 ....DLB-123
Lotichius Secundus, Petrus 1528-1560 ... DLB-179
Lott, Emeline ?-? DLB-166
Louisiana State University Press Y-97
The Lounger, no. 20 (1785), by Henry
  Mackenzie......................DLB-39
Lounsbury, Thomas R. 1838-1915 ....DLB-71
Louÿs, Pierre 1870-1925 ....DLB-123
Lovelace, Earl 1935- DLB-125; CDWLB-3
Lovelace, Richard 1618-1657...........DLB-131
Lovell, Coryell and Company..........DLB-49
Lovell, John W., Company DLB-49
Lover, Samuel 1797-1868.........DLB-159, 190
Lovesey, Peter 1936- DLB-87

Lovinescu, Eugen
  1881-1943 .... DLB-220; CDWLB-4
Lovingood, Sut
  (see Harris, George Washington)
Low, Samuel 1765-? DLB-37
Lowell, Amy 1874-1925............DLB-54, 140
Lowell, James Russell 1819-1891
  ...... DLB-1, 11, 64, 79, 189, 235; CDALB-2
Lowell, Robert 1917-1977 ..DLB-5, 169; CDALB-7
Lowenfels, Walter 1897-1976............DLB-4
Lowndes, Marie Belloc 1868-1947........DLB-70
Lowndes, William Thomas 1798-1843 ...DLB-184
Lownes, Humphrey [publishing house]... DLB-170
Lowry, Lois 1937- DLB-52
Lowry, Malcolm 1909-1957....DLB-15; CDBLB-7
Lowther, Pat 1935-1975.................DLB-53
Loy, Mina 1882-1966 ....DLB-4, 54
Lozeau, Albert 1878-1924 ....DLB-92
Lubbock, Percy 1879-1965 ....DLB-149
Lucan A.D. 39-A.D. 65 ....DLB-211
Lucas, E. V. 1868-1938 .... DLB-98, 149, 153
Lucas, Fielding, Jr. [publishing house] DLB-49
Luce, Clare Booth 1903-1987 ....DLB-228
Luce, Henry R. 1898-1967 ....DLB-91
Luce, John W., and Company..........DLB-46
Lucian circa 120-180 .... DLB-176
Lucie-Smith, Edward 1933- DLB-40
Lucilius circa 180 B.C.-102/101 B.C......DLB-211
Lucini, Gian Pietro 1867-1914 ....DLB-114
Lucretius circa 94 B.C.-circa 49 B.C.
  .... DLB-211; CDWLB-1
Luder, Peter circa 1415-1472.......... DLB-179
Ludlum, Robert 1927- Y-82
Ludus de Antichristo circa 1160 ....DLB-148
Ludvigson, Susan 1942- DLB-120
Ludwig, Jack 1922- DLB-60
Ludwig, Otto 1813-1865 ....DLB-129
Ludwigslied 881 or 882 ....DLB-148
Luera, Yolanda 1953- DLB-122
Luft, Lya 1938- DLB-145
Lugansky, Kazak Vladimir
  (see Dal', Vladimir Ivanovich)
Lukács, Georg (see Lukács, György)
Lukács, György
  1885-1971 .... DLB-215, 242; CDWLB-4
Luke, Peter 1919- DLB-13
Lummis, Charles F. 1859-1928 ....DLB-186
Lupton, F. M., Company...............DLB-49
Lupus of Ferrières
  circa 805-circa 862 ....DLB-148
Lurie, Alison 1926- DLB-2
Lustig, Arnošt 1926- DLB-232
Luther, Martin 1483-1546 ... DLB-179; CDWLB-2
Luzi, Mario 1914- DLB-128
L'vov, Nikolai Aleksandrovich 1751-1803 ...DLB-150
Lyall, Gavin 1932- DLB-87

Lydgate, John circa 1370-1450 .... DLB-146
Lyly, John circa 1554-1606......... DLB-62, 167
Lynch, Patricia 1898-1972 .... DLB-160
Lynch, Richard flourished 1596-1601 ....DLB-172
Lynd, Robert 1879-1949................ DLB-98
Lyon, Matthew 1749-1822 .... DLB-43
Lyotard, Jean-François 1924-1998 ...... DLB-242
Lysias circa 459 B.C.-circa 380 B.C...... .DLB-176
Lytle, Andrew 1902-1995.......... DLB-6; Y-95
Lytton, Edward
 (see Bulwer-Lytton, Edward)
Lytton, Edward Robert Bulwer
 1831-1891 .... DLB-32

M

Maass, Joachim 1901-1972 .... DLB-69
Mabie, Hamilton Wright 1845-1916 ..... DLB-71
Mac A'Ghobhainn, Iain (see Smith, Iain Crichton)
MacArthur, Charles 1895-1956 .....DLB-7, 25, 44
Macaulay, Catherine 1731-1791 .... DLB-104
Macaulay, David 1945- DLB-61
Macaulay, Rose 1881-1958............. DLB-36
Macaulay, Thomas Babington
 1800-1859........... DLB-32, 55; CDBLB-4
Macaulay Company.................. DLB-46
MacBeth, George 1932- DLB-40
Macbeth, Madge 1880-1965........... DLB-92
MacCaig, Norman 1910-1996 .... DLB-27
MacDiarmid, Hugh
 1892-1978.............. DLB-20; CDBLB-7
MacDonald, Cynthia 1928- DLB-105
MacDonald, George 1824-1905 ... DLB-18, 163, 178
MacDonald, John D. 1916-1986..... DLB-8; Y-86
MacDonald, Philip 1899?-1980 .... DLB-77
Macdonald, Ross (see Millar, Kenneth)
Macdonald, Sharman 1951- DLB-245
MacDonald, Wilson 1880-1967 .... DLB-92
Macdonald and Company (Publishers) .. DLB-112
MacEwen, Gwendolyn 1941-1987 ... DLB-53, 251
Macfadden, Bernarr 1868-1955 ...... DLB-25, 91
MacGregor, John 1825-1892 .... DLB-166
MacGregor, Mary Esther (see Keith, Marian)
Machado, Antonio 1875-1939......... DLB-108
Machado, Manuel 1874-1947 .... DLB-108
Machar, Agnes Maule 1837-1927 .... DLB-92
Machaut, Guillaume de
 circa 1300-1377...................... DLB-208
Machen, Arthur Llewelyn Jones
 1863-1947................DLB-36, 156, 178
MacInnes, Colin 1914-1976 .... DLB-14
MacInnes, Helen 1907-1985 .... DLB-87
Mac Intyre, Tom 1931- DLB-245
Mačiulis, Jonas (see Maironis, Jonas)
Mack, Maynard 1909- DLB-111
Mackall, Leonard L. 1879-1937 .... DLB-140
MacKaye, Percy 1875-1956 .... DLB-54

Macken, Walter 1915-1967 .... DLB-13
Mackenzie, Alexander 1763-1820........ DLB-99
Mackenzie, Alexander Slidell
 1803-1848 .... DLB-183
Mackenzie, Compton 1883-1972 .... DLB-34, 100
Mackenzie, Henry 1745-1831 .... DLB-39
Mackenzie, William 1758-1828........ DLB-187
Mackey, Nathaniel 1947- DLB-169
Mackey, Shena 1944- DLB-231
Mackey, William Wellington
 1937- DLB-38
Mackintosh, Elizabeth (see Tey, Josephine)
Mackintosh, Sir James 1765-1832....... DLB-158
Maclaren, Ian (see Watson, John)
Macklin, Charles 1699-1797 .... DLB-89
MacLean, Katherine Anne 1925- DLB-8
Maclean, Norman 1902-1990 .... DLB-206
MacLeish, Archibald 1892-1982
 ....DLB-4, 7, 45, 228; Y-82; CDALB-7
MacLennan, Hugh 1907-1990 .... DLB-68
MacLeod, Alistair 1936- DLB-60
Macleod, Fiona (see Sharp, William)
Macleod, Norman 1906-1985........... DLB-4
Mac Low, Jackson 1922- DLB-193
Macmillan and Company............ DLB-106
The Macmillan Company DLB-49
Macmillan's English Men of Letters,
 First Series (1878-1892) DLB-144
MacNamara, Brinsley 1890-1963 .... DLB-10
MacNeice, Louis 1907-1963 .... DLB-10, 20
MacPhail, Andrew 1864-1938 .... DLB-92
Macpherson, James 1736-1796 .... DLB-109
Macpherson, Jay 1931- DLB-53
Macpherson, Jeanie 1884-1946.......... DLB-44
Macrae Smith Company............... DLB-46
MacRaye, Lucy Betty (see Webling, Lucy)
Macrone, John [publishing house] DLB-106
MacShane, Frank 1927-1999........... DLB-111
Macy-Masius DLB-46
Madden, David 1933- DLB-6
Madden, Sir Frederic 1801-1873 .... DLB-184
Maddow, Ben 1909-1992 .... DLB-44
Maddux, Rachel 1912-1983 ....DLB-234; Y-93
Madgett, Naomi Long 1923- DLB-76
Madhubuti, Haki R. 1942- DLB-5, 41; DS-8
Madison, James 1751-1836............. DLB-37
Madsen, Svend Åge 1939- DLB-214
Maeterlinck, Maurice 1862-1949 .... DLB-192
Mafūz, Najīb 1911- Y-88
Magee, David 1905-1977 .... DLB-187
Maginn, William 1794-1842........DLB-110, 159
Magoffin, Susan Shelby 1827-1855 ..... DLB-239
Mahan, Alfred Thayer 1840-1914 .... DLB-47
Maheux-Forcier, Louise 1929- DLB-60
Mahin, John Lee 1902-1984 .... DLB-44

Mahon, Derek 1941- DLB-40
Maikov, Vasilii Ivanovich 1728-1778 .... DLB-150
Mailer, Norman 1923-
 ....DLB-2, 16, 28, 185; Y-80, Y-83, Y-97;
 DS-3; CDALB-6
Maillart, Ella 1903-1997 .... DLB-195
Maillet, Adrienne 1885-1963 .... DLB-68
Maillet, Antonine 1929- DLB-60
Maillu, David G. 1939- DLB-157
Maimonides, Moses 1138-1204 .... DLB-115
Main Selections of the Book-of-the-Month
 Club, 1926-1945 .... DLB-9
Main Trends in Twentieth-Century Book
 Clubs DLB-46
Mainwaring, Daniel 1902-1977......... DLB-44
Mair, Charles 1838-1927 .... DLB-99
Maironis, Jonas
 1862-1932 .... DLB-220; CDWLB-4
Mais, Roger 1905-1955 .....DLB-125; CDWLB-3
Major, Andre 1942- DLB-60
Major, Charles 1856-1913 .... DLB-202
Major, Clarence 1936- DLB-33
Major, Kevin 1949- DLB-60
Major Books....................... DLB-46
Makemie, Francis circa 1658-1708 .... DLB-24
The Making of Americans Contract............ Y-98
The Making of a People, by
 J. M. Ritchie..................... DLB-66
Maksimović, Desanka
 1898-1993 ....DLB-147; CDWLB-4
Malamud, Bernard 1914-1986
 ....DLB-2, 28, 152; Y-80, Y-86; CDALB-1
Mălăncioiu, Ileana 1940- DLB-232
Malerba, Luigi 1927- DLB-196
Malet, Lucas 1852-1931 .... DLB-153
Mallarmé, Stéphane 1842-1898 ....DLB-217
Malleson, Lucy Beatrice (see Gilbert, Anthony)
Mallet-Joris, Françoise 1930- DLB-83
Mallock, W. H. 1849-1923...........DLB-18, 57
"Every Man His Own Poet; or,
 The Inspired Singer's Recipe
 Book" (1877) DLB-35
Malone, Dumas 1892-1986 ....DLB-17
Malone, Edmond 1741-1812.......... DLB-142
Malory, Sir Thomas
 circa 1400-1410 - 1471 ... DLB-146; CDBLB-1
Malpede, Karen 1945- DLB-249
Malraux, André 1901-1976............. DLB-72
Malthus, Thomas Robert
 1766-1834................... DLB-107, 158
Maltz, Albert 1908-1985............. DLB-102
Malzberg, Barry N. 1939- DLB-8
Mamet, David 1947- DLB-7
Mamin, Dmitrii Narkisovich 1852-1912.. DLB-238
Manaka, Matsemela 1956- DLB-157
Manchester University Press DLB-112
Mandel, Eli 1922- DLB-53
Mandeville, Bernard 1670-1733 .... DLB-101

Mandeville, Sir John mid fourteenth century DLB-146

Mandiargues, André Pieyre de 1909- DLB-83

Manea, Norman 1936- DLB-232

Manfred, Frederick 1912-1994. . . . DLB-6, 212, 227

Manfredi, Gianfranco 1948- DLB-196

Mangan, Sherry 1904-1961 . . . . DLB-4

Manganelli, Giorgio 1922-1990 . . . . DLB-196

Manilius fl. first century A.D. DLB-211

Mankiewicz, Herman 1897-1953 . . . . DLB-26

Mankiewicz, Joseph L. 1909-1993 . . . . DLB-44

Mankowitz, Wolf 1924-1998 . . . . DLB-15

Manley, Delarivière 1672?-1724 . . . . DLB-39, 80

Preface to *The Secret History, of Queen Zarah, and the Zarazians* (1705) DLB-39

Mann, Abby 1927- DLB-44

Mann, Charles 1929-1998 . . . . Y-98

Mann, Heinrich 1871-1950 . . . . DLB-66, 118

Mann, Horace 1796-1859. . . . . DLB-1, 235

Mann, Klaus 1906-1949 . . . . DLB-56

Mann, Mary Peabody 1806-1887 . . . . DLB-239

Mann, Thomas 1875-1955 . . . . DLB-66; CDWLB-2

Mann, William D'Alton 1839-1920 . . . . . . DLB-137

Mannin, Ethel 1900-1984 . . . . DLB-191, 195

Manning, Emily (see Australie)

Manning, Laurence 1899-1972 . . . . DLB-251

Manning, Marie 1873?-1945 . . . . DLB-29

Manning and Loring DLB-49

Mannyng, Robert flourished 1303-1338. . . . . DLB-146

Mano, D. Keith 1942- DLB-6

Manor Books DLB-46

Mansfield, Katherine 1888-1923 . . . . DLB-162

Manuel, Niklaus circa 1484-1530 . . . . . . DLB-179

Manzini, Gianna 1896-1974 . . . . DLB-177

Mapanje, Jack 1944- DLB-157

Maraini, Dacia 1936- DLB-196

Marcel Proust at 129 and the Proust Society of America. Y-00

Marcel Proust's *Remembrance of Things Past*: The Rediscovered Galley Proofs Y-00

March, William 1893-1954 . . . . DLB-9, 86

Marchand, Leslie A. 1900-1999 . . . . DLB-103

Marchant, Bessie 1862-1941 . . . . DLB-160

Marchant, Tony 1959- DLB-245

Marchenko, Anastasiia Iakovlevna 1830-1880 . . . . DLB-238

Marchessault, Jovette 1938- DLB-60

Marcinkevičius, Justinas 1930- DLB-232

Marcus, Frank 1928- DLB-13

Marcuse, Herbert 1898-1979 . . . . DLB-242

Marden, Orison Swett 1850-1924 . . . . DLB-137

Marechera, Dambudzo 1952-1987 . . . . . . DLB-157

Marek, Richard, Books DLB-46

Mares, E. A. 1938- DLB-122

Margulies, Donald 1954- DLB-228

Mariani, Paul 1940- DLB-111

Marie de France flourished 1160-1178 . . . . DLB-208

Marie-Victorin, Frère 1885-1944 . . . . DLB-92

Marin, Biagio 1891-1985 . . . . DLB-128

Marincovič, Ranko 1913- DLB-147; CDWLB-4

Marinetti, Filippo Tommaso 1876-1944 . . . . DLB-114

Marion, Frances 1886-1973 . . . . DLB-44

Marius, Richard C. 1933-1999 . . . . Y-85

Markevich, Boleslav Mikhailovich 1822-1884 . . . . DLB-238

Markfield, Wallace 1926- DLB-2, 28

Markham, Edwin 1852-1940 . . . . DLB-54, 186

Markle, Fletcher 1921-1991 . . . . DLB-68; Y-91

Marlatt, Daphne 1942- DLB-60

Marlitt, E. 1825-1887 . . . . DLB-129

Marlowe, Christopher 1564-1593 . . . . DLB-62; CDBLB-1

Marlyn, John 1912- DLB-88

Marmion, Shakerley 1603-1639 . . . . DLB-58

Der Marner before 1230-circa 1287 . . . . . . DLB-138

Marnham, Patrick 1943- DLB-204

The *Marprelate Tracts* 1588-1589 . . . . DLB-132

Marquand, John P. 1893-1960 . . . . DLB-9, 102

Marqués, René 1919-1979 . . . . DLB-113

Marquis, Don 1878-1937 . . . . DLB-11, 25

Marriott, Anne 1913- DLB-68

Marryat, Frederick 1792-1848 . . . . DLB-21, 163

Marsh, Capen, Lyon and Webb DLB-49

Marsh, George Perkins 1801-1882 . . . . DLB-1, 64, 243

Marsh, James 1794-1842 . . . . DLB-1, 59

Marsh, Narcissus 1638-1713 . . . . DLB-213

Marsh, Ngaio 1899-1982 . . . . DLB-77

Marshall, Edison 1894-1967 . . . . DLB-102

Marshall, Edward 1932- DLB-16

Marshall, Emma 1828-1899 . . . . DLB-163

Marshall, James 1942-1992 . . . . DLB-61

Marshall, Joyce 1913- DLB-88

Marshall, Paule 1929- DLB-33, 157, 227

Marshall, Tom 1938- DLB-60

Marsilius of Padua circa 1275-circa 1342 . . . . DLB-115

Mars-Jones, Adam 1954- DLB-207

Marson, Una 1905-1965 . . . . DLB-157

Marston, John 1576-1634 . . . . DLB-58, 172

Marston, Philip Bourke 1850-1887 . . . . DLB-35

Martens, Kurt 1870-1945 . . . . DLB-66

Martial circa A.D. 40-circa A.D. 103 . . . . DLB-211; CDWLB-1

Martien, William S. [publishing house] DLB-49

Martin, Abe (see Hubbard, Kin)

Martin, Catherine ca. 1847-1937 . . . . DLB-230

Martin, Charles 1942- DLB-120

Martin, Claire 1914- DLB-60

Martin, Jay 1935- DLB-111

Martin, Johann (see Laurentius von Schnüffis)

Martin, Thomas 1696-1771 . . . . DLB-213

Martin, Violet Florence (see Ross, Martin)

Martin du Gard, Roger 1881-1958 . . . . DLB-65

Martineau, Harriet 1802-1876 . . . . DLB-21, 55, 159, 163, 166, 190

Martínez, Demetria 1960- DLB-209

Martínez, Eliud 1935- DLB-122

Martínez, Max 1943- DLB-82

Martínez, Rubén 1962- DLB-209

Martone, Michael 1955- DLB-218

Martyn, Edward 1859-1923 . . . . DLB-10

Marvell, Andrew 1621-1678 . . . . DLB-131; CDBLB-2

Marvin X 1944- DLB-38

Marx, Karl 1818-1883 . . . . DLB-129

Marzials, Theo 1850-1920 . . . . DLB-35

Masefield, John 1878-1967 . . . DLB-10, 19, 153, 160; CDBLB-5

Mason, A. E. W. 1865-1948 . . . . DLB-70

Mason, Bobbie Ann 1940- DLB-173; Y-87; CDALB-7

Mason, William 1725-1797 . . . . DLB-142

Mason Brothers DLB-49

Massey, Gerald 1828-1907 . . . . DLB-32

Massey, Linton R. 1900-1974 . . . . DLB-187

Massinger, Philip 1583-1640 . . . . DLB-58

Masson, David 1822-1907 . . . . DLB-144

Masters, Edgar Lee 1868-1950 . . . . DLB-54; CDALB-3

Masters, Hilary 1928- DLB-244

Mastronardi, Lucio 1930-1979 . . . . DLB-177

Matevski, Mateja 1929- . . . DLB-181; CDWLB-4

Mather, Cotton 1663-1728 . . . . DLB-24, 30, 140; CDALB-2

Mather, Increase 1639-1723 . . . . DLB-24

Mather, Richard 1596-1669 . . . . DLB-24

Matheson, Annie 1853-1924 . . . . DLB-240

Matheson, Richard 1926- DLB-8, 44

Matheus, John F. 1887- DLB-51

Mathews, Cornelius 1817-1889 . . . . DLB-3, 64, 250

Mathews, Elkin [publishing house] DLB-112

Mathews, John Joseph 1894-1979 . . . . DLB-175

Mathias, Roland 1915- DLB-27

Mathis, June 1892-1927 . . . . DLB-44

Mathis, Sharon Bell 1937- DLB-33

Matković, Marijan 1915-1985 . . . . DLB-181

Matoš, Antun Gustav 1873-1914 . . . . DLB-147

Matsumoto Seichō 1909-1992 . . . . DLB-182

The Matter of England 1240-1400 . . . . . . DLB-146

The Matter of Rome early twelfth to late fifteenth century DLB-146

Matthew of Vendôme circa 1130-circa 1200 . . . . DLB-208

Matthews, Brander 1852-1929 . . . . DLB-71, 78; DS-13

Matthews, Jack 1925- DLB-6	McClure, Michael 1932- DLB-16	McIntyre, James 1827-1906 .... DLB-99
Matthews, Victoria Earle 1861-1907..... DLB-221	McClure, Phillips and Company DLB-46	McIntyre, O. O. 1884-1938 .... DLB-25
Matthews, William 1942-1997 .... DLB-5	McClure, S. S. 1857-1949 .... DLB-91	McKay, Claude 1889-1948..... DLB-4, 45, 51, 117
Matthiessen, F. O. 1902-1950 .... DLB-63	McClurg, A. C., and Company DLB-49	The David McKay Company........... DLB-49
Matthiessen, Peter 1927- DLB-6, 173	McCluskey, John A., Jr. 1944- DLB-33	McKean, William V. 1820-1903......... DLB-23
Maturin, Charles Robert 1780-1824...... DLB-178	McCollum, Michael A. 1946 .... Y-87	McKenna, Stephen 1888-1967 .... DLB-197
Maugham, W. Somerset 1874-1965 ..... DLB-10, 36, 77, 100, 162, 195; CDBLB-6	McConnell, William C. 1917- DLB-88	The McKenzie Trust Y-96
Maupassant, Guy de 1850-1893 .... DLB-123	McCord, David 1897-1997 .... DLB-61	McKerrow, R. B. 1872-1940........... DLB-201
Mauriac, Claude 1914-1996 .... DLB-83	McCord, Louisa S. 1810-1879 .... DLB-248	McKinley, Robin 1952- DLB-52
Mauriac, François 1885-1970 .... DLB-65	McCorkle, Jill 1958- DLB-234; Y-87	McKnight, Reginald 1956- DLB-234
Maurice, Frederick Denison 1805-1872...................... DLB-55	McCorkle, Samuel Eusebius 1746-1811................. DLB-37	McLachlan, Alexander 1818-1896 ...... DLB-99
Maurois, André 1885-1967............. DLB-65	McCormick, Anne O'Hare 1880-1954.... DLB-29	McLaren, Floris Clark 1904-1978....... DLB-68
Maury, James 1718-1769.............. DLB-31	Kenneth Dale McCormick Tributes......... Y-97	McLaverty, Michael 1907- DLB-15
Mavor, Elizabeth 1927- DLB-14	McCormick, Robert R. 1880-1955....... DLB-29	McLean, John R. 1848-1916.......... DLB-23
Mavor, Osborne Henry (see Bridie, James)	McCourt, Edward 1907-1972 .... DLB-88	McLean, William L. 1852-1931 .... DLB-25
Maxwell, Gavin 1914-1969............ DLB-204	McCoy, Horace 1897-1955........... DLB-9	McLennan, William 1856-1904 .... DLB-92
Maxwell, H. [publishing house] DLB-49	McCrae, John 1872-1918 .... DLB-92	McLoughlin Brothers DLB-49
Maxwell, John [publishing house]....... DLB-106	McCullagh, Joseph B. 1842-1896 .... DLB-23	McLuhan, Marshall 1911-1980 .... DLB-88
Maxwell, William 1908- DLB-218; Y-80	McCullers, Carson 1917-1967......DLB-2, 7, 173, 228; CDALB-1	McMaster, John Bach 1852-1932 .... DLB-47
May, Elaine 1932- DLB-44	McCulloch, Thomas 1776-1843 .... DLB-99	McMurtry, Larry 1936- ...DLB-2, 143; Y-80, Y-87; CDALB-6
May, Karl 1842-1912 .... DLB-129	McDonald, Forrest 1927- DLB-17	McNally, Terrence 1939- DLB-7, 249
May, Thomas 1595 or 1596-1650 .... DLB-58	McDonald, Walter 1934- DLB-105, DS-9	McNeil, Florence 1937- DLB-60
Mayer, Bernadette 1945- DLB-165	"Getting Started: Accepting the Regions You Own–or Which Own You," ... DLB-105	McNeile, Herman Cyril 1888-1937 ..... DLB-77
Mayer, Mercer 1943- DLB-61	McDougall, Colin 1917-1984 .... DLB-68	McNickle, D'Arcy 1904-1977....... DLB-175, 212
Mayer, O. B. 1818-1891............. DLB-3, 248	McDowell, Katharine Sherwood Bonner 1849-1883 .... DLB-202, 239	McPhee, John 1931- DLB-185
Mayes, Herbert R. 1900-1987.......... DLB-137	McDowell, Obolensky DLB-46	McPherson, James Alan 1943- DLB-38, 244
Mayes, Wendell 1919-1992 .... DLB-26	McEwan, Ian 1948- DLB-14, 194	McPherson, Sandra 1943- Y-86
Mayfield, Julian 1928-1984........ DLB-33; Y-84	McFadden, David 1940- DLB-60	McWhirter, George 1939- DLB-60
Mayhew, Henry 1812-1887 ..... DLB-18, 55, 190	McFall, Frances Elizabeth Clarke (see Grand, Sarah)	McWilliams, Carey 1905-1980.........DLB-137
Mayhew, Jonathan 1720-1766.......... DLB-31	McFarlane, Leslie 1902-1977 .... DLB-88	Mda, Zakes 1948- DLB-225
Mayne, Ethel Colburn 1865-1941 ...... DLB-197	McFee, William 1881-1966............ DLB-153	Mead, L. T. 1844-1914.............. DLB-141
Mayne, Jasper 1604-1672 .... DLB-126	McGahern, John 1934- DLB-14, 231	Mead, Matthew 1924- DLB-40
Mayne, Seymour 1944- DLB-60	McGee, Thomas D'Arcy 1825-1868 ..... DLB-99	Mead, Taylor ?- DLB-16
Mayor, Flora Macdonald 1872-1932 ..... DLB-36	McGeehan, W. O. 1879-1933........DLB-25, 171	Meany, Tom 1903-1964...............DLB-171
Mayrocker, Friederike 1924- DLB-85	McGill, Ralph 1898-1969............. DLB-29	Mechthild von Magdeburg circa 1207-circa 1282 .... DLB-138
Mazrui, Ali A. 1933- DLB-125	McGinley, Phyllis 1905-1978 .... DLB-11, 48	Medieval French Drama............. DLB-208
Mažuranić, Ivan 1814-1890 .... DLB-147	McGinniss, Joe 1942- DLB-185	Medieval Travel Diaries.............. DLB-203
Mazursky, Paul 1930- DLB-44	McGirt, James E. 1874-1930........... DLB-50	Medill, Joseph 1823-1899............. DLB-43
McAlmon, Robert 1896-1956 .... DLB-4, 45; DS-15	McGlashan and Gill DLB-106	Medoff, Mark 1940- DLB-7
McArthur, Peter 1866-1924 .... DLB-92	McGough, Roger 1937- DLB-40	Meek, Alexander Beaufort 1814-1865 .... DLB-3, 248
McBride, Robert M., and Company...... DLB-46	McGrath, John 1935- DLB-233	Meeke, Mary ?-1816?................ DLB-116
McCabe, Patrick 1955- DLB-194	McGrath, Patrick 1950- DLB-231	Meinke, Peter 1932- DLB-5
McCaffrey, Anne 1926- DLB-8	McGraw-Hill DLB-46	Mejia Vallejo, Manuel 1923- DLB-113
McCarthy, Cormac 1933- DLB-6, 143	McGuane, Thomas 1939- DLB-2, 212; Y-80	Melanchthon, Philipp 1497-1560 ......DLB-179
McCarthy, Mary 1912-1989........ DLB-2; Y-81	McGuckian, Medbh 1950- DLB-40	Melançon, Robert 1947- DLB-60
McCay, Winsor 1871-1934............ DLB-22	McGuffey, William Holmes 1800-1873 ... DLB-42	Mell, Max 1882-1971 .... DLB-81, 124
McClane, Albert Jules 1922-1991 ....DLB-171	McGuinness, Frank 1953- DLB-245	Mellow, James R. 1926-1997 .... DLB-111
McClatchy, C. K. 1858-1936 .... DLB-25	McHenry, James 1785-1845 .... DLB-202	Mel'nikov, Pavel Ivanovich 1818-1883 .. DLB-238
McClellan, George Marion 1860-1934.... DLB-50	McIlvanney, William 1936- DLB-14, 207	Meltzer, David 1937- DLB-16
McCloskey, Robert 1914- DLB-22	McIlwraith, Jean Newton 1859-1938 ..... DLB-92	Meltzer, Milton 1915- DLB-61
McClung, Nellie Letitia 1873-1951 ...... DLB-92	McIntosh, Maria Jane 1803-1878 ... DLB-239, 248	Melville, Elizabeth, Lady Culross circa 1585-1640 ....DLB-172
McClure, Joanna 1930- DLB-16		

Melville, Herman
  1819-1891 ....DLB-3, 74, 250; CDALB-2
Memoirs of Life and Literature (1920),
  by W. H. Mallock [excerpt] DLB-57
Mena, María Cristina 1893-1965....DLB-209, 221
Menander 342-341 B.C.-circa 292-291 B.C.
  .... DLB 176; CDWLB-1
Menantes (see Hunold, Christian Friedrich)
Mencke, Johann Burckhard
  1674-1732 ....DLB-168
Mencken, H. L. 1880-1956
  .... DLB-11, 29, 63, 137, 222; CDALB-4
H. L. Mencken's "Berlin, February, 1917".... Y-00
Mencken and Nietzsche: An Unpublished
  Excerpt from H. L. Mencken's *My Life
  as Author and Editor*................... Y-93
Mendelssohn, Moses 1729-1786.........DLB-97
Mendes, Catulle 1841-1909............DLB-217
Méndez M., Miguel 1930- DLB-82
Mens Rea (or Something) Y-97
The Mercantile Library of New York Y-96
Mercer, Cecil William (see Yates, Dornford)
Mercer, David 1928-1980 ....DLB-13
Mercer, John 1704-1768.................DLB-31
Meredith, George
  1828-1909 .... DLB-18, 35, 57, 159; CDBLB-4
Meredith, Louisa Anne 1812-1895 ..DLB-166, 230
Meredith, Owen
  (see Lytton, Edward Robert Bulwer)
Meredith, William 1919- DLB-5
Mergerle, Johann Ulrich
  (see Abraham ä Sancta Clara)
Mérimée, Prosper 1803-1870.......DLB-119, 192
Merivale, John Herman 1779-1844 ....DLB-96
Meriwether, Louise 1923- DLB-33
Merlin Press......................DLB-112
Merriam, Eve 1916-1992 ....DLB-61
The Merriam Company DLB-49
Merril, Judith 1923-1997 ....DLB-251
Merrill, James 1926-1995........ DLB-5, 165; Y-85
Merrill and Baker....................DLB-49
The Mershon Company DLB-49
Merton, Thomas 1915-1968 ....DLB-48; Y-81
Merwin, W. S. 1927- DLB-5, 169
Messner, Julian [publishing house]........DLB-46
Mészöly, Miklós 1921- DLB-232
Metcalf, J. [publishing house]............DLB-49
Metcalf, John 1938- DLB-60
The Methodist Book Concern............DLB-49
Methuen and Company.................DLB-112
Meun, Jean de (see *Roman de la Rose*)
Mew, Charlotte 1869-1928 ....DLB-19, 135
Mewshaw, Michael 1943- Y-80
Meyer, Conrad Ferdinand 1825-1898 ....DLB-129
Meyer, E. Y. 1946- DLB-75
Meyer, Eugene 1875-1959 ....DLB-29
Meyer, Michael 1921-2000 ....DLB-155

Meyers, Jeffrey 1939- DLB-111
Meynell, Alice 1847-1922............DLB-19, 98
Meynell, Viola 1885-1956 ....DLB-153
Meyrink, Gustav 1868-1932 ....DLB-81
Mézières, Philipe de circa 1327-1405 .....DLB-208
Michael, Ib 1945- DLB-214
Michaëlis, Karen 1872-1950............DLB-214
Michaels, Leonard 1933- DLB-130
Micheaux, Oscar 1884-1951 ....DLB-50
Michel of Northgate, Dan
  circa 1265-circa 1340..............DLB-146
Micheline, Jack 1929-1998..............DLB-16
Michener, James A. 1907?-1997...........DLB-6
Micklejohn, George
  circa 1717-1818 ....DLB-31
Middle English Literature:
  An Introduction DLB-146
The Middle English Lyric DLB-146
Middle Hill Press....................DLB-106
Middleton, Christopher 1926- DLB-40
Middleton, Richard 1882-1911 ....DLB-156
Middleton, Stanley 1919- DLB-14
Middleton, Thomas 1580-1627 ....DLB-58
Miegel, Agnes 1879-1964...............DLB-56
Mieželaitis, Eduardas 1919-1997 ....DLB-220
Mihailović, Dragoslav 1930- DLB-181
Mihalić, Slavko 1928- DLB-181
Mikhailov, A. (see Sheller, Aleksandr
  Konstantinovich)
Mikhailov, Mikhail Larionovich
  1829-1865 ....DLB-238
Miles, Josephine 1911-1985 ....DLB-48
Miles, Susan (Ursula Wyllie Roberts)
  1888-1975 ....DLB-240
Miliković, Branko 1934-1961 ....DLB-181
Milius, John 1944- DLB-44
Mill, James 1773-1836 .... DLB-107, 158
Mill, John Stuart
  1806-1873 ....DLB-55, 190; CDBLB-4
Millar, Andrew [publishing house] DLB-154
Millar, Kenneth
  1915-1983 .... DLB-2, 226; Y-83; DS-6
Millay, Edna St. Vincent
  1892-1950..........DLB-45, 249; CDALB-4
Millen, Sarah Gertrude 1888-1968 ......DLB-225
Miller, Arthur 1915- DLB-7; CDALB-1
Miller, Caroline 1903-1992 ....DLB-9
Miller, Eugene Ethelbert 1950- DLB-41
Miller, Heather Ross 1939- DLB-120
Miller, Henry
  1891-1980 ....DLB-4, 9; Y-80; CDALB-5
Miller, Hugh 1802-1856 ....DLB-190
Miller, J. Hillis 1928- DLB-67
Miller, James [publishing house] DLB-49
Miller, Jason 1939- DLB-7
Miller, Joaquin 1839-1913 ....DLB-186
Miller, May 1899- DLB-41

Miller, Paul 1906-1991 ....DLB-127
Miller, Perry 1905-1963............ DLB-17, 63
Miller, Sue 1943- DLB-143
Miller, Vassar 1924-1998................DLB-105
Miller, Walter M., Jr. 1923- DLB-8
Miller, Webb 1892-1940 ....DLB-29
Millett, Kate 1934- DLB-246
Millhauser, Steven 1943- DLB-2
Millican, Arthenia J. Bates 1920- DLB-38
Milligan, Alice 1866-1953 ....DLB-240
Mills and Boon DLB-112
Milman, Henry Hart 1796-1868 ....DLB-96
Milne, A. A. 1882-1956......DLB-10, 77, 100, 160
Milner, Ron 1938- DLB-38
Milner, William [publishing house] DLB-106
Milnes, Richard Monckton (Lord Houghton)
  1809-1885 ....DLB-32, 184
Milton, John
  1608-1674 ....DLB-131, 151; CDBLB-2
Miłosz, Czesław 1911- DLB-215; CDWLB-4
Minakami Tsutomu 1919- DLB-182
Minamoto no Sanetomo 1192-1219......DLB-203
The Minerva Press DLB-154
Minnesang circa 1150-1280 ....DLB-138
Minns, Susan 1839-1938 ....DLB-140
Minor Illustrators, 1880-1914 ....DLB-141
Minor Poets of the Earlier Seventeenth
  Century......................DLB-121
Minton, Balch and Company DLB-46
Mirbeau, Octave 1848-1917........DLB-123, 192
Mirk, John died after 1414?........DLB-146
Miron, Gaston 1928- DLB-60
A Mirror for Magistrates DLB-167
Mishima Yukio 1925-1970.............DLB-182
Mitchel, Jonathan 1624-1668..........DLB-24
Mitchell, Adrian 1932- DLB-40
Mitchell, Donald Grant
  1822-1908..............DLB-1, 243; DS-13
Mitchell, Gladys 1901-1983............DLB-77
Mitchell, James Leslie 1901-1935.........DLB-15
Mitchell, John (see Slater, Patrick)
Mitchell, John Ames 1845-1918..........DLB-79
Mitchell, Joseph 1908-1996 .... DLB-185; Y-96
Mitchell, Julian 1935- DLB-14
Mitchell, Ken 1940- DLB-60
Mitchell, Langdon 1862-1935 ....DLB-7
Mitchell, Loften 1919- DLB-38
Mitchell, Margaret 1900-1949 ...DLB-9; CDALB-7
Mitchell, S. Weir 1829-1914 ....DLB-202
Mitchell, W. J. T. 1942- DLB-246
Mitchell, W. O. 1914- DLB-88
Mitchison, Naomi Margaret (Haldane)
  1897-1999 ....DLB-160, 191
Mitford, Mary Russell 1787-1855.... DLB-110, 116
Mitford, Nancy 1904-1973.............DLB-191

Cumulative Index

Mittelholzer, Edgar 1909-1965 .... DLB-117; CDWLB-3
Mitterer, Erika 1906- DLB-85
Mitterer, Felix 1948- DLB-124
Mitternacht, Johann Sebastian 1613-1679 .... DLB-168
Miyamoto, Yuriko 1899-1951 .... DLB-180
Mizener, Arthur 1907-1988 .... DLB-103
Mo, Timothy 1950- DLB-194
Modern Age Books DLB-46
"Modern English Prose" (1876), by George Saintsbury DLB-57
The Modern Language Association of America Celebrates Its Centennial Y-84
The Modern Library DLB-46
"Modern Novelists – Great and Small" (1855), by Margaret Oliphant DLB-21
"Modern Style" (1857), by Cockburn Thomson [excerpt] DLB-57
The Modernists (1932), by Joseph Warren Beach DLB-36
Modiano, Patrick 1945- DLB-83
Moffat, Yard and Company DLB-46
Moffet, Thomas 1553-1604 .... DLB-136
Mohr, Nicholasa 1938- DLB-145
Moix, Ana María 1947- DLB-134
Molesworth, Louisa 1839-1921 .... DLB-135
Möllhausen, Balduin 1825-1905 .... DLB-129
Molnár, Ferenc 1878-1952 .... DLB-215; CDWLB-4
Molnár, Miklós (see Mészöly, Miklós)
Momaday, N. Scott 1934- DLB-143, 175; CDALB-7
Monkhouse, Allan 1858-1936 .... DLB-10
Monro, Harold 1879-1932 .... DLB-19
Monroe, Harriet 1860-1936 .... DLB-54, 91
Monsarrat, Nicholas 1910-1979 .... DLB-15
Montagu, Lady Mary Wortley 1689-1762 .... DLB-95, 101
Montague, C. E. 1867-1928 .... DLB-197
Montague, John 1929- DLB-40
Montale, Eugenio 1896-1981 .... DLB-114
Montalvo, José 1946-1994 .... DLB-209
Monterroso, Augusto 1921- DLB-145
Montesquiou, Robert de 1855-1921 ..... DLB-217
Montgomerie, Alexander circa 1550?-1598 .... DLB-167
Montgomery, James 1771-1854 ...... DLB-93, 158
Montgomery, John 1919- DLB-16
Montgomery, Lucy Maud 1874-1942 .... DLB-92; DS-14
Montgomery, Marion 1925- DLB-6
Montgomery, Robert Bruce (see Crispin, Edmund)
Montherlant, Henry de 1896-1972 ...... DLB-72
The Monthly Review 1749-1844 .... DLB-110
Montigny, Louvigny de 1876-1955 ...... DLB-92
Montoya, José 1932- DLB-122

Moodie, John Wedderburn Dunbar 1797-1869 .... DLB-99
Moodie, Susanna 1803-1885 .... DLB-99
Moody, Joshua circa 1633-1697 .... DLB-24
Moody, William Vaughn 1869-1910 .... DLB-7, 54
Moorcock, Michael 1939- DLB-14, 231
Moore, Brian 1921-1999 .... DLB-251
Moore, Catherine L. 1911- DLB-8
Moore, Clement Clarke 1779-1863 ...... DLB-42
Moore, Dora Mavor 1888-1979 .... DLB-92
Moore, George 1852-1933 .... DLB-10, 18, 57, 135
Moore, Lorrie 1957- DLB-234
Moore, Marianne 1887-1972 .... DLB-45; DS-7; CDALB-5
Moore, Mavor 1919- DLB-88
Moore, Richard 1927- DLB-105
Moore, T. Sturge 1870-1944 .... DLB-19
Moore, Thomas 1779-1852 .... DLB-96, 144
Moore, Ward 1903-1978 .... DLB-8
Moore, Wilstach, Keys and Company DLB-49
Moorehead, Alan 1901-1983 .... DLB-204
Moorhouse, Geoffrey 1931- DLB-204
The Moorland-Spingarn Research Center DLB-76
Moorman, Mary C. 1905-1994 .... DLB-155
Mora, Pat 1942- DLB-209
Moraga, Cherríe 1952- DLB-82, 249
Morales, Alejandro 1944- DLB-82
Morales, Mario Roberto 1947- DLB-145
Morales, Rafael 1919- DLB-108
Morality Plays: *Mankind* circa 1450-1500 and *Everyman* circa 1500 .... DLB-146
Morante, Elsa 1912-1985 .... DLB-177
Morata, Olympia Fulvia 1526-1555 ..... DLB-179
Moravia, Alberto 1907-1990 .... DLB-177
Mordaunt, Elinor 1872-1942 .... DLB-174
Mordovtsev, Daniil Lukich 1830-1905 ... DLB-238
More, Hannah 1745-1833 .... DLB-107, 109, 116, 158
More, Henry 1614-1687 .... DLB-126
More, Sir Thomas 1477 or 1478-1535 .... DLB-136
Moreno, Dorinda 1939- DLB-122
Morency, Pierre 1942- DLB-60
Moretti, Marino 1885-1979 .... DLB-114
Morgan, Berry 1919- DLB-6
Morgan, Charles 1894-1958 .... DLB-34, 100
Morgan, Edmund S. 1916- DLB-17
Morgan, Edwin 1920- DLB-27
Morgan, John Pierpont 1837-1913 ...... DLB-140
Morgan, John Pierpont, Jr. 1867-1943 ... DLB-140
Morgan, Robert 1944- DLB-120
Morgan, Sydney Owenson, Lady 1776?-1859 .... DLB-116, 158
Morgner, Irmtraud 1933- DLB-75
Morhof, Daniel Georg 1639-1691 ...... DLB-164

Mori, Ōgai 1862-1922 .... DLB-180
Móricz, Zsigmond 1879-1942 .... DLB-215
Morier, James Justinian 1782 or 1783?-1849 .... DLB-116
Mörike, Eduard 1804-1875 .... DLB-133
Morin, Paul 1889-1963 .... DLB-92
Morison, Richard 1514?-1556 .... DLB-136
Morison, Samuel Eliot 1887-1976 .... DLB-17
Morison, Stanley 1889-1967 .... DLB-201
Moritz, Karl Philipp 1756-1793 .... DLB-94
Moriz von Craûn circa 1220-1230 .... DLB-138
Morley, Christopher 1890-1957 .... DLB-9
Morley, John 1838-1923 .... DLB-57, 144, 190
Morris, George Pope 1802-1864 .... DLB-73
Morris, James Humphrey (see Morris, Jan)
Morris, Jan 1926- DLB-204
Morris, Lewis 1833-1907 .... DLB-35
Morris, Margaret 1737-1816 .... DLB-200
Morris, Richard B. 1904-1989 .... DLB-17
Morris, William 1834-1896 ..... DLB-18, 35, 57, 156, 178, 184; CDBLB-4
Morris, Willie 1934-1999 .... Y-80
Morris, Wright 1910-1998 .... DLB-2, 206, 218; Y-81
Morrison, Arthur 1863-1945 .... DLB-70, 135, 197
Morrison, Charles Clayton 1874-1966 .... DLB-91
Morrison, Toni 1931- DLB-6, 33, 143; Y-81, Y-93; CDALB-6
Morrow, William, and Company DLB-46
Morse, James Herbert 1841-1923 .... DLB-71
Morse, Jedidiah 1761-1826 .... DLB-37
Morse, John T., Jr. 1840-1937 .... DLB-47
Morselli, Guido 1912-1973 .... DLB-177
Mortimer, Favell Lee 1802-1878 .... DLB-163
Mortimer, John 1923- DLB-13, 245; CDBLB-8
Morton, Carlos 1942- DLB-122
Morton, H. V. 1892-1979 .... DLB-195
Morton, John P., and Company DLB-49
Morton, Nathaniel 1613-1685 .... DLB-24
Morton, Sarah Wentworth 1759-1846 .... DLB-37
Morton, Thomas circa 1579-circa 1647 ... DLB-24
Moscherosch, Johann Michael 1601-1669 .... DLB-164
Moseley, Humphrey [publishing house] DLB-170
Möser, Justus 1720-1794 .... DLB-97
Mosley, Nicholas 1923- DLB-14, 207
Moss, Arthur 1889-1969 .... DLB-4
Moss, Howard 1922-1987 .... DLB-5
Moss, Thylias 1954- DLB-120
The Most Powerful Book Review in America [*New York Times Book Review*] Y-82
Motion, Andrew 1952- DLB-40
Motley, John Lothrop 1814-1877 .... DLB-1, 30, 59, 235

Motley, Willard 1909-1965 . . . . DLB-76, 143
Mott, Lucretia 1793-1880. . . . . .DLB-239
Motte, Benjamin Jr. [publishing house] . . .DLB-154
Motteux, Peter Anthony 1663-1718. . . . . . .DLB-80
Mottram, R. H. 1883-1971. . . . . .DLB-36
Mount, Ferdinand 1939- DLB-231
Mouré, Erin 1955- DLB-60
Mourning Dove (Humishuma) between
  1882 and 1888?-1936 . . . . DLB-175, 221
Movies from Books, 1920-1974 . . . . .DLB-9
Mowat, Farley 1921- DLB-68
Mowbray, A. R., and Company,
  Limited DLB-106
Mowrer, Edgar Ansel 1892-1977 . . . . .DLB-29
Mowrer, Paul Scott 1887-1971 . . . . .DLB-29
Moxon, Edward [publishing house]. DLB-106
Moxon, Joseph [publishing house]. DLB-170
Mphahlele, Es'kia (Ezekiel)
  1919- DLB-125; CDWLB-3
Mrożek, Sławomir 1930- . . .DLB-232; CDWLB-4
Mtshali, Oswald Mbuyiseni 1940- DLB-125
Mucedorus. DLB-62
Mudford, William 1782-1848 . . . . .DLB-159
Mueller, Lisel 1924- DLB-105
Muhajir, El (see Marvin X)
Muhajir, Nazzam Al Fitnah (see Marvin X)
Mühlbach, Luise 1814-1873. . . . . .DLB-133
Muir, Edwin 1887-1959 . . . . DLB-20, 100, 191
Muir, Helen 1937- DLB-14
Muir, John 1838-1914 . . . . .DLB-186
Muir, Percy 1894-1979. . . . . .DLB-201
Mujū Ichien 1226-1312 . . . . .DLB-203
Mukherjee, Bharati 1940- DLB-60, 218
Mulcaster, Richard
  1531 or 1532-1611 . . . . .DLB-167
Muldoon, Paul 1951- DLB-40
Müller, Friedrich (see Müller, Maler)
Müller, Heiner 1929-1995 . . . . .DLB-124
Müller, Maler 1749-1825 . . . . .DLB-94
Muller, Marcia 1944- DLB-226
Müller, Wilhelm 1794-1827 . . . . .DLB-90
Mumford, Lewis 1895-1990 . . . . .DLB-63
Munby, A. N. L. 1913-1974. . . . . .DLB-201
Munby, Arthur Joseph 1828-1910 . . . . .DLB-35
Munday, Anthony 1560-1633 . . . . . . DLB-62, 172
Mundt, Clara (see Mühlbach, Luise)
Mundt, Theodore 1808-1861 . . . . .DLB-133
Munford, Robert circa 1737-1783. . . . . . . .DLB-31
Mungoshi, Charles 1947- DLB-157
Munk, Kaj 1898-1944 . . . . .DLB-214
Munonye, John 1929- DLB-117
Munro, Alice 1931- DLB-53
Munro, George [publishing house] DLB-49
Munro, H. H.
  1870-1916 . . . . .DLB-34, 162; CDBLB-5

Munro, Neil 1864-1930 . . . . .DLB-156
Munro, Norman L. [publishing house] DLB-49
Munroe, James, and Company DLB-49
Munroe, Kirk 1850-1930. . . . . .DLB-42
Munroe and Francis. DLB-49
Munsell, Joel [publishing house] DLB-49
Munsey, Frank A. 1854-1925 . . . . .DLB-25, 91
Munsey, Frank A., and Company. DLB-49
Murakami Haruki 1949- DLB-182
Murav'ev, Mikhail Nikitich
  1757-1807. . . . . .DLB-150
Murdoch, Iris
  1919-1999 . . . . . . DLB-14, 194, 233; CDBLB-8
Murdoch, Rupert 1931- DLB-127
Murfree, Mary N. 1850-1922 . . . . . . .DLB-12, 74
Murger, Henry 1822-1861. . . . . .DLB-119
Murger, Louis-Henri (see Murger, Henry)
Murner, Thomas 1475-1537 . . . . .DLB-179
Muro, Amado 1915-1971. . . . . .DLB-82
Murphy, Arthur 1727-1805 . . . . .DLB-89, 142
Murphy, Beatrice M. 1908- DLB-76
Murphy, Dervla 1931- DLB-204
Murphy, Emily 1868-1933 . . . . .DLB-99
Murphy, Jack 1923-1980 . . . . .DLB-241
Murphy, John, and Company DLB-49
Murphy, John H., III 1916- DLB-127
Murphy, Richard 1927-1993 . . . . .DLB-40
Murray, Albert L. 1916- DLB-38
Murray, Gilbert 1866-1957 . . . . .DLB-10
Murray, Jim 1919-1998 . . . . .DLB-241
Murray, John [publishing house] DLB-154
Murry, John Middleton 1889-1957 . . . . . . .DLB-149
  "The Break-Up of the Novel" (1922) DLB-36
Murray, Judith Sargent 1751-1820. . . . DLB-37, 200
Murray, Pauli 1910-1985. . . . . .DLB-41
Musäus, Johann Karl August 1735-1787 . . .DLB-97
Muschg, Adolf 1934- DLB-75
The Music of *Minnesang*. DLB-138
Musil, Robert
  1880-1942 . . . . DLB-81, 124; CDWLB-2
Muspilli circa 790-circa 850. . . . . .DLB-148
Musset, Alfred de 1810-1857 . . . . . . .DLB-192, 217
Mussey, Benjamin B., and Company DLB-49
Mutafchieva, Vera 1929- DLB-181
Mwangi, Meja 1948- DLB-125
Myers, Frederic W. H. 1843-1901. . . . . . . .DLB-190
Myers, Gustavus 1872-1942 . . . . .DLB-47
Myers, L. H. 1881-1944 . . . . .DLB-15
Myers, Walter Dean 1937- DLB-33
Mykolaitis-Putinas, Vincas 1893-1967. . . .DLB-220
Myles, Eileen 1949- DLB-193

N

Na Prous Boneta circa 1296-1328 . . . . . . .DLB-208
Nabl, Franz 1883-1974. . . . . .DLB-81

Nabokov, Vladimir 1899-1977
  . . . . DLB-2, 244; Y-80, Y-91; DS-3; CDALB-1
The Vladimir Nabokov Archive
  in the Berg Collection Y-91
Nabokov Festival at Cornell Y-83
Nádaši, Ladislav (see Jégé)
Naden, Constance 1858-1889 . . . . .DLB-199
Nadezhdin, Nikolai Ivanovich
  1804-1856 . . . . .DLB-198
Naevius circa 265 B.C.-201 B.C. DLB-211
Nafis and Cornish .DLB-49
Nagai, Kafū 1879-1959. . . . . .DLB-180
Naipaul, Shiva 1945-1985 . . . . DLB-157; Y-85
Naipaul, V. S. 1932-
  . . . . .DLB-125, 204, 207; Y-85;
  CDBLB-8; CDWLB-3
Nakagami Kenji 1946-1992 . . . . .DLB-182
Nakano-in Masatada no Musume (see Nijō, Lady)
Nałkowska, Zofia 1884-1954. . . . . .DLB-215
Nancrede, Joseph [publishing house] DLB-49
Naranjo, Carmen 1930- DLB-145
Narezhny, Vasilii Trofimovich
  1780-1825 . . . . .DLB-198
Narrache, Jean 1893-1970 . . . . .DLB-92
Nasby, Petroleum Vesuvius (see Locke, David Ross)
Nash, Eveleigh [publishing house] DLB-112
Nash, Ogden 1902-1971 . . . . .DLB-11
Nashe, Thomas 1567-1601?. DLB-167
Nason, Jerry 1910-1986 . . . . .DLB-241
Nast, Conde 1873-1942 . . . . .DLB-91
Nast, Thomas 1840-1902. . . . . .DLB-188
Nastasijević, Momčilo 1894-1938 . . . . .DLB-147
Nathan, George Jean 1882-1958 . . . . .DLB-137
Nathan, Robert 1894-1985 . . . . .DLB-9
National Book Critics Circle Awards 2000 . . . Y-00
The National Jewish Book Awards Y-85
The National Theatre and the Royal
  Shakespeare Company: The
  National Companies DLB-13
Natsume, Sōseki 1867-1916 . . . . .DLB-180
Naughton, Bill 1910- DLB-13
Navarro, Joe 1953- DLB-209
Naylor, Gloria 1950- DLB-173
Nazor, Vladimir 1876-1949 . . . . .DLB-147
Ndebele, Njabulo 1948- DLB-157
Neagoe, Peter 1881-1960. . . . . .DLB-4
Neal, John 1793-1876 . . . . .DLB-1, 59, 243
Neal, Joseph C. 1807-1847 . . . . .DLB-11
Neal, Larry 1937-1981 . . . . .DLB-38
The Neale Publishing Company DLB-49
Nebel, Frederick 1903-1967. . . . . .DLB-226
Neely, F. Tennyson [publishing house] DLB-49
Negoițescu, Ion 1921-1993 . . . . .DLB-220
Negri, Ada 1870-1945 . . . . .DLB-114
"The Negro as a Writer," by
  G. M. McClellan DLB-50

Cumulative Index DLB 251

"Negro Poets and Their Poetry," by
 Wallace Thurman DLB-50

Neidhart von Reuental
 circa 1185-circa 1240 . . . . DLB-138

Neihardt, John G. 1881-1973 . . . . DLB-9, 54

Neilson, John Shaw 1872-1942 . . . . DLB-230

Neledinsky-Meletsky, Iurii Aleksandrovich
 1752-1828. . . . . DLB-150

Nelligan, Emile 1879-1941 . . . . DLB-92

Nelson, Alice Moore Dunbar 1875-1935 . . DLB-50

Nelson, Antonya 1961- DLB-244

Nelson, Kent 1943- DLB-234

Nelson, Thomas, and Sons [U.K.] DLB-106

Nelson, Thomas, and Sons [U.S.] DLB-49

Nelson, William 1908-1978 . . . . DLB-103

Nelson, William Rockhill 1841-1915 . . . . . DLB-23

Nemerov, Howard 1920-1991 . . . . . DLB-5, 6; Y-83

Németh, László 1901-1975 . . . . DLB-215

Nepos circa 100 B.C.-post 27 B.C. DLB-211

Nėris, Salomėja
 1904-1945 . . . . DLB-220; CDWLB-4

Nerval, Gerard de 1808-1855 . . . . DLB-217

Nesbit, E. 1858-1924 . . . . DLB-141, 153, 178

Ness, Evaline 1911-1986 . . . . DLB-61

Nestroy, Johann 1801-1862 . . . . DLB-133

Neugeboren, Jay 1938- DLB-28

Neukirch, Benjamin 1655-1729 . . . . DLB-168

Neumann, Alfred 1895-1952 . . . . DLB-56

Neumann, Ferenc (see Molnár, Ferenc)

Neumark, Georg 1621-1681 . . . . DLB-164

Neumeister, Erdmann 1671-1756 . . . . . . DLB-168

Nevins, Allan 1890-1971 . . . . DLB-17; DS-17

Nevinson, Henry Woodd 1856-1941 . . . . DLB-135

The New American Library DLB-46

New Approaches to Biography: Challenges
 from Critical Theory, USC Conference
 on Literary Studies, 1990 . . . . Y-90

New Directions Publishing Corporation . . . DLB-46

A New Edition of *Huck Finn* Y-85

New Forces at Work in the American Theatre:
 1915-1925 . . . . DLB-7

New Literary Periodicals:
 A Report for 1987 . . . . Y-87

New Literary Periodicals:
 A Report for 1988 . . . . Y-88

New Literary Periodicals:
 A Report for 1989 . . . . Y-89

New Literary Periodicals:
 A Report for 1990 . . . . Y-90

New Literary Periodicals:
 A Report for 1991 . . . . Y-91

New Literary Periodicals:
 A Report for 1992 . . . . Y-92

New Literary Periodicals:
 A Report for 1993 . . . . Y-93

The New Monthly Magazine
 1814-1884 . . . . DLB-110

The New Variorum Shakespeare Y-85

A New Voice: The Center for the Book's First
 Five Years Y-83

The New Wave [Science Fiction] DLB-8

New York City Bookshops in the 1930s and 1940s:
 The Recollections of Walter Goldwater . . . Y-93

Newbery, John [publishing house] DLB-154

Newbolt, Henry 1862-1938 . . . . DLB-19

Newbound, Bernard Slade (see Slade, Bernard)

Newby, Eric 1919- DLB-204

Newby, P. H. 1918- DLB-15

Newby, Thomas Cautley
 [publishing house] DLB-106

Newcomb, Charles King 1820-1894 . . . DLB-1, 223

Newell, Peter 1862-1924 . . . . DLB-42

Newell, Robert Henry 1836-1901 . . . . DLB-11

Newhouse, Samuel I. 1895-1979 . . . . DLB-127

Newman, Cecil Earl 1903-1976 . . . . DLB-127

Newman, David (see Benton, Robert)

Newman, Frances 1883-1928 . . . . Y-80

Newman, Francis William 1805-1897 . . . . DLB-190

Newman, John Henry
 1801-1890 . . . . DLB-18, 32, 55

Newman, Mark [publishing house] DLB-49

Newmarch, Rosa Harriet 1857-1940 . . . . DLB-240

Newnes, George, Limited DLB-112

Newsome, Effie Lee 1885-1979 . . . . DLB-76

Newspaper Syndication of American
 Humor DLB-11

Newton, A. Edward 1864-1940 . . . . DLB-140

Nexø, Martin Andersen 1869-1954 . . . . . DLB-214

Nezval, Vítěslav
 1900-1958 . . . . DLB-215; CDWLB-4

Ngugi wa Thiong'o
 1938- DLB-125; CDWLB-3

Niatum, Duane 1938- DLB-175

The *Nibelungenlied* and the *Klage*
 circa 1200 . . . . DLB-138

Nichol, B. P. 1944- DLB-53

Nicholas of Cusa 1401-1464 . . . . DLB-115

Nichols, Ann 1891?-1966 . . . . DLB-249

Nichols, Beverly 1898-1983 . . . . DLB-191

Nichols, Dudley 1895-1960 . . . . DLB-26

Nichols, Grace 1950- DLB-157

Nichols, John 1940- Y-82

Nichols, Mary Sargeant (Neal) Gove
 1810-1884 . . . . DLB-1, 243

Nichols, Peter 1927- DLB-13, 245

Nichols, Roy F. 1896-1973 . . . . DLB-17

Nichols, Ruth 1948- DLB-60

Nicholson, Edward Williams Byron
 1849-1912 . . . . DLB-184

Nicholson, Norman 1914- DLB-27

Nicholson, William 1872-1949 . . . . DLB-141

Ní Chuilleanáin, Eiléan 1942- DLB-40

Nicol, Eric 1919- DLB-68

Nicolai, Friedrich 1733-1811 . . . . DLB-97

Nicolas de Clamanges circa 1363-1437 . . . DLB-208

Nicolay, John G. 1832-1901 and
 Hay, John 1838-1905 . . . . DLB-47

Nicolson, Adela Florence Cory (see Hope, Laurence)

Nicolson, Harold 1886-1968 . . . . DLB-100, 149

Nicolson, Nigel 1917- DLB-155

Niebuhr, Reinhold 1892-1971 . . . . . DLB-17; DS-17

Niedecker, Lorine 1903-1970 . . . . DLB-48

Nieman, Lucius W. 1857-1935 . . . . DLB-25

Nietzsche, Friedrich
 1844-1900 . . . . DLB-129; CDWLB-2

Nievo, Stanislao 1928- DLB-196

Niggli, Josefina 1910- Y-80

Nightingale, Florence 1820-1910 . . . . DLB-166

Nijō, Lady (Nakano-in Masatada no Musume)
 1258-after 1306 . . . . DLB-203

Nijō Yoshimoto 1320-1388 . . . . DLB-203

Nikolev, Nikolai Petrovich
 1758-1815 . . . . DLB-150

Niles, Hezekiah 1777-1839 . . . . DLB-43

Nims, John Frederick 1913-1999 . . . . DLB-5

Nin, Anaïs 1903-1977 . . . . DLB-2, 4, 152

1985: The Year of the Mystery:
 A Symposium Y-85

The 1997 Booker Prize Y-97

The 1998 Booker Prize Y-98

Niño, Raúl 1961- DLB-209

Nissenson, Hugh 1933- DLB-28

Niven, Frederick John 1878-1944 . . . . DLB-92

Niven, Larry 1938- DLB-8

Nixon, Howard M. 1909-1983 . . . . DLB-201

Nizan, Paul 1905-1940 . . . . DLB-72

Njegoš, Petar II Petrović
 1813-1851 . . . . DLB-147; CDWLB-4

Nkosi, Lewis 1936- DLB-157

"The No Self, the Little Self, and the Poets,"
 by Richard Moore DLB-105

Noah, Mordecai M. 1785-1851 . . . . DLB-250

Nobel Peace Prize

The 1986 Nobel Peace Prize: Elie Wiesel Y-86

The Nobel Prize and Literary Politics Y-86

Nobel Prize in Literature

The 1982 Nobel Prize in Literature:
 Gabriel García Márquez Y-82

The 1983 Nobel Prize in Literature:
 William Golding Y-83

The 1984 Nobel Prize in Literature:
 Jaroslav Seifert Y-84

The 1985 Nobel Prize in Literature:
 Claude Simon Y-85

The 1986 Nobel Prize in Literature:
 Wole Soyinka Y-86

The 1987 Nobel Prize in Literature:
 Joseph Brodsky Y-87

The 1988 Nobel Prize in Literature:
 Najīb Mahfūz Y-88

The 1989 Nobel Prize in Literature:
 Camilo José Cela Y-89

The 1990 Nobel Prize in Literature:
 Octavio Paz Y-90

The 1991 Nobel Prize in Literature:
  Nadine Gordimer Y-91
The 1992 Nobel Prize in Literature:
  Derek Walcott..................... Y-92
The 1993 Nobel Prize in Literature:
  Toni Morrison Y-93
The 1994 Nobel Prize in Literature:
  Kenzaburō Ōe Y-94
The 1995 Nobel Prize in Literature:
  Seamus Heaney..................... Y-95
The 1996 Nobel Prize in Literature:
  Wisława Szymborsha Y-96
The 1997 Nobel Prize in Literature:
  Dario Fo Y-97
The 1998 Nobel Prize in Literature:
  José Saramago..................... Y-98
The 1999 Nobel Prize in Literature:
  Günter Grass...................... Y-99
The 2000 Nobel Prize in Literature:
  Gao Xingjian...................... Y-00
Nodier, Charles 1780-1844 ....DLB-119
Noel, Roden 1834-1894.................DLB-35
Nogami, Yaeko 1885-1985...............DLB-180
Nogo, Rajko Petrov 1945- DLB-181
Nolan, William F. 1928- DLB-8
Noland, C. F. M. 1810?-1858...........DLB-11
Noma Hiroshi 1915-1991 ....DLB-182
Nonesuch Press DLB-112
Noonan, Robert Phillipe (see Tressell, Robert)
Noonday Press.........................DLB-46
Noone, John 1936- DLB-14
Nora, Eugenio de 1923- DLB-134
Nordan, Lewis 1939- DLB-234
Nordbrandt, Henrik 1945- DLB-214
Nordhoff, Charles 1887-1947...........DLB-9
Norman, Charles 1904-1996 ....DLB-111
Norman, Marsha 1947- Y-84
Norris, Charles G. 1881-1945 ....DLB-9
Norris, Frank
  1870-1902 .... DLB-12, 71, 186; CDALB-3
Norris, Leslie 1921- DLB-27
Norse, Harold 1916- DLB-16
Norte, Marisela 1955- DLB-209
North, Marianne 1830-1890 ....DLB-174
North Point Press.....................DLB-46
Nortje, Arthur 1942-1970..............DLB-125
Norton, Alice Mary (see Norton, Andre)
Norton, Andre 1912- DLB-8, 52
Norton, Andrews 1786-1853 ....DLB-1, 235
Norton, Caroline 1808-1877....DLB-21, 159, 199
Norton, Charles Eliot 1827-1908 ...DLB-1, 64, 235
Norton, John 1606-1663 ....DLB-24
Norton, Mary 1903-1992................DLB-160
Norton, Thomas (see Sackville, Thomas)
Norton, W. W., and Company DLB-46
Norwood, Robert 1874-1932 ....DLB-92
Nosaka Akiyuki 1930- DLB-182
Nossack, Hans Erich 1901-1977.........DLB-69

Not Immediately Discernible . . . but Eventually
  Quite Clear: The *First Light* and *Final Years*
  of Hemingway's Centenary Y-99
A Note on Technique (1926), by
  Elizabeth A. Drew [excerpts].........DLB-36
Notker Balbulus circa 840-912.........DLB-148
Notker III of Saint Gall
  circa 950-1022.....................DLB-148
Notker von Zweifalten ?-1095 ....DLB-148
Nourse, Alan E. 1928- DLB-8
Novak, Slobodan 1924- DLB-181
Novak, Vjenceslav
  1859-1905 ....DLB-147
Novakovich, Josip 1956- DLB-244
Novalis 1772-1801 ....DLB-90; CDWLB-2
Novaro, Mario 1868-1944...............DLB-114
Novás Calvo, Lino
  1903-1983 ....DLB-145
"The Novel in [Robert Browning's] 'The Ring and
  the Book'" (1912), by Henry James ...DLB-32
The Novel of Impressionism,
  by Jethro Bithell DLB-66
Novel-Reading: *The Works of Charles Dickens,
  The Works of W. Makepeace Thackeray*
  (1879), by Anthony Trollope DLB-21
Novels for Grown-Ups Y-97
The Novels of Dorothy Richardson (1918),
  by May Sinclair DLB-36
Novels with a Purpose (1864), by
  Justin M'Carthy DLB-21
Noventa, Giacomo 1898-1960...........DLB-114
Novikov, Nikolai
  Ivanovich 1744-1818 ....DLB-150
Novomeský, Laco
  1904-1976 ....DLB-215
Nowlan, Alden 1933-1983...............DLB-53
Noyes, Alfred 1880-1958...............DLB-20
Noyes, Crosby S. 1825-1908 ....DLB-23
Noyes, Nicholas 1647-1717.............DLB-24
Noyes, Theodore W. 1858-1946..........DLB-29
N-Town Plays circa 1468 to early
  sixteenth century DLB-146
Nugent, Frank 1908-1965 ....DLB-44
Nugent, Richard Bruce 1906- DLB-151
Nušić, Branislav
  1864-1938 .... DLB-147; CDWLB-4
Nutt, David [publishing house] DLB-106
Nwapa, Flora 1931-1993 ....DLB-125; CDWLB-3
Nye, Bill 1850-1896...................DLB-186
Nye, Edgar Wilson (Bill) 1850-1896 ...DLB-11, 23
Nye, Naomi Shihab 1952- DLB-120
Nye, Robert 1939- DLB-14
Nyka-Niliūnas, Alfonsas
  1919- DLB-220

O

Oakes Smith, Elizabeth
  1806-1893 ....DLB-1, 239, 243
Oakes, Urian circa 1631-1681 ....DLB-24
Oakley, Violet 1874-1961 ....DLB-188

Oates, Joyce Carol 1938- ... DLB-2, 5, 130; Y-81
Ōba Minako 1930- DLB-182
Ober, Frederick Albion 1849-1913 .....DLB-189
Ober, William 1920-1993 .... Y-93
Oberholtzer, Ellis Paxson 1868-1936...DLB-47
Obradović, Dositej 1740?-1811 ....DLB-147
O'Brien, Charlotte Grace 1845-1909....DLB-240
O'Brien, Edna 1932- DLB-14, 231; CDBLB-8
O'Brien, Fitz-James 1828-1862..........DLB-74
O'Brien, Flann (see O'Nolan, Brian)
O'Brien, Kate 1897-1974...............DLB-15
O'Brien, Tim
  1946- DLB-152; Y-80; DS-9; CDALB-7
O'Casey, Sean 1880-1964 .....DLB-10; CDBLB-6
Occom, Samson 1723-1792 ....DLB-175
Ochs, Adolph S. 1858-1935.............DLB-25
Ochs-Oakes, George Washington
  1861-1931 ....DLB-137
O'Connor, Flannery 1925-1964
  .... DLB-2, 152; Y-80; DS-12; CDALB-1
O'Connor, Frank 1903-1966 ....DLB-162
Octopus Publishing Group DLB-112
Oda Sakunosuke 1913-1947 ....DLB-182
Odell, Jonathan 1737-1818............DLB-31, 99
O'Dell, Scott 1903-1989...............DLB-52
Odets, Clifford 1906-1963 ....DLB-7, 26
Odhams Press Limited DLB-112
Odoevsky, Aleksandr Ivanovich
  1802-1839 ....DLB-205
Odoevsky, Vladimir Fedorovich
  1804 or 1803-1869 ....DLB-198
O'Donnell, Peter 1920- DLB-87
O'Donovan, Michael (see O'Connor, Frank)
O'Dowd, Bernard 1866-1953 ....DLB-230
Ōe Kenzaburō 1935- DLB-182; Y-94
O'Faolain, Julia 1932- DLB-14, 231
O'Faolain, Sean 1900- DLB-15, 162
Off Broadway and Off-Off Broadway......DLB-7
Off-Loop Theatres.....................DLB-7
Offord, Carl Ruthven 1910- DLB-76
O'Flaherty, Liam 1896-1984 ... DLB-36, 162; Y-84
Ogilvie, J. S., and Company DLB-49
Ogilvy, Eliza 1822-1912...............DLB-199
Ogot, Grace 1930- DLB-125
O'Grady, Desmond 1935- DLB-40
Ogunyemi, Wale 1939- DLB-157
O'Hagan, Howard 1902-1982............DLB-68
O'Hara, Frank 1926-1966 ....DLB-5, 16, 193
O'Hara, John
  1905-1970 ....DLB-9, 86; DS-2; CDALB-5
John O'Hara's Pottsville Journalism Y-88
O'Hegarty, P. S. 1879-1955............DLB-201
Okara, Gabriel 1921- DLB-125; CDWLB-3
O'Keeffe, John 1747-1833..............DLB-89
Okes, Nicholas [publishing house]......DLB-170

Okigbo, Christopher 1930-1967............ DLB-125; CDWLB-3
Okot p'Bitek 1931-1982 .... DLB-125; CDWLB-3
Okpewho, Isidore 1941- DLB-157
Okri, Ben 1959- DLB-157, 231
Olaudah Equiano and Unfinished Journeys: The Slave-Narrative Tradition and Twentieth-Century Continuities, by Paul Edwards and Pauline T. Wangman DLB-117
Old English Literature: An Introduction................. DLB-146
Old English Riddles eighth to tenth centuries........... DLB-146
Old Franklin Publishing House DLB-49
Old German Genesis and *Old German Exodus* circa 1050-circa 1130 .... DLB-148
Old High German Charms and Blessings............ DLB-148; CDWLB-2
The *Old High German Isidor* circa 790-800 .... DLB-148
The Old Manse DLB-223
Older, Fremont 1856-1935............. DLB-25
Oldham, John 1653-1683.............. DLB-131
Oldman, C. B. 1894-1969............. DLB-201
Olds, Sharon 1942- DLB-120
Olearius, Adam 1599-1671 .... DLB-164
O'Leary, Ellen 1831-1889............. DLB-240
Oliphant, Laurence 1829?-1888 ..... DLB-18, 166
Oliphant, Margaret 1828-1897 ...... DLB-18, 190
Oliver, Chad 1928- DLB-8
Oliver, Mary 1935- DLB-5, 193
Ollier, Claude 1922- DLB-83
Olsen, Tillie 1912 or 1913- DLB-28, 206; Y-80; CDALB-7
Olson, Charles 1910-1970........ DLB-5, 16, 193
Olson, Elder 1909- DLB-48, 63
Omotoso, Kole 1943- DLB-125
Omulevsky, Innokentii Vasil'evich 1836 [or 1837]-1883.............. DLB-238
On Learning to Write..................... Y-88
Ondaatje, Michael 1943- DLB-60
O'Neill, Eugene 1888-1953..... DLB-7; CDALB-5
Eugene O'Neill Memorial Theater Center DLB-7
Eugene O'Neill's Letters: A Review Y-88
Onetti, Juan Carlos 1909-1994 .... DLB-113; CDWLB-3
Onions, George Oliver 1872-1961 ...... DLB-153
Onofri, Arturo 1885-1928 .... DLB-114
O'Nolan, Brian 1911-1966 .... DLB-231
Opie, Amelia 1769-1853 .... DLB-116, 159
Opitz, Martin 1597-1639............. DLB-164
Oppen, George 1908-1984 .... DLB-5, 165
Oppenheim, E. Phillips 1866-1946 ...... DLB-70
Oppenheim, James 1882-1932 .... DLB-28
Oppenheimer, Joel 1930-1988 ...... DLB-5, 193
Optic, Oliver (see Adams, William Taylor)
Oral History: B. W. Huebsch............. Y-99

Oral History Interview with Donald S. Klopfer......................... Y-97
Orczy, Emma, Baroness 1865-1947 ...... DLB-70
Oregon Shakespeare Festival Y-00
Origo, Iris 1902-1988 .... DLB-155
Orlovitz, Gil 1918-1973 .... DLB-2, 5
Orlovsky, Peter 1933- DLB-16
Ormond, John 1923- DLB-27
Ornitz, Samuel 1890-1957 .... DLB-28, 44
O'Rourke, P. J. 1947- DLB-185
Orten, Jiří 1919-1941 .... DLB-215
Ortese, Anna Maria 1914- DLB-177
Ortiz, Simon J. 1941- DLB-120, 175
Ortnit and *Wolfdietrich* circa 1225-1250.... DLB-138
Orton, Joe 1933-1967 .... DLB-13; CDBLB-8
Orwell, George 1903-1950 ...... DLB-15, 98, 195; CDBLB-7
The Orwell Year........................ Y-84
(Re-)Publishing Orwell Y-86
Ory, Carlos Edmundo de 1923- DLB-134
Osbey, Brenda Marie 1957- DLB-120
Osbon, B. S. 1827-1912................. DLB-43
Osborn, Sarah 1714-1796 .... DLB-200
Osborne, John 1929-1994..... DLB-13; CDBLB-7
Osgood, Francis Sargent 1811-1850 ..... DLB-250
Osgood, Herbert L. 1855-1918.......... DLB-47
Osgood, James R., and Company DLB-49
Osgood, McIlvaine and Company DLB-112
O'Shaughnessy, Arthur 1844-1881....... DLB-35
O'Shea, Patrick [publishing house]....... DLB-49
Osipov, Nikolai Petrovich 1751-1799..................... DLB-150
Oskison, John Milton 1879-1947 ....DLB-175
Osler, Sir William 1849-1919 .... DLB-184
Osofisan, Femi 1946- DLB-125; CDWLB-3
Ostenso, Martha 1900-1963 .... DLB-92
Ostrauskas, Kostas 1926- DLB-232
Ostriker, Alicia 1937- DLB-120
Osundare, Niyi 1947- DLB-157; CDWLB-3
Oswald, Eleazer 1755-1795 .... DLB-43
Oswald von Wolkenstein 1376 or 1377-1445 ....DLB-179
Otero, Blas de 1916-1979 .... DLB-134
Otero, Miguel Antonio 1859-1944 .... DLB-82
Otero, Nina 1881-1965................ DLB-209
Otero Silva, Miguel 1908-1985 .... DLB-145
Otfried von Weißenburg circa 800-circa 875? DLB-148
Otis, Broaders and Company........... DLB-49
Otis, James (see Kaler, James Otis)
Otis, James, Jr. 1725-1783 .... DLB-31
Ottaway, James 1911- DLB-127
Ottendorfer, Oswald 1826-1900......... DLB-23
Ottieri, Ottiero 1924- DLB-177
Otto-Peters, Louise 1819-1895 .... DLB-129
Otway, Thomas 1652-1685 .... DLB-80

Ouellette, Fernand 1930- DLB-60
Ouida 1839-1908 .... DLB-18, 156
Outing Publishing Company DLB-46
Outlaw Days, by Joyce Johnson........ DLB-16
Overbury, Sir Thomas circa 1581-1613 .... DLB-151
The Overlook Press................. DLB-46
Overview of U.S. Book Publishing, 1910-1945 .... DLB-9
Ovid 43 B.C.-A.D. 17........DLB-211; CDWLB-1
Owen, Guy 1925- DLB-5
Owen, John 1564-1622............... DLB-121
Owen, John [publishing house]......... DLB-49
Owen, Peter, Limited DLB-112
Owen, Robert 1771-1858 .... DLB-107, 158
Owen, Wilfred 1893-1918 .... DLB-20; DS-18; CDBLB-6
The Owl and the Nightingale circa 1189-1199 .... DLB-146
Owsley, Frank L. 1890-1956 ....DLB-17
Oxford, Seventeenth Earl of, Edward de Vere 1550-1604................DLB-172
Ozerov, Vladislav Aleksandrovich 1769-1816................. DLB-150
Ozick, Cynthia 1928- DLB-28, 152; Y-83
First Strauss "Livings" Awarded to Cynthia Ozick and Raymond Carver An Interview with Cynthia Ozick Y-83

P

Pace, Richard 1482?-1536 .... DLB-167
Pacey, Desmond 1917-1975 .... DLB-88
Pack, Robert 1929- DLB-5
Packaging Papa: *The Garden of Eden* Y-86
Padell Publishing Company DLB-46
Padgett, Ron 1942- DLB-5
Padilla, Ernesto Chávez 1944- DLB-122
Page, L. C., and Company............. DLB-49
Page, Louise 1955- DLB-233
Page, P. K. 1916- DLB-68
Page, Thomas Nelson 1853-1922 ....DLB-12, 78; DS-13
Page, Walter Hines 1855-1918........DLB-71, 91
Paget, Francis Edward 1806-1882 ...... DLB-163
Paget, Violet (see Lee, Vernon)
Pagliarani, Elio 1927- DLB-128
Pain, Barry 1864-1928 ....DLB-135, 197
Pain, Philip ?-circa 1666................ DLB-24
Paine, Robert Treat, Jr. 1773-1811 .... DLB-37
Paine, Thomas 1737-1809 .... DLB-31, 43, 73, 158; CDALB-2
Painter, George D. 1914- DLB-155
Painter, William 1540?-1594 .... DLB-136
Palazzeschi, Aldo 1885-1974 .... DLB-114
Paley, Grace 1922- DLB-28, 218
Palfrey, John Gorham 1796-1881 .. DLB-1, 30, 235
Palgrave, Francis Turner 1824-1897...... DLB-35

Palmer, Joe H. 1904-1952 . . . . DLB-171

Palmer, Michael 1943- DLB-169

Paltock, Robert 1697-1767 . . . . DLB-39

Paludan, Jacob 1896-1975 . . . . DLB-214

Pan Books Limited. DLB-112

Panama, Norman 1914- and
Frank, Melvin 1913-1988 . . . . DLB-26

Panaev, Ivan Ivanovich 1812-1862 . . . . . . DLB-198

Panaeva, Avdot'ia Iakovlevna
1820-1893 . . . . DLB-238

Pancake, Breece D'J 1952-1979 . . . . DLB-130

Panduro, Leif 1923-1977 . . . . DLB-214

Panero, Leopoldo 1909-1962. . . . . DLB-108

Pangborn, Edgar 1909-1976. . . . . DLB-8

"Panic Among the Philistines": A Postscript,
An Interview with Bryan Griffin. Y-81

Panizzi, Sir Anthony 1797-1879 . . . . DLB-184

Panneton, Philippe (see Ringuet)

Panshin, Alexei 1940- DLB-8

Pansy (see Alden, Isabella)

Pantheon Books. DLB-46

Papadat-Bengescu, Hortensia
1876-1955 . . . . DLB-220

Papantonio, Michael (see Kohn, John S. Van E.)

Paperback Library DLB-46

Paperback Science Fiction DLB-8

Paquet, Alfons 1881-1944 . . . . DLB-66

Paracelsus 1493-1541. . . . . DLB-179

Paradis, Suzanne 1936- DLB-53

Páral, Vladimír, 1932- DLB-232

Pardoe, Julia 1804-1862 . . . . DLB-166

Paredes, Américo 1915-1999 . . . . DLB-209

Pareja Diezcanseco, Alfredo 1908-1993 . . . DLB-145

Parents' Magazine Press DLB-46

Parise, Goffredo 1929-1986 . . . . DLB-177

Parisian Theater, Fall 1984: Toward
A New Baroque. Y-85

Parizeau, Alice 1930- DLB-60

Parke, John 1754-1789 . . . . DLB-31

Parker, Dan 1893-1967 . . . . DLB-241

Parker, Dorothy 1893-1967 . . . . DLB-11, 45, 86

Parker, Gilbert 1860-1932 . . . . DLB-99

Parker, J. H. [publishing house] DLB-106

Parker, James 1714-1770 . . . . DLB-43

Parker, John [publishing house] DLB-106

Parker, Matthew 1504-1575 . . . . DLB-213

Parker, Stewart 1941-1988. . . . . DLB-245

Parker, Theodore 1810-1860 . . . . DLB-1, 235

Parker, William Riley 1906-1968 . . . . DLB-103

Parkes, Bessie Rayner (Madame Belloc)
1829-1925 . . . . DLB-240

Parkman, Francis
1823-1893 . . . . DLB-1, 30, 183, 186, 235

Parks, Gordon 1912- DLB-33

Parks, Tim 1954- DLB-231

Parks, William 1698-1750 . . . . DLB-43

Parks, William [publishing house] DLB-49

Parley, Peter (see Goodrich, Samuel Griswold)

Parmenides
late sixth-fifth century B.C. DLB-176

Parnell, Thomas 1679-1718 . . . . DLB-95

Parnicki, Teodor 1908-1988 . . . . DLB-215

Parr, Catherine 1513?-1548 . . . . DLB-136

Parrington, Vernon L. 1871-1929 . . . . . DLB-17, 63

Parrish, Maxfield 1870-1966 . . . . DLB-188

Parronchi, Alessandro 1914- DLB-128

Parton, James 1822-1891 . . . . DLB-30

Parton, Sara Payson Willis
1811-1872 . . . . DLB-43, 74, 239

Partridge, S. W., and Company DLB-106

Parun, Vesna 1922- DLB-181; CDWLB-4

Pasinetti, Pier Maria 1913- DLB-177

Pasolini, Pier Paolo 1922- DLB-128, 177

Pastan, Linda 1932- DLB-5

Paston, George (Emily Morse Symonds)
1860-1936 . . . . DLB-149, 197

The Paston Letters 1422-1509 . . . . DLB-146

Pastorius, Francis Daniel
1651-circa 1720 . . . . DLB-24

Patchen, Kenneth 1911-1972 . . . . DLB-16, 48

Pater, Walter
1839-1894 . . . . DLB-57, 156; CDBLB-4

Aesthetic Poetry (1873) DLB-35

Paterson, A. B. "Banjo" 1864-1941 . . . . . . DLB-230

Paterson, Katherine 1932- DLB-52

Patmore, Coventry 1823-1896 . . . . DLB-35, 98

Paton, Alan 1903-1988 . . . . DS-17

Paton, Joseph Noel 1821-1901 . . . . DLB-35

Paton Walsh, Jill 1937- DLB-161

Patrick, Edwin Hill ("Ted") 1901-1964 . . . DLB-137

Patrick, John 1906-1995. . . . . DLB-7

Pattee, Fred Lewis 1863-1950 . . . . DLB-71

Pattern and Paradigm: History as
Design, by Judith Ryan DLB-75

Patterson, Alicia 1906-1963 . . . . DLB-127

Patterson, Eleanor Medill 1881-1948 . . . . . DLB-29

Patterson, Eugene 1923- DLB-127

Patterson, Joseph Medill 1879-1946 . . . . . . DLB-29

Pattillo, Henry 1726-1801 . . . . DLB-37

Paul, Elliot 1891-1958 . . . . DLB-4

Paul, Jean (see Richter, Johann Paul Friedrich)

Paul, Kegan, Trench, Trubner and
Company Limited DLB-106

Paul, Peter, Book Company DLB-49

Paul, Stanley, and Company Limited DLB-112

Paulding, James Kirke
1778-1860 . . . . DLB-3, 59, 74, 250

Paulin, Tom 1949- DLB-40

Pauper, Peter, Press DLB-46

Pavese, Cesare 1908-1950 . . . . DLB-128, 177

Pavić, Milorad 1929- DLB-181; CDWLB-4

Pavlov, Konstantin 1933- DLB-181

Pavlov, Nikolai Filippovich 1803-1864 . . . . . DLB-198

Pavlova, Karolina Karlovna 1807-1893 . . . . DLB-205

Pavlović, Miodrag
1928- DLB-181; CDWLB-4

Paxton, John 1911-1985 . . . . DLB-44

Payn, James 1830-1898 . . . . DLB-18

Payne, John 1842-1916 . . . . DLB-35

Payne, John Howard 1791-1852 . . . . DLB-37

Payson and Clarke DLB-46

Paz, Octavio 1914-1998. . . . . Y-90, Y-98

Pazzi, Roberto 1946- DLB-196

Peabody, Elizabeth Palmer 1804-1894 . . DLB-1, 223

Peabody, Elizabeth Palmer
[publishing house] DLB-49

Peabody, Josephine Preston 1874-1922 . . . DLB-249

Peabody, Oliver William Bourn
1799-1848 . . . . DLB-59

Peace, Roger 1899-1968 . . . . DLB-127

Peacham, Henry 1578-1644? DLB-151

Peacham, Henry, the Elder
1547-1634 . . . . DLB-172, 236

Peachtree Publishers, Limited DLB-46

Peacock, Molly 1947- DLB-120

Peacock, Thomas Love 1785-1866 . . . DLB-96, 116

Pead, Deuel ?-1727 . . . . DLB-24

Peake, Mervyn 1911-1968 . . . . DLB-15, 160

Peale, Rembrandt 1778-1860 . . . . DLB-183

Pear Tree Press DLB-112

Pearce, Philippa 1920- DLB-161

Pearson, H. B. [publishing house] DLB-49

Pearson, Hesketh 1887-1964 . . . . DLB-149

Pechersky, Andrei (see Mel'nikov, Pavel Ivanovich)

Peck, George W. 1840-1916 . . . . DLB-23, 42

Peck, H. C., and Theo. Bliss
[publishing house] DLB-49

Peck, Harry Thurston 1856-1914 . . . . . DLB-71, 91

Peden, William 1913-1999 . . . . DLB-234

Peele, George 1556-1596 . . . . DLB-62, 167

Pegler, Westbrook 1894-1969 . . . . DLB-171

Pekić, Borislav 1930-1992 . . . DLB-181; CDWLB-4

Pellegrini and Cudahy DLB-46

Pelletier, Aimé (see Vac, Bertrand)

Pelletier, Francine 1959- DLB-251

Pemberton, Sir Max 1863-1950 . . . . DLB-70

de la Peña, Terri 1947- DLB-209

Penfield, Edward 1866-1925 . . . . DLB-188

Penguin Books [U.K.] DLB-112

Penguin Books [U.S.] DLB-46

Penn Publishing Company DLB-49

Penn, William 1644-1718 . . . . DLB-24

Penna, Sandro 1906-1977 . . . . DLB-114

Pennell, Joseph 1857-1926 . . . . DLB-188

Penner, Jonathan 1940- Y-83

Pennington, Lee 1939- Y-82

Pepys, Samuel
1633-1703 . . . . DLB-101, 213; CDBLB-2

Percy, Thomas 1729-1811 . . . . DLB-104

Percy, Walker 1916-1990.....DLB-2; Y-80, Y-90
Percy, William 1575-1648..............DLB-172
Perec, Georges 1936-1982 .... DLB-83
Perelman, Bob 1947- DLB-193
Perelman, S. J. 1904-1979 .... DLB-11, 44
Perez, Raymundo "Tigre" 1946- DLB-122
Peri Rossi, Cristina 1941- DLB-145
Perkins, Eugene 1932- DLB-41
Perkoff, Stuart Z. 1930-1974........... DLB-16
Perley, Moses Henry 1804-1862 .... DLB-99
Permabooks DLB-46
Perovsky, Aleksei Alekseevich
 (Antonii Pogorel'sky) 1787-1836..... DLB-198
Perri, Henry 1561-1617 .... DLB-236
Perrin, Alice 1867-1934............... DLB-156
Perry, Bliss 1860-1954 .... DLB-71
Perry, Eleanor 1915-1981 .... DLB-44
Perry, Henry (see Perri, Henry)
Perry, Matthew 1794-1858 .... DLB-183
Perry, Sampson 1747-1823 .... DLB-158
Persius A.D. 34-A.D. 62............... DLB-211
Perutz, Leo 1882-1957 .... DLB-81
Pesetsky, Bette 1932- DLB-130
Pestalozzi, Johann Heinrich 1746-1827 .... DLB-94
Peter, Laurence J. 1919-1990 .... DLB-53
Peter of Spain circa 1205-1277 .... DLB-115
Peterkin, Julia 1880-1961 .... DLB-9
Peters, Lenrie 1932- DLB-117
Peters, Robert 1924- DLB-105
"Foreword to *Ludwig of Bavaria*" DLB-105
Petersham, Maud 1889-1971 and
 Petersham, Miska 1888-1960........ DLB-22
Peterson, Charles Jacobs 1819-1887 ...... DLB-79
Peterson, Len 1917- DLB-88
Peterson, Levi S. 1933- DLB-206
Peterson, Louis 1922-1998 .... DLB-76
Peterson, T. B., and Brothers DLB-49
Petitclair, Pierre 1813-1860............. DLB-99
Petrescu, Camil 1894-1957 .... DLB-220
Petronius circa A.D. 20-A.D. 66
 .... DLB-211; CDWLB-1
Petrov, Aleksandar 1938- DLB-181
Petrov, Gavriil 1730-1801.............. DLB-150
Petrov, Valeri 1920- DLB-181
Petrov, Vasilii Petrovich 1736-1799 ..... DLB-150
Petrović, Rastko
 1898-1949 ....DLB-147; CDWLB-4
Petruslied circa 854? DLB-148
Petry, Ann 1908-1997................. DLB-76
Pettie, George circa 1548-1589 .... DLB-136
Peyton, K. M. 1929- DLB-161
Pfaffe Konrad flourished circa 1172 ..... DLB-148
Pfaffe Lamprecht flourished circa 1150 .. DLB-148
Pfeiffer, Emily 1827-1890 .... DLB-199
Pforzheimer, Carl H. 1879-1957 .... DLB-140

Phaedrus circa 18 B.C.-circa A.D. 50 .... DLB-211
Phaer, Thomas 1510?-1560 .... DLB-167
Phaidon Press Limited DLB-112
Pharr, Robert Deane 1916-1992......... DLB-33
Phelps, Elizabeth Stuart 1815-1852...... DLB-202
Phelps, Elizabeth Stuart 1844-1911... DLB-74, 221
Philander von der Linde
 (see Mencke, Johann Burckhard)
Philby, H. St. John B. 1885-1960 .... DLB-195
Philip, Marlene Nourbese 1947- DLB-157
Philippe, Charles-Louis 1874-1909 .... DLB-65
Philips, John 1676-1708................ DLB-95
Philips, Katherine 1632-1664 .... DLB-131
Phillipps, Sir Thomas 1792-1872........ DLB-184
Phillips, Caryl 1958- DLB-157
Phillips, David Graham 1867-1911..... DLB-9, 12
Phillips, Jayne Anne 1952- Y-80
Phillips, Robert 1938- DLB-105
"Finding, Losing, Reclaiming: A Note
 on My Poems"................. DLB-105
Phillips, Sampson and Company DLB-49
Phillips, Stephen 1864-1915 .... DLB-10
Phillips, Ulrich B. 1877-1934........... DLB-17
Phillips, Wendell 1811-1884........... DLB-235
Phillips, Willard 1784-1873 .... DLB-59
Phillips, William 1907- DLB-137
Phillpotts, Adelaide Eden (Adelaide Ross)
 1896-1993 .... DLB-191
Phillpotts, Eden 1862-1960...DLB-10, 70, 135, 153
Philo circa 20-15 B.C.-circa A.D. 50......DLB-176
Philosophical Library DLB-46
Phinney, Elihu [publishing house] DLB-49
Phoenix, John (see Derby, George Horatio)
PHYLON (Fourth Quarter, 1950),
 The Negro in Literature:
 The Current Scene................ DLB-76
Physiologus circa 1070-circa 1150 ...... DLB-148
Piccolo, Lucio 1903-1969 .... DLB-114
Pickard, Tom 1946- DLB-40
Pickering, William [publishing house] ... DLB-106
Pickthall, Marjorie 1883-1922 .... DLB-92
Pictorial Printing Company DLB-49
Piercy, Marge 1936- DLB-120, 227
Pierro, Albino 1916- DLB-128
Pignotti, Lamberto 1926- DLB-128
Pike, Albert 1809-1891 .... DLB-74
Pike, Zebulon Montgomery
 1779-1813.................... DLB-183
Pillat, Ion 1891-1945................. DLB-220
Pilon, Jean-Guy 1930- DLB-60
Pinckney, Eliza Lucas 1722-1793 .... DLB-200
Pinckney, Josephine 1895-1957 .... DLB-6
Pindar circa 518 B.C.-circa 438 B.C.
 ....DLB-176; CDWLB-1
Pindar, Peter (see Wolcot, John)
Pineda, Cecile 1942- DLB-209

Pinero, Arthur Wing 1855-1934......... DLB-10
Pinget, Robert 1919-1997 .... DLB-83
Pinkney, Edward Coote 1802-1828 ..... DLB-248
Pinnacle Books...................... DLB-46
Piñon, Nélida 1935- DLB-145
Pinsky, Robert 1940- Y-82
Robert Pinsky Reappointed Poet Laureate.... Y-98
Pinter, Harold 1930- DLB-13; CDBLB-8
Piontek, Heinz 1925- DLB-75
Piozzi, Hester Lynch [Thrale]
 1741-1821.................DLB-104, 142
Piper, H. Beam 1904-1964.............. DLB-8
Piper, Watty........................ DLB-22
Pirckheimer, Caritas 1467-1532 ....DLB-179
Pirckheimer, Willibald 1470-1530 ....DLB-179
Pisar, Samuel 1929- Y-83
Pisemsky, Aleksai Feofilaktovich
 1821-1881 .... DLB-238
Pitkin, Timothy 1766-1847............ DLB-30
The Pitt Poetry Series: Poetry Publishing
 Today Y-85
Pitter, Ruth 1897- DLB-20
Pix, Mary 1666-1709 .... DLB-80
Pixerécourt, René Charles Guilbert de
 1773-1844..................... DLB-192
Plaatje, Sol T. 1876-1932 .... DLB-125, 225
Plante, David 1940- Y-83
Platen, August von 1796-1835 .... DLB-90
Plath, Sylvia
 1932-1963 .... DLB-5, 6, 152; CDALB-1
Plato circa 428 B.C.-348-347 B.C.
 ....DLB-176; CDWLB-1
Plato, Ann 1824?-? DLB-239
Platon 1737-1812.................... DLB-150
Platt and Munk Company DLB-46
Plautus circa 254 B.C.-184 B.C.
 ....DLB-211; CDWLB-1
Playboy Press....................... DLB-46
Playford, John [publishing house]........DLB-170
Plays, Playwrights, and Playgoers DLB-84
Playwrights on the Theater DLB-80
Der Pleier flourished circa 1250 .... DLB-138
Plenzdorf, Ulrich 1934- DLB-75
Plessen, Elizabeth 1944- DLB-75
Pletnev, Petr Aleksandrovich
 1792-1865..................... DLB-205
Pliekšāne, Elza Rozenberga (see Aspazija)
Pliekšāns, Jānis (see Rainis, Jānis)
Plievier, Theodor 1892-1955 .... DLB-69
Plimpton, George 1927- DLB-185, 241; Y-99
Pliny the Elder A.D. 23/24-A.D. 79 ..... DLB-211
Pliny the Younger
 circa A.D. 61-A.D. 112............ DLB-211
Plomer, William
 1903-1973...........DLB-20, 162, 191, 225
Plotinus 204-270.........DLB-176; CDWLB-1
Plowright, Teresa 1952- DLB-251

Plume, Thomas 1630-1704 . . . . DLB-213	Popov, Mikhail Ivanovich 1742-circa 1790 . . . . DLB-150	The Practice of Biography II: An Interview with B. L. Reid Y-83
Plumly, Stanley 1939- DLB-5, 193	Popović, Aleksandar 1929-1996 . . . . DLB-181	The Practice of Biography III: An Interview with Humphrey Carpenter Y-84
Plumpp, Sterling D. 1940- DLB-41	Popular Library DLB-46	The Practice of Biography IV: An Interview with William Manchester Y-85
Plunkett, James 1920- DLB-14	Porete, Marguerite ?-1310 . . . . DLB-208	
Plutarch circa 46-circa 120 . . . . . . DLB-176; CDWLB-1	Porlock, Martin (see MacDonald, Philip)	The Practice of Biography VI: An Interview with David Herbert Donald Y-87
Plymell, Charles 1935- DLB-16	Porpoise Press DLB-112	The Practice of Biography VII: An Interview with John Caldwell Guilds Y-92
Pocket Books DLB-46	Porta, Antonio 1935-1989 . . . . DLB-128	
Poe, Edgar Allan 1809-1849 . . . . DLB-3, 59, 73, 74, 248; CDALB-2	Porter, Anna Maria 1780-1832 . . . . . DLB-116, 159	The Practice of Biography VIII: An Interview with Joan Mellen Y-94
	Porter, David 1780-1843 . . . . DLB-183	
Poe, James 1921-1980 . . . . DLB-44	Porter, Eleanor H. 1868-1920 . . . . DLB-9	The Practice of Biography IX: An Interview with Michael Reynolds Y-95
The Poet Laureate of the United States Statements from Former Consultants in Poetry Y-86	Porter, Gene Stratton (see Stratton-Porter, Gene)	Prados, Emilio 1899-1962 . . . . DLB-134
	Porter, Henry ?-? DLB-62	Praed, Mrs. Caroline (see Praed, Rosa)
Pogodin, Mikhail Petrovich 1800-1875 . . . . DLB-198	Porter, Jane 1776-1850 . . . . DLB-116, 159	Praed, Rosa (Mrs. Caroline Praed) 1851-1935 . . . . DLB-230
Pogorel'sky, Antonii (see Perovsky, Aleksei Alekseevich)	Porter, Katherine Anne 1890-1980 . . . . . . DLB-4, 9, 102; Y-80; DS-12; CDALB-7	Praed, Winthrop Mackworth 1802-1839 . . . DLB-96
Pohl, Frederik 1919- DLB-8	Porter, Peter 1929- DLB-40	Praeger Publishers DLB-46
Poirier, Louis (see Gracq, Julien)	Porter, William Sydney 1862-1910 . . . . DLB-12, 78, 79; CDALB-3	Praetorius, Johannes 1630-1680 . . . . DLB-168
Poláček, Karel 1892-1945 . . . DLB-215; CDWLB-4		Pratolini, Vasco 1913-1991 . . . . DLB-177
Polanyi, Michael 1891-1976 . . . . DLB-100	Porter, William T. 1809-1858 . . . . . DLB-3, 43, 250	Pratt, E. J. 1882-1964 . . . . DLB-92
Pole, Reginald 1500-1558 . . . . DLB-132	Porter and Coates DLB-49	Pratt, Samuel Jackson 1749-1814 . . . . DLB-39
Polevoi, Nikolai Alekseevich 1796-1846 . . . . DLB-198	Portillo Trambley, Estela 1927-1998 . . . . . DLB-209	Preciado Martin, Patricia 1939- DLB-209
	Portis, Charles 1933- DLB-6	Preface to *The History of Romances* (1715), by Pierre Daniel Huet [excerpts] DLB-39
Polezhaev, Aleksandr Ivanovich 1804-1838 . . . . DLB-205	Posey, Alexander 1873-1908 . . . . DLB-175	
Poliakoff, Stephen 1952- DLB-13	Postans, Marianne circa 1810-1865 . . . . . . DLB-166	Préfontaine, Yves 1937- DLB-53
Polidori, John William 1795-1821 . . . . . . DLB-116	Postl, Carl (see Sealsfield, Carl)	Prelutsky, Jack 1940- DLB-61
Polite, Carlene Hatcher 1932- DLB-33	Poston, Ted 1906-1974 . . . . DLB-51	Premisses, by Michael Hamburger DLB-66
Pollard, Alfred W. 1859-1944 . . . . DLB-201	Potekhin, Aleksei Antipovich 1829-1908 . . DLB-238	Prentice, George D. 1802-1870 . . . . DLB-43
Pollard, Edward A. 1832-1872 . . . . DLB-30	Potok, Chaim 1929- DLB-28, 152	Prentice-Hall DLB-46
Pollard, Graham 1903-1976 . . . . DLB-201	A Conversation with Chaim Potok Y-84	Prescott, Orville 1906-1996 . . . . Y-96
Pollard, Percival 1869-1911 . . . . DLB-71	Potter, Beatrix 1866-1943 . . . . DLB-141	Prescott, William Hickling 1796-1859 . . . . DLB-1, 30, 59, 235
Pollard and Moss DLB-49	Potter, David M. 1910-1971 . . . . DLB-17	
Pollock, Sharon 1936- DLB-60	Potter, Dennis 1935-1994 . . . . DLB-233	The Present State of the English Novel (1892), by George Saintsbury DLB-18
Polonsky, Abraham 1910-1999 . . . . DLB-26	The Harry Potter Phenomenon Y-99	
Polotsky, Simeon 1629-1680 . . . . DLB-150	Potter, John E., and Company DLB-49	Prešeren, Francè 1800-1849 . . . . DLB-147; CDWLB-4
Polybius circa 200 B.C.-118 B.C. DLB-176	Pottle, Frederick A. 1897-1987 . . . . . DLB-103; Y-87	
Pomialovsky, Nikolai Gerasimovich 1835-1863 . . . . DLB-238	Poulin, Jacques 1937- DLB-60	Preston, Margaret Junkin 1820-1897 . . . . DLB-239, 248
	Pound, Ezra 1885-1972 . . . . DLB-4, 45, 63; DS-15; CDALB-4	Preston, May Wilson 1873-1949 . . . . DLB-188
Pomilio, Mario 1921-1990 . . . . DLB-177		Preston, Thomas 1537-1598 . . . . DLB-62
Ponce, Mary Helen 1938- DLB-122	Poverman, C. E. 1944- DLB-234	Price, Reynolds 1933- DLB-2, 218
Ponce-Montoya, Juanita 1949- DLB-122	Povich, Shirley 1905-1998 . . . . DLB-171	Price, Richard 1723-1791 . . . . DLB-158
Ponet, John 1516?-1556 . . . . DLB-132	Powell, Anthony 1905-2000 . . . DLB-15; CDBLB-7	Price, Richard 1949- Y-81
Poniatowski, Elena 1933- DLB-113; CDWLB-3	Dawn Powell, Where Have You Been All Our Lives? Y-97	Prideaux, John 1578-1650 . . . . DLB-236
		Priest, Christopher 1943- DLB-14, 207
Ponsard, François 1814-1867 . . . . DLB-192	Powell, John Wesley 1834-1902 . . . . DLB-186	Priestley, J. B. 1894-1984 . . . . DLB-10, 34, 77, 100, 139; Y-84; CDBLB-6
Ponsonby, William [publishing house] . . . DLB-170	Powell, Padgett 1952- DLB-234	
Pontiggia, Giuseppe 1934- DLB-196	Powers, J. F. 1917-1999 . . . . DLB-130	Primary Bibliography: A Retrospective Y-95
Pony Stories DLB-160	Powers, Jimmy 1903-1995 . . . . DLB-241	Prime, Benjamin Young 1733-1791 . . . . . . DLB-31
Poole, Ernest 1880-1950 . . . . DLB-9	Pownall, David 1938- DLB-14	Primrose, Diana floruit circa 1630 . . . . . . DLB-126
Poole, Sophia 1804-1891 . . . . DLB-166	Powys, John Cowper 1872-1963 . . . . DLB-15	Prince, F. T. 1912- DLB-20
Poore, Benjamin Perley 1820-1887 . . . . . . DLB-23	Powys, Llewelyn 1884-1939 . . . . DLB-98	Prince, Nancy Gardner 1799-? DLB-239
Popa, Vasko 1922-1991 . . . . . DLB-181; CDWLB-4	Powys, T. F. 1875-1953 . . . . DLB-36, 162	Prince, Thomas 1687-1758 . . . . DLB-24, 140
Pope, Abbie Hanscom 1858-1894 . . . . DLB-140	Poynter, Nelson 1903-1978 . . . . DLB-127	Pringle, Thomas 1789-1834 . . . . DLB-225
Pope, Alexander 1688-1744 . . . . . . DLB-95, 101, 213; CDBLB-2	The Practice of Biography: An Interview with Stanley Weintraub Y-82	Printz, Wolfgang Casper 1641-1717 . . . . . DLB-168
		Prior, Matthew 1664-1721 . . . . DLB-95

Prisco, Michele 1920- DLB-177

Pritchard, William H. 1932- DLB-111

Pritchett, V. S. 1900-1997......... DLB-15, 139

Probyn, May 1856 or 1857-1909 .... DLB-199

Procter, Adelaide Anne 1825-1864... DLB-32, 199

Procter, Bryan Waller 1787-1874 .... DLB-96, 144

Proctor, Robert 1868-1903............ DLB-184

Producing Dear Bunny, Dear Volodya: The Friendship and the Feud........................Y-97

The Profession of Authorship: Scribblers for Bread Y-89

Prokopovich, Feofan 1681?-1736 .... DLB-150

Prokosch, Frederic 1906-1989 .... DLB-48

The Proletarian Novel DLB-9

Pronzini, Bill 1943- DLB-226

Propertius circa 50 B.C.-post 16 B.C. DLB-211; CDWLB-1

Propper, Dan 1937- DLB-16

Prose, Francine 1947- DLB-234

Protagoras circa 490 B.C.-420 B.C. DLB-176

Proud, Robert 1728-1813 .... DLB-30

Proust, Marcel 1871-1922............. DLB-65

Prynne, J. H. 1936- DLB-40

Przybyszewski, Stanislaw 1868-1927 ..... DLB-66

Pseudo-Dionysius the Areopagite floruit circa 500...................... DLB-115

Public Domain and the Violation of Texts.....Y-97

The Public Lending Right in America Statement by Sen. Charles McC. Mathias, Jr. PLR and the Meaning of Literary Property Statements on PLR by American Writers........Y-83

The Public Lending Right in the United Kingdom Public Lending Right: The First Year in the United Kingdom Y-83

The Publication of English Renaissance Plays DLB-62

Publications and Social Movements [Transcendentalism].................. DLB-1

Publishers and Agents: The Columbia Connection........................Y-87

Publishing Fiction at LSU Press Y-87

The Publishing Industry in 1998: Sturm-und-drang.com Y-98

The Publishing Industry in 1999 ....Y-99

Pückler-Muskau, Hermann von 1785-1871 ....DLB-133

Pufendorf, Samuel von 1632-1694 ...... DLB-168

Pugh, Edwin William 1874-1930 .... DLB-135

Pugin, A. Welby 1812-1852 .... DLB-55

Puig, Manuel 1932-1990.... DLB-113; CDWLB-3

Pulitzer, Joseph 1847-1911 .... DLB-23

Pulitzer, Joseph, Jr. 1885-1955 .... DLB-29

Pulitzer Prizes for the Novel, 1917-1945 .... DLB-9

Pulliam, Eugene 1889-1975............ DLB-127

Purchas, Samuel 1577?-1626........... DLB-151

Purdy, Al 1918-2000.................. DLB-88

Purdy, James 1923- DLB-2, 218

Purdy, Ken W. 1913-1972 .... DLB-137

Pusey, Edward Bouverie 1800-1882...... DLB-55

Pushkin, Aleksandr Sergeevich 1799-1837.................... DLB-205

Pushkin, Vasilii L'vovich 1766-1830 .... DLB-205

Putnam, George Palmer 1814-1872..................DLB-3, 79, 250

G. P. Putnam's Sons [U.K.] DLB-106

G. P. Putnam's Sons [U.S.]............. DLB-49

A Publisher's Archives: G. P. Putnam Y-92

Putnam, Samuel 1892-1950 .... DLB-4

Puzo, Mario 1920-1999 .... DLB-6

Pyle, Ernie 1900-1945................ DLB-29

Pyle, Howard 1853-1911 .... DLB-42, 188; DS-13

Pym, Barbara 1913-1980 ...... DLB-14, 207; Y-87

Pynchon, Thomas 1937- DLB-2, 173

Pyramid Books...................... DLB-46

Pyrnelle, Louise-Clarke 1850-1907....... DLB-42

Pythagoras circa 570 B.C.-? DLB-176

Q

Quad, M. (see Lewis, Charles B.)

Quaritch, Bernard 1819-1899.......... DLB-184

Quarles, Francis 1592-1644 .... DLB-126

The Quarterly Review 1809-1967 .... DLB-110

Quasimodo, Salvatore 1901-1968....... DLB-114

Queen, Ellery (see Dannay, Frederic, and Manfred B. Lee)

Queen, Frank 1822-1882 .... DLB-241

The Queen City Publishing House DLB-49

Queneau, Raymond 1903-1976 .... DLB-72

Quennell, Sir Peter 1905-1993 ..... DLB-155, 195

Quesnel, Joseph 1746-1809............. DLB-99

The Question of American Copyright
  in the Nineteenth Century
  Preface, by George Haven Putnam
  The Evolution of Copyright, by Brander Matthews
  Summary of Copyright Legislation in the United States, by R. R. Bowker
  Analysis of the Provisions of the Copyright Law of 1891, by George Haven Putnam
  The Contest for International Copyright, by George Haven Putnam
  Cheap Books and Good Books, by Brander Matthews.......... DLB-49

Quiller-Couch, Sir Arthur Thomas 1863-1944 ....DLB-135, 153, 190

Quin, Ann 1936-1973............. DLB-14, 231

Quincy, Samuel, of Georgia ?-? DLB-31

Quincy, Samuel, of Massachusetts 1734-1789 .... DLB-31

Quinn, Anthony 1915- DLB-122

The Quinn Draft of James Joyce's Circe Manuscript.....................Y-00

Quinn, John 1870-1924............... DLB-187

Quiñónez, Naomi 1951- DLB-209

Quintana, Leroy V. 1944- DLB-82

Quintana, Miguel de 1671-1748 A Forerunner of Chicano Literature . DLB-122

Quintillian circa A.D. 40-circa A.D. 96 .... DLB-211

Quintus Curtius Rufus fl. A.D. 35 ...... DLB-211

Quist, Harlin, Books.................. DLB-46

Quoirez, Françoise (see Sagan, Françoise)

R

R-va, Zeneida (see Gan, Elena Andreevna)

Raabe, Wilhelm 1831-1910 .... DLB-129

Raban, Jonathan 1942- DLB-204

Rabe, David 1940- DLB-7, 228

Raboni, Giovanni 1932- DLB-128

Rachilde 1860-1953 .... DLB-123, 192

Racin, KoČo 1908-1943 ....DLB-147

Rackham, Arthur 1867-1939 .... DLB-141

Radauskas, Henrikas 1910-1970............ DLB-220; CDWLB-4

Radcliffe, Ann 1764-1823 ....DLB-39, 178

Raddall, Thomas 1903- DLB-68

Radford, Dollie 1858-1920............ DLB-240

Radichkov, Yordan 1929- DLB-181

Radiguet, Raymond 1903-1923 .... DLB-65

Radishchev, Aleksandr Nikolaevich 1749-1802..................... DLB-150

Radnóti, Miklós 1909-1944 ....DLB-215; CDWLB-4

Radványi, Netty Reiling (see Seghers, Anna)

Rahv, Philip 1908-1973 ....DLB-137

Raich, Semen Egorovich 1792-1855 ..... DLB-205

Raičković, Stevan 1928- DLB-181

Raimund, Ferdinand Jakob 1790-1836 .... DLB-90

Raine, Craig 1944- DLB-40

Raine, Kathleen 1908- DLB-20

Rainis, Jānis 1865-1929 .... DLB-220; CDWLB-4

Rainolde, Richard circa 1530-1606 .... DLB-136, 236

Rakić, Milan 1876-1938 .....DLB-147; CDWLB-4

Rakosi, Carl 1903- DLB-193

Ralegh, Sir Walter 1554?-1618........... DLB-172; CDBLB-1

Ralin, Radoy 1923- DLB-181

Ralph, Julian 1853-1903 .... DLB-23

Ramat, Silvio 1939- DLB-128

Rambler, no. 4 (1750), by Samuel Johnson [excerpt]........................ DLB-39

Ramée, Marie Louise de la (see Ouida)

Ramírez, Sergío 1942- DLB-145

Ramke, Bin 1947- DLB-120

Ramler, Karl Wilhelm 1725-1798 .... DLB-97

Ramon Ribeyro, Julio 1929- DLB-145

Ramos, Manuel 1948- DLB-209

Ramous, Mario 1924- DLB-128

Rampersad, Arnold 1941- DLB-111

Ramsay, Allan 1684 or 1685-1758 ..... DLB-95

Ramsay, David 1749-1815 .... DLB-30

Ramsay, Martha Laurens 1759-1811 ..... DLB-200

Ranck, Katherine Quintana 1942- DLB-122

Rand, Avery and Company DLB-49

Rand, Ayn 1905-1982 . . . . DLB-227; CDALB-7
Rand McNally and Company DLB-49
Randall, David Anton 1905-1975. . . . . DLB-140
Randall, Dudley 1914- DLB-41
Randall, Henry S. 1811-1876. . . . . DLB-30
Randall, James G. 1881-1953. . . . . DLB-17
The Randall Jarrell Symposium:
  A Small Collection of Randall Jarrells
  Excerpts From Papers Delivered at the
  Randall Jarrel Symposium. Y-86
Randolph, A. Philip 1889-1979 . . . . DLB-91
Randolph, Anson D. F.
  [publishing house] DLB-49
Randolph, Thomas 1605-1635 . . . . . . DLB-58, 126
Random House DLB-46
Ranlet, Henry [publishing house] DLB-49
Ransom, Harry 1908-1976. . . . . DLB-187
Ransom, John Crowe
  1888-1974 . . . . DLB-45, 63; CDALB-7
Ransome, Arthur 1884-1967 . . . . DLB-160
Raphael, Frederic 1931- DLB-14
Raphaelson, Samson 1896-1983 . . . . DLB-44
Rashi circa 1040-1105 . . . . DLB-208
Raskin, Ellen 1928-1984 . . . . DLB-52
Rastell, John 1475?-1536 . . . . DLB-136, 170
Rattigan, Terence
  1911-1977 . . . . DLB-13; CDBLB-7
Rawlings, Marjorie Kinnan 1896-1953
  . . . . DLB-9, 22, 102; DS-17; CDALB-7
Rawlinson, Richard 1690-1755 . . . . DLB-213
Rawlinson, Thomas 1681-1725 . . . . DLB-213
Raworth, Tom 1938- DLB-40
Ray, David 1932- DLB-5
Ray, Gordon Norton 1915-1986 . . . . DLB-103, 140
Ray, Henrietta Cordelia 1849-1916. . . . . . . DLB-50
Raymond, Ernest 1888-1974 . . . . DLB-191
Raymond, Henry J. 1820-1869 . . . . DLB-43, 79
Michael M. Rea and the Rea Award for the
  Short Story Y-97
Reach, Angus 1821-1856. . . . . DLB-70
Read, Herbert 1893-1968 . . . . DLB-20, 149
Read, Herbert, "The Practice of Biography," in
  The English Sense of Humour and
  Other Essays. DLB-149
Read, Martha Meredith DLB-200
Read, Opie 1852-1939. . . . . DLB-23
Read, Piers Paul 1941- DLB-14
Reade, Charles 1814-1884. . . . . DLB-21
Reader's Digest Condensed Books DLB-46
Readers Ulysses Symposium Y-97
Reading, Peter 1946- DLB-40
Reading Series in New York City Y-96
The Reality of One Woman's Dream:
  The de Grummond Children's
  Literature Collection Y-99
Reaney, James 1926- DLB-68
Rebhun, Paul 1500?-1546 . . . . DLB-179
Rèbora, Clemente 1885-1957. . . . . DLB-114

Rebreanu, Liviu 1885-1944 . . . . DLB-220
Rechy, John 1934- DLB-122; Y-82
The Recovery of Literature:
  Criticism in the 1990s: A Symposium. . . . Y-91
Redding, J. Saunders 1906-1988 . . . . . . DLB-63, 76
Redfield, J. S. [publishing house] DLB-49
Redgrove, Peter 1932- DLB-40
Redmon, Anne 1943- Y-86
Redmond, Eugene B. 1937- DLB-41
Redpath, James [publishing house] DLB-49
Reed, Henry 1808-1854. . . . . DLB-59
Reed, Henry 1914- DLB-27
Reed, Ishmael
  1938- DLB-2, 5, 33, 169, 227; DS-8
Reed, Rex 1938- DLB-185
Reed, Sampson 1800-1880. . . . . DLB-1, 235
Reed, Talbot Baines 1852-1893. . . . . DLB-141
Reedy, William Marion 1862-1920. . . . . . . DLB-91
Reese, Lizette Woodworth 1856-1935. . . . . DLB-54
Reese, Thomas 1742-1796 . . . . DLB-37
Reeve, Clara 1729-1807 . . . . DLB-39
Preface to The Old English Baron (1778) DLB-39
The Progress of Romance (1785) [excerpt] . . . DLB-39
Reeves, James 1909-1978 . . . . DLB-161
Reeves, John 1926- DLB-88
Reeves-Stevens, Garfield 1953- DLB-251
"Reflections: After a Tornado,"
  by Judson Jerome DLB-105
Regnery, Henry, Company DLB-46
Rehberg, Hans 1901-1963 . . . . DLB-124
Rehfisch, Hans José 1891-1960 . . . . DLB-124
Reich, Ebbe Kløvedal 1940- DLB-214
Reid, Alastair 1926- DLB-27
Reid, B. L. 1918-1990 . . . . DLB-111; Y-83
The Practice of Biography II:
  An Interview with B. L. Reid Y-83
Reid, Christopher 1949- DLB-40
Reid, Forrest 1875-1947 . . . . DLB-153
Reid, Helen Rogers 1882-1970 . . . . DLB-29
Reid, James ?-? DLB-31
Reid, Mayne 1818-1883. . . . . DLB-21, 163
Reid, Thomas 1710-1796 . . . . DLB-31
Reid, V. S. (Vic) 1913-1987 . . . . DLB-125
Reid, Whitelaw 1837-1912. . . . . DLB-23
Reilly and Lee Publishing Company DLB-46
Reimann, Brigitte 1933-1973 . . . . DLB-75
Reinmar der Alte
  circa 1165-circa 1205. . . . . DLB-138
Reinmar von Zweter
  circa 1200-circa 1250. . . . . DLB-138
Reisch, Walter 1903-1983 . . . . DLB-44
Reizei Family DLB-203
Remarks at the Opening of "The Biographical
  Part of Literature" Exhibition, by
  William R. Cagle Y-98
Remarque, Erich Maria
  1898-1970 . . . . DLB-56; CDWLB-2

Remington, Frederic
  1861-1909 . . . . DLB-12, 186, 188
Reminiscences, by Charles Scribner Jr. DS-17
Renaud, Jacques 1943- DLB-60
Renault, Mary 1905-1983 . . . . Y-83
Rendell, Ruth 1930- DLB-87
Rensselaer, Maria van Cortlandt van
  1645-1689 . . . . DLB-200
Repplier, Agnes 1855-1950 . . . . DLB-221
Representative Men and Women: A Historical
  Perspective on the British Novel,
  1930-1960 . . . . DLB-15
Research in the American Antiquarian Book
  Trade Y-97
Reshetnikov, Fedor Mikhailovich
  1841-1871 . . . . DLB-238
Rettenbacher, Simon 1634-1706 . . . . DLB-168
Reuchlin, Johannes 1455-1522. . . . . DLB-179
Revell, Fleming H., Company DLB-49
Reuter, Christian 1665-after 1712 . . . . DLB-168
Reuter, Fritz 1810-1874 . . . . DLB-129
Reuter, Gabriele 1859-1941 . . . . DLB-66
Reventlow, Franziska Gräfin zu
  1871-1918 . . . . DLB-66
Review of Nicholson Baker's Double Fold:
  Libraries and the Assault on Paper. Y-00
Review of Reviews Office DLB-112
Review of [Samuel Richardson's] Clarissa (1748),
  by Henry Fielding DLB-39
The Revolt (1937), by Mary Colum
  [excerpts] DLB-36
Rexroth, Kenneth 1905-1982
  . . . . . . DLB-16, 48, 165, 212; Y-82; CDALB-1
Rey, H. A. 1898-1977 . . . . DLB-22
Reynal and Hitchcock DLB-46
Reynolds, G. W. M. 1814-1879. . . . . DLB-21
Reynolds, John Hamilton 1794-1852. . . . . . DLB-96
Reynolds, Sir Joshua 1723-1792. . . . . DLB-104
Reynolds, Mack 1917- DLB-8
A Literary Archaeologist Digs On: A Brief
  Interview with Michael Reynolds by
  Michael Rogers Y-99
Reznikoff, Charles 1894-1976 . . . . DLB-28, 45
Rhett, Robert Barnwell 1800-1876. . . . . . . DLB-43
Rhode, John 1884-1964 . . . . DLB-77
Rhodes, James Ford 1848-1927 . . . . DLB-47
Rhodes, Richard 1937- DLB-185
Rhys, Jean 1890-1979
  . . . . DLB-36, 117, 162; CDBLB-7; CDWLB-3
Ricardo, David 1772-1823 . . . . DLB-107, 158
Ricardou, Jean 1932- DLB-83
Rice, Elmer 1892-1967. . . . . DLB-4, 7
Rice, Grantland 1880-1954 . . . . DLB-29, 171
Rich, Adrienne 1929- DLB-5, 67; CDALB-7
Richard de Fournival
  1201-1259 or 1260 . . . . DLB-208
Richard, Mark 1955- DLB-234
Richards, David Adams 1950- DLB-53
Richards, George circa 1760-1814 . . . . DLB-37

Cumulative Index

Richards, Grant [publishing house] DLB-112
Richards, I. A. 1893-1979 .... DLB-27
Richards, Laura E. 1850-1943 .... DLB-42
Richards, William Carey 1818-1892 ..... DLB-73
Richardson, Charles F. 1851-1913 ...... DLB-71
Richardson, Dorothy M. 1873-1957 ...... DLB-36
Richardson, Henry Handel
 (Ethel Florence Lindesay
 Robertson) 1870-1946 ....DLB-197, 230
Richardson, Jack 1935- DLB-7
Richardson, John 1796-1852 .... DLB-99
Richardson, Samuel
 1689-1761 .... DLB-39, 154; CDBLB-2
Introductory Letters from the Second
 Edition of *Pamela* (1741) DLB-39
Postscript to [the Third Edition of]
 Clarissa (1751) DLB-39
Preface to the First Edition of
 Pamela (1740) DLB-39
Preface to the Third Edition of
 Clarissa (1751) [excerpt] DLB-39
Preface to Volume 1 of *Clarissa* (1747) DLB-39
Preface to Volume 3 of *Clarissa* (1748) DLB-39
Richardson, Willis 1889-1977 .... DLB-51
Riche, Barnabe 1542-1617 .... DLB-136
Richepin, Jean 1849-1926 .... DLB-192
Richler, Mordecai 1931- DLB-53
Richter, Conrad 1890-1968 .... DLB-9, 212
Richter, Hans Werner 1908- DLB-69
Richter, Johann Paul Friedrich
 1763-1825 .... DLB-94; CDWLB-2
Rickerby, Joseph [publishing house] DLB-106
Rickword, Edgell 1898-1982 .... DLB-20
Riddell, Charlotte 1832-1906 .... DLB-156
Riddell, John (see Ford, Corey)
Ridge, John Rollin 1827-1867 .... DLB-175
Ridge, Lola 1873-1941 .... DLB-54
Ridge, William Pett 1859-1930 .... DLB-135
Riding, Laura (see Jackson, Laura Riding)
Ridler, Anne 1912- DLB-27
Ridruego, Dionisio 1912-1975 .... DLB-108
Riel, Louis 1844-1885 .... DLB-99
Riemer, Johannes 1648-1714 .... DLB-168
Rifbjerg, Klaus 1931- DLB-214
Riffaterre, Michael 1924- DLB-67
Riggs, Lynn 1899-1954 .... DLB-175
Riis, Jacob 1849-1914 .... DLB-23
Riker, John C. [publishing house] DLB-49
Riley, James 1777-1840 .... DLB-183
Riley, John 1938-1978 .... DLB-40
Rilke, Rainer Maria
 1875-1926 .... DLB-81; CDWLB-2
Rimanelli, Giose 1926- DLB-177
Rimbaud, Jean-Nicolas-Arthur
 1854-1891 .... DLB-217
Rinehart and Company DLB-46
Ringuet 1895-1960 .... DLB-68

Ringwood, Gwen Pharis 1910-1984 ...... DLB-88
Rinser, Luise 1911- DLB-69
Ríos, Alberto 1952- DLB-122
Ríos, Isabella 1948- DLB-82
Ripley, Arthur 1895-1961 .... DLB-44
Ripley, George 1802-1880 .....DLB-1, 64, 73, 235
The Rising Glory of America:
 Three Poems DLB-37
The Rising Glory of America:
 Written in 1771 (1786),
 by Hugh Henry Brackenridge and
 Philip Freneau DLB-37
Riskin, Robert 1897-1955 .... DLB-26
Risse, Heinz 1898- DLB-69
Rist, Johann 1607-1667 .... DLB-164
Ristikivi, Karl 1912-1977 .... DLB-220
Ritchie, Anna Mowatt 1819-1870 ..... DLB-3, 250
Ritchie, Anne Thackeray 1837-1919 ..... DLB-18
Ritchie, Thomas 1778-1854 .... DLB-43
Rites of Passage [on William Saroyan] Y-83
The Ritz Paris Hemingway Award Y-85
Rivard, Adjutor 1868-1945 .... DLB-92
Rive, Richard 1931-1989 .... DLB-125, 225
Rivera, José 1955- DLB-249
Rivera, Marina 1942- DLB-122
Rivera, Tomás 1935-1984 .... DLB-82
Rivers, Conrad Kent 1933-1968 .... DLB-41
Riverside Press DLB-49
Rivington, Charles [publishing house] ... DLB-154
Rivington, James circa 1724-1802 ...... DLB-43
Rivkin, Allen 1903-1990 .... DLB-26
Roa Bastos, Augusto 1917- DLB-113
Robbe-Grillet, Alain 1922- DLB-83
Robbins, Tom 1936- Y-80
Roberts, Charles G. D. 1860-1943 ...... DLB-92
Roberts, Dorothy 1906-1993 .... DLB-88
Roberts, Elizabeth Madox
 1881-1941 .... DLB-9, 54, 102
Roberts, James [publishing house] DLB-154
Roberts, Kenneth 1885-1957 .... DLB-9
Roberts, Michèle 1949- DLB-231
Roberts, Ursula Wyllie (see Miles, Susan)
Roberts, William 1767-1849 .... DLB-142
Roberts Brothers DLB-49
Robertson, A. M., and Company DLB-49
Robertson, Ethel Florence Lindesay
 (see Richardson, Henry Handel)
Robertson, William 1721-1793 .... DLB-104
Robins, Elizabeth 1862-1952 .... DLB-197
Robinson, A. Mary F. (Madame James
 Darmesteter, Madame Mary
 Duclaux) 1857-1944 .... DLB-240
Robinson, Casey 1903-1979 .... DLB-44
Robinson, Edwin Arlington
 1869-1935 .... DLB-54; CDALB-3
Robinson, Henry Crabb 1775-1867 ...... DLB-107
Robinson, James Harvey 1863-1936 ..... DLB-47

Robinson, Lennox 1886-1958 .... DLB-10
Robinson, Mabel Louise 1874-1962 ...... DLB-22
Robinson, Marilynne 1943- DLB-206
Robinson, Mary 1758-1800 .... DLB-158
Robinson, Richard circa 1545-1607 ..... DLB-167
Robinson, Therese 1797-1870 .... DLB-59, 133
Robison, Mary 1949- DLB-130
Roblès, Emmanuel 1914-1995 .... DLB-83
Roccatagliata Ceccardi, Ceccardo
 1871-1919 .... DLB-114
Roche, Billy 1949- DLB-233
Rochester, John Wilmot, Earl of
 1647-1680 .... DLB-131
Rochon, Esther 1948- DLB-251
Rock, Howard 1911-1976 .... DLB-127
Rockwell, Norman Perceval 1894-1978 .... DLB-188
Rodgers, Carolyn M. 1945- DLB-41
Rodgers, W. R. 1909-1969 .... DLB-20
Rodney, Lester 1911- DLB-241
Rodríguez, Claudio 1934-1999 .... DLB-134
Rodríguez, Joe D. 1943- DLB-209
Rodríguez, Luis J. 1954- DLB-209
Rodriguez, Richard 1944- DLB-82
Rodríguez Julia, Edgardo 1946- DLB-145
Roe, E. P. 1838-1888 .... DLB-202
Roethke, Theodore
 1908-1963 .... DLB-5, 206; CDALB-1
Rogers, Jane 1952- DLB-194
Rogers, Pattiann 1940- DLB-105
Rogers, Samuel 1763-1855 .... DLB-93
Rogers, Will 1879-1935 .... DLB-11
Rohmer, Sax 1883-1959 .... DLB-70
Roiphe, Anne 1935- Y-80
Rojas, Arnold R. 1896-1988 .... DLB-82
Rolfe, Frederick William
 1860-1913 .... DLB-34, 156
Rolland, Romain 1866-1944 .... DLB-65
Rolle, Richard circa 1290-1300 - 1340 ... DLB-146
Rölvaag, O. E. 1876-1931 .... DLB-9, 212
Romains, Jules 1885-1972 .... DLB-65
Roman, A., and Company DLB-49
Roman de la Rose: Guillaume de Lorris
 1200 to 1205-circa 1230, Jean de Meun
 1235-1240-circa 1305 .... DLB-208
Romano, Lalla 1906- DLB-177
Romano, Octavio 1923- DLB-122
Romero, Leo 1950- DLB-122
Romero, Lin 1947- DLB-122
Romero, Orlando 1945- DLB-82
Rook, Clarence 1863-1915 .... DLB-135
Roosevelt, Theodore 1858-1919 ...... DLB-47, 186
Root, Waverley 1903-1982 .... DLB-4
Root, William Pitt 1941- DLB-120
Roquebrune, Robert de 1889-1978 .... DLB-68
Rorty, Richard 1931- DLB-246
Rosa, João Guimarães 1908-1967 .... DLB-113

Rosales, Luis 1910-1992 . . . . .DLB-134

Roscoe, William 1753-1831 . . . . .DLB-163

Danis Rose and the Rendering of *Ulysses* Y-97

Rose, Reginald 1920- DLB-26

Rose, Wendy 1948- DLB-175

Rosegger, Peter 1843-1918 . . . . .DLB-129

Rosei, Peter 1946- DLB-85

Rosen, Norma 1925- DLB-28

Rosenbach, A. S. W. 1876-1952 . . . . .DLB-140

Rosenbaum, Ron 1946- DLB-185

Rosenberg, Isaac 1890-1918 . . . . .DLB-20, 216

Rosenfeld, Isaac 1918-1956 . . . . .DLB-28

Rosenthal, Harold 1914-1999 . . . . .DLB-241

Rosenthal, M. L. 1917-1996 . . . . .DLB-5

Rosenwald, Lessing J. 1891-1979 . . . . .DLB-187

Ross, Alexander 1591-1654 . . . . .DLB-151

Ross, Harold 1892-1951 . . . . .DLB-137

Ross, Leonard Q. (see Rosten, Leo)

Ross, Lillian 1927- DLB-185

Ross, Martin 1862-1915 . . . . .DLB-135

Ross, Sinclair 1908- DLB-88

Ross, W. W. E. 1894-1966 . . . . .DLB-88

Rosselli, Amelia 1930-1996 . . . . .DLB-128

Rossen, Robert 1908-1966 . . . . .DLB-26

Rossetti, Christina 1830-1894 . . . DLB-35, 163, 240

Rossetti, Dante Gabriel
  1828-1882 . . . . DLB-35; CDBLB-4

Rossner, Judith 1935- DLB-6

Rostand, Edmond 1868-1918 . . . . .DLB-192

Rosten, Leo 1908-1997 . . . . .DLB-11

Rostenberg, Leona 1908- DLB-140

Rostopchina, Evdokiia Petrovna
  1811-1858 . . . . .DLB-205

Rostovsky, Dimitrii 1651-1709 . . . . .DLB-150

Rota, Bertram 1903-1966 . . . . .DLB-201

  Bertram Rota and His Bookshop Y-91

Roth, Gerhard 1942- DLB-85, 124

Roth, Henry 1906?-1995 . . . . .DLB-28

Roth, Joseph 1894-1939 . . . . .DLB-85

Roth, Philip 1933-
  . . . . DLB-2, 28, 173; Y-82; CDALB-6

Rothenberg, Jerome 1931- DLB-5, 193

Rothschild Family DLB-184

Rotimi, Ola 1938- DLB-125

Routhier, Adolphe-Basile 1839-1920 . . . . . .DLB-99

Routier, Simone 1901-1987 . . . . .DLB-88

Routledge, George, and Sons DLB-106

Roversi, Roberto 1923- DLB-128

Rowe, Elizabeth Singer 1674-1737 . . . . .DLB-39, 95

Rowe, Nicholas 1674-1718 . . . . .DLB-84

Rowlands, Samuel circa 1570-1630 . . . . . .DLB-121

Rowlandson, Mary
  circa 1637-circa 1711 . . . . . . .DLB-24, 200

Rowley, William circa 1585-1626 . . . . .DLB-58

Rowse, A. L. 1903-1997 . . . . .DLB-155

Rowson, Susanna Haswell
  circa 1762-1824 . . . . DLB-37, 200

Roy, Camille 1870-1943 . . . . .DLB-92

Roy, Gabrielle 1909-1983 . . . . .DLB-68

Roy, Jules 1907- .DLB-83

The G. Ross Roy Scottish Poetry Collection
  at the University of South Carolina Y-89

The Royal Court Theatre and the English
  Stage Company DLB-13

The Royal Court Theatre and the New
  Drama DLB-10

The Royal Shakespeare Company
  at the Swan Y-88

Royall, Anne Newport 1769-1854 . . . .DLB-43, 248

The Roycroft Printing Shop DLB-49

Royde-Smith, Naomi 1875-1964 . . . . .DLB-191

Royster, Vermont 1914- DLB-127

Royston, Richard [publishing house] DLB-170

Różewicz, Tadeusz 1921- DLB-232

Ruark, Gibbons 1941- DLB-120

Ruban, Vasilii Grigorevich 1742-1795 . . . .DLB-150

Rubens, Bernice 1928- DLB-14, 207

Rudd and Carleton DLB-49

Rudd, Steele (Arthur Hoey Davis) DLB-230

Rudkin, David 1936- DLB-13

Rudolf von Ems circa 1200-circa 1254 . . .DLB-138

Ruffin, Josephine St. Pierre
  1842-1924 . . . . .DLB-79

Ruganda, John 1941- DLB-157

Ruggles, Henry Joseph 1813-1906 . . . . . . .DLB-64

Ruiz de Burton, María Amparo
  1832-1895 . . . . .DLB-209, 221

Rukeyser, Muriel 1913-1980 . . . . .DLB-48

Rule, Jane 1931- .DLB-60

Rulfo, Juan 1918-1986 . . . . . . DLB-113; CDWLB-3

Rumaker, Michael 1932- DLB-16

Rumens, Carol 1944- DLB-40

Rummo, Paul-Eerik 1942- DLB-232

Runyon, Damon 1880-1946 . . . . . DLB-11, 86, 171

Ruodlieb circa 1050-1075 . . . . .DLB-148

Rush, Benjamin 1746-1813 . . . . .DLB-37

Rush, Rebecca 1779-? DLB-200

Rushdie, Salman 1947- DLB-194

Rusk, Ralph L. 1888-1962 . . . . .DLB-103

Ruskin, John
  1819-1900 . . . . . . DLB-55, 163, 190; CDBLB-4

Russ, Joanna 1937- DLB-8

Russell, B. B., and Company DLB-49

Russell, Benjamin 1761-1845 . . . . .DLB-43

Russell, Bertrand 1872-1970 . . . . .DLB-100

Russell, Charles Edward 1860-1941 . . . . . .DLB-25

Russell, Charles M. 1864-1926 . . . . .DLB-188

Russell, Fred 1906- DLB-241

Russell, George William (see AE)

Russell, Countess Mary Annette Beauchamp
  (see Arnim, Elizabeth von)

Russell, R. H., and Son DLB-49

Russell, Willy 1947- DLB-233

Rutebeuf flourished 1249-1277 . . . . .DLB-208

Rutherford, Mark 1831-1913 . . . . .DLB-18

Ruxton, George Frederick 1821-1848 . . . .DLB-186

Ryan, Michael 1946- Y-82

Ryan, Oscar 1904- DLB-68

Ryder, Jack 1871-1936 . . . . .DLB-241

Ryga, George 1932- DLB-60

Rylands, Enriqueta Augustina Tennant
  1843-1908 . . . . .DLB-184

Rylands, John 1801-1888 . . . . .DLB-184

Ryleev, Kondratii Fedorovich
  1795-1826 . . . . .DLB-205

Rymer, Thomas 1643?-1713 . . . . .DLB-101

Ryskind, Morrie 1895-1985 . . . . .DLB-26

Rzhevsky, Aleksei Andreevich
  1737-1804 . . . . .DLB-150

S

The Saalfield Publishing Company DLB-46

Saba, Umberto 1883-1957 . . . . .DLB-114

Sábato, Ernesto 1911- DLB-145; CDWLB-3

Saberhagen, Fred 1930- DLB-8

Sabin, Joseph 1821-1881 . . . . .DLB-187

Sacer, Gottfried Wilhelm 1635-1699 . . . . .DLB-168

Sachs, Hans 1494-1576 . . . . . DLB-179; CDWLB-2

Sack, John 1930- DLB-185

Sackler, Howard 1929-1982 . . . . .DLB-7

Sackville, Lady Margaret 1881-1963 . . . . .DLB-240

Sackville, Thomas 1536-1608 . . . . .DLB-132

Sackville, Thomas 1536-1608
  and Norton, Thomas 1532-1584 . . . . . .DLB-62

Sackville-West, Edward 1901-1965 . . . . . .DLB-191

Sackville-West, V. 1892-1962 . . . . . . .DLB-34, 195

Sadlier, D. and J., and Company DLB-49

Sadlier, Mary Anne 1820-1903 . . . . .DLB-99

Sadoff, Ira 1945- DLB-120

Sadoveanu, Mihail 1880-1961 . . . . .DLB-220

Sáenz, Benjamin Alire 1954- DLB-209

Saenz, Jaime 1921-1986 . . . . .DLB-145

Saffin, John circa 1626-1710 . . . . .DLB-24

Sagan, Françoise 1935- DLB-83

Sage, Robert 1899-1962 . . . . .DLB-4

Sagel, Jim 1947- .DLB-82

Sagendorph, Robb Hansell 1900-1970 . . . .DLB-137

Sahagún, Carlos 1938- DLB-108

Sahkomaapii, Piitai (see Highwater, Jamake)

Sahl, Hans 1902- .DLB-69

Said, Edward W. 1935- DLB-67

Saigyō 1118-1190 . . . . .DLB-203

Saiko, George 1892-1962 . . . . .DLB-85

St. Dominic's Press DLB-112

Saint-Exupéry, Antoine de 1900-1944 . . . . .DLB-72

St. John, J. Allen 1872-1957 . . . . .DLB-188

St. Johns, Adela Rogers 1894-1988 . . . . . . .DLB-29

Cumulative Index

The St. John's College Robert Graves Trust . . Y-96
St. Martin's Press DLB-46
St. Omer, Garth 1931- DLB-117
Saint Pierre, Michel de 1916-1987 . . . . DLB-83
Sainte-Beuve, Charles-Augustin
  1804-1869 . . . . DLB-217
Saints' Lives DLB-208
Saintsbury, George 1845-1933 . . . . DLB-57, 149
Saiokuken Sōchō 1448-1532. . . . . DLB-203
Saki (see Munro, H. H.)
Salaam, Kalamu ya 1947- DLB-38
Šalamun, Tomaž 1941- . . . DLB-181; CDWLB-4
Salas, Floyd 1931- DLB-82
Sálaz-Marquez, Rubén 1935- DLB-122
Salemson, Harold J. 1910-1988. . . . . DLB-4
Salinas, Luis Omar 1937- DLB-82
Salinas, Pedro 1891-1951 . . . . DLB-134
Salinger, J. D.
  1919- DLB-2, 102, 173; CDALB-1
Salkey, Andrew 1928- DLB-125
Sallust circa 86 B.C.-35 B.C.
  . . . . DLB-211; CDWLB-1
Salt, Waldo 1914- DLB-44
Salter, James 1925- DLB-130
Salter, Mary Jo 1954- DLB-120
Saltus, Edgar 1855-1921 . . . . DLB-202
Saltykov, Mikhail Evgrafovich
  1826-1889 . . . . DLB-238
Salustri, Carlo Alberto (see Trilussa)
Salverson, Laura Goodman 1890-1970. . . . DLB-92
Samain, Albert 1858-1900. . . . . DLB-217
Sampson, Richard Henry (see Hull, Richard)
Samuels, Ernest 1903-1996. . . . . DLB-111
Sanborn, Franklin Benjamin
  1831-1917. . . . . DLB-1, 223
Sánchez, Luis Rafael 1936- DLB-145
Sánchez, Philomeno "Phil" 1917- DLB-122
Sánchez, Ricardo 1941-1995. . . . . DLB-82
Sánchez, Saúl 1943- DLB-209
Sanchez, Sonia 1934- DLB-41; DS-8
Sand, George 1804-1876. . . . . DLB-119, 192
Sandburg, Carl
  1878-1967. . . . . DLB-17, 54; CDALB-3
Sanders, Edward 1939- DLB-16, 244
Sandoz, Mari 1896-1966. . . . . DLB-9, 212
Sandwell, B. K. 1876-1954 . . . . DLB-92
Sandy, Stephen 1934- DLB-165
Sandys, George 1578-1644 . . . . DLB-24, 121
Sangster, Charles 1822-1893 . . . . DLB-99
Sanguineti, Edoardo 1930- DLB-128
Sanjōnishi Sanetaka 1455-1537. . . . . DLB-203
Sansay, Leonora ?-after 1823 . . . . DLB-200
Sansom, William 1912-1976 . . . . DLB-139
Santayana, George
  1863-1952 . . . . DLB-54, 71, 246; DS-13
Santiago, Danny 1911-1988 . . . . DLB-122

Santmyer, Helen Hooven 1895-1986 . . . . Y-84
Sanvitale, Francesca 1928- DLB-196
Sapidus, Joannes 1490-1561 . . . . DLB-179
Sapir, Edward 1884-1939 . . . . DLB-92
Sapper (see McNeile, Herman Cyril)
Sappho circa 620 B.C.-circa 550 B.C.
  . . . . DLB-176; CDWLB-1
Saramago, José 1922- Y-98
Sardou, Victorien 1831-1908 . . . . DLB-192
Sarduy, Severo 1937- DLB-113
Sargent, Pamela 1948- DLB-8
Saro-Wiwa, Ken 1941- DLB-157
Saroyan, William
  1908-1981 . . . . . DLB-7, 9, 86; Y-81; CDALB-7
Sarraute, Nathalie 1900-1999 . . . . DLB-83
Sarrazin, Albertine 1937-1967 . . . . DLB-83
Sarris, Greg 1952- DLB-175
Sarton, May 1912-1995 . . . . DLB-48; Y-81
Sartre, Jean-Paul 1905-1980 . . . . DLB-72
Sassoon, Siegfried
  1886-1967 . . . . DLB-20, 191; DS-18
Siegfried Loraine Sassoon:
  A Centenary Essay
  Tributes from Vivien F. Clarke and
  Michael Thorpe Y-86
Sata, Ineko 1904- DLB-180
Saturday Review Press DLB-46
Saunders, James 1925- DLB-13
Saunders, John Monk 1897-1940 . . . . DLB-26
Saunders, Margaret Marshall
  1861-1947. . . . . DLB-92
Saunders and Otley DLB-106
Saussure, Ferdinand de 1857-1913 . . . . . . DLB-242
Savage, James 1784-1873. . . . . DLB-30
Savage, Marmion W. 1803?-1872. . . . . DLB-21
Savage, Richard 1697?-1743 . . . . DLB-95
Savard, Félix-Antoine 1896-1982 . . . . DLB-68
Savery, Henry 1791-1842 . . . . DLB-230
Saville, (Leonard) Malcolm 1901-1982. . . DLB-160
Sawyer, Robert J. 1960- DLB-251
Sawyer, Ruth 1880-1970. . . . . DLB-22
Sayers, Dorothy L.
  1893-1957 . . . . . DLB-10, 36, 77, 100; CDBLB-6
Sayle, Charles Edward 1864-1924 . . . . . . DLB-184
Sayles, John Thomas 1950- DLB-44
Sbarbaro, Camillo 1888-1967 . . . . DLB-114
Scalapino, Leslie 1947- DLB-193
Scannell, Vernon 1922- DLB-27
Scarry, Richard 1919-1994 . . . . DLB-61
Schaefer, Jack 1907-1991. . . . . DLB-212
Schaeffer, Albrecht 1885-1950 . . . . DLB-66
Schaeffer, Susan Fromberg 1941- DLB-28
Schaff, Philip 1819-1893 . . . . DS-13
Schaper, Edzard 1908-1984 . . . . DLB-69
Scharf, J. Thomas 1843-1898 . . . . DLB-47
Schede, Paul Melissus 1539-1602. . . . . . . DLB-179
Scheffel, Joseph Viktor von 1826-1886. . . DLB-129

Scheffler, Johann 1624-1677 . . . . DLB-164
Schelling, Friedrich Wilhelm Joseph von
  1775-1854. . . . . DLB-90
Scherer, Wilhelm 1841-1886 . . . . DLB-129
Scherfig, Hans 1905-1979 . . . . DLB-214
Schickele, René 1883-1940 . . . . DLB-66
Schiff, Dorothy 1903-1989 . . . . DLB-127
Schiller, Friedrich
  1759-1805. . . . . DLB-94; CDWLB-2
Schirmer, David 1623-1687 . . . . DLB-164
Schlaf, Johannes 1862-1941 . . . . DLB-118
Schlegel, August Wilhelm 1767-1845 . . . . . DLB-94
Schlegel, Dorothea 1763-1839. . . . . DLB-90
Schlegel, Friedrich 1772-1829 . . . . DLB-90
Schleiermacher, Friedrich 1768-1834 . . . . . DLB-90
Schlesinger, Arthur M., Jr. 1917- DLB-17
Schlumberger, Jean 1877-1968 . . . . DLB-65
Schmid, Eduard Hermann Wilhelm
  (see Edschmid, Kasimir)
Schmidt, Arno 1914-1979 . . . . DLB-69
Schmidt, Johann Kaspar (see Stirner, Max)
Schmidt, Michael 1947- DLB-40
Schmidtbonn, Wilhelm August
  1876-1952. DLB-118
Schmitz, James H. 1911- DLB-8
Schnabel, Johann Gottfried
  1692-1760. DLB-168
Schnackenberg, Gjertrud 1953- DLB-120
Schnitzler, Arthur
  1862-1931 . . . . DLB-81, 118; CDWLB-2
Schnurre, Wolfdietrich 1920-1989 . . . . DLB-69
Schocken Books DLB-46
Scholartis Press. DLB-112
Scholderer, Victor 1880-1971 . . . . DLB-201
The Schomburg Center for Research
  in Black Culture. DLB-76
Schönbeck, Virgilio (see Giotti, Virgilio)
Schönherr, Karl 1867-1943 . . . . DLB-118
Schoolcraft, Jane Johnston 1800-1841. . . . DLB-175
School Stories, 1914-1960. . . . . DLB-160
Schopenhauer, Arthur 1788-1860 . . . . DLB-90
Schopenhauer, Johanna 1766-1838. . . . . . . DLB-90
Schorer, Mark 1908-1977 . . . . DLB-103
Schottelius, Justus Georg 1612-1676 . . . . . DLB-164
Schouler, James 1839-1920. . . . . DLB-47
Schrader, Paul 1946- DLB-44
Schreiner, Olive
  1855-1920 . . . . DLB-18, 156, 190, 225
Schroeder, Andreas 1946- DLB-53
Schubart, Christian Friedrich Daniel
  1739-1791. . . . . DLB-97
Schubert, Gotthilf Heinrich 1780-1860. . . . DLB-90
Schücking, Levin 1814-1883. . . . . DLB-133
Schulberg, Budd 1914- DLB-6, 26, 28; Y-81
Schulte, F. J., and Company DLB-49
Schulz, Bruno 1892-1942 . . . DLB-215; CDWLB-4
Schulze, Hans (see Praetorius, Johannes)

Schupp, Johann Balthasar 1610-1661.....DLB-164
Schurz, Carl 1829-1906................DLB-23
Schuyler, George S. 1895-1977.......DLB-29, 51
Schuyler, James 1923-1991..........DLB-5, 169
Schwartz, Delmore 1913-1966........DLB-28, 48
Schwartz, Jonathan 1938-................Y-82
Schwartz, Lynne Sharon 1939-........DLB-218
Schwarz, Sibylle 1621-1638............DLB-164
Schwerner, Armand 1927-1999.........DLB-165
Schwob, Marcel 1867-1905.............DLB-123
Sciascia, Leonardo 1921-1989.........DLB-177
Science Fantasy.......................DLB-8
Science-Fiction Fandom and Conventions...DLB-8
Science-Fiction Fanzines: The Time
 Binders...........................DLB-8
Science-Fiction Films.................DLB-8
Science Fiction Writers of America and the
 Nebula Awards....................DLB-8
Scot, Reginald circa 1538-1599........DLB-136
Scotellaro, Rocco 1923-1953..........DLB-128
Scott, Alicia Anne (Lady John Scott)
 1810-1900.......................DLB-240
Scott, Catharine Amy Dawson
 1865-1934.......................DLB-240
Scott, Dennis 1939-1991..............DLB-125
Scott, Dixon 1881-1915................DLB-98
Scott, Duncan Campbell 1862-1947......DLB-92
Scott, Evelyn 1893-1963.............DLB-9, 48
Scott, F. R. 1899-1985.................DLB-88
Scott, Frederick George 1861-1944......DLB-92
Scott, Geoffrey 1884-1929............DLB-149
Scott, Harvey W. 1838-1910............DLB-23
Scott, Lady Jane (see Scott, Alicia Anne)
Scott, Paul 1920-1978.............DLB-14, 207
Scott, Sarah 1723-1795................DLB-39
Scott, Tom 1918-......................DLB-27
Scott, Sir Walter 1771-1832
 ...... DLB-93, 107, 116, 144, 159; CDBLB-3
Scott, Walter, Publishing
 Company Limited................DLB-112
Scott, William Bell 1811-1890..........DLB-32
Scott, William R. [publishing house].....DLB-46
Scott-Heron, Gil 1949-................DLB-41
Scribe, Eugene 1791-1861.............DLB-192
Scribner, Arthur Hawley 1859-1932....DS-13, 16
Scribner, Charles 1854-1930.........DS-13, 16
Scribner, Charles, Jr. 1921-1995........Y-95
 Reminiscences.....................DS-17
Charles Scribner's Sons....DLB-49; DS-13, 16, 17
Scripps, E. W. 1854-1926..............DLB-25
Scudder, Horace Elisha 1838-1902....DLB-42, 71
Scudder, Vida Dutton 1861-1954........DLB-71
Scupham, Peter 1933-.................DLB-40
Seabrook, William 1886-1945............DLB-4
Seabury, Samuel 1729-1796............DLB-31
Seacole, Mary Jane Grant 1805-1881.....DLB-166

The Seafarer circa 970................DLB-146
Sealsfield, Charles (Carl Postl)
 1793-1864....................DLB-133, 186
Sears, Edward I. 1819?-1876...........DLB-79
Sears Publishing Company.............DLB-46
Seaton, George 1911-1979.............DLB-44
Seaton, William Winston 1785-1866.....DLB-43
Secker, Martin [publishing house].......DLB-112
Secker, Martin, and Warburg Limited....DLB-112
The Second Annual New York Festival
 of Mystery.........................Y-00
Second-Generation Minor Poets of the
 Seventeenth Century..............DLB-126
Sedgwick, Arthur George 1844-1915......DLB-64
Sedgwick, Catharine Maria
 1789-1867........DLB-1, 74, 183, 239, 243
Sedgwick, Ellery 1872-1930............DLB-91
Sedgwick, Eve Kosofsky 1950-.........DLB-246
Sedley, Sir Charles 1639-1701.........DLB-131
Seeberg, Peter 1925-1999.............DLB-214
Seeger, Alan 1888-1916................DLB-45
Seers, Eugene (see Dantin, Louis)
Segal, Erich 1937-......................Y-86
Šegedin, Petar 1909-.................DLB-181
Seghers, Anna 1900-1983......DLB-69; CDWLB-2
Seid, Ruth (see Sinclair, Jo)
Seidel, Frederick Lewis 1936-...........Y-84
Seidel, Ina 1885-1974..................DLB-56
Seifert, Jaroslav
 1901-1986........DLB-215; Y-84; CDWLB-4
Seigenthaler, John 1927-.............DLB-127
Seizin Press..........................DLB-112
Séjour, Victor 1817-1874..............DLB-50
Séjour Marcou et Ferrand, Juan Victor
 (see Séjour, Victor)
Sekowski, Józef-Julian, Baron Brambeus
 (see Senkovsky, Osip Ivanovich)
Selby, Bettina 1934-..................DLB-204
Selby, Hubert, Jr. 1928-............DLB-2, 227
Selden, George 1929-1989.............DLB-52
Selden, John 1584-1654...............DLB-213
Selected English-Language Little Magazines
 and Newspapers [France, 1920-1939]...DLB-4
Selected Humorous Magazines
 (1820-1950).......................DLB-11
Selected Science-Fiction Magazines and
 Anthologies........................DLB-8
Selenić, Slobodan 1933-1995..........DLB-181
Self, Edwin F. 1920-.................DLB-137
Self, Will 1961-.....................DLB-207
Seligman, Edwin R. A. 1861-1939.......DLB-47
Selim (see Woodworth, Samuel)
Selimović, Meša
 1910-1982..............DLB-181; CDWLB-4
Selous, Frederick Courteney
 1851-1917........................DLB-174
Seltzer, Chester E. (see Muro, Amado)
Seltzer, Thomas [publishing house].......DLB-46

Selvon, Sam 1923-1994......DLB-125; CDWLB-3
Semmes, Raphael 1809-1877...........DLB-189
Senancour, Etienne de 1770-1846.......DLB-119
Sendak, Maurice 1928-................DLB-61
Seneca the Elder
 circa 54 B.C.-circa A.D. 40........DLB-211
Seneca the Younger
 circa 1 B.C.-A.D. 65.....DLB-211; CDWLB-1
Senécal, Eva 1905-...................DLB-92
Sengstacke, John 1912-...............DLB-127
Senior, Olive 1941-..................DLB-157
Senkovsky, Osip Ivanovich
 (Józef-Julian Sekowski, Baron Brambeus)
 1800-1858........................DLB-198
Šenoa, August 1838-1881....DLB-147; CDWLB-4
"Sensation Novels" (1863), by
 H. L. Manse......................DLB-21
Sepamla, Sipho 1932-.............DLB-157, 225
Seredy, Kate 1899-1975................DLB-22
Sereni, Vittorio 1913-1983............DLB-128
Seres, William [publishing house].......DLB-170
Serling, Rod 1924-1975................DLB-26
Sernine, Daniel 1955-................DLB-251
Serote, Mongane Wally 1944-......DLB-125, 225
Serraillier, Ian 1912-1994.............DLB-161
Serrano, Nina 1934-..................DLB-122
Service, Robert 1874-1958.............DLB-92
Sessler, Charles 1854-1935............DLB-187
Seth, Vikram 1952-...................DLB-120
Seton, Elizabeth Ann 1774-1821........DLB-200
Seton, Ernest Thompson
 1860-1942...................DLB-92; DS-13
Setouchi Harumi 1922-................DLB-182
Settle, Mary Lee 1918-.................DLB-6
Seume, Johann Gottfried 1763-1810......DLB-94
Seuse, Heinrich 1295?-1366...........DLB-179
Seuss, Dr. (see Geisel, Theodor Seuss)
The Seventy-fifth Anniversary of the Armistice:
 The Wilfred Owen Centenary and
 the Great War Exhibit
 at the University of Virginia...........Y-93
Severin, Timothy 1940-...............DLB-204
Sewall, Joseph 1688-1769..............DLB-24
Sewall, Richard B. 1908-.............DLB-111
Sewall, Anna 1820-1878...............DLB-163
Sewall, Samuel 1652-1730.............DLB-24
Sex, Class, Politics, and Religion [in the
 British Novel, 1930-1959]...........DLB-15
Sexton, Anne 1928-1974...DLB-5, 169; CDALB-1
Seymour-Smith, Martin 1928-1998......DLB-155
Sgorlon, Carlo 1930-.................DLB-196
Shaara, Michael 1929-1988.............Y-83
Shabel'skaia, Aleksandra Stanislavovna
 1845-1921........................DLB-238
Shadwell, Thomas 1641?-1692..........DLB-80
Shaffer, Anthony 1926-................DLB-13
Shaffer, Peter 1926-......DLB-13, 233; CDBLB-8

Cumulative Index

Shaftesbury, Anthony Ashley Cooper, Third Earl of 1671-1713 .... DLB-101

Shairp, Mordaunt 1887-1939 .... DLB-10

Shakespeare, Nicholas 1957- DLB-231

Shakespeare, William 1564-1616 .... DLB-62, 172; CDBLB-1

The Shakespeare Globe Trust Y-93

Shakespeare Head Press DLB-112

Shakhovskoi, Aleksandr Aleksandrovich 1777-1846 .... DLB-150

Shange, Ntozake 1948- DLB-38, 249

Shapiro, Karl 1913-2000 .... DLB-48

Sharon Publications DLB-46

Sharp, Margery 1905-1991 .... DLB-161

Sharp, William 1855-1905 .... DLB-156

Sharpe, Tom 1928- DLB-14, 231

Shaw, Albert 1857-1947 .... DLB-91

Shaw, George Bernard 1856-1950 ....DLB-10, 57, 190; CDBLB-6

Shaw, Henry Wheeler 1818-1885 .... DLB-11

Shaw, Joseph T. 1874-1952 .... DLB-137

Shaw, Irwin 1913-1984 ...... DLB-6, 102; Y-84; CDALB-1

Shaw, Mary 1854-1929 .... DLB-228

Shaw, Robert 1927-1978 .... DLB-13, 14

Shaw, Robert B. 1947- DLB-120

Shawn, William 1907-1992 .... DLB-137

Shay, Frank [publishing house] DLB-46

Shchedrin, N. (see Saltykov, Mikhail Evgrafovich)

Shea, John Gilmary 1824-1892 .... DLB-30

Sheaffer, Louis 1912-1993 .... DLB-103

Shearing, Joseph 1886-1952 .... DLB-70

Shebbeare, John 1709-1788 .... DLB-39

Sheckley, Robert 1928- DLB-8

Shedd, William G. T. 1820-1894 .... DLB-64

Sheed, Wilfred 1930- DLB-6

Sheed and Ward [U.S.] DLB-46

Sheed and Ward Limited [U.K.] DLB-112

Sheldon, Alice B. (see Tiptree, James, Jr.)

Sheldon, Edward 1886-1946 .... DLB-7

Sheldon and Company DLB-49

Sheller, Aleksandr Konstantinovich 1838-1900 .... DLB-238

Shelley, Mary Wollstonecraft 1797-1851 ....DLB-110, 116, 159, 178; CDBLB-3

Shelley, Percy Bysshe 1792-1822 ...... DLB-96, 110, 158; CDBLB-3

Shelnutt, Eve 1941- DLB-130

Shenstone, William 1714-1763 .... DLB-95

Shepard, Clark and Brown DLB-49

Shepard, Ernest Howard 1879-1976 ..... DLB-160

Shepard, Sam 1943- DLB-7, 212

Shepard, Thomas I, 1604 or 1605-1649 ... DLB-24

Shepard, Thomas II, 1635-1677 .... DLB-24

Shepherd, Luke flourished 1547-1554 .... DLB-136

Sherburne, Edward 1616-1702 .... DLB-131

Sheridan, Frances 1724-1766 .... DLB-39, 84

Sheridan, Richard Brinsley 1751-1816 .... DLB-89; CDBLB-2

Sherman, Francis 1871-1926 .... DLB-92

Sherman, Martin 1938- DLB-228

Sherriff, R. C. 1896-1975 ....DLB-10, 191, 233

Sherrod, Blackie 1919- DLB-241

Sherry, Norman 1935- DLB-155

Sherry, Richard 1506-1551 or 1555 ..... DLB-236

Sherwood, Mary Martha 1775-1851 ..... DLB-163

Sherwood, Robert E. 1896-1955 ....DLB-7, 26, 249

Shevyrev, Stepan Petrovich 1806-1864 .... DLB-205

Shiel, M. P. 1865-1947 .... DLB-153

Shiels, George 1886-1949 .... DLB-10

Shiga, Naoya 1883-1971 .... DLB-180

Shiina Rinzō 1911-1973 .... DLB-182

Shikishi Naishinnō 1153?-1201 .... DLB-203

Shillaber, Benjamin Penhallow 1814-1890 .... DLB-1, 11, 235

Shimao Toshio 1917-1986 .... DLB-182

Shimazaki, Tōson 1872-1943 .... DLB-180

Shine, Ted 1931- DLB-38

Shinkei 1406-1475 .... DLB-203

Ship, Reuben 1915-1975 .... DLB-88

Shirer, William L. 1904-1993 .... DLB-4

Shirinsky-Shikhmatov, Sergii Aleksandrovich 1783-1837 .... DLB-150

Shirley, James 1596-1666 .... DLB-58

Shishkov, Aleksandr Semenovich 1753-1841 .... DLB-150

Shockley, Ann Allen 1927- DLB-33

Shōno Junzō 1921- DLB-182

Shore, Arabella 1820?-1901 and Shore, Louisa 1824-1895 .... DLB-199

Short, Peter [publishing house] DLB-170

Shorter, Dora Sigerson 1866-1918 ...... DLB-240

Shorthouse, Joseph Henry 1834-1903 .... DLB-18

Shōtetsu 1381-1459 .... DLB-203

Showalter, Elaine 1941- DLB-67

Shulevitz, Uri 1935- DLB-61

Shulman, Max 1919-1988 .... DLB-11

Shute, Henry A. 1856-1943 .... DLB-9

Shuttle, Penelope 1947- DLB-14, 40

Sibbes, Richard 1577-1635 .... DLB-151

Sibiriak, D. (see Mamin, Dmitrii Narkisovich)

Siddal, Elizabeth Eleanor 1829-1862 .... DLB-199

Sidgwick, Ethel 1877-1970 .... DLB-197

Sidgwick and Jackson Limited DLB-112

Sidney, Margaret (see Lothrop, Harriet M.)

Sidney, Mary 1561-1621 .... DLB-167

Sidney, Sir Philip 1554-1586 .... DLB-167; CDBLB-1

An Apologie for Poetrie (the Olney edition, 1595, of *Defence of Poesie*) DLB-167

Sidney's Press DLB-49

Sierra, Rubén 1946- DLB-122

Sierra Club Books DLB-49

Siger of Brabant circa 1240-circa 1284 ... DLB-115

Sigourney, Lydia Huntley 1791-1865 ......DLB-1, 42, 73, 183, 239, 243

Silkin, Jon 1930- DLB-27

Silko, Leslie Marmon 1948- DLB-143, 175

Silliman, Benjamin 1779-1864 .... DLB-183

Silliman, Ron 1946- DLB-169

Silliphant, Stirling 1918- DLB-26

Sillitoe, Alan 1928- DLB-14, 139; CDBLB-8

Silman, Roberta 1934- DLB-28

Silva, Beverly 1930- DLB-122

Silverberg, Robert 1935- DLB-8

Silverman, Kaja 1947- DLB-246

Silverman, Kenneth 1936- DLB-111

Simak, Clifford D. 1904-1988 .... DLB-8

Simcoe, Elizabeth 1762-1850 .... DLB-99

Simcox, Edith Jemima 1844-1901 .... DLB-190

Simcox, George Augustus 1841-1905 ..... DLB-35

Sime, Jessie Georgina 1868-1958 .... DLB-92

Simenon, Georges 1903-1989 ....DLB-72; Y-89

Simic, Charles 1938- DLB-105

"Images and 'Images,'" DLB-105

Simionescu, Mircea Horia 1928- DLB-232

Simmel, Johannes Mario 1924- DLB-69

Simmes, Valentine [publishing house] DLB-170

Simmons, Ernest J. 1903-1972 .... DLB-103

Simmons, Herbert Alfred 1930- DLB-33

Simmons, James 1933- DLB-40

Simms, William Gilmore 1806-1870 ....DLB-3, 30, 59, 73, 248

Simms and M'Intyre DLB-106

Simon, Claude 1913- DLB-83; Y-85

Simon, Neil 1927- DLB-7

Simon and Schuster DLB-46

Simons, Katherine Drayton Mayrant 1890-1969 .... Y-83

Simović, Ljubomir 1935- DLB-181

Simpkin and Marshall [publishing house] DLB-154

Simpson, Helen 1897-1940 .... DLB-77

Simpson, Louis 1923- DLB-5

Simpson, N. F. 1919- DLB-13

Sims, George 1923- DLB-87; Y-99

Sims, George Robert 1847-1922 ...DLB-35, 70, 135

Sinán, Rogelio 1904- DLB-145

Sinclair, Andrew 1935- DLB-14

Sinclair, Bertrand William 1881-1972 ..... DLB-92

Sinclair, Catherine 1800-1864 .... DLB-163

Sinclair, Jo 1913-1995 .... DLB-28

Sinclair, Lister 1921- DLB-88

Sinclair, May 1863-1946 .... DLB-36, 135

Sinclair, Upton 1878-1968 ..... DLB-9; CDALB-5

Sinclair, Upton [publishing house] DLB-46

Singer, Isaac Bashevis 1904-1991 ... DLB-6, 28, 52; Y-91; CDALB-1

Singer, Mark 1950- DLB-185

Singmaster, Elsie 1879-1958..............DLB-9

Sinisgalli, Leonardo 1908-1981 ....DLB-114

Siodmak, Curt 1902-2000 ....DLB-44

Sîrbu, Ion D. 1919-1989.................DLB-232

Siringo, Charles A. 1855-1928...........DLB-186

Sissman, L. E. 1928-1976..................DLB-5

Sisson, C. H. 1914- DLB-27

Sitwell, Edith 1887-1964...... DLB-20; CDBLB-7

Sitwell, Osbert 1892-1969 ....DLB-100, 195

Skácel, Jan 1922-1989 ....DLB-232

Skalbe, Kārlis 1879-1945 ....DLB-220

Skármeta, Antonio
   1940- DLB-145; CDWLB-3

Skavronsky, A. (see Danilevsky, Grigorii Petrovich)

Skeat, Walter W. 1835-1912 ....DLB-184

Skeffington, William
   [publishing house]................DLB-106

Skelton, John 1463-1529 ....DLB-136

Skelton, Robin 1925- DLB-27, 53

Škėma, Antanas 1910-1961 ....DLB-220

Skinner, Constance Lindsay
   1877-1939 ....DLB-92

Skinner, John Stuart 1788-1851 ....DLB-73

Skipsey, Joseph 1832-1903..............DLB-35

Skou-Hansen, Tage 1925- DLB-214

Škvorecký, Josef 1924- DLB-232; CDWLB-4

Slade, Bernard 1930- DLB-53

Slamnig, Ivan 1930- DLB-181

Slančeková, Božena (see Timrava)

Slater, Patrick 1880-1951...............DLB-68

Slaveykov, Pencho 1866-1912..........DLB-147

Slaviček, Milivoj 1929- DLB-181

Slavitt, David 1935- DLB-5, 6

Sleigh, Burrows Willcocks Arthur
   1821-1869 ....DLB-99

A Slender Thread of Hope:
   The Kennedy Center Black
   Theatre Project DLB-38

Slesinger, Tess 1905-1945 ....DLB-102

Slick, Sam (see Haliburton, Thomas Chandler)

Sloan, John 1871-1951 ....DLB-188

Sloane, William, Associates DLB-46

Small, Maynard and Company DLB-49

Small Presses in Great Britain and Ireland,
   1960-1985 ....DLB-40

Small Presses I: Jargon Society.............Y-84

Small Presses II: The Spirit That Moves
   Us Press Y-85

Small Presses III: Pushcart Press...........Y-87

Smart, Christopher 1722-1771 ....DLB-109

Smart, David A. 1892-1957 ....DLB-137

Smart, Elizabeth 1913-1986 ....DLB-88

Smedley, Menella Bute 1820?-1877 ......DLB-199

Smellie, William [publishing house]......DLB-154

Smiles, Samuel 1812-1904 ....DLB-55

Smiley, Jane 1949- DLB-227, 234

Smith, A. J. M. 1902-1980 ....DLB-88

Smith, Adam 1723-1790 ....DLB-104

Smith, Adam (George Jerome Waldo Goodman)
   1930- DLB-185

Smith, Alexander 1829-1867 ....DLB-32, 55

"On the Writing of Essays" (1862) DLB-57

Smith, Amanda 1837-1915..............DLB-221

Smith, Betty 1896-1972 ....Y-82

Smith, Carol Sturm 1938- Y-81

Smith, Charles Henry 1826-1903 ....DLB-11

Smith, Charlotte 1749-1806.........DLB-39, 109

Smith, Chet 1899-1973...................DLB-171

Smith, Cordwainer 1913-1966............DLB-8

Smith, Dave 1942- DLB-5

Smith, Dodie 1896- DLB-10

Smith, Doris Buchanan 1934- DLB-52

Smith, E. E. 1890-1965 ....DLB-8

Smith, Elder and Company DLB-154

Smith, Elihu Hubbard 1771-1798........DLB-37

Smith, Elizabeth Oakes (Prince)
   (see Oakes Smith, Elizabeth)

Smith, Eunice 1757-1823 ....DLB-200

Smith, F. Hopkinson 1838-1915 .... DS-13

Smith, George D. 1870-1920 ....DLB-140

Smith, George O. 1911-1981 ....DLB-8

Smith, Goldwin 1823-1910 ....DLB-99

Smith, H. Allen 1907-1976 ....DLB-11, 29

Smith, Harrison, and Robert Haas
   [publishing house]..................DLB-46

Smith, Harry B. 1860-1936 ....DLB-187

Smith, Hazel Brannon 1914- DLB-127

Smith, Henry circa 1560-circa 1591......DLB-136

Smith, Horatio (Horace) 1779-1849......DLB-116

Smith, Horatio (Horace) 1779-1849 and
   James Smith 1775-1839 ....DLB-96

Smith, Iain Crichton 1928- DLB-40, 139

Smith, J. Allen 1860-1924 ....DLB-47

Smith, J. Stilman, and Company DLB-49

Smith, Jessie Willcox 1863-1935 ....DLB-188

Smith, John 1580-1631..............DLB-24, 30

Smith, Josiah 1704-1781 ....DLB-24

Smith, Ken 1938- DLB-40

Smith, Lee 1944- DLB-143; Y-83

Smith, Logan Pearsall 1865-1946.........DLB-98

Smith, Margaret Bayard 1778-1844 ......DLB-248

Smith, Mark 1935- Y-82

Smith, Michael 1698-circa 1771 ....DLB-31

Smith, Pauline 1882-1959 ....DLB-225

Smith, Red 1905-1982 ....DLB-29, 171

Smith, Roswell 1829-1892 ....DLB-79

Smith, Samuel Harrison 1772-1845 ......DLB-43

Smith, Samuel Stanhope 1751-1819......DLB-37

Smith, Sarah (see Stretton, Hesba)

Smith, Sarah Pogson 1774-1870 ....DLB-200

Smith, Seba 1792-1868..........DLB-1, 11, 243

Smith, Stevie 1902-1971.................DLB-20

Smith, Sydney 1771-1845..............DLB-107

Smith, Sydney Goodsir 1915-1975........DLB-27

Smith, Sir Thomas 1513-1577 ....DLB-132

Smith, W. B., and Company DLB-49

Smith, W. H., and Son DLB-106

Smith, Wendell 1914-1972..............DLB-171

Smith, William flourished 1595-1597 ....DLB-136

Smith, William 1727-1803 ....DLB-31

A General Idea of the College of Mirania
   (1753) [excerpts] DLB-31

Smith, William 1728-1793 ....DLB-30

Smith, William Gardner 1927-1974 .....DLB-76

Smith, William Henry 1808-1872 ....DLB-159

Smith, William Jay 1918- DLB-5

Smithers, Leonard [publishing house] DLB-112

Smollett, Tobias
   1721-1771...........DLB-39, 104; CDBLB-2

Dedication, *Ferdinand Count
   Fathom* (1753) DLB-39

Preface to *Ferdinand Count Fathom* (1753) DLB-39

Preface to *Roderick Random* (1748).........DLB-39

Smythe, Francis Sydney 1900-1949......DLB-195

Snelling, William Joseph 1804-1848 .....DLB-202

Snellings, Rolland (see Touré, Askia Muhammad)

Snodgrass, W. D. 1926- DLB-5

Snow, C. P.
   1905-1980 .....DLB-15, 77; DS-17; CDBLB-7

Snyder, Gary 1930- ... DLB-5, 16, 165, 212, 237

Sobiloff, Hy 1912-1970.................DLB-48

The Society for Textual Scholarship and
   TEXT Y-87

The Society for the History of Authorship,
   Reading and Publishing Y-92

Soffici, Ardengo 1879-1964 ....DLB-114

Sofola, 'Zulu 1938- DLB-157

Solano, Solita 1888-1975 ....DLB-4

Soldati, Mario 1906-1999 ....DLB-177

Šoljan, Antun 1932-1993 ....DLB-181

Sollers, Philippe 1936- DLB-83

Sollogub, Vladimir Aleksandrovich
   1813-1882......................DLB-198

Sollors, Werner 1943- DBL-246

Solmi, Sergio 1899-1981 ....DLB-114

Solomon, Carl 1928- DLB-16

Solway, David 1941- DLB-53

Solzhenitsyn and America Y-85

Somerville, Edith Œnone 1858-1949.....DLB-135

Somov, Orest Mikhailovich
   1793-1833......................DLB-198

Sønderby, Knud 1909-1966..............DLB-214

Song, Cathy 1955- DLB-169

Sono Ayako 1931- DLB-182

Sontag, Susan 1933- DLB-2, 67

Sophocles 497/496 B.C.-406/405 B.C.
   .... DLB-176; CDWLB-1

Šopov, Aco 1923-1982................DLB-181

Sørensen, Villy 1929- DLB-214

Sorensen, Virginia 1912-1991 .... DLB-206

Sorge, Reinhard Johannes 1892-1916.... DLB-118

Sorrentino, Gilbert 1929- DLB-5, 173; Y-80

Sotheby, James 1682-1742 .... DLB-213

Sotheby, John 1740-1807................ DLB-213

Sotheby, Samuel 1771-1842 .... DLB-213

Sotheby, Samuel Leigh 1805-1861 ...... DLB-213

Sotheby, William 1757-1833 .... DLB-93, 213

Soto, Gary 1952- DLB-82

Sources for the Study of Tudor and Stuart Drama DLB-62

Souster, Raymond 1921- DLB-88

The *South English Legendary* circa thirteenth-fifteenth centuries DLB-146

Southerland, Ellease 1943- DLB-33

Southern, Terry 1924-1995 .... DLB-2

Southern Illinois University Press Y-95

Southern Writers Between the Wars DLB-9

Southerne, Thomas 1659-1746.......... DLB-80

Southey, Caroline Anne Bowles 1786-1854.................... DLB-116

Southey, Robert 1774-1843...... DLB-93, 107, 142

Southwell, Robert 1561?-1595 .... DLB-167

Southworth, E. D. E. N. 1819-1899 ..... DLB-239

Sowande, Bode 1948- DLB-157

Sowle, Tace [publishing house]..........DLB-170

Soyfer, Jura 1912-1939 .... DLB-124

Soyinka, Wole 1934- DLB-125; Y-86, Y-87; CDWLB-3

Spacks, Barry 1931- DLB-105

Spalding, Frances 1950- DLB-155

Spark, Muriel 1918- ... DLB-15, 139; CDBLB-7

Sparke, Michael [publishing house] DLB-170

Sparks, Jared 1789-1866 .... DLB-1, 30, 235

Sparshott, Francis 1926- DLB-60

Späth, Gerold 1939- DLB-75

Spatola, Adriano 1941-1988 .... DLB-128

Spaziani, Maria Luisa 1924- DLB-128

Special Collections at the University of Colorado at Boulder........................Y-98

The Spectator 1828- DLB-110

Spedding, James 1808-1881 .... DLB-144

Spee von Langenfeld, Friedrich 1591-1635 .... DLB-164

Speght, Rachel 1597-after 1630.......... DLB-126

Speke, John Hanning 1827-1864 .... DLB-166

Spellman, A. B. 1935- DLB-41

Spence, Catherine Helen 1825-1910..... DLB-230

Spence, Thomas 1750-1814 .... DLB-158

Spencer, Anne 1882-1975 .... DLB-51, 54

Spencer, Charles, third Earl of Sunderland 1674-1722..................... DLB-213

Spencer, Elizabeth 1921- DLB-6, 218

Spencer, George John, Second Earl Spencer 1758-1834..................... DLB-184

Spencer, Herbert 1820-1903............ DLB-57

"The Philosophy of Style" (1852) DLB-57

Spencer, Scott 1945- Y-86

Spender, J. A. 1862-1942 .... DLB-98

Spender, Stephen 1909-1995 .. DLB-20; CDBLB-7

Spener, Philipp Jakob 1635-1705 .... DLB-164

Spenser, Edmund circa 1552-1599 .... DLB-167; CDBLB-1

Envoy from *The Shepheardes Calender*..... DLB-167

"The Generall Argument of the Whole Booke," from *The Shepheardes Calender*. DLB-167

"A Letter of the Authors Expounding His Whole Intention in the Course of this Worke: Which for that It Giueth Great Light to the Reader, for the Better Vnderstanding Is Hereunto Annexed," from *The Faerie Qveene* (1590) DLB-167

"To His Booke," from *The Shepheardes Calender* (1579) DLB-167

"To the Most Excellent and Learned Both Orator and Poete, Mayster Gabriell Haruey, His Verie Special and Singular Good Frend E. K. Commendeth the Good Lyking of This His Labour, and the Patronage of the New Poete," from *The Shepheardes Calender*............ DLB-167

Sperr, Martin 1944- DLB-124

Spicer, Jack 1925-1965 .... DLB-5, 16, 193

Spielberg, Peter 1929- Y-81

Spielhagen, Friedrich 1829-1911 .... DLB-129

"*Spielmannsepen*" (circa 1152-circa 1500) .. DLB-148

Spier, Peter 1927- DLB-61

Spillane, Mickey 1918- DLB-226

Spink, J. G. Taylor 1888-1962 .... DLB-241

Spinrad, Norman 1940- DLB-8

Spires, Elizabeth 1952- DLB-120

Spitteler, Carl 1845-1924 .... DLB-129

Spivak, Lawrence E. 1900- DLB-137

Spofford, Harriet Prescott 1835-1921 .... DLB-74, 221

Spring, Howard 1889-1965 .... DLB-191

Squibob (see Derby, George Horatio)

Squier, E. G. 1821-1888 .... DLB-189

Stacpoole, H. de Vere 1863-1951 .... DLB-153

Staël, Germaine de 1766-1817...... DLB-119, 192

Staël-Holstein, Anne-Louise Germaine de (see Staël, Germaine de)

Stafford, Jean 1915-1979..............DLB-2, 173

Stafford, William 1914-1993......... DLB-5, 206

Stage Censorship: "The Rejected Statement" (1911), by Bernard Shaw [excerpts] ... DLB-10

Stallings, Laurence 1894-1968 ....DLB-7, 44

Stallworthy, Jon 1935- DLB-40

Stampp, Kenneth M. 1912- DLB-17

Stănescu, Nichita 1933-1983.......... DLB-232

Stanev, Emiliyan 1907-1979 .... DLB-181

Stanford, Ann 1916- DLB-5

Stangerup, Henrik 1937-1998 .... DLB-214

Stanitsky, N. (see Panaeva, Avdot'ia Iakovlevna)

Stankevich, Nikolai Vladimirovich 1813-1840 .... DLB-198

Stanković, Borisav ("Bora") 1876-1927............DLB-147; CDWLB-4

Stanley, Henry M. 1841-1904 ... DLB-189; DS-13

Stanley, Thomas 1625-1678 .... DLB-131

Stannard, Martin 1947- DLB-155

Stansby, William [publishing house]......DLB-170

Stanton, Elizabeth Cady 1815-1902 ...... DLB-79

Stanton, Frank L. 1857-1927........... DLB-25

Stanton, Maura 1946- DLB-120

Stapledon, Olaf 1886-1950............ DLB-15

Star Spangled Banner Office........... DLB-49

Stark, Freya 1893-1993............... DLB-195

Starkey, Thomas circa 1499-1538 ...... DLB-132

Starkie, Walter 1894-1976 .... DLB-195

Starkweather, David 1935- DLB-7

Starrett, Vincent 1886-1974 ....DLB-187

The State of Publishing Y-97

Statements on the Art of Poetry DLB-54

Stationers' Company of London, The DLB-170

Statius circa A.D. 45-A.D. 96 .... DLB-211

Stead, Robert J. C. 1880-1959 .... DLB-92

Steadman, Mark 1930- DLB-6

The Stealthy School of Criticism (1871), by Dante Gabriel Rossetti............ DLB-35

Stearns, Harold E. 1891-1943............ DLB-4

Stebnitsky, M. (see Leskov, Nikolai Semenovich)

Stedman, Edmund Clarence 1833-1908... DLB-64

Steegmuller, Francis 1906-1994 .... DLB-111

Steel, Flora Annie 1847-1929 ...... DLB-153, 156

Steele, Max 1922- Y-80

Steele, Richard 1672-1729.......... DLB-84, 101; CDBLB-2

Steele, Timothy 1948- DLB-120

Steele, Wilbur Daniel 1886-1970 .... DLB-86

Steere, Richard circa 1643-1721 .... DLB-24

Stefanovski, Goran 1952- DLB-181

Stegner, Wallace 1909-1993.....DLB-9, 206; Y-93

Stehr, Hermann 1864-1940 .... DLB-66

Steig, William 1907- DLB-61

Stein, Gertrude 1874-1946 .... DLB-4, 54, 86, 228; DS-15; CDALB-4

Stein, Leo 1872-1947.................. DLB-4

Stein and Day Publishers DLB-46

Steinbeck, John 1902-1968 ....DLB-7, 9, 212; DS-2; CDALB-5

John Steinbeck Research Center............Y-85

Steinem, Gloria 1934- DLB-246

Steiner, George 1929- DLB-67

Steinhoewel, Heinrich 1411/1412-1479....DLB-179

Steloff, Ida Frances 1887-1989 ....DLB-187

Stendhal 1783-1842................. DLB-119

Stephen Crane: A Revaluation Virginia Tech Conference, 1989 ....Y-89

Stephen, Leslie 1832-1904 ...... DLB-57, 144, 190

Stephen Vincent Benét Centenary Y-97

Stephens, A. G. 1865-1933. .... DLB-230

Stephens, Alexander H. 1812-1883 .... DLB-47

Stephens, Alice Barber 1858-1932 .... DLB-188

Stephens, Ann Sophia 1810-1886... DLB-3, 73, 250

Stephens, Charles Asbury 1844?-1931..... DLB-42

Stephens, James 1882?-1950 .... DLB-19, 153, 162

Stephens, John Lloyd 1805-1852 .... DLB-183, 250

Stephens, Michael 1946- DLB-234

Sterling, George 1869-1926 .... DLB-54

Sterling, James 1701-1763 .... DLB-24

Sterling, John 1806-1844 .... DLB-116

Stern, Gerald 1925- DLB-105

Stern, Gladys B. 1890-1973 .... DLB-197

Stern, Madeleine B. 1912- DLB-111, 140

Stern, Richard 1928- DLB-218; Y-87

Stern, Stewart 1922- DLB-26

Sterne, Laurence
  1713-1768. .... DLB-39; CDBLB-2

Sternheim, Carl 1878-1942.......... DLB-56, 118

Sternhold, Thomas ?-1549 and
  John Hopkins ?-1570 .... DLB-132

Steuart, David 1747-1824 .... DLB-213

Stevens, Henry 1819-1886............... DLB-140

Stevens, Wallace 1879-1955.... DLB-54; CDALB-5

Stevenson, Anne 1933- DLB-40

Stevenson, D. E. 1892-1973 .... DLB-191

Stevenson, Lionel 1902-1973 .... DLB-155

Stevenson, Robert Louis
  1850-1894 .... DLB-18, 57, 141, 156, 174;
                                  DS-13; CDBLB-5

"On Style in Literature:
  Its Technical Elements" (1885) DLB-57

Stewart, Donald Ogden
  1894-1980 .... DLB-4, 11, 26

Stewart, Dugald 1753-1828 .... DLB-31

Stewart, George, Jr. 1848-1906 .... DLB-99

Stewart, George R. 1895-1980............ DLB-8

Stewart, Maria W. 1803?-1879............ DLB-239

Stewart, Randall 1896-1964............. DLB-103

Stewart, Sean 1965- DLB-251

Stewart and Kidd Company DLB-46

Stickney, Trumbull 1874-1904........... DLB-54

Stieler, Caspar 1632-1707............... DLB-164

Stifter, Adalbert
  1805-1868 .... DLB-133; CDWLB-2

Stiles, Ezra 1727-1795 .... DLB-31

Still, James 1906- DLB-9

Stirling, S. M. 1954- DLB-251

Stirner, Max 1806-1856................. DLB-129

Stith, William 1707-1755................. DLB-31

Stock, Elliot [publishing house] DLB-106

Stockton, Frank R.
  1834-1902 .... DLB-42, 74; DS-13

Stockton, J. Roy 1892-1972 .... DLB-241

Stoddard, Ashbel [publishing house] DLB-49

Stoddard, Charles Warren
  1843-1909 .... DLB-186

Stoddard, Elizabeth 1823-1902 .... DLB-202

Stoddard, Richard Henry
  1825-1903 .... DLB-3, 64, 250; DS-13

Stoddard, Solomon 1643-1729........... DLB-24

Stoker, Bram
  1847-1912 .... DLB-36, 70, 178; CDBLB-5

Stokes, Frederick A., Company DLB-49

Stokes, Thomas L. 1898-1958 .... DLB-29

Stokesbury, Leon 1945- DLB-120

Stolberg, Christian Graf zu 1748-1821..... DLB-94

Stolberg, Friedrich Leopold Graf zu
  1750-1819 .... DLB-94

Stone, Herbert S., and Company......... DLB-49

Stone, Lucy 1818-1893 .... DLB-79, 239

Stone, Melville 1848-1929 .... DLB-25

Stone, Robert 1937- DLB-152

Stone, Ruth 1915- DLB-105

Stone, Samuel 1602-1663................ DLB-24

Stone, William Leete 1792-1844 .... DLB-202

Stone and Kimball DLB-49

Stoppard, Tom
  1937- DLB-13, 233; Y-85; CDBLB-8

Playwrights and Professors DLB-13

Storey, Anthony 1928- DLB-14

Storey, David 1933- DLB-13, 14, 207, 245

Storm, Theodor 1817-1888 .. DLB-129; CDWLB-2

Story, Thomas circa 1670-1742 .... DLB-31

Story, William Wetmore 1819-1895 ... DLB-1, 235

Storytelling: A Contemporary Renaissance... Y-84

Stoughton, William 1631-1701.......... DLB-24

Stow, John 1525-1605 .... DLB-132

Stowe, Harriet Beecher 1811-1896
  .. DLB-1, 12, 42, 74, 189, 239, 243; CDALB-3

Stowe, Leland 1899- DLB-29

Stoyanov, Dimitr Ivanov (see Elin Pelin)

Strabo 64 or 63 B.C.-circa A.D. 25 ...... DLB-176

Strachey, Lytton 1880-1932...... DLB-149; DS-10

Strachey, Lytton, Preface to Eminent
  Victorians DLB-149

Strahan, William [publishing house] DLB-154

Strahan and Company................. DLB-106

Strand, Mark 1934- DLB-5

The Strasbourg Oaths 842............. DLB-148

Stratemeyer, Edward 1862-1930 .... DLB-42

Strati, Saverio 1924- DLB-177

Stratton and Barnard DLB-49

Stratton-Porter, Gene
  1863-1924 .... DLB-221; DS-14

Straub, Peter 1943- Y-84

Strauß, Botho 1944- DLB-124

Strauß, David Friedrich 1808-1874 ..... DLB-133

The Strawberry Hill Press DLB-154

Streatfeild, Noel 1895-1986 .... DLB-160

Street, Cecil John Charles (see Rhode, John)

Street, G. S. 1867-1936................ DLB-135

Street and Smith..................... DLB-49

Streeter, Edward 1891-1976............ DLB-11

Streeter, Thomas Winthrop 1883-1965... DLB-140

Stretton, Hesba 1832-1911.......... DLB-163, 190

Stribling, T. S. 1881-1965 .... DLB-9

Der Stricker circa 1190-circa 1250....... DLB-138

Strickland, Samuel 1804-1867 .... DLB-99

Stringer, Arthur 1874-1950 .... DLB-92

Stringer and Townsend DLB-49

Strittmatter, Erwin 1912- DLB-69

Strniša, Gregor 1930-1987 .... DLB-181

Strode, William 1630-1645 .... DLB-126

Strong, L. A. G. 1896-1958 .... DLB-191

Strother, David Hunter (Porte Crayon)
  1816-1888 .... DLB-3, 248

Strouse, Jean 1945- DLB-111

Stuart, Dabney 1937- DLB-105

Stuart, Jesse 1906-1984 ..... DLB-9, 48, 102; Y-84

Stuart, Lyle [publishing house] DLB-46

Stuart, Ruth McEnery 1849?-1917 ...... DLB-202

Stubbs, Harry Clement (see Clement, Hal)

Stubenberg, Johann Wilhelm von
  1619-1663 .... DLB-164

Studio. DLB-112

The Study of Poetry (1880), by
  Matthew Arnold DLB-35

Stump, Al 1916-1995 .... DLB-241

Sturgeon, Theodore 1918-1985 ...... DLB-8; Y-85

Sturges, Preston 1898-1959 .... DLB-26

"Style" (1840; revised, 1859), by
  Thomas de Quincey [excerpt]....... DLB-57

"Style" (1888), by Walter Pater.......... DLB-57

Style (1897), by Walter Raleigh
  [excerpt] DLB-57

"Style" (1877), by T. H. Wright
  [excerpt] DLB-57

"Le Style c'est l'homme" (1892), by
  W. H. Mallock DLB-57

Styron, William
  1925- DLB-2, 143; Y-80; CDALB-6

Suárez, Mario 1925- DLB-82

Such, Peter 1939- DLB-60

Suckling, Sir John 1609-1641?....... DLB-58, 126

Suckow, Ruth 1892-1960............ DLB-9, 102

Sudermann, Hermann 1857-1928 .... DLB-118

Sue, Eugène 1804-1857 .... DLB-119

Sue, Marie-Joseph (see Sue, Eugène)

Suetonius circa A.D. 69-post A.D. 122 ... DLB-211

Suggs, Simon (see Hooper, Johnson Jones)

Sui Sin Far (see Eaton, Edith Maude)

Suits, Gustav 1883-1956 .... DLB-220; CDWLB-4

Sukenick, Ronald 1932- DLB-173; Y-81

Suknaski, Andrew 1942- DLB-53

Sullivan, Alan 1868-1947............... DLB-92

Sullivan, C. Gardner 1886-1965 .... DLB-26

Sullivan, Frank 1892-1976 .... DLB-11

Sulte, Benjamin 1841-1923 .... DLB-99

Sulzberger, Arthur Hays 1891-1968 ..... DLB-127

Sulzberger, Arthur Ochs 1926- DLB-127

Sulzer, Johann Georg 1720-1779 .... DLB-97

Sumarokov, Aleksandr Petrovich 1717-1777 .... DLB-150

Summers, Hollis 1916- DLB-6

A Summing Up at Century's End Y-99

Sumner, Charles 1811-1874 .... DLB-235

Sumner, Henry A. [publishing house] DLB-49

Surtees, Robert Smith 1803-1864 .... DLB-21

Survey of Literary Biographies Y-00

A Survey of Poetry Anthologies, 1879-1960 .... DLB-54

Surveys: Japanese Literature, 1987-1995 .... DLB-182

Sutherland, Efua Theodora 1924-1996 .... DLB-117

Sutherland, John 1919-1956 .... DLB-68

Sutro, Alfred 1863-1933 .... DLB-10

Svendsen, Hanne Marie 1933- DLB-214

Swados, Harvey 1920-1972 .... DLB-2

Swain, Charles 1801-1874 .... DLB-32

Swallow Press DLB-46

Swan Sonnenschein Limited DLB-106

Swanberg, W. A. 1907- DLB-103

Swenson, May 1919-1989 .... DLB-5

Swerling, Jo 1897- DLB-44

Swift, Graham 1949- DLB-194

Swift, Jonathan 1667-1745 .... DLB-39, 95, 101; CDBLB-2

Swinburne, A. C. 1837-1909 .... DLB-35, 57; CDBLB-4

Swineshead, Richard floruit circa 1350 .... DLB-115

Swinnerton, Frank 1884-1982 .... DLB-34

Swisshelm, Jane Grey 1815-1884 .... DLB-43

Swope, Herbert Bayard 1882-1958 .... DLB-25

Swords, T. and J., and Company DLB-49

Swords, Thomas 1763-1843 and Swords, James ?-1844 .... DLB-73

Sykes, Ella C. ?-1939 .... DLB-174

Sylvester, Josuah 1562 or 1563-1618 .... DLB-121

Symonds, Emily Morse (see Paston, George)

Symonds, John Addington 1840-1893 .... DLB-57, 144

"Personal Style" (1890) DLB-57

Symons, A. J. A. 1900-1941 .... DLB-149

Symons, Arthur 1865-1945 .... DLB-19, 57, 149

Symons, Julian 1912-1994 .... DLB-87, 155; Y-92

Julian Symons at Eighty Y-92

Symons, Scott 1933- DLB-53

A Symposium on *The Columbia History of the Novel* Y-92

Synge, John Millington 1871-1909 .... DLB-10, 19; CDBLB-5

Synge Summer School: J. M. Synge and the Irish Theater, Rathdrum, County Wiclow, Ireland Y-93

Syrett, Netta 1865-1943 .... DLB-135, 197

Szabó, Lőrinc 1900-1957 .... DLB-215

Szabó, Magda 1917- DLB-215

Szymborska, Wisława 1923- DLB-232, Y-96; CDWLB-4

T

Taban lo Liyong 1939?- DLB-125

Tabori, George 1914- DLB-245

Tabucchi, Antonio 1943- DLB-196

Taché, Joseph-Charles 1820-1894 ...... DLB-99

Tachihara Masaaki 1926-1980 .... DLB-182

Tacitus circa A.D. 55-circa A.D. 117 .... DLB-211; CDWLB-1

Tadijanović, Dragutin 1905- DLB-181

Tafdrup, Pia 1952- DLB-214

Tafolla, Carmen 1951- DLB-82

Taggard, Genevieve 1894-1948 .... DLB-45

Taggart, John 1942- DLB-193

Tagger, Theodor (see Bruckner, Ferdinand)

Taiheiki late fourteenth century DLB-203

Tait, J. Selwin, and Sons DLB-49

Tait's Edinburgh Magazine 1832-1861 ..... DLB-110

The Takarazaka Revue Company Y-91

Talander (see Bohse, August)

Talese, Gay 1932- DLB-185

Talev, Dimitr 1898-1966 .... DLB-181

Taliaferro, H. E. 1811-1875 .... DLB-202

Tallent, Elizabeth 1954- DLB-130

TallMountain, Mary 1918-1994 .... DLB-193

Talvj 1797-1870 .... DLB-59, 133

Tamási, Áron 1897-1966 .... DLB-215

Tammsaare, A. H. 1878-1940 .... DLB-220; CDWLB-4

Tan, Amy 1952- DLB-173; CDALB-7

Tandori, Dezső 1938- DLB-232

Tanner, Thomas 1673/1674-1735 .... DLB-213

Tanizaki Jun'ichirō 1886-1965 .... DLB-180

Tapahonso, Luci 1953- DLB-175

The Mark Taper Forum DLB-7

Taradash, Daniel 1913- DLB-44

Tarbell, Ida M. 1857-1944 .... DLB-47

Tardivel, Jules-Paul 1851-1905 .... DLB-99

Targan, Barry 1932- DLB-130

Tarkington, Booth 1869-1946 .... DLB-9, 102

Tashlin, Frank 1913-1972 .... DLB-44

Tasma (Jessie Couvreur) 1848-1897 .... DLB-230

Tate, Allen 1899-1979 .... DLB-4, 45, 63; DS-17

Tate, James 1943- DLB-5, 169

Tate, Nahum circa 1652-1715 .... DLB-80

Tatian circa 830 .... DLB-148

Taufer, Veno 1933- DLB-181

Tauler, Johannes circa 1300-1361 .... DLB-179

Tavčar, Ivan 1851-1923 .... DLB-147

Taverner, Richard ca. 1505-1575 .... DLB-236

Taylor, Ann 1782-1866 .... DLB-163

Taylor, Bayard 1825-1878 ...... DLB-3, 189, 250

Taylor, Bert Leston 1866-1921 .... DLB-25

Taylor, Charles H. 1846-1921 .... DLB-25

Taylor, Edward circa 1642-1729 .... DLB-24

Taylor, Elizabeth 1912-1975 .... DLB-139

Taylor, Henry 1942- DLB-5

Taylor, Sir Henry 1800-1886 .... DLB-32

Taylor, Jane 1783-1824 .... DLB-163

Taylor, Jeremy circa 1613-1667 .... DLB-151

Taylor, John 1577 or 1578 - 1653 .... DLB-121

Taylor, Mildred D. ?- DLB-52

Taylor, Peter 1917-1994 ..... DLB-218; Y-81, Y-94

Taylor, Susie King 1848-1912 .... DLB-221

Taylor, William Howland 1901-1966 ... DLB-241

Taylor, William, and Company DLB-49

Taylor-Made Shakespeare? Or Is "Shall I Die?" the Long-Lost Text of Bottom's Dream? Y-85

Teasdale, Sara 1884-1933 .... DLB-45

Telles, Lygia Fagundes 1924- DLB-113

Temple, Sir William 1628-1699 .... DLB-101

Temrizov, A. (see Marchenko, Anastasia Iakovlevna)

Tench, Watkin ca. 1758-1833 .... DLB-230

Tenn, William 1919- DLB-8

Tennant, Emma 1937- DLB-14

Tenney, Tabitha Gilman 1762-1837 .... DLB-37, 200

Tennyson, Alfred 1809-1892 .... DLB-32; CDBLB-4

Tennyson, Frederick 1807-1898 .... DLB-32

Tenorio, Arthur 1924- DLB-209

Tepliakov, Viktor Grigor'evich 1804-1842 .... DLB-205

Terence circa 184 B.C.-159 B.C. or after DLB-211; CDWLB-1

Terhune, Albert Payson 1872-1942 .... DLB-9

Terhune, Mary Virginia 1830-1922 .... DS-13, DS-16

Terry, Megan 1932- DLB-7, 249

Terson, Peter 1932- DLB-13

Tesich, Steve 1943-1996 .... Y-83

Tessa, Delio 1886-1939 .... DLB-114

Testori, Giovanni 1923-1993 .... DLB-128, 177

Tey, Josephine 1896?-1952 .... DLB-77

Thacher, James 1754-1844 .... DLB-37

Thackeray, William Makepeace 1811-1863 .. DLB-21, 55, 159, 163; CDBLB-4

Thames and Hudson Limited DLB-112

Thanet, Octave (see French, Alice)

Thatcher, John Boyd 1847-1909 .... DLB-187

Thaxter, Celia Laighton 1835-1894 ..... DLB-239

Thayer, Caroline Matilda Warren 1785-1844 .... DLB-200

The Theatre Guild DLB-7

The Theater in Shakespeare's Time DLB-62
Thegan and the Astronomer
    flourished circa 850..............DLB-148
Thelwall, John 1764-1834 ....DLB-93, 158
Theocritus circa 300 B.C.-260 B.C.......DLB-176
Theodorescu, Ion N. (see Arghezi, Tudor)
Theodulf circa 760-circa 821 ....DLB-148
Theophrastus circa 371 B.C.-287 B.C.....DLB-176
Theriault, Yves 1915-1983..............DLB-88
Thério, Adrien 1925- DLB-53
Theroux, Paul 1941- DLB-2, 218; CDALB-7
Thesiger, Wilfred 1910- DLB-204
They All Came to Paris................DS-16
Thibaudeau, Colleen 1925- DLB-88
Thielen, Benedict 1903-1965.........DLB-102
Thiong'o Ngugi wa (see Ngugi wa Thiong'o)
Third-Generation Minor Poets of the
    Seventeenth Century..............DLB-131
This Quarter 1925-1927, 1929-1932 ....DS-15
Thoma, Ludwig 1867-1921 ....DLB-66
Thoma, Richard 1902- DLB-4
Thomas, Audrey 1935- DLB-60
Thomas, D. M. 1935- ..DLB-40, 207; CDBLB-8
D. M. Thomas: The Plagiarism
    Controversy Y-82
Thomas, Dylan
    1914-1953 ....DLB-13, 20, 139; CDBLB-7
The Dylan Thomas Celebration Y-99
Thomas, Edward
    1878-1917 ....DLB-19, 98, 156, 216
Thomas, Frederick William 1806-1866...DLB-202
Thomas, Gwyn 1913-1981 ....DLB-15, 245
Thomas, Isaiah 1750-1831....... DLB-43, 73, 187
Thomas, Isaiah [publishing house].......DLB-49
Thomas, Johann 1624-1679...........DLB-168
Thomas, John 1900-1932................DLB-4
Thomas, Joyce Carol 1938- DLB-33
Thomas, Lorenzo 1944- DLB-41
Thomas, R. S. 1915-2000......DLB-27; CDBLB-8
Thomasîn von Zerclære
    circa 1186-circa 1259..............DLB-138
Thomasius, Christian 1655-1728........DLB-168
Thompson, Daniel Pierce 1795-1868.....DLB-202
Thompson, David 1770-1857............DLB-99
Thompson, Dorothy 1893-1961 ....DLB-29
Thompson, E. P. 1924-1993 ....DLB-242
Thompson, Flora 1876-1947 ....DLB-240
Thompson, Francis
    1859-1907 .... DLB-19; CDBLB-5
Thompson, George Selden (see Selden, George)
Thompson, Henry Yates 1838-1928 .....DLB-184
Thompson, Hunter S. 1939- DLB-185
Thompson, Jim 1906-1977...........DLB-226
Thompson, John 1938-1976............DLB-60
Thompson, John R. 1823-1873 ....DLB-3, 73, 248
Thompson, Lawrance 1906-1973........DLB-103

Thompson, Maurice 1844-1901 ...... DLB-71, 74
Thompson, Ruth Plumly 1891-1976......DLB-22
Thompson, Thomas Phillips 1843-1933 ...DLB-99
Thompson, William 1775-1833 ....DLB-158
Thompson, William Tappan
    1812-1882 ....DLB-3, 11, 248
Thomson, Edward William 1849-1924....DLB-92
Thomson, James 1700-1748 ....DLB-95
Thomson, James 1834-1882 ....DLB-35
Thomson, Joseph 1858-1895 ....DLB-174
Thomson, Mortimer 1831-1875.........DLB-11
Thon, Melanie Rae 1957- DLB-244
Thoreau, Henry David
    1817-1862 ....DLB-1, 183, 223; CDALB-2
The Thoreauvian Pilgrimage: The Structure of an
    American Cult...................DLB-223
Thorpe, Adam 1956- DLB-231
Thorpe, Thomas Bangs
    1815-1878 ....DLB-3, 11, 248
Thorup, Kirsten 1942- DLB-214
Thoughts on Poetry and Its Varieties (1833),
    by John Stuart Mill DLB-32
Thrale, Hester Lynch
    (see Piozzi, Hester Lynch [Thrale])
Thubron, Colin 1939- DLB-204, 231
Thucydides
    circa 455 B.C.-circa 395 B.C. DLB-176
Thulstrup, Thure de 1848-1930 ....DLB-188
Thümmel, Moritz August von
    1738-1817 ....DLB-97
Thurber, James
    1894-1961 .....DLB-4, 11, 22, 102; CDALB-5
Thurman, Wallace 1902-1934..........DLB-51
Thwaite, Anthony 1930- DLB-40
The Booker Prize
    Address by Anthony Thwaite,
    Chairman of the Booker Prize Judges
    Comments from Former Booker
    Prize Winners Y-86
Thwaites, Reuben Gold 1853-1913 ....DLB-47
Tibullus circa 54 B.C.-circa 19 B.C. DLB-211
Ticknor, George 1791-1871 .... DLB-1, 59, 140, 235
Ticknor and Fields....................DLB-49
Ticknor and Fields (revived) DLB-46
Tieck, Ludwig 1773-1853.....DLB-90; CDWLB-2
Tietjens, Eunice 1884-1944 ....DLB-54
Tilghman, Christopher circa 1948........DLB-244
Tilney, Edmund circa 1536-1610........DLB-136
Tilt, Charles [publishing house].........DLB-106
Tilton, J. E., and Company DLB-49
Time and Western Man (1927), by Wyndham
    Lewis [excerpts]...................DLB-36
Time-Life Books DLB-46
Times Books DLB-46
Timothy, Peter circa 1725-1782 ....DLB-43
Timrava 1867-1951 ....DLB-215
Timrod, Henry 1828-1867..........DLB-3, 248
Tindal, Henrietta 1818?-1879 ....DLB-199
Tinker, Chauncey Brewster 1876-1963 ...DLB-140

Tinsley Brothers DLB-106
Tiptree, James, Jr. 1915-1987.............DLB-8
Tišma, Aleksandar 1924- DLB-181
Titus, Edward William
    1870-1952 ....DLB-4; DS-15
Tiutchev, Fedor Ivanovich 1803-1873 ....DLB-205
Tlali, Miriam 1933- DLB-157, 225
Todd, Barbara Euphan 1890-1976.......DLB-160
Todorov, Tzvetan 1939- DLB-242
Tofte, Robert
    1561 or 1562-1619 or 1620.........DLB-172
Toklas, Alice B. 1877-1967.............DLB-4
Tokuda, Shūsei 1872-1943.............DLB-180
Tolkien, J. R. R.
    1892-1973 ....DLB-15, 160; CDBLB-6
Toller, Ernst 1893-1939................DLB-124
Tollet, Elizabeth 1694-1754 ....DLB-95
Tolson, Melvin B. 1898-1966 ....DLB-48, 76
Tolstoy, Aleksei Konstantinovich
    1817-1875.....................DLB-238
Tolstoy, Leo 1828-1910................DLB-238
Tom Jones (1749), by Henry Fielding
    [excerpt] DLB-39
Tomalin, Claire 1933- DLB-155
Tomasi di Lampedusa, Giuseppe
    1896-1957 ....DLB-177
Tomlinson, Charles 1927- DLB-40
Tomlinson, H. M. 1873-1958 ...DLB-36, 100, 195
Tompkins, Abel [publishing house].......DLB-49
Tompson, Benjamin 1642-1714..........DLB-24
Tomson, Graham R.
    (see Watson, Rosamund Marriott)
Ton'a 1289-1372 ....DLB-203
Tondelli, Pier Vittorio 1955-1991 ....DLB-196
Tonks, Rosemary 1932- DLB-14, 207
Tonna, Charlotte Elizabeth 1790-1846 ...DLB-163
Tonson, Jacob the Elder
    [publishing house] DLB-170
Toole, John Kennedy 1937-1969 ....Y-81
Toomer, Jean 1894-1967...DLB-45, 51; CDALB-4
Tor Books DLB-46
Torberg, Friedrich 1908-1979 ....DLB-85
Torrence, Ridgely 1874-1950.......DLB-54, 249
Torres-Metzger, Joseph V. 1933- DLB-122
Toth, Susan Allen 1940- Y-86
Tottell, Richard [publishing house] DLB-170
"The Printer to the Reader," (1557)
    by Richard Tottell................DLB-167
Tough-Guy Literature..................DLB-9
Touré, Askia Muhammad 1938- DLB-41
Tourgée, Albion W. 1838-1905..........DLB-79
Tournemir, Elizaveta Sailhas de (see Tur, Evgeniia)
Tourneur, Cyril circa 1580-1626..........DLB-58
Tournier, Michel 1924- DLB-83
Tousey, Frank [publishing house].........DLB-49
Tower Publications DLB-46
Towne, Benjamin circa 1740-1793 ....DLB-43

Cumulative Index   DLB 251

Towne, Robert 1936- DLB-44
The Townely Plays fifteenth and sixteenth centuries DLB-146
Townshend, Aurelian by 1583-circa 1651 .... DLB-121
Toy, Barbara 1908- DLB-204
Tracy, Honor 1913- DLB-15
Traherne, Thomas 1637?-1674 .... DLB-131
Traill, Catharine Parr 1802-1899 ...... DLB-99
Train, Arthur 1875-1945 .... DLB-86; DS-16
The Transatlantic Publishing Company ... DLB-49
The Transatlantic Review 1924-1925 .... DS-15
The Transcendental Club 1836-1840 .... DLB-223
Transcendentalism DLB-223
Transcendentalists, American DS-5
A Transit of Poets and Others: American Biography in 1982 .... Y-82
transition 1927-1938 .... DS-15
Translators of the Twelfth Century: Literary Issues Raised and Impact Created DLB-115
Travel Writing, 1837-1875 .... DLB-166
Travel Writing, 1876-1909 .... DLB-174
Travel Writing, 1910-1939 .... DLB-195
Traven, B. 1882? or 1890?-1969? DLB-9, 56
Travers, Ben 1886-1980 .... DLB-10, 233
Travers, P. L. (Pamela Lyndon) 1899-1996 .... DLB-160
Trediakovsky, Vasilii Kirillovich 1703-1769 .... DLB-150
Treece, Henry 1911-1966 .... DLB-160
Trejo, Ernesto 1950- DLB-122
Trelawny, Edward John 1792-1881 .... DLB-110, 116, 144
Tremain, Rose 1943- DLB-14
Tremblay, Michel 1942- DLB-60
Trends in Twentieth-Century Mass Market Publishing DLB-46
Trent, William P. 1862-1939 .... DLB-47
Trescot, William Henry 1822-1898 ..... DLB-30
Tressell, Robert (Robert Phillipe Noonan) 1870-1911 .... DLB-197
Trevelyan, Sir George Otto 1838-1928 .... DLB-144
Trevisa, John circa 1342-circa 1402 .... DLB-146
Trevor, William 1928- DLB-14, 139
Trierer Floyris circa 1170-1180 .... DLB-138
Trillin, Calvin 1935- DLB-185
Trilling, Lionel 1905-1975 .... DLB-28, 63
Trilussa 1871-1950 .... DLB-114
Trimmer, Sarah 1741-1810 .... DLB-158
Triolet, Elsa 1896-1970 .... DLB-72
Tripp, John 1927- DLB-40
Trocchi, Alexander 1925- DLB-15
Troisi, Dante 1920-1989 .... DLB-196
Trollope, Anthony 1815-1882 .... DLB-21, 57, 159; CDBLB-4
Trollope, Frances 1779-1863 .... DLB-21, 166
Trollope, Joanna 1943- DLB-207

Troop, Elizabeth 1931- DLB-14
Trotter, Catharine 1679-1749 .... DLB-84
Trotti, Lamar 1898-1952 .... DLB-44
Trottier, Pierre 1925- DLB-60
Troubadours, *Trobaíritz*, and Trouvères .. DLB-208
Troupe, Quincy Thomas, Jr. 1943- DLB-41
Trow, John F., and Company DLB-49
Trowbridge, John Townsend 1827-1916 . DLB-202
Trudel, Jean-Louis 1967- DLB-251
Truillier-Lacombe, Joseph-Patrice 1807-1863 .... DLB-99
Trumbo, Dalton 1905-1976 .... DLB-26
Trumbull, Benjamin 1735-1820 .... DLB-30
Trumbull, John 1750-1831 .... DLB-31
Trumbull, John 1756-1843 .... DLB-183
Truth, Sojourner 1797?-1883 .... DLB-239
Tscherning, Andreas 1611-1659 .... DLB-164
Tsubouchi, Shōyō 1859-1935 .... DLB-180
Tucholsky, Kurt 1890-1935 .... DLB-56
Tucker, Charlotte Maria 1821-1893 .... DLB-163, 190
Tucker, George 1775-1861 .... DLB-3, 30, 248
Tucker, James 1808?-1866? DLB-230
Tucker, Nathaniel Beverley 1784-1851 .... DLB-3, 248
Tucker, St. George 1752-1827 .... DLB-37
Tuckerman, Frederick Goddard 1821-1873 .... DLB-243
Tuckerman, Henry Theodore 1813-1871 .. DLB-64
Tumas, Juozas (see Vaižgantas)
Tunis, John R. 1889-1975 .... DLB-22, 171
Tunstall, Cuthbert 1474-1559 .... DLB-132
Tuohy, Frank 1925- DLB-14, 139
Tupper, Martin F. 1810-1889 .... DLB-32
Tur, Evgeniia 1815-1892 .... DLB-238
Turbyfill, Mark 1896- DLB-45
Turco, Lewis 1934- Y-84
Turgenev, Aleksandr Ivanovich 1784-1845 .... DLB-198
Turgenev, Ivan Sergeevich 1818-1883 ... DLB-238
Turnball, Alexander H. 1868-1918 ..... DLB-184
Turnbull, Andrew 1921-1970 .... DLB-103
Turnbull, Gael 1928- DLB-40
Turner, Arlin 1909-1980 .... DLB-103
Turner, Charles (Tennyson) 1808-1879 .... DLB-32
Turner, Ethel 1872-1958 .... DLB-230
Turner, Frederick 1943- DLB-40
Turner, Frederick Jackson 1861-1932 .... DLB-17, 186
Turner, Joseph Addison 1826-1868 ...... DLB-79
Turpin, Waters Edward 1910-1968 ...... DLB-51
Turrini, Peter 1944- DLB-124
Tutuola, Amos 1920-1997 .. DLB-125; CDWLB-3
Twain, Mark (see Clemens, Samuel Langhorne)
Tweedie, Ethel Brilliana circa 1860-1940 .... DLB-174

The 'Twenties and Berlin, by Alex Natan . DLB-66
Two Hundred Years of Rare Books and Literary Collections at the University of South Carolina Y-00
Twombly, Wells 1935-1977 .... DLB-241
Twysden, Sir Roger 1597-1672 .... DLB-213
Tyler, Anne 1941- DLB-6, 143; Y-82; CDALB-7
Tyler, Mary Palmer 1775-1866 .... DLB-200
Tyler, Moses Coit 1835-1900 .... DLB-47, 64
Tyler, Royall 1757-1826 .... DLB-37
Tylor, Edward Burnett 1832-1917 .... DLB-57
Tynan, Katharine 1861-1931 ...... DLB-153, 240
Tyndale, William circa 1494-1536 ...... DLB-132

U

Uchida, Yoshika 1921-1992 .... CDALB-7
Udall, Nicholas 1504-1556 .... DLB-62
Ugrêsić, Dubravka 1949- DLB-181
Uhland, Ludwig 1787-1862 .... DLB-90
Uhse, Bodo 1904-1963 .... DLB-69
Ujević, Augustin ("Tin") 1891-1955 ..... DLB-147
Ulenhart, Niclas flourished circa 1600 ... DLB-164
Ulibarrí, Sabine R. 1919- DLB-82
Ulica, Jorge 1870-1926 .... DLB-82
Ulivi, Ferruccio 1912- DLB-196
Ulizio, B. George 1889-1969 .... DLB-140
Ulrich von Liechtenstein circa 1200-circa 1275 .... DLB-138
Ulrich von Zatzikhoven before 1194-after 1214 .... DLB-138
Ulysses, Reader's Edition Y-97
Unaipon, David 1872-1967 .... DLB-230
Unamuno, Miguel de 1864-1936 .... DLB-108
Under, Marie 1883-1980 .... DLB-220; CDWLB-4
Under the Microscope (1872), by A. C. Swinburne DLB-35
Underhill, Evelyn 1875-1941 .... DLB-240
Ungaretti, Giuseppe 1888-1970 .... DLB-114
Unger, Friederike Helene 1741-1813 ..... DLB-94
United States Book Company DLB-49
Universal Publishing and Distributing Corporation DLB-46
The University of Iowa Writers' Workshop Golden Jubilee Y-86
The University of South Carolina Press Y-94
University of Wales Press DLB-112
University Press of Florida Y-00
University Press of Kansas Y-98
University Press of Mississippi Y-99
"The Unknown Public" (1858), by Wilkie Collins [excerpt] DLB-57
Uno, Chiyo 1897-1996 .... DLB-180
Unruh, Fritz von 1885-1970 .... DLB-56, 118
Unspeakable Practices II: The Festival of Vanguard Narrative at Brown University Y-93
Unsworth, Barry 1930- DLB-194

Unt, Mati 1944- DLB-232	van der Post, Laurens 1906-1996 ....DLB-204	Veríssimo, Erico 1905-1975............DLB-145
The Unterberg Poetry Center of the 92nd Street Y...................... Y-98	Van Dine, S. S. (see Wright, Williard Huntington)	Verlaine, Paul 1844-1896 ....DLB-217
Unwin, T. Fisher [publishing house] DLB-106	Van Doren, Mark 1894-1972..............DLB-45	Verne, Jules 1828-1905...............DLB-123
Upchurch, Boyd B. (see Boyd, John)	van Druten, John 1901-1957 ....DLB-10	Verplanck, Gulian C. 1786-1870 ....DLB-59
Updike, John 1932- DLB-2, 5, 143, 218, 227; Y-80, Y-82; DS-3; CDALB-6	Van Duyn, Mona 1921- DLB-5	Very, Jones 1813-1880................DLB-1, 243
	Van Dyke, Henry 1852-1933 .....DLB-71; DS-13	Vian, Boris 1920-1959.................DLB-72
John Updike on the Internet Y-97	Van Dyke, Henry 1928- DLB-33	Viazemsky, Petr Andreevich 1792-1878.....................DLB-205
Upīts, Andrejs 1877-1970 ....DLB-220	Van Dyke, John C. 1856-1932 ....DLB-186	Vicars, Thomas 1591-1638 ....DLB-236
Upton, Bertha 1849-1912 ....DLB-141	van Gulik, Robert Hans 1910-1967........ DS-17	Vickers, Roy 1888?-1965...............DLB-77
Upton, Charles 1948- DLB-16	van Itallie, Jean-Claude 1936- DLB-7	Vickery, Sukey 1779-1821 ....DLB-200
Upton, Florence K. 1873-1922..........DLB-141	Van Loan, Charles E. 1876-1919 ....DLB-171	Victoria 1819-1901 ....DLB-55
Upward, Allen 1863-1926 ....DLB-36	Van Rensselaer, Mariana Griswold 1851-1934.....................DLB-47	Victoria Press......................DLB-106
Urban, Milo 1904-1982................DLB-215		Vidal, Gore 1925- DLB-6, 152; CDALB-7
Urista, Alberto Baltazar (see Alurista)	Van Rensselaer, Mrs. Schuyler (see Van Rensselaer, Mariana Griswold)	Vidal, Mary Theresa 1815-1873 ....DLB-230
Urquhart, Fred 1912- DLB-139	Van Vechten, Carl 1880-1964............DLB-4, 9	Vidmer, Richards 1898-1978...........DLB-241
Urrea, Luis Alberto 1955- DLB-209	van Vogt, A. E. 1912-2000 ....DLB-8, 251	Viebig, Clara 1860-1952 ....DLB-66
Urzidil, Johannes 1896-1976 ....DLB-85	Vanbrugh, Sir John 1664-1726..........DLB-80	Viereck, George Sylvester 1884-1962.....................DLB-54
The Uses of Facsimile Y-90	Vance, Jack 1916?- DLB-8	
Usk, Thomas died 1388 ....DLB-146	Vančura, Vladislav 1891-1942 ....DLB-215; CDWLB-4	Viereck, Peter 1916- DLB-5
Uslar Pietri, Arturo 1906- DLB-113		Viets, Roger 1738-1811 ....DLB-99
Ussher, James 1581-1656...............DLB-213	Vane, Sutton 1888-1963 ....DLB-10	Viewpoint: Politics and Performance, by David Edgar DLB-13
Ustinov, Peter 1921- DLB-13	Vanguard Press.....................DLB-46	Vigil-Piñon, Evangelina 1949- DLB-122
Uttley, Alison 1884-1976 ....DLB-160	Vann, Robert L. 1879-1940 ....DLB-29	Vigneault, Gilles 1928- DLB-60
Uz, Johann Peter 1720-1796............DLB-97	Vargas Llosa, Mario 1936- DLB-145; CDWLB-3	Vigny, Alfred de 1797-1863...............DLB-119, 192, 217
V	Varley, John 1947- Y-81	Vigolo, Giorgio 1894-1983 ....DLB-114
Vac, Bertrand 1914- DLB-88	Varnhagen von Ense, Karl August 1785-1858......................DLB-90	The Viking Press....................DLB-46
Vācietis, Ojārs 1933-1983 ....DLB-232		Vilde, Eduard 1865-1933..............DLB-220
Vaičiulaitis, Antanas 1906-1992 ....DLB-220	Varnhagen von Ense, Rahel 1771-1833......................DLB-90	Vilinskaia, Mariia Aleksandrovna (see Vovchok, Marko)
Vaculík, Ludvík 1926- DLB-232	Varro 116 B.C.-27 B.C................DLB-211	
Vaičiūnaite, Judita 1937- DLB-232	Vasiliu, George (see Bacovia, George)	Villanueva, Alma Luz 1944- DLB-122
Vail, Laurence 1891-1968 ....DLB-4	Vásquez, Richard 1928- DLB-209	Villanueva, Tino 1941- DLB-82
Vailland, Roger 1907-1965..............DLB-83	Vásquez Montalbán, Manuel 1939- DLB-134	Villard, Henry 1835-1900 ....DLB-23
Vaižgantas 1869-1933 ....DLB-220	Vassa, Gustavus (see Equiano, Olaudah)	Villard, Oswald Garrison 1872-1949.....................DLB-25, 91
Vajda, Ernest 1887-1954 ....DLB-44	Vassalli, Sebastiano 1941- DLB-128, 196	Villarreal, Edit 1944- DLB-209
Valdés, Gina 1943- DLB-122	Vaughan, Henry 1621-1695 ....DLB-131	Villarreal, José Antonio 1924- DLB-82
Valdez, Luis Miguel 1940- DLB-122	Vaughan, Thomas 1621-1666 ....DLB-131	Villaseñor, Victor 1940- DLB-209
Valduga, Patrizia 1953-................DLB-128	Vaughn, Robert 1592?-1667 ....DLB-213	Villegas de Magnón, Leonor 1876-1955.....................DLB-122
Valente, José Angel 1929-2000 ....DLB-108	Vaux, Thomas, Lord 1509-1556........DLB-132	
Valenzuela, Luisa 1938- ...DLB-113; CDWLB-3	Vazov, Ivan 1850-1921 .....DLB-147; CDWLB-4	Villehardouin, Geoffroi de circa 1150-1215..................DLB-208
Valeri, Diego 1887-1976................DLB-128	Véa Jr., Alfredo 1950- DLB-209	
Valerius Flaccus fl. circa A.D. 92........DLB-211	Veblen, Thorstein 1857-1929...........DLB-246	Villemaire, Yolande 1949- DLB-60
Valerius Maximus fl. circa A.D. 31......DLB-211	Vega, Janine Pommy 1942- DLB-16	Villena, Luis Antonio de 1951- DLB-134
Valesio, Paolo 1939- DLB-196	Veiller, Anthony 1903-1965 ....DLB-44	Villiers, George, Second Duke of Buckingham 1628-1687............DLB-80
Valgardson, W. D. 1939- DLB-60	Velásquez-Trevino, Gloria 1949- DLB-122	
Valle, Víctor Manuel 1950- DLB-122	Veley, Margaret 1843-1887 ....DLB-199	Villiers de l'Isle-Adam, Jean-Marie Mathias Philippe-Auguste, Comte de 1838-1889..................DLB-123, 192
Valle-Inclán, Ramón del 1866-1936......DLB-134	Velleius Paterculus circa 20 B.C.-circa A.D. 30 ....DLB-211	
Vallejo, Armando 1949- DLB-122		Villon, François 1431-circa 1463? DLB-208
Vallès, Jules 1832-1885 ....DLB-123	Veloz Maggiolo, Marcio 1936- DLB-145	Vine Press DLB-112
Vallette, Marguerite Eymery (see Rachilde)	Vel'tman Aleksandr Fomich 1800-1870 ....DLB-198	Viorst, Judith ?- DLB-52
Valverde, José María 1926-1996 ....DLB-108		Vipont, Elfrida (Elfrida Vipont Foulds, Charles Vipont) 1902-1992............DLB-160
Van Allsburg, Chris 1949- DLB-61	Venegas, Daniel ?-? DLB-82	
Van Anda, Carr 1864-1945.............DLB-25	Venevitinov, Dmitrii Vladimirovich 1805-1827.....................DLB-205	Viramontes, Helena María 1954- DLB-122
	Vergil, Polydore circa 1470-1555........DLB-132	Virgil 70 B.C.-19 B.C....... DLB-211; CDWLB-1

Virtual Books and Enemies of Books Y-00	Waldman, Anne 1945- DLB-16	Ware, Henry, Jr. 1794-1843 . . . . DLB-235
Vischer, Friedrich Theodor 1807-1887 . . . DLB-133	Waldrop, Rosmarie 1935- DLB-169	Ware, William 1797-1852 . . . . DLB-1, 235
Vitruvius circa 85 B.C.-circa 15 B.C. DLB-211	Walker, Alice 1900-1982 . . . . DLB-201	Warfield, Catherine Ann 1816-1877 . . . . DLB-248
Vitry, Philippe de 1291-1361 . . . . DLB-208	Walker, Alice 1944- DLB-6, 33, 143; CDALB-6	Waring, Anna Letitia 1823-1910 . . . . DLB-240
Vivanco, Luis Felipe 1907-1975 . . . . DLB-108	Walker, Annie Louisa (Mrs. Harry Coghill) circa 1836-1907 . . . . DLB-240	Warne, Frederick, and Company [U.K.] . . . DLB-106
Viviani, Cesare 1947- DLB-128	Walker, George F. 1947- DLB-60	Warne, Frederick, and Company [U.S.] . . . DLB-49
Vivien, Renée 1877-1909 . . . . DLB-217	Walker, John Brisben 1847-1931 . . . . DLB-79	Warner, Anne 1869-1913 . . . . DLB-202
Vizenor, Gerald 1934- DLB-175, 227	Walker, Joseph A. 1935- DLB-38	Warner, Charles Dudley 1829-1900 . . . . . DLB-64
Vizetelly and Company DLB-106	Walker, Margaret 1915- DLB-76, 152	Warner, Marina 1946- DLB-194
Voaden, Herman 1903- DLB-88	Walker, Ted 1934- DLB-40	Warner, Rex 1905- DLB-15
Voß, Johann Heinrich 1751-1826 . . . . DLB-90	Walker and Company DLB-49	Warner, Susan 1819-1885 . . . DLB-3, 42, 239, 250
Voigt, Ellen Bryant 1943- DLB-120	Walker, Evans and Cogswell Company . . . DLB-49	Warner, Sylvia Townsend 1893-1978 . . . . DLB-34, 139
Vojnović, Ivo 1857-1929 . . . . . DLB-147; CDWLB-4	Wallace, Alfred Russel 1823-1913 . . . . . . DLB-190	Warner, William 1558-1609 . . . . DLB-172
Volkoff, Vladimir 1932- DLB-83	Wallace, Dewitt 1889-1981 and Lila Acheson Wallace 1889-1984 . . . . DLB-137	Warner Books DLB-46
Volland, P. F., Company DLB-46	Wallace, Edgar 1875-1932 . . . . DLB-70	Warr, Bertram 1917-1943 . . . . DLB-88
Vollbehr, Otto H. F. 1872?-1945 or 1946 . . . . DLB-187	Wallace, Lew 1827-1905 . . . . DLB-202	Warren, John Byrne Leicester (see De Tabley, Lord)
Vologdin (see Zasodimsky, Pavel Vladimirovich)	Wallace, Lila Acheson (see Wallace, Dewitt, and Lila Acheson Wallace)	Warren, Lella 1899-1982 . . . . Y-83
Volponi, Paolo 1924- DLB-177	Wallace, Naomi 1960- DLB-249	Warren, Mercy Otis 1728-1814 . . . . . DLB-31, 200
von der Grün, Max 1926- DLB-75	Wallant, Edward Lewis 1926-1962 . . . . DLB-2, 28, 143	Warren, Robert Penn 1905-1989 . . . . DLB-2, 48, 152; Y-80, Y-89; CDALB-6
Vonarburg, Élisabeth 1947- DLB-251	Waller, Edmund 1606-1687 . . . . DLB-126	Warren, Samuel 1807-1877 . . . . DLB-190
Vonnegut, Kurt 1922- DLB-2, 8, 152; Y-80; DS-3; CDALB-6	Walpole, Horace 1717-1797 . . . . . DLB-39, 104, 213	Die Wartburgkrieg circa 1230-circa 1280 . . . DLB-138
Voranc, Prežihov 1893-1950 . . . . DLB-147	Preface to the First Edition of The Castle of Otranto (1764) DLB-39	Warton, Joseph 1722-1800 . . . . DLB-104, 109
Vovchok, Marko 1833-1907 . . . . DLB-238	Preface to the Second Edition of The Castle of Otranto (1765) DLB-39	Warton, Thomas 1728-1790 . . . . DLB-104, 109
Voynich, E. L. 1864-1960 . . . . DLB-197	Walpole, Hugh 1884-1941 . . . . DLB-34	Warung, Price (William Astley) 1855-1911 . . . . DLB-230
Vroman, Mary Elizabeth circa 1924-1967 . . . . DLB-33	Walrond, Eric 1898-1966 . . . . DLB-51	Washington, George 1732-1799 . . . . DLB-31
W	Walser, Martin 1927- DLB-75, 124	Wassermann, Jakob 1873-1934 . . . . DLB-66
Wace, Robert ("Maistre") circa 1100-circa 1175 . . . . DLB-146	Walser, Robert 1878-1956 . . . . DLB-66	Wasserstein, Wendy 1950- DLB-228
Wackenroder, Wilhelm Heinrich 1773-1798 . . . . DLB-90	Walsh, Ernest 1895-1926 . . . . DLB-4, 45	Wasson, David Atwood 1823-1887 . . . DLB-1, 223
Wackernagel, Wilhelm 1806-1869 . . . . . . DLB-133	Walsh, Robert 1784-1859 . . . . DLB-59	Watanna, Onoto (see Eaton, Winnifred)
Waddell, Helen 1889-1965 . . . . DLB-240	Walters, Henry 1848-1931 . . . . DLB-140	Waterhouse, Keith 1929- DLB-13, 15
Waddington, Miriam 1917- DLB-68	Waltharius circa 825 . . . . DLB-148	Waterman, Andrew 1940- DLB-40
Wade, Henry 1887-1969 . . . . DLB-77	Walther von der Vogelweide circa 1170-circa 1230 . . . . DLB-138	Waters, Frank 1902-1995 . . . . DLB-212; Y-86
Wagenknecht, Edward 1900- DLB-103	Walton, Izaak 1593-1683 . . . . DLB-151, 213; CDBLB-1	Waters, Michael 1949- DLB-120
Wagner, Heinrich Leopold 1747-1779 . . . . . DLB-94	Wambaugh, Joseph 1937- DLB-6; Y-83	Watkins, Tobias 1780-1855 . . . . DLB-73
Wagner, Henry R. 1862-1957 . . . . DLB-140	Wand, Alfred Rudolph 1828-1891 . . . . . . DLB-188	Watkins, Vernon 1906-1967 . . . . DLB-20
Wagner, Richard 1813-1883 . . . . DLB-129	Waniek, Marilyn Nelson 1946- DLB-120	Watmough, David 1926- DLB-53
Wagoner, David 1926- DLB-5	Wanley, Humphrey 1672-1726 . . . . DLB-213	Watson, James Wreford (see Wreford, James)
Wah, Fred 1939- DLB-60	Warburton, William 1698-1779 . . . . DLB-104	Watson, John 1850-1907 . . . . DLB-156
Waiblinger, Wilhelm 1804-1830 . . . . DLB-90	Ward, Aileen 1919- DLB-111	Watson, Rosamund Marriott (Graham R. Tomson) 1860-1911 . . . . DLB-240
Wain, John 1925-1994 . . . DLB-15, 27, 139, 155; CDBLB-8	Ward, Artemus (see Browne, Charles Farrar)	Watson, Sheila 1909- DLB-60
Wainwright, Jeffrey 1944- DLB-40	Ward, Arthur Henry Sarsfield (see Rohmer, Sax)	Watson, Thomas 1545?-1592 . . . . DLB-132
Waite, Peirce and Company DLB-49	Ward, Douglas Turner 1930- DLB-7, 38	Watson, Wilfred 1911- DLB-60
Wakeman, Stephen H. 1859-1924 . . . . . . DLB-187	Ward, Mrs. Humphry 1851-1920 . . . . . . DLB-18	Watt, W. J., and Company DLB-46
Wakoski, Diane 1937- DLB-5	Ward, Lynd 1905-1985 . . . . DLB-22	Watten, Barrett 1948- DLB-193
Walahfrid Strabo circa 808-849 . . . . DLB-148	Ward, Lock and Company DLB-106	Watterson, Henry 1840-1921 . . . . DLB-25
Walck, Henry Z. DLB-46	Ward, Nathaniel circa 1578-1652 . . . . DLB-24	Watts, Alan 1915-1973 . . . . DLB-16
Walcott, Derek 1930- DLB-117; Y-81, Y-92; CDWLB-3	Ward, Theodore 1902-1983 . . . . DLB-76	Watts, Franklin [publishing house] DLB-46
Waldegrave, Robert [publishing house] . . . DLB-170	Wardle, Ralph 1909-1988 . . . . DLB-103	Watts, Isaac 1674-1748 . . . . DLB-95
		Waugh, Alec 1898-1981 . . . . DLB-191
		Waugh, Auberon 1939-2000 . . . DLB-14, 194; Y-00
		The Cult of Biography Excerpts from the Second Folio Debate:

"Biographies are generally a disease of
English Literature" Y-86

Waugh, Evelyn
1903-1966 . . . . . . DLB-15, 162, 195; CDBLB-6

Way and Williams DLB-49

Wayman, Tom 1945- DLB-53

We See the Editor at Work Y-97

Weatherly, Tom 1942- DLB-41

Weaver, Gordon 1937- DLB-130

Weaver, Robert 1921- DLB-88

Webb, Beatrice 1858-1943 and
Webb, Sidney 1859-1947 . . . . DLB-190

Webb, Frank J. ?-? DLB-50

Webb, James Watson 1802-1884 . . . . DLB-43

Webb, Mary 1881-1927 . . . . DLB-34

Webb, Phyllis 1927- DLB-53

Webb, Walter Prescott 1888-1963 . . . . DLB-17

Webbe, William ?-1591 . . . . DLB-132

Webber, Charles Wilkins 1819-1856? . . . DLB-202

Webling, Lucy (Lucy Betty MacRaye)
1877-1952 . . . . DLB-240

Webling, Peggy (Arthur Weston)
1871-1949 . . . . DLB-240

Webster, Augusta 1837-1894 . . . . DLB-35, 240

Webster, Charles L., and Company DLB-49

Webster, John
1579 or 1580-1634? DLB-58; CDBLB-1

John Webster: The Melbourne
Manuscript Y-86

Webster, Noah
1758-1843 . . . . DLB-1, 37, 42, 43, 73, 243

Weckherlin, Georg Rodolf 1584-1653 . . . . DLB-164

Wedekind, Frank
1864-1918 . . . . DLB-118; CDBLB-2

Weeks, Edward Augustus, Jr.
1898-1989 . . . . DLB-137

Weeks, Stephen B. 1865-1918 . . . . DLB-187

Weems, Mason Locke 1759-1825 . . DLB-30, 37, 42

Weerth, Georg 1822-1856 . . . . DLB-129

Weidenfeld and Nicolson DLB-112

Weidman, Jerome 1913-1998 . . . . DLB-28

Weiß, Ernst 1882-1940 . . . . DLB-81

Weigl, Bruce 1949- DLB-120

Weinbaum, Stanley Grauman 1902-1935 . . DLB-8

Weiner, Andrew 1949- DLB-251

Weintraub, Stanley 1929- DLB-111; Y82

The Practice of Biography: An Interview
with Stanley Weintraub Y-82

Weise, Christian 1642-1708 . . . . DLB-168

Weisenborn, Gunther 1902-1969 . . . . DLB-69, 124

Weiss, John 1818-1879 . . . . DLB-1, 243

Weiss, Peter 1916-1982 . . . . DLB-69, 124

Weiss, Theodore 1916- DLB-5

Weisse, Christian Felix 1726-1804 . . . . DLB-97

Weitling, Wilhelm 1808-1871 . . . . DLB-129

Welch, James 1940- DLB-175

Welch, Lew 1926-1971? DLB-16

Weldon, Fay 1931- DLB-14, 194; CDBLB-8

Wellek, René 1903-1995 . . . . DLB-63

Wells, Carolyn 1862-1942 . . . . DLB-11

Wells, Charles Jeremiah circa 1800-1879 . . . DLB-32

Wells, Gabriel 1862-1946 . . . . DLB-140

Wells, H. G.
1866-1946 . . . DLB-34, 70, 156, 178; CDBLB-6

Wells, Helena 1758?-1824 . . . . DLB-200

Wells, Robert 1947- DLB-40

Wells-Barnett, Ida B. 1862-1931 . . . . . DLB-23, 221

Welty, Eudora 1909-
. . . . DLB-2, 102, 143; Y-87; DS-12; CDALB-1

Eudora Welty: Eye of the Storyteller Y-87

Eudora Welty Newsletter Y-99

Eudora Welty's Ninetieth Birthday Y-99

Wendell, Barrett 1855-1921 . . . . DLB-71

Wentworth, Patricia 1878-1961 . . . . DLB-77

Wentworth, William Charles
1790-1872 . . . . DLB-230

Werder, Diederich von dem 1584-1657 . . DLB-164

Werfel, Franz 1890-1945 . . . . DLB-81, 124

Werner, Zacharias 1768-1823 . . . . DLB-94

The Werner Company DLB-49

Wersba, Barbara 1932- DLB-52

Wescott, Glenway 1901- DLB-4, 9, 102

Wesker, Arnold 1932- DLB-13; CDBLB-8

Wesley, Charles 1707-1788 . . . . DLB-95

Wesley, John 1703-1791 . . . . DLB-104

Wesley, Mary 1912- DLB-231

Wesley, Richard 1945- DLB-38

Wessels, A., and Company DLB-46

Wessobrunner Gebet circa 787-815 . . . . DLB-148

West, Anthony 1914-1988 . . . . DLB-15

West, Cornel 1953- DLB-246

West, Dorothy 1907-1998 . . . . DLB-76

West, Jessamyn 1902-1984 . . . . DLB-6; Y-84

West, Mae 1892-1980 . . . . DLB-44

West, Michele Sagara 1963- DLB-251

West, Nathanael
1903-1940 . . . . DLB-4, 9, 28; CDALB-5

West, Paul 1930- DLB-14

West, Rebecca 1892-1983 . . . . DLB-36; Y-83

West, Richard 1941- DLB-185

West and Johnson DLB-49

Westcott, Edward Noyes 1846-1898 . . . . . DLB-202

The Western Messenger 1835-1841 . . . . DLB-223

Western Publishing Company DLB-46

Western Writers of America Y-99

The Westminster Review 1824-1914 . . . . DLB-110

Weston, Arthur (see Webling, Peggy)

Weston, Elizabeth Jane circa 1582-1612 . . DLB-172

Wetherald, Agnes Ethelwyn 1857-1940 . . . . DLB-99

Wetherell, Elizabeth (see Warner, Susan)

Wetherell, W. D. 1948- DLB-234

Wetzel, Friedrich Gottlob 1779-1819 . . . . . . DLB-90

Weyman, Stanley J. 1855-1928 . . . . . DLB-141, 156

Wezel, Johann Karl 1747-1819 . . . . DLB-94

Whalen, Philip 1923- DLB-16

Whalley, George 1915-1983 . . . . DLB-88

Wharton, Edith 1862-1937
. . . . . DLB-4, 9, 12, 78, 189; DS-13; CDALB-3

Wharton, William 1920s?- Y-80

"What You Lose on the Swings You Make Up
on the Merry-Go-Round" Y-99

Whately, Mary Louisa 1824-1889 . . . . DLB-166

Whately, Richard 1787-1863 . . . . DLB-190

From Elements of Rhetoric (1828;
revised, 1846) DLB-57

What's Really Wrong With Bestseller Lists . . Y-84

Wheatley, Dennis Yates 1897-1977 . . . . DLB-77

Wheatley, Phillis
circa 1754-1784 . . . . DLB-31, 50; CDALB-2

Wheeler, Anna Doyle 1785-1848? DLB-158

Wheeler, Charles Stearns 1816-1843 . . . DLB-1, 223

Wheeler, Monroe 1900-1988 . . . . DLB-4

Wheelock, John Hall 1886-1978 . . . . DLB-45

Wheelwright, J. B. 1897-1940 . . . . DLB-45

Wheelwright, John circa 1592-1679 . . . . . . DLB-24

Whetstone, George 1550-1587 . . . . DLB-136

Whetstone, Colonel Pete (see Noland, C. F. M.)

Whicher, Stephen E. 1915-1961 . . . . DLB-111

Whipple, Edwin Percy 1819-1886 . . . . . . DLB-1, 64

Whitaker, Alexander 1585-1617 . . . . DLB-24

Whitaker, Daniel K. 1801-1881 . . . . DLB-73

Whitcher, Frances Miriam
1812-1852 . . . . DLB-11, 202

White, Andrew 1579-1656 . . . . DLB-24

White, Andrew Dickson 1832-1918 . . . . . . DLB-47

White, E. B. 1899-1985 . . . . DLB-11, 22; CDALB-7

White, Edgar B. 1947- DLB-38

White, Edmund 1940- DLB-227

White, Ethel Lina 1887-1944 . . . . DLB-77

White, Hayden V. 1928- DLB-246

White, Henry Kirke 1785-1806 . . . . DLB-96

White, Horace 1834-1916 . . . . DLB-23

White, Phyllis Dorothy James (see James, P. D.)

White, Richard Grant 1821-1885 . . . . DLB-64

White, T. H. 1906-1964 . . . . DLB-160

White, Walter 1893-1955 . . . . DLB-51

White, William, and Company DLB-49

White, William Allen 1868-1944 . . . . DLB-9, 25

White, William Anthony Parker
(see Boucher, Anthony)

White, William Hale (see Rutherford, Mark)

Whitchurch, Victor L. 1868-1933 . . . . DLB-70

Whitehead, Alfred North 1861-1947 . . . . . DLB-100

Whitehead, James 1936- Y-81

Whitehead, William 1715-1785 . . . . . . DLB-84, 109

Whitfield, James Monroe 1822-1871 . . . . . . DLB-50

Whitfield, Raoul 1898-1945 . . . . DLB-226

Whitgift, John circa 1533-1604 . . . . DLB-132

Whiting, John 1917-1963 . . . . DLB-13

Whiting, Samuel 1597-1679 . . . . DLB-24
Whitlock, Brand 1869-1934 . . . . DLB-12
Whitman, Albert, and Company DLB-46
Whitman, Albery Allson 1851-1901 . . . . . DLB-50
Whitman, Alden 1913-1990 . . . . Y-91
Whitman, Sarah Helen (Power)
  1803-1878 . . . . DLB-1, 243
Whitman, Walt
  1819-1892 . . . . DLB-3, 64, 224, 250; CDALB-2
Whitman Publishing Company DLB-46
Whitney, Geoffrey 1548 or 1552?-1601 . . DLB-136
Whitney, Isabella flourished 1566-1573 . . DLB-136
Whitney, John Hay 1904-1982 . . . . DLB-127
Whittemore, Reed 1919-1995 . . . . DLB-5
Whittier, John Greenleaf
  1807-1892 . . . . DLB-1, 243; CDALB-2
Whittlesey House DLB-46
Who Runs American Literature? Y-94
Whose *Ulysses?* The Function of Editing Y-97
Wickham, Anna (Edith Alice Mary Harper)
  1884-1947 . . . . DLB-240
Wicomb, Zoë 1948- DLB-225
Wideman, John Edgar 1941- DLB-33, 143
Widener, Harry Elkins 1885-1912 . . . . . . DLB-140
Wiebe, Rudy 1934- DLB-60
Wiechert, Ernst 1887-1950 . . . . DLB-56
Wied, Martina 1882-1957 . . . . DLB-85
Wiehe, Evelyn May Clowes (see Mordaunt, Elinor)
Wieland, Christoph Martin 1733-1813 . . . DLB-97
Wienbarg, Ludolf 1802-1872 . . . . DLB-133
Wieners, John 1934- DLB-16
Wier, Ester 1910- DLB-52
Wiesel, Elie
  1928- DLB-83; Y-86, 87; CDALB-7
Wiggin, Kate Douglas 1856-1923 . . . . DLB-42
Wigglesworth, Michael 1631-1705 . . . . . . DLB-24
Wilberforce, William 1759-1833 . . . . DLB-158
Wilbrandt, Adolf 1837-1911 . . . . DLB-129
Wilbur, Richard
  1921- DLB-5, 169; CDALB-7
Wild, Peter 1940- DLB-5
Wilde, Lady Jane Francesca Elgee
  1821?-1896 . . . . DLB-199
Wilde, Oscar 1854-1900
  . . . . DLB-10, 19, 34, 57, 141, 156, 190;
  CDBLB-5
"The Critic as Artist" (1891) DLB-57
Oscar Wilde Conference at Hofstra
  University Y-00
From "The Decay of Lying" (1889) DLB-18
"The English Renaissance of
  Art" (1908) DLB-35
"L'Envoi" (1882) DLB-35
Wilde, Richard Henry 1789-1847 . . . . . . DLB-3, 59
Wilde, W. A., Company DLB-49
Wilder, Billy 1906- DLB-26
Wilder, Laura Ingalls 1867-1957 . . . . DLB-22

Wilder, Thornton
  1897-1975 . . . . DLB-4, 7, 9, 228; CDALB-7
Thornton Wilder Centenary at Yale Y-97
Wildgans, Anton 1881-1932 . . . . DLB-118
Wiley, Bell Irvin 1906-1980 . . . . DLB-17
Wiley, John, and Sons DLB-49
Wilhelm, Kate 1928- DLB-8
Wilkes, Charles 1798-1877 . . . . DLB-183
Wilkes, George 1817-1885 . . . . DLB-79
Wilkins, John 1614-1672 . . . . DLB-236
Wilkinson, Anne 1910-1961 . . . . DLB-88
Wilkinson, Eliza Yonge
  1757-circa 1813 . . . . DLB-200
Wilkinson, Sylvia 1940- Y-86
Wilkinson, William Cleaver 1833-1920 . . . DLB-71
Willard, Barbara 1909-1994 . . . . DLB-161
Willard, Emma 1787-1870 . . . . DLB-239
Willard, Frances E. 1839-1898 . . . . DLB-221
Willard, L. [publishing house] DLB-49
Willard, Nancy 1936- DLB-5, 52
Willard, Samuel 1640-1707 . . . . DLB-24
Willeford, Charles 1919-1988 . . . . DLB-226
William of Auvergne 1190-1249 . . . . DLB-115
William of Conches
  circa 1090-circa 1154 . . . . DLB-115
William of Ockham circa 1285-1347 . . . . DLB-115
William of Sherwood
  1200/1205-1266/1271 . . . . DLB-115
The William Chavrat American Fiction Collection
  at the Ohio State University Libraries Y-92
Williams, A., and Company DLB-49
Williams, Ben Ames 1889-1953 . . . . DLB-102
Williams, C. K. 1936- DLB-5
Williams, Chancellor 1905- DLB-76
Williams, Charles 1886-1945 . . . . DLB-100, 153
Williams, Denis 1923-1998 . . . . DLB-117
Williams, Emlyn 1905-1987 . . . . DLB-10, 77
Williams, Garth 1912-1996 . . . . DLB-22
Williams, George Washington
  1849-1891 . . . . DLB-47
Williams, Heathcote 1941- DLB-13
Williams, Helen Maria 1761-1827 . . . . . . DLB-158
Williams, Hugo 1942- DLB-40
Williams, Isaac 1802-1865 . . . . DLB-32
Williams, Joan 1928- DLB-6
Williams, Joe 1889-1972 . . . . DLB-241
Williams, John A. 1925- DLB-2, 33
Williams, John E. 1922-1994 . . . . DLB-6
Williams, Jonathan 1929- DLB-5
Williams, Miller 1930- DLB-105
Williams, Nigel 1948- DLB-231
Williams, Raymond 1921- . . . DLB-14, 231, 242
Williams, Roger circa 1603-1683 . . . . DLB-24
Williams, Rowland 1817-1870 . . . . DLB-184
Williams, Samm-Art 1946- DLB-38
Williams, Sherley Anne 1944-1999 . . . . . DLB-41

Williams, T. Harry 1909-1979 . . . . DLB-17
Williams, Tennessee
  1911-1983 . . . . DLB-7; Y-83; DS-4; CDALB-1
Williams, Terry Tempest 1955- DLB-206
Williams, Ursula Moray 1911- DLB-160
Williams, Valentine 1883-1946 . . . . DLB-77
Williams, William Appleman 1921- . . . DLB-17
Williams, William Carlos
  1883-1963 . . . . . DLB-4, 16, 54, 86; CDALB-4
Williams, Wirt 1921- DLB-6
Williams Brothers DLB-49
Williamson, Henry 1895-1977 . . . . DLB-191
Williamson, Jack 1908- DLB-8
Willingham, Calder Baynard, Jr.
  1922-1995 . . . . DLB-2, 44
Williram of Ebersberg circa 1020-1085 . . DLB-148
Willis, Nathaniel Parker 1806-1867
  . . . . DLB-3, 59, 73, 74, 183, 250; DS-13
Willkomm, Ernst 1810-1886 . . . . DLB-133
Willumsen, Dorrit 1940- DLB-214
Wills, Garry 1934- DLB-246
Wilmer, Clive 1945- DLB-40
Wilson, A. N. 1950- DLB-14, 155, 194
Wilson, Angus 1913-1991 . . . . . . DLB-15, 139, 155
Wilson, Arthur 1595-1652 . . . . DLB-58
Wilson, August 1945- DLB-228
Wilson, Augusta Jane Evans 1835-1909 . . . DLB-42
Wilson, Colin 1931- DLB-14, 194
Wilson, Edmund 1895-1972 . . . . DLB-63
Wilson, Effingham [publishing house] . . . DLB-154
Wilson, Ethel 1888-1980 . . . . DLB-68
Wilson, F. P. 1889-1963 . . . . DLB-201
Wilson, Harriet E.
  1827/1828?-1863? DLB-50, 239, 243
Wilson, Harry Leon 1867-1939 . . . . DLB-9
Wilson, John 1588-1667 . . . . DLB-24
Wilson, John 1785-1854 . . . . DLB-110
Wilson, John Dover 1881-1969 . . . . DLB-201
Wilson, Lanford 1937- DLB-7
Wilson, Margaret 1882-1973 . . . . DLB-9
Wilson, Michael 1914-1978 . . . . DLB-44
Wilson, Mona 1872-1954 . . . . DLB-149
Wilson, Robert Charles 1953- DLB-251
Wilson, Robley 1930- DLB-218
Wilson, Romer 1891-1930 . . . . DLB-191
Wilson, Thomas 1524-1581 . . . . DLB-132, 236
Wilson, Woodrow 1856-1924 . . . . DLB-47
Wimsatt, William K., Jr. 1907-1975 . . . . . DLB-63
Winchell, Walter 1897-1972 . . . . DLB-29
Winchester, J. [publishing house] DLB-49
Winckelmann, Johann Joachim
  1717-1768 . . . . DLB-97
Winckler, Paul 1630-1686 . . . . DLB-164
Wind, Herbert Warren 1916- DLB-171
Windet, John [publishing house] DLB-170
Windham, Donald 1920- DLB-6

Wing, Donald Goddard 1904-1972 . . . . . . DLB-187

Wing, John M. 1844-1917 . . . . DLB-187

Wingate, Allan [publishing house] DLB-112

Winnemucca, Sarah 1844-1921 . . . . DLB-175

Winnifrith, Tom 1938- DLB-155

Winning an Edgar Y-98

Winsloe, Christa 1888-1944 . . . . DLB-124

Winslow, Anna Green 1759-1780 . . . . DLB-200

Winsor, Justin 1831-1897 . . . . DLB-47

John C. Winston Company DLB-49

Winters, Yvor 1900-1968 . . . . DLB-48

Winterson, Jeanette 1959- DLB-207

Winthrop, John 1588-1649 . . . . DLB-24, 30

Winthrop, John, Jr. 1606-1676 . . . . DLB-24

Winthrop, Margaret Tyndal 1591-1647 . . DLB-200

Winthrop, Theodore 1828-1861 . . . . DLB-202

Wirt, William 1772-1834 . . . . DLB-37

Wise, John 1652-1725 . . . . DLB-24

Wise, Thomas James 1859-1937 . . . . DLB-184

Wiseman, Adele 1928- DLB-88

Wishart and Company DLB-112

Wisner, George 1812-1849 . . . . DLB-43

Wister, Owen 1860-1938 . . . . DLB-9, 78, 186

Wister, Sarah 1761-1804 . . . . DLB-200

Wither, George 1588-1667 . . . . DLB-121

Witherspoon, John 1723-1794 . . . . DLB-31

Withrow, William Henry 1839-1908 . . . . . . DLB-99

Witkacy (see Witkiewicz, Stanisław Ignacy)

Witkiewicz, Stanisław Ignacy
    1885-1939 . . . . DLB-215; CDWLB-4

Wittig, Monique 1935- DLB-83

Wodehouse, P. G.
    1881-1975 . . . . DLB-34, 162; CDBLB-6

Wohmann, Gabriele 1932- DLB-75

Woiwode, Larry 1941- DLB-6

Wolcot, John 1738-1819 . . . . DLB-109

Wolcott, Roger 1679-1767 . . . . DLB-24

Wolf, Christa 1929- DLB-75; CDWLB-2

Wolf, Friedrich 1888-1953 . . . . DLB-124

Wolfe, Gene 1931- DLB-8

Wolfe, John [publishing house] DLB-170

Wolfe, Reyner (Reginald)
    [publishing house] DLB-170

Wolfe, Thomas
    1900-1938 . . . . DLB-9, 102, 229; Y-85;
                            DS-2, DS-16; CDALB-5

The Thomas Wolfe Collection at the University
    of North Carolina at Chapel Hill Y-97

Thomas Wolfe Centennial
    Celebration in Asheville Y-00

Fire at Thomas Wolfe Memorial Y-98

The Thomas Wolfe Society Y-97

Wolfe, Tom 1931- DLB-152, 185

Wolfenstein, Martha 1869-1906 . . . . DLB-221

Wolff, Helen 1906-1994 . . . . Y-94

Wolff, Tobias 1945- DLB-130

Wolfram von Eschenbach
    circa 1170-after 1220 . . . . DLB-138; CDWLB-2

Wolfram von Eschenbach's *Parzival*:
    Prologue and Book 3 . . . . DLB-138

Wolker, Jiří 1900-1924 . . . . DLB-215

Wollstonecraft, Mary
    1759-1797 . . . . DLB-39, 104, 158; CDBLB-3

Wondratschek, Wolf 1943- DLB-75

Wood, Anthony à 1632-1695 . . . . DLB-213

Wood, Benjamin 1820-1900 . . . . DLB-23

Wood, Charles 1932- DLB-13

Wood, Mrs. Henry 1814-1887 . . . . DLB-18

Wood, Joanna E. 1867-1927 . . . . DLB-92

Wood, Sally Sayward Barrell Keating
    1759-1855 . . . . DLB-200

Wood, Samuel [publishing house] DLB-49

Wood, William ?-? DLB-24

The Charles Wood Affair:
    A Playwright Revived Y-83

Woodberry, George Edward
    1855-1930 . . . . DLB-71, 103

Woodbridge, Benjamin 1622-1684 . . . . DLB-24

Woodcock, George 1912-1995 . . . . DLB-88

Woodhull, Victoria C. 1838-1927 . . . . DLB-79

Woodmason, Charles circa 1720-? DLB-31

Woodress, Jr., James Leslie 1916- DLB-111

Woods, Margaret L. 1855-1945 . . . . DLB-240

Woodson, Carter G. 1875-1950 . . . . DLB-17

Woodward, C. Vann 1908-1999 . . . . DLB-17

Woodward, Stanley 1895-1965 . . . . DLB-171

Woodworth, Samuel (Selim) 1785-1842 . . DLB-250

Wooler, Thomas 1785 or 1786-1853 . . . . . DLB-158

Woolf, David (see Maddow, Ben)

Woolf, Douglas 1922-1992 . . . . DLB-244

Woolf, Leonard 1880-1969 . . . . . . DLB-100; DS-10

Woolf, Virginia 1882-1941
    . . . . DLB-36, 100, 162; DS-10; CDBLB-6

Woolf, Virginia, "The New Biography," *New York
    Herald Tribune*, 30 October 1927 . . . . DLB-149

Woollcott, Alexander 1887-1943 . . . . DLB-29

Woolman, John 1720-1772 . . . . DLB-31

Woolner, Thomas 1825-1892 . . . . DLB-35

Woolrich, Cornell 1903-1968 . . . . DLB-226

Woolsey, Sarah Chauncy 1835-1905 . . . . . DLB-42

Woolson, Constance Fenimore
    1840-1894 . . . . DLB-12, 74, 189, 221

Worcester, Joseph Emerson
    1784-1865 . . . . DLB-1, 235

Worde, Wynkyn de [publishing house] . . . DLB-170

Wordsworth, Christopher 1807-1885 . . . . DLB-166

Wordsworth, Dorothy 1771-1855 . . . . DLB-107

Wordsworth, Elizabeth 1840-1932 . . . . DLB-98

Wordsworth, William
    1770-1850 . . . . DLB-93, 107; CDBLB-3

Workman, Fanny Bullock 1859-1925 . . . . DLB-189

The Works of the Rev. John Witherspoon
    (1800-1801) [excerpts] DLB-31

A World Chronology of Important Science
    Fiction Works (1818-1979) DLB-8

World Publishing Company DLB-46

World War II Writers Symposium
    at the University of South Carolina,
    12–14 April 1995 . . . . Y-95

Worthington, R., and Company DLB-49

Wotton, Sir Henry 1568-1639 . . . . DLB-121

Wouk, Herman 1915- Y-82; CDALB-7

Wreford, James 1915- DLB-88

Wren, Sir Christopher 1632-1723 . . . . DLB-213

Wren, Percival Christopher
    1885-1941 . . . . DLB-153

Wrenn, John Henry 1841-1911 . . . . DLB-140

Wright, C. D. 1949- DLB-120

Wright, Charles 1935- DLB-165; Y-82

Wright, Charles Stevenson 1932- DLB-33

Wright, Frances 1795-1852 . . . . DLB-73

Wright, Harold Bell 1872-1944 . . . . DLB-9

Wright, James
    1927-1980 . . . . DLB-5, 169; CDALB-7

Wright, Jay 1935- DLB-41

Wright, Louis B. 1899-1984 . . . . DLB-17

Wright, Richard
    1908-1960 . . . . . DLB-76, 102; DS-2; CDALB-5

Wright, Richard B. 1937- DLB-53

Wright, Sarah Elizabeth 1928- DLB-33

Wright, Willard Huntington ("S. S. Van Dine")
    1888-1939 . . . . DS-16

A Writer Talking: A Collage Y-00

Writers and Politics: 1871-1918,
    by Ronald Gray DLB-66

Writers and their Copyright Holders:
    the WATCH Project Y-94

Writers' Forum Y-85

Writing for the Theatre, by Harold Pinter . DLB-13

Wroth, Lawrence C. 1884-1970 . . . . DLB-187

Wroth, Lady Mary 1587-1653 . . . . DLB-121

Wurlitzer, Rudolph 1937- DLB-173

Wyatt, Sir Thomas circa 1503-1542 . . . . . DLB-132

Wycherley, William
    1641-1715 . . . . DLB-80; CDBLB-2

Wyclif, John
    circa 1335-31 December 1384 . . . . DLB-146

Wyeth, N. C. 1882-1945 . . . . DLB-188; DS-16

Wylie, Elinor 1885-1928 . . . . DLB-9, 45

Wylie, Philip 1902-1971 . . . . DLB-9

Wyllie, John Cook 1908-1968 . . . . DLB-140

Wyman, Lillie Buffum Chace
    1847-1929 . . . . DLB-202

Wymark, Olwen 1934- DLB-233

Wynne-Tyson, Esmé 1898-1972 . . . . DLB-191

X

Xenophon circa 430 B.C.-circa 356 B.C. . . . DLB-176

Y

Yasuoka Shōtarō 1920- DLB-182

Yates, Dornford 1885-1960 . . . . DLB-77, 153

Yates, J. Michael 1938- DLB-60

Yates, Richard
    1926-1992 . . . . DLB-2, 234; Y-81, Y-92

Yau, John 1950- DLB-234

Yavorov, Peyo 1878-1914 . . . . DLB-147

The Year in Book Publishing Y-86

The Year in Book Reviewing and the Literary
    Situation..........................Y-98
The Year in British Drama..........Y-99, Y-00
The Year in British Fiction..........Y-99, Y-00
The Year in Children's
    Books..........Y-92–Y-96, Y-98, Y-99, Y-00
The Year in Children's Literature..........Y-97
The Year in Drama........Y-82-Y-85, Y-87–Y-96
The Year in Fiction...Y-84–Y-86, Y-89, Y-94–Y-99
The Year in Fiction: A Biased View..........Y-83
The Year in Literary Biography...Y-83–Y-98, Y-00
The Year in Literary Theory..........Y-92–Y-93
The Year in London Theatre..............Y-92
The Year in the Novel.....Y-87, Y-88, Y-90–Y-93
The Year in Poetry........Y-83–Y-92, Y-94–Y-00
The Year in Science Fiction and Fantasy.....Y-00
The Year in Short Stories.................Y-87
The Year in the Short Story......Y-88, Y-90–Y-93
The Year in Texas Literature...............Y-98
The Year in U.S. Drama.................Y-00
The Year in U.S. Fiction..................Y-00
The Year's Work in American Poetry.......Y-82
The Year's Work in Fiction: A Survey.......Y-82
Yearsley, Ann 1753-1806..............DLB-109
Yeats, William Butler
    1865-1939...DLB-10, 19, 98, 156; CDBLB-5
Yep, Laurence 1948-..................DLB-52
Yerby, Frank 1916-1991................DLB-76
Yezierska, Anzia
    1880-1970...................DLB-28, 221
Yolen, Jane 1939-....................DLB-52
Yonge, Charlotte Mary 1823-1901...DLB-18, 163
The York Cycle circa 1376-circa 1569...DLB-146
A Yorkshire Tragedy..................DLB-58
Yoseloff, Thomas [publishing house].....DLB-46
Young, A. S. "Doc" 1919-1996.........DLB-241

Young, Al 1939-......................DLB-33
Young, Arthur 1741-1820..............DLB-158
Young, Dick 1917 or 1918 - 1987........DLB-171
Young, Edward 1683-1765..............DLB-95
Young, Frank A. "Fay" 1884-1957......DLB-241
Young, Francis Brett 1884-1954........DLB-191
Young, Gavin 1928-...................DLB-204
Young, Stark 1881-1963.......DLB-9, 102; DS-16
Young, Waldeman 1880-1938............DLB-26
Young, William [publishing house]......DLB-49
Young Bear, Ray A. 1950-...........DLB-175
Yourcenar, Marguerite
    1903-1987.................DLB-72; Y-88
"You've Never Had It So Good," Gusted by
    "Winds of Change": British Fiction in the
    1950s, 1960s, and After............DLB-14
Yovkov, Yordan 1880-1937..DLB-147; CDWLB-4

Z

Zachariä, Friedrich Wilhelm 1726-1777...DLB-97
Zagajewski, Adam 1945-..............DLB-232
Zagoskin, Mikhail Nikolaevich
    1789-1852....................DLB-198
Zajc, Dane 1929-....................DLB-181
Zālīte, Māra 1952-..................DLB-232
Zamora, Bernice 1938-................DLB-82
Zand, Herbert 1923-1970..............DLB-85
Zangwill, Israel 1864-1926......DLB-10, 135, 197
Zanzotto, Andrea 1921-..............DLB-128
Zapata Olivella, Manuel 1920-.........DLB-113
Zasodimsky, Pavel Vladimirovich
    1843-1912...................DLB-238
Zebra Books.......................DLB-46
Zebrowski, George 1945-...............DLB-8
Zech, Paul 1881-1946.................DLB-56
Zeidner, Lisa 1955-..................DLB-120
Zeidonis, Imants 1933-...............DLB-232

Zeimi (Kanze Motokiyo) 1363-1443.....DLB-203
Zelazny, Roger 1937-1995..............DLB-8
Zenger, John Peter 1697-1746........DLB-24, 43
Zepheria..........................DLB-172
Zesen, Philipp von 1619-1689..........DLB-164
Zhukovsky, Vasilii Andreevich
    1783-1852....................DLB-205
Zieber, G. B., and Company...........DLB-49
Ziedonis, Imants 1933-..............CDWLB-4
Zieroth, Dale 1946-..................DLB-60
Zigler und Kliphausen, Heinrich
    Anshelm von 1663-1697..........DLB-168
Zimmer, Paul 1934-....................DLB-5
Zinberg, Len (see Lacy, Ed)
Zindel, Paul 1936-........DLB-7, 52; CDALB-7
Zingref, Julius Wilhelm 1591-1635......DLB-164
Zinnes, Harriet 1919-................DLB-193
Zinzendorf, Nikolaus Ludwig von
    1700-1760....................DLB-168
Zitkala-Ša 1876-1938.................DLB-175
Zīverts, Mārtiņš 1903-1990...........DLB-220
Zlatovratsky, Nikolai Nikolaevich
    1845-1911....................DLB-238
Zola, Emile 1840-1902................DLB-123
Zolla, Elémire 1926-.................DLB-196
Zolotow, Charlotte 1915-..............DLB-52
Zschokke, Heinrich 1771-1848..........DLB-94
Zubly, John Joachim 1724-1781.........DLB-31
Zu-Bolton II, Ahmos 1936-............DLB-41
Zuckmayer, Carl 1896-1977.......DLB-56, 124
Zukofsky, Louis 1904-1978..........DLB-5, 165
Zupan, Vitomil 1914-1987.............DLB-181
Župančič, Oton 1878-1949...DLB-147; CDWLB-4
zur Mühlen, Hermynia 1883-1951.......DLB-56
Zweig, Arnold 1887-1968..............DLB-66
Zweig, Stefan 1881-1942..........DLB-81, 118

ISBN 0-7876-4668-7